13th Joint Conference on Lexical and Computational Semantics (*SEM 2024)

Mexico City, Mexico
20-21 June 2024

ISBN: 978-1-7138-9941-9

Printed from e-media with permission by:

Curran Associates, Inc.
57 Morehouse Lane
Red Hook, NY 12571

Association for Computational Linguistics
209 N. Eighth Street
Stroudsburg, Pennsylvania 18360

Phone: 1-570-476-8006
Fax: 1-570-476-0860

acl@aclweb.org

Additional copies of this publication are available from:

Curran Associates, Inc.
57 Morehouse Lane
Red Hook, NY 12571 USA
Phone: 845-758-0400
Fax: 845-758-2633
Email: curran@proceedings.com
Web: www.proceedings.com

StarSEM 2024

The 13th Joint Conference on Lexical and Computational Semantics

Proceedings of the Conference (*SEM 2024)

June 20-21, 2024

The StarSEM organizers gratefully acknowledge the support from the following sponsors.

Sponsored by

SIGLEX
ACL Special Interest Group

Preface by the Conference Organizers

We are excited to welcome you to *SEM 2024, the 13th Joint Conference on Lexical and Computational Semantics! We are pleased to present this volume containing the accepted long and short papers. *SEM 2024 is being held from June 20 to 21, 2024, in Mexico City, Mexico, co-located with NAACL 2024.

Since its first edition in 2012, *SEM has become a major venue to present recent advances in all areas of lexical and computational semantics, including semantic representations, theoretical semantics, multilingual semantics, and others. *SEM is sponsored by SIGLEX, the ACL Special Interest Group on the Lexicon.

*SEM 2024 accepted both papers submitted directly to *SEM and those already reviewed through ARR (ACL Rolling Review). We received submissions in 11 areas:

- Lexical Semantics
- Semantic Composition and Sentence-level Semantics
- Discourse, Dialogue and Generation
- Commonsense Reasoning and NLU
- Resources and Evaluation
- Theoretical and Formal Semantics
- Multilinguality
- Semantics in NLP Applications
- Psycholinguistics, Cognitive Linguistics, and Semantic Processing
- Social Biases and Ethics
- Interpretability and Explainability

We had 65 submissions this year combining both direct submissions and ARR commits. We compiled an exciting and wide-ranging program, accepting a total of 35 papers (27 long papers and 8 short papers). The submitted papers were carefully evaluated by a program committee led by 14 area chairs, who coordinated a large team of reviewers. The reviews were almost all of very high-quality, and for that we are extremely grateful! Area chairs then added meta-reviews to explain their accept/reject decisions. The final selection was made by the program co-chairs after a careful check of the reviews, meta-reviews, and discussions with the area chairs. We are also very excited to have two excellent keynote speakers: Greg Durrett from the University of Texas at Austin and Heng Ji from the University of Illinois Urbana-Champaign.

We are honored to serve as the organizing committee for *SEM 2024, and we absolutely could not have made this happen without a huge amount of help. First, tremendous thanks to all area chairs and reviewers for their invaluable help in selecting the program, for their engagement in thoughtful discussions, and for providing valuable feedback to authors. Second, thanks to our Publicity Chair Yi Zhou (Cardiff University) for taking care of the website and social media updates. Next, thanks to our Publication Chair Tom McCoy (Yale University) for putting together the proceedings, and to the NAACL 2024 workshop organizers for help and support with all organizational aspects of the conference. Finally, thank you to the authors and presenters for making *SEM 2024 such an engaging and exciting event! We hope that you will find the content of these proceedings as engaging as we do, and we hope to see you at future iterations of *SEM!

Danushka Bollegala and Vered Shwartz, co-Program Chairs
Jose Camacho-Collados, General Chair

Organizing Committee

General Chair

Jose Camacho-Collados, Cardiff University, UK

Program Chairs

Danushka Bollegala, Amazon and University of Liverpool, UK
Vered Shwartz, University of British Columbia and Vector Institute, Canada

Publicity Chair

Yi Zhou, Cardiff University, UK

Publication Chair

Tom McCoy, Yale University, USA

Program Committee

Area Chairs

Jackie Chi Kit Cheung, McGill University and Mila
Annemarie Friedrich, University of Augsburg
Hila Gonen, University of Washington
Masahiro Kaneko, MBZUAI and Tokyo Institute of Technology
Mamoru Komachi, Hitotsubashi University
Debjit Paul, EPFL
Enrico Santus, Bloomberg LP
Ryohei Sasano, Nagoya University and RIKEN
Asad Sayeed, University of Gothenburg
Dominik Schlechtweg, University of Stuttgart
Procheta Sen, University of Liverpool
Gabriel Stanovsky, The Hebrew University of Jerusalem
Elior Sulem, Ben-Gurion University of the Negev
Chris Tanner, Kensho Technologies and Massachusetts Institute of Technology

Program Committee

Sweta Agrawal, Instituto de Telecomunicações
Shafiuddin Rehan Ahmed, University of Colorado, Boulder
Kenichiro Ando, RIKEN
Marianna Apidianaki, University of Pennsylvania
Mohamad Hardyman Barawi, Universiti Malaysia Sarawak
Valerio Basile, University of Turin
Gábor Berend, University of Szeged
Uri Berger, Hebrew University of Jerusalem
Alexander Berman, Göteborg University
Eduardo Blanco, University of Arizona
Michael Bloodgood, The College of New Jersey
Davide Buscaldi, Ecole polytechnique
Elena Cabrio, Université Côte d'Azur
Aoife Cahill, Dataminr
Pierluigi Cassotti, Göteborg University
Akshay Chaturvedi, IRIT, Toulouse, France
Zhousi Chen, Hitotsubashi University
Emmanuele Chersoni, The Hong Kong Polytechnic University
Patricia Chiril, University of Chicago
Bonaventura Coppola, SAP Security Research
Shaobo Cui, EPFL - EPF Lausanne
Noam Dahan, Hebrew University of Jerusalem
Jad Doughman, Mohamed bin Zayed University of Artificial Intelligence
Yo Ehara, Tokyo Gakugei University
Luis Espinosa-Anke, Cardiff University
Francis Ferraro, University of Maryland, Baltimore County
Simona Frenda, University of Turin
Richard Futrell, University of California, Irvine
Voula Giouli, Aristotle University of Thessaloniki

Colin S. Gordon, Drexel University
Venkata Subrahmanyan Govindarajan, University of Texas, Austin
Ivan Habernal, Ruhr-Universität Bochum
Udo Hahn, Friedrich-Schiller Universität Jena
Yi Han, Nagoya University
Yoshihiko Hayashi, Waseda University
Mete Ismayilzada, EPFL - EPF Lausanne
Abhik Jana, IIT Bhubaneswar
Abhishek Kaushik, DkIT
Najoung Kim, Boston University
Thomas H Kober, Zalando SE
Patrick Lee, Montclair State University
Els Lefever, Ghent University
Alisa Liu, University of Washington
Chunhua Liu, University of Melbourne
Renze Lou, Pennsylvania State University
Qing Lyu, University of Pennsylvania
Alda Mari, CNRS
Eugenio Martínez-Cámara, Universidad de Jaén
Sahisnu Mazumder, Intel Labs, USA
Yisong Miao, National University of Singapore
Timothee Mickus, University of Helsinki
Amita Misra, Amazon
Moran Mizrahi, Hebrew University of Jerusalem
Nona Naderi, Université Paris-Saclay
Christina Niklaus, Universität St. Gallen
Ayana Niwa, Megagon Labs
Alexis Palmer, University of Colorado, Boulder
Emerson Cabrera Paraiso, Pontifícia Universidade Católica do Paraná
Alessandro Raganato, University of Milan - Bicocca
Sahithya Ravi, University of British Columbia
Michael Regan, University of Washington
Alla Rozovskaya, City University of New York
Irene Russo, Consiglio Nazionale delle Ricerche
Farig Sadeque, BRAC University
Steven Schockaert, Cardiff University
Sabine Schulte im Walde, University of Stuttgart
Sebastian Schuster, University College London, University of London
Esther Shizgal, Hebrew University of Jerusalem
Melanie Siegel, Darmstadt University of Applied Sciences
Egon Stemle, Masaryk University
Kevin Stowe, TU Darmstadt
Sara Stymne, Uppsala University
Aarne Talman, University of Helsinki
Andon Tchechmedjiev, IMT Mines Alès
Samia Touileb, University of Bergen
Enrica Troiano, Vrije Universiteit Amsterdam
Thinh Hung Truong, University of Melbourne
Sowmya Vajjala, National Research Council Canada
Eva Maria Vecchi, University of Stuttgart
Shira Wein, Georgetown University

Genta Indra Winata, Bloomberg
Tak-Lam Wong, Douglas College
Hanzi Xu, Temple University
He Zhou, Hong Kong Polytechnic University

Table of Contents

Program

Thursday, June 20, 2024

09:00 - 09:30	*Session 1: Opening Remarks*
09:30 - 10:30	*Invited Talk: Heng Ji*
10:30 - 11:00	*Break*
11:00 - 12:30	*Session 2: Applications*
12:30 - 14:00	*Lunch Break*
14:00 - 15:30	*Session 3: Discourse and Semantic Composition*
15:30 - 16:00	*Break*
16:00 - 17:30	*Session 4: In-Person Posters 1*

Friday, June 21, 2024

08:30 - 09:30	*Session 5: Virtual Poster Session*
09:30 - 10:30	*Invited Talk: Greg Durrett*
10:30 - 11:00	*Break*
11:00 - 12:30	*Session 6: Generation*
12:30 - 14:00	*Lunch Break*
14:00 - 15:30	*Session 7: In-Person Posters 2*
15:30 - 16:00	*Break*
16:00 - 17:00	*Session 8: Lexical Semantics and Closing Remarks*

MASSIVE Multilingual Abstract Meaning Representation: A Dataset and Baselines for Hallucination Detection

Michael Regan[†], **Shira Wein**[‡], **George Baker**[+], **Emilio Monti**[*]
[†]Paul G. Allen School of Computer Science & Engineering
[‡]Georgetown University
[+]University of Colorado Boulder
[*]Amazon, Cambridge, UK
mregan@cs.washington.edu,monti@amazon.co.uk

Abstract

Abstract Meaning Representation (AMR) is a semantic formalism that captures the core meaning of an utterance. There has been substantial work developing AMR corpora in English and more recently across languages, though the limited size of existing datasets and the cost of collecting more annotations are prohibitive. With both engineering and scientific questions in mind, we introduce MASSIVE-AMR, a dataset with more than 84,000 *text-to-graph annotations*, currently the largest and most diverse of its kind: AMR graphs for 1,685 information-seeking utterances mapped to 50+ typologically diverse languages. We describe how we built our resource and its unique features before reporting on experiments using large language models for multilingual AMR and SPARQL parsing as well as applying AMRs for hallucination detection in the context of knowledge base question answering, with results shedding light on persistent issues using LLMs for structured parsing.

1 Introduction

Knowledge base question answering (KBQA) has a long history in natural language processing, with the task of retrieving an answer from a knowledge base such as Wikidata or DBPedia (Lehmann et al., 2015) integral to many large-scale question answering systems (Kapanipathi et al., 2021). In KBQA, a question is converted into a structured query language such as SPARQL, an executable semantic parse. However, data to train models is expensive, few multilingual resources are available, and performance is limited for long-tail queries, a problem compounded by arbitrary variability in form-meaning mappings across languages (Croft, 2002).

Most notably, research in multilingual KBQA is hindered by lack of data (Usbeck et al., 2018; Cui et al., 2022; Perevalov et al., 2022). Following work using meaning representations for this problem, we create a dataset 20 times larger and with 5-6 times more languages than existing resources (Lee et al., 2022) (Table 1). For MASSIVE-AMR, we select 1685 QA utterances with manual translations from MASSIVE (FitzGerald et al., 2023) and manually compose Abstract Meaning Representation (AMR) graphs (Banarescu et al., 2013), amounting to 84,000 text-to-graph annotations, a significant boon to AMR and KBQA research.

	AMR3.0	QALD9-AMR	OURS
# of languages	1	9+	52
domain	various	QA	QA
# utterances	59K	508	1685
# utts-to-graphs	59K	5K	84K
mean tokens/utt	15.9	EN: 7.5	EN: 8.2
entities	-	not local	local
gold SPARQL	No	Yes	No

Table 1: Other AMR treebanks and ours, MASSIVE-AMR. Compared with QALD9-AMR (Lee et al., 2022), MASSIVE-AMR covers more languages, has more utterances, and has localized or translated entities for each language (see exs. Table 2).

Graphs with localized, language-specific entities (Table 2) and the long-tail utterances in MASSIVE-AMR (Appendix A.2) increase the challenge of our multilingual dataset (§3). To explore the resource's utility, we design and carry out experimentation leveraging AMRs to gauge a model's confidence in SPARQL query production (§4), reporting on multilingual structured parsing and SPARQL relation hallucination detection using large language models (LLMs) (§5).

Our research contributions thus include: (1) creation of the largest-scale multilingual AMR question corpus to date; (2) evaluation of LLMs on parsing of SPARQL and AMRs structures across languages; and (3) design, development, and evaluation of generative models leveraging AMRs for SPARQL relation hallucination detection.[1]

[1]We release the MASSIVE-AMR training and validation data at https://github.com/amazon-science/MASSIVE-AMR.

*Proceedings of the 13th Joint Conference on Lexical and Computational Semantics (*SEM 2024)*, pages 1 - 17
June 20-21, 2024

	Utterance	AMR
MASSIVE-AMR	when was obama born	(b / bear-02 :ARG1 (o / "obama") :time (u / unknown))
	quand est né sarkozy	(b / bear-02 :ARG1 (s / "sarkozy") :time (u / unknown))
	+50 langs.	+50 AMRs, local entities
QALD9-AMR	Who developed Skype? Qui a développé Skype?	(d / develop-02 :ARG0 (u / unknown) :ARG1 (s / "Skype"))
	9+ langs.	Same AMR, all langs.

Table 2: MASSIVE-AMR (top) has localized entities (English-US 'obama', French-FR 'sarkozy') and covers >5x more languages compared to QALD9-AMR (bottom). AMRs simplified to fit table.

2 Related Work

We present related work in QA, Knowledge base question answering (KBQA), the AMR formalism, AMRs for KBQA, and hallucination detection.

2.1 Question Answering

Question answering (QA) is the task of retrieving or predicting an answer to a natural language query given document(s), a list of answers, knowledge triples, or with a generative model. QA encompasses research in Information Retrieval (Lewis et al., 2020), Machine Reading Comprehension (MRC) (Das et al., 2018), and Open-Domain Question Answering (Lewis et al., 2021; Zhang et al., 2023). Research targeting model confidence for calibration of QA systems (Jiang et al., 2021; Kadavath et al., 2022) has aims similar to our own.

For research in multilingual dialogue systems, MASSIVE (FitzGerald et al., 2023) is a collection of 20K utterances with manual translations into 50+ typologically diverse languages (with 52 languages in v1.1). For our dataset, we select all QA utterances from MASSIVE and add AMR annotations (see Section 3).

2.2 Knowledge Base Question Answering

Knowledge base question answering (KBQA) is the task of retrieving answers from a knowledge base given a question. The challenges in retrieving textual information are fundamentally different from the primary challenge of KBQA: producing semantically accurate knowledge base queries.

Various approaches to KBQA have been proposed over the decades, including converting queries to logical forms, semantic parses, and decomposing complex questions (Zelle and Mooney, 1996; Zettlemoyer and Collins, 2005; Talmor and Berant, 2018). Scalable KBQA systems utilize structured representations (SPARQL) to query a knowledge base (e.g., DBPedia[2]), a collection of triples of form <subject, rel_j, object> with rel_j a semantic relation from ontology $\mathcal{R}$ (of various sizes, e.g., $|\mathcal{R}_{\text{DBPedia}}| > 2500$). Baselines for SPARQL parsing are available (Banerjee et al., 2022), with a central challenge being how to identify parsed queries not covered by a given $\mathcal{R}$, cases where models tend to hallucinate relations.

In the age of large language models, querying manually-curated knowledge bases provides numerous advantages such as: (1) factuality guarantees, (2) the ability to update information in real time, and (3) risk mitigation for users, reducing exposure to sensitive or toxic content. With these motivations in mind, we turn our attention to AMRs.

2.3 Abstract Meaning Representation

Abstract Meaning Representation (AMR) (Banarescu et al., 2013) is a linguistic formalism that represents utterance meaning as directed, mostly acyclic graphs. Graph nodes denote key concepts associated with the meaning of the utterance, targeting events and event participants. Nodes in turn are connected by labeled edges for event-event, event-entity, entity-entity, and other relations.

Early AMR research focused on text-to-AMR parsing, with the JAMR parser (Flanigan et al., 2014) paving the way for state-of-the-art models based on transitions (Drozdov et al., 2022), seq2seq approaches (Bevilacqua et al., 2021), and ensemble distillation (Lee et al., 2022). In lieu of such heavily engineered approaches, we target generative models with in-context learning and fine-tuning following recent work (Ettinger et al., 2023).

The original AMR reference-based metric is Smatch (Cai and Knight, 2013), a measure of overlapping triples, which has led to the newly optimized Smatch++ (Opitz, 2023) and S2match (Opitz et al., 2020) which uses embeddings to match concepts within triples. Wein and Schneider (2022) released multilingual AMR metrics such as XS2match using LaBSE embeddings (Feng et al., 2022) for cross-lingual AMR evaluation.

[2]https://www.dbpedia.org/

AMRs were not designed to function across languages (Banarescu et al., 2013), and while language has a measurable effect on AMR structure (Wein et al., 2022), efforts have been made to effectively represent the meaning of non-English sentences in AMRs (Xue et al., 2014; Hajič et al., 2014; Wein and Schneider, 2024). In typology, a Uniform Meaning Representation (Van Gysel et al., 2021) helps account for formal and semantic differences across languages more consistently than AMR, and work tying multilingual resources to a common formalism is ongoing (Navigli et al., 2022).

2.4 AMR for KBQA

Using symbolic representations for QA is well studied in NLP (Niu et al., 2023; Wang et al., 2023). A mapping of AMR nodes to SPARQL concepts and variables is shown to improve KBQA systems (Kapanipathi et al., 2021), and sequence-to-sequence models learn to apply these rules selectively for improved generalization (Bornea et al., 2022).

The multilingual QA resource most similar to ours is QALD9-AMR (Lee et al., 2022), which maps utterances from 9+ languages to the same English-only AMR and gold SPARQL queries (Usbeck et al., 2018). In comparison, graphs in MASSIVE-AMR consist of multilingual entities (Table 2) either translated or localized (e.g., a regional entity for where the language is spoken) for each of 50+ languages (Tables 2 and 3).

2.5 Hallucination detection

Hallucinations, the inclusion of flawed or incongruous assertions in synthetic text, represent a persistent problem with LLMs (Ji et al., 2023). Much research in hallucination detection targets the *text-to-text* paradigm, for example checking factuality or faithfulness of summarized texts (Gabriel et al., 2021; Qiu et al., 2023) or proposing mitigation strategies to make synthetic text attributable (Aksitov et al., 2023; Rashkin et al., 2023). In contrast, we examine *text-to-graph* systems that produce executable semantic parses, experimenting with AMRs to detect *easy* and *hard* cases of *semantic relation hallucination*, ranking parses of dual representation types in a joint space, as we will detail in Section 4.

3 Data: Corpus Creation

To create a corpus of multilingual AMR graphs, we started with an existing dataset of QA utterances, tailored AMR 3.0 guidelines to our use case, trained a team of professional annotators to create AMRs for English utterances, and then made automatic mappings to multilingual utterances using existing entity mention spans, a process which from start to finish took three months. In this section, we report details about the data we started with, guidelines, and annotation agreement scores.

Acquiring scaleable multilingual data. We wanted a resource targeting a wide distribution of QA utterances and thus selected 1685 English examples from MASSIVE (FitzGerald et al., 2023) including entity annotations like in the multilingual examples in Table 3.

Lang.	Example utterance
en-US	what is the population of [place: new york]
sl-SL	koliko prebivalcev ima [place: ljubljana]
it-IT	qual è la popolazione di [place: roma]
sq-AL	cila është popullësia e [place: tiranës]
cy-GB	beth yw poblogaeth [place: efrog newydd]
af-ZA	wat is die bevolking van [place: kaapstad]
is-IS	hver er íbúafjöldi [place: reykjavíkur]
az-AZ	[place: sumqayıtın] əhalisi nəqədərdir

Table 3: Example multilingual questions from MASSIVE (FitzGerald et al., 2023) about the populations of regional cities, with annotations for entity spans and types given.

Long-tail QA. Many utterances in MASSIVE are described as long-tail, that is, associated with low user feedback in interactions with a digital assistant. In some cases, it is clear what increases friction (an incomplete utterance, or a speech-to-text error). Examining translations of English utterances provides insight (Appendix A.2).

Localized entities. In comparable datasets (Cui et al., 2022; Perevalov et al., 2022), entities are shared across languages (e.g., English *Where did Abraham Lincoln die?* corresponds to German *Wo starb Abraham Lincoln?*). To address challenges of large-scale QA, MASSIVE entities are mostly language-specific, e.g. German questions target German entities (*wo starb otto von bismarck*[3]).

AMR datasets differ in composition: AMR 3.0 (Banarescu et al., 2013) is based on news and other written discourse and consists of relatively few factoid or information-seeking questions (less than 10%). In contrast, MASSIVE-AMR includes requests about currency conversions, quantities, comparative and superlatives, and simple arithmetic. For more details about how the corpora compare, see Appendix A and Table 11.

[3]MASSIVE utterances are uncased with no punctuation.

Annotation principles: Canonical forms. In keeping with original AMR guidelines, an AMR captures meaning, not form (Banarescu et al., 2019). We hence prefer canonical forms for utterances like currency conversion and arithmetic: e.g., 'how much is the euro versus the dollar' and 'what is the euro worth compared to the dollar' map to similar graphs. Likewise, arithmetic questions are associated with top node 'equal-01' even without token 'equal' present ('how much is two plus two' and 'sum of two and two' treated like 'what does two and two equal').

Question-imperative continuum. It proved difficult to reach agreement for annotations of question versus imperative forms. In English, 'could you tell me the price of google', 'what is the price of google', and 'tell me the price of google' share the same meaning. However, treating the imperative (e.g., an embedded question 'tell me what the price is') as a question is out-of-line with AMR 3.0. The guideline we adopt is to preserve imperative form and treat polite questions (e.g., English 'could you tell me the price') the same as base question forms (e.g., 'what is the price').

Annotation agreement scores. 4-5 trained annotators created AMRs for 1685 utterances, examining differences in batches of 200 weekly, with inter-annotator agreement ranging from 78-82% Smatch, comparable to reported agreement for AMR experts (Banarescu et al., 2013). We note that MASSIVE-AMR consists of many similar questions and simple utterances, with on average 50% fewer tokens compared to AMR 3.0 (Table 1). We select the single best AMR in candidate sets and manually retrofit to increase consistency.

For non-English entities, we replace AMR node labels using MASSIVE annotations. We note that not all utterances have annotations, and that a lack of entity alignments adds noise since often word order matters (e.g., currency conversion). To improve data quality, we manually curate validation and test sets (25% of total).

4 SPARQL Hallucination Detection

Our original motivation for creating a multilingual AMR dataset (§3) was to help improve large-scale QA systems. Scaleable QA systems often utilize structured representations (e.g., SPARQL) for knowledge base retrieval, pairing a natural language utterance with an executable semantic query. The SPARQL in the Wikidata or DBPedia case is straightforward: we get a question in, the system produces an answer out. However, in practice we simply need a system capable of judging if a given answer is correct, which using generative methods we study as *hallucination detection*.

Hallucinations. A problem in open-domain question-answering regards *hallucinations*, cases when effectively the target Ontology (in our case, DBPedia) does not have valid symbols for a given input question (see Figure 1). For example, if the relation 'crimeRate' does not exist, a SPARQL generation model may stumble on a question like 'What is the crime rate in LA?' by parsing a query with a non-existing relation, which we can verify with a set membership check. A harder case to detect is when the model predicts a relation for an utterance that is ambiguous, e.g., 'Who created Iron Man' may refer to its fictional (Tony Stark) or non-fictional (Stan Lee) creator. We would like to design and test methods for the detection of such cases using LLMs.

An advantage of AMR is that its ontology is open: i.e. if a given concept is missing, we can practically lemmatize the English. Or more often, AMR tends to be more granular, and more complex meanings (that in an Ontology might be collapsed into a single symbol) are split into several constituents (i.e. 'crimeRate' might be a single symbol in an Ontology, but it is instead split into constituents by AMR). Hence, hallucinations are much less of a problem in AMR.

We hypothesize that if we train a single semantic parser to parse both SPARQL and AMRs, simply mixing the training data (i.e. for multi-task learning), and produce multiple parse candidates in a target N-best, the inclusion of AMRs will allow us to detect SPARQL hallucinations. That is to say, a high confidence AMR and lower confidence SPARQL serve as a signal that a given utterance is not covered by an ontology or is in some way ambiguous, as in the examples in Figure 1.

We examine dual subtasks of SPARQL hallucination detection: (1) How accurate are models at the **easy** task of checking *set membership*, in our case, verifying produced relations are in a given relation set:

$$r_{pred} \overset{?}{\in} \mathcal{R}_{given}$$

and, (2) How good are models at flagging ambiguous queries (e.g., 'Who created Iron Man?'), the task of **hard** hallucination detection, detailed more in the next section.

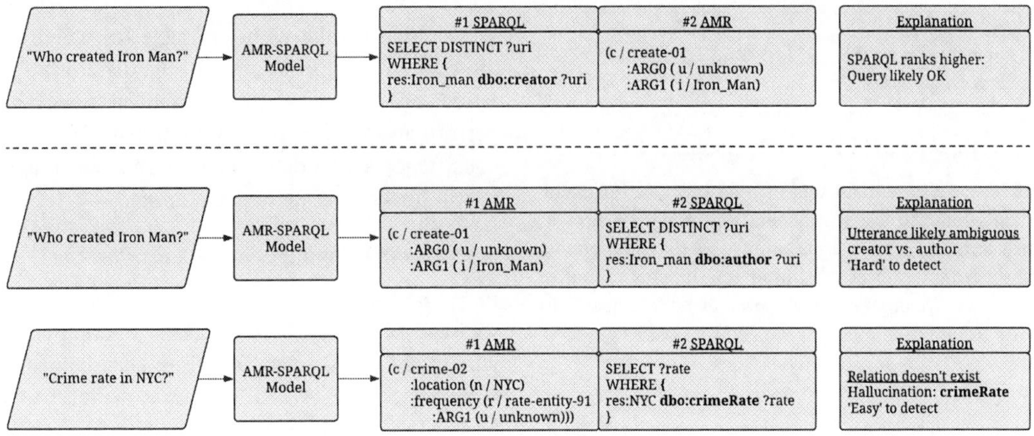

Figure 1: As a proxy for QA correctness, we test a joint AMR-SPARQL model, controlling for semantic relations (in **bold**). Given an utterance like *Who created Iron Man?*, a model outputs a N-best list of candidates of mixed representation types. When the relation **creator** is allowed (top), we expect the model to rank SPARQL higher than AMR. If the we change the ontology, the AMR may rank higher (middle), suggesting an ambiguity exists (**creator** $\approx$ **author**). Models also produce non-existent relations (bottom), detected via ranking or a look-up operation.

5 Experiments

To gain insight into our hypothesis that AMRs can help detect SPARQL relation hallucinations (§4), we first report on experiments in semantic representation parsing, a first-of-its-kind in a diverse multilingual setting. Next, we experimentally confirm models do indeed hallucinate relations, before moving on to our target task of hallucination detection. We compare in-context learning and fine-tuned LLMs, training and evaluating on an existing corpus of questions with gold AMRs and SPARQL and sampled MASSIVE-AMR. We are guided by the following **research questions**:

1. How effective are LLMs at parsing AMRs and SPARQL queries across languages?
2. How prevalent are SPARQL relation hallucinations with generative models?
3. How accurate are models at detecting hallucinated SPARQL relations?
4. Can we use a joint AMR-SPARQL model to do better relation hallucination detection?

The standard approach to study the coverage of a set of relations is use all the data associated with a relation set $\mathcal{R}$ to train semantic parser $SP_{\mathcal{R}}$; we then remove all examples that contain relation r_j and train $SP_{\{\mathcal{R}-r_j\}}$, measuring how well the model does for queries likely to require r_j.

An advantage of training a joint AMR-SPARQL model from scratch is having complete control over the input relations; a disadvantage is that, in the case we use a LLM, we have no knowledge about what relations the model may have seen in pretraining. For our early experiments, we use LLMs trained on 1000s of examples without hard constraints on allowed relations[4].

We define *hallucination detection* as the ability of an LLM to verify produced relations are members of a predefined set. We consider cases of *hard hallucination detection*, when a model produces a relation that may be imprecise, a case which occurs when the needed relation for a query is not covered by a given $\mathcal{R}$. For experiments, we compare in-context learning with fine-tuned LLMs.

5.1 In-context Learning

For in-context learning, we use GPT models (OpenAI, 2023) (GPT-3.5/GPT-4-0613) with prompts of length <2400 tokens (see Appendix C) composed employing strategies we describe in this section.

Strategy #1: Constrain and verify relations. Prompts include a list of allowed SPARQL relations with which we instruct the model to verify predicted relations. For in-context learning, we

[4] Ideally, this could be done at decoding time, setting logits of all non-relation tokens to `-inf` after a colon, an unambiguous signal of a SPARQL relation.

Relations	Subset descriptions
All observed	$\mathcal{R}_{\text{obs}}$
In-context	$\mathcal{R}_{\text{context}} \subset \mathcal{R}_{\text{obs}}$
Subsets similar	$\{\mathcal{R}_1^{\text{sim}}, \ldots, \mathcal{R}_j^{\text{sim}}\}, \mathcal{R}_i^{\text{sim}} \subset \mathcal{R}_{\text{obs}}$
Controlled	$r_{\text{cntl}} \in \mathcal{R}_i^{\text{sim}}, \notin \mathcal{R}_{\text{context}}$
Ground truth	$\{r_m, .., r_{\text{cntl}}, .., r_n\} \subset \mathcal{R}_{\text{obs}}$

Table 4: Different subsets of relations, $\mathcal{R}$, for experimentation. To test if a generation model adheres to instructions for allowed relations, we disallow one relation from a subset of similar relations as a control (4th row). We observe model performance for questions with ground truth relations we control (last row).

include eight examples of joint AMR-SPARQL predictions, with example hallucinations.

Strategy #2: Simulate missing relations. To control for relations (Table 4), we count DBPedia relations in QALD9-AMR training data, select the 140 more frequent relations, and set aside 1+ relations for utterances in prompt where the model should prefer AMR over SPARQL, ensuring examples abide by constraints. We define the more frequent relations as being observed >1 times, which is the case for about 50% of the data.

To test our *hard hallucination detection* hypothesis, we determine DBPedia relations to control for by manually grouping similar relations (e.g., 'creator,' 'writer,' and 'developer' are similar; Table 4, row 3) and select questions associated with any of these relations. We compare predictions allowing all relations versus the allowed list less the controlled relation (Table 4, row 4).

Strategy #3: Simulate ranking. We would like the model to rank without access to ground truth confidence scores, so we assign random confidence scores to in-context examples using a Dirichlet distribution (K=3), dropping the minimum value.[5] However, at decoding we consider only relative ranking, leaving a rigorous examination of confidence scores for future work.

Strategy #4: In-context examples of hallucination detection. Prompts (Appendix C) include cases of easy and hard hallucination detection, and we direct the model to specific cases where AMRs should rank higher.[6]

[5]The minimum value represents the probability density of bottom predictions in latent N-best ranking.

[6]The prompt reads: "Rank AMRs higher when predicted SPARQL is likely wrong, like in examples 5 and 8."

5.2 Additional Controls

We include results with an oracle, in which we direct the model's attention to the disallowed relation, providing an upper bound on achievable performance and giving insight into analysis. For consistency across datasets, we normalize all utterances (lower case, no punctuation).

5.3 Data: Language Subsets for Parsing

For experiments in AMR and SPARQL parsing, we identify a subset of languages: for comparison with QALD9, we select Indo-European languages from MASSIVE-AMR, the subset we refer to as **MASSIVE-**, and a more diverse sample with different scripts and less representation in Wikipedia, referred to as **MASSIVE+** (Table 5).

For structured parsing experiments using in-context learning, we sample about 100 utterances each from QALD9, MASSIVE-, and MASSIVE+ (e.g., the same 16 questions in 6 different languages), reporting average results across languages in each subset.

5.4 Fine-tuning

We fine-tune joint AMR-SPARQL models using publicly available LLMs: GPT-2-XL$_{\text{DISTILL}}$, a 1.5B parameter variant distilled on graph-structured knowledge (West et al., 2022) and LLaMA-13B (Touvron et al., 2023); for model fine-tuning details, consult Appendix B. For a challenging test set, we select same-sized samples from QALD9 and MASSIVE-AMR (900 each) of the same Indo-European languages (namely: English, Spanish, German, French, and Russian).

5.5 Evaluation Guidelines

For AMR parsing, we report Smatch (Cai and Knight, 2013), while for SPARQL we check (1) query executability (using the Python SPARQLWrapper) and (2) whether the query returns an answer from DBPedia. We do not check answer factuality, as our objective is to measure model confidence in semantic parse correctness, not the model's knowledge of the contents of a given knowledge base (given that knowledge bases change over time and many local entities do not have a DBPedia entry, for example).

For hallucination detection experiments using in-context learning, we employ quantitative and qualitative means of analysis. For perturbed examples (i.e., parse a query for a question likely to

	Language	# speakers	# Wiki pgs
QALD9/MASSIVE-	English	1.5b	58.7m
	French	320m	12.6m
	Russian	258m	7.7m
	German	76.5m	7.8m
	Italian	66m	7.7m
	Lithuanian	2.8m	0.5m
MASSIVE+	Vietnamese	85.2m	19.4m
	Japanese	125m	4.0m
	Korean	81.7m	3.1m
	Hungarian	8.2m	1.5m
	Urdu	91.5m	1.0m
	Amharic	31m	15k
	Azeri	24m	195k
	Finnish	5.1m	1.4m

Table 5: For AMR and SPARQL parsing, we assemble test sets selecting utterances from two subsets of languages: (1) The presumably easier subset MASSIVE- (top) covering the same Indo-European languages as QALD9, and (2) the more diverse MASSIVE+ (bottom), e.g., targeting different writing systems. Statistics are estimates, based on `https://meta.wikimedia.org/wiki/List_of_Wikipedias` and Google search results.

	Model	Data	Smatch ↑
Few-shot/EN	GPT-3.5	MASSIVE-EN	$0.43_{\pm 0.20}$
		QALD9-EN	$0.57_{\pm 0.17}$
	GPT-4	MASSIVE-EN	$0.53_{\pm 0.21}$
		QALD9-EN	$0.70_{\pm 0.16}$
Few-shot/non-EN	GPT-3.5	MASSIVE+	$0.33_{\pm 0.22}$
		MASSIVE-	$0.42_{\pm 0.20}$
		QALD9	$0.44_{\pm 0.20}$
	GPT-4	MASSIVE+	$0.46_{\pm 0.21}$
		MASSIVE-	$0.49_{\pm 0.20}$
		QALD9	$0.58_{\pm 0.22}$
SOTA	MBSE	QALD9-EN	0.90
		AMR 3.0	0.84

Table 6: AMR parsing results by model, dataset, and language subset, comparing in-context learning (top and middle) with SOTA (Lee et al., 2022) (bottom). Overall, in-context learning is less effective than more engineered approaches.

require a known disallowed relation), a predicted ranking is good if the model: (1) ranks the AMR higher, (2) ranks the SPARQL higher yet verifies the relation is not allowed, or (3) produces a valid alternative SPARQL. We stratify results by dataset, check executability and whether the query returns an existing record, and also evaluate manually.

For fine-tuned joint AMR-SPARQL, we use a diverse beam search (n=5) and different methods to determine relative ranking: (1) check the top-ranked produced sequence, (2) count the majority structure in the N-best ranking, and (3) compare transition scores for the first token produced.[7] Our hypothesis is models will prefer SPARQL over AMR for QALD9 and vice versa for MASSIVE-AMR. This is a reasonable hypothesis, as all QALD9 is known to be matched with ground truth SPARQL, while fewer queries in MASSIVE-AMR are likely convertible into an executable query, an assumption we assess qualitatively (Appendix A.2).

For evaluation, models output a queryable object (JSON) with three key-value pairs: parsed query, list of relations in query, and list of relation verifications (boolean values) (see Appendix C), with very few structural errors observed (<1% in our studies).

[7] Either 'AMR' or 'SPARQL,' or the first sub-token therein.

5.6 Results

We present results on in-context learning for AMR parsing (Table 6) and SPARQL queries (Table 7) across languages, report on SPARQL hallucinations (Table 8), followed by results in hallucination detection using in-context joint models (Table 9), as well as fine-tuned joint models (Table 10).

5.7 Analysis and Discussion

For **AMR parsing** (Research question 1), results (Table 6, examples and error analysis in Appendix D) show that state-of-the-art AMR systems still outperform in-context learning with margins between 10-20%, a display of the strengths of engineered modular systems, data augmentation, and AMR post-processing. Comparing few-shot models, GPT-4 outperforms GPT-3.5 by a margin of 10-13% F1, with performance on QALD9 14-17% F1 higher than MASSIVE-AMR, evidence of the challenge of the latter. Models perform 5-12% F1 higher for MASSIVE- compared to more diverse MASSIVE+ (see Section 5.3), the first reported AMR results we are aware of for many of these languages.

SPARQL parsing. Results of SPARQL query parsing with in-context learning (Table 7, examples in Appendix E) provide evidence that LLMs perform well in a few-shot setting, exceeding 90% F1 in executability across datasets and languages. However, as LLMs are not trained on up-to-date data, no more than 52% of queries for QALD9 and 32% of MASSIVE-AMR return existing DBPedia records. Additionally, models display good perfor-

	Data	Exec. ↑	Returns ↑
GPT-3.5	MASSIVE+	0.93	0.32
	MASSIVE-	0.94	0.41
	QALD9	0.97	0.53
GPT-4	MASSIVE+	0.94	0.34
	MASSIVE-	0.99	0.50
	QALD9	1.00	0.52

Table 7: Few-shot SPARQL parsing results across datasets and models. We report executability and how many return existing records. Overall, models produce structurally viable SPARQL across languages.

	Data	Perturb	#Utts	Halluc. ↓	Detects ↑
GPT-3.5	MASSIVE+	No	38	0.21	0.0
		Yes	62	**0.71**	0.04
	MASSIVE-	No	38	0.16	0.0
		Yes	62	**0.59**	0.0
	QALD9	No	110	0.22	0.09
		Yes	110	**0.84**	0.0
GPT-4	MASSIVE+	No	34	0.06	0.50
		Yes	66	**0.48**	0.09
	MASSIVE-	No	36	0.0	n/a
		Yes	64	**0.54**	0.14
	QALD9	No	50	0.04	0.0
		Yes	50	**0.46**	0.08

Table 8: Rates of SPARQL hallucination and hallucination detection with a SPARQL-only model. When we perturb a relation, hallucination is high, that is, models produce top-ranked queries with disallowed relations; in all settings, detection rates (gray) are consistently poor, that is models fail to verify relations are allowed or not.

mance for MASSIVE+, where AMR performance was observed to decrease, evidence that LLMs have more knowledge of SPARQL than AMR structures.

SPARQL relation hallucination rates (Research question 2). In Table 8, we examine if: (1) models hallucinate SPARQL relations when we remove some relations from an allowed list, and (2) models also can detect cases of generated relations not being allowed (i.e. hallucinations). In a nutshell, results confirm all models often hallucinate relations and yet fail at detection consistently.

Specifically, we find that under normal, non-perturbed conditions across languages (odd rows of Table 8), GPT-3.5 exhibits hallucination rates between 16-22%, which GPT-4 reduces to 0-6%. When we disallow a relation likely to be needed in the query (rows where Perturb=**Yes**), hallucination rates increase considerably: for GPT-3.5 to between 40-60%, and for GPT-4 between 42-54%.

Hallucination detection, non-joint model. With 2-shot SPARQL query parsing, models show poor rates of hallucination detection (Table 8), with GPT-4 detecting no more than 14% of all hallucinations. In a vast majority of cases (86-100%, gray column), models are deceptive, incorrectly reporting that disallowed relations are allowed (Ex. 2 in Appendix E), providing us with justification to test if we can do better with a joint AMR-SPARQL model.

Model	Oracle	#Perturb	Halluc. ↓	Detects ↑
GPT-3.5	no	60/120	0.58	0.07
GPT-4	no	60/120	0.39	0.17
GPT-4	yes	150/240	0.31	0.76

Table 9: Results of joint AMR-SPARQL detection with in-context learning (8-shot, GPTs), targeting 140 SPARQL relations and 8 languages. Hallucination occurs in at least 1 in 3 cases, and hallucination detection is not effective, except with an oracle (last row).

Hallucination detection, in-context joint model (Research question 3). Overall, in-context learning for hallucination detection is quite challenging. With oracle knowledge of which relation has been disallowed (Table 9), GPT-4 still misreports 24% of cases.

Nevertheless, we find evidence that GPT-4 with an oracle employs dual hallucination detection strategies in some cases: for 1 in 5 hallucinations, the model ranks AMRs higher, and, for 3 of 5, it parses queries with disallowed relations which it accurately verifies as non-existent.

Without an oracle, the rate of *deception* (i.e. *not* detecting a hallucinated relation) exceeds 80% in both cases tested, which proved challenging to overcome despite multiple prompt variations, including promised rewards for sticking to allowed relations, veiled (and unveiled) threats, repeated warnings, and legalese which bound the model to abide by restrictions, tactics the models consistently disregarded, suggesting space for future research into LLM confidence measures for QA as well as structural integrity metrics for a semantic critic.

Considering cases of ambiguous utterances (*hard hallucination detection*), GPT-4 mostly follows the rules (e.g., perhaps parsing ‘creator’ when disallowed for ‘who created iron man’ but verifying correctly the relation is fallacious). However, it is difficult in many cases to qualitatively determine query plausibility for various other relations parsed, as the correctness of any of a large range of queries that models actually produce depends on the target knowledge base, left implicit in our experiments.

Model	Langs.	Data	Top1	Top5	Token1
$\text{GPT2}_{\text{DISTILL}}$	EN	QALD9	0.50 ×	0.68 ✓	0.83 ✓
		MASSIVE-AMR	0.58	0.62	0.80
	Non-EN	QALD9	0.53 ×	0.55 ×	0.74 ✓
		MASSIVE-AMR	0.54	0.54	0.70
LLaMa-13B	EN	QALD9	0.82 ✓	0.95 ×	0.90 ~
		MASSIVE-AMR	0.76	0.95	0.88
	Non-EN	QALD9	0.78 ×	0.95 ×	0.82 ×
		MASSIVE-AMR	0.88	0.98	0.95

Table 10: The proportion of cases models prefer SPARQL over AMR structures for QALD9 and MASSIVE-AMR, comparing fine-tuned $\text{GPT2-xl}_{\text{DISTILL}}$ (top) and Llama-13B (bottom) with English (EN) and non-English data. The hypothesis in each case is that models will prefer SPARQL for QALD9, with a (✓) indicating evidence in support. Results from preliminary studies are overall inconclusive.

Hallucination detection, fine-tuned joint models (Research question 4). Results of fine-tuned models are inconclusive (Table 10). With $\text{GPT-2-XL}_{\text{distill}}$, preference between SPARQL vs AMR is mostly 50-50, with variation only observed with first token transition scores. LLaMa, in contrast, shows bias towards SPARQL under every condition (between 75-95%), and only in one setting (top-1) favoring SPARQL consistently for QALD9. Qualitative analysis shows LLaMa prefers AMR for incomplete utterances such as 'describe' and 'calculate this', yet it often misclassifies currency conversion utterances as having valid SPARQL.[8]

With our fine-tuned models, we examined an N-best space from multiple perspectives (top-1 prediction, majority, transition scores). We speculate that the proportion of AMRs versus SPARQL in fine-tuning likely has an effect: in our experiments, we include more AMRs than SPARQL (Appendix B), suggesting a study with varied proportions of training data is warranted as well as training with more data (we used <6k examples in fine-tuning).

6 Conclusion

We present MASSIVE-AMR, the largest and most diverse dataset of multilingual questions paired with Abstract Meaning Representation (AMR) graphs, which we publicly release for research purposes. We discuss the origins of the data, and detail the processes of dataset creation, curation, and quality control.

[8] In principle, currency conversion values could be stored in a knowledge base, but in practice knowledge bases are not updated in real-time.

To examine the utility of our dataset in controlled experimentation using large language models, we first consider the task of **structure parsing**, showing results for both AMR graph and SPARQL query parsing across languages. Overall, performance for AMR parsing with in-context learning is less effective compared with reported state-of-the-art using fine-tuning; still, qualitative assessment of produced structures reveals many coherent, correct graphs despite low similarity with a ground truth. In comparison, SPARQL parsing performance is high across languages, at least in small studies using the QALD9-AMR dataset.

One motivating factor behind the creation of MASSIVE-AMR was to be able to test the utility of AMRs for knowledge base question answering (KBQA), specifically ascertaining whether AMRs can help **detect incongruous SPARQL queries**, essentially serving as a proxy confidence measure for the correctness of an answer suggested by a QA system. In these experiments, we first confirm that the GPT models do indeed hallucinate semantic relations, and then discover that 'easy' hallucination detection—asking a model to verify relations are allowed—is actually quite challenging, even for GPT-4. Further, 'hard' hallucination detection—the identification of utterances that are likely ambiguous—is *also* challenging, with a joint AMR-SPARQL model only detecting 1 in 5 cases.

Beyond the AMR-for-KBQA investigations we performed in this work, we hope that the release of MASSIVE-AMR will support additional research into using structured meaning representations for multilingual QA and model interpretability.

7 Acknowledgements

We would like to thank Jack FitzGerald for help with the data and comments on early drafts, Nathan Schneider for feedback on writing and overall project clarity, and Meagan Vigus for thinking about data collection and discussing typological questions with us. We are grateful to Amazon Cambridge linguists and engineers Isabel Groves, Elizabeth Schett, Daraksha Parveen, and Wei-Wei Cheng for help building the dataset and compiling annotation guidelines. Our special thanks to the anonymous reviewers for insightful questions and critique helping us to achieve a more reader-friendly and scientific presentation of ideas. This work was supported through funding from Amazon and DARPA I2O (RA-21-02).

8 Ethical Considerations

Informed Consent: We ensured that all individuals providing annotations were fully informed about the purpose of the annotation task, how their data will be used, and what rights they have in relation to their data.

Fair Compensation: We ensured that individuals providing annotations were fairly compensated for their time and effort. For this project, professional annotators were compensated at least $30/hour, working between 20-80 hours each for the duration of data collection.

Transparency: We were transparent about the purpose and scope of the annotation task, as well as the potential benefits of the project, helping to build trust with individuals providing annotations and ensuring that they understood the significance of their contributions. We intend that through these practices data annotation efforts are overall more effective, resulting in a higher quality resource.

Environmental impact: We considered the environmental impact of the research, including the energy consumption of computing resources used. With GPT-4 inference, we limited input to 100s of examples to reduce costs. In-house fine-tuning was done using parameter efficient fine-tuning methods, allowing each experiment to be done on 1-2 NVIDIA Quadro RTX 8000 GPUs in <24 hours.

9 Limitations

1. Our work involved research into multilingual SPARQL and AMR parsing; though our dataset includes 52 languages, we report results on no more than 10-12 of these. Many of the languages we included are Indo-European, with only a few exceptions (Korean, Japanese, Amharic, Vietnamese).

2. No experiments in joint AMR-SPARQL parsing involved hypotheses about performance across languages, though some evidence of performance shifts has been observed.

3. Fine-tuning models was done with less than 6k AMRs and 3-4k SPARQL training examples. Test data was limited to 100s examples per language in order to allow for multiple iterations and explore hyperparameter settings. Increasing the sizes of training and test sets is left for future work.

4. Testing was limited to four large language models in this work (GPT-2-$XL_{distill}$, GPT-3.5, GPT-4, LLaMa). LLaMa does include multilingual data in training (Touvron et al., 2023), particularly languages using Latin and Cyrillic scripts. We did not test models explicitly trained for multilingual purposes and for other scripts, leaving such work for the future.

5. The MASSIVE-AMR dataset matches multilingual utterances to unique AMR graphs, making it the largest such dataset to date. However, unlike QALD9-AMR (Lee et al., 2022), MASSIVE-AMR does not include gold SPARQL queries. We emphasize that the use case we explore in this paper is only one of many possible, and we hope future research explores beyond this single application.

10 Bibliographical References

References

Renat Aksitov, Chung-Ching Chang, David Reitter, Siamak Shakeri, and Yunhsuan Sung. 2023. Characterizing attribution and fluency tradeoffs for retrieval-augmented large language models. *arXiv:2302.05578.*

Laura Banarescu, Claire Bonial, Shu Cai, Madalina Georgescu, Kira Griffitt, Ulf Hermjakob, Kevin Knight, Philipp Koehn, Martha Palmer, and Nathan Schneider. 2013. Abstract Meaning Representation for sembanking. In *Proceedings of the 7th Linguistic Annotation Workshop and Interoperability with Discourse*, pages 178–186, Sofia, Bulgaria. Association for Computational Linguistics.

Laura Banarescu, Claire Bonial, Shu Cai, Madalina Georgescu, Kira Griffitt, Ulf Hermjakob, Kevin Knight, Philipp Koehn, Martha Palmer, and Nathan Schneider. 2019. Abstract Meaning Representation (AMR) 1.2.6 specification. `https://github.com/amrisi/amr-guidelines/blob/master/amr.md`.

Debayan Banerjee, Pranav Ajit Nair, Jivat Neet Kaur, Ricardo Usbeck, and Chris Biemann. 2022. Modern baselines for SPARQL semantic parsing. In *Proceedings of the 45th International ACM SIGIR Conference on Research and Development in Information Retrieval*. ACM.

Michele Bevilacqua, Rexhina Blloshmi, and Roberto Navigli. 2021. One SPRING to rule them both: Symmetric AMR semantic parsing and generation without a complex pipeline. In *Proceedings of AAAI*.

Mihaela Bornea, Ramon Fernandez Astudillo, Tahira Naseem, Nandana Mihindukulasooriya, Ibrahim Abdelaziz, Pavan Kapanipathi, Radu Florian, and Salim Roukos. 2022. Learning to transpile amr into sparql. *arXiv:2112.07877.*

Shu Cai and Kevin Knight. 2013. Smatch: an evaluation metric for semantic feature structures. In *Proceedings of the 51st Annual Meeting of the Association for Computational Linguistics*, pages 748–752, Sofia, Bulgaria. Association for Computational Linguistics.

William Croft. 2002. *Typology and Universals*. Cambridge Textbooks in Linguistics. Cambridge University Press.

Ruixiang Cui, Rahul Aralikatte, Heather Lent, and Daniel Hershcovich. 2022. Compositional Generalization in Multilingual Semantic Parsing over Wikidata. *Transactions of the Association for Computational Linguistics*, 10:937–955.

Rajarshi Das, Tsendsuren Munkhdalai, Xingdi Yuan, Adam Trischler, and Andrew McCallum. 2018. Building dynamic knowledge graphs from text using machine reading comprehension. *arXiv:1810.05682*.

Andrew Drozdov, Jiawei Zhou, Radu Florian, Andrew McCallum, Tahira Naseem, Yoon Kim, and Ramón Astudillo. 2022. Inducing and using alignments for transition-based AMR parsing. In *Proceedings of the 2022 Conference of the North American Chapter of the Association for Computational Linguistics: Human Language Technologies*, pages 1086–1098, Seattle, United States. Association for Computational Linguistics.

Allyson Ettinger, Jena Hwang, Valentina Pyatkin, Chandra Bhagavatula, and Yejin Choi. 2023. "You are an expert linguistic annotator": Limits of LLMs as analyzers of Abstract Meaning Representation. In *Findings of the Association for Computational Linguistics: EMNLP 2023*, pages 8250–8263, Singapore. Association for Computational Linguistics.

Fangxiaoyu Feng, Yinfei Yang, Daniel Cer, Naveen Arivazhagan, and Wei Wang. 2022. Language-agnostic BERT Sentence Embedding. In *Proceedings of the 60th Annual Meeting of the Association for Computational Linguistics (Volume 1: Long Papers)*, pages 878–891, Dublin, Ireland. Association for Computational Linguistics.

Jack FitzGerald, Christopher Hench, Charith Peris, Scott Mackie, Kay Rottmann, Ana Sanchez, Aaron Nash, Liam Urbach, Vishesh Kakarala, Richa Singh, Swetha Ranganath, Laurie Crist, Misha Britan, Wouter Leeuwis, Gokhan Tur, and Prem Natarajan. 2023. MASSIVE: A 1M-example multilingual natural language understanding dataset with 51 typologically-diverse languages. In *Proceedings of the 61st Annual Meeting of the Association for Computational Linguistics (Volume 1: Long Papers)*, pages 4277–4302, Toronto, Canada. Association for Computational Linguistics.

Jeffrey Flanigan, Sam Thomson, Jaime Carbonell, Chris Dyer, and Noah A. Smith. 2014. A discriminative graph-based parser for the Abstract Meaning Representation. In *Proceedings of the 52nd Annual Meeting of the Association for Computational Linguistics (Volume 1: Long Papers)*, pages 1426–1436, Baltimore, Maryland. Association for Computational Linguistics.

Saadia Gabriel, Asli Celikyilmaz, Rahul Jha, Yejin Choi, and Jianfeng Gao. 2021. GO FIGURE: A meta evaluation of factuality in summarization. In *Findings of the Association for Computational Linguistics: ACL-IJCNLP 2021*, pages 478–487, Online. Association for Computational Linguistics.

Jan Hajič, Ondřej Bojar, and Zdeňka Urešová. 2014. Comparing Czech and English AMRs. In *Proceedings of Workshop on Lexical and Grammatical Resources for Language Processing*, pages 55–64, Dublin, Ireland. Association for Computational Linguistics and Dublin City University.

Ziwei Ji, Nayeon Lee, Rita Frieske, Tiezheng Yu, Dan Su, Yan Xu, Etsuko Ishii, Ye Jin Bang, Andrea Madotto, and Pascale Fung. 2023. Survey of hallucination in natural language generation. *ACM Comput. Surv.*, 55(12).

Zhengbao Jiang, Jun Araki, Haibo Ding, and Graham Neubig. 2021. How Can We Know When Language Models Know? On the Calibration of Language Models for Question Answering. *Transactions of the Association for Computational Linguistics*, 9:962–977.

Saurav Kadavath, Tom Conerly, Amanda Askell, Tom Henighan, Dawn Drain, Ethan Perez, Nicholas Schiefer, Zac Hatfield-Dodds, Nova DasSarma, Eli Tran-Johnson, Scott Johnston, Sheer El-Showk, Andy Jones, Nelson Elhage, Tristan Hume, Anna Chen, Yuntao Bai, Sam Bowman, Stanislav Fort, Deep Ganguli, Danny Hernandez, Josh Jacobson, Jackson Kernion, Shauna Kravec, Liane Lovitt, Kamal Ndousse, Catherine Olsson, Sam Ringer, Dario Amodei, Tom Brown, Jack Clark, Nicholas Joseph, Ben Mann, Sam McCandlish, Chris Olah, and Jared Kaplan. 2022. Language models (mostly) know what they know. *arXiv*.

Pavan Kapanipathi, Ibrahim Abdelaziz, Srinivas Ravishankar, Salim Roukos, Alexander Gray, Ramón Fernandez Astudillo, Maria Chang, Cristina Cornelio, Saswati Dana, Achille Fokoue, Dinesh Garg, Alfio Gliozzo, Sairam Gurajada, Hima Karanam, Naweed Khan, Dinesh Khandelwal, Young-Suk Lee, Yunyao Li, Francois Luus, Ndivhuwo Makondo, Nandana Mihindukulasooriya, Tahira Naseem, Sumit Neelam, Lucian Popa, Revanth Gangi Reddy, Ryan Riegel, Gaetano Rossiello, Udit Sharma, G P Shrivatsa Bhargav, and Mo Yu. 2021. Leveraging Abstract Meaning Representation for knowledge base question answering. In *Findings of the Association for Computational Linguistics: ACL-IJCNLP 2021*, pages 3884–3894, Online. Association for Computational Linguistics.

Young-Suk Lee, Ramón Astudillo, Hoang Thanh Lam, Tahira Naseem, Radu Florian, and Salim Roukos. 2022. Maximum Bayes Smatch ensemble distillation for AMR parsing. In *Proceedings of the 2022*

Conference of the North American Chapter of the Association for Computational Linguistics: Human Language Technologies, pages 5379–5392, Seattle, United States. ACL.

Jens Lehmann, Robert Isele, Max Jakob, Anja Jentzsch, Dimitris Kontokostas, Pablo N. Mendes, Sebastian Hellmann, Mohamed Morsey, Patrick van Kleef, Sören Auer, and Christian Bizer. 2015. DBpedia - a large-scale, multilingual knowledge base extracted from wikipedia. *Semantic Web Journal*, 6(2):167–195.

Patrick Lewis, Ethan Perez, Aleksandra Piktus, Fabio Petroni, Vladimir Karpukhin, Naman Goyal, Heinrich Küttler, Mike Lewis, Wen-tau Yih, Tim Rocktäschel, Sebastian Riedel, and Douwe Kiela. 2020. Retrieval-augmented generation for knowledge-intensive nlp tasks. In *Advances in Neural Information Processing Systems*, volume 33, pages 9459–9474. Curran Associates, Inc.

Patrick Lewis, Pontus Stenetorp, and Sebastian Riedel. 2021. Question and answer test-train overlap in open-domain question answering datasets. In *Proceedings of the 16th Conference of the European Chapter of the Association for Computational Linguistics: Main Volume*, pages 1000–1008, Online. Association for Computational Linguistics.

Roberto Navigli, Rexhina Blloshmi, and Abelardo Martinez Lorenzo. 2022. Babelnet Meaning Representation: A fully semantic formalism to overcome language barriers. In *Proceedings of the AAAI Conference on Artificial Intelligence*.

Yilin Niu, Fei Huang, Wei Liu, Jianwei Cui, Bin Wang, and Minlie Huang. 2023. Bridging the gap between synthetic and natural questions via sentence decomposition for semantic parsing. *Transactions of the Association for Computational Linguistics*, 11:367–383.

OpenAI. 2023. Gpt-4 technical report. *arXiv:2303.08774*.

Juri Opitz. 2023. SMATCH++: Standardized and extended evaluation of semantic graphs. In *Findings of the Association for Computational Linguistics: EACL 2023*, pages 1595–1607, Dubrovnik, Croatia. Association for Computational Linguistics.

Juri Opitz, Letitia Parcalabescu, and Anette Frank. 2020. AMR similarity metrics from principles. *Transactions of the Association for Computational Linguistics*, 8:522–538.

Aleksandr Perevalov, Dennis Diefenbach, Ricardo Usbeck, and Andreas Both. 2022. Qald-9-plus: A multilingual dataset for question answering over dbpedia and wikidata translated by native speakers. In *2022 IEEE 16th International Conference on Semantic Computing (ICSC)*.

Yifu Qiu, Yftah Ziser, Anna Korhonen, Edoardo Ponti, and Shay Cohen. 2023. Detecting and mitigating hallucinations in multilingual summarisation. In *Proceedings of the 2023 Conference on Empirical Methods in Natural Language Processing*, pages 8914–8932, Singapore. Association for Computational Linguistics.

Hannah Rashkin, Vitaly Nikolaev, Matthew Lamm, Lora Aroyo, Michael Collins, Dipanjan Das, Slav Petrov, Gaurav Singh Tomar, Iulia Turc, and David Reitter. 2023. Measuring Attribution in Natural Language Generation Models. *Computational Linguistics*, pages 1–64.

Alon Talmor and Jonathan Berant. 2018. The web as a knowledge-base for answering complex questions. In *Proceedings of the 2018 Conference of the North American Chapter of the Association for Computational Linguistics: Human Language Technologies, Volume 1 (Long Papers)*, pages 641–651, New Orleans, Louisiana. Association for Computational Linguistics.

Hugo Touvron, Thibaut Lavril, Gautier Izacard, Xavier Martinet, Marie-Anne Lachaux, Timothée Lacroix, Baptiste Rozière, Naman Goyal, Eric Hambro, Faisal Azhar, Aurelien Rodriguez, Armand Joulin, Edouard Grave, and Guillaume Lample. 2023. Llama: Open and efficient foundation language models. *arXiv:2302.13971*.

Ricardo Usbeck, Ria Gusmita, Axel-Cyrille Ngonga Ngomo, and Muhammad Saleem. 2018. 9th challenge on question answering over linked data (qald-9). In *Joint proceedings of the 4th Workshop on Semantic Deep Learning (SemDeep-4) and NLIWoD4*.

Jens Van Gysel, Meagan Vigus, Jayeol Chun, Kenneth Lai, Sarah Moeller, Jiarui Yao, Tim O'Gorman, Andrew Cowell, William Croft, Chu-Ren Huang, Jan Hajič, James Martin, Stephan Oepen, Martha Palmer, James Pustejovsky, Rosa Vallejos, and Nianwen Xue. 2021. Designing a uniform meaning representation for natural language processing. *Künstliche Intelligenz*.

Cunxiang Wang, Zhikun Xu, Qipeng Guo, Xiangkun Hu, Xuefeng Bai, Zheng Zhang, and Yue Zhang. 2023. Exploiting Abstract Meaning Representation for open-domain question answering. In *Findings of the Association for Computational Linguistics: ACL 2023*, pages 2083–2096, Toronto, Canada. Association for Computational Linguistics.

Shira Wein, Wai Ching Leung, Yifu Mu, and Nathan Schneider. 2022. Effect of source language on AMR structure. In *Proceedings of the 16th Linguistic Annotation Workshop (LAW-XVI) within LREC2022*, pages 97–102, Marseille, France. European Language Resources Association.

Shira Wein and Nathan Schneider. 2022. Accounting for language effect in the evaluation of cross-lingual AMR parsers. In *Proceedings of the 29th International Conference on Computational Linguistics*, pages 3824–3834, Gyeongju, Republic of Korea. International Committee on Computational Linguistics.

Shira Wein and Nathan Schneider. 2024. Assessing the Cross-linguistic Utility of Abstract Meaning Representation. *Computational Linguistics*, pages 1–55.

Peter West, Chandra Bhagavatula, Jack Hessel, Jena Hwang, Liwei Jiang, Ronan Le Bras, Ximing Lu, Sean Welleck, and Yejin Choi. 2022. Symbolic knowledge distillation: from general language models to commonsense models. In *Proceedings of the 2022 Conference of the North American Chapter of the Association for Computational Linguistics: Human Language Technologies*, pages 4602–4625, Seattle, United States. Association for Computational Linguistics.

Nianwen Xue, Ondřej Bojar, Jan Hajič, Martha Palmer, Zdeňka Urešová, and Xiuhong Zhang. 2014. Not an interlingua, but close: Comparison of English AMRs to Chinese and Czech. In *Proceedings of the Ninth International Conference on Language Resources and Evaluation (LREC'14)*, pages 1765–1772, Reykjavik. European Language Resources Association.

John M. Zelle and Raymond J. Mooney. 1996. Learning to parse database queries using inductive logic programming. In *Proceedings of the Thirteenth National Conference on Artificial Intelligence - Volume 2*, AAAI'96, page 1050–1055. AAAI Press.

Luke S. Zettlemoyer and Michael Collins. 2005. Learning to map sentences to logical form: Structured classification with probabilistic categorial grammars. In *Proceedings of the Twenty-First Conference on Uncertainty in Artificial Intelligence*, UAI'05, page 658–666, Arlington, Virginia, USA. AUAI Press.

Qin Zhang, Shangsi Chen, Dongkuan Xu, Qingqing Cao, Xiaojun Chen, Trevor Cohn, and Meng Fang. 2023. A survey for efficient open domain question answering. In *Proceedings of the 61st Annual Meeting of the Association for Computational Linguistics (Volume 1: Long Papers)*, pages 14447–14465, Toronto, Canada. Association for Computational Linguistics.

11 Appendices

A Characterizing Massive-AMR

A.1 AMR Top Nodes Across Datasets

AMR 3.0	#	QALD9-AMR	#	MASSIVE-AMR	#
and	7k	give-01	76	rate-01	105
say-01	3k	have-03	50	define-01	103
contrast-01	3k	have-degree	27	tell-01	94
multi-sentence	1.7k	have-org-role	21	have-quant	87
possible-01	1.7k	be-located-at	15	equal-01	86
cause-01	1.6k	die-01	14	price-01	70
state-01	1.5k	write-01	14	describe-01	66
have-concession	944	bear-02	13	be-located-at	64
think-01	901	marry-01	13	person	58
person	705	show-01	12	mean-01	50
have-03	618	locate-01	10	have-degree	50
have-condition	605	have-rel-role	10	bear-02	46
date-entity	538	person	9	have-org-role	32
know-01	451	name-01	9	show-01	21
have-degree	440	list-01	8	find-01	21

Table 11: 15 most frequent top AMR nodes in AMR 3.0, QALD9-AMR and MASSIVE-AMR, with counts for a single language (English).

A.2 Describing the MASSIVE Long Tail

We note long-tail characteristics of utterances in MASSIVE (FitzGerald et al., 2023).

- Outliers in terms of utterance length: some 1-2 tokens, others quite long (40+ tokens)
- Ambiguous referents ('chase' in 'is chase doing good' could be a bank, person, or activity)
- Incomplete arithmetic ('tell me what equals two three')
- Less frequent expressions ('who is the better half of obama')
- Incomplete questions ('synonym for word', 'is equal to', 'research someone')

B Model Details

For experiments in joint AMR-SPARQL hallucination and hallucination detection, we tested both fine-tuned models (Table 12) and in-context learning (Table 13).

	Element	Detail
Fine-tuning	Train set (QALD9/MASSIVE-AMR)	6000/2000
	Train set (SPARQL/AMR)	3000/5000
	Train set (langs)	1300 each, 6 lgs
	Test set (QALD9/MASSIVE-AMR)	700/500
	Test set (langs)	200 each, 6 lgs
	Block size (GPT-2/LlaMa)	512/2048
	Number epochs	8-16
	Learning rate	$3e^{-5}$
	Optimizer	AdamW
Inference	Number beams	20
	Beam size	5
	Number beam groups	10
	Diversity penalty	1.0
	Minimum length	8
	Maximum length	256

Table 12: Details about training and test splits (top), with model parameters for fine-tuning GPT-2-$XL_{distill}$ and LlaMa using Hugging Face transformers and PEFT.

Element	Detail
Number in-context exs.	8-12
Number tokens in prompt	2400
In-context langs.	English, Spanish
Test set (QALD9/MASSIVE-AMR)	150/150
Test set (langs)	20-40 each, 10 lgs
Temperature	1.0

Table 13: Details about in-context learning (GPT-3.5 and GPT-4-0613).

C Example prompts

C.1 SPARQL Parsing (Research question 1b)

```
{["messages": [
    {
        "role": "system",
        "content": "You are SPARQL-Predictor-GPT, a language model that predicts
                one SPARQL query for a given question."
    },
    {
        "role": "system",
        "content": "This is important! All relations in the predicted SPARQL query must be in
                the allowed_relation_list: ['abbreviation', 'accessioneudate', ... 'leadername']."
    },
    {
        "role": "system",
        "content": "Make a list of all the relations in the predicted SPARQL query.
                Verify that all relations are in allowed_relation_list,
                reporting True or False for each relation."
    },
    {
        "role": "system",
        "content": "Return the prediction in JSON form:
                {'sparql_query': str, 'relations': list(), 'verification': list()}"
    },
    {
        "role": "user",
        "content": "where did abraham lincoln die"
    },
    {
        "role": "assistant",
        "content": "{'sparql_query': 'PREFIX dbo: <http://dbpedia.org/ontology/>
                                PREFIX res: <http://dbpedia.org/resource/>
                                SELECT DISTINCT ?uri WHERE
                                { res:Abraham_Lincoln dbo:deathPlace ?uri. }',
                'relations': ['deathplace'],
                'verification': [True] }"
    },
    {
        "role": "user",
        "content": "give me all cosmonauts."
    }
],
"gold_sparql": "SELECT DISTINCT ?uri WHERE
                { ?uri a <http://dbpedia.org/ontology/Astronaut>
                { ?uri <http://dbpedia.org/ontology/nationality> <http://dbpedia.org/resource/Russia> }
                UNION
                { ?uri <http://dbpedia.org/ontology/nationality>
                <http://dbpedia.org/resource/Soviet_Union> } }",
"perturbed": 1,
"rel_excluded": "nationality",
"question": "give me all cosmonauts.",
"completion": "{'sparql_query': 'PREFIX dbo: <http://dbpedia.org/ontology/>
                            PREFIX rdf: <http://www.w3.org/1999/02/22-rdf-syntax-ns#>
                            SELECT DISTINCT ?cosmonaut WHERE
                            { ?cosmonaut rdf:type dbo:Astronaut. }',
                'relations': ['type'],
                'verification': [True] }",
"label": "qald9",
"hallucination": 0,
"hallucination-detection": 0,
"sparql_executable": 1,
"sparql_result": 1, "sparql_malformed": 0}
```

Figure 2: Example prompt for SPARQL parsing with generation completion and associated features. Our controlled setting for hallucination detection is then reduced to verifying all relations in a parsed query are in the given list, verification the model outputs along with the parsed SPARQL_QUERY. For considerations of space, we show only 3 (of 140) relations, the ALLOWED_RELATION_LIST (second system message in prompt).

D Parsed AMR Examples (GPT-4, 8-shot learning) with Error Analysis

Ex. 1 (QALD9, Spanish): cuánto pesa el satélite más ligero de júpiter (English: 'how much does jupiter's lightest moon weigh')

```
Reference

(h2 / heavy
   :quant (a / amr-unknown)
   :domain (m / moon
      :ARG1-of (h / have-degree-91
         :ARG2 (l / light-06
            :ARG1 m)
         :ARG3 (m2 / most)
         :ARG5 (m3 / moon
            :poss (p / planet
               :name (n / name
                  :op1 "Jupiter"))))))
```

```
Generated

(p / pesar-01
   :ARG1 (s / satellite
      :degree (m / more
         :quant (l / light))
      :location-of (j / planet
         :name (n / name
            :op1 "Júpiter"))))

F1: 0.3
Error: missing amr-unknown; non-English frame
```

Ex. 2 (QALD9, French): combien de théories albert einstein a-t-il produit (English: 'how many theories did albert einstein come up with')

```
Reference

(c / come-up-11
   :ARG0 (p / person
      :name (n / name
         :op1 "Albert"
         :op2 "Einstein"))
   :ARG1 (t / theory
      :quant (a / amr-unknown)))
```

```
Generated

(p / produce-01
   :ARG0 (p2 / person
      :name (n / name
         :op1 "Albert"
         :op2 "Einstein"))
   :ARG1 (t / theory
      :quant (c / count-01
         :op1 (a / amr-unknown))))

F1: 0.77
Diff: English come-up-11 vs French produce-01
Note: Better semantic similarity metric needed
```

Ex. 3 (Massive, English): what is the worlds record for the longest head of hair

```
Reference

(h / have-degree-91
    :ARG1 (h2 / hair
        :part-of (h3 / head)
        :mod (a / amr-unknown))
    :ARG2 (l / long-03
        :ARG1 h2)
    :ARG3 (m / most)
    :ARG5 (w2 / world)
    :ARG1-of (r / record-01))
```

```
Generated

(r / record-01
    :mod (w / world)
    :topic (l / long-02
        :degree (m / most)
        :ARG1 (h / hair-01
            :part-of (p / person))
        :duration (a / amr-unknown)))

F1: 0.38
Error: invents hair-01
Semantics of amr-unknown as 'duration'
Good: 'longest head of hair' = 'longest hair'
```

Errors in AMR parsing include:

- Lack of AMR token for questions 'amr-unknown' (33/100 examples, see Ex. 1); We note 6 of 8 examples in the prompt model this (2 of 8 are imperatives);
- 3/100 parses filtered by Smatch (missing parenthesis or nodes with duplicate variable name);
- Frequent errors with AMR -91 frames (Exs. 1 & 3), e.g., rate-entity-91, have-degree-91;
- 21 of 100 examples have F1<0.5 (Ex. 3); of these, 5 are QALD9 and 16 are MASSIVE-AMR
- Arithmetic problems are correct but do not follow canonical form, though we note there are no math examples in prompts; this suggests more than one reference graph would be helpful for evaluation.

E Results of SPARQL Parsing

```
Example 1: Massive- (Italian), Perturbed=False, Hallucination=False, Detection=False, Difficult=False

Question: quanti anni ha giorgia (English: `how old is giorgia`)

Completion: {'generated_sparql_query':
    'PREFIX dbo: <http://dbpedia.org/ontology/>
     PREFIX res: <http://dbpedia.org/resource/>
     SELECT (YEAR(NOW()) - YEAR(?birthDate)) AS ?age WHERE
        { res:Giorgia dbo:birthdate ?birthDate. }',
    'relations': ['birthdate'],
    'verification': [True]}

-------

Example 2: Massive+ (Hungarian), Perturbed=True, Hallucination=True, Detection=False, Difficult=False

Relation excluded: ['birthdate']

Question: milyen idos toth vera (English: `how old is toth vera`)

Completion: {'generated_sparql_query':
    'PREFIX dbo: <http://dbpedia.org/ontology/>
     PREFIX res: <http://dbpedia.org/resource/>
     SELECT (YEAR(NOW()) - YEAR(?birthdate)) WHERE
        { res:Toth_Vera dbo:birthDate ?birthdate. }',
    'relations': ['birthDate'],
    'verification': [True]}

-------

Example 3: Massive+ (Japanese), Perturbed=True, Hallucination=True, Detection=True, Difficult=False

Relation excluded: ['birthdate']

Question: 渡部篤郎の誕生日はいつ (English: `how old is atsuro watabe`)

Completion: {'generated_sparql_query':
    'PREFIX dbo: <http://dbpedia.org/ontology/>
     PREFIX res: <http://dbpedia.org/resource/>
     SELECT DISTINCT ?date WHERE
        { res:Atsuro_Watabe dbo:birthDate ?date. }',
    'relations': ['birthDate'],
    'verification': [False]}

-------

Example 4: Massive- (English), Perturbed=True, Hallucination=??, Detection=False, Difficult=True

Relation excluded: ['creator']

Question: who created the comic captain america?

{'generated_sparql_query':
    'PREFIX dbo: <http://dbpedia.org/ontology/>
    PREFIX res: <http://dbpedia.org/resource/>
    SELECT DISTINCT ?uri WHERE
        { res:Captain_America dbo:foundedby ?uri. }',
    'relations': ['foundedby'],
    'verification': [True]}
```

Figure 3: Examples of SPARQL parsing using GPT-3.5 showing hallucinations and hallucination detection.

How Does Stereotype Content Differ across Data Sources?

Kathleen C. Fraser, Svetlana Kiritchenko, and Isar Nejadgholi
National Research Council Canada, Ottawa, Canada
{kathleen.fraser,svetlana.kiritchenko,isar.nejadgholi}@nrc-cnrc.gc.ca

Abstract

For decades, psychologists have been studying stereotypes using specially-designed rating scales to capture people's beliefs and opinions about different social groups. Now, using NLP tools on extensive collections of text, we have the opportunity to study stereotypes "in the wild" and on a large scale. However, are we truly capturing the same information? In this paper we compare measurements along six psychologically-motivated, stereotype-relevant dimensions (Sociability, Morality, Ability, Assertiveness, Beliefs, and Status) for 10 groups, defined by occupation. We compute these measurements on stereotypical English sentences written by crowd-workers, stereotypical sentences generated by ChatGPT, and more general data collected from social media, and contrast the findings with traditional, survey-based results, as well as a spontaneous word-list generation task. We find that while the correlation with the traditional scales varies across dimensions, the free-text data can be used to specify the particular traits associated with each group, and provide context for numerical survey data.

1 Introduction

There is growing interest in the possibility of using NLP and large corpora to augment, complement, or even replace traditional psychological surveys to collect social sciences data (Goldstone and Lupyan, 2016; Argyle et al., 2022; Jackson et al., 2022; Dillion et al., 2023). One area where NLP research has started to contribute is in the study and analysis of *stereotypes*.

Stereotypes are "a set of cognitive generalizations (e.g., beliefs, expectations) about the qualities and characteristics of the members of a group or social category" (VandenBos, 2007). There are a number of properties of stereotypes that motivate the use of NLP tools to better study and understand them. First, stereotypes are often communicated and perpetuated through natural language (Beukeboom and Burgers, 2019). Second, they are by definition widely-held and pervasive, and so should be detectable in large samples of data (Garg et al., 2018). Third, they can lead to far-reaching negative consequences, and so there is practical interest in understanding how stereotypes are expressed "in the wild" in order to develop effective counter-strategies (Fraser et al., 2021). NLP researchers have begun to study methods of uncovering stereotype information in Twitter data (Marzouki et al., 2020; Fokkens et al., 2018), news texts and books (Garg et al., 2018), spoken conversations (Charlesworth et al., 2021), and large language models (Cao et al., 2022).

However, the question remains whether the information we can extract from these natural language datasets can actually replicate the information obtained from more traditional methods in social psychology; namely, rating scales. A common paradigm in stereotype research involves choosing a set of attributes, or dimensions, of interest, and then asking human participants (often college undergraduates) to rate social groups along those dimensions. The dimensions of interest vary according to different theoretical models, but can include, for example, *warmth* and *competence* in the Stereotype Content Model (Fiske et al., 2007), or *agency*, *beliefs*, and *communion* in the ABC Model (Koch et al., 2016). The social groups may be categorized based on gender, race, age, or any other social variable relevant to the research. As a result, for each social group, the researchers obtain annotations along each dimension.

In this work, we investigate the possibility of reproducing the results of such a scale-based study, using low-dimensional vector representations of natural language data to estimate the dimensions of interest. We consider six psychologically-motivated dimensions – Sociability, Morality, Ability, Assertiveness, Status, and Beliefs[1] – and a set

[1]See Appendix A for detailed definitions of each dimen-

*Proceedings of the 13th Joint Conference on Lexical and Computational Semantics (*SEM 2024)*, pages 18 - 34
June 20-21, 2024 ©2024 Association for Computational Linguistics

of ten groups defined by occupation. We conduct a detailed comparison of the kind of stereotype data we obtained through (1) direct stereotype elicitation from crowd-workers, (2) direct stereotype elicitation from a generative large language model, and (3) targeted data collection from Twitter (now known as 'X'). We compare these sources of information to two paradigms in the psychology literature: the traditional method using rating scales, as mentioned above, and a newer method involving spontaneous word list elicitation. We consider three research questions in the current study:

1. Can we reproduce the numerical, scale-based results from the social psychology literature through analysis of natural language? We explore this question using three different sources of text: crowd-workers, social media, and ChatGPT, and by transforming the data to a 6-dimensional representation such that each dimension corresponds to a scale measure.
2. Are all of the six aforementioned dimensions spontaneously mentioned in the free text, or are certain dimensions more frequently discussed than others?
3. Are there certain types of information which are available only from the ratings scales, or only in the natural language data? Or can we treat them equivalently?

Our findings suggest that particular dimensions can be estimated more reliably than others, with Morality and Status measurements being highly correlated with the traditional scales on all of the text datasets. The dimensions of Assertiveness and Beliefs were less accurately estimated; statements relevant to these dimensions were also less frequent in the data. However, the natural language texts were found to contain additional types of information not available in the scale-based dataset, adding detail and specificity to the stereotype descriptions.

2 Background

2.1 Psychological Models of Stereotypes

Stereotyping is an extensive area of research in social psychology. Numerous models have been developed to explain the underlying dimensions of social cognition, including stereotyping (Fiske et al., 2007; Koch et al., 2016; Abele and Wojciszke, 2007). Regardless of the specific dimensions in question, the measurements have almost always

sion.

been collected using scales or checklists (i.e., a *forced-choice* paradigm).

One recent study has questioned whether the exclusive use of forced-choice methods has limited, or even biased, the resulting information about how different social groups are viewed. Nicolas et al. (2022) propose a Spontaneous Stereotype Content Model, arguing that "free-response, open-ended stereotypes of social groups may best systematically reveal the complex contents that are spontaneously available to perceivers upon encountering a target." For a given dimension, the authors distinguish between *direction* (e.g., is the group perceived as friendly or unfriendly), which is measured directly by the scales and can be inferred from the open-ended responses, and *representativeness*, which measures how strongly a given dimension is associated with a group (regardless of polarity). In an example from Nicolas et al. (2022), doctors and nurses are both rated as being highly Warm and Competent on rating scales. However, when people spontaneously think about doctors and nurses, they think more about nurses' Warmth traits, and more about doctors' Competence traits. Such differences cannot be observed using the traditional, scale-based methods.

Nicolas et al. compare traditional, scaled-based methods against open-ended responses in the form of single words, and sets of words. We use their data as a baseline, and build on this basic premise by extending the types of open-ended responses to include full sentence stereotypes (generated either by humans or ChatGPT), and then further extending the analysis to the case of Twitter data (which is not specifically stereotypical in nature, but represents a large sample of public opinions on various topics).

2.2 NLP Methods for Analyzing Stereotypes

Numerous NLP methods have been used to extract, discover, and track stereotype content in naturally-occurring texts (Marzouki et al., 2020; Fokkens et al., 2018; Garg et al., 2018; Charlesworth et al., 2021; Fast et al., 2016). In some cases, stereotyping has been labelled as a subcategory of hate speech or offensive language, including gender stereotypes (Chiril et al., 2021; Parikh et al., 2019; Fersini et al., 2018) and stereotypes about immigrants (Sanguinetti et al., 2018; Sánchez-Junquera et al., 2021). For example, the EVALITA 2020 Hate Speech Detection Task involved a subtask

	Stereotypes?	All dimensions?	Human-generated?	Contextual?
Scales	✓	✓	✓	✗
Adjectives	✓	✗	✓	✗
Stereoset	✓	✗	✓	✓
ChatGPT	✓	✗	✗	✓
Tweets	✗	✗	✓	✓

Table 1: Summary of some relevant differences between the various data sources under consideration.

on detecting stereotypes targeting Muslims, Roma, and immigrants (Sanguinetti et al., 2020). Other closely-related work has compared stereotypical biases in large language models with human survey data (Cao et al., 2022). Our work is most similar to that of Fraser et al. (2022), which presents a computational model of Fiske et al.'s Stereotype Content Model (SCM), using the POLAR framework introduced by Mathew et al. (2020). We make use of a similar method to define an interpretable, psychologically-motivated, low-dimensional embedding space.

Other relevant NLP work has examined the verbs and adjectives which are mostly highly associated with certain social groups. Dong et al. (2019) collected words describing various social 'roles' from crowd-workers from different cultures, and also used NLP methods to predict the most likely social role, given a descriptor. Choenni et al. (2021) probed the stereotypes present in pretrained language models with prompts such as "Why are [TARGET GROUP] so [MASK]?" and observed the output attributes.

While similar in spirit to some of these earlier works, our work differs critically in our goal of trying to map *natural language sentences* down to six *numerical dimensions*, for direct comparison against the social psychology rating scales. Furthermore, we compare and contrast these different ways of collecting stereotypical beliefs to explore the types of information available from each source.

3 Methods

In the following section, we describe several different sources of survey and natural language data in English, namely: psychological rating scales (Sec 3.1) as well as lists of spontaneously-produced adjectives, crowd-sourced stereotypes from the Stereoset dataset (Nadeem et al., 2020), stereotypes prompted from ChatGPT, and tweets from Twitter (Sec 3.2). These data sources differ in many relevant aspects, summarized in Table 1. For example, were the writers of the text asked specifically to come up with stereotypes, or are they writing on a more general topic, that may or may not convey implicit stereotypes? Were the annotators required to make a judgement on every dimension, or did they comment only on the dimensions that most easily came to mind? Was the text generated by humans or by a language model? And does the format of the text provide context for the attributes being assigned, or must they be interpreted in isolation? We will discuss these aspects in relation to each dataset in the following.

To make a direct comparison across all the data sources, we first identify the subset of social groups for which data is available in all the existing datasets. The majority of this subset consists of different occupations: Politicians, Teachers, CEOs, Scientists, Bankers, Accountants, Engineers, Farmers, Lawyers, and Nurses. Thus we consider only these 10 target groups in the analysis.

Following our discussion of the datasets, in Section 3.3 we present the dimensionality-reduction method we use to reduce the free-text sentences in the four natural language datasets down to six dimensions, so that they can be compared directly to the 6-dimensional gold standard rating scale data.

3.1 Gold Standard Rating Scales

The gold-standard rating scale values are obtained from the supplemental materials for Experiment 1 in Nicolas et al. (2022). In that experiment, 400 Amazon Turk workers provided annotations for 43 social groups. Each annotator saw a random sample of six groups, and for each group provided six open-ended, free text responses describing "characteristics, traits, or descriptions of the group." Annotators were additionally informed that it was not necessary that they *personally* believe these characteristics to be true, in order to reduce social desirability bias. Most responses are single adjectives.

After annotators provided their free text responses, they were asked to provide a rating from 1 through 5 for "how society views the targets" along various dimensions: Sociability (measured by two subscales, *friendly* and *sociable*), Morality (*trustworthy* and *honest*), Ability (*competent* and *skilled*), Assertiveness (*confident* and *assertive*), Beliefs (*traditional* and *conservative*), and Status (*wealthy* and *high-status*).

In our analysis, we combine the two subscales for each dimension, and normalize the values to lie between -1 and +1, for better comparison with our computational models. We average the annotations for each group over all annotators (on average, 57 per group).

3.2 Alternative Data Sources

Spontaneous Adjectives As the first alternative data source, we consider the adjectives from Experiment 1, described above (Nicolas et al., 2022). The sets of adjectives represent an intermediate step between the rating scales and the spontaneously-produced sentences in the rest of the data sources. Additionally, the adjectives were provided by precisely the same annotators as the scale-based ratings. Thus, the information conveyed by the adjectives likely represents an upper bound for how well we can reproduce the scale ratings via language. Since our NLP analysis (described in Section 3.3) operates on the sentence level, we embed each adjective into a sentence template of the form: `These people are always ADJ`.

StereoSet We also consider data from the StereoSet dataset (Nadeem et al., 2020). This dataset was crowd-sourced on Mechanical Turk. [2] Annotators were asked to generate sentences about a particular group which were (1) stereotypical, (2) anti-stereotypical, and (3) neutral. In this work, we use the stereotypical sentences. There are approximately 55 sentences per target group. These data differ from the adjective sets in that they consist of complete sentences, of varying length and complexity. However, they were still generated in an artificial scenario, with the goal of communicating stereotype information.

ChatGPT As an additional source of data, we generate novel sentences using ChatGTP.[3] Unlike the other data sources, this text does not originate from human authors. However, other researchers have begun exploring the possibility of using large language models as potential sources of information for studying bias and stereotypes (Cao et al., 2022), or even as replacements for human participants in psychological studies (Argyle et al., 2022; Dillion et al., 2023).

We consider three prompts to ChatGPT: (1) `What are some adjectives people in North America use to describe GROUP?` This prompt attempts to directly replicate the open-response portion of Experiment 1 from Nicolas et al. (2) `In North America, what are some commonly held stereotypes about GROUP?` This prompt attempts to directly elicit stereotypes about various groups. (3) `What are some beliefs that many North Americans hold about GROUP?` After observing that many of the generations for the previous prompt focused on negative beliefs about groups, we added this prompt to elicit more neutral/positive characteristics. We re-run each prompt three times for each group, with the default temperature. Each response from ChatGPT contains a list of characteristics, each taken as a separate observation, resulting in an average of 81 sentences for each group.

Twitter Finally, we consider Twitter as a potential source of data about social groups. One significant difference between this dataset and the others is that the writers of the texts were not instructed to generate stereotypes, but rather had other communicative goals in mind. Another factor that may affect the Twitter data is *social desirability bias*. While someone might hold a belief privately, and even report it on an anonymous survey, it doesn't necessarily mean they will state that belief openly on a public forum. However, our hypothesis is that if we have a large data sample, the most common beliefs about different groups should emerge.

We used the Research API[4] to collect data containing the substring 'GROUP are' for the target groups of interest, from 1 January 2022, to 7 October 2022. We ignored re-tweets, duplicates, tweets with more than five hashtags, tweets with URLs, and tweets written by bots (user name or description contains 'bot') and other prolific users. This resulted in a large number of tweets, on average 118,768 per group.

To increase the likelihood of capturing relevant tweets, we then performed the following filtering steps: (1) filter by the user 'location' field to include only those tweets from the US and Canada;

[2] The annotators were all located in the USA, and the stereotypes were validated by an independent set of annotators to ensure that they represented commonly-held views.

[3] `https://chat.openai.com/chat`, GPT-3.5, September 25 2023 version

[4] Prior to the introduction of the data paywall.

(2) parse the sentence and include only those sentences where the target group is not modified by a quantifier or adjective (*Some lawyers are ..., Republican politicians are ...*), (3) using the sentence parse, include only those sentences where *are* is followed by an adjective (e.g., keep *Nurses are angry*, but discard *Nurses are going to go on strike*). This last filtering step is based on research that stereotype-consistent information tends to be communicated with abstract terms, like adjectives, while concrete terms like action verbs describe a particular, contextual behaviour that is not necessarily an essential trait that is present across situations (Beukeboom and Burgers, 2019). These filtering steps drastically reduce the amount of data available (to an average of 2,830 tweets per group), but with the goal of increasing the relevance.

3.3 POLAR Model

Here, we describe our methodology for embedding the text sentences into the six-dimensional social space. For each sentence, we begin by masking the target group name with the generic phrase *these people*. This is to avoid any bias in the sentence embeddings related to the group name (e.g., we want *Scientists are smart* and *Nurses are smart* to map to the same point, regardless of any intrinsic bias in the embedding model related to scientists and nurses). We represent each input sentence as a 1024-dimensional RoBERTa sentence embedding, and then reduce the embedding space to the six dimensions of interest using a variation on the method described by Fraser et al. (2022). The mathematical details are given in Appendix B, but essentially the method is as follows: For each dimension, collect a set of examples to define each pole of the axis. Here, since we want to reproduce the scale ratings of Nicolas et al. (2022), we use the same adjectives that were presented to the participants during data collection (e.g., for the dimension Sociability, they were shown *friendly* and *sociable*, for Morality they were shown *trustworthy* and *honest*, and so on). To define the negative pole, we used the direct antonym according to our own judgement (e.g., *unfriendly*, *unsociable*, *untrustworthy*, and *dishonest*). We then inserted those adjectives into the sentence template `These people are always ADJ`, to generate representative stereotypical sentences for the two poles of each dimension.

The positive examples are then averaged to define the positive direction, and the negative examples are averaged to define the negative direction. The difference between the positive and negative vectors, for each dimension, is then used to define a transformation matrix such that sentence embeddings in the high-dimensional embedding space can then be projected onto the interpretable, six-dimensional space. The dimension score for each sentence is simply the scalar projection of the sentence onto that dimension, ranging from -1 to 1. For each group, we then obtain the average dimension ratings over all sentences in the dataset.

The POLAR model has a small number of parameters that should be optimized for best performance. We validate the model on a hand-crafted lexicon of adjectives for each dimension (Nicolas et al., 2021). Our optimized model uses RoBERTa-NLI embeddings[5], Partial Least Squares (Rosipal and Krämer, 2005) to initially reduce the embedding dimensionality from 1024 to 30, and achieves an average accuracy of 95% at correctly predicting whether each word is positively or negatively associated with the relevant dimension. Further information about the validation process is available in Appendix C.

3.4 Word-Counting Baseline

We also consider a word-counting baseline. Although word-counting tends to be less effective in assessing sentence-level meaning due to negation, sarcasm, etc. (Fraser et al., 2022), we can use this as a baseline method in the case of the adjective lists. Nicolas et al. (2021) provides a set of lexicons for various psychologically-motivated dimensions, including the six dimensions studied here. Words in each lexicon are assigned either a positive (+1) or negative (-1) value according to their direction. Thus, the estimated score for each group on a given dimension is simply the average of all the lexicon values for the words associated with each group (ignoring words that are not in the lexicon for that dimension).

4 Results

4.1 Correlation with Rating Scales

To compare the scores from the text data sources with the gold-standard scale ratings, we measure correlation. Because the most important information is the *relative* differences between the groups,

[5] `https://huggingface.co/sentence-transformers/nli-roberta-large`

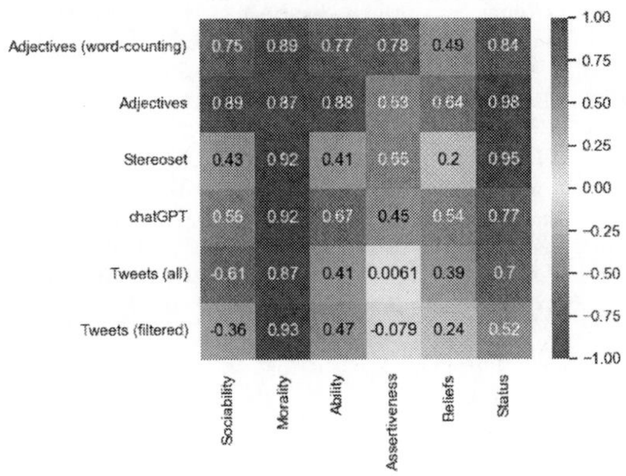

Figure 1: Spearman rank correlation with the scale-based measurement, for each dimension and dataset.

rather than absolute values, we compute Spearman's rank correlation. Correlation values for each dimension and each data source are shown in Figure 1 (full correlation matrices in Appendix D).

We begin by observing that the adjectives, elicited at the same time as the scales, are generally good (though not perfect) at approximating the scale values, and that our POLAR model is, in most cases, more effective than the word-counting approach at associating the adjectives with the scale values (first and second rows of Figure 1). One exception to both of these observations occurs in the case of Assertiveness, where our model achieves a correlation of only 0.53 with the scale values. As an example, we examine the data for farmers, the group ranked lowest on Assertiveness in the scale data, but second-highest in the adjectives data. The main underlying cause of the divergence seems to be that annotators interpreted the "Assertive" trait rather narrowly, as being *pushy* or *demanding*. However, when we look at the adjectives, many people mentioned words like *hard-working* or *strong*, which are also associated with Assertiveness in our model. As a result, farmers are rated higher than most other groups on this dimension.

Moving on to the free-text data sources, we observe that some dimensions are estimated more consistently across data sources. Morality in particular shows very high correlation across all data sources. Whether someone is judged as friend or foe, good or bad, has evolutionary significance and forms the basis of many of our social interactions (Fiske et al., 2007). Therefore it is not surprising that many of the data sources mention morality-related traits (more on this in Sec 4.2) and tend to agree on the direction and relative magnitude of those traits for different groups.

The estimates for Sociability show a somewhat different pattern, with the ChatGPT achieving a moderate correlation of 0.56, and Stereoset somewhat lower at 0.43. In the case of the Twitter data however, the correlation with the scales is actually negative. There are many possible explanations for this, stemming from the heterogeneity and diversity of topics in the Twitter dataset. For example, the scales rate nurses as high-Sociability and accountants as low-Sociability. Many of the tweets expressing low-Sociability traits in nurses are written in the context of the COVID-19 pandemic, such as *Nurses are frustrated and tired* or *Nurses are not ok!*. Conversely, some of the tweets expressing high Sociability for other groups are likely sarcastic, e.g. *Accountants are super fun haha.* In Sec 4.3, we perform topic modelling to disaggregate the different topics so they can be examined separately.

Considering now Assertiveness and Ability, sometimes considered two facets of a single dimension "Competence," we again observe a divergence in the results, with Ability estimates being more highly correlated with the scale ratings for all data sources except Stereoset. This may be an artifact of our particular dataset, as the Ability dimension is particularly relevant in the context of occupations. We also observe that in the Twitter data, groups with high Assertiveness on the traditional scales are often criticized as being ineffectual, e.g. *All politicians are spineless.*

For Beliefs, all data sources have only moderate correlation with the scales. In fact, Nicolas et al. (2022) found that very few of the spontaneously produced adjectives (around 5%) carried information about the Beliefs dimension. The data generated by ChatGPT has the best correlation score of the free-test data sources, specifically labelling accountants, bankers, and farmers as conservative.

Finally, the Status dimension shows reasonably high correlation between the scales and the text data. Again, this may be related to the fact that all of our target groups are based on occupation: in all data sources, we observe statements about CEOs and lawyers being rich, and teachers and nurses being underpaid.

4.2 Prevalence of Each Dimension

We now analyze how many of the texts in each dataset are directly relevant to each dimension. Un-

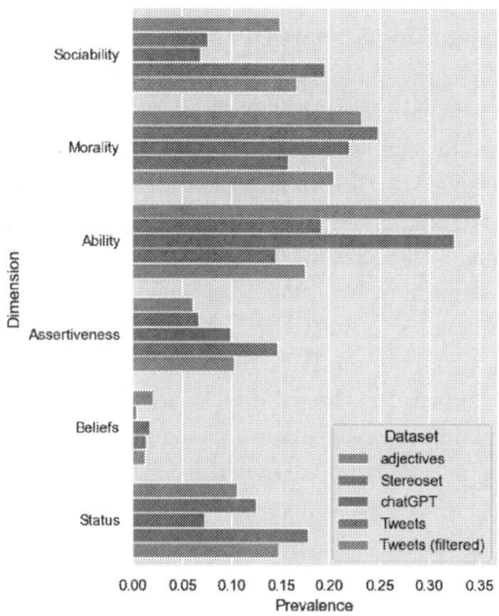

Figure 2: The proportion of text instances assigned an absolute value greater than 0.5. for each dimension.

like in the scale-based paradigm, there may be certain dimensions that simply are not mentioned, leading to difficulties in generating an accurate estimation. This is related to Nicolas et al.'s concept of *representativeness* (Section 2), except that we calculate it over all groups (for the results separated by group, see Appendix E).

Figure 2 shows the proportion of texts in each dataset that are assigned an absolute value greater than (or equal to) 0.5 on each dimension.[6] As hypothesized in the previous section, many of the sentences express Ability judgments, as expected when discussing groups based on occupation. The Morality dimension is mentioned quite often, consistent with the findings of Nicolas et al. (2022). A very small proportion of texts are relevant to the dimension of Beliefs, in all datasets.

However, we note that the trends do look different when considered on a group-by-group basis (Fig D.1). For example, Morality is mentioned in a much higher proportion of texts about politicians. Similarly, the Status dimension is described more frequently in texts about CEOs, bankers, and lawyers. The Ability dimension is the most prevalent dimension when discussing scientists, engineers, and accountants, while for teachers we observe that Ability and Sociability traits are mentioned equally often. The Belief dimension is brought up slightly more in texts about farmers (often described as being conservative).

[6]The threshold of 0.5 was chosen based on the validation set data, where it was observed that a score of 0.5 roughly differentiated the words associated with each dimension from words associated with other dimensions.

Group	Mor.	Soc.	Abil.	Ass.	Bel.	Stat.
Politicians	**-0.60**	0.17	-0.11	**0.50**	0.08	0.43
Teachers	**0.56**	**0.53**	0.46	0.30	0.26	-0.30
CEOs	-0.14	0.13	**0.50**	**0.64**	0.23	**0.73**
Scientists	0.48	0.04	**0.81**	0.49	-0.19	0.21
Bankers	-0.20	0.10	0.40	0.43	0.39	**0.59**
Accountants	0.29	0.02	**0.59**	0.32	0.43	0.22
Engineers	0.48	0.15	**0.86**	0.44	0.19	0.49
Farmers	**0.60**	0.36	0.46	0.23	**0.63**	-0.43
Lawyers	-0.47	-0.09	**0.50**	**0.60**	0.20	**0.64**
Nurses	**0.56**	**0.57**	**0.69**	0.40	0.23	-0.16

Table 2: Dimension estimates for each group, from the scale data, with most salient dimensions in boldface.

4.3 Topic Modeling

As we have seen in Section 4.1, our estimates of relevant psychological dimensions from text do *not* perfectly reproduce those obtained through traditional survey-based methods. However, the survey-based methods also have limited interpretability. For example, Nicolas et al. (2022) found in their original study that the limited set of dimensions did not always align well with people's perceptions of groups. When annotators were asked, "Which of the following characteristics fits best what you meant by [response]?" and given a choice of dimensions (Assertive, Friendly, etc.), "No Match" was actually the most common response. So when forced to make a choice, the annotators might rate politicians as being Sociable (because they are charismatic), but it doesn't really mean the same thing as rating nurses as highly Sociable (because they care deeply about other people). Therefore, in this section, we propose to use natural language resources as *complementary* data to explain and differentiate between the ratings obtained on the six-dimensional scales.

Our procedure is as follows: for each group, we defined the most 'salient' dimensions of the group stereotype as those dimensions with an average absolute scale-based estimate of 0.5 or greater (corresponding to an average response on the original survey of less than 2/5, or greater than 4/5). These dimensions are indicated with boldface in Table 2. We then seek to provide evidence, or further elucidation, of those dimensions by examining the topics arising in the free-text data sources.

For the topic modelling, we employ BERTopic

(Grootendorst, 2022), which uses the HDBSCAN clustering algorithm to remove outliers and concentrate on the most densely populated areas of the embedding space. This aligns with our understanding of stereotypes as being widely-held beliefs, rather than idiosyncratic opinions about a group.

Here, we want to find those topics that help explain the rating scales. Therefore, we then compute the centroid of each topic in the sentence embedding space, and then project the centroid down to the six-dimensional space using the same POLAR model. This allows us to compare the topics along the same dimensions as the rating scales.

We do not expect any single topic to be relevant to all six dimensions simultaneously; rather, we examine one dimension at a time, focusing on the most salient dimensions for each group (as defined above). For a given dimension, we first select all topics where the centroid projection has the same sign as the scale-based score. If there are multiple topics, we rank them according to their centroid projection along that dimension and keep the top three topics (i.e., three most positive or most negative) to analyze. These topics should be the most relevant to understanding why the group would be rated as they were along that dimension. Extended results are given in Appendix F, but we consider several illustrative cases in Table 3:

Differentiating similar groups One way that the text data can be useful is to provide information that differentiates groups that are similarly ranked along a given dimension. For example, scientists, CEOs, and nurses all have high Ability as a salient dimension. However, by examining the text data, we observe qualitative differences in what *aspects* of Ability stereotypically apply to each group (Table 3, Examples 1–3).

Increasing specificity of a stereotype In other cases, even within a particular group, looking at the text data gives a much more specific interpretation of the stereotype. In Example 4 in Table 3, we see that the stereotype of politicians as being low-Morality has a more precise interpretation: i.e., politicians are specifically seen as *corrupt*.

Different responses to stereotypes In other cases, even when there is agreement on the relevance of a dimension in the scale-based data, the text data can reveal different interpretations of that value. In Example 5 (Table 3), we see that teachers are rated as high-Morality. The related topic in the StereoSet data portrays this as *kindness*, while the high-morality topic in the ChatGPT data describes teachers as *strict* and concerned with *discipline*.

Finally, we briefly consider the set of topics not included in the above analysis; that is, those topics which are not strongly associated with one of the salient dimensions. As Nicolas et al. (2022) argue, not all of our social judgements are captured by the dimensions typically studied in social psychology. Aspects of social judgement not directly captured in the six dimensions used here include appearance, gender, and ethnicity, among others.

Table 4 shows examples of some common stereotypes which appear in the text data and are surfaced by the topic modelling, but are not identified with a salient dimension in Table 2. In Example 1 we see the stereotype that nurses are always women, as well as the associated stereotype of the "sexy nurse." In Example 2, in contrast, we see that scientists are stereotyped as being male. In that example, as well as in Example 3, we also see the stereotype that scientists and engineers are "nerdy." Nicolas et al. (2022) identified Appearance as one factor orthogonal to the original scales, and we find some evidence for a stereotype of bankers as being sharply dressed (Ex 4). More concerning, the Stereoset and Twitter data also reveal the offensive stereotype that all bankers are Jewish (Ex 5).

While we have presented only a handful of examples, many of the stereotypes in Table 4, which are not visible in the scale-based data, are arguably more harmful than those summarized in Table 3. Thus the information available in the free text responses provides a valuable and complementary perspective on how certain groups are stereotyped.

5 Conclusion

We conducted a comparison of stereotypes of 10 occupational groups across traditional survey-based data and various text sources. The answers to our research questions are summarized as follows: (1) While our computational analysis of the text data does not perfectly replicate the scale data, certain dimensions (e.g., Morality and Status) could be consistently estimated, with correlation values greater than 0.5 across all text sources. (2) This finding may be partially attributed to the fact that not all dimensions are mentioned spontaneously in the data sources we considered: in particular, adjectives and statements relating to the Beliefs dimension were infrequent. (3) Following from

Group	Dim.	Scales	Adjectives	StereoSet	ChatGPT	Twitter
1 Scientists	Ability	0.81	thoughtful, observant, careful	the scientist who developed this formula must have been smart	scientists are intelligent and analytical	scientists are usually inherently sane and intelligent
2 CEOs	Ability	0.50	savvy, cunning	he was ruthless and cunning	CEOs are strategic and decisive	CEOs are important to a business
3 Nurses	Ability	0.69	hard-working, tending, caring	a nurse has to be supportive to do their job well	nurses understand the physical and emotional needs of patients	nurses are essential to effective health care
4 Politicians	Morality	-0.60	sneaky, sly, lying	known for being corrupt	politicians are corrupt and dishonest	all politicians are corrupt at some level
5 Teachers	Morality	0.56	loyal, patient, strict	she was kind and maintained order in class	strict disciplinarians who enforced rules	these people are never inappropriate, abusive or violent

Table 3: Example stereotype words and sentences extracted using the topic modelling approach, associated with highly-salient dimensions in the scale-based data.

Group	Adjectives	StereoSet	ChatGPT	Twitter
1 Nurses	female, women, girls	she had a very short skirt while changing the iv	nurses are primarily female	nurses are the sexiest women alive
2 Scientists	male	he was middle aged man and was socially awkward	historically, there have been stereotypes associated with gender	cause scientists are all male and lonely
3 Engineers	awkward, nerdy, shy	geeks who are not good at social interaction	engineers are "nerds" or "geeks"	engineers are so weird
4 Bankers	shoes, suits, well-dressed	he wears a crisp suit and makes a lot of money	bankers are always wearing suits	*(none)*
5 Bankers	*(none)*	the person was a Jewish man	*(none)*	the left always assumes bankers are exclusively Jewish

Table 4: Example stereotype words and sentences extracted using the topic modelling approach, which are associated with traits not easily mapped to the six dimensions previously considered.

this, the scale data do contain important information not available in the text data, as participants are required to make a judgement for each dimension. However, the natural language data sources also contain useful information not available in the scale-based data, distinguishing between different groups that were rated similarly along a given dimension, and increasing the specificity of the stereotypes. In particular, topic modelling revealed specific beliefs about groups that were not captured by the abstract, high-level, numerical responses. Free text responses were able to distinguish between different groups that were rated similarly along a given dimension, and increase the specificity of the stereotypes.

Deepening our understanding of stereotypes can help in the development of effective counter-strategies. The work presented in this paper can support these goals in a number of ways. For example, if we consider the ratings of scientists and engineers on the scale-based data, it is not entirely clear what an appropriate counter-example should be (a scientist with low morality and low ability?). However, the natural language data helps surface the more specifically harmful stereotype that scientists are all male and anti-social. Challenging that aspect of the stereotype is more likely to be effective at increasing women's participation in science. At the same time, the scale-based data may provide information that is "hidden" in the social media data, such as the stereotypical idea that most farmers are religious and politically right-wing. This type of information, although essential in gaining a broader understanding of stereotypes, does not tend to be explicitly stated on social media. We also observed that the scale-based data, as well as the ChatGPT data, do not clearly communicate extremely negative or offensive stereotypes – even though these should be the highest priority for mitigation. Therefore, understanding the strengths and weaknesses of the information available in different datasets can have important real-world implications. Furthermore, future work could examine how the data from unconventional sources, such as social media or ChatGPT, may be used to augment more traditional sources, such as lexicons.

Limitations

In this study, we focused on English-language resources only. Further, the collected stereotypes in these resources (survey-based rating scales and word lists, StereoSet) may only be common in the North-American culture. Twitter has a biased demographic representation of users, with most users residing in the U.S. For a fair comparison, we also constrained the ChatGPT responses to the North-American context. Future studies should expand the language and cultural range of stereotype information, although data unavailability may pose a significant barrier.

We examined ten social groups based on occupation since they were common in all the considered data sources. However, stereotypes targeting groups based on other characteristics, such as gender, ethnicity, or socio-economic status, are also prevalent in online and offline communications and may result in severe consequences for the groups and the society at large. Future work should include a wide variety of social groups to investigate how well the results can generalize across the groups.

While social media presents a valuable data source for studying people's opinions and tracking common beliefs, the sheer volume of these data requires computational tools to process the data efficiently. In this study, we applied unsupervised topic modeling, but other unsupervised, semi-supervised, and supervised techniques should be explored and evaluated in this context and may result in different findings. Also, topic modeling and clustering methods tend to be sensitive to parameter settings, and re-running the analysis with different parameters may lead to different results.

Finally, the stereotype information in the different data sources was obtained from different population samples, each of which introducing its own sampling bias. Since for most data sources the information was collected as stereotypical beliefs *common in the society* (as opposed to individuals' beliefs), we expect the effects of sample bias to be small. Still, this may have contributed to the observed differences in findings. Complementary use of several data sources may provide a fuller and less biased view.

Ethics Statement

While collecting stereotype data is a necessary step in studying stereotyping, such resources could inadvertently propagate harmful beliefs or be misused by adversaries to target vulnerable populations. Another open issue is how to counter stereotypical beliefs and mitigate their negative effects. There is a tension between the right to free speech and respect for equality and dignity. Rigid prohibitive mechanisms (e.g., banning any stereotype information from public view) would likely be ineffective. Counter-strategies should work towards weakening stereotypical associations and emphasize the fact that individuals do not neatly fit in boxes prescribed by their demographic characteristics.

References

Andrea E Abele, Nicole Hauke, Kim Peters, Eva Louvet, Aleksandra Szymkow, and Yanping Duan. 2016. Facets of the fundamental content dimensions: Agency with competence and assertiveness—communion with warmth and morality. *Frontiers in Psychology*, 7:219720.

Andrea E Abele and Bogdan Wojciszke. 2007. Agency and communion from the perspective of self versus others. *Journal of Personality and Social Psychology*, 93(5):751.

Lisa P Argyle, Ethan C Busby, Nancy Fulda, Joshua Gubler, Christopher Rytting, and David Wingate. 2022. Out of one, many: Using language models to simulate human samples. *arXiv preprint arXiv:2209.06899*.

Camiel J Beukeboom and Christian Burgers. 2019. How stereotypes are shared through language: a review and introduction of the social categories and stereotypes communication (scsc) framework. *Review of Communication Research*, 7:1–37.

Marco Brambilla, Patrice Rusconi, Simona Sacchi, and Paolo Cherubini. 2011. Looking for honesty: The primary role of morality (vs. sociability and competence) in information gathering. *European Journal of Social Psychology*, 41(2):135–143.

Yang Cao, Anna Sotnikova, Hal Daumé III, Rachel Rudinger, and Linda Zou. 2022. Theory-grounded measurement of U.S. social stereotypes in English language models. In *Proceedings of the 2022 Conference of the North American Chapter of the Association for Computational Linguistics: Human Language Technologies*, pages 1276–1295, Seattle, United States. Association for Computational Linguistics.

Tessa ES Charlesworth, Victor Yang, Thomas C Mann, Benedek Kurdi, and Mahzarin R Banaji. 2021. Gender stereotypes in natural language: Word embeddings show robust consistency across child and adult language corpora of more than 65 million words. *Psychological Science*, 32(2):218–240.

Patricia Chiril, Farah Benamara, and Véronique Moriceau. 2021. "be nice to your wife! The restaurants are closed"': Can gender stereotype detection improve sexism classification? In *Findings of the Association for Computational Linguistics: EMNLP 2021*, pages 2833–2844.

Rochelle Choenni, Ekaterina Shutova, and Robert van Rooij. 2021. Stepmothers are mean and academics are pretentious: What do pretrained language models learn about you? In *Proceedings of the 2021 Conference on Empirical Methods in Natural Language Processing*, pages 1477–1491, Online and Punta Cana, Dominican Republic. Association for Computational Linguistics.

Danica Dillion, Niket Tandon, Yuling Gu, and Kurt Gray. 2023. Can AI language models replace human participants? *Trends in Cognitive Sciences*.

MeiXing Dong, David Jurgens, Carmen Banea, and Rada Mihalcea. 2019. Perceptions of social roles across cultures. In *Social Informatics: 11th International Conference, SocInfo 2019, Doha, Qatar, November 18–21, 2019, Proceedings 11*, pages 157–172. Springer.

Ethan Fast, Tina Vachovsky, and Michael Bernstein. 2016. Shirtless and dangerous: Quantifying linguistic signals of gender bias in an online fiction writing community. In *Proceedings of the International AAAI Conference on Web and Social Media*, volume 10, pages 112–120.

Elisabetta Fersini, Debora Nozza, Paolo Rosso, et al. 2018. Overview of the evalita 2018 task on automatic misogyny identification (AMI). In *CEUR Workshop Proceedings*, volume 2263, pages 1–9. CEUR-WS.

Susan T Fiske, Amy JC Cuddy, and Peter Glick. 2007. Universal dimensions of social cognition: Warmth and competence. *Trends in Cognitive Sciences*, 11(2):77–83.

Antske Fokkens, Nel Ruigrok, Camiel Beukeboom, Gagestein Sarah, and Wouter Van Atteveldt. 2018. Studying Muslim stereotyping through microportrait extraction. In *Proceedings of the Eleventh International Conference on Language Resources and Evaluation (LREC 2018)*.

Kathleen C Fraser, Svetlana Kiritchenko, and Isar Nejadgholi. 2022. Computational modeling of stereotype content in text. *Frontiers in Artificial Intelligence*, 5.

Kathleen C. Fraser, Isar Nejadgholi, and Svetlana Kiritchenko. 2021. Understanding and countering stereotypes: A computational approach to the stereotype content model. In *Proceedings of the 59th Annual Meeting of the Association for Computational Linguistics and the 11th International Joint Conference on Natural Language Processing (Volume 1: Long Papers)*, pages 600–616, Online. Association for Computational Linguistics.

Nikhil Garg, Londa Schiebinger, Dan Jurafsky, and James Zou. 2018. Word embeddings quantify 100 years of gender and ethnic stereotypes. *Proceedings of the National Academy of Sciences*, 115(16):E3635–E3644.

Felipe L Gewers, Gustavo R Ferreira, Henrique F De Arruda, Filipi N Silva, Cesar H Comin, Diego R Amancio, and Luciano da F Costa. 2021. Principal component analysis: A natural approach to data exploration. *ACM Computing Surveys (CSUR)*, 54(4):1–34.

Robert L Goldstone and Gary Lupyan. 2016. Discovering psychological principles by mining naturally occurring data sets. *Topics in Cognitive Science*, 8(3):548–568.

Maarten Grootendorst. 2022. BERTopic: Neural topic modeling with a class-based TF-IDF procedure. *arXiv preprint arXiv:2203.05794*.

Joshua Conrad Jackson, Joseph Watts, Johann-Mattis List, Curtis Puryear, Ryan Drabble, and Kristen A Lindquist. 2022. From text to thought: How analyzing language can advance psychological science. *Perspectives on Psychological Science*, 17(3):805–826.

Alex Koch, Roland Imhoff, Ron Dotsch, Christian Unkelbach, and Hans Alves. 2016. The ABC of stereotypes about groups: Agency/socioeconomic success, conservative–progressive beliefs, and communion. *Journal of Personality and Social Psychology*, 110(5):675.

Yousri Marzouki, Eliza Barach, Vidhushini Srinivasan, Samira Shaikh, and Laurie Beth Feldman. 2020. The dynamics of negative stereotypes as revealed by tweeting behavior in the aftermath of the charlie hebdo terrorist attack. *Heliyon*, 6(8):e04311.

Binny Mathew, Sandipan Sikdar, Florian Lemmerich, and Markus Strohmaier. 2020. The POLAR framework: Polar opposites enable interpretability of pretrained word embeddings. In *Proceedings of the Web Conference 2020*, pages 1548–1558.

Moin Nadeem, Anna Bethke, and Siva Reddy. 2020. Stereoset: Measuring stereotypical bias in pretrained language models. *arXiv preprint arXiv:2004.09456*.

Gandalf Nicolas, Xuechunzi Bai, and Susan T Fiske. 2021. Comprehensive stereotype content dictionaries using a semi-automated method. *European Journal of Social Psychology*, 51(1):178–196.

Gandalf Nicolas, Xuechunzi Bai, and Susan T Fiske. 2022. A spontaneous stereotype content model: Taxonomy, properties, and prediction. *Journal of Personality and Social Psychology*.

Pulkit Parikh, Harika Abburi, Pinkesh Badjatiya, Radhika Krishnan, Niyati Chhaya, Manish Gupta, and Vasudeva Varma. 2019. Multi-label categorization of accounts of sexism using a neural framework. In *Proceedings of the 2019 Conference on Empirical*

Methods in Natural Language Processing and the 9th International Joint Conference on Natural Language Processing (EMNLP-IJCNLP), pages 1642–1652, Hong Kong, China. Association for Computational Linguistics.

Roman Rosipal and Nicole Krämer. 2005. Overview and recent advances in partial least squares. In *Proceedings of the International Statistical and Optimization Perspectives Workshop "Subspace, Latent Structure and Feature Selection"*, pages 34–51. Springer.

Javier Sánchez-Junquera, Berta Chulvi, Paolo Rosso, and Simone Paolo Ponzetto. 2021. How do you speak about immigrants? Taxonomy and StereoImmigrants dataset for identifying stereotypes about immigrants. *Applied Sciences*, 11(8):3610.

Manuela Sanguinetti, Gloria Comandini, Elisa Di Nuovo, Simona Frenda, Marco Stranisci, Cristina Bosco, Tommaso Caselli, Viviana Patti, and Irene Russo. 2020. HaSpeeDe 2 evalita 2020: Overview of the evalita 2020 hate speech detection task. *Evaluation Campaign of Natural Language Processing and Speech Tools for Italian.*

Manuela Sanguinetti, Fabio Poletto, Cristina Bosco, Viviana Patti, and Marco Stranisci. 2018. An Italian Twitter corpus of hate speech against immigrants. In *Proceedings of the Eleventh International Conference on Language Resources and Evaluation (LREC 2018).*

Gary R VandenBos. 2007. *APA Dictionary of Psychology*. American Psychological Association.

A Stereotype Dimensions

We consider the same 6 psychological dimensions of stereotyping as Nicolas et al. (2022), to enable comparison against the ratings of the annotators in that study. These dimensions are: *Sociability, Morality, Ability, Assertiveness, Status,* and *Beliefs*. The dimensions are based on previous theories in the social psychology literature. Fiske et al. (2007) present the Stereotype Content Model ("SCM"), which posits that the two primary dimensions of stereotype content are Warmth and Competence. *Sociability* and *Morality* are two facets of Warmth, and *Ability* and *Assertiveness* are two facets of Competence. Koch et al. (2016) present a different, three-dimensional theory of stereotype content known as the "ABC Model," where A = Agency, B = Beliefs, and C = Communion. While Communion is similar to the concept of Warmth, the other two dimensions diverge from the SCM, with Agency being related to socioeconomic *Status*, and *Beliefs* capturing progressive versus conservative values. To compare the SCM and ABC models, Nicolas et al. (2022) included all 6 distinct dimensions, as did we in the current work.

In the instructions to annotators, Nicolas et al. (2022) define the dimensions with adjectives, as shown in Table A.1. Additional information for each dimension is as follows:

- **Sociability:** friendliness, likability; "pertains to cooperation and to forming connections with others" (Brambilla et al., 2011)
- **Morality:** fairness, honesty, trustworthiness; " being benevolent to people in ways that facilitate correct and principled relations with them by the adherence to ethics and important social values" (Abele et al., 2016)
- **Ability:** capability, intelligence, competence; relating to the capability to achieve goals (separately from the motivation to actively pursue those goals) (Abele et al., 2016)
- **Assertiveness:** ambition, confidence, activeness; related to the motivation to achieve goals (separately from the ability to do so) (Abele et al., 2016)
- **Beliefs:** measured across a continuum from progressive/liberal/modern to conservative/traditional; can encompass political as well as religious beliefs; "conservative-progressive beliefs are informative of mainstream society's views about a group's intention to preserve versus change the status quo" (Koch et al., 2016)
- **Status:** related to power, wealth, dominance, and social standing (Koch et al., 2016)

To give a few examples, society might stereotype a CEO as being intelligent (high-Ability), competitive (high-Assertiveness), right-wing (high-Beliefs), wealthy (high-Status) while at the same time uncaring (low-Sociability) and willing to cheat to get ahead (low-Morality). In contrast, an Asian high-schooler might be stereotyped as very smart (high-Ability) and honest (high-Morality), but passive (low-Assertiveness) and shy (low-Sociability). Some dimensions are more salient for certain social groups, as described in Appendix E below.

B POLAR Model

The following method is adapted from the POLAR framework introduced by Mathew et al. (2020).

Suppose we want to transform from the original sentence embedding space $\mathbb{E}$, $|\mathbb{E}| = D$, to the reduced embedding space $\mathbb{E}'$, $|\mathbb{E}'| = D'$, with $D' < D$.

In general, for each dimension $d \in \{1, 2, ..., D'\}$, we define the set of N_{d+} sentences associated with the positive pole of that dimension as $\mathbb{P}_{d+} = \{p^1_{d+}, p^2_{d+}, ..., p^{N_{d+}}_{d+}\}$, and a set of N_{d-} sentences associated with the negative pole of that dimension as $\mathbb{P}_{d-} = \{p^1_{d-}, p^2_{d-}, ..., p^{N_{d-}}_{d-}\}$. We obtain the POLAR directional vector for that dimension as follows:

$$\overrightarrow{dir_d} = \frac{1}{N_{d+}} \sum_{i=1}^{N_{d+}} \mathbb{V}_{p^i_{d+}} - \frac{1}{N_{d-}} \sum_{i=1}^{N_{d-}} \mathbb{V}_{p^i_{d-}} \quad (1)$$

where $\mathbb{V}_s$ represents the vector representation of the sentence s in the embedding space $\mathbb{E}$.

The set of POLAR direction vectors are then stacked to form $dir \in \mathbb{R}^{D' \times D}$, which represents the change of basis matrix for the new reduced-dimensional embedding subspace $\mathbb{E}'$. In the new subspace, a sentence s is represented by $\mathbb{V}'_s$, which is calculated using the following linear transformation:

$$\mathbb{V}'_s = (dir^T)^{-1} \mathbb{V}_s \quad (2)$$

Each dimension in $\mathbb{E}'$ can now be interpreted in terms of the polar opposites used to define $\overrightarrow{dir_1}$, $\overrightarrow{dir_2}$, ... $\overrightarrow{dir_{D'}}$.

Here, we transform from a high-dimensional RoBERTa sentence embedding space ($D = 1024$),

Dimension	Positive	Negative
Sociability	friendly, sociable	unfriendly, antisocial
Morality	trustworthy, honest	untrustworthy, dishonest
Ability	competent, skilled	incompetent, unskilled
Assertiveness	confident, assertive	meek, submissive
Beliefs	conservative, traditional	liberal, modern
Status	high-status, wealthy	low-status, poor

Table A.1: Adjectives used to define the poles of each dimension. Each adjective was embedded in the sentence template `These people are always <ADJ>.`

to a six-dimensional space, interpretable in terms of six psychologically-defined dimensions ($D' = 6$).

To define our six-dimensional model, we use 12 sets of seed words, each set containing two adjectives ($N_{d+} = N_{d-} = 2$ for $d = 1, 2, 3, 4, 5, 6$). The adjectives representing the positive poles of each dimension are taken from Nicolas et al. (2022). They are the same adjectives that the annotators saw when filling out the rating scales. For the set of adjectives defining the negative poles, we use the direct antonyms of the positive adjectives. See Table A.1 for the full set of adjectives used. Since we want a model that operates on the sentence level, each adjective is inserted in the sentence template `These people are always <ADJ>.` The sentences are then represented as sentence vectors using the 1024-dimensional RoBERTa embedding model, and the change of basis matrix is calculated according to the above.

C Validation Experiments

As a preliminary step to confirm that the POLAR model is capturing the expected information and to select the best parameters, we run a series of small experiments. Briefly, we use lexicons available from Nicolas et al. (2021) to create a validation set of words that should be associated with each dimension. These lexicons were created by hand, based on the existing literature in social psychology.

We then experiment with various parameters relating to the dimensionality reduction. Following Fraser et al. (2022), we consider the options:

- No dimensionality reduction
- Principal Components Analysis (Gewers et al., 2021), optimizing the number of dimensions between 10-100
- Partial Least Squares (Rosipal and Krämer, 2005), optimizing the number of dimensions between 10-100

We considered two evaluation criteria: (1) High accuracy (percentage of times a word was correctly associated with either the positive or negative direction of the salient dimension), (2) Low correlation between dimensions (while we expect some correlation between the dimensions, the POLAR model should represent them as separate, distinct concepts). Fortunately, the setting with the highest accuracy also resulted in the lowest correlation, and so in what follows we use the model with Partial Least Squares applied to reduce the embedding size to 30. This led to an average accuracy of 95% on the validation set, and a mean absolute correlation between the dimensions of 0.13.

We did not optimize the choice of word embeddings, as extensive exploration was previously documented by Fraser et al. (2022), and we use the RoBERTa-NLI embeddings[7] that they found to be optimal across multiple functional test cases.

D Correlations between Datasets

Figure C.1 shows the full correlation matrices for each dimension. In general, no unexpected patterns emerge. The two methods of processing the adjectives (our computational method and simple word-counting) tend to be correlated with each other, and the filtered and unfiltered Twitter datasets tend to be correlated with each other. Stereoset and ChatGPT (i.e., human and machine-generated stereotype sentences) are highly correlated ($\rho > 0.5$) for all dimensions except for Ability. The correlations between different datasets are almost always positive, with the notable exception of Sociability estimates based on Twitter, as discussed in the main text.

E Representativeness

In contrast to scale-based measures collected using a forced-choice methodology, when people are

[7] https://huggingface.co/sentence-transformers/nli-roberta-large

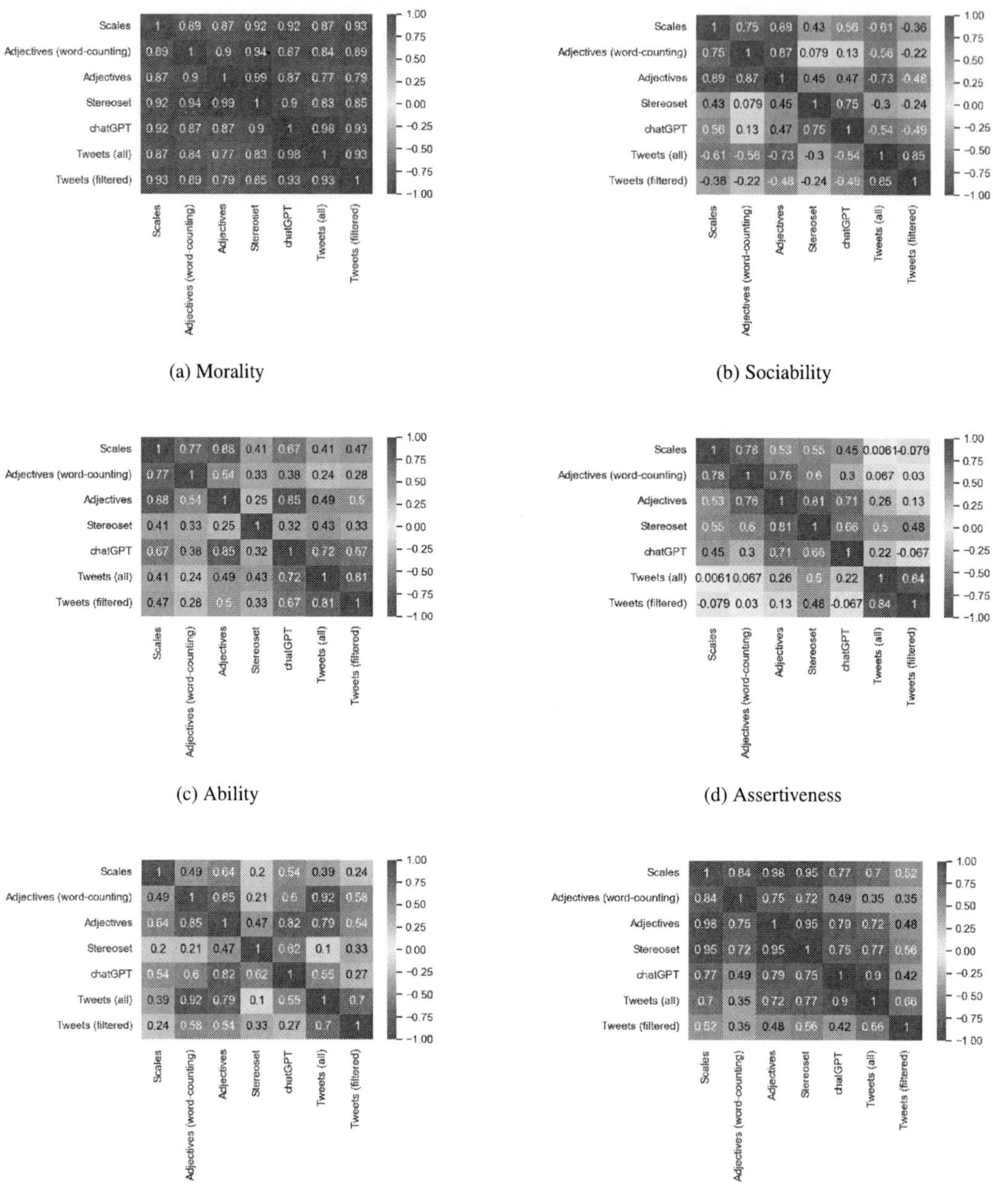

(a) Morality (b) Sociability (c) Ability (d) Assertiveness (e) Beliefs (f) Status

Figure C.1: Spearman rank correlations between estimates from each of the data sources, for each dimension.

generating spontaneous, free-text responses, they can choose which dimension(s) to focus on for any given group. This choice provides additional information about what stereotype dimensions are seen as being most relevant to each group. Nicolas et al. (2022) defined this as *representativeness*: "the prevalence of a stereotype dimension in perceivers' spontaneous beliefs about a social group." Here, we operationalize this as the proportion of text samples that are assigned an absolute value greater than 0.5 along a given dimension.[8] In the main text, we computed this proportion over all groups, and called it *prevalence*, with the goal of understanding more generally how many text samples make strong statements about the different dimensions. Here, we calculate the proportion per group, and thus call it *representativeness*, as it now captures the information about how representative, or important, any given dimension is perceived as being when describing each target group.

The values are shown in Figure D.1. Briefly, we observe that over 50% of the data in the adjectives dataset, Stereoset, and ChatGPT make statements about politicians' morality. This suggests that when people think about stereotypes of politicians, one of the first things they think about is their (im)morality. From a computational perspective, it also means our estimates of that dimension are based on a much larger dataset than our estimates for the other dimensions.

In contrast, for teachers, we see a more even distribution across the different dimensions. Still, dimensions like Assertiveness and Beliefs are more sparsely represented. CEOs have Morality and Ability as the most representative dimensions, with Status also mentioned 10-20% of the time. Scientists, accountants, engineers, farmers, and nurses all have Ability as the most representative dimension. For nurses, Sociability traits are also mentioned more often than for other groups.

Figure D.1 also shows that some data sources are more extreme in their representativeness values. In particular, the adjectives, Stereoset, and ChatGPT (all of which were collected by explicitly asking for stereotype information) have more extreme values, while the Twitter data is more uniformly distributed across dimensions. This reflects the more general nature of the Twitter data.

[8]The threshold of 0.5 was chosen based on the validation set data, where it was observed that a score of 0.5 roughly differentiated the words associated with each dimension from words associated with other dimensions.

F Topic-Modelling Results

BERTopic is available to install at `https://maartengr.github.io/BERTopic/index.html`. We used v0.13.0. For simplicity, we used the default parameters as much as possible.

We use the RoBERTa-NLI pre-trained embedding model, as mentioned in Appendix C. For the vectorizer model, we used the scikit-learn CountVectorizer method, removing English stopwords and ignoring terms that appear in less than 1% of the sentences (`min_df = 0.01`). To ensure reproducibility, we set `random_state = 42` in the UMAP model. For the HDBSCAN clustering algorithm, we specified the `min_samples = 1`, to promote less-conservative clustering.[9] Since we don't know *a priori* how many topics to expect for each group, we set `nr_topics = 'auto'`. For all the other parameters, the default settings of the BERTopic package were used.

G Data Licensing for Existing Datasets

The data associated with Nicolas et al. (2022) is freely available on the Open Science Framework: `https://osf.io/74rax/`. The OSF Terms of Use permit public data to be used for a wide range of non-commercial and commercial uses.

The StereoSet data is available here: `https://huggingface.co/datasets/stereoset` with License CC-BY-SA 4.0.

The Nicolas et al. data was collected with the intention of studying stereotypes. The StereoSet dataset was collected for the purpose of measuring stereotypical biases in language models. We believe our present research is in line with these purposes.

H ChatGPT Dataset

The CSV file containing the pre-processed text is available by contacting the authors.

I Twitter Dataset

The Twitter data was collected in November 2022, under an approved Academic Project on the Twitter developer portal. This was prior to the removal of the Research API and the introduction of a paywall in April 2023. Unfortunately, due to Twitter Terms of Service, we cannot redistribute the Twitter dataset.

[9]`https://hdbscan.readthedocs.io/en/latest/parameter_selection.html`

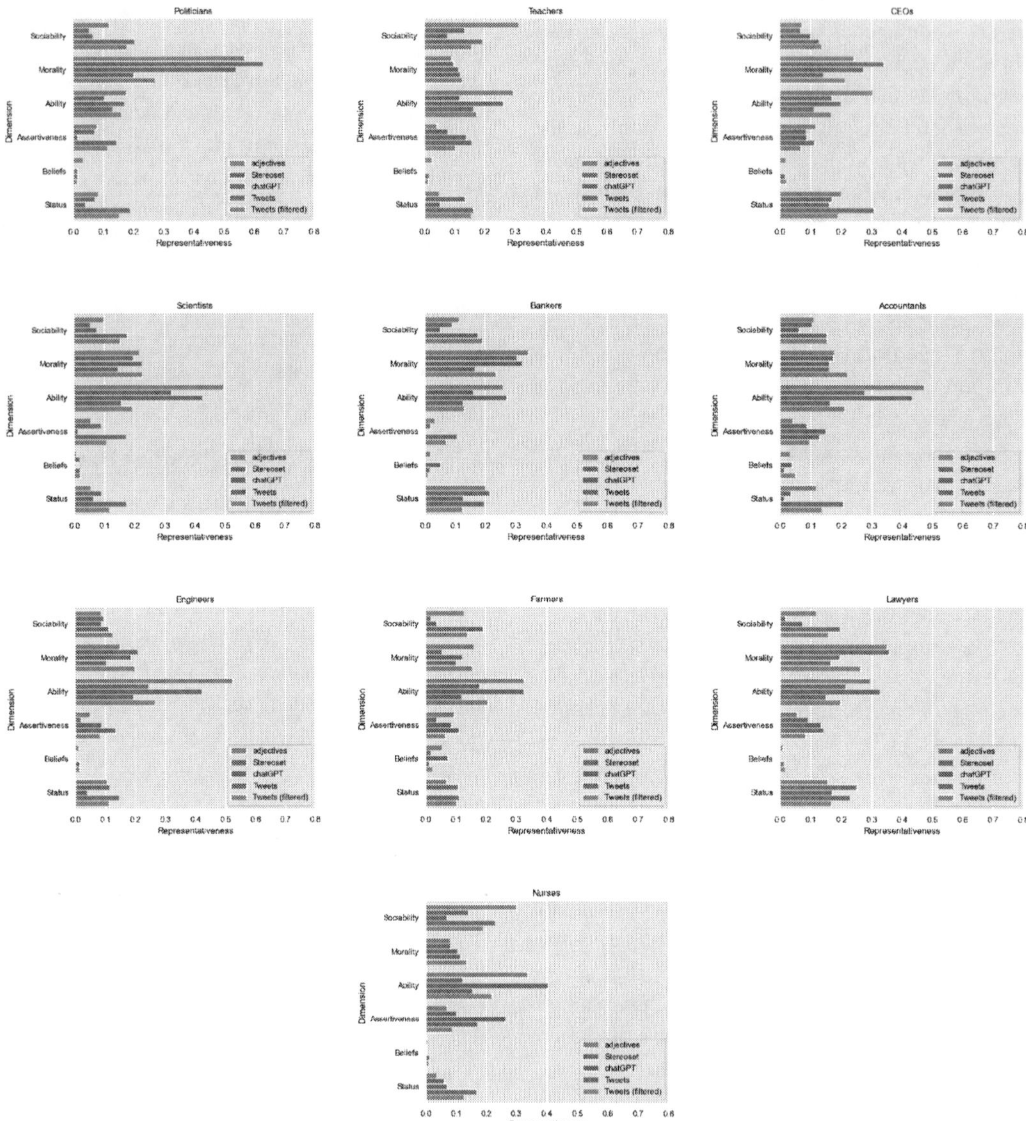

Figure D.1: The proportion of text instances assigned a value greater than 0.5, for each group, dimension, and data source.

Polysemy through the lens of psycholinguistic variables: a dataset and an evaluation of static and contextualized language models

Andrea Bruera
Cognition and Plasticity
Max Planck Institute for
Human Cognitive and
Brain Sciences
Leipzig, Germany
bruera@cbs.mpg.de

Farbod Zamani
Department of Computing
Goldsmiths
University of London
United Kingdom

Massimo Poesio
CogSci Research Group
School of Electronic Engineering
and Computer Science
Queen Mary
University of London
United Kingdom

Abstract

Polysemes are words that can have different senses depending on the context of utterance: for instance, 'newspaper' can refer to an organization (as in 'manage the newspaper') or to an object (as in 'open the newspaper'). Contrary to a large body of evidence coming from psycholinguistics, polysemy has been traditionally modelled in NLP by assuming that each sense should be given a separate representation in a lexicon (e.g. WordNet). This led to the current situation, where datasets used to evaluate the ability of computational models of semantics miss crucial details about the representation of polysemes, thus limiting the amount of evidence that can be gained from their use.

In this paper we propose a framework to approach polysemy as a continuous variation in psycholinguistic properties of a word in context. This approach accommodates different sense interpretations, without postulating clear-cut jumps between senses. First we describe a publicly available English dataset that we collected, where polysemes in context (verb-noun phrases) are annotated for their concreteness and body sensory strength. Then, we evaluate static and contextualized language models in their ability to predict the ratings of each polyseme in context, as well as in their ability to capture the distinction among senses, revealing and characterizing in an interpretable way the models' flaws.

1 Introduction

The meaning of individual words taken in isolation can look unambiguous. Take for instance the word *book*. If encountered on its own, it evokes the image of an object made of sheets of paper bound together. However, when put in context, such as in the phrase 'explain the book', it clearly does not refer to that same concrete object - rather, it denotes its immaterial, abstract content. A word like *book* is called a polyseme (Falkum and Benito, 2015; Vicente and Falkum, 2017; Haber and Poesio, 2023). Polysemes are easily understood when contrasted with monosemes (words with only one possible interpretation, like *leaf*) and homonyms (words that can that can take two completely unrelated interpretations, like *bat*): polysemes can take different interpretations - also called **senses** - which are related among them and that follow patterns that also apply to other words (so-called **regular polysemy**; Apresjan, 1974). In the case of *book*, for instance, the pattern is an alternation between a concrete object and an abstract meaning, which also characterizes other words like *newspaper* or *painting*.

In computational linguistics and Natural Language Processing (**NLP**), a large body of work has looked at polysemy. Mainly, the aim is that of finding out to what extent the distinctions between different senses can be captured by current models - either with a theoretical focus (Erk and Padó, 2010; Boleda et al., 2012; Del Tredici and Bel, 2015; Lopukhina and Lopukhin, 2016; Garí Soler and Apidianaki, 2021; Haber and Poesio, 2021; Li and Armstrong, 2023) or in applied tasks (word sense disambiguation Navigli, 2009; Bevilacqua et al., 2021; Loureiro et al., 2021 and induction Agirre and Soroa, 2007; Manandhar et al., 2010; Lau et al., 2012; Eyal et al., 2022). However, as pointed out in McCarthy et al. (2016); Haber and Poesio (2023), a fundamental conceptual limitation has characterized approaches to polysemy in NLP so far. Namely, they have (almost) exclusively assumed a traditional view of polysemy, the so-called **sense enumeration view** (Katz and Fodor, 1963), which has been shown to afford only limited explanatory power. According to this theory, each sense of a polysemous word like *book* should be given a separate, dedicated representation – like the meanings of distinct words like *leaf* and *curtain*. This is the way in which knowledge graphs like WordNet (Miller, 1995) or BabelNet (Navigli and Ponzetto, 2012), the resources that are most typ-

*Proceedings of the 13th Joint Conference on Lexical and Computational Semantics (*SEM 2024)*, pages 35 - 48
June 20-21, 2024 ©2024 Association for Computational Linguistics

ically used as the golden standard for polysemy in NLP, are structured: for *book*, we find multiple entries - e.g. <*noun.communication*> and <*noun.artifact*>. However, this view is challenged from a large body of work in cognitive psychology and psycholinguistics. Experimental approaches have rather proposed the so-called **one representation view** of polysemous nouns: different senses are not assumed not to be represented differently, but just to be different aspects or facets of the same semantic representation (among others, Klepousniotou, 2002; Rodd et al., 2004; Schumacher, 2013; see Falkum and Benito, 2015; Haber and Poesio, 2023 for comprehensive reviews).

As a reflection of this theoretical gap, the datasets typically used for the evaluation of computational models of language at capturing polysemy are built according the sense enumeration view. Lack of diverse evaluation approaches not only leaves a large amount of potential evidence untapped, but also obscures important insights that could emerge by taking a different perspective.

We concur with McCarthy et al. (2016); Haber and Poesio (2023) that, to investigate in depth the ability of current computational models of semantic to capture polysemy, it is necessary to go beyond the sense enumeration view. To this aim, we propose to take a hybrid approach. We break down regularized patterns of polysemy – from the sense enumeration view – in terms of psycholinguistic variables like concreteness – inspired by the one representation view. In this framework, the variation happening when varying the interpretation of *book* from <*noun.artifact*> to <*noun.communication*> can be captured by observing that the second is interpreted as a less concrete entity – which can be further characterized as a reduction in manipulability (touch) and readability (sight), possibly accompanied by an increase in its audibility (hearing). We build on previous work showing how hard distinctions between senses emerge from (and are contained by) complex representations of words (Pustejovsky, 1991; Cruse, 1995; Ortega-Andrés and Vicente, 2019). What we add is an explicit specification (i.e. in terms of psycholinguistic variables) of how sense alternations in polysemy take place. From previous approaches in NLP that rely on similarities in latent vector spaces (Boleda et al., 2012; McCarthy et al., 2016; Haber and Poesio, 2021), we retain the notion of using continuous measures of similarity/distance – i.e. a 'soft' approach to senses: however, while dimensions of language are not interpretable from a cognitive point of view, ours are. Importantly, this framework has been previously successfully applied to model how the brain processes fine-grained lexical meaning variations (Bruera et al., 2023). Since our framework revolves around cognitively motivated semantic features, it aims at fostering research connecting computational and cognitive models of language – with the broader goal of allowing to gain insights on how similar the two are, which is a fundamental open question in the field (Antonello and Huth, 2023; Beinborn and Hollenstein, 2023; Golan et al., 2023; Kanwisher et al., 2023).

Starting from this theoretical approach, in the current work we present two main contributions. First, we describe how we created an original dataset of examples of lexical polysemy. For each polyseme, the dataset provides ratings provided by human subjects in terms of concreteness and of sensory strength (with separate ratings for sight, hearing, touch, smell, taste) for phrases where the different senses are evoked. Our dataset is carefully crafted by controlling for psycholinguistic variables, with the aim of allowing its use both for *in silico* and cognitive experiments.

Secondly, we evaluate static and contextualized language models on their ability to predict the ratings provided by humans and to distinguish among different senses of polysemous words. We hypothesized that contextualized language models would consistently outperform static language models. Our results confirm our prediction, but they also show that there is large room for improvement in overall accuracy for contextualized language models too - indicating that polysemy is still a challenging semantic phenomenon for language models to capture.

We publish the dataset together with the code[1].

2 Data

2.1 Overview of the dataset

We select a set of 25 polysemic nouns admitting both an abstract and a concrete interpretation. Then, for each noun we select two verbs that, when combined with the noun in a verb-noun phrase, give rise to an abstract (e.g. 'explain the book', 'describe the picture', 'know the medicine') interpretation and two that evoke a concrete (e.g. 'open the book', 'carry the picture', 'swallow the medicine') read-

[1]they can be found at this link: https://osf.io/nfcuq/?view_only=9c7137bc88d543dbaaa17225cbfdef34

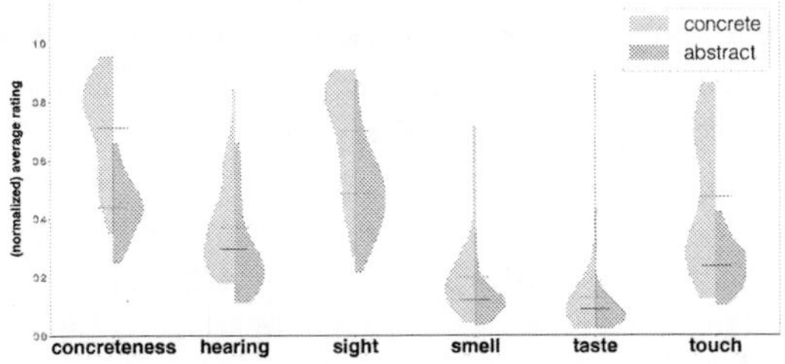

Figure 1: **Distribution of concreteness and sensory strength ratings for the 100 verb-noun polysemic phrases.** Ratings (y axis) are normalized in the range 0-1. As shown by the averages (horizontal coloured lines), concrete phrases show higher concreteness and stronger involvement of all types of sensory information.

ing of the noun. This is the process of so-called 'sense coercion' (Pustejovsky, 1991; Lauwers and Willems, 2011) or 'sense selection', where verbs make the interpretation of the noun go towards one sense or the other (Klepousniotou, 2002). In this way, phrases are equally divided into two mirrored sets of abstract and concrete senses.

Finally, we collect a set of psycholinguistic ratings for all of the nouns within each phrase. We collect ratings for concreteness – the most relevant cognitive dimension –and for the five body senses, since sensory strength can better characterize variation in meaning than simple concreteness (Lynott et al., 2020).

The main aim of this dataset is to fill a gap in existing resources that can be used to evaluate NLP models with respect to polysemy. Our hope is also to foster further research along these lines, with a strong focus on cognitive evaluation of computational models of semantics (Beinborn and Hollenstein, 2023). Therefore, we wanted our stimuli selection to be valid for further testing involving the collection of behavioural and brain data. In such studies, it is fundamental to control for experimental confounds which are not relevant for NLP models, but play an important role in human cognition. Such confounds can be related to non-semantic, low-level sensory properties of the stimuli (Hauk and Pulvermüller, 2004; Laszlo and Federmeier, 2014; Dufau et al., 2015) or, within semantics, to emotional processing (Kuperman et al., 2014; Hinojosa et al., 2020).

In the following we will describe the stimuli selection procedure in detail. A visualization of the distributions of the ratings, directly comparing abstract and concrete senses, is displayed in Figure 1.

2.2 Stimuli selection

2.2.1 Nouns

We selected the set of 25 polysemous nouns to be used among the polysemes annotated in CoreLex (Buitelaar, 1998). CoreLex is an annotation made on top of WordNet (Miller, 1995) specifically created for polysemy. In CoreLex, a number of polysemous nouns from WordNet are annotated according to their polysemy pattern - e.g. annotating with the same label all words that behave similarly to 'book'. For our purpose, the advantage of the annotation provided by CoreLex is that it allows to automatically isolate cases of polysemy where an alternation of a concrete and an abstract sense is present (cf. Boleda et al., 2012).

To extract the nouns, we therefore first looked at the types of nouns present in CoreLex (e.g. 'art'='artifact' or 'com'='informational content'; so-called 'Corelex basic types'). We annotated them according to whether they referred to 'concrete', 'abstract' or 'other' entities (where 'art'='concrete', 'com'='abstract'). From this list, we moved to the list of the polysemy classes ('CoreLex classes'), retaining only the classes where an alternation of an abstract and a concrete sense was present (e.g. a CoreLex class like 'cae', where both a 'art' and a 'com' sense are found). Finally, we chose our candidate nouns by taking the nouns which were annotated in CoreLex as instances of the selected polysemous classes - like 'book', which is a case of the CoreLex class 'cae'.

In parallel, we computed word (lemma) frequencies for the selected polysemous nouns from UKWaC (Baroni et al., 2009), a corpus reflecting general internet language use which has been validated as a corpus for psycholinguistic studies in previous work (Mandera et al., 2017). Since most words occurred with very low frequencies in the corpus, we selected as our candidate polysemes only the top 10% most frequent nouns . Among those, we tried to minimize variance in word length, so as to minimize this possible confounding factor which has a strong impact on cognitive processing (Hauk and Pulvermüller, 2004) . Given that word concreteness correlates negatively with word length (Reilly et al., 2017), we had to strike a balance, avoiding short (whose majority would be concrete) and long (overwhelmingly abstract) words. Therefore, we chose as a criterion to consider nouns between six and nine letters in length. This left us with 571 candidate polysemous nouns.

2.2.2 Verbs

Having thus reduced the set of polysemous nouns, we moved on to select the verbs to be used to create the phrases. We applied a procedure inspired by recent work on predicting concreteness from distributional semantics models (Bhaskar et al., 2017). First, we took the 40000 concreteness ratings for English words from (Brysbaert et al., 2014). Then, we filtered this list, considering only words whose most common POS was that of verb. To do so we used a corpus-based measure of POS prevalence provided by the same authors (Brysbaert et al., 2012). Then, to find verbs eliciting the concrete senses of the polysemes, we took the 1000 most concrete verbs; for the abstract senses, we took the 1000 least concrete verbs. We decided, here again, to reduce the variance in word length for the verbs. However, we kept a wider variance range (4-8 letters, extremes included), considering that we could balance length when choosing the final phrases. After this selection step, the number of concrete verbs was 811, and of abstract verbs 571 (incidentally, the same number of nouns retained from CoreLex).

2.2.3 Verb-noun phrases

Then we looked for the selected verbs' frequencies of co-occurrence with the polysemous nouns within the UKWaC corpus. The aim was that of obtaining a measure of the frequency of occurrence of each of the potential verb-noun phrases, so as to balance them for frequency across abstract and concrete senses. To do so, we exploited the POS annotation provided by UKWaC. We adapted the procedure already validated by Bruera et al. (2023) to extract verb-noun phrase mentions from corpora to be used with language models. We thus considered as relevant verb-noun co-occurrences (i.e. mentions of phrases) only cases where the (lemmatized) verb preceded the (lemmatized) polysemous noun, within a window of three words to the right (to be able to consider cases such as "open an old book", where the linear distance in words between the verb and the noun is three). Then, for each polyseme, we retained the 100 abstract and 100 concrete verbs that co-occurred the most with it. Finally, we proceeded to manually select the twenty-five nouns for which we could find clear cases of sense selection for two verbs and two nouns, thus obtaining the final set of 100 stimuli. We adjusted iteratively our choices so the resulting phrases did not differ statistically across abstract and concrete senses along relevant psycholinguistic variables. As statistical tests we used t-tests; reported p-values are not corrected for multiple comparisons - corrected p-values would be even more conservative. All differences among concrete and abstract phrases are not statistically significant. Since the nouns were the same in both conditions (abstract and concrete), for most variables it was enough to look at the verbs - the main exceptions being phrase frequency ($p = 0.952$) and phrase length ($p = 0.79$). Regarding verbs, we checked that no difference in valence ($p = 0.298$), arousal ($p = 0.103$), dominance ($p = 0.769$) was statistically significant, using the norms provided by (Warriner et al., 2013). Additionally, difference in frequency for concrete and abstract verbs is also not significant ($p = 0.0687$). By contrast, statistically significant differences between verbs emerge, as required by design, in concreteness ($p < 0.0001$).

2.3 Concreteness and sensory strength ratings

Given the 100 phrases selected following the procedure reported above, we then collected from 25 human volunteers ratings for concreteness and sensory strength in all of the five body senses. Sensory strength norms capture more precisely what drives the sense alternation in terms of semantic variables (e.g. the case of book can be explained in terms of variation in sight and touch, but no taste is involved). Participants were recruited among the communities of the authors' university departments, which are located in the same anglophone country. We did not require participants to be native speakers of English. Twenty-five (25) subjects, between 18 and 40 years of age, took part as volunteers to the rating experiment after giving their written consent. In the rating experiment, subjects were presented one by one with all of the 100 phrases, and asked to rate on a Likert scale from 1 to 5 how concrete the polysemous noun in that context was, as well as its so called sensory strength (Lynott et al., 2020). Before starting the experiment, participants were provided with an explanation for each variable, taken from previous rating experiments (Scott et al., 2019; Lynott et al., 2020) and with an example.

The distributions of the resulting ratings are reported in Figure 1. As it can be seen, the largest difference between distributions for concrete/abstract senses is found for concreteness, sight and touch (in all cases $p < 0.0001$), followed by hearing ($p = 0.0163$). The difference is also statistically significant for smell ($p = 0.00012$) and close to significance for taste ($p = 0.083$), however the ratings for the nouns are in both cases always low (averages after normalization: $abstract_{smell} = 0.12, concrete_{smell} = 0.198, abstract_{taste} = 0.088, concrete_{taste} = 0.128$).

We further compute the reliability of the scores provided by the raters. As a measure of interrater reliability we use the mean intra-class correlation (**ICC**, Shrout and Fleiss, 1979), which can take a value between 0 (random agreement) and 1 (perfect agreement). This is the recommended choice for cases like ours where multiple raters provide a single non-nominal score for the same set of items (Hallgren, 2012). We treat subjects as random effects, thus we report what is referred to as type 2 ICC, with 25 subjects – in the terminology of Shrout and Fleiss (1979), $ICC(2, k = 25)$. When aggregating all types of scores together (i.e. concreteness and all sensory modalities), $ICC = 0.945$, indicating excellent agreement (the lower threshold for excellence, according to the guidelines of Cicchetti, 1994; Hallgren, 2012, is $ICC > 0.75$). This confirms that the measurements contained in our dataset are reliable. To understand whether reliability is affected by each of the sensory modalities, we further compute the corresponding separate ICC scores. We find that reliability is highest for concreteness ($ICC_{concreteness} = 0.924$), touch ($ICC_{touch} = 0.913$) and sight ($ICC_{sight} = 0.895$. ICCs are slightly lower, but still indicate excellent agreement, for taste $ICC_{taste} = 0.87$, hearing ($ICC_{hearing} = 0.82$) and smell ($ICC_{smell} = 0.789$).

3 Models

A fine-grained semantic phenomenon like polysemy has proven particularly challenging to capture for language models. Older approaches (so-called **static** language models; Bommasani et al., 2020), were particularly unsuited to face its subtleties (Camacho-Collados and Pilehvar, 2018). Static language models learn fixed semantic representations for words, abstracted from specific contexts of usage. This made it hard to successfully model meaning of words in context - and consequently context-dependent phenomena such as polysemy (Schütze, 1998; Yaghoobzadeh and Schütze, 2016). The more recent language models, called **contextualized** language models (Rogers et al., 2021; Min et al., 2023)), should be in principle better equipped to face the challenge of polysemy. They are trained to create semantic representations of words which are context-specific. When focusing broadly on NLP tasks requiring to consider contextual semantic knowledge (e.g. natural language generation, inference, relation classification), contexualized models are clearly able to reach impressive performance, outperforming static models (Lenci et al., 2022). However, when zooming in through the lens of extremely specific semantic knowledge such as polysemy, synonymy, hypernymy and categorization, the picture changes: contextualized models appear to capture such phenomena only to a modest extent, leaving much room for improvement (Ravichander et al., 2020; Haber and Poesio, 2021; Lenci et al., 2022; Haber and Poesio, 2023).

To provide a better picture with regards to this, we use four models, including both static and contextualized language models (Lenci et al., 2022). In the following we will briefly describe each model, and how the vectors for the polysemous nouns in context were extracted from each one of them. In Appendix A we report an analysis measuring how similar the representations are across the models: the phrases that compose our dataset make notable differences emerge across different types of models, converging with our prediction and sense discrimination results (see Sections 5.1, 3, 4).

3.1 Baseline: count-based model

As a baseline model, we use a so-called count model, following previous work on using distributional models predicting concreteness ratings (Bhaskar et al., 2017). We used the same window size used for fasttext (Bojanowski et al., 2017) - therefore we counted word co-occurrences within a sliding window of ten words (five on the left and five on the right of the target word). As training corpus we used UKWaC. To reduce computational effort, we tried to keep vector dimensionality low by reducing the vocabulary size as done in Bhaskar et al. (2017); Charbonnier and Wartena (2019). Therefore, we reduced the vocabulary to the top 20% most frequent words that appeared in the concreteness norms of (Brysbaert et al., 2014), which makes vectors have 5220 dimensions. As is commonplace in the literature, we transform the raw co-occurrence counts using Pointwise-Mutual Information - therefore the model will be referred to as **count-pmi** (Levy et al., 2015).

We modelled the meaning of the polysemous

noun in the phrase by following the procedure validated in Bruera et al. (2023). It consists of adapting the noun's representation to the context by averaging it with the representation for the verb. Averaging was chosen because, despite its simplicity, it has been shown to be a strong baseline to compose the meaning of words both in NLP and in cognitive neuroscience (Dinu et al., 2013; Wu et al., 2022). We first extracted the pre-trained vector representations for each verb and noun present in the set of stimuli. Then, each phrase's vector representation was obtained by averaging the vectors for the verb and the noun.

3.2 fasttext

As a static model, we chose **fasttext**, using the pre-trained version for English, which is publicly available (Bojanowski et al., 2017; Grave et al., 2018). This version was trained on a combination of Common Crawl and Wikipedia and has 300-dimensional vectors. We extract word vectors for all nouns and verbs and create a phrase-specific representation for each noun as described for count-pmi.

3.3 ConceptNet Numberbatch

As discussed above, senses for polysemous are annotated explicitly in graph-based resources like WordNet. In recent years, ways to integrate graph- and vector- based approaches to semantic representation have been devised. To evaluate how the explicit knowledge about senses encoded in graph-based models can help language models, we used ConceptNet Numberbatch (in the following, **numberbatch**; Speer et al., 2017). Numberbatch is a widely used model that combines distributional and graph-based information: it brings together semantic knowledge from ConceptNet, a graph-based resource that includes WordNet annotations, and two word embeddings models (word2vec (Mikolov et al., 2013) and Glove (Pennington et al., 2014)) using the retrofitting procedure (Faruqui and Dyer, 2015). Recently, its performance has been shown to be superior to distributional-only models in modelling cognitive data (Turton et al., 2020; Alacam et al., 2022; Yang et al., 2024). We compose word vectors for the phrase using the same methodology as count-pmi and fasttext; the resulting phrase vectors have 300 dimensions.

3.4 XGLM

As a contextualized language model, we used XGLM, a recently proposed multilingual model (Lin et al., 2021). Since contextualized models are specialized for representation of language in context, and given previous results (Haber and Poesio, 2021; Bruera et al., 2023), we expect that XGLM should in principle provide the best performance at capturing polysemy. XGLM can beat a similarly-sized GPT-3, a monolingual model, at a number of NLP tasks – arguably thanks to the cross-linguistic transfer of semantic information (Lin et al., 2021). Also, it is publicly available and it has been already used in previous experiments with cognitive datasets (De Varda and Marelli, 2023). We experiment with different model sizes (as reported in the Section 5.3) and for the main comparisons we report results using the best layer (7) for the best-performing model, **XGLM-1.7B**.

To extract vectors for the phrases, we use HuggingFace's Transformers library (Wolf et al., 2020). We employed 'representation pooling', a methodology for creating 'static' representations in contextualized language models that was validated in (Bommasani et al., 2020; Vulić et al., 2020; Apidianaki, 2022) for NLP tasks and in (Bruera and Poesio, 2022, 2023; Bruera et al., 2023) for brain data. In our implementation, first we collected from UKWaC all the sentences containing each one of the selected phrases. To do so, we used the procedure described above for counting the frequencies of verb-noun co-occurrences during stimuli selection. Then, we used XGLM to encode all the sentences separately. Having done so, we extracted the hidden layers of the deep neural network, considering the tokens corresponding to the words contained in the phrase. We followed Bruera et al. (2023), where authors found that the best results with a causal language model like XGLM are obtained when considering all of the phrase tokens + 1, thus capturing both the meaning of the verb and the noun. In Section 5.3 we report results using different sizes of XGLM and all the layers. For the analyses reported in Sections 5.1 and 5.2 we use the layer and the model with the best performances (XGLM 1.7B, layer 7). For each mention of the phrase, we averaged vectors across layers and tokens. In this way, we could obtain a single contextualized vector for each phrase mention. Finally, we averaged, for each phrase, ten randomly sampled mention vectors, following (Vulić et al.,

2020). This allowed us to obtain one single vector capturing reliably the information encoded in XGLM for each phrase.

4 Evaluation

Having obtained the vectors for each verb-noun phrase, we measure to what extent it is possible to learn to predict the ratings obtained from human subjects. We use a cross-validated procedure, with a Ridge regression model (α is cross-validated within the train set among $0.01, 0.1, 1, 10, 100, 1000$). We employ a linear model, an efficient choice given the low number of data points (100; Lin et al., 2023). For cross-validation, we use Monte Carlo Cross-Validation (Kim, 2009) - which entails randomly sampling train and test sets many times (in our case, 20), in order to obtain a reliable average statistics. For the evaluation, we use two measures, explained below.

Correlation The first one simply measures the average Pearson correlation between predicted and real values, averaged across all 20 randomized train-test splits (proportion: 80% train - 20% test). This is the metric typically used in similar studies using language models to predict psycholinguistic variables (Bhaskar et al., 2017; Charbonnier and Wartena, 2019; Chersoni et al., 2020).

Sense discrimination The second measure, by contrast, is directly aimed at testing the ability of each language model to distinguish among different senses. It was originally introduced in cognitive neuroscience, to quantify how well a model could distinguish between two brain images referring to two different concepts (Mitchell et al., 2008; Pereira et al., 2018).

It works in the following way. First, as in Bruera et al. (2023), we consider each word and its two senses as a separate test set – consisting of two phrases for each sense. Suppose they are named $a = phr1_{sense1}, b = phr2_{sense1}, p = phr1_{sense2}, q = phr2_{sense2}$. At test time, the desired semantic variable for the four test items is predicted (e.g. for concreteness $\hat{a}_{conc}, \hat{b}_{conc}, \hat{p}_{conc}, \hat{q}_{conc}$). The predicted ratings are then used to quantify, with a binary accuracy metric, how well the model can distinguish between different senses. All possible pairs of phrases belonging to two different senses are taken (i.e. $\{a, p\}$, $\{b, p\}$, $\{a, q\}$, $\{b, q\}$). Intuitively, given a pair (e.g. $\{a, p\}$) we measure if the prediction $\hat{a}_{conc}$ is closer to the

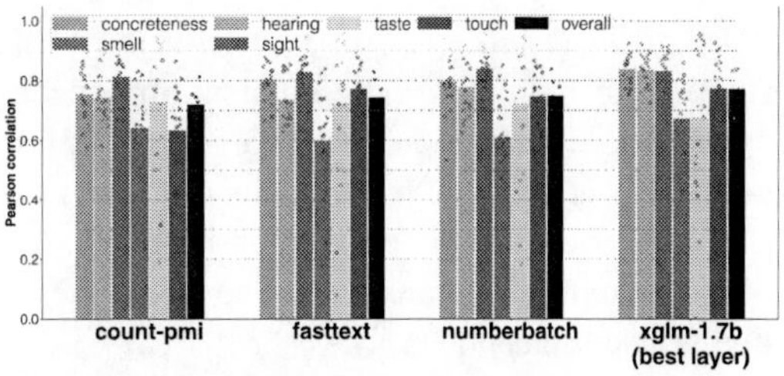

Figure 2: **Pearson correlation between predicted and true variables for each model.** We plot each cross-validation split as a separate scatter point. XGLM consistently provides the best correlation scores across all variables.

real value for its corresponding sense a_{conc} than it is to the other sense p_{conc}; and *vice versa*. If this is the case, then $accuracy = 1$ because the distinction between the two senses has been correctly captured; else, $accuracy = 0$.

More formally, $accuracy = 1$ if $abs(a_{conc} - \hat{a_{conc}}) + abs(p_{conc} - \hat{p_{conc}}) < abs(a_{conc} - \hat{p_{conc}}) + abs(p_{conc} - \hat{a_{conc}})$; else $accuracy = 0$. This evaluation is repeated for all combinations of phrases for the two senses of each word, then averaged; the final evaluation is the average of the scores for all the test sets. This procedure is repeated for all the semantic variables; overall results refer to their average. Since it is a binary accuracy measure, chance performance is at 0.5.

5 Results and discussion

5.1 Correlation analysis

In Figure 2 we report the average Pearson correlation between predicted and real ratings. XGLM (best performing layer and version: layer 7 of XGLM-1.7B; see Section 5.3) provides the best performance in all variables except taste ($XGLM_{sight} = 0.839, XGLM_{touch} = 0.774, XGLM_{hearing} = 0.837, XGLM_{smell} = 0.672$; best performance in taste by Conceptnet Numberbatch $numberbatch_{taste} = 0.725$). Overall low performance in taste and smell can be explained by the fact that, as shown in Figure 1, these two sensory variables had the smallest variance overall, and tended to cluster around low values – thus making it difficult to differentiate among values for different phrases.

Despite the superiority of XGLM, however, differences between different models are surprisingly small ($XGLM_{overall} = 0.771, count-pmi_{overall} = 0.72, fasttext_{overall} =$

$0.743, numberbatch_{overall} = 0.749$). This suggests that simpler, more efficient approaches can capture information about polysemy. Importantly, this concurs with the results of Lenci et al. (2022) in showing that even count-based models often can outperform much more complex ones at fine-grained semantic tasks.

The performance of our models are largely comparable to those obtained when predicting single-word semantic variables. For concreteness, Charbonnier and Wartena (2019) report scores for fasttext oscillating among 0.85 and 0.9, depending on the dataset; here fasttext is at 0.804 (the best performance is afforded by XGLM at 0.838). For sensory strength, Chersoni et al. (2020) report overall lower Spearman correlation for fasttext (average across body senses: 0.596) than us (body sensory average for fasttext: 0.731; top performance by XGLM at 0.758). We assume that such differences are due to the fact that our dataset is much smaller than those used for single-words evaluations, that range in the tens of thousands of words, and possibly to the different correlation metrics used (Spearman vs Pearson correlation).

Turning our approach on its head, our results show that it is possible to automatically obtain reliable concreteness and sensory ratings for phrases (an approach that has been recently advocated especially for low resource languages; Turton et al., 2020; Grand et al., 2022; Wang et al., 2023), and use those to *induce* word senses. In other words, our methodology can be used to automatically find in corpora contexts of use where the same polysemous word is used in different senses. This would also allow for an automated large scale expansion of the current dataset .

5.2 Sense discrimination analysis

While correlation scores provide a general evaluation of prediction performance, we separately assess the ability of the four models at discriminating among different senses of polysemous words using the dedicated pairwise evaluation (see above). We also run statistical significance t-tests against the chance baseline of 0.5. Results are reported in Figure 3. XGLM performs better overall ($XGLM_{overall} = 0.672, p = 0.0001; XGLM_{concreteness} = 0.88, p < 0.0001; XGLM_{hearing} = 0.62, p = 0.093; XGLM_{smell} = 0.61, p = 0.156; XGLM_{taste} = 0.35, p = 0.99$), as hypothesized. ConceptNet Numberbatch affords the best results only for sight ($numberbatch_{sight} = 0.81, p = 0.0002; XGLM_{sight} = 0.8, p = 0.0004$. The performance of the contextualized model is always better at capturing polysemy than both purely distributional models (count-pmi and fasttext), confirming previous reports (Haber and Poesio, 2021; Bruera et al., 2023). XGLM can also (in most cases) outperform ConceptNet Numberbatch, which incorporates hand-coded information about senses. This suggests that such fine-grained semantic knowledge can be alternatively captured by looking at linguistic contexts – i.e. at language in use. However, the fact that all models perform significantly above chance for the same variables, the small magnitude of the differences among models, and the rather low average performance taken together suggest that polysemy is still hard to capture.

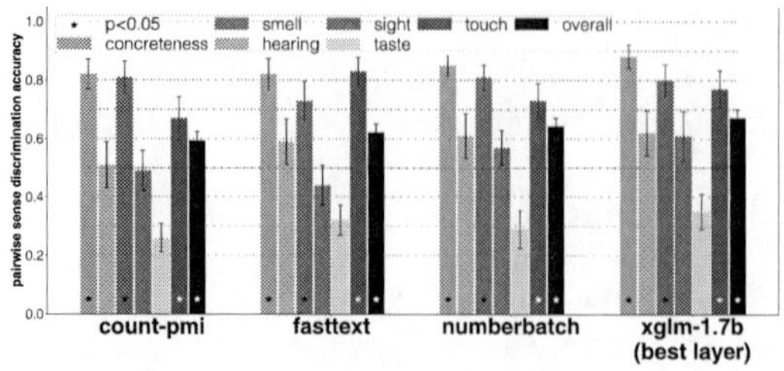

Figure 3: **Sense discrimination scores for each model, using all semantic variables.** Error bars indicate the standard error of the mean across test splits. Overall indicate that the sense discrimination task is challenging for all models.

5.3 In-depth evaluation of XGLM on sense discrimination

In Figure 4 we report the layer-by-layer results for the XGLM family of models (1.7B, 4.5B, 7.5B parameters). We plot overall performance – i.e. the average across all variables. In accordance with previous results on lexical information encoded in contextualized models, performance is better in earlier layers (Bommasani et al., 2020). A relatively small model (1.7B) can provide the best results overall, outperforming both static and larger-sized variants in almost all layers. This converges with previous results casting doubts over the need of ever-larger language models when it comes to modelling human cognition (Oh and Schuler (2023) for reading times, De Varda and Marelli (2023) for eye-tracking, Bruera et al. (2023) for fMRI; cf. Rogers et al., 2021).

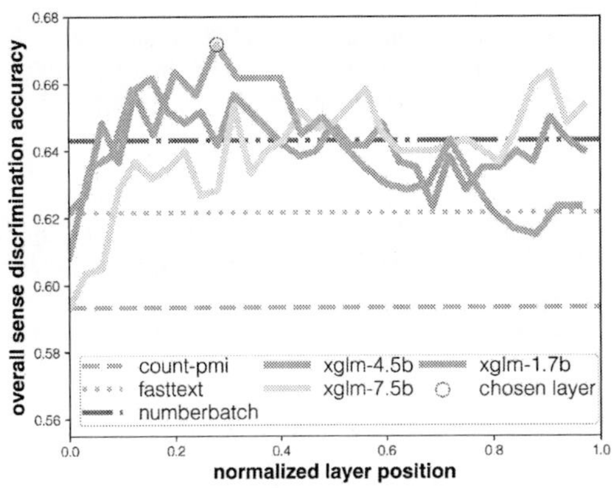

Figure 4: **Overall sense discrimination scores for a number of contextualized models, across all layers.** Overall, all versions of XGLM perform better in the first half of the layers. We indicate with a circle the layer used for the analyses reported above.

6 Limitations and future directions

The main limitation of our study is the size of the dataset, and the fact that we focus on only one case of regular polysemy. Future work could expand this dataset by considering more, and more specific types of polysemy that can be modelled within a similar framework – cases like *chicken* where another variable, taste, can explain sense alternations (animal vs taste; Boleda et al., 2012).

Another interesting direction could be investigating to what extent language models and human cognition align while processing these polysemes (e.g. using brain data; cf. Bruera et al., 2023).

References

Eneko Agirre and Aitor Soroa. 2007. Semeval-2007 task 02: Evaluating word sense induction and discrimination systems. In *Proceedings of the fourth international workshop on semantic evaluations (semeval-2007)*, pages 7–12.

Özge Alacam, Simeon Schüz, Martin Wegrzyn, Johanna Kißler, and Sina Zarrieß. 2022. Exploring semantic spaces for detecting clustering and switching in verbal fluency. In *Proceedings of the 29th International Conference on Computational Linguistics*, pages 178–191, Gyeongju, Republic of Korea. International Committee on Computational Linguistics.

Richard Antonello and Alexander Huth. 2023. Predictive coding or just feature discovery? an alternative account of why language models fit brain data. *Neurobiology of Language*, pages 1–16.

Marianna Apidianaki. 2022. From word types to tokens and back: A survey of approaches to word meaning representation and interpretation. *Computational Linguistics*, pages 1–60.

JD Apresjan. 1974. Regular polysemy. *Linguistics*, 12(142):5–32.

Marco Baroni, Silvia Bernardini, Adriano Ferraresi, and Eros Zanchetta. 2009. The wacky wide web: a collection of very large linguistically processed web-crawled corpora. *Language resources and evaluation*, 43:209–226.

Lisa Beinborn and Nora Hollenstein. 2023. *Cognitive Plausibility in Natural Language Processing.* Springer Nature.

Michele Bevilacqua, Tommaso Pasini, Alessandro Raganato, and Roberto Navigli. 2021. Recent trends in word sense disambiguation: A survey. In *Proceedings of the Thirtieth International Joint Conference on Artificial Intelligence, IJCAI-21*. International Joint Conference on Artificial Intelligence, Inc.

Sai Abishek Bhaskar, Maximilian Köper, Sabine Schulte Im Walde, and Diego Frassinelli. 2017. Exploring multi-modal text+ image models to distinguish between abstract and concrete nouns. In *Proceedings of the IWCS workshop on Foundations of Situated and Multimodal Communication.*

Piotr Bojanowski, Edouard Grave, Armand Joulin, and Tomas Mikolov. 2017. Enriching word vectors with subword information. *Transactions of the association for computational linguistics*, 5:135–146.

Gemma Boleda, Sebastian Padó, and Jason Utt. 2012. Regular polysemy: A distributional model. In ** SEM 2012: The First Joint Conference on Lexical and Computational Semantics–Volume 1: Proceedings of the main conference and the shared task, and Volume 2: Proceedings of the Sixth International Workshop on Semantic Evaluation (SemEval 2012)*, pages 151–160.

Rishi Bommasani, Kelly Davis, and Claire Cardie. 2020. Interpreting pretrained contextualized representations via reductions to static embeddings. In *Proceedings of the 58th Annual Meeting of the Association for Computational Linguistics*, pages 4758–4781.

Andrea Bruera and Massimo Poesio. 2022. Exploring the representations of individual entities in the brain combining eeg and distributional semantics. *Frontiers in Artificial Intelligence*, 5:796793.

Andrea Bruera and Massimo Poesio. 2023. Family lexicon: using language models to encode memories of personally familiar and famous people and places in the brain. *bioRxiv*, pages 2023–08.

Andrea Bruera, Yuan Tao, Andrew Anderson, Derya Çokal, Janosch Haber, and Massimo Poesio. 2023. Modeling brain representations of words' concreteness in context using gpt-2 and human ratings. *Cognitive Science*, 47(12):e13388.

Marc Brysbaert, Boris New, and Emmanuel Keuleers. 2012. Adding part-of-speech information to the subtlex-us word frequencies. *Behavior research methods*, 44:991–997.

Marc Brysbaert, Amy Beth Warriner, and Victor Kuperman. 2014. Concreteness ratings for 40 thousand generally known english word lemmas. *Behavior research methods*, 46:904–911.

Peter Paul Buitelaar. 1998. *CoreLex: systematic polysemy and underspecification.* Brandeis University.

Jose Camacho-Collados and Mohammad Taher Pilehvar. 2018. From word to sense embeddings: A survey on vector representations of meaning. *Journal of Artificial Intelligence Research*, 63:743–788.

Jean Charbonnier and Christian Wartena. 2019. Predicting word concreteness and imagery. In *Proceedings of the 13th International Conference on Computational Semantics-Long Papers*, pages 176–187.

Emmanuele Chersoni, Rong Xiang, Qin Lu, and Chu-Ren Huang. 2020. Automatic learning of modality exclusivity norms with crosslingual word embeddings. In *Proceedings of the Ninth Joint Conference on Lexical and Computational Semantics*, pages 32–38.

Domenic V Cicchetti. 1994. Guidelines, criteria, and rules of thumb for evaluating normed and standardized assessment instruments in psychology. *Psychological assessment*, 6(4):284.

D. A. Cruse. 1995. Polysemy and related phenomena from a cognitive linguistic viewpoint. In *Computational Lexical Semantics*, Studies in Natural Language Processing, page 33–49. Cambridge University Press.

Andrea De Varda and Marco Marelli. 2023. Scaling in cognitive modelling: A multilingual approach to human reading times. In *Proceedings of the 61st Annual Meeting of the Association for Computational Linguistics (Volume 2: Short Papers)*, pages 139–149.

Marco Del Tredici and Núria Bel. 2015. A word-embedding-based sense index for regular polysemy representation. In *Proceedings of the 1st Workshop on Vector Space Modeling for Natural Language Processing*, pages 70–78.

Georgiana Dinu, Marco Baroni, et al. 2013. General estimation and evaluation of compositional distributional semantic models. In *Proceedings of the Workshop on Continuous Vector Space Models and their Compositionality*, pages 50–58.

Stéphane Dufau, Jonathan Grainger, Katherine J Midgley, and Phillip J Holcomb. 2015. A thousand words are worth a picture: Snapshots of printed-word processing in an event-related potential megastudy. *Psychological science*, 26(12):1887–1897.

Katrin Erk and Sebastian Padó. 2010. Exemplar-based models for word meaning in context. In *Proceedings of the acl 2010 conference short papers*, pages 92–97.

Matan Eyal, Shoval Sadde, Hillel Taub-Tabib, and Yoav Goldberg. 2022. Large scale substitution-based word sense induction. In *Proceedings of the 60th Annual Meeting of the Association for Computational Linguistics (Volume 1: Long Papers)*, pages 4738–4752, Dublin, Ireland. Association for Computational Linguistics.

Ingrid Lossius Falkum and Agustín Vicente Benito. 2015. Polysemy: current perspectives and approaches. *Lingua: International review of general linguistics*, (157):1–16.

Manaal Faruqui and Chris Dyer. 2015. Non-distributional word vector representations. In *Proceedings of the 53rd Annual Meeting of the Association for Computational Linguistics and the 7th International Joint Conference on Natural Language Processing (Volume 2: Short Papers)*, pages 464–469.

Aina Garí Soler and Marianna Apidianaki. 2021. Let's play mono-poly: Bert can reveal words' polysemy level and partitionability into senses. *Transactions of the Association for Computational Linguistics*, 9:825–844.

Tal Golan, Matthew Siegelman, Nikolaus Kriegeskorte, and Christopher Baldassano. 2023. Testing the limits of natural language models for predicting human language judgements. *Nature Machine Intelligence*, 5(9):952–964.

Gabriel Grand, Idan Asher Blank, Francisco Pereira, and Evelina Fedorenko. 2022. Semantic projection recovers rich human knowledge of multiple object features from word embeddings. *Nature human behaviour*, 6(7):975–987.

Édouard Grave, Piotr Bojanowski, Prakhar Gupta, Armand Joulin, and Tomáš Mikolov. 2018. Learning word vectors for 157 languages. In *Proceedings of the Eleventh International Conference on Language Resources and Evaluation (LREC 2018)*.

Janosch Haber and Massimo Poesio. 2021. Patterns of polysemy and homonymy in contextualised language models. In *Findings of the Association for Computational Linguistics: EMNLP 2021*, pages 2663–2676.

Janosch Haber and Massimo Poesio. 2023. Polysemy-evidence from linguistics, behavioural science and contextualised language models. *Computational Linguistics*, pages 1–67.

Kevin A Hallgren. 2012. Computing inter-rater reliability for observational data: an overview and tutorial. *Tutorials in quantitative methods for psychology*, 8(1):23.

Olaf Hauk and Friedemann Pulvermüller. 2004. Effects of word length and frequency on the human event-related potential. *Clinical Neurophysiology*, 115(5):1090–1103.

José A Hinojosa, Eva M Moreno, and Pilar Ferré. 2020. Affective neurolinguistics: towards a framework for reconciling language and emotion. *Language, Cognition and Neuroscience*, 35(7):813–839.

Nancy Kanwisher, Meenakshi Khosla, and Katharina Dobs. 2023. Using artificial neural networks to ask 'why'questions of minds and brains. *Trends in Neurosciences*, 46(3):240–254.

Jerrold J Katz and Jerry A Fodor. 1963. The structure of a semantic theory. *language*, 39(2):170–210.

Ji-Hyun Kim. 2009. Estimating classification error rate: Repeated cross-validation, repeated hold-out and bootstrap. *Computational statistics & data analysis*, 53(11):3735–3745.

Ekaterini Klepousniotou. 2002. The processing of lexical ambiguity: Homonymy and polysemy in the mental lexicon. *Brain and language*, 81(1-3):205–223.

Nikolaus Kriegeskorte, Marieke Mur, and Peter A Bandettini. 2008. Representational similarity analysis-connecting the branches of systems neuroscience. *Frontiers in systems neuroscience*, page 4.

Victor Kuperman, Zachary Estes, Marc Brysbaert, and Amy Beth Warriner. 2014. Emotion and language: valence and arousal affect word recognition. *Journal of Experimental Psychology: General*, 143(3):1065.

Sarah Laszlo and Kara D Federmeier. 2014. Never seem to find the time: evaluating the physiological time course of visual word recognition with regression analysis of single-item event-related potentials. *Language, Cognition and Neuroscience*, 29(5):642–661.

Jey Han Lau, Paul Cook, Diana McCarthy, David Newman, and Timothy Baldwin. 2012. Word sense induction for novel sense detection. In *Proceedings of the 13th Conference of the European Chapter of the Association for Computational Linguistics*, pages 591–601.

Peter Lauwers and Dominique Willems. 2011. Coercion: Definition and challenges, current approaches, and new trends. *Linguistics*, 49(6):1219–1235.

Alessandro Lenci, Magnus Sahlgren, Patrick Jeuniaux, Amaru Cuba Gyllensten, and Martina Miliani. 2022. A comparative evaluation and analysis of three generations of distributional semantic models. *Language resources and evaluation*, 56(4):1269–1313.

Omer Levy, Yoav Goldberg, and Ido Dagan. 2015. Improving distributional similarity with lessons learned from word embeddings. *Transactions of the association for computational linguistics*, 3:211–225.

Jiangtian Li and Blair C Armstrong. 2023. Probing the representational structure of regular polysemy in a contextual word embedding model via sense analogy questions. In *Proceedings of the Annual Meeting of the Cognitive Science Society*, volume 45.

Xi Victoria Lin, Todor Mihaylov, Mikel Artetxe, Tianlu Wang, Shuohui Chen, Daniel Simig, Myle Ott, Naman Goyal, Shruti Bhosale, Jingfei Du, et al. 2021. Few-shot learning with multilingual language models. *arXiv preprint arXiv:2112.10668*.

Yu-Chen Lin, Si-An Chen, Jie-Jyun Liu, and Chih-Jen Lin. 2023. Linear classifier: An often-forgotten baseline for text classification. In *Proceedings of the 61st Annual Meeting of the Association for Computational Linguistics (Volume 2: Short Papers)*, pages 1876–1888, Toronto, Canada. Association for Computational Linguistics.

Anastasiya Lopukhina and Konstantin Lopukhin. 2016. Regular polysemy: from sense vectors to sense patterns. In *Proceedings of the 5th Workshop on Cognitive Aspects of the Lexicon (CogALex-V)*, pages 19–23.

Daniel Loureiro, Kiamehr Rezaee, Mohammad Taher Pilehvar, and Jose Camacho-Collados. 2021. Analysis and evaluation of language models for word sense disambiguation. *Computational Linguistics*, 47(2):387–443.

Dermot Lynott, Louise Connell, Marc Brysbaert, James Brand, and James Carney. 2020. The lancaster sensorimotor norms: multidimensional measures of perceptual and action strength for 40,000 english words. *Behavior Research Methods*, 52:1271–1291.

Suresh Manandhar, Ioannis Klapaftis, Dmitriy Dligach, and Sameer Pradhan. 2010. Semeval-2010 task 14: Word sense induction &disambiguation. In *Proceedings of the 5th international workshop on semantic evaluation*, pages 63–68.

Paweł Mandera, Emmanuel Keuleers, and Marc Brysbaert. 2017. Explaining human performance in psycholinguistic tasks with models of semantic similarity based on prediction and counting: A review and empirical validation. *Journal of Memory and Language*, 92:57–78.

Diana McCarthy, Marianna Apidianaki, and Katrin Erk. 2016. Word sense clustering and clusterability. *Computational Linguistics*, 42(2):245–275.

Tomas Mikolov, Kai Chen, Greg Corrado, and Jeffrey Dean. 2013. Efficient estimation of word representations in vector space. *arXiv preprint arXiv:1301.3781*.

George A Miller. 1995. Wordnet: a lexical database for english. *Communications of the ACM*, 38(11):39–41.

Bonan Min, Hayley Ross, Elior Sulem, Amir Pouran Ben Veyseh, Thien Huu Nguyen, Oscar Sainz, Eneko Agirre, Ilana Heintz, and Dan Roth. 2023.

Recent advances in natural language processing via large pre-trained language models: A survey. *ACM Computing Surveys*, 56(2):1–40.

Tom M Mitchell, Svetlana V Shinkareva, Andrew Carlson, Kai-Min Chang, Vicente L Malave, Robert A Mason, and Marcel Adam Just. 2008. Predicting human brain activity associated with the meanings of nouns. *science*, 320(5880):1191–1195.

Roberto Navigli. 2009. Word sense disambiguation: A survey. *ACM computing surveys (CSUR)*, 41(2):1–69.

Roberto Navigli and Simone Paolo Ponzetto. 2012. Babelnet: The automatic construction, evaluation and application of a wide-coverage multilingual semantic network. *Artificial intelligence*, 193:217–250.

Byung-Doh Oh and William Schuler. 2023. Why does surprisal from larger transformer-based language models provide a poorer fit to human reading times? *Transactions of the Association for Computational Linguistics*, 11:336–350.

Marina Ortega-Andrés and Agustín Vicente. 2019. Polysemy and co-predication. *Glossa: a journal of general linguistics*, 4(1).

Jeffrey Pennington, Richard Socher, and Christopher D Manning. 2014. Glove: Global vectors for word representation. In *Proceedings of the 2014 conference on empirical methods in natural language processing (EMNLP)*, pages 1532–1543.

Francisco Pereira, Bin Lou, Brianna Pritchett, Samuel Ritter, Samuel J Gershman, Nancy Kanwisher, Matthew Botvinick, and Evelina Fedorenko. 2018. Toward a universal decoder of linguistic meaning from brain activation. *Nature communications*, 9(1):963.

J Pustejovsky. 1991. The generative lexicon. *Computational Linguistics*, 17(4):409–441.

Abhilasha Ravichander, Eduard Hovy, Kaheer Suleman, Adam Trischler, and Jackie Chi Kit Cheung. 2020. On the systematicity of probing contextualized word representations: The case of hypernymy in bert. In *Proceedings of the Ninth Joint Conference on Lexical and Computational Semantics*, pages 88–102.

Jamie Reilly, Jinyi Hung, and Chris Westbury. 2017. Non-arbitrariness in mapping word form to meaning: Cross-linguistic formal markers of word concreteness. *Cognitive Science*, 41(4):1071–1089.

Jennifer M Rodd, M Gareth Gaskell, and William D Marslen-Wilson. 2004. Modelling the effects of semantic ambiguity in word recognition. *Cognitive science*, 28(1):89–104.

Anna Rogers, Olga Kovaleva, and Anna Rumshisky. 2021. A primer in bertology: What we know about how bert works. *Transactions of the Association for Computational Linguistics*, 8:842–866.

Petra B Schumacher. 2013. When combinatorial processing results in reconceptualization: toward a new approach of compositionality. *Frontiers in Psychology*, 4:677.

Hinrich Schütze. 1998. Automatic word sense discrimination. *Computational linguistics*, 24(1):97–123.

Graham G Scott, Anne Keitel, Marc Becirspahic, Bo Yao, and Sara C Sereno. 2019. The glasgow norms: Ratings of 5,500 words on nine scales. *Behavior research methods*, 51:1258–1270.

Patrick E Shrout and Joseph L Fleiss. 1979. Intraclass correlations: uses in assessing rater reliability. *Psychological bulletin*, 86(2):420.

Robyn Speer, Joshua Chin, and Catherine Havasi. 2017. Conceptnet 5.5: An open multilingual graph of general knowledge. In *Proceedings of the AAAI conference on artificial intelligence*, volume 31.

Jacob Turton, David Vinson, and Robert Smith. 2020. Extrapolating binder style word embeddings to new words. In *Proceedings of the second workshop on linguistic and neurocognitive resources*, pages 1–8.

Agustín Vicente and Ingrid L Falkum. 2017. Polysemy. In *Oxford research encyclopedia of linguistics*.

Ivan Vulić, Edoardo Maria Ponti, Robert Litschko, Goran Glavaš, and Anna Korhonen. 2020. Probing pretrained language models for lexical semantics. In *Proceedings of the 2020 Conference on Empirical Methods in Natural Language Processing (EMNLP)*, pages 7222–7240.

Shaonan Wang, Yunhao Zhang, Weiting Shi, Guangyao Zhang, Jiajun Zhang, Nan Lin, and Chengqing Zong. 2023. A large dataset of semantic ratings and its computational extension. *Scientific Data*, 10(1):106.

Amy Beth Warriner, Victor Kuperman, and Marc Brysbaert. 2013. Norms of valence, arousal, and dominance for 13,915 english lemmas. *Behavior research methods*, 45:1191–1207.

Thomas Wolf, Lysandre Debut, Victor Sanh, Julien Chaumond, Clement Delangue, Anthony Moi, Pierric Cistac, Tim Rault, Rémi Louf, Morgan Funtowicz, et al. 2020. Transformers: State-of-the-art natural language processing. In *Proceedings of the 2020 conference on empirical methods in natural language processing: system demonstrations*, pages 38–45.

Meng-Huan Wu, Andrew J Anderson, Robert A Jacobs, and Rajeev DS Raizada. 2022. Analogy-related information can be accessed by simple addition and subtraction of fmri activation patterns, without participants performing any analogy task. *Neurobiology of Language*, 3(1):1–17.

Yadollah Yaghoobzadeh and Hinrich Schütze. 2016. Intrinsic subspace evaluation of word embedding representations. In *Proceedings of the 54th Annual Meeting of the Association for Computational Linguistics (Volume 1: Long Papers)*, pages 236–246.

Yang Yang, Luan Li, Simon de Deyne, Bing Li, Jing Wang, and Qing Cai. 2024. Unraveling lexical semantics in the brain: Comparing internal, external, and hybrid language models. *Human Brain Mapping*, 45(1):e26546.

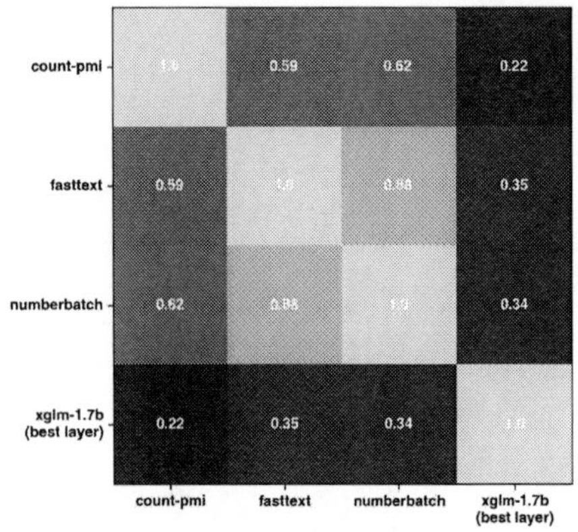

Figure 5: **Pairwise similarities as measured by Representational Similarity Analysis among models**. The scores reported in white are Pearson correlation scores, indicating a clear distinction between static and contextualized models.

A Appendix A: Representational Similarity Analysis of the models' representations

In order to gain some insights into how the models used in our work relate to each other, in Figure 5 we report a visualization of the similarity of the semantic representations across all pairs of models. We carry out the comparisons using the Representational Similarity Analysis (RSA) (Kriegeskorte et al., 2008) framework. RSA measures how similar two quantitative ways of representing the same stimuli are by looking at the similarity between the vectors of all pairwise similarities between individual representations in the space. We follow the traditional implementation and we measure similarity with Pearson correlation. As we can see, as it can be expected, static models are rather similar among each other ($corr_{count-pmi,\ fasttext} = 0.59$, $corr_{count-pmi,\ numberbatch} = 0.62$, $corr_{fasttext,\ numberbatch} = 0.88$), while the contextualized model has a different way of representing the phrases ($corr_{XGLM-7.5B,\ count-pmi} = 0.22$, $corr_{XGLM-7.5B,\ fasttext} = 0.35$, $corr_{XGLM-7.5B,\ numberbatch} = 0.34$).

Post-Hoc Answer Attribution for Grounded and Trustworthy Long Document Comprehension: Task, Insights, and Challenges

Abhilasha Sancheti[†,*] **Koustava Goswami**[‡], **Balaji Vasan Srinivasan**[‡]
[†]University of Maryland, College Park [‡]Adobe Research
sancheti@umd.edu, {koustavag,balsirini}@adobe.com

Abstract

Attributing answer text to its source document for information-seeking questions is crucial for building trustworthy, reliable, and accountable systems. We formulate a new task of post-hoc answer attribution for long document comprehension (LDC). Owing to the lack of long-form abstractive and information-seeking LDC datasets, we refactor existing datasets to assess the strengths and weaknesses of existing retrieval-based and proposed answer decomposition and textual entailment-based optimal selection attribution systems for this task. We throw light on the limitations of existing datasets and the need for datasets to assess the actual performance of systems on this task.

Input
Question: When does the next assasins creed come out?
Document: [1] Ubisoft has announced that its next Assassin's Creed game will be revealed in September 2022.
[2] Ubisoft shared the first trailer for the game on Saturday.
[3] Assassin's Creed Mirage, the next entry in Ubisoft's long-running action-adventure series, will arrive in 2023.
[4] The publisher announced the release date today during its Ubisoft Forward event. ...
Answer: The next Assassin's Creed game, Assassin's Creed Mirage, will arrive in 2023 according to Ubisoft's announcement during its Ubisoft Forward event. It will be released for Xbox ... The game will be revealed in September 2022.
Output
Attributed answer: The next Assassin's Creed game, Assassin's Creed Mirage, ... Ubisoft's announcement during its Ubisoft Forward event [3,4] ... The game will be revealed in September 2022 [1].

Table 1: An example taken from reformulated verifiability dataset (Liu et al., 2023) that includes a question, a document,[2] and an answer as inputs, and the document-grounded attributions for each sentence (some may not have any attribution) in the answer as output.

1 Introduction

Users now benefit from the help of automatic question-answering (QA) systems on a day-to-day basis when faced with an information need. Such systems are integrated into search engines (*e.g.*, BingAI[1]) and digital assistants (*e.g.*, ChatGPT). However, such systems are prone to generating answers lacking sufficient grounding to knowledge sources (Dziri et al., 2022; Ji et al., 2023), leading to the risks of misinformation and hallucination (Metzler et al., 2021; Shah and Bender, 2022; Huo et al., 2023). Therefore, attributing the generated answers to the respective sources is crucial for building trustworthy, reliable, verifiable, and accountable systems (Bohnet et al., 2022; Huang and Chang, 2023; Rashkin et al., 2023; Yue et al., 2023); by allowing users to verify outputs.

Existing works mainly consider generating attributed text in open-ended settings. These attributions are generated along with the answers either one per answer paragraph (Bohnet et al., 2022; Hu et al., 2024) or per answer sentence (Gao et al., 2023a,b; Malaviya et al., 2023). Evidence retrieval is used to select an answer in reading comprehension setting (Wang et al., 2019; Yadav et al., 2020; Cui et al., 2022) for short and extractive answers. Attribution becomes challenging when answers are abstractive such that each sentence could be composed of multiple sentences in the source document, requiring more sophisticated approaches. To address this gap, we aim to identify fine-grained attributions (*i.e.*, sentences grounded in a provided long document) for each sentence (unlike paragraph or article) of a long-form abstractive answer to an information-seeking question asked over a user-provided document (closed-domain). Such fine-grained attributions can lead to more trustworthy, reliable, and accountable systems. Specifically, we propose a new task (Table 1) of **post-hoc answer attribution for long document comprehension** wherein the input to a system is a **(question, answer, document)** triplet, and output is an **attributed answer** consisting of pointers to sentences in the document that provide supporting evi-

*This work was done when the author was at Adobe.
[1]https://www.microsoft.com/en-gb/bing?form=MW00X7
[2]A subset of sentences is shown due to space constraints.

*Proceedings of the 13th Joint Conference on Lexical and Computational Semantics (*SEM 2024)*, pages 49 - 57
June 20-21, 2024 ©2024 Association for Computational Linguistics

dence for each sentence in the answer.

Building systems for this task is challenging due to the unavailability of appropriate datasets as answers in existing information-seeking reading comprehension datasets (*e.g.*, Dasigi et al., 2021) are short and extractive. Moreover, obtaining attribution annotations is cognitively demanding, labor-intensive, and expensive as it requires expertise (Kamalloo et al., 2023). Thus, we (a) propose to reformulate existing datasets curated for evaluating citation verifiability in generative search engines (Liu et al., 2023), and generating attributed explanations in generative information-seeking systems (Kamalloo et al., 2023), and (b) assess the feasibility of using existing textual entailment models by proposing `ADiOSAA`– consisting of an answer decomposer and a textual entailment-based attributor that uses an optimal selection strategy to find attributions for each sentence of an answer.

This work **contributes** the following: (1) introduces the task of **post-hoc answer attribution for LDC** for building trustworthy, verifiable, reliable, and accountable QA systems (§2); (2) reformulates existing datasets for this task, owing to the lack of availability of long-form abstractive reading comprehension datasets (§2), and (3) assesses the strengths and weaknesses of existing retrieval-based systems, and proposed answer decomposition and textual entailment-based optimal selection system, `ADiOSAA` (§3), by adopting information retrieval measures (§4).

2 Adapting existing datasets for our task

Task Definition We formalize the task of post-hoc answer attribution for long document comprehension as: given a query Q, a set of sentences $S = s_1, \ldots, s_n$ from document D (namely, source sentences), and an answer (either generated from a system or ground-truth) to query Q, the goal is to identify supporting sentences (namely, attributions) $s_i \in S$ for each answer sentence $a_i \in A = a_1, \ldots, a_m$ (may be attributed to multiple source sentences or none). Since there are no datasets that match the needs of our task, we propose to reformulate the Citation Verifiability dataset (Liu et al., 2023) and Hagrid dataset (Kamalloo et al., 2023) for the proposed task.

Reformulation Citation Verifiability Dataset Citation verifiability dataset (Liu et al., 2023) consists of questions from NaturalQuestions (Kwiatkowski et al., 2019) and ELI5 (Fan et al., 2019) and answers are generated from different generative search engines; Bing Chat, NeevaAI, perplexity.ai, and YouChat. These answers are embedded with inline citations pointing to the web pages. Human annotators were shown a question and a verification-worthy sentence from the generated answer with its corresponding generated citations and were asked to judge if the citations *fully, partially, or do not support* the sentence. For sentences that are *fully* supported, annotators also provide sentences on the webpage that support the answer sentence. In this open-domian setup, the citations in an answer may belong to multiple web pages. To obtain a pseudo document for a question, we focus on questions anchored to a given document by combining fully supported web page contents cited for sentences. Hence, we have a corpus with questions, answers, a document to which questions are grounded, and ground truth attributions for sentences in an answer.

Split	Size	Avg. No. of source sentences	Avg. No. of attributions per sentence	Avg. No. of sentences per answer	Avg. No. of answers per question
		Verifiability/Hagrid			
Train	1138/1922	128.58/2.82	1.45/1.26	2.11/1.63	2.63/1.67
Dev	146/716	141.68/2.83	1.49/1.40	2.18/1.71	2.56/1.84
Test	136/–	130.03/–	1.60/–	2.13/–	2.75/–

Table 2: Dataset statistics. No test set in Hagrid.

Reformulating Hagrid Dataset Kamalloo et al. (2023) introduced Hagrid which is constructed based on human and LLM collaboration by first automatically collecting attributed answers (for information-seeking questions in MIRACL (Zhang et al., 2022) dataset) that follow an inline citation style using GPT-3.5. Then, asking human annotators to evaluate the LLM answers based on informativeness and attributability. We establish benchmarks for this dataset by considering the LLM-generated answers to be the gold-answers required as input (as opposed to the task formulation of Hagrid, wherein output is an attributed answer), attributability annotations as attributions for sentences in an answer, and labeled relevant passages as the document. We provide dataset statistics in Table 2.

3 Answer Decomposition and Optimal Selection for Answer Attribution

We propose an **A**nswer **D**ecompos**i**tion and **O**ptimal **S**election **A**nswer **A**ttribution system for

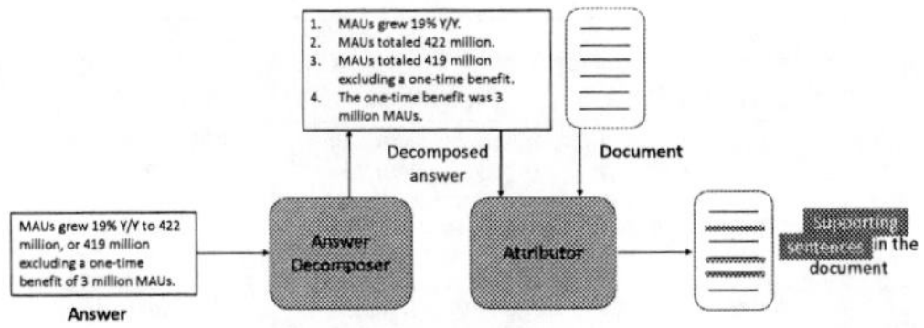

Figure 1: Overview of proposed answer attribution system, ADiOSAA. The **answer decomposer** breaks the given answer into *information units*, and the **attributor** finds the supporting sentences as attributions for each *information unit* in the answer.

the introduced task. ADiOSAA consists of two components (Figure 1): (1) An **answer decomposer** to break each sentence of an answer into one or more *information units* (Nenkova and Passonneau, 2004; Stanovsky et al., 2018; Ernst et al., 2021) as we believe that an answer sentence is composed of information from multiple sentences in the input document. (2) An **attributor** to find supporting sentences in the document for a given *information unit* in the answer sentence.

Answer Decomposer We prompt ("Please breakdown the following sentence into independent facts: ..") ChatGPT (OpenAI, 2023) to decompose the given answer into its information units, following Min et al. (2023) who found such decompositions to be effective and close to human. This decomposition resembles past frameworks derived from OpenIE (Stanovsky et al., 2018; Ernst et al., 2021) or Pyramid (Nenkova and Passonneau, 2004; Shapira et al., 2019), but avoids relying on annotated data and achieves greater flexibility by using ChatGPT. Such decomposition to information units has been successfully used for claim-verification (Kamoi et al., 2023) and propositional semantic representations (Chen et al., 2023).

Attributor Once the answer is decomposed into its information units, each unit needs to be mapped to sentences in the input document to provide the desired attributions. We pose this task of finding supporting sentences in the document for a given information unit as a textual entailment task. Textual entailment is the task of identifying if a given premise ($\mathcal{P}$) entails or does not entail the given hypothesis ($\mathcal{H}$). For our purpose, we consider sentence(s) in the document as the premise and an information unit as the hypothesis. We use

Algorithm 1 Optimal Selection Algorithm

```
Inputs: Information unit (iu), D = d_1, d_2 ... d_n, Attr(P, H), δ
Outputs: L = A list of supporting sentences in D which together attribute iu
L ← [], RS ← D, prev_score ← −1    // RS: remaining sentences; Initialization
while RS is not empty do
    curr_score ← max_{d_i ∈ RS} Attr(L + d_i, iu)
    d_max ← arg max_{d_i ∈ RS} Attr(L + d_i, iu)
    if curr_score > prev_score + δ then
        L += d_max
        RS −= d_max
        prev_score = curr_score
    else
        break
    end if
end while
```

RoBERTa-L (Liu et al., 2019) pretrained[3] on DocNLI (Yin et al., 2021) dataset (contains paragraph-level (premise, hypothesis) pairs, see §B for more details) as the entailment model (attributor) to predict if the given information unit can be inferred from the given sentence(s) from the document.

Optimal Selection An answer sentence could be attributed to multiple sentences in the provided document when: (a) the same information is available in the document at multiple places, and (b) pieces of information in the answer sentence is available in different parts of the document. (a) can be solved by considering the top k (premise hypothesis) pairs where the premise is the sentence from the document and the hypothesis is the sentence or information unit of the answer. To solve (b), it is required to check if a sentence or information unit of an answer can be entailed from a combination of sentences in the document as a premise. However, this becomes computationally expensive; for a document consisting of N sentences, there will be 2^N combinations. To address this issue, we propose an optimal selection approach that greedily selects sentences from the document that has the maximum probability of entailment as described in Algorithm 1. Attr($\mathcal{P}$,$\mathcal{H}$) refers to DocNLI-based attributor which takes sentences from the input document and the information unit (or sentence in an answer) and outputs the probability of entailment of $\mathcal{H}$ from $\mathcal{P}$. For each information unit in a sentence, Algorithm 1 iteratively selects a sentence from the set of remaining source sentences that maximizes the probability of entailment until the entailment score keeps increas-

[3]We use the official code and trained model available at https://github.com/salesforce/DocNLI.

Model	Verifiability			Hagrid		
	(P/R/F1)@1	(P/R/F1)@2	(P/R/F1)@4	(P/R/F1)@1	(P/R/F1)@2	(P/R/F1)@4
BM25	0.669/0.529/0.567	0.443/0.648/0.499	0.270/0.722/0.369	0.815/0.686/0.722	0.740/0.919/0.788	0.678/0.990/0.760
GTR	0.656/0.511/0.550	0.432/0.623/0.483	0.270/0.723/0.371	0.899/0.768/0.804	0.744/0.918/0.790	0.677/0.987/0.759
MonoT5	**0.698**/**0.552**/**0.593**	0.466/**0.675**/**0.522**	0.284/**0.757**/0.389	**0.962**/**0.827**/**0.864**	0.763/**0.946**/**0.811**	0.680/**0.993**/0.762
ADiOSAA	0.545/0.428/0.459	**0.484**/0.546/0.487	**0.476**/0.604/**0.499**	0.856/0.734/0.768	0.848/0.810/0.799	0.848/0.817/**0.801**
ADiOSAA - D	0.473/0.388/0.412	0.445/0.418/0.412	0.442/0.418/0.411	0.869/0.749/0.782	**0.861**/0.758/0.783	**0.861**/0.758/0.783
ADiOSAA - OS	0.375/0.295/0.317	0.280/0.333/0.284	0.256/0.360/0.276	0.793/0.679/0.710	0.745/0.783/0.736	0.743/0.830/0.752
ADiOSAA - D - OS	0.269/0.234/0.243	0.269/0.234/0.243	0.269/0.234/0.243	0.567/0.466/0.494	0.567/0.466/0.494	0.567/0.466/0.494

Table 3: Evaluation results: ADiOSAA systems use top 150 source sentences (see Table 6 in Appendix for results with GTR, MonoT5, and all the source sentences) retrieved using BM25 for the Verifiability dataset. D denotes Answer Decomposer, and OS refers to Optimal Selection.

ing above a threshold δ as compared to that in the previous iteration.

We reorder the attributions for each information unit based on their score and deduplicate (as different information units may be attributed to the same source sentence) them to obtain the predicted attributions for each sentence of an answer.

4 Evaluation

As answer sentence attribution to sentences in the source document could also be considered as an information retrieval task, we benchmark the performance of a range of retrieval-based systems: **(1) BM25 (sparse)**, **(2) GTR (dense)**, and **(3) MonoT5**, considering an answer sentence as the query, and the sentences/passages from the input document as the document (refer to §A). Because our task assumes the answer as an input, inline attribution-based systems like vanilla LLM prompting (Tay et al., 2022; Weller et al., 2023) and retrieve-and-read-based systems (Guu et al., 2020; Borgeaud et al., 2022; Izacard et al., 2022) do not fit here. For the Verifiability dataset, ADiOSAA system and its variants use top 150 retrieved sentences as the source sentences. As Hagrid has only 2.83 passages per question in total, we consider all the passages as the source sentences. Additionally, we perform ablation experiments to demonstrate the importance of decomposition and optimal selection in ADiOSAA in the following ways.

ADiOSAA - D considers an answer sentence as the information unit instead of decomposing it. This system establishes the importance of the answer decomposer in ADiOSAA.

ADiOSAA - OS decomposes each answer sentence into its information units, and then ranks source sentences based on their entailment probabilities from the Attr($\mathcal{P}$,$\mathcal{H}$) for each information unit. To obtain attributions for each sentence of the answer, it deduplicates and reorders the attributions for all the information units of the sentence based on the entailment probabilities.

ADiOSAA - D - OS neither uses the answer decomposer or the optimal selection algorithm rather for each sentence in the answer, it ranks source sentences based on their entailment probabilities from the Attr($\mathcal{P}$,$\mathcal{H}$). This system demonstrates the effectiveness of both the components in ADiOSSA.

Evaluation Measures We report precision (P), recall (R), and F1@k $\in \{1, 2, 4\}$ predicted attributions per sentence of an answer[4] for the test set of Verifiability dataset and development set of the Hagrid dataset (as no test set is available). We tune the threshold for attributor's entailment probability (=0.5) and δ (=0.3) in Algorithm 1 based on the Verifiability development set.

5 Results and Discussion

While MonoT5-based retrieval system outperforms (Table 3) others for the top-1 prediction, ADiOSAA variants attain the highest precision when top 2 or 4 predictions are considered. Having a high precision for top 2 or 4 predictions is important as the mean number of attributions per sentence > 1 (see Table 2) and with the increase in the number of predictions, recall may increase or remain the same however, precision may increase, decrease, or stay the same. ADiOSAA variants retain higher precision (as compared to retrieval-based systems) even with the increase in the number of predictions, indicating that retrieval-based systems are good at retrieving one attribution correctly but fail for the second (or more) one compared to our systems. This shows that our systems capture abstractive and compositional attributions more correctly. Optimal selection results in a significant improvement. Higher gains due to optimal selection under no decomposition (difference between ADiOSAA-D

[4]We filter out the instances where answer sentences were extracted directly from the documents.

and ADiOSAA-D-OS) than under decomposition (difference between ADiOSAA and ADiOSAA-OS) shows that the answer sentence is composed of multiple document sentences which are better captured with optimal selection. However, under decomposition, it is more likely that now the decomposed units could be attributed to a single sentence in the document. Decomposition also helps in better predictions (compare ADiOSAA-OS with ADiOSAA-D-OS) showing that compositional answers have multiple attributions to different sentences in the input document. Further, due to a small number of source sentences (avg. 2.83) in Hagrid, the precision and recall values are higher as compared to that in the Verifiability dataset.

Good performance of retrieval-based systems indicate that the existing datasets are less abstractive for long-form comprehension, suggesting the need for research in creating more challenging datasets to foster the development of trustworthy, reliable, and accountable systems that can be used in real-world information-seeking scenarios.

Quality of Decompositions Prior works have used ChatGPT for decomposing facts (Min et al., 2023) or claims (Kamoi et al., 2023) and have shown it to perform reasonably well. We manually examine a subset of decompositions and find that the decomposer might sometimes over-decompose a simple sentence, or generate hallucinated information units (see Table 4 in the appendix for examples). We leave a careful analysis of error categories, and ways to mitigate hallucinations and over-decompositions for future work.

6 Conclusion

We introduce a task of post-hoc answer attribution for long document comprehension, reformulate existing datasets, and asses the feasibility of existing textual entailment and retrieval-based systems in performing this task. Evaluation shows that retrieval-based systems are good at top one prediction however, our proposed answer decomposition and textual entailment-based optimal selection system, ADiOSAA, performs better when more than one predictions are considered. This further indicates the need for highly abstractive long-form reading comprehension datasets that can foster the development and evaluation of more sophisticated attribution systems.

7 Limitations

We note the following limitations of our work. (1) The decompositions are obtained without taking into consideration the source document which might result in unnecessary answer decompositions. This issue can be resolved if the information units are explicitly constrained in the input document, and (2) ADiOSAA is a post-hoc inference time attribution system which uses off-the-shelf trained model, DocNLI. However, future work may consider developing supervised systems for performing the task on the verifiability dataset, and building end-to-end systems where decomposition and optimal selection may happen in an interactive manner. (3) We acknowledge the performance dependence of ADiOSAA on the Attributor. Further investigation into the impact of NLI model's performance on the final results is an avenue for future work.

References

Bernd Bohnet, Vinh Q Tran, Pat Verga, Roee Aharoni, Daniel Andor, Livio Baldini Soares, Jacob Eisenstein, Kuzman Ganchev, Jonathan Herzig, Kai Hui, et al. 2022. Attributed question answering: Evaluation and modeling for attributed large language models. *arXiv preprint arXiv:2212.08037*.

Sebastian Borgeaud, Arthur Mensch, Jordan Hoffmann, Trevor Cai, Eliza Rutherford, Katie Millican, George Bm Van Den Driessche, Jean-Baptiste Lespiau, Bogdan Damoc, Aidan Clark, et al. 2022. Improving language models by retrieving from trillions of tokens. In *International conference on machine learning*, pages 2206–2240. PMLR.

Sihao Chen, Hongming Zhang, Tong Chen, Ben Zhou, Wenhao Yu, Dian Yu, Baolin Peng, Hongwei Wang, Dan Roth, and Dong Yu. 2023. Sub-sentence encoder: Contrastive learning of propositional semantic representations. *arXiv preprint arXiv:2311.04335*.

Yiming Cui, Ting Liu, Wanxiang Che, Zhigang Chen, and Shijin Wang. 2022. Expmrc: explainability evaluation for machine reading comprehension. *Heliyon*, 8(4).

Curation. 2020. Curation. 2020. curation corpus base.

Pradeep Dasigi, Kyle Lo, Iz Beltagy, Arman Cohan, Noah A Smith, and Matt Gardner. 2021. A dataset of information-seeking questions and answers anchored in research papers. *arXiv preprint arXiv:2105.03011*.

Nouha Dziri, Sivan Milton, Mo Yu, Osmar Zaiane, and Siva Reddy. 2022. On the origin of hallucinations in conversational models: Is it the datasets or the models? In *Proceedings of the 2022 Conference of the North American Chapter of the Association for*

Computational Linguistics: Human Language Technologies, pages 5271–5285, Seattle, United States. Association for Computational Linguistics.

Ori Ernst, Ori Shapira, Ramakanth Pasunuru, Michael Lepioshkin, Jacob Goldberger, Mohit Bansal, and Ido Dagan. 2021. Summary-source proposition-level alignment: Task, datasets and supervised baseline. In *Proceedings of the 25th Conference on Computational Natural Language Learning*, pages 310–322, Online. Association for Computational Linguistics.

Angela Fan, Yacine Jernite, Ethan Perez, David Grangier, Jason Weston, and Michael Auli. 2019. ELI5: Long form question answering. In *Proceedings of the 57th Annual Meeting of the Association for Computational Linguistics*, pages 3558–3567, Florence, Italy. Association for Computational Linguistics.

Luyu Gao, Zhuyun Dai, Panupong Pasupat, Anthony Chen, Arun Tejasvi Chaganty, Yicheng Fan, Vincent Zhao, Ni Lao, Hongrae Lee, Da-Cheng Juan, and Kelvin Guu. 2023a. RARR: Researching and revising what language models say, using language models. In *Proceedings of the 61st Annual Meeting of the Association for Computational Linguistics (Volume 1: Long Papers)*, pages 16477–16508, Toronto, Canada. Association for Computational Linguistics.

Tianyu Gao, Howard Yen, Jiatong Yu, and Danqi Chen. 2023b. Enabling large language models to generate text with citations. *arXiv preprint arXiv:2305.14627*.

Kelvin Guu, Kenton Lee, Zora Tung, Panupong Pasupat, and Mingwei Chang. 2020. Retrieval augmented language model pre-training. In *International conference on machine learning*, pages 3929–3938. PMLR.

Nan Hu, Jiaoyan Chen, Yike Wu, Guilin Qi, Sheng Bi, Tongtong Wu, and Jeff Z Pan. 2024. Benchmarking large language models in complex question answering attribution using knowledge graphs. *arXiv preprint arXiv:2401.14640*.

Jie Huang and Kevin Chen-Chuan Chang. 2023. Citation: A key to building responsible and accountable large language models. *arXiv preprint arXiv:2307.02185*.

Siqing Huo, Negar Arabzadeh, and Charles LA Clarke. 2023. Retrieving supporting evidence for llms generated answers. *arXiv preprint arXiv:2306.13781*.

Gautier Izacard, Patrick Lewis, Maria Lomeli, Lucas Hosseini, Fabio Petroni, Timo Schick, Jane Dwivedi-Yu, Armand Joulin, Sebastian Riedel, and Edouard Grave. 2022. Few-shot learning with retrieval augmented language models. *arXiv preprint arXiv:2208.03299*.

Ziwei Ji, Nayeon Lee, Rita Frieske, Tiezheng Yu, Dan Su, Yan Xu, Etsuko Ishii, Ye Jin Bang, Andrea Madotto, and Pascale Fung. 2023. Survey of hallucination in natural language generation. *ACM Computing Surveys*, 55(12):1–38.

Ehsan Kamalloo, Aref Jafari, Xinyu Zhang, Nandan Thakur, and Jimmy Lin. 2023. Hagrid: A human-llm collaborative dataset for generative information-seeking with attribution. *arXiv preprint arXiv:2307.16883*.

Ryo Kamoi, Tanya Goyal, Juan Diego Rodriguez, and Greg Durrett. 2023. Wice: Real-world entailment for claims in wikipedia. *arXiv preprint arXiv:2303.01432*.

Tom Kwiatkowski, Jennimaria Palomaki, Olivia Redfield, Michael Collins, Ankur Parikh, Chris Alberti, Danielle Epstein, Illia Polosukhin, Jacob Devlin, Kenton Lee, Kristina Toutanova, Llion Jones, Matthew Kelcey, Ming-Wei Chang, Andrew M. Dai, Jakob Uszkoreit, Quoc Le, and Slav Petrov. 2019. Natural questions: A benchmark for question answering research. *Transactions of the Association for Computational Linguistics*, 7:452–466.

Nelson F Liu, Tianyi Zhang, and Percy Liang. 2023. Evaluating verifiability in generative search engines. *arXiv preprint arXiv:2304.09848*.

Yinhan Liu, Myle Ott, Naman Goyal, Jingfei Du, Mandar Joshi, Danqi Chen, Omer Levy, Mike Lewis, Luke Zettlemoyer, and Veselin Stoyanov. 2019. Roberta: A robustly optimized bert pretraining approach. *arXiv preprint arXiv:1907.11692*.

Chaitanya Malaviya, Subin Lee, Sihao Chen, Elizabeth Sieber, Mark Yatskar, and Dan Roth. 2023. Expertqa: Expert-curated questions and attributed answers. *arXiv preprint arXiv:2309.07852*.

Donald Metzler, Yi Tay, Dara Bahri, and Marc Najork. 2021. Rethinking search: making domain experts out of dilettantes. In *Acm sigir forum*, volume 55, pages 1–27. ACM New York, NY, USA.

Sewon Min, Kalpesh Krishna, Xinxi Lyu, Mike Lewis, Wen-tau Yih, Pang Wei Koh, Mohit Iyyer, Luke Zettlemoyer, and Hannaneh Hajishirzi. 2023. Factscore: Fine-grained atomic evaluation of factual precision in long form text generation. *arXiv preprint arXiv:2305.14251*.

Ramesh Nallapati, Bowen Zhou, Caglar Gulcehre, Bing Xiang, et al. 2016. Abstractive text summarization using sequence-to-sequence rnns and beyond. *arXiv preprint arXiv:1602.06023*.

Ani Nenkova and Rebecca Passonneau. 2004. Evaluating content selection in summarization: The pyramid method. In *Proceedings of the Human Language Technology Conference of the North American Chapter of the Association for Computational Linguistics: HLT-NAACL 2004*, pages 145–152, Boston, Massachusetts, USA. Association for Computational Linguistics.

Yixin Nie, Adina Williams, Emily Dinan, Mohit Bansal, Jason Weston, and Douwe Kiela. 2019. Adversarial nli: A new benchmark for natural language understanding. *arXiv preprint arXiv:1910.14599*.

OpenAI. 2023. OpenAI. (2023). ChatGPT.

Colin Raffel, Noam Shazeer, Adam Roberts, Katherine Lee, Sharan Narang, Michael Matena, Yanqi Zhou, Wei Li, and Peter J Liu. 2020. Exploring the limits of transfer learning with a unified text-to-text transformer. *The Journal of Machine Learning Research*, 21(1):5485–5551.

Pranav Rajpurkar, Jian Zhang, Konstantin Lopyrev, and Percy Liang. 2016. Squad: 100,000+ questions for machine comprehension of text. *arXiv preprint arXiv:1606.05250*.

Hannah Rashkin, Vitaly Nikolaev, Matthew Lamm, Lora Aroyo, Michael Collins, Dipanjan Das, Slav Petrov, Gaurav Singh Tomar, Iulia Turc, and David Reitter. 2023. Measuring attribution in natural language generation models. *Computational Linguistics*, pages 1–66.

Chirag Shah and Emily M Bender. 2022. Situating search. In *Proceedings of the 2022 Conference on Human Information Interaction and Retrieval*, pages 221–232.

Ori Shapira, David Gabay, Yang Gao, Hadar Ronen, Ramakanth Pasunuru, Mohit Bansal, Yael Amsterdamer, and Ido Dagan. 2019. Crowdsourcing lightweight pyramids for manual summary evaluation. In *Proceedings of the 2019 Conference of the North American Chapter of the Association for Computational Linguistics: Human Language Technologies, Volume 1 (Long and Short Papers)*, pages 682–687, Minneapolis, Minnesota. Association for Computational Linguistics.

Gabriel Stanovsky, Julian Michael, Luke Zettlemoyer, and Ido Dagan. 2018. Supervised open information extraction. In *Proceedings of the 2018 Conference of the North American Chapter of the Association for Computational Linguistics: Human Language Technologies, Volume 1 (Long Papers)*, pages 885–895, New Orleans, Louisiana. Association for Computational Linguistics.

Yi Tay, Vinh Tran, Mostafa Dehghani, Jianmo Ni, Dara Bahri, Harsh Mehta, Zhen Qin, Kai Hui, Zhe Zhao, Jai Gupta, et al. 2022. Transformer memory as a differentiable search index. *Advances in Neural Information Processing Systems*, 35:21831–21843.

Hai Wang, Dian Yu, Kai Sun, Jianshu Chen, Dong Yu, David McAllester, and Dan Roth. 2019. Evidence sentence extraction for machine reading comprehension. *arXiv preprint arXiv:1902.08852*.

Orion Weller, Marc Marone, Nathaniel Weir, Dawn Lawrie, Daniel Khashabi, and Benjamin Van Durme. 2023. " according to..." prompting language models improves quoting from pre-training data. *arXiv preprint arXiv:2305.13252*.

Vikas Yadav, Steven Bethard, and Mihai Surdeanu. 2020. Unsupervised alignment-based iterative evidence retrieval for multi-hop question answering. In *Proceedings of the 58th Annual Meeting of the Association for Computational Linguistics*, pages 4514–4525, Online. Association for Computational Linguistics.

Wenpeng Yin, Dragomir Radev, and Caiming Xiong. 2021. DocNLI: A large-scale dataset for document-level natural language inference. In *Findings of the Association for Computational Linguistics: ACL-IJCNLP 2021*, pages 4913–4922, Online. Association for Computational Linguistics.

Xiang Yue, Boshi Wang, Kai Zhang, Ziru Chen, Yu Su, and Huan Sun. 2023. Automatic evaluation of attribution by large language models. *arXiv preprint arXiv:2305.06311*.

Xinyu Zhang, Nandan Thakur, Odunayo Ogundepo, Ehsan Kamalloo, David Alfonso-Hermelo, Xiaoguang Li, Qun Liu, Mehdi Rezagholizadeh, and Jimmy Lin. 2022. Making a miracl: Multilingual information retrieval across a continuum of languages. *arXiv preprint arXiv:2210.09984*.

Appendix

A Baseline Models

- **BM25 (sparse)** is a classical bag-of-words based sparse retrieval method that relies on lexical overlap, term frequency heuristics, inverse document frequency and document length for retrieval relevant passages given a query.
- **GTR (dense)** is a dense retrieval method that embeds both documents and queries into low-dimensional representations using T5-based (Raffel et al., 2020) dual encoders, with one of the encoders tailored to the queries and the other to the documents.
- **MonoT5** is a T5-based model that takes a query and a document, and outputs the probability of relevance of document with respect to the query. The documents are ranked based on this probability.

B Entailment model DocNLI

We have used RoBERTa-L model trained on DocNLI dataset as our go-to entailment model. DocNLI contains an array of reformulated versions of existing datasets (adversarial NLI (ANLI) (Nie et al., 2019), the question answering benchmark SQuAD (Rajpurkar et al., 2016) and three summarization benchmarks (CNN/DailyMail (Nallapati et al., 2016), DUC2001[5], and Curation (Curation, 2020))) by transforming various summarization and question answering datasets into natural language inference form to ensure that the premise and hypothesis are paragraph-level long and that the dataset does not contain any artifacts such as hypothesis length bias, direct overlap between premise and hypothesis. Table 5 reports the accuracy results of DocNLI on various NLI datasets.

C Additional Results

We present results on verifiability dataset when top 150 sentences retrieved using GTR and MonoT5 are used by `ADiOSAA` and when all the sentences in a document are used in Table 6. In all the cases, `ADiOSAA` outperforms all the ablations - removing decompose, optimal selection or both. This shows that each of the components of the proposed approach is important for the attribution task.

C.1 Implementation Details

The RoBERTa-L model contains 355 million parameters. We use off-the-shelf model so no training is required. We only perform inference on one NVIDIA T4 16GB GPU machine. All the reported scores are from one run of the model inference. Hyperparameter tuning is done for δ and entailment probability threshold using the development set of Verifiability dataset.

[5] `https://www-nlpir.nist.gov/projects/duc/guidelines/2001.html`

S.No.	Input	Output Decompositions
	Correct Decompositions	
1.	Based on the given contexts, the University Library of the Library of Congress in Washington D.C. is the biggest library in the world, with more than 167 million items including books, printed materials, recordings, photographs, maps, sheet music, and manuscripts.	The University Library of the Library of Congress is in Washington D.C. The University Library of the Library of Congress is the biggest library in the world. The University Library of the Library of Congress has more than 167 million items. The items include books, printed materials, recordings, photographs, maps, sheet music, and manuscripts.
2.	The Islamic Golden Age is traditionally dated from the 8th century to the 14th century.	The Islamic Golden Age is traditionally dated. The Islamic Golden Age is traditionally dated from the 8th century. The Islamic Golden Age is traditionally dated to the 14th century.
	Erroneous Decompositions	
1.	Ronnie Van Zant was born in Jacksonville, Florida.	Ronnie Van Zant was born. Ronnie Van Zant was born in Jacksonville, Florida
2.	The Beer Store, also known as Brewers Retail Inc, was founded in 1927.	The Beer Store is also known as Brewers Retail Inc. The Beer Store was founded in 1927. The Beer Store was founded in Ontario, Canada

Table 4: Sample outputs from the Answer Decomposer. 1. shows over-decomposition, and 2. shows hallucination error under Erroneous Decompositions.

FEVER	MCTest (v160)	MCTest (v500)	SciTail	MNLI
88.84	90.00	85.83	78.17	91.13

Table 5: Accuracy of DocNLI (used as the Attributor in our work) model on various NLI datasets. We report the numbers as-is from Yin et al. (2021).

Model	Top 1			Top 2			Top 4		
	P	R	F1	P	R	F1	P	R	F1
All + ADIOSAA	**0.537**	**0.422**	**0.452**	**0.479**	**0.540**	**0.482**	**0.471**	**0.598**	**0.494**
All + ADIOSAA - Decomposer	0.462	0.381	0.404	0.435	0.408	0.402	0.433	0.408	0.401
All + ADIOSAA - Optimal Selection	0.368	0.289	0.311	0.272	0.327	0.279	0.250	0.353	0.270
All + ADIOSAA - Decomposer - Optimal Selection	0.262	0.226	0.236	0.262	0.226	0.236	0.262	0.226	0.236
GTR + ADIOSAA	**0.538**	**0.423**	**0.453**	**0.479**	**0.541**	**0.483**	**0.471**	**0.598**	**0.494**
GTR + ADIOSAA - Decomposer	0.463	0.382	0.405	0.435	0.409	0.403	0.433	0.409	0.402
GTR + ADIOSAA - Optimal Selection	0.372	0.294	0.315	0.275	0.332	0.282	0.252	0.358	0.273
GTR + ADIOSAA - Decomposer - Optimal Selection	0.265	0.229	0.238	0.265	0.229	0.238	0.265	0.229	0.238
MonoT5 + ADIOSAA	**0.537**	**0.422**	**0.452**	**0.479**	**0.540**	**0.482**	**0.471**	**0.598**	**0.494**
MonoT5 + ADIOSAA - Decomposer	0.467	0.385	0.408	0.439	0.412	0.407	0.437	0.413	0.406
MonoT5 + ADIOSAA - Optimal Selection	0.371	0.292	0.314	0.274	0.330	0.281	0.251	0.356	0.272
MonoT5 + ADIOSAA - Decomposer - Optimal Selection	0.265	0.229	0.238	0.265	0.229	0.238	0.265	0.229	0.238

Table 6: Evaluation results with GTR, MonoT5 and all sentences for Verifiability dataset.

A Benchmark Suite of Japanese Natural Questions

Takuya Uematsu[1] **Hao Wang**[1] **Daisuke Kawahara**[1] **Tomohide Shibata**[2]
[1]Waseda University [2]LY Corporation
takuya1009@akane.waseda.jp conan1024hao@akane.waseda.jp
dkw@waseda.jp tomshiba@lycorp.co.jp

Abstract

To develop high-performance and robust natural language processing (NLP) models, it is important to have various question answering (QA) datasets to train, evaluate, and analyze them. Although there are various QA datasets available in English, there are only a few QA datasets in other languages. We focus on Japanese, a language with only a few basic QA datasets, and aim to build a Japanese version of Natural Questions (NQ) consisting of questions that naturally arise from human information needs. We collect natural questions from query logs of a Japanese search engine and build the dataset using crowdsourcing. We also re-define the dataset specification of the original NQ to construct Japanese Natural Questions (JNQ). Furthermore, we construct a Japanese version of BoolQ (JBoolQ), which is derived from NQ and consists of yes/no questions. JNQ consists of 16,871 questions, and JBoolQ consists of 6,467 questions. We also define two tasks from JNQ and one from JBoolQ and establish baselines using competitive methods drawn from related literature. We hope that these datasets will facilitate research on QA and NLP models in Japanese. We will make JNQ and JBoolQ publicly available.

1 Introduction

To develop high-performance and robust natural language processing (NLP) models, it is important to have various question answering (QA) datasets to train, evaluate, and analyze them. There are diverse extractive and generative QA datasets that require many techniques and knowledge to solve, such as multi-hop inference (Yang et al., 2018) and real-world knowledge (Dua et al., 2019). There have been some studies to solve many QA tasks in an integrated manner, rather than solving them individually, such as Unified QA (Khashabi et al., 2020) and FLAN (Wei et al., 2022). However, such an integrated analysis is possible only in English but not in other languages because of the lack of QA datasets. This study focuses on Japanese, which has only a few basic QA datasets, such as JSQuAD (Kurihara et al., 2022), JaQuAD (So et al., 2022), and JAQKET (Suzuki et al., 2020).

In this paper, we focus on Natural Questions (NQ) (Kwiatkowski et al., 2019), which consist of questions that arise naturally from human information needs, as a critical QA dataset that does not exist in Japanese. QA datasets such as SQuAD (Rajpurkar et al., 2016) have the problem of annotation artifacts (Gururangan et al., 2018) because the questions are manually created by annotators, which are not natural. In contrast, NQ uses queries entered by users in a search engine, which are considered natural questions. One possible approach to creating a Japanese version of NQ is translating the original NQ dataset into Japanese. However, we do not use translation due to concerns about the unnaturalness of translated sentences, which can result from differences in grammar and other linguistic factors, as well as potential cultural differences between Japan and other countries. Instead, we build and publish Japanese Natural Questions (JNQ) using query logs from a Japanese search engine. We also re-define the dataset specification of the original NQ to obtain a better NQ dataset. Kwiatkowski et al. (2019) have hired trained annotators to build the NQ dataset, but for JNQ, we use crowdsourcing to reduce costs. This method can be applied to any language in which search engine query logs are available.

In addition to JNQ, we build JBoolQ, a Japanese version of BoolQ (Clark et al., 2019). BoolQ is derived from NQ and consists of yes/no questions. JBoolQ questions and yes/no answers are collected in the same way as JNQ. In the original BoolQ, there are only two options: "yes" or "no". However, to make the setting more realistic, we add an option of "unable to answer" to JBoolQ, represented as "NONE". This makes our dataset more challenging than the original BoolQ.

*Proceedings of the 13th Joint Conference on Lexical and Computational Semantics (*SEM 2024)*, pages 58 - 68
June 20-21, 2024 ©2024 Association for Computational Linguistics

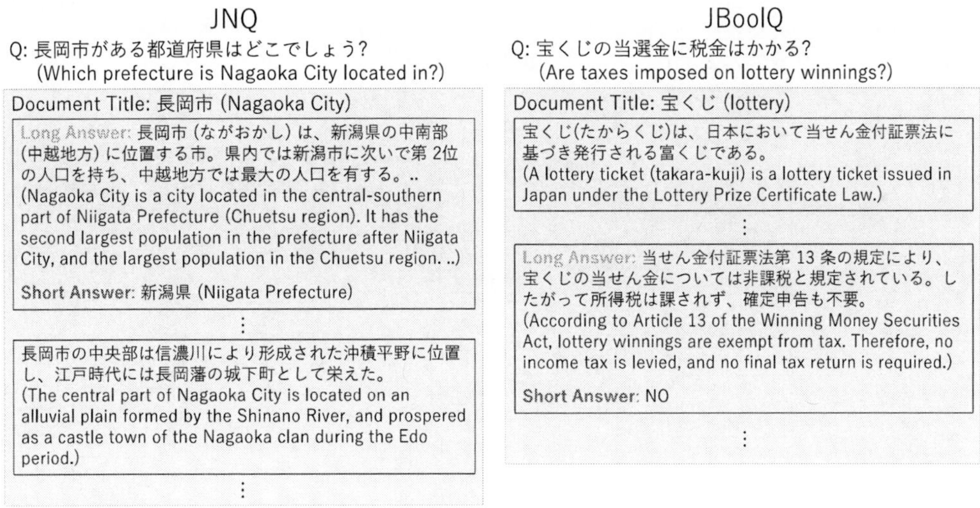

Figure 1: Examples of JNQ and JBoolQ.

In consequence, JNQ contains 16,871 queries and 80,288 paragraphs. JBoolQ, combined with the JNQ yes/no questions, contains 6,467 queries and 31,677 paragraphs. Examples of JNQ and JBoolQ are shown in Figure 1.

Furthermore, we define three tasks using the two datasets as a new QA benchmark in Japanese: long answer extraction, short answer extraction, and yes/no answer identification (BoolQ). We also evaluate these tasks with their respective baselines. JNQ and JBoolQ will be available online.

2 Related Work

Existing QA datasets can be broadly categorized into those where the questions are natural and those where they are not.

QA datasets where the questions are not natural mainly include SQuAD (Rajpurkar et al., 2016) and SQuAD 2.0 (Rajpurkar et al., 2018). The questions in these datasets are not natural because annotators create them after reading a paragraph. Therefore, annotation artifacts in the created questions and lexical overlap between questions and paragraphs are problematic when using these datasets.

Natural Questions (Kwiatkowski et al., 2019) and BoolQ (Clark et al., 2019) are QA datasets that contain natural questions. To build these datasets, search engine query logs are used to collect natural questions arising from human information needs. The documents are Wikipedia articles, and the answers consist of long answers (e.g., paragraphs or tables) and short answers (spans or Yes/No). Other datasets that collect questions from query logs include WikiQA (Yang et al., 2015) and MS MARCO (Bajaj et al., 2018). In these datasets, the answer format differs from NQ and BoolQ, with a single sentence in the document or a hand-crafted summary.

QA datasets whose questions are not derived from query logs but are claimed to be natural include TyDi QA (Clark et al., 2020), Icelandic NQ (Snæbjarnarson and Einarsson, 2022), and Russian BoolQ (Glushkova et al., 2021). In these datasets, annotators are given a prompt consisting of a part or summary of a document and asked to think of a question that cannot be answered by reading only the prompt. These questions are claimed to be "natural" because they are derived from what humans wanted to know about the prompt. However, they are not naturally occurring questions because the authors ask them to think of a question. Thus, we consider that they are not truly natural questions.

For non-English QA datasets, there are several multilingual QA datasets, such as TyDi QA (Clark et al., 2020), MLQA (Lewis et al., 2020), XOR QA (Asai et al., 2021), and XQuAD (Artetxe et al., 2020). However, only approximately half of them include Japanese. Due to the lack of diverse datasets in Japanese, we construct Japanese Natural Questions from scratch.

3 Japanese Natural Questions

Natural Questions (NQ) (Kwiatkowski et al., 2019) is a dataset that focuses on the ability to answer natural questions by reading documents. Each instance consists of a quadruple of a question, a document, a long answer, and a short answer. The

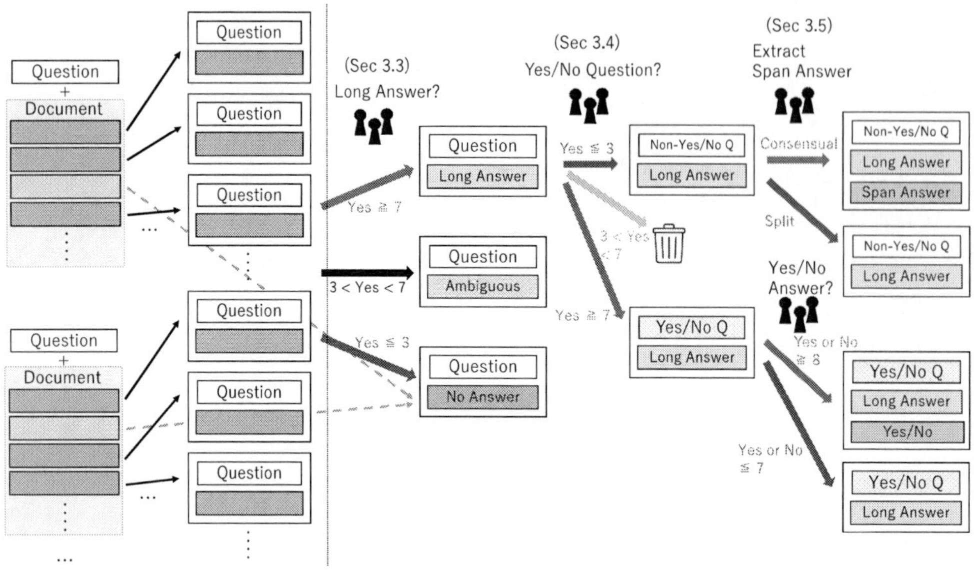

Figure 2: Construction flow of Japanese Natural Questions.

questions are collected from search engine query logs. The documents are Wikipedia articles, with one document provided for each question. The long answer is a paragraph or table in a document containing enough information to infer the answer. The short answer is the shortest possible answer to the question and is a span in the document.

Japanese Natural Questions (JNQ), like NQ, consists of quadruples of a question, a document, long answer(s), and short answer(s). The questions are extracted from search engine query logs, and the documents are Japanese Wikipedia articles. The long answers and short answers are obtained using crowdsourcing. By using crowdsourcing, it is possible to construct a dataset at a low cost and with some quality level without expert annotators. We limit the long answers only to paragraphs to simplify the task, considering that dataset construction is conducted using crowdsourcing. Although NQ has a strict restriction that there is at most one long answer in a document, there are often multiple paragraphs containing answers. Therefore, JNQ allows for scenarios with multiple long answers to a single question.

We describe each stage of building JNQ below. In crowdsourcing, 10 crowdworkers are assigned to deal with a task to build a high-quality benchmark. In cases where ambiguity is detected due to diverging opinions among crowdworkers at each stage, such instances are not incorporated into JNQ. We illustrate the construction flow in Figure 2.

3.1 Question and Document Collection

Question candidates of JNQ are taken from the search query logs accumulated by a company[1]. When people search, they sometimes use word sequences instead of full sentences. Such queries are specific to search engines and may include non-questions. Therefore, queries with spaces are excluded from the pool of question candidates[2]. Furthermore, short queries are often not in the form of questions; therefore, only queries composed of eight or more words are extracted[3]. Subsequently, we prepare the following question patterns and extract queries that match any of them.

1. Contains "は" (Japanese topic marker) + an interrogative word
2. The final character is "?"
3. Contains the specific word such as "意味" (meaning), "方法" (method), and "理由" (reason).

We perform a Google search with the question candidates obtained above. If there is a Wikipedia article within the top five search results, we select the top-ranked article as the document. Question candidates for which there are no Wikipedia articles within the top five search results are excluded.

[1]The name of the company will remain anonymous until the paper is accepted.

[2]Japanese is a language that does not use spaces between words, and Japanese sentences usually do not contain spaces.

[3]Word segmentation is performed using the morphological analyzer Juman++: https://github.com/ku-nlp/jumanpp.

3.2 Good Question Identification

The extracted question candidates contain non-questions and inappropriate questions. Therefore, we use crowdsourcing to obtain good questions. A good question is one that inquires about facts, methods, causes, or reasons. A bad question is ambiguous, based on incorrect assumptions, soliciting opinions, asking about the title of a work, or posing questions with answers that vary depending on the timing. 10 crowdworkers judge whether the given question is good or bad. Among the 10 crowdworkers, question candidates that are judged as good questions by six or more workers are adopted as questions for JNQ. Examples of good questions are provided in Appendix A. Examples judged as bad questions are "今日はどこに行こうか？" (Where shall we go today?) and "Amazon支払い方法が承認されません" (The Amazon payment method is not approved).

3.3 Long Answer Identification

Through crowdsourcing, we extract paragraphs from the document that contain sufficient information to answer a question and designate them as long answers. We provide crowdworkers with a maximum of five paragraphs to reduce annotation costs. These five paragraphs consist of the document's first paragraph and four paragraphs (excluding the first one) that have high relevance to the snippet obtained from the Google search conducted in Section 3.1. This is because the first paragraph, which usually provides an overview, and the paragraphs with high relevance to the snippet are likely to contain the answer. The paragraphs that are not included in these five paragraphs are identified as not containing the long answer and are accordingly labeled as "NONE". The relevance is calculated by the cosine similarity between the snippet and a paragraph, with both represented as bag-of-words vectors. We illustrate the paragraph selection process in Figure 3.

We provide a question and each paragraph to 10 crowdworkers, prompting them to make a binary choice on whether the paragraph contains "sufficient information to infer an answer to the question" or not. We classify the paragraphs into three groups based on the votes of the 10 workers. If seven or more "Yes" votes are collected, we categorize the paragraph as a long answer and assign it the label "EXIST". If four to six "Yes" votes are collected, we categorize the paragraph as ambiguous in terms of being a long answer and label it as "AMBIGUOUS". Excluding this paragraph during the training process can help reduce noise. If three or fewer votes are collected, we categorize the paragraph as lacking a long answer and label it as "NONE". Since the judgment is done on a per-paragraph basis, multiple paragraphs may be classified as long answers for a single question, or there may be no long answer at all. If none of the paragraphs within these five paragraphs qualifies as the long answer, we infer that the document does not contain a long answer to the question.

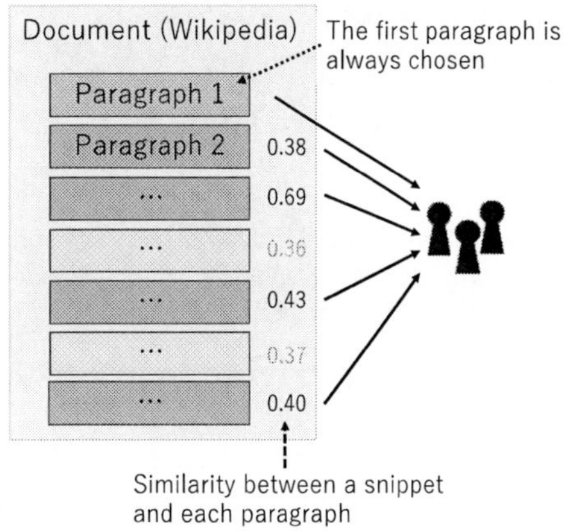

Figure 3: An illustration for choosing paragraphs from documents to ask crowdworkers whether they qualify as long answers.

3.4 Yes/No Question Identification

In the following step, detailed in Section 3.5, we extract short answers from paragraphs designated as long answers. The task of short answer extraction varies depending on whether the question is a yes/no question. Therefore, we first crowdsource the judgment of whether the question is a yes/no question. If seven or more crowdworkers judge the question to be a yes/no question, the question is considered as a yes/no question. If a question receives between four and six votes, we remove it from the dataset due to its ambiguity.

3.5 Short Answer Identification

We categorize the cases based on whether the question is a yes/no question. For each category, we obtain a short answer, i.e., a yes/no answer or a span answer, using the following procedure.

Yes/No Answer Identification If the question is a yes/no question, crowdworkers judge whether the answer is "YES" or "NO" based on the paragraph of a long answer. If more than seven crowdworkers judge the answer as either "YES" or "NO", the

	Number	Length (# of chars)		
		Mean	Max	Min
Question	16,871	17.7	50	8
Paragraph	192,514	159.0	999	10
Span answer	5,463	9.6	180	1

Table 1: Numbers and lengths of questions and paragraphs, and short answers in JNQ. The paragraphs in this table refer to all paragraphs, including unannotated paragraphs (i.e., considered as no long answer).

Long →	EXIST			AMBIGUOUS	NONE
Short →	Span	Yes/No	NONE		
	5,463	143	2,280	10,866	61,536

Table 2: Statistics of paragraphs in JNQ. The total number of paragraphs is 80,288.

answer is considered as a short answer. Paragraphs with seven or fewer "YES" or "NO" votes are considered ambiguous paragraphs, and a "NONE" label is assigned to the short answer. In other words, this paragraph is judged to have only a long answer.

Span Answer Identification If the question is not a yes/no question, we ask 10 crowdworkers to extract a span answer from the paragraph. If there is no span answer in the paragraph, crowdworkers judge it as "NONE". We aggregate the 10 answers by majority voting. As a pre-process, if one answer is subsumed by another, the votes are added to the shorter one. If there is a tie with multiple short answers receiving the most votes, the shortest one is chosen. Furthermore, answers that receive only one vote are considered unreliable and are not adopted.

4 Japanese BoolQ

BoolQ (Clark et al., 2019) is a QA dataset focusing on natural yes/no questions. It contains many non-factoid questions that require a wide range of inferential abilities to answer. Each instance consists of a question, a paragraph (equivalent to a long answer in NQ), and an answer (yes/no). The questions and paragraphs are extracted from search engine query logs and Wikipedia articles, like NQ. BoolQ adopts only the questions with either yes or no answers and pairs them with not a whole document but a paragraph to simplify the specification.

Japanese BoolQ (JBoolQ) consists of a question, a document, a long answer, and a yes/no answer, like yes/no questions in JNQ. Unlike BoolQ, each question may have multiple long answers, and the answers can include "NONE", which means unanswerable, in addition to yes/no. Therefore, it is more challenging than BoolQ, and a deeper understanding of the documents is required to answer the questions.

# of long answers	Number	Ratio
0	11,126	65.9%
1	4,117	24.4%
2	1,203	7.1%
3	344	2.0%
4	74	0.4%
5	7	0.04%
Total	16,871	100%

Table 3: Distribution of the number of long answers per question in JNQ.

We construct JBoolQ using basically the same procedure as JNQ. Since the ratio of yes/no questions in JNQ is only around 1%, for JBoolQ, we collect questions from a larger query log pool than JNQ. The construction procedure is as follows. The details of each step are described in Section 3.

1. Question and document collection[4]
2. Good question identification
3. Yes/No question identification
4. Long answer identification
5. Yes/No answer identification

Compared to JNQ, the order of yes/no question identification and long answer identification is reversed to narrow down the candidates to the target yes/no questions at an early stage and reduce the annotation cost later. Finally, we merge the yes/no questions in JNQ into JBoolQ.

5 Analysis

In this section, we analyze JNQ and JBoolQ.

5.1 JNQ

Statistics JNQ contains 16,871 questions. Table 1 shows the average, maximum, and minimum numbers of characters in the questions, paragraphs, and short answers. Statistics on the paragraphs are shown in Table 2. In JNQ, multiple paragraphs can be a long answer to a single question. The distribution of the number of long answers per question is shown in Table 3. Questions with multiple long answers account for approximately 10% of all questions and 28% of the questions with long answers.

[4]We change the conditions of JNQ to extract yes/no questions as follows: more than six words and ending with "?" or "か" (Japanese interrogative particle).

Type	Example
What	歌手「矢沢永吉」が1978年にヒットした曲は?
(39%)	What was the song that the singer Eikichi Yazawa had a hit with in 1978?
Where	「伯方の塩」で知られる伯方島があるのはどこ?
(12%)	Where is Hakata Island, known for "Hakata Salt"?
When	パスポートに菊が描かれたのはいつ
(4%)	When was the chrysanthemum depicted on passports?
Why	日本にはなぜ四季があるのか
(4%)	Why does Japan have four seasons?
Who	「青の時代」といった、20世紀を代表する画家は誰でしょう?
(3%)	Who is the iconic painter of the 20th century known for the 'Blue Period'?
How	スマートフォンでqrコードを読み取る方法
(31%)	How to read qr code with smartphone
Yes/No	源泉徴収票は市役所でもらえる?
(3%)	Can I obtain a withholding slip at the city hall?
Other	冬に卵を生で食べられる期間は何日
(4%)	How long can eggs be eaten raw in winter?

Table 4: Question types of JNQ.

	Number	Length (# of chars)		
		Mean	Max	Min
Question	6,467	11.4	48	6
Paragraph	27,954	171.7	988	21

Table 5: Numbers and lengths of questions and paragraphs in JBoolQ.

Long →	EXIST		AMBIGUOUS	NONE
Short →	Yes/No	NONE		
	1,742	833	3,723	25,379

Table 6: Statistics of paragraphs in JBoolQ. The total number of paragraphs is 31,677.

# of long answers	Number	Ratio
0	4,649	71.9%
1	1,252	19.4%
2	414	6.4%
3	117	1.8%
4	31	0.5%
5	4	0.06%
Total	6,467	100%

Table 7: Distribution of the number of long answers per question in JBoolQ.

Question Type We sampled 100 questions from JNQ and classified them according to which wh-word they begin with when translated into English. The results are shown in Table 4. The most common question type is "What", accounting for 39%. The next most common question is "How", accounting for 31%. Of the questions asking "How", 84% of the questions are about "How to". In NQ, questions starting with "How to" account for less than 1% of the total, and thus there are more "How to" questions in JNQ, which can be considered more difficult to answer than fact-seeking ones.

Lexical Overlap We investigated lexical overlap. Lexical overlap refers to the ratio of overlapping words between a paragraph and a question. It is reported that when this ratio is high, the model can easily provide answers (Clark et al., 2020). Each question and paragraph pair of JNQ was segmented at the word level[5], and lexical overlap was calculated. Lexical overlap of JNQ is 59.4%, which is much lower than 79.5% observed in Japanese SQuAD (JSQuAD). This result indicates that we address, to some extent, the issue of annotation artifacts, which are common in datasets such as SQuAD, where an annotator is asked to create a question after reading a paragraph.

[5]We used MeCab + IPAdic (https://taku910.github.io/mecab/) for word segmentation.

5.2 JBoolQ

Statistics JBoolQ contains 6,467 questions. Table 5 shows the average, maximum, and minimum numbers of characters in the questions and paragraphs. The average length of the questions is shorter than JNQ. This is because when extracting candidate questions from query logs, JNQ extracted queries with eight or more words, while JBoolQ extracted queries with six or more words to obtain more yes/no questions. Statistics on the paragraphs are shown in Table 6. The distribution of the number of long answers, shown in Table 7, is similar to JNQ.

Question Type We sampled 100 questions from JBoolQ and classified them according to their question types. We basically adopted the classification method used in BoolQ but added two categories: "Possibility" and "Necessity". The results are shown in Table 8. Questions asking facts about a specific entity occupy 31%, which is the most

Type	Example
Possibility	新幹線で携帯充電できる?
(23%)	Can I charge my cell phone on the Shinkansen?
Necessity	履歴書に印鑑は必要か
(11%)	Do I need a seal on my resume?
Definitional	ナショナルとパナソニックは同じ?
(7%)	Are "National" and "Panasonic" the same?
Existence	国会議事堂の中に保育園ある?
(4%)	Is there a daycare center in the Capitol?
Other General Fact	疲れで熱は出る?
(24%)	Does fatigue cause fever?
Other Entity Fact	久能山東照宮は神社?
(31%)	Kunouzan Toshogu is a shrine?

Table 8: Question types of JBoolQ.

Task	Train	Dev	Test
Long Answer Extraction	13,496	1,687	1,688
Short Answer Extraction	6,158	789	761
Yes/No Answer Identification	22,357	2,791	2,806

Table 9: Statistics of the three tasks. The number of long answer extraction refers to the number of questions, and the numbers of the other tasks refer to the number of instances.

common. Questions asking about "Possibility" and "Necessity", newly added categories in JBoolQ, account for 23% and 11%, respectively, corresponding to a total of 1/3 of the whole dataset.

6 Experiments

6.1 Experimental Setup

We define three tasks to use JNQ and JBoolQ as a benchmark for evaluating QA systems. From JNQ, we introduce the following two tasks: long answer extraction, short answer extraction. From JBoolQ, we introduce the task of yes/no answer identification. We also establish baselines using competitive methods drawn from related literature. We implement hyperparameter searches and report the best scores. We list the statistics of the tasks in Table 9.

Long Answer Extraction Unlike NQ, in our dataset, there can be multiple long answers or no long answer in a document. Thus, we consider long answer extraction as a paragraph-based multi-label classification task. *Given a question and a document, a system tries to select all paragraphs with long answers.* We use precision, recall, and F1 scores for evaluation metrics.

We introduce a baseline that considers the task a binary classification problem. For each paragraph in the document, we input the question-paragraph pair into the model and binarily decide whether the paragraph is a long answer. We use Japanese BERT (Devlin et al., 2019) and RoBERTa (Liu et al., 2019) as base models[6]. We use two kinds of training sets in our experiments: (1) the paragraphs collected in Section 3.3, which contain positive examples and hard negative examples (challenge candidates, which have high relevance to the snippet but are considered as no long answer), and (2) all paragraphs in the documents. The ambiguous paragraphs are excluded from both. For testing, we use all paragraphs in the documents, aiming to be close to real extraction scenarios.

We also evaluate human performance using crowdsourcing in the same way as the dataset construction process. We asked 10 annotators to answer. If seven or more annotators agree, it is considered that the paragraph is a long answer; otherwise, it is not. Due to cost reasons, we sampled 100 questions for human evaluation instead of using the whole test set.

Short Answer Extraction For short answer extraction, we target question-paragraph pairs labeled as being present for long answers. Following NQ, we exclude yes/no questions. In practice, we treat this task as a SQuAD 2.0 (Rajpurkar et al., 2018) like task. *Given a question-paragraph pair, a system tries to extract a span as the short answer from the paragraph.* If the paragraph has no short answer, we regard this question as unanswerable and make the target span an empty string. We use exact match (EM) and character-based F1 scores for evaluation metrics.

We treat short answer extraction as a classification problem of whether each token in a paragraph is an answer span's start/end position. We use BERT and RoBERTa as base models.

We also evaluate human performance using crowdsourcing on the whole test set. We asked three annotators to answer and average their scores.

Yes/No Answer Identification As described in Section 4, unlike BoolQ, our JBoolQ dataset contains three kinds of labels: "YES", "NO", and "NONE". This makes our task a multiclass classification problem. *Given a question-paragraph pair, a system tries to answer Yes/No/None.* We use precision, recall, and F1 scores on labels "YES" and "NO" for evaluation metrics.

We use BERT and RoBERTa as base models. Since the instances with yes/no answers are scarce, we oversample these instances five times.

[6]We use the transformers library provided by Hugging Face. https://github.com/huggingface/transformers

Model	Trained on Only Hard Negatives						Trained on All Data					
	Dev			Test			Dev			Test		
	P	R	F1	P	R	F1	P	R	F1	P	R	F1
Tohoku-BERT-base[1]	36.6	74.6	49.1	35.0	72.3	47.2	53.1	67.4	59.4	51.2	68.3	58.5
Tohoku-BERT-large[2]	39.6	70.9	50.8	42.1	72.1	53.2	53.9	67.5	59.9	56.8	66.2	61.2
Waseda-RoBERTa-base[3]	42.5	73.8	53.9	44.6	74.8	55.9	**63.7**	**73.0**	**68.0**	**64.2**	**73.4**	**68.5**
Waseda-RoBERTa-large[4]	**47.1**	**76.2**	**58.2**	**48.6**	**80.9**	**60.7**	57.9	51.4	54.5	57.9	48.3	52.7
Human	-	-	-	-	-	-	-	-	-	46.3	75.8	57.5

Table 10: Performance on long answer extraction. We list precision (P), recall (R), and F1 of baselines and human annotators. Human evaluation was conducted by sampling 100 questions from the test set.

Model	Dev		Test	
	EM	F1	EM	F1
Tohoku-BERT-base	23.3	33.4	23.1	31.3
Tohoku-BERT-large	23.1	32.9	23.3	31.0
Waseda-RoBERTa-base	41.1	49.9	41.7	50.1
Waseda-RoBERTa-large	**45.5**	**53.4**	**45.7**	**53.9**
Human	-	-	51.1	62.5

Table 11: Performance on short answer extraction.

Model	Dev			Test		
	P	R	F1	P	R	F1
Tohoku-BERT-base	63.4	**59.6**	61.4	62.5	52.5	57.0
Tohoku-BERT-large	66.0	54.1	59.5	65.1	50.6	56.9
Waseda-RoBERTa-base	58.1	56.8	57.5	59.5	56.2	57.8
Waseda-RoBERTa-large	**68.4**	57.9	**62.7**	**65.5**	**57.4**	**61.2**
Human	-	-	-	75.8	73.0	74.4

Table 12: Performance on yes/no answer identification.

We also evaluate human performance by asking 10 crowdworkers to conduct the following two tasks. First, they check if a paragraph is a long answer in a similar way to long answer extraction. Second, the workers judge "YES", "NO", or "NONE" for a paragraph that is judged to be a long answer. The answer with the most votes is adopted, and if the number of the most votes is the same, "NONE" is adopted.

6.2 Results

Long Answer Extraction We show the results of long answer extraction in Table 10. The models show high recall but low precision when trained on only hard negative examples. The models' precision becomes much higher when trained on all data, indicating unlabeled negative examples are also helpful to training.

Human annotators performed poorly in precision for this task. This also indicates the possibility of there being a few paragraphs with a long answer within the unlabeled paragraphs (except five paragraphs given to the crowdworkers). To tackle this problem, a possible way is to provide the crowdworkers with paragraphs except for the five paragraphs judged as "long answers" by the models and ask them to determine whether they are long answers. We leave this exploration for future work.

Short Answer Extraction We show the results of short answer extraction in Table 11. Waseda-RoBERTa-base and Waseda-RoBERTa-large perform well, but the scores are very inferior to the human performance. Tohoku-BERT-base and Tohoku-BERT-large perform poorly. When examining the outputs, we found that Tohoku-BERTs sometimes extract the entire paragraph as predictions, which leads to underperformance. Since the paragraph is a long answer, extracting the entire paragraph could also be considered correct, but it is wrong according to our task definition. We speculate that insufficient data caused this phenomenon, considering our data is only one-tenth of JSQuAD (Kurihara et al., 2022).

Yes/No Answer Identification We show the results of yes/no answer identification in Table 12. The models show high precision and relatively low recall scores, indicating that they predict a large proportion of yes/no instances as "NONE". "NONE" instances make our task more challenging than the original BoolQ, which makes our benchmark more valuable since advanced training techniques are needed to overcome the unbalanced data distribution and improve model performance.

Human annotators could recognize more yes/no answers correctly than the models. This leads to a higher recall.

7 Conclusion

We constructed two QA datasets: Japanese Natural Questions (JNQ) and Japanese BoolQ (JBoolQ). The questions in these datasets are collected from query logs from a Japanese search engine and are natural, derived from human information needs.

The annotation process was conducted through crowdsourcing. We also defined a total of three tasks, including long answer extraction, short answer extraction, and yes/no answer identification. We evaluated the performance of the baseline models. The constructed datasets can be used for training, evaluating, and analyzing QA and NLP models and are expected to facilitate these studies in Japanese.

Acknowledgements

This work was carried out in collaboration with LY Corporation and Waseda University.

References

Mikel Artetxe, Sebastian Ruder, and Dani Yogatama. 2020. On the cross-lingual transferability of monolingual representations. In *Proceedings of the 58th Annual Meeting of the Association for Computational Linguistics*, pages 4623–4637, Online. Association for Computational Linguistics.

Akari Asai, Jungo Kasai, Jonathan Clark, Kenton Lee, Eunsol Choi, and Hannaneh Hajishirzi. 2021. XOR QA: Cross-lingual open-retrieval question answering. In *Proceedings of the 2021 Conference of the North American Chapter of the Association for Computational Linguistics: Human Language Technologies*, pages 547–564, Online. Association for Computational Linguistics.

Payal Bajaj, Daniel Campos, Nick Craswell, Li Deng, Jianfeng Gao, Xiaodong Liu, Rangan Majumder, Andrew McNamara, Bhaskar Mitra, Tri Nguyen, Mir Rosenberg, Xia Song, Alina Stoica, Saurabh Tiwary, and Tong Wang. 2018. Ms marco: A human generated machine reading comprehension dataset.

Xilun Chen, Kushal Lakhotia, Barlas Oguz, Anchit Gupta, Patrick Lewis, Stan Peshterliev, Yashar Mehdad, Sonal Gupta, and Wen-tau Yih. 2022. Salient phrase aware dense retrieval: Can a dense retriever imitate a sparse one? In *Findings of the Association for Computational Linguistics: EMNLP 2022*, pages 250–262, Abu Dhabi, United Arab Emirates. Association for Computational Linguistics.

Christopher Clark, Kenton Lee, Ming-Wei Chang, Tom Kwiatkowski, Michael Collins, and Kristina Toutanova. 2019. BoolQ: Exploring the surprising difficulty of natural yes/no questions. In *Proceedings of the 2019 Conference of the North American Chapter of the Association for Computational Linguistics: Human Language Technologies, Volume 1 (Long and Short Papers)*, pages 2924–2936, Minneapolis, Minnesota. Association for Computational Linguistics.

Jonathan H. Clark, Eunsol Choi, Michael Collins, Dan Garrette, Tom Kwiatkowski, Vitaly Nikolaev, and Jennimaria Palomaki. 2020. TyDi QA: A benchmark for information-seeking question answering in typologically diverse languages. *Transactions of the Association for Computational Linguistics*, 8:454–470.

Jacob Devlin, Ming-Wei Chang, Kenton Lee, and Kristina Toutanova. 2019. BERT: Pre-training of deep bidirectional transformers for language understanding. In *Proceedings of the 2019 Conference of the North American Chapter of the Association for Computational Linguistics: Human Language Technologies, Volume 1 (Long and Short Papers)*, pages 4171–4186, Minneapolis, Minnesota. Association for Computational Linguistics.

Dheeru Dua, Yizhong Wang, Pradeep Dasigi, Gabriel Stanovsky, Sameer Singh, and Matt Gardner. 2019. DROP: A reading comprehension benchmark requiring discrete reasoning over paragraphs. In *Proceedings of the 2019 Conference of the North American Chapter of the Association for Computational Linguistics: Human Language Technologies, Volume 1 (Long and Short Papers)*, pages 2368–2378, Minneapolis, Minnesota. Association for Computational Linguistics.

Taisia Glushkova, Alexey Machnev, Alena Fenogenova, Tatiana Shavrina, Ekaterina Artemova, and Dmitry I. Ignatov. 2021. DaNetQA: A yes/no question answering dataset for the russian language. In *Lecture Notes in Computer Science*, pages 57–68. Springer International Publishing.

Suchin Gururangan, Swabha Swayamdipta, Omer Levy, Roy Schwartz, Samuel Bowman, and Noah A. Smith. 2018. Annotation artifacts in natural language inference data. In *Proceedings of the 2018 Conference of the North American Chapter of the Association for Computational Linguistics: Human Language Technologies, Volume 2 (Short Papers)*, pages 107–112, New Orleans, Louisiana. Association for Computational Linguistics.

Vladimir Karpukhin, Barlas Oguz, Sewon Min, Patrick Lewis, Ledell Wu, Sergey Edunov, Danqi Chen, and Wen-tau Yih. 2020. Dense passage retrieval for open-domain question answering. In *Proceedings of the 2020 Conference on Empirical Methods in Natural Language Processing (EMNLP)*, pages 6769–6781, Online. Association for Computational Linguistics.

Daniel Khashabi, Sewon Min, Tushar Khot, Ashish Sabharwal, Oyvind Tafjord, Peter Clark, and Hannaneh Hajishirzi. 2020. UNIFIEDQA: Crossing format boundaries with a single QA system. In *Findings of the Association for Computational Linguistics: EMNLP 2020*, pages 1896–1907, Online. Association for Computational Linguistics.

Kentaro Kurihara, Daisuke Kawahara, and Tomohide Shibata. 2022. JGLUE: Japanese general language understanding evaluation. In *Proceedings of the Thirteenth Language Resources and Evaluation Conference*, pages 2957–2966, Marseille, France. European Language Resources Association.

Tom Kwiatkowski, Jennimaria Palomaki, Olivia Redfield, Michael Collins, Ankur Parikh, Chris Alberti, Danielle Epstein, Illia Polosukhin, Jacob Devlin, Kenton Lee, Kristina Toutanova, Llion Jones, Matthew Kelcey, Ming-Wei Chang, Andrew M. Dai, Jakob Uszkoreit, Quoc Le, and Slav Petrov. 2019. Natural questions: A benchmark for question answering research. *Transactions of the Association for Computational Linguistics*, 7:452–466.

Patrick Lewis, Barlas Oguz, Ruty Rinott, Sebastian Riedel, and Holger Schwenk. 2020. MLQA: Evaluating cross-lingual extractive question answering. In *Proceedings of the 58th Annual Meeting of the Association for Computational Linguistics*, pages 7315–7330, Online. Association for Computational Linguistics.

Yinhan Liu, Myle Ott, Naman Goyal, Jingfei Du, Mandar Joshi, Danqi Chen, Omer Levy, Mike Lewis, Luke Zettlemoyer, and Veselin Stoyanov. 2019. Roberta: A robustly optimized bert pretraining approach.

Sewon Min, Jordan Boyd-Graber, Chris Alberti, Danqi Chen, Eunsol Choi, Michael Collins, Kelvin Guu, Hannaneh Hajishirzi, Kenton Lee, Jennimaria Palomaki, Colin Raffel, Adam Roberts, Tom Kwiatkowski, Patrick Lewis, Yuxiang Wu, Heinrich Küttler, Linqing Liu, Pasquale Minervini, Pontus Stenetorp, Sebastian Riedel, Sohee Yang, Minjoon Seo, Gautier Izacard, Fabio Petroni, Lucas Hosseini, Nicola De Cao, Edouard Grave, Ikuya Yamada, Sonse Shimaoka, Masatoshi Suzuki, Shumpei Miyawaki, Shun Sato, Ryo Takahashi, Jun Suzuki, Martin Fajcik, Martin Docekal, Karel Ondrej, Pavel Smrz, Hao Cheng, Yelong Shen, Xiaodong Liu, Pengcheng He, Weizhu Chen, Jianfeng Gao, Barlas Oguz, Xilun Chen, Vladimir Karpukhin, Stan Peshterliev, Dmytro Okhonko, Michael Schlichtkrull, Sonal Gupta, Yashar Mehdad, and Wen-tau Yih. 2021. Neurips 2020 efficientqa competition: Systems, analyses and lessons learned. In *Proceedings of the NeurIPS 2020 Competition and Demonstration Track*, volume 133 of *Proceedings of Machine Learning Research*, pages 86–111. PMLR.

Pranav Rajpurkar, Robin Jia, and Percy Liang. 2018. Know what you don't know: Unanswerable questions for SQuAD. In *Proceedings of the 56th Annual Meeting of the Association for Computational Linguistics (Volume 2: Short Papers)*, pages 784–789, Melbourne, Australia. Association for Computational Linguistics.

Pranav Rajpurkar, Jian Zhang, Konstantin Lopyrev, and Percy Liang. 2016. SQuAD: 100,000+ questions for machine comprehension of text. In *Proceedings of the 2016 Conference on Empirical Methods in Natural Language Processing*, pages 2383–2392, Austin, Texas. Association for Computational Linguistics.

Vésteinn Snæbjarnarson and Hafsteinn Einarsson. 2022. Natural questions in Icelandic. In *Proceedings of the Thirteenth Language Resources and Evaluation Conference*, pages 4488–4496, Marseille, France. European Language Resources Association.

ByungHoon So, Kyuhong Byun, Kyungwon Kang, and Seongjin Cho. 2022. JaQuAD: Japanese Question Answering Dataset for Machine Reading Comprehension.

Masatoshi Suzuki, Jun Suzuki, Koji Matsuda, Kyosuke Nishida, and Naoya Inoue. 2020. Jaqket: Construction of a japanese qa dataset on the subject of quizzes. *Proceedings of Annual Meeting of the Association for Natural Language Processing*, 26:237–240.

Jason Wei, Maarten Bosma, Vincent Zhao, Kelvin Guu, Adams Wei Yu, Brian Lester, Nan Du, Andrew M. Dai, and Quoc V Le. 2022. Finetuned language models are zero-shot learners. In *International Conference on Learning Representations*.

Yi Yang, Wen-tau Yih, and Christopher Meek. 2015. WikiQA: A challenge dataset for open-domain question answering. In *Proceedings of the 2015 Conference on Empirical Methods in Natural Language Processing*, pages 2013–2018, Lisbon, Portugal. Association for Computational Linguistics.

Zhilin Yang, Peng Qi, Saizheng Zhang, Yoshua Bengio, William Cohen, Ruslan Salakhutdinov, and Christopher D. Manning. 2018. HotpotQA: A dataset for diverse, explainable multi-hop question answering. In *Proceedings of the 2018 Conference on Empirical Methods in Natural Language Processing*, pages 2369–2380, Brussels, Belgium. Association for Computational Linguistics.

A Examples of Good Questions

Examples of good questions obtained in Section 3.2 are shown in Table 13.

Type	Example
Fact	ナスカの地上絵がある所はどこ?
	Where are the Nazca Lines?
Reason	ビール瓶の色が茶色なのはなぜでしょう?
	Why are beer bottles brown?
How to	ナスに油を吸わせない方法
	How to keep eggplant from absorbing oil?

Table 13: Examples of good questions.

B Open-Domain NQ

From JNQ, we additionally define the task of open-domain NQ tasks and establish baselines. We show the statistics of the task in Table 14.

Experimental Setup Following the EfficientQA competition (Min et al., 2021), which uses the NQ dataset for open-domain question answering, we use JNQ to conduct the same task. *Given a question, a system tries to output a short answer without reference.* We target questions labeled as being present for short answers and remove questions whose answers have more than three words because we considered these questions to be difficult to answer precisely. We use exact match (EM) for an evaluation metric.

We use retriever-reader models as baselines. We use TF-IDF and a DPR retriever (Karpukhin et al., 2020) for the retriever and a DPR reader for the reader. We first use the retriever to retrieve 100 relevant paragraphs to the question from a database of Wikipedia and then employ the reader to find the answer from the retrieved paragraphs. We use DPR checkpoints from the second AIO competition[7].

Results We show the results of open-domain NQ in Table 15. The TF-IDF retriever performs slightly better than DPR on the test set. We speculate that because the average length of the questions is relatively short, salient phrases and rare entities in the questions make DPR difficult to retrieve accurately (Chen et al., 2022). Additionally, we found that some questions are unsuitable for open-domain QA. For instance, there is no standard answer to questions such as "なぜ貧しい国はなくならないのか" (Why don't poor countries disappear?) and "男の子の髪の毛の切り方" (How to cut a boy's hair?). We plan to exclude these questions in future work.

Task	Train	Dev	Test
Open-Domain NQ	2,317	298	284

Table 14: Statistics of the task of open-domain NQ. The number refers to the number of instances.

	Dev	Test
	EM	
TF-IDF + DPR reader	30.2	**30.3**
DPR	**31.2**	29.9

Table 15: Performance on open-domain NQ.

[7]https://sites.google.com/view/project-aio/competition2

ROUGE-K: Do Your Summaries Have Keywords?

Sotaro Takeshita[1], Simone Paolo Ponzetto[1], Kai Eckert[2]
[1]Data and Web Science Group, University of Mannheim, Germany
[2]Mannheim University of Applied Sciences, Mannheim, Germany
{sotaro.takeshita, ponzetto}@uni-mannheim.de
k.eckert@hs-mannheim.de

Abstract

Keywords, that is, content-relevant words in summaries play an important role in efficient information conveyance, making it critical to assess if system-generated summaries contain such informative words during evaluation. However, existing evaluation metrics for extreme summarization models do not pay explicit attention to keywords in summaries, leaving developers ignorant of their presence. To address this issue, we present a keyword-oriented evaluation metric, dubbed ROUGE-K, which provides a quantitative answer to the question of – *How well do summaries include keywords?* Through the lens of this keyword-aware metric, we surprisingly find that a current strong baseline model often misses essential information in their summaries. Our analysis reveals that human annotators indeed find the summaries with more keywords to be more relevant to the source documents. This is an important yet previously overlooked aspect in evaluating summarization systems. Finally, to enhance keyword inclusion, we propose four approaches for incorporating word importance into a transformer-based model and experimentally show that it enables guiding models to include more keywords while keeping the overall quality.[1]

1 Introduction

Summarization systems compress long documents into shorter ones to convey important information more effectively to readers (Rush et al., 2015; Chopra et al., 2016). To convey all essential information correctly, it is crucial for summarization systems to include important, i.e., summary-relevant keywords. In our analysis, human annotators find that summaries with more keywords, words that are relevant for the summary (see Section 3), capture important information better than the ones with fewer keywords. However, existing evaluation metrics do not explicitly take such word importance into account. Table 1 shows an example. Two commonly used metrics, namely ROUGE (Lin, 2004) and BERTScore (Zhang et al., 2020), assign lower scores to the second hypothesis even though it contains an essential word that another summary misses. This discrepancy, namely that ROUGE assigns a lower score to a summary that contains more keywords and annotators find relevant, happens in 16.7% of the cases in our analysis.

Reference		
A novel, hybrid deep learning approach provides the best solution to a limited-data problem (which is important to the conservation of the Hawaiian language)		
	R-1	**BS**
Hypothesis 1: We propose two methods to solve the transliteration problem automatically, given that there were not enough data to train an end-to-end deep learning model.	27.45	0.8718
Hypothesis 2: We propose two methods to solve the Hawaiian orthography transliteration problem automatically using finite state transducers and a hybrid neural network.	26.09	0.8692

Table 1: An example where ROUGE and BERTScore (BS) can lead to misinterpretations. Although the incorrect generation (not including the word "Hawaiian") in the first hypothesis is more critical than the one in the second summary ("neural network" instead of "deep learning") to convey correct information, both metrics assign a higher score to the former summary.

In this paper, to shed light on this problem, we propose ROUGE-K, an extension of ROUGE which considers only those n-grams in the summaries that match a set of pre-defined keywords. We propose a simple heuristic that exploits the common structure of summarization datasets to extract keywords automatically, making it possible for our metric to scale in size and domain without additional annotation effort. Correlation analysis reveals that there is only a weak strength of dependence between our new metric and existing ones as well as summary lengths, thus demonstrating

[1]Our code: https://github.com/sobamchan/rougek.

*Proceedings of the 13th Joint Conference on Lexical and Computational Semantics (*SEM 2024)*, pages 69 - 79
June 20-21, 2024 ©2024 Association for Computational Linguistics

that our approach can complement, rather than replace, previous metrics. Through a manual evaluation, we find that human annotators show substantially higher agreement with ROUGE-K than with ROUGE and BERTScore on relevance, in other words, how well summaries include important information, which is one of four commonly assessed aspects in manual evaluations of summaries (Fabbri et al., 2021). This shows that while one still would use traditional ROUGE to assess the overall qualities, our metric can provide a better index for evaluating the relevance of summaries. As a showcase of this new metric, we evaluate both extractive (Liu and Lapata, 2019) and abstractive (Lewis et al., 2020; Dou et al., 2021; Saito et al., 2020) state-of-the-art models on two extreme summarization datasets from different domains, namely XSum (Narayan et al., 2018) and SciTLDR (Cachola et al., 2020), as well as a more traditional, non-extreme dataset, ScisummNet (Yasunaga et al., 2019). Besides news text (XSum), we choose summarization of scientific publications (ScisummNet and SciTLDR), since this is a domain where keyword inclusion within summaries plays a crucial role. Surprisingly, the results reveal that these strong baseline models often fail to include essential words in their summaries, and that ROUGE-K enables us to better distinguish systems' performance than alternative metrics. We also apply our ROUGE-K to the evaluations of recent large language models (LLMs) and show how our metric better accounts for the powerful capabilities of LLM-based summarizers when compared to traditional ROUGE metrics. Finally, As a first attempt to address the limitations on summary keyword inclusion, we introduce four ways to incorporate a lightweight word importance feature into existing transformer-based models. Experiments show that our methods can guide models to include more keywords without any additional annotations and negative effects on overall summarization quality. Our contributions are the following ones:

- We introduce **a new keyword-oriented evaluation metric, dubbed ROUGE-K**, which complements existing metrics by focusing on keywords.
- **We validate our metric**: a) against human judgments of summary relevance, b) by quantifying its correlation to existing metrics and summary lengths, and c) its ability to distinguish performance among different systems.
- Our experiments on three different datasets for summarization of scientific and news articles reveal that current **state-of-the-art models often fail to include important words** in summaries.
- We present experiments with **four approaches to incorporate word-importance scores** into BART and show that it can help to improve keyword inclusion without hurting the overall summarization qualities.

2 The need for another kind of ROUGE

ROUGE (Lin, 2004) is a long-running *de facto* standard evaluation metric for summarization systems. It is very popular due to its high correlation with human evaluation while keeping its simplicity and interpretability. However, several works report on its limitations (Akter et al., 2022; Fabbri et al., 2021), one of which is that it only takes the word surface into account and disregards semantics (Ng and Abrecht, 2015). Because it considers all n-gram matches to be equally important, ROUGE fails to detect salient words that underpin a summary's quality.

As an example, Table 1 shows two generated summaries of the same article from the SciTLDR dataset (Cachola et al., 2020) as well as their scores computed by ROUGE and BERTScore (Zhang et al., 2020), a pre-training language model based metric. Both metrics assign a higher score to the first summary even though it misses an important keyword that the second summary contains. In the case of ROUGE, this is because it favors the longer but nonessential n-gram overlaps in the first summary. This limitation of evaluation metrics can mislead the development of summarization systems towards including more of longer but less important words in summaries than truly essential keywords. When multiple reference summaries are available, ROUGE can assign higher scores to words potentially more important than others by counting n-grams that appear several times across references, which indirectly considers word importance. However, most commonly used datasets contain only one reference summary (Hermann et al., 2015; Narayan et al., 2018). In addition, because of its implicit nature, when a generated summary has a different textual style (even if the semantics of the summary did not change) from its reference summary, the ROUGE score can easily deflate.

SciTLDR (Cachola et al., 2020)

We show that autoregressive models can generate high fidelity images.
We introduce a new inductive bias that integrates tree structures in recurrent neural networks.

XSum (Narayan et al., 2018)

Opec, the oil producers' group is back in the driving seat.
Lenovo and Acer have both unveiled smartphones with much larger than normal batteries.

Table 2: Sample reference summaries with highlights on keywords extracted by our heuristic.

3 ROUGE-K

We present ROUGE-K, an extension of ROUGE that exclusively focuses on essential words in summaries. Its core idea is simple: ROUGE-K assesses the proportion of keywords from the reference summary that are included in the candidate summary. We compute ROUGE-K as:

$$\text{R-K} = \frac{\text{Count}(\text{kws} \cap \text{n-grams})}{\text{Count}(\text{kws})}$$

where kws is a set of pre-defined keywords and n-grams is a target hypothesis. This provides a direct understanding of how well system summaries contain essential pieces of information. ROUGE-K is essentially a recall-oriented metric since it computes *coverage* of keywords. While it is possible to complement this formula with another one to compute precision, this would give the proportion of keywords in the candidate summary. However, this metric would indicate how good the system is at extracting keywords, not its summarization capabilities, i.e., one could have a summary consisting only of keywords but only marginally overlapping with the reference summary.

Keyword extraction. An essential prerequisite of ROUGE-K is the availability of keywords. Ideally, we would like these keywords to be available for *any* summarization corpus to enable the wide applicability of our metric. A solution is thus to extract keywords from reference summaries heuristically. Nan et al. (2021), for instance, use words detected by a named entity recognition (NER) model to evaluate entity-level factual consistency in summaries. However, (1) not all keywords are named entities, (2) NER models accurate enough to be used for evaluation are not available for all domains (e.g., scholarly documents), (3) the accuracy of NER models for documents in summarization datasets is unknown.

	R-1	R-2	R-L	BS	R-K
SciTLDR	61.11	58.89	60.00	57.78	72.22
XSum	63.73	59.80	56.86	62.75	70.59

Table 3: Agreement ratios (%) of each metric and human annotator on summary relevance, computed as the proportion of documents for which a given metric gives the highest score to the summary judged as most relevant from humans.

In this paper, we present a simple and interpretable way to extract keywords. We define keywords as *the n-grams used in multiple reference summaries*, assuming that words used in multiple human-written summaries for the same document repeatedly should be included in system summaries as well. First, we tokenize and lowercase the reference summaries, extract n-grams, and then remove stopwords from the extracted n-grams. Next, we compare n-grams from multiple references and extract those that appear in multiple references. To capture multi-word keywords, the extraction process starts from 10-grams to unigrams. *When there is only one reference summary available, the corresponding title is used as a proxy reference* which is known to contain key information (Koto et al., 2022; Cachola et al., 2020). Table 2 shows examples of keywords extracted by our heuristic. We benchmark our heuristic against TF-IDF (Salton and Buckley, 1988) and TextRank (Mihalcea and Tarau, 2004). To this end, we take the first 100 samples of the SciTLDR development data and for each summary, we extract the same amount of keywords as the one from our method (i.e., we keep the recall level fixed). We then quantify for each method a) the average number of wrong keywords per summary and b) the overall false discovery rate FDR (for both, lower is better) – our hunch is that for humans, it is easier to judge whether something is not a keyword (i.e., a word is unquestionably not being essential to convey the information), as opposed to being one. In both cases, our heuristic achieves the best performance: 0.64 vs. 0.85 and 0.94 on average wrong extractions per summary and 0.13 vs. 0.16 and 0.21 FDR when compared against TF-IDF and TextRank, respectively.

Agreement with human judgments. We now perform a manual evaluation to test how well ROUGE-K aligns with human judgements on rating the relevance of summaries (we follow Fabbri et al. (2021) and define 'relevance' as the *selection* *of important content from the source*. We focus for manual evaluation on relevance only (as opposed to, e.g., Fabbri et al. (2021) considering three other aspects) because the purpose of ROUGE-K is to quantify how well summaries include essential words, and thus preserve important, i.e., relevant content, as opposed to, e.g., ROUGE taking into account style aspects.

Our dataset consists of pairs of summaries generated using different instances of the same model (BART), trained on each of SciTLDR and XSum with different random seeds. To avoid ties, we select a sample of 92 and 100, respectively from SciTLDR and XSum, summary pairs where the two models assign a different ROUGE-K score to each summary. We then ask four annotators from our CS graduate course to compare the summaries and rank them (i.e., label the best one among the two). We finally compute how often each evaluation metric assigns higher scores to the summaries preferred by the annotators. Results are shown in Table 3. In line with Fabbri et al. (2021), R-1 shows higher agreement than R-2 and R-L, and BERTScore marks a marginally lower score than ROUGE-1. Finally, ROUGE-K shows much higher agreement, indicating its strong ability to detect human-preferable summarization models.

Benchmarking BART with ROUGE-K. As a showcase of ROUGE-K, we evaluate BART (Lewis et al., 2020), a strong transformer-based generative language model on three different datasets: SciTLDR (Cachola et al., 2020), XSum (Narayan et al., 2018) and ScisummNet (Yasunaga et al., 2019). These cover different summarization tasks – i.e., extreme (SciTLDR, XSum) vs. non-extreme (ScisummNet) – as well as different domains – i.e., scholarly documents (SciTLDR, ScisummNet) vs. news (XSum). Datasets details are shown in Table 4. BART models are fine-tuned on the training set and early stopping is performed using validation data, and finally evaluated on the test split using the traditional ROUGE metrics and our ROUGE-K. Table 5 shows the results. Each score is an average of ten and three different random seeds, respectively, for SciTLDR and XSum/ScisummNet (a larger number of seeds is used for SciTLDR to obtain stable scores on its relatively small test dataset). Although one would consider the scores achieved by BART on ROUGE-1/-2/-L to be high, it only reaches 41.36% and 56.14% on ROUGE-K. In other words, a strong baseline model fails to include half of the essential n-grams in its summaries, unveiling a critical limitation previously missed by standard metrics.

Correlation with summary lengths. Since ROUGE-K is recall-oriented, it can potentially favor longer summaries, i.e., as suggested by the overall absolute scores obtained by BART in Table 5 on non-extreme summarization with ScisummNet data. To quantify this, we compute Pearson correlations between the number of words in summaries generated by BART and different evaluation scores. As Table 6 shows, ROUGE-K scores have marginally higher correlations with summary lengths than other ROUGE (F1) metrics, although they all are relatively weak, ranging from -0.07 to 0.17 on SciTLDR and even lower for XSum. These results are different from those from Sun et al. (2019), arguably because SciTLDR and XSum are extreme summarization datasets. On non-extreme summarization (ScisummNet), the results align instead with previous findings. However, we observe the same level of moderate correlation with the summary length between vanilla ROUGE and ROUGE-K.

Correlation with existing metrics. To better understand the relationship between ROUGE-K and other existing metrics, we perform an additional correlation analysis (Table 7). R-1 (avg) computes a R-1 for each reference given a sample and takes the average while R-1 (max) takes only the largest score. R-1 (avg) and R-1 (max) are the same for XSum and ScisummNet because there is only one reference summary in this dataset. The results indicate only a moderate strength of association between ROUGE-K and existing metrics, thus providing evidence that our metric can partially complement other metrics.

4 Importance-guided summarization

We next propose four ways to incorporate a soft guiding signal into BART to enforce the inclusion of keywords into the generated summaries.

Re-weighted encoding (RwEnc). The first approach is to modify the representations within the model with TF-IDF scores. Concretely, we compute the attention matrix in transformer layers as:

$$\text{attention matrix} = \text{softmax}(\frac{QK^\intercal}{\sqrt{d_k}} + T)V$$

	Documents		Summaries			Extracted keywords	
Dataset	# documents (train/val/test)	# words per doc on avg.	# words per summary on avg.	compress. ratio	# references on avg. (train/val/test)	# keywords on avg. (train/val/test)	average lengths (train/val/test)
SciTLDR	1,992 / 619 / 618	5,000	21.00	238.10	2.0 / 3.3 / 4.2	1.9 / 4.2 / 5.2	1.7 / 1.5 / 1.5
XSum	204K / 11K / 11K	431	23.26	18.53	2.0 / 2.0 / 2.0	2.9 / 2.9 / 2.9	1.5 / 1.5 / 1.5
ScisummNet	750 / 92 / 91	4,700	167.49	28.06	2.0 / 2.0 / 2.0	2.8 / 3.0 / 2.6	1.7 / 1.6 / 1.6

Table 4: Statistic of datasets and extracted keywords.

	R-1	R-2	R-L	R-K
SciTLDR	43.93	22.31	36.58	41.36
XSum	44.43	21.00	35.94	56.14
ScisummNet	50.75	47.80	49.73	68.95

Table 5: BART performance evaluated by ROUGE-1/-2/-L and our ROUGE-K.

	R-1	R-2	R-L	R-K
SciTLDR	-0.102	-0.070	-0.154	0.167
XSum	-0.003	-0.037	-0.075	0.057
ScisummNet	0.356	0.435	0.392	0.402

Table 6: Pearson Correlation between the number of words in summaries and evaluation metrics.

	R-1 (avg)	R-1 (max)	BS
SciTLDR	0.510	0.434	0.383
XSum	0.318	0.318	0.237
ScisummNet	0.288	0.288	0.413

Table 7: Pearson Correlation between ROUGE-K and ROUGE-1 average, ROUGE-1 max and BERTScore.

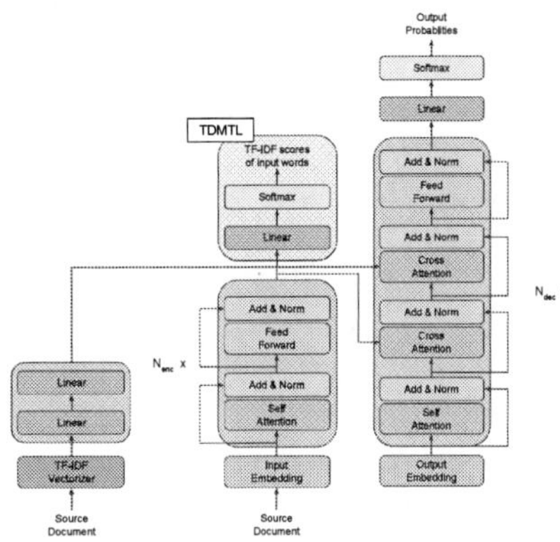

Figure 1: Overview of our TDSum model.

The first term within the softmax function is from the original transformer (Vaswani et al., 2017) where Q and K are query and key matrices respectively, and we introduce the second term T which is a matrix of TF-IDF scores over the input text. This enhances the model to propagate higher values for the important words to the upper layers. We apply this modification to the 0-, 4-, 8-th encoder layers, empirically selected on the dev data.

Re-weighted generation (RwGen). The second solution operates in the token selection phase. At each generation step, BART computes a probabilistic distribution over its vocabulary for the next token to produce. We modify this distribution by summing TF-IDF scores so that the words with higher scores are more likely to be selected:

$$\text{score}(y_{w_t}|w_{<t}, X, T)' = (1-\lambda) * \text{score}(y_{w_t}|w_{<t}, X) + \lambda * T$$

where score is a fine-tuned BART that takes previously generated words ($w_{<t}$) and the source document (X), and predicts scores which are further transformed to the probability for the next token at the time step t by a softmax function. We introduce the second term (T) which is a vector filled with TF-IDF values for the source document. λ is a hyperparameter with which we control how much we shift the distribution from vanilla BART.

Multi-Task Learning with TF-IDF (TDMTL). Another solution is to modify the objective function to ask the model to predict TF-IDF scores in parallel with generating summaries. For this, we compute the mean squared error as loss for TF-IDF score prediction L_{tfidf} and the standard cross entropy loss for summarization L_{sum}. The final loss we minimize is the linear interpolation of the two task-specific losses: $(1-\lambda)L_{sum} + \lambda L_{tfidf}$.

Injecting TF-IDF into the decoder (TDSum). Our last approach is inspired by Dou et al. (2021). Since their approach requires an explicit guidance signal (e.g., keywords), it uses additional models for keyword extraction leading to a drastic increase in computational costs. Instead, we propose to use light-weight TF-IDF scores as shown in Figure 1. TDSum equips two linear layers to process

TF-IDF scores for words in input documents and uses resulting word importance features in newly introduced cross-attention layers in each decoder layer to guide the model towards keyword-oriented summary generation. We train this model with the aforementioned TDMTL loss.

5 Experiments and results

5.1 Experimental setup

Datasets. We experiment on different domains and summarization tasks using SciTLDR (Cachola et al., 2020), XSum (Narayan et al., 2018) and ScisummNet (Yasunaga et al., 2019)

Baselines. We compare our models with three abstractive and one extractive summarizer:

- **BART** (Lewis et al., 2020) is a transformer-based generative language model, pre-trained with denoising objective function.
- **GSum** (Dou et al., 2021) is an extension of BART with additional parameters for processing textual guidance signals. Here, we input overlapping keywords, extracted as explained in Section 3.
- **MTL** (Saito et al., 2020) performs multitask training to predict keywords in source documents in addition to the summarization objective (we use our extracted keywords from Section 3).
- **PreSumm** (Liu and Lapata, 2019) is an extractive summarization model based on BERT (Devlin et al., 2019).

Hyperparameter tuning. We perform a grid search for each dataset and model using the development data and ROUGE-1 as a reference. We test for learning rate $\in \{1e-05, 2e-05, 3e-05\}$, gradient accumulation $\in \{4, 8\}$, number of beam search $\in \{2, 3\}$ and repetition penalty rate $\in \{0.8, 1.0\}$. We also explore $\lambda \in \{0.1, 0.2, 0.3\}$ for MTL and TDMTL and $\lambda \in \{30, 50\}$ for RwGen. During hyperparameter search, we use one random seed. The final reported results on the test data are the averaged performance over models fine-tuned with different random seeds. We use ten seeds for SciTLDR and ScisummNet and three for XSum. Our experiments are performed on RTX A6000 and utilize the implementation by Deutsch and Roth (2020) to compute ROUGE-1/2/L.

5.2 Results and discussion

We organize the discussion of our results around the following research questions:

- **RQ1:** Can models that incorporate TF-IDF scores increase the number of keywords in the summaries without degrading ROUGE scores?
- **RQ2:** Which kinds of keywords do models find hard to include in summaries?

RQ1: TF-IDF as guidance. We present our main results in Table 8. On the SciTLDR dataset, BART marginally outperforms two other baseline models on ROUGE-1/2/L. However, MTL performs the best on the ROUGE-K metric, thus showing its effectiveness of explicit training guidance. As reported by previous works (Cachola et al., 2020; Narayan et al., 2018), an extractive model considerably underperforms abstractive models on all the metrics in extreme summarization since it suffers from merging information across multiple input sentences into its outputs. Because keywords are also scattered over multiple sentences, it fails to include most keywords. Three out of four of our newly introduced TF-IDF-equipped models outperform vanilla BART on keyword inclusion, and TDSum significantly outperforms all the baselines on ROUGE-K while keeping its ROUGE scores on par with BART. TDMTL follows the same training procedure as MTL and learns to predict TF-IDF instead of keywords. While results still improve over BART, our results show that using hard signals (i.e., keywords) is preferable. RwGen is simple and fast to train, yet it includes more keywords than BART. On XSum, BART outperforms other baseline models on ROUGE-K. However, the MTL model exceeds other traditional ROUGE metrics showing that our metric can shed light on an aspect that other metrics cannot capture. Among our proposed methods, TDMTL performs well akin to the results on SciTLDR, outperforming BART on traditional ROUGE metrics, although the BART model still outperforms models with TF-IDF extensions on ROUGE-K.

We see similar trends for non-extreme summarization on ScisummNet, where our proposed models are on par (sometimes outperform) with baseline models on ROUGE metrics. All proposed methods outperform all baseline models on ROUGE-K, indicating that, even for longer summaries, TF-IDF can enhance keyword inclusion. One significant difference is that the extractive model (PreSumm) performs better than abstractive models on ROUGE-1/2. We speculate this is due to much longer output summaries (181.88 words on average for PreSumm vs. 48.01 for BART).

Model	SciTLDR				XSum				ScisummNet			
	R-1	R-2	R-L	R-K	R-1	R-2	R-L	R-K	R-1	R-2	R-L	R-K
BART	43.93	22.31	36.58	41.36	44.43	21.00	35.94	**56.14**	50.75	47.80	49.73	68.95
GSum	43.65	22.09	36.50	41.00	43.86	20.47	35.60	52.85	24.37	21.11	23.35	43.36
MTL	43.82	22.24	36.29	42.83	44.50	**21.05**	**36.10**	56.06	50.75	47.81	49.73	68.81
PreSumm	30.43	11.36	24.08	25.06	22.16	4.13	15.91	24.67	**60.58**	49.15	46.22	68.85
Std (1–4)	5.79	4.70	5.36	**7.25**	9.57	7.24	8.65	**13.12**	**13.45**	11.77	11.01	11.05
RwEnc	43.98	22.39	36.68	41.03	44.42	20.93	36.07	55.58	50.75	**47.92**	**49.89**	69.40
RwGen	43.96	22.35	36.59	41.60	**44.57**	21.04	36.09	56.03	50.38	47.78	49.54	69.19
TDMTL	**44.08**	**22.48**	**36.75**	41.85	44.50	**21.05**	**36.10**	56.06	50.64	47.75	49.67	**69.56**
TDSum	43.55	21.74	35.82	**43.04**	44.13	20.95	35.57	55.39	50.50	47.63	49.55	69.43
Std (all)	4.44	3.60	4.10	**5.59**	7.34	5.56	6.62	**10.23**	**9.72**	8.90	8.62	8.54

Table 8: Results on SciTLDR, XSum, and ScisummNet. Best results per metric are **bolded**. Scores with underline indicate that they significantly outperform all baseline models. We test for statistical significance using the Wilcoxon signed-rank test with $\alpha = 0.05$ (Dror et al., 2018).

Model	Dataset	IN-SRC	OUT-SRC
BART	SciTLDR	54.53	0.92
	XSum	73.78	30.34
	ScisummNet	75.21	8.17
TDSum	SciTLDR	56.75	1.37
	XSum	66.61	26.66
	ScisummNet	75.04	14.41

Table 9: ROUGE-K scores on keywords seen (IN-SRC) vs. unseen (OUT-SRC) in source documents.

RQ2: In search of missing keywords. We next focus on studying the relationship between a few specific characteristics of keywords and ROUGE-K scores. First, we look at *whether models can better include keywords if they appear in source documents*. We do this by splitting a list of pre-defined keywords into two lists, (1) an IN-SRC keyword list where all the keywords appear in the source documents, (2) an OUT-SRC keyword list where keywords cannot be found in the source documents, and then evaluate a model with ROUGE-K using each list. As Table 9 shows, on both datasets and models, ROUGE-K with OUT-SRC keywords is notably lower than IN-SRC ROUGE-K showing that when keywords are not in the source texts it is challenging for models to include them in summaries.

We next investigate whether there is a correlation between ROUGE-K and keyword length, that is, *whether longer keywords are more difficult to include.* Figure 2 shows that although there is one exceptional case ($N = 7$), ROUGE-K scores consistently decrease as keywords become longer, indicating the difficulty of including longer keywords in summaries. Another finding in this analysis is that while BART outperforms TDSum on XSum

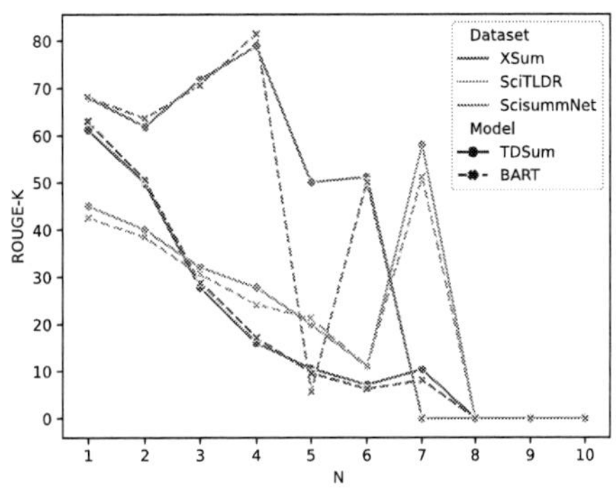

Figure 2: ROUGE-K and keyword length.

when keywords with all lengths are used when the n-grams are longer ($N >= 5$), TDSum starts to surpass BART on ROUGE-K.

LLMs on ROUGE-K To shed light on the summarization behaviour of recent large language models (LLMs), we evaluate an open-source model, namely instruction fine-tuned Llama 2 (Touvron et al., 2023) in two different sizes. The prompt used in our experiments is "Generate a summary of the following document in one sentence". Due to our limited computational resources, we cut off inputs and outputs at 512 and 128 tokens, respectively, and also truncate all the sentences after the first one in the generated summary, if longer. Results are shown in Table 10. While they perform remarkably well on both ROUGE and our ROUGE-K given that inferences are performed in zero-shot manner, we observe that more than half of the keywords are missing, calling for better prompting strategies. On traditional ROUGE scores, which consider the

Dataset	Llama2 7B				Llama2 13B			
	R-1	R-2	R-L	R-K	R-1	R-2	R-L	R-K
SciTLDR	35.9	13.9	26.7	44.1	36.3	14.6	27.8	44.4
XSum	21.8	5.6	15.5	34.7	22.0	5.6	15.9	35.9
SciNet	46.1	24.1	32.5	64.6	46.7	25.3	33.0	69.5

Table 10: Results with Llama2 7B and 13B.

Generated summary (a)
Input: Deep convolutional neural networks (CNNs) are known to be robust against label noise on extensive datasets. However, at the same time, CNNs are [...] (`https://openreview.net/forum?id=H1xmqiAqFm`)
TLDR: The authors challenge the CNNs robustness to label noise using ImageNet 1k tree of WordNet.
BART: We investigate the behavior of CNNs under class-dependently simulated label noise, which is generated based on the conceptual distance between classes of a large dataset.
TDSum: We show that CNNs are more robust to class-dependent label noise than class-independent label noise, which is generated based on the conceptual distance between classes of a large dataset.

Generated summary (b)
Input: We explore ways of incorporating bilingual dictionaries to enable semi-supervised neural machine [...] (`https://arxiv.org/abs/2004.02071`)
TLDR: We use bilingual dictionaries for data augmentation for neural machine translation.
BART: We propose a simple data augmentation technique to address both this shortcoming.
TDSum: We propose a simple data augmentation technique to enable semi-supervised neural machine translation.

Table 11: Summaries generated by our models.

words related to writing style, Llama performs noticeably worse than fine-tuned models because fine-tuning can help models learn reference styles from the dataset. However, results are comparable on ROUGE-K. This indicates that ROUGE-K can better account for the high quality of LLMs, despite different styles between generated and reference summaries, which has been noticed when evaluating zero-shot models (Goyal et al., 2022).

Model distinguishability. Most if not all recent summarization papers perform evaluations using multiple ROUGE metrics, yet the gap between systems is very small, making it hard to distinguish models' performance. Inspired by work from Xiao et al. (2022) on characterizing the distinguishability of datasets, we compute the standard deviation of scores from our models (cf. Section 5.1) for each metric, to see the distinguishability of ROUGE variants (larger deviation means higher distinguishability). As shown in Table 8, ROUGE-K achieves the highest standard deviation among other ROUGE metrics for two extreme summarization datasets, i.e., it differentiates models better when summaries are required to be very short. We highlight this by means of the sample output shown in Table 11. In (a), BART fails to include one of the keywords 'robust' which is necessary to convey the purpose of the paper. In (b), the summary by BART does not mention the task the paper worked on (in this case, neural machine translation) while TDSum successfully includes it.

6 Related work

In the context of factual consistency evaluation (Kryscinski et al., 2020; Scialom et al., 2021; Fabbri et al., 2022), Nan et al. (2021) propose to use a NER model to detect hallucinated named entities in summaries. While their approach also focuses on specific words in summaries as our ROUGE-K, it is limited because (1) not all critical information consists of named entities, (2) strong NER models are not available in many domains, and (3) NER performance is unknown for summarization datasets. Ng and Abrecht (2015) and Zhang et al. (2020) propose to use vector representations to compute semantic similarity between reference and candidate summaries. Eyal et al. (2019) instead propose to use a question-answering system to assess the summary quality. While these methods can exploit semantic knowledge stored in parameters in large models, as a side-effect, they introduce 'blackboxness' that hinders transparent model development. In contrast, we take a 'bottom-up' approach by proposing to focus on keyword availability.

7 Conclusion

In this paper, we proposed ROUGE-K, an extension of ROUGE to quantify how summary-relevant keywords are included in summaries. Using ROUGE-K, we showed human annotators prefer summaries with more keywords and how models often miss several essential keywords in their output. In a variety of experiments using the baseline provided by a large pre-trained language model (BART) we showed how ROUGE-K only moderately correlates with ROUGE and BERTScore, thus indicating that it can complement them, and correlates with the length of the generated summaries on a par with ROUGE F1 and BERTScore, despite being a recall-oriented metric. Finally, we proposed four ways to guide BART to include more keywords in its summaries. We plan in future work to further test our metric's applicability across different domains and languages, e.g., by relying on WikiLingua (Ladhak et al., 2020) and X-SciTLDR (Takeshita et al., 2022).

8 Limitations

This work has the following limitations: (1) Our new evaluation metric, ROUGE-K, uses a heuristic to extract keywords automatically. Although it enables to obtain better and more comprehensive keywords compared to other existing methods, some nonessential words are still included thus can bring some noise into the evaluation. (2) ROUGE-K does not take the context of keywords into consideration which leaves the possibility open that generated summaries with keywords still convey the meaning of keywords wrongly. (3) Like traditional ROUGE scores, ROUGE-K is based on hard string match, which cannot compensate for the semantics of, e.g., (near-)synonyms and paraphrases.

Acknowledgements

The work presented in this paper is funded by the German Research Foundation (DFG) under the VADIS (PO 1900/5-1; EC 477/7-1) project, and also supported by the state of Baden-Württemberg through bwHPC and the German Research Foundation (DFG) through grant INST 35/1597-1 FUGG.

References

Mousumi Akter, Naman Bansal, and Shubhra Kanti Karmaker. 2022. Revisiting automatic evaluation of extractive summarization task: Can we do better than ROUGE? In *Findings of the Association for Computational Linguistics: ACL 2022*, pages 1547–1560, Dublin, Ireland. Association for Computational Linguistics.

Isabel Cachola, Kyle Lo, Arman Cohan, and Daniel Weld. 2020. TLDR: Extreme summarization of scientific documents. In *Findings of the Association for Computational Linguistics: EMNLP 2020*, pages 4766–4777, Online. Association for Computational Linguistics.

Sumit Chopra, Michael Auli, and Alexander M. Rush. 2016. Abstractive sentence summarization with attentive recurrent neural networks. In *Proceedings of the 2016 Conference of the North American Chapter of the Association for Computational Linguistics: Human Language Technologies*, pages 93–98, San Diego, California. Association for Computational Linguistics.

Daniel Deutsch and Dan Roth. 2020. SacreROUGE: An open-source library for using and developing summarization evaluation metrics. In *Proceedings of Second Workshop for NLP Open Source Software (NLP-OSS)*, pages 120–125, Online. Association for Computational Linguistics.

Jacob Devlin, Ming-Wei Chang, Kenton Lee, and Kristina Toutanova. 2019. BERT: Pre-training of deep bidirectional transformers for language understanding. In *Proceedings of the 2019 Conference of the North American Chapter of the Association for Computational Linguistics: Human Language Technologies, Volume 1 (Long and Short Papers)*, pages 4171–4186, Minneapolis, Minnesota. Association for Computational Linguistics.

Zi-Yi Dou, Pengfei Liu, Hiroaki Hayashi, Zhengbao Jiang, and Graham Neubig. 2021. GSum: A general framework for guided neural abstractive summarization. In *Proceedings of the 2021 Conference of the North American Chapter of the Association for Computational Linguistics: Human Language Technologies*, pages 4830–4842, Online. Association for Computational Linguistics.

Rotem Dror, Gili Baumer, Segev Shlomov, and Roi Reichart. 2018. The hitchhiker's guide to testing statistical significance in natural language processing. In *Proceedings of the 56th Annual Meeting of the Association for Computational Linguistics (Volume 1: Long Papers)*, pages 1383–1392, Melbourne, Australia. Association for Computational Linguistics.

Matan Eyal, Tal Baumel, and Michael Elhadad. 2019. Question answering as an automatic evaluation metric for news article summarization. In *Proceedings of the 2019 Conference of the North American Chapter of the Association for Computational Linguistics: Human Language Technologies, Volume 1 (Long and Short Papers)*, pages 3938–3948, Minneapolis, Minnesota. Association for Computational Linguistics.

Alexander Fabbri, Chien-Sheng Wu, Wenhao Liu, and Caiming Xiong. 2022. QAFactEval: Improved QA-based factual consistency evaluation for summarization. In *Proceedings of the 2022 Conference of the North American Chapter of the Association for Computational Linguistics: Human Language Technologies*, pages 2587–2601, Seattle, United States. Association for Computational Linguistics.

Alexander R. Fabbri, Wojciech Kryściński, Bryan McCann, Caiming Xiong, Richard Socher, and Dragomir Radev. 2021. SummEval: Re-evaluating Summarization Evaluation. *Transactions of the Association for Computational Linguistics*, 9:391–409.

Tanya Goyal, Junyi Jessy Li, and Greg Durrett. 2022. News Summarization and Evaluation in the Era of GPT-3. ArXiv:2209.12356 [cs].

Karl Moritz Hermann, Tomas Kocisky, Edward Grefenstette, Lasse Espeholt, Will Kay, Mustafa Suleyman, and Phil Blunsom. 2015. Teaching machines to read and comprehend. In *Advances in Neural Information Processing Systems*, volume 28. Curran Associates, Inc.

Fajri Koto, Timothy Baldwin, and Jey Han Lau. 2022. LipKey: A large-scale news dataset for absent keyphrases generation and abstractive summarization. In *Proceedings of the 29th International Conference on Computational Linguistics*, pages 3427–3437, Gyeongju, Republic of Korea. International Committee on Computational Linguistics.

Wojciech Kryscinski, Bryan McCann, Caiming Xiong, and Richard Socher. 2020. Evaluating the factual consistency of abstractive text summarization. In *Proceedings of the 2020 Conference on Empirical Methods in Natural Language Processing (EMNLP)*, pages 9332–9346, Online. Association for Computational Linguistics.

Faisal Ladhak, Esin Durmus, Claire Cardie, and Kathleen McKeown. 2020. WikiLingua: A new benchmark dataset for cross-lingual abstractive summarization. In *Findings of the Association for Computational Linguistics: EMNLP 2020*, pages 4034–4048, Online. Association for Computational Linguistics.

Mike Lewis, Yinhan Liu, Naman Goyal, Marjan Ghazvininejad, Abdelrahman Mohamed, Omer Levy, Veselin Stoyanov, and Luke Zettlemoyer. 2020. BART: Denoising sequence-to-sequence pre-training for natural language generation, translation, and comprehension. In *Proceedings of the 58th Annual Meeting of the Association for Computational Linguistics*, pages 7871–7880, Online. Association for Computational Linguistics.

Chin-Yew Lin. 2004. ROUGE: A package for automatic evaluation of summaries. In *Text Summarization Branches Out*, pages 74–81, Barcelona, Spain. Association for Computational Linguistics.

Yang Liu and Mirella Lapata. 2019. Text summarization with pretrained encoders. In *Proceedings of the 2019 Conference on Empirical Methods in Natural Language Processing and the 9th International Joint Conference on Natural Language Processing (EMNLP-IJCNLP)*, pages 3730–3740, Hong Kong, China. Association for Computational Linguistics.

Rada Mihalcea and Paul Tarau. 2004. TextRank: Bringing order into text. In *Proceedings of the 2004 Conference on Empirical Methods in Natural Language Processing*, pages 404–411, Barcelona, Spain. Association for Computational Linguistics.

Feng Nan, Ramesh Nallapati, Zhiguo Wang, Cicero Nogueira dos Santos, Henghui Zhu, Dejiao Zhang, Kathleen McKeown, and Bing Xiang. 2021. Entity-level factual consistency of abstractive text summarization. In *Proceedings of the 16th Conference of the European Chapter of the Association for Computational Linguistics: Main Volume*, pages 2727–2733, Online. Association for Computational Linguistics.

Shashi Narayan, Shay B. Cohen, and Mirella Lapata. 2018. Don't give me the details, just the summary! topic-aware convolutional neural networks for extreme summarization. In *Proceedings of the 2018 Conference on Empirical Methods in Natural Language Processing*, pages 1797–1807, Brussels, Belgium. Association for Computational Linguistics.

Jun-Ping Ng and Viktoria Abrecht. 2015. Better summarization evaluation with word embeddings for ROUGE. In *Proceedings of the 2015 Conference on Empirical Methods in Natural Language Processing*, pages 1925–1930, Lisbon, Portugal. Association for Computational Linguistics.

Alexander M. Rush, Sumit Chopra, and Jason Weston. 2015. A neural attention model for abstractive sentence summarization. In *Proceedings of the 2015 Conference on Empirical Methods in Natural Language Processing*, pages 379–389, Lisbon, Portugal. Association for Computational Linguistics.

Itsumi Saito, Kyosuke Nishida, Kosuke Nishida, and Junji Tomita. 2020. Abstractive summarization with combination of pre-trained sequence-to-sequence and saliency models. *CoRR*, abs/2003.13028.

Gerard Salton and Chris Buckley. 1988. Term-weighting approaches in automatic text retrieval. *Inf. Process. Manag.*, 24(5):513–523.

Thomas Scialom, Paul-Alexis Dray, Sylvain Lamprier, Benjamin Piwowarski, Jacopo Staiano, Alex Wang, and Patrick Gallinari. 2021. QuestEval: Summarization asks for fact-based evaluation. In *Proceedings of the 2021 Conference on Empirical Methods in Natural Language Processing*, pages 6594–6604, Online and Punta Cana, Dominican Republic. Association for Computational Linguistics.

Simeng Sun, Ori Shapira, Ido Dagan, and Ani Nenkova. 2019. How to Compare Summarizers without Target Length? Pitfalls, Solutions and Re-Examination of the Neural Summarization Literature. In *Proceedings of the Workshop on Methods for Optimizing and Evaluating Neural Language Generation*, pages 21–29, Minneapolis, Minnesota. Association for Computational Linguistics.

Sotaro Takeshita, Tommaso Green, Niklas Friedrich, Kai Eckert, and Simone Paolo Ponzetto. 2022. X-SCITLDR: cross-lingual extreme summarization of scholarly documents. In *JCDL '22: The ACM/IEEE Joint Conference on Digital Libraries in 2022, Cologne, Germany, June 20 - 24, 2022*, page 4. ACM.

Hugo Touvron, Louis Martin, Kevin Stone, Peter Albert, Amjad Almahairi, Yasmine Babaei, Nikolay Bashlykov, Soumya Batra, Prajjwal Bhargava, Shruti Bhosale, Dan Bikel, Lukas Blecher, Cristian Canton Ferrer, Moya Chen, Guillem Cucurull, David Esiobu, Jude Fernandes, Jeremy Fu, Wenyin Fu, Brian Fuller, Cynthia Gao, Vedanuj Goswami, Naman Goyal, Anthony Hartshorn, Saghar Hosseini, Rui Hou, Hakan Inan, Marcin Kardas, Viktor Kerkez, Madian Khabsa,

Isabel Kloumann, Artem Korenev, Punit Singh Koura, Marie-Anne Lachaux, Thibaut Lavril, Jenya Lee, Diana Liskovich, Yinghai Lu, Yuning Mao, Xavier Martinet, Todor Mihaylov, Pushkar Mishra, Igor Molybog, Yixin Nie, Andrew Poulton, Jeremy Reizenstein, Rashi Rungta, Kalyan Saladi, Alan Schelten, Ruan Silva, Eric Michael Smith, Ranjan Subramanian, Xiaoqing Ellen Tan, Binh Tang, Ross Taylor, Adina Williams, Jian Xiang Kuan, Puxin Xu, Zheng Yan, Iliyan Zarov, Yuchen Zhang, Angela Fan, Melanie Kambadur, Sharan Narang, Aurelien Rodriguez, Robert Stojnic, Sergey Edunov, and Thomas Scialom. 2023. Llama 2: Open foundation and fine-tuned chat models.

Ashish Vaswani, Noam Shazeer, Niki Parmar, Jakob Uszkoreit, Llion Jones, Aidan N Gomez, Łukasz Kaiser, and Illia Polosukhin. 2017. Attention is All you Need. In *Advances in Neural Information Processing Systems*, volume 30, pages 5998–6008, Long Beach, CA, USA. Curran Associates, Inc.

Yang Xiao, Jinlan Fu, See-Kiong Ng, and Pengfei Liu. 2022. Are All the Datasets in Benchmark Necessary? A Pilot Study of Dataset Evaluation for Text Classification. In *Proceedings of the 2022 Conference of the North American Chapter of the Association for Computational Linguistics: Human Language Technologies*, pages 2930–2941, Seattle, United States. Association for Computational Linguistics.

Michihiro Yasunaga, Jungo Kasai, Rui Zhang, Alexander R Fabbri, Irene Li, Dan Friedman, and Dragomir R Radev. 2019. ScisummNet: A large annotated corpus and content-impact models for scientific paper summarization with citation networks. *Proc. Conf. AAAI Artif. Intell.*, 33:7386–7393. Publisher: Association for the Advancement of Artificial Intelligence (AAAI).

Tianyi Zhang, Varsha Kishore, Felix Wu, Kilian Q. Weinberger, and Yoav Artzi. 2020. Bertscore: Evaluating text generation with BERT. In *8th International Conference on Learning Representations, ICLR 2020, Addis Ababa, Ethiopia, April 26-30, 2020*. OpenReview.net.

Investigating Aspect Features in Contextualized Embeddings with Semantic Scales and Distributional Similarity

Yuxi Li[1,2] and **Emmanuele Chersoni**[1] and **Yu-Yin Hsu**[1]
[1]Chinese and Bilingual Studies, The Hong Kong Polytechnic University, Hong Kong, China
[2]School of Foreign Studies, Xi'an Jiaotong University, Xi'an, China

Abstract

Aspect, a linguistic category describing how actions and events unfold over time, is traditionally characterized by three semantic properties: *stativity*, *durativity* and *telicity*.

In this study, we investigate whether and to what extent these properties are encoded in the verb token embeddings of the contextualized spaces of two English language models – BERT and GPT-2. First, we propose an experiment using semantic projections to examine whether the values of the vector dimensions of annotated verbs for stativity, durativity and telicity reflect human linguistic distinctions. Second, we use distributional similarity to replicate the notorious Imperfective Paradox described by Dowty (1977), and assess whether the embedding models are sensitive to capture contextual nuances of the verb telicity.

Our results show that both models encode the semantic distinctions for the aspect properties of stativity and telicity in most of their layers, while durativity is the most challenging feature. As for the Imperfective Paradox, only the embedding similarities computed with the vectors from the early layers of the BERT model align with the expected pattern.

1 Introduction

Since the introduction of Transformer architectures in NLP (Vaswani et al., 2017; Devlin et al., 2019; Radford et al., 2019), their increasing success urged researchers to get more insights about the linguistic knowledge encoded in their internal representations. The literature on *probing tasks* is a clear example of this trend: a simple classification model is asked to solve a task requiring linguistic knowledge using embeddings representations extracted from a language model (LM) with little or minimal linguistic supervision, and if the classification model is successful, one can infer that the LM's representations do encode the targeted knowledge (e.g. Tenney et al. (2019); Hewitt and Liang (2019); Goldberg (2019); Jawahar et al. (2019); Wu et al. (2020); Ravichander et al. (2020); Madabushi et al. (2020); Chen et al. (2021); Koto et al. (2021); Belinkov (2022), *inter alia*).

An alternative approach, especially popular for probing the *semantic* knowledge contained in the embeddings, involves mapping them onto human-interpretable features (Chersoni et al., 2021; Proietti et al., 2022; Wang et al., 2023). Yet the probing methodology involves a trainable classifier, and therefore the relation between the probe results and the knowledge in the original representations is not always clear (Levy et al., 2023). Moderate correlations with human ratings/norms can sometimes be obtained even by using random vectors as features (Chersoni et al., 2020), and thus alternative methods for directly analysing/modifying the structure of the semantic space have been proposed (e.g. indicator tasks, Levy et al. (2023)). A recent study by Grand et al. (2022) introduced the usage of semantic projections to interpret the content of word embeddings, by constructing subspaces corresponding to human-interpretable semantic scales. Such semantic scales were shown to be very useful in modeling human judgements for a variety of concepts in the semantics of nominals (Grand et al., 2022; Diachek et al., 2023).

In our paper, we focus on *aspect*, a concept in verb semantics that characterizes the temporal relationship of actions and events. Aspect has been shown to be important in several NLP tasks, such as next event prediction (Chambers et al., 2014) and textual entailment (Kober et al., 2019). Combining the usage of semantic scales and embedding similarity measurements, in two experiments, we address the question of whether and to what the extent the contextualized word embeddings produced by LMs encode the aspectual properties of stativity, telicity and durativity. In the first experiment, we use semantic scales to quantify the values of the

*Proceedings of the 13th Joint Conference on Lexical and Computational Semantics (*SEM 2024)*, pages 80 - 92
June 20-21, 2024

three aspectual properties in the verb token embeddings produced by different hidden layers of BERT and GPT-2. We examine whether the projected scores reflect the binary distinction in the aspectual properties of the verbs described by Vendler (1957), assuming that verbs having different values for a property (e.g. telic vs. a) should have significantly different scores. To our knowledge, we are the first to adopt the semantic scales method for modeling verb semantics. In the second experiment, we examine the similarity between simple past and past progressive forms of telic and atelic verbs that express activities and accomplishments. According to the Imperfective Paradox in Dowty (1977), the past progressive of activity verb entails its simple past, while this entailment does not hold for accomplishment verbs. Again, we extracted the verb token embeddings from different internal layers: if a BERT/GPT-2 embedding from a given layer correctly encodes telicity, we expect that the similarity between past progressive and simple past of an activity verb will be higher - since the former entails the latter- than between the two corresponding past forms of an accomplishment verb.

We found that both LMs are capable of consistently encoding aspectual features, especially for stativity and telicity. However, BERT was more sensitive to the nuanced difference in telicity, as we found in the Imperfective Paradox experiment. Our findings reveal the extents to which prototypical LMs encode core verb properties, which has important implications for selecting LMs for downstream fine-tuning. For example, based on our results, we can hypothesize that fine-tuning BERT-family models may be proven more beneficial for improving the performance of textual entailment.

2 Related Work

In the semantics literature, verb aspect is generally characterized in terms of three properties: *stativity, telicity* and *durativity* (Moens and Steedman, 1988; Pruś et al., 2024).

Stativity refers to the distinction between states and events.Verbs of high stativity generally cannot be used in progressive forms: for example, it is not possible to use 'I am knowing/loving'. In comparison, verbs of low stativity can typically be used in progressive forms (e.g. 'I am running/swimming').

Telicity refers to whether an event unfolds in time in an homogeneous way, and whether any part of the process is of the same nature as the whole. Telic verbs can often be collocated with 'in' adverbial phrases but not with 'for' adverbial phrases; e.g. 'eat' can be used in 'He ate the apple in a minute' but not in 'He ate the apple for a minute'. Notice that verbs of this type describe actions/events with a natural end point (e.g. the moment in which the apple is finished). The use of 'in' signifies that the action (of eating the apple) is completed within a specific timeframe. In contrast, atelic verbs usually collocate with 'for' but not with 'in', e.g. 'He was running for an hour' but not 'He war running in an hour'.

Finally, **durativity** refers to how long an event lasts. Durative actions like 'love' can be questioned by 'How long have you loved her?', but punctual actions like 'recognize' cannot be questioned in a similar way ('How long have you recognized her?' sounds odd without additional context). These examples show that a verb can vary along the three dimensions. For example, 'love' is simultaneously stative, durative, and atelic.

The work conducted by Friedrich and Palmer (2014) focuses on the automatic classification of verb stativity in context, using a combination of distributional and manually crafted linguistic features. It is one of the first to introduce a dataset of annotated sentences specifically for this feature. Friedrich and Gateva (2017) expanded on this work, by releasing datasets also for telicity and durativity with gold and silver annotations; the latter was automatically extracted from a parallel corpus between English and Czech texts, exploiting the fact that Czech aspectual features are signaled with specific morphological markers. Kober et al. (2020) proposed an approach based on compositional distributional models to distinguish between stative and dynamic verbs, and between telic and atelic ones. Interestingly, their classification results confirmed that the tense is always a strong indicator of telicity; in particular, past tense is often correlated with telic events.

Cho et al. (2021) presented a study on using BERT surprisal to model human typicality ratings of the location arguments in natural language sentences, which were shown in the studies by Ferretti et al. (2001, 2007) to be strongly related to verb aspect: humans show priming effects for typical locations in sentences, but only when the tense of the main verb is progressive (or, in other words, the description of an action as ongoing makes the location argument more salient for human conceptual representations). BERT surprisal scores showed some sensitivity to the aspect of the verb, although they produced human-like patterns only when the entire sentence context other than the verb and the location were masked.

More recently, Metheniti et al. (2022) reported a classification experiment on telicity and durativity on English and French, suggesting that Transformer models encode a non-trivial amount of knowledge of aspect even before fine-tuning, although they have biases regards verb tense and word order. Finally, Liu and Chersoni (2023) presented a modeling study of the shortening effect that the usage of light verb constructions has on the perceived duration of event descriptions, and they also used the semantic scales method by Grand et al. (2022) to project BERT vectors onto interpretable dimensions. They showed that certain type of events (e.g. punctive) have smaller values in their DURATION-related dimensions when expressed in the light verb form (e.g. *to give a kiss* takes less time than *to kiss*).

3 Experiment 1: Measuring Aspect Properties with Semantic Scales

In the first experiment, we select a set of verbs from the study by Vendler (1957). For each of the three aspect properties, the verbs are divided into two groups: stative versus dynamic for stativity, telic versus atelic for telicity, and punctive versus durative for durativity.

Our primary goal is to construct a semantic scale for each property, and then to project the word embeddings of the verbs on the semantic scales, in order to assign them scores of stativity, telicity, and durativity. If the distributional space effectively captures the different value that a verb can express with respect to a given property (e.g. telicity), we expect the scores for the verbs of the two groups to be different (e.g. telic verbs should have considerably higher scores on the telicity scale compared to atelic verbs).

3.1 Verb Selection

To begin, we selected verbs based on the categorization in Vendler (1957) that divides verb into four classes: state, activity, accomplishment, and achievement. These classes often show differences in one crucial verb property while sharing similarities in other properties. For example, state verbs and activity verbs differ in stativity but are similar in terms of telicity and durativity. Therefore, state verbs and activity verbs can represent two extremes of stativity, with state verbs representing more stative nature and activity verbs more dynamic. Similarly, we used the 'accomplishment-activity' contrast to capture telicity, and the 'accomplishment-achievement' contrast to capture durativity. Selecting representative verbs for each extreme in this controlled manner can ensure that the constructed scales reflect the difference in the target property as much as possible. For each category, we prompted the ChatGPT online interface to generate 50 exemplars, and manually verified the results (See the Appendix for the full list of the experiment items).

3.2 Scale Construction

We followed Grand et al. (2022)'s method of identifying semantic scales from vector spaces. To obtain an 'out-of-context' representation for each target word, we averaged their contextualized embeddings from a sample of 20 randomly selected sentences from the British National Corpus (BNC) (Leech, 1992)[1]. If the target token was not included in the base vocabulary of a model and was split into sub-tokens, we used the average of the sub-tokens' embeddings as the representation for the target token. The same method was consistently applied in this study when extracting the representation for a target word in context.

Next, for each target property, we randomly sampled three words from the word lists to represent each extreme of the scale and we clustered their out-of-context embeddings, following the setup of the original study by Grand et al. (2022). For example, we sampled three words from the state verbs (e.g. *exist, lack, matter*) and three words from the activity verbs (*dance, walk, drive*) to represent the extremes of stativity. The authors recommend using this clustering step in order to avoid biases specific to the lexical meaning of a single word.

Finally, we constructed the scales by subtracting the embedding of one extreme by another extreme. This yielded a vector that represents the scale of values for a specific target property from one extreme to another. Since we had three target words for each extreme, we could construct nine scales based on different extreme pairings and average them to generate the final scale, which is meant

[1]Vulić et al. (2020) actually showed that sampling more than 10 contextualized instances leads to little differences in the representation. However, to ensure more robust results, we still chose to use 20 instances to build each out-of-context representations

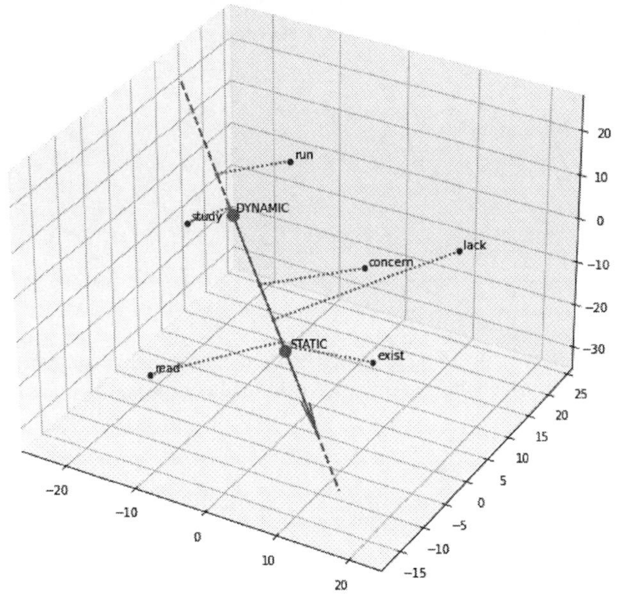

Figure 1: Semantic projection of verbs on stativity scale constructed by the 12th layer embeddings from BERT

to prevent the scale from being heavily influenced by the specific choice of antonym pairs (Grand et al., 2022). For example, if we used 'admire', 'appreciate' and 'dislike' to represent stative extreme, and 'swim', 'dance' and 'jog' to represent the dynamic extreme, we could have nine pairs, like ['admire' - 'swim'], ['admire' - 'dance'] and ['admire' - 'jog'], and subsequently average them to get the final scale.

3.3 Semantic Projection

After we constructed scales for the verb properties (henceforth as $\vec{stativity}$, $\vec{durativity}$, and $\vec{telicity}$), we assessed the validity of the scales by projecting other verbs onto the scales. Our hypothesis was that if the scale accurately reflected the semantic distinctions of the verbs in terms of the target property, the projection scores of one group of verbs would be significantly different from their semantic opposites. For example, we expected that the projection scores of the stative verbs on $\vec{stativity}$ to be significantly different from the projection scores of the dynamic verbs.

The projected verbs for projection are all the verbs in the original lists that are not used to build the scale extremes. For example, if we initially had fifty candidates for representing the one semantic extreme of a target property, we sampled three of them to represent the extreme, and then we used the remaining 47 words for projection. Therefore, for each property, we had in total 94 words for projection and difference testing.

To project the verbs on the scale, we used the standard scalar projection formula as follows:

$$Proj(\vec{target}) = \frac{\vec{target} \cdot \vec{property}}{||\vec{property}||}$$

The aggregated vector of each target event is denoted as $\vec{target}$. The result of projection is a scalar value, and a larger value indicates a higher degree of the property represented by the scale. Figure 1 provides a visualization of examples of semantic projection for the stative vs. dynamic opposition in a three-dimensional space.

After the projection, we analyzed the difference in the projection scores for the two verb groups for each scale, and we saw a significant difference as evidence that a model is able to set apart the verbs according to a specific semantic dimension (e.g. we expect stative and dynamic verb to differ significantly in their $\vec{stativity}$ scores). Specifically, we compared the projection scores of the verb groups for each scale by using the Mann-Whitney U statistical test (we chose a non-parametric test because the projected scores from some of our extraction

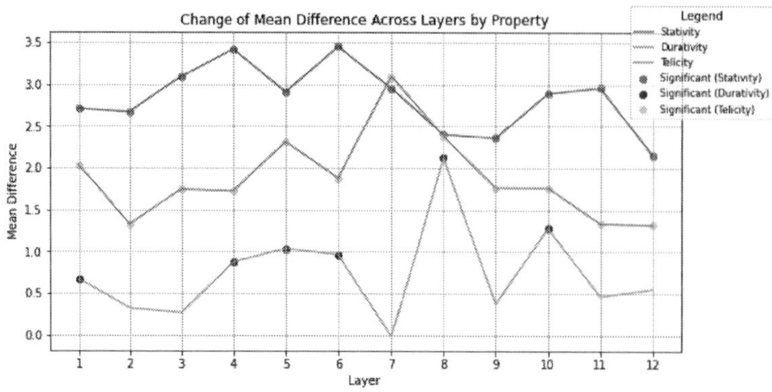

Figure 2: Layer-wise difference in the semantic projection score for stativity, durativity and telicity for each BERT layer. Dots mark the layers in which the scores for the two Vendler groups differ significantly.

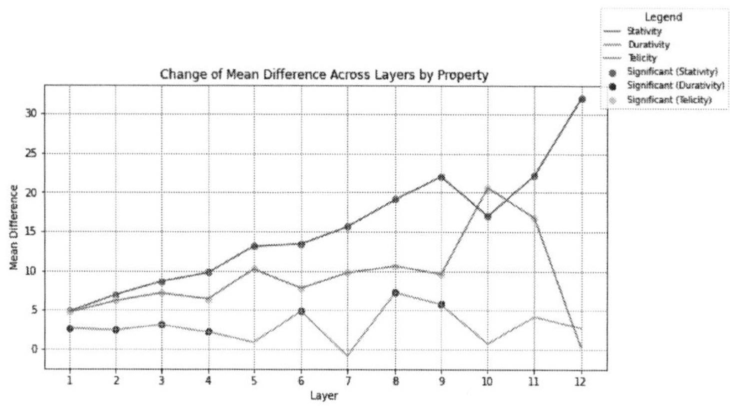

Figure 3: Layer-wise difference in the semantic projection score for stativity, durativity, and telicity for each GPT-2 layer. Dots mark the layers in which the scores for the two Vendler groups differ significantly.

experiments were not normally distributed).

3.4 Embedding Models

To obtain the contextualized embedding representations, we used the pre-trained BERT ('bert-base-uncased') (Devlin et al., 2019) and GPT-2 Base ('openai-community/gpt2') (Radford et al., 2019); both of them are available on HuggingFace[2]. The first model is a bidirectional, encoder-only Transformer, typically used for classification tasks, while GPT-2 is a unidirectional, decoder-only Transformer and it is often used for generation. The extraction of verb token embeddings was implemented in Pytorch. For verbs that were not included in the Transformers' vocabulary and were splitted in multiple subtokens, we obtained a single embedding via mean pooling of the embeddings of the subtokens. To have a finer-grained understanding of how Transformers encode verb properties, we ran the experiment by extracting the embeddings from all the 12 internal layers. As pointed out by Tenney et al. (2019), early Transformer layers tend to encode more permanent, 'out-of-context' features of a word (e.g. POS, syntax), while later layers tend to encode context-dependent semantics. Even if contextualized embeddings are able to model aspect properties, indeed, one may still be interested in understanding in what layers are best at separating the two verb groups for each property.

3.5 Results of Experiment 1

Figure 2 and Figure 3 show the layer-wise difference of projection scores of verbs of different groups on three semantic scales for BERT and GPT-2, respectively, and the dots indicate that a significant difference between the two groups at $p < 0.05$

[2]'bert-base-uncased' can be found at: https://huggingface.co/google-bert/bert-base-uncased, 'gpt2-base' can be found at: https://huggingface.co/openai-community/gpt2

for the Mann Whitney U Test. More detailed information for scale construction and projection can be found in Appendix A.

In both Transformer models, stativity is by far the property that is better encoded (blue line): it can be observed, indeed, that the differences between stative and dynamic verbs are almost always significant across layers. This is not a surprising finding, as the difference between states and events is probably one of the main distinction in verb semantics. In the BERT model, the absolute difference between the scores of the two groups is the largest across properties and it is statistically significant in all layers; in GPT-2 the difference widens in deeper layers and remains significant for all of them.

As for telicity (green line), although the projection scores of telic and atelic verbs are closer than stative and dynamic ones, the differences are still significant for all the BERT layers. For GPT-2, the difference in telicity becomes more salient as in deeper layers and finally drops in the last one, the only layer in which it is not significant. Durativity (orange line) is the most challenging property to model, with BERT managing to set the two groups apart in the first layer, around the middle layers (4-6) and in some of the later layers (8 and 10). The GPT-2 model can distinguish the two groups in the early (layer 1-4) and in the middle layers (layer 6; 8-9), but it fails to do so in the later layers.

It can be seen that later layers of both models are less consistent in discriminating the verb groups across different properties. Probably, in the later layers the embeddings become too context-specific to reflect the distinctions: the issue could be possibly related to the *anisotropy* of contextualized vector spaces (Ethayarajh, 2019), that is, the tendency for the representations to occupy just a small cone of the vector space, with the result that the similarities even between randomly sampled words tend to be very high. Interestingly, it has been reported than GPT-2 tends to have a much higher degree of anisotropy than bidirectional models in the later layers (Ethayarajh, 2019), which could explain why the performance of BERT is more stable and consistent across properties and layers.

4 Experiment 2: Modeling the Imperfective Paradox with Distributional Similarity

Our first experiment showed that the models generally have a good grasp of the semantic distinctions related to the three main aspectual properties. In our second experiment, we test if the distributional similarities between verb token embeddings reflect the entailment properties of telic and atelic verbs when we manipulate their tense. With this goal in mind, we aim at replicating the Imperfective Paradox described by Dowty (1977). In his work, Dowty focuses on the opposition of activities and accomplishments in the past progressive and in the simple past tense, as in the following example:

(1) a. *Maria **was singing** the national anthem* ⊨ *Maria **sang** the national anthem* (activity - atelic)

b. *The children **were building** a sandcastle* ⊭ *The children **built** a sandcastle* (accomplishment - telic)

Given that our models encode telicity in the embedding representations, we extract the token verb embeddings for the verbs in the provided sentence pairs in a. and b., and for each verb we measure the distributional similarity to itself when used in the other tense. Our hypothesis is that the similarity will reflect the entailment relation between the two statements. Specifically, we expect the similarity to be significantly higher for activities than accomplishments, since the simple past is entailed by the progressive in the former, but not in the latter case.

Similar to the previous experiment, we used the 'accomplishment-activity' contrast to define telicity, e.g. accomplishment verbs are telic while activity verbs are atelic. For these two groups, we used the same verbs from Experiment 1. For each group, we constructed 100 pairs of simple/progressive past sentence pairs, resulting in a total of 200 pairs.

Initially, we extracted sentences from the BNC that contained the target verbs in the simple past tense, and for each sentence we created an equivalent sentence in the past progressive by changing the verb's aspect. For telic verbs, we used word types from the 'accomplishment' verb class, while for atelic verbs, we used word types from the 'activity' verb class. In total, we collected 100 samples for each verb group. For each verb type in the lists, we randomly sampled 10 sentences in which the verbs are in the form of past particle, and filtered those sentences that are marked as passives rather than simple past sentences. The remaining sentences were evaluated by the authors and deemed less suitable for aspect conversion. We also made sure that each verb type occurred at most 5 times

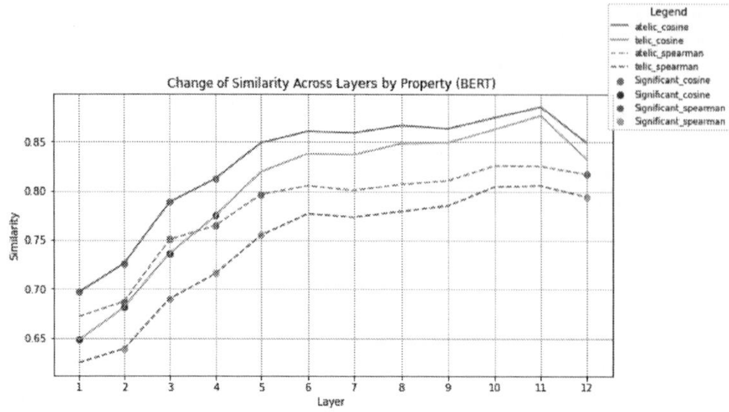

Figure 4: BERT: Layer-wise semantic similarity of the target words in simple past/past progressive pairs for the telic and atelic groups. Dots mark the layers in which the similarity scores differ significantly between two groups.

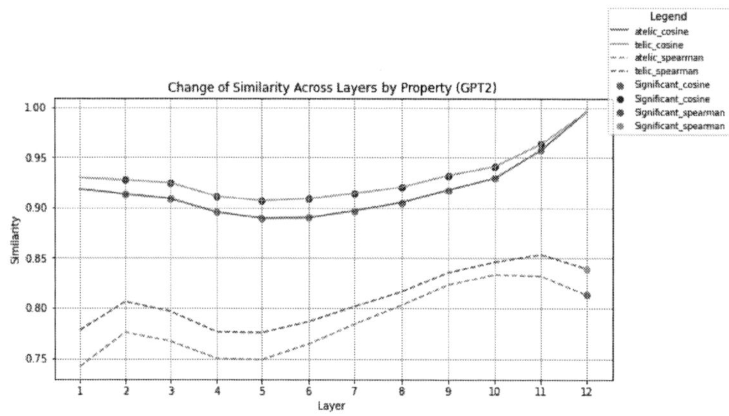

Figure 5: GPT-2: Layer-wise semantic similarity of the target words in simple past/past progressive pairs for the telic and atelic groups. Dots mark the layers in which the similarity scores differ significantly between two groups.

in the sample after filtering, to prevent the results from being too influenced by specific verb types.

As a result, we obtained 100 instances for the telic (32 verb types) and atelic group respectively (21 verb types). [3] The sentences in each pair are exactly the same, except for the main verb tense [4], and we also manually checked that they did not become incoherent due to the aspect conversion.Once obtained the sentence pairs, we extracted the verb embeddings from each of them by using Pytorch. For the sentences with the verb in the past progressive, we used the embedding of the progressive form, not including the auxiliary (e.g. from *The children were building a sandcastle*, we extract the embedding of *building*).Once again, embeddings for multi-token verbs were obtained via mean pooling of the embeddings of the subtokens. The similarity between embeddings was computed with the standard cosine metric and with Spearman correlation: we chose the latter as an additional measure because of the notorious issue of the anisotropy of contextualized vector spaces, as rank-based metrics were shown to be more robust to anisotropy and more consistently correlated with human similarity judgements (Timkey and van Schijndel, 2021).

[3]Notice that, after the filtering procedure, for several verb types we did not have any sentences left in the sample. Still, we considered the existing sample size as sufficient for statistical testing, and the diversity of verb types as high enough to make generalizations about the population.

[4]For a small number of cases (7 sentences in total) we had to adjust the additional context, as they have verbs linked by coordinate conjuctions, e.g., to convert 'shopped' in 'She walked and shopped' to 'was shopping' we had to change the aspect of 'walk' to make the sentence coherent.

4.1 Results of Experiment 2

Figure 4 and 5 show the two models' layer-wise semantic similarities of the target words in simple past/past progressive pairs for the telic and atelic groups, respectively; the dots on the figures indicate significant differences at threshold of $p < 0.05$. Unlike the previous experiment, more striking differences between BERT and GPT-2 are observed. Specifically, for BERT, the cosine similarity between the target words with different aspect features gradually increase across the layers. More importantly, the similarity in the telic group was constantly lower than the similarity in the atelic group, although the difference was only significant in the first four layers. This aligns with our hypothesis that telic verbs show difference in entailment compared to atelic verbs, and this difference is reflected by the distributional similarity between word vectors.

In contrast, GPT-2 embeddings behave in an unexpected way. The similarity in the telic group was almost always significantly higher than the atelic group across all the layers, except for the first and the final one. Additionally, the general similarity between the verbs in the two tenses is higher for GPT-2 than for BERT, and it gets very close to 1 in the later layers - which complies with Ethayarajh (2019)'s finding that the embeddings of autoregressive models are much more affected by anisotropy.

With Spearman, we observe that the scores are generally lower, which confirms the higher robustness to anisotropy of this metric. We can see that the similarities for BERT follow a similar pattern, with some additional significant differences in layer 5 and in the last, more contextualized layer; on the other hand, with GPT-2 the significance pattern is totally reversed, as it becomes significant only for the last layer. Once again, and surprisingly, telic verbs are more similar than atelic ones.

In general, the BERT model is the only one that approximates the expected behavior, with the atelic verbs having higher self-similarity in both tenses. Our results also confirm the recent finding that embeddings from autoregressive models are much weaker for similarity tasks, possibly because of anisotropy and of the lack of encoding of the information from later tokens (Springer et al., 2024). Specifically, GPT-2 similarities, indeed, appear to be more unstable across metrics and heavily affected by anisotropy (all the scores are increasingly close to 1 in the later layers).

Interestingly, in BERT, the difference tends to be significant only in the earlier, less contextualized layers. One possible explanation is that the model may be too "distracted" by the context in later layers. It has been reported that the capacity of BERT to reproduce human behavior in tasks related to verb semantics (e.g. selectional preference modeling, Metheniti et al. (2020); thematic fit estimation, Cho et al. (2021)) may improve by simply applying attention masks to the context words other than the verb and its arguments, which prevents the model from focusing on other elements of the sentence. Another possibility is that the semantics of these verbs in context is more ambiguous than traditionally assumed by linguists. In such cases, the decision about the existence of an entailment relation between progressive and simple past may not be straightforward even for humans (the results of Pruś et al. (2024) seem to go in this direction. Please also refer to the Limitations section).

We also conducted a qualitative analysis to identify cases whose similarity scores deviated from the majority examples. Specifically, we focused on BERT embeddings from layer 4, which was the last layer for which the difference in similarity was significant for both metrics. We defined outliers as data points with a z-score lower than -2 or higher than +2. Interestingly, we found no outliers for the telic group, while several outliers in the atelic group were found.

We further examined these outliers by projecting their past progressive form onto the three property scales, and found that besides being low in telicity, they generally have high durativity values (see also Figure 6 in the Appendix). Therefore, the conversion into the simple past form not only made them more 'bounded' by a natural end (i.e. increase in telicity), but also shortened their duration (i.e. decrease in durativity), which in turn led to lower similarity between the two aspectual forms. This finding is supported by an examination of the contexts of these outliers. For example, 'shop' in 'We were shopping in village stores as we went along, and my diary lists items of food bought rather than consumed' has low telicity and high durativity, but it has high telicity and low durativity in its simple past counterpart, as the former suggests that the shopping may last for the whole walk, while the latter suggest that they might be several times of quick shopping. Thus, in such cases telicity is not the only determinant of verb behaviour: the context might coerce the verb into wider meaning changes.

5 Conclusion

In our study, we presented an analysis of the contextualized verb embeddings of BERT and GPT-2 to assess to what extent they encode semantic distinctions related to the three aspectual properties of stativity, telicity, and durativity. Our first experiment, making use of the technique of the projection on a semantic scale by Grand et al. (2022), showed that both models could consistently distinguish verbs with different values for stativity and telicity, but faced more challenges with durativity, and gave less consistent results. To our knowledge, this study is the first that applies the method of semantic scales to analyse features of verb semantics.

As an additional contribution, we used the distributional similarities between the simple past and the past progressive of telic and atelic verbs to 'recreate' the Imperfective Paradox (Dowty, 1977) in a contextualized vector space. We showed that only the BERT model in the early layers reflects the distinction proposed by the theory – Progressive forms of atelic verbs, which entail their simple past, are more similar to the simple past than the corresponding forms of telic verbs.

Limitations

Our work suffers from some obvious limitations: first of all, we run our experiments on English, so we cannot be sure that Transformer models for other languages would show similar patterns in encoding aspect properties; secondly, we focused on two types of architectures, BERT and GPT-2, but due to the limitations of our computational resources we could not test the more recent Large Language Models (Wei et al., 2022).

Finally, both of our experiments assume binary distinctions in natural language semantics, with regards to the aspect properties in Experiment 1 (stative vs. dynamic verbs, telic vs. atelic, punctive vs. durative) and with regards to the entailment in Experiment 2 (either the past progressive of a verb entails its simple past, or it does not). However, this is likely to be just a simplifying assumption: for example, the ratings collected by Pruś et al. (2024) suggest that humans tends to disagree about the entailments of verbs with the same telicity features. Future studies on the topic might need to adopt a perspectivist approach to account for differences in human semantic intuitions (Cabitza et al., 2023).

Acknowledgements

We would like to thank the three anonymous reviewers for their constructive feedback.

References

Yonatan Belinkov. 2022. Probing Classifiers: Promises, Shortcomings, and Advances. *Computational Linguistics*, 48(1):207–219.

Federico Cabitza, Andrea Campagner, and Valerio Basile. 2023. Toward a Perspectivist Turn in Ground Truthing for Predictive Computing. In *Proceedings of AAAI*.

Nathanael Chambers, Taylor Cassidy, Bill McDowell, and Steven Bethard. 2014. Dense Event Ordering with a Multi-pass Architecture. *Transactions of the Association for Computational Linguistics*, 2:273–284.

Boli Chen, Yao Fu, Guangwei Xu, Pengjun Xie, Chuanqi Tan, Mosha Chen, and Liping Jing. 2021. Probing BERT in Hyperbolic Spaces. *arXiv preprint arXiv:2104.03869*.

Emmanuele Chersoni, Enrico Santus, Chu-Ren Huang, and Alessandro Lenci. 2021. Decoding Word Embeddings with Brain-based Semantic Features. *Computational Linguistics*, 47(3):663–698.

Emmanuele Chersoni, Rong Xiang, Qin Lu, and Chu-Ren Huang. 2020. Automatic Learning of Modality Exclusivity Norms with Crosslingual Word Embeddings. In *Proceedings of *SEM*.

Won Ik Cho, Emmanuele Chersoni, Yu-Yin Hsu, and Chu-Ren Huang. 2021. Modeling the Influence of Verb Aspect on the Activation of Typical Event Locations with BERT. In *Findings of ACL-IJCNLP*.

Jacob Devlin, Ming-Wei Chang, Kenton Lee, and Kristina Toutanova. 2019. BERT: Pre-training of Deep Bidirectional Transformers for Language Understanding. In *Proceedings of NAACL*.

Evgeniia Diachek, Sarah Brown-Schmidt, and Sean M Polyn. 2023. Items Outperform Adjectives in a Computational Model of Binary Semantic Classification. *Cognitive Science*, 47(9):e13336.

David R Dowty. 1977. Toward a Semantic Analysis of Verb Aspect and the English 'Imperfective' Progressive. *Linguistics and Philosophy*, pages 45–77.

Kawin Ethayarajh. 2019. How Contextual Are Contextualized Word Representations? Comparing the Geometry of BERT, ELMo, and GPT-2 Embeddings. In *Proceedings of EMNLP*.

Todd R Ferretti, Marta Kutas, and Ken McRae. 2007. Verb Aspect and the Activation of Event Knowledge. *Journal of Experimental Psychology: Learning, Memory, and Cognition*, 33(1):182.

Todd R Ferretti, Ken McRae, and Andrea Hatherell. 2001. Integrating Verbs, Situation Schemas, and Thematic Role Concepts. *Journal of Memory and Language*, 44(4):516–547.

Annemarie Friedrich and Damyana Gateva. 2017. Classification of Telicity Using Cross-linguistic Annotation Projection. In *Proceedings of EMNLP*.

Annemarie Friedrich and Alexis Palmer. 2014. Automatic Prediction of Aspectual Class of Verbs in Context. In *Proceedings of ACL*.

Yoav Goldberg. 2019. Assessing BERT's Syntactic Abilities. *arXiv preprint arXiv:1901.05287*.

Gabriel Grand, Idan Asher Blank, Francisco Pereira, and Evelina Fedorenko. 2022. Semantic Projection Recovers Rich Human Knowledge of Multiple Object Features from Word Embeddings. *Nature Human Behaviour*, 6(7):975–987.

John Hewitt and Percy Liang. 2019. Designing and Interpreting Probes with Control Tasks. In *Proceedings of EMNLP*.

Ganesh Jawahar, Benoît Sagot, and Djamé Seddah. 2019. What Does BERT Learn about the Structure of Language? In *Proceedings of ACL*.

Thomas Kober, Malihe Alikhani, Matthew Stone, and Mark Steedman. 2020. Aspectuality Across Genre: A Distributional Semantics Approach. In *Proceedings of COLING*.

Thomas Kober, Sander Bijl de Vroe, and Mark Steedman. 2019. Temporal and Aspectual Entailment. In *Proceedings of IWCS*.

Fajri Koto, Jey Han Lau, and Timothy Baldwin. 2021. Discourse Probing of Pretrained Language Models. In *Proceedings of NAACL*.

Geoffrey Neil Leech. 1992. 100 Million Words of English: The British National Corpus (BNC). *Language Research*.

Tal Levy, Omer Goldman, and Reut Tsarfaty. 2023. Is Probing All You Need? Indicator Tasks as an Alternative to Probing Embedding Spaces. In *Findings of EMNLP*.

Chenxin Liu and Emmanuele Chersoni. 2023. On Quick Kisses and How to Make Them Count: A Study on Event Construal in Light Verb Constructions with BERT. In *Proceedings of the EMNLP Workshop on Analysing and Interpreting Neural Networks (BlackBoxNLP)*.

Harish Tayyar Madabushi, Laurence Romain, Dagmar Divjak, and Petar Milin. 2020. CxGBERT: BERT Meets Construction Grammar. In *Proceedings of COLING*.

Eleni Metheniti, Tim Van de Cruys, and Nabil Hathout. 2020. How Relevant Are Selectional Preferences for Transformer-based Language Models? In *Proceedings of COLING*.

Eleni Metheniti, Tim Van De Cruys, and Nabil Hathout. 2022. About Time: Do Transformers Learn Temporal Verbal Aspect? In *Proceedings of the ACL Workshop on Cognitive Modeling and Computational Linguistics*.

Marc Moens and Mark Steedman. 1988. Temporal Ontology and Temporal Reference. *Computational Linguistics*.

Mattia Proietti, Gianluca E Lebani, and Alessandro Lenci. 2022. Does BERT Recognize an Agent? Modeling Dowty's Proto-Roles with Contextual Embeddings. In *Proceedings of COLING*.

Katarzyna Pruś, Mark Steedman, and Adam Lopez. 2024. Human Temporal Inferences Go Beyond Aspectual Class. In *Proceedings of EACL*.

Alec Radford, Jeffrey Wu, Rewon Child, David Luan, Dario Amodei, and Ilya Sutskever. 2019. Language Models Are Unsupervised Multitask Learners. *OpenAI Blog*, 1(8):9.

Abhilasha Ravichander, Eduard Hovy, Kaheer Suleman, Adam Trischler, and Jackie Chi Kit Cheung. 2020. On the Systematicity of Probing Contextualized Word Representations: The Case of Hypernymy in BERT. In *Proceedings of *SEM*.

Jacob Mitchell Springer, Suhas Kotha, Daniel Fried, Graham Neubig, and Aditi Raghunathan. 2024. Repetition Improves Language Model Embeddings. *arXiv preprint arXiv:2402.15449*.

Ian Tenney, Dipanjan Das, and Ellie Pavlick. 2019. BERT Rediscovers the Classical NLP Pipeline. In *Proceedings of ACL*.

William Timkey and Marten van Schijndel. 2021. All Bark and No Bite: Rogue Dimensions in Transformer Language Models Obscure Representational Quality. In *Proceedings of EMNLP*.

Ashish Vaswani, Noam Shazeer, Niki Parmar, Jakob Uszkoreit, Llion Jones, Aidan N Gomez, Lukasz Kaiser, and Illia Polosukhin. 2017. Attention Is All You Need. In *Advances in Neural Information Processing Systems*.

Zeno Vendler. 1957. Verbs and Times. *The Philosophical Review*, 66(2):143–160.

Ivan Vulić, Edoardo Maria Ponti, Robert Litschko, Goran Glavaš, and Anna Korhonen. 2020. Probing Pretrained Language Models for Lexical Semantics. In *Proceedings of EMNLP*.

Shaonan Wang, Yunhao Zhang, Weiting Shi, Guangyao Zhang, Jiajun Zhang, Nan Lin, and Chengqing Zong. 2023. A Large Dataset of Semantic Ratings and its Computational Extension. *Scientific Data*, 10(1):106.

Jason Wei, Yi Tay, Rishi Bommasani, Colin Raffel, Barret Zoph, Sebastian Borgeaud, Dani Yogatama, Maarten Bosma, Denny Zhou, Donald Metzler, et al. 2022. Emergent Abilities of Large Language Models. *arXiv preprint arXiv:2206.07682*.

Zhiyong Wu, Yun Chen, Ben Kao, and Qun Liu. 2020. Perturbed Masking: Parameter-free Probing for Analyzing and Interpreting BERT. In *Proceedings of ACL*.

A Verb Lists for Experiment 1

The verbs selected for Experiment 1 -divided into States, Activities, Accomplishments and Achievements- can be found in Table 1.

B Qualititative Analysis of Experiment 2

As a complement to the final qualitative analysis in Section 4.1, Figure 6 shows an illustration of the projection of the embeddings of Experiment 2 onto the three semantic scales that we used for Experiment 1. Outliers are displayed in red.

State	Activity	Accomplishment	Achievement
admire	dance	construct	discover
cherish	play	compose	recognize
dislike	jog	win	reach
fear	swim	deliver	spot
perceive	draw	encode	quit
pertain	sing	bond	forfeit
savor	cook	rebuild	explode
wish	travel	harvest	solve
disagree	study	decorate	die
deny	read	complete	notice
exist	run	bake	arrive
lack	chat	translate	find
concern	explore	repair	retire
depend	listen	fall	cure
equal	cycle	illustrate	hire
involve	push	produce	espouse
possess	hunt	train	score
rely	knit	freeze	break
signify	garden	thrive	invent
vary	exercise	drown	crack
value	sketch	organize	finalize
hope	juggle	renovate	overcome
weigh	weave	navigate	disappear
regret	drift	install	detect
know	browse	educate	unlock
appear	shop	cultivate	depart
imply	wait	assemble	ignite
matter	daydream	migrate	collide
include	hike	generate	elect
respect	fish	formulate	vanish
appreciate	wander	activate	baptize
resemble	babble	unveil	capture
contain	shiver	fabricate	resign
desire	walk	distill	convince
envy	glow	master	enlist
remember	lounge	establish	marry
forget	march	restore	quantify
mean	quarrel	digitize	provoke
believe	drive	synthesize	succumb
have	whisper	innovate	withdraw
suspect	celebrate	craft	originate
adore	drum	demolish	conquer
understand	giggle	export	divorce
belong	hum	forge	emerge
doubt	nap	launch	hop
owe	guard	implement	erupt
seem	rehearse	refurbish	plunge
prefer	watch	paint	shatter
consist	sail	upgrade	topple
need	relax	recover	unravel

Table 1: Verb list for Experiment 1

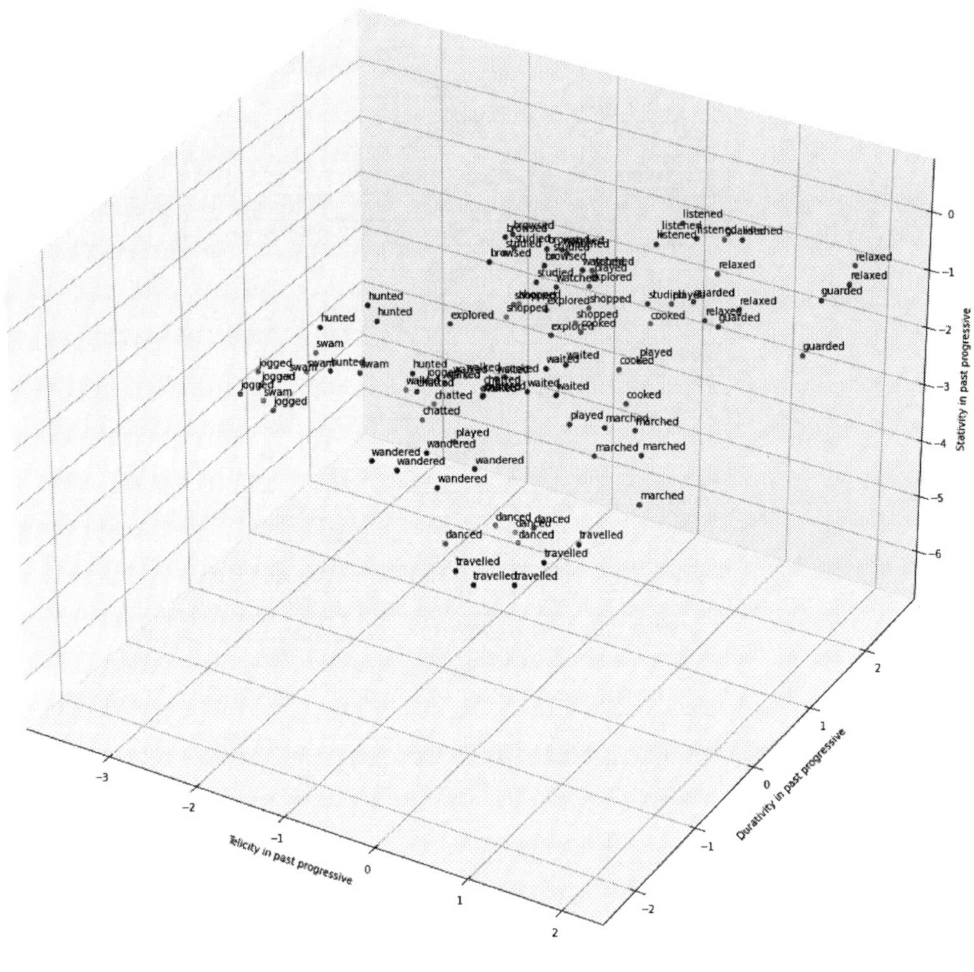

Figure 6: Visualization of aspect features of verbs in past progressive form, the red dots stand for the outliers

WikiScenes with Descriptions: Aligning Paragraphs and Sentences with Images in Wikipedia Articles

Özge Alaçam, Ronja Utescher, Hannes Grönner, Judith Sieker and Sina Zarrieß
Computational Linguistics, Dept. of Linguistics
University of Bielefeld, Germany
{oezge.alacam,hannes.groener,j.sieker,sina.zarriess}@uni-bielefeld.de

Abstract

Research in Language & Vision rarely uses naturally occurring multimodal documents as Wikipedia articles, since they feature complex image-text relations and implicit image-text alignments. In this paper, we provide one of the first datasets that provides ground-truth annotations of image-text alignments in multi-paragraph multi-image articles. The dataset can be used to study phenomena of visual language grounding in longer documents and assess retrieval capabilities of language models trained on, e.g., captioning data. Our analyses show that there are systematic linguistic differences between the image captions and descriptive sentences from the article's text and that intra-document retrieval is a challenging task for state-of-the-art models in L&V (CLIP, VILT, MCSE).

1 Introduction

Research in Language & Vision (L&V) aims at building models that ground language in the visual modality and therefore requires datasets that align text and images. To date, most work in L&V uses datasets that have been obtained via annotation of images in a way that image and text are aligned by construction as in, e.g., image captioning or VQA datasets (Thomee et al., 2016; Lin et al., 2014b; Young et al., 2014a). Multimodal image-text data that occurs "in the wild", as in, e.g., articles, recipes, comics, etc., is less commonly used since their image-text relations are much more complex (Bateman, 2008) and the alignment of images and text is often left implicit. Existing work on processing image-text alignment in multi-modal documents has usually been unsupervised, facing the challenge of missing evaluation and training data (Hessel et al., 2019). For this reason, it is unclear to what extent state-of-the-art (multi-modal) language models can discover text-image alignments in complex multi-image multi-paragraph documents and to what extent grounding capabilities in these models are biased by specific linguistic properties of annotated captions. With this work, we contribute to closing this gap and provide one of the first datasets that provide ground-truth annotations of image-text alignment in complex multimodal documents.[1]

Figure 1 shows a paragraph from the Wikipedia article on the *Reims Cathedral*[2], illustrating some of the complexities that can arise in text-image alignment in real multimodal documents. The paragraph contains highly descriptive sentences that refer to visual elements of the building shown in corresponding images. Thus, in this example, three sentences from the same paragraph *match* three different images, but there is no explicit alignment between sentences and images (e.g. through references). The paragraph also contains sentences that are not descriptive and do not match any of the images. At the same time, the images are accompanied by captions that briefly describe the image content and make it easier for the reader to establish its relation to the main text. Furthermore, this paragraph is embedded in a much longer document which contains many more, possibly matching images of this building. These alignment patterns between images and sentences in a longer text as well as captions of these images and corresponding sentences have, to date, not been extensively studied in L&V research and there is currently no available dataset that provides annotations for text-image alignments in Wikipedia articles.

In this paper, we conduct an annotation study on an existing dataset of multimodal Wikipedia articles on buildings, WikiScenes (Wu et al., 2021), and enrich the dataset with annotations of alignments between textual elements (sentences, paragraphs) and images. Since the articles in

[1] The dataset is available here: https://github.com/clause-bielefeld/wikiscenes_descriptions

[2] https://en.wikipedia.org/wiki/Reims_Cathedral

*Proceedings of the 13th Joint Conference on Lexical and Computational Semantics (*SEM 2024)*, pages 93 - 105
June 20-21, 2024

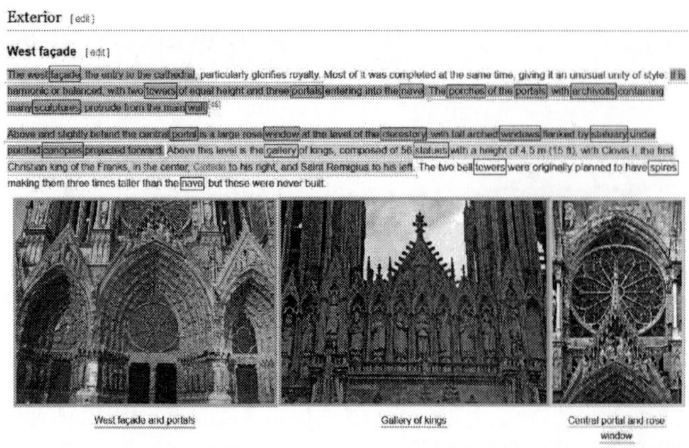

Figure 1: A highly descriptive paragraph and corresponding images from the Wikipedia article on the *Reims Cathedral*. Sentences that match an image are highlighted in the same color as the caption of the respective image.

Wikiscenes are about visual entities from the domain of historical buildings, they feature text that is at times highly descriptive and, thereby, comparable to caption-like descriptions (see, e.g., the mention of the facade of the *Reims Cathedral* in Figure 1). We restrict our annotation study to descriptive relations between text and images, i.e. textual elements that describe visual content shown in an image within the article, refraining from including more complex discourse relations involving complementary relations and others (Kruk et al., 2019). To deal with the fact that the articles are rather long and contain many images, we introduce a two-step annotation procedure, where we first ask annotators to skim the article for relations between paragraphs and images, and then annotate sentence-image alignments in a second step.

The dataset we obtain from our annotation setup, *WikiScenes with Descriptions*, can enhance research on visual language grounding in longer documents and assess grounding capabilities in language models. Our initial analyses in this paper focus on understanding how the descriptive sentences that occur within the main text and that match a particular image differ from captions of that image. We also experiment with baseline intra-document retrieval to evaluate L&V models on image-text alignment in our dataset. These analyses address the following research questions:

- Do descriptions of images in articles show different linguistic properties than captions of the corresponding images?
- Do the original captions in Wikipedia differ systematically from captions generated by captioning models?
- Can similarity-based retrieval based on the images' captions serve as a robust baseline for image-text alignment?
- How does image-sentence retrieval baselines with pretrained VILT (Kim et al., 2021) and CLIP (Radford et al., 2021) compare to caption-sentence retrieval?

Our analyses reveal systematic linguistic differences between the image captions on the one and descriptive sentences from the article's text at both linguistic and conceptual levels. We show that our dataset can serve as a challenging benchmark for image-text alignment in long documents.

2 Background

Our data collection is related to other efforts focused on multi-modal articles, e.g., WikiCaps (Schamoni et al., 2018) and WIT (Srinivasan et al., 2021), or datasets for news image captioning (Liu et al., 2020; Biten et al., 2019; Hollink et al., 2016). In comparison to these, our extension of Wu et al. (2021)'s*WikiScenes* features more detailed annotations of grounded text spans within sentences of the main text. Annotation of relations between spans or entities in longer text is generally challenging, as discussed in, e.g., work on coreference (Ghaddar and Langlais, 2016; Bamman et al., 2019). Annotation of multi-modal documents further comes with the significant complication that the number of possible combinations of text spans and images increases quadratically with the length of the text and the number of images.

There is some work on L&V datasets and tasks that capture more varied semantic or discursive relations between image and text: Kruk et al. (2019)

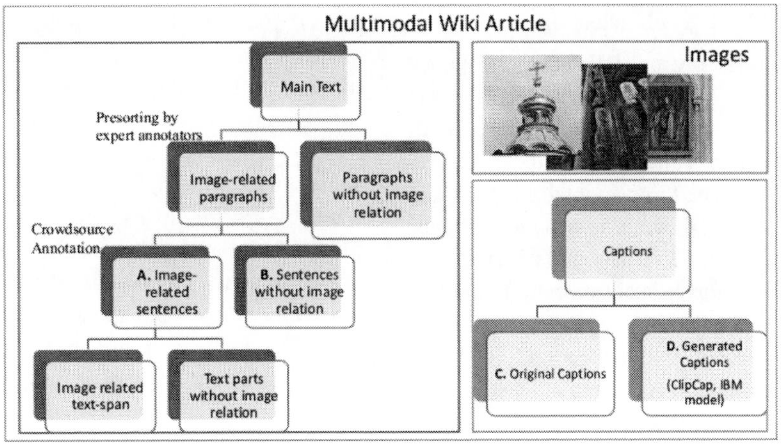

Figure 2: Illustration of the overall annotation procedure for the *WikiScenes with Descriptions* datasets, showing different levels and modalities of the annotation scheme

tag the image intent in multi-modal Twitter posts, distinguishing between intents like 'provocative', 'expressive' or 'promotive'. Their annotations assign a global label to the image which captures the relation to the text as a whole. This goes beyond literal image descriptions but still does not capture structurally diverse referential relations. Alikhani et al. (2019) investigate text-image coherence in recipe texts that describe sequences of consecutive actions in a cooking context. Structurally, the recipe text is already segmented, with an image aligned to each step. Alikhani et al. (2019) distinguish image-text relations concerning which part of the action is shown and whether all entities affected by an action are visible / mentioned in the text. Both papers work on naturally occurring texts, though these are still relatively short (tweets and 1-2 sentences per step respectively). Cheema et al. (2023) propose to combine frameworks from the area of semiotics with computational analysis of image-text relations, suggesting a framework for multimodal news analysis. In contrast to these accounts, our dataset features more or less uniform relations between texts centered on buildings and images, i.e. the texts stand in a descriptive relation to the content of images.

Muraoka et al. (2020) work with a more coarse-grained and somewhat simplified version of the problem discussed in this paper. Their task is to correctly predict the physical alignment of images and sections in Wikipedia articles. This approach utilizes the inherent document structure and consequently saves on expensive manual annotation. However, our observations call into question the presupposition that alignment in layout entails alignment in content. A similar text-image matching task is discussed in Hessel et al. (2019), where the authors seek to match the images in a document to the most relevant sentences in it (leaving out the captions). Their model is trained on collections of sentences and images from the same documents or different documents, for instances of non-relatedness. This information is used at test time to estimate the individual links between the sentences and images of a given document. Hessel et al. (2019) is highly relevant to the concerns discussed in this paper because it shows some success in handling comparatively large amounts of text in the genre of Wikipedia articles. Very recently, (Liu et al., 2023) presented the DocumentCLIP model designed to capture the interaction of text and images in longer multimodal documents. Importantly, they assume that images are, by default, aligned to the paragraph they co-occur with in the spatial document layout. This is a strong assumption and our dataset of ground-truth alignments between sentences, paragraphs, and images can be used to further test and benchmark such models.

3 Data collection

In this Section, we introduce our data collection and annotation procedures. Figure 2 shows an overview of the procedures, consisting of several stages with annotations completed at different levels, employing expert annotators and crowdsourcing. In the following, we detail each annotation stage.

3.1 Text and Paragraph Selection

From the *WikiScenes* corpus (Wu et al., 2021), we randomly sample 47 articles from the set of 98 articles. The first annotation step is a preselection of paragraphs and images that are candidates for text-image alignment. The three annotators annotated 1101 images and 1900 paragraphs. Due to the excessive number of possible paragraph-image combinations, thirty short to medium-length and one long articles were exhaustively annotated. Annotators were instructed (i) to make a snap judgment on whether a paragraph contained at least one reference to the image, (ii) to ignore non-photograph images such as plans, schemes, and paintings as well as aerial images and (iii) to consider only what is visible an image. The second and third instructions intend to exclude more complex image-paragraph correspondences and relations, that go beyond merely descriptive relations. As an example, given an image of a tower, annotators were instructed to consider sentences like *The tower was built in 1700.* as (potentially) related, while *The original altar was destroyed in the French Revolution.* is not related (even though it could be the case that the altar is inside the tower).

3.2 Fine-grained Image-Paragraph Annotations

The second annotation phase involves sentence & word-level annotations on the pre-selected paragraphs. 623 image-paragraph combinations were randomly sampled from the items collected in the previous annotation stage and evaluated by three annotators using crowd-sourcing. We recruited a group of 255 workers through Amazon Mechanical Turk. The annotators were given image and paragraph pairs, and instructed to highlight only text spans that describe something visible in the accompanying image. This ensures that the annotated text spans contain descriptions of the image or something in it. The annotation instruction are given in the Appendix, Figure 6. The average time per task was 137.6 seconds, workers were paid 0.35 $ per task.

The result of the annotation process is a collection of pairs of text spans (at sentence- and word-level) and captioned images that depict real-world objects.

Interrater agreement. At the sentence, level, if the majority of the annotators (two out of three) annotated at least one word in a sentence, the sentence is considered as depicted/matched to the respective image. We removed the cases where an annotator selects the entire paragraph instead of highlighting relevant parts. On average, the three crowd-workers who annotated each item agreed on the match or non-match of 65 % of sentences. While Wikipedia articles are aimed at a general audience, the annotation task is nonetheless non-trivial due to the complexity of the subject matter that requires a specialized vocabulary of the domain. For this reason, we believe this agreement to be of sufficient quality for further analysis. The dataset with the annotations and the generated captions at both sentence and text-span levels will be publicly available. For the rest of the paper, we present text-to-caption/image or caption/image-to-text at sentence-level alignment.

3.3 Captions

As illustrated in Figure 2, in addition to the original captions provided with the image in the wiki articles, we generated captions for the images using existing image captioning models, namely ClipCap (Mokady et al., 2021) and IBM-MAX.

ClipCap[3] (Mokady et al., 2021) is a lightweight caption generation model, based on CLIP encodings (Radford et al., 2021). It benefits from CLIP's rich semantic latent space shared by both visual and textual data trained on more than 400 M text-image pairs. In addition to the base model, we also further finetune it with several settings, the details of the finetuning are given in Appendix A.4. ClipCap-based models are listed as:

1. *clip-base*: It is the base ClipCap model without finetuning (using the CLIP Model ViT-B/32 and greedy search decoding)
2. *clip-ft*: It is created by finetuning the CLIP Image Encoder instead of the ClipCap model. 1270 unseen image-caption pairs are used for finetuning.
3. *clip-ft-gpt-20e*: It is obtained by finetuning the ClipCap model (both the prefix encoder and GPT-2 [4]

On the other hand, the IBM-MAX, inspired by Vinyals et al., 2017, does not use a transformer architecture or a large pretrained language model; instead, it utilizes an image encoder based on a

[3] `https://github.com/rmokady/CLIP_prefix_caption`

[4] with 10 epochs, prefix length 10, MLP Mapping with prefix size 512, lr 2e-5, with longer epochs (n=20)

deep convolutional net trained on MSCOCO images (Lin et al., 2014a), and an LSTM-based text decoder to generate the description. Both models generate a sentence describing the image content.

3.4 Data overview.

The dataset contains unique 3923 sentence-image-caption triples, with 1989 unique sentences. After the agreement analysis, we ended up with 683 matched sentences – image/caption pairs (A in Figure 2) and 1306 unmatched sentences (i.e. sentences from the same set of articles with no relation to any image (B in Figure 2).

4 Methods

This Section introduces the methods we use to analyze our dataset and to test L&V models on it. In our experiments, we look at two ways of aligning text and images: first, we study sentence-caption alignment, i.e. we investigate whether captions of images in an article are similar to sentences in the article's text that annotators marked as matching this image. Second, we study sentence-image alignment using multimodal L&V models.

4.1 Sentence – Caption Alignments

To explore the relations between sentences and captions, we investigate whether semantic similarities between image captions and matched/unmatched sentences constitute a promising baseline for automatic image-text alignments. We employ two types of sentence embeddings. First, we use text-only sentence representations extracted from the sentence transformer model (SBERT) from the Huggingface platform (Reimers and Gurevych, 2019). As the second method, we utilize pre-trained multimodal sentence representations (MCSE) provided by Zhang et al. (2022). MCSE are visually grounded sentence embeddings obtained by fine-tuning pre-trained models (e.g., ROBERTA-base (Liu et al., 2019)) in a contrastive learning framework. The sentence embeddings are enriched by training on a subset of Flickr30k (Young et al., 2014b) or MS-COCO (Lin et al., 2014b) image-caption dataset (30K images with multiple captions) and Wiki-1M text-only corpus. We used the pretrained weights using *flickr-mcse-roberta-base-uncased*[5]. We give each textual element as input to each pre-trained model and extract their CLS token embeddings.

[5]https://github.com/uds-lsv/MCSE

We compute text-image alignments in two directions and with different candidate sets: we retrieve captions (or images) based on the sentence (sentence-to-caption) or retrieve the sentence given the caption (caption-to-sentence). In both cases, we distinguish between the **match** condition, where the set of candidate sentences is restricted to sentences that match at least one of the images in the article, and the **all** condition where we include all sentences, i.e. un-matched sentences that are not grounded in any of the images.

Sentence-to-caption. For this condition, the retrieval analysis is conducted by calculating the ranking of each sentence in (i) paragraph-related captions, (ii) article-related captions, and (iii) all captions in the dataset. These are referred to as *caption-sets* for the following analysis. We have also calculated the paired sentence-caption similarities and presented them in the Appendix A.5.

Caption-to-sentence. In this condition, we measure the ranking of each caption in three respective sentence sets: (i) the sentences in the same paragraph, (ii) the sentences in the same article, and (iii) all sentences in the dataset.

4.2 Sentence – Image Alignments

In addition to comparing the sentence embeddings among various textual elements of the articles, we also analyze the similarities between image and textual element pairs (A to D separately, see Figure 2). To obtain image–text embeddings, we employ two state-of-the-art multimodal models with zero-shot capabilities: CLIP and VILT[6] .

VILT. VILT (Kim et al., 2021) is proposed as an efficient solution for real-time image retrieval or visual question-answering tasks. It handles the modalities in a single unified manner, instead of a simple fusion of the modalities, the training algorithm utilizes a more elaborate inter-modal interaction scheme, which in return could be very valuable for more complex vision-language tasks like our case. The efficiency comes from how they process and represent the images with convolution-free encoding. It is trained in a wide variety of datasets, including MSCOCO (Lin et al., 2014b) and Flickr30K (Young et al., 2014a).

[6]We also experimented with BLIP-2 model from the huggingface library https://huggingface.co/docs/transformers/main/en/model_doc/blip-2. Since the initial exploration indicates a similar performance to the CLIP with a longer calculation time, we abandoned it.

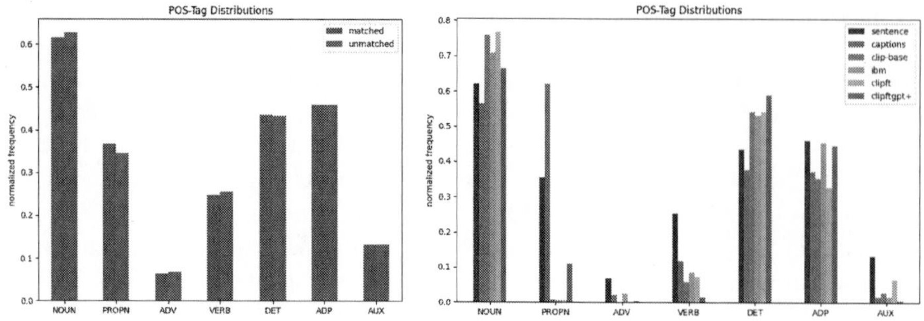

(a) Matched vs. unmatched sentences

(b) Sentences versus all caption types

Figure 3: POS tag distributions of matched vs. unmatched sentences, and sentences vs. captions (original Wiki captions and generated captions)

CLIP. The CLIP (Radford et al., 2021) model uses two separate encoders to embed text and images. It is trained on 400 M image–text pairs using contrastive learning utilizing Visual Transformers (Dosovitskiy et al., 2020). It is widely used for many L&V tasks, including zero-shot classification and retrieval.

Similar to the analysis of sentence-caption relations, we explored the sentence-image relations in two directions and distinguished the **match** condition (candidates restricted to matched sentences) and the **all** condition (all sentences).

Sentence-to-image. The ranking of each matched and unmatched sentence in two different sets of candidate lists to all images (i) from the same paragraph and (ii) from the same article. Due to the computational costs, we exclude the retrieval from the entire dataset for the multimodal models.

Image-to-sentence The ranking of each image in two different sets of candidate lists to all sentences (i) from the same paragraph and (ii) from the same article.

5 Results and Analysis

In this Section, we analyze the relationship between images, captions, and sentences from a linguistic and application perspective. Section 5.1 compares linguistic properties between captions and descriptions. Then we conduct experiments on intra-document retrieval using the methods for sentence–caption and sentence–image alignment in Section 4. , comparing the performance of unimodal and multimodal embedding models.

5.1 Analysis: Linguistic Differences between Sentences and Captions

To compare language use in descriptive sentences in the main text of an article to captions below images, we look at the distribution of tokens, PoS, and NER tags in sentences and captions.

Table 1 lists the number of unique captions and the average token length for each method. ClipCap produced 157 unique captions (such as *'English baroque structure on a sunny day'* for the image in Figure 1 but also the number of hallucinations or meaningless captions like *'a city in the smoke'* and *'a city is a city'* were not negligible. On the other hand, IBM-MAX generated 109 unique captions, significantly fewer compared to ClipCap. Yet, these are often visual descriptions such as *'a large building with a clock tower on top'* and *'a large cathedral with a clock on the wall'*.

As expected, the wiki captions are significantly shorter (7.43) than the sentences in the main text (28.47). ClipCap and IBM MAX models produce captions of lengths similar to the wiki captions (6.81 and 10.04). CLIP-base captions tend to be shorter, while IBM captions are slightly longer than the original captions. With CLIP fine-tuning, the generated captions get longer (8.09), but incorporating GPT-2 prefixes causes the model to generate fewer unique sentences (128). Because the main text sentences are significantly longer than any caption, the rest of the analysis is conducted on the

Table 1: Basic statistics on original and generated captions in *WikiScenes with Descriptions*

	Wiki	Clip-base	IBM	Clipft	Clip-ft-gpt-20
Unique captions	325	157	109	240	128
Average token count	7.43	6.81	10.04	7.22	8.09

normalized counts by the sentence length.

Figure 3 shows the distribution of POS and NER tags, obtained with spaCy's PoS and NER taggers (Honnibal and Johnson, 2015). To compare the distributions, we conducted statistical analysis on each parameter using the non-parametric Kruskal-Wallis test followed by the post-hoc Tukey test for pairwise comparisons. The analysis of PoS-tag distributions (Figure 3 (left)) does not show significant differences between matched and unmatched sentences from the article's main text. This suggests annotators did not exhibit a particular PoS preference when highlighting matched sentences. Yet, the POS-tag distribution of the main text sentences differs significantly from all kinds of captions. The details of the results are listed in Appendix Table 4. There are also significant differences between the captions types in terms of nouns, proper nouns, and determiners. The original captions are more distinct – they contain a noticeably higher proportion of proper names but a lower percentage of verbs, adverbs, and auxiliaries. The generated captions tend to have more nouns compared to human-generated captions. Just the opposite pattern is observed for the use of proper nouns. As expected, generated models avoid using this type and prefer generalized nouns. We observed no striking difference among the generated caption models except the clip-ft-gpt, which produces more proper nouns and fewer verbs.

The NER-tag analysis shows that human-generated wiki captions mostly contain entities that refer to a person, while generated captions avoid it. The IBM model's use of named entities is negligible in general. The details of the NER Distribution are presented in Figure 5 in the Appendix A.1.

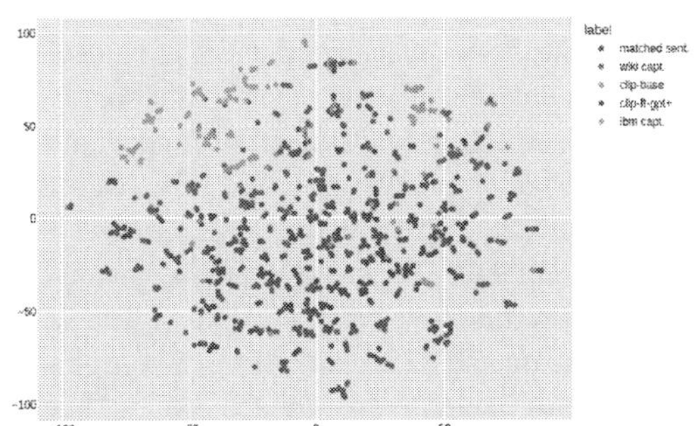

Figure 4: TSNE plot of SBERT sentence embeddings for matched sentences (blue), wiki captions (red), clip-base captions (green), clip-ft-gpt+ captions (purple) and IBM captions (orange)

To examine how sentences and captions are distributed in the semantic space, we plot their embeddings computed with SBERT, shown in Figure 4[7]. IBM-MAX captions cluster together and are located farther from the main text and ClipCap captions. Similarly, ClipCap captions are located in a specific area of the space, while original (wiki) captions, clip-ft-gpt+ captions, and matched sentences are distributed more widely. This corroborates the observation that captions show different linguistic properties and styles and sentences from the article's main text and, additionally, suggests that sentences may be more varied and linguistically diverse compared to generated captions.

5.2 Results: Intra-document Retrieval of Sentences and Images

We now compare different embedding models in terms of their ability to align sentences and captions, and sentences and images, using retrieval accuracies. We calculate the ranks of the target sentence, caption, or image (see Section 4) and report top-1 and top-5 accuracies. Additionally, the mean similarity scores between (un)matched sentences, captions, and images are presented in the Appendix Table 6 and Table 7.

The top-k accuracy scores for (i) sentence-to-caption/image and (ii) caption/image-to-sentence retrieval are presented in Table 2 and Table 3 respectively. Results from SBERT and MCSE are based on sentence-caption alignment, whereas CLIP and VILT results show sentence-image alignment. This allows us to compare unimodal to multimodal retrieval. We report retrieval accuracies on the paragraph-, text- and corpus level, as explained in Section 4.

In Table 2 and Table 3, we observe that the top-1 retrieval accuracy is overall very poor, even in the simpler match condition. On the paragraph level, the highest score for the matched sentences at top-1 is 0.66, achieved by multimodal retrieval with CLIP (in Table 2). The VILT model produces a slightly lower score, while the SBERT and MCSE models are notably low on aligning at paragraph level. For the article and corpus level, the top-1 accuracies are drastically low, in particular for caption/image-to-sentence alignment. Generally, caption/image-to-sentence retrieval is more complex than sentence-to-caption/image retrieval, regardless of the model.

[7]We use TSNE in scikit-learn: https://scikit-learn.org/stable/modules/generated/sklearn.manifold.TSNE.html

The top-5 accuracies look more promising across models and settings in the match condition, but it should also be noted that when retrieving from the paragraph-related sets the size of the candidate set is often less than five items. In the more realistic scenario of article-level retrieval, sentence embeddings (text-only and multimodal) perform better. The lowest retrieval accuracy is observed at the corpus level, as expected.

When we look at the retrieval scores of all sentences (column "all" in Table 2 and Table 3), the performance of SBERT and MCSE models further decreases, while average multimodal retrieval scores with CLIP and VILT is higher for all sentences than the matched sentences. This means that CLIP and VILT models will favor irrelevant images/sentences compared to relevant ones in top-1 and top-5 retrieval.

Finally, we look at the differences between various caption types and their similarities to the sentences. In sentence-to-caption conditions, for both SBERT and MCSE models, the generated captions are better at the paragraph and article level alignment. In contrast, the retrieval scored of wiki captions are higher at the entire set level. Among the generated captions, the clip-base model is a better fit for the task.

6 Discussion

We introduced a dataset for text–image alignment in multi-paragraph, multi-image documents, connecting captioned images with text spans from the main text which are depicted in the image. Our experiments show that these annotations provide a valuable benchmark dataset to evaluate the capabilities of zero-shot unimodal and multimodal pretrained models, that are challenged by image-text alignment in long and domain-specific documents. Based on the results, we revisit our research questions and possible implications of our experiments for future research on multimodal documents.

Do descriptions of images in articles show different linguistic properties than captions of the corresponding images? Yes. The analysis in Section 5.1 shows that descriptive, matched sentences from the main text exhibit different POS and NER distributions compared to the original captions written by Wikipedia authors. This highlights the importance of moving beyond the strong focus on captions in L&V research and indicates that different types of descriptions occurring within (and across) documents may exhibit different linguistic phenomena for visual language grounding.

Do the original captions in Wikipedia differ systematically from captions generated by captioning models? Partially. The analysis in Section 5.1 indicates that original captions written by Wikipedia authors differ in some aspects from the generated captions, which we expect to reflect the style of crowdsourced captions that many L&V models are currently trained on. This is not surprising but showcases that the style of captions collected in annotation and crowdsourcing experiments differs from naturally occurring captions found in real documents. This may bias or limit L&V models in a way that they do not encounter descriptive, visually grounded language in its full breadth in their pretraining data.

Are similarities between descriptive sentences within a text and captions robust enough to serve as a baseline for intra-document retrieval? Partially. The results in Section 5.2 show that intra-document retrieval for sentences and images via their captions works when the set of images/captions is restricted to the paragraph level, but drastically decreases at the article level. This holds for different types of captions. The retrieval score analysis shows inconclusive results in terms of the effect of captioning on different models.

How do image-sentence retrieval baselines compare to caption-sentence retrieval? The results in Section 5.2 show that sentence embeddings can distinguish more accurately between matched and unmatched sentences than multimodal models when looking at retrieval within an entire article. We believe that this may be because existing L&V models are typically trained on short texts that prioritize visually grounded language, but rarely on datasets of longer texts that include non-descriptive sentences. Generally, it appears that the multimodal models we tested lack awareness of depictability (i.e. detecting language that is visually grounded). Uni-modal sentence embedding models, on the other hand, seem to be less accurate in distinguishing grounded from non-grounded sentences at the more fine-grained paragraph level. For applications like intra-document retrieval in text-dominated documents, unimodal sentence embeddings still provide a better solution, but multimodal models have complementary strengths at the more fine-grained paragraph level distinctions. It

Table 2: Top-1 and Top-5 Retrieval Accuracy Scores for the sentence to caption/image conditions. The underlined scores represent the highest retrieval performance along the vertical axes. The match condition restricts candidate sentences to matched sentences.

		Top-1						Top-5					
		paragraph		article		entire set		paragraph		article		entire set	
	caption_type	**Match**	**All**	**Match**	**All**	**Match**	**All**	**Match**	**All**	**Match**	**All**	**Match**	**All**
SBERT	**wiki**	0.54	0.50	0.24	0.21	0.09	0.05	0.98	0.98	0.66	0.62	0.18	0.12
SBERT	**clip-base**	0.56	0.54	0.21	0.21	0.02	0.01	0.99	0.99	0.73	0.68	0.09	0.07
SBERT	**clip-ft-gpt+**	0.56	0.54	0.20	0.18	0.02	0.01	0.99	0.98	0.70	0.66	0.09	0.07
MCSE	**wiki**	0.52	0.50	0.20	0.19	0.05	0.03	0.99	0.99	0.68	0.63	0.11	0.08
MCSE	**clip-base**	0.58	0.53	0.23	0.19	0.01	0.01	1.00	0.99	0.71	0.68	0.09	0.06
MCSE	**clip-ft-gpt+**	0.55	0.53	0.19	0.18	0.01	0.01	0.99	0.99	0.68	0.67	0.08	0.06
CLIP	**wiki**	0.66	0.72	0.14	0.20	0.00	0.01	0.99	1.00	0.56	0.60	0.02	0.02
VILT	**wiki**	0.65	0.71	0.19	0.18	-	-	0.99	0.99	0.62	0.59	-	-

		Top-1						Top-5					
		paragraph		article		entire set		paragraph		article		entire set	
	caption_type	**Match**	**All**	**Match**	**All**	**Match**	**All**	**Match**	**All**	**Match**	**All**	**Match**	**All**
SBERT	**wiki**	0.24	0.14	0.08	0.04	0.04	0.02	0.85	0.73	0.25	0.17	0.09	0.05
SBERT	**clip-base**	0.22	0.15	0.04	0.03	0.00	0.00	0.83	0.73	0.15	0.13	0.01	0.01
SBERT	**clip-ft-gpt+**	0.21	0.15	0.04	0.03	0.00	0.00	0.83	0.73	0.17	0.12	0.02	0.00
MCSE	**wiki**	0.24	0.14	0.09	0.04	0.03	0.01	0.83	0.73	0.25	0.16	0.07	0.04
MCSE	**clip-base**	0.22	0.15	0.05	0.03	0.00	0.00	0.84	0.73	0.20	0.13	0.01	0.01
MCSE	**clip-ft-gpt+**	0.20	0.15	0.04	0.03	0.00	0.00	0.84	0.73	0.17	0.13	0.01	0.01
CLIP	**wiki**	0.16	0.16	0.01	0.03	-	-	0.76	0.75	0.09	0.13	-	-
VILT	**wiki**	0.15	0.16	0.01	0.03			0.76	0.75	0.09	0.13		

Table 3: Top-1 and Top-5 Retrieval Accuracy Scores for the caption/image to sentence conditions. The match condition restricts candidate sentences to matched sentences.

seems to be a promising direction for future work to explore models that exploit sentence-image and sentence-caption alignment in a joint fashion, and to develop multi-modal models that can handle text that includes non-descriptive language.

7 Conclusion

Wikipedia articles represent a genre of multimodal text that contains large amount of textual and visual information. Some foundational linguistic work on multimodal texts (Delin and Bateman, 2002; Hardy-Vallée, 2016) argues that in order to analyze multimodal texts, elements from different modalities should equally be treated as part of the document. With state-of-the-art L&V models being able to jointly represent text and image elements, this becomes increasingly feasible to do computationally as well. However, longer and more complex multimodal texts are not the norm in L&V research. With the collection of *WikiScenes with Descriptions*, we take a first step towards tackling the challenge of image-text alignment in naturally occurring, text-heavy, multi-image documents. This represents an important step in empirically-informed research on the topic of multimodal documents and provides a dataset for future modeling.

Limitations

Our extension of WikiScenes is a relatively small, domain-specific dataset so the results presented in this paper should not be assumed to necessarily generalize to other domains. The models used for the retrieval tasks were achieved with the respective base models and were not fine-tuned in our specific domain.

Ethics Statement

Images in the dataset are either under CC3.0 licenses or Open Domain. They are attributed via their identifications in Wikimedia Commons. We did not collect any personal information from annotators. Annotators were not presented with harmful materials during data collection. Crowdworkers were paid 0.35$ per item, which translates to an hourly wage of 9.01$.

Acknowledgement

The authors acknowledge financial support by the project "SAIL: SustAInable Life-cycle of Intelligent Socio-Technical Systems" (Grant ID NW21-059A), funded by the program "Netzwerke 2021" of the Ministry of Culture and Science of the State of Northrhine Westphalia, Germany.

References

Malihe Alikhani, Sreyasi Nag Chowdhury, Gerard de Melo, and Matthew Stone. 2019. Cite: A corpus of image-text discourse relations. *arXiv preprint arXiv:1904.06286*.

David Bamman, Olivia Lewke, and Anya Mansoor. 2019. An annotated dataset of coreference in english literature. *arXiv preprint arXiv:1912.01140*.

John Bateman. 2008. *Multimodality and genre: A foundation for the systematic analysis of multimodal documents*. Springer.

Ali Furkan Biten, Lluis Gomez, Marçal Rusinol, and Dimosthenis Karatzas. 2019. Good news, everyone! context driven entity-aware captioning for news images. In *Proceedings of the IEEE/CVF Conference on Computer Vision and Pattern Recognition*, pages 12466–12475.

Gullal S Cheema, Sherzod Hakimov, Eric Müller-Budack, Christian Otto, John A Bateman, and Ralph Ewerth. 2023. Understanding image-text relations and news values for multimodal news analysis. *Frontiers in Artificial Intelligence*, 6:1125533.

Judy Delin and John Bateman. 2002. Describing and critiquing multimodal documents. *Document Design*, 3:140–155.

Alexey Dosovitskiy, Lucas Beyer, Alexander Kolesnikov, Dirk Weissenborn, Xiaohua Zhai, Thomas Unterthiner, Mostafa Dehghani, Matthias Minderer, Georg Heigold, Sylvain Gelly, et al. 2020. An image is worth 16x16 words: Transformers for image recognition at scale. *arXiv preprint arXiv:2010.11929*.

Abbas Ghaddar and Philippe Langlais. 2016. Wikicoref: An english coreference-annotated corpus of wikipedia articles. In *Proceedings of the Tenth International Conference on Language Resources and Evaluation (LREC'16)*, pages 136–142.

Michel Hardy-Vallée. 2016. Text and image: a critical introduction to the visual/verbal divide by john a. bateman. *Visual Studies*, 31:366–368.

Jack Hessel, Lillian Lee, and David Mimno. 2019. Unsupervised discovery of multimodal links in multi-image, multi-sentence documents. In *Proceedings of the 2019 Conference on Empirical Methods in Natural Language Processing and the 9th International Joint Conference on Natural Language Processing (EMNLP-IJCNLP)*, pages 2034–2045, Hong Kong, China. Association for Computational Linguistics.

Laura Hollink, Adriatik Bedjeti, Martin Van Harmelen, and Desmond Elliott. 2016. A corpus of images and text in online news. In *Proceedings of the Tenth International Conference on Language Resources and Evaluation (LREC'16)*, pages 1377–1382.

Matthew Honnibal and Mark Johnson. 2015. An improved non-monotonic transition system for dependency parsing. In *Proceedings of the 2015 conference on empirical methods in natural language processing*, pages 1373–1378.

Wonjae Kim, Bokyung Son, and Ildoo Kim. 2021. Vilt: Vision-and-language transformer without convolution or region supervision. In *Proceedings of the 38th International Conference on Machine Learning*, volume 139 of *Proceedings of Machine Learning Research*, pages 5583–5594. PMLR.

Julia Kruk, Jonah Lubin, Karan Sikka, Xiao Lin, Dan Jurafsky, and Ajay Divakaran. 2019. Integrating text and image: Determining multimodal document intent in Instagram posts. In *Proceedings of the 2019 Conference on Empirical Methods in Natural Language Processing and the 9th International Joint Conference on Natural Language Processing (EMNLP-IJCNLP)*, pages 4622–4632, Hong Kong, China. Association for Computational Linguistics.

Tsung-Yi Lin, Michael Maire, Serge Belongie, James Hays, Pietro Perona, Deva Ramanan, Piotr Dollár, and C Lawrence Zitnick. 2014a. Microsoft coco: Common objects in context. In *Computer Vision–ECCV 2014: 13th European Conference, Zurich, Switzerland, September 6-12, 2014, Proceedings, Part V 13*, pages 740–755. Springer.

Tsung-Yi Lin, Michael Maire, Serge J. Belongie, Lubomir D. Bourdev, Ross B. Girshick, James Hays, Pietro Perona, Deva Ramanan, Piotr Dollár, and C. Lawrence Zitnick. 2014b. Microsoft COCO: common objects in context. *CoRR*, abs/1405.0312.

Fuxiao Liu, Hao Tan, and Chris Tensmeyer. 2023. Documentclip: Linking figures and main body text in reflowed documents. *arXiv preprint arXiv:2306.06306*.

Fuxiao Liu, Yinghan Wang, Tianlu Wang, and Vicente Ordonez. 2020. Visual news: Benchmark and challenges in news image captioning. *arXiv preprint arXiv:2010.03743*.

Yinhan Liu, Myle Ott, Naman Goyal, Jingfei Du, Mandar Joshi, Danqi Chen, Omer Levy, Mike Lewis, Luke Zettlemoyer, and Veselin Stoyanov. 2019. Roberta: A robustly optimized bert pretraining approach. *arXiv preprint arXiv:1907.11692*.

Ron Mokady, Amir Hertz, and Amit H Bermano. 2021. Clipcap: Clip prefix for image captioning. *arXiv preprint arXiv:2111.09734*.

Masayasu Muraoka, Ryosuke Kohita, and Etsuko Ishii. 2020. Image position prediction in multimodal documents. In *Proceedings of the Twelfth Language Resources and Evaluation Conference*, pages 4265–4274, Marseille, France. European Language Resources Association.

Alec Radford, Jong Wook Kim, Chris Hallacy, Aditya Ramesh, Gabriel Goh, Sandhini Agarwal, Girish Sastry, Amanda Askell, Pamela Mishkin, Jack Clark, et al. 2021. Learning transferable visual models from natural language supervision. In *International conference on machine learning*, pages 8748–8763. PMLR.

Nils Reimers and Iryna Gurevych. 2019. Sentence-bert: Sentence embeddings using siamese bert-networks. In *Proceedings of the 2019 Conference on Empirical Methods in Natural Language Processing*. Association for Computational Linguistics.

Shigehiko Schamoni, Julian Hitschler, and Stefan Riezler. 2018. A dataset and reranking method for multimodal MT of user-generated image captions. In *Proceedings of the 13th Conference of the Association for Machine Translation in the Americas (Volume 1: Research Track)*, pages 140–153, Boston, MA. Association for Machine Translation in the Americas.

Krishna Srinivasan, Karthik Raman, Jiecao Chen, Michael Bendersky, and Marc Najork. 2021. Wit: Wikipedia-based image text dataset for multimodal multilingual machine learning. In *Proceedings of the 44th International ACM SIGIR Conference on Research and Development in Information Retrieval*, pages 2443–2449, online.

Bart Thomee, David A Shamma, Gerald Friedland, Benjamin Elizalde, Karl Ni, Douglas Poland, Damian Borth, and Li-Jia Li. 2016. Yfcc100m: The new data in multimedia research. *Communications of the ACM*, 59(2):64–73.

Oriol Vinyals, Alexander Toshev, Samy Bengio, and Dumitru Erhan. 2017. Show and tell: Lessons learned from the 2015 mscoco image captioning challenge. *IEEE Transactions on Pattern Analysis and Machine Intelligence*, 39(4):652–663.

Xiaoshi Wu, Hadar Averbuch-Elor, Jin Sun, and Noah Snavely. 2021. Towers of Babel: Combining images, language, and 3D geometry for learning multimodal vision. In *ICCV*.

Peter Young, Alice Lai, Micah Hodosh, and Julia Hockenmaier. 2014a. From image descriptions to visual denotations: New similarity metrics for semantic inference over event descriptions. *TACL*, 2:67–78.

Peter Young, Alice Lai, Micah Hodosh, and Julia Hockenmaier. 2014b. From image descriptions to visual denotations: New similarity metrics for semantic inference over event descriptions. *Transactions of the Association for Computational Linguistics*, 2:67–78.

Miaoran Zhang, Marius Mosbach, David Adelani, Michael Hedderich, and Dietrich Klakow. 2022. MCSE: Multimodal contrastive learning of sentence embeddings. In *Proceedings of the 2022 Conference of the North American Chapter of the Association for Computational Linguistics: Human Language Technologies*, pages 5959–5969, Seattle, United States. Association for Computational Linguistics.

A Appendix

A.1 Text Analysis (Cont.)

Compared to the sentences, ClipCap captions contains similar amount of entities that refer to nationalities or religious or political groups (NORP), and significantly higher proportion of the dates or time periods (DATE). There is one named-entity category, ORGANIZATION was observed at similar rates among all textual elements.

Table 4: Statistical Difference between (i) matched and unmatched sentences and (ii) sentence, wiki captions and clip-ft-gpt20e captions in terms of POS- and NER-tag uses

	Sentence-Caption-Image
NOUN	554.19 (0.01 at all levels)
PROPN	105.79 (0.01 at all levels)
ADV	194.75 (0.01 sentence vs both captions)
VERB	765.87 (0.01 sentence vs both captions)
DET	494.13 (0.01 at all levels)
ADP	587.56 (0.01 at all levels)
AUX	636.11 (0.01 sentence vs both captions)
PERSON	84.92 (0.01 at all levels)
NORP	38.58 (0.01 at all levels)
DATE	120.86 (0.01 sentence vs both captions)
ORG	29.33 (0.01 clip-ft versus sent. and wiki capt.)

A.2 Annotation Instructions

Figure 6 shows the annotation instructions used for collecting annotations that align/match text spans and images from crowd workers.

A.3 Computational Resources

The experiments are conducted on a GPU workstation with NVIDIA® RTX™ A6000 (48GB). Table 5 list the approximate total time spent for ex-

Table 5: Analysis time (extracting embeddings and computing similarities) for each model on each condition

	sentence-to-caption/image	**image/caption-to-sentence**
SBERT	around 1 hours	3 hours
MCSE	around 2 hours	8 hours
CLIP	(all >32 hours) 4 hours[8]	10 hours
VILT	(all >2 days hours) 8 hours	19 hours

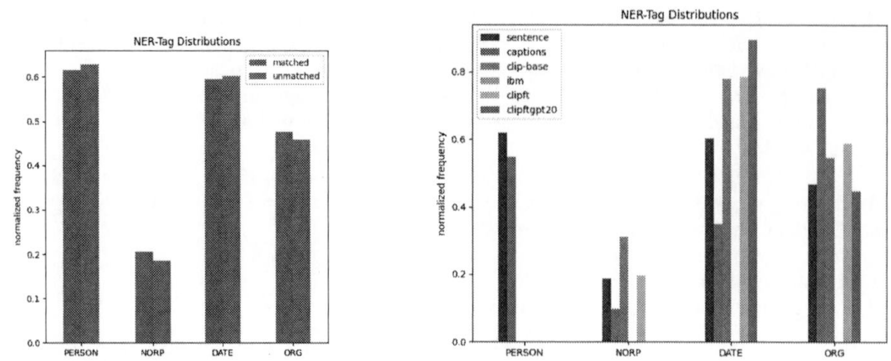

(a) NER tag distributions for matched and unmatched sentences

(b) NER tag distributions for matched sentences and captions

Figure 5: Comparing NER-tag distributions between textual elements

tracting the embeddings for each element (sentence, caption and image) and computing the similarities.

A.4 ClipCap finetuning

ClipCap finetuning follows the instructions from the original code repository: `https://github.com/rmokady/CLIP_prefix_caption`. First, the image is preprocessed using CLIP ("ViT-B/32") and mapped to a prefix vector. The prefix vector is projected into embedding space using a finetuned ClipCap model pretrained on Conceptual Captions. The prefix embedding is used as input for the GPT-2 model, as part of the ClipCap model. Greedy sampling with top-p=0.8 is used to generate the output sequence.

A.5 Similarity based Analysis

Table 6 and Table 7 present the average similarity scores of the target item against various candidate sets in two directions; sentence-to-caption/image and caption/image-to-sentence respectively.

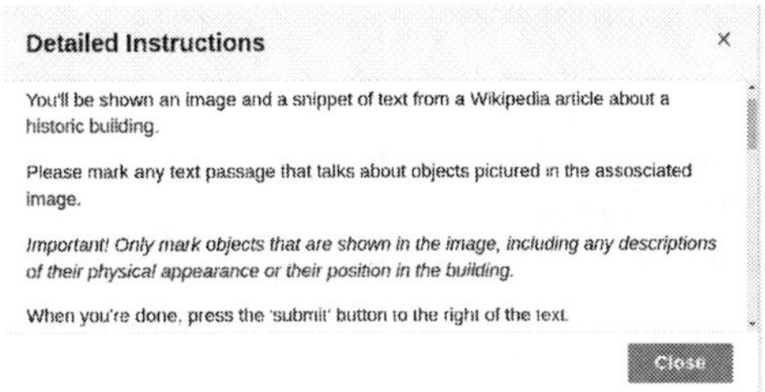

(a) Main instructions for paragraph-image alignment annotation

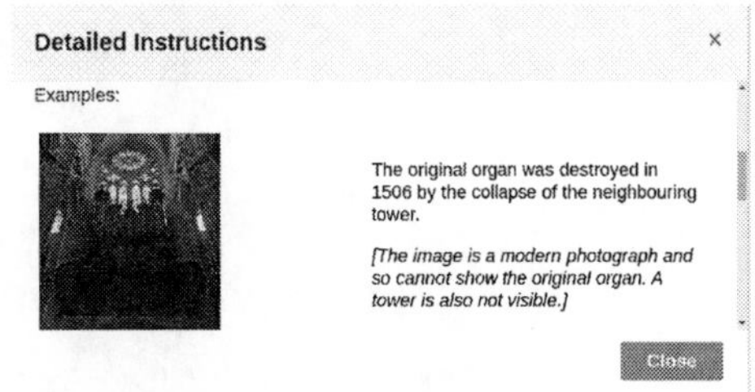

(b) Example shown in instructions for paragraph-image alignment annotation with none of the text spans matching the visual content of the image

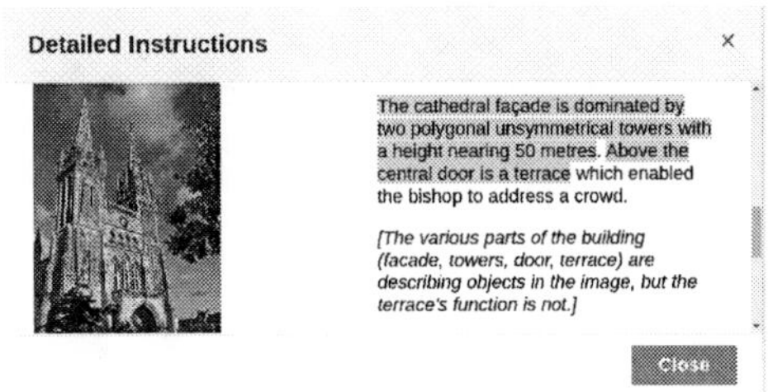

(c) Example shown in instructions for paragraph-image alignment annotation with a longer text span matching the visual content of the image

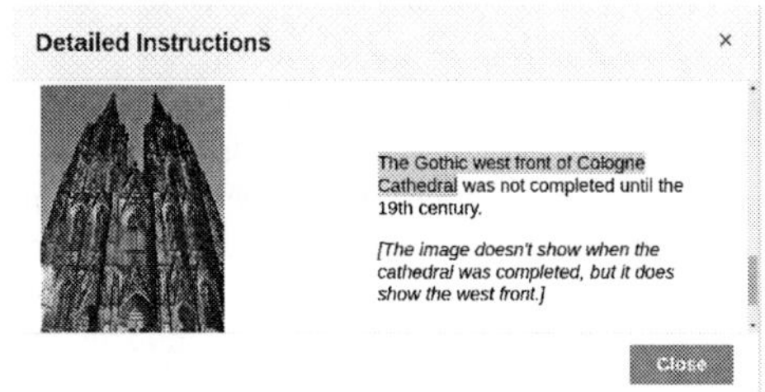

(d) Example shown in instructions for paragraph-image alignment annotation with a shorter text span matching the visual content of the image

Figure 6: Instructions used for the collection of annotations on paragraph-image alignments

Table 6: Average similarity scores for the sentence-to-caption or sentence-to-image conditions. Bold face represents the highest score along the horizontal axes, while the underlined text corresponds to highest score among the three caption types within each embedding space.

		paired		paragraph		article		entire	
		Unmatched	Matched	Unmatched	Matched	Unmatched	Matched	Unmatched	Matched
SBERT	**wiki**	0.754	**0.767**	0.754	**0.767**	0.745	0.752	0.733	0.738
SBERT	**clip-base**	0.744	**0.752**	0.743	0.751	0.739	0.746	0.726	0.731
SBERT	**clip-ft-gpt+**	0.752	**0.764**	0.752	0.762	0.750	0.759	0.739	0.746
MCSE	**wiki**	0.174	**0.216**	0.176	0.212	0.154	0.179	0.122	0.140
MCSE	**clip-base**	0.187	**0.221**	0.187	0.216	0.180	0.206	0.146	0.167
MCSE	**clip-ft-gpt+**	0.202	**0.235**	0.203	0.232	0.198	0.226	0.167	0.193
clip	**wiki**	**0.813**	0.772	0.810	0.780	0.803	0.785	0.791	0.775

Table 7: Average similarity scores for the caption-to-sentence or image-to-sentence conditions

		paired		paragraph		article		entire	
		Unmatched	Matched	Unmatched	Matched	Unmatched	Matched	Unmatched	Matched
SBERT	**wiki**	0.754	**0.767**	0.756	0.756	0.746	0.743	0.736	0.735
SBERT	**clip-base**	0.743	**0.751**	0.745	0.744	0.741	0.739	0.737	0.737
SBERT	**clip-ft-gpt+**	0.752	**0.764**	0.754	0.756	0.752	0.752	0.748	0.748
MCSE	**wiki**	0.174	**0.216**	0.180	0.186	0.158	0.154	0.135	0.132
MCSE	**clip-base**	0.187	**0.221**	0.192	0.196	0.184	0.182	0.175	0.175
MCSE	**clip-ft-gpt+**	0.202	**0.235**	0.207	0.213	0.204	0.200	0.192	0.189

Relevance, Diversity, and Exclusivity: Designing Keyword-augmentation Strategy for Zero-shot Text Classifiers

Taro Yano, Kunihiro Takeoka, Masafumi Oyamada
Data Science Laboratories, NEC Corporation
{taro_yano, k_takeoka, oyamada}@nec.com

Abstract

Zero-shot text classification involves categorizing text into classes without labeled data, typically using a pre-trained language model to compute the correlation between text and class names. This makes it essential for class names to contain sufficient information. Existing methods incorporate semantically similar keywords related to class names, but the properties of effective keywords remain unclear. We demonstrate that effective keywords should possess three properties: 1) keyword relevance to the task objective, 2) inter-class exclusivity, and 3) intra-class diversity. We also propose an automatic method for acquiring keywords that satisfy these properties without additional knowledge bases or data. Experiments on nine real-world datasets show our method outperforms existing approaches in fully zero-shot and generalized zero-shot settings. Ablation studies further confirm the importance of all three properties for superior performance.

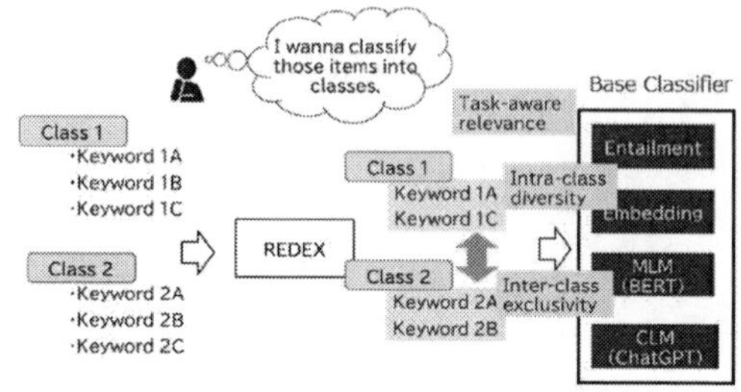

Figure 1: Overview of the proposed method REDEX. Zero-shot text classification needs proper assignment of keywords on each class. REDEX considers three properties regarding the nature of classification to assign the optimal keywords.

1 Introduction

Zero-shot text classification is the process of categorizing text into classes without any training data, which is essential in scenarios where creating a large amount of labeled data is impractical. To this end, most zero-shot classification techniques utilize signals that indicate the relationship between each instance and class, such as semantic textual similarity between instances and class names (Sappadla et al., 2016; Yin et al., 2019) or the contextual word co-occurrence of the instance and the class name found in large language models like BERT (Schick and Schütze, 2021) and T5 (Sanh et al., 2022; Wei et al., 2022).

The performance of zero-shot classifiers is heavily influenced by *keywords* related to each class (including the class name itself), as these classifiers use the keywords as queries to compute the similarity between each instance and class. For example, PET (Schick and Schütze, 2021) employs a masked language model like BERT to estimate the class of a text instance by synthesizing a sentence from the text using a template such as "${text} This text is about [MASK].", calculating token probabilities at the masked position, and aggregating the probabilities of keywords related to each class (e.g., token "news" for class "News" and token "finance" for class "Economics"). This *class to related keywords mapping* is sometimes referred to as a *verbalizer* (Schick and Schütze, 2021). Since determining optimal keywords for each class is hard, several works tried to determine proper related keywords for classes using external sources such as knowledge graphs (Hu et al., 2022) or language models (Zhao et al., 2023; Shi et al., 2022).

Regardless of whether it is manual or automatic, conventional ways to determine related keywords of each class often overlook *the nature of classification.* **(1) Keywords Relevance to the Objective:** First, the keywords attached to each class should be relevant to the classification objective, while the conventional method always attaches the same keywords for the same class name. For example, a class-keywords mapping { "Beauty" → ("mascara", "lipstick") } is suitable for product classification in E-commerce but may not be the best fit

*Proceedings of the 13th Joint Conference on Lexical and Computational Semantics (*SEM 2024)*, pages 106 - 119
June 20-21, 2024 ©2024 Association for Computational Linguistics

for movie classification. **(2) Intra-class Diversity of Keywords:** Second, the related keywords for a class should cover as broad a range of concepts as possible. Existing methods do not always consider the diversity of keywords within a class. **(3) Inter-class Exclusivity of Keywords:** Third, the related keywords for each class should be as distinct as possible, ensuring that two or more classes do not share similar keywords. For instance, the classes "Food" and "Cell Phone" might both have the keyword "apple," which can confuse zero-shot classifiers. Existing methods can produce such confusing class-keyword mappings because the keyword assignment for each class is performed independently.

In this paper, we explore the strategy of identifying optimal keywords for classes in zero-shot classifiers, considering the three properties mentioned above. Through extensive experiments, we found that considering all properties is necessary for obtaining better zero-shot classification performance in popular classifiers. To generate the optimal keywords automatically, we propose a new *generate-then-rerank* framework *REDEX* (REelevance, Diversity, EXclusivity) for keyword generation based on the concept of *maximal marginal relevance (MMR)* (Carbonell and Goldstein, 1998), which is often used in information retrieval. The extensive experiments demonstrate the effectiveness and versatility of the proposed method as it improved the performance of two types of state-of-the-art zero-shot classifiers drastically without any modifications to those methods (Zhang et al., 2022b; Yin et al., 2019; Zhang et al., 2022a; Geng and Liu, 2023; Holtzman et al., 2021) across all zero-shot settings, including generalized zero-shot text classification (GZTC) and fully-zero-shot text classification.

Our main contributions are as follows.

- We propose an automatic class-keyword mapping generation method *REDEX*, which generates keyword candidates by a generative language model and reranks them by considering three keyword properties: relevance to the objective of the classification, intra-class diversity of keywords, and inter-class exclusivity the keywords.

- Extensive experiments of REDEX for state-of-the-art zero-shot classifiers of fully or generalized zero-shot text classification in various domain datasets confirmed the effectiveness and versatility.

2 Proposed Method

2.1 Problem Setting

Zero-shot text classification is a task to estimate the optimal class $y_i \in \mathcal{K}$ of a test instance x_i, where $\mathcal{K} = \{1, 2, \ldots, K\}$ represents indices of all target classes. This paper assumes two types of zero-shot text classification: fully zero-shot setting and generalized zero-shot setting. The fully zero-shot setting provides only target class names to classify texts. The generalized zero-shot setting is where labeled data are available for a subset of target classes called seen classes, while those are not for the rest of the target classes called unseen classes. We assume that additional information, such as knowledge bases or unlabeled corpus, is unavailable.

2.2 Overview

Our method *REDEX* automatically finds keywords for each target class $k \in \mathcal{K}$ to improve classification performances. Through our experiments in Section 3, we found valuable keywords in enhancing the performance should possess three properties simultaneously: the semantic relatedness to class names, the intra-class diversity, and the inter-class exclusivity. The properties represent that keywords for a class should be not only related to the class name but also be diverse to cover features of instances belonging to the class and be semantically distant from keywords of the other classes to avoid misclassification.

Figure 2 illustrates our method, which generates keyword candidates for each class and reranks them to find valuable keywords with the aforementioned properties. The first step generates keyword candidates from a generative language model to obtain diverse and task-aware candidates without auxiliary information. The second step reranks keyword candidates to select keywords with the desired properties: semantic relatedness, intra-class diversity, and inter-class exclusivity.

2.3 Keyword Candidate Generation

In the first step of our method, we use a generative language model and prompting to generate keyword candidates. Compared to the conventional methods (Hu et al., 2022; Meng et al., 2020b) that find keywords from a knowledge base or in-domain

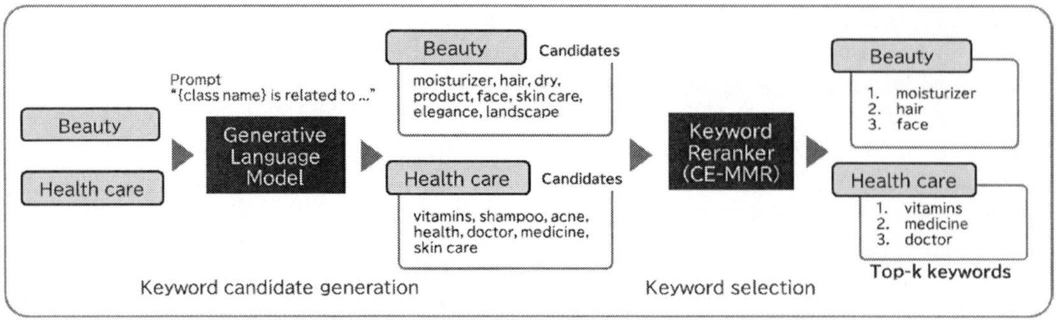

Figure 2: Overview of the proposed method REDEX for generating keyword candidates by a generative language model and reranking keyword candidates to select the suitable keywords for each class.

unlabeled data, our approach does not require any additional auxiliary information.

We manually construct prompts to input the model, such as "{class name} is related to"[1]. We then sample 20 texts using a generative language model and Nucleus Sampling (Holtzman et al., 2020). In our preliminary experiments, generating texts of more than 20 did not change most of the selected keyword candidates. We then extract phrases from generated texts by their term frequencies to acquire keyword candidates for each class. We select three times as many keyword candidates as the final number of target keywords. For details on hyperparameters and templates for generating texts, see Appendix A.

The proposed method can generate appropriate keywords by designing prompts depending on problem settings. In generalized zero-shot text classification, our method generates task-aware keywords for unseen classes using prompts that demonstrate task-aware keywords of seen classes. For instance, the task-aware keywords in the "Beauty" class in a product classification are "mascara" and "lipstick", and "elegance" and "landscapes" in a movie classification. We extract task-aware keywords for seen classes from labeled data using TF-IDF.

2.4 Reranking Keywords

Given sets of keyword candidates for classes $V = \{V_k\}_{k=1}^{|\mathcal{K}|}$, we rerank them to select suitable keywords P_k for each class k. While keyword candidates semantically relate to each class, without reranking candidate keywords, we do not capture the other properties of desirable keywords: the intra-class diversity of keywords for robust classification and the inter-class exclusivity of keywords

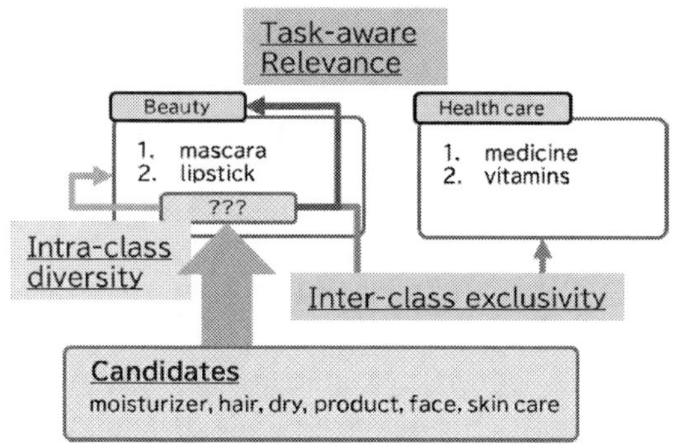

Figure 3: CE-MMR determines keywords for each class from its candidates incrementally in order of rank.

for preventing misclassification. To ensure these features of keywords, we propose class-exclusive maximal marginal relevance (CE-MMR) that extends maximal marginal relevance (MMR) for document retrieval to class-keyword reranking.

To consider the intra-class diversity, one can use maximal marginal relevance (MMR) (Carbonell and Goldstein, 1998), which reranks documents $\{d\}$ for a query q. MMR incrementally determines the rank of documents from top to bottom by the following scoring function:

$$S(d, q, R) = \lambda_1 \, s(d, q) - \lambda_2 \max_{d' \in R} s(d, d'), \quad (1)$$

where $s(d_1, d_2)$ is a function that returns a similarity of d_1 and d_2, R is a list of reranked documents, and $\lambda_1, \lambda_2 \in [0, 1]$ are hyperparameters controlling importance of the diversity of ranked documents and satisfy $\lambda_1 + \lambda_2 = 1$. This approach can be mapped to reranking keywords with their diversity. Considering a query and documents as a class name and its keyword candidates, MMR can be applied to the keyword reranking task. The formulation is

[1]The prompts to generate keyword candidates used in our experiments list in Appendix A.3.

Algorithm 1 Reranking keywords for all classes

Require: $\mathcal{C}, V$
Ensure: P

```
INITIALIZE ∀k, P_k ← list()
for rank = 1 → max_{k∈K} |V_k| do
    for k ∈ K do
        Select p_k^rank in a deterministic way by
        arg max_{v_k ∈ V_k \ P_k} S*(c_k, v_k, {P_k'}_{k'=1}^K)
        Append p_k^rank to P_k
    end for
end for
return P
```

as follows:

$$S(c_k, v_k, P_k) = \lambda_1 s(c_k, v_k) - \lambda_2 \max_{p_k \in P_k} s(v_k, p_k), \tag{2}$$

where c_k denotes the class name of k, $v_k (\in V_k \backslash P_k)$ does a keyword candidate for class k except for P_k, and P_k does the reranked keywords of class k. Using this extended MMR, we can incrementally rerank keywords to preserve the diversity of keywords for each class and class-keyword relevance.

However, the method does not consider the inter-class exclusivity of keywords in reranking. To prevent misclassification due to assigning a similar keyword to multiple classes, we use CE-MMR, which adds the inter-class exclusivity of keywords into the above method, as illustrated in Figure 3. Put the last term for inter-class exclusivity (marked in red), the scoring function of CE-MMR

$$\begin{aligned} S^\star(c_k, v_k, P) &= \alpha\, s(c_k, v_k) - \beta \max_{p_k \in P_k} s(v_k, p_k) \\ &- \gamma \max_{k' \in \mathcal{K} \backslash k} \max_{p_{k'} \in P_{k'}} s(v_k, p_{k'}), \end{aligned} \tag{3}$$

where α, β, and γ are hyperparameters for controlling the importance of the class-keyword relatedness, intra-class diversity, and inter-class exclusivity and satisfy $\alpha + \beta + \gamma = 1$.

For reranking class keywords with the CE-MMR scoring function, we take a greedy reranking approach as shown in Algorithm 1. This algorithm repeats the following steps: calculating scores for keywords, appending the top-scored keyword for a class to a list of reranked keywords for the class, and removing the keyword from candidates.

3 Experiments

3.1 Zero-shot Text Classification

We conduct fully zero-shot experiments to demonstrate the effectiveness of our method.

3.1.1 Experimental Setup

Datasets. We use widely used benchmark datasets for topic classification and sentiment analysis. Topic classification datasets are **AG News** (Zhang et al., 2015), a collection of news articles and their topic categories, **DBpedia** (Lehmann et al., 2015) consisting of contents and their ontology classes, and **Yahoo** (Zhang et al., 2015), a collection of question-answer pairs and their topic categories. Sentiment analysis datasets are Stanford Sentiment Treebank (**SST2**) (Socher et al., 2013), a widely used benchmark, and Rotten Tomatoes (**RT**) (Pang and Lee, 2005), a collection of movie reviews and their sentiments. Statistics of datasets are shown in Appendix A.1.

Preprocessing. We use the same class names and prompt templates as the previous work Shi et al. (2022); Min et al. (2023, 2022) described in Appendix A.1. For datasets of more than 3,000 instances, due to limited computational resources, we run the experiment for three times with a randomly selected subset of 3,000 with different seeds, as in prior work (Zhao et al., 2021; Lyu et al., 2022).

Evaluation Metrics. We use accuracy to evaluate methods as in Zhao et al. (2023).

3.1.2 Compared Methods

OPT-6.7b (Zhang et al., 2022a) and **OpenLLaMA-7b** (Geng and Liu, 2023; Computer, 2023) are baseline methods that classify texts using next-token prediction with score calibration (Zhao et al., 2021; Holtzman et al., 2021) and length normalization of log-likelihood (Brown et al., 2020) techniques to improve classification accuracy as in Min et al. (2022); Holtzman et al. (2021). Also, as a compared method, we utilize NPPrompt (Zhao et al., 2023) (indicated by **w/ NPPrompt** in tables) that selects top-k similar keywords to class names from the vocabulary of the language models based on cosine similarities of token embeddings. We experimented with two variants of NPPrompt, one using the same vocabulary and embedding vectors as the base model and the other using `roberta-large` vocabulary and embedding vectors as in Zhao et al. (2023), and adopted `roberta-large`, which

Table 1: Performance on zero-shot text classification. The best scores are marked in bold. OPT and OpenLLaMA with keywords selected by our method outperform methods without keywords and by NPPrompt.

Method	AG News	DBpedia	Yahoo	SST-2	RT	Avg.
OPT-6.7b	75.8	**50.7**	33.7	55.1	58.8	54.8
w/ NPPrompt	79.6	44.9	45.9	49.8	51.8	54.4
w/ Ours	**79.7**	49.4	**49.5**	**68.5**	**69.3**	**63.3** (↑ 8.5)
OpenLLaMA-7b	**65.7**	36.1	**45.1**	74.7	70.4	58.4
w/ NPPrompt	65.3	40.7	38.8	50.9	50.0	49.1
w/ Ours	61.9	**51.3**	36.9	**77.5**	**72.7**	**60.1** (↑1.7)

Table 2: Case studies of zero-shot text classification experiments using the Yahoo dataset. Keywords in a bold font have the largest scores in the correct class.

Text	Method	Prediction	Keywords for the Correct Class
what is the name the cartoon about the french cats?	w/ NPPrompt	politics	ent, ENT, ents, enting
	w/ Ours	✓entertainment	**cartoon**, theater, sport
Please answer this chem problem for me?	w/ NPPrompt	society	science, Science, scientific, technology
	w/ Ours	✓science	**chemistry**, iphone, scientist, experiment

showed better performances. Our method (indicated by **w/ Ours** in tables) generates keyword candidates by corresponding language models and reranks them to use in inference. In our reranking, we use the cosine similarity of `roberta-large` embedding vectors as the similarity $s(\cdot, \cdot)$. We set the number of keywords to five for w/ NPPrompt and w/ Ours. As another hyperparameters of reranking, we set $\alpha = \beta = \gamma = 1/3$ for w/ Ours because small changes in these values, such as 1/3 to 1/4, barely changed the selected keywords, resulting in a minor influence on the accuracy.

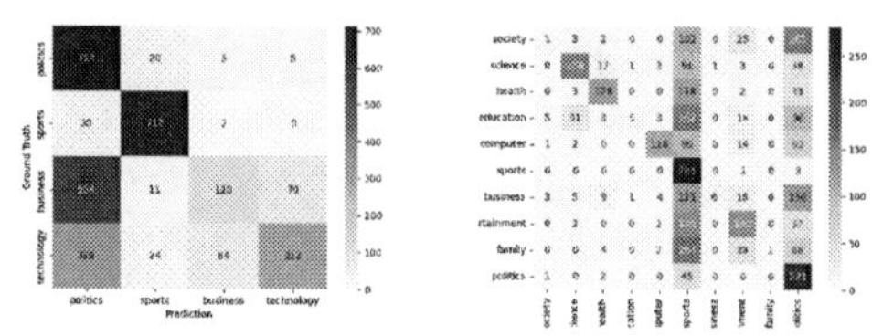

Figure 4: Error analysis for experimental results using OpenLLaMA-7b with our keywords. The left and right figures correspond to the AG News and Yahoo dataset results, respectively. OpenLLaMA-7b prefers to predict specific classes incorrectly due to the bias of giving higher scores to keywords of those incorrect classes.

3.1.3 Results

Overall Performances. Table 1 shows the experimental results of zero-shot text classification. In comparison to the baseline, our proposed method demonstrates an average accuracy improvement of 8.5 points (8.9 points compared to w/ NPPrompt) in OPT-6.7b, 1.7 points against the baseline (11.9 points compared to w/ NPPrompt) in OpenLLaMA-7b.

For some task-model combinations (Yahoo, AG News and OpenLLaMA-7b), the proposed method underperforms the vanilla OpenLLaMA-7b. To understand the reason for this, we show the confusion matrix in Figure 4. The figure shows that when the proposed method performs poorly, OpenLLaMA-7b prefers to predict specific classes incorrectly. For the case of the AG News dataset, OpenLLaMA-7b with our keywords prefers the "politics" class. We believe this is due to the bias of OpenLLaMA-7b to give higher scores to keywords in the "politics" class. In practice, we observed that OpenLLaMA-7b gave a high score to the keywords of the "politics" class even though the keywords seem to have no relationship with the input text. Although our proposed method subtracts the null prompt score to reduce the biases as in Zhao et al. (2021); Holtzman et al. (2021), there is still room for improvement regarding the score calibration method to alleviate the problem.

Case Studies. To further understand the disparity between NPPrompt and our method, we analyze the selected keywords and predictions on the Yahoo dataset. Table 2 shows that our diverse keywords can encourage a classifier to make a prediction based on the relatedness between a text and various semantics of the class. For example, the proposed method gives a high score to the keyword "chemistry" in the "science" class for the input text "Please answer this chem problem for me?". Thus,

Table 3: Relationship between the properties of keywords and accuracy. While considering only intra-class diversity or inter-class exclusivity underperform the vanilla model, considering both outperform in most cases.

Method	AG News	DBpedia	Yahoo	SST-2	RT	Avg.
OPT-6.7b	75.8	50.7	33.7	55.1	58.8	54.8
w/ Sim	**84.2**	**64.8**	47.6	56.0	58.3	62.1
w/ Sim + Exc	75.7	53.0	49.0	**68.6**	64.3	62.1
w/ Sim + Div	74.3	52.4	48.1	55.1	52.3	56.4
w/ Sim + Exc + Div	79.7	49.4	**49.5**	68.5	**69.3**	**63.3**

the proposed method correctly classifies the input text into the "science" class, while NPPrompt, which does not have the keyword "chemistry", fails to correctly classify the input text.

3.1.4 Analysis

To confirm the effectiveness of intra-class diversity and inter-class exclusivity in keyword reranking, we conduct experiments with varying keyword reranking methods. We compare four variants of CE-MMR with OPT-6.7b and vanilla OPT-6.7b as a baseline. For CE-MMR, we turn on and off three terms in Equation 3, where we denote the first, second, and third terms by **Sim**, **Div**, and **Exc**.

Table 3 shows the results. On average, Sim + Exc + Div, which considers intra-class diversity, inter-class exclusivity, and similarity to class names, achieves the highest accuracy. In sentiment analysis datasets, we find that inter-class exclusivity of keywords is more critical than intra-class diversity by comparing Sim+Exc to Sim+Div. This result suggests that when class names are antonyms such as "great" and "terrible", models are prone to give confusing keywords unless inter-class exclusivity is taken into account. Sim achieves the best results in the topic classification AG News and DBpedia. This result indicates that similarity is more important for some datasets and assigning reranking weights to exclusivity is sometimes semi-optimal. In practical applications, we can select the values of α, β, and γ according to the accuracy of the validation data. In addition, Sim + Div showed lower performance for all data in the zero-shot setting, while Sim + Exc + Div showed the best on average. This result suggests that it is not sufficient to consider only intra-class diversity, but it is essential to simultaneously consider inter-class exclusivity in order to achieve high accuracy.

3.2 Generalized Zero-shot Text Classification

We conduct experiments to confirm that our proposed method is also effective for the generalized zero-shot classification setting.

3.2.1 Datasets

We use four publicly available multi-class text classification datasets, including topic classification, intent classification, and emotion classification. The topic classification datasets are **Amazon** (McAuley et al., 2015), a collection of reviews for products and their categories, and **WoS** (Kowsari et al., 2017), a collection of academic papers and their research areas. The intent classification dataset is **Snips** (Coucke et al., 2018) that contains crowdsourced queries and their intent, such as "Book Restaurant". The emotion dataset is **Emotion** (Bostan and Klinger, 2018), a widely used benchmark for zero-shot text classification (Yin et al., 2019; Ye et al., 2020), a collection of short sequences and their emotion labels such as "joy" and "sad".

Preprocessing. We randomly select 50% from all classes as seen classes, the other 25% as unseen classes, and the other 25% as validation classes. Then, training data is selected from seen classes, validation data from seen and validation classes, and test data from the seen and unseen classes.

3.2.2 Compared Methods

We evaluate our methods, several baselines for GZSTC, and a method for a fully supervised setting as a reference. **LabelSim** (Sappadla et al., 2016) uses word embeddings to calculate similarities between an instance and class names. **LTA** (Zhang et al., 2022b) is a meta-learning method that rehearse on fake unseen classes selected from seen classes. **Entailment** (Yin et al., 2019) treats text classification tasks as textual entailment that predict whether a given text entails "This text is about {class name}." using a pre-trained language

Table 4: Harmonic mean accuracies of seen and unseen classes on generalized zero-shot text classification (seen and unseen class accuracies in the brackets). Bold values indicate the best results among GZSTC methods. Notice that LTA splits seen classes into fake seen and fake unseen classes, which is not applicable for datasets with a small number of seen classes, such as WoS and Snips. † Averaged on only Amazon and Emotion datasets.

Method	Amazon	WoS	Snips	Emotion	Avg
LabelSim	7.95 (7.83, 8.08)	40.5 (29.4, 65.3)	70.6 (75.7, 66.1)	6.46 (10.0, 22.3)	32.2 (33.8, 36.4)
LTA	53.5 (69.5, 43.5)	N/A	N/A	42.7 (37.9, **48.9**)	†48.1 (53.7, 46.2)
w/ Ours	66.6 (58.2, **77.7**)	N/A	N/A	35.6 (30.3, 43.3)	†51.1 (44.2, 60.5)
Entailment	63.2 (89.1, 49.0)	83.1 (**92.8**, 75.3)	98.9 (**99.8**, 98.1)	46.5 (**72.0**, 34.3)	72.9 (**88.4**, 64.1)
w/ Ours	**77.3** (**92.0**, 66.7)	**86.3** (92.0, **81.3**)	**99.2** (99.4, **98.9**)	**56.4** (69.0, 47.6)	**79.8** (88.1, **73.6**)
Fully Supervised					
BERT	92.4 (92.7, 92.0)	92.8 (89.2, 96.7)	99.7 (99.9, 99.6)	61.6 (68.4, 54.0)	86.6 (87.5, 85.5)

Table 5: Effectiveness of considering intra-class diversity and inter-class exclusivity on harmonic mean accuracies with seen and unseen class accuracies in brackets.

Method	Amazon	WoS	Snips	Emotion	Avg
No Reranking					
Term-Frequency	71.4 (91.6, 58.5)	79.8 (92.8, 69.9)	98.9 (100, 97.8)	54.4 (67.6, 45.5)	76.1 (88.0, 67.9)
Reranking					
w/ Sim	**77.3** (92.3, 66.5)	75.9 (92.5, 64.4)	97.7 (**100**, 95.5)	31.4 (68.1, 20.4)	70.6 (88.2, 61.7)
w/ Sim + Exc	74.0 (**92.7**, 61.5)	76.1 (**93.2**, 64.3)	97.4 (**100**, 94.9)	25.3 (**74.6**, 15.2)	68.2 (**90.1**, 59.0)
w/ Sim + Div	68.7 (92.2, 54.8)	83.8 (92.4, 76.7)	92.1 (87.4, 97.3)	**60.3** (69.7, **53.1**)	76.2 (85.4, 70.5)
w/ Sim + Exc + Div	**77.3** (92.0, **66.7**)	**86.3** (92.0, **81.3**)	**99.2** (99.4, **98.9**)	56.4 (69.0, 47.6)	**79.8** (88.1, **73.6**)

model. In addition to these baselines, we denote our method combined with baselines as **w/ Ours**. We combine Entailment, LTA and the proposed method by simply replacing a class name with the keyword expanded class name "{class name} such as {keyword1}, {keyword2}, {keyword3} , {keyword4}" because we found this simple method to be sufficient for improving performance, as it requires the same order of computation as the vanilla method.

To find out how much room for improvement is left compared to the *fully supervised setting*, we compare **BERT** trained on the training data for seen classes and training data for unseen classes that is not available for GZSTC methods.

3.2.3 Experimental Setup

Evaluation Metrics. We use accuracies of seen and unseen classes and their harmonic mean as evaluation metrics as in Zhang et al. (2022b). We use the harmonic mean to measure overall performances since there is a trade-off between seen and unseen class accuracy.

Implementation Details. We use `bert-base-uncased` (Devlin et al., 2019) as a pre-trained language model for Entailment, Entailment w/ ours, LTA, and Supervised BERT. For Entailment, we do not conduct pre-finetuning on an NLI dataset suggested in the original paper (Yin et al., 2019) since the original BERT without pre-finetuning shows better performances in our experiments. Our method uses GPT-J-6B (Wang and Komatsuzaki, 2021) as a generative language model. Furthermore, for reranking keywords, we use the cosine similarity of embeddings obtained by the BERT encoder as similarities in Equation 3 and select the top-4 keywords per class. For LabelSim, we use the bi-gram of public fastText (Grave et al., 2018) embeddings trained on the Wikipedia corpus. Please refer to Appendix A for other implementation details.

Hyperparameters. To validate the model, we use validation data that consists of labeled data of seen classes and validation classes. Search spaces and determined values of hyperparameters are described in Appendix A.2.

3.2.4 Results

Table 4 shows the results of the end-to-end experiments. In comparison, Entailment overperformes

Table 6: Effectiveness of task-aware keyword generation on harmonic mean accuracies of seen and unseen classes (seen and unseen class accuracies in the brackets). Bold values indicate the best results among methods.

Generation Method	Amazon	WoS	Snips	Emotion	Avg
Language Model	**78.5**$_{(\mathbf{90.5},\ \mathbf{69.3})}$	84.5$_{(\mathbf{92.5},\ 77.8)}$	98.0$_{(\mathbf{100},\ 96.1)}$	47.8$_{(\mathbf{69.7},\ 36.4)}$	77.2$_{(\mathbf{88.2},\ 69.9)}$
In-Context	77.3$_{(92.0,\ 66.7)}$	**86.3**$_{(92.0,\ \mathbf{81.3})}$	**99.2**$_{(99.4,\ \mathbf{98.9})}$	**56.4**$_{(69.0,\ \mathbf{47.6})}$	**79.8**$_{(88.1,\ \mathbf{73.6})}$

the other baselines, and Entailment and LTA with our extension overperformes methods without using our extension on average. The results suggest that the Entailment method generalizes better than the dual-encoder approach (LTA), as pointed out in the few-shot settings in Müller et al. (2022). Also, the results suggest that keywords selected with our method help improve unseen class accuracy due to the keywords complementing the lack of information on unseen classes. Compared to the result of the fully supervised method, there is a little room for improvement.

3.2.5 Analysis

We analyze the contribution of each component of our method by conducting additional experiments.

Keyword Reranking Methods. To confirm the effectiveness of reranking keywords by the intra-class diversity and inter-class exclusivity in the generalized zero-shot settings, we conduct ablation studies on reranking methods similar to Section 3.1.4. We use the Entailment method without reranked keywords as a baseline and compare four reranking methods to the baseline.

Table 5 shows the comparison results of keyword reranking methods. Consistent with the analysis in Section 3.1, the method considering all the characteristics is the best among compared methods on average. An inconsistent trend with the fully zero-shot setting is that intra-class diversity is more important than inter-class exclusivity in the generalized zero-shot setting. We hypothesize that the classifier learns to ignore noisy keywords and concentrate only on relevant ones through model training.

Keyword Candidate Generation Methods. To study the effectiveness of task-aware keywords described in Section 2.3 compared to task-unaware keywords, we compare keyword candidate generation technique that uses in-context demonstrations of class name and keyword pairs of seen classes (**In-Context**) to generate task-aware keywords and keyword candidates generation technique that uses only class names to generate task-unawware keyword candidates (**Language Model**). Implementation details are described in Appendix A. In the experiment, we use our keyword reranking method described in Section 2.4 to rerank keyword candidates and Entailment as the base classifier. Table 6 shows the experimental results to confirm the effectiveness of task-aware keywords. In-Context outperforms Language Model by 2.6 points on the harmonic mean of accuracies on average. This result indicates that task-aware keywords generated with in-context learning are more effective than task-unaware keywords generated with only class names.

4 Related Work

Zero-shot Text Classification. Zero-shot text classification is a text classification task in a special situation where some target classes do not have any training data. Existing methods for zero-shot text classification decide the class y of an input instance x based on the relationship between a class name and an instance (Sappadla et al., 2016; Yin et al., 2019) such as semantic similarity. Recent methods use a pre-trained language model (PLM) to calculate the similarity (Holtzman et al., 2021; Xia et al., 2022; Sun et al., 2022) of the class and the instance. For example, Schick and Schütze (2021) transforms similarity calculations into the predictions of masked token probabilities such as "Good movie! [SEP] The sentiment of this review is [MASK].". If the likelihood of "great" is higher than "bad" for "[MASK]", one can classify "Good movie!" into the positive class. At this time, it is necessary to associate the vocabulary of the PLMs and the target classes.

When training data for a part of target classes are available, the task is *generalized zero-shot text classification* (GZSTC). Similar to zero-shot text classification, Pushp and Srivastava (2017) predicts the relatedness between texts and classes by a trained neural network with the training data, and Yin et al. (2019) proposes a textual entailment-based method with PLMs, where textual entailment-based methods show effectiveness in other zero-shot tasks such as stance detection (Xu et al., 2022) and ultra-fine entity typing (Li et al., 2022). LTA (Zhang et al., 2022b) applies meta-learning for GZSTC, which learns how to adapt the encoder to new classes by episodic training on fake unseen classes selected from seen classes.

In another line of work, when a large amount of unlabeled data for target classes is available, the task is called *weakly supervised text classification* and has been studied in (Meng et al., 2018; Mekala and Shang, 2020; Mekala et al., 2022; Zhang et al., 2021; Wang et al., 2021). X-Class (Wang et al., 2021) uses class-adaptive embedding representations of instances to obtain high-quality pseudo-labeled data. Zhang et al. (2023) proposes PIEClass that iteratively trains two types of classifiers, a prompt-based classifier, and a head-token classifier, to correct pseudo-label errors with each other. Since the existing weakly supervised text classification methods require a large amount of in-domain unlabeled data that are unavailable for unseen classes in zero-shot scenarios, those methods are not applicable in our problem settings.

Class-keyword Mapping Construction. What keywords are associated with the target classes is crucial. In PET (Schick and Schütze, 2021), a mapping from keywords to classes is designed by users. For instance, in sentiment analysis, the word "terrible" is associated with the negative class, and "great" is associated with the positive class. However, since manually constructing class-keyword mappings is costly, methods to automate the process have been proposed (Schick et al., 2020; Shin et al., 2020; Shi et al., 2022; Hu et al., 2022; Zhao et al., 2023). If training data is available, they can be utilized in the construction method (Schick et al., 2020; Shin et al., 2020). When a large amount of unlabeled corpus is available, weakly supervised methods (Meng et al., 2020c,a,b) are practical to acquire keywords. LOTClass (Meng et al., 2020b) masks class names in unlabeled data and obtains mask tokens predicted by the mask language model as keywords associated with the class names. As in our problem setting, when both labeled and unlabeled data are unavailable, one approach is to select words that resemble the class name based on embedding similarity (Zhao et al., 2023).

While the conventional methods select keywords for each class independently, the attached keywords ignore the nature of classification as described in Figure 1. To avoid choosing such keywords, our proposed method selects keywords carefully by considering intra-class diversity and inter-class exclusivity of keywords.

5 Conclusion

This paper proposes a novel method for improving zero-shot text classification that finds keywords related to classes properly. Our method generates diverse keyword candidates by a generative language model and reranks the candidates by an extended maximal marginal relevance method to acquire the keywords that are diverse within a class and exclusive among different classes. Experimental results on fully zero-shot and generalized zero-shot text classification tasks demonstrate the effectiveness of the proposed method.

6 Limitations

We used a limited variety of language models in the experiments, but further work will be needed to confirm that our results are maintained for other models, such as multi-lingual models or larger-sized models. Even if we use our proposed method, it is still necessary to provide appropriate seed class names manually. Also, our proposed method is applicable to few-shot learning, so we need to investigate whether the proposed method is effective in these settings.

7 Acknowledgements

We thank three anonymous reviewers for their helpful comments and suggestions.

References

Laura Ana Maria Bostan and Roman Klinger. 2018. An analysis of annotated corpora for emotion classification in text. In *Proceedings of the 27th International Conference on Computational Linguistics, COLING 2018, Santa Fe, New Mexico, USA, August 20-26, 2018*, pages 2104–2119. Association for Computational Linguistics.

Tom B. Brown, Benjamin Mann, Nick Ryder, Melanie Subbiah, Jared Kaplan, Prafulla Dhariwal, Arvind Neelakantan, Pranav Shyam, Girish Sastry, Amanda Askell, Sandhini Agarwal, Ariel Herbert-Voss, Gretchen Krueger, Tom Henighan, Rewon Child, Aditya Ramesh, Daniel M. Ziegler, Jeffrey Wu, Clemens Winter, Christopher Hesse, Mark Chen, Eric Sigler, Mateusz Litwin, Scott Gray, Benjamin Chess, Jack Clark, Christopher Berner, Sam McCandlish, Alec Radford, Ilya Sutskever, and Dario Amodei.

2020. Language models are few-shot learners. In *Advances in Neural Information Processing Systems 33: Annual Conference on Neural Information Processing Systems 2020, NeurIPS 2020, December 6-12, 2020, virtual.*

Jaime G. Carbonell and Jade Goldstein. 1998. The use of mmr, diversity-based reranking for reordering documents and producing summaries. In *SIGIR '98: Proceedings of the 21st Annual International ACM SIGIR Conference on Research and Development in Information Retrieval, August 24-28 1998, Melbourne, Australia*, pages 335–336. ACM.

Together Computer. 2023. Redpajama-data: An open source recipe to reproduce llama training dataset.

Alice Coucke, Alaa Saade, Adrien Ball, Théodore Bluche, Alexandre Caulier, David Leroy, Clément Doumouro, Thibault Gisselbrecht, Francesco Caltagirone, Thibaut Lavril, Maël Primet, and Joseph Dureau. 2018. Snips voice platform: an embedded spoken language understanding system for private-by-design voice interfaces. *CoRR*, abs/1805.10190.

Jacob Devlin, Ming-Wei Chang, Kenton Lee, and Kristina Toutanova. 2019. BERT: Pre-training of deep bidirectional transformers for language understanding. In *Proceedings of the 2019 Conference of the North American Chapter of the Association for Computational Linguistics: Human Language Technologies, Volume 1 (Long and Short Papers)*, pages 4171–4186, Minneapolis, Minnesota. Association for Computational Linguistics.

Xinyang Geng and Hao Liu. 2023. Openllama: An open reproduction of llama.

Edouard Grave, Piotr Bojanowski, Prakhar Gupta, Armand Joulin, and Tomás Mikolov. 2018. Learning word vectors for 157 languages. In *Proceedings of the Eleventh International Conference on Language Resources and Evaluation, LREC 2018, Miyazaki, Japan, May 7-12, 2018*. European Language Resources Association (ELRA).

Maarten Grootendorst. 2022. Bertopic: Neural topic modeling with a class-based TF-IDF procedure. *CoRR*, abs/2203.05794.

Ari Holtzman, Jan Buys, Li Du, Maxwell Forbes, and Yejin Choi. 2020. The curious case of neural text degeneration. In *8th International Conference on Learning Representations, ICLR 2020, Addis Ababa, Ethiopia, April 26-30, 2020*. OpenReview.net.

Ari Holtzman, Peter West, Vered Shwartz, Yejin Choi, and Luke Zettlemoyer. 2021. Surface form competition: Why the highest probability answer isn't always right. In *Proceedings of the 2021 Conference on Empirical Methods in Natural Language Processing*, pages 7038–7051, Online and Punta Cana, Dominican Republic. Association for Computational Linguistics.

Shengding Hu, Ning Ding, Huadong Wang, Zhiyuan Liu, Jingang Wang, Juanzi Li, Wei Wu, and Maosong Sun. 2022. Knowledgeable prompt-tuning: Incorporating knowledge into prompt verbalizer for text classification. In *Proceedings of the 60th Annual Meeting of the Association for Computational Linguistics (Volume 1: Long Papers)*, pages 2225–2240, Dublin, Ireland. Association for Computational Linguistics.

Kamran Kowsari, Donald E. Brown, Mojtaba Heidarysafa, Kiana Jafari Meimandi, Matthew S. Gerber, and Laura E. Barnes. 2017. Hdltex: Hierarchical deep learning for text classification. In *16th IEEE International Conference on Machine Learning and Applications, ICMLA 2017, Cancun, Mexico, December 18-21, 2017*, pages 364–371. IEEE.

Jens Lehmann, Robert Isele, Max Jakob, Anja Jentzsch, Dimitris Kontokostas, Pablo N. Mendes, Sebastian Hellmann, Mohamed Morsey, Patrick van Kleef, Sören Auer, and Christian Bizer. 2015. Dbpedia - A large-scale, multilingual knowledge base extracted from wikipedia. *Semantic Web*, 6(2):167–195.

Bangzheng Li, Wenpeng Yin, and Muhao Chen. 2022. Ultra-fine entity typing with indirect supervision from natural language inference. *Transactions of the Association for Computational Linguistics*, 10:607–622.

Xinxi Lyu, Sewon Min, Iz Beltagy, Luke Zettlemoyer, and Hannaneh Hajishirzi. 2022. Z-ICL: zero-shot in-context learning with pseudo-demonstrations. *CoRR*, abs/2212.09865.

Julian J. McAuley, Christopher Targett, Qinfeng Shi, and Anton van den Hengel. 2015. Image-based recommendations on styles and substitutes. In *Proceedings of the 38th International ACM SIGIR Conference on Research and Development in Information Retrieval, Santiago, Chile, August 9-13, 2015*, pages 43–52. ACM.

Dheeraj Mekala, Chengyu Dong, and Jingbo Shang. 2022. LOPS: learning order inspired pseudo-label selection for weakly supervised text classification. In *Findings of the Association for Computational Linguistics: EMNLP 2022, Abu Dhabi, United Arab Emirates, December 7-11, 2022*, pages 4894–4908. Association for Computational Linguistics.

Dheeraj Mekala and Jingbo Shang. 2020. Contextualized weak supervision for text classification. In *Proceedings of the 58th Annual Meeting of the Association for Computational Linguistics, ACL 2020, Online, July 5-10, 2020*, pages 323–333. Association for Computational Linguistics.

Yu Meng, Jiaxin Huang, Guangyuan Wang, Zihan Wang, Chao Zhang, Yu Zhang, and Jiawei Han. 2020a. Discriminative topic mining via category-name guided text embedding. In *WWW '20: The Web Conference 2020, Taipei, Taiwan, April 20-24, 2020*, pages 2121–2132. ACM / IW3C2.

Yu Meng, Jiaming Shen, Chao Zhang, and Jiawei Han. 2018. Weakly-supervised neural text classification. In *Proceedings of the 27th ACM International Conference on Information and Knowledge Management, CIKM 2018, Torino, Italy, October 22-26, 2018*, pages 983–992. ACM.

Yu Meng, Yunyi Zhang, Jiaxin Huang, Chenyan Xiong, Heng Ji, Chao Zhang, and Jiawei Han. 2020b. Text classification using label names only: A language model self-training approach. In *Proceedings of the 2020 Conference on Empirical Methods in Natural Language Processing, EMNLP 2020, Online, November 16-20, 2020*, pages 9006–9017. Association for Computational Linguistics.

Yu Meng, Yunyi Zhang, Jiaxin Huang, Yu Zhang, Chao Zhang, and Jiawei Han. 2020c. Hierarchical topic mining via joint spherical tree and text embedding. In *KDD '20: The 26th ACM SIGKDD Conference on Knowledge Discovery and Data Mining, Virtual Event, CA, USA, August 23-27, 2020*, pages 1908–1917. ACM.

Sewon Min, Mike Lewis, Hannaneh Hajishirzi, and Luke Zettlemoyer. 2022. Noisy channel language model prompting for few-shot text classification. In *Proceedings of the 60th Annual Meeting of the Association for Computational Linguistics (Volume 1: Long Papers)*, pages 5316–5330, Dublin, Ireland. Association for Computational Linguistics.

Sewon Min, Weijia Shi, Mike Lewis, Xilun Chen, Wentau Yih, Hannaneh Hajishirzi, and Luke Zettlemoyer. 2023. Nonparametric masked language modeling. In *Findings of the Association for Computational Linguistics: ACL 2023*, pages 2097–2118, Toronto, Canada. Association for Computational Linguistics.

Thomas Müller, Guillermo Pérez-Torró, and Marc Franco-Salvador. 2022. Few-shot learning with Siamese networks and label tuning. In *Proceedings of the 60th Annual Meeting of the Association for Computational Linguistics (Volume 1: Long Papers)*, pages 8532–8545, Dublin, Ireland. Association for Computational Linguistics.

Bo Pang and Lillian Lee. 2005. Seeing stars: Exploiting class relationships for sentiment categorization with respect to rating scales. In *ACL 2005, 43rd Annual Meeting of the Association for Computational Linguistics, Proceedings of the Conference, 25-30 June 2005, University of Michigan, USA*, pages 115–124. The Association for Computer Linguistics.

Pushpankar Kumar Pushp and Muktabh Mayank Srivastava. 2017. Train once, test anywhere: Zero-shot learning for text classification. *CoRR*, abs/1712.05972.

Victor Sanh, Albert Webson, Colin Raffel, Stephen H. Bach, Lintang Sutawika, Zaid Alyafeai, Antoine Chaffin, Arnaud Stiegler, Arun Raja, Manan Dey, M Saiful Bari, Canwen Xu, Urmish Thakker, Shanya Sharma Sharma, Eliza Szczechla, Taewoon Kim, Gunjan Chhablani, Nihal V. Nayak, Debajyoti Datta, Jonathan Chang, Mike Tian-Jian Jiang, Han Wang, Matteo Manica, Sheng Shen, Zheng Xin Yong, Harshit Pandey, Rachel Bawden, Thomas Wang, Trishala Neeraj, Jos Rozen, Abheesht Sharma, Andrea Santilli, Thibault Févry, Jason Alan Fries, Ryan Teehan, Teven Le Scao, Stella Biderman, Leo Gao, Thomas Wolf, and Alexander M. Rush. 2022. Multitask prompted training enables zero-shot task generalization. In *The Tenth International Conference on Learning Representations, ICLR 2022, Virtual Event, April 25-29, 2022*. OpenReview.net.

Prateek Veeranna Sappadla, Jinseok Nam, Eneldo Loza Mencía, and Johannes Fürnkranz. 2016. Using semantic similarity for multi-label zero-shot classification of text documents. In *24th European Symposium on Artificial Neural Networks, ESANN 2016, Bruges, Belgium, April 27-29, 2016*.

Timo Schick, Helmut Schmid, and Hinrich Schütze. 2020. Automatically identifying words that can serve as labels for few-shot text classification. In *Proceedings of the 28th International Conference on Computational Linguistics*, pages 5569–5578, Barcelona, Spain (Online). International Committee on Computational Linguistics.

Timo Schick and Hinrich Schütze. 2021. Exploiting cloze-questions for few-shot text classification and natural language inference. In *Proceedings of the 16th Conference of the European Chapter of the Association for Computational Linguistics: Main Volume*, pages 255–269, Online. Association for Computational Linguistics.

Weijia Shi, Julian Michael, Suchin Gururangan, and Luke Zettlemoyer. 2022. Nearest neighbor zero-shot inference. In *Proceedings of the 2022 Conference on Empirical Methods in Natural Language Processing*, pages 3254–3265, Abu Dhabi, United Arab Emirates. Association for Computational Linguistics.

Taylor Shin, Yasaman Razeghi, Robert L. Logan IV, Eric Wallace, and Sameer Singh. 2020. AutoPrompt: Eliciting Knowledge from Language Models with Automatically Generated Prompts. In *Proceedings of the 2020 Conference on Empirical Methods in Natural Language Processing (EMNLP)*, pages 4222–4235, Online. Association for Computational Linguistics.

Richard Socher, Alex Perelygin, Jean Wu, Jason Chuang, Christopher D. Manning, Andrew Y. Ng, and Christopher Potts. 2013. Recursive deep models for semantic compositionality over a sentiment treebank. In *Proceedings of the 2013 Conference on Empirical Methods in Natural Language Processing, EMNLP 2013, 18-21 October 2013, Grand Hyatt Seattle, Seattle, Washington, USA, A meeting of SIGDAT, a Special Interest Group of the ACL*, pages 1631–1642. ACL.

Yi Sun, Yu Zheng, Chao Hao, and Hangping Qiu. 2022. NSP-BERT: A prompt-based few-shot learner through an original pre-training task —— next sentence prediction. In *Proceedings of the 29th International Conference on Computational Linguistics*, pages 3233–3250, Gyeongju, Republic of Korea. International Committee on Computational Linguistics.

Ben Wang and Aran Komatsuzaki. 2021. GPT-J-6B: A 6 Billion Parameter Autoregressive Language Model. `https://github.com/kingoflolz/mesh-transformer-jax`.

Zihan Wang, Dheeraj Mekala, and Jingbo Shang. 2021. X-class: Text classification with extremely weak supervision. In *Proceedings of the 2021 Conference of the North American Chapter of the Association for Computational Linguistics: Human Language Technologies, NAACL-HLT 2021, Online, June 6-11, 2021*, pages 3043–3053. Association for Computational Linguistics.

Jason Wei, Maarten Bosma, Vincent Y. Zhao, Kelvin Guu, Adams Wei Yu, Brian Lester, Nan Du, Andrew M. Dai, and Quoc V. Le. 2022. Finetuned language models are zero-shot learners. In *The Tenth International Conference on Learning Representations, ICLR 2022, Virtual Event, April 25-29, 2022*. OpenReview.net.

Mengzhou Xia, Mikel Artetxe, Jingfei Du, Danqi Chen, and Veselin Stoyanov. 2022. Prompting ELECTRA: Few-shot learning with discriminative pre-trained models. In *Proceedings of the 2022 Conference on Empirical Methods in Natural Language Processing*, pages 11351–11361, Abu Dhabi, United Arab Emirates. Association for Computational Linguistics.

Hanzi Xu, Slobodan Vucetic, and Wenpeng Yin. 2022. Openstance: Real-world zero-shot stance detection. In *Proceedings of the 26th Conference on Computational Natural Language Learning, CoNLL 2022, Abu Dhabi, United Arab Emirates (Hybrid Event), December 7-8, 2022*, pages 314–324. Association for Computational Linguistics.

Zhiquan Ye, Yuxia Geng, Jiaoyan Chen, Jingmin Chen, Xiaoxiao Xu, SuHang Zheng, Feng Wang, Jun Zhang, and Huajun Chen. 2020. Zero-shot text classification via reinforced self-training. In *Proceedings of the 58th Annual Meeting of the Association for Computational Linguistics*, pages 3014–3024, Online. Association for Computational Linguistics.

Wenpeng Yin, Jamaal Hay, and Dan Roth. 2019. Benchmarking zero-shot text classification: Datasets, evaluation and entailment approach. In *Proceedings of the 2019 Conference on Empirical Methods in Natural Language Processing and the 9th International Joint Conference on Natural Language Processing (EMNLP-IJCNLP)*, pages 3914–3923, Hong Kong, China. Association for Computational Linguistics.

Lu Zhang, Jiandong Ding, Yi Xu, Yingyao Liu, and Shuigeng Zhou. 2021. Weakly-supervised text classification based on keyword graph. In *Proceedings of the 2021 Conference on Empirical Methods in Natural Language Processing, EMNLP 2021, Virtual Event / Punta Cana, Dominican Republic, 7-11 November, 2021*, pages 2803–2813. Association for Computational Linguistics.

Susan Zhang, Stephen Roller, Naman Goyal, Mikel Artetxe, Moya Chen, Shuohui Chen, Christopher Dewan, Mona T. Diab, Xian Li, Xi Victoria Lin, Todor Mihaylov, Myle Ott, Sam Shleifer, Kurt Shuster, Daniel Simig, Punit Singh Koura, Anjali Sridhar, Tianlu Wang, and Luke Zettlemoyer. 2022a. OPT: open pre-trained transformer language models. *CoRR*, abs/2205.01068.

Xiang Zhang, Junbo Jake Zhao, and Yann LeCun. 2015. Character-level convolutional networks for text classification. In *Advances in Neural Information Processing Systems 28: Annual Conference on Neural Information Processing Systems 2015, December 7-12, 2015, Montreal, Quebec, Canada*, pages 649–657.

Yiwen Zhang, Caixia Yuan, Xiaojie Wang, Ziwei Bai, and Yongbin Liu. 2022b. Learn to adapt for generalized zero-shot text classification. In *Proceedings of the 60th Annual Meeting of the Association for Computational Linguistics (Volume 1: Long Papers)*, pages 517–527, Dublin, Ireland. Association for Computational Linguistics.

Yunyi Zhang, Minhao Jiang, Yu Meng, Yu Zhang, and Jiawei Han. 2023. PIEClass: Weakly-supervised text classification with prompting and noise-robust iterative ensemble training. In *Proceedings of the 2023 Conference on Empirical Methods in Natural Language Processing*, pages 12655–12670, Singapore. Association for Computational Linguistics.

Xuandong Zhao, Siqi Ouyang, Zhiguo Yu, Ming Wu, and Lei Li. 2023. Pre-trained language models can be fully zero-shot learners. In *Proceedings of the 61st Annual Meeting of the Association for Computational Linguistics (Volume 1: Long Papers)*, pages 15590–15606, Toronto, Canada. Association for Computational Linguistics.

Zihao Zhao, Eric Wallace, Shi Feng, Dan Klein, and Sameer Singh. 2021. Calibrate before use: Improving few-shot performance of language models. In *Proceedings of the 38th International Conference on Machine Learning, ICML 2021, 18-24 July 2021, Virtual Event*, volume 139 of *Proceedings of Machine Learning Research*, pages 12697–12706. PMLR.

A Other Experimental Details.

A.1 Datasets

Table 7 and Table 8 are statistics of datasets used in experiments of Section 3.1 and Section 3.2, respectively.

Table 9 shows class names and templates used in our experiments.

Table 7: Statistics of datasets used in the zero-shot experiments.

	#Instances	#Classes	Domain
AG News[2]	3000	4	News
DBpedia[3]	3000	14	Wikipedia
Yahoo[4]	3000	10	Yahoo Answers
SST-2[5]	872	2	Movie review
RT[6]	1066	2	Movie review

Table 8: Statistics of datasets used in the experiments before splitting into seen and unseen classes.

	#Instances	#Classes	Domain
Amazon[7]	24,000	24	Product Review
WoS[8]	46,985	7	Academic Paper
Snips	13,802	7	Voice Assistant
Emotion	36,463	10	Mixed

A.2 Hyperparameters

Table 10 shows the hyperparameters used for model training in Section 3.2. We use the same values of hyperparameters in the original papers, except for parameters that the original papers use different values for different datasets. We use the same hyperparameters as the vanilla LTA or Entailment for our methods combined with LTA or Entailment.

In addition to the hyperparameters described in the table, parameters that are unique for each method are set as follows.

LTA We use the hyperparameters for LTA in the original paper as $d_h = 768, d_a = 768, \alpha = 10.0, \tau = 10.0, N^{s_i} = N^{u_i} = 2, K = 5, d_r = 32$.

Entailment For the template to generate a hypothesis, we use "This text is about {class name}." as suggested in the original paper.

Ours When generating sequences that contain keyword candidates in our method, the temperature parameters that control the generation probabilities, top_p parameter (the threshold for top-p sampling), and generation length are manually set to 0.9, 0.8, and 16, respectively. We generate 20 sequences for each class and extract 24 keyword candidates with the highest Term-Frequency value per class.

A.3 Templates for Generating Keyword Candidates

Zero-Shot Text Classification. We use the following templates to generate keyword candidates for experiments in Section 3.1.

- "{class name} such as "
- "{class name}: "
- "examples of {class name} are "
- "{class name} also "
- "{class name} and "

Generalized Zero-Shot Text Classification. We use the following templates to generate keyword candidates for experiments in Section 3.2.

- "{class name} such as {keyword candidate1}, {keyword candidate2}, $\cdots$",
- "{class name}: {keyword candidate1}, {keyword candidate2}, $\cdots$",
- "examples of {class name} are {keyword candidate1}, {keyword candidate2}, $\cdots$",

where a {keyword candidate} is a keyword of the seen class extracted from training data. We concatenate the class-keyword pairs of several seen classes with a line break "\n" in between and add instructions of the same format to generate the unseen class keywords on the last line. When retrieving keyword candidates from training data for seen classes, we aggregate training data for each class and use TF-IDF to retrieve class-specific keywords, which is similar to class-based TF-IDF (Grootendorst, 2022).

Table 9: Templates and class names used in our experiments.

Dataset	Class Name		Template
AG News	"politics", "sports", "business", "technology"		"{text}topic: "
DBpedia	"Company", "school", "Artist", "Athlete", "OfficeHolder", "transportation", "Building", "Mountain", "Village", "Animal", "Plant", "Album", "Film", "book"	1	"{title}{content}{title} is a "
Yahoo	"society", "science", "health", "education", "computer", "sports", "business", "entertainment", "amily", "politics"	1	"{question title}topic: "
SST-2	"terrible", "great"		"{text}It was "
RT	"terrible", "great"		"{text}It was "
Amazon	(seen) "Apps for Android", "Baby", "Beauty", "Clothing Shoes and Jewelry", "Digital Music", "Electronics", "Movies and TV", "Patio Lawn and Garden", "Pet Supplies", "Tools and Home Improvement", "Toys and Games", "Video Games" (unseen) "Amazon Instant Video", "CDs and Vinyl", "Cell Phones and Accessories", "Grocery and Gourmet Food", "Kindle Store", "Office Productsy" (valid) "Automotive", "Books", "Health and Personal Care", "Home and Kitchen", "Musical Instruments", "Sports and Outdoors"	1	"{text}This text is about {class name}"
WoS	(seen) "Civil Engineering", "Computer Science", "Mechanical Engineering" (unseen) "Electrical Engineering", "Medical Science" (valid) "Psychology", "biochemistry"	1	"{text}This text is about {class name}"
Snips	(seen) "book", "movie", "playlist", (unseen) "music", "restaurant" (valid) "search", "weather"	1	"{text}This text is about {class name}"
Emotion	(seen) "anger", "fear", "love", "no emotion" (unseen) "disgust", "sadness", "shame" (valid) "guilt", "joy", "surprise"	1	"{text}This text is about {class name}"

Table 10: Hyperparameters for fine-tuning. Notice that the batch size of LTA (step2) is determined by K, N^{s_i}, and N^{u_i}.

Hyperparameter	LTA (step1)	LTA (step2)	Entailment
# of maximum epochs	10	300	3
Model selection	early stopping (3epochs)	early stopping (30epochs)	best epoch
Learning rate	1e-3	1e-5	1e-5
Scheduler	None	None	linear
Optimizer	Adam	Adam	AdamW
Adam epsilon	1e-08	1e-08	1e-08
Adam beta weights	0.9, 0.999	0.9, 0.999	0.9, 0.999
Weight decay	0.0	0.0	0.01
Batch size	64	N/A	32

Lexical Substitution as Causal Language Modeling

Ning Shi **Bradley Hauer** **Grzegorz Kondrak**
Alberta Machine Intelligence Institute (Amii)
Department of Computing Science
University of Alberta, Edmonton, Canada
{ning.shi,bmhauer,gkondrak}@ualberta.ca

Abstract

Causal language models such as the GPT series have achieved significant success across various domains. However, their application to the lexical substitution task (LST) remains largely unexplored due to inherent limitations in autoregressive decoding. Our work is motivated by our observation that existing LST approaches tend to suffer from a misalignment between the pre-training objectives of the language models that they employ, and their subsequent fine-tuning and application for substitute generation. We introduce PromptSub, the first system to use causal language modeling (CLM) for LST. Through prompt-aware fine-tuning, PromptSub not only enriches the given context with additional knowledge, but also leverages the unidirectional nature of autoregressive decoding. PromptSub consistently outperforms GeneSis, the best previously published supervised LST method. Further analysis demonstrates the potential of PromptSub to further benefit from increased model capacity, expanded data resources, and retrieval of external knowledge. By framing LST within the paradigm of CLM, our approach indicates the versatility of general CLM-based systems, such as ChatGPT, in catering to specialized tasks, including LST.[1]

1 Introduction

Lexical substitution task (LST) is to identify appropriate replacements for a designated target word in context while maintaining the contextual meaning and coherence of the text (McCarthy, 2002; McCarthy and Navigli, 2007). For example, given the sentence "Let me *begin* again", an LST system would be expected to provide words such as *start* or *commence* as substitutes for *begin*. LST is an important task due to its numerous applications, including word sense disambiguation (Hou et al., 2020), word sense induction (Eyal et al., 2022),

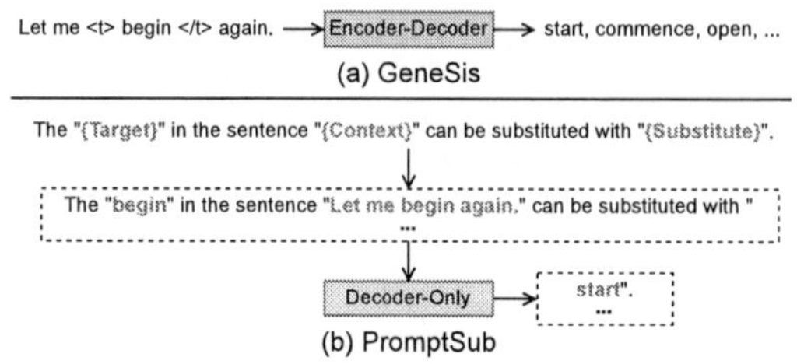

Figure 1: Comparison between (a) GeneSis (Lacerra et al., 2021b) and (b) our proposed PromptSub.

lexical simplification (Aumiller and Gertz, 2022), adversarial attacks and defenses (Li et al., 2021), semantic change detection (Card, 2023), and natural language watermarking (Yang et al., 2022).

Recent prior work on LST leverages pre-trained language models (PLMs), specifically *masked* language models (MLMs) (Lin et al., 2022; Michalopoulos et al., 2022; Omarov and Kondrak, 2023), of which BERT (Devlin et al., 2019) is a well-known example. Since MLMs are trained on the task of predicting likely words in a context where a single word is masked, they seem to be a natural fit for LST. However, masking a word is an information-losing process. As a result, the predicted substitutes may fit the context well, but can significantly alter the original meaning of the sentence.

As an alternative to masked language modeling, we propose to employ *causal* language modeling instead. While MLMs first encode the entire context around the mask and then decode output from this encoding, causal language models (CLMs) are trained to predict the next token in a sequence given *only the previous tokens* as context (Radford et al., 2018). This linear processing of text is referred to as *auto-regressive decoding*; by eschewing the need for discrete encoding and decoding phases, these models can achieve high performance in generative tasks, without an encoder that increases the number of parameters. These *decoder-only* models include

[1]Our code and data are publicly available on GitHub: https://github.com/ShiningLab/PromptSub

*Proceedings of the 13th Joint Conference on Lexical and Computational Semantics (*SEM 2024)*, pages 120 - 132
June 20-21, 2024 ©2024 Association for Computational Linguistics

the well-known GPT series (Brown et al., 2020), which powers popular language generation tools such as ChatGPT (OpenAI, 2023). However, prior methods for applying a pre-trained CLM to LST go no further than simple prompting (Lee et al., 2021).

In this paper, we present the first method to efficiently reduce LST to causal language modeling: PromptSub, a system based on lexical substitution via prompt-aware fine-tuning. Our approach bridges the gap between the pre-training of CLMs and their fine-tuning for LST via the same training objective (i.e., to predict the next token). By way of an innovative prompting strategy, PromptSub empowers a decoder-only CLM to leverage the full bidirectional context of a given LST instance, and also seamlessly integrate external knowledge into an auto-regressive language modeling strategy.

In our experiments, PromptSub consistently surpasses the previous best supervised method, GeneSis (Lacerra et al., 2021b), across all datasets, metrics, and settings. Figure 1 illustrates how GeneSis and PromptSub employ encoder-decoder (Sutskever et al., 2014) and decoder-only models respectively. Our extensive evaluations indicate that PromptSub either matches or exceeds previously published methods, establishing a new state of the art on the most recent LST benchmark, SWORDS (Lee et al., 2021). Notably, PromptSub outperforms MLM-based approaches, previously recognized state-of-the-art, by a large margin (Yang et al., 2022; Wada et al., 2022). Our detailed analysis highlights the robustness and extensibility of PromptSub, showing that it can take advantage of greater model capacity, leverage a broad array of resources, and benefit from external knowledge through retrieval-augmented generation (RAG; Lewis et al., 2020b).

2 Related Work

Conventional LST techniques predominantly capitalize on external knowledge bases (Hassan et al., 2007; Szarvas et al., 2013a; Hintz and Biemann, 2016) and learned word embeddings to identify and rank potential substitution candidates based on predefined metrics (Melamud et al., 2015b,a; Garí Soler et al., 2019). These methods often depend heavily on external resources like WordNet (Miller, 1995), with additional processes such as the manual ranking and rule construction often required to optimize outcomes. Recognizing these limitations, recent initiatives have emerged to harness the advantages of PLMs.

Prior work indicates that contextualized representations obtained from PLMs can be applied to LST by incorporating context-based scores (Seneviratne et al., 2022) and decontextualized embeddings (Wada et al., 2022). In an effort to augment PLMs with knowledge derived from lexical resources, Lin et al. (2022) proposed involving gloss matching in pre-training. Michalopoulos et al. (2022) advocate for the incorporation of structured knowledge from lexical databases.

On the one hand, certain of these approaches utilize PLMs primarily as feature extractors. Thus, the complete potential of PLMs remains untapped due to the disconnect between their pre-training objectives and subsequent applications. On the other hand, to align with pre-training, others (Zhou et al., 2019) estimate the probability distribution of potential replacements through masked language modeling (Devlin et al., 2019). This inclination towards MLMs, as opposed to CLMs, has led to the over-representation of encoder-only PLMs, leaving the application of decoder-only architectures largely unexplored.

Similarly, while prior work has explored the ideas of enriching LST inputs with target words (Arefyev et al., 2020) and semantic knowledge (Omarov and Kondrak, 2023), how to inject such knowledge into PLMs remains an open question. This issue is particularly true within the prevailing trend of unsupervised methods that exclude the fine-tuning stage.

Supervised approaches to LST, such as those by Szarvas et al. (2013a,b), were initially limited by data scarcity until the advent of GeneSis (Lacerra et al., 2021a,b) and ParaLS (Qiang et al., 2023). GeneSis adopts a sequence-to-sequence model, generating substitutes given the context and marked target word. By concatenating multiple datasets, fine-tuning a PLM specifically for LST was made viable, achieving strong results despite the scarcity of annotated data in the domain. ParaLS produces substitutes through a paraphraser, utilizing a heuristics-based decoding strategy. This facilitates fine-tuning PLMs on paraphrase data, which is available in relatively large quantities.

However, in both GeneSis and ParaLS, a discernible gap persists between the pre-training of PLMs and their subsequent fine-tuning. Furthermore, they are both rooted in an encoder-decoder framework (Lewis et al., 2020a), depending on external resources, and require post-processing steps

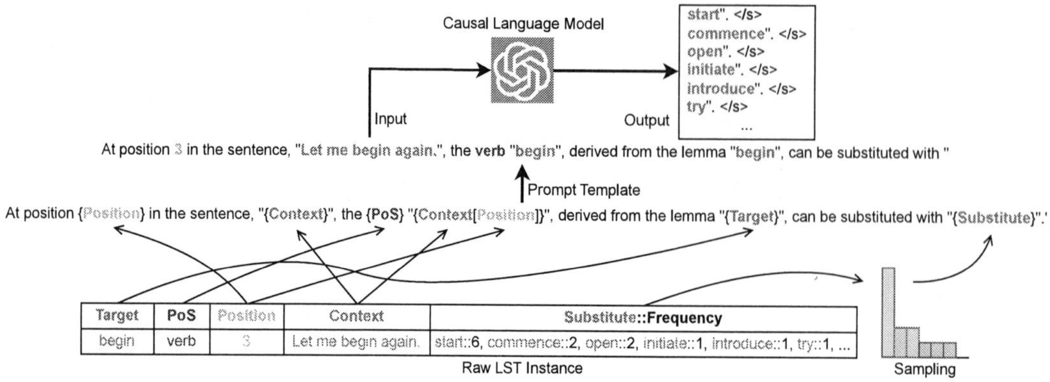

Figure 2: An illustration of PromptSub. An LST instance is transformed into a description by populating a prompt with details. A CLM estimates the probability distribution of potential substitutes at the final placeholder.

that involve adjustable heuristics and thresholds. This raises a pivotal question: does LST have to be approached in a two-step manner, where substitutions are first generated and then reranked using manually designed scores? Or, is it possible to create a single-step, end-to-end, generative solution, that also sidesteps the need for external resources and manually-crafted heuristics? In presenting PromptSub, we argue for the latter: a first-of-its-kind single-step approach to generating substitutions via a decoder-only language model.

3 Methodology

In this section, we formally define LST and CLM, outline our sampling strategy, and detail our prompt engineering techniques.

3.1 Definitions

We introduce our theoretical framework that reduces LST to CLM, building upon two binary problems we defined.

Lexical substitution task (LST) involves identifying suitable replacements for target words while preserving the contextual meaning of the sentence. Formally, given an input sentence $S = w_1^n$ containing a target word w_x, the objective of LST is to return a ranked list of m appropriate replacements for w_x, which are selected from a vocabulary $\mathcal{V}$. For example, consider *begin* as the target word w_x in the sentence $S =$ *"Let me begin again"*. If we are to specify $m = 3$ substitutes, a reasonable output would be ["start", "commence", "open"].

Causal language modeling (CLM) refers to prediction of the next word in a sequence given the preceding words. Formally, given a sequence of words $s = w_1^n$ of length n, the objective of CLM is to model the conditional probability distribution of the next word: $p(w_{n+1} \mid w_1^n)$. CLM is autoregressive: words are predicted one at a time, conditioned on the context of the previous words. By applying a decoder-only model repeatedly, CLM can be used to model the probability of any sequence of words: $p(w_{n+1}^{n+k} \mid w_1^n)$.

We define a binary decision problem of lexical substitution (LexSub) which returns TRUE if two words are lexical substitutes in a given sentence, and FALSE otherwise (Hauer and Kondrak, 2023):

LexSub(S, w_x, w_y) := "the word w_x can be replaced by the word w_y in the sentence S without altering its meaning"

Similarly, we define a binary decision problem of word prediction (WP) as:

WP(S, w) := "the word w has the same meaning as the masked word in the sentence S"

LexSub is thus reducible to WP in a straightforward way:

$$\text{LexSub}(S, w_x, w_y) \Leftrightarrow \text{WP}(S, w_x) \wedge \text{WP}(S, w_y)$$

In practice, implementations of methods for LexSub or WP may return a probability value instead of a Boolean. LST datasets often require a ranked list of substitutes for each instance. To satisfy this, given a method for solving WP as we defined, we can simply rank each word w in the vocabulary by the probability returned by WP(S, w). To apply CLM to LST, we constrain the word to be identified (in WP) or replaced (in LexSub) to appear at the end of the context. We can thus model LexSub and WP as *autoregressive* language modeling tasks suitable for use with decoder-only models.

3.2 PromptSub definition

The most direct application of CLM to LST would entail modeling the probability distribution at the position of the target word given only the preceding words, denoted as $p(w_x \mid w_1^{x-1})$, where $w_x \in \mathcal{V}$. However, this would omit w_{x+1}^n, the part of the sentence *after* w_x, which may contain vital information. An example can be found in Appendix B.

We therefore propose **PromptSub**, the first LST method to give CLMs access to the full context of an LST instance. PromptSub uses carefully constructed prompts which allow a CLM to produce a substitute based on the full context, including the target word w_x itself.

The following prompt template illustrates how a CLM can be fine-tuned for LST:

The "w_x" in "S" can be
substituted with "y". </s>

where S is the input sentence, w_x the target word, and y a selected gold substitute. The underlined part is what the decoder-only model is fine-tuned to predict. Formally, given an LST instance, we construct a prompt s by filling in the placeholders in a prompt template with w_x and S. This reconstruction allows us to reframe LST as CLM, where the objective is to model the probability of: $p(s_{z+1}^{z+4} \mid s_1, \cdots, \{w_x\}, \cdots, \{S\}, \cdots, s_z)$. To ensure the generation of appropriate substitutes, we fix the last five tokens as follows:

- s_z: an open quotation mark
- s_{z+1}: a sampled gold substitute y
- s_{z+2}: a close quotation mark
- s_{z+3}: a period
- s_{z+4}: the end of sentence symbol </s>

Using static quotation marks and a period effectively aids in extracting the eventual substitutes from the generated text. In practice, we notice no adverse effects on loss or performance, and outputs always reliably incorporate these punctuation marks before the sentence concludes.

We then fine-tune the decoder-only model to specifically minimize the cross-entropy loss on s_{z+1}, s_{z+2}, s_{z+3}, and s_{z+4}, where s_{z+4} is included for the model to learn the end of inference. We can then generate a list of potential substitutes $\hat{y}$ by sampling from the probability distribution at $s_{z+1} \in \mathcal{V}$. Consider again our LST example from Section 3.1. We construct the filled prompt as follows:

The "begin" in "let me begin again." can
be substituted with "start". </s>

3.3 Sampling strategy

Generating a corpus from an LST dataset for fine-tuning CLMs is not straightforward, since LST instances often have multiple substitute options (often ranked), creating many choices for verbalizing these instances. We therefore introduce two sampling strategies, described below:

TopSub selects only the top-ranked substitute. By doing so, we aim to capture the most probable and relevant substitute for the given context.

FreqSub exploits the frequency information associated with gold substitutes in LST datasets, where frequency is determined by the number of annotations in agreement for each substitute. These frequencies, gathered during the dataset annotation process, are often overlooked in previous methods. Applying a softmax function to these frequencies creates a probability distribution over the gold substitutes, reflecting their likelihood of selection. We then sample one substitute from this distribution, ensuring the model encounters substitutes in proportion to their data-driven frequencies.

3.4 Prompt engineering

This section outlines the prompt engineering for corpus construction, grounded in integrating contextual information into the templates. From an informational standpoint, we operate under the assumption that enriching prompts with more relevant information leads to improved outcomes. Instead of manual, iterative adjustments, we focus on demonstrating the impact of prompts by contrasting several distinct variants. Examples of each template, filled with a single shared LST instance, can be found in Table 1.

BaseP, shown in Figure 1, is the basic prompt template from Section 3.2. It provides the model only the target word and its context. It serves as the foundation for developing more complex prompts.

InfoP seeks to harness the comprehensive information available in LST data. Traditional approaches often focus on the target word and its immediate context, while LST instances often provide additional details that can be valuable. In InfoP, as exemplified in Figure 2, we incorporate three additional attributes of the target word: its position in the sentence, its part of speech (PoS) tag, and its lemma form. These additions work as enriched contextual cues, guiding the model to produce more appropriate substitutions. It is important to note that these attributes utilized in InfoP are

Instance:	let me begin again.
BaseP:	the "begin" in the sentence "let me begin again." can be substituted with "start".
InfoP:	at position 3 in the sentence, "let me begin again.", the verb "begin", derived from the lemma "begin", can be substituted with "start".
AugP (Train):	at position 3 in the sentence, "let me begin again.", the verb "begin", derived from the lemma "begin", can be substituted with "start", "commence", "open", "bring about", "carry on", "initiate", "introduce", "originate", "restart", "try".
AugP (Test):	at position 3 in the sentence, "let me begin again.", the verb "begin", derived from the lemma "begin", can be best substituted with "start".
ExP (Train):	at position 3 in the sentence, "let me begin again.", the verb "begin", derived from the lemma "begin" with synonyms "commence", "get", "get down", "lead off", "set about", "set out", "start", "start out", can be substituted with "start", "commence", "open", "bring about", "carry on", "initiate", "introduce", "originate", "restart", "try".
ExP (Test):	at position 3 in the sentence, "let me begin again.", the verb "begin", derived from the lemma "begin" with synonyms "commence", "get", "get down", "lead off", "set about", "set out", "start", "start out", can be best substituted with "start".

Table 1: Comparative overview of prompting strategies for a given LST instance. Notably, AugP and ExP utilize distinct prompts for training and inference phases. The masked sentence portion, highlighted in blue, is used for loss calculation during training and autoregressive decoding in testing.

exclusively derived from the LST datasets, without reliance on external resources. Furthermore, as evidenced in Section 5, PromptSub remains flexible, allowing for the incorporation of external knowledge if needed.

AugP is designed to boost the diversity of the generated corpus by further augmenting InfoP. In LST tasks, there is often a need to delineate both the best or "top-1" substitute, and a list of the top 10 substitutes. We therefore specifically embed the term "best" into the prompt, where only the top-ranked gold substitute is presented. To incorporate multiple possible substitutes, we exclude the word "best", instead including the top 10 gold substitutes, as determined by the weighted sampling strategy, following the open quotation mark s_n. This means multiple $y \in \mathbf{y}$ will occupy the s_{n+1} slot, rather than just one; substitutes are separated by a comma followed by a space. During the training phase, the fine-tuning prompt is drawn randomly from templates that either include or exclude the term "best". For inference, potential substitutes are solely sampled using the "best" prompt, the intuition being that this will help the model to produce substitutes that are not only acceptable but optimal. This strategy offers deeper insights into the efficacy of our approach when melded with advanced prompt techniques, such as prompt augmentation.

4 Experiments

In this section, we describe our empirical comparison of PromptSub to the top-performing previously published LST methods. After brief descriptions of the benchmark datasets (Section 4.1) and our experimental setup (Section 4.2), we proceed with a comparative analysis of PromptSub and GeneSis, two supervised generative approaches (Section 4.3). We then extend this experiment to include more methods and test of the full suite of datasets (Section 4.4). Unless stated otherwise, we apply PromptSub with FreqSub sampling and AugP for corpus generation, as these settings gave the best performance in our development experiments. Further sensitivity analysis will be presented in Section 5.

4.1 Datasets

LST datasets are few in number and small in size, presenting a challenge for supervised approaches. Thus, we adopt the strategy used by Lacerra et al. (2021b) of merging multiple LST resources for fine-tuning and evaluating on the remainder.

LS07 facilitates comparison with GeneSis, as we can directly compare the results reported by the authors to those we obtain using PromptSub. We carefully follow the dataset construction procedure described in the GeneSis paper.

LS14 includes the CoInCo (Kremer et al., 2014) training set combined with LST and TWSI (Biemann, 2012), as well as a subset of SWORDS (se-

Backbone	Size	Method	best	best-m	oot	oot-m	P@1
bart-large	406M	GeneSis	$19.2_{\pm 0.6}$	$31.1_{\pm 1.5}$	$45.7_{\pm 3.7}$	$60.0_{\pm 4.6}$	$47.9_{\pm 1.1}$
		GeneSis+WN	$20.6_{\pm 0.8}$	$33.2_{\pm 1.7}$	$50.0_{\pm 2.4}$	$65.1_{\pm 2.4}$	$49.2_{\pm 1.9}$
gpt2-medium	345M	PromptSub (ours)	$21.4_{\pm 0.2}$	$35.8_{\pm 0.3}$	$50.5_{\pm 0.2}$	$66.2_{\pm 0.4}$	$50.4_{\pm 0.3}$
		PromptSub+ (ours)	$\mathbf{21.5}_{\pm 0.2}$	$\mathbf{35.9}_{\pm 0.4}$	$\mathbf{51.1}_{\pm 0.2}$	$\mathbf{67.0}_{\pm 0.5}$	$\mathbf{50.7}_{\pm 0.3}$

Table 2: Evaluation results on LS07. For all the metrics, the higher, the better. The best are bolded.

lected to avoid overlap with the CoInCo test set). The dataset is divided into training (90%) and validation (10%) splits. The CoInCo test set is provided for testing.

LS21 follows a similar procedure, but with the SWORDS training set combined with LST and TWSI. A section of CoInCo is added, again ensuring no overlap with the SWORDS test set. The dataset is partitioned into 90% for training and 10% for validation. The original SWORDS test set is preserved for evaluation.

4.2 Experimental setup

Per established practices, we evaluate model performance on LS07 and LS14 using the metrics from the SemEval-2007 task (McCarthy and Navigli, 2007). We use `best` and out-of-ten (`oot`), along with their modal variations `best-m` and `oot-m`, to assess the top-1 and top-10 predictions, respectively. These metrics weight the gold substitutes according to their selection frequency by annotators. For the more recent LS21 dataset, we follow the evaluation protocol developed for the SWORDS benchmark (Lee et al., 2021). We use the F^{10} score, the harmonic mean of precision and recall, for the top 10 predictions against both acceptable ($\mathtt{F^{10}}_a$) and conceivable ($\mathtt{F^{10}}_c$) gold substitutes. SWORDS assigns a score to each substitute to indicate its appropriateness, defining acceptable substitutes as those with scores above 50%, and conceivable substitutes as those with scores above 0%. For thoroughness, we also report a variety of metrics: top-1 precision (`P@1`), top-3 precision (`P@3`), and top-10 recall (`R@10`). Our results, including standard deviations, are averages from five iterations with random seeds 0 to 4.

We utilize GPT-2 (Radford et al., 2019) as our primary CLM. In particular, we use gpt2-medium, except where otherwise specified. This decision stems from constraints related to computational resources and the restrictions on access to more advanced models like GPT-3 (Brown et al., 2020), as well as the desire to compare PromptSub to GeneSis using models with comparable numbers of parameters.

To evaluate the impact of fine-tuning data size on PromptSub, after determining the optimal hyperparameters, we repeat the fine-tuning process on the concatenation of the training and validation sets. We refer to this more fine-tuned variant of PromptSub as PromptSub+. To reiterate, the only distinction between PromptSub and PromptSub+ lies in the training data volume.

To optimize GPU memory utilization on the Nvidia Tesla V100 we use for training, we employ a batch size of 16 with mixed precision training and gradient accumulation. For fine-tuning, we use the AdamW optimizer (Loshchilov and Hutter, 2019) with a learning rate $1e^{-5}$ and an ℓ_2 gradient clipping of 1.0, following Pascanu et al. (2013). To prevent overfitting, we use early stopping with respect to `P@1` on validation for a maximum of 8 epochs (Prechelt, 1998). We set the dropout rate to 0.2, following Srivastava et al. (2014). During inference, we use a beam search with a width of 50, in line with prior methods (Zhou et al., 2019; Lacerra et al., 2021b). All implementations are executed using PyTorch (Paszke et al., 2019), with pre-trained models sourced from the HuggingFace repository (Wolf et al., 2020).

4.3 Experiments on LS07

In evaluating GeneSis, Lacerra et al. (2021b) introduces a set of post-processing steps to the system's output. To ensure a fair comparison, we apply the same post-processing steps to the output of PromptSub. We also test its enhanced variant GeneSis+WN with two extra tricks applied: Fallback strategy (FS) ensures at least ten substitutes are returned by first including previously discarded substitutes and, if necessary, adding more from the vocabulary ranked by cosine similarity to the target, until 10 substitutes are obtained. Vocabulary cut (VC) limits the model to a specified output vocabulary; it discards any generated substitutes outside this vocabulary. It is noteworthy that both FS and

Method	best	best-m	oot	oot-m	P@1
BalAdd	5.6	11.9	20.0	33.8	11.8
SubstituteVector	8.1	17.4	26.7	46.2	–
BERT	14.5	33.9	45.9	69.9	56.3
GeneSis	13.8	30.4	45.6	72.3	58.8
LexSubCon	11.3	23.8	33.6	54.4	41.3
GR-RoBERTa	13.1	28.8	40.9	66.6	48.8
ParaLS	13.8	29.5	41.7	65.6	50.0
ParaLS*	**16.8**	**35.4**	**48.3**	**75.0**	<u>57.8</u>
PromptSub (ours)	14.5	33.1	46.2	72.9	57.7
PromptSub+ (ours)	<u>14.9</u>	<u>33.9</u>	<u>47.0</u>	<u>73.9</u>	**59.5**

Table 3: Evaluation results on LS14. The upper section presents the complete system outcomes, while the lower focuses on the generation step. Results for BalAdd (Melamud et al., 2015b) and SubstituteVector (Melamud et al., 2015a) are sourced from BERT (Zhou et al., 2019). LexSubCon (Michalopoulos et al., 2022), GR-RoBERTa (Lin et al., 2022), ParaLS, and ParaLS* are reported by Qiang et al. (2023). The best are in bold, with the second-best underlined.

Method	F^{10}_a	F^{10}_c
BERT (Zhou et al., 2019)	17.4	27.5
GeneSis (Lacerra et al., 2021b)	23.3	43.0
GPT-3 (Lee et al., 2021)	22.7	36.3
WordTune (Lee et al., 2021)	23.4	33.2
CALS (Yang et al., 2022)	16.7	28.4
mBERT (Wada et al., 2022)	12.4	22.6
SpanBERT (Wada et al., 2022)	20.9	34.0
MPNet (Wada et al., 2022)	22.0	34.1
XLNet (Wada et al., 2022)	23.3	37.4
ELECTRA (Wada et al., 2022)	23.2	36.7
DeBERTa-V3 (Wada et al., 2022)	24.5	39.9
BART (Wada et al., 2022)	23.5	37.2
ParaLS (Qiang et al., 2023)	23.5	38.6
ParaLS* (Qiang et al., 2023)	24.9	40.1
GPT-3 (Lee et al., 2021)	22.2	34.3
WordTune (Lee et al., 2021)	22.8	32.1
BERT (Wada et al., 2022)	20.7	34.4
BERT-K (Wada et al., 2022)	15.7	24.4
BERT-M (Wada et al., 2022)	10.7	16.5
CILex3 (Seneviratne et al., 2022)	19.9	31.5
ParaLS* (Qiang et al., 2023)	22.8	37.0
PromptSub (ours)	23.2	45.4
PromptSub+ (ours)	**24.0**	**46.4**

Table 4: Evaluation results on LS21. The upper section presents the performance of their complete systems, while the lower section reports that of the generation step only. Results of BERT (Zhou et al., 2019), CALS (Yang et al., 2022), and GPT-3 (Lee et al., 2021) are borrowed from Wada et al. (2022). That of CILex3 (Seneviratne et al., 2022) is reported by Qiang et al. (2023). The best are bolded.

VC rely on external resources such as WordNet (Miller, 1995), while PromptSub does not. However, we still incorporate GeneSis+WN for a thorough comparison.

In Table 2, PromptSub outperforms GeneSis across all metrics. Using gpt2-medium, a model with 15% fewer parameters than the bart-large model used by GeneSis, our PromptSub method yields better results, attaining for example 21.5 in `best` and 50.7 in `P@1`. With both FS and VC enabled, GeneSis+WN is still outperformed by PromptSub, even when the former leverages WordNet for post-processing. The results support the hypothesis that PromptSub can benefit from additional training data, as evidenced by the improvements of PromptSub+ over the standard PromptSub.

Another salient point is the pronounced stability exhibited by PromptSub, evident from the reduced variance we observed across random seeds. For instance, PromptSub shows a variance of 0.2, markedly less than the 3.7 of Genesis, in terms of `oot`. This can be attributed to the fact that PromptSub generates substitutes through greedy sampling from a single-step probability distribution, leading to a more stable and consistent output. In contrast, GeneSis relies on multiple decoding steps, resulting in higher variability across runs.

4.4 Experiments on LS14 and LS21

As detailed in Section 4.3, we follow the same evaluation procedure as in GeneSis to ensure a fair comparison. Other competing systems were tested under different experimental configurations, complicating the comparison. Moreover, existing approaches typically involve multiple stages, such as substitute generation and contextualized reranking. This complicates the isolation and evaluation of the specific impact of PromptSub, which is a single-stage end-to-end generative approach, as opposed to the "pipeline" approaches of the methods we compare to. To address this, we expand our evaluation scope to include LS14 and LS21, emphasizing the substitute generation aspect. In Tables 3 and 4, we compare PromptSub (and PromptSub+) to previously published methods on LS14 and LS21 respectively. Results reported in the second part of each table (below the double horizontal line) evaluate performance after the generation stage, with no post-processing. To further verify the advantages of our PromptSub, we re-implement GeneSis using the same configurations, maintaining gpt2-medium for PromptSub and bart-large for GeneSis.

For results on LS14 (Table 3), PromptSub+

yields competitive performance, ranking first or second on all metrics. A standout observation is the prowess of PromptSub+ in the P@1 metric, where it achieves the top result by a wide margin. We find that this disparity between P@1 and other metrics is attributed to annotator preference induced by the weighted task metrics of SemEval-2007 (McCarthy and Navigli, 2007). This thus suggests that certain methods, such as ParaLS*, may be biased toward the substitutes preferred by annotators.

Turning to LS21 (Table 4), both PromptSub and PromptSub+ outperform prior methods, including GeneSis, setting a new state of the art. Specifically, PromptSub+ achieves an unprecedented F^{10}_c of 46.4, surpassing the previous best by almost 10. It also achieves the best F^{10}_a at 24.0 using PromptSub+. Notably, despite using gpt2-medium, PromptSub and PromptSub+ are able to outperform GPT-3 by a substantial margin, demonstrating the utility of the knowledge-rich prompting techniques we built into PromptSub. Based on these results, we speculate that, with full access to GPT-3 (or even more powerful models), and additional labeled LST data for fine-tuning, PromptSub could yield even stronger results.

4.5 Error examples

In this section, we discuss the most frequent types of errors made by our method.

The first such category that we identified involves instances where the substitutes provided by annotators include phrases rather than single words. For example, one test instance from LS21 has the context "That is why I cannot take payment"; the target word *take* is annotated with substitutions including *accept* and *ask for*. While *accept* is a single element of the vocabulary, *ask for* is a phrase that models trained predominantly to predict single-word substitutes may not generate.

Besides, we observed some potential omissions in the datasets. One example involves substituting the target word *voice* in the context "How should I reply? Her voice had grown quiet". The top prediction of PromptSub, *sound*, is not among the provided substitutes, and so is considered incorrect. However, the annotations include *talk*, *utterance*, and *tongue*, which are, arguably, less suitable as substitutes than *sound*. This highlights the need for benchmarks which are more comprehensive, and which have more consistent criteria for substitutes.

Method	Backbone	LS14				LS21	
		best	best-m	oot	oot-m	F^{10}_a	F^{10}_c
PromptSub	gpt2	13.8	31.7	43.8	68.8	22.1	42.6
	gpt2-medium	14.5	33.1	46.2	72.9	23.2	45.4
	gpt2-large	14.7	34.5	46.2	72.4	23.8	46.7
PromptSub+	gpt2	14.1	32.4	44.3	69.4	22.8	44.3
	gpt2-medium	14.9	33.9	**47.0**	**73.9**	**24.0**	46.4
	gpt2-large	**15.1**	**34.9**	46.8	72.9	23.8	**47.6**

Table 5: Analysis results of PromptSub on LS14 and LS21, showing the impact of varying model capacity.

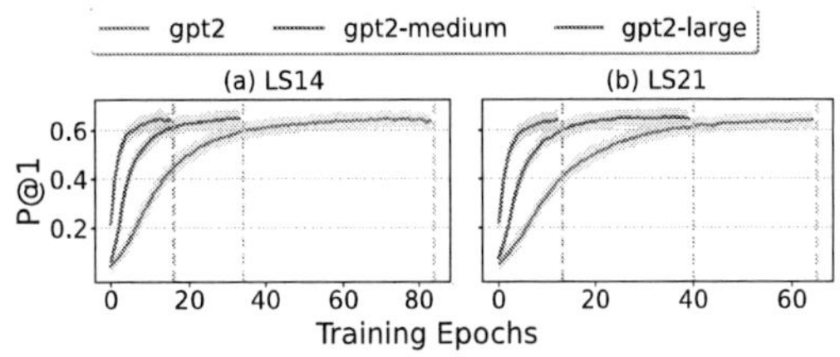

Figure 3: Learning curve of PromptSub for various model sizes on LS14 and LS21 validation sets. Vertical dotted lines indicate the last training epoch before early stopping.

5 Analysis

We now present a sensitivity analysis of our method. We measure the impact of various aspects of our experimental setup, including training size, model capacity, sampling strategy, prompt engineering, and external knowledge. We maintain the same experimental setup, modifying one aspect of our methods to observe the resulting performance change on LS21. The random seed is held constant at 0.

Training size Regarding training data size, we have introduced PromptSub+, a variant of PromptSub, that includes the validation set in its training data. Across all experiments, PromptSub+ consistently outperforms PromptSub on the test data, demonstrating its ability to benefit from additional data. This finding underscores the challenge posed by limited data resources in most existing LST benchmarks, which affects the broader application of PromptSub and other supervised methods (Lacerra et al., 2021a,b).

Model capacity We tested three GPT2 model sizes to measure the impact of model capacity (i.e. number of parameters). As reported in Table 5, the results demonstrate the trend of improved performance, across most evaluation metrics, as we scale from gpt2 to gpt2-medium, then to gpt2-large. Figure 3 depicts the learning curve in relation to model capacity, showing a drop in the number of

Sampling	F_a^{10}	F_c^{10}	P@1	P@3	R@10
TopSub	20.9	39.9	69.4	57.8	40.1
FreqSub	**22.0**	**42.3**	**71.0**	**60.7**	**42.5**

Table 6: Analysis results of gpt2 under PromptSub on LS21, obtained by varying the sampling strategy to fill in the prompt template with label substitutes.

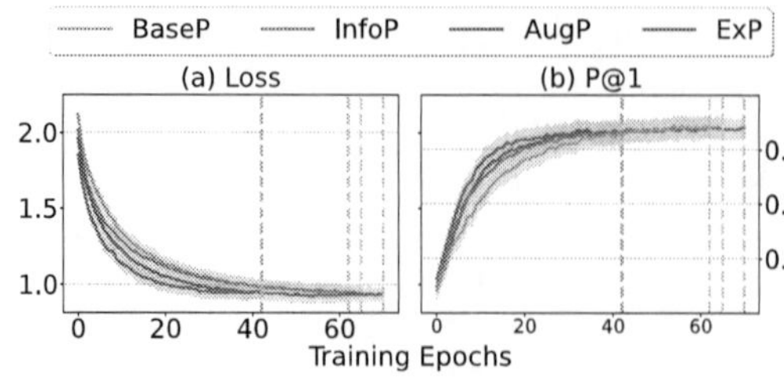

Figure 4: Training dynamics of gpt2 under PromptSub, showing the average loss (a) and P@1 (b) across different prompt templates on the validation set of LS21. Vertical dotted lines mark the early stopping epochs.

training epochs before early stopping is triggered. It also becomes apparent that larger models are more prone to overfitting the training set. This trend again reflects the challenge posed by limited data resources in LST, particularly when deploying PLMs in scale.

Sampling strategy In Section 3.3, we considered two different sampling techniques, TopSub and FreqSub. The results obtained by our method with each sampling strategy are presented in Table 6. We observe a constant improvement from TopSub to FreqSub, hence its usage in our principal experiments. These results support that FreqSub successfully addresses the one-to-many mapping issue during corpus generation and facilitates the generation of more accurate and diverse substitutes.

Prompt engineering We next quantify the impact of different prompt templates (Section 3.4) on PromptSub. Table 7 shows that InfoP generally outperforms BaseP, validating the value of extra contextualized cues. AugP outperforms both, aligning with our expectations as the information provided to the language model by AugP is a superset of what InfoP provides. This comparison effectively serves as an ablation study, showcasing the significance of incorporating additional knowledge into prompts. Interestingly, although augmented prompt templates are not used during inference, their inclusion in the training phase still leads to noticeable performance improvements.

External knowledge To validate the efficacy of incorporating external knowledge in PromptSub, we introduce a new prompting strategy, ExP, as a simple form of retrieval-augmented generation (RAG; Lewis et al., 2020b). Building upon AugP, ExP utilizes WordNet as an external knowledge base, retrieving WordNet synsets for the word to be substituted, and which share the same part of speech. These synsets are integrated into the prompt templates as descriptions, following a similar approach to that used for other information. Comparison with AugP in Table 7 reveals the superiority of ExP in P@1 and P@3, indicating that high-quality substitutes are more likely to be near the top of the list produced by PromptSub. Training results in Figure 4 also demonstrate the advantages of ExP, with lower loss, higher P@1, and earlier convergence. These results indicate the potential benefits of grounding PromptSub on external sources of knowledge through RAG.

Prompt	F_a^{10}	F_c^{10}	P@1	P@3	R@10
BaseP	21.1	37.6	72.7	58.3	38.6
InfoP	20.7	38.4	72.3	59.0	39.5
AugP	**22.1**	42.2	71.9	62.0	**43.6**
ExP	22.0	**42.3**	**73.0**	**62.6**	43.4

Table 7: Analysis results of gpt2 under PromptSub on LS21, obtained by varying the prompt templates.

6 Conclusion

We have presented PromptSub, a framework for recasting LST as CLM, which overcomes the limitations of earlier methods by bridging the gap between pre-training and fine-tuning. PromptSub is flexible and extensible: it allows for variations in the prompt template, facilitating the inclusion of additional knowledge; further analysis reveals the potential for further improvement through scaling up model capacity and data size, applying prompt engineering, and retrieving external knowledge via RAG. Our extensive experiments found that PromptSub consistently outperforms the previous generative approach, GeneSis, on LS07, and establishes a new overall state of the art. As the first attempt to fine-tune decoder-only PLMs for LST, our work highlights the broader applicability of PLMs to semantic tasks.

Limitations

While PromptSub is a significant step forward in LST, it is not without its limitations. Firstly, its effectiveness is limited by the quality and diversity of its training data, a common challenge in supervised methods. This is particularly relevant given the data scarcity in LST, restricting our ability to scale with data extension. Furthermore, PromptSub has not been tested with the latest PLMs due to limited computing resources and closed-source constraints. The computational demands for fine-tuning large-scale language models may limit its practicality, especially in resource-constrained environments.

Acknowledgements

This research was supported by the Natural Sciences and Engineering Research Council of Canada (NSERC), and the Alberta Machine Intelligence Institute (Amii).

References

Nikolay Arefyev, Boris Sheludko, Alexander Podolskiy, and Alexander Panchenko. 2020. Always keep your target in mind: Studying semantics and improving performance of neural lexical substitution. In *Proceedings of the 28th International Conference on Computational Linguistics*, pages 1242–1255, Barcelona, Spain (Online). International Committee on Computational Linguistics.

Dennis Aumiller and Michael Gertz. 2022. UniHD at TSAR-2022 shared task: Is compute all we need for lexical simplification? In *Proceedings of the Workshop on Text Simplification, Accessibility, and Readability (TSAR-2022)*, pages 251–258, Abu Dhabi, United Arab Emirates (Virtual). Association for Computational Linguistics.

Chris Biemann. 2012. Turk bootstrap word sense inventory 2.0: A large-scale resource for lexical substitution. In *Proceedings of the Eighth International Conference on Language Resources and Evaluation (LREC'12)*, pages 4038–4042, Istanbul, Turkey. European Language Resources Association (ELRA).

Tom Brown, Benjamin Mann, Nick Ryder, Melanie Subbiah, Jared D Kaplan, Prafulla Dhariwal, Arvind Neelakantan, Pranav Shyam, Girish Sastry, Amanda Askell, Sandhini Agarwal, Ariel Herbert-Voss, Gretchen Krueger, Tom Henighan, Rewon Child, Aditya Ramesh, Daniel Ziegler, Jeffrey Wu, Clemens Winter, Chris Hesse, Mark Chen, Eric Sigler, Mateusz Litwin, Scott Gray, Benjamin Chess, Jack Clark, Christopher Berner, Sam McCandlish, Alec Radford, Ilya Sutskever, and Dario Amodei. 2020. Language models are few-shot learners. In *Advances in Neural Information Processing Systems*, volume 33, pages 1877–1901. Curran Associates, Inc.

Dallas Card. 2023. Substitution-based semantic change detection using contextual embeddings. In *Proceedings of the 61st Annual Meeting of the Association for Computational Linguistics (Volume 2: Short Papers)*, pages 590–602, Toronto, Canada. Association for Computational Linguistics.

Jacob Devlin, Ming-Wei Chang, Kenton Lee, and Kristina Toutanova. 2019. BERT: Pre-training of deep bidirectional transformers for language understanding. In *Proceedings of the 2019 Conference of the North American Chapter of the Association for Computational Linguistics: Human Language Technologies, Volume 1 (Long and Short Papers)*, pages 4171–4186, Minneapolis, Minnesota. Association for Computational Linguistics.

Matan Eyal, Shoval Sadde, Hillel Taub-Tabib, and Yoav Goldberg. 2022. Large scale substitution-based word sense induction. In *Proceedings of the 60th Annual Meeting of the Association for Computational Linguistics (Volume 1: Long Papers)*, pages 4738–4752, Dublin, Ireland. Association for Computational Linguistics.

Aina Garí Soler, Anne Cocos, Marianna Apidianaki, and Chris Callison-Burch. 2019. A comparison of context-sensitive models for lexical substitution. In *Proceedings of the 13th International Conference on Computational Semantics - Long Papers*, pages 271–282, Gothenburg, Sweden. Association for Computational Linguistics.

Samer Hassan, Andras Csomai, Carmen Banea, Ravi Sinha, and Rada Mihalcea. 2007. UNT: SubFinder: Combining knowledge sources for automatic lexical substitution. In *Proceedings of the Fourth International Workshop on Semantic Evaluations (SemEval-2007)*, pages 410–413, Prague, Czech Republic. Association for Computational Linguistics.

Bradley Hauer and Grzegorz Kondrak. 2023. Taxonomy of problems in lexical semantics. In *Findings of the Association for Computational Linguistics: ACL 2023*, pages 9833–9844, Toronto, Canada.

Gerold Hintz and Chris Biemann. 2016. Language transfer learning for supervised lexical substitution. In *Proceedings of the 54th Annual Meeting of the Association for Computational Linguistics (Volume 1: Long Papers)*, pages 118–129, Berlin, Germany. Association for Computational Linguistics.

Bairu Hou, Fanchao Qi, Yuan Zang, Xurui Zhang, Zhiyuan Liu, and Maosong Sun. 2020. Try to substitute: An unsupervised Chinese word sense disambiguation method based on HowNet. In *Proceedings of the 28th International Conference on Computational Linguistics*, pages 1752–1757, Barcelona, Spain (Online). International Committee on Computational Linguistics.

Gerhard Kremer, Katrin Erk, Sebastian Padó, and Stefan Thater. 2014. What substitutes tell us - analysis of an "all-words" lexical substitution corpus. In *Proceedings of the 14th Conference of the European Chapter of the Association for Computational Linguistics*, pages 540–549, Gothenburg, Sweden. Association for Computational Linguistics.

Caterina Lacerra, Tommaso Pasini, Rocco Tripodi, and Roberto Navigli. 2021a. Alasca: an automated approach for large-scale lexical substitution. In *Proceedings of the Thirtieth International Joint Conference on Artificial Intelligence, IJCAI-21*, pages 3836–3842. International Joint Conferences on Artificial Intelligence Organization. Main Track.

Caterina Lacerra, Rocco Tripodi, and Roberto Navigli. 2021b. GeneSis: A Generative Approach to Substitutes in Context. In *Proceedings of the 2021 Conference on Empirical Methods in Natural Language Processing*, pages 10810–10823, Online and Punta Cana, Dominican Republic. Association for Computational Linguistics.

Mina Lee, Chris Donahue, Robin Jia, Alexander Iyabor, and Percy Liang. 2021. Swords: A benchmark for lexical substitution with improved data coverage and quality. In *Proceedings of the 2021 Conference of the North American Chapter of the Association for Computational Linguistics: Human Language Technologies*, pages 4362–4379, Online. Association for Computational Linguistics.

Mike Lewis, Yinhan Liu, Naman Goyal, Marjan Ghazvininejad, Abdelrahman Mohamed, Omer Levy, Veselin Stoyanov, and Luke Zettlemoyer. 2020a. BART: Denoising sequence-to-sequence pre-training for natural language generation, translation, and comprehension. In *Proceedings of the 58th Annual Meeting of the Association for Computational Linguistics*, pages 7871–7880, Online. Association for Computational Linguistics.

Patrick Lewis, Ethan Perez, Aleksandra Piktus, Fabio Petroni, Vladimir Karpukhin, Naman Goyal, Heinrich Küttler, Mike Lewis, Wen-tau Yih, Tim Rocktäschel, Sebastian Riedel, and Douwe Kiela. 2020b. Retrieval-augmented generation for knowledge-intensive nlp tasks. In *Advances in Neural Information Processing Systems*, volume 33, pages 9459–9474. Curran Associates, Inc.

Dianqi Li, Yizhe Zhang, Hao Peng, Liqun Chen, Chris Brockett, Ming-Ting Sun, and Bill Dolan. 2021. Contextualized perturbation for textual adversarial attack. In *Proceedings of the 2021 Conference of the North American Chapter of the Association for Computational Linguistics: Human Language Technologies*, pages 5053–5069, Online. Association for Computational Linguistics.

Yu Lin, Zhecheng An, Peihao Wu, and Zejun Ma. 2022. Improving contextual representation with gloss regularized pre-training. In *Findings of the Association for Computational Linguistics: NAACL 2022*, pages 907–920, Seattle, United States. Association for Computational Linguistics.

Ilya Loshchilov and Frank Hutter. 2019. Decoupled weight decay regularization. In *International Conference on Learning Representations*.

Diana McCarthy. 2002. Lexical substitution as a task for WSD evaluation. In *Proceedings of the ACL-02 Workshop on Word Sense Disambiguation: Recent Successes and Future Directions*, pages 089–115. Association for Computational Linguistics.

Diana McCarthy and Roberto Navigli. 2007. SemEval-2007 task 10: English lexical substitution task. In *Proceedings of the Fourth International Workshop on Semantic Evaluations (SemEval-2007)*, pages 48–53, Prague, Czech Republic. Association for Computational Linguistics.

Oren Melamud, Ido Dagan, and Jacob Goldberger. 2015a. Modeling word meaning in context with substitute vectors. In *Proceedings of the 2015 Conference of the North American Chapter of the Association for Computational Linguistics: Human Language Technologies*, pages 472–482, Denver, Colorado. Association for Computational Linguistics.

Oren Melamud, Omer Levy, and Ido Dagan. 2015b. A simple word embedding model for lexical substitution. In *Proceedings of the 1st Workshop on Vector Space Modeling for Natural Language Processing*, pages 1–7, Denver, Colorado. Association for Computational Linguistics.

George Michalopoulos, Ian McKillop, Alexander Wong, and Helen Chen. 2022. LexSubCon: Integrating knowledge from lexical resources into contextual embeddings for lexical substitution. In *Proceedings of the 60th Annual Meeting of the Association for Computational Linguistics (Volume 1: Long Papers)*, pages 1226–1236, Dublin, Ireland. Association for Computational Linguistics.

George A Miller. 1995. Wordnet: a lexical database for english. *Communications of the ACM*, 38(11):39–41.

Talgat Omarov and Grzegorz Kondrak. 2023. Grounding the lexical substitution task in entailment. In *Findings of the Association for Computational Linguistics: ACL 2023*, pages 2854–2869, Toronto, Canada. Association for Computational Linguistics.

OpenAI. 2023. ChatGPT. `https://openai.com/chatgpt`. Version 4.0.

Razvan Pascanu, Tomas Mikolov, and Yoshua Bengio. 2013. On the difficulty of training recurrent neural networks. In *Proceedings of the 30th International Conference on International Conference on Machine Learning - Volume 28*, ICML'13, page III–1310–III–1318. JMLR.org.

Adam Paszke, Sam Gross, Francisco Massa, Adam Lerer, James Bradbury, Gregory Chanan, Trevor Killeen, Zeming Lin, Natalia Gimelshein, Luca

Antiga, Alban Desmaison, Andreas Kopf, Edward Yang, Zachary DeVito, Martin Raison, Alykhan Tejani, Sasank Chilamkurthy, Benoit Steiner, Lu Fang, Junjie Bai, and Soumith Chintala. 2019. Pytorch: An imperative style, high-performance deep learning library. In *Advances in Neural Information Processing Systems*, volume 32. Curran Associates, Inc.

Lutz Prechelt. 1998. Early stopping-but when? In *Neural Networks: Tricks of the trade*, pages 55–69. Springer.

Jipeng Qiang, Kang Liu, Yun Li, Yunhao Yuan, and Yi Zhu. 2023. ParaLS: Lexical substitution via pretrained paraphraser. In *Proceedings of the 61st Annual Meeting of the Association for Computational Linguistics (Volume 1: Long Papers)*, pages 3731–3746, Toronto, Canada. Association for Computational Linguistics.

Alec Radford, Karthik Narasimhan, Tim Salimans, Ilya Sutskever, et al. 2018. Improving language understanding by generative pre-training. Technical report, OpenAI.

Alec Radford, Jeffrey Wu, Rewon Child, David Luan, Dario Amodei, Ilya Sutskever, et al. 2019. Language models are unsupervised multitask learners. *OpenAI blog*, 1(8):9.

Colin Raffel, Noam Shazeer, Adam Roberts, Katherine Lee, Sharan Narang, Michael Matena, Yanqi Zhou, Wei Li, and Peter J. Liu. 2020. Exploring the limits of transfer learning with a unified text-to-text transformer. *Journal of Machine Learning Research*, 21(140):1–67.

Sandaru Seneviratne, Elena Daskalaki, Artem Lenskiy, and Hanna Suominen. 2022. CILex: An investigation of context information for lexical substitution methods. In *Proceedings of the 29th International Conference on Computational Linguistics*, pages 4124–4135, Gyeongju, Republic of Korea. International Committee on Computational Linguistics.

Nitish Srivastava, Geoffrey Hinton, Alex Krizhevsky, Ilya Sutskever, and Ruslan Salakhutdinov. 2014. Dropout: A simple way to prevent neural networks from overfitting. *Journal of Machine Learning Research*, 15(56):1929–1958.

Ilya Sutskever, Oriol Vinyals, and Quoc V Le. 2014. Sequence to sequence learning with neural networks. In Z. Ghahramani, M. Welling, C. Cortes, N. D. Lawrence, and K. Q. Weinberger, editors, *Advances in Neural Information Processing Systems 27*, pages 3104–3112. Curran Associates, Inc.

György Szarvas, Chris Biemann, and Iryna Gurevych. 2013a. Supervised all-words lexical substitution using delexicalized features. In *Proceedings of the 2013 Conference of the North American Chapter of the Association for Computational Linguistics: Human Language Technologies*, pages 1131–1141, Atlanta, Georgia. Association for Computational Linguistics.

György Szarvas, Róbert Busa-Fekete, and Eyke Hüllermeier. 2013b. Learning to rank lexical substitutions. In *Proceedings of the 2013 Conference on Empirical Methods in Natural Language Processing*, pages 1926–1932, Seattle, Washington, USA. Association for Computational Linguistics.

Takashi Wada, Timothy Baldwin, Yuji Matsumoto, and Jey Han Lau. 2022. Unsupervised lexical substitution with decontextualised embeddings. In *Proceedings of the 29th International Conference on Computational Linguistics*, pages 4172–4185, Gyeongju, Republic of Korea. International Committee on Computational Linguistics.

Thomas Wolf, Lysandre Debut, Victor Sanh, Julien Chaumond, Clement Delangue, Anthony Moi, Pierric Cistac, Tim Rault, Remi Louf, Morgan Funtowicz, Joe Davison, Sam Shleifer, Patrick von Platen, Clara Ma, Yacine Jernite, Julien Plu, Canwen Xu, Teven Le Scao, Sylvain Gugger, Mariama Drame, Quentin Lhoest, and Alexander Rush. 2020. Transformers: State-of-the-art natural language processing. In *Proceedings of the 2020 Conference on Empirical Methods in Natural Language Processing: System Demonstrations*, pages 38–45, Online. Association for Computational Linguistics.

Xi Yang, Jie Zhang, Kejiang Chen, Weiming Zhang, Zehua Ma, Feng Wang, and Nenghai Yu. 2022. Tracing text provenance via context-aware lexical substitution. *Proceedings of the AAAI Conference on Artificial Intelligence*, 36(10):11613–11621.

Wangchunshu Zhou, Tao Ge, Ke Xu, Furu Wei, and Ming Zhou. 2019. BERT-based lexical substitution. In *Proceedings of the 57th Annual Meeting of the Association for Computational Linguistics*, pages 3368–3373, Florence, Italy. Association for Computational Linguistics.

A PromptSub vs. T5

Our approach distinguishes itself from T5 (Raffel et al., 2020) in several key aspects:
Architecture. Unlike the encoder-decoder framework of T5, PromptSub leverages a decoder-only model to reframe LST as CLM, taking advantage of its inherent strengths in generating text.
Prompting. T5 utilizes a short prefix to specify each task. One example is "cola sentence: " for the CoLA dataset. In contrast, PromptSub employs in-context placeholder prompts that not only verbalize raw LST data instances but also provide a descriptive context for CLM.
Method. The text-to-text format has inherent limitations, thus, aside from GeneSis, there has been no effective method to address LST within this framework. PromptSub, however, offers a fresh perspective and demonstrates a new solution.
Task. PromptSub has successfully adapted causal language models to LST, a domain where, to the best of our knowledge, T5 has not been demonstrated to operate.
Performance. Empirical evidence show that PromptSub outperforms GeneSis, which takes BART as the backbone. Given that GeneSis uses an encoder-decoder framework akin to T5, it stands to reason that PromptSub could extend its advantages over approaches that merely transition from BART to T5.

B MLM & CLM

Consider the following example illustrating the direct application of MLM and CLM to LST:

- Sentence: I live in a beautiful house .
- MLM: I live in a [MASK] house .
- CLM: I live in a [MASK] [MASK] [MASK]

The target word (i.e., "beautiful") is masked for the model to predict it, potentially leading to a substitute (e.g., "big") that fits the context but does not preserve the original sentence semantics due to the absence of the target word information.

Paraphrase Identification via Textual Inference

Ning Shi Bradley Hauer Jai Riley Grzegorz Kondrak
Alberta Machine Intelligence Institute (Amii)
Department of Computing Science
University of Alberta, Edmonton, Canada
{ning.shi,bmhauer,jrbuhr,gkondrak}@ualberta.ca

Abstract

Paraphrase identification (PI) and natural language inference (NLI) are two important tasks in natural language processing. Despite their distinct objectives, an underlying connection exists, which has been notably under-explored in empirical investigations. We formalize the relationship between these semantic tasks and introduce a method for solving PI using an NLI system, including the adaptation of PI datasets for fine-tuning NLI models. Through extensive evaluations on six PI benchmarks, across both zero-shot and fine-tuned settings, we showcase the efficacy of NLI models for PI through our proposed reduction. Remarkably, our fine-tuning procedure enables NLI models to outperform dedicated PI models on PI datasets. In addition, our findings provide insights into the limitations of current PI benchmarks.[1]

1 Introduction

Semantic relationships have been the subject of extensive research, and play pivotal roles in natural language processing (Burdick et al., 2022; Hauer and Kondrak, 2023; Pàmies et al., 2023; Peng et al., 2023a; Wahle et al., 2023), including the study and evaluation of the reasoning capabilities of language models (Liu et al., 2019; Yang et al., 2019). Two important tasks that depend on semantic relations between sentences are paraphrase identification (PI; Bai et al., 2023; Peng et al., 2023b) and natural language inference (NLI; Williams et al., 2018; Nie et al., 2020; Williams et al., 2022). PI is the task of deciding whether two sentences are in the paraphrase relation, that is, whether they convey the same meaning (Bhagat and Hovy, 2013). NLI involves three labels that describe the relationship between two sentences: entailment, contradiction, and neutral (MacCartney, 2009).

Our focus is specifically on detecting textual entailment, as indicated by the first of these categories

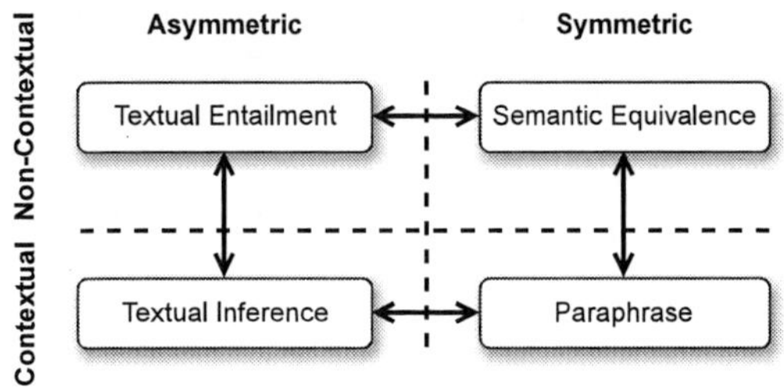

Figure 1: Four sentence-level relations in terms of symmetry and contextuality. Arrows indicate interdependence between the relations (Section 2).

(Bos and Markert, 2005; Dagan et al., 2005; Poliak, 2020), or, more generally, textual inference (Manning, 2006), which is the relation between sentences where one can be inferred from the other in a given context. Take the example from SNLI (Bowman et al., 2015); while the premise "this man is surfing" does not always entail the hypothesis "a man is on water", the broader context may make it clear that the word *surfing* refers to an aquatic activity rather than website browsing, and so the latter sentence can be inferred from the former.

Prior work has hypothesized that paraphrasing corresponds to bidirectional textual entailment; see, for example, the surveys of Androutsopoulos and Malakasiotis (2010) and Madnani and Dorr (2010). However, to the best of our knowledge, the only work that empirically investigates the connection between these two tasks is Seethamol and Manju (2017). They incorporate a blend of modules, including word sense disambiguation for sentence similarity and a Markov logic network for probabilistic inference, which complicates the analysis of the interplay between paraphrases and entailment. Moreover, their approach aligns more with traditional PI methods than with our approach, and lacks any theoretical formalization.

In this work, we formalize prior informal observations on the relationship between textual entail-

[1]We make our code and data publicly available on GitHub: https://github.com/ShiningLab/PI2NLI

*Proceedings of the 13th Joint Conference on Lexical and Computational Semantics (*SEM 2024)*, pages 133 - 141
June 20-21, 2024 ©2024 Association for Computational Linguistics

ment and paraphrasing into a coherent theoretical framework (Figure 1). We formally define four semantic relations and classify them according to two criteria: symmetry and contextuality. This formalization implies a practical reduction of PI to NLI, which we empirically validate by employing two widely used pre-trained transformer-based language models, RoBERTa and XLNet. We introduce a dataset adaptation process for fine-tuning an NLI model for PI, and test our implementation on six PI benchmarks. Our results indicate that in the fine-tuned setting, our PI to NLI reduction can actually yield better performance compared to the direct application of a PI system. This provides strong support for the utility of our reduction, and the theoretical model upon which it is based.

2 Methodology

In this section, we present our theoretical framework linking four semantic relations. We also introduce a novel method for fine-tuning an NLI model for PI, proposing a dataset adaptation procedure that converts PI datasets to labeled NLI instances.

2.1 Equivalence and Paraphrasing

We define the *semantic equivalence relation* (SEQ) as follows:

SEQ(S_1, S_2) := "the sentences S_1 and S_2 convey the same meaning"

The *paraphrase relation* (PR) between sentences is related to semantic equivalence; specifically, SEQ implies PR. Our definition of PR is *contextual*, so that it also admits semantic equivalence in a broader context, which may include common sense and world knowledge.

PR(C, S_1, S_2) := "the sentences S_1 and S_2 convey the same meaning given the context C"

Bhagat and Hovy (2013) refer to this type of paraphrases as *quasi-paraphrases*; for example:

- S_1: *We must work hard to win this election.*
- S_2: *The Democrats must work hard to win this election.*

We postulate the following relationship between the semantic equivalence and paraphrase relations:

$$\text{SEQ}(S_1, S_2) \Leftrightarrow \forall C : \text{PR}(C, S_1, S_2)$$

2.2 Entailment and Inference

Textual entailment (TE) is a directional relation between sentences which holds if the truth of one sentence follows from another sentence (Dagan and Glickman, 2004):

TE(S_1, S_2) := "the sentence S_2 can be inferred from the sentence S_1"

The proposition that T entails H is denoted as $T \models H$. The entailment relation is not symmetric: $T \models H$ does *not* imply $H \models T$.

Following prior work, we assume that sentences are semantically equivalent if and only if each entails the other:

$$\text{SEQ}(S_1, S_2) \Leftrightarrow \text{TE}(S_1, S_2) \wedge \text{TE}(S_2, S_1)$$

Finally, we define *textual inference* (TI) as a contextual generalization of textual entailment which takes into account the broad context of the statements, which may include common sense and world knowledge (Manning, 2006):

TI(C, S_1, S_2) := "the sentence S_2 can be inferred from the sentence S_1 given the context C"

Intuitively, $TI(C, S_1, S_2)$ expresses the following inference property: $(C + S_1) \models S_2$.

Analogous to the relationship between SEQ and PR, we postulate the following relationship between TE and TI:

$$\text{TE}(S_1, S_2) \Leftrightarrow \forall C : \text{TI}(C, S_1, S_2)$$

The following proposition establishes a connection between PR and TI:

Proposition 1 *Given context C, sentences S_1 and S_2 are paraphrases if and only if they can be mutually inferred from each other.*

$$\text{PR}(C, S_1, S_2) \Leftrightarrow \text{TI}(C, S_1, S_2) \wedge \text{TI}(C, S_2, S_1)$$

Thus, the paraphrase relation can be viewed as the conjunction of the inference relation in both directions.

2.3 Dataset Adaptation

Building on our theoretical formalization, we posit that the task of PI, which depends on detecting the PR relation, can be reduced to NLI, specifically the detection of the TI relation. To implement and test our PI to NLI reduction – henceforth PI2NLI – we present a novel fine-tuning procedure that allows an NLI model to be fine-tuned for solving PI instances. Our goal is to mitigate biases stemming from the transfer learning and any domain-specific disparities or other properties of the data that may degrade performance on PI datasets. Our dataset adaptation procedure transforms PI datasets to be compatible with NLI systems so as to facilitate fine-tuning on adapted PI data.

We convert each positive PI instance into two distinct positive NLI instances, one in each direction, indicating mutual TI between two paraphrases, as postulated in Proposition 1. Conversely, since determining in which direction TI fails to hold in a negative PI instance is not straightforward, we generate a negative NLI instance in a random direction. While this heuristic is not theoretically justified, we found that it works well in practice.

3 Experiments

The experiments in this section are aimed at validating the proposed theoretical framework. Additional data specifics and training details can be found in Appendices B and C.

3.1 Models

We implement and test our reduction with each of two freely available transformer-based (Vaswani et al., 2017) language models, RoBERTa (Liu et al., 2019) and XLNet (Yang et al., 2019). Specific model names have been provided in the footnotes. We choose them because of their low hardware requirements, and their status as well-known and well-studied models (Peng et al., 2022). The primary distinction between them lies in their design: RoBERTa is an autoencoding-based model, while XLNet is an autoregressive model. Note that the prior works we will mainly compare to are as recent as 2022, thus we gain no advantage from our choice of models.

In our implementation, we apply the NLI classification head because pre-trained NLI models are readily available (Nie et al., 2020). We consider the relation labeled as "entailment" in the NLI datasets as TI rather than TE because the positive instances typically require broader contextual knowledge, as exemplified by the "surfing" instance in Section 1. Since NLI models are not typically trained on paraphrase data (PI being an entirely separate task from NLI), this maintains a sound experimental setup.

Since recognizing TI is a binary task (outputs are positive or negative), while NLI is a ternary task (outputs are entailment, neutral, or contradiction), we require a means of converting labeled TI instances to NLI instances (so that we can fine-tune NLI models), and NLI outputs to TI outputs (so that we can evaluate them). We map positive TI labels to "entailment" NLI labels and negative TI labels to "neutral" or "contradiction" labels at random. We map "entailment" NLI output to a positive TI classification, and "neutral" or "contradiction" to a negative TI classification. Further details and discussion can be found in Appendix A.

Data	#Train.	#Valid.	#Test	Test Pos.%
PIT	11,530	4,142	838	20.88
QQP	384,290	10,000	10,000	50.00
MSRP	3,668	408	1,725	66.49
PAWS QQP	11,988	8,000	677	28.21
PAWS Wiki	49,401	8,000	8,000	44.20
PARADE	7,550	1,275	1,357	47.90

Table 1: Statistics of all six benchmarks, including the positive rate of the test set (Test Pos.%).

For the zero-shot application of PI2NLI, $\text{pi2nli}_{\text{zero}}$, we employ two trained NLI models: $\text{RoBERTa}_{\text{nli}}$[2] and $\text{XLNet}_{\text{nli}}$[3]. For the fine-tuned version, pi2nli, these models undergo fine-tuning on the NLI dataset derived from the corresponding PI dataset through dataset adaptation (Section 2.3). This yields a TI (or, more accurately, NLI) model adapted for PI following our PI2NLI reduction.

3.2 Setup

Data We test our reduction on six PI benchmarks: PIT (Xu et al., 2015), QQP (Iyer et al., 2017), MSRP (Dolan and Brockett, 2005), PAWS QQP (Zhang et al., 2019), PAWS Wiki (Zhang et al., 2019), and PARADE (He et al., 2020). We follow the data processing established by prior work (He et al., 2020; Peng et al., 2022). Detailed specifications of each dataset are provided in Table 1.

Baselines We adopt baselines from previous studies, citing each source for reference. Beyond referencing prior work, we set new benchmarks pi by training dedicated PI models using the same language models as pi2nli, alongside vanilla RoBERTa and XLNet.[4] Furthermore, we ensure that all classification heads are initialized from scratch. This facilitates a controlled comparison to isolate the distinct contributions of the PI2NLI reduction from the language models used. We meticulously follow the experimental setups and data preprocessing detailed in the referenced works, particularly aligning with the protocol established by Peng et al. (2022) for hyperparameter tuning.

[2] roberta-large-snli_mnli_fever_anli_R1_R2_R3-nli

[3] xlnet-large-cased-snli_mnli_fever_anli_R1_R2_R3-nli

[4] roberta-large, xlnet-large-cased

Backbone	Method	PIT	QQP	MSRP	PAWS QQP	PAWS Wiki	PARADE
–	Random	27.18	50.31	56.47	35.01	46.94	51.22
$\text{BERT}_{\text{base}}$	Reimers and Gurevych (2019)	$52.03_{\pm1.44}$	$90.78_{\pm0.09}$	$81.67_{\pm0.46}$	$66.01_{\pm0.45}$	$81.57_{\pm0.53}$	–
	Peng et al. (2021)	$59.11_{\pm0.93}$	$90.41_{\pm0.09}$	$81.70_{\pm0.17}$	$66.22_{\pm0.75}$	$81.14_{\pm0.81}$	–
	Peng et al. (2022)	$59.19_{\pm1.85}$	$90.74_{\pm0.06}$	$83.42_{\pm0.23}$	$68.85_{\pm0.73}$	$82.60_{\pm0.18}$	–
$\text{BERT}_{\text{large}}$	He et al. (2020)	74.60	87.70	89.30	–	93.30	70.90
$\text{RoBERTa}_{\text{base}}$	Reimers and Gurevych (2019)	$52.67_{\pm2.75}$	$90.79_{\pm0.09}$	$81.69_{\pm0.53}$	$67.35_{\pm0.97}$	$81.42_{\pm0.93}$	–
	Peng et al. (2022)	$59.50_{\pm2.74}$	$90.76_{\pm0.03}$	$83.22_{\pm0.46}$	$69.68_{\pm0.72}$	$82.87_{\pm0.35}$	–
$\text{RoBERTa}_{\text{large}}$	pi (Liu et al., 2019)	$81.20_{\pm0.89}$	$91.66_{\pm0.22}$	$91.17_{\pm0.15}$	$88.92_{\pm1.09}$	$\mathbf{94.05_{\pm0.22}}$	$71.10_{\pm7.18}$
$\text{XLNet}_{\text{large}}$	pi (Yang et al., 2019)	$56.39_{\pm32.39}$	$73.19_{\pm40.92}$	$87.51_{\pm4.36}$	$89.83_{\pm1.24}$	$74.91_{\pm41.88}$	$59.02_{\pm32.82}$
$\text{RoBERTa}_{\text{nli}}$	pi (Nie et al., 2020)	$79.64_{\pm1.72}$	$91.62_{\pm0.28}$	$91.48_{\pm0.68}$	$\mathbf{90.06_{\pm1.81}}$	$93.89_{\pm0.22}$	$74.65_{\pm0.64}$
	$\text{pi2nli}_{\text{zero}}$ (ours)	10.70	53.03	35.92	61.36	71.40	27.00
	pi2nli (ours)	$\mathbf{83.64_{\pm1.44}}$	$\mathbf{92.27_{\pm0.14}}$	$\mathbf{92.38_{\pm0.30}}$	$88.67_{\pm1.84}$	$93.87_{\pm0.18}$	$\mathbf{75.04_{\pm0.85}}$
$\text{XLNet}_{\text{nli}}$	pi (Nie et al., 2020)	$78.80_{\pm0.82}$	$91.27_{\pm0.30}$	$91.00_{\pm0.63}$	$89.68_{\pm0.38}$	$93.66_{\pm0.24}$	$73.97_{\pm0.21}$
	$\text{pi2nli}_{\text{zero}}$ (ours)	18.46	60.28	50.38	56.00	69.97	33.74
	pi2nli (ours)	$82.07_{\pm1.31}$	$91.95_{\pm0.20}$	$91.41_{\pm0.40}$	$87.55_{\pm1.26}$	$93.90_{\pm0.35}$	$74.24_{\pm0.75}$

Table 2: F1 scores (%) of PI2NLI in zero-shot ($\text{pi2nli}_{\text{zero}}$) and fine-tuned (pi2nli) settings, compared with the Random and pi baselines we implemented, as well as prior methods cited. Scores highlighted in bold signify the best performance with a p-value < 0.005, denoting high statistical significance.

Metrics To address the inherent class imbalance in most datasets and follow prior work (Peng et al., 2022), we use the F1 score as our primary evaluation metric. We run each method on each dataset five times, using each integer from 0 to 4 as a random seed, and report the average F1 score.

3.3 Results

We present our results in Table 2.

Zero-shot The zero-shot performance of PI2NLI is erratic, with highly variable F1 scores across datasets. Indeed, $\text{pi2nli}_{\text{zero}}$ outperforms the random baseline on only half of the datasets. Our analysis reveals that this is not indicative of a flaw in our PI2NLI reduction but rather due to inherent flaws in the PI benchmarks. Specifically, the annotations in these datasets do not strictly conform to the criteria imposed by our hypothesis. Table 3 highlights instances where paraphrasing-induced information loss disrupts mutual TI, leading to discrepancies between the original PI labels (Y_{PI}) and the outputs ($\hat{Y}_{\text{PI}}$) derived from the PI2NLI hypothesis. In essence, our results suggest that PI2NLI is able to identify and rectify inconsistencies in PI benchmarks. Such inconsistencies also suggest that context information essentially represents the dataset-specific distribution in practice: a paraphrase identified in one dataset might not necessarily be considered a valid paraphrase in the other. Taken together, these findings strongly suggests the need for a dataset adaptation procedure, to prepare the model for the unique properties of each dataset.

Fine-tuning Contrariwise, the fine-tuned version of our PI2NLI reduction yields consistently high F1 scores, outperforming the reported results obtained by prior work on all six datasets. In particular, the F1 score of the $\text{RoBERTa}_{\text{large}}$-based PI2NLI implementation increases from 10.70 to 83.64 on the PIT dataset. Notably, our top performances of 92.27 on QQP and 75.04 on PARADE also surpass the 89.6 (Peng et al., 2023b) and 74.06 (Bai et al., 2023) reported by the latest work respectively. This demonstrates that our dataset adaptation procedure successfully empowers NLI models to adapt to the peculiarities of various PI datasets and to yield state-of-the-art results. Moreover, our experiments show that PI2NLI consistently outperforms dedicated PI models using the same underlying language models on four of six datasets. This controlled experiment therefore confirms that the performance gains achieved can be attributed to our PI2NLI reduction, rather than other factors like the differing model capacities.

Pre-training Another critical observation is that pre-training[5] on additional NLI data leads to better and more stable fine-tuned performance on PI tasks. This observation is especially evident when transitioning pi from $\text{XLNet}_{\text{large}}$ to $\text{XLNet}_{\text{nli}}$. While it is a common belief that pre-training on additional tasks (e.g., NLI) could inherently improve performance on one certain task (e.g., PI), this is

[5]We regard "pre-training" as any foundational training conducted prior to our task-specific fine-tuning in this work.

Input	$S_1 \models S_2$	$S_2 \models S_1$	$\hat{Y}_{PI}$	Y_{PI}
S_1: The district also sent letters yesterday informing parents of the situation . S_2: Parents received letters informing them of the possible contamination yesterday .	T	T	T	T
S_1: Two kids from Michigan are in today 's third round . S_2: Both will compete in today 's third round , which is all oral examination .	F	F	F	F
S_1: Pacific Northwest has more than 800 employees , and Wells Fargo has 2,400 in Washington . S_2: It has 800 employees , compared with Wells Fargo 's 2,400 .	T	F	F	T
S_1: Six Democrats are vying to succeed Jacques and have qualified for the Feb. 3 primary ballot . S_2: Six Democrats and two Republicans are running for her seat and have qualified for the Feb. 3 primary ballot .	F	T	F	T

Table 3: Four PI instances that differ in the detected entailment direction. Although all eight individual TI outputs are arguably correct, the last two instances are counted as false negatives.

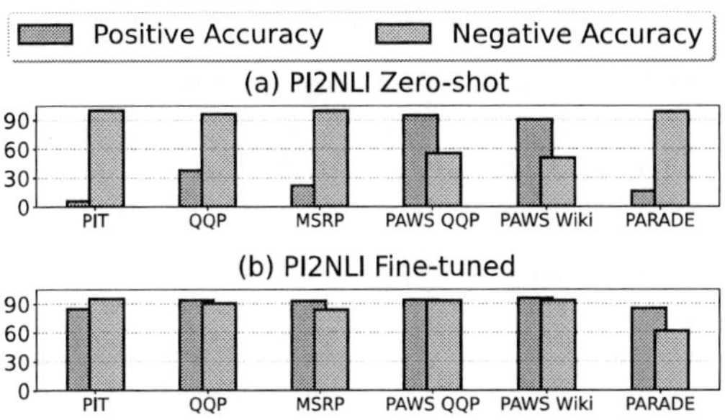

Figure 2: The results of (a) $\text{pi2nli}_{\text{zero}}$ and (b) pi2nli using $\text{RoBERTa}_{\text{nli}}$ in Table 2, separated into positive and negative accuracy.

not always a given. Several factors could potentially lead to a negative impact after such additional pre-training. These include domain mismatches, biases inherent in the pre-training data, and the phenomenon of catastrophic forgetting (McCloskey and Cohen, 1989). Following NLI pre-training, the improved performance of PI serves as a positive indicator. They support our hypothesis of a closely related and synergistic relationship between PI and NLI. This synergy is not automatic but is indicative of the effective transfer of relevant skills and knowledge from NLI to PI tasks.

Boundary In Figure 2, we split the results into positive and negative accuracy. In (a), $\text{pi2nli}_{\text{zero}}$ tends to have relatively higher negative accuracy, leading to a lower likelihood of classifying sentences as paraphrases. In (b), both positive and negative accuracy of pi2nli increase and become more balanced. This supports our earlier findings that, in order to perform better in the PI task, NLI models can correct their decision boundaries after fine-tuning. We view this adjustment as the process of how models learn the context inherent in each PI dataset.

PAWS Our error analysis reveals that the results of pi2nli on PAWS QQP and PAWS Wiki are due to the presence of adversarial examples (Zhang et al., 2019). This becomes particularly evident when comparing the QQP results with those of PAWS QQP, as both derive from the same source. These PAWS datasets are augmented with paraphrase adversaries to offer refined versions of the original datasets, presenting a challenge for models to predict the correct outcomes. Applying PI2NLI requires an NLI model to predict the TI relation in each direction. Therefore, the impact of the paraphrase adversaries becomes more apparent due to error accumulation from making two predictions.

4 Conclusion

We have presented a novel theoretical and empirical study of the relationship between two important semantic tasks, PI and NLI, a topic that has remained largely unexplored. Our experiments provide strong evidence that our innovative PI2NLI reduction, combined with fine-tuning on the NLI data facilitated by our dataset adaptation procedure, yields substantial F1 improvements on the PI task, outperforming dedicated PI models on benchmark PI datasets. The variable outcomes observed when applying PI2NLI in a zero-shot setting also offer insights into the existing limitations of the current PI datasets. In addition to advancing the state of the art, our findings offer valuable insights into the relation between PI and NLI, and set the stage for further investigation.

Limitations

While our work has made significant strides in understanding the four semantic relations, it is not without its limitations.

Firstly, our zero-shot results suggest mismatches between our theoretical proposition and existing

PI benchmarks. These benchmarks may not adequately capture the bidirectional inference relation integral to genuine paraphrase identification.

Secondly, our study focuses on the application of NLI models in solving PI tasks through the PI2NLI reduction, but there are still avenues left to explore. For instance, augmenting the PI dataset with an NLI one could potentially yield new insights.

Finally, our study has been NLI-centric so far, allowing us to delve deeply into the potential of NLI models in PI tasks. However, there is an opportunity for future research to explore the relationship from a PI-centric perspective. This could include investigating the capability of PI models in solving NLI tasks. A more balanced exploration would provide a more comprehensive understanding of the four semantic relations.

Acknowledgements

This research was supported by the Natural Sciences and Engineering Research Council of Canada (NSERC), and the Alberta Machine Intelligence Institute (Amii).

References

Ion Androutsopoulos and Prodromos Malakasiotis. 2010. A survey of paraphrasing and textual entailment methods. *Journal of Artificial Intelligence Research*, 38:135–187.

Jun Bai, Chuantao Yin, Hanhua Hong, Jianfei Zhang, Chen Li, Yanmeng Wang, and Wenge Rong. 2023. Permutation invariant training for paraphrase identification. In *ICASSP 2023 - 2023 IEEE International Conference on Acoustics, Speech and Signal Processing (ICASSP)*, pages 1–5.

Rahul Bhagat and Eduard Hovy. 2013. What is a paraphrase? *Computational Linguistics*, 39(3):463–472.

Johan Bos and Katja Markert. 2005. Recognising textual entailment with logical inference. In *Proceedings of Human Language Technology Conference and Conference on Empirical Methods in Natural Language Processing*, pages 628–635, Vancouver, British Columbia, Canada.

Samuel R. Bowman, Gabor Angeli, Christopher Potts, and Christopher D. Manning. 2015. A large annotated corpus for learning natural language inference. In *Proceedings of the 2015 Conference on Empirical Methods in Natural Language Processing*, pages 632–642, Lisbon, Portugal.

Laura Burdick, Jonathan K. Kummerfeld, and Rada Mihalcea. 2022. Using paraphrases to study properties of contextual embeddings. In *Proceedings of the 2022 Conference of the North American Chapter of the Association for Computational Linguistics: Human Language Technologies*, pages 4558–4568, Seattle, United States. Association for Computational Linguistics.

Ido Dagan and Oren Glickman. 2004. Probabilistic textual entailment: Generic applied modeling of language variability. *Learning Methods for Text Understanding and Mining*, 2004(26-29):2–5.

Ido Dagan, Oren Glickman, and Bernardo Magnini. 2005. The pascal recognising textual entailment challenge. In *Machine learning challenges workshop*, pages 177–190. Springer.

William B. Dolan and Chris Brockett. 2005. Automatically constructing a corpus of sentential paraphrases. In *Proceedings of the Third International Workshop on Paraphrasing (IWP2005)*.

Bradley Hauer and Grzegorz Kondrak. 2023. Taxonomy of problems in lexical semantics. In *Findings of the Association for Computational Linguistics: ACL 2023*, pages 9833–9844, Toronto, Canada.

Yun He, Zhuoer Wang, Yin Zhang, Ruihong Huang, and James Caverlee. 2020. PARADE: A New Dataset for Paraphrase Identification Requiring Computer Science Domain Knowledge. In *Proceedings of the 2020 Conference on Empirical Methods in Natural Language Processing (EMNLP)*, pages 7572–7582, Online. Association for Computational Linguistics.

Shankar Iyer, Nikhil Dandekar, and Kornél Csernai. 2017. Quora question pairs. *First Quora Dataset Release: Question Pairs*.

Yinhan Liu, Myle Ott, Naman Goyal, Jingfei Du, Mandar Joshi, Danqi Chen, Omer Levy, Mike Lewis, Luke Zettlemoyer, and Veselin Stoyanov. 2019. Roberta: A robustly optimized bert pretraining approach. *arXiv preprint arXiv:1907.11692*.

Ilya Loshchilov and Frank Hutter. 2019. Decoupled weight decay regularization. In *International Conference on Learning Representations*.

Bill MacCartney. 2009. *Natural language inference*. Stanford University.

Nitin Madnani and Bonnie J. Dorr. 2010. Generating phrasal and sentential paraphrases: A survey of data-driven methods. *Computational Linguistics*, 36(3):341–387.

Christopher D Manning. 2006. Local textual inference: it's hard to circumscribe, but you know it when you see it–and nlp needs it. Technical report, Stanford University.

Michael McCloskey and Neal J Cohen. 1989. Catastrophic interference in connectionist networks: The sequential learning problem. In *Psychology of learning and motivation*, volume 24, pages 109–165. Elsevier.

Yixin Nie, Adina Williams, Emily Dinan, Mohit Bansal, Jason Weston, and Douwe Kiela. 2020. Adversarial NLI: A new benchmark for natural language understanding. In *Proceedings of the 58th Annual Meeting of the Association for Computational Linguistics*, pages 4885–4901, Online.

Marc Pàmies, Joan Llop, Francesco Multari, Nicolau Duran-Silva, César Parra-Rojas, Aitor Gonzalez-Agirre, Francesco Alessandro Massucci, and Marta Villegas. 2023. A weakly supervised textual entailment approach to zero-shot text classification. In *Proceedings of the 17th Conference of the European Chapter of the Association for Computational Linguistics*, pages 286–296, Dubrovnik, Croatia.

Adam Paszke, Sam Gross, Francisco Massa, Adam Lerer, James Bradbury, Gregory Chanan, Trevor Killeen, Zeming Lin, Natalia Gimelshein, Luca Antiga, Alban Desmaison, Andreas Kopf, Edward Yang, Zachary DeVito, Martin Raison, Alykhan Tejani, Sasank Chilamkurthy, Benoit Steiner, Lu Fang, Junjie Bai, and Soumith Chintala. 2019. Pytorch: An imperative style, high-performance deep learning library. In *Advances in Neural Information Processing Systems*, volume 32. Curran Associates, Inc.

Qiwei Peng, David Weir, and Julie Weeds. 2021. Structure-aware sentence encoder in bert-based Siamese network. In *Proceedings of the 6th Workshop on Representation Learning for NLP (RepL4NLP-2021)*, pages 57–63, Online.

Qiwei Peng, David Weir, and Julie Weeds. 2023a. Testing paraphrase models on recognising sentence pairs at different degrees of semantic overlap. In *Proceedings of the 12th Joint Conference on Lexical and Computational Semantics (*SEM 2023)*, pages 259–269, Toronto, Canada. Association for Computational Linguistics.

Qiwei Peng, David Weir, Julie Weeds, and Yekun Chai. 2022. Predicate-argument based bi-encoder for paraphrase identification. In *Proceedings of the 60th Annual Meeting of the Association for Computational Linguistics (Volume 1: Long Papers)*, pages 5579–5589, Dublin, Ireland.

Rui Peng, Zhiling Jin, and Yu Hong. 2023b. GBT: Generative boosting training approach for paraphrase identification. In *Findings of the Association for Computational Linguistics: EMNLP 2023*, pages 6094–6103, Singapore. Association for Computational Linguistics.

Adam Poliak. 2020. A survey on recognizing textual entailment as an NLP evaluation. In *Proceedings of the First Workshop on Evaluation and Comparison of NLP Systems*, pages 92–109, Online.

Lutz Prechelt. 1998. Early stopping-but when? In *Neural Networks: Tricks of the trade*, pages 55–69. Springer.

Nils Reimers and Iryna Gurevych. 2019. Sentence-BERT: Sentence embeddings using Siamese BERT-networks. In *Proceedings of the 2019 Conference on Empirical Methods in Natural Language Processing and the 9th International Joint Conference on Natural Language Processing (EMNLP-IJCNLP)*, pages 3982–3992, Hong Kong, China.

S Seethamol and K Manju. 2017. Paraphrase identification using textual entailment recognition. In *2017 International Conference on Intelligent Computing, Instrumentation and Control Technologies (ICICICT)*, pages 1071–1074. IEEE.

Ashish Vaswani, Noam Shazeer, Niki Parmar, Jakob Uszkoreit, Llion Jones, Aidan N Gomez, Ł ukasz Kaiser, and Illia Polosukhin. 2017. Attention is all you need. In I. Guyon, U. V. Luxburg, S. Bengio, H. Wallach, R. Fergus, S. Vishwanathan, and R. Garnett, editors, *Advances in Neural Information Processing Systems 30*, pages 5998–6008. Curran Associates, Inc.

Jan Philip Wahle, Bela Gipp, and Terry Ruas. 2023. Paraphrase types for generation and detection. In *Proceedings of the 2023 Conference on Empirical Methods in Natural Language Processing*, pages 12148–12164, Singapore. Association for Computational Linguistics.

Alex Wang, Amanpreet Singh, Julian Michael, Felix Hill, Omer Levy, and Samuel Bowman. 2018. GLUE: A multi-task benchmark and analysis platform for natural language understanding. In *Proceedings of the 2018 EMNLP Workshop BlackboxNLP: Analyzing and Interpreting Neural Networks for NLP*, pages 353–355, Brussels, Belgium.

Adina Williams, Nikita Nangia, and Samuel Bowman. 2018. A broad-coverage challenge corpus for sentence understanding through inference. In *Proceedings of the 2018 Conference of the North American Chapter of the Association for Computational Linguistics: Human Language Technologies, Volume 1 (Long Papers)*, pages 1112–1122, New Orleans, Louisiana. Association for Computational Linguistics.

Adina Williams, Tristan Thrush, and Douwe Kiela. 2022. ANLIzing the adversarial natural language inference dataset. In *Proceedings of the Society for Computation in Linguistics 2022*, pages 23–54, online. Association for Computational Linguistics.

Thomas Wolf, Lysandre Debut, Victor Sanh, Julien Chaumond, Clement Delangue, Anthony Moi, Pierric Cistac, Tim Rault, Remi Louf, Morgan Funtowicz, Joe Davison, Sam Shleifer, Patrick von Platen, Clara Ma, Yacine Jernite, Julien Plu, Canwen Xu, Teven Le Scao, Sylvain Gugger, Mariama Drame, Quentin Lhoest, and Alexander Rush. 2020. Transformers: State-of-the-art natural language processing. In *Proceedings of the 2020 Conference on Empirical Methods in Natural Language Processing: System Demonstrations*, pages 38–45, Online.

Wei Xu, Chris Callison-Burch, and Bill Dolan. 2015. SemEval-2015 task 1: Paraphrase and semantic similarity in Twitter (PIT). In *Proceedings of the 9th International Workshop on Semantic Evaluation (SemEval 2015)*, pages 1–11, Denver, Colorado.

Zhilin Yang, Zihang Dai, Yiming Yang, Jaime Carbonell, Russ R Salakhutdinov, and Quoc V Le. 2019. Xlnet: Generalized autoregressive pretraining for language understanding. In *Advances in Neural Information Processing Systems*, volume 32. Curran Associates, Inc.

Yuan Zhang, Jason Baldridge, and Luheng He. 2019. PAWS: Paraphrase adversaries from word scrambling. In *Proceedings of the 2019 Conference of the North American Chapter of the Association for Computational Linguistics: Human Language Technologies, Volume 1 (Long and Short Papers)*, pages 1298–1308, Minneapolis, Minnesota. Association for Computational Linguistics.

A Dataset Adaptation

The alignment of PI data with NLI data starts with converting PI data to NLI format, as outlined in Section 2.3. While converting positive PI instances to positive NLI instances is straightforward, that for negative NLI instances is not. A negative PI instance is transformed into a negative NLI instance in one direction. When fine-tuning the NLI model, both "contradiction" and "neutral" are used to represent these negative NLI instances. In this context, a FALSE label is randomly assigned as either "contradiction" or "neutral" in NLI. This is justified in the context of our work because both labels can align with a negative TI relation.

Determining the precise TI direction and corresponding NLI class without additional resources or explicit human judgment presents a significant challenge. Hence, we adopted random sampling as a practical solution in our research. However, we recognize that further refining this aspect, such as using a pre-trained NLI model for more granular annotation of negative NLI instances, could enhance the performance of PI2NLI. We believe this represents a promising direction for future research.

B Training

The AdamW optimizer (Loshchilov and Hutter, 2019) is employed with an initial learning rate of 1e-5 and a batch size of 32. We tune the learning rate within the range of [1e-5, 2e-5, 5e-5] and choose the batch size to optimize the GPU memory utilization on a single Nvidia Tesla V100. To prevent overfitting, we adopt early stopping on the F1 score of validation for 6 epochs (Prechelt, 1998). All implementations are executed using PyTorch (Paszke et al., 2019), with pre-trained models sourced from the HuggingFace repository (Wolf et al., 2020).

In our implementation, we transitioned from a standard PI pipeline consistent with established practices in existing literature (Peng et al., 2022). to our PI2NLI. This strategic shift was executed with an emphasis on ensuring fairness and comparability across tests. Thus, our setup may even slightly favor the PI baselines. While more precise tuning of training configurations might enhance the performance of PI2NLI, our primary focus has been on validating our hypothesis. Our future work will explore optimizing these configurations to further improve performance.

C Data

The Paraphrase and Semantic Similarity in Twitter (PIT) dataset is sourced from Twitter's trending service and annotated using Amazon Mechanical Turk (Xu et al., 2015). The labels range from 0 to 5. We follow the suggested binary data processing where labels 4 and 5 indicate a paraphrase, and labels 0 through 2 do not.[6]

The Quora Question Pairs (QQP) dataset originates from the question-and-answer platform Quora, consisting of question pairs annotated for potential duplicity (Iyer et al., 2017). The dataset labels are binary, indicating whether question pairs are duplicates (TRUE) or not (FALSE).[7]

The Microsoft Research Paraphrase Corpus (MSRP) is derived from sentence pairs generated by clustering news articles using heuristic extraction and an SVM classifier, with human annotations provided (Dolan and Brockett, 2005). For this study, we adhere to the GLUE benchmark standards for processing and splitting the data (Wang et al., 2018).[8]

The PARAphrase identification based on Domain knowledgE (PARADE) dataset is tailored for PI in computer science, requiring in-depth domain knowledge (He et al., 2020). It challenges models to identify paraphrases that, despite minimal lexical and syntactic overlap, are semantically equivalent due to the specialized context of computer science. The dataset offers annotations in both four-class and binary formats, provided by annotators with domain expertise.[9] In this work, we use binary labels to maintain consistency with prior studies.

The Paraphrase Adversaries from Word Scrambling (PAWS) benchmark, including PAWS QQP and PAWS Wiki, is proposed to test models to discern semantic relationships despite superficial lexical similarities (Zhang et al., 2019). These datasets utilize word scrambling and back-translation to create adversarial examples that, while sharing high lexical overlap, differ significantly in meaning. PAWS QQP draws questions from the QQP corpus and PAWS Wiki is based on sentences from Wikipedia.[10] Labels are provided in binary format, and we follow the standard data processing protocols as originally released.[11]

[6] https://github.com/cocoxu/SemEval-PIT2015

[7] https://huggingface.co/datasets/quora

[8] https://huggingface.co/datasets/nyu-mll/glue

[9] https://github.com/heyunh2015/PARADE_dataset

[10] https://dumps.wikimedia.org/

[11] https://github.com/google-research-datasets/paws

Identifying Emotional and Polar Concepts via Synset Translation

Logan Woudstra, Moyo Dawodu, Frances Igwe
Senyu Li, Ning Shi, Bradley Hauer, Grzegorz Kondrak
Alberta Machine Intelligence Institute (Amii)
Department of Computing Science
University of Alberta, Edmonton, Canada
{lwoudstr,mdawodu,figwe,senyu,ning.shi,bmhauer,gkondrak}@ualberta.ca

Abstract

Emotion identification and polarity classification seek to determine the sentiment expressed by a writer. Sentiment lexicons that provide classifications at the word level fail to distinguish between different senses of polysemous words. To address this problem, we propose a translation-based method for labeling each individual lexical concept and word sense. Specifically, we translate synsets into 20 different languages and verify the sentiment of these translations in multilingual sentiment lexicons. By applying our method to all WordNet synsets, we produce SentiSynset, a synset-level sentiment resource containing 12,429 emotional synsets and 15,567 polar synsets, which is significantly larger than previous resources. Experimental evaluation shows that our method outperforms prior automated methods that classify word senses, in addition to outperforming ChatGPT. We make the resulting resource publicly available on GitHub.

1 Introduction

Emotion identification is the semantic task of analyzing a piece of text to identify a set of underlying emotions from a predefined inventory (de Albornoz et al., 2012). *Polarity classification* is the closely related task of determining the polarity of a text, which can be positive, negative, or neutral (Pang and Lee, 2004; Turney, 2002). These two tasks are variations on *sentiment analysis*, the extraction of sentiment that a writer expresses toward some object (Jurafsky and Martin, 2009). Following Kakkonen and Galić Kakkonen (2011), we refer to a text, a word token, or a lexical concept as *sentimental* if it is associated with any emotion or non-neutral polarity.

The scope of sentiment analysis can be a single word (Pennebaker et al., 2001; Mohammad and Turney, 2010, 2013), a sentence (Abdul-Mageed and Ungar, 2017; Sosea and Caragea, 2020), or longer texts such as Twitter posts and customer reviews (Liew and Turtle, 2016; Dini and Bittar, 2016; Hu and Liu, 2004). In this paper, we focus on *sense-level sentiment*; knowing the sentiment of the individual words in a text can help determine its overall sentiment.

Emotion identification is more informative than polarity classification, but it is also more subjective in the sense that we would expect more disagreement among annotators. For example, determining that the word *murder* has a negative polarity is more objective than deciding which combination of emotions, such as anger, disgust, fear, and sadness, best relate to the word. This subjectivity is only heightened by the lack of consensus on the set of basic human emotions. Researchers have proposed inventories of six (Ekman, 1992), eight (Plutchik, 1962), or more fundamental emotions. Therefore, while we explore both tasks, we place greater emphasis on polarity classification.

Since many emotion-bearing words are polysemous, we focus our attention on word senses and lexical concepts. Senses are associated with one specific meaning of a word, so classifying sentiments at the level of senses avoids the ambiguity that arises from words having multiple meanings. In WordNet (Miller, 1995), sets of words that express the same concept are grouped together in *synsets*, each uniquely corresponding to a single concept. For example, the synset that contains the words *sadness*, *sorrow*, and *sorrowfulness* corresponds to the concept which is defined as "the state of being sad". Synsets in WordNet are connected via various relations. A word can convey different sentiments depending on its sense in a given context; we assume that the sentiment associated with a specific sense/synset/concept is fixed. While it is true that the sentiment of a sense can too change depending on the context in which it is used, this ambiguity is much less prevalent among senses than it is among words. Thus, by labeling a synset,

*Proceedings of the 13th Joint Conference on Lexical and Computational Semantics (*SEM 2024)*, pages 142 - 152
June 20-21, 2024 ©2024 Association for Computational Linguistics

we provide a single emotional label for all word senses in the synset.

Furthermore, we hypothesize that the sentiment of a given concept is likely to be the same in other languages. For example, the concept mentioned above is also expressed by the Spanish word *tristeza* and the Yoruba word *ibanuje*. We test this hypothesis by developing methods that classify English word senses by leveraging multilingual translations. Conversely, we leverage English sentiment labels for other languages.

In this paper, we outline the development of an automatic method that leverages multilinguality to identify sentimental concepts. Unlike existing resources that were constructed by expanding a core of manually-annotated synsets, we propose a fully automatic method that can provide labels for a significantly larger number of synsets. Our method achieves a precision of 96.0% and 92.0% on identifying emotional and polar synsets, respectively. Of those, a correct emotional label is assigned with an accuracy of 84.3%, and a correct polarity label is assigned with an accuracy of 95.8%. The resulting resource, which we call *SentiSynset*, contains 12,429 emotional and 15,567 polar synset labels. When used in conjunction with word sense disambiguation techniques, the resource could be useful for the downstream application of sentiment analysis at the level of sentences and documents. SentiSynset is publicly available on GitHub, together with our code.[1]

2 Related Work

In this section, we provide an overview of the related work on emotion identification and polarity classification at the synset level. Our focus is on the resources based on the Princeton WordNet (Miller, 1995), which consists of 117,659 synsets, each corresponding to a specific concept defined by its *gloss*.

Emotion identification WordNet-Affect (Strapparava and Valitutti, 2004; Strapparava et al., 2006) and SentiSense (de Albornoz et al., 2012; Carrillo-de Albornoz and Plaza, 2013) associate a subset of WordNet synsets with emotional classifications. WordNet-Affect contains 2,874 synsets, each associated with one or more of 32 emotions. It was constructed by first manually annotating a relatively small "core" of emotional synsets, which was later expanded by leveraging inter-synset relations in WordNet. SentiSense encompasses 2,190 synsets labeled with one of 14 emotional categories. While its development is similar to that of WordNet-Affect, they differ in their specific sets of manually annotated synsets and the WordNet relations chosen for extension.

WordNet-Affect and SentiSense are built upon emotional inventories that are not only mutually incompatible but also rooted in separate psychological theories of emotion. This misalignment complicates data integration, consistency maintenance, and interpretation. Meanwhile, reconciling the two resources by mapping their distinct emotion inventories remains problematic. For example, senses of the words *abashed* and *upset* are both identified with *anxiety* in WordNet-Affect, but are respectively labeled with *disgust* and *anger* in SentiSense; however, senses of the words *embarrassment* and *nausea* are both identified with *disgust* in SentiSense, but are respectively labeled with *shame* and *general-dislike* in WordNet-Affect. These discrepancies highlight the inherent subjectivity in emotion identification, thus motivating our prioritization of the more objective task of polarity classification. Additionally, both resources provide limited coverage of WordNet of less than 3,000 synsets each; this limited coverage arises from their semi-automatic construction. We aim to address this problem by developing a scalable automatic method that can classify a much larger proportion of WordNet synsets.

Polarity classification SentiWordNet (Esuli and Sebastiani, 2006; Baccianella et al., 2010) stands as a prominent resource for polarity classification. It assigns each synset a positive, negative, and objective score, with values ranging from 0.0 to 1.0, summing up to 1 across the three categories. These scores are produced by a committee of classifiers which leverage synset glosses. Since the method is entirely automated, polarity scores are assigned to every WordNet synset. Contrariwise, our method, while automated, is focused on precision, rather than coverage; we do not seek to label every synset, but rather aim to label as many synsets as possible with high confidence.

ML-SentiCon (Cruz et al., 2014) attains polarity labels for synsets using a variation of the method used to create SentiWordNet. As such, the resource has the same drawbacks as SentiWordNet. In addition to the synset labels, ML-Senticon also contains

[1]https://github.com/UAlberta-NLP/SentiSynset

lemma-level lexicons for English, Spanish, Catalan, Basque, and Galician that were developed by averaging the polarity values of all synsets belonging to a lemma. While these are useful lexicons, particularly because of the inclusion of low-resource languages, assigning labels to lemmas introduces issues with polysemy.

Multilinguality Chen and Skiena (2014) leverage multilingual information to develop word-level polarity lexicons for 136 major world languages. They create graphs connecting words from these languages, considering both cross-language links, such as translations and transliterations, and intra-language links, such as synonyms and antonyms. They propagate English word-level polarity labels across the graphs to create lexicons for the non-English languages. While these automatically developed lexicons have high levels of agreement with human-annotated lexicons, they still retain the ambiguity that arises when sentiment labels are assigned to words rather than senses.

Applications of Synset Lexicons Synset-level lexicons can be used for sentiment analysis at the broader levels of sentences and documents (Hung and Chen, 2016; Pamungkas and Putri, 2017). These works find that using synset lexicons in conjunction with word sense disambiguation techniques for English texts results in more precise sentiment predictions than those achieved using word-level lexicons. Similar improvements were observed using synset lexicons to classify non-English text as well (Denecke, 2008). Thus, the resource we develop can be used with these existing methods to perform downstream sentiment analysis tasks in multilingual settings.

3 Methodology

Our method to create a large set of sentiment-labeled synsets (SentiSynset) consists of two main stages. The first stage is to identify a set of emotional or polar synsets that we refer to as the *core*. In the second stage, this core is extended via WordNet relations that preserve sentiment. Our approach differs from prior works in that we create our core automatically, rather than manually. While assigning labels, we follow the precedent established in previously mentioned related works to map a synset to only one sentiment label.

3.1 Leveraging Word-Level Lexicons

To automatically develop the core of SentiSynset, we leverage existing multilingual sentiment lexicons created for sentiment analysis tasks at the *word* level. Sentiment labels for polysemous words may be inaccurate, due to different senses having different associated sentiments. We aim to resolve this ambiguity by leveraging translations, based on the observation that different senses of a word may translate differently. For example, *lick* translates into three distinct Dutch words, *ranselen*, *likken*, and *oplossen*, depending on the sense in which it is used. The sentiment labels associated with each Dutch translation can therefore be used to determine the appropriate label for each sense of *lick*.

While our method is bootstrapped from emotion lexicons, we make no assumptions about the languages or emotion inventories. Thus, our method is flexible and can be applied to other lexicons, potentially with larger vocabularies, or pertaining to specific domains. While emotional inventories vary, polarity labels are positive or negative.

Translating polysemous words into another language is not guaranteed to resolve *all* ambiguities that exist in word-level lexicons. For example, the two senses of *star* meaning "a celestial body of hot gases that radiates energy" and "someone who is dazzlingly skilled in a field" (definitions from WordNet) can both be translated as *estrella* in Spanish. This phenomenon is particularly prevalent among closely related languages; it is therefore advisable to perform translations into multiple languages with varying levels of similarity to English.

3.2 Developing the Core

Our method is designed to generate a core of high-precision synsets, which contain multiple words that are known to express a given sentiment. When labeling a synset, we consider the number of languages that contain sentimental lemmas belonging to the synset. For a lemma in a language other than English to be considered sentimental, it must share a sentiment label with an English lemma in the synset. For example, since the Indonesian lemmas in Figure 1 are associated with a disjoint set of emotions and polarity with respect to the English lemmas, they are disregarded when processing this synset.

To provide an emotional label (from a given emotion inventory) or polarity label (positive or negative), our method takes in a synset and finds all

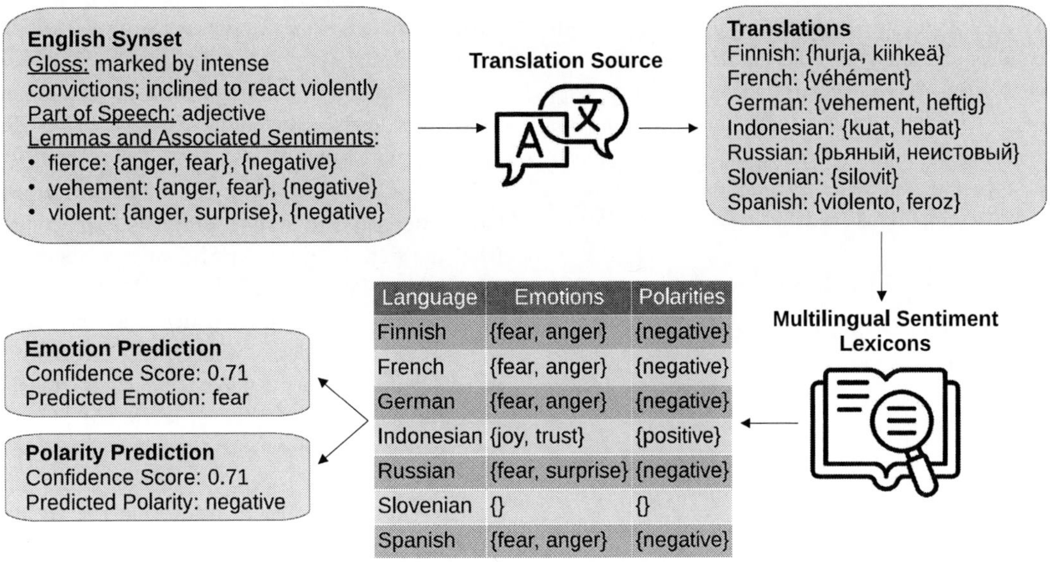

Figure 1: Illustration of performing emotion identification and polarity classification on a synset.

corresponding lemmas in the selected languages. We then determine which sentiments are associated with these lemmas using multilingual word-level lexicons. We finally associate the synset with the sentiment class which is associated with the highest number of translations. For example, since the synset in Figure 1 is associated with *fear* in 5 languages, *anger* in 4 languages, and *surprise* in 1 language, the synset is labeled with *fear*. Through a similar process, the synset is also associated with a negative polarity.

We calculate the confidence score of each candidate synset as the ratio of languages with sentimental lemmas to the total number of languages for which the synset has translations. For example, since the synset in Figure 1 has translations in seven languages, and lemmas that are considered emotional in five of the languages, it receives a confidence score of $5/7 \approx 0.71$.

Since each synset is assigned a single label, we proceed to break any ties that exist between sentiments that share the highest number of associated languages. For emotion identification, this is done by finding sentence embeddings for the gloss of the target synset and gloss for the most frequent sense of each of the top emotions. The synset is identified with the single emotion that has the most similar sentence embedding. For polarity identification, when a synset is associated with positive and negative polarities in the same number of languages, a similar process using sentence embeddings is applied to break the tie. We perform a comparison to this embedding-based approach as a baseline in Section 5.2.

3.3 Extending the Core

To expand the set of core synsets, we leverage WordNet's graph-based structure, which connects synsets through both semantic and lexical relations. Specifically, we propagate sentiment labels from the core to neighboring synsets via sentiment-preserving relations. If a synset is related to multiple core synsets with differing sentiments, we resolve this conflict with the embedding-based tie-breaking algorithm described in Section 3.2. In order to maintain high precision, we do not apply this procedure recursively or transitively.

We adopt the comprehensive set of sentiment-preserving relations used by WordNet-Affect, which differs slightly from the one used by SentiSense, and contains the following WordNet relations: *antonym*, *similar to*, *derived from*, *pertains to*, *attribute*, and *also-sees*. For example, the synset in Figure 1 is classified as having negative polarity, and is associated with the emotion of fear. The synset containing the adverbial sense of *fiercely* is related to this synset by the WordNet *pertains to* relation, and so is also labeled with negative polarity and the emotion of fear.

The relation of *antonymy* is unique in that it connects synsets that convey the *opposite* rather than identical sentiments. We follow Plutchik (1962) by identifying the following pairs of antonymic emotions: *anger/fear, anticipation/surprise, disgust/trust, and joy/sadness.* If a core synset is labeled with one of these sentiments, its antonyms are labeled with the opposite sentiment. Similarly, if a synset is labeled with positive or negative polarity, its antonyms are labeled with the opposite.

4 Experimental Setup

In this section, we provide details of our implementation and the datasets that we use.

4.1 Datasets

The NRC Word-Emotion Association Lexicon (EmoLex) (Mohammad and Turney, 2010, 2013), is a word-level sentiment lexicon which contains 14,182 English words tagged with emotional and polar labels by human annotators. Of those words, 4,454 are tagged with one or more of Plutchik's 8 fundamental emotions: *anger, anticipation, disgust, fear, joy, sadness, surprise*, and *trust.* As well, 5,543 of these words are tagged with positive and/or negative polarity. EmoLex was originally developed in English but has since been translated into 108 different languages. It is these translations that we use as our multilingual sentiment lexicons.

To evaluate the quality of SentiSynset, we construct both a validation set and a test set, each containing 1,000 synsets. Each set includes a random sample of 500 synsets from the SentiSense resource; these constitute the sentimental instances. Each also includes a random sample of 500 synsets that have no emotional or polar lemmas according to EmoLex or the LIWC dictionary (Pennebaker et al., 2001); these provide non-sentimental instances. We ensure that the validation and test sets are disjoint.

4.2 Synsets and Translations

The core of SentiSynset is found by applying the multilingual method described in Section 3.2 to all 117,659 WordNet synsets for the two independent tasks. We use the NLP library spaCy[2] to obtain sentence embeddings (c.f., Section 3.2).

Our method also requires a way of obtaining, for each synset, a set of words in various languages which lexicalize the concept to which that synset corresponds; for brevity, we refer to these multilingual terms as translations. We use translations for WordNet synsets in 20 languages covered by EmoLex: Chinese, Dutch, Estonian, Finnish, French, German, Greek, Indonesian, Korean, Lithuanian, Norwegian, Polish, Romanian, Russian, Slovak, Slovenian, Spanish, Swedish, Turkish, and Ukrainian.

During development, we considered two translation sources. The first set of translations comes from the multilingual lexical database BabelNet (Navigli and Ponzetto, 2010). BabelNet was built by integrating various large lexical databases such as WordNet, Wikipedia, and Open Multilingual WordNet among others, alongside machine translation. We make use of BabelNet version 5.1, which covers over 500 languages; however, it does not contain translations for every synset in every language. On average, each of the selected 20 languages has BabelNet translations for 70.7% of all WordNet synsets. WordNet synsets have BabelNet translations in 14 of the selected languages on average, and 99.9% of all WordNet synsets have a BabelNet translation in at least one of the 20 selected languages.

The second set of translations comes from Google Translate (GT). To obtain sense-accurate translations, we translate an example sentence associated with the synset. WordNet provides such sentences for some synsets. For synsets without examples, we construct an example using the WordNet gloss. For instance, for the synset in Figure 1, we would construct the following sentence: "to be *fierce* is to be marked by intense convictions; inclined to react violently." Note that the templates used to construct sentences differ slightly depending on the synset's part of speech. We compile all the English sentences together and use the document translator on the GT online interface to attain the sentence translations. We then use the alignment system SimAlign (Jalili Sabet et al., 2020) to find the translation of the target word in the translated sentences. GT provides translations for every synset in every language, but not all translations are correct.

After obtaining translations from both BabelNet and GT, we lemmatize the translations using the Simplemma[3] library This step is skipped for languages such as Chinese and Korean where lemmatization is not applicable.

We consider four approaches to obtaining synset translations: GT alone, BabelNet alone, BabelNet supplemented with GT (i.e., BabelNet is used if

[2]https://spacy.io

[3]https://github.com/adbar/simplemma

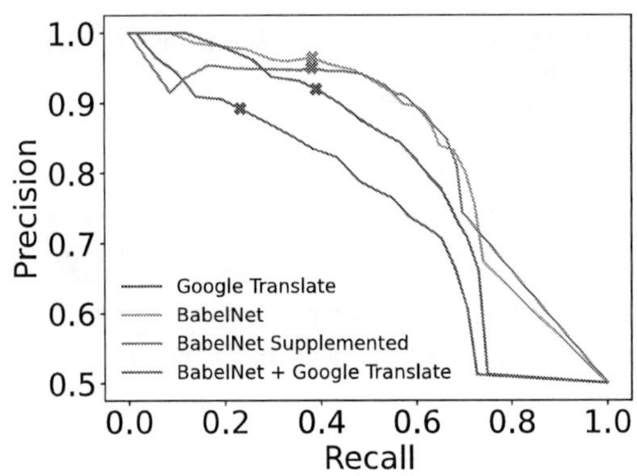

Figure 2: Precision-recall curve across various translation sources. Each curve is marked with a point corresponding to a high-confidence threshold of 0.70.

Sentiment	#Synsets
Anger	1891
Anticipation	1192
Disgust	1078
Fear	1939
Joy	1048
Sadness	1877
Surprise	391
Trust	3013
Positive	7081
Negative	8486

Table 1: Number of synsets associated with different sentiments in SentiSynset.

translations exist for a synset, otherwise GT is used), and the union of BabelNet and GT. On the validation set, we calculate the 11-point interpolated average precision (11-PIAP) (Manning et al., 2008) for each of these approaches and find that BabelNet alone results in the highest 11-PIAP of 83.9%, while GT, BabelNet Supplemented, and the union of BabelNet and GT result in the 11-PIAP's of 74.5%, 82.8% and 70.5% respectively. We also considered the precision and recall scores that the four translation approaches achieve on the validation set in the task of detecting emotional synsets (see Figure 2). Therefore, we use the best-performing method of BabelNet alone as the source of synset translations.

5 Results

In this section, we evaluate our method's performance in the desired tasks and discuss the newly created resource.

5.1 Core Synsets

To determine the confidence threshold of the method, we look at the experimental results of using BabelNet translations on the validation set (as shown in Figure 2). Since we want high-precision predictions, we choose the confidence threshold with a precision above 0.95 which has the highest recall. We find that a confidence threshold of 0.70 satisfies this condition, and thus all synsets that are predicted to be sentimental with a confidence score of 0.70 or above are added to the core of SentiSynset.

With the high-confidence threshold set, running the method on all WordNet synsets for the tasks of emotion identification and polarity classification results in a core containing 6,056 synsets that are predicted to be emotional and a core containing 8,519 synsets that are predicted to be polar. After extending these cores through the use of sentiment-preserving WordNet relations, SentiSynset contains a total of 12,429 emotional synsets and a total of 15,567 polar synsets. Information regarding the distribution of sentiments and parts of speech in these synset sets is shown in Tables 1 and 2.

5.2 Emotion Identification

To evaluate the quality of our newly constructed emotion resource, we measure the proportion of correct sentiment labels. We consider synsets in the intersection of our emotion resource and the test set. If a synset labeled as sentimental is in the intersection, we consider this a true positive. If a non-sentimental synset is in the intersection, we consider this a false positive. Using these classifications, we find that our method achieves a precision of 96.0% and a recall of 57.2% in the task of detecting emotional synsets.

To determine the accuracy of the emotion labels given by our method, three native English-speaking authors of this paper independently annotated all true positive synsets in the test set with one of the 8 fundamental emotions. The annotators achieved an average pairwise Cohen's kappa coefficient of 0.60, suggesting substantial agreement between the annotations. Similarly, at least 2 annotators agreed on a label for 92.3% of the synsets, and all 3 annotators agreed on a label for 53.3% of the synsets. For the 7.7% of synsets that all three annotators disagreed

POS	Emotional	Polar
Adjective	4531	5879
Adverb	144	237
Noun	5301	6464
Verb	2453	2987
Total	12,429	15,567

Table 2: Number of synsets associated with different parts of speech (POS) in SentiSynset.

Method	Emotion	Polarity
Random EmoLex	34.5	82.0
Sentence Embeddings	41.5	85.4
SentiWordNet	–	91.3
ChatGPT	79.0	93.1
Ours	**82.4**	**95.8**

Table 3: Accuracy of our method versus other approaches on the test set (in %).

on, the annotators were asked to reconsider their labels after being shown the emotions assigned to the synsets by the other annotators. Once all synsets had a single emotion that the majority of annotators agreed upon, these emotions were taken as the true labels.

We compare our method to several approaches. As a baseline, we find all emotions related to the English lemmas of a synset in EmoLex, then label a synset with a random emotion from this set. *Sentence Embeddings* takes these same emotions found in the English lexicon, computes sentence embeddings for the gloss of the target synset and for the gloss of the most frequent sense of each of these emotions, and labels the synset with the most similar emotion. We also prompt GPT-3.5 (Brown et al., 2020) to provide emotional labels for the synsets based on gloss and the lemmas. Finally, we classify synsets with the emotion labels assigned by our multilingual method. The accuracy of these different approaches can be found in Table 3, and we find that our method achieves the best performance.

No comparisons are made between the emotion labels assigned by our method and those of an existing resource because of the incongruent emotional inventories used between different synset-level resources; neither WordNet-Affect nor SentiSense uses Plutchik's 8 fundamental emotions as we do.

5.3 Polarity Classification

We evaluate the quality of our newly constructed polarity resource through a similar process used to evaluate our performance in emotion identification. When comparing the intersection of the test set and our polarity resource, we find that our method achieves a precision of 92.0% and a recall of 67.0% in the task of detecting polar synsets. We compare our polarity resource to SentiWordNet. Since SentiWordNet assigns synsets polarity scores in the range [0.0, 1.0], we assign synsets a single polarity label based on these scores. We do so by associating a synset with the polarity category (positive, negative, or objective) with the highest score. For the intersection between the test set and polar SentiWordNet synsets, SentiWordNet achieves a precision of 91.6% and recall of 41.6%.

To determine the accuracy of the polarity labels given by different methods, we convert the emotional labels given to the synsets by SentiSense to polarity labels. The emotions of *calmness, hope, joy, like,* and *love* are associated with positive polarity, while *anger, despair, disgust, fear, hate,* and *sadness* are associated with negative polarity. We disregard synsets associated with the emotions of *ambiguity, anticipation,* or *surprise* since synsets labeled with these emotions are not strongly correlated to either polarity. These emotion-to-polarity mappings, alongside equivalent polarity labels, are considered the true positives.

The methods that we compare for polarity classification are similar to those for emotion identification. Our baseline is to assign synsets with a random polarity that is associated with the English lemmas in EmoLex. We also compare to Sentence Embeddings, SentiWordNet, and ChatGPT. As shown in the rightmost column of Table 3, our method again achieves the best performance.

5.4 Polysemous Words

We investigate how well our method can resolve the ambiguity of polysemous words. To do so, we identify pairs of synsets in the test set that share a lemma but have opposite sentiments (polar and non-polar, emotional and non-emotional). Since our method focuses on precision over accuracy, we only consider pairs of synsets that share a polysemous word when at least one of the synsets is predicted to be sentimental.

We find 18 pairs of synsets with polar and non-polar labels in the test set, and our method provides correct classifications for both senses with 94.4% accuracy. The only pair of synsets that the method fails to correctly classify contains the polar and non-polar senses of *sublime* meaning "of high moral or intellectual value" and to "vaporize and then condense right back again" (WordNet). Our method identifies both senses as being positive, while this is only true for the first sense.

Our method is 100.0% accurate on 10 pairs of synsets with emotional and non-emotional labels that exist in the test set. For example, given the senses of *plume* meaning to "be proud of" and "(of a bird) to clean with one's beak" our method correctly identifies the first one as emotional and associated with joy, and the second one as non-emotional.

6 Error Analysis

In this section, we investigate incorrect labels produced by our method and discuss possible causes and solutions for such errors.

6.1 Parallel Polysemy

Our method struggles to correctly label concepts that exhibit parallel polysemy across many of the selected languages. For example, two nominal senses of *resistance* meaning "the action of opposing something that you disapprove or disagree with" and "a material's opposition to the flow of electric current; measured in ohms" share the same translation in French (*résistance*), German (*widerstehen*), Polish (*opór*), and 12 other languages. This causes the first sentimental sense to be viewed the same as the second non-sentimental sense, leading to an incorrect classification.

Although our selected languages do not all come from the same language family, the majority of them are European. This relatedness means they are more susceptible to exhibiting parallel polysemy than if we were to use more non-European languages. However, most non-European languages have considerably fewer lexical resources available than European languages, even for widely spoken non-European languages. For example, Estonian has 1.1 million speakers while Yoruba has 44.0 million speakers (Eberhard et al., 2023); nevertheless, BabelNet has translations available in Estonian for 6.4 times as many synsets than those that are available in Yoruba.

If synset translations were more readily available for languages such as Yoruba or Igbo, parallel polysemy would present less of a problem. Regarding the example of *resistance* above, the two senses would be translated to *atako* and *resistance* in Yoruba. In Igbo, the first sense translates to *iguzogide* while the second does not translate to a single word. Thus, translations from either language would help disambiguate the sentiment of the senses.

6.2 EmoLex Errors

The multilingual versions of EmoLex are translations of the original English EmoLex, so some translation errors exist in these translated lexicons. Words are typically translated as their most frequent sense (MFS), which causes issues when the MFS is non-sentimental. For example, the MFS of *waffle* is the non-sentimental nominal sense meaning "pancake batter baked in a waffle iron." However, *waffle* is considered sentimental in English Emolex due to the verbal sense meaning to "pause or hold back in uncertainty or unwillingness" (WordNet). When EmoLex is translated to other languages, *waffle* is translated as the non-sentimental MFS, but retains the sentiments associated with the verbal sense. Therefore, errors arise such as the Slovak word *vafle* being associated with the emotion of sadness and a negative polarity, despite the word referring strictly to the food item. These translation errors in EmoLex result in the MFS of *waffle* being incorrectly classified as sentimental.

6.3 Subjectivity

Other errors arise from the inherently subjective nature of the given tasks. It is very possible that one person may view a synset as sentimental, while another person views the same synset as non-sentimental. This causes issues when the method correctly determines which word sense EmoLex references, but the accuracy of the EmoLex annotation itself is debatable. For example, *bee* is associated with the emotions of anger and fear in EmoLex, with this annotation most likely referring to the MFS of the word meaning "any of numerous hairy-bodied insects including social and solitary species" (WordNet). Since the method bases its classifications on EmoLex, this sense of *bee* is associated with fear. However, some people may feel that this classification is inappropriate, instead viewing the synset as non-emotional. This opposing view is supported by the fact that *wasp* is not

Language Pair		Emotion	Polarity
Igbo	Yoruba	0.446	0.360
Chinese	Igbo	0.410	0.166
Chinese	Yoruba	0.390	0.401
Polish	Chinese	0.334	0.105
Polish	Igbo	0.353	0.354
Polish	Yoruba	0.292	0.355

Table 4: Cohen's kappa coefficient between emotion and polarity labels for different languages.

associated with any emotions in EmoLex, despite this term being very similar to *bee*.

Subjectivity is also influenced by cultural differences. While an English-speaking annotator labeled *bee* with the negative emotions of anger and fear in EmoLex, people from other cultures may associate bees with positive emotions as they are often considered hard-working creatures. This contrasting sentiment of the word that exists in English may be projected onto sentiment lexicons in other languages because of the virtual hegemony of English resources.

6.4 Cultural Differences

Our multilingual method hinges upon the idea that the sentiments associated with synsets tend to be universal across languages and cultures. However, the *bee* example demonstrates that this is not always the case. We therefore perform a multilingual analysis to quantify the influence of cultural differences on synset classifications.

We utilize plWordNet (Maziarz et al., 2016), a Polish wordnet that contains over 30,000 word senses that have been manually annotated with emotion and polarity labels (Zaśko-Zielińska et al., 2015). Of these labeled synsets, many have mappings onto Princeton WordNet, thus allowing us to investigate the effect of cultural differences on synset labels. There are 1,729 polar synsets and 1,506 emotional synsets that have sentiment labels in both our resource and plWordNet. The polarity and emotional labels have 94.9% and 73.3% agreement, respectively, between the two resources.

Authors of this paper who are native Chinese, Igbo, Polish, and Yoruba speakers labeled 40 polar synsets and 60 emotional synsets, which are among those that plWordNet and SentiSynset disagree on. The annotators were provided with the lemmas and glosses of synsets in their native language, with this information coming from BabelNet when available and Google Translate when not. For the Polish annotator, lemmas and glosses for all synsets were available from plWordNet.

The results of this experiment are shown in Table 4. The average Cohen's Kappa coefficient between the annotations for Polish and the three other languages (the last three rows of the table) are 0.326 and 0.271 for emotion and polarity, respectively. The Cohen's Kappa coefficient between our Polish annotator and plWordNet are 0.387 and 0.203 for emotion and polarity, respectively. Thus, the agreement between our Polish annotator and plWordNet for these contentious synsets is at a similarly low level as the agreement between annotators from different cultures.

7 Conclusion

We have presented a novel method that leverages multilingual translations to shift the sentimental classifications of word-level lexicons from words to synsets. The method is sufficiently general to be applied to the related yet independent tasks of emotion identification and polarity classification. The method outperforms existing methods used to automatically construct resources for the task of polarity classification. With our method, we constructed SentiSynset, which is substantially larger than comparable English sentiment resources. The large number of labeled synsets, and the high precision of labeling demonstrate the method's usefulness. The new resource can be paired with word-sense disambiguation techniques for the downstream task of sentiment analysis at the level of sentences or documents. Since our method is not dependent on EmoLex, it could also leverage information from multiple word-level lexicons, which could further improve the quality and size of SentiSynset.

Acknowledgements

This research was supported by the Natural Sciences and Engineering Research Council of Canada (NSERC), and the Alberta Machine Intelligence Institute (Amii).

References

Muhammad Abdul-Mageed and Lyle Ungar. 2017. EmoNet: Fine-grained emotion detection with gated recurrent neural networks. In *Proceedings of the 55th Annual Meeting of the Association for Computational Linguistics (Volume 1: Long Papers)*, pages 718–728,

Vancouver, Canada. Association for Computational Linguistics.

Stefano Baccianella, Andrea Esuli, and Fabrizio Sebastiani. 2010. SentiWordNet 3.0: An enhanced lexical resource for sentiment analysis and opinion mining. In *Proceedings of the Seventh International Conference on Language Resources and Evaluation (LREC'10)*, Valletta, Malta. European Language Resources Association (ELRA).

Tom B. Brown, Benjamin Mann, Nick Ryder, Melanie Subbiah, Jared Kaplan, Prafulla Dhariwal, Arvind Neelakantan, Pranav Shyam, Girish Sastry, Amanda Askell, Sandhini Agarwal, Ariel Herbert-Voss, Gretchen Krueger, Tom Henighan, Rewon Child, Aditya Ramesh, Daniel M. Ziegler, Jeffrey Wu, Clemens Winter, Christopher Hesse, Mark Chen, Eric Sigler, Mateusz Litwin, Scott Gray, Benjamin Chess, Jack Clark, Christopher Berner, Sam McCandlish, Alec Radford, Ilya Sutskever, and Dario Amodei. 2020. Language models are few-shot learners. *CoRR*, abs/2005.14165.

Jorge Carrillo-de Albornoz and Laura Plaza. 2013. An emotion-based model of negation, intensifiers, and modality for polarity and intensity classification. *Journal of the American Society for Information Science and Technology*, 64(8):1618–1633.

Yanqing Chen and Steven Skiena. 2014. Building sentiment lexicons for all major languages. In *Proceedings of the 52nd Annual Meeting of the Association for Computational Linguistics (Volume 2: Short Papers)*, pages 383–389, Baltimore, Maryland. Association for Computational Linguistics.

Fermín Cruz, José Troyano, Beatriz Pontes, and F. Javier Ortega. 2014. Ml-senticon: A multilingual, lemma-level sentiment lexicon. *Procesamiento de Lenguaje Natural*, 53:113–120.

Jorge Carrillo de Albornoz, Laura Plaza, and Pablo Gervás. 2012. SentiSense: An easily scalable concept-based affective lexicon for sentiment analysis. In *Proceedings of the Eighth International Conference on Language Resources and Evaluation (LREC'12)*, pages 3562–3567, Istanbul, Turkey. European Language Resources Association (ELRA).

Kerstin Denecke. 2008. Using sentiwordnet for multilingual sentiment analysis. In *2008 IEEE 24th International Conference on Data Engineering Workshop*, pages 507–512.

Luca Dini and André Bittar. 2016. Emotion analysis on Twitter: The hidden challenge. In *Proceedings of the Tenth International Conference on Language Resources and Evaluation (LREC'16)*, pages 3953–3958, Portorož, Slovenia. European Language Resources Association (ELRA).

David M. Eberhard, Gary F. Simons, and Charles D. Fennig, editors. 2023. *Ethnologue: Languages of the World*, twenty-sixth edition. SIL International, Dallas, Texas.

Paul Ekman. 1992. An argument for basic emotions. *Cognition and Emotion*, 6(3-4):169–200.

Andrea Esuli and Fabrizio Sebastiani. 2006. SENTIWORDNET: A publicly available lexical resource for opinion mining. In *Proceedings of the Fifth International Conference on Language Resources and Evaluation (LREC'06)*, Genoa, Italy. European Language Resources Association (ELRA).

Minqing Hu and Bing Liu. 2004. Mining and summarizing customer reviews. In *Proceedings of the Tenth ACM SIGKDD International Conference on Knowledge Discovery and Data Mining*, KDD '04, page 168–177, New York, NY, USA. Association for Computing Machinery.

Chihli Hung and Shiuan-Jeng Chen. 2016. Word sense disambiguation based sentiment lexicons for sentiment classification. *Knowledge-Based Systems*, 110:224–232.

Masoud Jalili Sabet, Philipp Dufter, François Yvon, and Hinrich Schütze. 2020. SimAlign: High quality word alignments without parallel training data using static and contextualized embeddings. In *Findings of the Association for Computational Linguistics: EMNLP 2020*, pages 1627–1643, Online. Association for Computational Linguistics.

Daniel Jurafsky and James H. Martin. 2009. *Speech and Language Processing*, 2nd edition. Prentice Hall.

Tuomo Kakkonen and Gordana Galić Kakkonen. 2011. SentiProfiler: Creating comparable visual profiles of sentimental content in texts. In *Proceedings of the Workshop on Language Technologies for Digital Humanities and Cultural Heritage*, pages 62–69, Hissar, Bulgaria. Association for Computational Linguistics.

Jasy Suet Yan Liew and Howard R. Turtle. 2016. Exploring fine-grained emotion detection in tweets. In *Proceedings of the NAACL Student Research Workshop*, pages 73–80, San Diego, California. Association for Computational Linguistics.

Christopher D. Manning, Prabhakar Raghavan, and Hinrich Schutze. 2008. *Introduction to information retrieval*. Cambridge University Press.

Marek Maziarz, Maciej Piasecki, Ewa Rudnicka, Stan Szpakowicz, and Paweł Kędzia. 2016. plWordNet 3.0 – a comprehensive lexical-semantic resource. In *Proceedings of COLING 2016, the 26th International Conference on Computational Linguistics: Technical Papers*, pages 2259–2268, Osaka, Japan. The COLING 2016 Organizing Committee.

George A Miller. 1995. Wordnet: a lexical database for english. *Communications of the ACM*, 38(11):39–41.

Saif Mohammad and Peter Turney. 2010. Emotions evoked by common words and phrases: Using Mechanical Turk to create an emotion lexicon. In *Proceedings of the NAACL HLT 2010 Workshop on Computational Approaches to Analysis and Generation of Emotion in Text*, pages 26–34, Los Angeles, CA. Association for Computational Linguistics.

Saif M. Mohammad and Peter D. Turney. 2013. Crowdsourcing a word–emotion association lexicon. *Computational Intelligence*, 29(3):436–465.

Roberto Navigli and Simone Paolo Ponzetto. 2010. BabelNet: Building a very large multilingual semantic network. In *Proceedings of the 48th Annual Meeting of the Association for Computational Linguistics*, pages 216–225, Uppsala, Sweden. Association for Computational Linguistics.

Endang Wahyu Pamungkas and Divi Galih Prasetyo Putri. 2017. Word sense disambiguation for lexicon-based sentiment analysis. In *Proceedings of the 9th International Conference on Machine Learning and Computing*, ICMLC '17, page 442–446, New York, NY, USA. Association for Computing Machinery.

Bo Pang and Lillian Lee. 2004. A sentimental education: Sentiment analysis using subjectivity summarization based on minimum cuts. In *Proceedings of the 42nd Annual Meeting of the Association for Computational Linguistics (ACL-04)*, pages 271–278, Barcelona, Spain.

James W Pennebaker, Martha E Francis, and Roger J Booth. 2001. Linguistic inquiry and word count: Liwc 2001. *Mahway: Lawrence Erlbaum Associates*, 71(2001):2001.

Robert Plutchik. 1962. *The emotions: Facts, theories, and a new model.* Random House.

Tiberiu Sosea and Cornelia Caragea. 2020. CancerEmo: A dataset for fine-grained emotion detection. In *Proceedings of the 2020 Conference on Empirical Methods in Natural Language Processing (EMNLP)*, pages 8892–8904, Online. Association for Computational Linguistics.

Carlo Strapparava and Alessandro Valitutti. 2004. WordNet affect: an affective extension of WordNet. In *Proceedings of the Fourth International Conference on Language Resources and Evaluation (LREC'04)*, Lisbon, Portugal. European Language Resources Association (ELRA).

Carlo Strapparava, Alessandro Valitutti, and Oliviero Stock. 2006. The affective weight of lexicon. In *Proceedings of the Fifth International Conference on Language Resources and Evaluation (LREC'06)*, Genoa, Italy. European Language Resources Association (ELRA).

Peter Turney. 2002. Thumbs up or thumbs down? semantic orientation applied to unsupervised classification of reviews. In *Proceedings of the 40th Annual Meeting of the Association for Computational Linguistics*, pages 417–424, Philadelphia, Pennsylvania, USA. Association for Computational Linguistics.

Monika Zaśko-Zielińska, Maciej Piasecki, and Stan Szpakowicz. 2015. A large Wordnet-based sentiment lexicon for Polish. In *Proceedings of the International Conference Recent Advances in Natural Language Processing*, pages 721–730, Hissar, Bulgaria.

A Closer Look at Claim Decomposition

Miriam Wanner*, **Seth Ebner***, **Zhengping Jiang**,
Mark Dredze, **Benjamin Van Durme**

Johns Hopkins University

{mwanner5,seth,zjiang31,mdredze,vandurme}@jhu.edu

Abstract

As generated text becomes more commonplace, it is increasingly important to evaluate how well-supported such text is by external knowledge sources. Many approaches for evaluating textual support rely on some method for decomposing text into its individual subclaims which are scored against a trusted reference. We investigate how various methods of claim decomposition—especially LLM-based methods—affect the result of an evaluation approach such as the recently proposed FACTSCORE, finding that it is sensitive to the decomposition method used. This sensitivity arises because such metrics attribute overall textual support to the model that generated the text even though error can also come from the metric's decomposition step. To measure decomposition quality, we introduce an adaptation of FACTSCORE, which we call DECOMPSCORE. We then propose an LLM-based approach to generating decompositions inspired by Bertrand Russell's theory of logical atomism and neo-Davidsonian semantics and demonstrate its improved decomposition quality over previous methods.

1 Introduction

Recent work uses claim decomposition to determine how well supported a claim is for applications in factual precision of generated text (Min et al., 2023), entailment of human generated text (Kamoi et al., 2023; Chen et al., 2023b), and claim verification (Chen et al., 2023a; Li et al., 2023; Milbauer et al., 2023; Tang et al., 2024), with similar ideas going back over a decade (Hickl and Bensley, 2007). In each of these cases, a claim is decomposed into natural language subclaims,[1] typically using a large language model (LLM), and each subclaim is then scored or aligned to information from external sources using a task-specific metric.

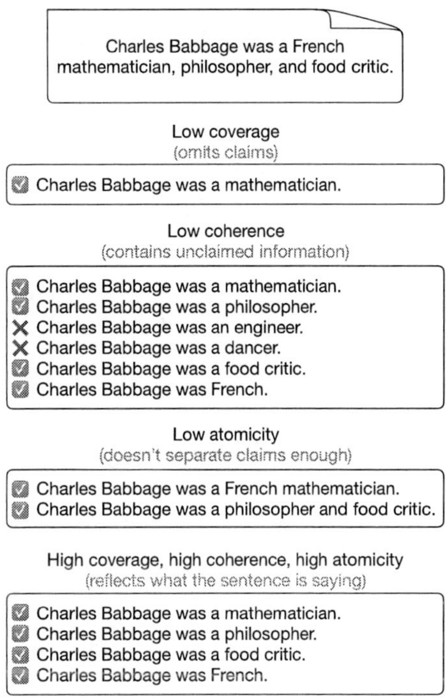

Figure 1: Modes of claim decomposition. The extent to which textual support can be determined depends on how the generated text (yellow box) is decomposed into its subclaims (white boxes). Higher quality decompositions enable more complete identification of discrepancies between generated text and a reference (not shown), which consequently increases the reliability of the downstream textual support metric. Checks and Xs denote that the statement is claimed or is not claimed, respectively, by the generated text.

Claim decompositions with various characteristics are shown in Figure 1. Coverage denotes how much of the information in the claim is present in the subclaims, coherence denotes whether the information in the subclaims accurately reflects what is stated in the claim, and atomicity denotes how

*Equal contribution

[1]The terms "atomic fact" and "atomic proposition" are also used for similar concepts.

*Proceedings of the 13th Joint Conference on Lexical and Computational Semantics (*SEM 2024)*, pages 153 - 175
June 20-21, 2024 ©2024 Association for Computational Linguistics

separated the information in each subclaim is.

Evaluating subclaims individually, as opposed to the entire claim at once, we can assign partial credit to a claim (e.g., for partial support), identify which parts of the claim differ from reference texts (such as a retrieved or pre-specified document or passage), and more easily identify relevant source material for each part of the claim.[2] Claims can come from human-authored text based on cited documents (Kamoi et al., 2023; Chen et al., 2023b,c) or from machine-generated text based on dynamically provided grounding text or text observed during pre-training (Min et al., 2023).

Since claim decomposition determines the number and scope of each evaluated subclaim, any analysis or resulting metric will be inherently tied to the decomposition method. Nevertheless, prior work has left decomposition itself largely untested. How do different decomposition strategies affect downstream analysis? What are their qualitative and quantitative similarities and differences?

We show that a downstream metric of textual support such as FACTSCORE (Min et al., 2023) is sensitive to the decomposition method it uses (Figure 2). While FACTSCORE aims to measure the factual precision of generated text, the number and nature of the subclaims it evaluates from that text depend on the metric's claim decomposition method. The higher the quality of the decomposition method, and the better we understand its characteristics, the more we can attribute the factual precision that FACTSCORE aims to measure to the text generation model rather than to artifacts of the decomposition.

Finding that the method of claim decomposition matters, we introduce DECOMPSCORE, an adaptation of FACTSCORE that measures decomposition quality, an important step in determining the reliability of the downstream metric. DECOMPSCORE measures the number of subclaims supported by the original claim that was decomposed. Because a decomposition with high atomicity and coverage will have more subclaims than a decomposition that doesn't, we then favor the decomposition method with the greatest DECOMPSCORE, especially when coupled with qualitative evidence of high atomicity and coverage.

With a way to compare decomposition methods in hand, we propose an LLM-based decomposition approach inspired by Bertrand Russell's theory of logical atomism and neo-Davidsonian semantics. Our approach gives far more subclaims than other methods while maintaining high coherence with the claim being decomposed, and thus results in greater confidence in the entire pipeline for evaluating the level of textual support.

Our contributions are:

1. Empirical evidence that the method of claim decomposition affects a downstream metric of textual support;

2. Quantitative and qualitative comparisons of claim decomposition methods;

3. A method for claim decomposition inspired by philosophical and semantic theories that outperforms previous methods.

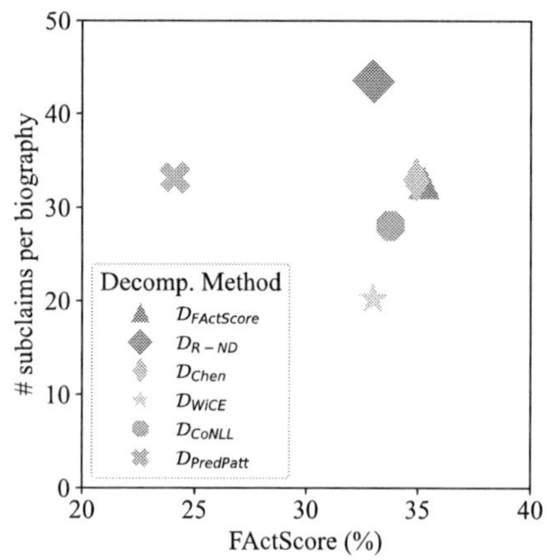

Figure 2: FACTSCORE (macro-averaged across LM_{SUBJ}) using different decomposition methods. The same underlying set of documents is assigned different FACTSCORE values depending on the decomposition method used.

2 Localized Textual Support

FACTSCORE (Min et al., 2023) and WICE (Kamoi et al., 2023) are representative examples of current LLM-based approaches for determining support for particular claims for different downstream use cases. Broadly, methods of this type decompose a claim into its subclaims, evaluate each subclaim for its level of support based on external sources,

[2]For example, separating the claim "Charles Babbage was a French mathematician" into the atomic subclaims "Charles Babbage was French" and "Charles Babbage was a mathematician" enables a claim verification system to determine that the subclaim about his occupation is supported by trusted reference documents and that the subclaim about his nationality is not supported. The non-atomic original claim as written, however, is not supported.

Name	Instruction	In-Context Examples			
		Static	Dynamic	Sentences	Decompositions
$\mathcal{D}_{\text{FActScore}}$	"Please breakdown the following sentence into independent facts:" (Min et al., 2023)	7	1	Min et al. (2023)	Min et al. (2023)
$\mathcal{D}_{\text{WiCE}}$	"Segment the following sentence into individual facts:" (Kamoi et al., 2023)	6	0	Kamoi et al. (2023)	Kamoi et al. (2023)
$\mathcal{D}_{\text{Chen et al.}}$	"Given the following sentence, tell me what claims they are making. Please split the sentence as much as possible, but do not include information not in the sentence:" (Chen et al., 2023c)	7	1	Min et al. (2023)	Min et al. (2023)
$\mathcal{D}_{\text{CoNLL-U}}$	"The sentence below is given in CoNLL-U format. Word lines contain the annotation of a word/token/node in 10 fields separated by single tab characters. Sentences consist of one or more word lines. Please break down the following sentence given in CoNLL-U format into independent facts:"	1	1	Min et al. (2023) + CoNLL-U Parse	Min et al. (2023)
$\mathcal{D}_{\text{R-ND}}$	"Please decompose the following sentence into individual facts:"	7	1	Min et al. (2023)	**Manual (ours)**

Table 1: Summary of LLM prompted claim decomposition methods used in this work (method names are prefixed with $\mathcal{D}$ for "decomposer"). The prompt given to the LLM is a concatenation of the instruction, statically and dynamically selected in-context examples, and the sentence to be decomposed. The in-context decomposition examples used in our approach ($\mathcal{D}_{\text{R-ND}}$) are based on Russellian and neo-Davidsonian theories (§5).

and then aggregate results to give a single score or label for the entire claim. Since each subclaim is evaluated, we get a localized view of which parts of the claim are supported. The more atomic the subclaims are, the more precisely we can localize the information in the claim that differs from a trusted reference. Since these approaches rely on decomposition, the better the decomposition method the more reliable the results.

FACTSCORE (Min et al., 2023) measures factual precision of model-generated text with respect to a knowledge source. A generated passage is split into sentences, which are decomposed into subclaims by an LLM. The percentage of subclaims supported by a retrieved knowledge source (e.g., Wikipedia excerpts) is the FACTSCORE for the passage. FAITHSCORE (Jing et al., 2023) takes a similar approach for evaluating the outputs of vision-language models, in which the knowledge source against which the subclaims are evaluated is an image. They additionally require that the subclaims fit into certain domain-specific categories such as color and count.

The WICE dataset (Kamoi et al., 2023) contains annotations for whether subclaims in human-written text are supported, partially supported, or not supported by external reference documents, from which claim-level support labels are derived. Kamoi et al. (2023) also apply their LLM-based Claim-Split approach to entailment classification, in which entailment scores for each subclaim are aggregated to give an entailment score for the whole claim.

3 Evaluating Decomposition Quality

Previous work on evaluating the veracity of generated text attributes the resulting score to the quality of the generation, overlooking the role of metric's decomposition step. However, higher quality decompositions mean that we can more reliably measure the quality of the generation. Depending on the characteristics of the decomposition method (e.g., how atomic its decompositions are), a metric like FACTSCORE can change for the same underlying generated text (Figure 2). Furthermore, FACTSCORE implicitly assumes complete and coherent decompositions. However, the decomposition step can introduce unclaimed information or omit existing (possibly incorrect) claims, which introduces measurement error into FACTSCORE.

3.1 Qualitative Evaluation

What makes a decomposition higher quality? The subclaims must be faithful to the original claim. In other words, they must cohere with (are supported or entailed by) the original claim.[3] To be of

[3]In contrast to the coherence theory of truth, the correspondence theory deems a statement to be true if it matches a situation in reality. It is not in the purview of a decomposition model to determine whether a claim agrees with a knowledge source; that is the purpose of the validator. In other words,

the greatest use for localizing discrepancies with a trusted reference, the subclaims should cover all parts of the claim and also be as atomic as possible. Different methods decompose claims to various degrees, with some methods producing more or fewer subclaims. We explore these various characteristics across decomposition methods in §8.1.

3.2 Quantitative Evaluation: DECOMPSCORE

We develop a measure of decomposition method quality by utilizing the same procedure as FACTSCORE, namely using an LLM to assign a binary judgment of support for every subclaim. Rather than providing an external knowledge source as context for the validator, we provide the original sentence that was decomposed, thus identifying the subclaims that are supported by the original sentence.

The DECOMPSCORE of a decomposition method is the average number of supported subclaims per passage produced by that decomposition method. This metric indicates which method generates the most subclaims that cohere with the sentence being decomposed. For example, if a text is decomposed into a large number of subclaims but DECOMPSCORE is low, we can infer that the subclaims produced by the decomposition method are not of good quality. The optimal value of DECOMPSCORE for a particular passage is difficult to determine because we do not have a set of reference decompositions, but in general, methods that produce decompositions with high atomicity and coverage will achieve higher DECOMPSCORE.

Entailment is another notion of coherence that could be used to evaluate whether a subclaim is a valid part of the decomposition. In practice, we find high correlation (Figure 7 in Appendix C) between DECOMPSCORE and the average number of subclaims entailed by the original claim using a strong natural language inference (NLI) model (Nie et al., 2020).[4]

the validator is the "fact checker". A validator that appeals to a knowledge source is actually following a coherence theory of truth (where the given set of statements is the information contained in the knowledge source). The validator's adherence to a coherence theory of truth is apparent if we consider a case in which the subclaims are not grounded in reality but rather derived from a work of fiction. We can judge a statement like "Sherlock Holmes lives at 221B Baker Street" to be true even though it is false in reality.

[4]https://huggingface.co/ynie/roberta-large-snli_mnli_fever_anli_R1_R2_R3-nli

4 Methods of Claim Decomposition

We study three types of claim decomposition methods, which are discussed below.

4.1 LLM prompting

Much of the recent work for claim decomposition utilizes a prompted LLM-based method, typically with in-context example decompositions (Min et al., 2023; Kamoi et al., 2023; Chen et al., 2023c; Jing et al., 2023; Mohri and Hashimoto, 2024). The in-context examples can be dynamically selected using a retrieval model (Min et al., 2023). We use three instructions from prior work (Min et al., 2023; Chen et al., 2023c; Kamoi et al., 2023) and one of our own, with various static and retrieved in-context examples. Notably, our approach uses manually decomposed in-context examples based on philosophical and linguistic theories, which are discussed in §5. The approaches' configurations are outlined in Table 1.

The LLM prompting approach is flexible and unstructured, allowing for the generation of arbitrary text. This text generation nature of LLMs produces fluent natural language decompositions by incorporating words outside the original sentence (in contrast to, e.g., PROPSEGMENT (Chen et al., 2023b)), but this also permits hallucinations and forces us to relinquish control over the model's outputs due to the large output space. We can adapt the instructions and in-context examples to encourage certain characteristics in the output (such as coherence and atomicity), but ultimately there is no mechanism to guarantee they are reflected in the output. However, in-context examples that are dynamically chosen based on high similarity with the claim to be decomposed could encourage similar styles of decomposition, which may provide some amount of controllability. A simple prompt-in, subclaims-out interface also avoids issues of parsing into and generating out of an explicit intermediate semantic representation, designing such a representation in the first place, and overcoming any structural weaknesses in such a representation.

4.2 Shallow semantic parsing

Rather than relying on an LLM for the decomposition, we can use a more structured analysis of the text. We use PredPatt (White et al., 2016; Zhang et al., 2017), a rule-based system for extracting predicate-argument sub-structures from a syntactic dependency parse. We take these sub-structures as representing the propositional content of subclaims. Goyal and Durrett (2020) use similar intuitions about a correspondence between syntactic dependency arcs and semantic units to decompose a claim based on arcs in a dependency parse.

The resulting subclaims contain only words from the original sentence, and are often not grammatical sentences.[5] The subclaims in a valid decomposition should be full sentences in order to be validated by DECOMPSCORE and FACTSCORE, and for this reason, we use an LLM (`gpt-3.5-turbo-instruct`) to convert the PredPatt outputs into fluent, natural language. Details are given in Appendix B. Although the resulting strings are often full grammatical sentences, the LLM does not guarantee this behavior.[6]

4.3 LLM prompting with parse

Combining syntactic structure with the flexibility of text generation could support a more grounded decomposition from an LLM. We use an LLM prompting method, but this time supplied with a parsed version of the original sentence. We use Trankit (Nguyen et al., 2021), a state-of-the-art dependency parser, to obtain dependency parses (Zeman et al., 2019) (in the CoNLL-U format) of each claim as well as each in-context learning example. Because CoNLL-U formatted parses (Nivre et al., 2017) are token-heavy, fewer in-context examples are provided. Prompt details can be found in Table 1.

This method inherits the fluency and flexibility of LLM prompting while grounding the LLM's response in a syntactic analysis, resulting in (hopefully) a higher quality decomposition. While we hope the added structure imposes controllability, LLMs can still generate subclaims that do not cohere with the original claim.

5 Russellian and Neo-Davidsonian decomposition

The notion of claim decomposition has roots in the philosophical literature. We draw inspiration from Bertrand Russell's theory of logical atomism for how claims should be decomposed into their atomic components.

Russell defines atomic facts as properties of individuals or relations between individuals from which all other facts are composed (Russell, 1918b).[7, 8] We take individuals to be entities and eventualities mentioned in the sentence. This kind of Russellian analysis accords with neo-Davidsonian analysis (Castañeda, 1967; Parsons, 1990) (building on Davidson (1967)), in which the logical form of a sentence is decomposed fully to a conjunction of unary predicates (akin to properties of individuals) and binary predicates (akin to relations between individuals).

We manually decompose the 21 in-context examples from Min et al. (2023) into lists of such Russellian atomic propositions that we further decompose following neo-Davidsonian intuitions into unary and binary relations to obtain the smallest units that are claimed in each sentence: each subclaim designates a property of an individual or a relation between two individuals.[9] Our decompositions are listed in Table 10. These in-context examples are retrieved in the same way as the examples are retrieved for the FACTSCORE prompt.

6 Data

We use the released data from Min et al. (2023), which consists of biographies of 500 individuals generated from each of 12 LMs (following their notation, we call the text generation models LM_{SUBJ}).[10] We do not modify the biographies generated by Min et al. (2023), nor do we generate

[5] PredPatt can add short strings like "is/are" and "poss" to indicate being and possession, respectively, but these additions do not make the propositions fluent.

[6] A model for determining grammatical acceptability could be included in this approach to filter out ungrammatical strings or send them back for rewriting (Warstadt et al., 2019).

[7] Ludwig Wittgenstein theorizes a similar idea of elementary propositions that assert atomic "states of affairs". On the whole, we find Wittgenstein's theory to be less actionable than Russell's. Incidentally, Wittgenstein later abandoned this theory in part due to the color exclusion problem, which we avoid by not requiring independence of subclaims, instead requiring only that each subclaim is claimed by the sentence.

[8] For Russell, "facts" are "the kind of thing that makes a proposition true or false" (Russell, 1918a), and for Wittgenstein they are states of affairs. In both cases, they are not propositions but rather conditions of the world. Russell and Wittgenstein use the terms "atomic proposition" and "elementary proposition", respectively, to refer to the corresponding truth function or expression of an atomic fact. The NLP literature uses the term "atomic fact" to mean the corresponding proposition, typically written in natural language.

[9] We do not include existence as a property of entities. Consider the sentences: "Allan Pinkerton was a detective who worked in the United States." and "Sherlock Holmes was a detective who worked in London." From just the sentences alone and without external knowledge, there is no way to tell that one of these people existed and one didn't.

[10] GPT-4 (OpenAI, 2023); ChatGPT; InstructGPT; Alpaca 7B, 13B, 65B (Taori et al., 2023); Vicuna 7B, 13B (Chiang et al., 2023); Dolly 12B (Biderman et al., 2023); StableLM-tuned-alpha 7B (Taori et al., 2023; Chiang et al., 2023; Anand et al., 2023); Oasst-pythia 12B; and MPT Chat 7B.

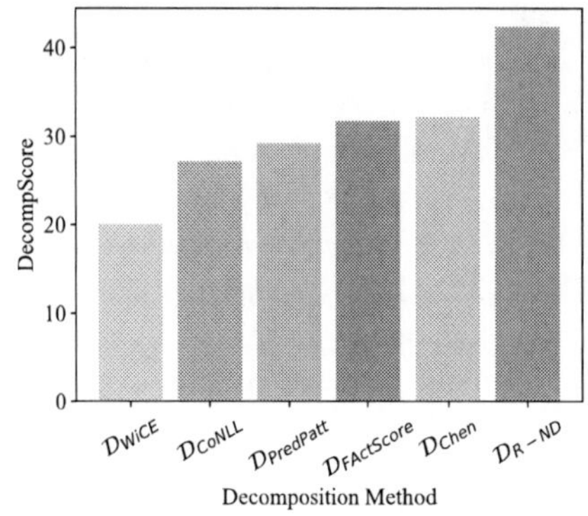

Figure 3: DECOMPSCORE (macro-averaged across LM_{SUBJ}) of different decomposition methods. A higher DECOMPSCORE is better.

additional ones. We treat them as static documents to investigate various decomposition methods applied to the sentences in the biographies.

7 Experiments

We use the data described in §6 for sentence-level decomposition with the methods outlined in §4 and §5. Model specifications are listed in Appendix B. We evaluate using DECOMPSCORE with Inst-LLAMA from Min et al. (2023) (LLAMA trained on Super Natural Instructions (Wang et al., 2022; Touvron et al., 2023)) and FACTSCORE with the Inst-LLAMA + retrieval + NPM setting. In total, generating decompositions took 120 GPU-hours, computing DECOMPSCORE took 250 GPU-hours, and computing FACTSCORE took 450 GPU-hours, all using a Quadro RTX 6000.

8 Results

DECOMPSCORE results are shown in Figure 3, with full results in Table 2 (Appendix A). $\mathcal{D}_{\text{R-ND}}$ attains the highest DECOMPSCORE (i.e., highest average number of supported subclaims per biography) with 42.3, followed by $\mathcal{D}_{\text{Chen et al.}}$ and $\mathcal{D}_{\text{FActScore}}$, both with around 32. $\mathcal{D}_{\text{WiCE}}$ produces the fewest average supported subclaims, with a DECOMPSCORE of 20.0, less than half that of $\mathcal{D}_{\text{R-ND}}$. The DECOMPSCOREs of $\mathcal{D}_{\text{PredPatt}}$ and $\mathcal{D}_{\text{CoNLL-U}}$ fall between $\mathcal{D}_{\text{WiCE}}$ and $\mathcal{D}_{\text{FActScore}}$, with $\mathcal{D}_{\text{PredPatt}}$ achieving a slightly higher DECOMPSCORE (29.2) than $\mathcal{D}_{\text{CoNLL-U}}$ (27.1).

FACTSCORE results are shown in Figure 2, with full results in Table 4 and Figure 4 (Appendix A). Undesirably, the FACTSCORE values vary based on the decomposition method used.

8.1 Qualitative Analysis

We analyze all decomposition methods on two sentences generated by GPT-4: one about Alfred Hitchcock and one about John Nash.[11] The decompositions, alongside our own manual decompositions, are shown in Table 8 and Table 9 in Appendix D. The evaluation criteria we use are coherence to the original sentence, coverage of the information claimed, and atomicity.

We observe that for the sentence about Alfred Hitchcock (Table 8), no decomposition method separates the date into month, day, and year or the location into city and state. No method generates the subclaim "Alfred Hitchcock passed away", opting to always include the date or location. Additionally, no method outputs all four combinations arising from the conjunction of "captivate" and "inspire" with "audiences" and "filmmakers". $\mathcal{D}_{\text{R-ND}}$ is the only method to separate "suspenseful" from "thrilling"; every other method keeps them as one unit. Similarly, many methods keep "captivate and inspire" as one unit; $\mathcal{D}_{\text{R-ND}}$ and $\mathcal{D}_{\text{FActScore}}$ are the only ones to always split this conjunction.

We see that for the sentence about John Nash (Table 9), $\mathcal{D}_{\text{R-ND}}$, $\mathcal{D}_{\text{FActScore}}$, and $\mathcal{D}_{\text{Chen et al.}}$ all output a large number of subclaims. However, many of the subclaims generated by $\mathcal{D}_{\text{FActScore}}$ and $\mathcal{D}_{\text{Chen et al.}}$ incrementally add information to their other subclaims, which makes them non-atomic. This behavior of incrementally adding information can be expected given that it occurs in the in-context examples used by Min et al. (2023). This incrementality makes it more difficult to localize errors in the original claim because the textual support of the new information in the subclaim undesirably depends on the re-used information also being supported. All methods except for $\mathcal{D}_{\text{WiCE}}$ generate non-atomic subclaims that combine Nash's bachelor's and master's degrees. $\mathcal{D}_{\text{R-ND}}$, $\mathcal{D}_{\text{CoNLL-U}}$, and $\mathcal{D}_{\text{PredPatt}}$ mention the degrees without the additional information that they were for mathematics, which increases atomicity; the other methods describe them always as "degree[s] in mathematics".

In our experiments, $\mathcal{D}_{\text{FActScore}}$ and $\mathcal{D}_{\text{Chen et al.}}$ use the same in-context examples with slightly dif-

[11]"Alfred Hitchcock passed away on April 29, 1980, in Bel-Air, California, leaving behind a rich legacy of suspenseful and thrilling films that continue to captivate and inspire audiences and filmmakers alike." and "Nash demonstrated a natural aptitude for mathematics from a young age and earned his bachelor's and master's degrees in mathematics from the Carnegie Institute of Technology (now Carnegie Mellon University) in 1948."

ferent instructions and generate similar decompositions on the two sentences (identical decompositions on the Nash sentence). This behavior suggests that the in-context examples influence the decomposition more than the instruction does.

Takeaways For both sentences, we observe that many subclaims in our manual decompositions are missed by the decomposition methods, but the methods with the most coverage are $\mathcal{D}_{\text{R-ND}}$, $\mathcal{D}_{\text{Chen et al.}}$, $\mathcal{D}_{\text{FActScore}}$, and $\mathcal{D}_{\text{WiCE}}$. All methods but $\mathcal{D}_{\text{PredPatt}}$ have perfect coherence for both sentences. In general, we observe that $\mathcal{D}_{\text{WiCE}}$ has low atomicity,[12] as does $\mathcal{D}_{\text{CoNLL-U}}$ because it does not split conjunctions. $\mathcal{D}_{\text{PredPatt}}$ exhibits many issues: its subclaims are not atomic, often not fluent (despite using an LLM to make them more fluent), and not coherent with the original claim (e.g., "The bachelor possessed a master's degree").

8.2 Quantitative Analysis

Even though all decomposition methods are run on the same set of static biographies, they differ in FACTSCORE and number of subclaims generated (averaged over LM_{SUBJ}: Figure 2, per LM_{SUBJ}: Table 4). This finding indicates that FACTSCORE is sensitive to the method of decomposition that is used. The most reliable estimate of the generated text's "true" factual precision is the FACTSCORE achieved by the highest quality decomposition method.

We hypothesize that $\mathcal{D}_{\text{PredPatt}}$'s FACTSCORE is low because it produces subclaims not likely to be supported by the external knowledge source,[13] while also being constrained to using only the words in the sentence and missing implicit subclaims not extractable as predicate-argument structures from the dependency parse. Additionally, only 86% of the subclaims it produces are supported by the original claim (Table 6 in Appendix A), which agrees with our previous observation that its outputs have low coherence.

$\mathcal{D}_{\text{FActScore}}$ and $\mathcal{D}_{\text{Chen et al.}}$ both achieve a DECOMPSCORE around 32, and since they use the same in-context examples in our experiments, this further suggests that the decompositions are robust to the wording of the instruction in the prompt. Additionally, the similarity of the configuration of $\mathcal{D}_{\text{R-ND}}$ to those of $\mathcal{D}_{\text{FActScore}}$ and $\mathcal{D}_{\text{Chen et al.}}$ suggests that it is the manually decomposed in-context examples used in $\mathcal{D}_{\text{R-ND}}$ that are responsible for its higher DECOMPSCORE.

Because the in-context examples seem to have a larger effect on the decompositions than the instructions do and because we provide fewer examples in $\mathcal{D}_{\text{CoNLL-U}}$ due to the large token count of the parses, we evaluate the effect on decomposition of the number of in-context examples given. We use the same prompt specifications as in $\mathcal{D}_{\text{FActScore}}$ in Table 1, but use the same number of static examples as in $\mathcal{D}_{\text{CoNLL-U}}$ (one). We find that using fewer examples produces around the same number of subclaims (+1.3 subclaims on average), and achieves similar DECOMPSCORE (-0.69%) and FACTSCORE (+0.06%). Overall, using fewer in-context examples does not appear to have much impact on either decomposition quality or factual precision.

When evaluating FACTSCORE on only the *supported* subclaims (as determined in the calculation of DECOMPSCORE), in most cases, this subset of subclaims yields a higher FACTSCORE (Table 4, Table 5, Figure 4, Figure 5 in Appendix A),[14] indicating that subclaims which do not cohere with the original sentence are likely also not supported by the knowledge source. Although simple, this filtering step removes potential errors introduced during decomposition. The fewest amount of subclaims (0.2 on average) are removed from $\mathcal{D}_{\text{WiCE}}$'s decompositions (compare Table 2 and Table 3 in Appendix A), indicating very high coherence, and the most are removed from $\mathcal{D}_{\text{PredPatt}}$'s decompositions (4 subclaims per biography on average), suggesting low coherence to the original sentence. On average, 1.2 out of 43.5 subclaims are removed from $\mathcal{D}_{\text{R-ND}}$'s decompositions.

To ensure that decompositions have high coherence, we recommend that subclaims produced by a decomposition method that are not supported by the original claim be filtered out (giving full coherence by construction). In doing so, unclaimed information that is introduced during the decomposition step is removed and not incorrectly attributed back to the generated text being evaluated.

Takeaways Despite $\mathcal{D}_{\text{WiCE}}$ having high coherence and coverage, it has the lowest DECOMP-

[12] The instructions given to annotators for evaluating WICE's Claim-Split decomposition method include an example that explicitly states that one of its subclaims can be further decomposed but to ignore that issue, which suggests atomicity is not prioritized in that method.

[13] For example, the mention of "civil rights" results in the subclaim "Rights are civil", which is likely not explicitly asserted in the retrieved Wikipedia passages.

[14] There are 4 exceptions out of 84 cases, and the maximum decrease in FACTSCORE is 0.2%.

SCORE because it has low atomicity, which makes it undesirable as a decomposition method for use in a localized textual support metric.

Achieving a higher FACTSCORE with a particular decomposition method does not necessarily mean the decompositions are also of high quality. Although $\mathcal{D}_{\text{R-ND}}$ achieves lower FACTSCORE than most of the other methods, it has a far higher DECOMPSCORE than the other methods, which we hypothesize is due to our manually decomposed in-context examples. Such a method that produces a large number of supported subclaims that (qualitatively) have high coverage and atomicity is far more favorable in the textual support evaluation setting because it increases confidence in the results obtained from the downstream metric.

9 Related Work

Evaluation We evaluated decomposition methods that produce subclaims in sentential natural language, primarily by using contemporary technologies like large language models (§4). We review other methods of decomposition used in evaluation of textual support here.

Question answering (Wang et al., 2020; Durmus et al., 2020; Scialom et al., 2021; Fabbri et al., 2022) has been used for evaluating abstractive summarization. These methods generally ask questions only about noun phrases, require generating questions (the decomposition step), and require extracting answer spans, after which (typically lexical) heuristics determine if the answers between the summary and reference agree. Higher decomposition quality in this paradigm would involve generating a large number of highly focused questions, which would give better localized coverage of the claims made in the summary.

Goodrich et al. (2019) evaluate summarization by extracting relation tuples from a model-generated summary which are compared to relations extracted from a ground-truth summary. Fan et al. (2023) improve upon this approach by extracting fact tuples using semantic role labeling. Goyal and Durrett (2020) evaluate the factuality of model-generated text by obtaining entailment labels on each arc in a dependency parse, which assumes a correspondence between syntactic dependency arcs and semantic units (the same core assumption made by PredPatt).

In addition to evaluating *whether* text is supported, there has also been work on evaluating types of textual errors (Pagnoni et al., 2021; Devaraj et al., 2022; Mishra et al., 2024) and evaluating ambiguously supported claims (Glockner et al., 2024). Although designed to be used at the sentence-level, such methodologies can also be applied to subclaims. For further discussion about identifying and mitigating errors in model-generated text, such as hallucinations, we refer the reader to Ji et al. (2023) and Ye et al. (2023).

NLI Decomposition is also used for sub-sentence level NLI. PROPSEGMENT (Chen et al., 2023b) identifies subclaims by marking tokens in a claim that are part of the subclaim. They use propositional-level NLI to detect hallucinations by comparing tokens in entailed and non-entailed propositions. Sub-sentence entailment judgments can also be combined to make sentence-level or paragraph-level entailment judgments more interpretable and robust (Stacey et al., 2022, 2023; Kamoi et al., 2023).

Fact Verification Verifying the accuracy of statements depends on high quality decompositions to facilitate evidence retrieval. Chen et al. (2023a) build a system for complex claim verification by generating lists of yes/no questions that align to specific aspects of a claim. Chen et al. (2022) build a similar system that also asks implied subquestions. Li et al. (2023) and Milbauer et al. (2023) align generated claims with statements in documents that entail or contradict the claim. Similarly, Ernst et al. (2021) align propositions between reference summaries and source documents—which is similar to the fact verification task. A model trained on their dataset was later used to cluster propositions in a system for multi-document summarization (Ernst et al., 2022). Chen et al. (2023c) use decomposition to find matching subclaims ("atomic propositions") across sentences to train proposition-level representations using contrastive learning. The proposition representations are used for retrieving propositions from a corpus that support a given proposition.

10 Conclusion

We observe that a downstream metric of textual support, namely factual precision as measured by FACTSCORE, is sensitive to the method it uses to decompose a claim into its subclaims. This finding leads us to measure decomposition quality using our proposed metric DECOMPSCORE so that we can use the most appropriate decomposition method among those we consider.

We show that an LLM prompted with in-context learning examples that we manually decompose by following intuitions from logical atomism and neo-Davidsonian semantics outperforms other methods. Decompositions generated by our method contain the greatest number of subclaims supported by the original claim among the methods we consider. Qualitative analysis and comparison to manual decompositions demonstrate that all the decomposition methods we consider still miss subclaims and many generate non-atomic subclaims, indicating there still remains room for improvement.

Limitations

Metrics like FACTSCORE and DECOMPSCORE are able to evaluate only information that is claimed in a generated text. Information relevant to an upstream query may be absent in the text, whether accidentally or intentionally, and these evaluation approaches cannot account for that.

This study is limited to the domain of entity biographies, so it is not representative of all use cases. Additionally, the data is monolingual (English), and we do not know if these results hold across other languages.

Running LLMs can be expensive. Because of this, we chose to use LLAMA instead of ChatGPT as the validator, but even running that model is not financially feasible for everyone to use.

Ethics Statement

LLMs are well-known to hallucinate information, and mitigation of hallucination is still an active area of research. Using LLMs to decompose a claim into subclaims can introduce new factual errors. Despite attempts to remove such errors (for example, by filtering out subclaims that are not supported by the original claim according to DECOMPSCORE), errors can still persist. Caution must be taken when relying on text generated from a model.

Acknowledgements

We thank Nathaniel Weir, Kate Sanders, and Anqi Liu for helpful discussions, as well as the anonymous reviewers for their feedback. This work has been supported in part by the U.S. National Science Foundation under grant No. 2204926.

References

Yuvanesh Anand, Zach Nussbaum, Brandon Duderstadt, Benjamin Schmidt, and Andriy Mulyar. 2023. Gpt4all: Training an assistant-style chatbot with large scale data distillation from gpt-3.5-turbo. https://github.com/nomic-ai/gpt4all.

Stella Biderman, Hailey Schoelkopf, Quentin Gregory Anthony, Herbie Bradley, Kyle O'Brien, Eric Hallahan, Mohammad Aflah Khan, Shivanshu Purohit, Usvsn Sai Prashanth, Edward Raff, Aviya Skowron, Lintang Sutawika, and Oskar Van Der Wal. 2023. Pythia: A suite for analyzing large language models across training and scaling. In *Proceedings of the 40th International Conference on Machine Learning*, volume 202 of *Proceedings of Machine Learning Research*, pages 2397–2430. PMLR.

Héctor-Neri Castañeda. 1967. Comments on D. Davidson's 'The logical form of action sentences'. In Nicholas Rescher, editor, *The Logic of Decision and Action*, pages 104–112. University of Pittsburgh Press.

Jifan Chen, Grace Kim, Aniruddh Sriram, Greg Durrett, and Eunsol Choi. 2023a. Complex claim verification with evidence retrieved in the wild. *arXiv preprint arXiv:2305.11859*.

Jifan Chen, Aniruddh Sriram, Eunsol Choi, and Greg Durrett. 2022. Generating literal and implied subquestions to fact-check complex claims. In *Proceedings of the 2022 Conference on Empirical Methods in Natural Language Processing*, pages 3495–3516, Abu Dhabi, United Arab Emirates. Association for Computational Linguistics.

Sihao Chen, Senaka Buthpitiya, Alex Fabrikant, Dan Roth, and Tal Schuster. 2023b. PropSegmEnt: A large-scale corpus for proposition-level segmentation and entailment recognition. In *Findings of the Association for Computational Linguistics: ACL 2023*, pages 8874–8893, Toronto, Canada. Association for Computational Linguistics.

Sihao Chen, Hongming Zhang, Tong Chen, Ben Zhou, Wenhao Yu, Dian Yu, Baolin Peng, Hongwei Wang, Dan Roth, and Dong Yu. 2023c. Sub-sentence encoder: Contrastive learning of propositional semantic representations. *arXiv preprint arXiv:2311.04335*.

Wei-Lin Chiang, Zhuohan Li, Zi Lin, Ying Sheng, Zhanghao Wu, Hao Zhang, Lianmin Zheng, Siyuan Zhuang, Yonghao Zhuang, Joseph E. Gonzalez, Ion Stoica, and Eric P. Xing. 2023. Vicuna: An Open-Source Chatbot Impressing GPT-4 with 90%* ChatGPT Quality.

Donald Davidson. 1967. The logical form of action sentences. In Nicholas Rescher, editor, *The Logic of Decision and Action*, pages 81–95. University of Pittsburgh Press.

Ashwin Devaraj, William Sheffield, Byron Wallace, and Junyi Jessy Li. 2022. Evaluating factuality in text simplification. In *Proceedings of the 60th Annual Meeting of the Association for Computational Linguistics (Volume 1: Long Papers)*, pages 7331–7345, Dublin, Ireland. Association for Computational Linguistics.

Esin Durmus, He He, and Mona Diab. 2020. FEQA: A question answering evaluation framework for faithfulness assessment in abstractive summarization. In *Proceedings of the 58th Annual Meeting of the Association for Computational Linguistics*, pages 5055–5070, Online. Association for Computational Linguistics.

Ori Ernst, Avi Caciularu, Ori Shapira, Ramakanth Pasunuru, Mohit Bansal, Jacob Goldberger, and Ido Dagan. 2022. Proposition-level clustering for multi-document summarization. In *Proceedings of the 2022 Conference of the North American Chapter of the Association for Computational Linguistics: Human Language Technologies*, pages 1765–1779, Seattle, United States. Association for Computational Linguistics.

Ori Ernst, Ori Shapira, Ramakanth Pasunuru, Michael Lepioshkin, Jacob Goldberger, Mohit Bansal, and Ido Dagan. 2021. Summary-source proposition-level alignment: Task, datasets and supervised baseline. In *Proceedings of the 25th Conference on Computational Natural Language Learning*, pages 310–322, Online. Association for Computational Linguistics.

Alexander Fabbri, Chien-Sheng Wu, Wenhao Liu, and Caiming Xiong. 2022. QAFactEval: Improved QA-based factual consistency evaluation for summarization. In *Proceedings of the 2022 Conference of the North American Chapter of the Association for Computational Linguistics: Human Language Technologies*, pages 2587–2601, Seattle, United States. Association for Computational Linguistics.

Jing Fan, Dennis Aumiller, and Michael Gertz. 2023. Evaluating factual consistency of texts with semantic role labeling. In *Proceedings of the 12th Joint Conference on Lexical and Computational Semantics (*SEM 2023)*, pages 89–100, Toronto, Canada. Association for Computational Linguistics.

Max Glockner, Ieva Staliūnaitė, James Thorne, Gisela Vallejo, Andreas Vlachos, and Iryna Gurevych. 2024. AmbiFC: Fact-Checking Ambiguous Claims with Evidence. *Transactions of the Association for Computational Linguistics*, 12:1–18.

Ben Goodrich, Vinay Rao, Peter J. Liu, and Mohammad Saleh. 2019. Assessing the factual accuracy of generated text. In *Proceedings of the 25th ACM SIGKDD International Conference on Knowledge Discovery & Data Mining*, KDD '19, page 166–175, New York, NY, USA. Association for Computing Machinery.

Tanya Goyal and Greg Durrett. 2020. Evaluating factuality in generation with dependency-level entailment. In *Findings of the Association for Computational Linguistics: EMNLP 2020*, pages 3592–3603, Online. Association for Computational Linguistics.

Andrew Hickl and Jeremy Bensley. 2007. A discourse commitment-based framework for recognizing textual entailment. In *Proceedings of the ACL-PASCAL Workshop on Textual Entailment and Paraphrasing*, pages 171–176, Prague. Association for Computational Linguistics.

Ziwei Ji, Nayeon Lee, Rita Frieske, Tiezheng Yu, Dan Su, Yan Xu, Etsuko Ishii, Ye Jin Bang, Andrea Madotto, and Pascale Fung. 2023. Survey of hallucination in natural language generation. *ACM Comput. Surv.*, 55(12).

Liqiang Jing, Ruosen Li, Yunmo Chen, Mengzhao Jia, and Xinya Du. 2023. Faithscore: Evaluating hallucinations in large vision-language models.

Ryo Kamoi, Tanya Goyal, Juan Diego Rodriguez, and Greg Durrett. 2023. WiCE: Real-world entailment for claims in Wikipedia. In *Proceedings of the 2023 Conference on Empirical Methods in Natural Language Processing*, pages 7561–7583, Singapore. Association for Computational Linguistics.

Miaoran Li, Baolin Peng, and Zhu Zhang. 2023. Self-checker: Plug-and-play modules for fact-checking with large language models. *arXiv preprint arXiv:2305.14623*.

Jeremiah Milbauer, Ziqi Ding, Zhijin Wu, and Tongshuang Wu. 2023. NewsSense: Reference-free verification via cross-document comparison. In *Proceedings of the 2023 Conference on Empirical Methods in Natural Language Processing: System Demonstrations*, pages 422–430, Singapore. Association for Computational Linguistics.

Sewon Min, Kalpesh Krishna, Xinxi Lyu, Mike Lewis, Wen-tau Yih, Pang Koh, Mohit Iyyer, Luke Zettlemoyer, and Hannaneh Hajishirzi. 2023. FActScore: Fine-grained atomic evaluation of factual precision in long form text generation. In *Proceedings of the 2023 Conference on Empirical Methods in Natural Language Processing*, pages 12076–12100, Singapore. Association for Computational Linguistics.

Abhika Mishra, Akari Asai, Vidhisha Balachandran, Yizhong Wang, Graham Neubig, Yulia Tsvetkov, and Hannaneh Hajishirzi. 2024. Fine-grained hallucination detection and editing for language models. *arXiv preprint arXiv:2401.06855*.

Christopher Mohri and Tatsunori Hashimoto. 2024. Language models with conformal factuality guarantees. *arXiv preprint arXiv:2402.10978*.

Minh Van Nguyen, Viet Dac Lai, Amir Pouran Ben Veyseh, and Thien Huu Nguyen. 2021. Trankit: A light-weight transformer-based toolkit for multilingual natural language processing. In *Proceedings of the 16th Conference of the European Chapter of the Association for Computational Linguistics: System Demonstrations*, pages 80–90, Online. Association for Computational Linguistics.

Yixin Nie, Adina Williams, Emily Dinan, Mohit Bansal, Jason Weston, and Douwe Kiela. 2020. Adversarial NLI: A new benchmark for natural language understanding. In *Proceedings of the 58th Annual Meeting of the Association for Computational Linguistics*, pages 4885–4901, Online. Association for Computational Linguistics.

Joakim Nivre, Daniel Zeman, Filip Ginter, and Francis Tyers. 2017. Universal Dependencies. In *Proceedings of the 15th Conference of the European Chapter of the Association for Computational Linguistics: Tutorial Abstracts*, Valencia, Spain. Association for Computational Linguistics.

OpenAI. 2023. Gpt-4 technical report.

Artidoro Pagnoni, Vidhisha Balachandran, and Yulia Tsvetkov. 2021. Understanding factuality in abstractive summarization with FRANK: A benchmark for factuality metrics. In *Proceedings of the 2021 Conference of the North American Chapter of the Association for Computational Linguistics: Human Language Technologies*, pages 4812–4829, Online. Association for Computational Linguistics.

Terence Parsons. 1990. *Events in the Semantics of English: A Study in Subatomic Semantics*. MIT Press.

Bertrand Russell. 1918a. The philosophy of logical atomism, lecture 1. *The Monist*, 28.

Bertrand Russell. 1918b. The philosophy of logical atomism, lecture 2. *The Monist*, 28.

Thomas Scialom, Paul-Alexis Dray, Sylvain Lamprier, Benjamin Piwowarski, Jacopo Staiano, Alex Wang, and Patrick Gallinari. 2021. QuestEval: Summarization asks for fact-based evaluation. In *Proceedings of the 2021 Conference on Empirical Methods in Natural Language Processing*, pages 6594–6604, Online and Punta Cana, Dominican Republic. Association for Computational Linguistics.

Joe Stacey, Pasquale Minervini, Haim Dubossarsky, Oana-Maria Camburu, and Marek Rei. 2023. Logical reasoning for natural language inference using generated facts as atoms. *arXiv preprint arXiv:2305.13214*.

Joe Stacey, Pasquale Minervini, Haim Dubossarsky, and Marek Rei. 2022. Logical reasoning with span-level predictions for interpretable and robust NLI models. In *Proceedings of the 2022 Conference on Empirical Methods in Natural Language Processing*, pages 3809–3823, Abu Dhabi, United Arab Emirates. Association for Computational Linguistics.

Liyan Tang, Philippe Laban, and Greg Durrett. 2024. Minicheck: Efficient fact-checking of llms on grounding documents. *arXiv preprint arXiv:2404.10774*.

Rohan Taori, Ishaan Gulrajani, Tianyi Zhang, Yann Dubois, Xuechen Li, Carlos Guestrin, Percy Liang, and Tatsunori B. Hashimoto. 2023. Stanford alpaca: An instruction-following llama model. `https://github.com/tatsu-lab/stanford_alpaca`.

Hugo Touvron, Thibaut Lavril, Gautier Izacard, Xavier Martinet, Marie-Anne Lachaux, Timothée Lacroix, Baptiste Rozière, Naman Goyal, Eric Hambro, Faisal Azhar, Aurelien Rodriguez, Armand Joulin, Edouard Grave, and Guillaume Lample. 2023. Llama: Open and efficient foundation language models. *arXiv preprint arXiv:2302.13971*.

Alex Wang, Kyunghyun Cho, and Mike Lewis. 2020. Asking and answering questions to evaluate the factual consistency of summaries. In *Proceedings of the 58th Annual Meeting of the Association for Computational Linguistics*, pages 5008–5020, Online. Association for Computational Linguistics.

Yizhong Wang, Swaroop Mishra, Pegah Alipoormolabashi, Yeganeh Kordi, Amirreza Mirzaei, Atharva Naik, Arjun Ashok, Arut Selvan Dhanasekaran, Anjana Arunkumar, David Stap, Eshaan Pathak, Giannis Karamanolakis, Haizhi Lai, Ishan Purohit, Ishani Mondal, Jacob Anderson, Kirby Kuznia, Krima Doshi, Kuntal Kumar Pal, Maitreya Patel, Mehrad Moradshahi, Mihir Parmar, Mirali Purohit, Neeraj Varshney, Phani Rohitha Kaza, Pulkit Verma, Ravsehaj Singh Puri, Rushang Karia, Savan Doshi, Shailaja Keyur Sampat, Siddhartha Mishra, Sujan Reddy A, Sumanta Patro, Tanay Dixit, and Xudong Shen. 2022. Super-NaturalInstructions: Generalization via declarative instructions on 1600+ NLP tasks. In *Proceedings of the 2022 Conference on Empirical Methods in Natural Language Processing*, pages 5085–5109, Abu Dhabi, United Arab Emirates. Association for Computational Linguistics.

Alex Warstadt, Amanpreet Singh, and Samuel R. Bowman. 2019. Neural network acceptability judgments. *Transactions of the Association for Computational Linguistics*, 7:625–641.

Aaron Steven White, Drew Reisinger, Keisuke Sakaguchi, Tim Vieira, Sheng Zhang, Rachel Rudinger, Kyle Rawlins, and Benjamin Van Durme. 2016. Universal Decompositional Semantics on Universal Dependencies. In *Proceedings of the 2016 Conference on Empirical Methods in Natural Language Processing*, pages 1713–1723, Austin, Texas. Association for Computational Linguistics.

Hongbin Ye, Tong Liu, Aijia Zhang, Wei Hua, and Weiqiang Jia. 2023. Cognitive mirage: A review of hallucinations in large language models. *arXiv preprint arXiv:2309.06794*.

Daniel Zeman, Joakim Nivre, Mitchell Abrams, Noëmi Aepli, Željko Agić, Lars Ahrenberg, Gabrielė Aleksandravičiūtė, Lene Antonsen, Katya Aplonova, Maria Jesus Aranzabe, Gashaw Arutie, Masayuki Asahara, Luma Ateyah, Mohammed Attia, Aitziber Atutxa, Liesbeth Augustinus, Elena Badmaeva, Miguel Ballesteros, Esha Banerjee, Sebastian Bank, Verginica Barbu Mititelu, Victoria Basmov, Colin Batchelor, John Bauer, Sandra Bellato, Kepa Bengoetxea, Yevgeni Berzak, Irshad Ahmad Bhat, Riyaz Ahmad Bhat, Erica

Biagetti, Eckhard Bick, Agnė Bielinskienė, Rogier Blokland, Victoria Bobicev, Loïc Boizou, Emanuel Borges Völker, Carl Börstell, Cristina Bosco, Gosse Bouma, Sam Bowman, Adriane Boyd, Kristina Brokaitė, Aljoscha Burchardt, Marie Candito, Bernard Caron, Gauthier Caron, Tatiana Cavalcanti, Gülşen Cebiroğlu Eryiğit, Flavio Massimiliano Cecchini, Giuseppe G. A. Celano, Slavomír Čéplö, Savas Cetin, Fabricio Chalub, Jinho Choi, Yongseok Cho, Jayeol Chun, Alessandra T. Cignarella, Silvie Cinková, Aurélie Collomb, Çağrı Çöltekin, Miriam Connor, Marine Courtin, Elizabeth Davidson, Marie-Catherine de Marneffe, Valeria de Paiva, Elvis de Souza, Arantza Diaz de Ilarraza, Carly Dickerson, Bamba Dione, Peter Dirix, Kaja Dobrovoljc, Timothy Dozat, Kira Droganova, Puneet Dwivedi, Hanne Eckhoff, Marhaba Eli, Ali Elkahky, Binyam Ephrem, Olga Erina, Tomaž Erjavec, Aline Etienne, Wograine Evelyn, Richárd Farkas, Hector Fernandez Alcalde, Jennifer Foster, Cláudia Freitas, Kazunori Fujita, Katarína Gajdošová, Daniel Galbraith, Marcos Garcia, Moa Gärdenfors, Sebastian Garza, Kim Gerdes, Filip Ginter, Iakes Goenaga, Koldo Gojenola, Memduh Gökırmak, Yoav Goldberg, Xavier Gómez Guinovart, Berta González Saavedra, Bernadeta Griciūtė, Matias Grioni, Normunds Grūzītis, Bruno Guillaume, Céline Guillot-Barbance, Nizar Habash, Jan Hajič, Jan Hajič jr., Mika Hämäläinen, Linh Hà Mỹ, Na-Rae Han, Kim Harris, Dag Haug, Johannes Heinecke, Felix Hennig, Barbora Hladká, Jaroslava Hlaváčová, Florinel Hociung, Petter Hohle, Jena Hwang, Takumi Ikeda, Radu Ion, Elena Irimia, Ọlájídé Ishola, Tomáš Jelínek, Anders Johannsen, Fredrik Jørgensen, Markus Juutinen, Hüner Kaşıkara, Andre Kaasen, Nadezhda Kabaeva, Sylvain Kahane, Hiroshi Kanayama, Jenna Kanerva, Boris Katz, Tolga Kayadelen, Jessica Kenney, Václava Kettnerová, Jesse Kirchner, Elena Klementieva, Arne Köhn, Kamil Kopacewicz, Natalia Kotsyba, Jolanta Kovalevskaitė, Simon Krek, Sookyoung Kwak, Veronika Laippala, Lorenzo Lambertino, Lucia Lam, Tatiana Lando, Septina Dian Larasati, Alexei Lavrentiev, John Lee, Ph01AF01A1ng Lê Hồng, Alessandro Lenci, Saran Lertpradit, Herman Leung, Cheuk Ying Li, Josie Li, Keying Li, KyungTae Lim, Maria Liovina, Yuan Li, Nikola Ljubešić, Olga Loginova, Olga Lyashevskaya, Teresa Lynn, Vivien Macketanz, Aibek Makazhanov, Michael Mandl, Christopher Manning, Ruli Manurung, Cătălina Mărănduc, David Mareček, Katrin Marheinecke, Héctor Martínez Alonso, André Martins, Jan Mašek, Yuji Matsumoto, Ryan McDonald, Sarah McGuinness, Gustavo Mendonça, Niko Miekka, Margarita Misirpashayeva, Anna Missilä, Cătălin Mititelu, Maria Mitrofan, Yusuke Miyao, Simonetta Montemagni, Amir More, Laura Moreno Romero, Keiko Sophie Mori, Tomohiko Morioka, Shinsuke Mori, Shigeki Moro, Bjartur Mortensen, Bohdan Moskalevskyi, Kadri Muischnek, Robert Munro, Yugo Murawaki, Kaili Müürisep, Pinkey Nainwani, Juan Ignacio Navarro Horñiacek, Anna Nedoluzhko, Gunta Nešpore-Bērzkalne, L01AF01A1ng Nguyễn Thị, Huyền Nguyễn Thị Minh, Yoshihiro Nikaido, Vitaly Nikolaev, Rattima Nitisaroj, Hanna Nurmi, Stina Ojala, Atul Kr. Ojha, Adédayọ00D2 Olúòkun, Mai Omura, Petya Osenova, Robert Östling, Lilja Øvrelid, Niko Partanen, Elena Pascual, Marco Passarotti, Agnieszka Patejuk, Guilherme Paulino-Passos, Angelika Peljak-Łapińska, Siyao Peng, Cenel-Augusto Perez, Guy Perrier, Daria Petrova, Slav Petrov, Jason Phelan, Jussi Piitulainen, Tommi A Pirinen, Emily Pitler, Barbara Plank, Thierry Poibeau, Larisa Ponomareva, Martin Popel, Lauma Pretkalniņa, Sophie Prévost, Prokopis Prokopidis, Adam Przepiórkowski, Tiina Puolakainen, Sampo Pyysalo, Peng Qi, Andriela Rääbis, Alexandre Rademaker, Loganathan Ramasamy, Taraka Rama, Carlos Ramisch, Vinit Ravishankar, Livy Real, Siva Reddy, Georg Rehm, Ivan Riabov, Michael Rießler, Erika Rimkutė, Larissa Rinaldi, Laura Rituma, Luisa Rocha, Mykhailo Romanenko, Rudolf Rosa, Davide Rovati, Valentin Roșca, Olga Rudina, Jack Rueter, Shoval Sadde, Benoît Sagot, Shadi Saleh, Alessio Salomoni, Tanja Samardžić, Stephanie Samson, Manuela Sanguinetti, Dage Särg, Baiba Saulīte, Yanin Sawanakunanon, Nathan Schneider, Sebastian Schuster, Djamé Seddah, Wolfgang Seeker, Mojgan Seraji, Mo Shen, Atsuko Shimada, Hiroyuki Shirasu, Muh Shohibussirri, Dmitry Sichinava, Aline Silveira, Natalia Silveira, Maria Simi, Radu Simionescu, Katalin Simkó, Mária Šimková, Kiril Simov, Aaron Smith, Isabela Soares-Bastos, Carolyn Spadine, Antonio Stella, Milan Straka, Jana Strnadová, Alane Suhr, Umut Sulubacak, Shingo Suzuki, Zsolt Szántó, Dima Taji, Yuta Takahashi, Fabio Tamburini, Takaaki Tanaka, Isabelle Tellier, Guillaume Thomas, Liisi Torga, Trond Trosterud, Anna Trukhina, Reut Tsarfaty, Francis Tyers, Sumire Uematsu, Zdeňka Urešová, Larraitz Uria, Hans Uszkoreit, Andrius Utka, Sowmya Vajjala, Daniel van Niekerk, Gertjan van Noord, Viktor Varga, Eric Villemonte de la Clergerie, Veronika Vincze, Lars Wallin, Abigail Walsh, Jing Xian Wang, Jonathan North Washington, Maximilan Wendt, Seyi Williams, Mats Wirén, Christian Wittern, Tsegay Woldemariam, Tak-sum Wong, Alina Wróblewska, Mary Yako, Naoki Yamazaki, Chunxiao Yan, Koichi Yasuoka, Marat M. Yavrumyan, Zhuoran Yu, Zdeněk Žabokrtský, Amir Zeldes, Manying Zhang, and Hanzhi Zhu. 2019. Universal dependencies 2.5. LINDAT/CLARIAH-CZ digital library at the Institute of Formal and Applied Linguistics (ÚFAL), Faculty of Mathematics and Physics, Charles University.

Sheng Zhang, Rachel Rudinger, and Benjamin Van Durme. 2017. An evaluation of PredPatt and open IE via stage 1 semantic role labeling. In *Proceedings of the 12th International Conference on Computational Semantics (IWCS) — Short papers*.

A Full Results

FACTSCORE evaluation is outlined in §2, and full results are reported in Table 4 and Figure 4. DECOMPSCORE evaluation is discussed in §3.2, and full results are reported in Table 2. Unlike FACTSCORE, we do not impose a length penalty in DECOMPSCORE because shorter passages naturally contain fewer subclaims. Percentages of subclaims that are judged to be supported (i.e., the coherence of each method) are shown in Table 6 and Figure 6.

FACTSCORE results based on the subclaims judged to cohere with the original claim (based on judgments obtained when computing DECOMPSCORE) are shown in Table 5 and Figure 5. The average numbers of subclaims per biography are reported in Table 3, and the average numbers of supported subclaims (i.e., the DECOMPSCORE) are reported in Table 2.

It is important to note the special cases and conditions placed on these results:

- The released data from Min et al. (2023) includes uninformative LM responses (e.g. "I'm sorry, I don't have any information on a person named..."). Including these generations is valuable for evaluating factuality of a language model, however results in noise when evaluating decomposition quality. These uninformative responses are still processed by the decomposition methods we wish to evaluate, however the quality of decomposition is unaffected.

- Different language models are trained on different versions of Wikipedia, which introduces inconsistencies from the Wikipedia context used for fact-checking. This can affect FACTSCORE but does not affect DECOMPSCORE because it does not make use of external knowledge sources.

B Model Details

To reduce cost using the `text-davinci-003` model used by Min et al. (2023), we instead use InstructGPT (`gpt-3.5-turbo-instruct`) as the LLM for decomposition with 4K token context window, 512 `max_tokens` and a temperature of 0.7. This model costs $0.0015 per 1K input tokens and $0.0020 per 1K output tokens. `gpt-3.5-turbo-instruct` achieves Pearson correlation coefficients of over 0.97 for both FACTSCORE and number of subclaims generated compared to results reported by Min et al. (2023) (Table 7).

Inst-LLAMA is LLAMA trained on Super Natural Instructions (Wang et al., 2022; Touvron et al., 2023), and is used for all FACTSCORE and DECOMPSCORE evaluations. We use `max_sequence_length` of 2048 and `max_output_length` of 128.

For $\mathcal{D}_{\text{PredPatt}}$, we use `Trankit` for generating the dependency parse for each sentence. This parse is then used by `PredPatt` with the following flags: relative clauses, appositional modifiers, adjectival modifiers, conjunction, possessives, borrow_arg_for_relcl and strip all set to True, with the remaining flags (simple, cut, and big_args) set to False. We use `PredPatt` with Universal Dependencies v2.

We use `gpt-3.5-turbo-instruct` with the settings enumerated above for converting PredPatt outputs into natural language sentences with the following prompt:

```
Please turn my input utterances into a grammatically correct natural English sentence by resolving tense, fixing grammatical errors, and reordering words without changing meanings. Your output should not contain "is/are" or "poss". Your output should contain no hallucinated information and no redundant sentences. Just the modified utterance.

Input: born 1908 community leader
Output: The community leader was born in 1908.

Input: date of death is/are unknown
Output: The date of death is unknown.

Input: was an African - American social worker activist
Output: They were an African-American social worker activist.

Input: <subclaim>
Output:
```

When a prompt in the $\mathcal{D}_{\text{CoNLL-U}}$ approach exceeds the length allowed for the context window, examples are incrementally removed until the prompt fits. When a zero-shot prompt (no in-context examples) exceeds the size of the context window, we backoff and set the entire original sentence as the subclaim. In practice, we backoff 0.05% of the time: across 6000 passages (500 passages generated by each of 12 LM_{SUBJ}), twice we use one example and once we use the original sentence. We leave it to future work to reduce the size of the parses used in the prompt.

DecompScore							
LM_{SUBJ}	$\mathcal{D}_{\mathcal{D}_{\text{R-ND}}}$	$\mathcal{D}_{\text{Chen}}$	$\mathcal{D}_{\text{WiCE}}$	$\mathcal{D}_{\text{FS}}$	$\mathcal{D}_{\text{FS2}}$	$\mathcal{D}_{\text{CoNLL}}$	$\mathcal{D}_{\text{PP}}$
Alpaca 7B	**21.9**	17.7	11.2	17.2	18.8	15.4	15.2
Alpaca 13B	**21.6**	16.9	10.5	16.5	18.2	15.0	14.9
Alpaca 65B	**21.9**	17.3	10.8	16.7	18.5	15.2	14.8
ChatGPT	**43.0**	32.5	20.2	32.4	33.9	27.3	29.0
Dolly 12B	**32.1**	24.9	15.2	24.3	26.8	21.9	20.5
GPT4	**76.0**	57.5	35.9	57.2	58.5	47.0	54.8
InstructGPT	**35.5**	27.6	17.2	26.9	28.8	23.4	23.1
MPT-Chat 7B	**47.7**	36.5	22.7	35.9	37.4	30.2	33.1
Oasst-pythia 12B	**56.7**	41.6	25.4	40.9	42.3	34.8	39.7
StableLM 7B	**38.2**	29.5	18.9	29.3	30.6	25.5	28.1
Vicuna 7B	**58.4**	43.8	27.4	43.4	45.4	36.7	41.1
Vicuna 13B	**54.6**	39.8	24.9	39.9	41.5	33.1	36.2
Macro-average	**42.3**	32.1	20.0	31.7	33.4	27.1	29.2

Table 2: DecompScore for each decomposition method and LM_{SUBJ}. Average number of subclaims generated per biography that are determined to be supported by the original sentence.

# Subclaims							
LM_{SUBJ}	$\mathcal{D}_{\mathcal{D}_{\text{R-ND}}}$	$\mathcal{D}_{\text{Chen}}$	$\mathcal{D}_{\text{WiCE}}$	$\mathcal{D}_{\text{FS}}$	$\mathcal{D}_{\text{FS2}}$	$\mathcal{D}_{\text{CoNLL}}$	$\mathcal{D}_{\text{PP}}$
Alpaca 7B	**22.2**	17.9	11.3	17.3	19.0	15.7	16.4
Alpaca 13B	**22.0**	17.2	10.6	16.6	18.4	15.3	16.2
Alpaca 65B	**22.2**	17.5	10.9	16.9	18.6	15.5	16.0
ChatGPT	**44.2**	33.0	20.4	33.0	34.6	28.5	33.2
Dolly 12B	**33.0**	25.2	15.4	24.7	27.2	22.9	23.4
GPT4	**77.7**	58.2	36.2	57.9	59.2	48.6	63.6
InstructGPT	**36.3**	27.9	17.3	27.2	29.1	23.9	25.6
MPT-Chat 7B	**49.0**	37.0	22.9	36.3	37.8	31.1	37.4
Oasst-pythia 12B	**57.7**	41.8	25.5	41.2	42.6	35.4	44.6
StableLM 7B	**40.4**	30.7	19.4	30.4	32.0	27.4	33.4
Vicuna 7B	**59.8**	44.3	27.6	43.9	45.9	37.7	46.3
Vicuna 13B	**57.3**	44.6	25.1	45.8	42.8	34.8	42.2
Macro-average	**43.5**	32.9	20.2	32.6	33.9	28.1	33.2

Table 3: Average number of subclaims generated per biography.

FACTSCORE (%)							
LM_{SUBJ}	$\mathcal{D}_{\mathcal{D}_{\text{R-ND}}}$	$\mathcal{D}_{\text{Chen}}$	$\mathcal{D}_{\text{WICE}}$	$\mathcal{D}_{\text{FS}}$	$\mathcal{D}_{\text{FS2}}$	$\mathcal{D}_{\text{CoNLL}}$	$\mathcal{D}_{\text{PP}}$
Alpaca 7B	35.0	36.9	33.7	36.9	37.5	34.9	27.4
Alpaca 13B	38.9	40.3	35.1	40.8	41.1	38.3	30.0
Alpaca 65B	44.0	47.0	42.8	46.9	47.3	45.0	36.5
ChatGPT	48.2	52.1	51.4	52.2	52.2	50.7	36.8
Dolly 12B	16.5	16.3	13.9	16.7	17.2	15.5	10.4
GPT4	51.1	56.1	54.8	55.9	54.9	53.3	35.6
InstructGPT	40.1	43.2	43.2	43.6	43.4	41.7	31.5
MPT-Chat 7B	24.8	25.9	24.4	26.2	25.2	25.1	16.1
Oasst-pythia 12B	20.1	20.8	19.2	21.2	21.1	20.5	11.7
StableLM 7B	13.8	13.1	11.6	13.5	13.4	13.3	8.2
Vicuna 7B	32.4	34.5	34.0	35.2	34.9	33.8	21.7
Vicuna 13B	31.1	32.8	31.8	34.1	35.7	33.1	23.3
Macro-average	33.0	34.9	33.0	35.3	35.3	33.8	24.1

Table 4: FACTSCORE of biographies generated by each LM_{SUBJ} and decomposed with each method. Note: For evaluating decomposition quality, a larger FACTSCORE is not necessarily better; we care about high confidence that FACTSCORE is correct.

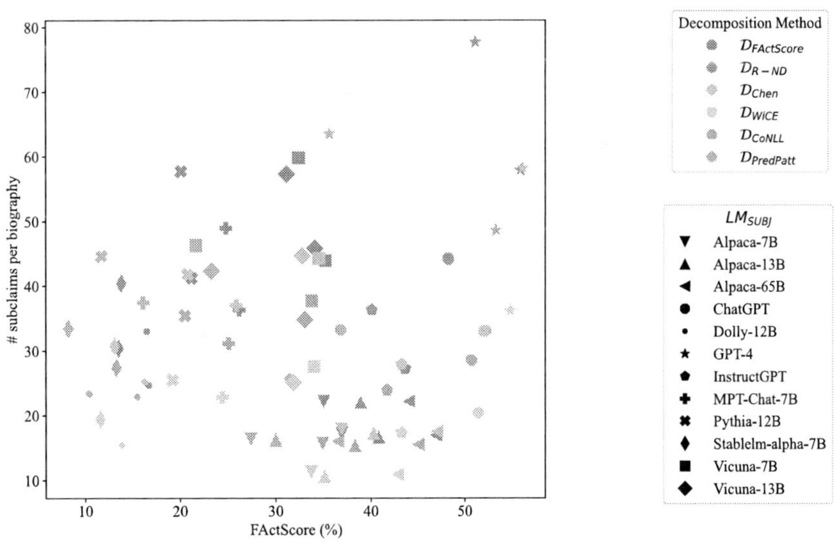

Figure 4: FACTSCORE results for all claim decomposition methods and LM_{SUBJ}.

FACTSCORE (%) After Filtering Out Unsupported Subclaims							
$\mathrm{LM_{SUBJ}}$	$\mathcal{D}_{\mathcal{D}_{\text{R-ND}}}$	$\mathcal{D}_{\text{Chen}}$	$\mathcal{D}_{\text{WICE}}$	$\mathcal{D}_{\text{FS}}$	$\mathcal{D}_{\text{FS2}}$	$\mathcal{D}_{\text{CoNLL}}$	$\mathcal{D}_{\text{PP}}$
Alpaca 7B	34.9	36.7	36.1	36.8	37.6	35.8	29.1
Alpaca 13B	40.1	40.8	40.2	41.4	41.2	39.9	31.3
Alpaca 65B	45.0	48.4	47.0	47.6	47.9	46.3	39.4
ChatGPT	55.8	60.5	60.2	59.9	59.9	59.1	45.1
Dolly 12B	17.1	17.1	16.1	17.6	17.7	16.9	12.2
GPT4	57.0	62.6	61.4	62.0	61.0	59.9	43.8
InstructGPT	40.7	43.5	43.6	44.0	44.0	42.6	34.3
MPT-Chat 7B	27.0	28.3	27.5	28.7	27.6	28.0	19.5
Oasst-pythia 12B	20.4	21.2	20.2	21.4	21.4	21.0	12.8
StableLM 7B	16.0	15.6	14.6	16.0	15.8	15.9	8.9
Vicuna 7B	35.7	38.6	38.4	38.8	38.4	37.6	25.3
Vicuna 13B	37.7	41.7	41.3	41.7	41.1	40.6	29.3
Macro-average	35.6	37.9	37.2	38.0	37.8	37.0	27.6

Table 5: FACTSCORE of biographies after filtering out subclaims determined to be not supported by the original sentence (using DECOMPSCORE judgments). Note: For evaluating decomposition quality, a larger FACTSCORE is not necessarily better; we care about high confidence that FACTSCORE is correct.

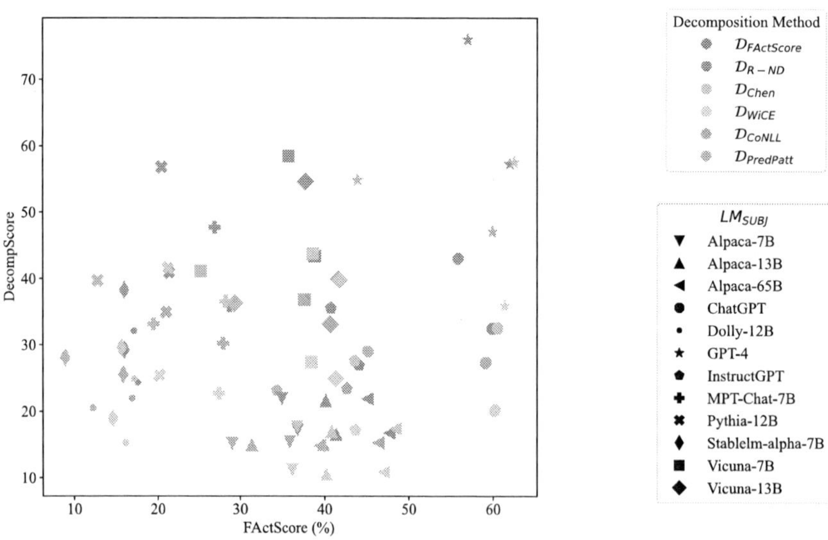

Figure 5: FACTSCORE results after filtering out subclaims determined to be not supported by the original sentence (using DECOMPSCORE judgments) for all claim decomposition methods and $\mathrm{LM_{SUBJ}}$.

% Subclaims Supported							
LM_{SUBJ}	$\mathcal{D}_{\mathcal{D}_{R\text{-}ND}}$	$\mathcal{D}_{Chen}$	$\mathcal{D}_{WiCE}$	$\mathcal{D}_{FS}$	$\mathcal{D}_{FS2}$	$\mathcal{D}_{CoNLL}$	$\mathcal{D}_{PP}$
Alpaca 7B	98.7	98.9	**99.2**	99.1	99.1	98.4	93.6
Alpaca 13B	98.6	99.0	**99.4**	99.0	99.2	98.2	93.2
Alpaca 65B	98.6	99.3	**99.4**	99.2	99.3	98.5	93.7
ChatGPT	93.0	95.9	96.7	**99.4**	94.5	89.0	80.0
Dolly 12B	97.4	98.7	**99.0**	98.7	98.6	96.5	89.6
GPT4	96.2	97.4	**98.3**	97.4	97.2	94.2	83.2
InstructGPT	98.1	99.1	**99.3**	99.0	99.0	98.0	90.8
MPT-Chat 7B	96.5	97.6	**98.4**	97.6	97.8	95.4	86.9
Oasst-pythia 12B	98.3	99.3	**99.4**	99.3	99.3	98.4	89.4
StableLM 7B	89.2	90.7	**94.1**	90.5	89.4	84.8	74.4
Vicuna 7B	94.8	97.0	**98.1**	96.3	96.5	92.9	84.1
Vicuna 13B	88.9	93.3	**95.4**	90.8	88.1	82.6	72.6
Macro-average	96.0	97.2	**98.1**	97.2	96.5	93.9	86.0

Table 6: Percentage of subclaims from each decomposition method and LM_{SUBJ} that are judged to be supported by (cohere with) the original claim.

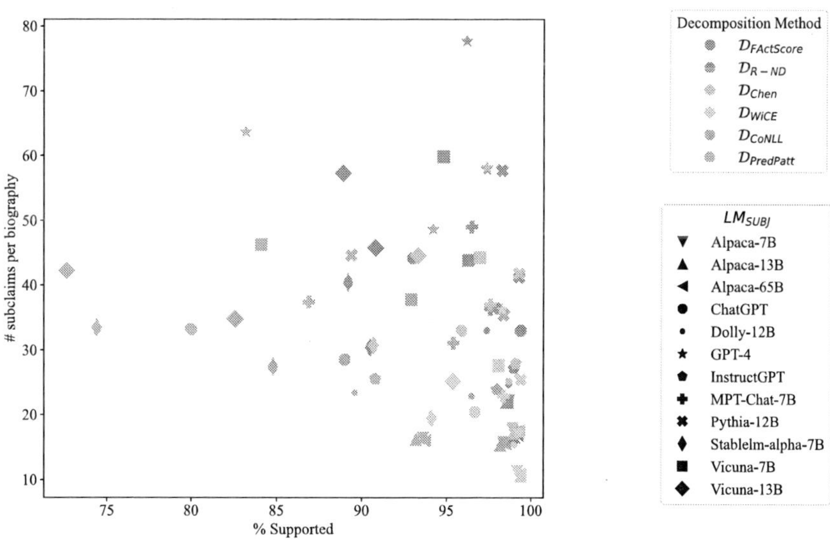

Figure 6: Percentage of subclaims that are supported by (cohere with) the original claim.

	FACTSCORE	Reported FACTSCORE	# subclaims	Reported # subclaims
Alpaca 7B	36.9	36.5	17.3	17.4
Alpaca 13B	40.8	40.3	16.6	16.6
Alpaca 65B	46.9	46.3	16.9	17.1
ChatGPT	52.2	60.4	33.0	37.0
Dolly 12B	16.7	17.1	24.7	24.6
GPT4	55.9	59.9	57.9	60.8
InstructGPT	43.6	41.7	27.2	27.7
MPT-Chat 7B	26.2	27.9	36.3	37.3
Oasst-pythia 12B	21.2	20.8	41.2	39.7
StableLM 7B	13.5	16.3	30.4	38.0
Vicuna 7B	35.2	36.9	43.9	45.6
Vicuna 13B	34.1	40.7	45.8	50.9
ρ	0.9786		0.9821	

Table 7: Pearson correlation coefficients (ρ) between our setup for computing FACTSCORE (using `gpt-3.5-turbo-instruct` for subclaim generation) and results reported by Min et al. (2023) (using `text-davinci-003` for subclaim generation).

C NLI Entailment

The numbers of subclaims that are judged to be entailed by the original sentence are highly correlated with the numbers of subclaims judged by an LLM to be supported by the original sentence (DECOMPSCORE), achieving a Pearson correlation coefficient of 0.9978 (Figure 7).

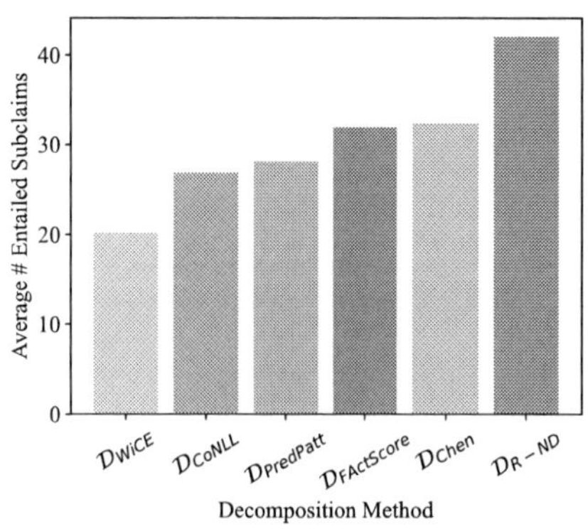

Figure 7: Average number of subclaims per passage that are entailed by their original sentential claim, as determined by an NLI model (Nie et al., 2020). Values are macro-averaged across LM_{SUBJ}.

D Decomposition Examples

We include examples of two sentences decomposed manually and by all claim decomposition methods evaluated. Table 8 contains the decompositions for the sentence "Alfred Hitchcock passed away on April 29, 1980, in Bel-Air, California, leaving behind a rich legacy of suspenseful and thrilling films that continue to captivate and inspire audiences and filmmakers alike." Table 9 contains the decompositions for the sentence "Nash demonstrated a natural aptitude for mathematics from a young age and earned his bachelor's and master's degrees in mathematics from the Carnegie Institute of Technology (now Carnegie Mellon University) in 1948."

E Russellian/Neo-Davidsonian In-context Learning Examples

The manually decomposed sentences used as in-context examples for $\mathcal{D}_{\text{R-ND}}$ are shown in Table 10.

Method	Decomposition
Manual	- Alfred Hitchcock passed away. - Alfred Hitchcock's death occurred in April. - Alfred Hitchcock's death occurred on the 29th day of a month. - Alfred Hitchcock's death occurred in 1980. - Alfred Hitchcock's death occurred in Bel-Air. - Bel-Air is in California. - Alfred Hitchcock left behind a legacy. - Alfred Hitchcock's legacy is rich. - Alfred Hitchcock's legacy contains films. - The films in Alfred Hitchcock's legacy are suspenseful. - The films in Alfred Hitchcock's legacy are thrilling. - The films in Alfred Hitchcock's legacy captivate audiences. - The films in Alfred Hitchcock's legacy captivate filmmakers. - The films in Alfred Hitchcock's legacy inspire audiences. - The films in Alfred Hitchcock's legacy inspire filmmakers.
$\mathcal{D}_{\text{R-ND}}$	- Alfred Hitchcock passed away on April 29, 1980. - His death occurred in Bel-Air, California. - Alfred Hitchcock had a legacy. - Alfred Hitchcock's legacy contains suspenseful films. - Alfred Hitchcock's legacy contains thrilling films. - Alfred Hitchcock's films continue to captivate audiences. - Alfred Hitchcock's films continue to inspire filmmakers. - Alfred Hitchcock left behind his legacy.
$\mathcal{D}_{\text{Chen et al.}}$	- Alfred Hitchcock passed away on April 29, 1980. - Alfred Hitchcock passed away in Bel-Air, California. - Alfred Hitchcock left behind a rich legacy. - Alfred Hitchcock's legacy includes suspenseful and thrilling films. - Alfred Hitchcock's films continue to captivate and inspire audiences. - Alfred Hitchcock's films continue to captivate and inspire filmmakers.
$\mathcal{D}_{\text{WICE}}$	- Alfred Hitchcock passed away on April 29, 1980. - He passed away in Bel-Air, California. - He left behind a rich legacy of suspenseful and thrilling films. - His films continue to captivate and inspire audiences. - His films continue to inspire filmmakers.
$\mathcal{D}_{\text{FACTSCORE}}$	- Alfred Hitchcock passed away on April 29, 1980. - Alfred Hitchcock passed away in Bel-Air, California. - Alfred Hitchcock left behind a legacy of films. - Alfred Hitchcock's films were suspenseful and thrilling. - Alfred Hitchcock's films continue to captivate audiences. - Alfred Hitchcock's films continue to inspire filmmakers.
$\mathcal{D}_{\text{CoNLL-U}}$	- Alfred Hitchcock passed away on April 29, 1980. - He passed away in Bel-Air, California. - He left behind a rich legacy. - His legacy includes suspenseful and thrilling films. - His films continue to captivate and inspire audiences and filmmakers.
$\mathcal{D}_{\text{PredPatt}}$	- Alfred Hitchcock passed away on April 29 , 1980 , in Bel - Air. - Bel - Air is/are in California - Alfred Hitchcock left behind a rich legacy of suspenseful and thrilling films that continue to captivate and inspire audiences and filmmakers alike - The legacy of suspenseful and thrilling films that continue to captivate and inspire audiences and filmmakers alike is/are rich - The films that continue to captivate and inspire audiences and filmmakers alike are suspenseful - Suspenseful and thrilling films continue to captivate audiences. - Suspenseful and thrilling films continue to captivate filmmakers alike. - That continue to inspire.

Table 8: Decomposition comparison for the sentence "Alfred Hitchcock passed away on April 29, 1980, in Bel-Air, California, leaving behind a rich legacy of suspenseful and thrilling films that continue to captivate and inspire audiences and filmmakers alike."

Manual	- Nash demonstrated an aptitude for mathematics. - Nash's aptitude for mathematics was natural. - Nash's demonstration of an aptitude for mathematics began at a young age. - Nash earned his bachelor's degree. - Nash's bachelor's degree is in mathematics. - Nash's bachelor's degree is from the Carnegie Institute of Technology. - Nash's bachelor's degree was earned in 1948. - Nash earned his master's degree. - Nash's master's degree is in mathematics. - Nash's master's degree is from the Carnegie Institute of Technology. - Nash's master's degree was earned in 1948. - The Carnegie Institute of Technology is now Carnegie Mellon University.
$\mathcal{D}_{\text{R-ND}}$	- Nash demonstrated a natural aptitude for mathematics. - His natural aptitude for mathematics was evident from a young age. - He earned a bachelor's degree in mathematics. - He earned a master's degree in mathematics. - He earned his degrees from the Carnegie Institute of Technology. - The Carnegie Institute of Technology is now known as Carnegie Mellon University. - He earned his degrees in 1948. - He earned his bachelor's degree in mathematics in 1948. - He earned his master's degree in mathematics in 1948.
$\mathcal{D}_{\text{Chen et al.}}$	- Nash demonstrated a natural aptitude for mathematics. - Nash demonstrated a natural aptitude for mathematics from a young age. - Nash earned his bachelor's degree in mathematics. - Nash earned his master's degree in mathematics. - Nash earned his bachelor's and master's degrees in mathematics. - Nash earned his bachelor's and master's degrees in mathematics from the Carnegie Institute of Technology. - The Carnegie Institute of Technology is now Carnegie Mellon University. - Nash earned his bachelor's and master's degrees in mathematics from the Carnegie Institute of Technology (now Carnegie Mellon University). - Nash earned his bachelor's and master's degrees in mathematics from the Carnegie Institute of Technology (now Carnegie Mellon University) in 1948.
$\mathcal{D}_{\text{WICE}}$	- Nash demonstrated a natural aptitude for mathematics from a young age. - Nash earned his bachelor's degree in mathematics from the Carnegie Institute of Technology in 1948. - Nash earned his master's degree in mathematics from the Carnegie Institute of Technology in 1948. - The Carnegie Institute of Technology is now known as Carnegie Mellon University.
$\mathcal{D}_{\text{FACTSCORE}}$	- Nash demonstrated a natural aptitude for mathematics. - Nash demonstrated a natural aptitude for mathematics from a young age. - Nash earned his bachelor's degree in mathematics. - Nash earned his master's degree in mathematics. - Nash earned his bachelor's and master's degrees in mathematics. - Nash earned his bachelor's and master's degrees in mathematics from the Carnegie Institute of Technology. - Carnegie Institute of Technology is now called Carnegie Mellon University. - Nash earned his bachelor's and master's degrees in mathematics from the Carnegie Institute of Technology (now Carnegie Mellon University). - Nash earned his bachelor's and master's degrees in mathematics from the Carnegie Institute of Technology (now Carnegie Mellon University) in 1948.
$\mathcal{D}_{\text{CoNLL-U}}$	- Nash demonstrated an aptitude for mathematics. - Nash earned his bachelor's and master's degrees in mathematics. - Nash's degrees were from Carnegie Institute of Technology. - The institute is now known as Carnegie Mellon University. - Nash received his degrees in 1948.
$\mathcal{D}_{\text{PredPatt}}$	- Nash demonstrated a natural aptitude for mathematics from a young age. - Aptitude for mathematics is natural. - They were young. - Nash earned his bachelor 's and master 's degrees in mathematics from the Carnegie Institute of Technology in 1948. - He had a bachelor 's and master 's degrees in mathematics. - The bachelor possessed a master's degree. - The Carnegie Institute of Technology is now Carnegie Mellon University.

Table 9: Decomposition comparison for the sentence "Nash demonstrated a natural aptitude for mathematics from a young age and earned his bachelor's and master's degrees in mathematics from the Carnegie Institute of Technology (now Carnegie Mellon University) in 1948."

He made his acting debut in the film The Moon is the Sun's Dream (1992), and continued to appear in small and supporting roles throughout the 1990s.
- He has an acting debut.
- He acted in a film.
- His acting debut was in a film.
- His acting debut was in The Moon is the Sun's Dream.
- He acted in The Moon is the Sun's Dream.
- The Moon is the Sun's Dream is a film.
- The Moon is the Sun's Dream was released in 1992.
- His acting debut occurred in 1992.
- He appeared in small roles.
- He appeared in supporting roles.
- His small roles occurred throughout the 1990s.
- His supporting roles occurred throughout the 1990s.
- His appearance in small roles occurred after his acting debut.
- His appearance in supporting roles occurred after his acting debut.

He is also a successful producer and engineer, having worked with a wide variety of artists, including Willie Nelson, Tim McGraw, and Taylor Swift.
- He is a producer.
- He is successful at being a producer.
- He is an engineer.
- He is successful at being an engineer.
- He has worked with a wide variety of artists.
- Willie Nelson is an artist.
- He has worked with Willie Nelson.
- Tim McGraw is an artist.
- He has worked with Tim McGraw.
- Taylor Swift is an artist.
- He has worked with Taylor Swift.

In 1963, Collins became one of the third group of astronauts selected by NASA and he served as the back-up Command Module Pilot for the Gemini 7 mission.
- NASA selected a third group of astronauts.
- Collins belonged to the third group of astronauts.
- Collins was selected by NASA.
- Collins's selection by NASA occurred in 1963.
- The Gemini 7 mission has a back-up Command Module Pilot.
- Collins's role in the Gemini 7 mission was as the back-up Command Module Pilot.
- Collins participated in the Gemini 7 mission.

In addition to his acting roles, Bateman has written and directed two short films and is currently in development on his feature debut.
- Bateman has acting roles.
- Bateman has written short films.
- The number of short films Bateman has written is two.
- Bateman has directed short films.
- The number of short films Bateman has directed is two.
- Bateman is currently in development on his feature debut.
- The two short films were made before his feature debut.
- His acting roles came before his feature debut.

Michael Collins (born October 31, 1930) is a retired American astronaut and test pilot who was the Command Module Pilot for the Apollo 11 mission in 1969.
- Michael Collins was born in October.
- Michael Collins was born on the 31st day of a month.
- Michael Collins was born in 1930.
- Michael Collins is retired.
- Michael Collins is American.
- Michael Collins was an astronaut.
- Michael Collins was a test pilot.
- Michael Collins participated in the Apollo 11 mission.
- Michael Collins's participation in the Apollo 11 mission occurred in 1969.
- The Apollo 11 mission was active in 1969.
- The day of Michael Collins's birth occurred before his year of participation in the Apollo 11 mission.
- The Apollo 11 mission had a Command Module Pilot.
- Michael Collins's role in the Apollo 11 mission was as the Command Module Pilot.

He was an American composer, conductor, and musical director.
- He was American.
- He was a composer.
- He was a conductor.
- He was a musical director.

She currently stars in the romantic comedy series, Love and Destiny, which premiered in 2019.
- She stars in Love and Destiny.
- Love and Destiny is a series.
- Love and Destiny is a romantic comedy.
- Love and Destiny premiered in 2019.

His music has been described as a mix of traditional Mexican and Latin American styles, as well as jazz, folk, and rock.
- He has music.
- His music has been described.
- His music has been described as a mix of styles.
- His music has been described as containing elements of traditional styles of music.
- His music has been described as containing elements of Mexican style of music.
- His music has been described as containing elements of Latin American style of music.
- His music has been described as containing elements of jazz music.
- His music has been described as containing elements of folk music.
- His music has been described as containing elements of rock music.

He also serves as an ambassador for the charity Leonard Cheshire Disability.
- He has a role in Leonard Cheshire Disability.
- His role in Leonard Cheshire Disability is as an ambassador.
- Leonard Cheshire Disability is a charity.

He began his career in Nashville in the late 1950s and has since released numerous albums, including a greatest hits collection in 1999.
- He has a career.
- His career began in Nashville.
- His career began in the late 1950s.
- He has released albums.
- His released albums are numerous.
- He released a collection.
- His collection contains greatest hits.
- His collection was released in 1999.
- The release of his albums occurred after he began his career.

He has been performing since the age of 8, when he joined a band in his hometown of Guadalajara and has since gone on to record six studio albums and several singles of his own original material.
- He has been performing.
- He started performing at the age of 8.
- He joined a band.
- He joined a band at the age of 8.
- His band was in Guadalajara.
- His hometown is Guadalajara.
- He has recorded studio albums.
- The number of studio albums he has recorded is six.
- He has recorded singles.
- He has several singles.
- His studio albums are his own original material.
- His singles are his own original material.
- His recording of studio albums occurred after he joined a band.
- His recording of singles occurred after he joined a band.

She is also the former President of the Malaysian Chinese Association (MCA) from 2010 to 2013.
- She had a role in the Malaysian Chinese Association.
- Her role in the Malaysian Chinese Association was as its President.
- Her tenure as President of the Malaysian Chinese Association started in 2010.
- Her tenure as President of the Malaysian Chinese Association ended in 2013.
- MCA is another name for the Malaysian Chinese Association.

During his professional career, McCoy played for the Broncos, the San Diego Chargers, the Minnesota Vikings, and the Jacksonville Jaguars.
- McCoy had a professional career.
- McCoy played for the Broncos.
- McCoy played for the San Diego Chargers.
- The Chargers are from San Diego.
- McCoy played for the Minnesota Vikings.
- The Vikings are from Minnesota.
- McCoy played for the Jacksonville Jaguars.
- The Jaguars are from Jacksonville.

Miller has been described as the architect of Trump's controversial immigration policies, and has previously worked for Alabama Senator Jeff Sessions on immigration issues.
- Miller has been described.
- Miller has been described as an architect.
- Miller has been described as an architect of Trump's controversial immigration policies.
- Trump has immigration policies.
- Trump's immigration policies are controversial.
- Miller worked for Jeff Sessions.
- Jeff Sessions is a Senator.
- Jeff Sessions represents Alabama.
- Miller worked on immigration issues.
- Miller's work for Jeff Sessions involved immigration issues.

Her work is often described as whimsical and dreamlike.
- She has work.
- Her work has been described.
- Her work is described as whimsical.
- Her work is described as dreamlike.
- The description of her work as whimsical has occurred often.
- The description of her work as dreamlike has occurred often.

He graduated from the United States Military Academy in 1952, and then went on to serve in the United States Air Force.
- He graduated from the United States Military Academy.
- His graduation from the United States Military Academy occurred in 1952.
- He served in the United States Air Force.
- His service in the United States Air Force occurred after his graduation from the United States Military Academy.

He is best known for his roles in the films Memories of Murder (2003), The Host (2006), (...) and Parasite (2019).
- He had a role in Memories of Murder.
- Memories of Murder is a film.
- Memories of Murder was released in 2003.
- He had a role in The Host.
- The Host is a film.
- The Host was released in 2006.
- He had a role in Parasite.
- Parasite is a film.
- Parasite was released in 2009.
- His role in Memories of Murder is one of his best known.
- His role in The Host is one of his best known.
- His role in Parasite is one of his best known.

Song Kang-ho was born in Gongju, South Korea in 1967.
- Song Kang-ho was born.
- Song Kang-ho's birth occurred in Gongju.
- Song Kang-ho's birth occurred in South Korea.
- Song Kang-ho's birth occurred in 1967.
- Gongju is in South Korea.

He studied theater at Chung-Ang University in Seoul.
- He studied.
- He studied theater.
- He studied at Chung-Ang University.
- His study of theater occurred at Chung-Ang University.
- Chung-Ang University is located in Seoul.

His breakthrough came with the leading role in the acclaimed crime-drama film Memories of Murder in 2003.
- He had a breakthrough.
- His breakthrough was based on a leading role.
- His breakthrough was based on his role in Memories of Murder.
- His breakthrough occurred in 2003.
- He had a leading role.
- He had a leading role in Memories of Murder.
- Memories of Murder is a film.
- The genre of Memories of Murder is crime-drama.
- Memories of Murder is acclaimed.
- Memories of Murder was released in 2003.

This was followed by the monster movie The Host in 2006, which became the highest-grossing film in Korean history at the time.
- This was followed by The Host.
- The Host is a movie.
- The Host was released in 2006.
- The genre of The Host is monster movie.
- The Host became the highest-grossing film in Korean history.

Table 10: Manually decomposed examples used for in-context examples by $\mathcal{D}_{\text{R-ND}}$.

Speedy Gonzales: A Collection of Fast Task-Specific Models for Spanish

José Cañete
Department of Computer Science, University of Chile
jose.canete@ug.uchile.cl

Felipe Bravo-Marquez
Department of Computer Science, University of Chile
National Center for Artificial Intelligence (CENIA)
Millennium Institute for Foundational Research on Data (IMFD)
fbravo@dcc.uchile.cl

Abstract

Large language models (LLM) are now a very common and successful path to approach language and retrieval tasks. While these LLM achieve surprisingly good results it is a challenge to use them on more constrained resources. Techniques to compress these LLM into smaller and faster models have emerged for English or Multilingual settings, but it is still a challenge for other languages. In fact, Spanish is the second language with most native speakers but lacks of these kind of resources. In this work, we evaluate all the models publicly available for Spanish on a set of 6 tasks and then, by leveraging on Knowledge Distillation, we present Speedy Gonzales, a collection of inference-efficient task-specific language models based on the ALBERT architecture. All of our models (fine-tuned and distilled) are publicly available on: https://huggingface.co/dccuchile.

1 Introduction

The utilization of learned dense representations of text is nowadays a common and successful approach for different kind of information retrieval (IR) tasks (Yates et al., 2021). These learned representations are usually obtained by training a language model using large collections of texts from the web. Two key aspects to watch to make the most of these models are size and speed of them.

The size of these models has grown overtime and now very large language models (LLM) are common, with models that range from hundred of millions to billions of parameters. These pre-trained models are not only heavy on memory requirements but also on the operations they do on every inference, which is a bottleneck when trying to deploy these models for tasks that are expected to be fast such as question answering or semantic search.

These LLMs are usually trained on English by big technology companies using web-scale datasets and substantial computational resources. Prominent examples include the well-known GPT-3 model (Brown et al., 2020). For languages other than English the available models are typically variants of BERT (Devlin et al., 2019), RoBERTa (Liu et al., 2019) or ALBERT (Lan et al., 2020). In the case of Spanish, which is one of the five most spoken languages in the world and the second with most native speakers, the available models range from 5M to 335M of parameters. In Figure 1 we showed how different Spanish pre-trained models compare in terms of model size (number of parameters) and inference speed (MACs).

Despite the remarkable performance of these LLMs across a range of tasks, it remains a challenge to utilize them effectively in computing environments that are constrained by limited resources, such as web or mobile applications.

New techniques to address this problem have emerged for English (Tang et al., 2019; Turc et al., 2019; Sanh et al., 2019; Wang et al., 2020; Jiao et al., 2020) or Multilingual (Jiao et al., 2021) models. These typically leverage on different kinds of Knowledge Distillation (Hinton et al., 2015) to compress the results of a large and performant model into another one which is typically lighter and more inference efficient. For other languages this is still an open challenge, where we lack from this kind of resources.

In this work we try to close this gap with new resources (inference-efficient models) for the Spanish language. Our contributions are the following:

- We perform a comprehensive evaluation of all publicly available Spanish pre-trained models, which are trained on general-domain corpora, by fine-tuning them across six different tasks and eight datasets.

- By selecting the best model on each evaluated dataset, we distilled its knowledge into lighter

*Proceedings of the 13th Joint Conference on Lexical and Computational Semantics (*SEM 2024)*, pages 176 - 189
June 20-21, 2024 ©2024 Association for Computational Linguistics

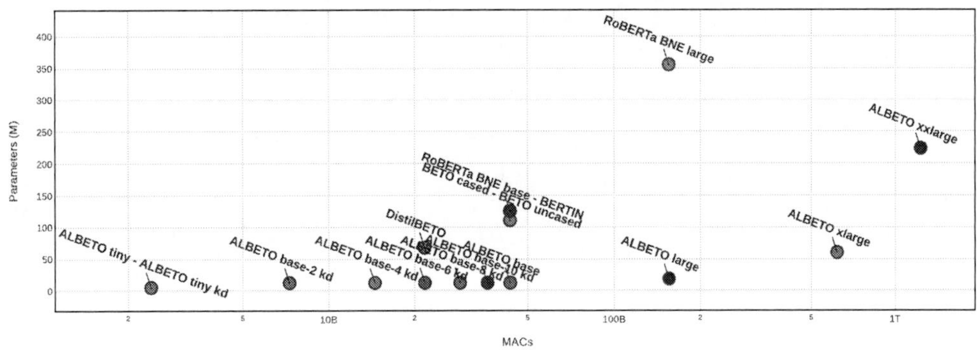

Figure 1: The size (number of parameters) and speed (MACs) of every Spanish model evaluated on this work. MACs are measured using a single sequence of length 512, which is the maximum sequence length of all the evaluated models.

ALBERT models, achieving more lighter and inference efficient models, while retaining most of the task performance of the bigger counterparts.

- We make our newly created resource, Speedy Gonzales, consisting of over 140 fine-tuned and distilled models, publicly accessible on the HuggingFace Hub at: `https://huggingface.co/dccuchile`.

2 Related Work

Transformers, introduced by Vaswani et al. (2017) have become the default architecture for text-related tasks. Transformer encoders like BERT (Devlin et al., 2019), RoBERTa (Liu et al., 2019) or ALBERT (Lan et al., 2020) are some of the most popular, by its ability to encode complex relations on texts by training on large collections of texts, with the training task consisting of corrupt some parts of a text sequence and train a model to reconstruct the correct sequence.

While models with billions of parameters have become common for English language (Brown et al., 2020), it is not the case for most other languages, which are typically restricted to hundreds of millions of parameters. For Spanish language, which is one of the most spoken languages in the world, the models available follow the BERT (Devlin et al., 2019), RoBERTa (Liu et al., 2019) or ALBERT (Lan et al., 2020) architecture and are described in further detail in Section 4.2.

Several ways to compress these models have been proposed through the years. The most common ones are quantization (Gholami et al., 2021), pruning (Blalock et al., 2020) and knowledge distillation (Hinton et al., 2015).

Network quantization compresses the original network by reducing the number of bits required to represent each weight, resulting in a lighter model. In the case of BERT, examples of these kinds of methods are TernaryBERT (Zhang et al., 2020) and BinaryBERT (Bai et al., 2021) where they were able to reduce the weight size to 2 and 1 bit respectively, while maintaining most of the original BERT performance.

The technique of pruning aims to reduce the number of connections (weights) in a neural network, which results in a reduction of the model size and also a very sparse pattern of the weights. Frankle and Carbin (2019) showed that in most feed-forward neural networks it is possible to find a subnetwork that achieves similar or better accuracy.

In Knowledge Distillation (KD) (Hinton et al., 2015) the knowledge learned by a big and strong model, the teacher model, is transferred to a lighter model, the student model, by forcing this student to mimic the teacher. Multiples ways of knowledge distillation have been proposed (Gou et al., 2021).

Tang et al. (2019) uses KD to transfer the knowledge from BERT to lighter RNNs. Turc et al. (2019) proposes pre-training compact BERT models and then using task-specific KD to achieve better results. Sanh et al. (2019) introduces a task-agnostic scheme where KD is used on the pre-training task. Wang et al. (2020) and Jiao et al. (2020) proposed different methods exclusive for

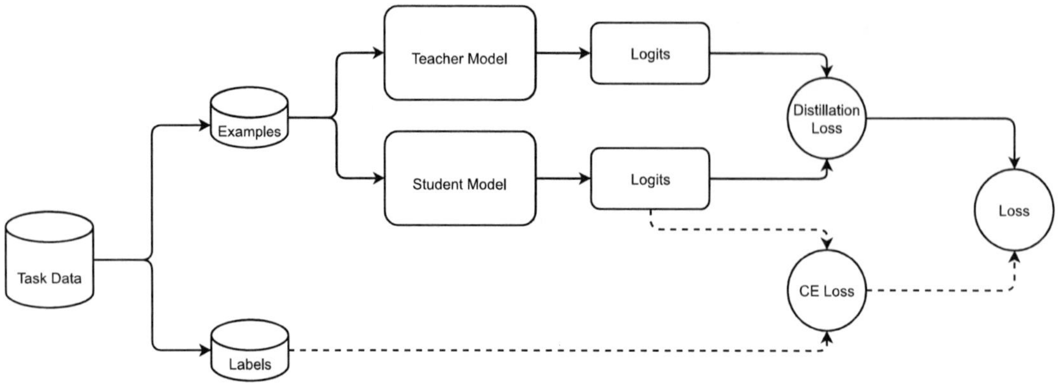

Figure 2: The figure provides a visual representation of the Knowledge Distillation framework applied in this work. In line with common practices, the framework includes both a distillation loss between the teacher and student models and a cross-entropy loss between the gold labels and the student's predictions, as indicated by the dashed line.

Transformers, to directly distill the knowledge from the self-attention layers of the teacher model to the student model.

Our work is similar to Turc et al. (2019) by proposing the use of compact Transformers but we use the ALBERT architecture instead of the BERT one. We also use the idea from Sanh et al. (2019) of reusing the layers of a pre-trained model, instead of random initializing a new one. Differently from that work, that has to choose which layers to reuse, we only adjust the number of layers (and thus, the inference speed) since all the ALBERT layers are shared. Another difference with those two works is that in our work we skip pre-training (or KD on the pre-training task) and directly apply KD on the task-specific phase.

3 Methodology

In pursuit of our goal to have efficient models for Spanish in various tasks, we employ the method of Knowledge Distillation. This method will be further elaborated in the subsequent section.

3.1 Knowledge Distillation

The technique of Knowledge Distillation aims to transfer the knowledge learned from a big and capable model, usually called the teacher model, say M_T, to a more restricted model, called the student model, say M_S. To achieve this objective, we train M_S to imitate M_T. There are multiple ways to imitate M_T (Gou et al., 2021), in this work we use the simple, yet powerful approach, of directly mimic the output of M_T given a input text.

Formally, we define the distillation objective as L_{KD}:

$$L_{KD} = L_O(M_T(x), M_S(x))$$

Where L_O is a loss function that works on the logits of M_T and M_S. The most common choices for this loss are the cross entropy loss, the KL-divergence loss and the mean-squared error loss. In the case of KL-divergence or cross-entropy loss is it a common practice to use soft-targets (Hinton et al., 2015) instead of direct logits, which means to apply a softmax with temperature T (with $T >= 1$) to $M_T(x)$ and $M_S(x)$ in order to produce a soft probability distribution over the classes.

Also, typically we use not only the output of M_T but also the gold labels from the training dataset. The complete loss, accounting these labels can be seen as:

$$L = \alpha L_{CE} + (1 - \alpha) L_{KD}$$

Where L_{CE} is the traditional cross-entropy loss against gold labels and α defines the weight of each loss.

An overview of the entire framework is shown in Figure 2.

3.2 Approach

Our approach has two stages, in the first one, we fine-tune a set of candidate teacher models in a set of tasks of interest. Then, for each task we select the best teacher model (which we define as the model with minimum validation loss among all candidate models) as the teacher model for that task. In stage two, we apply KD using these teachers models and a set of students models.

The complete set of evaluated tasks and possible teacher models is described in Section 4.

3.3 Student Models

For the student models, we rely on the ALBERT (Lan et al., 2020) architecture. This architecture is lighter in terms of parameters because all layers are weight-tied. Specifically, we adopt ALBETO models (Cañete et al., 2022) models, adhering to the ALBERT architecture and exclusively trained for the Spanish language. We considered ALBETO *tiny*, which is the lightest models of all ALBETO models and also, inspired by Sanh et al. (2019) we propose models with less layers (and thus faster) that match the configuration of ALBETO *base*, except on the number of layers. These lighter ALBERTs are then initialized with the weights of ALBETO *base*. These models are noted in the tables as ALBETO *base-n*, where *n* is the number of layers of the model.

3.4 Implementation Details

All our code uses Python and PyTorch (Paszke et al., 2019) as machine learning framework and is publicly available on GitHub[1].

The evaluation of the inference speed of the proposed models is performed through the utilization of the Multiply-Accumulate (MACs) metric, which provides a hardware-agnostic evaluation and is thus considered to be a more robust evaluation criterion. This measurement is conducted using the THOP[2] library, which operates on PyTorch models, to accurately measure MACs. In addition, to provide a more intuitive understanding of the models' performance, actual inference speeds on commonly used hardware configurations are also reported in Section 3.5.

For KD, we first experimented using the three different losses, with different parameters α and T using Optuna (Akiba et al., 2019). These experiments showed that the best results where using $\alpha = 0$ and $T = 1$. With that parameters, while the three different losses works well, KL-divergence was slightly better, so we conducted the rest of the experiments using that configuration.

For both stages of our approach, the only preprocessing applied was tokenization of the input texts according to the subword vocabulary of every model.

For the first stage, which is fine-tuning of the possible teacher models we rely heavily on the HuggingFace Transformers (Wolf et al., 2020) library. For all models and tasks, we run a grid search over the hyperparameters batch size = {16, 32, 64} and epochs = {2, 3, 4}. We experimented with learning rate = {1e-5, 2e-5, 3e-5, 5e-5} for all models except ALBETO *large*, *xlarge*, and *xxlarge*, where we used learning rate = {1e-6, 2e-6, 3e-6, 5e-6}, which are the same hyperparameters used on (Cañete et al., 2022).

For the second stage, which is applying KD, the implementation depended on the task. For text classification tasks we do the KD between the pooled output of both models. For sequence tagging and question answering tasks, we aligned the first token of every word (because the vocabulary of both models is not always the same, which implies that the subword tokenization can result in a different number of tokens) and then we do the KD using the sequence of representations of first tokens for every word in the text between the two models. We note that this approach is not new and is almost the same applied on the original BERT (Devlin et al., 2019) for sequence tagging tasks, that was adapted to work on KD.

For the experiments on this second stage we did a grid search using the hyperparameters: learning rate = {5e-5, 1e-4}, batch sizes = {16, 32, 64} and epochs = 50, we also use early stopping with a tolerance of 10 epochs of no improving.

To accelerate experimentation, we employ a teacher output cache, with its impact on training times discussed in Appendix C.

In Tables 2 and 3 we report results of the models on the test set of each dataset. These models were selected based on the best results on the validation set among the grid search experiments. These models are also the ones publicly available on the HuggingFace Hub.

3.5 Inference Speed on Common Hardware

In our work we measure inference speed in terms of Multiply-Accumulate (MAC) operations. This metric is advantageous as it is agnostic to hardware variations. However, it can be useful to also report the actual inference speed of models on common hardware, as this can provide a more intuitive understanding of their performance.

Table 1 presents the average number of inferences per second that can be achieved on two different hardware platforms, a CPU with an In-

[1]https://github.com/dccuchile/speedy-gonzales
[2]https://github.com/Lyken17/pytorch-OpCounter

Model	Inferences per second	
	CPU	**GPU**
Fine-tuning		
BETO *uncased*	3.96	107.19
BETO *cased*	4.26	109.02
DistilBETO	9.12	217.40
ALBETO *tiny*	32.53	539.61
ALBETO *base*	4.50	108.62
ALBETO *large*	1.29	33.62
ALBETO *xlarge*	0.35	11.72
ALBETO *xxlarge*	0.14	6.60
BERTIN	3.99	109.39
RoBERTa BNE *base*	3.82	107.77
RoBERTa BNE *large*	1.18	33.65
Task-specific Knowledge Distillation		
ALBETO *tiny*	32.53	539.61
ALBETO *base-2*	31.08	625.30
ALBETO *base-4*	15.16	319.32
ALBETO *base-6*	10.45	213.53
ALBETO *base-8*	6.82	160.66
ALBETO *base-10*	6.01	128.38

Table 1: The number of inferences per second of each model on two different hardware settings, CPU and GPU.

tel Core i7-11700K and a GPU with a NVIDIA GeForce RTX 3090. To account for variance in the measurements, we first conducted 10 warm-up inferences followed by 100 real measures for each model. We then applied an aggressive outlier filtering method based on the modified Z-Score (Iglewicz and Hoaglin, 1993) with a threshold of 0.75, which resulted in the removal of approximately 40-45% of the measures. The remaining 55-60% of the measures were used to calculate, with very low variance, the average inference speed (in milliseconds) and the number of inferences that could be performed in one second, which serves as a clearer illustration of the model's inference speed.

It is worth noting that the difference in speed between the larger models and the proposed models trained using task-specific KD is substantial. Specifically, on the CPU setting, which is representative of popular serverless platforms used in industry, the best model found in this study in terms of task performance, ALBETO *xxlarge*, would take several seconds for a single inference, making it unsuitable for real-time user-facing applications. On the other hand, if we consider our proposed faster models, we can observe that ALBETO *base-6* is capable of executing more than 10 inferences per second, which is a much more acceptable latency for a real-time application.

4 Evaluating Spanish Pre-trained Language Models

In order to achieve our goal of have efficient models for Spanish in a variety of tasks we first define a set of tasks to evaluate those models. These tasks are the same evaluated by Cañete et al. (2022) and are described in Section 4.1. We then define a set of possible teacher models, in particular, we wanted to try every model that was pre-trained on general domain Spanish text and is publicly available, therefore we exclude RigoBERTa (Serrano et al., 2022), which is a DeBERTa (He et al., 2021) model for Spanish that is not public and RoBERTuito (Pérez et al., 2022) which is a RoBERTa-like model for Spanish that was trained on Twitter datasets and should be better suited for social media related tasks. All considered models are described in Section 4.2. After evaluating all models on each task, we selected the model with lowest validation loss as the teacher model for the task. The list of selected models can be found in Appendix A.

4.1 Tasks and Data

4.1.1 Document Classification

The task of document classification consists on the assignment of an entire document to a category according to its semantic meaning. For our evaluation we are using the Spanish portion of MLDoc (Schwenk and Li, 2018) which is a multilingual dataset for document classification in eight languages. MLDoc is based on the Reuters Corpus (Lewis et al., 2004) and has four different categories for its documents, which are: Corporate/Industrial, Economics, Government/Social and Markets.

4.1.2 Paraphrase Identification

On Paraphrase Identification we aim to assess whether two sentences share the same semantic meaning. To evaluate our models in this task we are using the Spanish subset of PAWS-X (Yang et al., 2019). This dataset can be seen as a translation to six different languages of the PAWS (Zhang et al., 2019) dataset, where the train set is machine translated and the validation and test sets were translated professionally by humans.

Model	Text Classification (Accuracy)			Sequence Tagging (F1 Score)		Question Answering (F1 Score / Exact Match)		
	MLDoc	**PAWS-X**	**XNLI**	**POS**	**NER**	**MLQA**	**SQAC**	**TAR / XQuAD**
Fine-tuning								
BETO *uncased*	96.38	84.25	77.76	97.81	80.85	64.12 / 40.83	72.22 / 53.45	74.81 / 54.62
BETO *cased*	96.65	89.80	81.98	98.95	**87.14**	67.65 / 43.38	78.65 / 60.94	77.81 / 56.97
DistilBETO	96.35	75.80	76.59	97.67	78.13	57.97 / 35.50	64.41 / 45.34	66.97 / 46.55
ALBETO *tiny*	95.82	80.20	73.43	97.34	75.42	51.84 / 28.28	59.28 / 39.16	66.43 / 45.71
ALBETO *base*	96.07	87.95	79.88	98.21	82.89	66.12 / 41.10	77.71 / 59.84	77.18 / 57.05
ALBETO *large*	92.22	86.05	78.94	97.98	82.36	65.56 / 40.98	76.36 / 56.54	76.72 / 56.21
ALBETO *xlarge*	95.70	89.05	81.68	98.20	81.42	68.26 / 43.76	78.64 / 59.26	**80.15 / 59.66**
ALBETO *xxlarge*	96.85	89.85	**82.42**	98.43	83.06	**70.17 / 45.99**	**81.49** / 62.67	79.13 / 58.40
BERTIN	96.47	88.65	80.50	**99.02**	85.66	66.06 / 42.16	78.42 / 60.05	77.05 / 57.14
RoBERTa BNE *base*	96.82	89.90	81.12	99.00	86.80	67.31 / 44.50	80.53 / **62.72**	77.16 / 55.46
RoBERTa BNE *large*	**97.00**	**90.00**	51.62	61.83	21.47	67.69 / 44.88	80.41 / 62.14	77.34 / 56.97
Task-specific Knowledge Distillation								
ALBETO *tiny*	96.40	85.05	75.99	97.36	72.51	54.17 / 32.22	63.03 / 43.35	67.47 / 46.13
ALBETO *base-2*	96.20	76.75	73.65	97.17	69.69	48.62 / 26.17	58.40 / 39.00	63.41 / 42.35
ALBETO *base-4*	96.35	86.40	78.68	97.60	74.58	62.19 / 38.28	71.41 / 52.87	73.31 / 52.43
ALBETO *base-6*	96.40	88.45	81.66	97.82	78.41	66.35 / 42.01	76.99 / 59.00	75.59 / **56.72**
ALBETO *base-8*	96.70	89.75	**82.55**	97.96	80.23	67.39 / 42.94	77.79 / 59.63	77.89 / **56.72**
ALBETO *base-10*	**96.88**	**89.95**	82.26	**98.00**	**81.10**	**68.29 / 44.29**	**79.89 / 62.04**	**78.21** / 56.21

Table 2: Results of every evaluated model on the test set of each task. On Text Classification datasets (MLDoc, PAWS-X, XNLI) we use Accuracy as metric. For POS and NER, which are Sequence Tagging tasks, we report the F1 Score. On Question Answering, we report two metrics, noted as F1 Score / Exact Match.

Model	Parameters	Speedup	Score
Fine-tuning			
BETO *uncased*	110M	1.00x	81.02
BETO *cased*	110M	1.00x	84.82
DistilBETO	67M	2.00x	76.73
ALBETO *tiny*	**5M**	**18.05x**	74.97
ALBETO *base*	12M	0.99x	83.25
ALBETO *large*	18M	0.28x	82.02
ALBETO *xlarge*	59M	0.07x	84.13
ALBETO *xxlarge*	223M	0.03x	**85.17**
BERTIN	125M	1.00x	83.97
RoBERTa BNE *base*	125M	1.00x	84.83
RoBERTa BNE *large*	355M	0.28x	68.42
Task-specific Knowledge Distillation			
ALBETO *tiny*	**5M**	**18.05x**	76.49
ALBETO *base-2*	12M	5.96x	72.98
ALBETO *base-4*	12M	2.99x	80.06
ALBETO *base-6*	12M	1.99x	82.70
ALBETO *base-8*	12M	1.49x	83.78
ALBETO *base-10*	12M	1.19x	**84.32**

Table 3: The summary of results of every evaluated model in terms of parameters, inference speedup and overall score across tasks. The speedup is relative to BETO models. The score column shows the average of the metrics on all tasks.

4.1.3 Natural Language Inference

In the task of Natural Language Inference we are given two sentences, an "hypothesis" and a "premise", and our task is to determine if one entails the other one, contradicts it or is neutral to it. For this task we use the Spanish subset of XNLI (Conneau et al., 2018), which, very similarly to PAWS-X, offers a machine translated train set from MultiNLI (Williams et al., 2018) and professionally translated validation and test sets to 15 languages.

4.1.4 Part of Speech Tagging

The objective of the task of Part of Speech Tagging is to label words within a sentence according to its corresponding syntactic categories. There are different categories of parts of speech, for example, nouns, verbs, adjectives, adverbs, pronouns, etc. In this task the dataset used was AnCora (Taulé et al., 2008) which is included on the Spanish part of Universal Dependencies (de Marneffe et al., 2021) Treebank.

4.1.5 Named Entity Recognition

Named Entity Recognition is a sequence labeling task in which the goal is to classify entities within a text with their corresponding type. These types are usually names of people, places, organizations or miscellaneous. These entities can be formed by more than one word, that is why the datasets typically adopt the BIO annotation, which means for a word that it can be the beggining (B) of a entity, inside (I) a entity or out (O) of it. For this task the dataset used as evaluation is from the shared task of CoNLL-2002 (Tjong Kim Sang, 2002), we use the Spanish subset of it.

4.1.6 Question Answering

There are different types of Question Answering tasks. In this evaluation our focus is Extractive Question Answering, that is, given a context text and question about that context, point out the span of words that fully answers the question. On this task we considered four different datasets, which are, MLQA (Lewis et al., 2020), SQAC (Gutiérrez-Fandiño et al., 2022), TAR (Carrino et al., 2020) and XQuAD (Artetxe et al., 2020). MLQA is a multilingual dataset created by using English QA instances and then professionally translated them to six different languages, from these they provide a validation and a test set, but they also provide a machine translated version of SQuAD v1.1 (Rajpurkar et al., 2016) as train set to each of the languages, we use the Spanish subsets of it. TAR offers a different machine translated dataset from SQuAD v1.1 to Spanish. XQuAD provides a test set obtained from SQuAD v1.1 and professionally translated to 11 different languages. Following the setup by (Cañete et al., 2020) we pair the train and validation sets from TAR and the Spanish test set from XQuAD as a single evaluation dataset. Finally, SQAC is the only dataset evaluated that was built exclusively for Spanish.

4.2 Models

4.2.1 BETO

BETO (Cañete et al., 2020) is the first Transformer encoder pre-trained exclusively on Spanish corpora. It is BERT-base sized model that has two versions available, *uncased* and *cased*. They have an approximate of 110M parameters and each have a vocabulary of 31K BPE (Sennrich et al., 2016) subwords which was constructed using SentencePiece (Kudo and Richardson, 2018). Both models were trained for 2M optimization steps on the SUC (Cañete, 2019) dataset.

4.2.2 ALBETO

ALBETO (Cañete et al., 2022) is a series of ALBERT (Lan et al., 2020) models for Spanish. There are 5 different sizes, that range from 5M to 223M parameters, which are *tiny*, *base*, *large*, *xlarge* and *xxlarge*. The *tiny* model is similar to the one trained on Chinese [3], the rest follow closely the configurations trained on the original ALBERT work. They share a vocabulary of 31K lowercase BPE (Sennrich et al., 2016) subwords created using SentencePiece (Kudo and Richardson, 2018). All ALBETO models were trained on SUC (Cañete, 2019).

4.2.3 DistilBETO

DistilBETO (Cañete et al., 2022) is a lighter Transformer encoder based on the weights of BETO and further pre-trained using the knowledge distillation technique presented by (Sanh et al., 2019) on DistilBERT. It has 67M parameters and uses the same lowercase vocabulary from BETO *uncased*.

4.2.4 RoBERTa-BNE

RoBERTa-BNE (Gutiérrez-Fandiño et al., 2022) are two different sized RoBERTa (Liu et al., 2019) models trained on Spanish using the National Library of Spain (BNE) (Gutiérrez-Fandiño et al., 2022) corpus which is also the larger Spanish corpus of this type to this date. The *base* model has 125M parameters while the *large* version has 355M. Both version share a vocabulary of 50K BPE (Sennrich et al., 2016) subwords.

4.2.5 BERTIN

BERTIN (de la Rosa et al., 2022) is a RoBERTa-base model trained on the Spanish portion of the mC4 (Raffel et al., 2020) dataset. It has the same size, configuration and vocabulary of the RoBERTa-BNE *base* model.

5 Results

Table 2 presents the results of each model across all evaluated tasks. A general observation is that there are two distinct behaviors among the tasks. Firstly, there is minimal variation in performance between smaller and larger models in certain tasks, as evidenced by the comparable high scores achieved by all models in the MLDoc and POS tasks. It is hypothesized that these tasks are relatively simple, and as a result, the utilization of larger models results in overparameterization.

Secondly, there are tasks where there is a notable difference in performance between smaller and bigger models. This is evident in tasks such as Paraphrase Identification (PAWS-X), Natural Language Inference (XNLI), Named Entity Recognition (NER) and Question Answering (MLQA,

[3] https://github.com/ckiplab/ckip-transformers

SQAC, TAR/XQuAD), where the larger models tend to outperform the smaller models. This suggests that these tasks are more complex and require a greater model capacity. Overall, the results of this evaluation demonstrate the importance of considering the appropriate model size for a given task, as overparameterization can lead to suboptimal inference performance.

5.1 Text Classification

In our experiments on text classification tasks, we observed that models with a depth of 8 or more layers exhibit performance comparable to the best larger models, while also demonstrating significant improvements in inference time. Specifically, for the XNLI dataset, we found that the ALBETO *base-8* model outperforms all other models evaluated in our study.

5.2 Sequence Tagging

On NER we observe a significant difference between our faster models and the *cased* models (BETO, BERTIN, RoBERTa-BNE), especially with BETO *cased*, which was the best model on the task. Furthermore, we observe a difference of almost 4.1 percentual difference (pd) between ALBETO *xxlarge*, and BETO *cased*, even though ALBETO *xxlarge* is one of the largest models in the fine-tuning setting. Additionally, we find a difference of almost 6.3 pd between the *cased* and *uncased* versions of BETO. Based on these observations, we posit that the difference in performance between *cased* and *uncased* models can be attributed to the additional hints provided by capitalization for solving the NER task. Specifically, the names of persons, organizations, and places typically begin with a capital letter. Furthermore, our results from models trained using knowledge distillation (KD) suggest that this hint is not easily replicable in an uncased model.

5.3 Question Answering

The performance on Question Answering datasets, as indicated in the final three columns of the table, follows a pattern similar to that observed in text classification tasks. The larger models, specially ALBETO *xxlarge* and *xlarge*, exhibit higher performance, while our proposed models featuring 8 or more layers present results similar to those of the base-sized models.

5.4 Discussion and Summary

It should be noted that some models performed significantly worse than the others. Specifically, the utilization of RoBERTa-BNE *large* on XNLI, POS, and NER tasks produced subpar results. This deviation from the performance of the same model on other tasks, as well as the results reported by Gutiérrez-Fandiño et al. (2022), suggests that RoBERTa-BNE *large* may be particularly sensitive to hyperparameter selection and may benefit from additional hyperparameter tuning.

Our results show a general progression in performance of our proposed models as the number of layers increases. A clear trade-off between task performance and inference speed is observed, with a more pronounced effect in text classification and question answering tasks, and a weaker effect in sequence tagging. Additionally, at equal inference speed, our models trained with task-specific distillation exhibit improved performance compared to DistilBETO, which was trained with task-agnostic distillation, despite having significantly fewer parameters.

A similar effect can be observed when comparing ALBETO *base-{8-10}* to the original 12-layer ALBETO *base* fine-tuned using standard techniques, the former exhibits improved performance. This underscores the vital role of task-specific knowledge distillation in obtaining improved performance for these faster models. Additional experiments comparing straightforward fine-tuning and the application of knowledge distillation on these more compact and faster models are presented in Appendix B.

Table 3 summarizes our findings. Following the methodology of GLUE (Wang et al., 2018), we compute a global score that encompasses all tasks, which is displayed in the third column. The score is the simple mean of the individual task results. In the instance of Question Answering, which provides two metrics, we opted for the F1 Score as the representative score for the task. The ALBETO *xxlarge* model achieved the best overall performance, although it was also the slowest and had the second largest number of parameters. With a mere 0.35 performance drop from the top model, the RoBERTa BNE *base* and BETO *cased* models exhibited comparable results. The ALBETO *base-10*, exhibiting a 19% improvement in speed compared to BETO models, is our strongest proposed model with a difference of approximately 0.5

performance drop from the aforementioned models. Our remaining models display varying degrees of improved inference speed, at the expense of slight reductions in task performance.

6 Conclusion and Future Work

In this work, we introduce Speedy Gonzales, a novel resource for the Spanish NLP and IR communities comprising a collection of computationally efficient language models trained on six tasks and eight datasets. By applying the Knowledge Distillation technique, our models achieve comparable performance to state-of-the-art models, while showing faster inference speeds.

The full collection of models, including our proposed models and all the teacher models fine-tuned on the tasks considered, are made publicly available for further research.

We believe that the availability of these models and the expansion of the Knowledge Distillation method to additional tasks will drive the widespread utilization of large language models in the Spanish speaking community, particularly for individuals and organizations seeking to tackle crucial information retrieval challenges, such as question answering, text similarity and semantic search, in both academic and industrial settings.

Potential directions for future research include exploring the use of multiple teachers in the distillation process and developing metrics to formally evaluate the balance between inference speed and task performance.

Acknowledgements

This work was supported by ANID Millennium Science Initiative Program Code ICN17_002 and the National Center for Artificial Intelligence CENIA FB210017, Basal ANID.

References

Takuya Akiba, Shotaro Sano, Toshihiko Yanase, Takeru Ohta, and Masanori Koyama. 2019. Optuna: A next-generation hyperparameter optimization framework. In *Proceedings of the 25th ACM SIGKDD International Conference on Knowledge Discovery & Data Mining, KDD 2019, Anchorage, AK, USA, August 4-8, 2019*, pages 2623–2631. ACM.

Mikel Artetxe, Sebastian Ruder, and Dani Yogatama. 2020. On the cross-lingual transferability of monolingual representations. In *Proceedings of the 58th Annual Meeting of the Association for Computational Linguistics*, pages 4623–4637, Online. Association for Computational Linguistics.

Haoli Bai, Wei Zhang, Lu Hou, Lifeng Shang, Jin Jin, Xin Jiang, Qun Liu, Michael Lyu, and Irwin King. 2021. BinaryBERT: Pushing the limit of BERT quantization. In *Proceedings of the 59th Annual Meeting of the Association for Computational Linguistics and the 11th International Joint Conference on Natural Language Processing (Volume 1: Long Papers)*, pages 4334–4348, Online. Association for Computational Linguistics.

Davis Blalock, Jose Javier Gonzalez Ortiz, Jonathan Frankle, and John Guttag. 2020. What is the state of neural network pruning? In *Proceedings of Machine Learning and Systems*, volume 2, pages 129–146.

Tom Brown, Benjamin Mann, Nick Ryder, Melanie Subbiah, Jared D Kaplan, Prafulla Dhariwal, Arvind Neelakantan, Pranav Shyam, Girish Sastry, Amanda Askell, Sandhini Agarwal, Ariel Herbert-Voss, Gretchen Krueger, Tom Henighan, Rewon Child, Aditya Ramesh, Daniel Ziegler, Jeffrey Wu, Clemens Winter, Chris Hesse, Mark Chen, Eric Sigler, Mateusz Litwin, Scott Gray, Benjamin Chess, Jack Clark, Christopher Berner, Sam McCandlish, Alec Radford, Ilya Sutskever, and Dario Amodei. 2020. Language models are few-shot learners. In *Advances in Neural Information Processing Systems*, volume 33, pages 1877–1901. Curran Associates, Inc.

José Cañete, Sebastian Donoso, Felipe Bravo-Marquez, Andrés Carvallo, and Vladimir Araujo. 2022. ALBETO and DistilBETO: Lightweight Spanish language models. In *Proceedings of the Thirteenth Language Resources and Evaluation Conference*, pages 4291–4298, Marseille, France. European Language Resources Association.

Casimiro Pio Carrino, Marta R. Costa-jussà, and José A. R. Fonollosa. 2020. Automatic Spanish translation of SQuAD dataset for multi-lingual question answering. In *Proceedings of the Twelfth Language Resources and Evaluation Conference*, pages 5515–5523, Marseille, France. European Language Resources Association.

José Cañete. 2019. Compilation of Large Spanish Unannotated Corpora.

José Cañete, Gabriel Chaperon, Rodrigo Fuentes, Jou-Hui Ho, Hojin Kang, and Jorge Pérez. 2020. Spanish pre-trained bert model and evaluation data. In *PML4DC at ICLR 2020*.

Alexis Conneau, Ruty Rinott, Guillaume Lample, Adina Williams, Samuel Bowman, Holger Schwenk, and Veselin Stoyanov. 2018. XNLI: Evaluating cross-lingual sentence representations. In *Proceedings of the 2018 Conference on Empirical Methods in Natural Language Processing*, pages 2475–2485, Brussels, Belgium. Association for Computational Linguistics.

Javier de la Rosa, Eduardo G Ponferrada, Paulo Villegas, Pablo González de Prado Salas, Manu Romero, and Maria Grandury. 2022. Bertin: Efficient pre-training of a spanish language model using perplexity sampling. *Procesamiento del Lenguaje Natural*, 68(0):13–23.

Marie-Catherine de Marneffe, Christopher D. Manning, Joakim Nivre, and Daniel Zeman. 2021. Universal Dependencies. *Computational Linguistics*, 47(2):255–308.

Jacob Devlin, Ming-Wei Chang, Kenton Lee, and Kristina Toutanova. 2019. BERT: Pre-training of deep bidirectional transformers for language understanding. In *Proceedings of the 2019 Conference of the North American Chapter of the Association for Computational Linguistics: Human Language Technologies, Volume 1 (Long and Short Papers)*, pages 4171–4186, Minneapolis, Minnesota. Association for Computational Linguistics.

Jonathan Frankle and Michael Carbin. 2019. The lottery ticket hypothesis: Finding sparse, trainable neural networks. In *International Conference on Learning Representations*.

Amir Gholami, Sehoon Kim, Zhen Dong, Zhewei Yao, Michael W. Mahoney, and Kurt Keutzer. 2021. A survey of quantization methods for efficient neural network inference. *CoRR*, abs/2103.13630.

Jianping Gou, Baosheng Yu, Stephen J. Maybank, and Dacheng Tao. 2021. Knowledge distillation: A survey. *Int. J. Comput. Vision*, 129(6):1789–1819.

Asier Gutiérrez-Fandiño, Jordi Armengol Estapé, Marc Pàmies, Joan Llop Palao, Joaquin Silveira Ocampo, Casimiro Pio Carrino, Carme Armentano Oller, Carlos Rodriguez Penagos, Aitor Gonzalez Agirre, and Marta Villegas. 2022. Maria: Spanish language models. *Procesamiento del Lenguaje Natural*, 68.

Pengcheng He, Xiaodong Liu, Jianfeng Gao, and Weizhu Chen. 2021. Deberta: decoding-enhanced bert with disentangled attention. In *9th International Conference on Learning Representations, ICLR 2021, Virtual Event, Austria, May 3-7, 2021*. OpenReview.net.

Geoffrey Hinton, Oriol Vinyals, Jeff Dean, et al. 2015. Distilling the knowledge in a neural network. *arXiv preprint arXiv:1503.02531*, 2(7).

Boris Iglewicz and David C Hoaglin. 1993. *Volume 16: how to detect and handle outliers*. Quality Press.

Xiaoqi Jiao, Yichun Yin, Lifeng Shang, Xin Jiang, Xiao Chen, Linlin Li, Fang Wang, and Qun Liu. 2020. TinyBERT: Distilling BERT for natural language understanding. In *Findings of the Association for Computational Linguistics: EMNLP 2020*, pages 4163–4174, Online. Association for Computational Linguistics.

Xiaoqi Jiao, Yichun Yin, Lifeng Shang, Xin Jiang, Xiao Chen, Linlin Li, Fang Wang, and Qun Liu. 2021. Lightmbert: A simple yet effective method for multilingual bert distillation. *arXiv preprint arXiv:2103.06418*.

Taku Kudo and John Richardson. 2018. SentencePiece: A simple and language independent subword tokenizer and detokenizer for neural text processing. In *Proceedings of the 2018 Conference on Empirical Methods in Natural Language Processing: System Demonstrations*, pages 66–71, Brussels, Belgium. Association for Computational Linguistics.

Zhenzhong Lan, Mingda Chen, Sebastian Goodman, Kevin Gimpel, Piyush Sharma, and Radu Soricut. 2020. ALBERT: A lite BERT for self-supervised learning of language representations. In *8th International Conference on Learning Representations, ICLR 2020, Addis Ababa, Ethiopia, April 26-30, 2020*. OpenReview.net.

David D. Lewis, Yiming Yang, Tony G. Rose, and Fan Li. 2004. RCV1: A new benchmark collection for text categorization research. *J. Mach. Learn. Res.*, 5:361–397.

Patrick Lewis, Barlas Oguz, Ruty Rinott, Sebastian Riedel, and Holger Schwenk. 2020. MLQA: Evaluating cross-lingual extractive question answering. In *Proceedings of the 58th Annual Meeting of the Association for Computational Linguistics*, pages 7315–7330, Online. Association for Computational Linguistics.

Yinhan Liu, Myle Ott, Naman Goyal, Jingfei Du, Mandar Joshi, Danqi Chen, Omer Levy, Mike Lewis, Luke Zettlemoyer, and Veselin Stoyanov. 2019. Roberta: A robustly optimized BERT pretraining approach. *CoRR*, abs/1907.11692.

Adam Paszke, Sam Gross, Francisco Massa, Adam Lerer, James Bradbury, Gregory Chanan, Trevor Killeen, Zeming Lin, Natalia Gimelshein, Luca Antiga, Alban Desmaison, Andreas Kopf, Edward Yang, Zachary DeVito, Martin Raison, Alykhan Tejani, Sasank Chilamkurthy, Benoit Steiner, Lu Fang, Junjie Bai, and Soumith Chintala. 2019. Pytorch: An imperative style, high-performance deep learning library. In *Advances in Neural Information Processing Systems*, volume 32. Curran Associates, Inc.

Juan Manuel Pérez, Damián Ariel Furman, Laura Alonso Alemany, and Franco M. Luque. 2022. RoBERTuito: a pre-trained language model for social media text in Spanish. In *Proceedings of the Thirteenth Language Resources and Evaluation Conference*, pages 7235–7243, Marseille, France. European Language Resources Association.

Colin Raffel, Noam Shazeer, Adam Roberts, Katherine Lee, Sharan Narang, Michael Matena, Yanqi Zhou, Wei Li, and Peter J. Liu. 2020. Exploring the limits of transfer learning with a unified text-to-text transformer. *Journal of Machine Learning Research*, 21(140):1–67.

Pranav Rajpurkar, Jian Zhang, Konstantin Lopyrev, and Percy Liang. 2016. SQuAD: 100,000+ questions for machine comprehension of text. In *Proceedings of the 2016 Conference on Empirical Methods in Natural Language Processing*, pages 2383–2392, Austin, Texas. Association for Computational Linguistics.

Victor Sanh, Lysandre Debut, Julien Chaumond, and Thomas Wolf. 2019. Distilbert, a distilled version of BERT: smaller, faster, cheaper and lighter. *CoRR*, abs/1910.01108.

Holger Schwenk and Xian Li. 2018. A corpus for multilingual document classification in eight languages. In *Proceedings of the Eleventh International Conference on Language Resources and Evaluation (LREC 2018)*, Miyazaki, Japan. European Language Resources Association (ELRA).

Rico Sennrich, Barry Haddow, and Alexandra Birch. 2016. Neural machine translation of rare words with subword units. In *Proceedings of the 54th Annual Meeting of the Association for Computational Linguistics (Volume 1: Long Papers)*, pages 1715–1725, Berlin, Germany. Association for Computational Linguistics.

Alejandro Vaca Serrano, Guillem García Subies, Helena Montoro Zamorano, Nuria Aldama Garcia, Doaa Samy, David Betancur Sánchez, Antonio Moreno-Sandoval, Marta Guerrero Nieto, and Álvaro Barbero Jiménez. 2022. Rigoberta: A state-of-the-art language model for spanish. *CoRR*, abs/2205.10233.

Raphael Tang, Yao Lu, Linqing Liu, Lili Mou, Olga Vechtomova, and Jimmy Lin. 2019. Distilling task-specific knowledge from BERT into simple neural networks. *CoRR*, abs/1903.12136.

Mariona Taulé, M. Antònia Martí, and Marta Recasens. 2008. AnCora: Multilevel annotated corpora for Catalan and Spanish. In *Proceedings of the Sixth International Conference on Language Resources and Evaluation (LREC'08)*, Marrakech, Morocco. European Language Resources Association (ELRA).

Erik F. Tjong Kim Sang. 2002. Introduction to the CoNLL-2002 shared task: Language-independent named entity recognition. In *COLING-02: The 6th Conference on Natural Language Learning 2002 (CoNLL-2002)*.

Iulia Turc, Ming-Wei Chang, Kenton Lee, and Kristina Toutanova. 2019. Well-read students learn better: On the importance of pre-training compact models. *arXiv preprint arXiv:1908.08962v2*.

Ashish Vaswani, Noam Shazeer, Niki Parmar, Jakob Uszkoreit, Llion Jones, Aidan N Gomez, Ł ukasz Kaiser, and Illia Polosukhin. 2017. Attention is all you need. In *Advances in Neural Information Processing Systems*, volume 30. Curran Associates, Inc.

Alex Wang, Amanpreet Singh, Julian Michael, Felix Hill, Omer Levy, and Samuel Bowman. 2018. GLUE: A multi-task benchmark and analysis platform for natural language understanding. In *Proceedings of the 2018 EMNLP Workshop BlackboxNLP: Analyzing and Interpreting Neural Networks for NLP*, pages 353–355, Brussels, Belgium. Association for Computational Linguistics.

Wenhui Wang, Furu Wei, Li Dong, Hangbo Bao, Nan Yang, and Ming Zhou. 2020. Minilm: Deep self-attention distillation for task-agnostic compression of pre-trained transformers. In *Proceedings of the 34th International Conference on Neural Information Processing Systems*, NIPS'20, Red Hook, NY, USA. Curran Associates Inc.

Adina Williams, Nikita Nangia, and Samuel Bowman. 2018. A broad-coverage challenge corpus for sentence understanding through inference. In *Proceedings of the 2018 Conference of the North American Chapter of the Association for Computational Linguistics: Human Language Technologies, Volume 1 (Long Papers)*, pages 1112–1122, New Orleans, Louisiana. Association for Computational Linguistics.

Thomas Wolf, Lysandre Debut, Victor Sanh, Julien Chaumond, Clement Delangue, Anthony Moi, Pierric Cistac, Tim Rault, Remi Louf, Morgan Funtowicz, Joe Davison, Sam Shleifer, Patrick von Platen, Clara Ma, Yacine Jernite, Julien Plu, Canwen Xu, Teven Le Scao, Sylvain Gugger, Mariama Drame, Quentin Lhoest, and Alexander Rush. 2020. Transformers: State-of-the-art natural language processing. In *Proceedings of the 2020 Conference on Empirical Methods in Natural Language Processing: System Demonstrations*, pages 38–45, Online. Association for Computational Linguistics.

Yinfei Yang, Yuan Zhang, Chris Tar, and Jason Baldridge. 2019. PAWS-X: A cross-lingual adversarial dataset for paraphrase identification. In *Proceedings of the 2019 Conference on Empirical Methods in Natural Language Processing and the 9th International Joint Conference on Natural Language Processing (EMNLP-IJCNLP)*, pages 3687–3692, Hong Kong, China. Association for Computational Linguistics.

Andrew Yates, Rodrigo Nogueira, and Jimmy Lin. 2021. Pretrained transformers for text ranking: BERT and beyond. In *Proceedings of the 2021 Conference of the North American Chapter of the Association for Computational Linguistics: Human Language Technologies: Tutorials*, pages 1–4, Online. Association for Computational Linguistics.

Wei Zhang, Lu Hou, Yichun Yin, Lifeng Shang, Xiao Chen, Xin Jiang, and Qun Liu. 2020. TernaryBERT: Distillation-aware ultra-low bit BERT. In *Proceedings of the 2020 Conference on Empirical Methods in Natural Language Processing (EMNLP)*, pages 509–521, Online. Association for Computational Linguistics.

Yuan Zhang, Jason Baldridge, and Luheng He. 2019. PAWS: Paraphrase adversaries from word scrambling.

In *Proceedings of the 2019 Conference of the North American Chapter of the Association for Computational Linguistics: Human Language Technologies, Volume 1 (Long and Short Papers)*, pages 1298–1308, Minneapolis, Minnesota. Association for Computational Linguistics.

A Selected Teacher Models

Table 4 presents the teacher models selected for each task. The selection process is based on the lowest validation loss achieved among the candidate teacher models that were fine-tuned for each task.

Dataset	Teacher Model
MLDoc	RoBERTa BNE *large*
PAWS-X	ALBETO *xxlarge*
XNLI	ALBETO *xxlarge*
POS	RoBERTa BNE *base*
NER	RoBERTa BNE *base*
MLQA	ALBETO *xxlarge*
SQAC	ALBETO *xxlarge*
TAR / XQuAD	ALBETO *xxlarge*

Table 4: The teacher models selected for each task.

B Importance of Knowledge Distillation

In addition to other experiments, we conducted ablation experiments to evaluate the contribution of Task-Specific Knowledge Distillation to the results of our faster models based on ALBETO.

Tables 5, 6, and 7 compare the performance of each of our proposed models under two training settings: regular fine-tuning (FT) and task-specific knowledge distillation (KD). For fine-tuning and KD we followed the settings described in Section 3.4.

Overall, our results indicate that training using KD generally yields better results than simple fine-tuning, except for sequence tagging tasks (POS, NER), where the results are mixed.

Table 5 presents the results of text classification tasks, where we observe that KD outperforms fine-tuning. In MLDoc, which is hypothesized as an easier task, the performance is similar for both training schemes and different models. However, in PAWS-X and XNLI, we observe a significant difference between the fine-tuning and KD training schemes.

Table 6 presents the results for sequence tagging tasks, where the performance of models under the KD and fine-tuning settings are mixed. Unlike other types of tasks, where the KD training method is the clear winner, the results here vary. In the case of NER, faster models perform better under the fine-tuning setting, while those with larger compute requirements perform better under the KD setting.

Finally, Table 7 presents the results for question answering, where we observe that models trained using KD generally exhibit better performance than those trained using simple fine-tuning, with a significant difference of around 3-4 percentage points, depending on the model and dataset.

In summary, our results underscore the significance of KD, particularly for harder tasks where the effect is more pronounced, allowing for lighter and faster models to achieve better task performance.

C Effect of Caching Teacher Outputs During Training

A significant challenge in our experimental study is the use of large and costly language models as teacher models for our faster and lighter models. Despite this, as discussed in Appendix B, the importance of these teacher models is essential for achieving better results with our proposed models.

Thus, the use of these teacher models poses challenges in terms of experimentation, particularly when working with restricted budgets, as is often the case in research outside big tech companies. To mitigate this issue, we implement a cache for the outputs of the teacher model, which allows us to train and experiment more efficiently.

The idea behind this approach is straightforward: since the teacher model is fixed during training, its outputs on an input x remain unchanged during different epochs, allowing us to compute them once and reuse them in subsequent epochs.

Formally, suppose F_t and F_s represent the computational cost of the forward pass for the teacher and student models, respectively, on an entire dataset, and E is the number of epochs used to train our proposed models. By caching the teacher's output, the total cost of computing the forward pass reduces from $O(E \cdot (F_t + F_s))$ to $O(F_t + E \cdot F_s)$.

It is worth noting that typically $F_t >> F_s$, and the number of epochs used in knowledge distillation is often higher than that used in simple fine-tuning. To illustrate, our fine-tuning experiments employ between 2 and 4 epochs, while our knowledge distillation experiments use a maximum of 50 epochs.

Model	MLDoc		PAWS-X		XNLI	
	FT	KD	FT	KD	FT	KD
ALBETO *tiny*	95.82	**96.40**	80.20	**85.05**	73.43	**75.99**
ALBETO *base-2*	94.67	**96.20**	73.45	**76.75**	72.08	**73.65**
ALBETO *base-4*	95.88	**96.35**	82.90	**86.40**	75.83	**78.68**
ALBETO *base-6*	95.88	**96.40**	85.20	**88.45**	78.42	**81.66**
ALBETO *base-8*	95.82	**96.70**	87.30	**89.75**	79.44	**82.55**
ALBETO *base-10*	95.65	**96.88**	88.80	**89.95**	79.62	**82.26**

Table 5: Comparison of the performance of our proposed models on text classification tasks on two settings: fine-tuning and task-specific knowledge distillation.

Model	POS		NER	
	FT	KD	FT	KD
ALBETO *tiny*	97.34	**97.36**	**75.42**	72.51
ALBETO *base-2*	**97.46**	97.17	**71.70**	69.69
ALBETO *base-4*	**97.87**	97.60	**76.18**	74.58
ALBETO *base-6*	**98.03**	97.82	78.10	**78.41**
ALBETO *base-8*	**98.18**	97.96	79.46	**80.23**
ALBETO *base-10*	**98.17**	98.00	80.46	**81.10**

Table 6: Comparison of the performance of our proposed models on sequence tagging tasks on two settings: fine-tuning and task-specific knowledge distillation.

To evaluate the impact of our cache implementation, we compare the training times of our proposed models on the XNLI dataset, which is the largest dataset considered in this study, for only 5 epochs (1/10 of the epochs used in our primary experiments) when using the cache and when not using it. Table 8 reports the results of this experiment, presenting the mean (noted as M) and standard deviation (noted as SD) over three runs. As expected, the use of the cache reduces the training time significantly, with results indicating that training time is approximately 1/4 of the time required to train without a cache. This reduction in training time is expected since the forward pass of the teacher model is the most costly operation and is computed only in the first epoch and then retrieved in the next 4 epochs. Furthermore, this difference will increase as the number of epochs increases.

In conclusion, while our cache implementation is a simple engineering trick, it has a significant impact on our experimentation phase in terms of training time and required compute.

Model	MLQA		SQAC		TAR, XQuAD	
	FT	KD	FT	KD	FT	KD
ALBETO *tiny*	51.84 / 28.28	**54.17 / 32.22**	59.28 / 39.16	**63.03 / 43.35**	66.43 / 45.71	**67.47 / 46.13**
ALBETO *base-2*	45.97 / 23.60	**48.62 / 26.17**	53.32 / 34.34	**58.40 / 39.00**	61.82 / 40.67	**63.41 / 42.35**
ALBETO *base-4*	59.99 / 35.69	**62.19 / 38.28**	65.66 / 45.54	**71.41 / 52.87**	68.91 / 49.07	**73.31 / 52.43**
ALBETO *base-6*	63.75 / 38.58	**66.35 / 42.01**	72.22 / 53.61	**76.99 / 59.00**	74.33 / 52.68	**75.59 / 54.95**
ALBETO *base-8*	64.99 / 40.58	**67.39 / 42.94**	75.22 / 56.43	**77.79 / 59.63**	75.47 / 54.11	**77.89 / 56.72**
ALBETO *base-10*	66.29 / 41.69	**68.29 / 44.29**	77.14 / 59.21	**79.89 / 62.04**	77.06 / **56.47**	**78.21** / 56.21

Table 7: Comparison of the performance of our proposed models on question answering on two settings: fine-tuning and task-specific knowledge distillation.

Model	Training Time (hours)			
	Cache		No Cache	
	M	SD	M	SD
ALBETO *tiny*	3.8	3.1×10^{-2}	16.2	3.1×10^{-3}
ALBETO *base-2*	3.8	1.6×10^{-3}	16.3	3.6×10^{-3}
ALBETO *base-4*	4.2	3.3×10^{-4}	16.6	2.6×10^{-3}
ALBETO *base-6*	4.5	1.5×10^{-3}	17.0	1.5×10^{-3}
ALBETO *base-8*	4.8	1.9×10^{-4}	17.3	5.8×10^{-3}
ALBETO *base-10*	5.3	9.6×10^{-3}	17.6	5.6×10^{-3}

Table 8: Training times when using teacher cache vs not using it. Table report the mean (M) and standard deviation (SD) over three runs.

Exploring Factual Entailment with NLI: A News Media Study

Guy Mor-Lan
Hebrew University of Jerusalem
guy.mor@mail.huji.ac.il

Effi Levi
Hebrew University of Jerusalem
efle@cs.huji.ac.il

Abstract

We explore the relationship between factuality and Natural Language Inference (NLI) by introducing FactRel – a novel annotation scheme that models *factual* rather than *textual* entailment, and use it to annotate a dataset of naturally occurring sentences from news articles. Our analysis shows that 84% of factually supporting pairs and 63% of factually undermining pairs do not amount to NLI entailment or contradiction, respectively, suggesting that factual relationships are more apt for analyzing media discourse. We experiment with models for pairwise classification on the new dataset, and find that in some cases, generating synthetic data with GPT-4 on the basis of the annotated dataset can improve performance. Surprisingly, few-shot learning with GPT-4 yields strong results on par with medium LMs (DeBERTa) trained on the labelled dataset. We hypothesize that these results indicate the fundamental dependence of this task on both world knowledge and advanced reasoning abilities.

1 Introduction

In recent years, the concept of factuality in news media has garnered increasing attention. Studies increasingly examine the relation between facts - as presented in news coverage - and phenomena such as political polarization, misinformation and fake news (Roy and Goldwasser, 2020; Levy, 2021; Bakshy et al., 2015; Garimella et al., 2021). As a result, the ability to model factual relations between claims becomes increasingly important. This has led to a line of work on automated fact-checking, which involves textual pipelines for detecting and evaluating factual claims (Zeng et al., 2021).

In automatic fact-checking, fact verification is predominantly addressed via the Natural Language Inference (NLI) task, also known as Recognizing Textual Entailment (RTE) (Zeng et al., 2021; Arana-Catania et al., 2022; Nie et al., 2018; Sathe et al., 2020), which has been used for decades for evaluating natural language understanding capabilities (Poliak, 2020). NLI is traditionally formulated as a categorical classification task between a premise p and a hypothesis h, where p can either contradict, entail or be neutral with respect to h. Large NLI datasets such as SNLI and MNLI (Bowman et al., 2015; Williams et al., 2018) have become highly popular, leading NLI to be adapted to various uses such as zero-shot classification (Yin et al., 2019) and semantic similarity (Reimers and Gurevych, 2019). In fact verification, NLI is used to evaluate the relations between a candidate fact and trusted pieces of evidence (Zeng et al., 2021).

However, the adequacy of NLI for analyzing factual relationships in news media is hindered by two primary reasons, relating to the nature of the task as well as to the characteristics of commonly used NLI datasets. First, large NLI datasets such SNLI and MNLI define the pairwise relationship in terms of necessity of meaning (Bowman et al., 2015; Williams et al., 2018). Thus, in MNLI an entailment is defined to be the case whereby a hypothesis "is necessarily true or appropriate whenever the premise is true", and similarly a contradiction is when the hypothesis "is necessarily false or inappropriate whenever the premise is true" (Williams et al., 2018). However, these types of relationships may be too restrictive for the analysis of media discourse, where explicit contradictions and entailments are likely to be rare, as such discourse tends take place in the margins of plausibility.

Secondly, texts in popular NLI datasets considerably differ from news texts. While sentences in NLI datasets tend to be short, simple, highly generic and convey a single idea or statement, media sentences tend to be longer, more complex, more specific and convey multiple pieces of information.

A common feature of NLI datasets such as RTE, SNLI and MNLI is that while premises are naturally occurring texts, the hypotheses are specifically

*Proceedings of the 13th Joint Conference on Lexical and Computational Semantics (*SEM 2024)*, pages 190 - 199
June 20-21, 2024

written to correspond to the categories (Chatzikyriakidis et al., 2017; Williams et al., 2018). While this method is effective in generating large amounts of data, constructed hypotheses are likely to express a simple relationship to the premise and thus not resemble pairs of naturally occurring sentences. Additionally, Chatzikyriakidis et al. (2017) notes that these datasets feature strictly logical relationships and stresses the need for datasets capturing other sorts of inferential relationships.

In this work, we set out to examine the relationship between NLI and textual factuality. For this purpose, we have developed a novel annotation scheme that expresses *factual* rather than *textual* entailment, encoding each pair of sentences with the relation of factual support, factual undermining, or neither. We have annotated a new dataset of naturally occurring sentence pairs from news media using both our factual entailment scheme and NLI, enabling a comparison of the schemes on news media. We also check the ability of recent generative LLMs (GPT-4) to generate such pairs correctly. We end with a set of experiments that demonstrate the ability to learn the factual entailment task using fine-tuned models as well as generative LLMs, and draw conclusions regarding the task's relation to real world knowledge in comparison to NLI. Overall, we analyze differences between NLI and factual entailment in their scope, relevance to news text and dependence on world knowledge, and show potential for new ways to model factual relations.

2 Factual Entailment

For the purpose of exploring the relationship between factual relations and textual entailment, we have developed FactRel, a novel annotation scheme encoding the *factual entailment* between pairs of sentences. Similarly to NLI, FactRel is a 3-category pairwise classification task. Given a premise p and a hypothesis h, p can either factually support h (*SUPPORT*), factually undermine h (*UNDERMINING*), or be factually neutral w.r.t h (*NEUTRAL*). p is said to factually support h when p being true would make h more plausible or likely to be true, compared to a situation in which the truth value of p is unknown. p is said to factually undermine h when p being true would make h less plausible or likely to be true, compared to a situation in which the truth value of p is unknown. Finally, p is said to be factually neutral w.r.t to p when p's truth has no bearing on the plausibility of h, and the likelihood of h would not change if p was known to be either true or false.

While both NLI and FactRel encode a ternary entailment relation between pairs of sentences, the factual relation encoded by FactRel is quite different from the one encoded by NLI. For example, consider the following pair of sentences:

(1) *p.* "You can't run a festival or you can't run a nightclub or a live-music gig with social distancing," Lord said.

h. Peter Marks, the CEO of Rekom, Britain's largest specialist late-night bar operator, told Insider the company's venues were set to open on June 21 "without COVID measures."

The above example exhibits a relation of factual *SUPPORT* while its NLI label is *NEUTRAL*. The hypothesis matches the premise and exemplifies it, but the premise does not necessitate the hypothesis.

A parallel example can be observed in the following pair of sentences:

(2) *p.* FILE – In this April 12, 2021 file photo, people queue outside a Hermes store in Mayfair in London.

h. Sales of luxury apparel, jewelry, leather goods and beauty products plunged to 217 billion euros in the pandemic year of 2020, from 281 billion euros in 2019, shedding six years of growth.

This example exhibits a relation of factual *UNDERMINING* while its NLI label is *NEUTRAL*. There is factual tension between the premise and hypothesis, as the premise can be considered a counter-example to the hypothesis, but it does not necessitate the hypothesis' falsity.

There are, however, cases in which the two schemes converge to the same relation. For example,

(3) *p.* Woman accused of attempted murder after driving into President Trump supporters in Southern California

h. The vast majority of those cases tallied by Weil involved motorists who ran into those demonstrating for causes aligned with the Black Lives Matter movement, Weil said.

Item	Agreement %	Kappa
Factual Entailment	95.2%	0.93
NLI	95.2%	0.85

Table 1: Intercoder reliability for annotations of NLI and factual entailment, showing raw agreement rate and Cohen's Kappa.

This example is factually *NEUTRAL*, and its NLI label is *NEUTRAL* as well.

3 Dataset

3.1 Construction

The core dataset comprises 1,507 sentence pairs sampled from 211 news articles appearing in diverse English-language digital news outlets in the period 2020-2022. Pairs were sampled from the same news article in order to increase the likelihood of the pairs having a non-neutral relationship. The sentence pairs were independently labelled by two annotators – one of the authors and a research assistant – with a subset annotated by both for calculating inter-coder reliability (Table 1). Annotators are instructed to categorize only non-negligible relations of support and undermining as such. Conflicts were resolved by committee consultation.

The core dataset is augmented by two additions. First, a subset of 500 sentence pairs from the MNLI dataset was annotated with factual entailment, for the purpose of examining differences between the MNLI dataset and the proposed dataset. Secondly, a synthetic dataset was generated using GPT-4 on the basis of the training set split from the core dataset. Each sentence pair in the training set was sent to GPT-4 accompanied by an explanation of the factual relationship task, the annotated label for that pair, and the definition of the label. GPT-4 was asked to generate 10 diverse examples possessing the same label, modelled on the sentence pair from the annotated dataset (see appendix A for prompts). Thus, the synthesized addendum is 10 times larger than the core training set and consists of 12,050 pairs. A subset of 500 GPT generated pairs was randomly sampled for manual validation, showing that in 98.4% of the pairs the manual labelling is consistent with GPT.

3.2 Analysis

In the core dataset, 93% of sentence pairs are NLI-neutral, whereas a smaller share of 70% are factually neutral (see Table 2). This indicates that

Factual / NLI	Contra.	Entail.	Neutral
Support	0	48	245
Undermining	67	0	113
Neutral	0	0	1130

Table 2: Cross-tabulation between NLI and Factual Entailment, core dataset.

Factual / NLI	Contra.	Entail.	Neutral
Support	5	155	67
Undermining	174	1	2
Neutral	17	10	69

Table 3: Cross-tabulation between NLI and Factual Entailment, MNLI subset.

non-neutral factual relationships are significantly more common in news media than non-neutral NLI relationships. In terms of length, we observe a significant difference between FactRel and NLI datasets – the average number of tokens per sentence in FactRel is 20.2, compared to 10.1 and 15.01 in the respective training splits of SNLI and MNLI.

The dual annotation of the dataset with factual entailment and NLI labels allows us to examine the relationship between the two. We examine the correlation between the labels utilizing Cramér's V association measure for discrete variables. While factual categories are strongly correlated with the categories in the MNLI subset ($\phi_c = 0.72$), the correlation is lower in the core dataset of news sentence pairs ($\phi_c = 0.49$). In the core dataset, 84% of factually supporting pairs and 63% of factually undermining pairs do not amount to entailment or contradiction, respectively (Table 2). In the MNLI subset, the numbers are respectively 32% and 2% (Table 3). This discrepancy likely indicates how in real news discourse, factual relations are increasingly untangled from semantic necessity, compared to datasets such as MNLI which contain sentences specifically written to form relations of semantic necessity.

4 Experiments

We tackle the task of factual entailment with several types and sizes of language models.

Baseline model. As a simple baseline, we embed the premise and hypothesis using the UAE-Large-V1 encoder (Li and Li, 2023) and calculate the cosine similarity between them, on which we train a decision tree with a max depth of 10.

Model	$F1_{MAC}$	ACC
Baseline (Cosine similarity)	0.38	0.61
Stock NLI (no training)	0.54	0.72
GPT-4 zero-shot	0.65	0.80
GPT-4 3-shot	**0.70**	**0.81**
Fine-tuned GPT-3.5	0.69	0.78
DeBERTa-NLI / Focal loss	0.68	0.8

Table 4: Top performing models, core training set

Zero shot and Few Shot (no training). We use two models in a zero-shot setting. First, we utilize a state-of-the-art NLI model trained on many NLI datasets (Laurer et al., 2022). The NLI model, based on DeBERTa V3 large (He et al., 2021), was used as if the NLI categories are equivalent to FactRel categories (e.g., *CONTRADICTION* equals *UNDERMINING*). Second, we utilize GPT-4 in a zero-shot setting provided only with a description of the task and the categories. We additionaly use GPT-4 in a 3-shot setting, adding three example pairs, one for each category.

Trained Models. We fine-tune several encoder models: RoBERTa-base (Liu et al., 2019), DeBERTa V3 large (He et al., 2021), and DeBERTa V3 SOTA NLI checkpoint (Laurer et al., 2022). Training variants included training with class weights and utilizing focal loss. We also fine-tune GPT-3.5 using OpenAI's API with the recommended settings. All the models were tested using two types of training sets – the core training set, and the augmented set with GPT-4 synthetic pairs added. Full technical details of the training setup are laid out in appendix B.

Macro-F1 results on the validation set for the baseline model, the stock NLI model and the top performing models are reported in Table 4 (see appendix C for full results). Table 5 examines the effect of adding synthetic data to the training set. Overall, the results show that while the task is learnable, it is not easy even for large pre-trained models. GPT-4 performs surprisingly well in both zero-shot and 3-shot settings, with GPT-4 3-shot being the most performant model, matching the Macro-F1 of finetuned DeBERTa with slightly better accuracy. The inclusion of synthetic data enhances the performance of the baseline model and DeBERTa-NLI, but decreases the performance of fine-tuned GPT-3.5.

Model	$F1_{MAC}$	ACC
Baseline (Cosine similarity)	0.44	0.63
Fine-tuned GPT-3.5	0.63	0.77
DeBERTa-NLI / Focal loss	**0.70**	**0.79**

Table 5: Top trained models, augmented training set

5 Conclusion

In this paper we explored the relationship between NLI and factual relations. For this purpose, we designed a new annotation scheme for factual entailment, FactRel; examined it in comparison to NLI on a sample of annotated pairs from news coverage; and examined the performance of various models on the task. We have shown that factual entailment relations are significantly more common in news articles in comparison to semantic entailment, thus underlining the shortcomings of NLI when applied to naturally occurring text.

We have also shown that GPT-4 performs better in a few-shot setting than smaller models trained on the entire training set. Moreover, GPT-4's performance even in a zero-shot setting is competitive with other models. The success of these LLMs, even with significantly less data, can give us insight on the challenge involved in the FactRel task and how it differs from NLI.

NLI is a fundamentally semantic task, as determining whether p entails or contradicts h hinges on understanding the meaning of the words and concepts employed in both. Thus, if p semantically entails h, then h itself must be included either explicitly or implicitly in p itself. The relations are therefore to be found in the meaning of the words. Modelling factual relationships, on the other hand, also requires a significant amount of background knowledge on the referents of the words, a detailed world model, and nuanced reasoning abilities. Thus, in order to identify that the premise "Twitter has locked Trump's account for 12 hours, and required the removal of the tweets" supports the hypothesis "Facebook locked Trump's account for 24 hours following two policy violations", it is required to not only understand the words and concepts, but to also be able to infer why a social network might lock one's account, and why such actions on two social networks are likely to co-occur. It is thus hypothesized that LLMs that have broad world knowledge, and especially those that excel at reasoning such as GPT-4, are well placed for this task, and their world knowledge and reasoning capabilities can compensate for decreased exposure to training data.

Finally, the addition of synthesized data improves performance of the top medium size LM, showing that data synthesis can be successfully employed on this task. However, this improvement is not consistent for all configurations.

Limitations

In line with NLI datasets, FactRel uses discrete classification labels. While the dataset distinguishes between semantic entailment and contradiction and (mere) factual support and undermining, it does not quantify the amount of support or undermining. However, the modelling of factual relationships can benefit from a probabilistic framework, which we leave to future research.

Acknowledgements

This work was supported by the Israel Science Foundation (Grant no. 2501/22). We thank Hagar Kaminer for diligent research assistance as well as insightful comments and suggestions during the annotation process. We extend deep gratitude to Shaul R. Shenhav and Tamir Sheafer for their invaluable guidance, support and advice.

References

Miguel Arana-Catania, Elena Kochkina, Arkaitz Zubiaga, Maria Liakata, Robert Procter, and Yulan He. 2022. Natural language inference with self-attention for veracity assessment of pandemic claims. In *Proceedings of the 2022 Conference of the North American Chapter of the Association for Computational Linguistics: Human Language Technologies*, pages 1496–1511, Seattle, United States. Association for Computational Linguistics.

Eytan Bakshy, Solomon Messing, and Lada A Adamic. 2015. Exposure to ideologically diverse news and opinion on facebook. *Science*, 348(6239):1130–1132.

Samuel R. Bowman, Gabor Angeli, Christopher Potts, and Christopher D. Manning. 2015. A large annotated corpus for learning natural language inference. In *Proceedings of the 2015 Conference on Empirical Methods in Natural Language Processing*, pages 632–642, Lisbon, Portugal. Association for Computational Linguistics.

Stergios Chatzikyriakidis, Robin Cooper, Simon Dobnik, and Staffan Larsson. 2017. An overview of natural language inference data collection: The way forward? In *Proceedings of the Computing Natural Language Inference Workshop*.

Kiran Garimella, Tim Smith, Rebecca Weiss, and Robert West. 2021. Political polarization in online news consumption. In *Proceedings of the International AAAI Conference on Web and Social Media*, volume 15, pages 152–162.

Pengcheng He, Jianfeng Gao, and Weizhu Chen. 2021. Debertav3: Improving deberta using electra-style pretraining with gradient-disentangled embedding sharing.

Moritz Laurer, Wouter van Atteveldt, Andreu Salleras Casas, and Kasper Welbers. 2022. Less annotating, more classifying – addressing the data scarcity issue of supervised machine learning with deep transfer learning and bert - nli. Preprint.

Ro'ee Levy. 2021. Social media, news consumption, and polarization: Evidence from a field experiment. *American economic review*, 111(3):831–870.

Xianming Li and Jing Li. 2023. Angle-optimized text embeddings.

Yinhan Liu, Myle Ott, Naman Goyal, Jingfei Du, Mandar Joshi, Danqi Chen, Omer Levy, Mike Lewis, Luke Zettlemoyer, and Veselin Stoyanov. 2019. Roberta: A robustly optimized BERT pretraining approach. *CoRR*, abs/1907.11692.

Yixin Nie, Haonan Chen, and Mohit Bansal. 2018. Combining fact extraction and verification with neural semantic matching networks.

Adam Poliak. 2020. A survey on recognizing textual entailment as an NLP evaluation. In *Proceedings of the First Workshop on Evaluation and Comparison of NLP Systems*, pages 92–109, Online. Association for Computational Linguistics.

Nils Reimers and Iryna Gurevych. 2019. Sentence-BERT: Sentence embeddings using Siamese BERT-networks. In *Proceedings of the 2019 Conference on Empirical Methods in Natural Language Processing and the 9th International Joint Conference on Natural Language Processing (EMNLP-IJCNLP)*, pages 3982–3992, Hong Kong, China. Association for Computational Linguistics.

Shamik Roy and Dan Goldwasser. 2020. Weakly supervised learning of nuanced frames for analyzing polarization in news media. In *Proceedings of the 2020 Conference on Empirical Methods in Natural Language Processing (EMNLP)*, pages 7698–7716, Online. Association for Computational Linguistics.

Aalok Sathe, Salar Ather, Tuan Manh Le, Nathan Perry, and Joonsuk Park. 2020. Automated fact-checking of claims from Wikipedia. In *Proceedings of the Twelfth Language Resources and Evaluation Conference*, pages 6874–6882, Marseille, France. European Language Resources Association.

Adina Williams, Nikita Nangia, and Samuel Bowman. 2018. A broad-coverage challenge corpus for sentence understanding through inference. In *Proceedings of the 2018 Conference of the North American*

Chapter of the Association for Computational Linguistics: Human Language Technologies, Volume 1 (Long Papers), pages 1112–1122, New Orleans, Louisiana. Association for Computational Linguistics.

Wenpeng Yin, Jamaal Hay, and Dan Roth. 2019. Benchmarking zero-shot text classification: Datasets, evaluation and entailment approach. In *Proceedings of the 2019 Conference on Empirical Methods in Natural Language Processing and the 9th International Joint Conference on Natural Language Processing (EMNLP-IJCNLP)*, pages 3914–3923, Hong Kong, China. Association for Computational Linguistics.

Xia Zeng, Amani S Abumansour, and Arkaitz Zubiaga. 2021. Automated fact-checking: A survey. *Language and Linguistics Compass*, 15(10):e12438.

A Synthetic Dataset

The synthetic component was created by generating 10 synthetic examples for each annotated sample in the training set, using GPT-4.

The following system prompt was used:

> **SYSTEM PROMPT**
>
> You are an advanced synthetic dataset generator.

For factual support samples, the following prompt was used:

> **FACTUAL SUPPORT PROMPT**
>
> 'Factual support' is a relationship between sentences A and B whereby A being true increases the likelihood of B being true.
>
> For example:
> A: {premise}
> B: {hypothesis}
>
> Generate 10 more pairs of sentences with a factual support relationship. The sentences should be diverse and reflect the type of real life sentences normally found in news discourse. The sentences should resemble the provided example but should also vary. Like the provided example, the generated samples should not be overly simple. Each sentence pair should be separated with two newlines.
>
> Within each pair, the sentences should be separated with a single newline. Each sentence should start with 'A: ' or 'B: '. Apart from that do not generate any other output.

For factual undermining samples, the following prompt was used:

> **FACTUAL UNDERMINING PROMPT**
>
> 'Factual undermining' is a relationship between sentences A and B whereby A being true decreases the likelihood of B being true.

For example:
A: {premise}
B: {hypothesis}

Generate 10 more pairs of sentences with a factual undermining relationship. The sentences should be diverse and reflect the type of real life sentences normally found in news discourse. The sentences should resemble the provided example but should also vary. Like the provided example, the generated samples should not be overly simple. Each sentence pair should be separated with two newlines.

Within each pair, the sentences should be separated with a single newline. Each sentence should start with 'A: ' or 'B: '. Apart from that do not generate any other output.

For factually neutral samples, the the following prompt was used:

FACTUAL NEUTRALITY PROMPT

'Factual neutrality' is a relationship between sentences A and B whereby has no effect on the likelihood of B being true.

For example:
A: {premise}
B: {hypothesis}

Generate 10 more pairs of sentences with a factual neutrality relationship. The sentences should be diverse and reflect the type of real life sentences normally found in news discourse. The sentences should resemble the provided example but should also vary. Like the provided example, the generated samples should not be overly simple. Each sentence pair should be separated with two newlines.

Within each pair, the sentences should be separated with a single newline. Each sentence should start with 'A: ' or 'B: '. Apart from that do not generate any other output.

B Training Setup

The core dataset was randomly split to a training set (80%) and a validation set (20%). The core training set comprises 1205 samples, and the validation set comprises 302 samples. With the addition of the synthetically generated data and 500 pairs from the MNLI dataset, the training dataset comprises 12,249 sentence pairs.

Training was performed on an Nvidia A100 GPU, using Huggingface Transformers (v4.34.0) and PyTorch (v2.0.1). Fine-tuning was for 6 epochs, using early stopping on the validation loss. Best performing checkpoint on the validation set was kept. Otherwise, training used the default huggingface hyperparameters. GPT-3.5 was finetuned via the OpenAI API with the recommended default settings.

C Full Experimental Results

Table 6: Model results. Each entry indicates a single run.

Gradient Training	Model	Data	Method	$F1_{MAC}$	ACC
V	DeBERTa-large-NLI	Core + Synthetic	Focal Loss	**0.7**	0.79
V	DeBERTa-large-NLI	Core + Synthetic	Class Weights	0.65	0.77
V	DeBERTa-large-NLI	Core + Synthetic	Regular	0.61	0.74
V	DeBERTa-large-V3	Core + Synthetic	Focal Loss	0.37	0.58
V	DeBERTa-large-V3	Core + Synthetic	Class Weights	0.61	0.75
V	DeBERTa-large-V3	Core + Synthetic	Regular	0.28	0.71
V	RoBERTa-base	Core + Synthetic	Focal Loss	0.57	0.72
V	RoBERTa-base	Core + Synthetic	Class Weights	0.6	0.73
V	RoBERTa-base	Core + Synthetic	Regular	0.59	0.74
V	DeBERTa-large-NLI	Core	Focal Loss	0.68	0.8
V	DeBERTa-large-NLI	Core	Class Weights	0.66	0.75
V	DeBERTa-large-NLI	Core	Regular	0.67	0.78
V	DeBERTa-large-V3	Core	Focal Loss	0.61	0.75
V	DeBERTa-large-V3	Core	Class Weights	0.47	0.56
V	DeBERTa-large-V3	Core	Regular	0.54	0.71
V	RoBERTa-base	Core	Focal Loss	0.4	0.7
V	RoBERTa-base	Core	Class Weights	0.45	0.61
V	RoBERTa-base	Core	Regular	0.41	0.68
X	GPT-4	None	Zero-Shot	0.65	0.8
X	GPT-4	3-shot	Few-shot	**0.7**	**0.81**
V	GPT-3.5	Core	Regular	0.69	0.78
V	GPT-3.5	Core + Synthetic	Regular	0.63	0.77
X	DeBERTa-large-NLI	None	No training	0.54	0.72
X	Baseline	Core	Cos. Sim. + DecisionTree	0.38	0.61
X	Baseline	Core + Synthetic	Cos. Sim. + DecisionTree	0.44	0.63

D Zero-Shot and 3-shot Prompts

For zero-shot classification with GPT-4, the following system prompt was used:

> **SYSTEM PROMPT**
>
> You are an advanced classifier.

And the following instruction prompt:

> **ZERO-SHOT CLASSIFICATION PROMPT**
>
> You will classify the factual relationship between sentences A and B. The factual relationship can be either 'SUPPORTS', 'UNDERMINES', or 'NEUTRAL'. 'SUPPORTS' means that A factually supports B - if A is true, B is more plausible or likely to be true. 'UNDERMINES' means that A factually undermines B - if A is true, then B is less plausible or less likely to be true. 'NEUTRAL' means that the truthness of A has no implication on the likelihood of B being true.
>
> Here is a pair of sentences:
> A: {premise}
> B: {hypothesis}
>
> Classify their factual relation. Respond with 'SUPPORTS', 'UNDERMINES' or 'NEUTRAL', and nothing else.

For 3-shot classification, the same system prompt was used, in conjunction with the following instruction prompt:

> **3-SHOT CLASSIFICATION PROMPT**
>
> You will classify the factual relationship between sentences A and B. The factual relationship can be either 'SUPPORTS', 'UNDERMINES', or 'NEUTRAL'. 'SUPPORTS' means that A factually supports B - if A is true, B is more plausible or likely to be true. 'UNDERMINES' means that A factually undermines B - if A is true, then B is less plausible or less likely to be true. 'NEUTRAL' means that the truthness of A has no implication on the likelihood of B being true.
>
> Here's an example of two sentences with a 'NEUTRAL' relationship:
> A: And with us having so much money invested into our honeymoon, we had no other choice but to board the ship.
> B: The memory that will stick with her, she said, is when the ship stopped in Sri Lanka to refuel.
>
> Here are two sentences with a 'SUPPORTS' relationship:
> A: Industry experts say the increase in milking cows has come from expansion of longstanding dairies, the launch of milking operations at existing farms that have diversified, and also from the relocation of dairy operations to South Dakota from states such as California.
> B: As in other agricultural industries, dairy farmers are increasingly using genetics, data monitoring, technology and robotics to boost the production of each individual animal while implementing an economies-of-scale approach to the size of their farms, raising the efficiency and profitability of their operations.

And here are two sentences with an 'UNDERMINES' relationship:
A: Guinea had announced late Wednesday that it was canceling its participation to protect the health of its athletes.
B: North Korea is the only country to pull out of the Tokyo Olympics, also citing concerns related to COVID-19.

Here is a new pair of sentences:
A: {premise}
B: {hypothesis}

Classify their factual relation. Respond with 'SUPPORTS', 'UNDERMINES' or 'NEUTRAL', and nothing else.

The Emergence of High-Level Semantics in a Signaling Game

Timothée Bernard
Université Paris Cité
France
timothee.bernard
@u-paris.fr

Timothee Mickus
University of Helsinki
Finland
timothee.mickus
@helsinki.fi

Hiroya Takamura
AIST, Tokyo
Japan
takamura.hiroya
@aist.go.jp

Abstract

The symbol grounding problem—how to connect a symbolic system to the outer world—is a longstanding question in AI that has recently gained prominence with the progress made in NLP in general and surrounding large language models in particular. In this article, we study the emergence of semantic categories in the communication protocol developed by neural agents involved in a well-established type of signaling game. In its basic form, the game requires one agent to retrieve an image based on a message produced by a second agent. We first show that the agents are able to, and do, learn to communicate high-level semantic concepts rather than low-level features of the images even from very indirect training signal to that end. Second, we demonstrate that the introduction of an adversarial agent in the game fosters the emergence of semantics by producing an appropriate training signal when no other method is available.

1 Introduction

How would it be possible to acquire and represent the meaning of words, not simply their function in language but also their connection to the outer world? A cogent account of this question, known as the problem of *symbol grounding*, is that of Harnad (1990). In the case where all we ever have access to is pure linguistic data, Harnad likens the question of attributing meaning representations to a never-ending chain of dictionary look-ups. Harnad's approach to circumvent this problem is to require agents to deal with *iconic* and *categorical* representations, in addition to manipulating symbols. Iconic representations are nonsymbolic representations of perceptual inputs; categorical representations are nonsymbolic representations of categories or concepts. Together, they form the basis of the interface between the agent's symbolic system and the outer world, and it is this interface that gives meaning to, or grounds, the symbols manipulated by the agent. Since Harnad's article, researchers in AI and NLP have often stressed supplementary requirements beyond perceptual data for the development of meaningful and grounded representations, mentioning embodiment (e.g., Steels, 2008), intent (e.g., Bender and Koller, 2020) or interactions with other agents as well as the environment (Chandu et al., 2021). In effect, there is a growing consensus that meaningful representations can only emerge in goal-driven interactive situations.

The study of *emergent communication* is the study of how interacting agents (human or otherwise) can successfully establish effective communication protocols (Kirby, 2002), and under which conditions this is possible. Recently, much interest has been devoted to emergent communication between *neural* agents involved in signaling games (e.g., Lazaridou et al., 2017), in which the agents have to cooperate through information exchange in order to retrieve some target. Such setups have the advantage that they can provide a very tight control on experimental conditions. In the present paper, we focus on a two-agents single-round signaling game, in which the two agents, playing the role of a *sender* and a *receiver*, are to cooperate by exchanging sequences of arbitrary symbols so that the receiver successfully retrieves an image based on one that was shown to the sender. We propose to study what conditions are necessary to the emergence of semantic categories in neural agents in this setting through two sets of experiments.

It has been shown that under certain circumstances, neural agents trained in similar setups develop "trivial" strategies, describing low-level features of their input (Bouchacourt and Baroni, 2018). Accordingly, we hypothesize that in the absence of any form of pressure towards generalization capabilities, the agents will not tend towards conveying high-level information, but will rather settle on exchanging about low-level image-

*Proceedings of the 13th Joint Conference on Lexical and Computational Semantics (*SEM 2024)*, pages 200 - 211
June 20-21, 2024 ©2024 Association for Computational Linguistics

specific information. We test this assumption in our first set of experiments by contrasting emergent communication protocols in three different environments: in the first, agents have a direct training signal towards learning to communicate categorical information; in the second, an indirect signal is given, but categorical information is not necessary to solve the task at hand; in the third, agents have no explicit information about categories. To our surprise, we observe that, given enough (training) time, the agents in the second type of environments reliably pick up the indirect signal about the existence of categories and spontaneously shift from communicating low-level features to high-level information (even though they are equally useful to solve the training task). In the third type of environments, semantic categories might be recovered but to a much lesser extent.

This leads us to our second set of experiments, where we study whether a category-level training signal can be synthesized by introducing an *adversarial* agent. This adversary aims to exploit the message sent by the sender to fool the receiver, and thereby implicitly guides the sender away from communicating information that is too easily falsifiable. We observe that introducing such an adversarial agent in the game can significantly bolster the emergence of high-level semantics in the agents' communication.

2 Related works

Grounding, viz., how to relate the symbols of a symbolic system (e.g., a language) to other aspects of the world, has been a fecund domain of research over the past decades. In particular, Harnad (1990) provides an insightful thought experiment, inspired by Searle's controversial Chinese Room argument, and aimed at showing the necessity of grounding: "Suppose you had to learn Chinese as a *first* language and the only source of information you had was a Chinese/Chinese dictionary! This is more like the actual task faced by a purely symbolic model of the mind" (pp.339–40). He also outlines a cogent program towards practical implementations of grounded hybrid systems, involving trained nonsymbolic input and categorical representations interfacing a symbolic system with the outer world.

More recent discussions on this concept have been written by Bender and Koller (2020), who emphasize the role of speakers' intent, or Steels (2008), who stresses the importance of embodied usages of symbols. Note, however, that it has been shown that some structures of the outer world can be found in the topology of the embedding space of ungrounded language models (e.g., Abdou et al. 2021 with color terms). There is now sustained interest in establishing if and how symbol grounding can occur within modern large language models, and to what extent their productions match our expectations for situated, intentional and semantically coherent communication (Patel and Pavlick, 2022; Tenney et al., 2019; Hwang et al., 2021; Ghaffari and Krishnaswamy, 2023). Many works focus on harnessing the boons that come with systems handling multiple channels of inputs, be it to create generalist agents (e.g., Reed et al., 2022; Ni et al., 2021), to enrich their inputs (e.g., Jia et al., 2021), or to facilitate human-robot interactions (e.g., Shichman et al., 2023).

However, practitioners of NLP rarely study the multi-agent aspects of grounding (Chandu et al., 2021), despite them being outlined as a crucial component; Steels (2008) goes as far as stating that standard supervised learning alone, possibly involving multiple modalities but without proper agent-agent or agent-environment interaction, cannot solve the symbol grounding problem. At the same time, there is also a growing interest in using multimodal neural networks as models of how perceptual information is used in humans (esp. Khorrami and Räsänen, 2021; Nikolaus and Fourtassi, 2021); this line of work could therefore benefit from developments on multi-agents NLP system.

In that respect, previous works that include simulations of how language and communication can emerge (Kirby, 2002) is especially useful in that they provide data and define a framework to test hypotheses related to symbol grounding. These works generally involve multiple agents negotiating the use of symbols in order to solve a task through the interaction with nonlinguistic data. While prior work has studied multi-turn communication (a.o., Jorge et al., 2016; Evtimova et al., 2018), populations and generations of agents (e.g., Kirby et al., 2014; Foerster et al., 2016; Ren et al., 2020; Chaabouni et al., 2022) or nonsymbolic communication channels (e.g., Mihai and Hare, 2021), we focus on a straightforward signaling game (Lewis, 1969) involving multiple agents communicating through a symbolic channel (Sukhbaatar et al., 2016; Havrylov and Titov, 2017; Lazaridou et al., 2017, 2018). More precisely, our starting point is the setup of Bernard and Mickus (2023), where we introduced a computer-generated image dataset, studied the impact of many design choices of the learning process (pertaining to the loss function and regularization, the selection of training instances, and pretraining methods) on a two-agent signaling game, and defined several metrics used to study the properties of the emergent languages.

The work of Mu and Goodman (2021) is close to ours in that they study how the choice of training instances in a signaling game can improve the systematicity of the emergent languages. However, they mainly do so by explicitly strengthening the training signal pertaining to semantic classes (through the use of sets of images instantiating these classes), while we try to achieve similar effects without relying on a priori known semantic classes.

One novelty of the present work is the introduction of an adversary agent in the signaling game. Relevant precedents in the literature include non-cooperative language games, such as the competitive setup of Noukhovitch et al. (2021). To our knowledge, the present work is the first to introduce a GAN-like agent (Goodfellow et al., 2014) in an emergent communication setting.

3 Signaling game definition

We start by presenting the basics of the signaling game that we study in this section. We document departures from this base setup where relevant.

Data. Our dataset (see Bernard and Mickus, 2023) consists of images each depicting an object on a gray background (with varying shade); the objects varies in shape (`cube` or `sphere`), size (`large` or `small`), color (`red` or `blue`), and vertical (`top` or `bottom`) and horizontal position (`left` or `right`). Two images are considered to be of the same category if and only if they agree on these five object features.[1]

We use only 22 of the 32 categories during training (*base categories*), the 10 remaining ones are only used during evaluation (*generalization categories*).[2] Evaluation involves only images not seen during training. More precisely, 20% of each base category is reserved for evaluation; these images plus all images from generalization categories are used during evaluation.

Game definition. We study a signaling game involving a sender, who sees one *original image* I_o and then produces a message m_{I_o}; and a receiver, that receives this message m_{I_o} along with a *target image* I_t and a *distractor image* I_D, and must decide which of the two is the target through the production of a probability distribution over these two images. In such a setting, the relation between the three images involved can provide more or less (even no) signal about the categories to the agents.

Both agents are neural networks that contain a convolutional image encoder; in addition, the sender contains an LSTM message decoder while the receiver contains an LSTM message encoder. We use for these sub-networks the same architectures as Bernard and Mickus (2023). The symbols of the message are selected from a vocabulary of size 16.

We train the receiver to assign a higher probability to the target than to the distractor by minimizing its negative log-likelihood. Writing $p_{\text{receiver}}(I_i \mid I_1, \ldots, I_n, m_{I_o})$ for the probability assigned by the receiver to image I_i based on message m_{I_o} when confronted to images $I_1, \ldots, I_n$, this loss is:

$$-\log(p_{\text{receiver}}(I_t \mid I_t, I_d, m_{I_o})). \quad (1)$$

In contrast, the sender is trained with REINFORCE (Williams, 1992) by assigning a reward of value $+1$ to each symbol production action when the receiver correctly retrieves the target, and a reward of value -1 when it fails to do so. For each training batch, the sum of the sender's REINFORCE loss and of the receiver's negative log-likelihood loss is minimized (with RMSProp; Hinton et al., 2012).

4 Influence of target and distractor choice

The goal of the present work is to establish what training signal is necessary for categorical information to appear in the communication protocols developed by the agents. This requires modifying

[1]Two images from the same category may not only differ on background color but also on the position of the light source used to render the scene, and the specific shade of blue/red, vertical and horizontal position, and 3D orientation, of the object.

[2]In Bernard and Mickus (2023), we partitioned the set of categories in such a way that two distinct base categories never differ on just a single feature. This makes it possible for the agents to achieve perfect performance during training while ignoring entirely one of the five features; a possibility they do take advantage of to some extent. In contrast, we are here interested in the agents communicating about category-level information as much as possible, and thus partition the categories differently: we take as generalization categories (`cube`, `small`, `blue`, `down`, `left`)—chosen arbitrarily—and all 10 categories differing from it on exactly three features.

the environment in which the agents interact so that its categorical structure is more or less obvious.

4.1 Three types of environments

If we provide the sender with an image I_o from some category C, then we can either provide as target image I_t for the receiver either this very same image ($I_o = I_t$) or a different image of the same category; the latter option provides a clear signal that different images should be construed as part of the same category. When using the former option ($I_o = I_t$), selecting the distractor image I_d such that it always belongs to a category $C' \neq C$ still induces a training signal pertaining to the categorization of images, albeit a much more indirect one. These two choices compound to three types of environments for our agents, which are illustrated (along with a variant introduced in Section 5.1) in Figure 1.

Direct signal environments. In *direct signal environments*, we provide as the receiver's target image I_t an image randomly sampled from the category of the original image, and select the distractor image I_d from a different category ($I_o, I_t \in C$, $I_d \in C'$ and $C \neq C'$). As a result, the message produced by the sender cannot focus solely on low-level, image-specific, features of the original image (e.g., the average brightness of the image), as they might not match with the target. In other words, the selection of a target image I_t that differs from the original image I_o but shares the same category provides these models with an explicit signal towards learning high-level semantic information. Hence, the performance of these models indicates what sort of communication protocol emerges under optimal conditions for retrieving categorical information.

While a successful game in this environment requires that the receiver be able to derive category-level information in its messages, this does not prevent the sender from describing its input image. Indeed, the sender could go as far as to purely convey enough image-specific information and let the receiver infer the relevant category. This would however arguably lead to a remarkably complex communication protocol, whereas having the sender infer and describe the category ought to lead to a much simpler solution.

Indirect signal environments. Models trained in *indirect signal environments* only differ from those trained in direct signal environments in that the target is exactly the original image ($I_t = I_o$). In this setting, describing low-level, image-specific, features of the original image, such as the background color, is a perfectly viable strategy. We expect this strategy to be favored by the sender as low-level features are intuitively easier to recognize than high-level (category-level) ones (e.g., shape or size of the object depicted).

Remark that in such environment, we still sample the distractor image I_d from a category C' distinct from that of the target image ($C \neq C'$). As such, this environment does provide some means by which categorical information can be recovered: Implicitly, receivers are only ever presented pairs of images that belong to different categories, and may very well learn to segregate them along their categories. This could in turn provide a weak, indirect training signal for the sender. We however expect image-specific information to be more straightforward, although inductive biases in the agents' neural architectures could also shape the emergent communication towards category-level descriptions.

No signal environments. Our ability to train models in direct signal and, to a lesser extent, indirect signal environments hinges on the existence of well-defined semantic categories in our dataset. However, natural pictures of everyday scenes, for instance, do not readily come with such annotations. We therefore also study models that can be trained without such information, so as to determine what are the minimal requirements for non-trivial semantics to emerge. Accordingly, in *no signal environments*, we use the sender's original input image as the target image for the receiver to retrieve ($I_o = I_t$) and select a distractor image at random, regardless of which category it comes from.[3]

In this last type of environment, no training signal about the categories in the dataset is given to the agents. If category-specific information does emerge in the communication protocol, this would have to be pinned on inductive biases present in our architectures.

4.2 Automatic evaluation metrics

To assess whether settings are conducive to the emergence of semantic categories, we use two automated metrics as our primary means of evaluation: *abstractness* and *category communication*

[3]As a result, for some training instances, the target and the distractor belong to the same category.

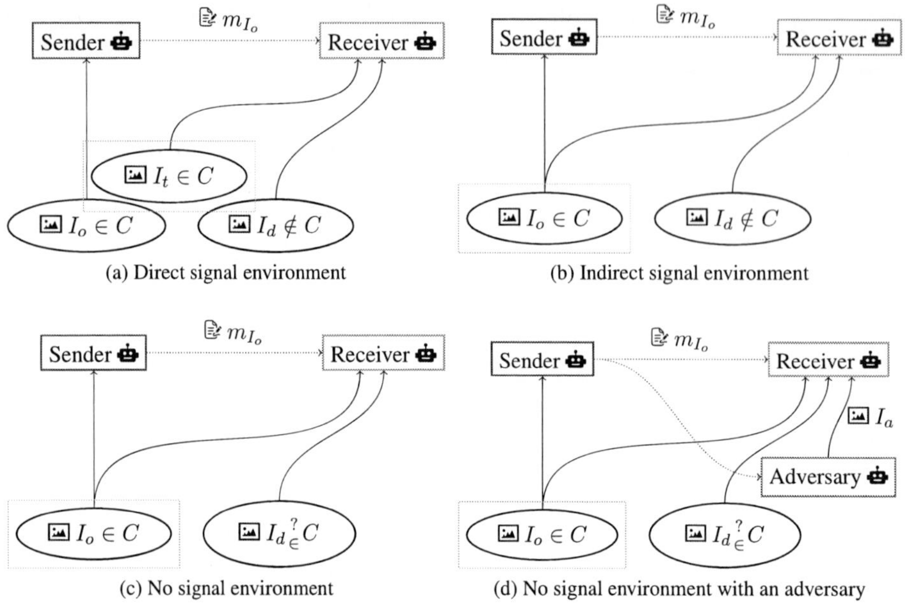

(a) Direct signal environment

(b) Indirect signal environment

(c) No signal environment

(d) No signal environment with an adversary

Figure 1: The four training setups. C is an image category sampled randomly and uniformly. The green frame indicates which image is the target for the receiver agent. (a)-(c) are introduced in Section 4.1; (d) is introduced in Section 5.1.

efficiency.[4]

Abstractness (abs.). We define this measure as

$$2 \cdot p_{\text{receiver}}(I_t \mid I_o, I_t, m_{I_o}), \qquad (2)$$

where I_o and I_t are two images from the same category. This measure quantifies the use of image-specific information by the sender-receiver system: Abstractness scores near 0 indicate that the message m_{I_o} contains image-specific information that the receiver uses to accurately distinguish I_o from I_t, whereas scores near 1 suggest that the message does not include such information.

Category communication efficiency (c.c.e.). We define this measure as

$$p_{\text{receiver}}(I_t \mid I_t, I_d, m_{I_o}), \qquad (3)$$

where I_o and I_t are two images of the same category, and I_d is an image of a different category. This measure corresponds exactly to the objective maximized in direct signal environment. It is relevant to make a distinction between *category* communication efficiency and a notion of *image* communication efficiency (i.c.e.), defined as $p_{\text{receiver}}(I_o \mid I_o, I_d, m_{I_o})$, which corresponds to the objective maximized in indirect signal environment.

[4]The definitions below are given based on a single evaluation instance; the values reported later are averaged over a large number of such instances.

A sender-receiver system with both low abstractness and low c.c.e. only communicates image-level information (low abstractness) that does not generalize to other images of the same category (low c.c.e.). A system with low abstractness but high c.c.e. communicates at least image-specific information; nothing, however, can be concluded a priori about category-level information because, as two images of the same category tend to be more similar than two images of different categories, image-specific information may be enough to achieve high c.c.e. A system with high abstractness but low c.c.e. does not communicate about image-specific neither category-level information (such a system is not properly trained). Only for a system with both high abstractness and high c.c.e. can we conclude about the emergence of high-level semantics: The system does not communicate image-specific information (high abstractness) but must then communicate category-level information (high c.c.e.).

For finer-grained analyses, we consider other metrics: meaning-form correlation (Brighton and Kirby, 2006), as well as scrambling resistance and semantic probes accuracy (Bernard and Mickus, 2023); see Appendix A for further details.

4.3 Experimental results

Training & evaluation procedure Models are used with a baseline term in the sender's loss and no entropy term; we pretrain all image encoders and decoders on an auto-encoding task (without freezing their parameters afterwards).[5] For each of the three environment types, we select the learning rate through a grid search, ran on 10 runs per settings (trained for 200 epochs each; 1000 batch updates per epoch; batches of 128 instances) so as to maximize c.c.e. We then use these optimal learning rates to train 40 models in each environment for 1000 epochs.[6] Each run is evaluated once every 1000 batch updates. Unless otherwise stated, we keep the values of the metrics obtained when the c.c.e. is maximal so as to focus our observations on effective communication protocols, and report medians over the 40 runs for any given setup.

Direct signal environments. We first begin by looking at models trained in direct signal environments (first row of Table 1). We observe very high c.c.e. and abstractness scores; in other words, messages produced by the senders tend to contain only category-level information, and no image-specific information. This is expected, since the receivers in these models are tasked with retrieving a target that is not the original image. We can also point out that these models often develop protocols that appear compositional, even though they likely remain simplistic: They achieve a high scrambling resistance of 82.2% (suggesting that the information carried by a symbol is independent of its position in the message), as well as a relatively high MFC score of $\rho = 0.39$. In line with this analysis, we observe perfect probing accuracy for all features except shape (64.2% accuracy): This suggests that most relevant categorical information is robustly encoded in senders' messages. In short, there is reasonably strong evidence that direct signal environments allow models to learn to link symbols to the values of the five features.

Indirect signal environments. Turning to models trained in indirect signal environments (second row of Table 1), we observe both a very high median c.c.e. score and a high median abstractness score. As pointed out earlier, a high c.c.e. score could be due to the presence of category-level information in the message, but also to enough image-specific information—as two images from the same category resemble each other more than two images from different categories. As for the high abstractness score, it shows that the receiver assigns a similar probability mass to the image based on which the sender produces the message, and to another image of the same category. More precisely, 0.853 corresponds to assigning a probability of $p_{\text{receiver}}(I_t \mid I_o, I_t, m_{I_o})) = \frac{0.853}{2} = 0.4265$ to the target image, and $1 - 0.4265 = 0.5735$ to the original image, i.e., roughly a 4-to-5 odds. Even if two images of the same category resemble each other, they are however clearly distinct from a low-level perspective, and if the sender were sending enough low-level information, it would not be hard for the receiver to confidently distinguish between the original image and another from the same category. Furthermore, the high performance of the semantic probes does confirm that all five high-level features of the images are reliably encoded in the sender's messages. This suggests that the sender mainly conveys category-level information. Our hypothesis—that the sender does not communicate category-level information if other strategies are available—appears thus to be disproved. Furthermore, the fact that the sender only conveys little image-specific information on top of the category-level information it communicates is surprising, as nothing in this setting seems to prevent the sender from communicating more image-specific information (e.g., background color).[7]

Figure 2 shows the evolution of abstractness, c(ategory).c.e and i(mage).c.e. (see Section 4.2) during training in indirect signal environments. We observe that i.c.e converges much more rapidly than c.c.e. and abstractness; the agents learn fairly quickly to communicate about specific images but also gradually shift to communicating about image categories themselves.

Interestingly, even though the messages do contain some image-specific information that ought

[5]Using the notation suggested in (Bernard and Mickus, 2023), the setups considered here correspond to $\langle +P_{AE}, -F, -A, -H, -C, +B\rangle$.

[6]For no signal environments, we report results after 200 epochs as preliminary results indicate further training to have very limited impact.

[7]Somewhat paradoxically, models trained in indirect signal environments obtain a higher median c.c.e. than those trained in direct signal environments, despite the latter being directly trained to maximize c.c.e. scores. This is likely due to the little bit of image-specific information included in the messages along with category-level information, reinforcing the ability of the receiver to recognize the target.

Env.	c.c.e.	abs.	s.r.	semantic probes					MFC
				shape	size	color	h. pos.	v. pos.	
Direct signal	0.986	0.992	0.822	0.642	0.996	0.998	0.999	0.999	0.387
Indirect signal	0.992	0.853	0.949	0.818	0.993	0.993	0.999	0.999	0.439
No signal	0.771	0.511	0.898	0.624	0.869	0.677	0.812	0.754	0.265
No signal + adv.	0.768	0.594	0.859	0.609	0.901	0.601	0.867	0.838	0.243

Table 1: Summary of performances observed at maximal c.c.e., according to the training environment. Direct/Indirect/No signal environments are introduced in Section 4.1; the adversary agent is introduced in Section 5.1.

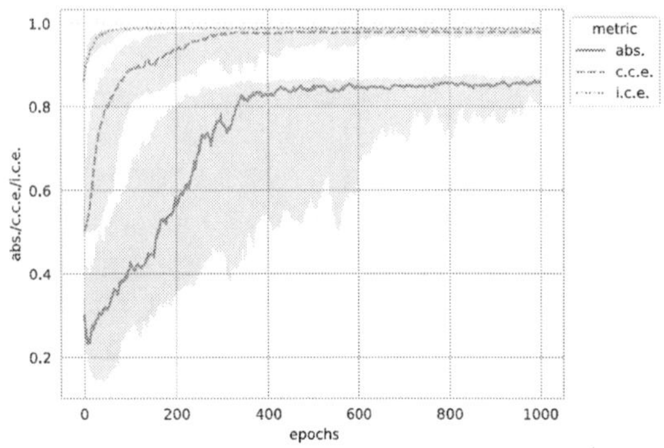

Figure 2: Evolution of the abstractness, c.c.e. and i.c.e. scores over 1000 epochs of training in indirect signal environments. Median over all runs, interquartile intervals shaded; exponential moving average with $\alpha = 0.1$.

to deteriorate MFC scores (as evidenced by the lower than 1 abstractness), the MFC is higher than what we observe for models in direct signal environments ($\rho = 0.439$). This is probably explained by communication protocols in this setting having very high scrambling resistance (94.9%), suggesting that receivers treat messages as orderless bags-of-symbols. Indeed, we compute MFC based on Jaccard indices; therefore, distances between messages are not sensitive to symbol order.

No signal environments. If we now study models trained in no signal environments (third row of Table 1), we can observe a sharp decrease in abstractness, although performances remain non-trivial (an abstractness of 0.511 corresponds to assigning a fourth of the probability mass on a target image of the same category).

Likewise, while it remains firmly above a random chance threshold of 0.5, c.c.e. drops to 0.771. This shows that the sender not only communicates more about image-specific information, but also communicates less about category-level features. Looking at semantic probes accuracy, we find more evidence of the same trend—all probes perform worse than what we saw thus far; shape and color appear especially unreliably encoded.

5 Fostering the emergence of high-level semantics

As we just saw, encoding category-level information systematically seems to require the agents to have access (directly or indirectly) to category-level information. We now turn to whether we can dispense from including this explicit information while retaining category-level information in the messages.

Spike (2017, §.5) suggests that noisy inputs can foster more robust and effective communication channels: Adding noise to input images would prevent agents from communicating about very low-level information (e.g., specific pixel brightness), since this information may not match with what the receiver would perceive. Such a procedure is therefore a natural candidate to explore. However, preliminary experiments involving the addition of normal noise to the images showed this technique to only make the training process less reliable, without any observable benefit.

Instead, we focus on a more involved approach: incorporating an agent playing an adversarial role to discourage the sender and receiver to exchange image-specific information.

5.1 An adversary agent

In this section, we introduce a third agent in the signaling game. This *adversary* agent is implemented with an LSTM message encoder (like the receiver) and a convolutional image decoder. In this setting, the message produced by the sender is also passed to the adversary, which outputs an *adversary image* $I_a = \text{adversary}(m_{I_o})$ intended to fool the receiver. Our intuition is that messages that convey low-level information can easily be counterfeited by this adversary, and therefore should be disfavored by the receiver, and therefore by the sender—thereby creating an implicit training signal towards communicating high-level semantic information.[8]

As in previous settings, the sender is trained with REINFORCE using rewards determined by the ability of the receiver to distinguish between the target and the distractor only. Unlike in previous settings, however, receivers in adversary settings are trained to distinguish the target from both the distractor and the adversary image by minimizing the negative log-likelihood of the target image considering the three images:

$$-\log(p_{\text{receiver}}(I_t \mid I_t, I_d, I_a, m_{I_o})). \quad (4)$$

We use an adversarial scheme (Goodfellow et al., 2014) to train the adversary to generate an image that the receiver cannot distinguish from the target; i.e., the adversary is trained to minimize the negative log-likelihood of the adversary image:

$$-\log(p_{\text{receiver}}(I_a \mid I_d, I_a, m_{I_o})). \quad (5)$$

To foster the diversity of adversary images, we add Gaussian noise to the output of the adversary's message encoder before feeding it into the image decoder.

To perform the optimization, each agent's loss is scaled by a factor that depends on the agent' performance. Let us define

$$\begin{aligned} s_{\text{sender}} &= p_{\text{receiver}}(I_t \mid I_t, I_d, m_{I_o}), \\ s_{\text{receiver}} &= p_{\text{receiver}}(I_t \mid I_t, I_d, I_a, m_{I_o}), \\ s_{\text{adversary}} &= p_{\text{receiver}}(I_a \mid I_t, I_a, m_{I_o}). \end{aligned}$$

Over the course of training, we compute moving averages of these values, noted "$\hat{s}_a$" for "s_a". Now consider the following values:

$$\begin{aligned} w_{\text{sender}} &= 2 \cdot \hat{s}_{\text{sender}} - 1, \\ w_{\text{receiver}} &= 3 \cdot \hat{s}_{\text{receiver}} - 1, \\ w_{\text{adversary}} &= 2 \cdot \hat{s}_{\text{adversary}}. \end{aligned}$$

Except in pathological situations (that we have not observed), each of these values is nonnegative. These weights are normalized using the softmax function and a "temperature" hyperparameter τ, and then used to scale each of the three losses:

$$\frac{\exp\left(-w_a/\tau\right)}{\sum\limits_{a' \in \text{ agents}} \exp\left(-w_{a'}/\tau\right)} \cdot \mathcal{L}_a.$$

[8]This adversary agent can also be seen as an auxiliary module of the receiver: one devoted to formulating plausible alternative targets that the receiver has yet to learn to discriminate.

This scaling of the losses (and therefore of the gradients) entails that training focuses on the agents that perform the worst at their task. Note that to avoid updating agents with gradients derived from their adversaries' loss, the losses are not summed: Each agent's loss is minimized by a distinct optimizer that only updates this agent's parameters.

Finally, because image-generation is a particularly challenging task, when the adversary is present, we send the target and distractor images through a pretrained auto-encoder before showing them to the receiver. Indeed, convolution image decoders like the one used to produce the adversary images are very likely to generate visual artifacts that a receiver can easily use to distinguish between neurally generated images and images from the dataset (which lack such artifacts). If the adversary images were to be spotted in this trivial manner, the additional agent would be rendered entirely ineffective. Using auto-encoded versions of the target and distractor images, then exhibiting similar artefacts, we make it technically possible (though still quite challenging) for the adversary to fool the receiver. We implement this auto-encoder using the same image encoding architecture as the sender and receiver agents, and the same image decoding architecture as the distractor agent. This network is trained beforehand and its parameters are frozen during the signaling game.

5.2 Experimental results

Training & evaluation procedure Unless otherwise specified, we rely on the same implementation choices as in Section 4.3. As previously (but with the temperature τ as an additional hyperparameter), we employ a grid search with 10 runs per settings over 200 epochs to maximize c.c.e. We then use these optimal learning rates to train 40 models in each environment (still on 200 epochs as preliminary experiments show that further training brings no improvements).

Adversary agents. In the last (fourth) row of Table 1, we list the performances of models in no-signal environments that involve an adversary agent. Compared with similar environments but without an adversary, we notice a boost in terms of abstractness (from 0.511 to 0.594). This boost is unlikely to be due to random variation only, as indicated by a Pitman permutation test targeting the difference of abstractness scores (p-value $\simeq 0.02$). C.c.e. scores are comparable (the difference is

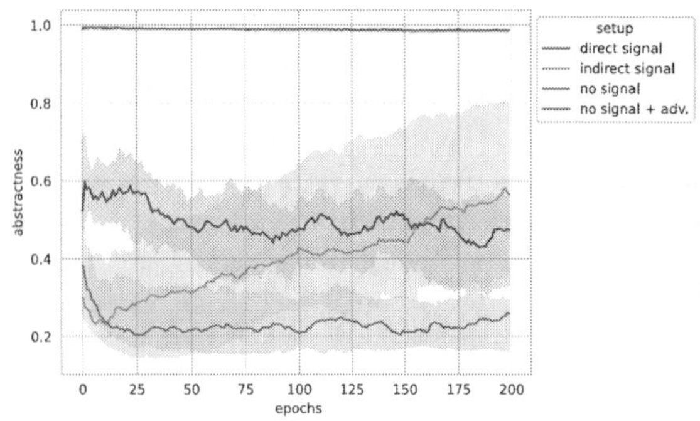

Figure 3: Evolution of the abstractness scores over 200 epochs of training in the four setups studied. For each setup, median over all runs, interquartile intervals shaded; exponential moving average with $\alpha = 0.1$.

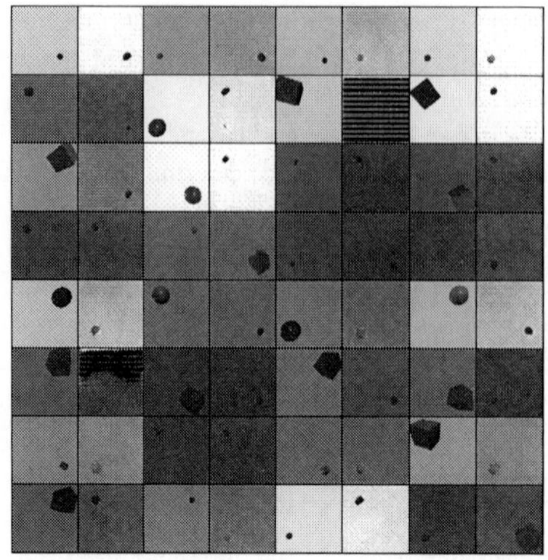

Figure 4: Original and adversary images (no signal environment). Each image in an even column is an adversary image crafted from the sender's message for the original image immediately on its left.

not statistically significant, p-value $\simeq 0.5$), which demonstrates that the presence of an adversary agent tends to remove image-specific information in the sender's messages with no impact on the receiver's ability to retrieve a target selected from the original image category. The accuracy of the semantic probes suggests that the sender and receiver rely less on the color and shape of the object when an adversary is present, and more on its size and its position (both horizontal and vertical).

Figure 3 shows the evolution of abstractness during training in all four setups. The information about categories provided in indirect signal environments has a very progressive effect on abstractness, which starts low and raises gradually. In contrast, the presence of an adversary immediately limits the reliance of the sender and receiver agents on image-specific information. Additional experiments not presented here in details due to space constraints show that in indirect signal environments, while the presence of an adversary agent does not lead to an increase in abstractness in the long run, it clearly fosters higher abstractness scores in the early stages of training.

Adversary images. We include a grid of selected examples from one model in Figure 4. We can observe many images with severe defects, but also that in most images, the background color and even some higher-level features are properly recreated. It is important to keep in mind that the rationale behind introducing the adversary was not to produce high quality images, but to drive the sender and receiver away from communicating only about low-level features of the image, such as the background color. As indicated by the increase in abstractness, this goal has been achieved. These images contribute to explain how: The fact that adversary images often faithfully reproduce the original images' background indicates that the sender and the receiver used to rely on this feature to retrieve the target; the adversary then prevents them from relying only on this feature.

6 Conclusions

Do agents learning to identify images through symbolic communication develop a language able to describe category-level features of these images? Interestingly, indirect signal environments provide evidence that models are able to develop high-level semantics even when the only relevant training signal is extremely tenuous.

The results of models in no signal environments suggest, however, that one cannot expect the sender to encode category-level information systematically without an appropriate training signal.

Our last experiment shows that even without relying on the availability of semantic categories—as is often the case with natural images—, fostering the emergence of high-level semantics is possible via the introduction of an adversarial agent.

In the future, we would be interested in studying whether this technique is effective on other datasets that the one used here, and in whether improvements of the (delicate) training procedure of the adversary may lead to a stronger impact on the emergent languages.

Acknowledgments

We thank Emmanuel Chemla for fruitful discussions on this work.

This work was supported by an Émergence 2021 grant (SYSNEULING project) from IdEx Université Paris Cité.

This work is part of the FoTran project, funded by the European Research Council (ERC) under the EU's Horizon 2020 research and innovation program (agreement № 771113). We also thank the CSC-IT Center for Science Ltd., for computational resources. Preliminary results were obtained from project JPNP15009, commissioned by the New Energy and Industrial Technology Development Organization (NEDO), using the computational resources of the AI Bridging Cloud Infrastructure (ABCI), provided by the National Institute of Advanced Industrial Science and Technology (AIST), Japan.

References

Mostafa Abdou, Artur Kulmizev, Daniel Hershcovich, Stella Frank, Ellie Pavlick, and Anders Søgaard. 2021. Can Language Models Encode Perceptual Structure Without Grounding? A Case Study in Color. In *Proceedings of the 25th Conference on Computational Natural Language Learning*, pages 109–132, Online. Association for Computational Linguistics.

Emily M. Bender and Alexander Koller. 2020. Climbing towards NLU: On meaning, form, and understanding in the age of data. In *Proceedings of the 58th Annual Meeting of the Association for Computational Linguistics*, pages 5185–5198, Online. Association for Computational Linguistics.

Timothée Bernard and Timothee Mickus. 2023. So many design choices: Improving and interpreting neural agent communication in signaling games. In *Findings of the Association for Computational Linguistics: ACL 2023*, pages 8399–8413, Toronto, Canada. Association for Computational Linguistics.

Diane Bouchacourt and Marco Baroni. 2018. How agents see things: On visual representations in an emergent language game. In *Proceedings of the 2018 Conference on Empirical Methods in Natural Language Processing*, pages 981–985, Brussels, Belgium. Association for Computational Linguistics.

Henry Brighton and Simon Kirby. 2006. Understanding linguistic evolution by visualizing the emergence of topographic mappings. *Artif. Life*, 12(2):229–242.

Rahma Chaabouni, Eugene Kharitonov, Diane Bouchacourt, Emmanuel Dupoux, and Marco Baroni. 2020. Compositionality and generalization in emergent languages. In *Proceedings of the 58th Annual Meeting of the Association for Computational Linguistics*, pages 4427–4442, Online. Association for Computational Linguistics.

Rahma Chaabouni, Florian Strub, Florent Altché, Eugene Tarassov, Corentin Tallec, Elnaz Davoodi, Kory Wallace Mathewson, Olivier Tieleman, Angeliki Lazaridou, and Bilal Piot. 2022. Emergent communication at scale. In *International Conference on Learning Representations*.

Khyathi Raghavi Chandu, Yonatan Bisk, and Alan W Black. 2021. Grounding 'grounding' in NLP. In *Findings of the Association for Computational Linguistics: ACL-IJCNLP 2021*, pages 4283–4305, Online. Association for Computational Linguistics.

Katrina Evtimova, Andrew Drozdov, Douwe Kiela, and Kyunghyun Cho. 2018. Emergent communication in a multi-modal, multi-step referential game. In *International Conference on Learning Representations*.

Jakob Foerster, Ioannis Alexandros Assael, Nando de Freitas, and Shimon Whiteson. 2016. Learning to communicate with deep multi-agent reinforcement learning. In D. D. Lee, M. Sugiyama, U. V. Luxburg, I. Guyon, and R. Garnett, editors, *Advances in Neural Information Processing Systems 29*, pages 2137–2145. Curran Associates, Inc.

Sadaf Ghaffari and Nikhil Krishnaswamy. 2023. Grounding and distinguishing conceptual vocabulary through similarity learning in embodied simulations.

Ian Goodfellow, Jean Pouget-Abadie, Mehdi Mirza, Bing Xu, David Warde-Farley, Sherjil Ozair, Aaron Courville, and Yoshua Bengio. 2014. Generative Adversarial Nets. In Z. Ghahramani, M. Welling, C. Cortes, N. D. Lawrence, and K. Q. Weinberger, editors, *Advances in Neural Information Processing Systems 27*, pages 2672–2680. Curran Associates, Inc.

Stevan Harnad. 1990. The symbol grounding problem. *Physica D: Nonlinear Phenomena*, 42(1):335 – 346.

Serhii Havrylov and Ivan Titov. 2017. Emergence of language with multi-agent games: Learning to communicate with sequences of symbols. In *Advances in Neural Information Processing Systems*, volume 30. Curran Associates, Inc.

Geoffrey Hinton, Nitish Srivastava, and Kevin Swersky. 2012. Coursera lectures slides, lecture 6.

Jena D. Hwang, Chandra Bhagavatula, Ronan Le Bras, Jeff Da, Keisuke Sakaguchi, Antoine Bosselut, and Yejin Choi. 2021. Comet-atomic 2020: On symbolic and neural commonsense knowledge graphs. In *AAAI*.

Paul Jaccard. 1912. The distribution of the flora in the alpine zone. *New Phytologist*, 11(2):37–50.

Chao Jia, Yinfei Yang, Ye Xia, Yi-Ting Chen, Zarana Parekh, Hieu Pham, Quoc Le, Yun-Hsuan Sung, Zhen Li, and Tom Duerig. 2021. Scaling up visual and vision-language representation learning with noisy text supervision. In *International Conference on Machine Learning*, pages 4904–4916. PMLR.

Emilio Jorge, Mikael Kågebäck, and Emil Gustavsson. 2016. Learning to play guess who? and inventing a grounded language as a consequence.

Khazar Khorrami and Okko Räsänen. 2021. Can phones, syllables, and words emerge as side-products of cross-situational audiovisual learning? - a computational investigation. *Language Development Research*, 1(1):123–191.

Simon Kirby. 2002. Natural language from artificial life. *Artif. Life*, 8(2):185–215.

Simon Kirby, Tom Griffiths, and Kenny Smith. 2014. Iterated learning and the evolution of language. *Curr. Opin. Neurobiol.*, 28:108–114.

Angeliki Lazaridou, Karl Moritz Hermann, Karl Tuyls, and Stephen Clark. 2018. Emergence of linguistic communication from referential games with symbolic and pixel input. In *International Conference on Learning Representations*.

Angeliki Lazaridou, Alexander Peysakhovich, and Marco Baroni. 2017. Multi-agent cooperation and the emergence of (natural) language. In *International Conference on Learning Representations*.

David Lewis. 1969. *Convention: a philosophical study*. Harvard University Press Cambridge.

Timothee Mickus, Timothée Bernard, and Denis Paperno. 2020. What meaning-form correlation has to compose with: A study of MFC on artificial and natural language. In *Proceedings of the 28th International Conference on Computational Linguistics*, pages 3737–3749, Barcelona, Spain (Online). International Committee on Computational Linguistics.

Daniela Mihai and Jonathon Hare. 2021. Learning to draw: Emergent communication through sketching. In *Advances in Neural Information Processing Systems*, volume 34, pages 7153–7166. Curran Associates, Inc.

Jesse Mu and Noah Goodman. 2021. Emergent communication of generalizations. In *Advances in Neural Information Processing Systems*, volume 34, pages 17994–18007. Curran Associates, Inc.

Minheng Ni, Haoyang Huang, Lin Su, Edward Cui, Taroon Bharti, Lijuan Wang, Dongdong Zhang, and Nan Duan. 2021. M3p: Learning universal representations via multitask multilingual multimodal pretraining. In *Proceedings of the IEEE/CVF conference on computer vision and pattern recognition*, pages 3977–3986.

Mitja Nikolaus and Abdellah Fourtassi. 2021. Modeling the interaction between perception-based and production-based learning in children's early acquisition of semantic knowledge. In *Proceedings of the 25th Conference on Computational Natural Language Learning*, pages 391–407.

Michael Noukhovitch, Travis LaCroix, Angeliki Lazaridou, and Aaron Courville. 2021. Emergent communication under competition. In *Proceedings of the 20th International Conference on Autonomous Agents and MultiAgent Systems*, AAMAS '21, page 974–982, Richland, SC. International Foundation for Autonomous Agents and Multiagent Systems.

Roma Patel and Ellie Pavlick. 2022. Mapping language models to grounded conceptual spaces. In *International Conference on Learning Representations*.

Scott Reed, Konrad Zolna, Emilio Parisotto, Sergio Gómez Colmenarejo, Alexander Novikov, Gabriel Barth-maron, Mai Giménez, Yury Sulsky, Jackie Kay, Jost Tobias Springenberg, Tom Eccles, Jake Bruce, Ali Razavi, Ashley Edwards, Nicolas Heess, Yutian Chen, Raia Hadsell, Oriol Vinyals, Mahyar Bordbar, and Nando de Freitas. 2022. A generalist agent. *Transactions on Machine Learning Research*. Featured Certification.

Yi Ren, Shangmin Guo, Matthieu Labeau, Shay B. Cohen, and Simon Kirby. 2020. Compositional languages emerge in a neural iterated learning model. In *International Conference on Learning Representations*.

John R. Searle. 1980. Minds, brains, and programs. *Behavioral and Brain Sciences*, 3(3):417–457. 06894.

Mollie Shichman, Claire Bonial, Austin Blodgett, Taylor Hudson, Francis Ferraro, and Rachel Rudinger. 2023. Use defines possibilities: Reasoning about object function to interpret and execute robot instructions. In *Proceedings of the 15th International Conference on Computational Semantics (IWCS 2023)*.

Matthew Spike. 2017. *Minimal requirements for the cultural evolution of language*. Ph.D. thesis, University of Edinburgh.

Luc Steels. 2008. The symbol grounding problem has been solved, so what's next? In *Symbols and Embodiment: Debates on meaning and cognition*. Oxford University Press.

Sainbayar Sukhbaatar, Arthur Szlam, and Rob Fergus. 2016. Learning multiagent communication with backpropagation. In *Advances in Neural Information Processing Systems*, volume 29. Curran Associates, Inc.

Ian Tenney, Patrick Xia, Berlin Chen, Alex Wang, Adam Poliak, R Thomas McCoy, Najoung Kim, Benjamin Van Durme, Sam Bowman, Dipanjan Das, and Ellie Pavlick. 2019. What do you learn from context? probing for sentence structure in contextualized word representations. In *International Conference on Learning Representations*.

Ronald J. Williams. 1992. Simple statistical gradient-following algorithms for connectionist reinforcement learning. *Mach. Learn.*, 8(3–4):229–256.

A Supplementary metrics

To further evaluate the communication protocols that emerge from our various models, we rely on abstractness and c.c.e., as well as three metrics previously proposed in the literature.

Meaning–form correlation (MFC), also known as topographic similarity (Brighton and Kirby, 2006), consists in evaluating whether changes in form are commensurate to changes in meaning. The metric was originally proposed as a means of quantifying compositionality, but see Mickus et al. (2020); Chaabouni et al. (2020) for discussions. In our specific case, we use Jaccard distance (Jaccard, 1912) as a form metric and Hamming distance between categories as a meaning distance. Noting $|m|_x$ for the number of occurrences of symbol x in message m, the Jaccard distance between two messages m and m' is defined as

$$1 - \frac{\sum_{x \in \mathit{Alphabet}} \min(|m|_x, |m'|_x)}{\sum_{x \in \mathit{Alphabet}} \max(|m|_x, |m'|_x)}. \tag{6}$$

For instance, the Jaccard distance between "A A B A C" and "A B C D" is $1 - \frac{1+1+1+0}{3+1+1+1}$, i.e., $\frac{1}{2}$. The Hamming distance between two categories c and c' is simply the number of features (i.e., among color, size, shape, h. pos., v. pos.) on which c and c' disagree.

The two other metrics are borrowed from Bernard and Mickus (2023). *Scrambling resistance* (s.r.), quantifies how sensitive to symbol ordering receivers are: Values close to 1 indicate that each symbol is interpreted independently of its position in the message, whereas values close to 0 indicate that the message is only interpreted as a whole. We also rely on *semantic probes* to detect how much each of the five category-level features is communicated in the sender's messages. In practice, they are implemented as a decision tree per feature, trained to predict the corresponding value for the original image based on a bag-of-symbol representation of the sender's message (i.e., a vector in $\mathbb{N}^{16}$).

PDDLEGO: Iterative Planning in Textual Environments

Li Zhang[1*] **Peter Jansen**[3] **Tianyi Zhang**[1]
Peter Clark[2] **Chris Callison-Burch**[1] **Niket Tandon**[2]
[1]University of Pennsylvania [2]Allen Institute for Artificial Intelligence
[3]The University of Arizona
{zharry}@upenn.edu {nikett}@allenai.org

Abstract

Planning in textual environments have been shown to be a long-standing challenge even for current models. A recent, promising line of work uses LLMs to generate a formal representation of the environment that can be solved by a symbolic planner. However, existing methods rely on a fully-observed environment where all entity states are initially known, so a one-off representation can be constructed, leading to a complete plan. In contrast, we tackle partially-observed environments where there is initially no sufficient information to plan for the end-goal. We propose PDDLEGO that **iteratively** construct a planning representation that can lead to a partial plan for a given sub-goal. By accomplishing the sub-goal, more information is acquired to augment the representation, eventually achieving the end-goal. We show that plans produced by few-shot PDDLEGO are 43% more efficient than generating plans end-to-end on the Coin Collector simulation, with strong performance (98%) on the more complex Cooking World simulation where end-to-end LLMs fail to generate coherent plans (4%).[1]

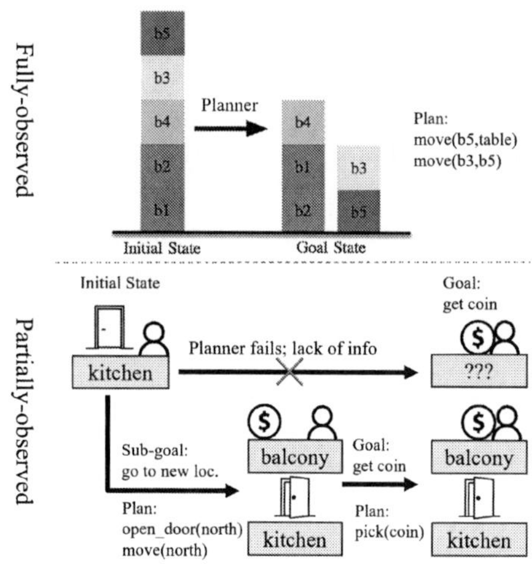

Figure 1: A fully-observed environment like BlocksWorld (upper, to rearrange objects from and to a given configuration) can be tackled by generating a PDDL problem file, while a partially observed one like Coin Collector (lower, to look for an object in an unknown location) cannot until sufficient exploration.

1 Introduction

Planning with LLMs has witnessed a surge of interest in the NLP community, not only because it showcases AI systems' ability to reason about complex events, but also because of the need of many downstream applications like goal-driven robotics (Huang et al., 2022a,b) and intelligent planning assistants (Lyu et al., 2021). The most intuitive approach of this task is using LLMs as planners to produce a sequence of actions executed to arrive at a goal state (Valmeekam et al., 2023a; Stein and Koller, 2023). While applicable in many domains, this LLM-based approach is found to underperform in textual simulated environments (Valmeekam et al., 2023c,b) and to lack interpretability compared to symbolic planning methods that derive a plan from a formal representation of the environment. We join the efforts that combine both approaches, effectively translating the textual input into a symbolic representation expressed in the planning domain definition language (PDDL) (see Appendix A for an introduction), which can then be solved by a symbolic planner (Collins et al., 2022; Lyu et al., 2023; Liu et al., 2023; Xie et al., 2023; Wong et al., 2023). This neurosymbolic approach has gained popularity as it combines LLMs' flexibility to understand rich NL and classical planners' determinism and faithfulness.

All previous work on LLM generating PDDL has only experimented on **fully-observed** environments where all entity states are initially known, thus requiring no exploration. Take BlocksWorld, a

[*] Work done as an intern at AI2.

[1]Our code can be found at `https://anonymous.4open.science/r/nl-to-pddl-4FBE/`.

*Proceedings of the 13th Joint Conference on Lexical and Computational Semantics (*SEM 2024)*, pages 212 - 221
June 20-21, 2024 ©2024 Association for Computational Linguistics

common benchmark for such work, as an example (Figure 1, upper), both the initial and goal states are initially spelled out, in which case the LLM's job is akin to translating the textual descriptions of the environment into a PDDL problem file which specifies the initial and goal entity states. Assuming also a domain file, a one-off plan can be found and executed to reach the end-goal. In contrast, many real-world environments are **partially-observed** (Figure 1, lower), where the entity states dynamically get uncovered during exploration. Since the necessary initial and goal states might also be unknown (e.g., looking for an item without knowing where it is), the previous approach falls apart due to the impossibility to specify a complete problem file. This causes a chicken-and-egg problem where a plan is required for exploration, while exploration is required to build PDDL that results in a plan. Given this challenge, past work on partially-observed environments has only used LLMs to directly generate plans (Shinn et al., 2023; Majumder et al., 2023), but not a planning representation.

To break the above stalemate, we propose PDDLEGO, a methodology to use LLMs to iteratively build a PDDL problem file from textual observations from the environment. In this problem file, the initial states (or rather current states) reflect the current knowledge of the environment, while the goal states can be dynamically adjusted. In case the problem file does not contain sufficient information to plan for the end-goal (e.g., find a coin), PDDLEGO recursively falls back to a provided sub-goal (e.g., go to an unvisited room). This way, a plan can be found to reach the sub-goal, leading to new observations by exploring the environment, and iteratively refine the problem file until a plan can be found for the end-goal.

We evaluate PDDLEGO on benchmarks of textual interactive virtual environments akin to the robotic planning simulations where PDDL is known for. Our PDDL-induced plans are 43% more efficient than LLMs generating plans directly on the Coin Collector simulation. On one setting of the more complex Cooking World simulation PDDLEGO achieves near-perfect 98% success rate where LLMs that predict action achieves only 4%, while on a more challenging setting, 46% over 0%.

2 Methodology

Our approach is illustrated in Figure 2. We operate in a partially-observed, textual, simulated environment which functions as a multi-turn interaction between the environment and the agent (e.g., *a game to find an item*). Specifically, the environment provides an observation (*objects in a room*) along with a list of permitted actions (*move, pick up*). Then, the agent selects on of these actions, and repeats. The environment can be seen as a finite state machine where each state consists of the conjunction of all entity states and determines the permitted actions. The agent succeeds when a goal state is reached (*the sought item is in hand*); it fails when it cannot possibly reach goal state.

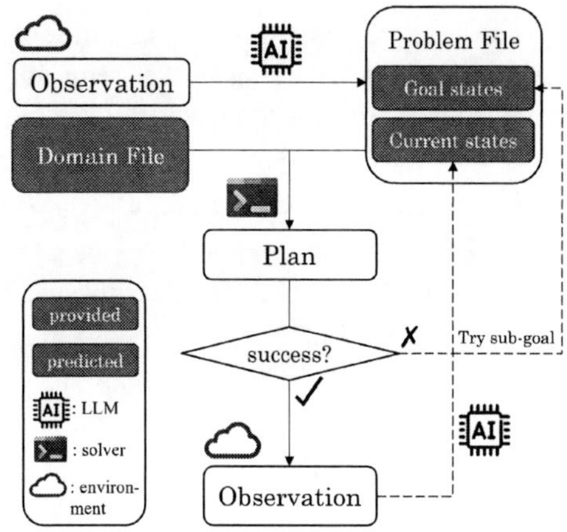

Figure 2: The pipeline of PDDLEGO. A PDDL problem file is iteratively built during exploration.

Like most prior work in using LLMs to generate a planning representation like PDDL, we assume that a domain file that defines the available actions is provided; this domain file can solve a problem file that defines the initial and goal entity states (*where the agent is, where the item is, how are these two locations connected*) when possible to result in a plan (*go west, pick up item*). We also assume a sub-goal structure, namely, an array of goal states defined in PDDL that a model can fall back to when the current goal is unattainable.

Formally, we are initially presented with the first observation o_1 with the end-goal G. We use an LLM to construct an initial problem file PF_1 ({current states, goal states}) to plan for this end-goal.

$$PF_1 = \{LLM(o_1), G\} \quad (1)$$

If this problem file can be solved by the provided domain file with a solver, a plan containing one or more actions is found.

$$Plan_1 := (a_1^1, a_1^2, \dots) = solver(DF, PF_1) \quad (2)$$

If a plan cannot be found due to a lack of information in the problem file, the goal G is swapped out by an immediate sub-goal G', and the solver retries. The actions in the plan are then sequentially executed in the current environment E, resulting in a list of new observations.

$$(E, o_2^1, o_2^2, \dots) = exec(E, a_1^1, a_1^2, \dots) \quad (3)$$

Thus begins the second iteration. Using the new observations, the previous problem file is regenerated (referred to as **PDDL-gen**).

$$PF_2 = \{LLM(PF_1, o_2), G\} \quad (4)$$

The process goes on until one observation fulfills the termination condition.

Unlike prior work that generates the problem file once, PDDLEGO's having LLMs iteratively generating the problem file often result in inconsistencies and errors (e.g., missing a connectivity relation between two rooms, using the name a room in a relation without declaring the room, missing a parenthesis, etc.). To tackle this, we have the LLMs only predict the change in the problem file (i.e., the change of entity states), which we deterministically applied to the previous problem file (referred to as **PDDL-edit**).

$$\Delta_2 = LLM(PF_1, o_2),\ PF_2 = PF_1 + \Delta_2 \quad (4')$$

We will compare our two approaches above with the baseline where LLMs directly generate an action (referred to as **Action-gen**).

$$Plan_i = LLM(o_i) \quad (2')$$

3 Environments

We experiment with two goal-oriented, partially-observed simulated environments, or text games, that span a variety of difficulty and flavor.

Coin Collector (Yuan et al., 2019) focuses on navigation, which is an indispensable element of most simulations. The agent's task is to explore rooms, some connected by locked doors, and find a coin, similar to the running example above. Just as previously discussed, the previous approach on generating a PDDL problem file cannot be applied to Coin Collector because the location of the coin is unknown until the agent enters the same room as the coin. Therefore, the sub-goal structure for this tasks is defined as:

1. pick up coin (requires the location of the coin)
2. go to a room that has not been visited (reveals location of the coin)

The sub-goal of "going to an unvisited room" results in monotonously increasing progress to the end-goal of "finding the coin". In similar search-related tasks, this singular sub-goal or strategy suffices, though it may not work for all situations.

Cooking World (Madotto et al., 2020) subsumes Coin Collector with more complex tasks. The agent' task is to first explore rooms to find ingredients required by a recipe, much like Coin Collector. Next, it should cook the ingredient in some specified location using some specified appliance. Finally, when all ingredients are cooked correctly, a meal can be successfully prepared. Therefore, the sub-goal structure for this tasks is defined as:

1. prepare meal (requires having obtained each ingredient and located relevant appliances)
2. pick up each ingredient (requires the location of each ingredient; obtains ingredients)
3. go to a room that has not been visited (reveals location of ingredients and appliances)

To better understand these simulations, example trajectories are shown in Appendix D.

4 Evaluation

For both simulations, we use the implementation from Jansen and Côté (2022). For Coin Collector, we use the most complex setting; for Cooking World, we consider an easy and a hard setting with varying number of locations and ingredients. See more details in Appendix C. For the choice of LLM, we consider `gpt-3.5-turbo-1106` (GPT 3.5 Turbo) and `gpt-4-1106-preview` (GPT 4 Turbo) across baseline methods (i.e., Action-gen, PDDL-gen, and PDDL-edit). For Action-gen, we prompt the LLM with a full description of the simulation, and for PDDL methods, with a hand-annotated domain file containing well-defined actions. For the PDDL-edit setting, we prompt the LLM to generate templated edits (add, replace, and delete lines in the problem file). The prompt of each method include a 1-shot demonstration of the output format. See details of prompt design and domain file annotation in the Appendix B.

Regarding **performance**, Table 1 shows a drastic performance degradation of Action-gen moving from Coin Collector (only 2 valid actions: move, open door each with 4 direction arguments) to the much more complex Cooking World (with 8 more actions with infinite possible arguments, like processing an ingredient). Moreover, in Cooking World, an agent would fail if an ingredient is processed incorrectly (e.g., fried instead of grilled, was not chopped before roasted). Therefore, LLMs generating actions on the fly are more likely to make irrevocable mistakes and fail the task. In con-

	random	GPT 3.5 Turbo			GPT 4 Turbo		
		Action-gen	PDDL-gen†	PDDL-edit†	Action-gen	PDDL-gen†	PDDL-edit†
Coin	4%	68%	26%	28%	**94%**	58%	78%
Cooking (easy)	0%	0%	70%	68%	4%	94%	**98%**
Cooking (hard)	0%	0%	4%	6%	0%	16%	**46%**

Table 1: The percentage where the agent succeeds by taking no more than the maximum steps on the test set. The † sign specifies methods under our proposed PDDLEGO methodology.

trast, our two-stage PDDL generation approaches ensure the correctness of the plan to process the ingredients (in the second stage) *assuming* that the ingredients are gathered and that the appliances are identified (in the first stage). Logically, the failures of PDDLEGO indicates an inconsistency between the environmental observation and the problem file. For example, the connectivity of the rooms may not be updated correctly upon entrance to a new room, causing no plan or invalid plans to be found. By lessen the burden on LLMs, PDDL-edit notably ameliorates but cannot eliminate this issue. On Coin Collector, issues frequently arise in a loop, where opening a new door leads to a visited room. Notably, GPT3.5 is far worse than GPT4 in generating PDDL, in line with the observations by Anonymous (2023) and Silver et al. (2023).

Regarding **efficiency**, Figure 3 shows that on Coin Collector, PDDL-edit is no less efficient than Action-gen on 7 out 8 examples (red crosses are often lower than the blue circles) in the development set where PDDL-edit terminates successfully. Scaling up to the entire test set, with GPT4, PDDL-edit has an average step to success of 7.8 compared to Action-gen's 13.6 among successful attempts, a 43% improvement on efficiency. Among these steps, 3.3 of Action-gen are invalid (e.g., moving through a closed door) compared to merely 0.2 of PDDLEGO, a significant difference when trials and errors are expensive. PDDLEGO also shows better **stability**. In Figure 3, PDDL-edit exhibits a much smaller variance across runs than Action-gen. For example, if the coin happens to be immediately to the west of the initial room, deciding to go west initially would result in a prompt success, while exploring the east portion initially would result in a notable detour. Our approach of PDDL generation leaves only the task of parsing environmental configuration to the LLM, while the planning task is done deterministically by the solver, leading to more consistent plans across runs.

Regarding **interpretability** and **correctability**, the black-box nature of LLMs results in no faithful

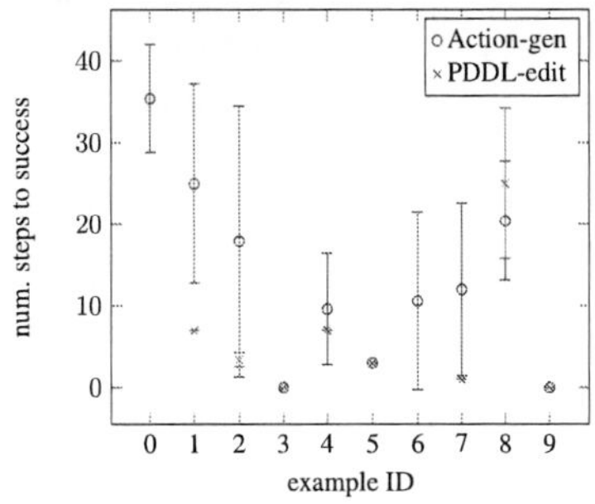

Figure 3: On Coin Collector, the mean and standard deviation of number of steps to success (less is better) for each development example, each over 5 trials with different random seeds of `gpt-4-1106-preview`, comparing Action-gen and PDDL-edit. The error bar represents the sample standard deviation. On example 0 and 6, PDDL-edit fails and thus not shown.

interpretation behind the decisions (c.f., thought-process). In Coin Collector, for example, if the coin has not be found at the maximum permitted steps, a problematic Action-gen trajectory is almost impossible to manually correct unless a human is to plot a map and keep track of the exploration. On the other hand, both PDDL-gen and PDDL-edit guarantees the correctness of the plan assuming that the generated or edited problem file is correct. Hence, upon failure, a human only needs to inspect and correct the most recent observation and the PDDL. For PDDL-edit, the job is even easier as only the change in the problem needs to be considered. An example learned problem file can be found in Appendix E.

5 Conclusion

We propose PDDLEGO, the first approach to use LLMs to iteratively learn a planning representation while exploring partially-observed environments. We quantitatively show the improvement of performance, efficiency and stability, while qualitatively argue the benefit of interpretability and correctability. Future work might remove the assumption of a domain file and a sub-goal structure.

Limitations

Despite the many benefits of PDDLEGO, it also poses the following shortcomings compared to having LLMs directly generating the plan or actions.

The first is speed and cost, as both the input and output become much longer to include PDDL code. For the OpenAI model we experiment with, PDDL-gen and PDDL-edit are on average about 5x slower than Action-gen. On the other hand, it is difficult to compare the cost which is highly dependent on prompt design. In our work, Action-gen keeps appending the chosen action, new observation and valid actions to the prompt, resulting in a longer input and higher cost for every exploration step. However, our PDDL methods only retain the most recent observation and problem file, so the input length, though initially longer, is roughly constant.

The second is flexibility, which is the strongsuit of methods leveraging LLMs to do most of the work. For each environment we experiment with, a certain extent of hard-coding is required for our methods to work, hindering generalization. In our case, the domain file and sub-goals of one or more problem file for each environment must be manually annotated. Doing so presumes some prior insight into the environment, and therefore PDDLEGO is not truly a zero-shot methodology.

While the aim of this work is to show the preliminary gains of generating PDDL while exploring partially-observed environments, there could be stronger Action-gen baselines, such as using chain-of-thought to formulate a plan first instead of selecting actions on the fly, or more advanced methods in the literature.

Acknowledgements

This work is supported in part by the DARPA KAIROS Program (contract FA8750-19-2-1004), AFRL (contract FA8750-23-C-0507), the Office of the Director of National Intelligence (ODNI) via the IARPA HIATUS Program (contract 2022-22072200005), the NSF (Award 1928631), and gifts from Roblox and Salesforce. Approved for Public Release, Distribution Unlimited. The views and conclusions contained herein are those of the authors and should not be interpreted as necessarily representing the official policies, either expressed or implied, of DARPA, ODNI, IARPA, NSF, AFRL, the U.S. Government, or of Roblox or Salesforce. The U.S. Government is authorized to reproduce and distribute reprints for governmental purposes notwithstanding any copyright annotation therein.

References

Katherine M. Collins, Catherine Wong, Jiahai Feng, Megan Wei, and Joshua B. Tenenbaum. 2022. Structured, flexible, and robust: benchmarking and improving large language models towards more human-like behavior in out-of-distribution reasoning tasks.

Malik Ghallab, Adele Howe, Craig Knoblock, Drew McDermott, Ashwin Ram, Manuela Veloso, Daniel Weld, and David Wilkins. 1998. PDDL - the planning domain definition language. Technical Report "CVC TR-98-003/DSC TR-1165", Yale Center for Computational Vision and Control.

Wenlong Huang, Pieter Abbeel, Deepak Pathak, and Igor Mordatch. 2022a. Language models as zero-shot planners: Extracting actionable knowledge for embodied agents. In *International Conference on Machine Learning*, pages 9118–9147. PMLR.

Wenlong Huang, Fei Xia, Ted Xiao, Harris Chan, Jacky Liang, Pete Florence, Andy Zeng, Jonathan Tompson, Igor Mordatch, Yevgen Chebotar, Pierre Sermanet, Noah Brown, Tomas Jackson, Linda Luu, Sergey Levine, Karol Hausman, and Brian Ichter. 2022b. Inner monologue: Embodied reasoning through planning with language models. In *arXiv preprint arXiv:2207.05608*.

Peter A. Jansen and Marc-Alexandre Côté. 2022. Textworldexpress: Simulating text games at one million steps per second. *arXiv*.

Bo Liu, Yuqian Jiang, Xiaohan Zhang, Qiang Liu, Shiqi Zhang, Joydeep Biswas, and Peter Stone. 2023. Llm+ p: Empowering large language models with optimal planning proficiency. *arXiv preprint arXiv:2304.11477*.

Qing Lyu, Shreya Havaldar, Adam Stein, Li Zhang, Delip Rao, Eric Wong, Marianna Apidianaki, and Chris Callison-Burch. 2023. Faithful chain-of-thought reasoning. *arXiv preprint arXiv:2301.13379*.

Qing Lyu, Li Zhang, and Chris Callison-Burch. 2021. Goal-oriented script construction. In *Proceedings of the 14th International Conference on Natural Language Generation*, pages 184–200, Aberdeen, Scotland, UK. Association for Computational Linguistics.

Andrea Madotto, Mahdi Namazifar, Joost Huizinga, Piero Molino, Adrien Ecoffet, Huaixiu Zheng, Alexandros Papangelis, Dian Yu, Chandra Khatri, and Gokhan Tur. 2020. Exploration based language learning for text-based games. In *Proceedings of the Twenty-Ninth International Joint Conference on Artificial Intelligence, IJCAI-20*, pages 1488–1494. International Joint Conferences on Artificial Intelligence Organization. Main track.

Bodhisattwa Prasad Majumder, Bhavana Dalvi Mishra, Peter Jansen, Oyvind Tafjord, Niket Tandon, Li Zhang, Chris Callison-Burch, and Peter Clark. 2023. Clin: A continually learning language agent for rapid task adaptation and generalization.

Noah Shinn, Federico Cassano, Edward Berman, Ashwin Gopinath, Karthik Narasimhan, and Shunyu Yao. 2023. Reflexion: Language agents with verbal reinforcement learning.

Tom Silver, Soham Dan, Kavitha Srinivas, Joshua B. Tenenbaum, Leslie Pack Kaelbling, and Michael Katz. 2023. Generalized planning in pddl domains with pretrained large language models.

Katharina Stein and Alexander Koller. 2023. Autoplanbench:: Automatically generating benchmarks for llm planners from pddl. *arXiv preprint arXiv:2311.09830*.

Karthik Valmeekam, Matthew Marquez, Alberto Olmo, Sarath Sreedharan, and Subbarao Kambhampati. 2023a. Planbench: An extensible benchmark for evaluating large language models on planning and reasoning about change. In *Thirty-seventh Conference on Neural Information Processing Systems Datasets and Benchmarks Track*.

Karthik Valmeekam, Matthew Marquez, Sarath Sreedharan, and Subbarao Kambhampati. 2023b. On the planning abilities of large language models–a critical investigation. *arXiv preprint arXiv:2305.15771*.

Karthik Valmeekam, Alberto Olmo, Sarath Sreedharan, and Subbarao Kambhampati. 2023c. Large language models still can't plan (a benchmark for llms on planning and reasoning about change).

Lionel Wong, Jiayuan Mao, Pratyusha Sharma, Zachary S Siegel, Jiahai Feng, Noa Korneev, Joshua B Tenenbaum, and Jacob Andreas. 2023. Learning adaptive planning representations with natural language guidance. *arXiv preprint arXiv:2312.08566*.

Yaqi Xie, Chen Yu, Tongyao Zhu, Jinbin Bai, Ze Gong, and Harold Soh. 2023. Translating natural language to planning goals with large-language models. *arXiv preprint arXiv:2302.05128*.

Xingdi Yuan, Marc-Alexandre Côté, Alessandro Sordoni, Romain Laroche, Remi Tachet des Combes, Matthew Hausknecht, and Adam Trischler. 2019. Counting to explore and generalize in text-based games.

A Formulation of PDDL

As shown in Figure 4, an instance of PDDL (Ghallab et al., 1998) consists of a domain file, describing the actions, and a problem file, describing the initial and goal states of entities. A well-formed pair of domain and problem files can be solved by a symbolic planner, whose output is a sequence of actions.

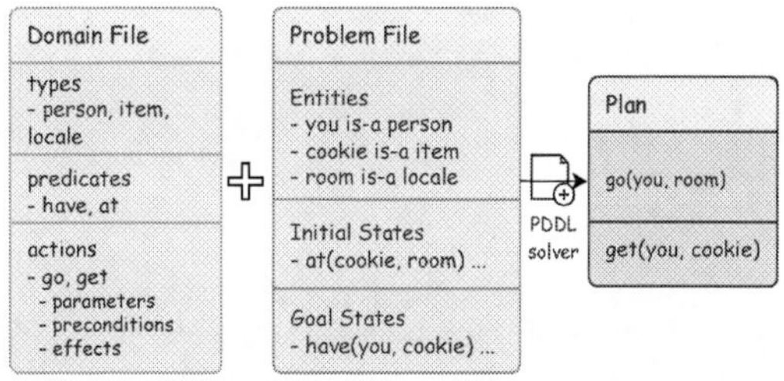

Figure 4: A PDDL solver produces a plan based on a minimal domain file and problem file. Previous work assumes the domain file as given, while we predict the action definitions in the domain file.

B Annotated Domain Files and Prompts

PDDLEGO is a method to iteratively construct problem files based on a provided domain file. Figure 5 and 6 show the annotated domain files for Coin Collector and Cooking World, respectively. Note that the actions and their parameter lists in the domain file strictly maps to the permitted actions in the simulations, so that a PDDL plan can be mapped onto executable actions in the environment. Based on the domain file, our prompts for either generating (PDDL-gen) or editing (PDDL-edit) the problem file are simply (for Coin Collector):

> You will continue to build a PDDL representation of an environment while exploring it. We will be using the following domain file: «domain file» For example, for the given observation:
>
> You are in the kitchen. To the South you see a closed wooden door.
>
> Your task is to go to a location you have not been yet. You will generate the following problem file: «example domain file»
>
> Now, let's start afresh.

For PDDL-edit, a few more details are appended.

> «the above prompt»
>
> Let's work with an example. Say you're given this observation: You are in the kitchen. To the South you see a closed wooden door. To the East you see a closed glass door.
>
> You will modify the above problem file using add, replace, and delete operations (in a JSON format). You SHOULD NOT provide a problem file directly.

```
{
  "objects": {
    "add": [
      "loc1 - location",
      "loc2 - location"
    ],
    "replace": {},
    "delete": []
  },
  "init": {
    "add": [
      "(connected kitchen loc1 south)",
      "(closed_door kitchen loc1)",
      "(connected kitchen loc2 east)",
```

```
    "(closed_door kitchen loc2)"
  ],
  "replace": {},
  "delete": []
 }
}
```

Note a couple of things:

1. When you see a closed door, you would use a placeholder for the room behind the door.

2. When you enter a room, you learn the name of the room and will replace the placeholder with the name. You should also make sure to replace that name for all relations under "init".

3. When you enter a room, you're "at" the room and it becomes "visited". You should also delete other "at" conditions because you can only be at one room.

4. You should never delete the "visited" relations, because once a room is visited, it will remain that way.

For Cooking World, the prompt is mostly the same for the first stage (looking for ingredients), with an additional LLM instance to identify closed containers, and their contents once opened. As described above, all found ingredients are mechanically picked up (hard-coded).

For Action-gen, the prompt is simply a description of the simulation, providing as much information as specified in the above domain files. For Coin Collector, it is:

> You will play a game where your goal is to collect a coin. You need to move through rooms explore them. Sometimes, two rooms are connected by closed door that you need to open before you can go from one to another. You should also keep track of which room you have visited, and the direction at which you enter a room.
>
> I will provide you with a description of the environment, and you will take one of the valid actions. Ready?

For Cooking World, it is:

> You will play a game where your goal is to read a recipe, find ingredients, cook a meal, and eat the meal. The recipe includes the ingredients that you'll need to collect. The ingredients are scattered around rooms and may be found in containers. After you find the ingredients, you need to process them as required in the recipe. Here are how the ingredients are processed:
>
> - slice: use a knife to slice the ingredient
>
> - chop: use a knife to chop the ingredient
>
> - dice: use a knife to dice the ingredient
>
> - grill: use a toaster or a barbeque to cook the ingredient will grill it
>
> - roast: use an oven to cook the ingredient will roast it
>
> - fry: use a stove to cook the ingredient will fry it
>
> You have to process the ingredients as specified in the recipe, otherwise you will fail. Once the ingredients are processed, you can cook the meal and eat the meal in the kitchen, so make sure you go back to the kitchen at that point.
>
> Now, I will provide you with a description of the environment, and you will take one of the valid actions. Ready?

```
(define (domain environment)
  (:requirements :strips :typing :negative-preconditions :disjunctive-
        preconditions)
  (:types
    location
    direction
  )
  (:predicates
    (at ?loc - location)
    (visited ?loc - location)
    (connected ?loc1 - location ?loc2 - location ?dir - direction)
    (closed_door ?loc1 - location ?loc2 - location)
  )

  (:action move
    :parameters (?loc1 - location ?loc2 - location ?dir - direction)
    :precondition (and (at ?loc1) (connected ?loc1 ?loc2 ?dir) (not (
          closed_door ?loc1 ?loc2)))
    :effect (and (not (at ?loc1)) (at ?loc2))
  )

  (:action open_door
    :parameters (?loc1 - location ?loc2 - location)
    :precondition (and (at ?loc1) (closed_door ?loc1 ?loc2))
    :effect (not (closed_door ?loc1 ?loc2))
  )
)
```

Figure 5: Annotated domain file for Coin Collector.

C Hyperparameters

For both simulations, we use the implementation from Jansen and Côté (2022). For Coin Collector, we use the most complex setting supported by the system of 11 rooms with random connectivity, allowing up to 50 exploration steps. For Cooking World, we consider an easy setting with 2 rooms and 2 ingredients up to 20 steps and a hard setting of 5 rooms and 5 ingredients up to 50 steps. For both datasets, we vary the random random seed to generate randomize environment configurations, and use 0-9 as the development set, and 10-59 as the test set.

For the choice of LLM, we consider `gpt-3.5-turbo-1106` (GPT 3.5 Turbo) and `gpt-4-1106-preview` (GPT 4 Turbo) across baseline methods (i.e., Action-gen, PDDL-gen, and PDDL-edit). We set the temperature to 1 to study stability. For Action-gen, we prompt the LLM with a full description of the simulation with the aim that a human player can learn to succeed. For the PDDL approaches, whenever the generated or edited problem cannot be solved by the domain file, indicating an error, the model is allowed to retry up to 5 times before failing the task. Models are provided with a hand-annotated domain file for each task contains permitted actions (e.g., move,

```
(define (domain environment)
  (:requirements :strips :typing :negative-preconditions :disjunctive-
        preconditions)

  (:types
    ingredient container knife toaster stove oven barbeque - object
    location
    direction
  )

  (:predicates
    (at ?loc - location)
    (obj_at ?obj - object ?loc - location)
    (visited ?loc - location)
    (connected ?loc1 - location ?loc2 - location ?dir - direction)
    (closed_door ?loc1 - location ?loc2 - location)

    (grilled ?ing - ingredient)
    (roasted ?ing - ingredient)
    (fried ?ing - ingredient)
    (chopped ?ing - ingredient)
    (sliced ?ing - ingredient)
    (diced ?ing - ingredient)
    (have ?obj - object)
  )

  (:action move
    :parameters (?loc1 - location ?loc2 - location ?dir - direction)
    :precondition (and (at ?loc1) (connected ?loc1 ?loc2 ?dir) (not (
          closed_door ?loc1 ?loc2)))
    :effect (and (not (at ?loc1)) (at ?loc2))
  )

  (:action open_door
    :parameters (?loc1 - location ?loc2 - location)
    :precondition (and (at ?loc1) (closed_door ?loc1 ?loc2))
    :effect (not (closed_door ?loc1 ?loc2))
  )

  (:action use_stove
    :parameters (?ing - ingredient ?loc - location ?sto - stove)
    :precondition (and (at ?loc) (obj_at ?sto ?loc) (have ?ing))
    :effect (fried ?ing)
  )

  (:action use_toaster
    :parameters (?ing - ingredient ?loc - location ?toa - toaster)
    :precondition (and (at ?loc) (obj_at ?toa ?loc) (have ?ing))
    :effect (grilled ?ing)
  )

  (:action use_oven
    :parameters (?ing - ingredient ?loc - location ?ove - oven)
    :precondition (and (at ?loc) (obj_at ?ove ?loc) (have ?ing))
    :effect (roasted ?ing)
  )

  (:action use_barbeque
    :parameters (?ing - ingredient ?loc - location ?bbq - barbeque)
    :precondition (and (at ?loc) (obj_at ?bbq ?loc) (have ?ing))
    :effect (grilled ?ing)
  )

  (:action chop
    :parameters (?ing - ingredient ?kni - knife)
    :precondition (and (have ?ing) (have ?kni))
    :effect (chopped ?ing)
  )

  (:action slice
    :parameters (?ing - ingredient ?kni - knife)
    :precondition (and (have ?ing) (have ?kni))
    :effect (sliced ?ing)
  )

  (:action dice
    :parameters (?ing - ingredient ?kni - knife)
    :precondition (and (have ?ing) (have ?kni))
    :effect (diced ?ing)
  )
)
```

Figure 6: Annotated domain file for Cooking World.

open door, pick up) with well-defined types and predicates, parameters, pre-conditions, and effects. For the PDDL-edit setting, we prompt the LLM to generate edits (add, replace, and delete lines in the problem file) in JSON with the force-JSON flag set. The prompt of each method include a 1-shot demonstration of the output format (i.e., an action, a problem file, or edits to a problem file). See details of prompt design and domain file annotation in the Appendix B.

D Example Trajectories

A sample trajectory by GPT 4 Turbo with PDDL-edit on Cooking World (hard) is shown in Figure 7. The navigation portion of the interaction (look around, open door, move) is inherited from Coin Collector.

E Generated Problem Files

Figure 8 demonstrates a PDDL problem file learned throughout exploration in Coin Collector that indicates the existence and connectivity of all rooms the agent has access to before finding the coin.

F Results on the Development Set

Table 2 is the counterpart of Table 1 showcasing the results on the development set.

```
< examine cookbook
> Gather all following ingredients and follow the directions to prepare this tasty meal.
Ingredients:
  black pepper, block of cheese, salt, red apple, yellow potato
Directions:
  slice the block of cheese, dice the red apple, chop the yellow potato, grill the yellow potato, prepare meal
< look around
> You are in the kitchen. In one part of the room you see a stove. There is also an oven. You also see a fridge that is closed. In another part of the
      room you see a counter that has a knife, a red apple, a raw yellow potato, and a cookbook on it. In one part of the room you see a kitchen
      cupboard that is closed. There is also a cutlery drawer that is closed. You also see a trash can that is closed. In another part of the room you
      see a dishwasher that is closed. In one part of the room you see a dining chair, that has nothing on it.
To the South you see a closed plain door. To the West you see the corridor.
< open fridge
> You open the fridge. The fridge contains a block of cheese.
< take block of cheese
> You take the block of cheese.
< take knife
> You take the knife.
< take red apple
> You take the red apple.
< take yellow potato
> You take the yellow potato.
< open kitchen cupboard
> You open the kitchen cupboard. It's empty inside.
< open cutlery drawer
> You open the cutlery drawer. It's empty inside.
< open trash can
> You open the trash can. It's empty inside.
< open dishwasher
> You open the dishwasher. It's empty inside.
< move west
> You are in the corridor. In one part of the room you see a key holder, that has nothing on it. There is also a shoe cabinet that is closed. You also
      see a umbrella stand, that has nothing on it. In another part of the room you see a hat rack, that has nothing on it. In one part of the room you
      see a coat hanger, that has nothing on it.
To the North you see a closed wood door. To the East you see the kitchen. To the West you see a closed sliding patio door.
< open shoe cabinet
> You open the shoe cabinet. It's empty inside.
< open door to north
> You open the wood door, revealing the bedroom.
< move north
> You are in the bedroom. In one part of the room you see a dressing table, that has nothing on it. There is also a desk chair, that has nothing on it.
      You also see a desk, that has nothing on it. In another part of the room you see a chest of drawers that is closed. In one part of the room you
      see a wardrobe that is closed. There is also a night stand, that has nothing on it. You also see a bed, that has nothing on it.
Through an open wood door, to the South you see the corridor.
< open chest of drawers
> You open the chest of drawers. It's empty inside.
< open wardrobe
> You open the wardrobe. It's empty inside.
< move south
> You are in the corridor. (description omitted)
< open door to west
> You open the sliding patio door, revealing the backyard.
< move west
> You are in the backyard. In one part of the room you see a barbeque. There is also a workbench, that has nothing on it. You also see a patio chair,
      that has nothing on it. In another part of the room you see a patio table, that has nothing on it. In one part of the room you see a clothes line
      , that has nothing on it. There is also a garden, that has nothing on it.
Through an open sliding patio door, to the East you see the corridor.
< move east
> You are in the corridor. (description omitted)
< move east
> You are in the kitchen. (description omitted)
< open door to south
> You open the plain door, revealing the pantry.
< move south
> You are in the pantry. In one part of the room you see a folding chair, that has nothing on it. There is also a shelf that has some black pepper, and
      some salt on it.
Through an open plain door, to the North you see the kitchen.
< take black pepper
> You take the black pepper.
< take salt
> You take the salt.
< dice red apple
> You dice the red apple.
< slice block of cheese
> You slice the block of cheese.
< chop yellow potato
> You chop the yellow potato.
< move north
> You are in the kitchen. (description omitted)
Through an open plain door, to the South you see the pantry. To the West you see the corridor.
< move west
> You are in the corridor. (description omitted)
< move west
> You are in the backyard. (description omitted)
< cook yellow potato in barbeque
> You grill the yellow potato with the barbeque.
< move east
> You are in the corridor. (description omitted)
< move east
> You are in the kitchen. (description omitted)
< prepare meal
> Adding the meal to your inventory.
< eat meal
> You eat the meal. It is delicious.
```

Figure 7: An example trajectory performed by GPT 4 Turbo and PDDL-edit on Cooking World (hard).

	random	GPT 3.5 Turbo			GPT 4 Turbo		
		Action-gen	PDDL-gen†	PDDL-edit†	Action-gen	PDDL-gen†	PDDL-edit†
Coin	20%	80%	30%	70%	**90%**	50%	80%
Cooking (easy)	0%	0%	100%	70%	10%	90%	**100%**
Cooking (hard)	0%	0%	0%	0%	0%	0%	**50%**

Table 2: The percentage where the agent succeeds by taking no more than the maximum steps on the development set. The † sign specifies methods under our proposed PDDLEGO methodology.

```
(define (problem exploration)
  (:domain environment)
  (:objects
    kitchen corridor backyard driveway street supermarket
    laundry_room bathroom living_room 16 111 - location
    north south east west - direction
  )
  (:init
    (at backyard)
    (visited kitchen)
    (visited corridor)
    (visited backyard)
    (visited driveway)
    (visited street)
    (visited supermarket)
    (visited laundry_room)
    (visited bathroom)
    (visited living_room)
    (connected kitchen corridor west)
    (connected corridor backyard north)
    (connected corridor laundry_room south)
    (connected corridor kitchen east)
    (connected corridor bathroom west)
    (connected backyard corridor south)
    (connected backyard driveway east)
    (connected backyard living_room west)
    (connected driveway backyard west)
    (connected driveway street east)
    (connected street driveway west)
    (connected street supermarket south)
    (connected supermarket street north)
    (connected laundry_room corridor north)
    (connected bathroom living_room north)
    (connected bathroom corridor east)
    (connected living_room bathroom south)
    (connected living_room backyard east)
    (connected living_room 111 west)
    (closed_door living_room 111)
  )
```

Figure 8: An example PDDL problem file learned throughout exploration in Coin Collector.

VOLIMET: A Parallel Corpus of Literal and Metaphorical Verb-Object Pairs for English–German and English–French

Prisca Piccirilli[1] and **Alexander Fraser**[2,3] and **Sabine Schulte im Walde**[1]
[1]Institute for Natural Language Processing, University of Stuttgart, Germany
[2]School of Computation, Information and Technology, TUM, Germany
[3]Munich Centre for Machine Learning, Germany
{prisca.piccirilli,schulte}@ims.uni-stuttgart.de

Abstract

The interplay of cultural and linguistic elements that characterizes metaphorical language poses a substantial challenge for both human comprehension and machine processing. This challenge goes beyond monolingual settings and becomes particularly complex in translation, even more so in automatic translation. We present VOLIMET, a corpus of 2,916 parallel sentences containing gold standard alignments of metaphorical verb-object pairs and their literal paraphrases, e.g., *tackle/address question*, from English to German and French. On the one hand, the parallel nature of our corpus enables us to explore monolingual patterns for metaphorical vs. literal uses in English. On the other hand, we investigate different aspects of cross-lingual translations into German and French and the extent to which metaphoricity and literalness in the source language are transferred to the target languages. Monolingually, our findings reveal clear preferences in using metaphorical or literal uses of verb-object pairs. Cross-lingually, we observe a rich variability in translations as well as different behaviors for our two target languages[1].

Figure 1: Example of gold standard alignments for a source English sentence containing the metaphorical verb-object *tackle challenge* to German and French.

1 Introduction

Metaphor is a figurative device which allows us to understand and experience one (typically abstract) domain in terms of another (typically more concrete) domain (Lakoff and Johnson, 1980). For example, in the sentence *I'll tackle the challenging problem of metaphors in translation*, the abstract domain of dealing with a problem is expressed in terms of the more concrete domain of physically seizing and throwing down something/someone. Metaphorical language has long been recognized as a challenge for both human understanding and machine processing (Tong et al., 2021) and is not confined to monolingual settings. It extends into cross-lingual territory, particularly in the realm of translation, where metaphors represent a hard nut to crack: they are not only very flexible in their structures and meanings, but also strongly depend on the involved languages and cultures (Schäffner, 2004; Kövecses, 2010). While the effort to automate the translation of figurative language using machine translation (MT) systems is underway, limited MT research explores the **contrast between metaphorical and literal language in translation** and its potential effect on translatability (van den Broek, 1981) and variability (Tong et al., 2021) in language production and generation.

To bridge this gap, we create VOLIMET, a parallel corpus of English–German and English–French sentences containing gold standard alignments of paraphrased metaphorical and literal uses of verb-object (VO) pairs (see example in Fig. 1). The corpus provides insights on the translation of metaphorical VO pairs and their corresponding literal paraphrases from the source language (SL) English, to the target languages (TL) French and German. For instance, given the metaphorical VO *tackle question*, is its literal VO counterpart *address question* equally frequent in natural language? How is it translated into other languages

[1]All data and guidelines are available at https://github.com/priscapiccirilli/VOLIMET

*Proceedings of the 13th Joint Conference on Lexical and Computational Semantics (*SEM 2024)*, pages 222 - 237
June 20-21, 2024 ©2024 Association for Computational Linguistics

and to which extent is the metaphoricity transferred or preserved in the translation from SL to TL? How many different translations of this VO do humans produce, i.e., do we find one-to-one or one-to-many mappings between source and target languages?

In this paper, we present a comprehensive account of the corpus construction process and perform extensive monolingual and cross-lingual analyses. Monolingually, we seek to uncover patterns in the use of metaphorical vs. literal VOs. We find that considering the verb and its object as a unit provides a more nuanced representation than considering the verb on its own, crucial for accurate automatic processing. Cross-lingually, we observe a rich tapestry of translation variability, indicating one-to-many mappings between the source VOs and their target translations, where both metaphorical and literal uses are prevalent in the TLs. We further uncover differences in translations between the TLs, highlighting the need for flexible MT systems capable of reproducing this diversity.

Overall, our parallel corpus is meticulously crafted to encapsulate all these intricacies and represents a key resource in the endeavor to tackle the challenges posed by metaphorical language. In the future, it will also be of great use for machine translation research on metaphors.

2 Related Work

Translation Studies Metaphorical language represents an extremely common phenomenon (Shutova and Teufel, 2010) and has been of interest in translation studies when prescribing conditions for translating metaphors (van den Broek, 1981; Schäffner, 2004). As of today, the three translation modes from van den Broek (1981) remain the core choices in TL translations of SL metaphors: (1) a translation "sensu stricto" as in *le jour tombe–der Tag fällt* (lit. *the day falls*), which might lead to a semantic anomaly or innovation if the metaphor vehicles in SL and TL differ, (2) an onomasiological translation referred to as "substitution" where the SL and TL vehicles are translation equivalents sharing the same tenor, as in *le jour tombe–die Nacht bricht (her)ein* (lit. *the night falls in*); and (3) a discursive, non-metaphorical translation "paraphrase" as in *le jour tombe–es wird Abend* (lit. *it is becoming night*).

Machine Translation MT research incorporating figurative language has mainly been restricted to studies on the translation of structurally or semantically less flexible expressions, such as idioms (Huet and Langlais, 2013; Fadaee and Monz, 2018) and multi-word-expressions (e.g., noun compounds such as *flea market*; particle verbs such as *give up*; support verb constructions such as *play a role*) (Carpuat and Diab, 2010; Gamallo et al., 2019).

Cognitive Linguistics Stefanowitsch (2008) and Martin (2008) provide evidence for the cognitive function of metaphors in contrast to their literal counterparts, by demonstrating that people tend to use metaphors to explicate things. Metaphorical language tends to also be more emotionally-loaded than literal language (Citron and Goldberg, 2014; Mohammad et al., 2016; Piccirilli and Schulte im Walde, 2022) and may influence the way people conceptualize the world (Thibodeau and Boroditsky, 2011). Overall, there is empirical evidence for differences in using metaphorical in contrast to literal language, which we explore from a cross-lingual perspective in this work.

NLP Research has mainly focused on metaphor *detection* (Mu et al., 2019; Dankers et al., 2020) and *interpretation* (Bizzoni and Lappin, 2018; Mao et al., 2018), with the predominant idea to generate literal paraphrases for metaphorical expressions. More recently and more closely related to the current interest of this present work, we built a dataset of verb–object and subject–verb metaphorical vs. literal expressions used in large context and collected via crowd-sourcing annotations (Piccirilli and Schulte im Walde, 2021). In further work, we compared adapted computational models for discourse metaphor/literal interactions; the results from the human judgements showed the equal importance of metaphorical and literal usages, a behavior that computational models fail at mimicking (Piccirilli and Schulte im Walde, 2022). This reinforces the necessity for a more nuanced approach and attests limitations of word representations for metaphorically-used language.

Overall, rich interdisciplinary research offers insights on metaphors in monolingual settings, but less so in cross-lingual settings. Our work contributes to filling this gap by looking at the contrast of metaphorical and literal language, both from a monolingual and cross-lingual perspective.

3 Creating VOLIMET

We create VOLIMET, a comprehensive linguistic resource comprising various components that are necessary to enhance not only our understanding of metaphorical language use but also its effect on translated text. VOLIMET encompasses an **extensive collection of English metaphorical and literal VO pairs**, as in *tackle vs. address question*, thoughtfully curated to provide paraphrases of one another (§3.1). VOLIMET also significantly enhances its contribution by **offering English sentences featuring these VO pairs**, meticulously extracted from parallel data (§3.2). The parallel nature of VOLIMET allows on the one hand **monolingual analyses** of metaphorical and literal VO pairs in context. On the other hand, it also enables a **cross-lingual exploration** of how these VOs are translated into German and French, making VOLIMET the first resource of metaphorical and literal VOs and their respective translations.

3.1 VO Pairs: Collection

At its core, VOLIMET consists of a set of metaphorical and literal verb-object pairs, which we (i) obtained from previous work and (ii) semi-automatically augmented.

Original Pairs As a starting point, we collected a seed of 47 metaphorical VOs and their literal paraphrases from previous work (Mohammad et al., 2016; Shutova, 2010; Piccirilli and Schulte im Walde, 2021; Stowe et al., 2022), cf. Appendix A. For example, the basic sense of the verb *tackle* is used in the context of "to catch and knock down someone who is running",[2] which makes the idea of *tackling a question* physically impossible. The VO *tackle question* was therefore judged as being metaphorical, and *address question* was proposed as its literal paraphrase. Note that because the verb and its object are considered as a unit, there is no semantic ambiguity: no matter the context in which the VO occurs, *tackle question* is always used metaphorically, while *address question* is always used literally. Each VO pair in our original seed is composed of (i) a metaphorical verb and its literal paraphrase (*tackle/address*) and (ii) a direct-object noun (*question*) which makes the pair as a whole (verb-object) considered synonymous.

Extended Pairs As we expect that our verb pairs naturally occur with more than one common object, we expanded the range of direct objects co-occurring with each of our 47 seed verb pairs. For example, the verbs in the pair *tackle/address* both subcategorize *question* as a direct object but may also occur with *issue, challenge, matter*, to name just a few. Each of these nouns is not only a direct object of both verbs but also does not affect the paraphrase reading. We minimized human involvement for this task and applied a semi-automatic approach. Assuming that a direct object (*dobj*) occurring with both verbs within the same parsed corpus is likely to be a valid candidate, we automatically extracted all *dobjs* nouns if occurring with both verbs of a verb pair within the ENCOW corpus (Schäfer and Bildhauer, 2012; Schäfer, 2015). We first collected 157,437 additional arguments across our 47 pairs and then applied restrictions to reduce potential noise: We defined a frequency threshold of 15 for each object to occur with each of the two verbs, and discarded extracted nouns of less than two characters or labeled as "unknown" or "proper noun". Finally, we retained the 50 most frequent extracted objects for each verb pair. We automatically obtained 2,325 additional objects, from which we manually selected up to 10 valid candidates per verb pair. On average, each verb pair was augmented with six objects (max=11, min=1)[3], resulting in a total of 297 VO pairs. Note that the verb pairs remain the same, and the augmentation only applies to the nominal objects. For example, the original VO pair *drown/forget trouble* was augmented with the additional objects {*pain, problem, feeling*}. In Appendix A, we provide the original VO pairs and the sets of extended objects.

3.2 VO Pairs: Parallel Sentence Extraction and VO Alignments

The second part of the data collection consists of extracting natural English data containing any of our VO pairs. Because we aim to explore metaphors and their literal counterparts from both a mono- and cross-lingual perspective, we extracted data from parallel corpora.

Source and Target Languages We chose English as our SL. As our TLs we chose German and French, two high-resource languages.

Parallel Corpus Using existing parallel corpora such as the Europarl Parallel Corpus (Koehn, 2005) seemed the most straightforward approach, as it offers large amounts of data for our language pairs English–German (*en2de*) and English–French

[2] https://dictionary.cambridge.org/dictionary/english/tackle

[3] No additional valid *dobj* was found for four of our VO pairs, namely *push/sell drugs, wear/have smile, flood/saturate market, shipwreck/ruin career.*

(*en2fr*). However, a major limitation of existing large parallel corpora is the (lack of) information regarding the language-pair direction. For example, the Europarl *en2de* corpus does not reliably ensure that the English text is always the actual SL nor that the parallel German text is the TL obtained *from* translating the SL English. This is problematic within the scope of our work: metaphorical language is a specific cognitive and linguistic phenomenon that is language- and culture-specific (Schäffner, 2004; Kövecses, 2010), hence the necessity to be aware of the original SL and the corresponding TLs. This limitation was previously noticed and addressed in Rabinovich et al. (2018), who publicly released a subset of the Europarl corpus providing accurate and reliable indications of translation directions. Their corpus contains 217,344 *en2fr* and 225,089 *en2de* parallel sentences, representing about 16% of the respective original Europarl datasets. We decided to use this corpus to build VOLIMET.

Extraction and Gold Standard Alignments We extracted all parallel sentences in which the source texts contain any of our 297 VO pairs, and performed word alignments using `fast-align` (Dyer et al., 2013). We ideally wanted to automatically obtain translations of the components of the pairs, but the accuracy of automatic alignments was rather sub-optimal, and resulted in many partial alignments. It also missed some crucial linguistic information or provided erroneous alignments; in fact, as soon as the translator took some creative liberty, the aligner generally failed to provide an alignment.

We therefore hired three German and two French speakers to correct potential errors in the automatically-obtained alignments. We defined clear guidelines on what and how to align. Note that we did not correct the word alignments of the *full* sentences, but focused only on the alignments between the SL *verb* and *object* of our VO pairs and their corresponding translations. This was a necessary and valuable step in creating VOLIMET: 66% and 90% of the *en2fr* metaphorical and literal parallel texts, respectively, needed their alignments to be corrected. For the *en2de* parallel texts, 92% and 85% of the metaphorical and literal data, respectively, had their alignments corrected.

Thanks to this human effort, we obtain **gold standard alignments** between metaphorical and literal English VO pairs and all their German and French human-produced translations. We release the annotation guidelines and the gold standard *en2fr* and *en2de* alignments for our metaphorical vs. literal VO pairs at `https://github.com/priscapiccirilli/VOLIMET`.

	Met. VOs		Lit. VOs		Total
# instances	730	(12.59)	961	(10.92)	1,691
# VO pairs	58	(27)	88	(32)	31
# inflected VOs	135	(2.33)	203	(2.31)	–
Avg. sent. length	30.08	–	34.16	–	–

Table 1: Statistics on extracted monolingual English data: number of instances containing metaphorical and literal VOs (avg. instances per VO), number of extracted VOs (verb-specific) and number of inflected variants (avg. per VO) as well as average sentence length.

4 Quantitative Analyses

VOLIMET encompasses close to 3,000 *en2fr* and *en2de* parallel sentences containing a total of 114 metaphorical and literal VO pairs. We first perform in-depth monolingual (§ 4.1) and cross-lingual (§ 4.2) quantitative analyses. Monolingually, we shed light on the frequency of our VOs, their syntactic (non-)fixedness and the contrast in their metaphorical vs. literal usages. Cross-lingually, we look at the variability across translations. Then we explore whether metaphoricity vs. literalness in English is transferred to French and German during the translation process, and how the findings differ between the two TLs.

4.1 Monolingual (English) Analyses

The parallel nature of our corpora enables us to first perform quantitative analyses regarding the use of metaphorical and literal VO pairs in a monolingual setting, namely English. This way, we shed light on properties of metaphorical vs. literal language use in natural language. All statistics are reported in Table 1.

Starting with a set of 297 VOs, we wanted to see how **frequently** they occur in natural language, and whether we observe a **clear distinction between metaphorical VOs and their literal counterparts**. We extracted a total of 1,691 English sentences, 730 of them containing 58 **metaphorical VOs** (27 verbs-only[4]), and 961 sentences containing 88 **literal VOs** (32 verbs-only). We observe imbalances in the frequencies of VOs, e.g., we retrieved only two instances of *shape outcome*, but

[4]For example, *tackle question* and *tackle challenge* are 2 metaphorical VOs with 1 verb-only.

169 instances of *tackle problem*. Independently of their metaphoricity, each VO occurred with an average of 2.5 inflections (max=8) regarding both components (verb and/or object), e.g., *follow(ing) activity(ies), cause(s) death(s)*. We did not observe any major differences in sentence length, and the average sentence length is ≈30 words, both in the metaphorical and literal data.

The first 10 most frequent metaphorical and literal VOs represent 84% and 77% of the data, respectively (Table 2). The only pairs that seem to be equally frequent in their metaphorical and literal forms all stem from the same verb pair, i.e., *tackle* vs. *address (problem/question/issue)*. Paraphrased pairs are not equally frequent; in other words, either the metaphorical use or the literal alternative occurs in our data, e.g., *clause debate* is amongst the 10 most frequent VOs while its counterpart *end debate* does not occur once in our data at all. Out of the 58 metaphorical and 88 literal retrieved VOs, 31 of them are actual paraphrased pairs whose frequencies can be compared. We report in Figure 2 the proportions of frequencies for these 31 pairs. As we can see, only six of these pairs show equal frequencies of their metaphorical and literal uses (e.g., *break/end agreement*). There are 13 of them for which the literal use is more frequent than its metaphorical counterpart (e.g., *stimulate/fuel debate*) and 12 of them for which the metaphorical use is more frequent than its literal alternative (e.g., *boost/improve economy*). We will develop this observation in Section 5.

Quite a few additional verbs also display high frequencies when they are considered regardless of their objects. For example, the metaphorical VO *breathe life* is not part of the 10 most frequent metaphorical VOs but the verb *breathe* is, if we gather all its instances regardless of its objects (*life, confidence, value, hope*, etc.).

4.2 Cross-Lingual Analyses

VOLIMET is a valuable resource to exploit the annotations cross-lingually and analyze metaphorical vs. literal properties of translations. In this section, we quantify our findings for each language pair – *en2fr* and *en2de* – containing metaphorical vs. literal VOs. We provide qualitative analyses of these findings in Section 5. A detailed summary of the discussed statistics of VOLIMET can be found in Table 3.

Size and Frequency VOLIMET consists of 1,701 *en2de* and 1,215 *en2fr* parallel sentences, containing 114 of our source VOs. The obtained data is overall balanced for *en2de* regarding the amount of parallel sentences containing source metaphorical and literal VOs. However, the *en2fr* parallel dataset containing source metaphorical VOs is twice as large as the one containing source literal VOs. This is due to the fact that we had more German annotators; we aim to correct more *en2fr* alignments, in order to reach a balanced dataset.

Across the metaphorical and literal parallel datasets and language pairs, we find an average of 11 parallel sentences for each VO. This number however varies greatly across VOs. For instance, for the metaphorical *en2fr* dataset, we obtained only one parallel sentence containing the source VO *break contract* but 102 parallel sentences containing the source VO *find way*.

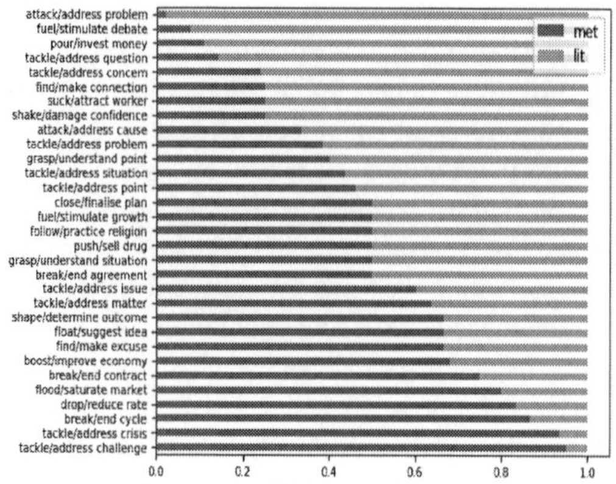

Figure 2: Proportions of VO pairs: metaphorical (blue) vs. literal (orange).

Met.		Lit.	
VO	verb-only	VO	verb-only
find way	tackle	address problem	address
tackle problem	find	make remark	make
tackle issue	close	address question	pose
tackle challenge	break	address issue	improve
close debate	boost	pose question	invest
tackle question	*float*	make comment	*reduce*
boost economy	*mount*	invest money	*understand*
tackle crisis	attack	improve situation	*get*
break cycle	*breathe*	address concern	stimulate
close case	*shape*	stimulate debate	*cause*

Table 2: The first 10 most frequent metaphorical and literal VOs in the SL English texts, in descending order. Underlined are the metaphorical vs. literal VO pairs that are equally frequent. In *italics* are the verbs that enter the top-10 when considered regardless of their objects.

	Met. VOs				Lit. VOs				Total
	en2de		en2fr		en2de		en2fr		
# parallel sentences	719	(12.40)	394	(8.76)	982	(11.55)	821	(11.40)	2,916
# VO pairs	58	(27)	45	(25)	85	(32)	72	(28)	114/297
# inflected VO pairs	133	(2.29)	103	(2.29)	198	(2.33)	154	(2.14)	–
# total translations	560	(9.66)	296	(6.58)	832	(9.79)	534	(7.42)	–
# unique translations	290	(5.67)	176	(4.44)	417	(5.48)	239	(3.82)	–
# Fig. translations (%)	109	(37.59)	112	(63.64)	128	(30.70)	88	(36.82)	–
# Lit. translations (%)	147	(50.59)	53	(30.11)	245	(58.75)	127	(53.14)	–

Table 3: Statistics on parallel datasets containing literal vs. metaphorical VO pairs: number of parallel sentences, VO pair inflections, all and unique (=type) translations (mean in brackets), the number of VO pairs covered in our datasets (unique verbs in brackets), and whether the respective VO translations were judged figurative or literal by humans (% in brackets). For example, the *en2de* dataset contains 719 **parallel sentences** with 58 **metaphorical VO pairs** (27 **verbs-only**[4]). We obtained 560 **total translations** for these 58 VO pairs (avg. 9.66 **translations per VO**), 327 **unique translations** (avg. 5.67 **translations per VO**), for which 42.41% of the **translations** were judged **figurative** and 57.59% **literal**.

Syntactic Variation Across language pairs and datasets, each VO presents on average two inflections (max=7 for *en2fr*, max=11 for *en2de*), from both components (verb and/or object), e.g., *found/finding excuse(s)*.

Variability in Translation We obtain a large array of translations with an average of eight translations per source VO, irrespective of the metaphoricity and the TL. These numbers are cut in half when looking at the number of unique translations. This still results in large variations in translations as each VO is aligned on average to four different individual translations for each language pair. Out of an average of 280 unique translations across language pairs, we find only 19 *en2fr* and 27 *en2de* translations that are translations of several metaphorical VOs, e.g., *répondre à question* is found as a translation for both *tackle challenge* and *tackle issue*, and 27 *en2fr* and 42 *en2de* translations that are translations of several literal VOs.

Similarly to the number of instances retrieved per VO, the number of unique translations varies across VOs: out of the 302 *en2de* parallel sentences containing the VO *address problem*, we observe up to 79 different (unique) translations. The number of instances per VO is highly correlated with the number of translations (average Spearman's correlation ρ=0.99 for *en2de* and ρ=0.88 for *en2fr*), i.e., the more a VO appears in natural language, the more (unique) translations are produced. As a matter of fact, none of the source metaphorical VOs for the *en2de* language pair results in only one translation, and only three source metaphorical VOs produce one *en2fr* translation. A few source literal VOs obtain only one French/German translation (see Appendix B).

	FRENCH			GERMAN	
	Anno2	Anno3		Anno2	Anno3
Anno1	0.36	0.35	Anno1	0.42	0.36
Anno2	–	0.53	Anno2	–	0.43

Table 4: Cohen's κ scores across French and German annotators on judging the figurativeness of French and German translations, respectively, of metaphorical and literal English VOs.

Lost in Translation Beyond the *variability* in translation we described above, it is crucial to also quantify the *diversity* we encounter in translation: is metaphoricity/literalness transferred to the TLs, i.e., are metaphorical vs. literal VOs translated as metaphors vs. literal phrases, respectively?

We presented all unique German and French translations to three German and French native speakers and expert linguists, respectively, and asked them for a binary decision whether they judged each phrase[5] to be figurative[6] or literal. We

[5]We do not use the term "translation" in this annotation study, as we want to obtain judgements independently of the corresponding source text.

[6]We use the more general term "figurative language" for this annotation study, as the translations represent different *types* of figurative language, e.g., a metaphor, metonymy, an idiom, etc.

	FRENCH				GERMAN			
	Anno1	Anno2	Anno3	Maj. Vote	Anno1	Anno2	Anno3	Maj. Vote
Fig.	145 (41.31%)	178 (50.71%)	199 (56.70%)	178	320 (55.65%)	171 (29.74%)	181 (31.48%)	215
Lit.	206 (58.68%)	173 (49.29%)	152 (43.30%)	173	255 (44.35%)	404 (70.26%)	394 (68.52%)	360
Total	351				575			

Table 5: Human judgements (three expert French and German native speakers, respectively) regarding figurativeness for French (left) and German (right) translations, as well as the majority judgements.

report in Appendix C a detailed description of the annotation instructions.

Table 5 presents the number of translations that are judged figurative vs. literal, across annotators, as well as the majority vote. Overall, out of the 351 French translations, the judgements are rather balanced, i.e., the translations into French do not seem to be *clearly* figurative or literal, and this observation holds across annotators. The picture is different for translations into German: 2/3 of them are judged literal.

Judging figurative language is a difficult task (Zayed et al., 2019; Piccirilli and Schulte im Walde, 2021; Zhou et al., 2021), and we therefore observe disagreements across annotators on both languages. For example, the French VOs *plonger économie, jeter doute* (lit. *dive in economy, throw doubt*) and *comprendre signification, investir fond* (lit. *understand meaning, invest fund*) are unanimously judged figurative and literal, respectively. However, the VOs *trouver voie/moyen/issue/excuse* (lit. *find path/way (out)/excuse*) or *évoquer idée/question* (lit. *evoke idea/question*) were source of disagreement. Despite the difficulty of such a task, we obtain however fair-to-moderate inter-annotator agreement (IAA), with an average $\kappa = 0.41$ for both *en2fr* and *en2de*. Table 4 reports all κ scores between all annotators for both languages. We discuss in Section 5 some aspects on collecting human judgements regarding figurativeness which might have consequences for the analysis.

In the bottom part of Table 3, we also report the judgements regarding figurativeness of the translations with respect to the metaphoricity of the source phrases. The assumption that source metaphorical VOs are more likely to be translated figuratively and that literal source VOs are more likely to be translated with literal equivalences is confirmed for French. In fact, 63% of the translations from source metaphorical phrases are judged figurative, e.g., "float idea": *lancer idée* (lit. *throw idea*) rather than its literal paraphrase *suggérer idée* (lit. *suggest idea*), and more than half of the translations from source literal phrases are judged literal (53%), e.g., "address question": *considérer question* (lit. *consider question*) rather than *s'attaquer à question* (lit. *attack question*), the figurative paraphrase. We observe different results for German translations. Even though literal translations from literal source phrases are largely favored (59%), e.g., "address crisis": *etw. gegen Krise tun* (lit. *do sth against crisis*), rather than *Krise bekämpfen* (lit. *fight crisis*), this correlation is not noted for source metaphorical phrases being translated figuratively. As a matter of fact, half of the translations of metaphorical source phrases are judged literal, e.g., "find excuse": *Entschuldigung haben* (lit. *have excuse*), and not *als Entschuldigung nehmen* (lit. *take excuse*), its figurative alternative.

5 Discussion

VOs Frequency From our original 297 metaphorical vs. literal VO pairs, there were more literal VOs which were extracted from the source part of our parallel corpus (75 vs. 58). For some VO pairs we find clear preferences for one option over the other, i.e., either the metaphorical or the literal VO of a pair is clearly more frequent. For instance, the metaphorical VOs *tackle crisis/challenge* are nine times more frequent than their literal paraphrases *address crisis/challenge*. One might think that this phenomenon has to do with the verb only, e.g., *tackle* is always favored over *address*. This is however not the case as *address* is favored over *tackle* when combined with other objects (e.g., *problem, concern*). For computational tasks such as text generation or machine translation, this finding gives support to the necessity to consider a verb along with its object: when considering paraphrases, one cannot rely on the frequency of the verb only, as more nuance might be brought by whichever argument is used along with that verb.

This finding should be taken with a grain of salt because we are lacking data points to generalize across VO pairs. For instance, the verb pair *grasp/understand* only occurs with the object *point* in our data, and while the metaphorical usage *grasp* is favored over its literal counterpart, we do not know whether we would observe similar behaviors with other objects (e.g., *meaning, concern*, etc.) of that verb pair.

VOs Syntactic Variation Looking at syntactic variations can shed light on (i) whether there are some clearly lexicalized VOs, but also (ii) whether there exist discrepancies between the paraphrase VO pairs, where one variant is more lexicalized than its paraphrase. Unlike idioms, metaphors are considered (syntactically) more flexible expressions that retain their metaphorical meaning if they undergo syntactic variations (Fazly et al., 2009; Kövecses, 2010). For example, *It's raining cats and dogs* cannot be replaced by *It's raining a cat and a dog* without losing its idiomatic interpretation. We however expect to observe a metaphorical VO such as *tackle question* in different morpho-syntactic forms, as in *tackling the questions* or *the question was tackled*, where the (metaphorical) meaning remains intact.

We have observed that both metaphorical and literal VOs that appear more than once in the data present up to eight different syntactic variations (three on average). None of the VOs therefore presents clear signs of syntactic fixedness, but there also exists no clear discrepancy in syntactic flexibility between metaphorical and literal VOs. In other words, this finding suggests that amongst our paraphrased pairs, there is complete consistency in terms of (non-)lexicalization.

Variability in Translation As we discussed in the two previous paragraphs, we observe quite some diversity in the use of metaphorical vs. literal VO pairs in the source language, both in terms of frequency and syntactic variations. Indeed, we saw that some VOs present a preference for either the metaphorical or literal variant (see Figure 2), and that VOs display many inflections. Is this diversity encountered in the SL also observed in the French and German translations, respectively? We observe many syntactic variations in translation for both *en2fr* and *en2de*, indicating that the syntactic structure of the source VO is therefore not necessarily respected in the translation process. For example, the verb-object construction *break agreement* is translated as a noun-preposition-noun construction into French (*rupture de accord*, lit. *breaking of agreement*). Regarding variability, we have seen that each source VO, regardless of its metaphoricity, is on average aligned to four translations, in both language pairs. Only very few VOs occurring more than once in the parallel corpus correspond to a one-to-one translation. Not only does this confirm that there are many ways to transfer one concept from one language to another, but also that humans tend to be very creative in the way they produce language. In other words, we generally find (large) variability in translation per SL concept (see Section 4.2).

We also notice slightly less variability in translation per literal VO than per metaphorical VO, i.e., one-to-many translations are more frequent for metaphorical VOs than for literal VOs. For example, the metaphorical concept of *boost* in *boost economy* does not have a *sensu stricto* metaphorical translation in French; we observed seven different translations for the 15 instances of the source metaphorical VO. However, we found only one (sensu stricto) French translation of the literal paraphrase *improve economy*. It therefore seems that if a metaphor in the SL does not have an equivalent in the TL, translators seem to show more creativity in their translation process. This perspective is especially interesting to keep in mind for natural language processing downstream tasks such as MT. Unlike the translation of idioms, which is either right or wrong (Volk, 1998; Huet and Langlais, 2013; Salton et al., 2014), efforts should be focused on building MT systems which are able to be more nuanced with respect to the use of metaphors.

Lost in Translation To which extent is metaphoricity/literalness transferred from source to target in the translation process, and does the language pair matter? We observe a clear divergence in behavior between the two TLs, according to expert judgements. In French, metaphorical vs. literal uses in the SL tend to be preserved in translation, i.e., source metaphorical VOs tend to be translated into figurative phrases, and source literal VOs tend to be translated into literal phrases. This is however not the case for translations into German: overall, they have been judged more literal, even if the source text contained a metaphorical VO. Further investigation is needed in order to find the reasons behind this behavior.

Indeed, judging metaphoricity is a difficult task (Zayed et al., 2019; Zhou et al., 2021; Piccirilli and Schulte im Walde, 2021, 2022) for which many aspects need to be taken into account and where the community has yet to find an optimal way to collect human judgements, e.g., number of annotators, binary vs. scale decision, but also the level of conventionality of metaphorical vs. literal phrases.

6 Conclusion

We presented VOLIMET, the first parallel corpus of English–German and English–French paraphrased metaphorical and literal verb-object pairs. Besides offering a novel lexicon of 297 metaphorical vs. literal VO paraphrase pairs, VOLIMET also provides their cross-lingual contexts at the sentence level.

We conducted substantial human work to provide gold standard alignments of source VOs to all their corresponding translations. We performed quantitative and qualitative analyses from both a monolingual and cross-lingual perspective. Monolingually, we showed that for some VO pairs, there exists a clear preference for either the metaphorical or the literal variant. It is however crucial to consider the verb and its object as a unit, as we observed apparent differences in behaviors when the verb is considered with or without its object. Cross-lingually, our findings revealed substantial variability in translations, i.e., one-to-many mappings between source VOs and their target translations. Finally, we investigated the extent to which metaphoricity/literalness gets preserved in the translation process. We found different behaviors between our two target languages, where French translations show equal use of metaphorical and literal language, while German tends to favor literal translations by a large margin.

Ethical Considerations

In the context of our annotation tasks, we collected judgements from human participants. For this, the participants were provided an Informed Consent Letter with the name and the contact of the investigators; the title, purpose and procedure of the study; risks and benefits for participating in the study; confirmation of confidential anonymous data handling; and confirmation that participation in the study is paid (12€/hour). The Informed Consent Letter was signed before the participants took part in the study.

Limitations

The creation of the VOLIMET parallel corpus and the research conducted represent significant advancements in understanding monolingual and cross-lingual metaphorical and literal language use and subsequently handling metaphors in machine translation. However, some limitations should be acknowledged. First, the corpus focuses on English–German and English–French translations and therefore does not fully capture the diversity of languages and translation challenges in other language combinations. Additionally, even though we provided clear instructions and examples of metaphorical vs. literal language, the human judgments collected for figurativeness and literalness in translations remain potentially subjective and may not represent the full spectrum of possible interpretations. Finally, the corpus' size and coverage as well as the number of verb-object pairs we used, might not encompass all possible metaphorical constructs and translation variations, requiring further expansion and exploration. These limitations highlight the need for ongoing research and the development of more comprehensive resources to enhance metaphor-aware machine translation systems.

Acknowledgements

This research was supported by the DFG Research Grants SCHU 2580/4-1 (*MUDCAT: Multimodal Dimensions and Computational Applications of Abstractness*) and SCHU 2580/7-1 and FR 2829/8-1 (*MeTRapher: Learning to Translate Metaphors*). Prisca Piccirilli is also supported by the Studienstiftung des deutschen Volkes.

References

Yuri Bizzoni and Shalom Lappin. 2018. Predicting Human Metaphor Paraphrase Judgments with Deep Neural Networks. In *Proceedings of the Workshop on Figurative Language Processing*, pages 45–55, New Orleans, Louisiana. Association for Computational Linguistics.

Marine Carpuat and Mona Diab. 2010. Task-based Evaluation of Multiword Expressions: a Pilot Study in Statistical Machine Translation. In *Proceedings of the Annual Conference of the North American Chapter of the Association for Computational Linguistics*, pages 242–245, Los Angeles, California. Association for Computational Linguistics.

Francesca M.M. Citron and Adele E. Goldberg. 2014. Metaphorical Sentences Are More Emotionally Engaging Than Their Literal Counterparts. *Journal of cognitive neuroscience*, 26(11):2585–2595.

Verna Dankers, Karan Malhotra, Gaurav Kudva, Volodymyr Medentsiy, and Ekaterina Shutova. 2020. Being Neighbourly: Neural Metaphor Identification in Discourse. In *Proceedings of the Second Workshop on Figurative Language Processing*, pages 227–234, Online. Association for Computational Linguistics.

Chris Dyer, Victor Chahuneau, and Noah A. Smith. 2013. A Simple, Fast, and Effective Reparameterization of IBM Model 2. In *Proceedings of the 2013 Conference of the North American Chapter of the Association for Computational Linguistics: Human Language Technologies*, pages 644–648, Atlanta, Georgia. Association for Computational Linguistics.

Marzieh Fadaee and Christof Monz. 2018. Examining the Tip of the Iceberg: A Data Set for Idiom Translation. In *Proceedings of the 11th International Conference on Language Resources and Evaluation*, Miyazaki, Japan.

Afsaneh Fazly, Paul Cook, and Suzanne Stevenson. 2009. Unsupervised Type and Token Identification of Idiomatic Expressions. *Computational Linguistics*, 35(1):61–103.

Pablo Gamallo, Susana Sotelo, José Ramom Pichel, and Mikel Artetxe. 2019. Contextualized Translations of Phrasal Verbs with Distributional Compositional Semantics and Monolingual Corpora. *Computational Linguistics*, 45(3):395–421.

Stéphane Huet and Philippe Langlais. 2013. Translation of Idiomatic Expressions Across Different Languages: A Study of the Effectiveness of TransSearch. In A. Neustein and J. A. Markowitz, editors, *Where Humans Meet Machines: Innovative Solutions to Knotty Natural Language Problems*, pages 185–209. New York: Springer.

Philipp Koehn. 2005. Europarl: A Parallel Corpus for Statistical Machine Translation. In *Proceedings of the 10th Machine Translation Summit*, pages 79–86, Phuket, Thailand.

Zoltan Kövecses. 2010. *Metaphor: A Practical Introduction*, 2nd edition. Oxford University Press, New York.

George Lakoff and Mark Johnson. 1980. *Metaphors We Live By*. University of Chicago Press, Chicago.

Rui Mao, Chenghua Lin, and Frank Guerin. 2018. Word Embedding and WordNet Based Metaphor Identification and Interpretation. In *Proceedings of the 56th Annual Meeting of the Association for Computational Linguistics*, pages 1222–1231, Melbourne, Australia. Association for Computational Linguistics.

James H. Martin. 2008. A Corpus-based Analysis of Context Effects on Metaphor Comprehension. In A. Stefanowitsch and S. Th. Gries, editors, *Corpus-Based Approaches to Metaphor and Metonymy*, pages 214–236. De Gruyter Mouton.

Saif Mohammad, Ekaterina Shutova, and Peter Turney. 2016. Metaphor as a Medium for Emotion: An Empirical Study. In *Proceedings of the Fifth Joint Conference on Lexical and Computational Semantics*, pages 23–33, Berlin, Germany. Association for Computational Linguistics.

Jesse Mu, Helen Yannakoudakis, and Ekaterina Shutova. 2019. Learning Outside the Box: Discourse-level Features Improve Metaphor Identification. In *Proceedings of the 2019 Conference of the North American Chapter of the Association for Computational Linguistics: Human Language Technologies*, pages 596–601, Minneapolis, Minnesota. Association for Computational Linguistics.

Prisca Piccirilli and Sabine Schulte im Walde. 2021. Synonymous Pairs of Metaphorical and Literal Expressions in Context: An Empirical Study and Dataset *to tackle* or *to address the question*. In *Proceedings of the Workshop DiscAnn*, Tübingen, Germany.

Prisca Piccirilli and Sabine Schulte im Walde. 2022. Features of Perceived Metaphoricity on the Discourse Level: Abstractness and Emotionality. In *Proceedings of the 13th Conference on Language Resources and Evaluation*, pages 5261–5273, Marseille, France. European Language Resources Association.

Ella Rabinovich, Shuly Wintner, and Ofek Luis Lewinsohn. 2018. A Parallel Corpus of Translationese. In *Proceedings of the 17th International Conference on Computational Linguistics and Intelligent Text Processing*, pages 140–155, Konya, Turkey. Springer International Publishing.

Giancarlo Salton, Robert Ross, and John Kelleher. 2014. Evaluation of a Substitution Method for Idiom Transformation in Statistical Machine Translation. In *Proceedings of the 10th Workshop on Multiword Expressions*, pages 38–42, Gothenburg, Sweden. Association for Computational Linguistics.

Roland Schäfer. 2015. Processing and Querying Large Web Corpora with the COW14 Architecture. Proceedings of the 3rd Workshop on Challenges in the Management of Large Corpora, pages 28–34, Mannheim, Germany. Institut für Deutsche Sprache.

Roland Schäfer and Felix Bildhauer. 2012. Building Large Corpora from the Web Using a New Efficient Tool Chain. In *Proceedings of the 8th International Conference on Language Resources and Evaluation*, pages 486–493, Istanbul, Turkey. European Language Resources Association.

Christina Schäffner. 2004. Metaphor and Translation: Some Implications of a Cognitive Approach. *Journal of Pragmatics*, 36(7):1253–1269.

Ekaterina Shutova. 2010. Automatic Metaphor Interpretation as a Paraphrasing Task. In *Proceedings of the Annual Conference of the North American Chapter of the Association for Computational Linguistics: Human Language Technologies:*, pages 1029–1037, Los Angeles, California. Association for Computational Linguistics.

Ekaterina Shutova and Simone Teufel. 2010. Metaphor Corpus Annotated for Source - Target Domain Mappings. In *Proceedings of the 7th International Conference on Language Resources and Evaluation*, Valletta, Malta. European Language Resources Association.

Anatol Stefanowitsch. 2008. *Words and Their Metaphors: A Corpus-Based Approach*, pages 63–105. De Gruyter Mouton.

Kevin Stowe, Prasetya Utama, and Iryna Gurevych. 2022. IMPLI: Investigating NLI Models' Performance on Figurative Language. In *Proceedings of the 60th Annual Meeting of the Association for Computational Linguistics*, pages 5375–5388, Dublin, Ireland. Association for Computational Linguistics.

Paul H. Thibodeau and Lera Boroditsky. 2011. Metaphors We Think With: The Role of Metaphor in Reasoning. *PLOS one*, 6(2).

Xiaoyu Tong, Ekaterina Shutova, and Martha Lewis. 2021. Recent Advances in Neural Metaphor Processing: A Linguistic, Cognitive and Social Perspective. In *Proceedings of the Conference of the North American Chapter of the Association for Computational Linguistics: Human Language Technologies*, pages 4673–4686, Online. Association for Computational Linguistics.

Raymond van den Broek. 1981. The Limits of Translatability Exemplified by Metaphor Translation. *Poetics Today*, 1(4):73–87.

Martin Volk. 1998. The Automatic Translation of Idioms. Machine Translation vs. Translation Memory Systems. Technical report, University of Zürich.

Yorick Wilks. 1978. Making Preferences More Active. *Artificial Intelligence*, 11(3):197–223.

Omnia Zayed, John P. McCrae, and Paul Buitelaar. 2019. Crowd-Sourcing A High-Quality Dataset for Metaphor Identification in Tweets. In *Proceedings of the 2nd Conference on Language, Data, and Knowledge*, pages 1–17, Leipzig, Germany.

Jianing Zhou, Hongyu Gong, and Suma Bhat. 2021. PIE: A Parallel Idiomatic Expression Corpus for Idiomatic Sentence Generation and Paraphrasing. In *Proceedings of the 17th Workshop on Multiword Expressions*, pages 33–48, Online. Association for Computational Linguistics.

A Verb-Object Pairs

See Table 6.

B VOs: One-only Translations

See Table 7.

Original met/lit VO-pairs	Extended sets of objects
absorb/assimilate knowledge	information, idea, culture, material, lesson, fact, content, experience, concept, thought
absorb/pay costs	fee, bill, tax, debt, interest, expense
abuse/misuse alcohol	drug, substance, medication, product
attack/address problem	issue, need, question, challenge, point, situation, topic, change, cause, matter
boost/improve economy	service, system, situation, process, education, work, business, result, number
break/end agreement	cycle, relationship, contract, marriage, process, pattern
breathe/instill life	sense, confidence, value, spirit, love, hope, idea, passion
buy/believe story	word, lie
cast/cause doubt	issue, fear
catch/get disease	idea, chance, information, result, message, point, call, problem, opportunity
close/end investigation	season, deal, case, debate, operation, story
close/finaliz(s)e deal	case, plan, arrangement, agreement, project
cloud/impair memory	ability, judgement, judgment, mind, vision, thinking, perception, understanding
colo(u)r/affect judgement	decision, choice, perception, experience, interpretation
deflate/reduce economy	cost, price, value, supply, wage, market, currency
devour/read book	article, story, page, novel, information, chapter, news
digest/comprehend information	meaning, material, fact, text, concept, idea, word, content, situation, message
disown/reject past	idea, policy, responsibility
drop/reduce price	cost, rate, temperature
drown/forget trouble	pain, problem, feeling
dull/decrease appetite	pain, sense, noise, feeling
find/make excuse	way, connection
float/suggest idea	theory, concept
flood/saturate market	X
follow/practis(c)e profession	religion, activity
frame/pose question	problem, challenge, issue, debate, concern, argument, idea, hypothesis
fuel/stimulate debate	growth, economy, interest, discussion, demand, activity, imagination, creativity, conversation
grasp/understand meaning	concept, issue, point, problem, situation, reason, language, idea, risk, question
juggle/manage job	project, work, life, career, school
kill/cancel proposal	project, bill, program, process, agreement, deal
leak/disclose report	information, document, story
mount/organiz(s)e production	event, campaign, conference, exhibition, demonstration, protest
poison/corrupt mind	system, process, soul, relationship
pour/invest money	fortune
push/sell drug	X
recapture/recall feeling	memory, moment, experience
shake/damage confidence	foundation
shape/determine result	life, outcome, success, strategy
shipwreck/ruin career	X
sow/cause doubt	death, confusion, chaos, conflict, panic, fear, violence, uncertainty, terror, hatred
stir/cause excitement	confusion, reaction, feeling, emotion
suck/attract worker	talent
tackle/address question	issue, problem, concern, challenge, situation, point, crisis, matter, inequality, task
taste/experience freedom	pain, life, joy
throw/make remark	comment
twist/misinterpret word	fact, meaning, comment, situation, information, message
wear/have smile	X

Table 6: Original metaphorical/literal VO-pairs and their sets of extended arguments. X means that no further objects were found according to our criteria (see Section 3.1 for a description of our extended pairs' selection).

	English	→ German	English	→ French
Met.			find excuse	trouver excuse
			flood market	inonder marché
			shake confidence	ébranler confiance
Lit.	organise production	Produktion organisieren	address challenge	relever défi
	read book	Buch lesen	end agreement	mettre terme à accord
			organise conference	organiser conférence
			organise production	organiser production
			pose problem	poser problème
			suggest idea	suggérer idée
			understand problem	comprendre problème
			understand reason	comprendre raison

Table 7: English metaphorical and literal VOs for which only one German/French translation was suggested.

C Annotation Study: Guidelines

The purpose of this human annotation study was to evaluate the figurativeness of German and French translations of metaphorical and literal English phrases. We wanted to quantify the diversity we encounter in translation, for answering the question: are metaphorical vs. literal VOs translated as metaphors vs. literal phrases, respectively?
Using Google Forms, we compiled the 351 unique French and 575 German translated phrases, and asked three native French and German speakers and expert linguists, respectively, to judge whether the phrases were *figurative* or *literal*. For each phrase, we also provided one sentence containing that phrase, in case more context was needed for the binary decision. We estimated the task to take 3–5 hours, and we paid the annotators the (German) legal minimum wage of 12€/hour.

Description of the research study In this project, we are interested in annotating whether French phrases are figurative or literal.

Purpose of the research study The gold standard annotations will be used as training data for modeling the detection of figurative language.

What is figurative language? As opposed to **literal** language, whose interpretation does not deviate from the word's defined and most frequent senses, the meaning of a **figurative** phrase is not simply composed of the common meanings of its components: its surface form and its underlying semantics do not directly correspond to each other. This is for example very clear when a phrase is an **idiom**: *"It's raining cats and dogs"*. This can be a bit more subtle when dealing with other forms of figurative language, such as **metaphors**, when one concept is viewed in terms of the properties of another: *"Let's kill the process"*, where the computational process is viewed as a living being. A **figurative** word/phrase can be recognized if it represents a violation of **selectional preference** in a given context: e.g., the verb "drink" normally requires a grammatical subject of type ANIMATE and a grammatical object of type LIQUID, as in (1-a). As a result, "drink" taking a "car" as a subject in (1-b) is an anomaly, indicative a figurative use of the verb.

(1) a. "She *drinks* tea"
b. "My car *drinks* gasoline" (Wilks, 1978)

Your task You will evaluate whether phrases in French/German are figurative or literal.

- You will be given a list of French phrases. For each phrase, you will judge whether it is figurative or literal. Note that there is no ambiguity, i.e., each phrase has only one interpretation (figurative or literal).
- The phrases might not be as clear-cut as in the example (1). Do your best to make a judgement, based on the intuition you get from the explanation given above. There is no "right" or "wrong" answer!
- You can make use of whatever external resource you think might be helpful, e.g., dictionaries, etc.
- The phrase context (minimum two words) should be enough to emit a judgement. However, for each phrase, we provide one sentence containing the phrase, in case it helps you make a final decision.
- Do not leave any blank: always provide a judgement, i.e., Figurative or Literal
- We provide an example in Figure 3 (Note that this is a random annotation).

Phrases	Figurative or Literal?	Sentences
contracter maladie	Figurative	Si l' un des animaux contracte la maladie , pourquoi faut -il abattre tout le troupeau ?
poursuivre remarque	Figurative	Pouvez -vous répondre à ma question avant que je ne poursuive mes remarques ?
remédier à situation	Literal	Espérons que ce rapport , ainsi que la directive sur l' emploi , permettront de remédier à cette situation .

Figure 3: Example of the annotation task set up for judging figurativeness of VO translations.

Improving Word Sense Induction through Adversarial Forgetting of Morphosyntactic Information

Deniz Ekin Yavas[*,1], **Timothée Bernard**[2], **Laura Kallmeyer**[1], **Benoît Crabbé**[2]
Heinrich Heine University Düsseldorf[1], Université Paris Cité[2]
{deniz.yavas, laura.kallmeyer}@hhu.de[1]
{timothee.bernard, benoit.crabbe}@u-paris.fr[2]

Abstract

This paper addresses the problem of word sense induction (WSI) via clustering of word embeddings. It starts from the hypothesis that contextualized word representations obtained from pre-trained language models (LMs), while being a valuable source for WSI, encode more information than what is necessary for the identification of word senses and some of this information affect the performance negatively in unsupervised settings. We investigate whether using contextualized representations that are invariant to these 'nuisance features' can increase WSI performance. For this purpose, we propose an adaptation of the adversarial training framework proposed by Jaiswal et al. (2020) to erase specific information from the representations of LMs, thereby creating *feature-invariant representations*. We experiment with erasing (i) morphological and (ii) syntactic features. The results of subsequent clustering for WSI show that these features indeed act like noise: Using feature-invariant representations, compared to using the original representations, increases clustering-based WSI performance. Furthermore, we provide an in-depth analysis of how the information about the syntactic and morphological features of words relate to and affect WSI performance.

1 Introduction

Words in their different senses occur in different contexts. Contextualized word representations obtained from transformer based pre-trained language models (LMs) such as BERT (Devlin et al., 2019) are especially suitable for Word Sense Disambiguation (WSD) because they capture the sentential context of a word and thereby oftentimes allow to distinguish different senses of a word. They have indeed been successfully used for WSD in recent work (Hadiwinoto et al., 2019; Loureiro et al., 2021; Vandenbussche et al., 2021).

However, in both unsupervised WSD, where the goal is to identify the instances of a specific sense, and word sense induction (WSI), which allows the discovery of novel senses, using the LM representations alone does not yield satisfactory results (Pilehvar and Camacho-Collados, 2019; Samih and Kallmeyer, 2023). In both, similarity of the representations plays a crucial role, and this similarity is determined by many features. Indeed, the contextualized representation of a word usually encodes a wide range of linguistic information about the word in its context, such as its syntactic function, its morphological properties, its position, its casing, and the identity of its neighbouring words (Sajjad et al., 2022). However, most of the encoded information that determines the similarity of the representations is not relevant to word senses (Yavas, 2024). Note that this is not a problem for supervised WSD, as a supervised model can learn to ignore those features that are not discriminative for word senses.

Building on these insights, we focus on WSI and aim at investigating the relationship between specific types of information encoded in contextualized representations of LMs and WSI performance. Concretely, we examine whether erasing certain information from the representations of LMs can lead to an increase in performance for a simple clustering-based WSI system. Our investigation examines two types of information that have been observed to affect the word sense clustering performance negatively. Yavas (2024) have shown that in word sense clustering with BERT representations on SemCor (Miller et al., 1993), word instances are frequently clustered together based on the similarities between their morphological and syntactic features (more specifically, *syntactic role* of the word) rather than their semantic similarities. For example, past tense instances of a specific verb, or all instances of a specific noun occurring as direct objects, are clustered together.

We adapt the adversarial training framework of

*This work was conducted during the author's visit to Université Paris Cité.

*Proceedings of the 13th Joint Conference on Lexical and Computational Semantics (*SEM 2024)*, pages 238 - 251
June 20-21, 2024 ©2024 Association for Computational Linguistics

Jaiswal et al. (2020) in order to train a forget-gate that erases information from the representations of LMs, resulting in *feature-invariant representations*. We experiment with the BERT model and create feature-invariant representations for both of the above-mentioned types of features (morphological and syntactic). Finally, we evaluate the performance of WSI on SemCor with different feature-invariant representations, comparing them to the original word representations obtained from BERT. Furthermore, we conduct an in-depth analysis of how the information about the syntactic and morphological features of words relate to and affect WSI performance.[1]

Our results show that words' morphological and syntactic features indeed act like noise that negatively affects clustering performance and syntax- and morphology-invariant representations are better suited to WSI than the original BERT representations. Furthermore, a more detailed analysis of the relation between these information types and WSI performance shows that even though syntactic features are more correlated to word senses than morphological features are, they still affect the WSI performance negatively overall.

This paper makes several contributions. First, we propose an adaptation of the framework proposed by Jaiswal et al. (2020) to erase unwanted information from the representations of LMs. Secondly, we use this method to generate syntax- and morphology-invariant representations from the word representations of the BERT model and achieve better performance in clustering-based WSI. Lastly, we provide an in-depth analysis of how the morphological and syntactic features of words affect WSI performance.

The paper is structured as follows: We review related work in Section 2, then we introduce our framework for creating feature-invariant representations in Section 3 and report the results of the creation process. Finally in Section 4, we report the experiments on WSI with an analysis of the relation between the information types and WSI performance.

[1]We also experimented with positional information. In our experiments, we successfully removed the positional information from the representations, however, these representations exhibited unexpected behaviour in clustering experiments. As a result, we decided to exclude this feature type. We intend to investigate the underlying reasons in the future.

2 Related Work

Word Sense and Information Encoded in Contextualized Representations. Contextualized representations of pre-trained LMs encode more contextual information than what is necessary for the identification of word senses and this information can affect the similarity of the representations in an unwanted way. Sajjad et al. (2022) have shown that semantic, morphological, and syntactic concepts are encoded in contextualized representations. These concepts include words' POS tags, CCG super-tags, ngrams, casings, WordNet concepts, and so on. Furthermore, clustering of contextualized word representations reveal these similarities between the words.

In their detailed qualitative analysis, Yavas (2024) have shown that word sense clustering with BERT's representations on SemCor is heavily and negatively affected by information encoded in the representations from the sentence context that is insignificant to WSD, such as some morphological features of the words, their syntactic role, the presence of some punctuation marks and function words in the sentence (e.g. 'not', 'then', etc.). In the present study, we aim to investigate whether the effects of some of these features can be controlled and whether doing so can increase performance in WSI on the same dataset.

Similar effects have been found in lexical semantic change detection. Laicher et al. (2021) have observed that BERT representations are influenced by the orthographic form of words. Consequently, this affects how the representations are clustered. They have shown that removal of this bias increases the clustering performance. In order to do so, they preprocess the input data by lemmatizing the target word in each sentence before feeding it to the model.

Adversarial Training for Invariant Representation Learning. Invariant representation learning aims to create representations that do not encode certain unwanted features of data, such as nuisances, biases, or domain-specific features. Nuisances are features in the data that have no or little relevance to the task but influence model performance, like facial expressions in face recognition (Bronstein et al., 2003) or orientation in image recognition (Khotanzad and Hong, 1990). The creation of representations invariant to nuisances aims to increase model performance and robustness.

In this study, we consider morphological and

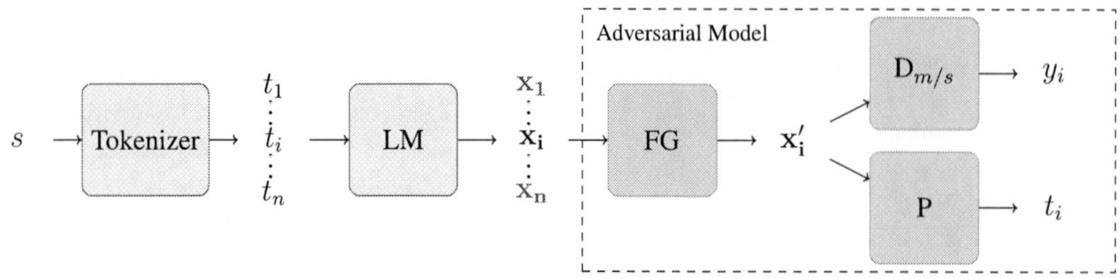

Figure 1: Framework for training a forget-gate (FG) to create feature-invariant representations from the representations of a pre-trained model. The FG is trained as a part of an adversarial model. The *LM* is only used as a feature extractor and its parameters are frozen.

syntactic features of words as nuisance features for WSI because they are not directly related to different senses of words but affect performance. We acknowledge that the syntactic features of words are, to some extent, relevant to WSI, but while these features may aid in identifying the senses of some words, we hypothesize that it introduces noise overall.

Invariant representation learning is widely used to create representations that are invariant to nuisance features in Computer Vision (Louizos et al., 2017; Xie et al., 2017; Jaiswal et al., 2018, 2020). However, in NLP, most applications of this technique center around learning domain-invariant representations (Louizos et al., 2017; Jaiswal et al., 2018; Peng and Zhang, 2020; Xin et al., 2022) . As for our knowledge, there has been no attempt to create contextualized representations invariant to any linguistic information.

Jaiswal et al. (2020) propose a framework for learning invariant representations through adversarial training in a Computer Vision context. They train an encoder (and a decoder) to generate representations for a set of inputs. At the same time, a *forget-gate* is trained to generate masks meant to be applied to the representations in order to create invariant representations. The forget-gate is trained as part of an adversarial model, in which a *discriminator* predicts the unwanted information from the masked representation while a *predictor* predicts some task-related information. Our framework for learning invariant representations is inspired by Jaiswal et al. (2020) while showing clear differences. We do not train an encoder-decoder model but, instead, we utilize LMs and create invariant representations from their representations. Furthermore, forgetting is not done by masking but by transforming the LM representations through a feed-forward network.

3 Creating Feature-Invariant Representations via Adversarial Training

In order to obtain contextualized representations that are invariant to certain features, we propose to add a forget-gate on top of a pre-trained LM. The forget-gate applies a nonlinear transformation and thereby selectively removes the unwanted information from the original contextualized representations. It is trained as a part of an adversarial model inspired by Jaiswal et al. (2020). Concretely, we train two forget-gates to create feature-invariant representations for syntactic and morphological features. We will refer to the respective resulting representations as *syntax-invariant*, and *morphology-invariant representations*.

3.1 Framework

Our framework is illustrated in Figure 1. We define a neural network named *forget-gate* (FG). This network is implemented as a feedforward neural network with two hidden layers with ReLU activation function. It applies a transformation to the representations obtained from a pre-trained LM to create representations that are invariant to specific information. The input of FG ($\mathbf{x}$) is the representation we aim to transform, namely the token embedding from the pre-trained LM. The output of FG ($\mathbf{x}'$) is the feature-invariant representation.

Given a sentence s, we first tokenize it with the LM tokenizer and then pass the tokenized sentence $(t_1, ..., t_i, ..., t_n)$ to the LM in order to extract the token embeddings $(\mathbf{x_1}, ..., \mathbf{x_i}, ..., \mathbf{x_n})$, obtained from the last layer of the LM (i.e., the LM acts as a feature extractor). Each of these embeddings constitutes one input data point to the FG. We use the BERT (*base-cased*) model.[2]

[2]The embeddings are extracted using the Transformers library (Wolf et al., 2020).

The forget-gate FG is trained as part of an adversarial model with two auxiliary modules; a discriminator (D) and a predictor (P). During training, the representation produced by the forget-gate ($\mathbf{x}'_\mathrm{i} = FG(\mathbf{x}_\mathrm{i})$ for token t_i) is given to P and D. D is tasked with probing for unwanted information (some label y_i for token t_i) in the embedding $\mathbf{x}'_\mathrm{i}$, and P is tasked with recovering the identity of the token (t_i) from $\mathbf{x}'_\mathrm{i}$. The adversarial model is trained on the representations of both masked and unmasked tokens (i.e., we sometimes substitute the [MASK] token for t_i in the input of the LM).

The training of the adversarial model alternates between three types of batch, each batch containing training data for only one of the three subnetworks of the adversarial model. On the first type of batch, the parameters of D, on the second type of batch, the parameters of P, and on the third type of batch, the parameters of FG are updated. There are two batches of the first type (for D) for one batch of the second and one batch of the third type. So, D is trained more than the rest of the network. The parameters of FG are updated based on the combined loss L_{FG} of D and P as indicated in (1). The loss of D is given as negative since we want to increase it.[3]

$$\begin{aligned} L_{FG}(x, y, t) &= -L_D(D(x'), y) \\ &\quad + L_P(P(x'), t) \end{aligned} \tag{1}$$

For each feature type (morphological and syntactic), we train an adversarial model with a unique discriminator to obtain a feature-specific forget-gate.[4] The discriminators, D_m and D_s, are trained as classification models and towards labelling tokens with POS tags (from the Penn Treebank tagset, Marcus et al., 1993 — these tags are fine-grained and provide morphological information such as number for nouns and tense for verbs) and (incoming) dependency labels respectively; the training labels are predicted, see Section 3.3. For each feature type, the corresponding discriminator aims to probe for this specific feature, while the forget-gate simultaneously aims to erase it. The details about the architecture of the different modules of the adversarial model and their loss functions can be found in Appendix A.

We train the adversarial models for 800 epochs creating checkpoints every 100th epoch and select the best checkpoint a posteriori based on the evaluation results (see next section). The details about the hyperparameters and the training of the adversarial model can be found in Appendix B. As a result of training the two adversarial models, we obtain two different forget gates, FG_m and FG_s. These forget gates, when applied to a BERT word embedding, yield the respective feature-invariant representations.

3.2 Evaluation

In order to evaluate this method, we create representations using the trained forget-gates for each type of information and use these representations to train two models from scratch: one for word (i.e., token) prediction and the other for unwanted information probing. The performance of these models on the test data tells us whether the feature-invariant representation creation was successful.

We compare the performances of these models to a lower and an upper bounds. The upper bound for a task is defined as the performance of a similar system trained using the original BERT representations. The lower bound is defined differently for the two types of information. For syntactic information, the probing model is trained using the non-contextualized word representations used by BERT as input to its first layer. For morphological information, the lower bound is given by the most frequent POS baseline. It is calculated for each grammatical category (i.e. noun, verb, and so on.) by predicting the most frequent POS tag for that category and averaged for all categories.

The probing models for morphological and syntactic features are similar to the respective discriminators in the adversarial models: They share the same architecture, training and test data. The word predictors are also similar to the respective predictors in the adversarial models, in regard to their architecture, training and test data.

We compare the performances of different models on the test data. We use perplexity as the metric to evaluate the word predictors and accuracy for the probing models. We select the best forget-gate for each feature type aiming at a low probing performance (close to the lower bound): We evaluate all checkpoints and pick the forget-gate with the lowest probing scores (if not lower than the lower

[3] In Jaiswal et al. (2020)'s framework, forgetting is not done by using the opposite of D's loss on the correct labels, but by using D's loss on random labels.

[4] We target morphological and syntactic information independently, even though theoretically, they are interrelated. However, this does not affect the relevance of our method, but only some linguistic interpretations of the results.

bound). Details about the hyperparameters and the training of the lower bound and upper models, evaluation models (probing and word prediction), and the selected forget-gates are given in Appendix B.[5]

3.3 Data

For the training and evaluation of the models, we use the Brown corpus (Kučera et al., 1967). We extract the token representations by BERT of each sentence. These token representations are then used as the input for the forget-gate. Since words are tokenized into WordPiece subwords by the BERT tokenizer, we work with these subwords rather than entire words.

In cases a word is split in multiple parts, we only take the first subword into account, i.e. we only erase information from the first subword a word and we only use this subword for WSI. We expect the first subwords to encode more relevant information for WSI because they are more likely to align with the stems of the words as opposed to suffixes (e.g. 'booklets' is tokenized into 'booklet' and 's' by the model tokenizer).

We assign two labels to each token; one for the discriminator (or probe) and another for the predictor. The predictor's label corresponds to the token ID assigned by the BERT's tokenizer to the token. The discriminator's label varies depending on the feature type: the label is either the label of the incoming syntactic dependency or the POS tag (of the word associated with the token). We get these labels automatically using spaCy.[6]

The dataset for morphological information only contains tokens of words belonging to grammatical categories that exhibit inflection in English: nouns, verbs, adjectives, adverbs, and pronouns. No such restrictions apply to syntactic information. This process yields datasets containing 2,341,954 tokens for syntactic information, and 1,315,988 tokens for morphological information. All datasets are split to train, development, and test data with the ratio 80:10:10.

3.4 Results

Both feature-invariant representations achieve good results in word prediction and probing tasks; the unwanted information is erased from the representations while their word prediction capabilities are intact. The lower bounds and upper bounds for all tasks and the evaluation results for feature-invariant representations can be seen in Table 1.

	Word Prediction	Probing
Syntactic Information		
Upper Bound	3.0	85.0
Lower Bound	-	70.2
Invariant Rep.	4.1	72.1
Morphological Information		
Upper Bound	3.0	89.1
Lower Bound	-	62.1
Invariant Rep.	7.1	75.9

Table 1: Evaluation results for the feature-invariant representations with comparison to the upper and lower bounds of the tasks. *Accuracy* is given for probing (in this context, lower is better) and *perplexity* is given for word prediction results (lower is better).

Erasing morphological information impacts the performance of word prediction more. This is expected because the morphological features of words (for instance grammatical number for nouns) are strongly correlated with their word forms.

4 Word Sense Induction Performance

Our aim is to investigate whether using feature-invariant contextualized representations can improve WSI performance. For this purpose, we compare the performance on WSI of three variants of the same system, respectively using three different representations; 1) the original contextualized representations of the BERT model, 2) syntax-invariant, and 3) morphology-invariant contextualized representations, where the latter two are obtained by applying our trained forget-gates FG_m and FG_s to the BERT representations. Furthermore, we provide a detailed analysis of the relation between the morphological and syntactic features of words and WSI and how the erasure of this information affects the WSI performance.

4.1 Data

We evaluate our WSI systems on SemCor. SemCor is based on a subset of the Brown Corpus and it provides sentences in which a word, the *target word*, is labelled with a WordNet sense (Fellbaum, 1998) as shown in (1). We focus on nouns and verbs and exclude other grammatical categories. We further exclude the words that have only one sense, and the senses that occur in less than 10 sentences.

[5]The code for this project is available at: `https://github.com/yavasde/Adversarial-Forgetting-of-Morphosyntactic-Information`.

[6]`https://spacy.io/`, model: *en_core_web_trf*.

(1) officer:

a. "An officer with a squad of men had been waiting on the bank."
(officer.n.01)

b. "And the policy officer has the hounds of time snapping at his heels."
(officer.n.02)

One of the advantages of using SemCor for WSI is that it is a subset of a bigger corpus (Brown Corpus), that we can use to train the forget-gates. The forget-gates are then trained on the same kind of texts that the ones used for WSI, which helps ensuring the quality of the invariant representations used during clustering. There is no methodological problem in doing so as the gold clusters are not used at any time during the training of the forget-gates. This approach can be applied to any dataset by training a forget-gate and performing WSI on the same data. Note that while the training of the forget-gates requires feature annotation, this does not limit the applicability of our approach as we perform it automatically.

4.2 Method

We cluster instances of words using their representations (BERT, syntax-invariant or morphology-invariant) in the sentences. We tokenize each sentence with the BERT tokenizer and give the tokenized sentence to the model to extract the representations of the target word from the last layer of the BERT model. In cases where the words are tokenized into subwords, we only use the first subword token. We create feature-invariant representations from the original representations of BERT for each information type using the information-specific forget-gate (FG_s or FG_m). We apply normalization to all embeddings before clustering.

We use the K-Means algorithm for clustering.[7] K-Means requires the cluster number as a hyperparameter. To determine the optimal number of clusters for each word, we run the algorithm with different cluster numbers between 2 and 6 and select the one with the highest silhouette score.[8]

We evaluate the clustering performance by comparing cluster assignments and the WordNet senses of word instances and average the result over all words. The evaluation metric used is the *Adjusted Rand Index* (ARI) (Hubert and Arabie, 1985). ARI measures the similarity between two clusterings by counting the pairs that are assigned to the same or different clusters in both the gold clusters and predicted clusters. It is adjusted to account for chance agreement and gives a score between -1 and 1 where 1 indicates perfect agreement between the two clusterings, while scores below 0 suggest that the match is worse than random chance. For the ARI formula and different clustering evaluation metrics see Appendix C.

We compare the WSI performance with 3 different types of representations. We run the clustering algorithm 5 times for each type of representation with different random states. We report the mean of 5 runs. We apply unpaired t-test to determine if the performance difference is statistically significant. We compare the overall performance and the performance based on grammatical category (verbs and nouns).

	Overall	nouns	verbs
BERT	0.210 (8×10^{-4})	0.251 (1×10^{-3})	0.174 (1×10^{-3})
Syn-Inv	**0.221** (1×10^{-3})	**0.263** (4×10^{-4})	**0.185** (2×10^{-3})
Morph-Inv	**0.232** (1×10^{-3})	**0.267** (1×10^{-3})	**0.201** (2×10^{-3})

Table 2: WSI performance with different representation types. The performance is measured using *ARI*. Results are presented for all words in the dataset, as well as for verbs and nouns individually. The mean results over 5 runs are given with standard deviation in brackets. The scores that surpass the BERT representations are in bold.

4.3 Results

Results are shown in Table 2. WSI is performed better with feature-invariant representations than with the original BERT representations for both feature types, with statistically significant differences observed through unpaired t-tests (p-value: 0.0001). The best results are obtained with morphology-invariant representations overall. The largest gain in the performance happens for verbs with morphology-invariant representations. For a more detailed evaluation of the clustering performance using different metrics see Appendix C. Further analysis of the specific cases and reasons behind performance increases and decreases are addressed in the following section.

[7]The algorithms are implemented using the Scikit-learn library (Pedregosa et al., 2011).

[8]The silhouette score measures how similar a sample is to its cluster compared to other clusters. It's calculated for each sample and then averaged for the entire dataset.

	Syntax						Morphology					
	#	T_L	T_U	Sense	BERT	Invariant	#	T_L	T_U	Sense	BERT	Invariant
MI	-	9.4	27.8	14.7	26.4	23.1	-	4.7	40.5	9.4	41.8	25.4
Case 1	59	-	-	-	**0.34**	0.33	11	-	-	-	**0.66**	065
Case 2	34	-	-	-	0.07	**0.10**	80	-	-	-	0.04	**0.09**
Case 3	53	-	-	-	**0.19**	0.18	55	-	-	-	0.28	**0.29**

Table 3: Relation between the feature types and the WSI performance. MI scores for the association between linguistic features and sense or cluster assignments are given. T_L and T_U refers to the lower and upper threshold for MI. For each *Case*, ARI scores for BERT clusters and the clusters formed by the feature-invariant representations are given. Performance increases are in bold.

4.4 Analysis of the Relation Between the Information Types and WSI Performance

Our aim is to determine in which cases the erasure of these information types helps the WSI process. More specifically, we aim to investigate whether, for individual words, word senses are distinguishable by the word's morphological and syntactic features and therefore, whether the existence or the erasure of the related information helps the WSI process. Even though the overall WSI performance improves with feature-invariant representations, it is possible that for some words, the information erased is actually useful for sense identification. In these cases, the information erasure would negatively affect the WSI process.

In order to investigate this, we identify the three following cases and assess the performance with the original BERT representations and feature-invariant representations for each case:

- *Case 1:* The senses of a word are distinguishable by the word's morphological, or syntactic features. In this case, we expect the performance with invariant representations to be lower than with the original BERT representations.
- *Case 2:* The senses of a word are *not* distinguishable by the word's morphological, or syntactic features, but clusters of BERT representations are distinguishable by these features — which then can be assumed to be noise for clustering-based WSI. In this case, we expect the performance with invariant representations to be higher than with the original BERT representations.
- *Case 3:* The senses of a word are *not* distinguishable by the morphological, or syntactic features of the word, and clusters of BERT representations are also *not* distinguishable by these features. In this case, we expect the performance with invariant representations to be the same as with the original BERT representations.

4.4.1 Method

We measure the association between the features of the word instances and their sense or cluster assignments using *Mutual Information* (MI).[9] We use this information to automatically categorize words into the three cases outlined above.

In order to determine the features of the word instances, we use again the POS tags and dependency labels obtained from spaCy. [10] We refer to them as *linguistic labels*. For each word and for each type of feature we compute three MI scores. Firstly, we calculate the MI score between the linguistic labels of the instances and their gold WordNet sense labels (*Sense MI*). Secondly, we calculate the MI score between the linguistic labels of the instances and their cluster labels, considering the clusters formed by the BERT representations *(BERT MI)*. Lastly, we assess the MI score between the linguistic labels of the instances and their cluster labels, considering this time the clusters formed by the feature-invariant representations (*Invariant MI*).

We compare the MI scores to lower (T_L) and upper thresholds (T_U). The lower and upper threshold are calculated for each feature type as the first quartile and third quartile for all MI scores for this feature. We interpret scores below the lower threshold as indicating no association, and scores above

[9]The mutual information between two variables X and Y is defined as follows:

$$MI(X;Y) = \sum_{x \in \mathcal{X}} \sum_{y \in \mathcal{Y}} p(x,y) \log \left(\frac{p(x,y)}{p(x)p(y)} \right) \quad (2)$$

[10]For some instances of words, the target word is not found in the sentence due to a lemmatization error. We discard these words and experiment with 540 words in total (out of 567).

the upper threshold as indicating an association. We then automatically categorise word types. *Case 1* words have high Sense MI scores, *Case 2* words have low Sense MI and high BERT MI scores, and finally, *Case 3* words have low Sense MI and low BERT MI scores. We compute the average ARI score for each word within each case and compare their performances.

4.4.2 Results

The results of the analysis can be seen in Table 3. MI scores show that the linguistic labels are more strongly associated with BERT clusters than with the sense groups. This suggests that these features are dominant in the BERT clusters more than necessary. This and the fact that ARI performance is lowest for the *Case 2* words indicate that these features introduce noise that affects WSI performance negatively. With the feature-invariant representations, this effect is limited to some extent.

Regarding different *Cases*, the results mostly align with our expectations. Clustering performance with *Case 1* words is slightly higher with original BERT representations. Clustering performance with *Case 2* words is increased with feature-invariant representations. However, the increase for *Case 2* words is much higher than the decrease for *Case 1* words, showing that the erasure of syntactic and morphological information benefits the WSI performance overall. Finally, with *Case 3* words, there is a slight increase or decrease in performance depending on the different feature types.

Regarding different feature types, we observe that the morphological features of words introduce a lot of noise to WSI performance (Sense MI vs. BERT MI). Only for 11 words (out of 540), morphological features of words are found to be associated with different senses (*Case 1*). For 80 words, these features are found to be associated with different BERT clusters, even though they are not relevant to different senses (*Case 2*), therefore introducing noise. Similarly, the average BERT MI score for morphological features surpasses the upper threshold (T_U) of association, showing that there is a high level of association between morphological features and BERT clusters. Conversely, syntactic features of words have more relevance to word senses. For 59 words, these features show associations with different senses, and both the Sense MI score is higher, and the difference between Sense and BERT MI scores is lower for this feature type. These differences are also evident

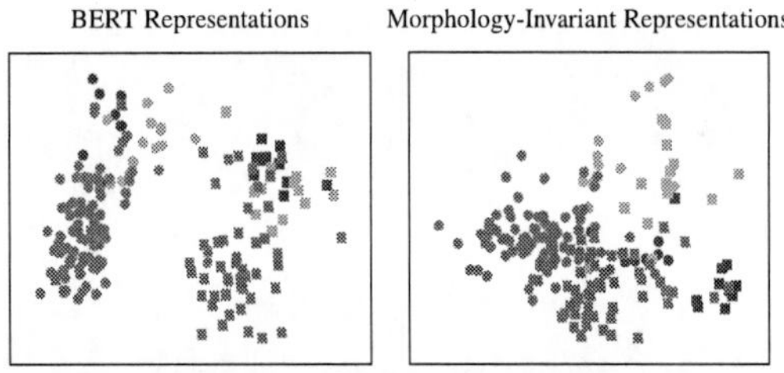

Figure 2: PCA visualizations of BERT representations (left) and morphology-invariant representations (right) of different sense instances of 'area'. Different data point colors refer to different senses. Different marker styles refer to instances with different morphological features, i.e. grammatical number; *circles* for *singular nouns*, *squares* for *plural nouns*.

in the WSI performance. Erasing morphological information benefits WSI performance more than erasing syntactic information (Table 2).

Let us illustrate these findings with a few examples. The noun 'area' has 3 senses in the data. WSI performs worse with BERT representations than with morphology-invariant representations on this word (BERT ARI: 0.03, INV ARI: 0.49). With BERT representations, we observe that two clusters are formed and that they are formed mostly based on the grammatical number of the instances, although there is no association between grammatical number and the senses of the word (Sense MI: 0.0, BERT MI: 57.7, Invariant MI: 4.2). With morphology-invariant representations, we observe that this pattern is broken. Grammatical number does not affect the similarity of the representations and the instances of each sense are closer to each other. Singular and plural instances of the third sense are successfully clustered together. Even though first and second sense instances form only one cluster, instances of each sense are closer to each other and the senses are more separable. See Figure 2 for the PCA visualization of the different representations of 'area' instances. For a more detailed plot see Figure 4 in Appendix D.

Let's consider a contrasting example. The noun 'field' has 4 senses in the data. WSI performs better with BERT representations than syntax-invariant representations (BERT ARI: 0.62, INV ARI: 0.26) and senses are associated with the syntactic features of the word (Sense MI: 40.3, BERT MI: 43.7, Invariant MI: 11.0). The 3rd sense of 'field' has the meaning 'somewhere (away from a studio or office or library or laboratory) where practical work is done or data is collected' and almost all of its

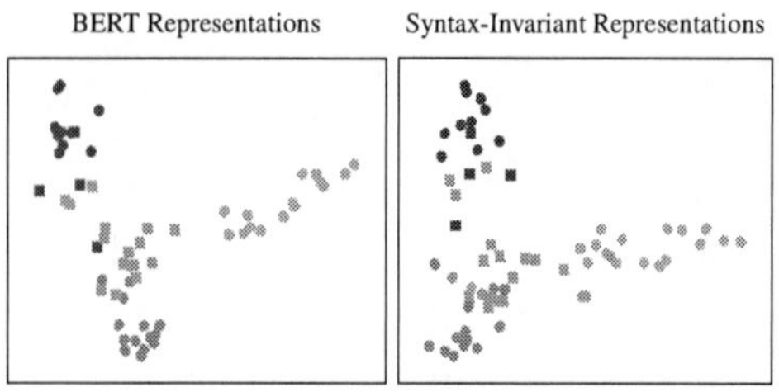

Figure 3: PCA visualizations of BERT representations (left) and syntax-invariant representations (right) of different sense instances of 'field'. Different data point colors refer to different senses. *Light blue* data points represent the 3rd sense instances of the noun. Different marker styles refer to instances with different syntactic roles; *squares* for *compounds heads*, *circles* for others.

instances are heads of a compound as in example (2).

(2) a. They will give suggestions that can be worked up into **field** procedures.
  b. Actually, none of these papers says much directly about **field** techniques.

The 3rd sense instances are clustered together when BERT representations are used. After the erasure of syntactic information, their representations are closer to the representations of other sense instances. As a result, they are clustered with other sense instances when syntax-invariant representations are used, resulting in poor performance. See Figure 3 for the PCA visualization of the different representations of 'field' instances. For a more detailed plot see Figure 5 in Appendix D.

5 Conclusion

We adapt the framework proposed by Jaiswal et al. (2020) in order to erase specific information from the representations of LMs. With this method, we create two types of representations from BERT embeddings: invariant to either (i) morphological features or (ii) syntactic features. Our results show that the resulting feature-invariant representations are more suitable for the WSI task. Furthermore, we show that even though some syntactic features provide valuable information for WSI, both types of features introduce noise that, overall, negatively impacts the performance of clustering-based WSI.

6 Acknowledgement

This study is funded by Labex EFL and the DFG project "Coercion and Copredication as Flexible Frame Composition". We would like to thank the anonymous reviewers for their valuable comments.

References

Enrique Amigó, Julio Gonzalo, Javier Artiles, and Felisa Verdejo. 2009. A comparison of extrinsic clustering evaluation metrics based on formal constraints. *Information retrieval*, 12:461–486.

Amit Bagga and Breck Baldwin. 1998. Entity-based cross-document coreferencing using the vector space model. In *COLING 1998 Volume 1: The 17th International Conference on Computational Linguistics*.

Alexander M Bronstein, Michael M Bronstein, and Ron Kimmel. 2003. Expression-invariant 3d face recognition. In *international conference on Audio-and video-based biometric person authentication*, pages 62–70. Springer.

Jacob Devlin, Ming-Wei Chang, Kenton Lee, and Kristina Toutanova. 2019. BERT: Pre-training of deep bidirectional transformers for language understanding. In *Proceedings of the 2019 Conference of the North American Chapter of the Association for Computational Linguistics: Human Language Technologies, Volume 1 (Long and Short Papers)*, pages 4171–4186, Minneapolis, Minnesota. Association for Computational Linguistics.

Christiane Fellbaum. 1998. *WordNet: An electronic lexical database*. MIT press.

Christian Hadiwinoto, Hwee Tou Ng, and Wee Chung Gan. 2019. Improved word sense disambiguation using pre-trained contextualized word representations. In *Proceedings of the 2019 Conference on Empirical Methods in Natural Language Processing and the 9th International Joint Conference on Natural Language Processing (EMNLP-IJCNLP)*, pages 5297–5306, Hong Kong, China. Association for Computational Linguistics.

Lawrence Hubert and Phipps Arabie. 1985. Comparing partitions. *Journal of classification*, 2:193–218.

Ayush Jaiswal, Daniel Moyer, Greg Ver Steeg, Wael AbdAlmageed, and Premkumar Natarajan. 2020. Invariant representations through adversarial forgetting. In *Proceedings of the AAAI Conference on Artificial Intelligence*, volume 34, pages 4272–4279.

Ayush Jaiswal, Rex Yue Wu, Wael Abd-Almageed, and Prem Natarajan. 2018. Unsupervised adversarial invariance. *Advances in neural information processing systems*, 31.

Alireza Khotanzad and Yaw Hua Hong. 1990. Rotation invariant image recognition using features selected via a systematic method. *Pattern recognition*, 23(10):1089–1101.

Henry Kučera, Winthrop Francis, William Freeman Twaddell, Mary Lois Marckworth, Laura M Bell, and John Bissell Carroll. 1967. Computational analysis of present-day american english. *Brown University Press, Providence, RI.*

Severin Laicher, Sinan Kurtyigit, Dominik Schlechtweg, Jonas Kuhn, and Sabine Schulte im Walde. 2021. Explaining and improving BERT performance on lexical semantic change detection. In *Proceedings of the 16th Conference of the European Chapter of the Association for Computational Linguistics: Student Research Workshop*, pages 192–202, Online. Association for Computational Linguistics.

Christos Louizos, Kevin Swersky, Yujia Li, Max Welling, and Richard Zemel. 2017. The variational fair autoencoder.

Daniel Loureiro, Kiamehr Rezaee, Mohammad Taher Pilehvar, and Jose Camacho-Collados. 2021. Analysis and evaluation of language models for word sense disambiguation. *Computational Linguistics*, 47(2):387–443.

Mitchell P. Marcus, Beatrice Santorini, and Mary Ann Marcinkiewicz. 1993. Building a large annotated corpus of English: The Penn Treebank. *Computational Linguistics*, 19(2):313–330.

George A. Miller, Claudia Leacock, Randee Tengi, and Ross T. Bunker. 1993. A semantic concordance. In *Human Language Technology: Proceedings of a Workshop Held at Plainsboro, New Jersey, March 21-24, 1993.*

Fabian Pedregosa, Gaël Varoquaux, Alexandre Gramfort, Vincent Michel, Bertrand Thirion, Olivier Grisel, Mathieu Blondel, Peter Prettenhofer, Ron Weiss, Vincent Dubourg, Jake Vanderplas, Alexandre Passos, David Cournapeau, Matthieu Brucher, Matthieu Perrot, and Édouard Duchesnay. 2011. Scikit-learn: Machine learning in python. *Journal of Machine Learning Research*, 12(85):2825–2830.

Minlong Peng and Qi Zhang. 2020. Weighed domain-invariant representation learning for cross-domain sentiment analysis. In *Proceedings of the 28th International Conference on Computational Linguistics*, pages 251–265, Barcelona, Spain (Online). International Committee on Computational Linguistics.

Mohammad Taher Pilehvar and Jose Camacho-Collados. 2019. WiC: the word-in-context dataset for evaluating context-sensitive meaning representations. In *Proceedings of the 2019 Conference of the North American Chapter of the Association for Computational Linguistics: Human Language Technologies, Volume 1 (Long and Short Papers)*, pages 1267–1273, Minneapolis, Minnesota. Association for Computational Linguistics.

Andrew Rosenberg and Julia Hirschberg. 2007. V-measure: A conditional entropy-based external cluster evaluation measure. In *Proceedings of the 2007 joint conference on empirical methods in natural language processing and computational natural language learning (EMNLP-CoNLL)*, pages 410–420.

Hassan Sajjad, Nadir Durrani, Fahim Dalvi, Firoj Alam, Abdul Khan, and Jia Xu. 2022. Analyzing encoded concepts in transformer language models. In *Proceedings of the 2022 Conference of the North American Chapter of the Association for Computational Linguistics: Human Language Technologies*, pages 3082–3101, Seattle, United States. Association for Computational Linguistics.

Younes Samih and Laura Kallmeyer. 2023. Unsupervised semantic frame induction revisited. In *Proceedings of the 15th International Conference on Computational Semantics*, pages 89–93, Nancy, France. Association for Computational Linguistics.

Pierre-Yves Vandenbussche, Tony Scerri, and Ron Daniel Jr. 2021. Word sense disambiguation with transformer models. In *Proceedings of the 6th Workshop on Semantic Deep Learning (SemDeep-6)*, pages 7–12, Online. Association for Computational Linguistics.

Thomas Wolf, Lysandre Debut, Victor Sanh, Julien Chaumond, Clement Delangue, Anthony Moi, Pierric Cistac, Tim Rault, Remi Louf, Morgan Funtowicz, Joe Davison, Sam Shleifer, Patrick von Platen, Clara Ma, Yacine Jernite, Julien Plu, Canwen Xu, Teven Le Scao, Sylvain Gugger, Mariama Drame, Quentin Lhoest, and Alexander Rush. 2020. Transformers: State-of-the-art natural language processing. In *Proceedings of the 2020 Conference on Empirical Methods in Natural Language Processing: System Demonstrations*, pages 38–45, Online. Association for Computational Linguistics.

Qizhe Xie, Zihang Dai, Yulun Du, Eduard Hovy, and Graham Neubig. 2017. Controllable invariance through adversarial feature learning. *Advances in neural information processing systems*, 30.

Ji Xin, Chenyan Xiong, Ashwin Srinivasan, Ankita Sharma, Damien Jose, and Paul Bennett. 2022. Zero-shot dense retrieval with momentum adversarial domain invariant representations. In *Findings of the Association for Computational Linguistics: ACL 2022*, pages 4008–4020, Dublin, Ireland. Association for Computational Linguistics.

Deniz Ekin Yavas. 2024. Assessing the significance of encoded information in contextualized representations to word sense disambiguation. In *Proceedings of the Third Workshop on Understanding Implicit and Underspecified Language*, pages 42–53, Malta. Association for Computational Linguistics.

Ying Zhao and George Karypis. 2001. Criterion functions for document clustering: Experiments and analysis.

A Model Architectures

- **Discriminator for Synactic Information:** 2-layer nonlinear neural network for classification. ReLU is used as the activation function. Given a token embedding, it predicts the dependency label of the token. Output dimension is the number of classes. Cross-entropy loss is used as the loss function and Adam is used as the optimizer.
- **Discriminator for Morphological Information:** 2-layer nonlinear neural network for classification. ReLU is used as the activation function. Given a token embedding, it predicts the fine-grained POS tag of the token. Output dimension is the number of classes found in the dataset. Cross-entropy loss is used as the loss function and Adam is used as the optimizer.
- **Predictor:** 3-layer linear neural network that maps the token embedding to the vocabulary of BERT with size 30522. 2nd layer is for normalization and drop-out (0.1) is applied before the output layer. Cross-entropy loss is used as the loss function and Adam is used as the optimizer.
- **Forget-Gate:** 3-layer nonliner neural network that transforms the input embedding. ReLU is used as the activation function. Cross-entropy loss is used as the loss function and Adam is used as the optimizer.

B Model Training Procedures

Adversarial Models. All adversarial models are trained with batch size 128 and learning rate 10^{-6} for the predictor, 10^{-5} for the discriminator, and 10^{-4} for the forget gate. All the models are trained for 800 epochs.

Upper Bounds.

- **Probing for syntactic information:** 74 epochs, batch size 128, learning rate 10^{-5}.
- **Probing for morphological information:** 66 epochs, batch size 128, learning rate 10^{-5}.
- **Word prediction:** 132 epochs, batch size 128, learning rate 10^{-6}.

Lower Bounds.

- **Probing for syntactic information:** 9 epochs, batch size 128, learning rate 10^{-4}.

Feature-Invariant Representations Evaluation.

- **Morphology-Invariant Representations:** The word predictor is trained for 30 epochs with batch size 128, learning rate 10^{-5}. The probing model is trained for 22 epochs with batch size 128, learning rate 10^{-4}. The best forget-gate is obtained from the 400th epoch of the adversarial model's training.
- **Syntax-Invariant Representations:** The word predictor is trained for 20 epochs with batch size 128, learning rate 10^{-5}. The probing model is trained for 37 epochs with batch size 128, learning rate 10^{-4}. The best forget-gate is obtained from the 500th epoch of the adversarial model's training.

C Clustering Performance Details

We evaluate the clustering performance using metrics from 4 different categories based on the categorization in Amigó et al. (2009) because different categories have different strengths in measuring clustering quality; metrics based on set matching (*Purity*, *Inverse Purity* (Zhao and Karypis, 2001) and their harmonic mean *PIF*), metrics based on entropy (*V-Measure* (Rosenberg and Hirschberg, 2007)), metrics based on counting pairs (*Adjusted Rand Index* (Hubert and Arabie, 1985)), and BCubed metrics (*BCubed Precision, Recall* and *F-score* (Bagga and Baldwin, 1998)).

C being the set of clusters and L being the true grouping, *Purity* and *Inverse Purity* are calculated as follows:

$$\text{Purity} = \sum_i \frac{|C_i|}{N} \max_j \text{Precision}(C_i, L_j) \quad (3)$$

$$\text{Inverse Purity} = \sum_i \frac{|L_i|}{N} \max_j \text{Precision}(L_i, C_j) \quad (4)$$

V-measure is calculated based on the homogeneity and completeness. Homogeneity measures how much each cluster contains only data points that are members of a single class. Completeness measures how much all data points that are members of a given class are assigned to the same cluster. It is calculated as follows:

	ARI	V-M	PU	IPU	PIF	P-Bcubed	R-Bcubed	F-Bcubed
BERT	0.210 (0.0008)	0.265 (0.0007)	0.732 (0.0007)	0.658 (0.001)	0.670 (0.001)	0.652 (0.0006)	0.575 (0.0008)	0.580 (0.0004)
Syn-Invariant	0.221 (0.001)	0.274 (0.001)	0.732 (0.0006)	0.682 (0.0009)	0.684 (0.0008)	0.653 (0.0007)	0.599 (0.001)	0.594 (0.0008)
Morph-Invariant	0.232 (0.001)	0.283 (0.0006)	0.736 (0.0004)	0.683 (0.001)	0.688 (0.0007)	0.657 (0.0004)	0.598 (0.0008)	0.597 (0.0005)

Table 4: Clustering evaluation results with different representations with different metrics for all words in the data. The mean results over 5 runs are given with standard deviation in brackets.

	ARI	V-M	PU	IPU	PIF	P-Bcubed	R-Bcubed	F-Bcubed
BERT	0.251 (0.001)	0.309 (0.001)	0.769 (0.0007)	0.689 (0.002)	0.707 (0.001)	0.699 (0.0004)	0.607 (0.001)	0.623 (0.0008)
Syn-Invariant	0.263 (0.0004)	0.320 (0.0005)	0.772 (0.0006)	0.682 (0.001)	0.706 (0.001)	0.703 (0.0003)	0.600 (0.001)	0.622 (0.0009)
Morph-Invariant	0.267 (0.001)	0.322 (0.001)	0.772 (0.001)	0.682 (0.001)	0.705 (0.001)	0.704 (0.001)	0.598 (0.001)	0.620 (0.001)

Table 5: Clustering evaluation results with different representations with different metrics for nouns. The mean results over 5 runs are given with standard deviation in brackets.

	ARI	V-M	PU	IPU	PIF	P-Bcubed	R-Bcubed	F-Bcubed
BERT	0.174 (0.001)	0.227 (0.001)	0.699 (0.001)	0.632 (0.001)	0.638 (0.0008)	0.611 (0.001)	0.547 (0.0006)	0.542 (0.0001)
Syn-Invariant	0.185 (0.002)	0.233 (0.002)	0.698 (0.001)	0.681 (0.002)	0.665 (0.001)	0.608 (0.001)	0.598 (0.001)	0.570 (0.001)
Morph-Invariant	0.201 (0.002)	0.248 (0.002)	0.705 (0.001)	0.684 (0.002)	0.672 (0.002)	0.616 (0.001)	0.599 (0.002)	0.576 (0.002)

Table 6: Clustering evaluation results with different representations with different metrics for verbs. The mean results over 5 runs are given with standard deviation in brackets.

$$\mathrm{V} = 2 \times \frac{\text{Homogeneity} \times \text{Completeness}}{\text{Homogeneity} + \text{Completeness}} \quad (5)$$

Adjusted Rand Index (ARI) adjusts the *Rand Index* (RI) to account for chance agreement. *RI* calculates the similarity between two clusterings by considering pairs of samples and determining whether they are assigned to the same cluster or different clusters in both clusterings. They are calculated as follows:

$$\mathrm{RI} = \frac{\text{correct similar pairs + correct dissimilar pairs}}{\text{total number of pairs}} \quad (6)$$

$$\mathrm{ARI} = \frac{\max(RI) - \text{Expected\_RI}}{RI - \text{Expected\_RI}} \quad (7)$$

Correctness is the relation between e and e' in the distribution, where $C(e)$ denotes the cluster and $L(e)$ true grouping of the item. Correctness means that both items have the same category and belong to the same cluster. The overall *Precision BCubed* and *Recall BCubed* are obtained by averaging the precision and recall scores of all items in the dataset as follows:

$$\text{Precision BCubed} = Avg_e[Avg'_{e \cdot C(e)=C(e')}[Correctness(e, e')]] \quad (8)$$

$$\text{Recall BCubed} = Avg_e[Avg'_{e \cdot L(e)=L(e')}[Correctness(e, e')]] \quad (9)$$

The detailed evaluation of the clustering performance with different metrics for all words can be seen in Table 4, for nouns in Table 5 and verbs in Table 6. The mean results over 5 runs are given.

D Clustering Visualizations

The PCA visualizations of the BERT representations and morphology-invariant representations of ‘area’ instances can be seen in Figure 4. Similarly, the PCA visualizations of the BERT representations and syntax-invariant representations of ‘field’ instances can be seen in Figure 5.

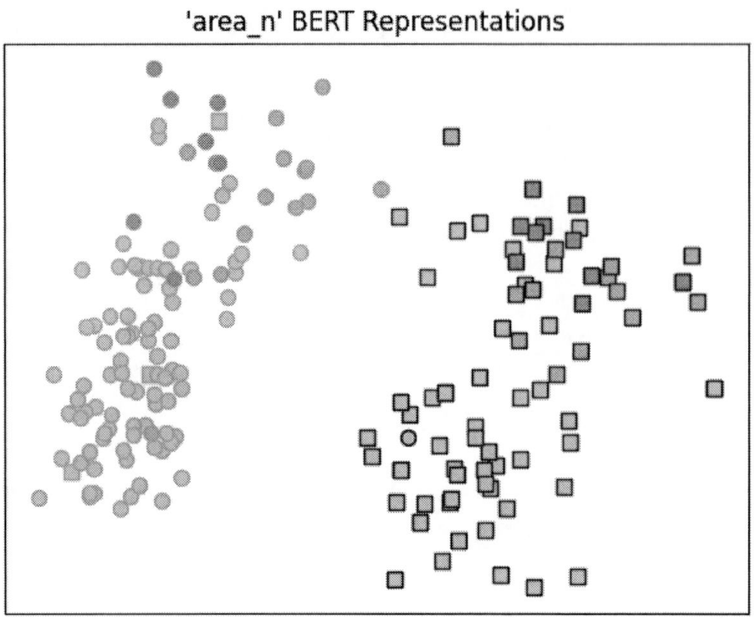

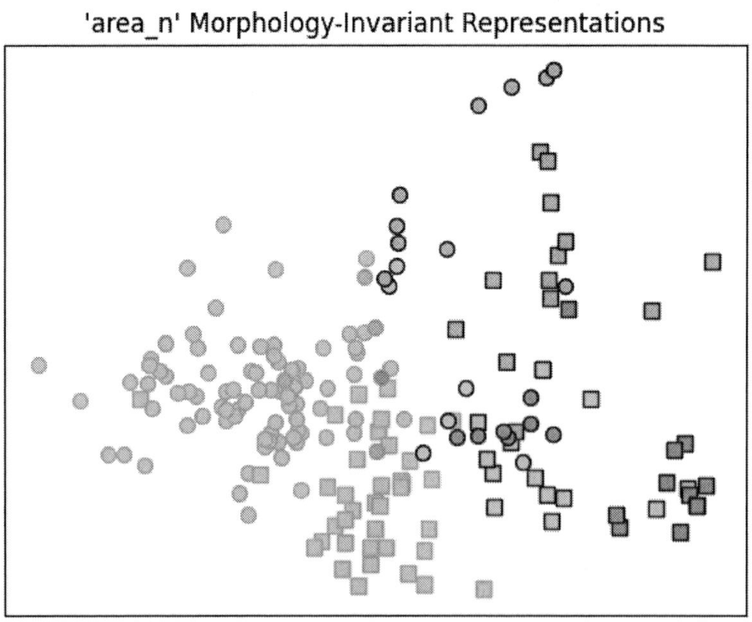

Figure 4: PCA visualizations of BERT representations (top) and morphology-invariant representations (bottom) of different sense instances of 'area'. Different data point colors refer to different senses, and different border colors refer to different clusters. Additionally, different marker styles refer to instances with different morphological features, i.e. grammatical number; *circles* for *singular nouns*, *squares* for *plural nouns*.

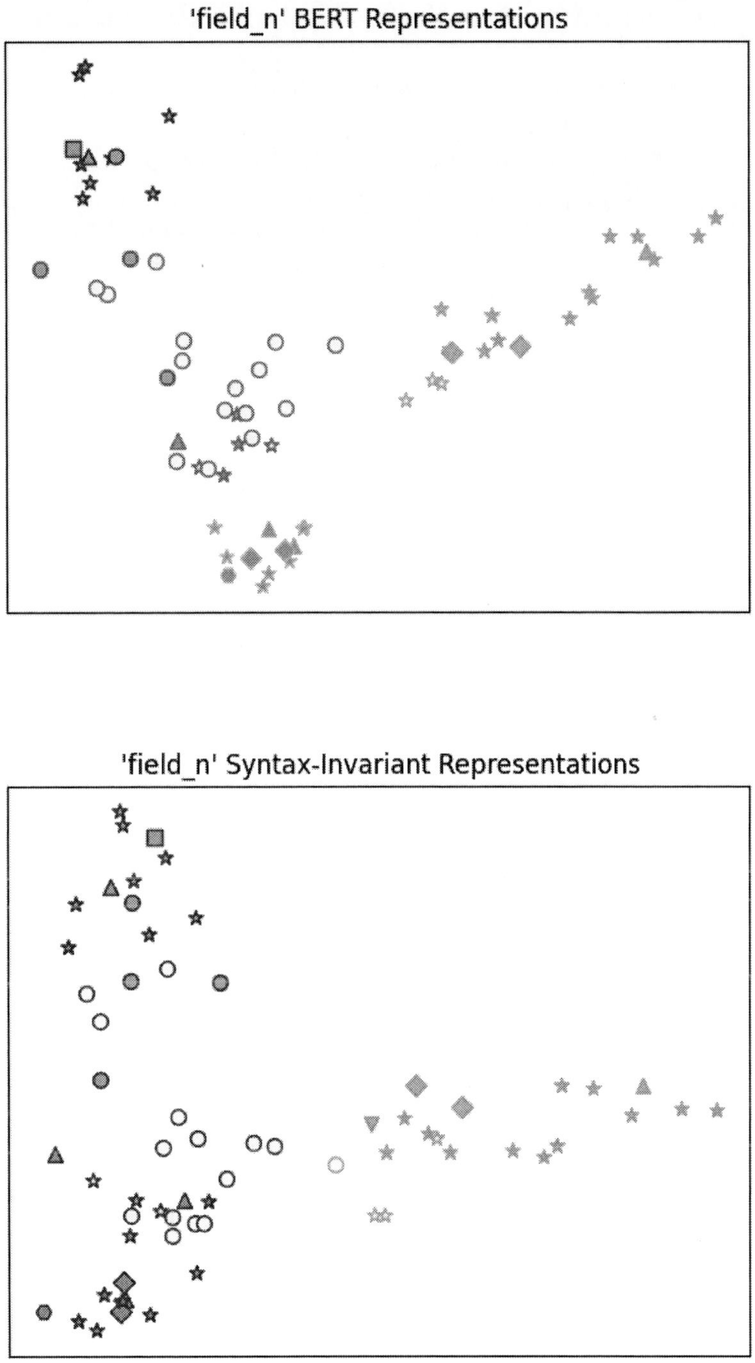

Figure 5: PCA visualizations of BERT representations (top) and syntax-invariant representations (bottom) of different sense instances of 'field'. Different data point colors refer to different senses, and different border colors refer to different clusters. Additionally, different marker styles refer to instances with different syntactic roles; *circles* for *compound heads*, *stars* for *prepositional objects*, *triangles* for *direct objects*, *diamonds* for *subjects*, *reversed triangles* for *passive subjects*, and *hexagons* for *attributes*.

What's wrong with your model?
A Quantitative Analysis of Relation Classification

Elisa Bassignana **Rob van der Goot** **Barbara Plank**
IT University of Copenhagen, Denmark
Pioneer Center for Artificial Intelligence, Denmark
Center for Information and Language Processing, LMU Munich, Germany
elba@itu.dk robv@itu.dk b.plank@lmu.de

Abstract

With the aim of improving the state-of-the-art (SOTA) on a target task, a standard strategy in Natural Language Processing (NLP) research is to design a new model, or modify the existing SOTA, and then benchmark its performance on the target task. We argue in favor of enriching this chain of actions by a preliminary error-guided analysis: *First*, explore weaknesses by analyzing the hard cases where the existing model fails, and *then* target the improvement based on those. Interpretable evaluation has received little attention for structured prediction tasks. Therefore we propose the first in-depth analysis suite for Relation Classification (RC), and show its effectiveness through a case study. We propose a set of potentially influential attributes to focus on (e.g., entity distance, sentence length). Then, we bucket our datasets based on these attributes, and weight the importance of them through correlations. This allows us to identify highly challenging scenarios for the RC model. By exploiting the findings of our analysis, with a carefully targeted adjustment to our architecture, we effectively improve the performance over the baseline by >3 Micro-F1.

1 Introduction

A major trend in NLP research aims at designing more sophisticated setups and model architectures in order to improve the state-of-the-art (SOTA) on a target task. The improvements are usually based on intuitions that target limitations of the previous SOTA on the task. The most common procedure follows the steps of *(1)* intuition, *(2)* modeling, *(3)* experiments, *(4)* results, and *(5)* analysis of the results. The latter is occasionally enriched with ablation or case studies with the main aim of proving the validity of the initial intuition and the effectiveness of the proposed methodology. We claim that conducting a preliminary in-depth analysis can help find good intuitions, and therefore guide better modeling and reducing the probability of negative experiments, usually not reported in the paper. Following previous error-guided analysis (Ribeiro et al., 2020; Fu et al., 2020a; Das et al., 2022), we argue in favor of changing the standard chain of actions listed above: *First* perform an exhaustive quantitative analysis of the previous SOTA to identify failure cases and challenging scenarios, and *then* effectively target the baseline improvement in order to tackle those.

We introduce an in-depth performance analysis suite in the context of Relation Classification (RC). Within the field of Information Extraction (IE), which broadly aims at extracting structured knowledge from unstructured text, the goal of RC aims at classifying the semantic relation between two named entities. We pick this task because, despite its popularity, the task is far from being solved or reaching high performance, especially when considering realistic challenging setups—e.g. cross-domain (Bassignana and Plank, 2022), or document-level (Popovic and Färber, 2022). We inspect the research approach of some of the most cited papers in the field from recent years, on top of which current SOTA are based: Baldini Soares et al. (2019) introducing the widely adopted entity markers, Zhong and Chen (2021) introducing the typed entity markers and proposing a pipeline approach for end-to-end Relation Extraction (RE), and Ye et al. (2022) at the time of writing holding the SOTA on three of the most established datasets in the field. We also inspect the research approach of papers published in the last year at major NLP conferences (ACL, NAACL, EMNLP, AACL, EACL) that propose new SOTA models for RC, or for the related tasks of end-to-end RE and few-shot RC (Tan et al., 2022; Liu et al., 2022; Zhou and Chen, 2022; Wang et al., 2022b; Zhenzhen et al., 2022; Guo et al., 2022; Wang et al., 2022c; Zhang et al., 2022b; Zhang and Lu, 2022; Tang et al., 2022; Zhang et al., 2022a; Wang et al., 2022a; Duan et al., 2022; Guo et al., 2023; Wan

*Proceedings of the 13th Joint Conference on Lexical and Computational Semantics (*SEM 2024)*, pages 252 - 263
June 20-21, 2024

et al., 2023). We find that that the common procedure consists of the five steps earlier mentioned. Specifically, we found that in most cases, the intuition (step 1) that is used as a starting point and as a motivation for the model improvement is based on generic observations of the model architecture, instead of on a quantitative analysis which could lead to more effective targeted improvements.

In this work, we propose a systematic quantitative analysis of a SOTA RC model to detect sets of challenging instances sharing common characteristics (e.g., entity distance). The goal is to identify hard-to-handle setups for the SOTA architecture. Importantly, our approach is easily reproducible in future setups with different models, and/or on different datasets. The relevance of performing an in-depth analysis is supported by a demonstration of how the acquired information can help to effectively address the weaknesses of the baseline and design a new SOTA. Our contributions are:[1]

- We provide a tool for comprehensive quantitative analyses of RC model performance.
- We exploit the proposed analysis for investigating the performance of a SOTA RC architecture across 36 in- and cross-domain setups.
- Based on the findings of the analysis, we perform a case study improving the previous SOTA by over 3 points Micro-F1.

2 Related Work

Analysis of NLP Models In this study, we are inspired by the recent trend targeting the evaluation of NLP models. Ribeiro et al. (2020) propose a task-agnostic methodology for testing general linguistic capabilities of NLP models by generating ad-hoc test instances; they test their approach over three tasks: sentiment analysis, Quora question pair, machine comprehension. Liu et al. (2021a) presents a software package for diagnosing the strengths and weaknesses of a single system, allowing for interpretation of relationships between multiple systems, and examining prediction results. They go a bit deeper into the task specificity, therefore their system currently supports the tasks of text classification (sentiment, topic, intention), aspect sentiment classification, Natural Language Inference (NLI), Named Entity Recognition (NER), Part-of-Speech (POS) tagging, chunking, Chinese Word Segmentation (CWS), semantic parsing, summarization, and machine translation. Furthermore, Fu et al. (2020a) and Fu et al. (2020b) introduce the concept of interpretable task-specific evaluation. The first target the comparison of a set of NER systems. The latter, instead, perform a deep evaluation of CWS systems proving that despite the excellent performance achieved on some datasets, there is no perfect system for CWS. This concept has also been applied by Fu et al. (2021) for interpreting the results over a set of sequence tagging setups (NER, CWS, POS, chunking). Within the field of Information Extraction, previous work explored error-driven analysis for the automatic categorization of model prediction errors (Das et al., 2022).

Analysis of RC Models Error analysis and in-depth evaluations of NLP systems are tied to specific tasks because of the peculiarities of each of them in terms of linguistic challenges, input type, and expected output. Relation Classification and related tasks (e.g., end-to-end RE) have received little attention in the context of systematic quantitative evaluation. Pre-Large Language Models, Katiyar and Cardie (2016) performed a manual evaluation of bi-directional LSTMs for the extraction of opinion entities and relations ("is-from", "is-about") by discussing the model output of a couple of instances. The same authors (Katiyar and Cardie, 2017) performed an error analysis, also based on a manual evaluation, comparing their model with Miwa and Bansal (2016). More recently, instead, some work has inspected the quality of RC corpora. Alt et al. (2020) analyze the impact of potentially noisy crowd-based annotations in the widely adopted TACRED (Zhang et al., 2017). Lee et al. (2022) target the specific problem of overlapping instances between train and test sets in two popular RC benchmarks, namely NYT (Riedel et al., 2010) and WebNLG (Gardent et al., 2017).

Driven by the popularity of the task, and the contrasting lack of in-depth quantitative evaluation of RC systems, we fill this gap with an evaluation analysis suite for RC, and a case study including 36 in- and cross-domain setups.

3 Background

3.1 Cross-domain Relation Classification

Given a sentence and two entity spans within it, the task of RC aims at classifying the semantic relation between them into a type from a pre-defined label

[1]Project repository: `https://github.com/mainlp/RC-analysis`

Attribute	Description	Value Type		Computation		Level		
		DISCR.	CONT.	LOCAL	AGGR.	ENT.	REL.	SENT.
`entity type`*	the types of *e1* and *e2*							
`relation type`	the type of *r*							
`IV entities`	in-vocabulary entities: the amount of entities which appear in the train set (values 0, 1, or 2)							
`entity length`	the sum of the number of tokens in *e1* and *e2*							
`entity distance`	the number of tokens separating *e1* from *e2*							
`sentence length`	the number of tokens in *s*							
`entity density`	the total number of entities in *s* over the `sentence length` (in percentage)							
`relation density`	the total number of semantic relations in *s* over the `sentence length` (in percentage)							
`OOV token density`	the amount of out-of-vocabulary tokens in *s* with respect to the train set over the `sentence length` (in percentage)							
`entity type frequency`*	the frequencies of the types of *e1* and *e2* in the train set							
`relation type frequency`	the frequency of the type of *r* in the train set							

Table 1: **Relation Classification Attributes.** Description of the 11 RC attributes and categorization in DISCRETE/CONTINUOUS value type, LOCAL/AGGREGATE computation, and ENTITY/RELATION/SENTENCE level. ($\star$): We map the original 36 domain-specific entity types defined by Liu et al. (2021b) into five more generic types shared across domains, see Appendix B for details.

set. The task is currently far from being solved, in particular when considering realistic challenging setups, for example document-level RC (Yao et al., 2019), or few-shot RC (Han et al., 2018; Gao et al., 2019). In this study, we consider the cross-domain setup, where the challenge lies in different text types and label distributions from train to evaluation set. The cross-domain setup is important for testing the robustness of models aginst data shift. Despite the research in this direction from previous years, mainly evaluated on ACE (Doddington et al., 2004) where the domains are not particularly distinctive (Fu et al., 2017; Pouran Ben Veyseh et al., 2019), recent work on more challenging scenarios show very low performance due to data sparsity across domains. For example, cross-dataset (Popovic and Färber, 2022), or evaluated on the recently published CrossRE dataset (Bassignana and Plank, 2022) which consists of data from six diverse text domains. In this study, we aim at improving the CrossRE baseline by systematically identifying challenging scenarios for the model.

3.2 Experimental Setup

CrossRE (Bassignana and Plank, 2022),[2] is a manually-annotated dataset for cross-domain RC including 17 relation types spanning over six diverse text domains: artificial intelligence, literature, music, news, politics, natural science. The dataset was annotated on top of CrossNER (Liu et al., 2021b), a Named Entity Recognition (NER) dataset. Appendix A reports the statistics of CrossRE.

We use the baseline model of the original paper.[3] Following the architecture proposed by Baldini Soares et al. (2019), the model by Bassignana and Plank (2022) augments the sentence with four entity markers e_1^{start}, e_1^{end}, e_2^{start}, e_2^{end} surrounding the two entities. The augmented sentence is then passed through a pre-trained encoder, and the classification made by a linear layer over the concatenation of the start markers $[\hat{s}_{e_1^{start}}, \hat{s}_{e_2^{start}}]$. We run our experiments over five random seeds and report the average performance. See Appendix C for reproducibility details.

4 Attribute Guided Analysis

We propose a systematic quantitative analysis of the performance of the CrossRE baseline model's performance across the 36 in- and cross-domain setups derived from training and testing the model on the six domains included in CrossRE. The analysis is performed over the development sets of the dataset. Inspired by the work of Fu et al. (2020a) on Named Entity Recognition, we introduce the first evaluation suite for RC, opening the way to other similar structured prediction tasks. The analysis evaluates the performance of the model over

[2]Released with a GNU General Public License v3.0.

[3]https://github.com/mainlp/CrossRE

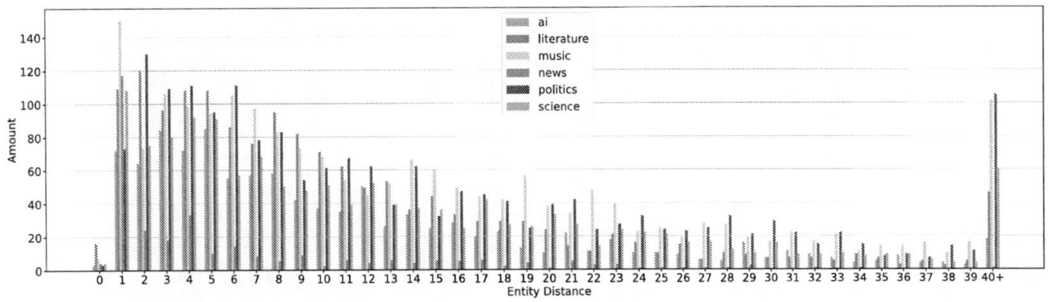

Figure 1: **`entity distance` Distribution.** Distribution of the `entity distance` values across the six development sets of CrossRE (Bassignana and Plank, 2022).

instances grouped by common values of potentially influential attributes (e.g., entity distance, sentence length). In what follows, we will describe the attributes considered and the bucketing strategy employed for splitting the evaluation instances based on the attribute values. Last, we go through the results of our correlation analysis.

4.1 Attributes

In our analysis, we consider 11 different attributes. These are characteristics of the RC instances that could challenge the model and influence its performance. Given an RC instance defined by a triplet *(e1, e2, r)* where *e1* is the head entity, *e2* is the tail entity, and *r* is the relation type connecting *e1* with *e2*; and given a sentence *s* expressing the relation *r* between *e1* and *e2*, we define the attributes listed in Table 1. We categorize each of them in the following three divisions:

- **Value Type:** If the values of the attribute belong to a set of pre-defined values the attribute is DISCRETE (e.g., the entity type), otherwise it is CONTINUOUS (e.g., the entity distance).
- **Computation:** If the attribute is computed by only considering the current instance it is LOCAL, if it is computed over aggregated properties of the train set, it is AGGREGATE; for example, the frequency of entity and relation types refers to the training statistics.
- **Level:** If the attribute value depends on the entities it is at ENTITY LEVEL, if it depends on properties of the entity pair it is at RELATION LEVEL, last if it is related to characteristics of the sentence *s* it is at SENTENCE LEVEL.

As an attribute example, Figure 1 shows the `entity distance` distribution, measured as number of tokens separating *e1* from *e2*. The plot reveals some domain-specific peculiarities, e.g., music and politics have the longest distances. This is mostly due to the long lists present in these domains, where the head entity is mentioned at the beginning and linked to all the elements in the list. For example, a music genre and a list of musical artists representing it; or the artifacts (i.e., songs and albums) of a band. We use the attribute values in order to group the evaluation instances with similar characteristics. We discuss the bucketing strategy in the next section.

4.2 Methodology

Once identified the potential influential attributes for the task of RC, the next step is splitting the evaluation sets depending on the attributes values (i.e., bucketing). For the attributes with DISCRETE value types (see Table 1) the bucketing creates one subset for each attribute values—e.g., one subset for each entity type for the `entity type` attribute. For the attributes with CONTINUOUS value types, instead, we set the number of buckets to four in order to maintain a reasonable size for each bucket. We then split the instances by equally distributing them across subsets—except for the two AGGREGATE attributes, which by definition are computed over properties of the train set. Note that the `entity type` and `entity type frequency` have each instance placed into two buckets, one considering the type of *e1* and one considering the type of *e2*.

We measure the performance of the model over the subsets, and compute the Spearman's rank correlation coefficient with respect to the average attribute values of the buckets. Since `entity type` and `relation type` have categorical values, we cannot compute the correlation coefficient and analyze these two attributes separately in Section 4.3.1.

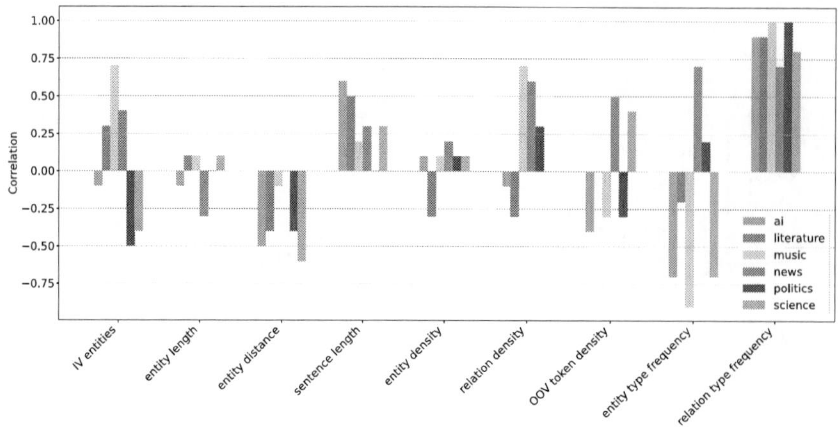

Figure 2: **Per-domain Correlation Analysis.** Spearman's rank correlation coefficient of the the 36 considered setups, averaged over the dev sets.

	IV entities	entity length	entity distance	sentence length	entity density	relation density	OOV token density	entity type frequency	relation type frequency
avg. correl	0.1	0.0	-0.4	0.3	0.1	0.2	0.0	-0.3	0.9
avg. stdev	22.2	7.1	6.1	6.4	7.0	5.9	9.9	14.6	24.9

Table 2: **Overall Results.** Average correlation and average standard deviation of the Micro-F1 scores of the buckets (within attribute), averaged over the 36 train-test setups.

4.3 Results

In this section we are going to present the results of our analysis, first looking at the overall correlation study, and then at the per-domain results.

Overall Table 2 reports the correlations for the proposed attributes (Section 4.1) averaged across all 36 setups. We also report the average standard deviation across the Micro-F1 scores achieved within attribute and computed separately for each train-test setup. The `relation type frequency` is by far the most influential attribute: It reports the highest absolute correlation value, and the highest standard deviation between buckets including low- and high-frequent relations types in the train sets. In the current setups with relatively small training sets (see CrossRE statistics in Appendix A) the amount of training instances have an high impact on the final performance of the model. In addition, this is also influenced by the cross-domain setup, with diverse relation label distributions over the six domains (see Figure 3). The second most relevant attribute is `entity distance`, with the second highest absolute value in correlation and a 6.1 average standard deviation across buckets containing entity pairs at different distances. The `entity type frequency` presents a weaker correlation, confirming the findings that we will discuss in Section 4.3.1 about the `entity type`. All the other attributes report an absolute correlation value ranging between 0.2 and 0.0 indicating that within the overall overview of the considered setups they have a lower impact on the model's performance.

Domain Level We visualize the average across the test domains in Figure 2. As previously noted, the `relation type frequency` trend confirms that the amount of training instances is the most influential attribute within the current setup. The `entity distance` and `sentence length` also present a similar trend across all six domains. The negative correlation of the first indicates that, as we could intuitively expect, it is more challenging to identify the semantic relation connecting two entities which are far apart in the sentence, with respect to entity pairs separated by only a couple of tokens. The positive trend within the `sentence length` attribute, instead, suggests that entity pairs belonging to long sentences (i.e., where more context is given) are easier to classify than the ones from short sentences. The `entity density`, and `relation density` attributes present a general positive trend in correlation, but with some outliers (literature and AI). High values in these attributes refer to sentences with many instances, e.g., lists of

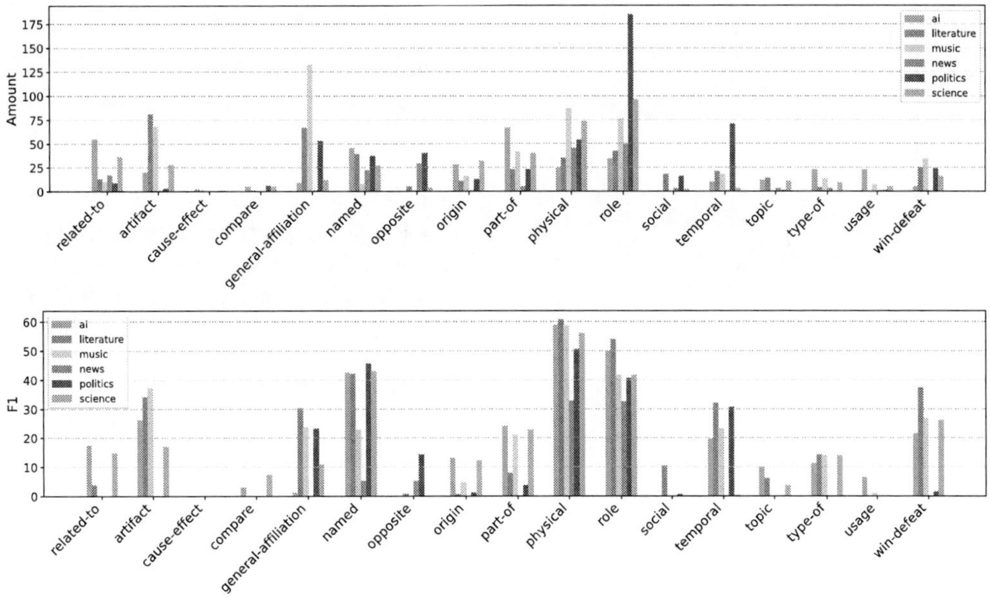

Figure 3: **`relation type` Analysis.** Distribution of the relation types in the train sets of CrossRE (Bassignana and Plank, 2022) (above), and F1 per label (bottom).

entities which are all linked to an head entity with a similar structure and (most likely) with the same relation type. For example, in the music domain, a list of songs authored by a music artist, or by a band. We speculate these to be easy patterns to identify and learn by a deep learning model.

News is often an outlier with respect to the other domains. When training on this domain the performance drops with higher values of `entity length` (instead of improving as for most of the other domains), and for `entity type frequency` is exactly the reverse. The latter is probably due to the entity type hierarchy adopted, which maps the domain-specific entity types defined by Liu et al. (2021b) for the other five domains into the types included in the news domain. However, it should be noted that news comes from a different data source and has ~4 times fewer relations compared to the other domains, which makes the results more unstable (Bassignana and Plank, 2022).

4.3.1 Categorical analysis

For the two categorical attributes it is not possible to compute the correlation coefficients.

`relation type` The results in Figure 3 reveal that some of the types are easier to learn across all domains than others (i.e. have higher scores, despite their lower frequency). These can be explained because they occur in very similar linguistic constructions, like "named", which often connects an entity to the consecutive acronym in brackets. Or because they mostly occur with the same entity types, like "temporal" with "event" and "physical" with "location". On the other hand, some relation labels have different performances across domains. For example "win-defeat" which in the domains of AI, literature, music, and science mostly links a person winning an award. In the politics domain, instead, it refers to more complex scenarios where one out of multiple mentioned political parties wins the election. Or, in a completely different semantic context, a country wins a war against another country. Unsurprisingly the most difficult are clearly the infrequent ones, like "cause-effect".

`entity type` The results in Figure 4 show that there is not a strong link between the amount of training instances and the performance achieved, confirming the findings from Figure 2. This is because in the CrossRE guidelines there are no constraints linking the relation types to specific entity types. The higher scoring types are mostly the ones that are implicitly associated with specific relation types, e.g., "location" with the "physical" relation type, and "event" with "temporal". On the other hand, the most varied category "misc" is the most challenging (see entity mapping in Table 5).

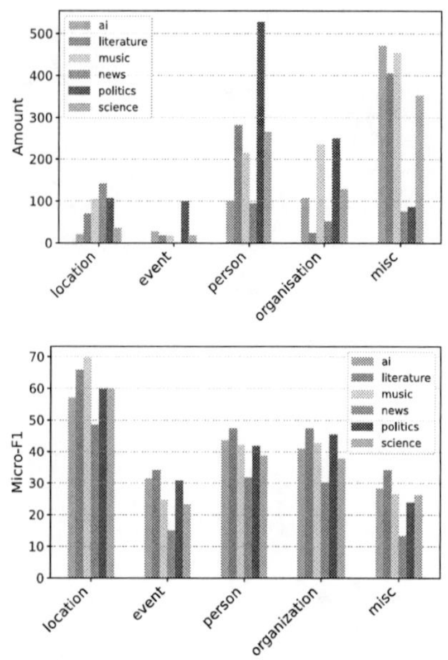

Figure 4: **`entity type` Analysis.** Distribution of the entity types in the train sets of CrossRE (Bassignana and Plank, 2022) (above), and Micro-F1 achieved on each bucket (bottom).

	TRAIN	ai	literature	music	news	politics	science	avg.
BASELINE	ai	46.4	32.9	27.5	44.6	36.4	35.3	37.2
	literature	28.0	63.1	55.5	34.7	49.0	35.4	44.3
	music	25.3	44.2	70.8	38.8	37.2	29.9	41.0
	news	12.6	15.8	16.4	52.6	33.5	21.6	25.4
	politics	20.1	34.0	40.6	40.5	55.8	31.2	37.0
	science	35.9	29.0	30.0	41.4	37.8	38.0	35.3
	avg.							36.7
FIRST-TWO	ai	45.2	33.2	28.4	40.7	35.8	33.7	36.2
	literature	25.7	66.4	64.2	37.8	53.6	35.8	**47.3**
	music	27.5	48.4	71.6	36.9	42.2	30.6	**42.8**
	news	14.1	17.0	18.9	43.6	35.5	23.2	25.3
	politics	18.4	33.4	41.3	43.2	56.6	31.1	**37.3**
	science	36.8	28.6	30.2	40.7	36.3	38.6	35.2
	avg.							**37.4**
LAST-TWO	ai	45.0	35.1	31.7	41.4	39.7	34.6	**37.9**
	literature	25.1	68.9	68.7	38.6	51.5	34.8	**47.9**
	music	28.6	57.6	73.2	38.2	39.1	32.4	**44.8**
	news	9.9	14.4	17.7	33.3	29.8	19.4	20.8
	politics	15.7	28.7	38.6	42.2	55.6	29.9	35.1
	science	33.2	31.0	35.8	42.0	41.6	40.9	**37.4**
	avg.							**37.3**
ALL-FOUR	ai	46.5	36.2	32.2	48.1	42.0	37.5	**40.4**
	literature	25.8	69.4	68.2	40.1	53.9	35.8	**48.9**
	music	29.6	59.1	74.6	37.7	46.0	33.6	**46.8**
	news	12.8	16.3	20.5	41.4	32.9	21.4	24.2
	politics	19.4	32.9	41.9	43.7	58.3	33.1	**38.2**
	science	38.0	31.8	34.2	45.8	44.9	41.3	**39.3**
	avg.							**39.6**

Table 3: **Performance Comparison Across Setups.** Micro-F1 scores achieved with the baseline architecture, and with the three proposed variants. (**bold**): Scores beating the baseline; (underline): Highest scores within the four setups.

5 Application: Model Improvement

As mentioned in the introduction, our final aim is to guide better modeling by targeting quantitatively measured weaknesses of the model. Here we present a case study which exploits the findings of our proposed analysis. From the overall results in Table 2 we can derive that the most influential attribute is the `relation type frequency`, with a correlation of 0.9 and the highest standard deviation of 24.9. Targeting this factor would mean obtaining additional training data by manual annotation or via some data augmentation techniques. Within this case study, we aim to focus on improving the model architecture. Therefore, here we target the `entity distance` attribute, which holds the second highest absolute correlation (0.4), for improving the model performance.

5.1 Improved Experimental Setting

The fact that the `entity distance` (i.e., the number of tokens separating *e1* from *e2*) has a high influence on the RC model performance, means that the tokens between *e1* and *e2* can somehow mislead the prediction. In order to target this issue, we aim at moving the two involved entities closer to each other. We repeat the entities at the end of the original sentence representation augmented with the entity markers. Then, similar to the original CrossRE baseline (Section 3.2), we pass the input through a pre-trained encoder and extract a representation on which we do the classification of the relation with a linear layer. We test out three different representations as illustrated in Figure 5:

- FIRST-TWO concatenation of the representation of the first two entity markers start, as in the original baseline setup;
- LAST-TWO concatenation of the representation of the last two entity markers start, the ones introduced after the [SEP] token;
- ALL-FOUR concatenation of the representation of all four entity markers start, the original ones and the newly introduced.

In what follows, we show the effectiveness of moving the entities closer to each other, and compare the three classification strategies described above. The new model architectures are also included in our project repository.[4]

[4] https://anonymous.4open.science/r/RC-analysis-sSEM-3B2A

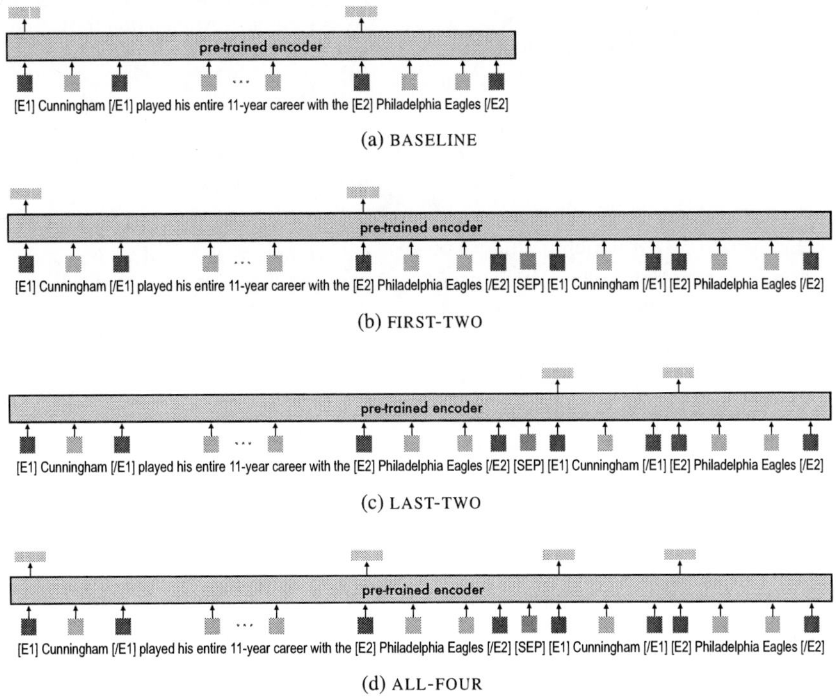

Figure 5: **Proposed Setups.** Representation of the baseline architecture (a) and of the three proposed setups (b, c, d) which include the repetition of *e1* and *e2* at the end of the sentence.

5.2 New SOTA Results

Table 3 compares the performance of the original baseline architecture with our proposed settings. In general, performances are higher with the repeated entities, except for the news domain, which achieves the least stable results across all our analyses. As pointed out by the authors of the dataset, this is the most challenging domain because it comes from a different data source and contains the least amount of instances, making the scores more unstable with respect to the other domains (Bassignana and Plank, 2022). Furthermore, ALL-FOUR consistently outperforms FIRST-TWO and LAST-TWO. The gain of the overall average is even larger compared to the sum of both individual gains, suggesting that they provide highly complementary insights. The obtained improvements are substantial (> 3 points on average), and come at negligible costs—e.g., without drastically increasing the training time with pre-training steps. We perform significance testing in Appendix D.

6 Conclusion

We present a tool for systematic quantitative analysis of the performance of RC models, and conduct the first in-depth analysis of an RC system, across 36 in- and cross-domain setups. We identify potentially influential attributes, and correlate their value with model performance. Our findings highlight the influence of data scarcity of relation types over the model performance. The second most correlated attribute is the distance between the two entities: The further away, the more challenging it is to classify the semantic relation between them.

Last, we provide a case study exploiting the findings of the analysis for improving the baseline architecture with a simple yet effective method. We target the entity distance weakness, and by repeating the entities closer to each other at the end of the sentence we achieve a new SOTA on CrossRE, with an average improvement > 3 points Micro-F1. We provide code for reproducing the proposed analysis on other RC setups (or related tasks, e.g., end-to-end RE). And we also release the code of the new SOTA architecture.

Our aim is to encourage preliminary quantitative analysis of models prior to designing new architectures. Future work includes expanding the set of attributes proposed in this work for RC in order to comprise other tasks, with different challenges.

Ethics Statement

We do not foresee any potential risk related to this work. The data we use is published freely by Liu et al. (2021b) and Bassignana and Plank (2022).

Limitations

In this work we report a case study of our proposed evaluation suite over CrossRE which includes six datasets covering six text domains. We focused mainly on the current SOTA model, future work could consider more models and datasets. The set of attributes is mostly bound to the RC task, but other relation-based tasks could employ similar attributes. More aspects could be included in the analysis in order to inspect specific strengths and weaknesses of the model, or in order to adapt it to other related structured prediction tasks. Last, with respect to the model improvement in Section 5, we focus on the architecture of the RC model, but given the high impact of the `relation type frequency` attribute, data augmentation techniques could be explored in order to further improve the performance of the model.

Acknowledgements

We thank the NLPnorth group at ITU and the MaiNLP group at LMU for feedback on an earlier version of this paper. EB and BP are supported by the Independent Research Fund Denmark (Danmarks Frie Forskningsfond; DFF) Sapere Aude grant 9063-00077B. BP is in parts supported by the European Research Council (ERC) grant agreement No. 101043235.

References

Christoph Alt, Aleksandra Gabryszak, and Leonhard Hennig. 2020. TACRED revisited: A thorough evaluation of the TACRED relation extraction task. In *Proceedings of the 58th Annual Meeting of the Association for Computational Linguistics*, pages 1558–1569, Online. Association for Computational Linguistics.

Livio Baldini Soares, Nicholas FitzGerald, Jeffrey Ling, and Tom Kwiatkowski. 2019. Matching the blanks: Distributional similarity for relation learning. In *Proceedings of the 57th Annual Meeting of the Association for Computational Linguistics*, pages 2895–2905, Florence, Italy. Association for Computational Linguistics.

Elisa Bassignana and Barbara Plank. 2022. CrossRE: A cross-domain dataset for relation extraction. In *Findings of the Association for Computational Linguistics: EMNLP 2022*, pages 3592–3604, Abu Dhabi, United Arab Emirates. Association for Computational Linguistics.

C.E. Bonferroni. 1936. *Teoria statistica delle classi e calcolo delle probabilità*. Pubblicazioni del R. Istituto superiore di scienze economiche e commerciali di Firenze. Seeber.

Aliva Das, Xinya Du, Barry Wang, Kejian Shi, Jiayuan Gu, Thomas Porter, and Claire Cardie. 2022. Automatic error analysis for document-level information extraction. In *Proceedings of the 60th Annual Meeting of the Association for Computational Linguistics (Volume 1: Long Papers)*, pages 3960–3975, Dublin, Ireland. Association for Computational Linguistics.

Eustasio Del Barrio, Juan A Cuesta-Albertos, and Carlos Matrán. 2018. An optimal transportation approach for assessing almost stochastic order. In *The Mathematics of the Uncertain*, pages 33–44. Springer.

George Doddington, Alexis Mitchell, Mark Przybocki, Lance Ramshaw, Stephanie Strassel, and Ralph Weischedel. 2004. The automatic content extraction (ACE) program – tasks, data, and evaluation. In *Proceedings of the Fourth International Conference on Language Resources and Evaluation (LREC'04)*, Lisbon, Portugal. European Language Resources Association (ELRA).

Rotem Dror, Segev Shlomov, and Roi Reichart. 2019. Deep dominance - how to properly compare deep neural models. In *Proceedings of the 57th Annual Meeting of the Association for Computational Linguistics*, pages 2773–2785, Florence, Italy. Association for Computational Linguistics.

Zhichao Duan, Xiuxing Li, Zhenyu Li, Zhuo Wang, and Jianyong Wang. 2022. Not just plain text! fuel document-level relation extraction with explicit syntax refinement and subsentence modeling. In *Findings of the Association for Computational Linguistics: EMNLP 2022*, pages 1941–1951, Abu Dhabi, United Arab Emirates. Association for Computational Linguistics.

Jinlan Fu, Liangjing Feng, Qi Zhang, Xuanjing Huang, and Pengfei Liu. 2021. Larger-context tagging: When and why does it work? In *Proceedings of the 2021 Conference of the North American Chapter of the Association for Computational Linguistics: Human Language Technologies*, pages 1463–1475, Online. Association for Computational Linguistics.

Jinlan Fu, Pengfei Liu, and Graham Neubig. 2020a. Interpretable multi-dataset evaluation for named entity recognition. In *Proceedings of the 2020 Conference on Empirical Methods in Natural Language Processing (EMNLP)*, pages 6058–6069, Online. Association for Computational Linguistics.

Jinlan Fu, Pengfei Liu, Qi Zhang, and Xuanjing Huang. 2020b. RethinkCWS: Is Chinese word segmentation a solved task? In *Proceedings of the 2020 Conference on Empirical Methods in Natural Language Processing (EMNLP)*, pages 5676–5686, Online. Association for Computational Linguistics.

Lisheng Fu, Thien Huu Nguyen, Bonan Min, and Ralph Grishman. 2017. Domain adaptation for relation extraction with domain adversarial neural network. In *Proceedings of the Eighth International Joint Conference on Natural Language Processing (Volume 2: Short Papers)*, pages 425–429, Taipei, Taiwan. Asian Federation of Natural Language Processing.

Tianyu Gao, Xu Han, Hao Zhu, Zhiyuan Liu, Peng Li, Maosong Sun, and Jie Zhou. 2019. FewRel 2.0: Towards more challenging few-shot relation classification. In *Proceedings of the 2019 Conference on Empirical Methods in Natural Language Processing and the 9th International Joint Conference on Natural Language Processing (EMNLP-IJCNLP)*, pages 6250–6255, Hong Kong, China. Association for Computational Linguistics.

Claire Gardent, Anastasia Shimorina, Shashi Narayan, and Laura Perez-Beltrachini. 2017. Creating training corpora for NLG micro-planners. In *Proceedings of the 55th Annual Meeting of the Association for Computational Linguistics (Volume 1: Long Papers)*, pages 179–188, Vancouver, Canada. Association for Computational Linguistics.

Jia Guo, Stanley Kok, and Lidong Bing. 2023. Towards integration of discriminability and robustness for document-level relation extraction. In *Proceedings of the 17th Conference of the European Chapter of the Association for Computational Linguistics*, pages 2606–2617, Dubrovnik, Croatia. Association for Computational Linguistics.

Qiushi Guo, Xin Wang, and Dehong Gao. 2022. Dependency position encoding for relation extraction. In *Findings of the Association for Computational Linguistics: NAACL 2022*, pages 1601–1606, Seattle, United States. Association for Computational Linguistics.

Xu Han, Hao Zhu, Pengfei Yu, Ziyun Wang, Yuan Yao, Zhiyuan Liu, and Maosong Sun. 2018. FewRel: A large-scale supervised few-shot relation classification dataset with state-of-the-art evaluation. In *Proceedings of the 2018 Conference on Empirical Methods in Natural Language Processing*, pages 4803–4809, Brussels, Belgium. Association for Computational Linguistics.

Arzoo Katiyar and Claire Cardie. 2016. Investigating LSTMs for joint extraction of opinion entities and relations. In *Proceedings of the 54th Annual Meeting of the Association for Computational Linguistics (Volume 1: Long Papers)*, pages 919–929, Berlin, Germany. Association for Computational Linguistics.

Arzoo Katiyar and Claire Cardie. 2017. Going out on a limb: Joint extraction of entity mentions and relations without dependency trees. In *Proceedings of the 55th Annual Meeting of the Association for Computational Linguistics (Volume 1: Long Papers)*, pages 917–928, Vancouver, Canada. Association for Computational Linguistics.

Juhyuk Lee, Min-Joong Lee, June Yong Yang, and Eunho Yang. 2022. Does it really generalize well on unseen data? systematic evaluation of relational triple extraction methods. In *Proceedings of the 2022 Conference of the North American Chapter of the Association for Computational Linguistics: Human Language Technologies*, pages 3849–3858, Seattle, United States. Association for Computational Linguistics.

Pengfei Liu, Jinlan Fu, Yang Xiao, Weizhe Yuan, Shuaichen Chang, Junqi Dai, Yixin Liu, Zihuiwen Ye, and Graham Neubig. 2021a. ExplainaBoard: An explainable leaderboard for NLP. In *Proceedings of the 59th Annual Meeting of the Association for Computational Linguistics and the 11th International Joint Conference on Natural Language Processing: System Demonstrations*, pages 280–289, Online. Association for Computational Linguistics.

Yang Liu, Jinpeng Hu, Xiang Wan, and Tsung-Hui Chang. 2022. A simple yet effective relation information guided approach for few-shot relation extraction. In *Findings of the Association for Computational Linguistics: ACL 2022*, pages 757–763, Dublin, Ireland. Association for Computational Linguistics.

Zihan Liu, Yan Xu, Tiezheng Yu, Wenliang Dai, Ziwei Ji, Samuel Cahyawijaya, Andrea Madotto, and Pascale Fung. 2021b. Crossner: Evaluating cross-domain named entity recognition. *Proceedings of the AAAI Conference on Artificial Intelligence*, 35(15):13452–13460.

Makoto Miwa and Mohit Bansal. 2016. End-to-end relation extraction using LSTMs on sequences and tree structures. In *Proceedings of the 54th Annual Meeting of the Association for Computational Linguistics (Volume 1: Long Papers)*, pages 1105–1116, Berlin, Germany. Association for Computational Linguistics.

Nicholas Popovic and Michael Färber. 2022. Few-shot document-level relation extraction. In *Proceedings of the 2022 Conference of the North American Chapter of the Association for Computational Linguistics: Human Language Technologies*, pages 5733–5746, Seattle, United States. Association for Computational Linguistics.

Amir Pouran Ben Veyseh, Thien Nguyen, and Dejing Dou. 2019. Improving cross-domain performance for relation extraction via dependency prediction and information flow control. In *Proceedings of the Twenty-Eighth International Joint Conference on Artificial Intelligence, IJCAI-19*, pages 5153–5159. International Joint Conferences on Artificial Intelligence Organization.

Marco Tulio Ribeiro, Tongshuang Wu, Carlos Guestrin, and Sameer Singh. 2020. Beyond accuracy: Behavioral testing of NLP models with CheckList. In *Proceedings of the 58th Annual Meeting of the Association for Computational Linguistics*, pages 4902–4912, Online. Association for Computational Linguistics.

Sebastian Riedel, Limin Yao, and Andrew McCallum. 2010. Modeling relations and their mentions without labeled text. In *Joint European Conference on Machine Learning and Knowledge Discovery in Databases*, pages 148–163, Berlin, Heidelberg. Springer Berlin Heidelberg.

Qingyu Tan, Ruidan He, Lidong Bing, and Hwee Tou Ng. 2022. Document-level relation extraction with adaptive focal loss and knowledge distillation. In *Findings of the Association for Computational Linguistics: ACL 2022*, pages 1672–1681, Dublin, Ireland. Association for Computational Linguistics.

Wei Tang, Benfeng Xu, Yuyue Zhao, Zhendong Mao, Yifeng Liu, Yong Liao, and Haiyong Xie. 2022. UniRel: Unified representation and interaction for joint relational triple extraction. In *Proceedings of the 2022 Conference on Empirical Methods in Natural Language Processing*, pages 7087–7099, Abu Dhabi, United Arab Emirates. Association for Computational Linguistics.

Dennis Ulmer, Christian Hardmeier, and Jes Frellsen. 2022. deep-significance-easy and meaningful statistical significance testing in the age of neural networks. *arXiv preprint arXiv:2204.06815*.

Zhen Wan, Fei Cheng, Qianying Liu, Zhuoyuan Mao, Haiyue Song, and Sadao Kurohashi. 2023. Relation extraction with weighted contrastive pre-training on distant supervision. In *Findings of the Association for Computational Linguistics: EACL 2023*, pages 2580–2585, Dubrovnik, Croatia. Association for Computational Linguistics.

Fengqi Wang, Fei Li, Hao Fei, Jingye Li, Shengqiong Wu, Fangfang Su, Wenxuan Shi, Donghong Ji, and Bo Cai. 2022a. Entity-centered cross-document relation extraction. In *Proceedings of the 2022 Conference on Empirical Methods in Natural Language Processing*, pages 9871–9881, Abu Dhabi, United Arab Emirates. Association for Computational Linguistics.

Shusen Wang, Bosen Zhang, Yajing Xu, Yanan Wu, and Bo Xiao. 2022b. RCL: Relation contrastive learning for zero-shot relation extraction. In *Findings of the Association for Computational Linguistics: NAACL 2022*, pages 2456–2468, Seattle, United States. Association for Computational Linguistics.

Yiwei Wang, Muhao Chen, Wenxuan Zhou, Yujun Cai, Yuxuan Liang, and Bryan Hooi. 2022c. GraphCache: Message passing as caching for sentence-level relation extraction. In *Findings of the Association for Computational Linguistics: NAACL 2022*, pages 1698–1708, Seattle, United States. Association for Computational Linguistics.

Yuan Yao, Deming Ye, Peng Li, Xu Han, Yankai Lin, Zhenghao Liu, Zhiyuan Liu, Lixin Huang, Jie Zhou, and Maosong Sun. 2019. DocRED: A large-scale document-level relation extraction dataset. In *Proceedings of the 57th Annual Meeting of the Association for Computational Linguistics*, pages 764–777, Florence, Italy. Association for Computational Linguistics.

Deming Ye, Yankai Lin, Peng Li, and Maosong Sun. 2022. Packed levitated marker for entity and relation extraction. In *Proceedings of the 60th Annual Meeting of the Association for Computational Linguistics (Volume 1: Long Papers)*, pages 4904–4917, Dublin, Ireland. Association for Computational Linguistics.

Liang Zhang, Jinsong Su, Yidong Chen, Zhongjian Miao, Min Zijun, Qingguo Hu, and Xiaodong Shi. 2022a. Towards better document-level relation extraction via iterative inference. In *Proceedings of the 2022 Conference on Empirical Methods in Natural Language Processing*, pages 8306–8317, Abu Dhabi, United Arab Emirates. Association for Computational Linguistics.

Peiyuan Zhang and Wei Lu. 2022. Better few-shot relation extraction with label prompt dropout. In *Proceedings of the 2022 Conference on Empirical Methods in Natural Language Processing*, pages 6996–7006, Abu Dhabi, United Arab Emirates. Association for Computational Linguistics.

Yuhao Zhang, Victor Zhong, Danqi Chen, Gabor Angeli, and Christopher D. Manning. 2017. Position-aware attention and supervised data improve slot filling. In *Proceedings of the 2017 Conference on Empirical Methods in Natural Language Processing*, pages 35–45, Copenhagen, Denmark. Association for Computational Linguistics.

Yunqi Zhang, Yubo Chen, and Yongfeng Huang. 2022b. RelU-net: Syntax-aware graph U-net for relational triple extraction. In *Proceedings of the 2022 Conference on Empirical Methods in Natural Language Processing*, pages 4208–4217, Abu Dhabi, United Arab Emirates. Association for Computational Linguistics.

Li Zhenzhen, Yuyang Zhang, Jian-Yun Nie, and Dongsheng Li. 2022. Improving few-shot relation classification by prototypical representation learning with definition text. In *Findings of the Association for Computational Linguistics: NAACL 2022*, pages 454–464, Seattle, United States. Association for Computational Linguistics.

Zexuan Zhong and Danqi Chen. 2021. A frustratingly easy approach for entity and relation extraction. In *Proceedings of the 2021 Conference of the North American Chapter of the Association for Computational Linguistics: Human Language Technologies*, pages 50–61, Online. Association for Computational Linguistics.

Wenxuan Zhou and Muhao Chen. 2022. An improved baseline for sentence-level relation extraction. In *Proceedings of the 2nd Conference of the Asia-Pacific Chapter of the Association for Computational Linguistics and the 12th International Joint Conference on Natural Language Processing (Volume 2: Short Papers)*, pages 161–168, Online only. Association for Computational Linguistics.

A CrossRE Statistics

We report in Table 4 the dataset statistics of CrossRE (Bassignana and Plank, 2022).

B Entity Type Mapping

The CrossRE dataset adopts the 39 domain-specific entity types initially proposed by Liu et al. (2021b) in CrossNER. When dealing with the `entity type` and `entity type frequency` attributes, in order to perform our cross-domain analysis, we map the original 39 entity types into five domain-agnostic meta entity types as illustrated in Table 5.

C Reproducibility

We report in Table 6 the hyperparameter setting of our RC model (see Section 3.2). All experiments were ran on an NVIDIA® A100 SXM4 40 GB GPU and an AMD EPYC™ 7662 64-Core CPU.

D Significance Testing

We compare our setups using the Almost Stochastic Order test (ASO; Del Barrio et al. (2018); Dror et al. (2019)) implementation by Ulmer et al. (2022). The method computes a score (ϵ_{min}) which represents how far the first is from being significantly better in respect to the second. The possible scenarios are therefore $\epsilon_{min} = 0.0$ (*truly stochastic dominance*), and $\epsilon_{min} < 0.5$ (*almost stochastic dominance*). Table 7 reports the ASO scores with a confidence level of $\alpha = 0.05$ adjusted by using the Bonferroni correction (Bonferroni, 1936). See Section 5 for the setup details.

	SENTENCES				RELATIONS			
	train	dev	test	**tot.**	train	dev	test	**tot.**
AI	100	350	431	881	350	1,006	1,127	2,483
literature	100	400	416	916	397	1,539	1,591	3,527
music	100	350	399	849	496	1,861	2,333	4,690
news	164	350	400	914	175	300	396	871
politics	101	350	400	851	502	1,616	1,831	3,949
science	103	351	400	854	355	1,340	1,393	3,088
tot.	668	2,151	2,446	**5,265**	2,275	7,662	8,671	**18,608**

Table 4: **CrossRE Statistics.** Number of sentences and number of relations for each domain of CrossRE (Bassignana and Plank, 2022).

person	**location**	**miscellaneous**	
researcher	country	field	program language
writer		task	product
musical artist		algorithm	metrics
politician		book	literary genre
scientist		award	poem
organization	**event**	magazine	music genre
university	election	song	album
band	conference	musical instrument	discipline
political party		enzyme	chemical element
		chemical compound	protein
		astronomical object	theory
		academic journal	

Table 5: **Entity Hierarchy.** Mapping of the original 39 domain-specific entity types by Liu et al. (2021b) into five domain-agnostic meta types.

Parameter	**Value**
Encoder	`bert-base-cased`
Classifier	1-layer FFNN
Loss	Cross Entropy
Optimizer	Adam optimizer
Learning rate	$2e^{-5}$
Batch size	32
Seeds	4012, 5096, 8257, 8824, 9908

Table 6: **Hyperparameters Setting.** Model details for reproducibility of the experiments.

	BASELINE	FIRST-TWO	LAST-TWO	ALL-FOUR
BASELINE	1.0	0.8	0.8	0.9
FIRST-TWO	**0.0**	1.0	**0.1**	1.0
LAST-TWO	**0.0**	**0.3**	1.0	1.0
ALL-FOUR	**0.0**	**0.0**	**0.0**	1.0

Table 7: **Significance Testing.** ASO scores comparing the experimental setups described in Section 5. Read as row → column.

Disambiguating Emotional Connotations of Words Using Contextualized Word Representations

Akram Sadat Hosseini
University of Stuttgart
Stuttgart, Germany
akram-sadat.hosseini@ki.uni-stuttgart.de

Steffen Staab
University of Stuttgart
Stuttgart, Germany
University of Southampton
Southampton, UK
Steffen.Staab@ki.uni-stuttgart.de

Abstract

Understanding emotional nuances in written content is crucial for effective communication; however, the context-dependent nature of language poses challenges in precisely discerning emotions in text. This study contributes to the understanding of how the emotional connotations of a word are influenced by the sentence context in which it appears. Leveraging the contextual understanding embedded in contextualized word representations, we conduct an empirical investigation to (i) evaluate the varying abilities of these representations in distinguishing the diverse emotional connotations evoked by the same word across different contexts, (ii) explore potential biases in these representations toward specific emotions of a word, and (iii) assess the capability of these representations in estimating the number of emotional connotations evoked by a word in diverse contexts. Our experiments, utilizing four popular models—BERT, RoBERTa, XLNet, and GPT-2—and drawing on the GoEmotions and SemEval 2018 datasets, demonstrate that these models effectively discern emotional connotations of words. RoBERTa, in particular, shows superior performance and greater resilience against biases. Our further analysis reveals that disambiguating the emotional connotations of words significantly enhances emotion identification at the sentence level.

1 Introduction

Understanding the emotional nuances conveyed by words is crucial for effective communication. This insight enhances the design of conversational agents that emulate human empathy, enabling responses that accurately reflect the emotions conveyed by word choice (Raji and de Melo, 2021). Psycholinguistics leverages this understanding to identify depression and suicidality, where specific word usage on social media posts may indicate underlying distress (Aragón et al., 2019). Moreover, comprehending these emotional subtleties alongside literal meanings of words can deepen second language comprehension for non-native speakers (Dewaele, 2010).

In cognitive linguistics, the concept of `emotional connotation` refers to the emotion attributed to a specific word, transcending its explicit meaning (Stubbs, 1995). Take, for instance, the word 'damn', which is rated by humans as *anger* (Mohammad and Kiritchenko, 2018), likely stemming from its frequent use in expressions of anger. However, a word may take on various emotional connotations depending on the context in which it appears. Consider the word 'damn' in the following sentences sourced from the GoEmotions dataset (Demszky et al., 2020):

S1. Wash your damn hands. [Anger]
S2. Damn [NAME] is KILLING it. [Joy]
S3. I damn near broke down! [Sadness]
S4. Damn, that's dark here! [Fear]

In S1, the word 'damn' expresses anger, while in S2, it is used in a positive context to convey joy. Both S3 and S4 exemplify its usage in other negative contexts.

Research on determining the emotional connotations of lexical items has typically utilized crowdsourcing methods, leading to the development of diverse lexicons of words with predefined emotions (Hofmann et al., 2020). These lexicons, however, provide static and generalized ratings for words, regardless of the context in which they are used (De Bruyne et al., 2022). Additionally, despite attempts to ensure consistency in word ratings through anchoring, implicit biases may persist in the rating process (Semeraro et al., 2023). Efforts to address these limitations have mainly focused on distinguishing the polarity of words (Hellrich et al., 2019). In a domain-specific corpus (soccer), Braun et al. (2022) relied on human judgments to measure the differences between the positivity and negativ-

*Proceedings of the 13th Joint Conference on Lexical and Computational Semantics (*SEM 2024)*, pages 264 - 277
June 20-21, 2024 ©2024 Association for Computational Linguistics

ity of words with and without a sentence context. Moreover, adopting automatic methods as an alternative to manual acquisition has been limited to extending the lexicon's word coverage (Sedoc et al., 2017) or developing domain-specific polarity lexicons (Hamilton et al., 2016).

Recently, contextualized word representations, exemplified by BERT (Devlin et al., 2019), have been frequently evaluated on word relatedness benchmarks, such as word sense disambiguation (Wiedemann et al., 2019), which is the task of identifying the correct sense of a word's usage from a fixed inventory of sense identifiers (Hadiwinoto et al., 2019). Studies on textual emotion analysis have utilized these representations particularly for *sentence-level* emotion classification tasks (Chen et al., 2023; Fan et al., 2022; Huang et al., 2021; Alhuzali and Ananiadou, 2023).

What is particularly intriguing about contextualized word representations is their ability to generate unique embeddings for a word based on its context (Saravia et al., 2018). Our objective is to leverage this property of contextualized word representations to disentangle the emotional connotations of words that evoke various emotions within different sentence contexts. Let W be the set of all words, where $w \in W$ represents a target word, which evokes different emotions depending on its surrounding context. $\mathcal{S}$ is the set of all possible sentences, and $\mathbb{N}$ is the set of natural numbers representing the position in a sentence where we aim to analyze the emotional connotation of the word w. The function f, $f(S, i) = e$, categorizes the dominant emotional connotation of w at position i in sentence S. The signature of this function is given by $f : \mathcal{S} \times \mathbb{N} \rightarrow \mathcal{E}$, where $\mathcal{E}$ is the set of all possible emotion categories.

We conduct an empirical investigation to:

(i) Evaluate the varying abilities of contextual word representations in distinguishing the diverse emotional connotations evoked by the same word across different contexts;

(ii) Explore the existence of potential biases in these representations toward specific emotional connotations of a word; in this context, bias refers to the likelihood of models incorrectly associating a word linked to $emotion_k$ with $emotion_j$;

(iii) Assess the capability of these representations in estimating the number of emotions a word can evoke in various contexts; and

(iv) Investigate the impact of disambiguating the emotional connotations of words on the accuracy of sentence-level emotion classification.

Focusing on emotional words that evoke various emotions across diverse contexts, we obtain contextualized representations of these words within emotion-annotated sentences in the GoEmotions and the SemEval 2018 (Mohammad et al., 2018) datasets. We then cluster these representations and assess the alignment degree between the resulting clusters and the emotions of the words in question. Our analysis of various models—BERT, RoBERTa, XLNet, and GPT-2—showcases their capability to capture the emotional connotations of words. We find that not all models are equally effective in discerning these emotional nuances. Our findings also reveal biases towards specific emotions in these representations, with different models exhibiting biases towards different emotions for a given word. Moreover, our experiments indicate that disambiguating the emotional connotations of a small number of words significantly improves the accuracy of sentence-level emotion classification.

2 Related work

Textual emotion recognition has typically involved either the utilization of lexicons—lists of words with pre-assigned emotions—without the need for extensive labeled data (Semeraro et al., 2023), or contextualized word representations, known for their domain-agnostic adaptability, when sufficient labeled data is available (Öhman et al., 2020).

Methods that rely on lexicons view texts as word collections and use word ratings from lexicons for emotion identification (Ma et al., 2018; Hosseini and Staab, 2023). However, the static nature of these word ratings limits a comprehensive understanding of emotions, as they disregard contextual nuances (De Bruyne et al., 2022). For instance, in a domain-specific corpus (soccer), Braun et al. (2022) demonstrated that pragmatic and semantic shifts in context can significantly influence word polarity in lexicons. To address this limitation, researchers often explore the identification of negations, diminishers, and intensifiers (Reitan et al., 2015; Hutto and Gilbert, 2014), or they develop domain-specific lexicons (Amir et al., 2015), which have mainly focused on distinguishing polarity of words in a specific domain (Hellrich et al., 2019).

Recent methods in textual emotion analysis have increasingly leveraged contextual word representations like BERT, particularly for sentence-level emotion classification (Alhuzali and Ananiadou, 2023; Li et al., 2021; Mao et al., 2023). These methods enhance model training by fine-tuning these embeddings with emotion-labeled datasets. For instance, Batbaatar et al. (2019) applied these representations in a Convolutional Neural Network to discern semantic relationships between words, and Kassner and Schütze (2020) focused on refining the understanding of contradictory sentiment words within these representations for binary sentiment classification. Some studies have integrated emotional lexicons into these representations, enabling these models to achieve a more nuanced understanding of emotional words (Aduragba et al., 2021; Ke et al., 2020; Wang et al., 2020). For example, Sosea and Caragea (2021) proposed a pre-training objective for BERT, which increases masking probabilities for emotional words in sentences using emotion lexicons, while Zhou et al. (2020) developed a BERT model from scratch using Yelp and Amazon reviews by increasing the masking probability for positive and negative words. However, these approaches exhibit high sensitivity to both the training corpus and the lexical resources employed (Shah et al., 2023), which suffer from ambiguity (Wang et al., 2021). Certain studies, such as Wang and Zong (2021), focused on semantic role labeling for emotions, modeling the semantics and interrelatedness of emotion labels by learning representations for emotion classes from annotated data. However, these representations do not generalize to other datasets and label formats (Campagnano et al., 2022).

Previous studies have primarily utilized contextualized representations for *sentence-level* emotion classification tasks. In contextualized word representations, each input word is represented as a vector dependent on the context of its occurrence (Saravia et al., 2018). This approach captures both semantic and syntactic nuances within the surrounding context of words, rendering these models particularly intriguing for investigating the emotional connotations of words across diverse contexts. This paper exploits these representations to conduct an empirical study, aiming to scrutinize their efficacy in distinguishing different emotional connotations evoked by the same word in various contexts. To achieve this, we adopt a clustering-based approach, wherein the representation vectors of the word, obtained from emotion-annotated sentences, are clustered using a Gaussian Mixture Model. Further, we evaluate potential biases in different representation models toward certain emotional connotations of words and assess whether clustering is a viable method for predicting the number of emotions a word can evoke in diverse contexts.

3 Methodology

To investigate the effectiveness of contextualized word representations in discerning the various emotional connotations of words that evoke different emotions depending on the sentence context, we propose a method comprising the following steps:
1. *Target Word Identification:* Identify a subset of emotional words within an emotion lexicon that evoke diverse emotions across different contexts.
2. *Sample Sentence Extraction:* Retrieve sentences featuring the target words from emotion-annotated resources to compile a representative set of instances showcasing the words in diverse contexts.
3. *Contextualized Representation Generation:* Obtain contextualized representation vectors for the target words in the set of sample sentences.
4. *Word Representation Clustering.* Apply clustering to the contextualized representations using a Gaussian Mixture Model (GMM) and find a mapping between the resulting clusters and the emotions of target words that maximizes the overall number of accurate matches, with the match rate serving as the evaluation metric.

The next sections detail the target word identification phase, the word representations used in our study, and the clustering of these representations.

3.1 Target Word Identification

The task of identifying emotional words that can evoke multiple emotions in different contexts relies on two foundational assumptions:

Assumption 1: The subset of emotional words eliciting diverse emotions is significantly smaller than the set of words maintaining consistent emotional connotations across various contexts (Wang et al., 2021; Gollapalli et al., 2020).

Assumption 2: The emotional connotation of a word can be inferred by analyzing its frequency within a corpus of annotated text. If an emotional word frequently appears in sentences expressing a specific emotion, it is reasonable to deduce that it is commonly employed to convey that emotion (Liu, 2022; Hosseini, 2017).

To identify words that evoke various emotions based on context, the inherent emotionality of a word is a prerequisite for our study. We utilized the

NRC-Affect lexicon (Mohammad and Kiritchenko, 2018), a well-established resource in emotion analysis, to extract emotional words from annotated datasets. This lexicon, annotated manually, comprises 4,192 English words and their associations with four basic emotions (*anger, fear, sadness, and joy*) with scores ranging from 0 to 1. It encompasses common English terms and terms prevalent on social media platforms.

The initial step involved extracting words from the NRC-Affect lexicon that were present in various emotional classes of the annotated datasets. We then calculated the proportion of the word's frequency in each emotional class to its total frequency across all sentences, as shown in (1):

$$\text{Proportion}(w, e) = \frac{\text{freq}(w, e)}{\sum_e \text{freq}(w, e)} \quad (1)$$

Here, $\text{freq}(w, e)$ denotes the frequency of candidate word w in emotion category e, where e represents each emotion category in the dataset. Formula (1) generates values between 0 and 1, with the sum equal to 1, indicating the normalized frequency of extracted words in distinct categories, irrespective of dataset size. For a word w to be considered a target word, a minimum normalized frequency of 0.2 in each emotion category is required. This criterion reduces noise in the identification process and strikes a balance between being stringent enough to filter out less relevant words while remaining practical for analysis.

We refined the target word selection process further by requiring a minimum occurrence in the 25 annotated sentences for each emotion. For example, the word 'crazy' met this criterion, appearing in 75 sentences expressing *anger* and 40 sentences expressing *joy*. In contrast, 'abortion' did not meet the criteria, as it appeared in sentences expressing various emotions (anger, fear, and sadness) but lacked the required number of annotated sentences per emotion. Setting a minimum occurrence criterion ensures the identified words have a robust presence in the dataset. To ensure a balanced distribution of sentences across emotions and prevent bias towards more frequent emotion classes, we imposed a maximum limit of 100 sentences per emotion. In line with Assumption 2, we associated the emotions of the identified target words with the emotion expressed within sentences.

3.2 Contextual Representation Generation

This section provides an overview of the contextualized word representations used in this paper, e.g., BERT, RoBERTa, XLNet, and GPT-2. These models were selected based on their prevalent use in sentiment analysis and text emotion analysis (Chen et al., 2023; Fan et al., 2022; Mao et al., 2023). They embody a broad spectrum of transformer architectures, with unique objectives and pre-training methods. The coverage includes bidirectional models (BERT, RoBERTa, XLNet) and a unidirectional model (GPT-2), incorporating various language modeling approaches such as masked language modeling and autoregressive language modeling. Table 1 summarizes their differences in corpus size, parameters, embedding dimensions, and layers. We used publicly available pre-trained versions of these models specified by 'bert- large-uncased,' 'roberta-large,' 'xlnet-base-cased' and 'gpt2' on Hugging Face.

- **BERT** (Devlin et al., 2019) employs masked language modeling and next-sentence prediction to generate bidirectional text representations, considering both preceding and succeeding context.
- **RoBERTa** (Liu et al., 2019), built on BERT's architecture, omits the next-sentence prediction task and introduces dynamic masking, which generates unique masking patterns for each sentence during training rather than using a fixed masked token.
- **XLNet** (Yang et al., 2019) is an autoregressive language model that employs permutation-based training to predict random tokens in both directions, allowing for bidirectional context capture.
- **GPT-2** (Radford et al., 2019) is a unidirectional autoregressive language model that employs the Transformer decoder architecture for its generative pre-training, specializing in predicting the next word in a sentence by considering preceding words.

Model	Params.	Corpus Size	Tokenization	Dims.	Layers
BERT	340M	16GB	WordPiece	1024	24
RoBERTa	355M	160GB	Byte-Pair		
XLNet	340M	158GB	SentencePiece		
GPT-2	345M	40GB	Byte-Pair		

Table 1: Details of contextualized word representations used in this study.

3.3 Word Representation Clustering

We utilized the Gaussian Mixture Model (GMM) from scikit-learn for clustering the generated contextualized word vectors, selecting the 'spherical' covariance type, which assumes equal diagonal elements in a diagonal covariance matrix. The GMM can adapt to clusters with diverse shapes and sizes while employing a probabilistic method for clustering (Melnykov and Maitra, 2010). Through an optimization strategy, we then identified a mapping between the resulting clusters and the emotions of the target words that maximize the overall number of accurate matches. Using the match rate as the evaluation metric leads to a more refined measure of clustering quality.

The match rate quantifies the alignment between the resulting clusters and the emotions of target words. We determined this rate by constructing a contingency table with `pandas.crosstab` (denoted as C), where each cell C_{ij} counts the instances in cluster i associated with emotion label j. Initially, we assigned an emotion label to each cluster based on the predominant emotion of the instances within that cluster, following a majority voting principle. Subsequently, we refined this alignment by employing the Hungarian algorithm (Kuhn, 1955) to establish an optimal one-to-one mapping between clusters and target words' emotions. This optimization seeks a permutation π that minimizes mismatch costs, thereby maximizing the alignment between clusters and emotions. The match rate was then calculated by normalizing the sum of correctly matched labels, according to the optimal mapping π, by the total count of instances n, as follows:

$$\text{Match Rate} = \frac{\sum_{i=1}^{k} C_{i,\pi(i)}}{n} \quad (2)$$

Here, k denotes the number of clusters, and $\pi(i)$ represents the label matched with cluster i through the optimal matching.

4 Experiments

In this section, we first investigate the ability of various contextualized word representations to distinguish between the different emotional connotations evoked by the same word in different contexts (Section 4.2). Then, we explore the presence of emotional biases in these representations (Section 4.3). Finally, we evaluate the accuracy of these representations in quantifying the range of emotions elicited by each word (Section 4.4).

4.1 Datasets

We used the GoEmotions and SemEval 2018 datasets, sourced from Reddit and Twitter, respectively, as emotion-annotated datasets.

- **GoEmotions** (Demszky et al., 2020) is the largest manually annotated dataset of 58k English Reddit comments from popular subreddits. At least three raters assessed each comment, resulting in significant inter-rater agreement. Comments range from 3 to 30 tokens, with a median length of 12 tokens. We utilized the version of the dataset annotated for six emotions: joy, anger, fear, sadness, disgust, and surprise.

- **SemEval 2018** (Mohammad et al., 2018) comprises 10,983 tweets annotated for 11 emotions: anger, anticipation, disgust, fear, joy, love, optimism, pessimism, sadness, surprise, and trust. At least seven raters assessed each tweet, ensuring reliable annotation with strong inter-rater correlation. The tweets range from 1 to 36 tokens, with a median length of 16 tokens.

We followed the procedure outlined in Section 3.1 for target word identification. In the GoEmotions dataset, we identified 133 words with an average of 2.5 distinct emotions, and in the SemEval dataset, 113 words with an average of 2.3 emotions per word. For evaluation, we selected 90 and 80 words from the GoEmotions and SemEval datasets, respectively, as the test set, reserving the remaining words for parameter fine-tuning in the development set. The emotional labels for these words were assigned based on the emotions expressed in the sentences, including anger, fear, sadness, and joy. Emotions like *surprise*, although present in the datasets, did not meet the criteria outlined in Section 3.1 and were thus excluded from our analysis. We then retrieved example sentences associated with these words from the datasets, with an average of 58.37 annotated sentences per emotion in GoEmotions and 32.17 in SemEval.

4.2 Emotional Connotations Distinction

This section investigates the effectiveness of various contextualized representations in identifying varied emotional connotations evoked by a single word in different contexts. To ensure the robustness of our experiments, we conducted five clustering trials with different random seeds and selected the result with the highest likelihood.

Figure 1 presents a comparative analysis of macro-average match rates across all words for individual layers within four representation models on the development set, using the GoEmotions and SemEval datasets. This empirical evidence reveals

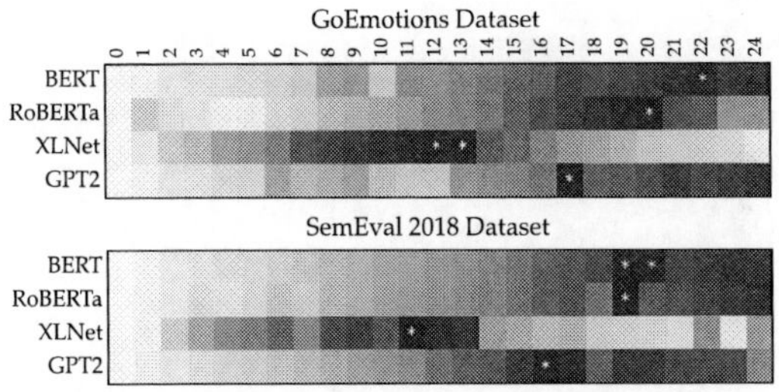

Figure 1: Layer-wise comparison of macro-average match rates across models on the development set for GoEmotions and SemEval datasets. Blue shading highlights the best-performing layers, marked with ⋆.

Model	GoEmotions		SemEval 2018	
	Dev	Test	Dev	Test
BERT	0.694 (22)	0.689 (22)	0.631 (20)	0.623 (20)
RoBERTa	**0.718** (20)	**0.707** (20)	**0.665** (19)	**0.656** (19)
XLNet	0.662 (13)	0.639 (13)	0.643 (11)	0.631 (11)
GPT-2	0.618 (17)	0.598 (17)	0.595 (16)	0.587 (16)

Table 2: Macro-average match rates of the highest-scoring development layers (in brackets) and their corresponding test set scores across models. Bold values represent the top scores for each datasets.

significant variation in layer effectiveness across different models, indicating that selecting an optimal layer is model-specific. The final layer (Layer 24), typically associated with encoding semantic knowledge, consistently underperforms across all models. A hierarchical performance pattern is observed in BERT and RoBERTa models, with higher match rates in the upper layers. In contrast, the XLNet and GPT-2 models perform best in layers closer to the middle rather than in the final layer.

Table 2 presents the macro-average match rates of the top-performing layers during development and their corresponding scores on the test set. Given the diverse contextualization approaches, objectives, and pre-training strategies of the models in question, significant variations were noted in their ability to discern the emotional nuances conveyed by the same words across different contexts. RoBERTa emerged as the leading model in terms of scores on both datasets, underscoring its superior ability to differentiate emotional connotations of words and position them into distinct embedding space regions. Following RoBERTa, XLNet and BERT—both employing bidirectional architectures—demonstrated strong performance. Conversely, GPT-2, which operates on a unidirectional autoregressive language model framework, recorded the lowest scores on both datasets.

4.3 Bias Analysis

This section investigates the presence of biases toward specific emotional connotations of a word in contextualized representations, aiming to enhance our understanding of their behavior in distinguishing different emotions of the same word.

We aim to measure $Bias(w, j)$, related to the j-th emotion ($emotion_j$), for a word w that evokes multiple emotions (n). This involves assessing c_{ij}, the count of instances where the correct label is $emotion_i$ but is erroneously identified as $emotion_j$ ($i \neq j$). First, we determine the extent of bias from emotion i to emotion j ($bias_{ij}$) by normalizing c_{ij}, dividing it by the total number of instances gold-labeled as $emotion_i$, denoted as $\sum_j c_{ij}$. We then compute the overall bias towards a specific emotion, $Bias(w, j)$, as follows:

$$Bias(w, j) = \frac{1}{n-1} \sum_{i=1, i \neq j}^{n} \left(\frac{c_{ij}}{\sum_j c_{ij}} \right) \quad (3)$$

The value of $Bias(w, j)$ represents the likelihood of models incorrectly identifying a word associated with $emotion_k$ as $emotion_j$ when $k \neq j$ (Loureiro et al., 2021). This value ranges from 0 to 1, where a value close to 1 indicates a stronger bias towards $emotion_j$. We calculate the maximum bias value ($\max(Bias(w, j))$) towards different emotions of a word, with j ranging across the emotions associated with the word ($j \in [1, n]$). Table 3 shows the average of these maximum bias values across all words for the four models. Consistent with the findings in Section 4.2, our analysis indicates RoBERTa is more robust against biases, maintaining a bias value below 0.3 in both datasets.

Table 4 presents the average $Bias(w, j)$ scores from equation 3 for different emotions across all words. This breakdown analysis reveals biases in word representations toward specific emotions, with variations observed across different models. Although models generally exhibit similar behavior, they do not uniformly exhibit identical bias toward the same emotions. For instance, in the GoEmotions dataset, RoBERTa is biased toward *Anger*, whereas XLNet and GPT-2 lean towards *Joy*. Moreover, the models consistently show low biases, below 0.2, towards *Fear* and *Sadness* emotions.

The radar charts in Figure 2 illustrate biases towards different emotions in several representative cases. For instance, the words 'Freak', 'Damn', and

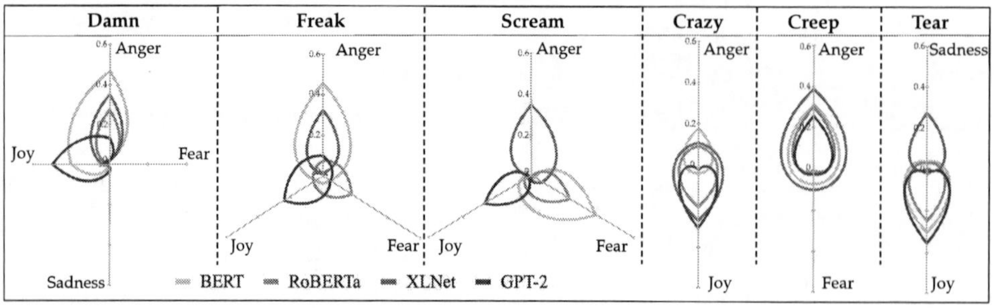

Figure 2: Analysis of bias towards different emotions for a few representative cases.

Dataset	BERT	RoBERTa	XLNet	GPT-2
GoEmotions	0.310	**0.257**	0.331	0.396
SemEval 2018	0.380	**0.286**	0.349	0.422

Table 3: Average bias values across models for the GoEmotions and SemEval datasets.

Model	Anger	Fear	Sadness	Joy
GoEmotions Dataset				
BERT	**0.283**	0.091	0.186	0.251
RoBERTa	**0.267**	0.116	0.103	0.233
XLNet	0.241	0.118	0.191	**0.281**
GPT-2	0.287	0.141	0.149	**0.322**
SemEval 2018 Dataset				
BERT	**0.387**	0.135	0.118	0.285
RoBERTa	**0.297**	0.054	0.152	0.276
XLNet	**0.353**	0.114	0.112	0.275
GPT-2	0.390	0.145	0.148	**0.415**

Table 4: Breakdown analysis of bias values toward various emotions across different models and datasets.

'Creep' exhibit a bias towards *Anger*, and 'Scream' is skewed toward *Fear*, showcasing a preference for the more prevalent emotions of these words. This reflects biases present during the models' pre-training, meaning they encountered the target word with the prevalent emotion more frequently than with other emotions. Thus, they may overlook the word's emotional nuance in varied contexts. For example, these models associated the word 'damn' with more negative emotions due to its frequent co-occurrence with words like 'fuck' and 'shit' during pre-training, potentially missing the word's positive connotations in different contexts. Moreover, different models exhibit varying biases for the same word; for instance, RoBERTa shows a bias toward *Anger* for 'Freak', whereas GPT-2 leans towards *Joy*. Similarly, for the word 'Crazy', BERT, RoBERTa, and GPT-2 tend to misclassify *Anger* as *Joy*, whereas XLNet does the opposite.

4.4 Number of Emotions Estimation

In prior experiments, we analyzed words that evoke diverse emotions and provided the Gaussian Mixture Model with the number of emotions present in sample sentences. The current experiment aims to assess the models' accuracy in estimating the number of emotional connotations of words. By including words that elicit only a single emotion alongside those evoking multiple emotions, we enhance the robustness of our evaluation.

For the implementation of this experiment, we matched the number of additional words to the quantity used in Section 4.2. This approach resulted in parameter tuning with 86 and 66 words in the development set for GoEmotions and SemEval datasets, respectively. For the test set evaluation, we utilized 180 words for the GoEmotions and 160 words for the SemEval dataset.

We utilized an adjusted version of the Bayesian Information Criterion (ABIC) (Schwarz, 1978) as the criterion for model selection to determine the optimal number of clusters, which align with the number of emotions elicited by each word. The ABIC fine-tunes the model for the best fit to the data by considering both model complexity and mitigating overfitting, as specified by the formula:

$$\text{ABIC} = c \cdot p \cdot \ln(N) - 2\ln(\hat{L}) \quad (4)$$

Here, $\hat{L}$ denotes the maximum likelihood of the model, N is the sample size, p is the number of model parameters, and c is a constant to adjust the penalty term, $c \cdot p \cdot \ln(N)$. The penalty term penalizes model complexity based on the number of parameters and discourages excessive increases in the number of clusters. We increment c from 1 in 0.1 steps until the total number of emotions and the estimated number of clusters are as close as possible

Model	GoEmotions			SemEval 2018		
	ρ	Accuracy	RMSE	ρ	Accuracy	RMSE
BERT	0.513	0.572	1.133	0.231	0.503	1.254
RoBERTa	**0.648**	**0.617**	**1.002**	**0.437**	**0.569**	**1.142**
XLNet	0.359	0.521	1.211	0.327	0.519	1.239
GPT-2	0.189	0.465	1.291	0.151	0.434	1.303

Table 5: Comparison of different models in estimating the number of emotions using Spearman's (ρ), accuracy, and Root Mean Square Error (RMSE).

in the development set. For the GoEmotions and SemEval datasets, the optimal c values were identified as 3.6 and 3.2, respectively. In the GMM, each cluster encompasses a mean, a spherical covariance matrix, and a mixture weight. The parameter count for the GMM is given by $p = [N_c \times (D + 2)] - 1$, where N_c is the number of clusters, and D the data dimensionality. The term $(D + 2)$ accounts for the mean and covariance parameters, and subtracting 1 corrects for the constraints, ensuring the sum of parameters equals 1 for mixture weights (Murphy, 2012; Yamada et al., 2021).

Table 5 presents the performance of various models on estimating the number of emotions and clusters in both datasets, using accuracy, Spearman's rank correlation coefficient (ρ), and root mean square error (RMSE) metrics. RMSE quantifies the error magnitude between estimated cluster counts and the actual emotion counts per word. The findings indicate that RoBERTa surpasses other models in accurately estimating the number of emotions for over 60% of the words analyzed. RoBERTa achieved the lowest RMSE and the highest ρ values—0.648 and 0.437 for the GoEmotions and SemEval datasets, respectively—suggesting a strong alignment between the actual number of emotions and model estimates. Figure 3 in the Appendix A further illustrates RoBERTa's performance through confusion matrices, analyzing its emotion count estimates for words with a single emotion and those with context-dependent multiple emotions.

5 Sentence-level Emotion Classification

This section explores the impact of disambiguating the emotional connotation of words that evoke different emotions depending on the context, on the accuracy of sentence-level emotion detection. We evaluate sentences containing at least one identified target word, as those without these words remain unaffected. Sentences are divided into stratified training (80%) and test (20%) splits based on emotions through random sampling.

Our initial experiments involve comparing the original NRC-Affect lexicon and its modified versions in a *before-and-after* manner. Here, *modified lexicon* refers to the disambiguation of emotional connotations associated with target words in the original NRC-Affect lexicon, achieved by utilizing various contextualized word representations. The probability values from the Gaussian Mixture Model indicate the extent to which each instance of a target word belongs to each of the GMM clusters, which have been mapped to specific emotions. We computed the average probability for all instances of a target word within an emotion's cluster to ascertain its disambiguated ratings. For example, while the original lexicon associated 'damn' exclusively with *anger*, with a score of 0.7, the modified lexicon provides a nuanced view of the different emotional connotations—joy, sadness, and fear, in addition to anger—that 'damn' evokes across various contexts in the GoEmotions dataset. Building on the lexicon-based classifier design outlined in (De Bruyne et al., 2022), we utilized the information from both the original NRC-Affect lexicon and its modified versions as features in a logistic regression classifier for emotion prediction, detailed in Appendix B. Table 6 presents the results using F1-macro scores, demonstrating substantial improvements with the modified lexicons compared to the original. This underscores the crucial role of addressing ambiguous emotional words and considering context in determining their emotional connotations for accurate emotion classification.

Method	GoEmotions	SemEval 2018
Original NRC-Affect	0.324	0.361
Modified NRC-Affect using		
├─ BERT	0.377	0.396
├─ RoBERTa	**0.382**	**0.408**
├─ XLNet	0.372	0.406
└─ GPT-2	0.356	0.390

Table 6: The F1-macro scores for sentence-level emotion classification using lexicons.

Method	GoEmotions	SemEval 2018
BERT	0.593	0.532
RoBERTa	*0.621*	*0.561*
XLNet	0.614	0.543
GPT-2	0.461	0.503
RoBERTa + Original NRC-Affect	0.631	0.569
RoBERTa + Modified NRC-Affect (RoBERTa)	**0.636**	**0.573**

Table 7: The F1-macro scores for sentence-level emotion classification using pre-trained models.

In the second series of experiments, we evaluated the ability of pre-trained transformer models—BERT, RoBERTa, XLNet, and GPT-2—to classify emotions in sentences with target words. We applied a uniform set of hyperparameters across all models, adhering to the settings recommended by Demszky et al. (2020): four epochs, a batch size of 16, and a learning rate 5e-5. As expected, the results in Table 7 demonstrate that these models significantly outperformed the lexicon-based approach, which depended solely on lexicon features, with RoBERTa achieving the highest F1-macro scores across both datasets. Building on prior research that indicates incorporating lexicon information into linguistic models further enhances the understanding of emotional nuances in pre-trained models (Baziotis et al., 2018), we integrated features derived from the original and top-performing modified lexicons as auxiliary inputs into the highest-performing pre-trained model. Specifically, we concatenated the auxiliary features with the output vector from the last hidden layer of the pre-trained model, appending them to the sequence embedding since the features aggregate across the entire text. The concatenated vector was then fed into the final decision-making layer, and we adjusted the dimensionality of the final layer to accommodate the additional inputs. Our findings, detailed in the second set of entries in Table 7, revealed that including modified lexicon features, in addition to the models, enhances classification performance beyond what is achieved with original lexicon information. Appendix C further discusses the enhanced ability of RoBERTa, compared to other models in discerning emotions.

Overall performance. Table 8 compares our method, using the modified NRC-Affect lexicon and RoBERTa embeddings, with state-of-the-art approaches across the entire GoEmotions and SemEval datasets, covering sentences both with and without identified target words. We compare our results with various models, such as the TCS model, which uses dual BiLSTM networks for tweet encoding (Meisheri and Dey, 2018); the DATN model, which employs a dual attention mechanism within a transfer learning setup (Yu et al., 2018); the BERT+DK, that integrates domain knowledge into BERT (Ying et al., 2019); the Seq2Emo, which leverages a bi-directional decoder in a sequence-to-emotion framework without relying on external data(Huang et al., 2021); and the UCCA-GAT and Dep-GAT models (Ameer et al., 2023) that integrate semantic and syntactic information into graph attention networks via Universal Conceptual Cognitive Annotation and dependency trees, respectively. Our approach surpasses most competing models, though it falls slightly behind the UCCA-GAT on the SemEval dataset. These findings highlight the efficacy of contextualized representations to disambiguate emotional connotations of words and adapt to varying contexts, thereby enhancing emotion detection at the sentence level.

Method	F1-macro
SemEval 2018 Dataset	
TCS Research (Meisheri and Dey, 2018)	0.530
DATN (Yu et al., 2018)	0.544
BERT-Large + DK (Ying et al., 2019)	0.563
Seq2Emo (Huang et al., 2021)	0.519
UCCA-GAT (Ameer et al., 2023)	**0.600 (1)**
Dep-GAT (Ameer et al., 2023)	**0.578 (3)**
RoBERTa + Modified NRC-Affect (RoBERTa)	**0.583 (2)**
GoEmotions Dataset	
BERT (Demszky et al., 2020)	**0.640 (2)**
UCCA-GAT (Ameer et al., 2023)	**0.639 (3)**
Dep-GAT (Ameer et al., 2023)	0.611
RoBERTa + Modified NRC-Affect (RoBERTa)	**0.653 (1)**

Table 8: Comparison of our method using modified NRC-Affect lexicon and RoBERTa embeddings with state-of-the-art approaches. Rankings (1), (2), and (3) denote the top three results.

6 Conclusion

In this study, we have explored disentangling the emotional connotations of words within diverse sentence contexts, leveraging contextualized word representations. We evaluated these representations' ability to differentiate the diverse emotions of words, identify potential biases in predicting emotional connotations, and accurately estimate the multiplicity of words' emotional connotations. Our methodology involved clustering based on contextualized representations of words that evoke different emotions in various contexts and assessing the alignment between the generated clusters and the words' emotions. Our evaluation of BERT, RoBERTa, XLNet, and GPT-2 models revealed that contextualized representations can effectively disambiguate the emotional connotations of words, with RoBERTa showing superior performance and greater resilience against biases. Further analysis indicated that addressing a small subset of ambiguous emotional words and considering the context in determining their emotional connotations are crucial for accurately determining sentence emotion.

7 Limitations

The empirical results presented in this paper highlighted that many commonly used linguistic models can significantly improve word emotion induction methods. However, our experiments were conducted exclusively on English-language datasets. Consequently, the effectiveness of the proposed method in diverse corpora and multilingual resources remains to be determined. Additionally, we employed the NRC-Affect lexicon as a resource to identify target emotional words that evoke different emotions depending on the context. However, this lexicon may not encompass all emotional words, such as emerging slang terms in social media. The inclusion of a more comprehensive spectrum of emotional words should be a priority in future research. These investigations will be essential for evaluating the applicability of our method across different languages and are expected to advance us toward the goal of automatically constructing high-quality emotional lexical resources with broader linguistic coverage for under-resourced languages or specific domains.

References

Olanrewaju Tahir Aduragba, Jialin Yu, Alexandra I Cristea, and Lei Shi. 2021. Detecting fine-grained emotions on social media during major disease outbreaks: health and well-being before and during the covid-19 pandemic. In *AMIA annual symposium proceedings*, volume 2021, page 187. American Medical Informatics Association.

Hassan Alhuzali and Sophia Ananiadou. 2023. Improving textual emotion recognition based on intra- and inter-class variations. *IEEE Transactions on Affective Computing*, 14(2):1297–1307.

Iqra Ameer, Necva Bölücü, Grigori Sidorov, and Burcu Can. 2023. Emotion classification in texts over graph neural networks: Semantic representation is better than syntactic. *IEEE Access*, 11:56921–56934.

Silvio Amir, Ramon F. Astudillo, Wang Ling, Bruno Martins, Mario J. Silva, and Isabel Trancoso. 2015. INESC-ID: A regression model for large scale Twitter sentiment lexicon induction. In *Proceedings of the 9th International Workshop on Semantic Evaluation (SemEval 2015)*, pages 613–618, Denver, Colorado. Association for Computational Linguistics.

Mario Ezra Aragón, Adrián Pastor López Monroy, Luis Carlos González-Gurrola, and Manuel Montes. 2019. Detecting depression in social media using fine-grained emotions. In *Proceedings of the 2019 conference of the North American chapter of the association for computational linguistics: human language technologies, volume 1 (long and short papers)*, pages 1481–1486.

Erdenebileg Batbaatar, Meijing Li, and Keun Ho Ryu. 2019. Semantic-emotion neural network for emotion recognition from text. *IEEE Access*, 7:111866–111878.

Christos Baziotis, Athanasiou Nikolaos, Alexandra Chronopoulou, Athanasia Kolovou, Georgios Paraskevopoulos, Nikolaos Ellinas, Shrikanth Narayanan, and Alexandros Potamianos. 2018. NTUA-SLP at SemEval-2018 task 1: Predicting affective content in tweets with deep attentive RNNs and transfer learning. In *Proceedings of the 12th International Workshop on Semantic Evaluation*, pages 245–255, New Orleans, Louisiana. Association for Computational Linguistics.

Lisa Beinborn and Yuval Pinter. 2023. Analyzing cognitive plausibility of subword tokenization. In *Proceedings of the 2023 Conference on Empirical Methods in Natural Language Processing*, pages 4478–4486, Singapore. Association for Computational Linguistics.

Nadine Braun, Martijn Goudbeek, and Emiel Krahmer. 2022. Affective words and the company they keep: Studying the accuracy of affective word lists in determining sentence and word valence in a domain-specific corpus. *IEEE Transactions on Affective Computing*, 13(3):1440–1451.

Cesare Campagnano, Simone Conia, and Roberto Navigli. 2022. SRL4E – Semantic Role Labeling for Emotions: A unified evaluation framework. In *Proceedings of the 60th Annual Meeting of the Association for Computational Linguistics (Volume 1: Long Papers)*, pages 4586–4601, Dublin, Ireland. Association for Computational Linguistics.

Chih Yao Chen, Tun Min Hung, Yi-Li Hsu, and Lun-Wei Ku. 2023. Label-aware hyperbolic embeddings for fine-grained emotion classification. In *Proceedings of the 61st Annual Meeting of the Association for Computational Linguistics (Volume 1: Long Papers)*, pages 10947–10958, Toronto, Canada. Association for Computational Linguistics.

Luna De Bruyne, Pepa Atanasova, and Isabelle Augenstein. 2022. Joint emotion label space modeling for affect lexica. *Computer Speech Language*, 71:101257.

Dorottya Demszky, Dana Movshovitz-Attias, Jeongwoo Ko, Alan Cowen, Gaurav Nemade, and Sujith Ravi. 2020. GoEmotions: A dataset of fine-grained emotions. In *Proceedings of the 58th Annual Meeting of the Association for Computational Linguistics*, pages 4040–4054, Online. Association for Computational Linguistics.

Jacob Devlin, Ming-Wei Chang, Kenton Lee, and Kristina Toutanova. 2019. Bert: Pre-training of deep bidirectional transformers for language understanding. In *North American Chapter of the Association for Computational Linguistics*.

Jean-Marc Dewaele. 2010. *Emotions in multiple languages*. Springer.

Shuai Fan, Chen Lin, Haonan Li, Zhenghao Lin, Jinsong Su, Hang Zhang, Yeyun Gong, JIan Guo, and Nan Duan. 2022. Sentiment-aware word and sentence level pre-training for sentiment analysis. In *Proceedings of the 2022 Conference on Empirical Methods in Natural Language Processing*, pages 4984–4994, Abu Dhabi, United Arab Emirates. Association for Computational Linguistics.

Sujatha Das Gollapalli, Polina Rozenshtein, and See-Kiong Ng. 2020. ESTeR: Combining word co-occurrences and word associations for unsupervised emotion detection. In *Findings of the Association for Computational Linguistics: EMNLP 2020*, pages 1043–1056, Online. Association for Computational Linguistics.

Christian Hadiwinoto, Hwee Tou Ng, and Wee Chung Gan. 2019. Improved word sense disambiguation using pre-trained contextualized word representations. In *Proceedings of the 2019 Conference on Empirical Methods in Natural Language Processing and the 9th International Joint Conference on Natural Language Processing (EMNLP-IJCNLP)*, pages 5297–5306, Hong Kong, China. Association for Computational Linguistics.

William L. Hamilton, Kevin Clark, Jure Leskovec, and Dan Jurafsky. 2016. Inducing domain-specific sentiment lexicons from unlabeled corpora. In *Proceedings of the 2016 Conference on Empirical Methods in Natural Language Processing*, pages 595–605, Austin, Texas. Association for Computational Linguistics.

Johannes Hellrich, Sven Buechel, and Udo Hahn. 2019. Modeling word emotion in historical language: Quantity beats supposed stability in seed word selection. In *Proceedings of the 3rd Joint SIGHUM Workshop on Computational Linguistics for Cultural Heritage, Social Sciences, Humanities and Literature*, pages 1–11, Minneapolis, USA. Association for Computational Linguistics.

Jan Hofmann, Enrica Troiano, Kai Sassenberg, and Roman Klinger. 2020. Appraisal theories for emotion classification in text. In *Proceedings of the 28th International Conference on Computational Linguistics*, pages 125–138, Barcelona, Spain (Online). International Committee on Computational Linguistics.

Akram Sadat Hosseini. 2017. Sentence-level emotion mining based on combination of adaptive meta-level features and sentence syntactic features. *Engineering Applications of Artificial Intelligence*, 65:361–374.

Akram Sadat Hosseini and Steffen Staab. 2023. Emotional framing in the spreading of false and true claims. In *Proceedings of the 15th ACM Web Science Conference 2023*, WebSci '23, page 96–106, New York, NY, USA. Association for Computing Machinery.

Chenyang Huang, Amine Trabelsi, Xuebin Qin, Nawshad Farruque, Lili Mou, and Osmar Zaïane. 2021. Seq2Emo: A sequence to multi-label emotion classification model. In *Proceedings of the 2021 Conference of the North American Chapter of the Association for Computational Linguistics: Human Language Technologies*, pages 4717–4724, Online. Association for Computational Linguistics.

C. Hutto and Eric Gilbert. 2014. Vader: A parsimonious rule-based model for sentiment analysis of social media text. *Proceedings of the International AAAI Conference on Web and Social Media*, 8(1):216–225.

Nora Kassner and Hinrich Schütze. 2020. Negated and misprimed probes for pretrained language models: Birds can talk, but cannot fly. In *Proceedings of the 58th Annual Meeting of the Association for Computational Linguistics*, pages 7811–7818, Online. Association for Computational Linguistics.

Pei Ke, Haozhe Ji, Siyang Liu, Xiaoyan Zhu, and Minlie Huang. 2020. SentiLARE: Sentiment-aware language representation learning with linguistic knowledge. In *Proceedings of the 2020 Conference on Empirical Methods in Natural Language Processing (EMNLP)*, pages 6975–6988, Online. Association for Computational Linguistics.

Harold W Kuhn. 1955. The hungarian method for the assignment problem. *Naval research logistics quarterly*, 2(1-2):83–97.

Zhengyan Li, Yicheng Zou, Chong Zhang, Qi Zhang, and Zhongyu Wei. 2021. Learning implicit sentiment in aspect-based sentiment analysis with supervised contrastive pre-training. In *Proceedings of the 2021 Conference on Empirical Methods in Natural Language Processing*, pages 246–256, Online and Punta Cana, Dominican Republic. Association for Computational Linguistics.

Bing Liu. 2022. *Sentiment analysis and opinion mining*. Springer Nature.

Yinhan Liu, Myle Ott, Naman Goyal, Jingfei Du, Mandar Joshi, Danqi Chen, Omer Levy, Mike Lewis, Luke Zettlemoyer, and Veselin Stoyanov. 2019. Roberta: A robustly optimized bert pretraining approach. *arXiv preprint arXiv:1907.11692*.

Daniel Loureiro, Kiamehr Rezaee, Mohammad Taher Pilehvar, and José Camacho-Collados. 2021. Analysis and evaluation of language models for word sense disambiguation. *Computational Linguistics*, 47:387–443.

Yukun Ma, Haiyun Peng, and Erik Cambria. 2018. Targeted aspect-based sentiment analysis via embedding commonsense knowledge into an attentive lstm. *Proceedings of the AAAI Conference on Artificial Intelligence*, 32(1).

Rui Mao, Qian Liu, Kai He, Wei Li, and Erik Cambria. 2023. The biases of pre-trained language models: An empirical study on prompt-based sentiment analysis and emotion detection. *IEEE Transactions on Affective Computing*, 14(3):1743–1753.

Hardik Meisheri and Lipika Dey. 2018. Tcs research at semeval-2018 task 1: Learning robust representations using multi-attention architecture. In *Proceedings of The 12th International Workshop on Semantic Evaluation*, pages 291–299.

Volodymyr Melnykov and Ranjan Maitra. 2010. Finite mixture models and model-based clustering.

Saif Mohammad, Felipe Bravo-Marquez, Mohammad Salameh, and Svetlana Kiritchenko. 2018. SemEval-2018 task 1: Affect in tweets. In *Proceedings of the 12th International Workshop on Semantic Evaluation*, pages 1–17, New Orleans, Louisiana. Association for Computational Linguistics.

Saif Mohammad and Svetlana Kiritchenko. 2018. Understanding emotions: A dataset of tweets to study interactions between affect categories. In *Proceedings of the Eleventh International Conference on Language Resources and Evaluation (LREC 2018)*, Miyazaki, Japan. European Language Resources Association (ELRA).

Kevin P Murphy. 2012. *Machine learning: a probabilistic perspective*. MIT press.

Emily Öhman, Marc Pàmies, Kaisla Kajava, and Jörg Tiedemann. 2020. XED: A multilingual dataset for sentiment analysis and emotion detection. In *Proceedings of the 28th International Conference on Computational Linguistics*, pages 6542–6552, Barcelona, Spain (Online). International Committee on Computational Linguistics.

Alec Radford, Jeffrey Wu, Rewon Child, David Luan, Dario Amodei, Ilya Sutskever, et al. 2019. Language models are unsupervised multitask learners. *OpenAI blog*, 1(8):9.

Shahab Raji and Gerard de Melo. 2021. Guilt by association: Emotion intensities in lexical representations. In *Proceedings of the 2021 Conference on Empirical Methods in Natural Language Processing*, pages 9911–9917, Online and Punta Cana, Dominican Republic. Association for Computational Linguistics.

Johan Reitan, Jørgen Faret, Björn Gambäck, and Lars Bungum. 2015. Negation scope detection for Twitter sentiment analysis. In *Proceedings of the 6th Workshop on Computational Approaches to Subjectivity, Sentiment and Social Media Analysis*, pages 99–108, Lisboa, Portugal. Association for Computational Linguistics.

Elvis Saravia, Hsien-Chi Toby Liu, Yen-Hao Huang, Junlin Wu, and Yi-Shin Chen. 2018. CARER: Contextualized affect representations for emotion recognition. In *Proceedings of the 2018 Conference on Empirical Methods in Natural Language Processing*, pages 3687–3697, Brussels, Belgium. Association for Computational Linguistics.

Gideon Schwarz. 1978. Estimating the dimension of a model. *The Annals of Statistics*, 6(2):461–464.

João Sedoc, Daniel Preoţiuc-Pietro, and Lyle Ungar. 2017. Predicting emotional word ratings using distributional representations and signed clustering. In *Proceedings of the 15th Conference of the European Chapter of the Association for Computational Linguistics: Volume 2, Short Papers*, pages 564–571, Valencia, Spain.

Alfonso Semeraro, Salvatore Vilella, Saif Mohammad, Giancarlo Ruffo, and Massimo Stella. 2023. Emoatlas: An emotional profiling tool merging psychological lexicons, artificial intelligence and network science.

Sapan Shah, Sreedhar Reddy, and Pushpak Bhattacharyya. 2023. Retrofitting light-weight language models for emotions using supervised contrastive learning. In *Proceedings of the 2023 Conference on Empirical Methods in Natural Language Processing*, pages 3640–3654, Singapore. Association for Computational Linguistics.

Tiberiu Sosea and Cornelia Caragea. 2021. emlm: A new pre-training objective for emotion related tasks. In *Annual Meeting of the Association for Computational Linguistics*, pages 286–293.

Michael Stubbs. 1995. Collocations and semantic profiles: On the cause of the trouble with quantitative studies. *Functions of Language*, 2(1):23–55.

Shuai Wang, Guangyi Lv, Sahisnu Mazumder, and Bing Liu. 2021. Detecting domain polarity-changes of words in a sentiment lexicon. In *Findings of the Association for Computational Linguistics: ACL-IJCNLP 2021*, pages 3657–3668, Online. Association for Computational Linguistics.

Shuo Wang, Aishan Maoliniyazi, Xinle Wu, and Xiaofeng Meng. 2020. Emo2vec: Learning emotional embeddings via multi-emotion category. *ACM Trans. Internet Technol.*, 20(2).

Xiangyu Wang and Chengqing Zong. 2021. Distributed representations of emotion categories in emotion space. In *Proceedings of the 59th Annual Meeting of the Association for Computational Linguistics and the 11th International Joint Conference on Natural Language Processing (Volume 1: Long Papers)*, pages 2364–2375.

Gregor Wiedemann, Steffen Remus, Avi Chawla, and Chris Biemann. 2019. Does bert make any sense? interpretable word sense disambiguation with contextualized embeddings. *arXiv preprint arXiv:1909.10430*.

Kosuke Yamada, Ryohei Sasano, and Koichi Takeda. 2021. Verb sense clustering using contextualized word representations for semantic frame induction.

In *Findings of the Association for Computational Linguistics: ACL-IJCNLP 2021*, pages 4353–4362, Online. Association for Computational Linguistics.

Zhilin Yang, Zihang Dai, Yiming Yang, Jaime Carbonell, Russ R Salakhutdinov, and Quoc V Le. 2019. Xlnet: Generalized autoregressive pretraining for language understanding. In *Advances in Neural Information Processing Systems*, volume 32. Curran Associates, Inc.

Wenhao Ying, Rong Xiang, and Qin Lu. 2019. Improving multi-label emotion classification by integrating both general and domain-specific knowledge. In *Proceedings of the 5th Workshop on Noisy User-generated Text (W-NUT 2019)*, pages 316–321, Hong Kong, China. Association for Computational Linguistics.

Jianfei Yu, Luís Marujo, Jing Jiang, Pradeep Karuturi, and William Brendel. 2018. Improving multi-label emotion classification via sentiment classification with dual attention transfer network. In *Proceedings of the 2018 Conference on Empirical Methods in Natural Language Processing*, pages 1097–1102, Brussels, Belgium. Association for Computational Linguistics.

Jie Zhou, Junfeng Tian, Rui Wang, Yuanbin Wu, Wenming Xiao, and Liang He. 2020. Sentix: A sentiment-aware pre-trained model for cross-domain sentiment analysis. In *Proceedings of the 28th international conference on computational linguistics*, pages 568–579.

A Appendix

The confusion matrices presented in Figure 3 depict the analysis of how the RoBERTa model estimates the number of emotions for words with single emotions versus those with context-dependent multiple emotions. The model reliably identifies single-emotion words across datasets in most cases. However, it occasionally overestimates the number of emotions, suggesting 2 or 3 clusters. For words that elicit 2 or 3 emotions, the model provides reasonably accurate estimates but often underestimates the actual count, indicating a lower number of emotions. As the number of emotions increases to 4, the reliability of the model's estimations decreases, leading to a wider range of possibilities.

B Appendix

We provide more details on the features utilized in the design of the lexicon-based classifier outlined in (De Bruyne et al., 2022). We employed statistical features of emotional words and a logistic regression classifier in the learning model for emotion prediction experiments. We trained

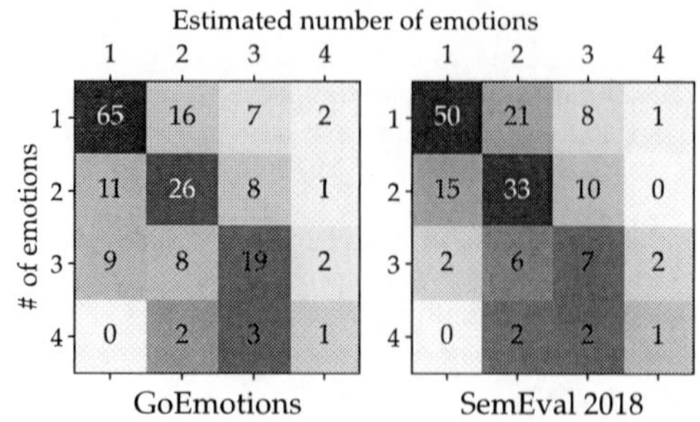

Figure 3: Confusion matrices for estimating the number of emotions using the RoBERTa model.

the classifier with the statistical features derived from both the original NRC-Affect lexicon and its modified versions. Given a sequence of words $s = (w_1, \ldots, w_k)$, statistical features quantify the proportion of a given emotion e_i within the sentence s as $P(s, e_i)$, calculated by:

$$P(s, e_i) = \frac{1}{k} \sum_{j=1}^{k} \phi_{e_i}(w_j) \quad (5)$$

where $\phi_{e_i}(w_j)$ represents the emotion score of the word w_j for the emotion e_i, derived from the lexicons. Here, e_i belongs to the set $\{e_{\text{anger}}, e_{\text{fear}}, e_{\text{sadness}}, e_{\text{joy}}\}$.

The logistic regression classifier uses a liblinear solver with L2 regularization and a regularization strength of $C = 1.0$. The choice of L2 regularization helps prevent model overfitting by penalizing the size of the coefficients, with $C = 1.0$ providing an optimal balance between regularization intensity and model complexity based on either empirical evidence. We deploy separate binary classifiers for each of the categories and aggregate the predictions afterward by selecting the highest probability, thereby identifying the most dominant emotion in the sentence.

C Appendix

This appendix provides a detailed discussion on the superior performance of RoBERTa over other models—BERT, XLNet, and GPT-2—on the task of disambiguating emotional connotations. Notably, all models in our experiments were trained under identical conditions, using the same hyperparameters such as batch size, learning rate, and dataset sizes. This uniform setup ensures that any observed performance differences are due to architectural or training method variations. RoBERTa, the most

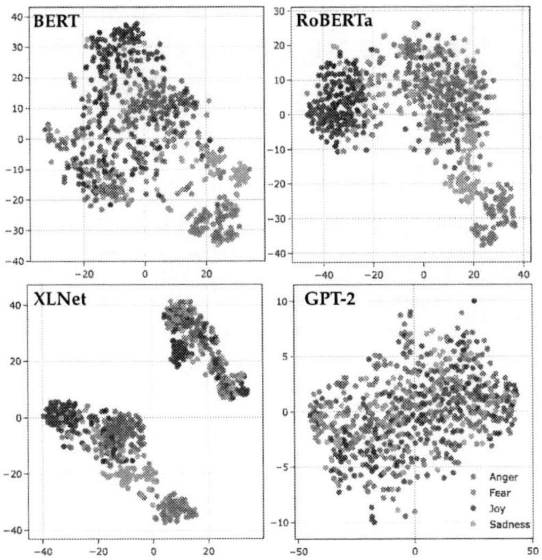

Figure 4: The t-SNE projection of BERT, RoBERTa, XLNet, and GPT-2 representations of the word *damn* in sentences expressing various emotions in GoEmotions dataset.

advanced transformer among the considered models, possesses the highest number of parameters (355M) as detailed in Table 1. Its dynamic masking technique, which alters mask patterns with each data pass, provides a training advantage over the static masking used by BERT. Additionally, the tokenization approach of models significantly impacts their performance. In our evaluation, tokenization was consistent with the method used during pre-training. RoBERTa employs Byte-Pair Encoding (BPE), which effectively captures frequent subword units compared to BERT's WordPiece or XLNet's SentencePiece. BPE constructs its vocabulary by merging frequently occurring character pairs or combinations, thus improving the capture of rare or out-of-vocabulary words (Beinborn and Pinter, 2023).

Additionally, empirical evidence from the layer-wise comparison of macro-average match rates in Section 4.2 revealed that the ability to capture emotional connotations varies significantly across layers of selected models, indicating that optimal layer selection is model-specific. RoBERTa consistently excelled in identifying the varying emotional connotations of words, particularly in its upper layers, which are typically associated with semantic knowledge encoding. Figure 4 showcases t-SNE projections of contextualized representations from the most effective layer of each model, using the word 'damn' in various sentences sourced from the GoEmotions dataset. These visualizations highlight the distinctive distribution of RoBERTa's representations, further emphasizing its ability to capture emotion evoked by 'damn' in each example.

Length-Aware Multi-Kernel Transformer for Long Document Classification

Guangzeng Han[†] **Jack Tsao**[‡] **Xiaolei Huang**[†*]
[†] Department of Computer Science, University of Memphis, United States
[‡] Department of Neurology, Langone School of Medicine, New York University, United States
ghan@memphis.edu, jack.tsao@nyulangone.org, xiaolei.huang@memphis.edu

Abstract

Lengthy documents pose a unique challenge to neural language models due to substantial memory consumption. While existing state-of-the-art (SOTA) models segment long texts into equal-length snippets (e.g., 128 tokens per snippet) or deploy sparse attention networks, these methods have new challenges of context fragmentation and generalizability due to sentence boundaries and varying text lengths. For example, our empirical analysis has shown that SOTA models consistently overfit one set of lengthy documents (e.g., 2000 tokens) while performing worse on texts with other lengths (e.g., 1000 or 4000). In this study, we propose a **L**ength-**A**ware **M**ulti-**K**ernel **T**ransformer (*LAMKIT*) to address the new challenges for the long document classification. LAMKIT encodes lengthy documents by diverse transformer-based kernels for bridging context boundaries and vectorizes text length by the kernels to promote model robustness over varying document lengths. Experiments on five standard benchmarks from health and law domains show LAMKIT outperforms SOTA models up to an absolute 10.9% improvement. We conduct extensive ablation analyses to examine model robustness and effectiveness over varying document lengths. [1]

1 Introduction

Lengthy documents widely exist in many fields, while the input limit of transformer models prevents developing powerful pre-trained language models on those long documents, such as BERT (Devlin et al., 2019) and RoBERTa (Liu et al., 2019). For example, a recent study shows that clinical documents have grown over 60% longer in a decade (Rule et al., 2021). Truncation is a common strategy to handle long documents and fit the input limit of BERT-based classifiers, however, the method may lose many critical contexts beyond the first 512 tokens and hurdle model effectiveness. Auto-regressive large language models (LLMs), such as ChatGPT (OpenAI, 2022) show their great ability at processing long documents, however the training object of these LLMs is to prediction the next token, which is inconsistent with the text classification task. In other words, supervised fine-tuning on these domain specific data may not improve the performance of LLMs on these classification task. Therefore, researchers focus on prompting methods (Wei et al., 2022; Chen et al., 2023a; Song et al., 2023; Sun et al., 2024; Zhang et al., 2024) or decoding strategies (Wang et al., 2023) rather than fine-tuning (Xiong et al., 2024) to help the LLMs categorize text better. This reality makes LLMs limited in this scenario. Compare with these methods, developing discriminative transformer models that can model long documents is a more direct and effective solution to handle the long document classification task.

Among existing transformer-based models, long document modeling has two major directions, hierarchical transformer and sparse attention (Dong et al., 2023; Qin et al., 2023). The hierarchical approach (Wu et al., 2021; Chalkidis et al., 2022; Dai et al., 2022; Li et al., 2023a; Chalkidis et al., 2023) splits document into small text chunks (e.g., 128 tokens) so that long document models can take shorter input per step. As the self-attention in transformer-style models causes quadratic complexity $O(n^2)$, the sparse attention aims to lower the complexity to linear and reduce context fragmentation caused by the segments (Beltagy et al., 2020; Zaheer et al., 2020; Guo et al., 2022; Zhang et al., 2023). For example, sparse attention in Longformer (Beltagy et al., 2020) lifts up the input limit from 512 tokens to 4096 tokens. Popular evaluation benchmarks also switch from social media data (e.g., IMDb and Amazon reviews (Wu

* Corresponding author

[1] Code available at https://github.com/trust-nlp/LAMKIT

*Proceedings of the 13th Joint Conference on Lexical and Computational Semantics (*SEM 2024)*, pages 278 - 290
June 20-21, 2024

Dataset	Length-Quantile			L-mean	Size	|Label|	Splits		
	25%	50%	75%				Train	Valid	Test
Diabetes	408	608	945	720	1,265	10	885	190	190
MIMIC	1,432	2,022	2,741	2,200	11,368	50	8,066	1,753	1,729
ECtHR A/B	668	1,328	2,627	2,139	11,000	11	9,000	1,000	1,000
SCOTUS	3,723	7,673	12,275	9,840	7,800	14	5,000	1,400	1,400

Table 1: Statistics of average token count per document (L-mean), data size (Size), and unique labels (|Label|).

et al., 2021)) to more complex data in health and legal domains (Qin et al., 2023; Chalkidis et al., 2022). For example, the median document length of IMDb is only 225 tokens (Li et al., 2023a), which is much smaller than the lengths in Table 1. Indeed, document lengths vary across datasets, and model performance can vary across length-varied corpora (Li et al., 2023a). However, very few studies have examined if long document models can handle varying-length texts, ranging from short to extremely long. A common question is: *will a long document model be capable to maintain robust performance across varying-length data?* Our analysis on SOTA baselines in Figure 1 says "No."

To understand the length effects and encounter the long document challenges, we conduct extensive analysis and propose **L**ength-**A**ware **M**ulti-**K**ernel **T**ransformer (*LAMKIT*) for robust long document classification. LAMKIT diversifies learning processes by a multi-kernel encoding (MK) so that the model can capture contexts from different perspectives. The MK contains multiple neural encoders with diverse kernel sizes and can relieve context fragmentation caused by a unique segment encoder on short text chunks. LAMKIT promotes model robustness over varying-length documents by a length-aware vectorization (LaV) module. The LaV encodes length information in a hierarchical way, position embedding on segment and length vectors on document level. We compare LAMKIT with 8 domain-specific models on five datasets (MIMIC-III (Johnson et al., 2016), SCOTUS (Chalkidis et al., 2022), ECtHR-A (Chalkidis et al., 2019) and ECtHR-B (Chalkidis et al., 2021), Diabetes (Stubbs et al., 2019)) from health and legal domains evaluated by F1 and AUC metrics. Additionally, we also conduct a case study on the performance of ChatGPT in these tasks. Classification results demonstrate that our LAMKIT approach's outperforms competitive baselines by an absolute improvement of up to 10.9%. We conduct further experiments on the length-varying effects and ablation analysis to examine the effectiveness of our individual modules.

2 Data

We have retrieved five publicly available dataset, Diabetes (Stubbs et al., 2019), MIMIC-III (Johnson et al., 2016), ECtHR-A (Chalkidis et al., 2019), ECtHR-B (Chalkidis et al., 2021)and SCOTUS (Chalkidis et al., 2022), which are popular benchmarks for the long document classification. We obtained *Diabetes* (Stubbs et al., 2019) from the 2018 National NLP Clinical Challenges (n2c2) shared task with a collection of longitudinal patient records and 13 selection criteria annotations. We exclude 3 annotations due to less than 0.5 inter-rater agreements and discard documents with fewer than 40 tokens. *MIMIC-III* (Medical Information Mart for Intensive Care) (Johnson et al., 2016) is a relational database that contains patients admitted to the Intensive Care Unit (ICU) at the Beth Israel Deaconess Medical Center from 2001 to 2012. We follow previous work (Mullenbach et al., 2018; Vu et al., 2021) to select discharge summaries and use the top 50 frequent labels of International Classification of Disease codes (9th Edition, ICD-9), which are types of procedures and diagnoses during patient stay in the ICU. *ECtHR-A* collects facts and articles from law case descriptions from the European Court of Human Rights' public database (Chalkidis et al., 2019). Each case is mapped to the articles it was found to have violated in the ECHR, while in *ECtHR-B* (Chalkidis et al., 2021), cases are mapped to a set of allegedly violated articles. *SCOTUS* is a data collection of US Supreme Court (the highest US federal court) opinions and the US Supreme Court Database (SCDB) (Spaeth et al., 2020) with cases from 1946 to 2020. SCOTUS has 14 issue areas, such as Criminal Procedure, Civil Rights, and Economic Activity. We summarize data statistics and splits in Table 1.

Table 1 shows each data has a varying length

range, a critical yet under-explored question is: does the varying length effect model performance or will models be generalizable across all lengths? For example, the document length in Table 1 is either less than a few hundred or over ten thousand tokens surpassing input limitations of regular transformer-style models (e.g., BERT), and there are significant length variations across the data. While studies (Dong et al., 2023) have achieved improving performance overall to encode more contexts beyond the 512 token limit, there is very few work examining the effects of varying document lengths over model robustness. To answer the question, we conduct an exploratory analysis of existing state-of-the-art (SOTA) models and evaluate their performance.

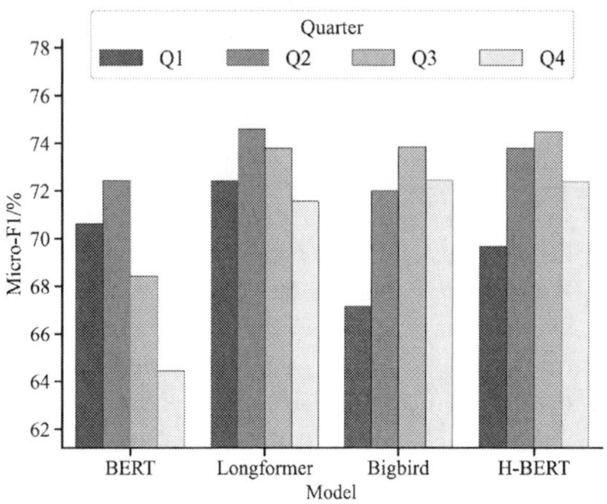

Figure 1: Average performance on quarter splits for four state-of-the-art baselines. The length boundaries of quarters are shown in Table 1. Detailed performance scores are presented in Table 3

Our exploratory analysis follows existing studies (Mullenbach et al., 2018; Dai et al., 2022; Chalkidis et al., 2022; Qin et al., 2023) to split data, includes three state-of-the-art transformer classifiers (BigBird, Longformer, and Hierarchical BERT (H-BERT)) for long document and a BERT classifier, and evaluates models performance by F1-micro (F1-μ) score. We refer to the details of experimental settings and SOTA baselines under the Experiments section. For each quarter, we maintain similar data sizes and run the classifier multiple times to take average performance scores. Finally, we visualize the relation between model performance and document lengths in Figure 1.

Figure 1 shows that model performance varies across document lengths, posing a unique challenge to build robust models on varying lengthy data. For example, while the SOTA classifiers achieve better scores on mid-lengthy texts, the performance drops significantly in either short (e.g., 400 tokens) or super long (e.g., 10K tokens) documents. The consistent observations can suggest that: 1) varying length can be a critical factor to make models perform better; 2) length-based splits are important to understand the capacity of classifiers on long documents. The findings inspire us to propose the **L**ength-**A**ware **M**ulti-**K**ernel **T**ransformer (*LAMKIT*) to encounter the length factor.

2.1 Ethic and Privacy Concern

All data used in this research is publicly accessible and has been stripped of identifying information. Our investigation is centered on computational techniques, and we do not gather data directly from individuals. Our institution's review board has confirmed that this research does not mandate an IRB approval.

3 Length-Aware Multi-Kernel Transformer

This section presents our Length-Aware Multi-Kernel Transformer (*LAMKIT*) for robust long document classification in Figure 2. LAMKIT consists of three major modules, 1) multi-kernel encoding, 2) length-aware vectorization, and 3) hierarchical integration, aiming to solve context fragmentation and augment model robustness on lengthy documents. We deploy different encoding kernels to diversify text segments with various contexts. Incorporating length as vectors can adapt classifiers across varying-length documents. Finally, we elaborate on how to learn robust document representations via a hierarchical integration.

3.1 Multi-kernel Encoding

Multi-kernel Encoding (MK) aims to diversify context to segment and encode documents from multiple perspectives. The mechanism is to solve the challenge of existing long document modeling methods (Beltagy et al., 2020; Wu et al., 2021; Dai et al., 2022; Dong et al., 2023) — splitting and vectorizing each document by a fixed size, which has been analyzed in our previous data section. Our MK mechanism gets inspirations from TextCNN (Kim, 2014), which uses kernels of different sizes to convolve text representations. In contrast, our MK mechanism encodes each document into various sizes of text segments to obtain

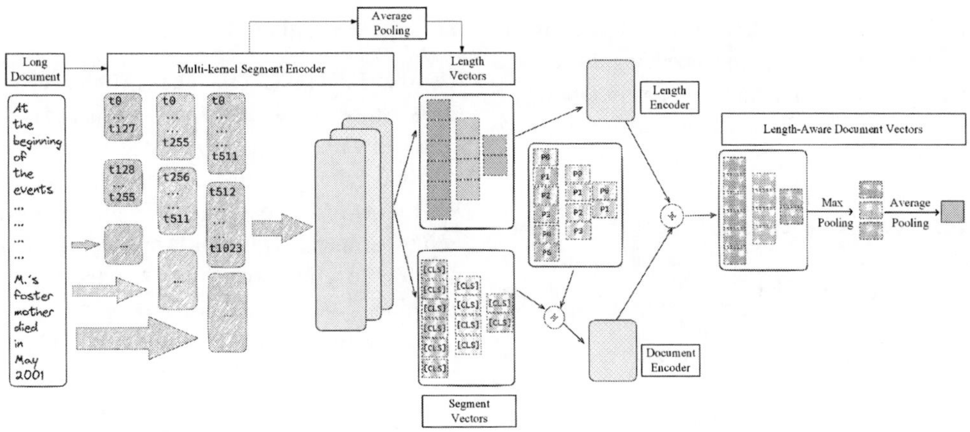

Figure 2: LAMKIT diagram overview. Our approach consists of three main components: multi-kernel encoding, length-aware vectorization, and hierarchical integration. We denote one color of segments and vectors per kernel. The arrows indicate model workflows, $\bigoplus$ is a sum operation.

various feature representations. By learning diverse document features with varying-size text chunks, we can enrich representations of lengthy documents with various sizes.

Specifically, we empirically choose a set of kernel sizes (e.g. $m = \{128, 256, 512\}$ for the MIMIC dataset) to split and vectorize the long documents. Following the CNN, we tried the stride ranging between $(2/3 * m, m)$, but we did not get significant improvements. Therefore the stride of all kernels is set to its kernel size such that two adjacent segments do not overlap. In the later section, our ablation analysis shows that the major performance drops come from the number of kernels. We infer the performance of kernel and stride sizes as encoding contexts with different kernels is more critical to augment classifiers on lengthy documents. For each chunk size of text, we deploy a pre-trained RoBERTa model (Liu et al., 2019) so that our MK has enriched representations for the varied text chunks. While our MK mechanism allows other Transformer variants, we choose the RoBERTa to keep consistent with existing SOTA approaches (Chalkidis et al., 2022; Li et al., 2023c; Dong et al., 2023) for fair comparisons. We take the embedding of the "[CLS]" token from each text chunk to represent its segment vector and feed to the following operation, combining with the segment position embedding of length-aware vectorization.

3.2 Length-aware Vectorization

We propose the Length-aware Vectorization (*LaV*) to incorporate lengthy contexts and augment model generalizability, as our Figure 1 presents that the model performance varies across document lengths. LaV achieves the grand goal by two levels: text chunk and document. On the text chunk level, we encode length information by the segment position embedding, and on the document level, we vectorize text length with MK outputs.

Segment Position Embedding vectorizes positions of text chunks into a learnable embedding by a Transformer encoder in Equation 1, where $|d|$ refers to the embedding size, i is the column index of a vector scalar, and *pos* is the index of the text chunk. For example, if we segment a 1024-token document into 15 chunks (with a stride) by the 128 kernel encoder, the total will be the 15 and the second chunk's index (pos) will be 2. Similarly, we can obtain segment position embeddings for other multi-kernel encoders and equip the segment vectors from the MK step with the length information, segment position. Finally, we sum the segment position embeddings up with the segment vectors and feed them to the document encoder.

$$PE_{(pos,i)} = \begin{cases} \sin\left(\frac{pos}{10000^{2i/|d|}}\right), & \text{if } i \text{ is even} \\ \cos\left(\frac{pos}{10000^{2i/|d|}}\right), & \text{if } i \text{ is odd} \end{cases} \quad (1)$$

Note that, our position embedding **differs** from previous studies. For example, majority of long document classifiers (Wu et al., 2021; Li et al., 2023b; Zhang et al., 2023) deploy position embeddings for tokens rather than the segment. There is one close study (Dai et al., 2022) that utilizes segment position embedding in classification models. In contrast, our position embedding diversifies segment positions from multiple kernels, aiming to incorporate text lengths and augment model generalizability over varying text lengths.

Length Vectors encode document length information into feature vectors. Instead of directly encoding a length scalar into a vector, we obtain the length vectors by applying averaging pooling over each MK encoder's outputs and vectorizing the chunk sizes per document by the position embedding. The length vectors not only encode document lengths by chunk sizes but also implicitly incorporate lengthy contexts from the MK encoders. Finally, we feed the length vectors into the length encoder to obtain learnable length-aware vectors, which will be integrated with the document encoder's outputs.

3.3 Hierarchical Integration

We obtain length-aware document representations through the hierarchical integration process from segment and length vectors. The integration process starts with a document encoder to encode segment vectors and a length encoder to encode length vectors. Both modules are Transformer (Vaswani et al., 2017) encoders but serve different purposes — while both encoders take length-related vectors, the document encoder focuses on learning diversified contexts from the MK encoders and the length encoder focuses on incorporating varying length features. We then combine the two encoders' outputs by a sum operation and feed the integration to a hierarchical pooling process to obtain length-aware document vectors.

Hierarchical pooling operations has two major processes in order, max pooling and average pooling. The max pooling aims to squeeze length-aware multidimensional representations of text chunks from the length and document encoders. We concatenate the pooling outputs and feed them to the average pooling operation. The average pooling aggregates the length-aware segment features into the length-aware document vectors. Finally we feed the document vectors to linear layer for classification. Our tasks cover both binary and multi-label classifications. We deploy a sigmoid function for binary prediction and a softmax function for the multi-label task.

4 Experiments

We follow the previous studies (Mullenbach et al., 2018; Stubbs et al., 2019; Chalkidis et al., 2022) on lengthy document to preprocess data and split data into training, validation, and test, as in Table 1. We follow SOTA baselines to set up our evaluation experiments. Our results include F1 and AUC metrics, covering both micro (μ) and macro (m) variations.

Our evaluation presents performance comparisons and ablation analysis to understand the length effects and the models better. More details of the hyperparameter settings for the baselines and LAMKIT are in the Appendix A, which allows for experiment replications.

4.1 Baselines

To demonstrate the effectiveness of LAMKIT, we compare it against both hierarchical transformer and sparse attention transformer SOTA baselines for long-document modeling, as well as with regular BERT. Although our LAMKIT has no theoretical length limit, we set the text length to 4096 for all experiments for a fair comparison, except for BERT which is 512.

Our experiments utilize baseline hyperparameters that achieved their best results in the previous studies. For example, we take publicly released models or source codes to train long document classifiers. As our data come from health and legal domains, we choose the pre-trained models on the domain data. For example, we report the performance of Clinical-Longformer (Li et al., 2023c) and Legal-Longformer (Chalkidis et al., 2023) on health and legal data, respectively, instead of the vanilla Longformer (Beltagy et al., 2020).

BERT includes classifiers built on domain-specific pre-trained BERT models. Specifically, we include two types of pre-trained BERT model, *Legal-BERT* (Chalkidis et al., 2020) for the legal data and *RoBERTa-PM-M3* (Lewis et al., 2020) for the clinical data, which achieved the best performance on broad text classification tasks in legal and clinical domains. Due to the input limit, the BERT baselines truncate and only take 512 tokens per entry. We experiment two types of truncation, first and last 512 tokens of each data entry, and name the two types as $BERT_{First}$ and $BERT_{Last}$.

Hierarchical BERT (*H-BERT*) splits long document into equal-length segments, hierarchically

Model	Diabetes				MIMIC				ECtHR-A				ECtHR-B				SCOTUS			
	F1-μ	F1-m	AUC-μ	AUC-m	F1-μ	F1-m	AUC-μ	AUC-m	F1-μ	F1-m	AUC-μ	AUC-m	F1-μ	F1-m	AUC-μ	AUC-m	F1-μ	F1-m	AUC-μ	AUC-m
BERT_{First}	<u>72.0</u>	43.2	86.9	72.4	56.8	47.0	87.1	84.0	64.2	52.6	91.6	88.6	73.3	67.6	93.1	91.4	73.9	61.6	<u>95.9</u>	90.0
BERT_{Last}	68.7	39.1	87.2	72.2	51.3	41.5	84.8	81.4	66.1	59.1	93.7	91.3	75.1	65.7	94.5	93.0	66.9	53.1	93.6	87.2
Longformer	71.5	41.2	<u>88.4</u>	71.6	<u>67.2</u>	58.2	92.5	89.8	<u>71.4</u>	59.0	95.4	93.3	<u>79.6</u>	<u>73.1</u>	95.2	94.0	74.3	62.9	95.6	89.9
BigBird	71.9	42.5	**88.5**	**76.4**	65.3	56.8	92.3	89.7	70.2	<u>61.8</u>	93.8	91.8	78.9	70.3	<u>95.5</u>	93.8	72.3	60.6	94.3	89.7
H-BERT	70.4	<u>46.0</u>	83.2	69.7	66.9	<u>60.6</u>	<u>92.6</u>	<u>90.2</u>	70.4	57.7	<u>95.7</u>	<u>93.9</u>	79.2	72.0	95.4	<u>94.4</u>	<u>76.6</u>	**68.0**	95.5	**95.0**
LAMKIT	**73.4**	**49.9**	<u>88.4</u>	<u>74.5</u>	**69.5**	**63.7**	**93.3**	**91.2**	**73.0**	**65.0**	**96.0**	**94.7**	**80.2**	**74.4**	**95.8**	**94.7**	**78.5**	<u>67.8</u>	**97.1**	<u>94.9</u>
$\overline{\Delta}$	↑2.5	↑6.9	↑1.6	↑2.0	↑8.0	↑10.9	↑3.4	↑4.2	↑4.5	↑7.0	↑2.0	↑2.9	↑3.0	↑4.7	↑1.1	↑1.4	↑5.7	↑6.6	↑2.1	↑4.5

Table 2: Overall performance in percentages of F1 and AUC metrics, both micro (μ) and macro (m). We **bolden** the best performance and <u>underline</u> the second best value. $\overline{\Delta}$ denotes the absolute improvement of LAMKIT over the baselines average.

integrate segment features into document vectors, and yield predictions on the document vectors (Dai et al., 2022; Qin et al., 2023; Dong et al., 2023). We follow the existing SOTA studies that achieved the best results using the H-BERT in health (Dai et al., 2022) and legal (Chalkidis et al., 2022) domains. The H-BERT models are close to our hierarchical architecture, while the H-BERT models do not incorporate our proposed multi-kernel mechanism (MK) and length vectors. If LAMKIT achieves better performance, the improvements over the H-BERT can prove the effectiveness of adapting varying-length texts.

Longformer (Beltagy et al., 2020) solves the 512-length limit by replacing self-attention with a local (sliding window) attention and unidirectional global attention and thus can process sequences up to 4096 tokens. We deploy domain-specific Longformer to keep consistent experimental settings. Specifically, we utilize *Clinical-Longformer* (Li et al., 2023c) and *Legal-Longformer* (Chalkidis et al., 2023) to build our document classifiers for the health and legal data, respectively.

BigBird deploys a block sparse attention to relieve the length limit that reduces the Transformer quadratic dependency to linear (Zaheer et al., 2020). BigBird utilizes a fusion of local, global, and random attention, extending the maximum processable sequence length to 4096 tokens. We utilize its domain-specific variants, Clinical-BigBird (Li et al., 2023c) and Legal-Bigbird (Dassi and Kwate, 2021) to conduct experiments.

5 Result Analysis

This section reports the performance of SOTA baselines and LAMKIT in terms of F1 and AUC metrics, both micro (μ) and macro (m) modes. Besides the overall performance, we examine varying-length effects and conduct ablation analysis on our individual modules (e.g., MK and LaV). The results show that LAMKIT not only surpasses the baselines by a large margin on long documents from both health and legal domains but also shows more stable performance on documents of varying lengths.

5.1 Overall Performance

We present the results of long document classification benchmarks in Table 2 that our LAMKIT significantly outperforms the other SOTA baselines. For example, compared to the baselines' average performance, LAMKIT shows an improvement of 4.7% in F1-micro and 7.2% in F1-macro. Long document models do not perform better than regular BERT models on shorter texts. For example, $BERT_{first}$ outperforms most of the SOTA baselines on Diabetes, of which 50% clinical notes are less than 608 tokens. In contrast, we can observe our LAMKIT is robust on both shorter and longer text documents, highlighting the unique contribution and effectiveness of our approach.

Document characteristics of health and legal data can impact baselines performance. For example, we find that H-BERT performs better on the SCOTUS compared to models with sparse attention networks (e.g., Longformer and BigBird), while its performance on other datasets is comparable. We infer this as the SCOTUS dataset has clear segment boundaries that H-BERT can utilize the boundaries as segments, however, other data is compressed and dense, which can cause context fragmentation (Beltagy et al., 2020) and weaken effectiveness of H-BERT. *However*, our LAMKIT demonstrates superior performance on the issue, and we think the MK and length-aware vectors play critical roles, which is shown in our ablation analysis.

5.2 Performance on Varying-length Splits

To assess the model's robustness and generalizability across documents of varying lengths, we follow the approach described in the Data Section, dividing each dataset into quarters based on the lengths of the documents, ensuring similar data sizes in

Model	Diabetes				MIMIC				ECtHR-A				ECtHR-B				SCOTUS			
	Q-1	Q-2	Q-3	Q-4	Q-1	Q-2	Q-3	Q-4	Q-1	Q-2	Q-3	Q-4	Q-1	Q-2	Q-3	Q-4	Q-1	Q-2	Q-3	Q-4
BERT_{First}	65.7	**74.1**	73.4	74.2	57.9	63.0	57.5	52.9	74.9	73.4	62.6	54.4	79.6	77.3	70.7	70.7	**75.0**	74.3	80.9	70.0
BERT_{Last}	63.4	66.9	71.6	71.8	51.6	57.8	50.3	48.4	72.6	73.0	62.5	61.6	77.8	79.5	73.4	73.0	68.8	64.4	69.4	66.0
Longformer	64.6	72.7	72.2	75.8	63.8	71.0	68.1	66.4	79.0	74.0	72.4	65.7	**84.4**	**81.9**	79.4	76.4	69.3	73.4	76.9	74.5
BigBird	61.0	72.1	71.7	**79.9**	62.9	70.2	66.3	62.6	68.8	65.9	73.9	**70.7**	77.8	81.4	80.1	77.0	65.3	70.4	77.2	72.1
H-BERT	61.2	67.6	74.2	77.8	62.1	69.6	66.8	66.5	79.1	**75.3**	69.1	64.1	81.7	80.7	79.4	77.1	64.2	75.8	82.9	76.5
LAMKIT	**66.0**	71.2	**77.0**	78.1	**66.4**	**72.6**	**70.4**	**68.0**	**79.7**	74.6	**74.3**	67.5	79.4	80.8	**80.3**	**80.0**	72.2	**76.4**	**83.0**	**78.5**
$\overline{\Delta}$	↑2.8	↑0.5	↑4.4	↑2.2	↑6.7	↑6.3	↑8.6	↑8.6	↑4.8	↑2.3	↑6.2	↑4.2	↓-0.9	↑0.6	↑3.7	↑5.2	↑3.7	↑4.7	↑5.5	↑6.7

Table 3: F1-micro scores across four quarters following our Figure 1. We **bolden** the best performance and underline the second best value. $\overline{\Delta}$ refers to the absolute improvement of LAMKIT over the average of baselines.

each quarter.

Table 3 presents F1-micro scores across four quarters of each dataset that LAMKIT outperforms baselines on most quarters across the datasets. Surprisingly, SOTA baselines tend to favor and overfit one quarter data with a specific length, which does not exceed their input limit (e.g., 4096 for Longformer). In contrast, our LAMKIT shows more generalizable performance across varying-length documents. The stable performance of our LAMKIT highlights the effectiveness of our multi-kernel and length vectors in adapting classifiers on varying lengths and promoting classification robustness on the health and legal domains.

5.3 Ablation Study

We conduct an ablation analysis to assess the effectiveness of individual LAMKIT modules focusing on the multi-kernel mechanism (MK) and length-aware vectorization (LaV). Table 4 shows the results of our anylysis. *w/o MK* replaces multi-kernel encoders with a single kernel encoder (RoBERTa) and shrinks segment vectors accordingly. *w/o LaV* removes length-related vectors and encoders from LAMKIT. And, *w/o MK and LaV* removes both MK mechanism and length-related encoding.

We can observe that removing one of the modules or removing all modules can significantly reduce model performance. Replacing the MK mechanism can result in a 1.3% and 1.9% drop in F1-micro and F1-macro on average, respectively. The performance drop indicates multi-kernel encoding mechanism can relieve context fragmentation to promote model performance by diversifying document representations. Removing LaV leads to 1.3% and 2.4% drops in F1-micro and F1-macro on average, respectively. The performance drop shows that the length information can be critical to building robust classifiers on the health and legal data.

We can observe the most significant performance drop in LAMKIT after removing both MK and LaV modules, with F1-micro and F1-macro scores decreasing by 2.8% and 3.5%, and AUC-micro and AUC-macro scores by 1.5% and 1.8%, respectively, demonstrating the effectiveness of these modules.

6 Case Study on ChatGPT

Large language models (LLMs) have achieved impressive performance on many generative tasks, such as long text summarization or long text QA. However, long text classification is a natural language understanding task, which makes fine-tuning the large model on such a task not a guaranteed improvement in classification accuracy. Thus the dominant paradigms for text classification in LLMs are zero-shot learning and few-shot learning (Lou et al., 2023). To examine the ability of LLMs on the long document classification task, we utilize representative GPT-3.5-Turbo via *ChatCompletion API*[2] in a zero-shot prompting strategy with multiple templated instructions summarized by (Lou et al., 2023; Chalkidis, 2023; Chen et al., 2023b), and report the best performing template results. Due to privacy concerns and data usage agreement, we do not test ChatGPT (OpenAI, 2022) on MIMIC and Diabetes. The results in Table 5 suggest that compared to our LAMKIT and also the chosen baseline models, ChatGPT still underperforms on long text classification tasks. For the prompt template, we refer more details in the Appendix Figure 3.

7 Related Work

7.1 Transformers for Text Classification

Pretrained language models (PLMs) based on vanilla self-attention, such as BERT (Devlin et al., 2019) and its variants (Nerella et al., 2023; He et al., 2021; Zhou et al., 2022; Ma et al., 2021; Alsentzer et al., 2019; Jin and Wang, 2023), have achieved state-of-the-art (SOTA) results in regular text classification tasks. However, with their input typically

[2] https://platform.openai.com/docs/guides/gpt/chat-completions-api

Model	Diabetes				MIMIC				ECtHR-A				ECtHR-B				SCOTUS			
	F1-μ	F1-m	AUC-μ	AUC-m	F1-μ	F1-m	AUC-μ	AUC-m	F1-μ	F1-m	AUC-μ	AUC-m	F1-μ	F1-m	AUC-μ	AUC-m	F1-μ	F1-m	AUC-μ	AUC-m
LAMKIT	73.4	49.3	88.4	74.5	69.5	63.7	93.3	91.2	73.0	65.0	96.0	94.7	80.2	74.4	95.8	94.7	78.5	67.8	97.1	94.9
w/o MK	72.1	47.6	88.2	72.3	68.5	61.9	92.8	90.5	72.0	62.7	95.5	93.9	79.0	72.3	95.8	94.2	76.7	66.3	97.0	93.3
w/o LaV	71.5	42.1	87.5	72.7	68.4	62.9	93.0	90.8	71.5	64.2	95.6	94.3	79.2	72.4	95.4	94.6	77.6	66.6	97.1	93.1
w/o MK and LaV	69.9	46.6	85.3	71.1	66.3	60.0	92.3	89.9	70.4	61.3	94.9	93.4	78.0	70.7	94.1	93.4	76.0	63.9	96.4	93.6

Table 4: Ablation performance of LAMKIT modules in F1 and AUC, both micro (μ) and macro (m), shown in percentages.

Model	ECtHR-A		ECtHR-B		SCOTUS	
	F1-μ	F1-m	F1-μ	F1-m	F1-μ	F1-m
ChatGPT	51.1	47.7	54.0	60.8	49.9	42.0

Table 5: F1 metrics (in %) of ChatGPT on Legal Data.

limited to 512 tokens, truncation becomes necessary when handling long texts (Ding et al., 2020). Such truncation might cause the text to lose a significant amount of valuable information, thereby affecting the model's performance. Another option is to use the generative LLMs to categorize text, however, their architecture and training methods make them unsuitable for fine-tuning directly on text categorization tasks, thus previous studies have focused more on their zero-shot and few-shot performance(Han et al., 2024; Pan et al., 2024; Srivastava et al., 2023). Compare with these methods, long document modeling serves as a more directly solution to handle the long document classification task.

7.2 Long Document Modeling

To enable transformers to accept longer sequences, two primary approaches have been employed in long document modeling: efficient transformers (e.g., sparse attention transformers) and hierarchical transformers (Dong et al., 2023). Hierarchical transformer models (Li et al., 2023a; Ruan et al., 2022; Chalkidis et al., 2023) rely on chunking the text into slices of equal size and obtaining the document representation based on the representations of these slices, ensuring that the model's input does not exceed the limit in each instance. For example, HiPool (Li et al., 2023a) employs Transformers for sentence modeling and then uses Graph Convolutional Neural Networks for document information modeling. HiStruct+ (Ruan et al., 2022) encodes the hierarchical structure information of the document and infuses it into the hierarchical attention model. Due to the full-rank attention mechanism in transformer models leading to quadratic computational complexity, efficient transformers (Beltagy et al., 2020; Zaheer et al., 2020; Choromanski et al., 2021; Zhang et al., 2023) aim to use sparse attention or low-rank methods to reduce the complexity and minimize context fragmentation caused by segmentation. For instance, to reduce computational complexity from $O(n^2)$ to $O(n)$, Longformer (Beltagy et al., 2020) employs a mix of local attention (through a sliding window) and global attention on certain special tokens. Similarly, BigBird (Zaheer et al., 2020) incorporates both these attention mechanisms and introduces an additional random attention strategy. Both models have expanded their input limits to 4096 tokens. However, they do not perform well on documents of all lengths.

Prior research (Li et al., 2023a) has noted that document lengths differ among datasets, and model performance can be inconsistent across corpora with varying lengths. Studies (Dai et al., 2022) have also shown that segmenting documents inevitably leads to issues of context fragmentation. However, no previous work has centered on the aforementioned two inherent issues of long document models: context fragmentation and generalizability across varying text lengths. In this study, we propose a novel approach Length-Aware Multi-Kernel Transformer (*LAMKIT*). By using multi-kernel encoding (MK), LAMKIT obtains multi-perspective context representations to mitigate the context fragmentation issue caused by using a unique chunk size. LAMKIT also enhances model robustness for documents of varying lengths through its Length-Aware Vectorization (LaV) module. This LaV module encodes length information hierarchically, using segment position embedding at the segment level and length vectors from the MK outputs at the document level.

8 Conclusion

In this study, we posit that for long document classification tasks, the length of the text might be a pivotal determinant for model performance. Our exploratory experiments demonstrate that the current state-of-the-art models display inconsistent results across samples of differing lengths, suggesting their lack of robustness and affirming our hypothesis.

To address this issue and the inherent problem of context fragmentation in long-text models, we propose Length-Aware Multi-Kernel Transformer. Through extensive experiments, LAMKIT consistently outperforms all baseline models across five standard long document classification benchmarks. Moreover, we follow our exploratory experiments to examine model robustness over varying document lengths. We also conduct ablation studies on two modules. The results show that LAMKIT exhibits better robustness and stability across different lengths.

Additionally, the case study on ChatGPT (OpenAI, 2022) reveals that LLMs still underperform discriminative models on long document classification tasks, suggesting that the paradigm of solving classification problems through generation still needs to be enhanced.

Limitations

LAMKIT has a flexibility to be applicable on other tasks by changing its prediction layer, while we experiment it on the text classification task. Dong et al. demonstrated the importance of long document modeling in other NLP scenarios. We plan to explore this direction for a more comprehensive understanding on long document modeling.

9 Acknowledgement

This work was partially supported by the National Science Foundation by award number CNS-2318210. We thank anonymous reviewers for their insightful feedback.

References

Emily Alsentzer, John Murphy, William Boag, Wei-Hung Weng, Di Jindi, Tristan Naumann, and Matthew McDermott. 2019. Publicly available clinical BERT embeddings. In *Proceedings of the 2nd Clinical Natural Language Processing Workshop*, pages 72–78, Minneapolis, Minnesota, USA. Association for Computational Linguistics.

Iz Beltagy, Matthew E. Peters, and Arman Cohan. 2020. Longformer: The long-document transformer. *arXiv preprint arXiv:2004.05150*.

Ilias Chalkidis. 2023. ChatGPT May Pass the Bar Exam Soon, but Has a Long Way to Go for the LexGLUE Benchmark. *SSRN Electronic Journal*.

Ilias Chalkidis, Ion Androutsopoulos, and Nikolaos Aletras. 2019. Neural legal judgment prediction in English. In *Proceedings of the 57th Annual Meeting of the Association for Computational Linguistics*, pages 4317–4323, Florence, Italy. Association for Computational Linguistics.

Ilias Chalkidis, Manos Fergadiotis, Prodromos Malakasiotis, Nikolaos Aletras, and Ion Androutsopoulos. 2020. LEGAL-BERT: The muppets straight out of law school. In *Findings of the Association for Computational Linguistics: EMNLP 2020*, pages 2898–2904, Online. Association for Computational Linguistics.

Ilias Chalkidis, Manos Fergadiotis, Dimitrios Tsarapatsanis, Nikolaos Aletras, Ion Androutsopoulos, and Prodromos Malakasiotis. 2021. Paragraph-level rationale extraction through regularization: A case study on European court of human rights cases. In *Proceedings of the 2021 Conference of the North American Chapter of the Association for Computational Linguistics: Human Language Technologies*, pages 226–241, Online. Association for Computational Linguistics.

Ilias Chalkidis, Nicolas Garneau, Catalina Goanta, Daniel Katz, and Anders Søgaard. 2023. LeXFiles and LegalLAMA: Facilitating English multinational legal language model development. In *Proceedings of the 61st Annual Meeting of the Association for Computational Linguistics (Volume 1: Long Papers)*, pages 15513–15535, Toronto, Canada. Association for Computational Linguistics.

Ilias Chalkidis, Abhik Jana, Dirk Hartung, Michael Bommarito, Ion Androutsopoulos, Daniel Katz, and Nikolaos Aletras. 2022. LexGLUE: A benchmark dataset for legal language understanding in English. In *Proceedings of the 60th Annual Meeting of the Association for Computational Linguistics (Volume 1: Long Papers)*, pages 4310–4330, Dublin, Ireland. Association for Computational Linguistics.

Jiuhai Chen, Lichang Chen, Heng Huang, and Tianyi Zhou. 2023a. When do you need chain-of-thought prompting for chatgpt? *arXiv preprint arXiv:2304.03262*.

Jiuhai Chen, Lichang Chen, Chen Zhu, and Tianyi Zhou. 2023b. How many demonstrations do you need for in-context learning? In *Findings of the Association for Computational Linguistics: EMNLP 2023*, pages 11149–11159, Singapore. Association for Computational Linguistics.

Krzysztof Marcin Choromanski, Valerii Likhosherstov, David Dohan, Xingyou Song, Andreea Gane, Tamas Sarlos, Peter Hawkins, Jared Quincy Davis, Afroz Mohiuddin, Lukasz Kaiser, David Benjamin Belanger, Lucy J Colwell, and Adrian Weller. 2021. Rethinking attention with performers. In *International Conference on Learning Representations*, Vienna, Austria.

Xiang Dai, Ilias Chalkidis, Sune Darkner, and Desmond Elliott. 2022. Revisiting transformer-based models for long document classification. In *Findings of the*

Association for Computational Linguistics: EMNLP 2022, pages 7212–7230, Abu Dhabi, United Arab Emirates. Association for Computational Linguistics.

Loic Kwate Dassi and Loic Kwate. 2021. Legal-bigbird: An adapted long-range transformer for legal documents. In *Proceedings of the 35th International Conference on Neural Information Processing Systems, Black in AI Workshop*. Curran Associates, Inc.

Jacob Devlin, Ming-Wei Chang, Kenton Lee, and Kristina Toutanova. 2019. BERT: Pre-training of deep bidirectional transformers for language understanding. In *Proceedings of the 2019 Conference of the North American Chapter of the Association for Computational Linguistics: Human Language Technologies, Volume 1 (Long and Short Papers)*, pages 4171–4186, Minneapolis, Minnesota. Association for Computational Linguistics.

Ming Ding, Chang Zhou, Hongxia Yang, and Jie Tang. 2020. Cogltx: Applying bert to long texts. In *Advances in Neural Information Processing Systems*, volume 33, pages 12792–12804, Vancouver, British Columbia, Canada. Curran Associates, Inc.

Zican Dong, Tianyi Tang, Lunyi Li, and Wayne Xin Zhao. 2023. A survey on long text modeling with transformers. *arXiv preprint arXiv:2302.14502*.

Mandy Guo, Joshua Ainslie, David Uthus, Santiago Ontanon, Jianmo Ni, Yun-Hsuan Sung, and Yinfei Yang. 2022. LongT5: Efficient text-to-text transformer for long sequences. In *Findings of the Association for Computational Linguistics: NAACL 2022*, pages 724–736, Seattle, United States. Association for Computational Linguistics.

Guangzeng Han, Weisi Liu, Xiaolei Huang, and Brian Borsari. 2024. Chain-of-interaction: Enhancing large language models for psychiatric behavior understanding by dyadic contexts. *arXiv preprint arXiv:2403.13786*.

Pengcheng He, Xiaodong Liu, Jianfeng Gao, and Weizhu Chen. 2021. Deberta: Decoding enhanced bert with disentangled attention. In *International Conference on Learning Representations*.

Xin Jin and Yuchen Wang. 2023. Understand legal documents with contextualized large language models. *arXiv preprint arXiv:2303.12135*.

Alistair EW Johnson, Tom J Pollard, Lu Shen, Li-wei H Lehman, Mengling Feng, Mohammad Ghassemi, Benjamin Moody, Peter Szolovits, Leo Anthony Celi, and Roger G Mark. 2016. Mimic-iii, a freely accessible critical care database. *Scientific Data*, 3:160035.

Yoon Kim. 2014. Convolutional neural networks for sentence classification. In *Proceedings of the 2014 Conference on Empirical Methods in Natural Language Processing (EMNLP)*, pages 1746–1751, Doha, Qatar. Association for Computational Linguistics.

Patrick Lewis, Myle Ott, Jingfei Du, and Veselin Stoyanov. 2020. Pretrained language models for biomedical and clinical tasks: Understanding and extending the state-of-the-art. In *Proceedings of the 3rd Clinical Natural Language Processing Workshop*, pages 146–157, Online. Association for Computational Linguistics.

Irene Li, Aosong Feng, Dragomir Radev, and Rex Ying. 2023a. HiPool: Modeling long documents using graph neural networks. In *Proceedings of the 61st Annual Meeting of the Association for Computational Linguistics (Volume 2: Short Papers)*, pages 161–171, Toronto, Canada. Association for Computational Linguistics.

Xianming Li, Zongxi Li, Xiaotian Luo, Haoran Xie, Xing Lee, Yingbin Zhao, Fu Lee Wang, and Qing Li. 2023b. Recurrent attention networks for long-text modeling. In *Findings of the Association for Computational Linguistics: ACL 2023*, pages 3006–3019, Toronto, Canada. Association for Computational Linguistics.

Yikuan Li, Ramsey M Wehbe, Faraz S Ahmad, Hanyin Wang, and Yuan Luo. 2023c. A comparative study of pretrained language models for long clinical text. *Journal of the American Medical Informatics Association*, 30(2):340–347.

Yinhan Liu, Myle Ott, Naman Goyal, Jingfei Du, Mandar Joshi, Danqi Chen, Omer Levy, Mike Lewis, Luke Zettlemoyer, and Veselin Stoyanov. 2019. Roberta: A robustly optimized bert pretraining approach. *arXiv preprint arXiv:1907.11692*.

Ilya Loshchilov and Frank Hutter. 2019. Decoupled weight decay regularization. In *International Conference on Learning Representations*.

Renze Lou, Kai Zhang, and Wenpeng Yin. 2023. Is prompt all you need? no. a comprehensive and broader view of instruction learning. *arXiv preprint arXiv:2303.10475*.

Weicheng Ma, Kai Zhang, Renze Lou, Lili Wang, and Soroush Vosoughi. 2021. Contributions of transformer attention heads in multi- and cross-lingual tasks. In *Proceedings of the 59th Annual Meeting of the Association for Computational Linguistics and the 11th International Joint Conference on Natural Language Processing (Volume 1: Long Papers)*, pages 1956–1966, Online. Association for Computational Linguistics.

James Mullenbach, Sarah Wiegreffe, Jon Duke, Jimeng Sun, and Jacob Eisenstein. 2018. Explainable prediction of medical codes from clinical text. In *Proceedings of the 2018 Conference of the North American Chapter of the Association for Computational Linguistics: Human Language Technologies, Volume 1 (Long Papers)*, pages 1101–1111, New Orleans, Louisiana. Association for Computational Linguistics.

Subhash Nerella, Sabyasachi Bandyopadhyay, Jiaqing Zhang, Miguel Contreras, Scott Siegel, Aysegul Bumin, Brandon Silva, Jessica Sena, Benjamin Shickel, Azra Bihorac, et al. 2023. Transformers in healthcare: A survey. *arXiv preprint arXiv:2307.00067*.

OpenAI. 2022. Chatgpt: Optimizing language models for dialogue. `https://openai.com/blog/chatgpt/`. Accessed: 2023-07-24.

Zhenyu Pan, Haozheng Luo, Manling Li, and Han Liu. 2024. Chain-of-action: Faithful and multimodal question answering through large language models. *arXiv preprint arXiv:2403.17359*.

Adam Paszke, Sam Gross, Francisco Massa, Adam Lerer, James Bradbury, Gregory Chanan, Trevor Killeen, Zeming Lin, Natalia Gimelshein, Luca Antiga, Alban Desmaison, Andreas Kopf, Edward Yang, Zachary DeVito, Martin Raison, Alykhan Tejani, Sasank Chilamkurthy, Benoit Steiner, Lu Fang, Junjie Bai, and Soumith Chintala. 2019. Pytorch: An imperative style, high-performance deep learning library. In *Advances in Neural Information Processing Systems*, volume 32, pages 8024–8035. Curran Associates, Inc.

Guanghui Qin, Yukun Feng, and Benjamin Van Durme. 2023. The NLP task effectiveness of long-range transformers. In *Proceedings of the 17th Conference of the European Chapter of the Association for Computational Linguistics*, pages 3774–3790, Dubrovnik, Croatia. Association for Computational Linguistics.

Qian Ruan, Malte Ostendorff, and Georg Rehm. 2022. HiStruct+: Improving extractive text summarization with hierarchical structure information. In *Findings of the Association for Computational Linguistics: ACL 2022*, pages 1292–1308, Dublin, Ireland. Association for Computational Linguistics.

Adam Rule, Steven Bedrick, Michael F. Chiang, and Michelle R. Hribar. 2021. Length and Redundancy of Outpatient Progress Notes Across a Decade at an Academic Medical Center. *JAMA Network Open*, 4(7):e2115334–e2115334.

Xingchen Song, Di Wu, Binbin Zhang, Zhendong Peng, Bo Dang, Fuping Pan, and Zhiyong Wu. 2023. Zeroprompt: Streaming acoustic encoders are zero-shot masked lms. In *Proc. INTERSPEECH 2023*, pages 1648–1652.

Harold J. Spaeth, Lee Epstein, Andrew D. Martin, Jeffrey A. Segal, Theodore J. Ruger, and Sara C. Benesh. 2020. Supreme Court Database, Version 2020 Release 01. `http://Supremecourtdatabase.org`. Accessed: [2021-01-01].

Saurabh Srivastava, Chengyue Huang, Weiguo Fan, and Ziyu Yao. 2023. Instance needs more care: Rewriting prompts for instances yields better zero-shot performance. *arXiv preprint arXiv:2310.02107*.

Amber Stubbs, Michele Filannino, Ergin Soysal, Samuel Henry, and Özlem Uzuner. 2019. Cohort selection for clinical trials: n2c2 2018 shared task track 1. *Journal of the American Medical Informatics Association*, 26(11):1163–1171.

Chuanneng Sun, Zeeshan Ahmed, Yingyi Ma, Zhe Liu, Lucas Kabela, Yutong Pang, and Ozlem Kalinli. 2024. Contextual biasing of named-entities with large language models. In *ICASSP 2024 - 2024 IEEE International Conference on Acoustics, Speech and Signal Processing (ICASSP)*, pages 10151–10155.

Ashish Vaswani, Noam Shazeer, Niki Parmar, Jakob Uszkoreit, Llion Jones, Aidan N Gomez, Ł ukasz Kaiser, and Illia Polosukhin. 2017. Attention is all you need. In *Advances in Neural Information Processing Systems*, volume 30, Long Beach, California, United States. Curran Associates, Inc.

Thanh Vu, Dat Quoc Nguyen, and Anthony Nguyen. 2021. A label attention model for icd coding from clinical text. In *Proceedings of the Twenty-Ninth International Joint Conference on Artificial Intelligence*, IJCAI'20, pages 3335–3341. International Joint Conferences on Artificial Intelligence Organization. Main track.

Xuezhi Wang, Jason Wei, Dale Schuurmans, Quoc Le, Ed Chi, Sharan Narang, Aakanksha Chowdhery, and Denny Zhou. 2023. Self-consistency improves chain of thought reasoning in language models. *arXiv preprint arXiv:2203.11171*.

Jason Wei, Xuezhi Wang, Dale Schuurmans, Maarten Bosma, brian ichter, Fei Xia, Ed Chi, Quoc V Le, and Denny Zhou. 2022. Chain-of-thought prompting elicits reasoning in large language models. In *Advances in Neural Information Processing Systems*, volume 35, pages 24824–24837. Curran Associates, Inc.

Thomas Wolf, Lysandre Debut, Victor Sanh, Julien Chaumond, Clement Delangue, Anthony Moi, Pierric Cistac, Tim Rault, Remi Louf, Morgan Funtowicz, Joe Davison, Sam Shleifer, Patrick von Platen, Clara Ma, Yacine Jernite, Julien Plu, Canwen Xu, Teven Le Scao, Sylvain Gugger, Mariama Drame, Quentin Lhoest, and Alexander Rush. 2020. Transformers: State-of-the-art natural language processing. In *Proceedings of the 2020 Conference on Empirical Methods in Natural Language Processing: System Demonstrations*, pages 38–45, Online. Association for Computational Linguistics.

Chuhan Wu, Fangzhao Wu, Tao Qi, and Yongfeng Huang. 2021. Hi-transformer: Hierarchical interactive transformer for efficient and effective long document modeling. In *Proceedings of the 59th Annual Meeting of the Association for Computational Linguistics and the 11th International Joint Conference on Natural Language Processing (Volume 2: Short Papers)*, pages 848–853, Online. Association for Computational Linguistics.

Siheng Xiong, Ali Payani, Ramana Kompella, and Faramarz Fekri. 2024. Large language models can learn temporal reasoning. *arXiv preprint arXiv:2401.06853*.

Manzil Zaheer, Guru Guruganesh, Avinava Dubey, Joshua Ainslie, Chris Alberti, Santiago Ontanon, Philip Pham, Anirudh Ravula, Qifan Wang, Li Yang, and Amr Ahmed. 2020. Big bird: Transformers for longer sequences. In *Proceedings of the 34th International Conference on Neural Information Processing Systems*, volume 33, pages 17283–17297, Red Hook, NY, USA. Curran Associates Inc.

Xuanyu Zhang, Zhepeng Lv, and Qing Yang. 2023. Adaptive attention for sparse-based long-sequence transformer. In *Findings of the Association for Computational Linguistics: ACL 2023*, pages 8602–8610, Toronto, Canada. Association for Computational Linguistics.

Ye Zhang, Kailin Gui, Mengran Zhu, Yong Hao, and Haozhan Sun. 2024. Unlocking personalized anime recommendations: Langchain and llm at the forefront. *Journal of Industrial Engineering and Applied Science*, 2(2):46–53.

Yucheng Zhou, Xiubo Geng, Tao Shen, Guodong Long, and Daxin Jiang. 2022. Eventbert: A pre-trained model for event correlation reasoning. In *Proceedings of the ACM Web Conference 2022*, WWW '22, page 850–859, New York, NY, USA. Association for Computing Machinery.

A Experimental Details

For all baseline models, we maintain the same model architecture and optimization parameters as described in their respective papers. For Longformer (Beltagy et al., 2020), Bigbird (Zaheer et al., 2020), and BERT(Devlin et al., 2019), we fine-tune the pre-trained models obtained from huggingface transformers (Wolf et al., 2020) library based on their given configurations and produce predictions. For H-BERT(Dai et al., 2022), we train using the code released by the authors and obtain our results.

For our proposed *LAMKIT* model. The kernel sizes are set to {32, 64, 128} in the ECTHR dataset and {128, 256, 512} in the other three datasets. The corresponding segment numbers are set to {128, 64, 32} and {32, 16, 8} to ensure that the input length of LAMKIT is 4096 tokens, the same as the other baselines. The kernel stride is set by default to be equal to the kernel size. To make the results reproducible, we set the random seed in training to 1. For the MIMIC-III and Diabetes datasets, we employ pretrained Roberta-PM-M3-base (Lewis et al., 2020) as our multi-kernel encoder. For SCOTUS and ECtHR, we opt for pretrained Legal-BERT-base (Chalkidis et al., 2020). Both encoders have 12 layers, 12 attention heads, and hidden states of 768 dimensions. Additionally, we set a Transformer (Vaswani et al., 2017) encoder with 1 layer, 12 attention heads, and 768-dimensional hidden states as the length encoder, and another with 2 layers, 12 attention heads, and 768-dimensional hidden states as the document encoder. The dropout between the two linear layers of the classifier is set at 0.1. Due to our limited computational resources, we empirically set the learning rate and tried two batch sizes: 32 and 16. Each experiment is set with a maximum of 20 training epochs and an early stopping patience of 3. We utilize the AdamW (Loshchilov and Hutter, 2019) optimizer, with a weight decay of 0.01. To expedite model convergence, we make use of 16-bit float point numbers (half-precision). Finally, we select the best-performing model based on F1-micro on the validation set. The chosen hyperparameters for the model are presented in table 6.

Dataset	Learing Rate	Batch Size	Kernel Size		
MIMIC	3.5e-5	16	128	256	512
ECtHR	1.0e-5	32	32	64	128
SCOTUS	3.5e-5	16	128	256	512
Diabetes	2.5e-5	16	128	256	512

Table 6: Chosen hyperparameters for LAMKIT.

All experiments are conducted on a device equipped with an NVIDIA 3090 GPU with 24GB memory, running the Ubuntu system, and utilizing the PyTorch (Paszke et al., 2019) framework.

Data	Long Document Input [X]	Template T + Input[X]	Output [Y]
ECtHR (A/B)	The applicants are former members……had in fact been fleeing the State forces.	*Task Definition:* **Given the following facts from a European Court of Human Rights (ECtHR) case.** *Test Instance:* **Input [X]** *Labels Presentation :* **Which article(s) of ECHR (have been violated) / (are related) , if any, out of the following options:** **Article 2** **…..** **Article 1** Output: [Y]	[Article 2, Article 3]
SCOTUS	Messrs. Thomas J. Hughes, of Detroit…… Charles River Bridge v. Proprietors of Warren Bridge	*Task Definition:* **Given the following opinion from the Supreme Court of USA (SCOTUS):** *Test Instance:* **Input [X]** *Labels Presentation:* **Which topics are relevant out of the following options:** **Criminal Procedure** **……** **Civil Rights** Output: [Y]	[Criminal Procedure]

Figure 3: The best performing zero-shot template of the legal data.

B Prompt Template of Case Study

For ChatGPT (OpenAI, 2022), we set the temperature to 0, and the Top P sampling value to 1. The prompt template is shown in Figure 3.

Investigating Wit, Creativity, and Detectability of Large Language Models in Domain-Specific Writing Style Adaptation of Reddit's Showerthoughts

Tolga Buz*, **Benjamin Frost***, **Nikola Genchev***,
Moritz Schneider, **Lucie-Aimée Kaffee**, **Gerard de Melo**
Hasso Plattner Institute / University of Potsdam, Germany
tolga.buz@hpi.de, gdm@demelo.org

Abstract

Recent Large Language Models (LLMs) have shown the ability to generate content that is difficult or impossible to distinguish from human writing. We investigate the ability of differently-sized LLMs to replicate human writing style in short, creative texts in the domain of *Showerthoughts*, thoughts that may occur during mundane activities. We compare GPT-2 and GPT-Neo fine-tuned on Reddit data as well as GPT-3.5 invoked in a zero-shot manner, against human-authored texts. We measure human preference on the texts across the specific dimensions that account for the quality of creative, witty texts. Additionally, we compare the ability of humans versus fine-tuned RoBERTa classifiers to detect AI-generated texts. We conclude that human evaluators rate the generated texts slightly worse on average regarding their creative quality, but they are unable to reliably distinguish between human-written and AI-generated texts. We further provide a dataset for creative, witty text generation based on Reddit Showerthoughts posts.

1 Introduction

As Large Language Models (LLMs) continue to advance, it becomes increasingly challenging for humans to distinguish AI-generated and human-written text. Generated text may appear surprisingly convincing, inciting debates whether new forms of evaluating models are necessary (Sejnowski, 2023). The high quality of LLM outputs can benefit diverse use cases, while also increasing the risk of enabling more sophisticated spam, misinformation, and hate speech bots (Manduchi et al., 2024). LLMs are known to master various aspects of grammar and basic semantics. Yet, one goal that still has proven non-trivial using LLMs is that of generating creative text (Chakrabarty et al., 2023a), especially in the realm of humour (Jentzsch and Kersting, 2023).

*Equal contribution

We seek to understand the ability of differently-sized LLMs to replicate human writing style in short and creative texts as shared in the *Showerthoughts* community on Reddit, which exhibits humour, cleverness, and creativity – often in a single sentence. The Showerthoughts community (Reddit's 11th largest) provides a unique dataset of short texts with a characteristic writing style drawing from general creative qualities. To understand how well models of different sizes can replicate such witty Reddit posts, we fine-tuned two LLMs, GPT-2 (Medium) and GPT-Neo, on posts from this online community. Additionally, we used GPT-3.5-turbo as a zero-shot model, i.e., without additional fine-tuning for our specific task. We evaluated how well the AI-generated texts emulate the style of Showerthoughts. To this end, we employed a mixed-method approach: We compare genuine, human-authored posts with generated Showerthoughts based on various lexical characteristics as well as in their similarity in sentence embeddings. Furthermore, we conducted a human evaluation study to assess the human evaluators' perception of the creative quality (specifically, logical validity, creativity, humour, and cleverness) and to measure how easily AI-generated texts can be detected.

We find that participants cannot reliably detect AI-generated texts, as the LLMs come close to human-level quality. Generating humour remains a challenging task, but shows a promising future for the generation of short, witty, and creative statements. We find that a machine learning (ML) classifier, trained on Showerthoughts, succeeds at robustly distinguishing human-authored from AI-written text. Thus, there remains potential for current AI-generated content to be identified, even in the ambiguous realm of humour and creative text.

We summarize our contributions in this paper as follows: (1) A new dataset for creative, witty text generation based on Reddit Showerthoughts

*Proceedings of the 13th Joint Conference on Lexical and Computational Semantics (*SEM 2024)*, pages 291 - 307
June 20-21, 2024 ©2024 Association for Computational Linguistics

posts.[1] (2) Experiments with three different models for the generation of creative, witty text. (3) Evaluation of human perception of creative language generation through a survey. (4) Experiments on automated authorship identification of the text as human-written or AI-generated.

2 Background and Related Work

Reddit and Showerthoughts Reddit is a social media platform that is organized in communities called *subreddits*, which exist for a plethora of topics – all written, curated, voted, and commented on by the community. This provides a diverse and valuable research subject; each subreddit is characterized by a distinct writing style and type of content (Agrawal et al., 2022; Buz et al., 2024).

Our work is centered on the r/Showerthoughts subreddit[2], which defines *Showerthought* as "a loose term that applies to the types of thoughts you might have while carrying out a routine task like showering, driving, or daydreaming. At their best, Showerthoughts are universally relatable and find the amusing/interesting within the mundane." In general, popular Showerthoughts exhibit wit (or cleverness), creativity, and sometimes humour, which come from the realization of matters that lie in everyday life's banality, which are well thought out but tend to go unnoticed. They condense various intellectual qualities into short texts that often allude to a deeper context – these qualities can be facilitators of a text's success in various other settings, including posting on social media or copywriting for marketing purposes. One of the community's most successful post goes as follows: "When you're a kid, you don't realize you're also watching your mom and dad grow up."[3]

To the best of our knowledge, there is only one related paper focused on Showerthoughts, which covers a neuro-scientific perspective (Crawford, 2020). Limited research exists that uses Showerthoughts data among other subreddits, but on completely different topics, e.g., detection of suicidal thoughts (Aladağ et al., 2018), predicting conversations (Kim et al., 2023), or changes of the community (Lin et al., 2017). Our work is the first to analyse the texts that are shared in this community from a perspective of computational linguistics and the first to publish a Showerthoughts dataset.

Creative Quality in Natural Language Generation Early work on computational creativity found that while computers can aid in the creative process, it has long remained difficult to achieve novelty and quality with such systems (Gervás, 2009). More recent LLMs possess a remarkable ability to produce entirely novel content, but Chakrabarty et al. (2022a) find that they have limited capabilities w.r.t. figurative language, and that full stories generated by LLMs seem to be of far inferior quality compared to those written by professional authors (Chakrabarty et al., 2023a). Further, popular LLMs such as ChatGPT have been found to be subpar at writing creative and humourous content such as jokes (Jentzsch and Kersting, 2023). For many creative tasks, such as writing convincing poems, human intervention may be needed to create high-quality text (Chakrabarty et al., 2022b), and the temperature hyperparameter may have a significant impact on the creativity of LLM-generated texts (Davis et al., 2024). AI-assisted writing may lead to improved results (Roemmele, 2021) and LLMs have been perceived as writing collaborators by professional writers (Chakrabarty et al., 2023b). However, it is yet to be seen how the generation of creative, witty text without human intervention can be improved to agree with human preferences.

Authorship Identification There have been significant advancements in LLMs generating grammatically correct sentences adhering to semantic rules, even purportedly attaining human levels (Köbis and Mossink, 2021; Clark et al., 2021). This presents opportunities in areas such as accessibility of information and education, and enhanced productivity (Dwivedi et al., 2023; Noy and Zhang, 2023). However, it also poses a threat to the credibility of information (Kreps et al., 2022; Kumar and Shah, 2018), especially as social media users often fail to detect bots (Kenny et al., 2022), while such bots continue to evolve and spread misinformation (Abokhodair et al., 2015; Shao et al., 2018). Indeed, Ippolito et al. (2020) found that even trained participants struggle to identify AI-generated texts. Köbis and Mossink (2021) further found that while completely random texts could be detected, cherry-picked texts could not be distinguished by humans. The model size used to generate texts affects participants' performance – both studies used smaller models (GPT-2 with 355M, 774M, and 1.5B parameters, respectively), whereas

[1] Dataset accessible via our GitHub repository.

[2] `www.reddit.com/r/Showerthoughts`

[3] Accessible via `https://www.reddit.com/awd10u/`

participants confronted with never models such as GPT-3 performed significantly worse in a similar study (Clark et al., 2021; Brown et al., 2020). With larger model sizes, humans require more time to decide, and their accuracy declines (Brown et al., 2020). In very recent work, Chen and Shu (2024) find that LLM-generated misinformation can be more deceptive than when written by human authors, and Muñoz-Ortiz et al. (2023) identify measurable differences between AI-generated and human-written texts.

As LLMs advance rapidly, it becomes crucial to understand what type of generated content humans can detect and how to detect generated content automatically. For automatic authorship identification, Wani and Jabin (2017) use ML classifiers to detect bots. Ippolito et al. (2020) use a fine-tuned BERT-based binary classifier to label texts as human-written or AI-generated. However, their model lacks generalizability – when trained on top-k samples and evaluated on non-truncated random samples, the model only achieves 43.8% accuracy. The sharp increase in discussions about misuse and plagiarism using tools such as ChatGPT has shifted researchers' focus on this area, e.g., Mitchell et al. (2023) proposed DetectGPT, a zero-shot model for detecting AI-generated text, and Deng et al. (2023) proposed a Bayesian Surrogate Model, claiming to outperform DetectGPT. Tang et al. (2024) provide an overview of further detection techniques.

3 Data Compilation

To create the Showerthoughts dataset, we used the publicly available Pushshift API (Clark et al., 2021; Brown et al., 2020) to extract submissions from the Showerthoughts subreddit from April 2020 to November 2022, resulting in an initial collection of 1.3 million posts.[4] We discard posts that have been deleted or removed (often due to rule violation) as well as those that contain images or additional explanations in their body text (as the community's rules require the full Showerthought to be contained in the title). Accordingly, we only use each post's title for our experiments, resulting in a dataset of 411,189 Showerthoughts. An analysis of the most frequent choices of words reveals that they are often about people, life, common objects, and the world in general. A frequent word analysis indicates that they often compare things using, e.g., "more", "other", "old", "good".

In order to obtain a ground truth about the lexical characteristics of the dataset and later compare them with the generated texts, we conducted several tests on 5,000 randomly selected examples, focusing on sentence complexity, length, grammar, and vocabulary, the results of which are summarized in Table 1 (in the first row 'Genuine'). The complexity score is based on the Flesch-Kincaid grade level, which quantifies a text's complexity based on the number of words per sentence and syllables per word (Kincaid et al., 1975). For example, a score of 7.0 indicates that a 7th-grade student (or a person with at least seven years of education) would typically be able to read and understand the respective text.[5]

4 Experimental Setup

In the following, we detail our experimental setup for addressing our three research questions. We explain our process for generating Reddit Showerthoughts-like texts with differently sized selected LLMs. These texts are subsequently evaluated through a survey, assessing several textual aspects. Additionally, we compare the ability of humans and fine-tuned BERT-based classifiers in detecting originality. An overview of this experimental setup is given in Figure 1.

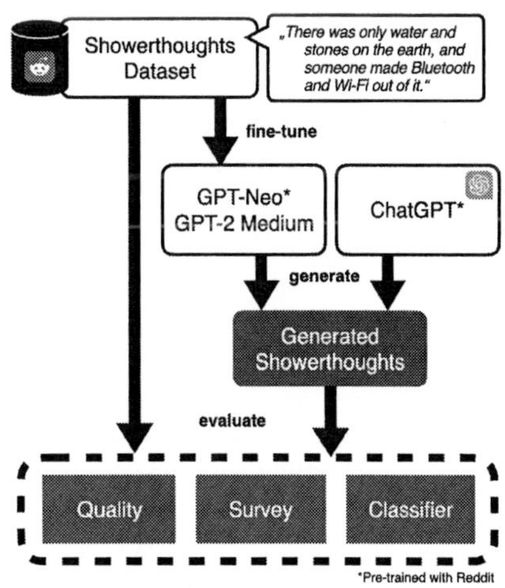

Figure 1: Overview of our experimental setup

[4]In mid 2023, Reddit changed their API guidelines, forcing Pushshift to restrict its access to Reddit moderators only. Our datasets were collected before this change occurred.

[5]Tests are conducted with the `textstat`, `language_tool_python`, and `nltk` libraries.

4.1 LLM Fine-Tuning and Prompting

We consider two setups for the generation of Showerthoughts; (1) two models of different sizes are fine-tuned; (2) ChatGPT (based on GPT-3.5-turbo) is invoked to generate Showerthoughts in a zero-shot setting.

Fine-tuning GPT-2 and GPT-Neo For the fine-tuned models, we select GPT-2 Medium (355M parameters) and GPT-Neo (2.7B parameters) and fine-tune them on the aforementioned Showerthoughts dataset. To later be able to induce the models to generate Showerthoughts, each instance is wrapped around two previously unseen tokens, <|showerthought|> and <|endoftext|>. These serve as prompt and end-of-text markers, respectively, during generation. We use the standard parameters for text generation for both models, including a temperature value of 0.9.

GPT-2 Medium[6] is a unidirectional causal language model that generates text sequences, using 355 million parameters. This was the smallest LLM still able to generate sensible results in our initial evaluation during LLM selection. We use AdamW for optimization, the `GPT2Tokenizer`, a maximum learning rate of 3×10^{-5} with 5,000 warm-up steps, a batch size of 16, and train the model for five epochs on the task of next token prediction.

GPT-Neo is an architecturally upgraded model compared to GPT-2 that closely resembles GPT-3, with 2.7 billion parameters and trained on the Pile dataset (Gao et al., 2020). We selected the same hyperparameters as for GPT-2 besides using Adafactor optimization, which provides manual control over the learning rate and has better memory efficiency (Shazeer and Stern, 2018). We used a learning rate of 2×10^{-5}, which is reduced to 7×10^{-6} over five epochs, and a batch size of 32.

Zero-shot Text Generation with ChatGPT In initial experiments, we found that a basic prompt (*"Please generate 10 Showerthoughts"*) results in repetition of content and structure in generated texts, in accordance with the findings of Jentzsch and Kersting (2023). We therefore extended the prompt by including a definition of Showerthoughts, alongside instructions for enhancing wit, creativity, and humour, and varying sentence structure. This resulted in the following prompt:

"Please generate 100 Showerthoughts, which are inspired by the Reddit community r/Showerthoughts. Vary the sentence structure between the different sentences, and try to be clever, creative, and funny. The Showerthoughts should be relatable and connected to things that people might encounter during mundane tasks."

This process was repeated 50 times to sample a total of 5,000 Showerthoughts. We use the standard settings for text generation, including a temperature value of 0.7.

4.2 Survey of Human Preferences

We evaluated the results of the text generation models by means of a survey. The participants were randomly split into two groups to evaluate a larger number of Showerthoughts while ensuring an adequate number of responses per Showerthought and a reasonable completion time (around 25 minutes). Each group evaluated 15 human-written and ten AI-generated Showerthoughts, each from GPT-2, GPT-Neo, and ChatGPT. Participants were not informed about the distribution of the sources and received the texts in a random order to prevent evaluation bias. The Showerthoughts were selected randomly and manually filtered to exclude posts harboring vulgarity or a "not safe for work" (NSFW) topic.

The survey starts with a briefing on Reddit and r/Showerthoughts, and we informed participants that they will evaluate 45 Showerthoughts, some of which are written by humans and some generated by LLMs. We further ask demographic questions, including age group and the level of experience with Reddit, Showerthoughts, and Machine Learning on a five-point scale. Then, participants were asked to evaluate a series of 45 Showerthoughts by rating along six dimensions (each on a six-point Likert scale): (1) "I like this Showerthought", (2) "It makes a true/valid/logical statement", (3) "It is creative", (4) "It is funny", (5) "It is clever", and (6) "I believe this Showerthought has been written by a real person". These criteria were selected to capture the quality of a Showerthought from diverse angles, and are also applicable to comparable short texts such as social media posts and marketing texts. For evaluation, we consider the average scores of the selected Likert scale from 1 (lowest) to 6 (highest). This method is widely used, e.g., in Tang et al. (2021). Finally, the participants could optionally provide a free-text explanation or reasoning on how they decided.

[6]Accessible via `https://huggingface.co/gpt2-medium`

4.3 Authorship Identification

As a counterpart to the human evaluators on the task of authorship identification, we fine-tuned a total of four RoBERTa-based models[7] (Liu et al., 2019) for binary classification of each input Showerthought as either human-written or AI-generated. For the training and testing of the three LLM-specific RoBERTa classifiers, we used 10,000 randomly selected Showerthoughts per class (i.e., genuine, generated) for GPT-2 and GPT-Neo, and 5,000 examples for the ChatGPT version (due to the smaller generated dataset size). In addition, we trained and tested another RoBERTa classifier on a combined set of 15,000 examples per class (i.e., 5,000 per LLM source). All datasets were randomly split at a 80–20 ratio for training and testing. We assessed the classifiers in three setups; (1) evaluating the three LLMs' outputs compared to human-written (genuine) text separately; (2) evaluating all three LLMs' outputs combined compared to human-written text; (3) training the classifier on one LLM's outputs (GPT-Neo) and evaluating it on another LLM's outputs (GPT-2, ChatGPT, and all combined).

All versions of the classifier were trained with the tokenizer of RoBERTa-Base, AdamW optimization, a learning rate of 2×10^{-5}, batch size of 32, and a linear scheduler with 300 warm-up steps. To compute the loss for a given prediction, the model receives the tokenized Showerthought and the corresponding label indicating whether the Showerthought was genuine or generated.

5 Results

This section presents our experimental results. Section 5.1 compares lexical characteristics, showing that the LLMs come close to human quality. Next, Section 5.2 explores the survey results, providing insights into crucial Showerthought attributes such as logical validity and creativity. Lastly, Section 5.3 reports on our authorship identification, including patterns to distinguish between human-written and AI-generated Showerthoughts.

5.1 Characteristics of Generated Showerthoughts

To assess the quality and similarity of generated to original Showerthoughts, we apply the linguistic metrics described in Section 3 to the AI-generated Showerthoughts utilizing 5,000 random samples per source (for ChatGPT we use all 5,000 texts generated). Table 1 shows that human-written (genuine) Showerthoughts have a larger vocabulary, are slightly more complex, and contain more difficult words and grammar mistakes. Based on these metrics, GPT-Neo's generated texts are closer to genuine texts compared to the significantly smaller GPT-2. ChatGPT ranks closest to the human reference regarding average complexity and length, slightly behind GPT-Neo regarding vocabulary size, but farthest away from the reference in terms of difficult words and grammar mistakes. We find that the models produce a negligible amount of duplicate Showerthoughts (GPT-2: 13 of 10,000, GPT-Neo: 162 of 10,000, ChatGPT: 6 of 5,000).

Source	Genuine	GPT-Neo	GPT-2	ChatGPT
Compl.[1]	7.4 ± 3.4	6.8 ± 3.0	6.3 ± 2.7	6.9 ± 2.4
Length[1]	81 ± 38	88 ± 39	87 ± 33	81 ± 21
Vocab.[2]	13,000	8,700	4,900	7,200
Diffic.[3]	1.2	0.7	0.4	0.36
Errors[3]	0.3	0.2	0.1	0.05

[1] Mean linguistic complexity (Flesch-Kincaid grade level) and length with standard deviation.

[2] Vocabulary size in number of unique words.

[3] Number of difficult words and grammatical errors per sentence.

Table 1: Comparison of common lexical characteristics (based on 5,000 random samples per source)

Comparison of Sentence Embeddings How semantically diverse are Showerthoughts and are our LLMs able to match this diversity? To answer this, we employ sentence embeddings[8] for comparing the similarity between human-written and AI-generated content, and to measure the linguistic distance to texts from other subreddits. We have reviewed the embeddings of 1,000 randomly sampled Showerthoughts per source visualized with the t-SNE algorithm (Van der Maaten and Hinton, 2008); GPT-2 and GPT-Neo produce more diverse texts than zero-shot ChatGPT, which matches human-written Showerthoughts based on their output distributing across the same semantic clusters as the human-written texts (Figure 2, in Appendix). When comparing these embeddings to 1,000 randomly selected titles from different, similarly large and popular subreddits, we find that every subreddit has a distinct focus, and the generated and genuine Showerthoughts being in the same cluster indicates

[7]Specifically: *RoBERTaForSequenceClassification*.

[8]SBERT embeddings in their default, pre-trained configuration (`all-MiniLM-L6-v2`)

that the models are successful in replicating the distinct writing of each subreddit (Figure 3, in Appendix).

5.2 Survey Results

A total of 56 human evaluators took our survey (25 participants in Group A and 31 in Group B), resulting in an accumulated 2,520 ratings for the full set of 90 Showerthoughts and an average of 28 ratings per item, as each group reviewed a completely different set of 45 texts.

Demographics of Survey Participants The participants' demographics are influenced by the channels the survey was shared in: The majority of the participants are younger than 30 years old, with 8.5% above 30 years. 89.4% of respondents have some degree of machine learning (ML) experience, 42.6% have trained an ML model at least once, and some of these even work with ML models daily. Only 10.6% indicated little to no experience with ML. 53.1% of participants rarely or never visit Reddit, while the rest visit monthly (8.5%), weekly (38.3%), or daily (27.7%). 31.2% had never heard of r/Showerthoughts before, while 68.7% visited the community at least once in the past – 16.6% are subscribed and follow it regularly, with 6.2% even occasionally engaging in the community.

It is clear that this demographic distribution is not representative for the broader population, but a result of the distribution channels used for the survey: the professional and university networks of the authors. From a statistical perspective, this is likely to introduce a bias – however, we find it highly interesting to study this group of individuals nonetheless, as many are experienced with ML and approximately half are familiar with Reddit, which we hypothesize to potentially improve their abilities.

Source	Genuine	GPT-2	GPT-Neo	ChatGPT
Score	**3.71**	2.42	<u>3.40</u>	3.23
Log. Val.	**4.20**	3.10	<u>3.96</u>	3.55
Creativity	**3.63**	2.42	3.23	<u>3.45</u>
Humour	**3.18**	2.10	2.74	<u>2.85</u>
Cleverness	**3.41**	2.19	<u>3.15</u>	3.07

Table 2: Mean score (on a six-point scale) for the Showerthought quality criteria (Log. Val. = Logical Validity); best score bold, best model underlined

Overview of Showerthought Ratings Table 2 displays the average response scores for the first five evaluation criteria. None of the LLMs is able to beat or match the scores of human-written Showerthoughts, but some of them get remarkably close.

Among the models, GPT-Neo achieves the best ratings for general score, logical validity, and cleverness, while ChatGPT (based on GPT-3.5-turbo) performs better on creativity and humour. It appears that the general ability to write a convincing, logical, and clever Showerthought can be learned in fine-tuning, but more abstract abilities like creativity and humour improve with model size.

The smallest model, GPT-2, performs the worst, consistently short of human-written Showerthoughts, exhibiting an approximately 30% worse performance. GPT-Neo and ChatGPT achieve a much smaller margin with an overall average disparity of 6% and 7%, respectively. The evaluators consistently prefer human-written texts – however, the margins are small and this does not necessarily have implications for the task of authorship identification, as we show below.

Manual Authorship Identification From the survey responses regarding authorship of a text, we consider answers between 1 and 3 as a vote for AI-generated, and answers between 4 and 6 as a vote for human-written text. Table 3 displays the average accuracy of the survey's participants in correctly identifying each Showerthought's source. For a more granular evaluation, we additionally display the responses by the participants' experience in Reddit, machine learning (ML), and Showerthoughts.[9]

We find that the survey participants were not able to consistently identify whether a Showerthought was human-written or AI-generated; Between all human-written (genuine) and GPT-2, GPT-Neo, and ChatGPT generated Showerthoughts the survey participants were only able to correctly identify 63.8%, 73.1%, 48.1%, and 46.2%, respectively. For GPT-Neo and ChatGPT, this is worse than (balanced) random guessing, i.e., a strategy that would choose one of the two classes in 50% of cases. This indicates that GPT-Neo and ChatGPT already generate Showerthoughts sufficiently convincing to mislead human evaluators. Experience with Reddit and Showerthoughts improves the participants' ability to identify human-written Show-

[9]The participants were considered 'experienced' in one of the given categories if they chose one of the top two answers (e.g., visiting Reddit 'Weekly' or 'Daily') and 'unexperienced' if they chose one of the bottom two answers (e.g., visiting Reddit 'Never' or 'Rarely').

Model	Overall	Reddit Experience		ML Experience		Showerthoughts Experience	
		Yes	No	Yes	No	Yes	No
Genuine	63.8 %	71.3 %	60.2 %	63.2 %	62.3 %	81.6 %	62.0 %
GPT-2	73.1 %	71.3 %	72.2 %	74.0 %	74.0 %	60.0 %	72.4 %
GPT-Neo	48.1 %	49.0 %	46.6 %	48.0 %	53.5 %	55.0 %	45.7 %
ChatGPT	46.2 %	43.9 %	45.1 %	46.8 %	44.0 %	42.5 %	44.3 %
No. Participants	56	21	30	25	7	5	45

Table 3: Survey participants' accuracy in correctly identifying the Showerthought's source

		Prec.	Rec.	F1	Support
GPT-2	Generated	0.91	1.00	0.95	2,000
	Genuine	1.00	0.90	0.95	2,000
	Accuracy			0.95	4,000
	Average	0.96	0.95	0.95	4,000
GPT-Neo	Generated	0.84	0.99	0.91	2,000
	Genuine	0.99	0.82	0.90	2,000
	Accuracy			0.90	4,000
	Average	0.92	0.90	0.90	4,000
ChatGPT	Generated	0.91	0.99	0.95	400
	Genuine	0.99	0.91	0.94	400
	Accuracy			0.95	800
	Average	0.95	0.95	0.95	800
Combined	Generated	0.82	0.95	0.88	3,000
	Genuine	0.94	0.79	0.86	3,000
	Accuracy			0.87	6,000
	Average	0.88	0.87	0.87	6,000

Table 4: Precision, Recall, F1, and Support of the RoBERTa models trained for Showerthoughts authorship identification (LLM-specific models and one combined model for all LLMs)

erthoughts, but does not improve their ability to detect AI-generated texts consistently.

To investigate whether evaluators are more accurate with higher confidence, we evaluated high-confidence answers only (i.e., 1 – 2 and 4 – 6). However, detection accuracy did not improve. In these cases GPT-2 was detected with an accuracy of 79.6%, while there were only small improvements in detecting the other sources. The detection accuracy regarding GPT-Neo and ChatGPT remained below the random-guess baseline. Similar to the overall results, experience with Reddit or Showerthoughts only helped in identifying genuine texts. This shows that independent of their size GPT-Neo and ChatGPT are able to mislead evaluators with the quality of their generated texts.

Participants' Reasoning for Detecting AI-Generated Texts At the end of the survey, participants could add explanations for their evaluation. Within the 42 responses, the primary factors were: illogical statements, common sense, good grammar, lack of humour / depth / creativity, and repetitive word or syntax usage. Endowing machines with commonsense knowledge has been a long-standing goal in AI (Tandon et al., 2017), which LLMs address to a significant degree. The finding that 'good grammar' was frequently mentioned is noteworthy, as many participants believed that machines excel at grammar while errors indicate human authorship. These findings are consistent with prior research by Dugan et al. (2022), who identified similar factors as the most commonly cited indicators of AI-generated content.

5.3 Automated Authorship Identification

This section presents the evaluation results of the four different RoBERTa classifiers introduced in Section 4.3 – three LLM-specific classifiers and one trained on the combined texts of all three models. The classification reports presented in Table 4 show that the classifiers trained per model achieve an overall accuracy ranging from 90% to 95%, with the single model trained for all LLMs scoring an accuracy of 87% (Table 4). Across all classifiers, recall for LLM-generated instances approaches 100% with lower precision, while precision for the genuine human-authored class is nearly perfect but with lower recall. These findings indicate the following: (1) These classifiers outperform human evaluators on authorship identification.[10], (2) The

[10]Note: While human evaluators receive a more general instruction at the beginning of the survey, the classification models are fine-tuned for the task. Nonetheless, we consider this a realistic setup, as almost 70% of the evaluators have responded to have prior experience with the Showerthoughts community. For future work, human evaluators could be presented with human-written and AI-generated examples at the beginning of the survey.

classifiers consistently misclassify a portion of genuine Showerthoughts as generated, which are either lower-quality examples or similar to generated texts in some regard. (3) The models perform well in detecting the AI-generated texts, with the combined RoBERTa model achieving an average F1 score of 0.87. (4) Current (GPT-based) language models, independent of their size, appear to utilize similarly transparent techniques for language generation and are therefore similarly easy to detect for an ML classifier, even when trained on a different GPT-based model.

In an additional experiment, we trained a classifier to distinguish texts of GPT-Neo from genuine ones but evaluate its performance on texts of the other LLMs. The results in Table 5 show that the classifier's average performance on the texts of other models can achieve a relatively high value of 0.86 when a single model's texts are utilized for evaluation. However, the results are significantly worse when texts of various models, of which most were not part of the training, are included for evaluation, suggesting fine-tuning with texts from multiple LLMs for better detection performance.

Our evaluation of the fine-tuned RoBERTa models shows that none of the classifiers attain 100% accuracy, emphasizing caution when using detection tools, particularly in cases with serious consequences such as academic failure or job loss. In a real-world setting, the specific LLM invoked to generate and spread texts will likely be unknown, and, therefore, cannot provide training samples, which requires robust generalizable classifiers and non-GPT-based LLMs – important questions requiring investigation in future work. Nonetheless, our results suggest that the models have learned patterns that strongly indicate whether a given Showerthought is AI-generated, which proves valuable for evaluating the tokens and patterns that contribute the most to the classification results, which we do in the following section.

Tokens with Greatest Contribution towards Class Prediction We use the LLM explainability library `transformers-interpret` to identify the most influential tokens per RoBERTa model. For evaluating correctly and falsely classified texts, we select the top four contributing tokens to each Showerthought's predicted class, then aggregate and normalize each token's significance relative to the dataset.

The results for the three LLMs are similar – significant contributors are (1) tokens at the beginning of a sentence, as they start with a capitalized first letter ('If', 'The', 'You' and 'We' seem to be frequent in generated texts) and (2) punctuation ('.' and ',' specifically). Punctuation and specific stop words (e.g., 'you', 'the') seem to be tokens with high attribution scores for the genuine class, indicating that a critical difference between the two classes is the placement of these tokens. ChatGPT shows slightly different top contributors, especially 'Why' and '?' – this model seems to generate questions more frequently and seems to have a unique usage of the word 'is'. Differences between ChatGPT and the other models may result from ChatGPT's pre-training data including a different subset of Reddit data and the model's much larger size.

		Prec.	Rec.	F1	Support
GPT-2	Generated	0.83	0.90	0.86	2,000
	Genuine	0.89	0.82	0.85	2,000
	Accuracy			0.86	4,000
	Average	0.86	0.86	0.86	4,000
ChatGPT	Generated	0.99	0.74	0.85	400
	Genuine	0.79	0.99	0.88	400
	Accuracy			0.86	800
	Average	0.89	0.86	0.86	800
All models	Generated	0.75	0.54	0.62	3,000
	Genuine	0.64	0.82	0.72	3,000
	Accuracy			0.68	6,000
	Average	0.69	0.68	0.67	6,000

Table 5: Evaluation of the RoBERTa model trained on on GPT-Neo's generated texts when evaluated on texts from other sources

Furthermore, our results indicate that those human-written Showerthoughts falsely classified as AI-generated by GPT-2 and GPT-Neo share the characteristics identified of generated texts, e.g., starting sentences with 'You', 'The', and 'We'. ChatGPT shows fewer distinct patterns in contributor variety and overlap between correct and incorrect human classifications. Showerthoughts mistaken as human-written ones use punctuation and blank spaces in a similar way as the genuine texts, while the misclassified human-written texts use words that may occur rarely, or seem to originate from another language. We provide more detailed results in the Appendix. In summary, RoBERTa classifiers have difficulties in cases where the characteristic writing styles of the classes overlap (especially for GPT-2 and GPT-Neo) or the misclassified Showerthought contains rarely-used or foreign words.

6 Conclusion

In this study, we demonstrate that relatively small, GPT-based LLMs can be fine-tuned to replicate the writing style of short texts of high creative quality, using the Showerthoughts subreddit as an example. While it remains to be investigated to what extent the creativity stems from observations encountered in the pretraining corpus as opposed to novel creations, we find that large numbers of diverse texts can be produced with great ease. Human raters confirm that the generated texts exhibit wit, creativity, and humour. This paves the way for diverse applications in productivity, creative work, and entertainment, and is relevant for practitioners deploying small LLMs to be cost-efficient.

We find that human evaluators rate the generated texts on average slightly lower regarding creativity, humour, cleverness. This does not seem to aid in authorship detection ("I believe this Showerthought has been written by a real person"), as we find that evaluators could not reliably distinguish AI-generated texts from human-written ones. Additionally, the quality of human-written Showerthoughts varies, with bad ones often being mislabeled as AI-generated.

Nonetheless, the possibility to abuse these models to produce spam, misinformation, or other harmful content is a growing concern. Our RoBERTa-based authorship identification classifiers performs well after fine-tuning, revealing interesting hidden patterns that help in detecting the texts generated by specific LLMs. While ML classifiers can currently detect AI-generated texts (when fine-tuned for the task), we can assume that the text generation quality of LLMs will further improve, making this task more difficult. Additionally, differently designed models may pursue other strategies for generating texts, necessitating their inclusion when training general-purpose classifiers.

Our work extends existing work that LLMs can learn to generate specific types of texts (when fine-tuned on high-quality data) to the domain of creative and witty texts, as exhibited by Showerthoughts, but not limited to those. For example, practitioners who would like to utilize such a LLM for marketing or copy-writing, could not only prompt it for general Showerthoughts about a random topic, but also add the start of a text or topic to their prompt for the LLM to complete. Alternatively, generated texts can be clustered by topic to identify the right topics for a specific use case. Simultaneously, we strongly recommend further research on detection mechanisms – while training detection models using generated texts of known LLMs and those fine-tuned on known datasets seems feasible, the task becomes more difficult when there is an exceedingly high number of LLMs to consider and even more so if the author-LLM's architecture or the training dataset is not known.

Ethics Statement

As the dataset proposed in this paper (see Section 3) is based on real user-submitted data from the Reddit Showerthoughts community, it is important to handle it with care. It should not be used to identify individuals and might contain offensive text or wrong information. This should be considered in future use of the dataset. For the survey (see Section 4.2), we manually removed inappropriate content to make it appropriate for the context of where the survey was distributed, e.g., university mailing lists. The type of survey conducted here is exempt from an ethics board review at our institution, as we have carefully designed it to be transparently described and to avoid collection of personal data.

References

Norah Abokhodair, Daisy Yoo, and David W. McDonald. 2015. Dissecting a Social Botnet: Growth, Content and Influence in Twitter. In *Proceedings of the 18th ACM Conference on Computer Supported Cooperative Work & Social Computing*, CSCW '15, page 839–851, New York, NY, USA. Association for Computing Machinery.

Pratik Agrawal, Tolga Buz, and Gerard de Melo. 2022. WallStreetBets beyond GameStop, YOLOs, and the Moon: The unique traits of Reddit's finance communities. In *Proceedings of AMCIS 2022*. Association for Information Systems.

Ahmet Emre Aladağ, Serra Muderrisoglu, Naz Berfu Akbas, Oguzhan Zahmacioglu, and Haluk O Bingol. 2018. Detecting Suicidal Ideation on Forums: Proof-of-Concept Study. *Journal of Medical Internet Research*, 20(6):e9840.

Tom Brown, Benjamin Mann, Nick Ryder, Melanie Subbiah, Jared D Kaplan, Prafulla Dhariwal, Arvind Neelakantan, Pranav Shyam, Girish Sastry, Amanda Askell, Sandhini Agarwal, Ariel Herbert-Voss,

Gretchen Krueger, Tom Henighan, Rewon Child, Aditya Ramesh, Daniel Ziegler, Jeffrey Wu, Clemens Winter, Chris Hesse, Mark Chen, Eric Sigler, Mateusz Litwin, Scott Gray, Benjamin Chess, Jack Clark, Christopher Berner, Sam McCandlish, Alec Radford, Ilya Sutskever, and Dario Amodei. 2020. Language Models are Few-Shot Learners. In *Advances in Neural Information Processing Systems*, volume 33, pages 1877–1901. Curran Associates, Inc.

Tolga Buz, Moritz Schneider, Lucie-Aimée Kaffee, and Gerard de Melo. 2024. Highly Regarded Investors? Mining Predictive Value from the Collective Intelligence of Reddit's WallStreetBets. In *ACM Web Science Conference (Websci '24), May 21–24, 2024, Stuttgart, Germany*, page 11. ACM, New York, NY, USA.

Tuhin Chakrabarty, Yejin Choi, and Vered Shwartz. 2022a. It's not Rocket Science: Interpreting Figurative Language in Narratives. *Transactions of the Association for Computational Linguistics*, 10:589–606.

Tuhin Chakrabarty, Philippe Laban, Divyansh Agarwal, Smaranda Muresan, and Chien-Sheng Wu. 2023a. Art or Artifice? Large Language Models and the False Promise of Creativity. *CoRR*, abs/2309.14556.

Tuhin Chakrabarty, Vishakh Padmakumar, Faeze Brahman, and Smaranda Muresan. 2023b. Creativity Support in the Age of Large Language Models: An Empirical Study Involving Emerging Writers. *arXiv preprint arXiv:2309.12570*.

Tuhin Chakrabarty, Vishakh Padmakumar, and He He. 2022b. Help me write a poem: Instruction Tuning as a Vehicle for Collaborative Poetry Writing. *arXiv preprint arXiv:2210.13669*.

Canyu Chen and Kai Shu. 2024. Can LLM-Generated Misinformation Be Detected? *arXiv preprint arXiv:2309.13788*.

Elizabeth Clark, Tal August, Sofia Serrano, Nikita Haduong, Suchin Gururangan, and Noah A. Smith. 2021. "All That's 'Human' Is Not Gold: Evaluating Human Evaluation of Generated Text". In *Proceedings of the 59th Annual Meeting of the Association for Computational Linguistics and the 11th International Joint Conference on Natural Language Processing (Volume 1: Long Papers)*, pages 7282–7296, Online. Association for Computational Linguistics.

Kevin Crawford. 2020. Daydreaming of Genius: Insight and the Wandering Mind. *Scientific Kenyon: The Neuroscience Edition*, 4(1):55–62.

Joshua Davis, Liesbet Van Bulck, Brigitte N Durieux, and Charlotta Lindvall. 2024. "The Temperature Feature of ChatGPT: Modifying Creativity for Clinical Research". *JMIR Hum Factors*, 11.

Zhijie Deng, Hongcheng Gao, Yibo Miao, and Hao Zhang. 2023. Efficient Detection of LLM-generated Texts with a Bayesian Surrogate Model. *arXiv preprint arXiv:2305.16617*.

Liam Dugan, Daphne Ippolito, Arun Kirubarajan, Sherry Shi, and Chris Callison-Burch. 2022. Real or Fake Text?: Investigating Human Ability to Detect Boundaries Between Human-Written and Machine-Generated Text. *arXiv preprint arXiv:2212.12672*.

Yogesh K Dwivedi, Nir Kshetri, Laurie Hughes, Emma Louise Slade, Anand Jeyaraj, Arpan Kumar Kar, Abdullah M Baabdullah, Alex Koohang, Vishnupriya Raghavan, Manju Ahuja, et al. 2023. "So what if ChatGPT wrote it?" Multidisciplinary perspectives on opportunities, challenges and implications of generative conversational AI for research, practice and policy. *International Journal of Information Management*, 71:102642.

Leo Gao, Stella Biderman, Sid Black, Laurence Golding, Travis Hoppe, Charles Foster, Jason Phang, Horace He, Anish Thite, Noa Nabeshima, et al. 2020. The Pile: An 800GB Dataset of Diverse Text for Language Modeling. *arXiv preprint arXiv:2101.00027*.

Pablo Gervás. 2009. Computational Approaches to Storytelling and Creativity. *AI Magazine*, 30(3):49–49.

Daphne Ippolito, Daniel Duckworth, Chris Callison-Burch, and Douglas Eck. 2020. Automatic Detection of Generated Text is Easiest when Humans are Fooled. In *Proceedings of the 58th Annual Meeting of the Association for Computational Linguistics*, pages 1808–1822, Online. Association for Computational Linguistics.

Sophie F. Jentzsch and Kristian Kersting. 2023. ChatGPT is fun, but it is not funny! Humor is still challenging Large Language Models. pages 325–340.

Ryan Kenny, Baruch Fischhoff, Alex Davis, Kathleen M Carley, and Casey Canfield. 2022. Duped by Bots: Why Some are Better than Others at Detecting Fake Social Media Personas. *Human factors*, page 00187208211072642.

Jinhyeon Kim, Jinyoung Han, and Daejin Choi. 2023. Predicting continuity of online conversations on Reddit. *Telematics and Informatics*, 79:101965.

J Peter Kincaid, Robert P Fishburne Jr, Richard L Rogers, and Brad S Chissom. 1975. Derivation of new readability formulas (automated readability index, fog count and flesch reading ease formula) for navy enlisted personnel.

Sarah Kreps, R. Miles McCain, and Miles Brundage. 2022. All the News That's Fit to Fabricate: AI-Generated Text as a Tool of Media Misinformation. *Journal of Experimental Political Science*, 9(1):104–117.

Srijan Kumar and Neil Shah. 2018. False Information on Web and Social Media: A Survey. *arXiv preprint arXiv:1804.08559*.

Nils Köbis and Luca D. Mossink. 2021. Artificial intelligence versus Maya Angelou: Experimental evidence that people cannot differentiate AI-generated from human-written poetry. *Computers in Human Behavior*, 114:106553.

Zhiyuan Lin, Niloufar Salehi, Bowen Yao, Yiqi Chen, and Michael Bernstein. 2017. Better When It Was Smaller? Community Content and Behavior After Massive Growth. In *Proceedings of the International AAAI Conference on Web and Social Media*, volume 11, pages 132–141.

Yinhan Liu, Myle Ott, Naman Goyal, Jingfei Du, Mandar Joshi, Danqi Chen, Omer Levy, Mike Lewis, Luke Zettlemoyer, and Veselin Stoyanov. 2019. RoBERTa: A Robustly Optimized BERT Pretraining Approach. *arXiv preprint arXiv:1907.11692*.

Laura Manduchi, Kushagra Pandey, Robert Bamler, Ryan Cotterell, Sina Däubener, Sophie Fellenz, Asja Fischer, Thomas Gärtner, Matthias Kirchler, Marius Kloft, Yingzhen Li, Christoph Lippert, Gerard de Melo, Eric Nalisnick, Björn Ommer, Rajesh Ranganath, Maja Rudolph, Karen Ullrich, Guy Van den Broeck, Julia E Vogt, Yixin Wang, Florian Wenzel, Frank Wood, Stephan Mandt, and Vincent Fortuin. 2024. On the challenges and opportunities in generative ai.

Eric Mitchell, Yoonho Lee, Alexander Khazatsky, Christopher D Manning, and Chelsea Finn. 2023. DetectGPT: Zero-Shot Machine-Generated Text Detection using Probability Curvature. *arXiv preprint arXiv:2301.11305*.

Alberto Muñoz-Ortiz, Carlos Gómez-Rodríguez, and David Vilares. 2023. Contrasting Linguistic Patterns in Human and LLM-Generated Text.

Shakked Noy and Whitney Zhang. 2023. Experimental evidence on the productivity effects of generative artificial intelligence. *Science*, 381(6654):187–192.

Melissa Roemmele. 2021. Inspiration through Observation: Demonstrating the Influence of Automatically Generated Text on Creative Writing.

Terrence J Sejnowski. 2023. Large Language Models and the Reverse Turing Test. *Neural computation*, 35(3):309–342.

Chengcheng Shao, Giovanni Luca Ciampaglia, Onur Varol, Kai-Cheng Yang, Alessandro Flammini, and Filippo Menczer. 2018. The spread of low-credibility content by social bots. *Nature communications*, 9(1):1–9.

Noam Shazeer and Mitchell Stern. 2018. Adafactor: Adaptive Learning Rates with Sublinear Memory Cost. In *International Conference on Machine Learning*, pages 4596–4604. PMLR.

Niket Tandon, Aparna Varde, and Gerard de Melo. 2017. Commonsense knowledge in machine intelligence. *SIGMOD Record*, 46(4):49–52.

Ruixiang Tang, Yu-Neng Chuang, and Xia Hu. 2024. The Science of Detecting LLM-Generated Text. *Communications of the ACM*, 67(4):50–59.

Xiangru Tang, Alexander Fabbri, Haoran Li, Ziming Mao, Griffin Thomas Adams, Borui Wang, Asli Celikyilmaz, Yashar Mehdad, and Dragomir Radev. 2021. Investigating Crowdsourcing Protocols for Evaluating the Factual Consistency of Summaries. *arXiv preprint arXiv:2109.09195*.

Laurens Van der Maaten and Geoffrey Hinton. 2008. Visualizing data using t-SNE. *Journal of machine learning research*, 9(11).

Mudasir Ahmad Wani and Suraiya Jabin. 2017. A sneak into the Devil's Colony-Fake Profiles in Online Social Networks. *arXiv preprint arXiv:1705.09929*.

A Appendix

A.1 Simulation of Human Preference with GPT-4

We conducted an additional experiment using OpenAI's GPT-4 API investigating its ability to learn from the survey results to simulate the preferences of the human evaluators on a larger set of Showerthoughts. For this purpose, we defined a system prompt that includes a set of survey-evaluated examples and their average scores for all six categories to provide guidance for the model. To measure whether the few-shot prompting has a genuine effect and how the number of few-shot examples affects the results, we experimented with different amounts of examples, starting with three (3% of all survey items), 45 (50%), and 72 (80%), while using the rest of the survey items for testing.

We measured the coherence of GPT-4's test outputs with the Pearson Correlation metric, which shows a significant increase in correlation when increasing the number of examples shown to GPT-4 in the system prompt: after three examples (train), GPT-4's ratings obtain a Pearson correlation of 0.28 with the remaining human evaluations (test), whereas the correlation is 0.49 after 45 examples (50%), and 0.70 after 72 examples (which is a 80–20 train–test split). In order to further validate these results, we perform tenfold cross-validation using all 90 evaluated Showerthoughts, i.e., by splitting up the evaluated examples into groups of nine and using each group as a test set in a separate iteration, while all other groups are shown to the model as few-shot examples.

The system prompt is defined as follows:

> *Act like a frequent visitor of Reddit, and its r/Showerthoughts community in par-*

ticular. You participate in a scientific survey and utilize your experience to rate Showerthoughts across five dimensions: general score, validity, creativity, funniness, cleverness - with scores from 1 (low) to 6 (high). Additionally, you make a guess on a range from 1 to 6 whether the Showerthought was written by a human author (6) or generated by a language model (1). In order to learn how to score the Showerthoughts, you will receive examples, which have been rated by a team of human annotators. Your task is to rate Showerthoughts as similar to the human annotators as possible.

Here are the examples:
1 Most drivers of the Honda Fit are in fact not fit 3,8 3,4 4 4,28 3,2 4,28
...

For the evaluation of a larger set of 2,000 Showerthoughts per source, we provide all human-labelled items as examples within the system prompt to maximize the model's ability to simulate human preference.

A.2 Visualization of Sentence Embeddings

Figures 2 and 3 show the distribution of the SBERT embeddings for the different Showerthoughts compared to each other and compared to different subreddits selected for their similarity, respectively. These indicate that the fine-tuned LLMs in fact reproduce all topics that the original Showerthoughts cover, while ChatGPT is limited to a subset of the topics.

A.3 Further Survey Details

This section provides additional information on the conducted survey.

A.3.1 Participant Briefing

All survey participants were briefed with the following text:

"We are a group of students from the Hasso Plattner Institute in Potsdam who are taking part in the research seminar 'Recent Trends in AI and Deep Learning'. As part of the project, we have trained a Machine Learning model that is able to generate short texts in the style of the Reddit community 'Showerthoughts'. This survey aims to evaluate the quality of the generated texts compared to the original examples."

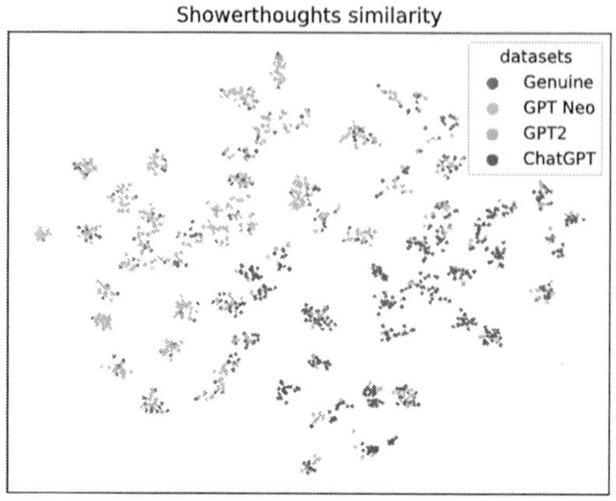

Figure 2: Semantic diversity of the different Showerthoughts datasets (t-SNE visualization of SBERT embeddings)

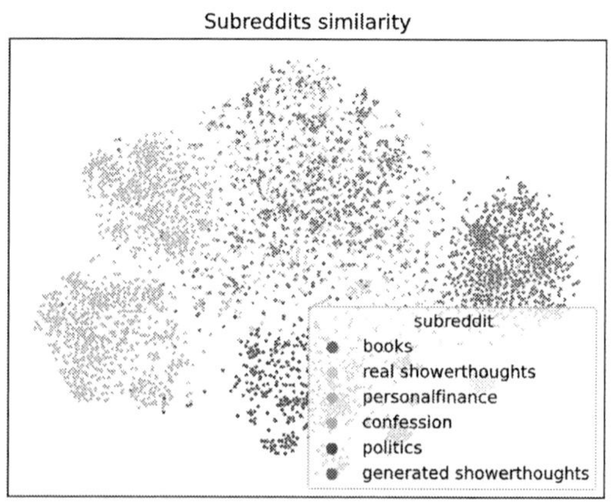

Figure 3: Comparison of genuine and generated Showerthoughts embeddings to other relevant subreddits

Definition

- **Reddit** is a social media platform that is organized in sub-communities called "subreddits". Any user can create a subreddit that revolves around any specific topic, e.g., world news, formula 1, a specific computer game, or the newest Apple iPhone. Users interested in a community can subscribe and interact within the community by posting content (self-written texts, images, videos, or links to external websites), commenting on posts, or up-/downvoting other posts and comments. Each subreddit usually has a self-defined set of rules and guidelines and is managed by a group of moderators.
- The community of **r/showerthoughts** describes itself as a "subreddit for sharing those miniature epiphanies you have that highlight the oddities within the familiar." They define a "Showerthought" as "a loose term that applies to the type of thoughts you might have while carrying out a routine task like showering, driving, or daydreaming. At their best, showerthoughts are universally relatable and find the amusing/interesting within the mundane."

Survey Setup After a few demographic questions, you will be presented with Showerthoughts, of which some are real examples from the community, and some are generated by one of three Machine Learning models (GPT-2, GPT Neo, and ChatGPT). The survey results will be anonymised and utilised only in this research project and the resulting paper. This survey consists of 5 demographics-related questions, followed by the 45 Showerthoughts, which have to be rated regarding a set of criteria each. Finally, you can optionally describe what your thinking process was like / what criteria you used to distinguish genuine from generated Showerthoughts. We estimate that the survey will take you between 20 and 30 minutes to complete.

A.3.2 Survey Questions

After the demographic questions shown in Table 6, the participants were presented a list of 45 Showerthoughts, each with six questions to answer on a six-step Likert scale (from 1= Strongly disagree to 6 = Strongly agree):

1. I like this Showerthought.
2. It makes a true/valid/logical statement.
3. It is creative.
4. It is funny.
5. It is clever.
6. I believe this Showerthought has been written by a real person.

At the end of the survey, we asked the participants a final optional question that could be answered with a free text: "When you tried to distinguish genuine from generated Showerthoughts, was there anything specific (e.g., bad grammar, or logical errors) that unveiled the generated ones?"

A.3.3 Retrieving Random Genuine Showerthoughts

In order to retrieve random genuine Showerthoughts we used an endpoint Reddit provides with its API[11]. To retrieve Showerthoughts specifically we used `GET /r/Showerthoughts/random`.

A.3.4 Statistics of Demographic Question Results

Figures 4 – 7 illustrate the survey participants' demographics and levels of familiarity with machine learning, Reddit, and the Showerthoughts subreddit.

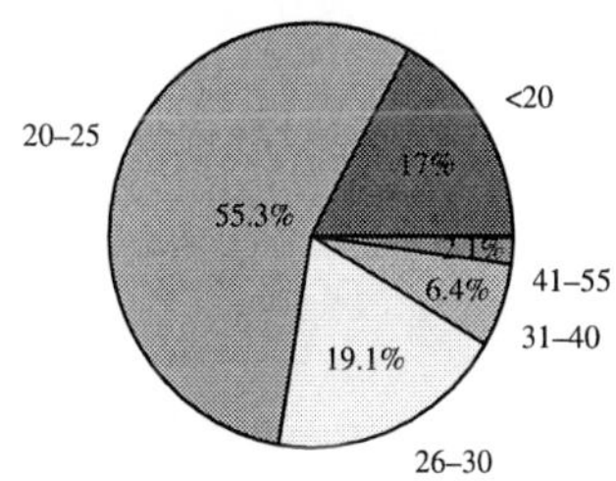

Figure 4: Age

A.3.5 Statistics on Showerthought Ratings

The box plots in Figures 8 – 13 illustrate the evaluations provided by the survey participants regarding the Showerthoughts, grouped by statement and model.

A.4 RoBERTa Interpretability Results

Figures 14 – 19 depict which tokens had the highest influence towards the predicted class.

[11] `www.reddit.com/dev/api/#GET_random`

Question	Answer Options
How old are you?	<20 / 20–25 / 26–30 / 31–40/ 41–55/ >55
How often do you visit Reddit?	Never / Rarely / Monthly / Weekly / Daily
Are you familiar with the r/Showerthoughts community?	No never heard of it / Visited sometime in the past / Subscribed and regularly following / Interact (post, up/downvote, or comment) rarely / Interact (post, up/downvote, or comment) regularly
How experienced are you in using Machine Learning models?	No experience / Using a product with AI or Machine Learning-based features / Played around with AI tools (e.g., ChatGPT) / Trained a ML model at least once / Working with ML models regularly

Table 6: Demographic Survey Questions and Answer Options

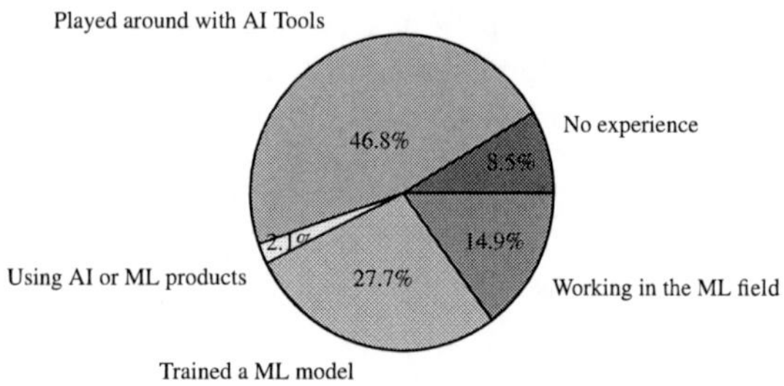

Figure 5: Experience in ML

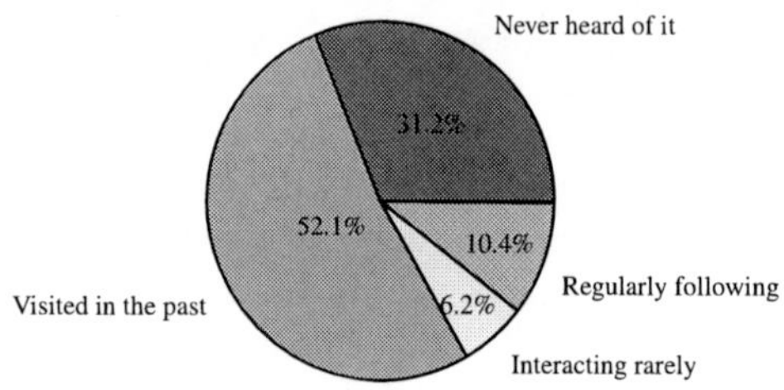

Figure 7: Familarity with Showerthoughts

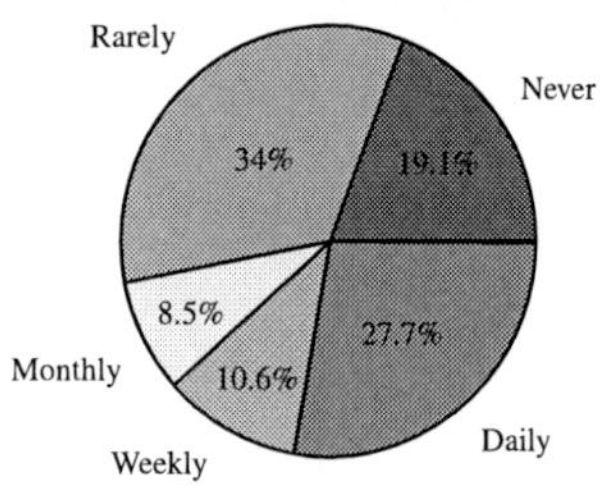

Figure 6: Reddit usage

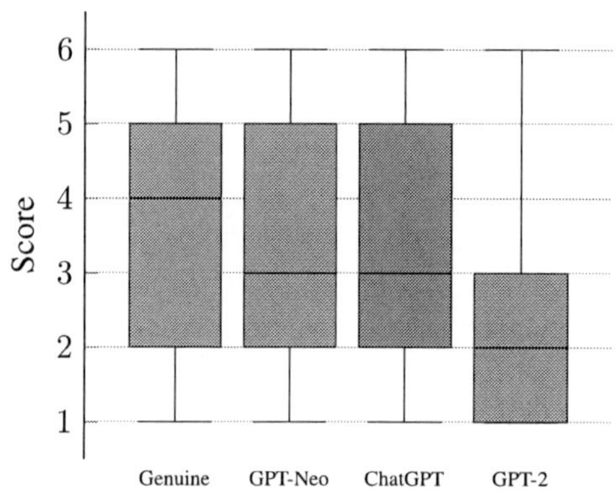

Figure 8: General Score

For instance, Figures 14a, 15a, and 16a depict the most significant contributors for predicting the generated class in the training data for each of the model-specific RoBERTa classifiers.

For an additional perspective, Figures 17, 18, and 19 show the most relevant contributors for misclassified Showerthoughts, i.e., the features that influenced the respective RoBERTa classifier to predict the wrong class.

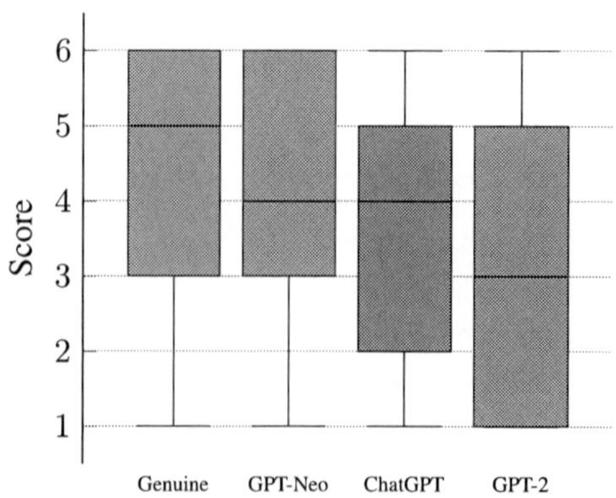

Figure 9: Logical Validity

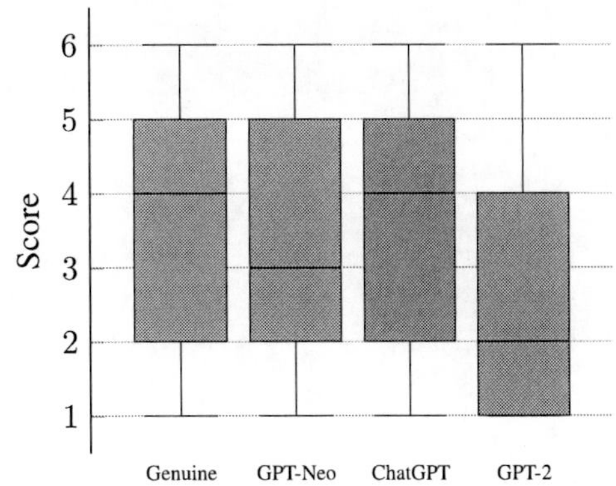

Figure 10: Creativity

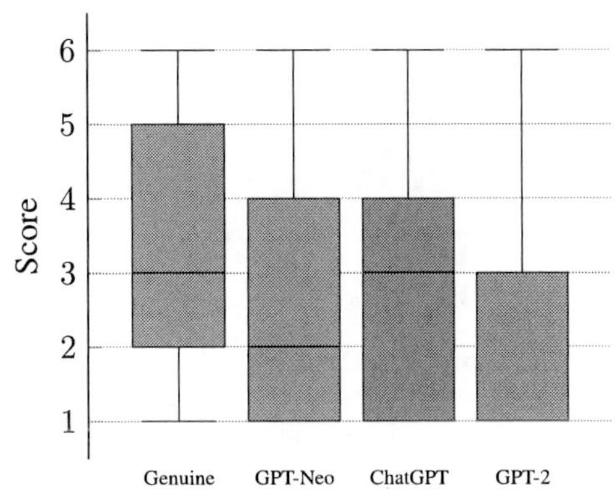

Figure 11: Funniness

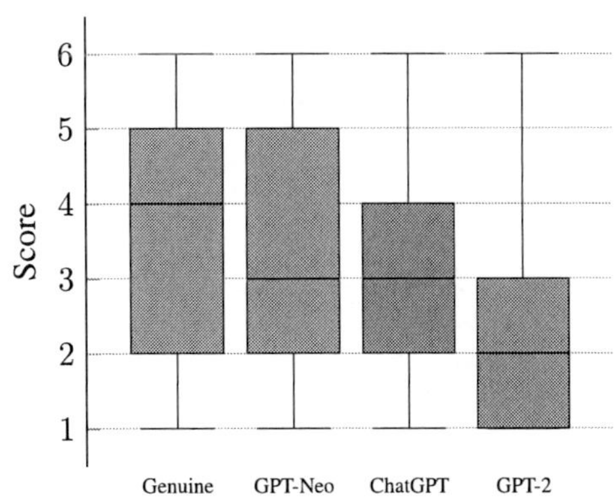

Figure 12: Cleverness

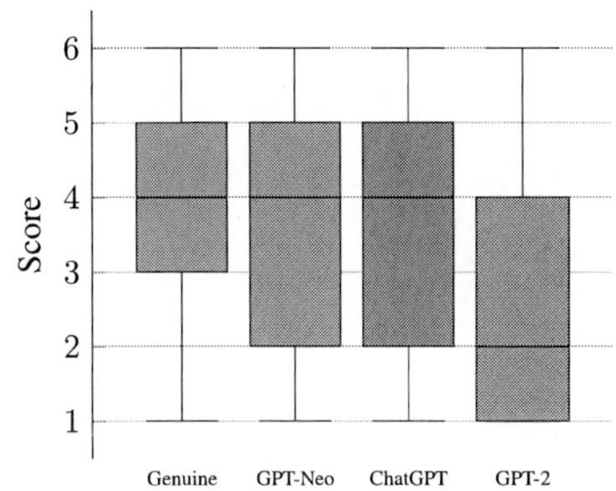

Figure 13: "I believe this Showerthought has been written by a real person"

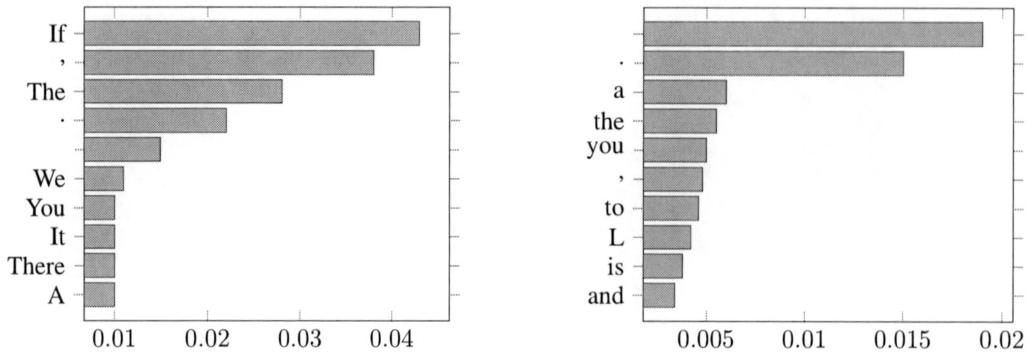

(a) Predicted "generated" class

(b) Predicted "genuine" class

Figure 14: Tokens with highest attribution scores towards the predicted class (GPT-2)

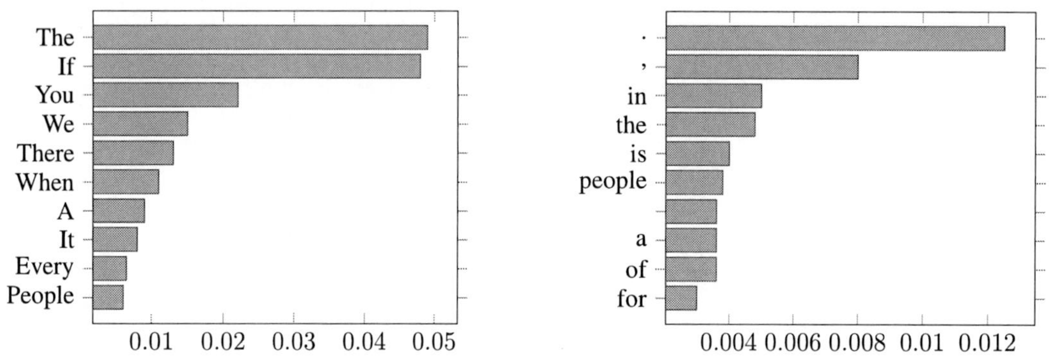

(a) Predicted "generated" class

(b) Predicted "genuine" class

Figure 15: Tokens with highest attribution scores towards the predicted class (GPT-Neo)

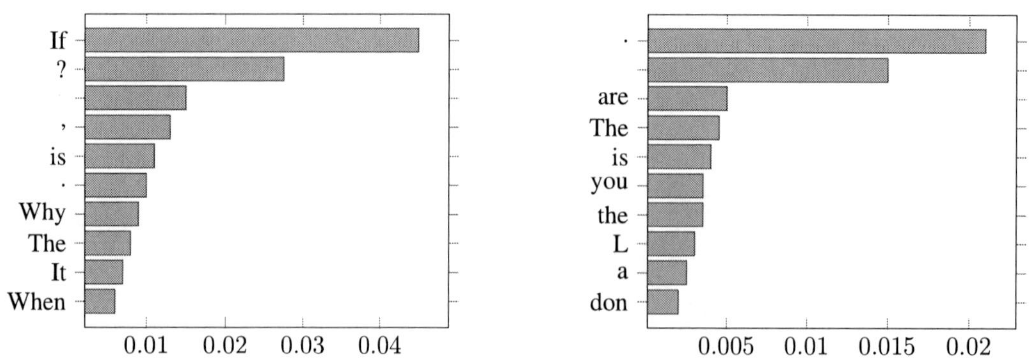

(a) Predicted "generated" class

(b) Predicted "genuine" class

Figure 16: Tokens with highest attribution scores towards the predicted class (ChatGPT)

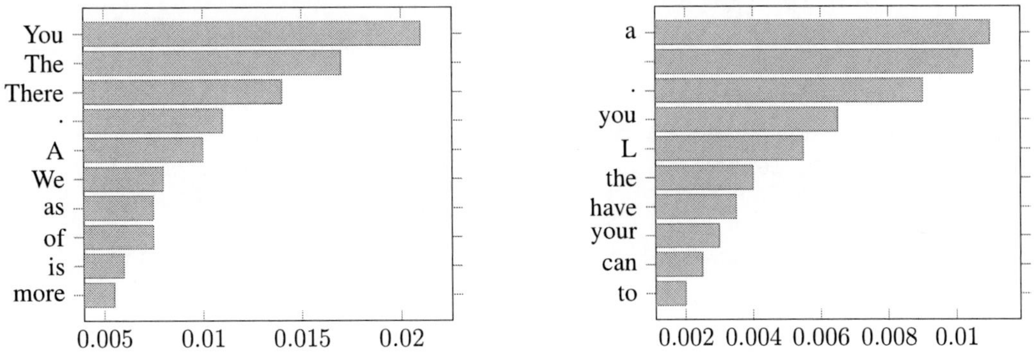

(a) Predicted "generated" class

(b) Predicted "genuine" class

Figure 17: Tokens with highest attribution scores towards the predicted class when misclassified (GPT-2)

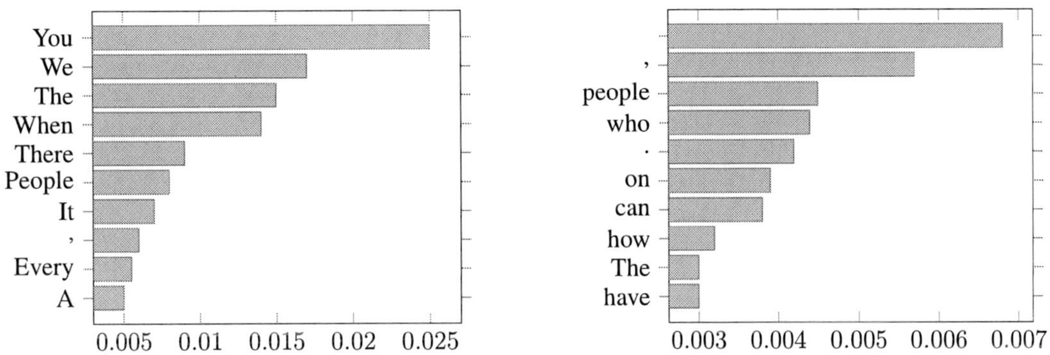

(a) Predicted "generated" class

(b) Predicted "genuine" class

Figure 18: Tokens with highest attribution scores towards the predicted class when misclassified (GPT-Neo)

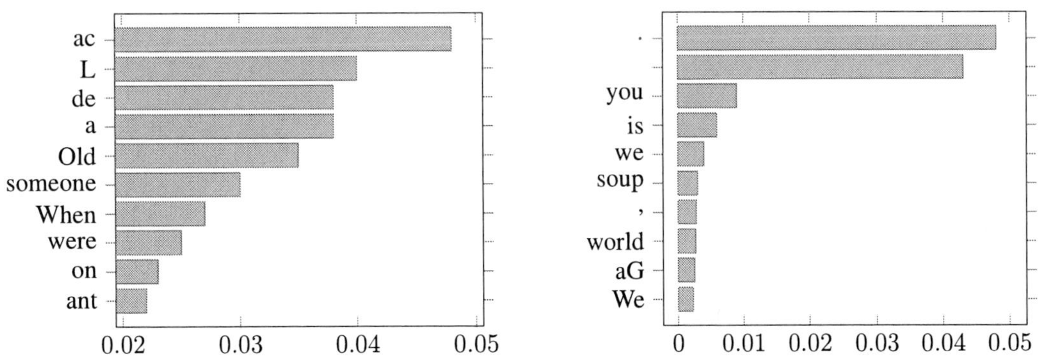

(a) Predicted "generated" class

(b) Predicted "genuine" class

Figure 19: Tokens with highest attribution scores towards the predicted class when misclassified (ChatGPT)

Multilingual and Code-Switched Sentence Ordering

Alexandre Salle
VTEX, Porto Alegre, RS, Brazil
alex@alexsalle.com

Shervin Malmasi
Amazon.com, Inc., Seattle, WA, USA
malmasi@amazon.com

Abstract

Sentence Ordering (SO) is a linguistic task which requires re-ordering of shuffled sentences into a coherent paragraph. SO has downstream applications, but also serves as a semantic probe for computational models as this capability is essential for understanding narrative structures, causal and temporal relations within texts. Despite its importance, prior research has been limited to predictable English language structures and has not thoroughly addressed the complexities of multilingual and varied narrative contexts. To fill this gap, we introduce a novel and comprehensive Multilingual Sentence Ordering task that extends SO to diverse narratives across 12 languages, including challenging code-switched texts. We have developed MULTISO, a new benchmark dataset that represents these challenges. Our findings reveal that both specialized sentence ordering models and advanced Large Language Models like GPT-4 face significant challenges with this task.

1 Introduction

Advances in Language Models (LMs) have increased focus on general language understanding through increasingly sophisticated tasks requiring a deeper understanding of meaning in text. These advances are underpinned by improved representation learning of core linguistic units (morphemes, words, sentences) via methods like subword tokenization, masked LMs, and next sentence prediction - combined with significant increases in model size. At the sentence level, the self-supervised task of re-ordering shuffled tokens and sentences to recover the original sequence has been used, e.g., in BART (Lewis et al., 2020).

Sentence Ordering (SO)[1] is a task that extends the permutation recovery approach to the paragraph level by shuffling sentence order. Originally studied outside of computational linguistics, SO has been used in studies of understanding human cognition (Delis et al., 1983), as well as language learning assessment and testing (Alderson, 2000). Along the same lines, understanding longer texts has always been an overarching goal in NLP, and SO serves as a semantic probe for assessing model understanding of causal and temporal relations, and ability to reason over longer texts.

Numerous computational approaches to SO have been explored (Lapata, 2003; Logeswaran et al., 2018). However, there are several shortcomings. To our knowledge, all SO research has been on English. Further, most work uses sentences from paper abstracts or text describing entities, and recent work has shown that these texts have similar and highly regular structures, allowing models to learn simple shallow cues that result in shortcut learning (Basu Roy Chowdhury et al., 2021).

To address these gaps, we propose a comprehensive multilingual SO task using varied narratives spanning several domains and 12 languages, including challenging code-switched passages. Our proposed multilingual SO task is depicted in Figure 1. Experiments on MULTISO, a new benchmark dataset that we have created, show that both models trained specifically for SO, as well as state-of-art LLMs (GPT-4), struggle on this task.

In sum, our contributions include:

- Proposing a novel comprehensive Multilingual Sentence Ordering task;
- Releasing MULTISO, a new public dataset to advance SO research;[2]
- Evaluating MULTISO with LMs and LLMs to establish benchmarks.

[1] Sometimes called sentence arrangement or re-ordering.

[2] https://github.com/alexandres/mso

*Proceedings of the 13th Joint Conference on Lexical and Computational Semantics (*SEM 2024)*, pages 308 - 313
June 20-21, 2024

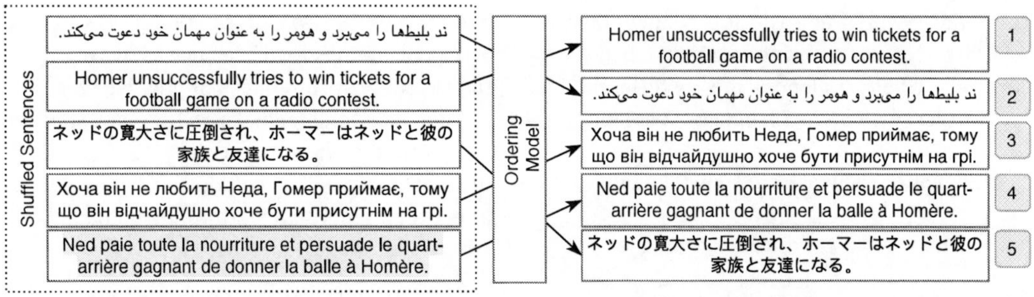

Figure 1: An example of the Code-Switched Sentence Ordering task spanning 5 languages (FA, EN, JA, UK, and FR). English versions of sentences: (2) Ned wins the tickets and invites Homer as his guest. (3) Although he dislikes Ned, Homer accepts because he desperately wants to attend the game. (4) Ned pays for all of the food and persuades the winning quarterback to give the game ball to Homer. (5) Overwhelmed by Ned's generosity, Homer becomes friends with Ned and his family.

2 Related Work

Sentence Ordering is a longstanding task within Natural Language Processing research (Lapata, 2003). SO also has more direct downstream applications in text summarization (Nallapati et al., 2017), retrieval-dependent QA (Yu et al., 2018), and concept-to-text generation (Schwartz et al., 2017). More recently, the task has gained attention with the rise of neural language models (Chen et al., 2016; Cui et al., 2018). For a comprehensive overview of the work in the area, we refer the reader to the recent survey by Shi et al. (2024).

Research on SO is nascent, and there is a paucity of benchmark tasks and datasets. Datasets such as ROC Stories (Mostafazadeh et al., 2016) provide well-structured, simple narratives composed of five sentences, purposely crafted to model coherent story progression in a strictly monolingual (English) context. Similarly, datasets based on abstracts from NIPS, ACL, and arXiv papers (Chen et al., 2016; Logeswaran et al., 2018) focus on the logical sequence of scientific ideas, yet are confined to English language scholarly texts. These datasets predominantly support tasks that require understanding simple, linear narrative structures in solely English contexts. Contrasting this, our work extends beyond the monolingual framework by introducing a novel, multilingual dataset that includes code-switching, addressing the complexities of interlaced linguistic elements. Additionally, our dataset encompasses a broader spectrum of intricate narration styles, thereby challenging models to grasp and generate more sophisticated narratives.

While SO is intrinsically interesting, it is also relevant to research on using LMs to generate semantic representations of text: Lewis et al. (2020) find that SO is an important pretraining task for downstream task performance in a monolingual setting. We hypothesize that Multilingual SO, particularly a Code-Switched variant, may help align semantic representations across languages.

Our work tries to address some of the above shortcomings by proposing a new multilingual SO task, and developing a new corresponding dataset (MULTISO) to further research in this area.

3 Multilingual Sentence Ordering

To address current gaps in the literature, we design a new SO task which is more challenging. We focus on the following areas:

- **Multilinguality**: while all previous work is on English, we expand SO to 11 new languages.
- **Challenging Data**: we work with diversely-structured narratives covering many themes.
- **Cross-lingual transfer and Code-Switching**: we define settings for zero-shot transfer, and are the first to propose mixed-language SO.

3.1 MULTISO Dataset

We have created MULTISO, a new **Multi**lingual **S**entence **O**rdering benchmark dataset[3] that includes the following monolingual, multilingual, and code-switched subtasks:

(A) **Monolingual Task**: given a shuffled narrative, the original sentence ordering must be recovered. Eight languages are included.

(B) **Cross-lingual Transfer Task**: similar to (A), but using data from 4 languages where we provide no training data (zero-shot).

[3]Available at https://github.com/alexandres/mso

(C) **Code-Switching Task**: this challenging subtask requires ordering code-switched narratives where sentences are in different languages, with up to 5 languages per story.

Examples of each task are shown in Table 1.

• The story concerns King Charlemagne, who has gotten lost and detached from his retinue in a storm. • He is forced to take refuge in the home of a collier named "Rauf". • While Rauf is more or less hospitable, he does not realize his guest is the king, and so treats him somewhat roughly.
• Родина Тернерів вирішила переселитися до штату Вірджинія. • Дорогою вони підбирають бежатнього собаку - колі Лессі. • РЛессі стає членом родини, й особливо допомагає підліткові Мету, рятуючи його в скрутних ситуаціях.
• Романтичний фільм обертався навколо рокера і глухого хлопчика. • 一人は沈黙の中で暮らし、もう一方は騒音と恐怖の中で生きている。 • The two met in a Baguio camp where hearing kids were mixed with non-hearing kids to find their common ground, which is their love for music.

Table 1: Example narratives from our data: *The Tale of Ralph the Collier* (EN), *Lassie* (UK), and *If I Knew What You Said* (Code-Switched UK+JA+EN).

Languages Our task is multilingual, spanning 12 languages: DE, EN, ES, FA, FR, IT, PT, UK, JA, SV, TR, and ZH. Detailed statistics are shown in Table 2.

Language	Train	Valid	Test	Sents/Story	Tokens/Sent
German (DE)	20k	4.6k	4.6k	5.5 ± 3.0	17.7 ± 8.2
English (EN)	20k	12.3k	12.3k	4.7 ± 2.8	20.3 ± 8.9
Spanish (ES)	20k	2.7k	2.7k	3.9 ± 2.2	22.9 ± 9.8
Farsi (FA)	5.6k	0.7k	0.7k	4.0 ± 2.5	20.9 ± 9.6
French (FR)	20k	4.7k	4.7k	3.9 ± 2.2	19.4 ± 9.1
Italian (IT)	20k	4.2k	4.2k	4.1 ± 2.4	22.2 ± 9.8
Portuguese (PT)	14.9k	1.9k	1.9k	4.0 ± 2.2	21.7 ± 9.3
Ukrainian (UK)	16.9k	2.1k	2.1k	4.8 ± 2.8	14.9 ± 7.4
Japanese (JA)	0	0.9k	7.5k	3.2 ± 1.5	55.5 ± 31.9
Swedish (SV)	0	1.3k	11.7k	4.0 ± 2.2	17.5 ± 8.1
Turkish (TR)	0	0.5k	4.7k	5.0 ± 3.0	14.5 ± 7.5
Chinese (ZH)	0	0.8k	7.2k	3.8 ± 2.1	48.0 ± 27.9
Code-Switched (CS)	20k	2.5k	2.5k	4.7 ± 2.8	16.6 ± 11.4
CS English Control (CS-EN)	20k	2.5k	2.5k	4.7 ± 2.8	20.4 ± 8.9
English Books (EN-Books)	0	0	240	6.5 ± 4.3	16.9 ± 11.1
Books Code-Switched (CSB)	0	0	240	6.5 ± 4.3	15.9 ± 10.8
Translated Books (CSB-MT)	0	0	240	6.5 ± 4.3	16.0 ± 10.7

Table 2: Per-split data statistics, with mean±std number of sentences per story (Sents/Story) and mean±std tokens (characters for JA, ZH) per sentence (Tokens/Sent). We are collecting more languages and narrative types.

Our data focuses on narratives describing stories from creative works (e.g., movies, books, TV shows). Unlike existing data used for SO (text from paper abstracts, descriptions of persons and entities), these narratives have a less regular structure, and can include any subject matter (e.g., sci-fi). Our data generation process is described below.

Monolingual Narratives (Task A) Parsing Wikipedia dumps for 12 languages, we extract narrative sections from pages of creative works. We take the first paragraph, which is often a short summary of the story with a clear start and end. We filter paragraphs that are too short (< 2 sents) or long (> 20 sents). We perform monolingual evaluation on DE, EN, ES, FA, FR, IT, PT, UK.

Cross-lingual Transfer (Task B) For JA, SV, TR, & ZH, we provide no training data and evaluate cross-lingual, zero-shot transfer.

Code-Switched Data (Task C) These are narratives where the sentences can be from up to 5 languages: EN, FR, FA, UK, & JA. As aligning the monolingual stories is noisy and challenging, we apply Machine Translation (MT) to monolingual data to create code-switched narratives.

Books Data To assess the impact of MT used in constructing Task C, we use aligned human translations of out-of-copyright books[4] in EN, DE, ES, HU, & IT to a create a Code-Switched Books (CSB) corpus. We apply MT on the English-only version of this corpus – Books (EN) – to create a MT Code-switched Books corpus (CSB-MT) for comparison to Code-Switched Books (CSB). Although this corpus is two orders of magnitude smaller than the Wikipedia-based data, its sole use here is to assess the impact of MT on the task.

Data Validation We randomly sampled 80 EN, DE, and FR monolingual narratives; 97% were found to be valid stories by native speakers.

4 Experiments and Results

Models We use the SO model from Shen and Baldwin (2021) and employ both BERT and Multilingual BERT as the underlying encoder. We also test ChatGPT models (`gpt-3.5-turbo`, `gpt-4`) in a zero-shot setting, with a prompt instructing it to order the input story. We align the output to the original story by matching generated sentences to the original input using Longest Common Subsequence (LCS), where a match between a pair of sentences (s, t) occurs when $|LCS(s,t)|/max(|s|,|t|)) \geq 0.7$. When we fail to match each sentence in the original story to a one in the generated story, we consider this a parse error and penalize the model by randomly permuting the original story to compute the metrics.

[4] https://opus.nlpl.eu/Books.php

	Monolingual (Task A)										Cross-lingual (Task B)						Code-Switched (Task C)			
	EN		DE		IT		FA		UK		EN→DE		ES→IT		EN→FA		CS		CS-EN	
	τ	PMR	τ	PMR	τ	PMR	τ	PMR	τ	PMR	τ	PMR	τ	PMR	τ	PMR	τ	PMR	τ	PMR
BERT	**0.80**	21.08	0.59	11.94	0.61	12.51	0.48	11.27	0.46	8.57	-	-	-	-	-	-	0.47	9.47	0.78	19.33
mBERT	0.78	20.26	**0.80**	21.03	**0.79**	21.03	**0.72**	20.38	**0.77**	19.80	**0.77**	**18.64**	**0.74**	**19.13**	**0.76**	**22.28**	**0.72**	16.16	**0.81**	23.04
GPT-3.5	0.39	13.88	0.30	10.45	0.37	15.61	0.25	12.60	0.25	10.53	-	-	-	-	-	-	0.16	8.96	0.39	16.30
GPT-4	0.68	**24.35**	0.68	**23.60**	0.72	**24.71**	0.66	**20.95**	0.67	**23.21**	-	-	-	-	-	-	0.58	**16.41**	0.69	**24.59**

Table 3: Pilot results for our three subtasks, using models based on BERT, Multilingual BERT, and ChatGPT (zero-shot).

	EN-Books		CSB		CSB-MT	
	τ	PMR	τ	PMR	τ	PMR
mBERT	**0.56**	**8.05**	**0.43**	**6.77**	**0.43**	**6.69**
GPT-3.5	0.06	5.64	0.04	4.50	-0.01	4.35
GPT-4	0.16	7.04	0.09	6.54	0.07	6.16

Table 4: Results on English Books, Code-switched Books (CSB), and Translated Code-Switched Books (CSB-MT).

Metrics We utilize two standard metrics from the SO literature: (1) *Kendall's Tau* (τ) (Kendall, 1938) which measures the correlation between the correct and predicted orderings in terms of inversions; and (2) *Perfect Match Ratio* (PMR) which is the proportion of predicted orderings which are absolutely correct (equal to the correct ordering). As evidenced in Table 2, sentence counts per story vary greatly with language. To control for this and allow for direct comparison between language results, rather than averaging τ and PMR across all stories, we stratify narratives by length and compute mean τ and PMR across strata, and finally compute an unweighted mean over strata means.

4.1 Main Results

Pilot results from all models on a subset of languages are shown in Table 3. We leave evaluation on all languages for future work.

Monolingual Performance (Task A) We trained BERT and mBERT models for 5 languages. mBERT has reasonable results for all languages, with higher resource languages performing better. The monolingual BERT model performs poorly on non-EN languages, demonstrating the need for multilingual (or monolingual in the target language) encoders. Overall performance on our data is much lower than existing work leveraging narrative text such as ROCStories (Mostafazadeh et al., 2016), where reported PMRs can exceed 80% (Basu Roy Chowdhury et al., 2021). This highlights the relative difficulty of our dataset.

Cross-lingual Transfer (Task B) We apply zero-shot transfer between typologically similar and diverse languages. Transfer between similar source-target pairs (EN→DE, ES→IT) achieves similar results as monolingual models: the drop in metrics is under 10%. Interestingly, training on high-resource EN data and testing on low-resource FA data increases performance over the monolingual FA model, which has a much smaller training set. This finding demonstrates that cross-lingual transfer works well for SO.

Code-switched Performance (Task C) We create a code-switched corpus (CS) where each narrative can have up to 5 languages. This data is translated from EN, and we retain the original monolingual data as a control set (CS-EN). The Code-Switched results show that it is indeed the most challenging setting, with a 30% drop in PMR and an 11% drop in τ compared to the equivalent non-code-switched corpus (CS-EN). This result is not surprising as code-mixed tasks are usually much more difficult (Fetahu et al., 2021; Malmasi et al., 2022), but it highlights that using a pretrained multilingual Transformer model is a weak baseline, and possible efforts to address this create interesting new research directions in semantic, multilingual sentence and document representation.

ChatGPT To control for costs, we sampled 500 stories from each dataset using stratified sampling by number of sentences (to better match our metrics which are macro averaged by number of sentences). Surprisingly, despite significant prompt engineering effort, GPT-3.5 struggles on all data. In contrast, GPT-4 has the highest PMR on all datasets. Interestingly, its τ is lower than both BERT and mBERT, indicating an all or nothing approach to the task: its high PMR shows that it tends to get the ordering correct more frequently than other models, but when it fails, it is a complete failure (this all-or-nothing effect is even more pronounced for GPT-3.5; in Task A IT, it has a higher PMR than BERT, but a τ nearly 40% lower). Given its difficulty, we hope further experiments with our dataset will shed some light on the degree to which SO is emergent in LLMs (Wei et al., 2022).

4.2 Impact of Translation (Books)

Table 4 shows translation does not impact SO performance; this matches our observations in validating the translated narratives. Results on Books are lower than all results in Wikipedia: this is due to different and much more varied narrative structure, domain shift, and longer sentences.

4.3 LLM Memory Test

It is reasonable to expect LLMs such as GPT-3.5/4 to be able to recall from memory plots from Wikipedia and out-of-copyright books which are used in our dataset. We test this by randomly sampling 50 EN-plot and 50 EN-books containing at least 10 sentences. We then prompt both models with the first 5 sentences of each plot in order, and check whether they are able to recall the next 5 sentences in the correct order. Generated sentences are matched to the original sentences using the same LCS technique described in section 4. Surprisingly, GPT4 is only able to recall 14/100 instances (all correctly recalled stories are from Books), and GPT3.5 even fewer, only 3/100 (also from Books).

Focusing on GPT-4, we tested whether it could perform the SO task on the 14 stories it *can* recall perfectly from memory. It fails to do so, with a PMR of 0.0 and a Kendall's Tau close to 0. Recent work shows that LLMs suffer from the Reversal Curse (Berglund et al., 2023): GPT-4 is able to answer "Who is Tom Cruise's mother? [A: Mary Lee Pfeiffer]" but fails to answer the reverse "Who is Mary Lee Pfeiffer's son?". This might be connected to the failure in the memory test: GPT4 can recall the stories if prompted in the original order, but runs into a failure when prompted out of order. Further investigation is needed to understand the cause of this failure.

5 Conclusion and Future Work

We proposed a multilingual SO task and dataset, and showed that it is challenging, particularly for code-switched data. Although based on a well explored monolingual SO task, our research is the first to address the gap in research covering non-English and code-switched languages.

Our MULTISO dataset uses narratives describing stories from creative works, making it varied and providing a challenge for language models. This dataset is the first to explore the multilingual and mixed-language directions. We expect this task and data will facilitate research in several areas. The task enables evaluation of LM representations and model reasoning over longer language units and sequences. Each task also covers multiple languages, making it possible to study cross-lingual transfer using MULTISO.

In future work, we plan to: (1) expand the dataset with more languages and narrative types to further provide researchers with valuable resources for enhancing multilingual language models (2) perform a deeper investigation on using models to solve the task, in particular LLMs.

Ethics Statement

In accordance with the ACM Code of Ethics and Professional Conduct, our work adheres to the principles of respecting privacy and honoring confidentiality by ensuring that the data used complies with the licenses of the original sources (CC-BY-SA for Wikipedia and out-of-copyright for Books) (§1.6 and 1.7). Furthermore, our study confirms that the data does not contain any personal information or harmful content (§1.2), thereby avoiding potential harm and minimizing negative consequences. We strive to maintain high standards of professional competence, conduct, and ethical practice (§2.2) throughout our research. Our commitment to ethical conduct also involves transparency and full disclosure of our data sources and limitations (§1.3). By following these ethical guidelines, we aim to contribute to the public good and uphold the principles of responsible computing (§1.1).

References

Charles J Alderson. 2000. *Assessing Reading*. Cambridge University Press.

Somnath Basu Roy Chowdhury, Faeze Brahman, and Snigdha Chaturvedi. 2021. Is Everything in Order? A Simple Way to Order Sentences. In *Proceedings of the 2021 Conference on Empirical Methods in Natural Language Processing*, pages 10769–10779, Online and Punta Cana, Dominican Republic. Association for Computational Linguistics.

Lukas Berglund, Meg Tong, Max Kaufmann, Mikita Balesni, Asa Cooper Stickland, Tomasz Korbak, and Owain Evans. 2023. The reversal curse: Llms trained on" a is b" fail to learn" b is a". *arXiv preprint arXiv:2309.12288*.

Xinchi Chen, Xipeng Qiu, and Xuanjing Huang. 2016. Neural sentence ordering. *arXiv preprint arXiv:1607.06952*.

Baiyun Cui, Yingming Li, Ming Chen, and Zhongfei Zhang. 2018. Deep attentive sentence ordering network. In *Proceedings of the 2018 Conference on Empirical Methods in Natural Language Processing*, pages 4340–4349.

Dean C. Delis, Wendy Wapner, Howard Gardner, and James A. Moses. 1983. The Contribution of the Right Hemisphere to the Organization of Paragraphs. *Cortex*, 19(1):43–50.

Besnik Fetahu, Anjie Fang, Oleg Rokhlenko, and Shervin Malmasi. 2021. Gazetteer enhanced named entity recognition for code-mixed web queries. In *Proceedings of the 44th International ACM SIGIR Conference on Research and Development in Information Retrieval*, SIGIR '21, page 1677–1681, New York, NY, USA. Association for Computing Machinery.

M. G. Kendall. 1938. A new measure of rank correlation. *Biometrika*, 30(1/2):81–93.

Mirella Lapata. 2003. Probabilistic text structuring: Experiments with sentence ordering. In *Proceedings of the 41st Annual Meeting of the Association for Computational Linguistics*, pages 545–552, Sapporo, Japan. Association for Computational Linguistics.

Mike Lewis, Yinhan Liu, Naman Goyal, Marjan Ghazvininejad, Abdelrahman Mohamed, Omer Levy, Veselin Stoyanov, and Luke Zettlemoyer. 2020. BART: Denoising sequence-to-sequence pre-training for natural language generation, translation, and comprehension. In *Proceedings of the 58th Annual Meeting of the Association for Computational Linguistics*, pages 7871–7880, Online. Association for Computational Linguistics.

Lajanugen Logeswaran, Honglak Lee, and Dragomir Radev. 2018. Sentence ordering and coherence modeling using recurrent neural networks. In *Proceedings of the AAAI Conference on Artificial Intelligence*, volume 32.

Shervin Malmasi, Anjie Fang, Besnik Fetahu, Sudipta Kar, and Oleg Rokhlenko. 2022. MultiCoNER: A large-scale multilingual dataset for complex named entity recognition. In *Proceedings of the 29th International Conference on Computational Linguistics*, pages 3798–3809, Gyeongju, Republic of Korea. International Committee on Computational Linguistics.

Nasrin Mostafazadeh, Nathanael Chambers, Xiaodong He, Devi Parikh, Dhruv Batra, Lucy Vanderwende, Pushmeet Kohli, and James Allen. 2016. A corpus and cloze evaluation for deeper understanding of commonsense stories. In *Proceedings of the 2016 Conference of the North American Chapter of the Association for Computational Linguistics: Human Language Technologies*, pages 839–849, San Diego, California. Association for Computational Linguistics.

Ramesh Nallapati, Feifei Zhai, and Bowen Zhou. 2017. Summarunner: A recurrent neural network based sequence model for extractive summarization of documents. In *Proceedings of the AAAI conference on artificial intelligence*, volume 31.

Roy Schwartz, Maarten Sap, Ioannis Konstas, Leila Zilles, Yejin Choi, and Noah A. Smith. 2017. The effect of different writing tasks on linguistic style: A case study of the ROC story cloze task. In *Proceedings of the 21st Conference on Computational Natural Language Learning (CoNLL 2017)*, pages 15–25, Vancouver, Canada. Association for Computational Linguistics.

Aili Shen and Timothy Baldwin. 2021. A simple yet effective method for sentence ordering. In *Proceedings of the 22nd Annual Meeting of the Special Interest Group on Discourse and Dialogue*, pages 154–160, Singapore and Online. Association for Computational Linguistics.

Yunmei Shi, Haiying Zhang, Ning Li, and Teng Yang. 2024. An overview of sentence ordering task. *International Journal of Data Science and Analytics*, pages 1–18.

Jason Wei, Yi Tay, Rishi Bommasani, Colin Raffel, Barret Zoph, Sebastian Borgeaud, Dani Yogatama, Maarten Bosma, Denny Zhou, Donald Metzler, et al. 2022. Emergent abilities of large language models. *arXiv preprint arXiv:2206.07682*.

Adams Wei Yu, David Dohan, Quoc Le, Thang Luong, Rui Zhao, and Kai Chen. 2018. Fast and accurate reading comprehension by combining self-attention and convolution. In *International Conference on Learning Representations*.

HANS, are you clever? Clever Hans Effect Analysis of Neural Systems

Leonardo Ranaldi and Fabio Massimo Zanzotto
Università degli studi Roma Tor Vergata, Italy
[first_name].[last_name]@uniroma2.it

Abstract

Large Language Models (LLMs) have been exhibiting outstanding abilities to reason around cognitive states, intentions, and reactions of all people involved, letting humans guide and comprehend day-to-day social interactions effectively. In fact, several multiple-choice questions (MCQ) benchmarks have been proposed to construct solid assessments of the models' abilities. However, earlier works demonstrate the presence of inherent "order bias" in LLMs, posing challenges to the appropriate evaluation.

In this paper, we investigate LLMs' resilience abilities through a series of probing tests using four MCQ benchmarks. Introducing adversarial examples, we show a significant performance gap, mainly when varying the order of the choices, which reveals a selection bias and brings into discussion reasoning abilities. Following a correlation between first positions and model choices due to positional bias, we hypothesized the presence of structural heuristics in the decision-making process of the LLMs, strengthened by including significant examples in few-shot scenarios. Finally, by using the Chain-of-Thought (CoT) technique, we elicit the model to reason and mitigate the bias by obtaining more robust models.

1 Introduction

The intensifying dispute on AI abilities has led to the evolution of robust evaluation methods to assess the actual limits of LLMs. Recently, many anecdotal examples have been used to suggest that LLMs such as GPTs (OpenAI, 2023), Llamas (Touvron et al., 2023a), and other well-known models are proficient at understanding that people have ideas, thoughts, emotions, and preferences, which is referred to the Neural Theory of Mind (N-ToM) (Sap et al., 2022).

Although these abilities have been observed, earlier works advance conflicting conclusions showing that many solved tasks rely on memorization (Ranaldi et al., 2024a) and superficial heuristics (Shapira et al., 2024), as well-known as *Clever Hans Effect*.

In fact, it seems that LLMs are very sensitive to the arrangement of components in prompts (Zhu et al., 2023), as it directly affects the evaluation of their ability to understand and reason about specific tasks (Ranaldi et al., 2023a,d; Wang et al., 2023a; Lu et al., 2023). Given these findings, our research question arises: Do LLMs have N-ToM abilities, or is it a *Clever Hans Effect*?

In this paper, we propose a systematic evaluation using several benchmarks with the multiple-choice questions (MCQ) format to investigate the interplay between N-ToM and Clever Hans Effect. In order to probe the real abilities of LLMs, we introduce different adversarial strategies by varying the order and altering the content of choices in zero- and few-shot scenarios.

We conduct different experiments using two versions of Llama (Touvron et al., 2023a,b), Vicuna (Chiang et al., 2023), and Falcon (Almazrouei et al., 2023) on four different MCQ benchmarks. Hence, by using PIQA (Bisk et al., 2019), OpenBookQA (Mihaylov et al., 2018), CommonsenseQA (Talmor et al., 2019), Social IQA (Sap et al., 2019) we demonstrate that LLMs have particular N-ToM abilities, but they are not robust.

More specifically, behind in-depth analyses in a zero-shot scenario, we discover a substantial sensitivity gap between the original and adversarial benchmarks. Following, we tested different settings in a few-shot scenario, where we observed that introducing examples in the input prompt led to marginal improvements in the robustness of the LLMs. These results led us to hypothesize that considerable sensitivity in prompting emerges from LLMs' positional bias in that they tend to favor specific structures. Therefore, Clever Hans' heuristics emerge as the choice is not made through reasoning ability.

*Proceedings of the 13th Joint Conference on Lexical and Computational Semantics (*SEM 2024)*, pages 314 - 325
June 20-21, 2024 ©2024 Association for Computational Linguistics

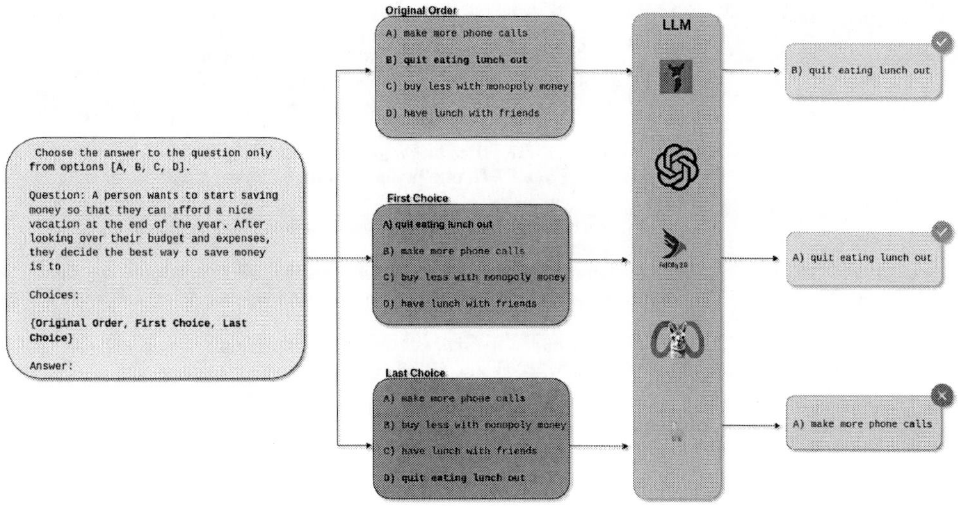

Figure 1: We proposed three different prompts: the original prompt consisting of the `Question` and the `Choices` and two adversarial prompts consisting of the `Question` and different `Choices` order (the example is taken from the OpenBookQA).

Nevertheless, the integration of demonstrations within the input prompts has manifested as a salient mechanism, markedly enhancing the predictive accuracy of LLMs. The impact of the Chain-of-Thought paradigm elucidates bifurcated advantages: it fortifies both the robustness and interpretative stability inherent to the models while concurrently attenuating the positional bias. These methodological augmentations suggest emergent N-ToM abilities, indicating a more profound and contextually attuned linguistic grasp.

Our findings can be summarized as follows:

- LLMs, while lacking robust N-ToM abilities, often resort to structural heuristics;
- When instructed appropriately via few-shot demonstrations, the stability of LLMs improves considerably;
- Hiring a step-by-step methodology boosts enriched reasoning abilities within LLMs, resulting in more consistent results.

Via these studies, we have contributed to a deeper understanding of how the order of options influences the decision-making process of LLMs in multiple-choice questions and offer practical solutions to increase robustness and reliability in such tasks.

2 Empirical Investigation & Analysis

Intending to empirically assess the incline between the Neural Theory of Mind abilities and Clever Hans traps into which Large Language Models (LLMs) could fall, we propose a series of experiments where we use four question-answering benchmarks presented in Section 2.1 and several adversarial experiments introduced in Section 2.2).

2.1 Speculative Benchmark

An essential component of the Theory of Mind (ToM) is the ability to reason about the intentions and reactions of participants to social interactions. To measure it in LLMs, i.e., Neural-ToM (N-ToM) with empirical methods, Sap et al. (2022) was used Social IQa (Sap et al., 2019).

In our work, we extend the study by also considering: PIQA (Bisk et al., 2019), OpenBookQA (Mihaylov et al., 2018), CommonsenseQA (Talmor et al., 2019). Table 1 shows one example for each dataset. The common factor in these datasets is the type of question-answering format, as they are multiple-choice questions (MCQ). This format makes it easier to edit the prompt and observe the output. In particular, the selected datasets deal with the following topics:

OpenBookQA is a resource that contains questions requiring multi-step reasoning, common knowledge, and rich text comprehension. It is mod-

Dataset	Example
OpenBookQA (Mihaylov et al., 2018)	*When birds migrate south for the winter, they do it because* **A) they are genetically called to.** B) their children ask them to. C) it is important to their happiness. D) they decide to each.
Social IQa (Sap et al., 2019)	*Taylor gave help to a friend who was having trouble keeping up with their bills. What will their friend want to do next?* A) Help the friend find a higher paying job. **B) Thank Taylor for the generosity.** C) pay some of their late employees.
PIQA (Bisk et al., 2019)	*How do you attach toilet paper to a glass jar?* **A) Press a piece of double-sided tape to the glass jar and then press the toilet paper onto the tape.** B) Spread mayonnaise all over the jar with your palms and then roll the jar in toilet paper.
CommonsenseQA (Talmor et al., 2019)	*Aside from water and nourishment what does your dog need?* A) bone. B) charm. C) petted. **D) lots of attention.** E) walked.

Table 1: Examples of the datasets used in this paper.

Model	Backbone
Alpaca-13b (Taori et al., 2023)	Llama
Vicuna-13b (Chiang et al., 2023)	Llama
Instruct-Falcon 7b (Almazrouei et al., 2023)	Falcon
Llama2-chat 13b (Touvron et al., 2023b)	Llama2

Table 2: Models used in our work, found on huggingface.co. We used all the default configurations proposed in the repositories for each model.

Model	Available Hugging Face
Alpaca-13b (Taori et al., 2023)	tolen/alpaca-lora-13b
Vicuna-13b (Chiang et al., 2023)	lmsys/vicuna-13b
Instruct-Falcon 7b (Almazrouei et al., 2023)	tiiuae/falcon-7b-instruct
Llama2-chat 13b (Touvron et al., 2023b)	meta-llama/Llama-2-13b-chat

Table 3: In this table, we list the versions of the models proposed in this work, which can be found on huggingface.co. We used all the default configurations proposed in the repositories for each model.

eled behind open-book exams for evaluating human understanding of a topic.

CommonsenseQA is one of the best-known datasets of answers to multiple-choice questions dealing with different types of general commonsense knowledge.

Physical Interaction Question Answering (PIQA) is a resource consisting of a series of everyday situations with a pair of typical or atypical solutions. The choice of the most appropriate solution is binary.

Social Interaction Question Answering (Social IQa) is a benchmark focusing on reasoning about people's actions and social implications. The actions in Social IQa cover various social situations and candidates for plausible and not plausible answers.

Hence, we select benchmarks with the same structure, MCQ, by the number of different choices, which range from the five choices of CommonsenseQA to the four of OpenBookQA, three of Social IQa, and finally, the two of PIQA. This choice allows us to conduct different types of analysis.

2.2 Adversarial Shuffling

The LLMs' impressive knowledge and desirable N-ToMs abilities can be empirically assessed through a series of benchmarks. However, these abilities should persist in the presence of alterations such as the order of choices in MCQ. To probe robustness, we introduce probing experiments by changing the order of the target choices. In particular, we propose two different versions wherein, in the first, we insert the target choice as first, and in the second, we insert the target choice as last, which we defined as "First Target" and "Last Target", as showed in the blue and red block in Figure 1.

3 Experiments

To investigate the open question of social intelligence and Theory of Mind in modern NLP models from an empirical viewpoint, we extended the evaluations of Sap et al. (2022) to a series of Speculative Benchmarks (Section 2.1) altered with appropriately constructed Adversarial Shuffling (Section 2.2) prompts. Then, to assess the factual abilities of the Large Language Models (LLMs), we set up several baseline models (Section 3.1), which we probed with different approaches (Section 3.2). Hence, we performed a series of systematic evaluations to observe the impact of the proposed methods.

3.1 Instruction-tuned LLMs

In this paper, we use four instruction-tuned methods to produce an empirical analysis of the objective ability of different Large Language Models (LLMs). Their power seems to be in the form of a novel tuning called instruction-tuning. These LLMs are fine-tuned LLMs on Instruction-following demonstrations (Ouyang et al., 2022) and how an important part of the currently in-vogue LLMs have at their base a decoder-only architecture. Therefore, we experiment with models of different families of LLMs with similar sizes to avoid creating critical differences. In particular, Alpaca-Lora, fine-tuned on Standford Intruction-following demonstrations (Taori et al., 2023) that has at its backbone Llama-13b (Touvron et al., 2023a), Llama-2-chat-13b fine-tuned on custom data (Touvron et al., 2023b), Vicuna-13b (Chiang et al., 2023) fine-tuned on ShareGPT data and Falcon-7b-instruct (Almazrouei et al., 2023) fine-tuned on Refinedweb data (Penedo et al., 2023). For simplicity of notation in the following experiments, the models will be named as follows: Alpaca (Alpaca-Lora), Falcon (Falcon-7b-instruct), Vicuna (Vicuna-13b), Llama2 (Llama-2-chat-13b). These selected models, summarized in Table 2, are all accessible open-source on the Hugging Face platform (Table 3).

3.2 Experimental Setup & Evaluation

LLMs seem to have interesting abilities as well as introduced in Section 5. However, LLMs seem to be sensitive to the input required. They produce satisfactory answers if they are rightly prompted. To investigate whether their abilities are attributable to Coincidental correlations or inherited N-ToM abilities, we standardized the probing techniques to conduct systematic analyses that yield robust empirical results.

Multiple-Choice Prompting We set the prompts by structuring them as follows: `"Choose the answer to the question only from options [A, B, C, and D]. Question: {question}.` and after the line character the `"Choices: {options}."` also appropriately separated by the return character and finally `"Answer:"`.

Zero- & Few-shot Prompting Furthermore, we conducted the experiments in a zero-shot and one-shot scenario. In the first case, the prompt consists of the introduction of the task, the question, and the possible choices (see Figure 1). In the second case, a prompt like the previous one was constructed in which an example with the corresponding target was inserted (see Figure 6).

Chain-of-Thought Prompting Finally, to elicit the reasoning abilities of the proposed models, we adopted the Chain-of-Thought (CoT) approach (Wei et al., 2023) by prompting the input query after `"Answer:"` the formula `"Let's think step by step"` (see Figure 6). Although we are aware of the limitations of this method on models with a few billion parameters (with more than 60B parameters as stated by Wei et al. (2023)), we decided to test it anyway because, as we will see later in the experiments, it delivered more stability to the models used.

Evaluation The most commonly used evaluation methods for MCQ tasks are language-model probing, where the option with the highest probability is chosen (Brown et al., 2020), and multiple-choice probing, where models are asked to respond. The evaluation in the former case is done with a function that takes the max value, while in the latter case, a string matching. The second method is widely used in recent evaluations because it applies to models such as GPT-x (GPT-3.5 and GPT-4) (OpenAI, 2023) that do not produce probabilities.

We could use both methods in our experiments, but we selected the second method for a comparable and scalable pipeline. We performed a string matching of the generated outputs and the target choice.

4 Results

Looking for evidence that Theory of Mind (ToM) has been inherited from Neural Minds is like looking for a drop in the ocean. The results in Table 4 show the fluctuations in the performances obtained from Instruction-tuned Large Language Models (LLMs) on more straightforward patterns (Section 4.1). However, although the evident gaps seem to be order-dependent, the performances obtained from the few-shot scenario are encouraging (Section 4.2). These data presaged a strong inclination toward Clever Hans's effects. Therefore, we analyzed the impact of elicitation on the reasoning of LLMs using promting techniques (Section 4.3) that showed strong improvements.

Models	OpenBookQA			Social IQa			CommonsenseQA			PIQA		
	Origin	First	Last	Origin	First	Last	Origin	First	Last	Origin	First	Last
Alpaca	36.2	+11.7	-9.2	48.2	+8.5	-18.6	55.2	+8.4	-11.7	62.7	+2.3	-1.8
Falcon	54.8	+3.2	-13.6	57.5	+3.6	-14.5	60.2	+5.3	-7.8	68.6	+1.7	-0.9
Vicuna	58.1	+3.9	-8.6	60.3	+3.1	-6.4	66.4	+6.3	-6.4	74.2	+1.9	-1.2
Llama2	61.2	+3.6	-5.8	65.6	+4.3	-5.2	80.5	+2.3	-4.6	82.5	+1.6	-1.2

Table 4: Accuracy on the benchmarks introduced in Section 2.1 performs on the original order of the choices 'Origin', shifting the target choice respectively as first 'First' last 'Last'. The specific position of the target choice causes drastic fluctuations in performance.

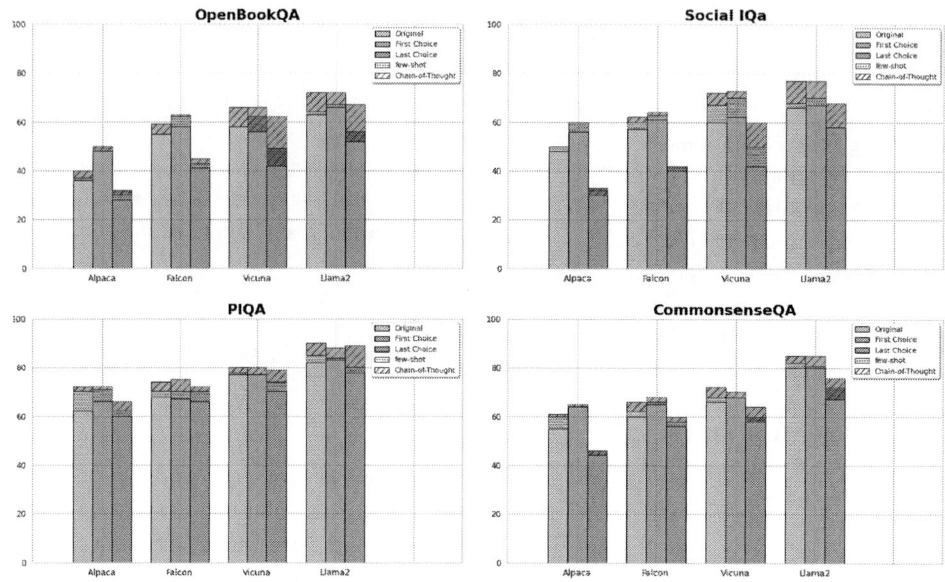

Figure 2: Evaluation results on proposed benchmarks. First means that the target is the first choice. Last means that the target is the last choice.

Choose the answer to the question only from options A, B, C, D.

Question: Which of these would stop a car quicker?

A) a wheel with wet brake pads
B) a wheel without brake pads
C) a wheel with worn brake pads
D) a wheel with dry brake pads
Answer: **Let's think step by step**

Table 5: This is an example of our Chain-of-Thought prompting approach.

Fine-grained analysis revealed critical issues about the robustness of LLMs and their tendency to Clever Hans effects; however, elicitation to reasoning produced thrilling results that opened the way for new hypotheses about the Neural-ToM abilities inherited by LLMs.

4.1 Does the Order Matter?

The order of the input parameters seems to have a considerable impact on the choices of the LLMs. In fact, as shown in Table 4, there are significant imbalances in accuracy as the target options change (see the differences in the Firsts and Lasts columns). This positional bias manifests more in zero-shot scenarios, as also showed in (Robinson et al., 2023; Zheng et al., 2023a). Furthermore, the gaps differ between the benchmarks; e.g., in PIQA, there are no significant differences as there are only two possible choices.

In addition to highlighting the presence of a bias

```
Choose the answer to the question
only from options A, B, C, D.

Question: Which of these would stop a car
quicker?

A) a wheel with wet brake pads
B) a wheel without brake pads
C) a wheel with worn brake pads
D) a wheel with dry brake pads
Answer: D) a wheel with dry brake pads

Choose the answer to the question
only from options A, B, C, D.

Question: What animal eats plants?
A) eagles
B) robins
C) owls
D) leopards
Answer:
```

Table 6: This is an example of our one-shot prompting approach.

toward order, this phenomenon presages factual evidence that models are prone to adopt shallow heuristics when faced with several choices. For this reason, we analyzed in Section 4.4 whether the performances on the original benchmarks are partly supported by the instances with the first choice, i.e., option 'A)', as the original target.

4.2 Could Few-shot Prompting be a solution?

Although the LLMs are affected by order bias, they should also be sensitive to the structure of the prompt. Hence, we conduct experiments in a few-shot scenario, particularly one-shot. As introduced in Section 3.2, we constructed the prompt by providing a random pair instance-target of the benchmark under evaluation, for example, as Figure 6.

As shown in Figure 2, constructing prompts with question-answer demonstrations helped reduce the order bias predominantly for the adversarial versions of the benchmarks considered (see the red columns in Figure 2). However, although the results were encouraging, providing examples in a few-shot scenario is not an optimal strategy for two reasons: firstly, it is not possible to analyze the proper knowledge and abilities of the LLMs; secondly, providing examples very close to the question the model is supposed to answer could cause the model to fall into Clever Hans effects (Shapira et al., 2023).

4.3 N-ToM Abilities or Prompting Techniques?

Stimulating the generative abilities of LLMs could be the key. Figure 2 shows that the performance of models where Chain-of-Thought prompting has been done is more stable and significantly better. In particular, Llama2 and Vicuna have benefitted best from this technique.

Hence, constructing prompts with strategically placed choices facilitates shallow heuristics, and providing examples produces Clever Hans Effects elicitation to step-by-step reasoning prompts the LLMs to consider the whole question with choices. Moreover, the production of the choice between the various seems more robust as the model seems less uncertain. However, this strategy does not always seem to have positive effects. Alpaca-Alpaca-Lora and Falcon do not have the same sound effects as the other two models.

4.4 Ablation Study

Downstreaming our analysis, we observed the presence of a bias in the order of choices. Indeed, as discussed in Section 4.1, there is a strong bias towards the first choice, i.e., 'A)'. Therefore, we examined whether this bias supports the performances of the original benchmarks. We then reproduced all the experiments by eliminating the instances that target the first choice. In this experiment, we did not consider PIQA as it only has two choices; therefore, the results are irrelevant for this experiment.

Our experiment in Figure 3 reveals a gap between the performances obtained without the 'simple' instances. This result shows that, indeed, the performance of the evaluation benchmarks is affected by positional bias. However, these are more dramatic than denying all experiments but must be considered as they could distort many evaluations.

5 Related Work

5.1 Evaluation of Large Language Models

Increasing confidence in LLMs requires a fundamental empirical assessment part. Traditional evaluation methods assess the ability to respond to instructions by calculating metrics such as BLEU,

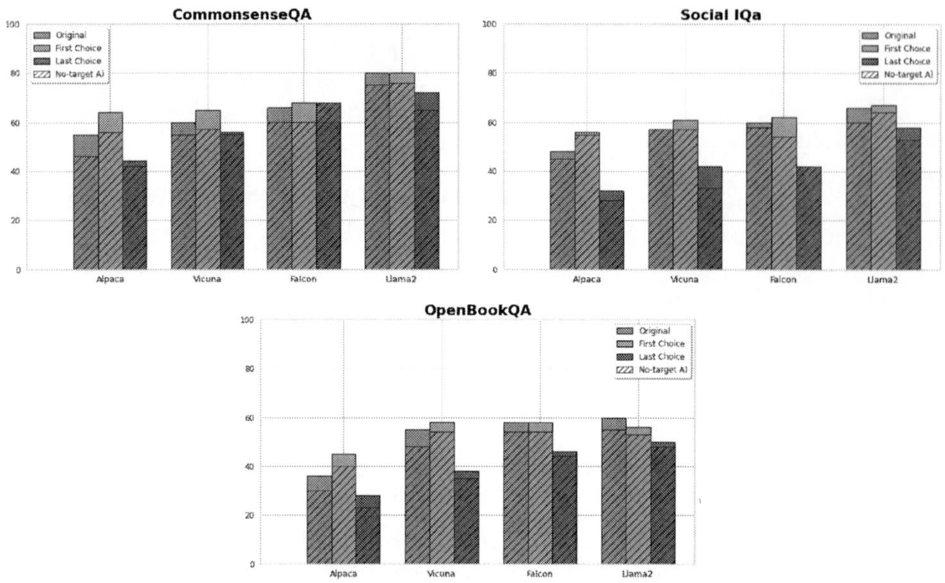

Figure 3: Accuracy on original benchmarks vs. corrupted benchmarks. They stem from the original ones without instances where the target choice is the first among the multiples.

ROUGE, or BERTScore to compare the generated response with a reference response. However, these metrics need to adequately measure the alignment of the generated response with human intent (He et al., 2023). Although human evaluation is considered the most accurate measure of model performance, it is expensive and time-consuming to perform at scale. Therefore, researchers have begun using LLMs to evaluate generative models' ability to follow human instructions (Zheng et al., 2023b; Lu et al., 2023). Zheng et al. (2023b) used GPT-4 (OpenAI, 2023) as an arbiter to compare the answers of the two models. However, Wang et al. (2023c,b) demonstrated several weaknesses in this method, giving rise to a proliferation of skepticism that has been reinforced by a series of works highlighting sensitivity to prompting (Lu et al., 2023) and instability to response generation (Wang et al., 2023b; Zhu et al., 2023).

5.2 Question-answering Benchmark

In parallel with the multiple validation techniques, numerous Question-answering benchmarks have arisen consisting of multiple subtasks characterized by multiple-choice questions. These benchmarks have been introduced as a method to assess reasoning skills and (Artetxe et al., 2019; Lewis et al., 2020; Hendrycks et al., 2021; Suzgun et al., 2022) factual abilities (Elsahar et al., 2018; Petroni et al., 2019). Despite the difficulties present in these tasks, great strides have been made with language models achieving human-like performance in various benchmarks (OpenAI, 2023; Savelka et al., 2023; Liévin et al., 2023). However, the effective use of these tasks to effectively probe reasoning and other knowledge presents substantial challenges that deserve further investigation.

5.3 Clever Hans Effect & Neural Theory of Mind

Large Language Models psychotherapy seems to be an emerging field (Hewitt et al., 2023; Meng et al., 2023; Lamparth and Reuel, 2023) Recent studies on the emerging abilities of Large Language Models have proposed numerous theories (Wei et al., 2022; Kasneci et al., 2023). Some of these have been empirically proven, while others have remained only hypotheses and conjectures that are difficult to prove. Numerous studies have shown that LLMs can inherit certain Theories of Mind (ToM) from learning, defining this as Neural-ToM abilities (Le et al., 2019; Sap et al., 2019). However, numerous works have refuted these theories by scapegoating the Clever Hans Effect (Shapira et al., 2023). The latter phenomenon has manifested in multiple forms on numerous well-known benchmarks (Webson and Pavlick, 2022; Carlini et al., 2023).

In our contribution, we analyzed whether several open-source LLMs can defend themselves against the traps of the Clever Hans Effect by proposing a series of experiments. Behind extensive analysis, we discovered that LLMs are prone to adopt superficial heuristics when they are facilitated in their decisions.

On the other side of the coin, they can apply robust mechanisms when prompted to reason. This opens up different attractive scenarios on the promising approaches of Chain-of-Thought techniques (Wei et al., 2023).

6 Future Works

In future work, we plan to extend our experimentation to different models and observe whether this phenomenon can be mitigated through downstream model distillation techniques. Hence, we will extend our work to different models, including GPT-3.5 and GPT-4. On the other hand, we study the impact and robustness of the variation of backbone model parameters (as done in (Ranaldi and Pucci, 2024)) and how it affects further trained models through refinement techniques using teacher-student approaches (Ranaldi and Freitas, 2024) and multi- and cross-lingual techniques (Ranaldi and Pucci, 2023a; Ruzzetti et al., 2023; Ranaldi et al., 2023b, 2022a). At the same time, it will be of interest to us to analyze whether prompt engineering techniques are affected by this phenomenon, such as Chain-of-Thought in contexts with few-shots and Tree-of-Thought in cross-lingual contexts (Ranaldi et al., 2024b). Addressing these studies will allow us to look at the problem from multiple perspectives and investigate the consequences of shallow heuristics.

Finally, we will analyze the impact of a further injection of bias into the best-known benchmarks to observe whether the capabilities of LLMs can overcome challenging scenarios in order to understand whether these phenomena are indeed related to structural representations (Zanzotto et al., 2020; Ranaldi and Pucci, 2023b; Ranaldi et al., 2023c) handed down by the models or are merely the result of structural features of Large Language Models (Onorati et al., 2023; Ranaldi et al., 2022b).

7 Conclusion

The Large Language Models (LLMs) have been demonstrating interesting abilities in real-world understanding. Empirically assessing these abilities is a challenging task. In our contribution, we propose systematic evaluations through multiple-choice questions (MCQ) benchmarks. However, our study revealed an inherent order-bias in these models. Through adversarial testing, we observed a significant discrepancy in performance, particularly when altering the sequence of options, underlining a prevailing selection bias that challenges the reasoning abilities of the LLMs. We identified a link between positional preferences and model selections, which led us to theorize the existence of structural heuristics guiding the decision-making process. By incorporating relevant examples in few-shot contexts, this notion was further strengthened. Using Chain-of-Thought approaches allowed us to make the model introspect its decisions, thus reducing observed bias and resulting in more reliable and robust LLMs.

Our results revealed some limitations regarding robustness in zero-shot scenarios but simultaneously showed that the CoT approach enhances stability. Our future research will focus on proposing definitely unseen benchmarks to evaluate real abilities without the presence of distorted glass.

Limitations

In our study, we conducted extensive analyses to evaluate order bias in open-source Large Language Models (LLMs) using multiple-choice questions (MCQ) benchmarks. Following the performed analyses and the results obtained, we observed the presence of order bias and proposed methods to mitigate this phenomenon. However, our analysis needs to be completed, as more robust models were not tested, as the primary purpose was to analyze these phenomena in smaller, countable contexts. We plan to scale our approach to more extensive and robust LLMs in future developments. In addition, we plan to include further benchmarks in our analyses to observe whether the effect also manifests itself with different task types.

Ethical Statement

We have observed the highest ethical standards in our research and development. We want to emphasize the following points regarding the sources and methods used:

- Use of open-source benchmarks: All benchmarks and datasets used in our work come from open-access public repositories. We have ensured the transparency of our methods by relying on commonly accepted and widely recognized resources.

- Content sensitivity: We have consciously refrained from using datasets or benchmarks that could be associated with controversial, derogatory, or potentially harmful content. We aim to ensure that our work is inclusive and respects the diverse perspectives of all stakeholders.
- Avoiding harmful contexts: In selecting benchmarks and datasets, we have prioritized those not linked to contexts where someone could be offended or harmed. We strive to contribute positively to the community without causing unintended harm or inconvenience.

References

Ebtesam Almazrouei, Hamza Alobeidli, Abdulaziz Alshamsi, Alessandro Cappelli, Ruxandra Cojocaru, Merouane Debbah, Etienne Goffinet, Daniel Heslow, Julien Launay, Quentin Malartic, Badreddine Noune, Baptiste Pannier, and Guilherme Penedo. 2023. Falcon-40B: an open large language model with state-of-the-art performance.

Mikel Artetxe, Sebastian Ruder, and Dani Yogatama. 2019. On the cross-lingual transferability of monolingual representations. In *Annual Meeting of the Association for Computational Linguistics*.

Yonatan Bisk, Rowan Zellers, Ronan Le Bras, Jianfeng Gao, and Yejin Choi. 2019. Piqa: Reasoning about physical commonsense in natural language.

Tom B. Brown, Benjamin Mann, Nick Ryder, Melanie Subbiah, Jared Kaplan, Prafulla Dhariwal, Arvind Neelakantan, Pranav Shyam, Girish Sastry, Amanda Askell, Sandhini Agarwal, Ariel Herbert-Voss, Gretchen Krueger, Tom Henighan, Rewon Child, Aditya Ramesh, Daniel M. Ziegler, Jeffrey Wu, Clemens Winter, Christopher Hesse, Mark Chen, Eric Sigler, Mateusz Litwin, Scott Gray, Benjamin Chess, Jack Clark, Christopher Berner, Sam McCandlish, Alec Radford, Ilya Sutskever, and Dario Amodei. 2020. Language models are few-shot learners.

Nicholas Carlini, Daphne Ippolito, Matthew Jagielski, Katherine Lee, Florian Tramer, and Chiyuan Zhang. 2023. Quantifying memorization across neural language models.

Wei-Lin Chiang, Zhuohan Li, Zi Lin, Ying Sheng, Zhanghao Wu, Hao Zhang, Lianmin Zheng, Siyuan Zhuang, Yonghao Zhuang, Joseph E. Gonzalez, Ion Stoica, and Eric P. Xing. 2023. Vicuna: An open-source chatbot impressing gpt-4 with 90%* chatgpt quality.

Hady Elsahar, Pavlos Vougiouklis, Arslen Remaci, Christophe Gravier, Jonathon Hare, Frederique Laforest, and Elena Simperl. 2018. T-REx: A large scale alignment of natural language with knowledge base triples. In *Proceedings of the Eleventh International Conference on Language Resources and Evaluation (LREC 2018)*, Miyazaki, Japan. European Language Resources Association (ELRA).

Tianxing He, Jingyu Zhang, Tianle Wang, Sachin Kumar, Kyunghyun Cho, James Glass, and Yulia Tsvetkov. 2023. On the blind spots of model-based evaluation metrics for text generation. In *Proceedings of the 61st Annual Meeting of the Association for Computational Linguistics (Volume 1: Long Papers)*, pages 12067–12097, Toronto, Canada. Association for Computational Linguistics.

Dan Hendrycks, Collin Burns, Steven Basart, Andy Zou, Mantas Mazeika, Dawn Song, and Jacob Steinhardt. 2021. Measuring massive multitask language understanding.

John Hewitt, John Thickstun, Christopher D. Manning, and Percy Liang. 2023. Backpack language models.

Enkelejda Kasneci, Kathrin Sessler, Stefan Küchemann, Maria Bannert, Daryna Dementieva, Frank Fischer, Urs Gasser, Georg Groh, Stephan Günnemann, Eyke Hüllermeier, Stephan Krusche, Gitta Kutyniok, Tilman Michaeli, Claudia Nerdel, Jürgen Pfeffer, Oleksandra Poquet, Michael Sailer, Albrecht Schmidt, Tina Seidel, Matthias Stadler, Jochen Weller, Jochen Kuhn, and Gjergji Kasneci. 2023. Chatgpt for good? on opportunities and challenges of large language models for education. *Learning and Individual Differences*, 103:102274.

Max Lamparth and Anka Reuel. 2023. Analyzing and editing inner mechanisms of backdoored language models.

Matthew Le, Y-Lan Boureau, and Maximilian Nickel. 2019. Revisiting the evaluation of theory of mind through question answering. In *Proceedings of the 2019 Conference on Empirical Methods in Natural Language Processing and the 9th International Joint Conference on Natural Language Processing (EMNLP-IJCNLP)*, pages 5872–5877, Hong Kong, China. Association for Computational Linguistics.

Patrick Lewis, Barlas Oguz, Ruty Rinott, Sebastian Riedel, and Holger Schwenk. 2020. MLQA: Evaluating cross-lingual extractive question answering. In *Proceedings of the 58th Annual Meeting of the Association for Computational Linguistics*, pages 7315–7330, Online. Association for Computational Linguistics.

Valentin Liévin, Christoffer Egeberg Hother, and Ole Winther. 2023. Can large language models reason about medical questions?

Qingyu Lu, Baopu Qiu, Liang Ding, Liping Xie, and Dacheng Tao. 2023. Error analysis prompting enables human-like translation evaluation in large language models: A case study on chatgpt.

Kevin Meng, David Bau, Alex Andonian, and Yonatan Belinkov. 2023. Locating and editing factual associations in gpt.

Todor Mihaylov, Peter Clark, Tushar Khot, and Ashish Sabharwal. 2018. Can a suit of armor conduct electricity? a new dataset for open book question answering. In *EMNLP*.

Dario Onorati, Elena Sofia Ruzzetti, Davide Venditti, Leonardo Ranaldi, and Fabio Massimo Zanzotto. 2023. Measuring bias in instruction-following models with P-AT. In *Findings of the Association for Computational Linguistics: EMNLP 2023*, pages 8006–8034, Singapore. Association for Computational Linguistics.

OpenAI. 2023. Gpt-4 technical report.

Long Ouyang, Jeff Wu, Xu Jiang, Diogo Almeida, Carroll L. Wainwright, Pamela Mishkin, Chong Zhang, Sandhini Agarwal, Katarina Slama, Alex Ray, John Schulman, Jacob Hilton, Fraser Kelton, Luke Miller, Maddie Simens, Amanda Askell, Peter Welinder, Paul Christiano, Jan Leike, and Ryan Lowe. 2022. Training language models to follow instructions with human feedback.

Guilherme Penedo, Quentin Malartic, Daniel Hesslow, Ruxandra Cojocaru, Alessandro Cappelli, Hamza Alobeidli, Baptiste Pannier, Ebtesam Almazrouei, and Julien Launay. 2023. The refinedweb dataset for falcon llm: Outperforming curated corpora with web data, and web data only.

Fabio Petroni, Tim Rocktäschel, Patrick Lewis, Anton Bakhtin, Yuxiang Wu, Alexander H. Miller, and Sebastian Riedel. 2019. Language models as knowledge bases?

Federico Ranaldi, Elena Sofia Ruzzetti, Dario Onorati, Leonardo Ranaldi, Cristina Giannone, Andrea Favalli, Raniero Romagnoli, and Fabio Massimo Zanzotto. 2024a. Investigating the impact of data contamination of large language models in text-to-sql translation.

Leonardo Ranaldi, Francesca Fallucchi, and Fabio Massimo Zanzotto. 2022a. Dis-cover ai minds to preserve human knowledge. *Future Internet*, 14(1).

Leonardo Ranaldi and Andre Freitas. 2024. Aligning large and small language models via chain-of-thought reasoning. In *Proceedings of the 18th Conference of the European Chapter of the Association for Computational Linguistics (Volume 1: Long Papers)*, pages 1812–1827, St. Julian's, Malta. Association for Computational Linguistics.

Leonardo Ranaldi, Aria Nourbakhsh, Elena Sofia Ruzzetti, Arianna Patrizi, Dario Onorati, Michele Mastromattei, Francesca Fallucchi, and Fabio Massimo Zanzotto. 2023a. The dark side of the language: Pre-trained transformers in the DarkNet. In *Proceedings of the 14th International Conference on Recent Advances in Natural Language Processing*, pages 949–960, Varna, Bulgaria. INCOMA Ltd., Shoumen, Bulgaria.

Leonardo Ranaldi and Giulia Pucci. 2023a. Does the English matter? elicit cross-lingual abilities of large language models. In *Proceedings of the 3rd Workshop on Multi-lingual Representation Learning (MRL)*, pages 173–183, Singapore. Association for Computational Linguistics.

Leonardo Ranaldi and Giulia Pucci. 2023b. Knowing knowledge: Epistemological study of knowledge in transformers. *Applied Sciences*, 13(2).

Leonardo Ranaldi and Giulia Pucci. 2024. When large language models contradict humans? large language models' sycophantic behaviour.

Leonardo Ranaldi, Giulia Pucci, and Andre Freitas. 2023b. Empowering cross-lingual abilities of instruction-tuned large language models by translation-following demonstrations.

Leonardo Ranaldi, Giulia Pucci, Federico Ranaldi, Elena Sofia Ruzzetti, and Fabio Massimo Zanzotto. 2024b. Empowering multi-step reasoning across languages via tree-of-thoughts.

Leonardo Ranaldi, Giulia Pucci, and Fabio Massimo Zanzotto. 2023c. Modeling easiness for training transformers with curriculum learning. In *Proceedings of the 14th International Conference on Recent Advances in Natural Language Processing*, pages 937–948, Varna, Bulgaria. INCOMA Ltd., Shoumen, Bulgaria.

Leonardo Ranaldi, Federico Ranaldi, Francesca Fallucchi, and Fabio Massimo Zanzotto. 2022b. Shedding light on the dark web: Authorship attribution in radical forums. *Information*, 13(9).

Leonardo Ranaldi, Elena Sofia Ruzzetti, and Fabio Massimo Zanzotto. 2023d. PreCog: Exploring the relation between memorization and performance in pre-trained language models. In *Proceedings of the 14th International Conference on Recent Advances in Natural Language Processing*, pages 961–967, Varna, Bulgaria. INCOMA Ltd., Shoumen, Bulgaria.

Joshua Robinson, Christopher Michael Rytting, and David Wingate. 2023. Leveraging large language models for multiple choice question answering.

Elena Sofia Ruzzetti, Federico Ranaldi, Felicia Logozzo, Michele Mastromattei, Leonardo Ranaldi, and Fabio Massimo Zanzotto. 2023. Exploring linguistic properties of monolingual BERTs with typological classification among languages. In *Findings of the Association for Computational Linguistics: EMNLP 2023*, pages 14447–14461, Singapore. Association for Computational Linguistics.

Maarten Sap, Ronan Le Bras, Daniel Fried, and Yejin Choi. 2022. Neural theory-of-mind? on the limits of social intelligence in large LMs. In *Proceedings of the 2022 Conference on Empirical Methods in Natural Language Processing*, pages 3762–3780, Abu Dhabi, United Arab Emirates. Association for Computational Linguistics.

Maarten Sap, Hannah Rashkin, Derek Chen, Ronan Le Bras, and Yejin Choi. 2019. Social IQa: Commonsense reasoning about social interactions. In *Proceedings of the 2019 Conference on Empirical Methods in Natural Language Processing and the 9th International Joint Conference on Natural Language Processing (EMNLP-IJCNLP)*, pages 4463–4473, Hong Kong, China. Association for Computational Linguistics.

Jaromir Savelka, Arav Agarwal, Christopher Bogart, and Majd Sakr. 2023. Large language models (gpt) struggle to answer multiple-choice questions about code.

Natalie Shapira, Mosh Levy, Seyed Hossein Alavi, Xuhui Zhou, Yejin Choi, Yoav Goldberg, Maarten Sap, and Vered Shwartz. 2023. Clever hans or neural theory of mind? stress testing social reasoning in large language models.

Natalie Shapira, Mosh Levy, Seyed Hossein Alavi, Xuhui Zhou, Yejin Choi, Yoav Goldberg, Maarten Sap, and Vered Shwartz. 2024. Clever hans or neural theory of mind? stress testing social reasoning in large language models. In *Proceedings of the 18th Conference of the European Chapter of the Association for Computational Linguistics (Volume 1: Long Papers)*, pages 2257–2273, St. Julian's, Malta. Association for Computational Linguistics.

Mirac Suzgun, Nathan Scales, Nathanael Schärli, Sebastian Gehrmann, Yi Tay, Hyung Won Chung, Aakanksha Chowdhery, Quoc V Le, Ed H Chi, Denny Zhou, , and Jason Wei. 2022. Challenging big-bench tasks and whether chain-of-thought can solve them. *arXiv preprint arXiv:2210.09261*.

Alon Talmor, Jonathan Herzig, Nicholas Lourie, and Jonathan Berant. 2019. CommonsenseQA: A question answering challenge targeting commonsense knowledge. In *Proceedings of the 2019 Conference of the North American Chapter of the Association for Computational Linguistics: Human Language Technologies, Volume 1 (Long and Short Papers)*, pages 4149–4158, Minneapolis, Minnesota. Association for Computational Linguistics.

Rohan Taori, Ishaan Gulrajani, Tianyi Zhang, Yann Dubois, Xuechen Li, Carlos Guestrin, Percy Liang, and Tatsunori B. Hashimoto. 2023. Stanford alpaca: An instruction-following llama model. `https://github.com/tatsu-lab/stanford_alpaca`.

Hugo Touvron, Thibaut Lavril, Gautier Izacard, Xavier Martinet, Marie-Anne Lachaux, Timothée Lacroix, Baptiste Rozière, Naman Goyal, Eric Hambro, Faisal Azhar, Aurelien Rodriguez, Armand Joulin, Edouard Grave, and Guillaume Lample. 2023a. Llama: Open and efficient foundation language models.

Hugo Touvron, Louis Martin, Kevin Stone, Peter Albert, Amjad Almahairi, Yasmine Babaei, Nikolay Bashlykov, Soumya Batra, Prajjwal Bhargava, Shruti Bhosale, Dan Bikel, Lukas Blecher, Cristian Canton Ferrer, Moya Chen, Guillem Cucurull, David Esiobu, Jude Fernandes, Jeremy Fu, Wenyin Fu, Brian Fuller, Cynthia Gao, Vedanuj Goswami, Naman Goyal, Anthony Hartshorn, Saghar Hosseini, Rui Hou, Hakan Inan, Marcin Kardas, Viktor Kerkez, Madian Khabsa, Isabel Kloumann, Artem Korenev, Punit Singh Koura, Marie-Anne Lachaux, Thibaut Lavril, Jenya Lee, Diana Liskovich, Yinghai Lu, Yuning Mao, Xavier Martinet, Todor Mihaylov, Pushkar Mishra, Igor Molybog, Yixin Nie, Andrew Poulton, Jeremy Reizenstein, Rashi Rungta, Kalyan Saladi, Alan Schelten, Ruan Silva, Eric Michael Smith, Ranjan Subramanian, Xiaoqing Ellen Tan, Binh Tang, Ross Taylor, Adina Williams, Jian Xiang Kuan, Puxin Xu, Zheng Yan, Iliyan Zarov, Yuchen Zhang, Angela Fan,

Melanie Kambadur, Sharan Narang, Aurelien Rodriguez, Robert Stojnic, Sergey Edunov, and Thomas Scialom. 2023b. Llama 2: Open foundation and fine-tuned chat models.

Jindong Wang, Xixu Hu, Wenxin Hou, Hao Chen, Runkai Zheng, Yidong Wang, Linyi Yang, Haojun Huang, Wei Ye, Xiubo Geng, Binxin Jiao, Yue Zhang, and Xing Xie. 2023a. On the robustness of chatgpt: An adversarial and out-of-distribution perspective.

Jiongxiao Wang, Zichen Liu, Keun Hee Park, Muhao Chen, and Chaowei Xiao. 2023b. Adversarial demonstration attacks on large language models.

Peiyi Wang, Lei Li, Liang Chen, Zefan Cai, Dawei Zhu, Binghuai Lin, Yunbo Cao, Qi Liu, Tianyu Liu, and Zhifang Sui. 2023c. Large language models are not fair evaluators.

Albert Webson and Ellie Pavlick. 2022. Do prompt-based models really understand the meaning of their prompts? In *Proceedings of the 2022 Conference of the North American Chapter of the Association for Computational Linguistics: Human Language Technologies*, pages 2300–2344, Seattle, United States. Association for Computational Linguistics.

Jason Wei, Yi Tay, Rishi Bommasani, Colin Raffel, Barret Zoph, Sebastian Borgeaud, Dani Yogatama, Maarten Bosma, Denny Zhou, Donald Metzler, Ed H. Chi, Tatsunori Hashimoto, Oriol Vinyals, Percy Liang, Jeff Dean, and William Fedus. 2022. Emergent abilities of large language models.

Jason Wei, Xuezhi Wang, Dale Schuurmans, Maarten Bosma, Brian Ichter, Fei Xia, Ed Chi, Quoc Le, and Denny Zhou. 2023. Chain-of-thought prompting elicits reasoning in large language models.

Fabio Massimo Zanzotto, Andrea Santilli, Leonardo Ranaldi, Dario Onorati, Pierfrancesco Tommasino, and Francesca Fallucchi. 2020. KERMIT: Complementing transformer architectures with encoders of explicit syntactic interpretations. In *Proceedings of the 2020 Conference on Empirical Methods in Natural Language Processing (EMNLP)*, pages 256–267, Online. Association for Computational Linguistics.

Chujie Zheng, Hao Zhou, Fandong Meng, Jie Zhou, and Minlie Huang. 2023a. On large language models' selection bias in multi-choice questions.

Lianmin Zheng, Wei-Lin Chiang, Ying Sheng, Siyuan Zhuang, Zhanghao Wu, Yonghao Zhuang, Zi Lin, Zhuohan Li, Dacheng Li, Eric. P Xing, Hao Zhang, Joseph E. Gonzalez, and Ion Stoica. 2023b. Judging llm-as-a-judge with mt-bench and chatbot arena.

Kaijie Zhu, Jindong Wang, Jiaheng Zhou, Zichen Wang, Hao Chen, Yidong Wang, Linyi Yang, Wei Ye, Neil Zhenqiang Gong, Yue Zhang, and Xing Xie. 2023. Promptbench: Towards evaluating the robustness of large language models on adversarial prompts.

Exploring Semantics in Pretrained Language Model Attention

Frédéric Charpentier[1,2] and **Jairo Cugliari**[1] and **Adrien Guille**[1]
[1]Université Lyon 2, Laboratoire ERIC, Lyon, France
[2]Cabot Financial France
{frederic.charpentier, jairo.cugliari, adrien.guille}@univ-lyon2.fr

Abstract

Abstract Meaning Representations (AMRs) encode the semantics of sentences in the form of graphs. Vertices represent instances of concepts, and labeled edges represent semantic relations between those instances. Language models (LMs) operate by computing weights of edges of per layer complete graphs whose vertices are words in a sentence or a whole paragraph. In this work, we investigate the ability of the attention heads of two LMs, RoBERTa and GPT-2, to detect the semantic relations encoded in an AMR. This is an attempt to show semantic capabilities of those models without finetuning. To do so, we apply both unsupervised and supervised learning techniques.

1 Introduction

An AMR graph, as specified by Banarescu et al. (2013), is a representation of the meaning of a sentence in the form of a directed acyclic graph, involving concepts from neo-Davidsonian semantics (Davidson, 1969). A number of datasets of sentences and their corresponding hand-crafted AMRs have been published, and various techniques have been developed to automatically build AMR graphs from sentences in natural language. These include graph based approaches, which directly predict nodes and edges from the sentences, (Flanigan et al., 2014, Zhang et al., 2019), and algorithms based on transition systems (Nivre, 2008), inspired by dependency parsing algorithms (CAMR: Wang et al., 2015, AMR-Eager: Damonte et al., 2017). The most recent solutions combine an encoder-decoder pair of a transformer network (Vaswani et al., 2017) to adapt it to the task of transition-based AMR parsing, as StructBART does (Zhou et al., 2021).

AMR graphs abstract away meaning from syntactic representations. This is evidenced by the fact that one AMR graph can encode several differently worded sentences, even with different syntaxes. (Banarescu et al., 2013)

Transformer-based language models, introduced by Vaswani et al. (2017), have shown remarkable performance in solving many problems related to automatic natural language processing, but the interpretability of their computations is still subject to active research: Clark et al. (2019) studied the ability of certain attention heads in the BERT network (Devlin et al., 2019) to classify several syntactic relations between words and to resolve coreference, without finetuning BERT for any specific task. Luo (2021) studied how constituency grammar is captured by different attention heads in BERT. We complement their work and explore the ability of attention heads to classify semantic relations between two words as described by the edge type between two vertices of an AMR.

We study a representative bidirectional pretrained language model, without finetuning: RoBERTa (Liu et al., 2019), and compare it to GPT-2 (Radford et al., 2019), a pretrained conditional model, using both unsupervised and supervised techniques. Our study reveals a striking correlation of these networks' attention heads with semantics. We observed that RoBERTa showed conspicuously better results than GPT-2, probably because of the bidirectional nature of the former. To reproduce our experiments, we made our code publicly available.[1]

2 Dataset Design and Experimental Setup

In a nutshell, an AMR encodes in a rooted directed acyclic graph **who** is doing **what** to **whom**, **where**, **when** and **how**, in a manner that abstracts away semantics from syntax. In particular, a single AMR graph can encode several syntactically different sentences, like "the bears invaded Sicily" (a whole clause), "the bears' invasion of Sicily" (a noun

[1]https://anonymous.4open.science/r/sem_LM_att-322F/

*Proceedings of the 13th Joint Conference on Lexical and Computational Semantics (*SEM 2024)*, pages 326 - 333
June 20-21, 2024

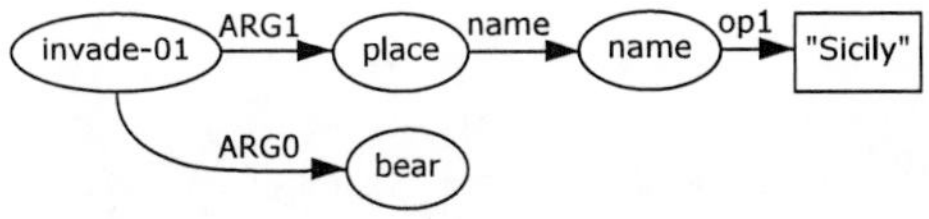

Figure 1: AMR for several wordings: "The bears invaded Sicily", "The bears' invasion of Sicily", "The invasion of Sicily by the bears" and "The invasion of the bears in Sicily".

phrase), "the invasion of Sicily by the bears", or "the invasion of the bears in Sicily". See Figure 1. In so doing, an AMR encodes instances of concepts as vertices in the graph, using PropBank framesets (Palmer et al., 2005) wherever possible[2]. Relations between instances of concepts are encoded as directed labeled edges in the graph. Those relations can be the frame arguments, following PropBank conventions (`ARG0`, `ARG1`,...), or other general semantic relations (`time`, `cause`, `location`, *etc.*).

Blodgett and Schneider (2021) published a dataset of automatic alignments between AMRs and the corresponding English sentences in the LDC2020T02 dataset (Knight et al., 2020), which comprises 59,255 sentences. We took advantage of those alignments and built a **dataset of edges** to test the capability of an LM's attention mechanism to retrieve the semantic relation encoded in a edge from the two connected vertices.

In their work, Blodgett and Schneider labeled their alignments across several categories: • **subgraph alignments**, a mutually exclusive alignment between consecutive spans of words and subgraphs of the AMR, • **duplicate subgraph alignments**, to account for elliptical construction, where several identical subgraphs in the AMR are mapped to the same word span, • **relation alignments**, providing alignments between a span and a single relation, (an arc in the AMR), such as "when" $\rightarrow$ `:time`, and • **reentrancy alignments**, accounting for reentrancy, (the fact that an AMR node may have multiple incoming edge). Reentrancy alignments provide alignments between reentrant arcs and a word span that triggers the reentrancy. (Pronouns, control verb, etc.) We selected the "subgraph alignments", sorting them to keep only those alignments involving a single word in the sentence and a single-vertex subgraph. Next, we had the sentences processed by the tokenizers of two pretrained language models with 12 layers and 12 heads per layer : • **RoBERTa**, a bidirectional encoder (Liu et al., 2019), and • **GPT-2**, a conditional decoder (Radford et al., 2019). To deal with the case of words split across several tokens, we aligned the sequences of words with the sequences of tokens, keeping only alignments involving a single word aligned with a single token.

[2]For example, the noun "invasion" and the verb "invaded" are both encoded using the PropBank frame `invade-01`.

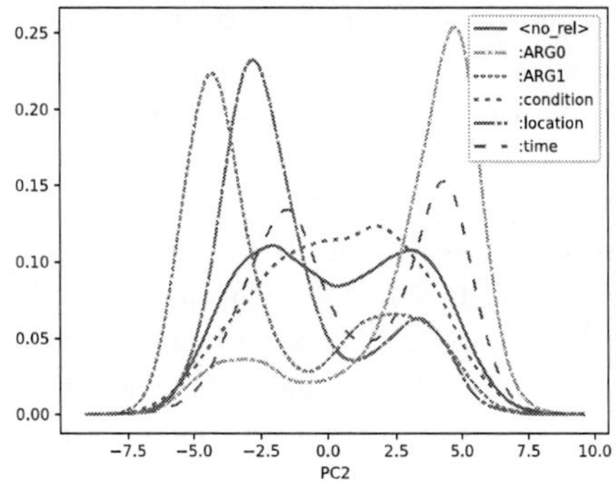

Figure 2: Distributions of six relations on the RoBERTa encoder, projected on PC2.

We thus created a dataset of pairs of tokens aligned with vertices of AMR graphs, linked by a semantic relation. To assess the ability to detect the absence of a semantic relation, we included random pairs of tokens corresponding to vertices in the AMRs with no edge between them, to create a category "<no_rel>". We then ran the transformers with all sentences as input and computed their representations. For each pair of words, there are possibly two attention directions to be computed: attention from one word to the other, or conversely. We call them ST and TS, as they represent attention from the source to the target or from the target to the source, where "target" and "source" denote the direction of the edge in the AMR graph. Each of those two attentions is represented by 144 scalars, as there are 12 layers, and 12 attention heads per layer.

In a transformer, the attention weight from a source token Q to a target token K is obtained by taking two affine transformations of the embeddings of Q and K, computing the inner product of those, and taking the softmax of that product with respect to all other target tokens. The features we use throughout this study are actually those inner products, before application of the softmax.

2.1 Illustration

As an example, let us consider the sentence "Establishing Models in Industrial Innovation". Its

AMR displays an edge ":ARG1" between the node "innovate-01" and the node "Industry". The alignments indicate a subgraph-alignment between the node "innovate-01" and the word "innovation", and another alignment between the node "industry" and the word "industrial". Both words "industrial" and "innovation" correspond to a token in the transformer model, therefore the edge labeled ":ARG1" could be kept in the dataset. The corresponding entry consists of the 144 features of attention from the token "industrial" to the token "innovation", and the 144 features from the token "innovation" to the token "innovation". The label is ARG1.

3 Unsupervised Analysis: PCA

The first step of our study was to apply a simple dimension reduction technique to the dataset. We chose to compute a principal component analysis on the inner product dataset. For the dataset computed with RoBERTa, we found that keeping 4 principal components enabled us to explain about 52% of the total variance.

We filtered the dataset by relation, and computed kernel density estimations of the distribution of different relations, and looked for dissimilarities between those. To do so, we selected a few relations to be plotted overlaid : (<no_rel>, ARG0, ARG1, condition, location, time, ARG2, quant, polarity, mod, and poss). We found that the first six relations could easily be distinguished by examining only the projection on the second principal component, as their distributions seem very different, although somewhat overlapped (See Figure 2).

The most conspicuous separation is between ARG0 and ARG1. However, no pair of relations presented completely distinct distributions. The separation of the relations quant, mod and poss is less obvious, and can best be seen on the projection on the fourth principal component. As for the pair of relations (ARG1, ARG2), they can hardly be distinguished. (Plots can be seen on appendix A.1)

For the dataset computed with the decoder GPT-2, we found that keeping 4 principal components enabled us to explain 70% of the total variance. (18% more than with RoBERTa). In spite of this difference, we found that GPT-2 was less effective than RoBERTa in distinguishing relations. As an illustration, in Figure 3, we plotted the distributions of the three easiest to distinguish relations for RoBERTa and GPT-2 on the most distinctive axis

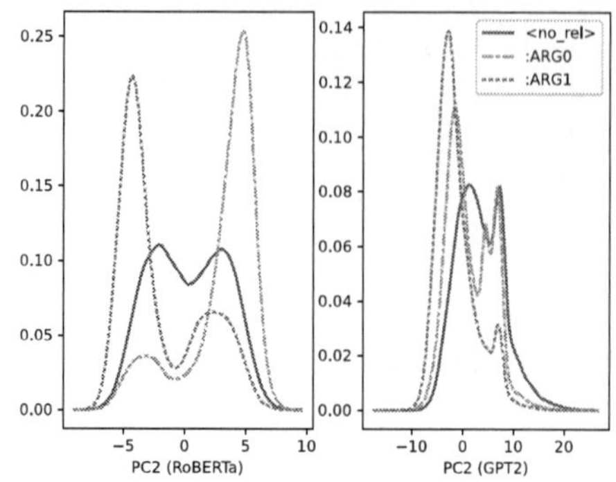

Figure 3: Distributions of relations <no_rel>, ARG0 and ARG1 on RoBERTa and GPT-2, showing the better separation of RoBERTa.

PC2. (See appendix A.2 for more GPT-2 plots.)

This first step tends to show that it is possible to use the attention heads of a transformer network to observe different distributions for pairs of different semantic relations. This behavior of a transformer is more prevalent for a bidirectional encoder (like RoBERTa) than for a conditional decoder (like GPT-2).

4 Supervised Analysis: Logistic Classifier

On the strength of these results, we trained a logistic model to classify the semantic relations of our datasets. To do so, we modified the datasets in the following way :

1. For RoBERTa, we included both ST and TS attention features, thus amounting to 288 features per sample.

2. We left out from the dataset some relations which we deemed irrelevant for semantics : snt-n, used to point to numbered independent clauses in a sentence, op-n, used for coordination with conjunctions like "and", "or", or commas, or for numbering the parts of a composite named entity, and polarity, whose target is almost always the constant "negative", and not an instance of a concept.[3]

3. Since the dataset is highly unbalanced, we grouped every relation with fewer than 1000 samples under the general category <other>, gathering 2.1% of our data.

[3]polarity is used to signal that a sentence is negative.

4.1 RoBERTa Language Model

Eventually, we obtained for the RoBERTa dataset 375,335 samples divided into 18 semantic relations to be classified. We then trained a Logistic classifier, using class weighting to compensate for the imbalance. The global balanced accuracy on test data is 0.62.[4] Detailed results are shown in the left column of Table 1.

Classes `ARG0`, `ARG1`, `time`, `mod`, `quant` exhibit the best F1 scores, with respectively 0.74, 0.63, 0.63, 0.63 and 0.60. Besides `<other>`, `ARG3`, `ARG4` and `topic` are the classes showing the worst F1 scores (0.09, 0.13 and 0.17). This is probably because `ARG3` and `ARG4` are used in some PropBank frames to describe a role where other AMR relations could arguably have been used. (`price`, `instrument`, `reason`, `location`). Relations `topic` and `condition` also exhibit a poor F1 score of 0.17 and 0.20. Interestingly enough, a careful scrutiny of the confusion matrix shows that many false positives for `topic` are confusions with `ARG1`, `mod` and `<no_rel>`, entailing a poor precision for this relation. The recall is otherwise good. This is also the case for `condition`. (See Appendix C.1 for the confusion matrix.)

4.2 GPT-2 Language Model

For the case of GPT-2, the very nature of a decoder does not allow attention to be computed in both directions, but only from a subsequent token to its predecessors. Therefore, we could only take advantage of 144 features. The global balanced accuracy is 0.44, and individual F1 scores are reported in Table 1. They are much poorer than the results obtained with RoBERTa, with which we used the full number of 288 features. We made the hypothesis that the reduced number of features due to causal self-attention is detrimental to a good detection of the semantics. To confirm this idea, we modified the implementation[5] to output the full inner products tensors used in computing attention before masking, without altering the network's operation. We trained another logistic classifier on this new dataset, and reported the results in the right column of Table 1. Every single F1 score is better than the scores obtained on the plain GPT-2, and the global balanced accuracy amounts to 0.56, a gain of more than 11 points.

Relation	Freq	RoBERTa	GPT2	GPT2 aug.
ARG0	16%	0.74	0.60	0.69
ARG1	33%	0.63	0.34	0.55
time	3%	0.63	0.29	0.54
mod	12%	0.63	0.44	0.57
quant	1%	0.60	0.40	0.56
<no_rel>	17%	0.59	0.44	0.49
degree	1%	0.54	0.35	0.52
poss	1%	0.47	0.20	0.32
location	1%	0.45	0.22	0.37
part	0.4%	0.37	0.11	0.24
manner	1%	0.36	0.16	0.28
ARG2	8%	0.33	0.20	0.29
purpose	1%	0.31	0.18	0.23
condition	1%	0.20	0.14	0.16
<other>	2%	0.18	0.08	0.15
topic	1%	0.17	0.11	0.14
ARG4	0.5%	0.13	0.07	0.10
ARG3	1%	0.09	0.08	0.11

Table 1: F1 scores per class of the Logistic classifier trained on the three datasets: RoBERTa, GPT2 and GPT2 augmented.

4.3 Influence of the Heads on the Results

The nature of a Logistic classifier allows us to interpret the contribution of the different heads to the detection of a relation by analyzing the coefficients of the classifier. Specifically, we can determine if an increment in the response of a particular head increases or decreases the ratio of probabilities of two relations.The following study was conducted on RoBERTa, we left GPT-2 aside. First, we analyzed the ratio of all probabilities with respect to the probability of `<no_rel>`. For that purpose, we computed the differences between the coefficients of all linear predictors and the coefficients of the linear predictor for `<no_rel>`. We noticed that for head 3 in layer 4, (head `H3L4`), as well as heads `H1L6` and `H2L3` of the TS product, all those differences were negative. This means that any positive shift in the inner product computed by one of those heads induces an increase of every ratio $\frac{\mathbb{P}[y=\texttt{<no\_rel>}]}{\mathbb{P}[y=y_k]}$, for all $y_k \neq$ `<no_rel>`. Conversely, we noticed that a positive shift in heads `H5L8` or `H3L9` (both for ST attention) induced an increase of the inverse ratio. We can conclude that those heads are specialized in determining a semantic relation, or absence thereof.

We further analyzed the contribution of every head to the probability ratio of any pair of relations: for each possible pair of relations, we recorded the k most contributional heads to the direct probability ratio, as well as the top k heads for the inverse

[4]In comparison, random forests and MLP classifiers have slightly poorer precision.

[5]We used minGPT, (https://github.com/karpathy/minGPT), which we deemed the easiest to modify, while providing a complete implementation.

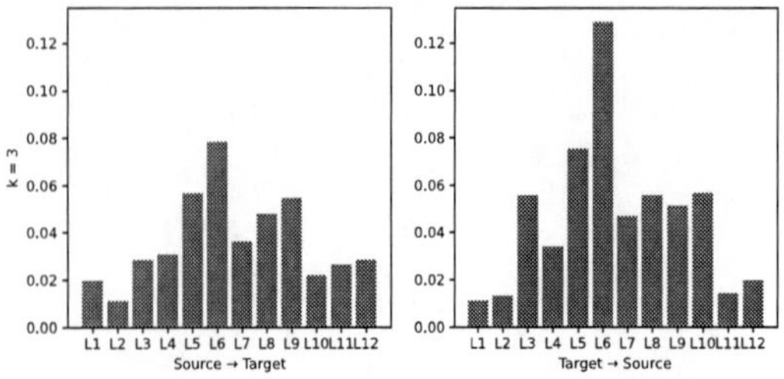

Figure 4: Distribution against layer index of the location of the top $k = 3$ most contributional heads to the distinction of pairs of relations.

probability ratio, and grouped them by layer index. For different values of k, we found that the most distinctive heads were predominantly located in layers of average depth. It appears for example that heads in Layer 6 of the TS attention often contribute the most to determining between two relations. This is also the case for layers 5 to 9 in the ST attention. For $k = 3$, for example, 13% of the top three heads are located in layer 6 of the TS attention. See Figure 4. We could also notice the imbalance in favor of TS attention for holding the top k heads for low values of k. This imbalance decreases as k increases. (See appendix B.)

5 Conclusion

Pre-trained LMs can, to some extent, code semantic relations in their attention mechanism without need of specialization. Bidirectional networks, as RoBERTa, show better ability to distinguish between different semantic roles than conditional networks, as GPT-2. Linear methods used in this work unveils an important fact. Pre-trained LMs encode not only the syntactic structure, but also the semantic structure of the text so that it can be exploited in a linear fashion.

References

Laura Banarescu, Claire Bonial, Shu Cai, Madalina Georgescu, Kira Griffitt, Ulf Hermjakob, Kevin Knight, Philipp Koehn, Martha Palmer, and Nathan Schneider. 2013. Abstract Meaning Representation for sembanking. In *Proceedings of the 7th Linguistic Annotation Workshop and Interoperability with Discourse*, pages 178–186, Sofia, Bulgaria. Association for Computational Linguistics.

Austin Blodgett and Nathan Schneider. 2021. Probabilistic, Structure-Aware Algorithms for Improved Variety, Accuracy, and Coverage of AMR Alignments. In *Proceedings of the 59th Annual Meeting of the Association for Computational Linguistics and the 11th International Joint Conference on Natural Language Processing (Volume 1: Long Papers)*, pages 3310–3321, Online. Association for Computational Linguistics.

Kevin Clark, Urvashi Khandelwal, Omer Levy, and Christopher D. Manning. 2019. What does BERT look at? An analysis of BERT's attention. In *Proceedings of the 2019 ACL workshop BlackboxNLP: Analyzing and interpreting neural networks for NLP*, pages 276–286, Florence, Italy. Association for Computational Linguistics.

Marco Damonte, Shay B. Cohen, and Giorgio Satta. 2017. An Incremental Parser for Abstract Meaning Representation. In *Proceedings of the 15th Conference of the European Chapter of the Association for Computational Linguistics: Volume 1, Long Papers*, pages 536–546, Valencia, Spain. Association for Computational Linguistics.

Donald Davidson. 1969. The individuation of events. In Nicholas Rescher, editor, *Essays in Honor of Carl G. Hempel*, pages 216–34. Reidel.

Jacob Devlin, Ming-Wei Chang, Kenton Lee, and Kristina Toutanova. 2019. BERT: Pre-training of deep bidirectional transformers for language understanding. In *Proceedings of the 2019 conference of the north American chapter of the association for computational linguistics: Human language technologies, volume 1 (long and short papers)*, pages 4171–4186, Minneapolis, Minnesota. Association for Computational Linguistics.

Jeffrey Flanigan, Sam Thomson, Jaime Carbonell, Chris Dyer, and Noah A. Smith. 2014. A Discriminative Graph-Based Parser for the Abstract Meaning Representation. In *Proceedings of the 52nd Annual Meeting of the Association for Computational Linguistics (Volume 1: Long Papers)*, pages 1426–1436, Baltimore, Maryland. Association for Computational Linguistics.

Kevin Knight, Bianca Badarau, Laura Baranescu, Claire Bonial, Madalina Bardocz, Kira Griffitt, Ulf Hermjakob, Daniel Marcu, Martha Palmer, Tim O'Gorman, and Schneider Nathan. 2020. Abstract meaning representation (amr) annotation release 3.0 ldc2020t02. *Linguistic Data Consortium.*

Yinhan Liu, Myle Ott, Naman Goyal, Jingfei Du, Mandar Joshi, Danqi Chen, Omer Levy, Mike Lewis, Luke Zettlemoyer, and Veselin Stoyanov. 2019. RoBERTa: A Robustly Optimized BERT Pretraining Approach. ArXiv:1907.11692 [cs].

Ziyang Luo. 2021. Have Attention Heads in BERT Learned Constituency Grammar? In *Proceedings of the 16th Conference of the European Chapter of the Association for Computational Linguistics: Student Research Workshop*, pages 8–15, Online. Association for Computational Linguistics.

Joakim Nivre. 2008. Algorithms for Deterministic Incremental Dependency Parsing. *Computational Linguistics*, 34(4):513–553.

Martha Palmer, Daniel Gildea, and Paul Kingsbury. 2005. The Proposition Bank: An annotated corpus of semantic roles. *Computational Linguistics*, 31(1):71–106.

Alec Radford, Jeff Wu, Rewon Child, David Luan, Dario Amodei, and Ilya Sutskever. 2019. Language models are unsupervised multitask learners.

Ashish Vaswani, Noam Shazeer, Niki Parmar, Jakob Uszkoreit, Llion Jones, Aidan N Gomez, Łukasz Kaiser, and Illia Polosukhin. 2017. Attention is all you need. In *Advances in neural information processing systems*, volume 30. Curran Associates, Inc.

Chuan Wang, Nianwen Xue, and Sameer Pradhan. 2015. A Transition-based Algorithm for AMR Parsing. In *Proceedings of the 2015 Conference of the North American Chapter of the Association for Computational Linguistics: Human Language Technologies*, pages 366–375, Denver, Colorado. Association for Computational Linguistics.

Sheng Zhang, Xutai Ma, Kevin Duh, and Benjamin Van Durme. 2019. AMR parsing as sequence-to-graph transduction. In *Proceedings of the 57th annual meeting of the association for computational linguistics*, pages 80–94, Florence, Italy. Association for Computational Linguistics.

Jiawei Zhou, Tahira Naseem, Ramón Fernandez Astudillo, Young-Suk Lee, Radu Florian, and Salim Roukos. 2021. Structure-aware fine-tuning of sequence-to-sequence transformers for transition-based AMR parsing. In *Proceedings of the 2021 conference on empirical methods in natural language processing*, pages 6279–6290, Online and Punta Cana, Dominican Republic. Association for Computational Linguistics.

A Plots of the densities of different relations

The following figures are plots of the densities (estimated through kernel density estimation) of different relations, projected onto the first four principal components.

A.1 RoBERTa Language Model

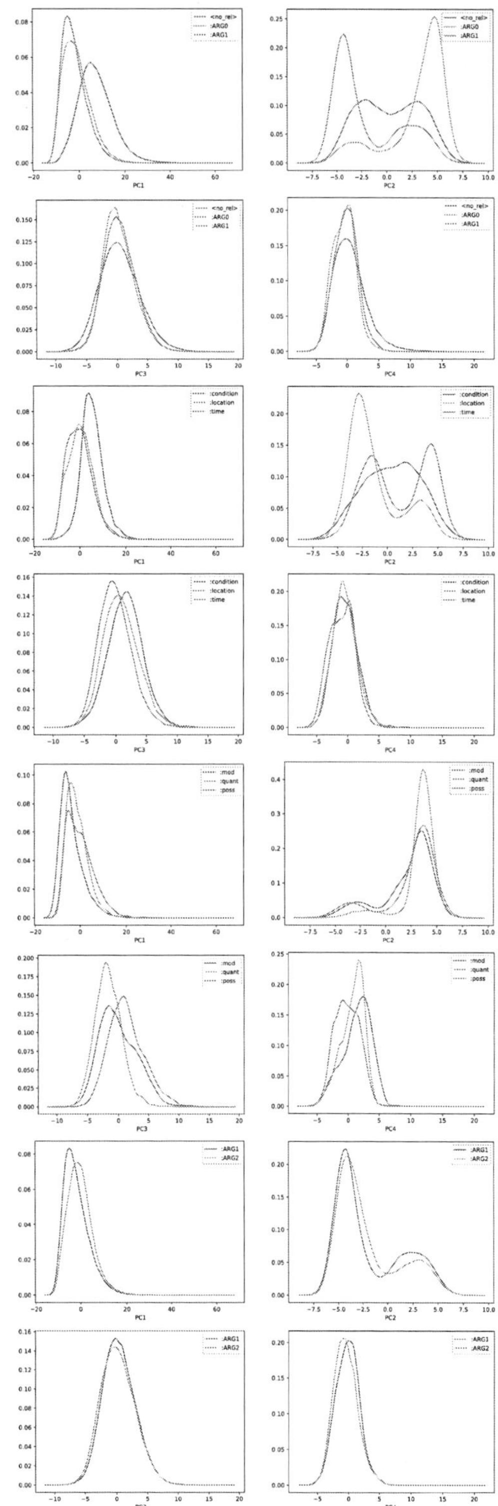

A.2 GPT-2 Language Model

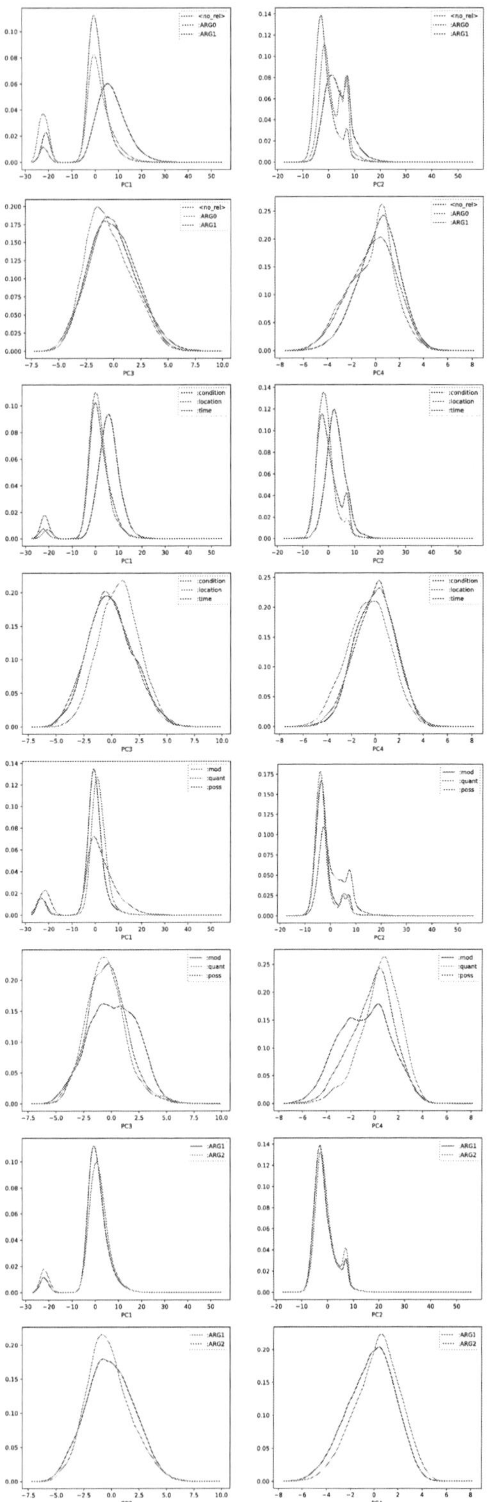

B Evolution of the distribution of the top k heads

The following figures present the evolution of the distribution against layer index of the location of the top k most contributional heads to the distinction of pairs of relations. As k increases from 1 to 5, the imbalance in favor of the TS attention decreases.

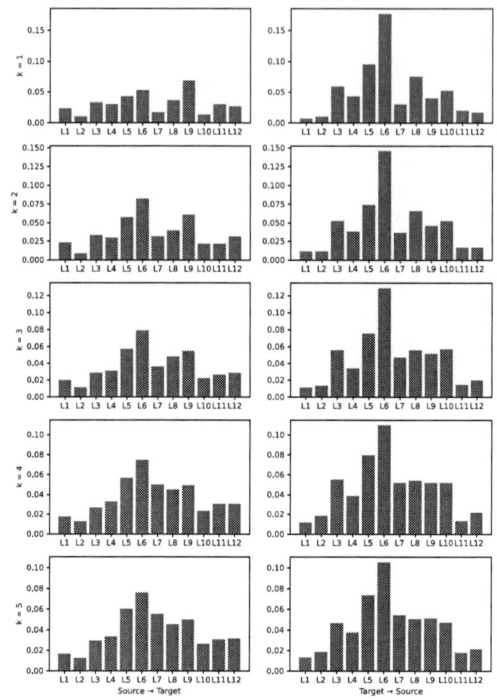

C Confusion Matrices of the Logistic Classsifiers

C.1 Confusion Matrix for RoBERTa LM

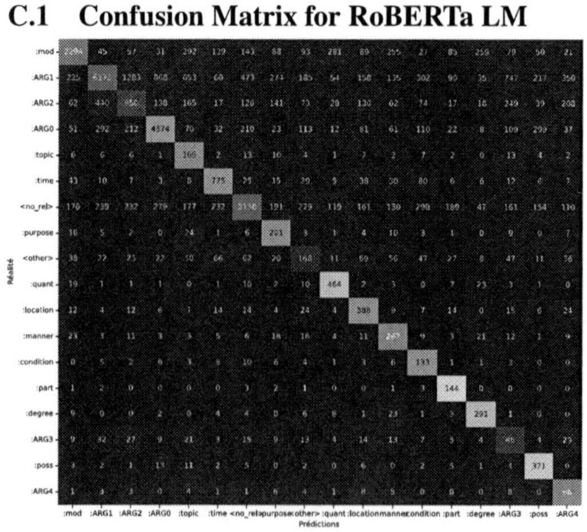

C.2 Confusion Matrix for GPT-2 LM

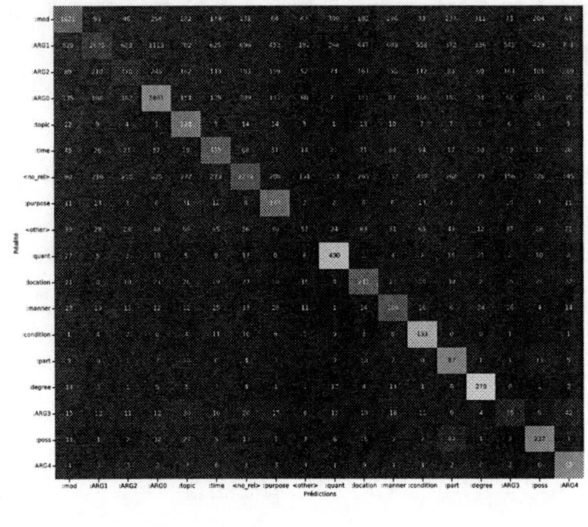

C.3 Confusion Matrix for Augmented GPT-2 LM

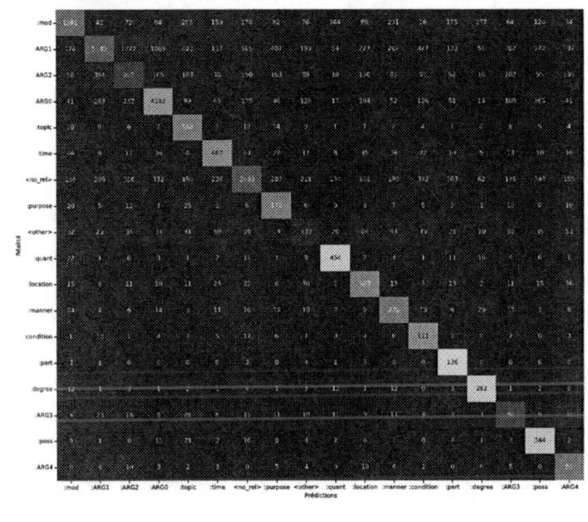

Enhancing Self-Attention via Knowledge Fusion: Deriving Sentiment Lexical Attention from Semantic-Polarity Scores

Dongjun Jang
Department of Linguistics
Seoul National University
qwer4107@snu.ac.kr

Jinwoong Kim
Graduate School of Data Science
Seoul National University
kjw900106@snu.ac.kr

Hyopil Shin
Department of Linguistics
Seoul National University
hpshin@snu.ac.kr

Abstract

In recent years, pre-trained language models have demonstrated exceptional performance across various natural language processing (NLP) tasks. One fundamental component of these models is the self-attention mechanism, which has played a vital role in capturing meaningful relationships between tokens. However, a question still remains as to whether injecting lexical features into the self-attention mechanism can further enhance the understanding and performance of language models. This paper presents a novel approach for injecting semantic-polarity knowledge, referred to as Sentiment Lexical Attention, directly into the self-attention mechanism of Transformer-based models. The primary goal is to improve performance on sentiment classification task. Our approach involves consistently injecting Sentiment Lexical Attention derived from the lexicon corpus into the attention scores throughout the training process. We have conducted empirical analysis on our approach using the NSMC, a benchmark for Korean sentiment classification, where it demonstrated substantial performance enhancements and secured state-of-the-art achievements. Furthermore, our approach demonstrates robustness and effectiveness in out-of-domain tasks, indicating its potential for broad applicability. Additionally, we analyze the impact of Sentiment Lexical Attention on the view of the CLS token's attention distribution. Our method offers a fresh perspective on synergizing lexical features and attention scores, thereby encouraging further investigations in the realm of knowledge injection utilizing the lexical features.

1 Introduction

In recent years, pre-trained language models such as BERT (Devlin et al., 2018), XLNet (Yang et al., 2019b), BART (Lewis et al., 2019), and GPT-3 (Brown et al., 2020) have demonstrated remarkable performance across various downstream tasks in NLP. These language models (LMs) are characterized by a vast number of trainable parameters, which many researchers believe encode valuable knowledge during the processing of contextualized token embeddings (Wang et al., 2020; Incitti et al., 2023). Among these parameters, self-attention mechanisms play a crucial role and are widely considered as the foundation of nearly all language models. Many studies have led to performance improvements by attempting to inject knowledge into self-attention, based on the understanding that it learns based on relationships between tokens (Hu et al., 2023; Kaddari and Bouchentouf, 2023; Xie et al., 2023; Zhao et al., 2024). However, an important question remains: Can we leverage the sentiment lexical features to enhance the self-attention mechanism and gain a deeper understanding of the relationships between semantically meaningful tokens?

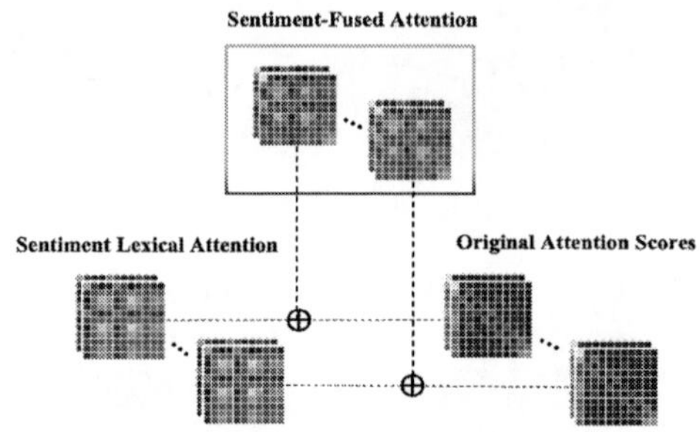

Figure 1: The Sentiment-Fused Attention, induced by forming a linear combination of the Sentiment Lexical Attention and the Original Attention Scores.

Many studies have investigated the methods of knowledge fusion on LMs to enhance performance in natural language understanding tasks (Sun et al., 2019; Liu et al., 2020; Wang et al., 2023). Knowledge injection techniques can be applied to any part of the LMs (Colon-Hernandez et al., 2021; Wei et al., 2021). Among the many methods, we introduce a method to convert lexical sentiment features

*Proceedings of the 13th Joint Conference on Lexical and Computational Semantics (*SEM 2024)*, pages 334 - 344
June 20-21, 2024 ©2024 Association for Computational Linguistics

into a computable matrix (Sentiment Lexical Attention), which is then induced into a linear combination with the Self-Attention. We denote this fused attention mechanism as Sentiment-Fused Attention (Figure 1). For injecting Sentiment-Fused Attention well on attention score, we partially follow Xia et al. (2021)'s way, which proposes a method of guiding the attention output by injecting similarity knowledge into the attention score.

In Section 3, we suggest our novel approach of injection, pointing out Xia et al. (2021)'s injection methods might have the potential to distort the relationships of tokens. Furthermore, the process of extracting Sentiment Lexical Features from the Polarity Score of the Lexicon Corpus and deriving them into a fusible matrix is elaborately described in Section 3. We believe our method of injection is meticulously formulated to augment the weights between tokens with similar sentiment features. In Section 4, we substantiate the effectiveness of our injection method through experiments, simultaneously empirically demonstrating that it yields stable performance improvements, unlike Xia et al. (2021)'s approach. To the best of our knowledge, our results represent the state-of-the-art on the Naver Sentiment Movie Corpus (NSMC)[1], which is widely regarded as the leading benchmark for sentiment analysis in the Korean language. Additionally, experimental observations reveal the effectiveness of sentiment lexical features in out-of-domain tasks. In Section 6, we investigate the impact of Sentiment-Fused Attention on attention by statistically examining the attention dynamics of the CLS token (serving as the classifier) and demonstrate through analysis that it exerts significant influence.

The main contribution of our work are as follows:

- We propose the way of inducing Sentiment Lexical Attention from the semantic-polarity score, which means that any corpus containing the polarity information could follow our work for the enhancement on downstream tasks.
- We establish a mathematical formula that combines two different attention matrix. The theoretical underpinnings and empirical evidence supporting this approach are demonstrated through experiments.
- We achieve a state-of-the-art performance on NSMC benchmark.

[1]`https://github.com/e9t/nsmc`

2 Related Work

Previous research has extensively investigated the injection of knowledge into self-attention based language models to augment its language representation prowess (Wang et al., 2023). In this chapter, we introduce prior research on knowledge graph-based approaches, which are most commonly utilized for Knowledge Injection, and discuss how knowledge integration has been approached from the perspective of Lexical Semantics. Finally, we justify the validity of our research by introducing prior studies related to self-attention distributions.

Infusing Knowledge Graph into the Self-Attention Mechanism Zhang et al. (2019) pioneered the development of the ERNIE model, an innovative approach that employs knowledge integration to enhance language representation. Liu et al. (2020) propose K-BERT with knowledge graphs, in which triples are injected into the sentences as domain knowledge. Peters et al. (2019) present KnowBERT, a model that integrates knowledge bases (KBs) into the pre-trained BERT model. Xu et al. (2020) utilize external entity descriptions to provide contextual information for knowledge understanding task. Yu et al. (2022) propose JAKET, the framework to model both the knowledge graph and language model. Ostendorff et al. (2019) combine text representations with metadata and knowledge graph embeddings to enhance BERT performance for document classification tasks.

Lexical Semantics Approach Xia et al. (2021) induce Word Similarity Matrix based on the similarity of lexical pair from the semantics role in WordNet. They inject Word Similarity Matrix directly into BERT's attention. Zhang et al. (2020) propose SemBERT, which integrates explicit contextual semantics from pre-trained semantic role labeling. Wu et al. (2021) also introduce SIFT, which incorporate explicit semantic structures into the training paradigm. Yin et al. (2020) propose SentiBERT, which incorporates contextualized representation with binary constituency parse tree to capture semantic composition.

Distribution of Self-Attention Several studies explore the characteristics of self-attention distribution and their implications for enhancing transformer-based Pre-trained Language Models (PLMs). Gong et al. (2019) investigate the self-attention distribution within BERT models, demonstrating that the distribution tends to be focused around the token's position and the start-of-sentence token. They also find striking similarities in the attention distributions across the lower and upper layers. Kovaleva et al. (2019) propose that selectively disabling attention in certain heads can actually enhance the performance of fine-tuned BERT models. This discovery suggests the potential redundancy and over-complexity in the current attention mechanism. Additionally, Shi et al. (2021) present empirical evidence that the diagonal elements of the self-attention matrix, representing the attention of each token to itself, can be removed without compromising model performance. This finding further emphasizes the importance of inter-token attention over self-attention in PLMs.

3 Direct Injection of Sentiment Lexical Attention into Self-Attention

In this investigation, we enhance the existing Self-Attention mechanism by embedding Sentiment Lexical Attention within its attention matrix, thereby integrating sentiment-related connections among tokens. Sentiment Lexical Attention is conceptualized through the quantification of semantic-polarity similarity among token pairs, established via the dot product computation of their context polarity vectors. This process engenders a semantic-polarity similarity matrix that meticulously delineates the sentiment linkages inherent in tokens within a specific input sequence, ensuring a nuanced comprehension of these interrelations. Notably, a pronounced amplification of polarity similarities is observed among tokens sharing analogous sentiment properties, with the similarity values delineated within a spectrum ranging from 0 to 1.

By leveraging this semantic-polarity similarity as Sentiment Lexical Attention, we could directly inject this information into attention scores. This methodology enables us to potentially refine the attention mechanism by injecting sentiment-associated values between tokens. Consequently, this process facilitates the generation of a more informed representation of the sentiment relationships within sentences.

3.1 Knowledge-Guided Attention Approach Proposed by Xia et al. (2021)

Xia et al. (2021) proposed a methodology for directly incorporating knowledge into the self-attention mechanism by utilizing a Word Similarity Matrix. Their main objective is to enhance the focus of BERT on word pairs that demonstrate semantic similarity. To calculate the Attention Weight, they utilize the Similarity Matrix, which allows the model to assign higher weights to tokens with high similarity. The conventional definition of Self Attention can be described as follows:

$$\mathit{SelfAttention}(Q, K, V) = \mathrm{softmax}\left(\frac{QK^T}{\sqrt{d_k}}\right) V,$$

where Q represents the query matrix, K represents the key matrix, V represents the value matrix, and d_k represents the dimensionality of the key matrix. Xia (2021)'s Knowledge-Guided Attention calculates the Hadamard product of the QK^T using the similarity matrix S:

$$\mathit{score} = QK^T \odot S$$

$$\mathit{SelfAttention}(Q, K, V) = \mathrm{softmax}\left(\frac{\mathit{score}}{\sqrt{d_k}}\right) V.$$

However, the Hadamard product of S and QK^T in the self-attention mechanism can potentially lead to issues, particularly when negative values are present in the attention score output. The nature of the Hadamard product can cause the loss of significance of certain elements if negative attention scores exist. This can dampen the importance of positive similarity values and result in an unintentional representation of token relationships. To address this, non-linear transformations or the addition of bias terms to the attention scores is necessary to ensure more reliable and stable attention distributions.

3.2 Sentiment-Fused Attention

We propose a novel concept called **Sentiment-Fused Attention**, which presents an advanced formulation for incorporating sentiment knowledge into the self-attention mechanism. Building upon the work of Xia et al. (2021), we modify the injection of knowledge to mitigate the risks associated with the Hadamard product. Instead of using the Hadamard product, we employ a summation operation to combine the Sentiment Lexical Attention with the attention scores. This alteration effectively integrates the knowledge without distorting token relationships. By using summation, we retain the positive characteristics of the original model while addressing the issues related to negative attention

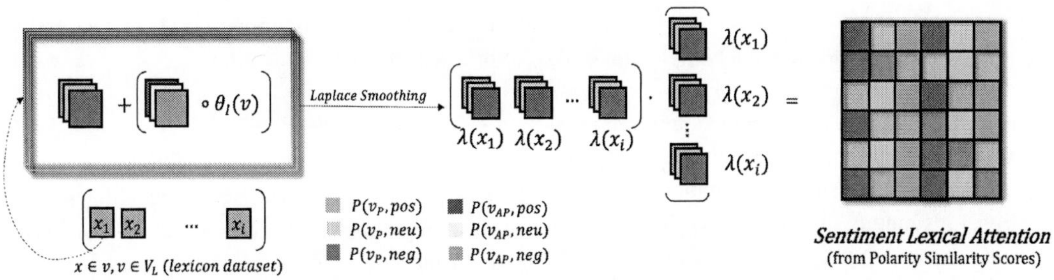

Figure 2: Pictorial Illustration of Sentiment Lexical Attention Induction from Input Variables Using Sentiment Information Sourced from the Lexicon Dataset

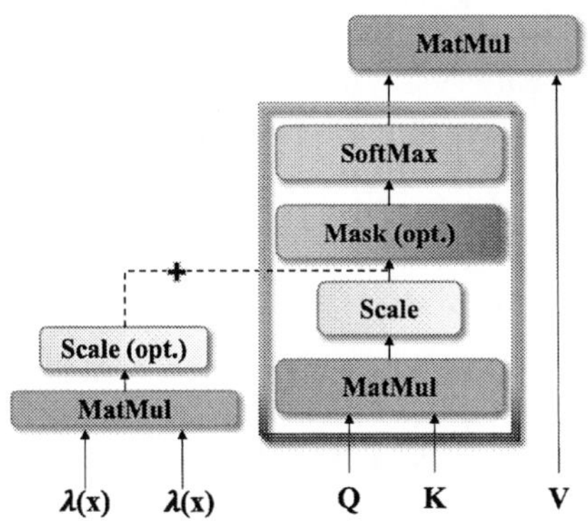

Figure 3: Visualizing the Linear Combination of Sentiment Lexical Attention and Original Attention Score Matrix

scores. This approach ensures a more accurate and stable representation of token relationships, resulting in more reliable attention distributions.

3.2.1 Leveraging Semantic-Polarity Similarity Score as Sentiment Lexical Attention

To leverage semantic-polarity similarity, we introduce the notion of Total Sentiment, denoted as $\boldsymbol{\lambda}(x) \in \mathbb{R}^3_{(0,1)}$, for each token x in an input sentence. The context polarity $\boldsymbol{\lambda}(x)$ is defined as a combination of aspect polarity vectors $\boldsymbol{\theta}_{AP}$, aspect-agnostic polarity vectors $\boldsymbol{\theta}_P$, and intensity values θ_I of words or phrases containing x. We compute Total Sentiment by Laplace smoothing the aggregate of aspect polarity vectors $\boldsymbol{\theta}_{AP}$ and taking the product of aspect-agnostic polarity vectors $\boldsymbol{\theta}_P$ and intensity values θ_I. We denote $V_{L,x}(\subset V_L)$ as a set of words or phrases containing token x, then Total Sentiment of the token is represented as follows,

$$\boldsymbol{\lambda}(x) = LS(\sum_{v \in S_L} (\boldsymbol{\theta}_P(v) + \theta_I(v)\boldsymbol{\theta}_{AP}(v)) I_{V_{L,x}}(v))$$

These modifications allow us to incorporate Sentiment Lexical Attention effectively, leading to improved attention mechanisms that provide a more accurate and stable representation of token relationships.

If there is no word or phrase containing a token x in S_L, we set $\boldsymbol{\lambda}(x)$ to a neutral sentiment vector, $(\frac{1}{3}, \frac{1}{3}, \frac{1}{3})$. This can be expressed as follows:

$$\begin{cases} LS(\sum_{v \in V_{L,x}} \boldsymbol{\lambda}(v)) & \text{if } V_{L,x} \neq \emptyset, \\ (\frac{1}{3}, \frac{1}{3}, \frac{1}{3}) & \text{if otherwise.} \end{cases}$$

Additionally, we define the semantic-polarity similarity σ_{ij} (represented as $\sigma(x_i, x_j)$) as the product of the context polarities $\boldsymbol{\lambda}(x_i)$ and $\boldsymbol{\lambda}(x_j)$ for tokens x_i and x_j, respectively (Figure 2).

$$\sigma_{ij} = \sigma(x_i, x_j) = \boldsymbol{\lambda}(x_i) \cdot \boldsymbol{\lambda}(x_j)$$

3.2.2 Injection of Sentiment Lexical Attention into Attention Scores for Sentiment-Fused Attention

The formulation of Sentiment-Fused Attention involves a linear combination of Sentiment Lexical Attention, denoted as σ_{ij}, and the initial attention score, represented by $\frac{QK^T}{\sqrt{d_k}}$. This combination takes place during the forward propagation of $\frac{QK^T}{\sqrt{d_k}}$, prior to its non-linear activation through the $softmax$ function (Figure 3). The formula for the attention distribution is as follows:

$$softmax\left(\frac{QK^T}{\sqrt{d_k}} + \sigma_{ij}\right) \cdot V.$$

To stabilize the range of σ_{ij}, we include a scaling factor, $\sqrt{d_k}$, in the denominator. This architectural design ensures that the distribution of the original attention score outputs is preserved while mitigating the impact of Sentiment Lexical Attention.

$$softmax\left(\frac{QK^T}{\sqrt{d_k}} + \frac{\sigma_{ij}}{\sqrt{d_k}}\right) \cdot V$$

Throughout the training process, σ_{ij} consistently promotes similar tokens to have higher values. To ensure this consistency, we set σ_{ij} as a constant, thereby providing the model with a unidirectional stream of information. By doing so, σ_{ij} continues to provide consistent information about the relationships among similar tokens to the model. During the training procedure, σ_{ij} consistently induces high values for similar tokens, maintaining a reliable signal throughout the training process.

3.3 CARBD-ko dataset

CARBD-ko (A Korean Contextually Annotated Review Benchmark) dataset (Jang et al., 2024) is a comprehensive dataset ($S_L = \{X_i, \theta_i\}$) that includes reviews (X_i) paired with corresponding sets of sentiment factors (θ_i) for words or phrases (v_j) in the reviews. These sets consist of aspect-agnostic polarity attribute vectors ($\boldsymbol{\theta}_P(v_j)$), aspect polarity attribute vectors ($\boldsymbol{\theta}_{AP}(v_j)$), and associated intensity information of polarity values ($\theta_I(v_j)$) for each word or phrase (v_j) within the reviews. Both the aspect-agnostic and aspect polarity vectors are represented as three-dimensional one-hot vectors, which correspond to the polarity values of -1, 0, or 1. For example, a polarity value of 1 is represented by the vector $(1, 0, 0)$. The set of all words or phrases having sentiment factors is denoted as V_L. Leveraging the CARBD-ko dataset, our approach focuses on the extraction of context polarity vectors.

4 Experiments

4.1 Sentiment Classification Task

Our study focuses on conducting experiments in the domain of Sentiment Analysis, which provides a natural application for leveraging pre-existing knowledge in the field of natural language understanding. Sentiment classification tasks typically involve binary classification, distinguishing between positive and negative sentiments. Transformer-based models have shown high performance on such tasks. In our case, we evaluate the language model's performance on Sentiment Classification using the NSMC (Naver Sentiment Movie Corpus) benchmark dataset, which is widely used in Korean sentiment analysis work. The dataset consists of 200K reviews, with 150K reviews for the training set and 50K reviews for the test set. To assess the broader implications of our approach, we examine the effectiveness of Sentiment-Fused Attention in tasks that extend beyond sentiment classification.

4.2 Out-of-Domain Tasks

In addition to sentiment classification, we conduct experiments on diverse out-of-domain downstream tasks, including KorNLI (Ham et al., 2020), PAWS-ko (Yang et al., 2019a), Hate Speech Detection (Moon et al., 2020), and Question-Pair benchmark[2]. These tasks are commonly used to evaluate the overall performance of Korean language models. By evaluating our approach on these tasks, we aim to determine the generalizability and applicability of the Sentiment Lexical Attention and understand its impact on performance across various out-of-domain tasks.

4.3 Scaling Factor and Attention Head Configuration

We design a suite of experiments consisting of four distinct scenarios on NSMC benchmark. These scenarios involve different configurations of the scaling factor $\sqrt{d_k}$ and the injection scope of the Sentiment Lexical Attention. The objective is to quantify the influence of the Sentiment Lexical Attention on attention mechanisms.

The first setting involves the direct injection of values from the Sentiment Lexical Attention into all attention heads across all layers without normalization by $\sqrt{d_k}$. The second setting modifies the approach by normalizing the Sentiment Lexical Attention values σ_{ij} with $\sqrt{d_k}$ to constrain their range. The third and fourth scenarios exclusively inject the Sentiment Lexical Attention σ_{ij} into the final attention head (Att_{last}) across all layers. The fourth scenario further reduces the range of the external knowledge values through the application of $\sqrt{d_k}$.

Our working hypothesis suggests that if the use of $\sqrt{d_k}$ leads to superior results compared to alternative approaches, there may be a positive correlation between the efficacy of σ_{ij} and overall model performance. On the other hand, if enhanced performance is observed when solely activating the last attention head, it could indicate that a more targeted application of σ_{ij} yields outputs that are more representative of the context, contributing to more effective convergence of the model's objective loss.

[2]`https://github.com/songys/Question_pair`

NSMC	ko-electra	kr-electra	kc-electra	xlm-roberta-base	kr-bert
Baseline	90.63	91.17	91.97	89.49	90.1
Xia et al. (2021)	90.06(-0.57)	91.11(-0.06)	92.10(+0.13)	89.17(-0.32)	89.35(-0.75)
$\sum Att + \sqrt{d_k}$	91.18(+0.55)	91.73(+0.56)	92.6(+0.63)	90.42(+0.93)	90.19(+0.09)
$\sum Att$	**91.32**(+0.69)	**91.82**(+0.65)	92.56(+0.59)	90.47(+0.98)	90.17(+0.07)
$Att_{last} + \sqrt{d_k}$	91.17(+0.54)	91.78(+0.61)	92.56(+0.59)	**90.55**(+1.06)	**90.3**(+0.2)
Att_{last}	91.24(+0.61)	**91.82**(+0.65)	**92.65**(+0.68)	90.33(+0.84)	90.23(+0.13)

Table 1: Accuracy of Performance on NSMC dataset

Model	μ	σ	σ^2
$\sum Att + \sqrt{d_k}$	0.596	0.109	0.33
$\sum Att$	0.552	0.091	0.301
$Att_{last} + \sqrt{d_k}$	0.582	**0.071**	**0.267**
Att_{last}	**0.600**	0.094	0.306

Table 2: Analysis of Performance Variations via Statistical Configuration

We will employ statistical analysis to identify the scenarios that yield acceptable performance. Subsequently, we intend to assess the performance of these optimized scenarios in other out-of-domain contexts.

4.4 Models and Hyper-Parameters

To conduct our experiments, we utilize four prominent Korean Transformer Encoder-based pretrained language models (ko-electra (Park, 2020), kr-electra (Lee and Shin, 2022), kc-electra (Lee, 2021), kr-bert (Lee et al., 2020)), as well as a multilingual model (Conneau et al., 2019). The baseline performance of each model on the NSMC task is shown in Table 1, which serves as our initial reference point for comparison. To further improve the performance of our models, we engage in hyperparameter tuning. This involves adjusting the learning rate within a range of 1e-5 to 5e-5 and extending the number of training epochs from 3 to 10. By employing this rigorous setup, we aim to ensure that our experimental results accurately capture the potential benefits of our proposed approach.

4.5 $\lambda(x)$ Initialization

In our experimental setup, we extract the context polarity $\lambda(v)$ from the CARBD-ko dataset to initialize the context polarity $\lambda(x)$ for individual tokens x_i, aligned with the appropriate tokenizer for each language model. However, in real-world datasets, it is possible for previously unseen tokens x_i to appear. For such cases, we initialize all $\lambda(x_i)$ to $\frac{1}{3}$, as described in Section 3.3.1.

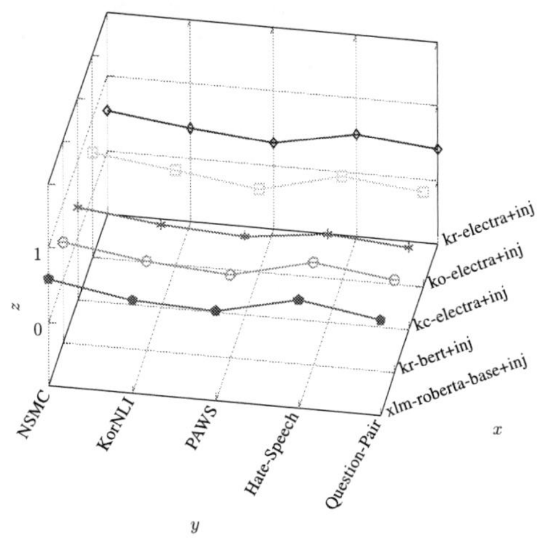

Figure 4: Appearance Rates of Initialized Tokens across 5 Downstream Tasks

When a significant number of tokens are initialized with $\frac{1}{3}$, it becomes challenging to establish a clear correlation between improved model performance and the use of σ_{ij}. Figure 4 provides insights into the appearance rates of tokens that have been initialized by σ_{ij} across five different tasks. As depicted in Figure 4, there are minimal variations observed between tasks and models, with most of the rates centered around 50%. Notably, the results on the NSMC dataset exhibit consistent stability. This finding underscores the significance of Sentiment Lexical Attention on attention, emphasizing that its impact cannot be disregarded.

5 Result

5.1 NSMC

The evidence in Table 1 emphatically underscores the advantage of injecting Sentiment Lexical Attention during fine-tuning, leading to a consistent improvement in performance across all four scenarios enumerated in Section 4.3, as compared to the baseline models and Xia et al. (2021)'s way. An intriguing observation lies in the fact that Xia et al.

Downstream Tasks		ko-electra	kr-electra	kc-electra	xlm-roberta-base	kr-bert
KorNLI	baseline	82.24	82.51	82.12	79.92	77.13
	+injection	**+83.25**(+1.01)	82.48(-0.03)	82.07(-0.05)	80.07(+0.15)	79.3(+2.17)
PAWS	baseline	84.45	82.05	76.5	82.95	80.35
	+injection	**85.35**(+0.9)	81.3(-0.75)	76.9(+0.4)	83.1(+0.15)	80.65(+0.3)
Hate-Speech	baseline	67.45	73.2	**73.67**	64.06	66.45
	+injection	67.73(+0.28)	73.04(-0.16)	73.46(-0.21)	66.02(+1.96)	66.67(+0.22)
Question-Pair	baseline	95.25	95.51	95.12	93.8	94.591
	+injection	95.51(+0.26)	95.51(0)	**96.04**(+0.92)	94.06(+0.26)	94.591(0)

Table 3: Accuracy of Performance Evaluation of Models on Four Out-of-Domain Tasks. We inject σ_{ij} exclusively into the last attention head of each layer with scaling factor $\sqrt{d_k}$

(2021)'s injection method and our approach yield entirely distinct outcomes. As previously noted in Section 3.2, we pointed out the potential for distortion in the mathematical derivations of Xia et al. (2021)'s method, and this has manifested in empirical results (Table 1).

Among the models, the xlm-roberta-base model illustrates the most substantial performance enhancement, whereas the kr-bert model exhibits a modest performance gain. The remaining three models demonstrate performance amplifications exceeding 0.5% across all investigated scenarios. When considering the magnitude of the NSMC benchmark's test dataset (50K), these improvements are of considerable significance, indicating a potential escalation in the number of correct predictions varying from an average of 250 to almost 500 sentences.

Notably, the kc-electra model, upon the injection of Sentiment Lexical Attention into ATT_{last} without the utilization of $\sqrt{d_k}$, achieves an accuracy metric of 92.65%. To the best of our knowledge, this represents a state-of-the-art (SoTA) result for the NSMC benchmark. These findings highlight the effectiveness of directly injecting sentiment knowledge into the attention mechanism during the training phase, leading to improved model performance.

5.2 Other Downstream Task

Table 2 indicates that, on average, the Att_{last} scenario results in the most significant performance improvements. The configuration of Att_{last}+$\sqrt{d_k}$ demonstrates the smallest standard deviation and variance, indicating its stability across a diverse range of models. Therefore, we adopt the Att_{last}+$\sqrt{d_k}$ configuration to inject knowledge into out-of-domain tasks.

In Table 3, out of the 20 cases examined, 13 show an increase in performance, 5 show a decrease, and 2 maintain their performance. Interestingly, these performance increases in different domains occur despite the absence of a direct correlation between the domain and the σ_{ij} values established in our experiments. This suggests that the similarity between tokens can facilitate a model's decision-making processes. However, the lack of consistent performance gains across all models, as seen in the NSMC benchmark, highlights the need for task-specific knowledge development. One notable aspect of our results is the variability and model-dependency observed in the injection of the sentiment knowledge. Performance decreases are exclusively observed in the kr-electra and kc-electra models, while other models either maintain or improve their performance. It is worth mentioning that both the kr-electra and kc-electra models consistently exhibit stable performance enhancements on the NSMC task.

Based on these findings, we conclude that directly injecting sentiment knowledge into the training process may lead to varying performance outcomes depending upon the specific model. If the knowledge, however, is logically structured and has a direct causal link with the task, it has the potential to yield stable performance improvements.

6 Dissecting the Impact of σ_{ij} on Attention Dynamics: An In-depth Analysis Centered on the CLS Token

In this section, we investigate the differences in standard deviation between the baseline model and the Att_{last} + $\sqrt{d_k}$ model concerning the CLS token at each layer. Our approach involves the direct injection of Sentiment Lexical Attention into the attention scores. We hypothesize that this injection of knowledge will lead to alterations in the relationship centered on the CLS token, which serves as

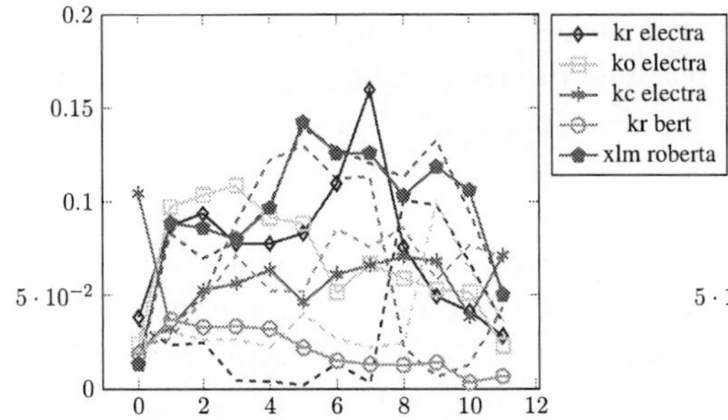

(a) Standard Deviation (σ^2) of CLS Token's Attention towards Other Tokens

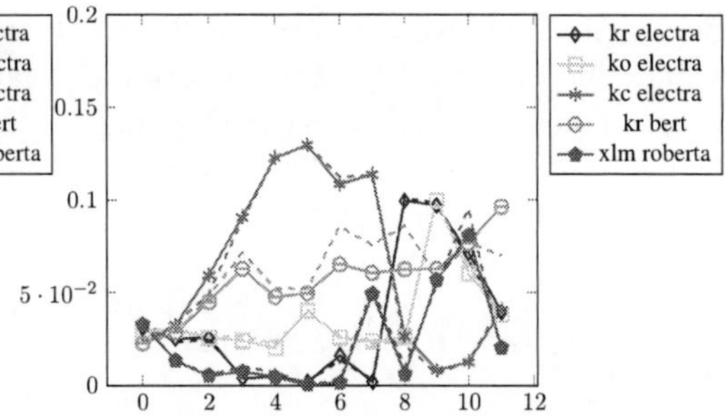

(b) Standard Deviation (σ^2) of the Other Token's Attention towards CLS Tokens

Figure 5: Layer-wise Distributional Differences in Five Baseline Models and the $Att_{last} + \sqrt{d_k}$ Models, Centered on CLS Tokens. The dashed line represents the baseline models, while the solid line corresponds to the $Att_{last} + \sqrt{d_k}$ model.

the representative vector for the subsequent classifier. To test this hypothesis, we conduct an analysis of the standard deviation of attention scores surrounding the CLS token at each layer, aiming to understand the impact of σ_{ij}.

For statistical analysis, we examine the standard deviation of attention scores between the CLS token and other tokens in both the baseline model and the Att_{last} + $\sqrt{d_k}$ model. We conduct this analysis layer-by-layer while processing the 50K test dataset from the NSMC dataset. By comparing the standard deviation of attention scores, we aim to understand how the attention patterns of the CLS token change when Sentiment Lexical Attention is incorporated into the model. This analysis provides insights into the impact of knowledge injection on the attention mechanism and its effect on the relationship between the CLS token and other tokens.

Figure 5 demonstrates that the deviation between the baseline models and the Att_{last} + $\sqrt{d_k}$ model, specifically regarding the CLS tokens, primarily manifests in the alterations in the distribution of attention scores between the CLS token and other tokens. The presence of such disparities between models that differ solely based on the injection of σ_{ij} in their training processes strongly suggests a significant influence of σ_{ij} on the dispersion of attention scores. Interestingly, the distribution of attention scores from other tokens towards the CLS token remains mostly unchanged.

These findings can be attributed to the fact that the CLS token does not derive its context polarity $\boldsymbol{\lambda}(x)$ from $\boldsymbol{\lambda}(v)$, resulting in minimal differences in the attention weights towards the CLS token compared to the baseline models. On the other hand, tokens other than the CLS token, influenced by $\boldsymbol{\lambda}(v)$, consistently induce modifications in the attention score distribution throughout the training process, which likely affects the final attention distribution of the model. Through this analysis, we propose that these shifts in attention distribution serve as the primary catalyst for the performance alterations depicted in Tables 1 and 2.

7 Discussion

In this paper, we have introduced a novel approach for enhancing the self-attention mechanism of Transformer-based models through the injection of Sentiment Lexical Attention, derived from semantic-polarity scores. Our results demonstrate significant improvements in sentiment classification, particularly in the Korean language context. However, the applicability and challenges of this method across different tasks and languages, as well as its technical novelty, warrant further discussion.

7.1 Applicability to Other Languages

Our approach's effectiveness in the Korean language context opens up intriguing prospects for its applicability to other languages. Firstly, the fundamental principle of leveraging semantic-polarity scores for Sentiment Lexical Attention is language-agnostic and can be adapted to any language with available sentiment lexicons. However, the adaptation process requires careful consideration of linguistic nuances and sentiment expression in target languages. It involves meticulous curation of sentiment lexicons that accurately reflect the sentiment polarity in diverse linguistic contexts. Future work will explore the cross-linguistic applicability of our method, focusing on curating high-quality sentiment lexicons and adjusting the model to account for language-specific sentiment expression patterns.

7.2 Addressing Tasks Beyond Sentiment Analysis

The current study focuses on sentiment classification, leveraging semantic-polarity scores. While this is a direct application of Sentiment Lexical Attention, extending our approach to tasks without a clear relevance to sentiment poses challenges. To enhance the versatility and scalability of our approach, we are exploring strategies to generalize the concept of lexical feature-based attention. Future research could investigate domain-specific knowledge injection, where domain-related lexical features are derived and injected similarly to sentiment features. Additionally, integrating multiple types of lexical knowledge simultaneously could lead to a more robust and versatile model applicable across a wider range of tasks.

7.3 Technical Novelty and Contribution

While our approach builds upon existing work by Xia et al. (2021), it introduces significant innovations that extend beyond their framework. Specifically, the method of deriving Sentiment Lexical Attention from semantic-polarity scores and integrating it into the self-attention mechanism represents a novel contribution to the field. Our approach also presents a comprehensive empirical analysis across multiple architectures and tasks, establishing the effectiveness and robustness of our method. The novelty of our work lies in the specific application of lexical sentiment knowledge in enhancing the attention mechanism.

8 Conclusion

In our study, we introduced a new approach to inject sentiment knowledge into the self-attention mechanism of Transformer-based models. This approach yielded significant improvements, particularly in Korean sentiment classification benchmark, where we achieved a new state-of-the-art performance. Moreover, the promising results obtained across various out-of-domain tasks highlighted the general applicability of our method. Although the observed performance variations were task- and model-dependent, they underscored the substantial potential of incorporating human-derived knowledge into Transformer-based language models. Furthermore, in our examination of the CLS token, we could ascertain the direct impact of knowledge injection on the layer-wise attention distribution. The approach presented in this study opens the door for further exploration of effective techniques for injecting human knowledge into language models.

Limitations

Despite the promising results obtained in our study, it is important to acknowledge several limitations that should be addressed. Firstly, the application of the Sentiment Lexical Attention in our method assumes a direct relevance of the semantic-polarity scores to the specific task being addressed. This assumption limits the versatility and scalability of our approach, as the selection and application of relevant knowledge may require careful consideration and may not be readily available for all tasks. Secondly, the variation in performance observed across different models indicates that the efficacy of our approach may not be uniform across all types of Transformer-based models. It is necessary to conduct preliminary tests to assess the compatibility and effectiveness of our method with a given model before deploying it in real-world scenarios.

Thirdly, the success of our approach relies heavily on the quality and accuracy of the Sentiment Lexical Attention being employed. Tasks that require high-precision or complex human knowledge can be challenging, as even small inaccuracies in the knowledge may lead to significant deviations in performance. Careful attention should be given to the selection and curation of the Sentiment Lexical Attention to ensure its reliability and relevance to the task at hand.

Lastly, while we have made progress in understanding how to integrate pre-annotated sentiment values into Transformer models, there is still much to explore and understand about the precise influence of this knowledge on the model's training and decision-making processes. Further research and analysis are needed to gain a comprehensive understanding of these dynamics, particularly in complex real-world applications. Future work could focus on addressing these limitations by developing more adaptable knowledge injection mechanisms or conducting a more comprehensive analysis of how sentiment information influences model behavior.

By addressing these limitations, we can further enhance the effectiveness and applicability of integrating Sentiment Lexical Attention into Transformer-based models, opening up new avenues for advancements in NLP and related fields.

Ethics Statement

This research study follows ethical guidelines for conducting experiments following ACL rules. It utilizes publicly available datasets and sentiment lexicons, ensuring user privacy and avoiding any ethical concerns. The focus is on enhancing language models through the injection of the semantic-polarity scores, without manipulation or deception. The research does not involve human subjects or human-generated data. The study acknowledges potential biases and takes steps to mitigate them. Transparency and ethical considerations are paramount in the research process.

References

Tom Brown, Benjamin Mann, Nick Ryder, Melanie Subbiah, Jared D Kaplan, Prafulla Dhariwal, Arvind Neelakantan, Pranav Shyam, Girish Sastry, Amanda Askell, et al. 2020. Language models are few-shot learners. *Advances in neural information processing systems*, 33:1877–1901.

Pedro Colon-Hernandez, Catherine Havasi, Jason Alonso, Matthew Huggins, and Cynthia Breazeal. 2021. Combining pre-trained language models and structured knowledge. *arXiv preprint arXiv:2101.12294*.

Alexis Conneau, Kartikay Khandelwal, Naman Goyal, Vishrav Chaudhary, Guillaume Wenzek, Francisco Guzmán, Edouard Grave, Myle Ott, Luke Zettlemoyer, and Veselin Stoyanov. 2019. Unsupervised cross-lingual representation learning at scale. *arXiv preprint arXiv:1911.02116*.

Jacob Devlin, Ming-Wei Chang, Kenton Lee, and Kristina Toutanova. 2018. Bert: Pre-training of deep bidirectional transformers for language understanding. *arXiv preprint arXiv:1810.04805*.

Linyuan Gong, Di He, Zhuohan Li, Tao Qin, Liwei Wang, and Tieyan Liu. 2019. Efficient training of bert by progressively stacking. In *International conference on machine learning*, pages 2337–2346. PMLR.

Jiyeon Ham, Yo Joong Choe, Kyubyong Park, Ilji Choi, and Hyungjoon Soh. 2020. KorNLI and KorSTS: New benchmark datasets for Korean natural language understanding. In *Findings of the Association for Computational Linguistics: EMNLP 2020*, pages 422–430, Online. Association for Computational Linguistics.

Linmei Hu, Zeyi Liu, Ziwang Zhao, Lei Hou, Liqiang Nie, and Juanzi Li. 2023. A survey of knowledge enhanced pre-trained language models. *IEEE Transactions on Knowledge and Data Engineering*.

Francesca Incitti, Federico Urli, and Lauro Snidaro. 2023. Beyond word embeddings: A survey. *Information Fusion*, 89:418–436.

Dongjun Jang, Jean Seo, Sungjoo Byun, Taekyoung Kim, Minseok Kim, and Hyopil Shin. 2024. Carbd-ko: A contextually annotated review benchmark dataset for aspect-level sentiment classification in korean.

Zakaria Kaddari and Toumi Bouchentouf. 2023. A novel self-attention enriching mechanism for biomedical question answering. *Expert Systems with Applications*, 225:120210.

Olga Kovaleva, Alexey Romanov, Anna Rogers, and Anna Rumshisky. 2019. Revealing the dark secrets of bert. *arXiv preprint arXiv:1908.08593*.

Junbum Lee. 2021. Kcelectra: Korean comments electra. `https://github.com/Beomi/KcELECTRA`.

Sangah Lee, Hansol Jang, Yunmee Baik, Suzi Park, and Hyopil Shin. 2020. Kr-bert: A small-scale korean-specific language model. *ArXiv*, abs/2008.03979.

Sangah Lee and Hyopil Shin. 2022. Kr-electra: a korean-based electra model. `https://github.com/snunlp/KR-ELECTRA`.

Mike Lewis, Yinhan Liu, Naman Goyal, Marjan Ghazvininejad, Abdelrahman Mohamed, Omer Levy, Ves Stoyanov, and Luke Zettlemoyer. 2019. Bart: Denoising sequence-to-sequence pre-training for natural language generation, translation, and comprehension. *arXiv preprint arXiv:1910.13461*.

Weijie Liu, Peng Zhou, Zhe Zhao, Zhiruo Wang, Qi Ju, Haotang Deng, and Ping Wang. 2020. K-bert: Enabling language representation with knowledge graph. In *Proceedings of the AAAI Conference on Artificial Intelligence*, volume 34, pages 2901–2908.

Jihyung Moon, Won Ik Cho, and Junbum Lee. 2020. BEEP! Korean corpus of online news comments for toxic speech detection. In *Proceedings of the Eighth International Workshop on Natural Language Processing for Social Media*, pages 25–31, Online. Association for Computational Linguistics.

Malte Ostendorff, Peter Bourgonje, Maria Berger, Julian Moreno-Schneider, Georg Rehm, and Bela Gipp. 2019. Enriching bert with knowledge graph embeddings for document classification. *arXiv preprint arXiv:1909.08402*.

Jangwon Park. 2020. Koelectra: Pretrained electra model for korean. `https://github.com/monologg/KoELECTRA`.

Matthew E Peters, Mark Neumann, Robert L Logan IV, Roy Schwartz, Vidur Joshi, Sameer Singh, and Noah A Smith. 2019. Knowledge enhanced contextual word representations. *arXiv preprint arXiv:1909.04164*.

Han Shi, Jiahui Gao, Xiaozhe Ren, Hang Xu, Xiaodan Liang, Zhenguo Li, and James Tin-Yau Kwok. 2021. Sparsebert: Rethinking the importance analysis in self-attention. In *International Conference on Machine Learning*, pages 9547–9557. PMLR.

Yu Sun, Shuohuan Wang, Yukun Li, Shikun Feng, Xuyi Chen, Han Zhang, Xin Tian, Danxiang Zhu, Hao Tian, and Hua Wu. 2019. Ernie: Enhanced representation through knowledge integration. *arXiv preprint arXiv:1904.09223*.

Shirui Wang, Wenan Zhou, and Chao Jiang. 2020. A survey of word embeddings based on deep learning. *Computing*, 102:717–740.

Yuqi Wang, Wei Wang, Qi Chen, Kaizhu Huang, Anh Nguyen, Suparna De, and Amir Hussain. 2023. Fusing external knowledge resources for natural language understanding techniques: A survey. *Information Fusion*, 92:190–204.

Xiaokai Wei, Shen Wang, Dejiao Zhang, Parminder Bhatia, and Andrew Arnold. 2021. Knowledge enhanced pretrained language models: A compreshensive survey. *arXiv preprint arXiv:2110.08455*.

Zhaofeng Wu, Hao Peng, and Noah A Smith. 2021. Infusing finetuning with semantic dependencies. *Transactions of the Association for Computational Linguistics*, 9:226–242.

Tingyu Xia, Yue Wang, Yuan Tian, and Yi Chang. 2021. Using prior knowledge to guide bert's attention in semantic textual matching tasks. In *Proceedings of the Web Conference 2021*, pages 2466–2475.

Yifeng Xie, Zhihong Zhu, Xuxin Cheng, Zhiqi Huang, and Dongsheng Chen. 2023. Syntax matters: Towards spoken language understanding via syntax-aware attention. In *Findings of the Association for Computational Linguistics: EMNLP 2023*, pages 11858–11864.

Yichong Xu, Chenguang Zhu, Ruochen Xu, Yang Liu, Michael Zeng, and Xuedong Huang. 2020. Fusing context into knowledge graph for commonsense question answering. *arXiv preprint arXiv:2012.04808*.

Yinfei Yang, Yuan Zhang, Chris Tar, and Jason Baldridge. 2019a. PAWS-X: A cross-lingual adversarial dataset for paraphrase identification. In *Proceedings of the 2019 Conference on Empirical Methods in Natural Language Processing and the 9th International Joint Conference on Natural Language Processing (EMNLP-IJCNLP)*, pages 3687–3692, Hong Kong, China. Association for Computational Linguistics.

Zhilin Yang, Zihang Dai, Yiming Yang, Jaime Carbonell, Russ R Salakhutdinov, and Quoc V Le. 2019b. Xlnet: Generalized autoregressive pretraining for language understanding. *Advances in neural information processing systems*, 32.

Da Yin, Tao Meng, and Kai-Wei Chang. 2020. Sentibert: A transferable transformer-based architecture for compositional sentiment semantics. *arXiv preprint arXiv:2005.04114*.

Donghan Yu, Chenguang Zhu, Yiming Yang, and Michael Zeng. 2022. Jaket: Joint pre-training of knowledge graph and language understanding. In *Proceedings of the AAAI Conference on Artificial Intelligence*, volume 36, pages 11630–11638.

Zhengyan Zhang, Xu Han, Zhiyuan Liu, Xin Jiang, Maosong Sun, and Qun Liu. 2019. Ernie: Enhanced language representation with informative entities. *arXiv preprint arXiv:1905.07129*.

Zhuosheng Zhang, Yuwei Wu, Hai Zhao, Zuchao Li, Shuailiang Zhang, Xi Zhou, and Xiang Zhou. 2020. Semantics-aware bert for language understanding. In *Proceedings of the AAAI Conference on Artificial Intelligence*, volume 34, pages 9628–9635.

Ying Zhao, Tingyu Xia, Yunqi Jiang, and Yuan Tian. 2024. Enhancing inter-sentence attention for semantic textual similarity. *Information Processing & Management*, 61(1):103535.

Handling Ontology Gaps in Semantic Parsing

Andrea Bacciu[1,2], Marco Damonte[1], Marco Basaldella[1], Emilio Monti[1]
[1]Amazon
[2]Sapienza University of Rome
{andbac, dammarco, mbbasald, monti}@amazon.com

Abstract

The majority of Neural Semantic Parsing (NSP) models are developed with the assumption that there are no concepts outside the ones such models can represent with their target symbols (closed-world assumption). This assumption leads to generate hallucinated outputs rather than admitting their lack of knowledge. Hallucinations can lead to wrong or potentially offensive responses to users. Hence, a mechanism to prevent this behavior is crucial to build trusted NSP-based Question Answering agents. To that end, we propose the Hallucination Simulation Framework (HSF), a general setting for stimulating and analyzing NSP model hallucinations. The framework can be applied to any NSP task with a closed-ontology. Using the proposed framework and KQA Pro as the benchmark dataset, we assess state-of-the-art techniques for hallucination detection. We then present a novel hallucination detection strategy that exploits the computational graph of the NSP model to detect the NSP hallucinations in the presence of ontology gaps, out-of-domain utterances, and to recognize NSP errors, improving the F1-Score respectively by $\sim$21%, $\sim$24% and $\sim$1%. This is the first work in closed-ontology NSP that addresses the problem of recognizing ontology gaps. We release our code and checkpoints at `https://github.com/amazon-science/handling-ontology-gaps-in-semantic-parsing`.

1 Introduction

Semantic Parsing (SP) is one of the long-standing tasks in Natural Language Understanding, aiming at mapping complex natural language to machine-readable languages (e.g., SQL, SPARQL, KoPL (Cao et al., 2022), and so on). These languages, which we will refer to as Meaning Representation Languages (MRLs), are designed to be precise representations of the natural language's intent, enabling efficient querying of a Knowledge Base (KB) to retrieve pertinent answers in a Question Answering (QA) agent. Despite the advent of the Transformer architecture (Vaswani et al., 2017), which has enabled semantic parsers to achieve extraordinary performance (Cao et al., 2022; Bai et al., 2022; Conia et al., 2021), Semantic Parsing's crux remains the handling of out-of-ontology queries; in other words, since SP models and tasks (such as KQA-PRO (Cao et al., 2022), LC-QUAD 2.0 (Dubey et al., 2019), and QALD-9 (Cui et al., 2022)) hold a closed-world assumption, they will always try to map an utterance to a MRL *even if there is no valid representation for that utterance in the target ontology*, leading to wrong answers to be delivered to the model's users, called hallucinations.

In fact, the closed-ontology task formulation enforces NSP models to always produce interpretations without an option to admit their lack of knowledge, inducing the models to hallucinate. Therefore, the resulting models produce hallucinated outputs when they receive an utterance that requires symbols outside of their ontology, resulting in a wrong and potentially offensive answer. It is then of paramount importance to develop a system able to detect and prevent these hallucinations, so that users are not exposed to such mistakes. Hallucinations in NSP differs with the notion of hallucinations in Natural Language Generation, we report the differences in Appendix A.

To better understand different types of hallucinations in NSP, we classify errors into four macro categories. Given a semantic Q&A parsing task $\mathcal{T}$, a dataset $\mathcal{D}$, and an ontology $\mathcal{O}$, hallucinations of a model trained over $\mathcal{D}$ are classified as:

- **in-ontology NSP errors**: utterances within the scope of $\mathcal{T}$ and where $\mathcal{O}$ contains all the symbols required to produce the correct MRLs, but for which the NSP model produces an incorrect MRL. For example, the utterance *"What is the capital of France?"* is in-ontology

*Proceedings of the 13th Joint Conference on Lexical and Computational Semantics (*SEM 2024)*, pages 345 - 359
June 20-21, 2024 ©2024 Association for Computational Linguistics

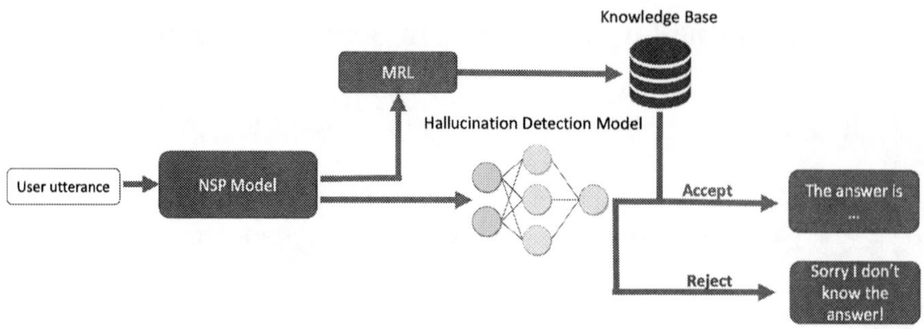

Figure 1: The proposed pipeline: (1) the NSP model (KQA-PRO Bart model) receives the question from the user and produces the corresponding MRL; (2) the Hallucination Detection Model extracts features from the NSP model and decides whether to deliver the MRL to the user or not.

if $\mathcal{O}$ contains the symbols for "*France*" and "*capital of*". However, if the NSP model erroneously translates the utterance to an MRL referencing e.g. a symbol for *"weather of"* instead of *"capital of"*, this type of hallucination is categorized as in-ontology NSP error. We will refer to this kind of errors as **NSP errors** for brevity.

- **out-of-ontology**: utterances that are within $\mathcal{T}$ but for which $\mathcal{O}$ does not contain all the symbols required to produce the correct MRLs (ontology gap). For example, *"What is the crime rate of France?"*, is out-of-ontology if $\mathcal{O}$ does not contain a symbol for the predicate "*crime-rate-of*". In this case, the NSP model will hallucinate another symbol, e.g. it could generate the MRL for *"what is the population of France"* instead.
- **out-of-domain (OOD)**: utterances outside the scope of $\mathcal{T}$. For example, if $\mathcal{T}$ = factual QA, *"Switch on the lights!"* is OOD because it is not a factual question. We expect an empty MRL because $\mathcal{O}$ does not have the necessary symbols to satisfy the out-of-ontology user utterance and the NSP model is trained to perform the task $\mathcal{T}$.
- **non-executable output**: in this case, the NSP model will output a MRL that cannot be executed and it thus cannot lead to an answer.

We show actual closed ontology Semantic Parsing hallucination examples in Figure 2 and we report more in Appendix H. High performance in detecting OOD utterances in NSP can be achieved (Lukovnikov et al., 2021; Lang et al., 2023), and non-executable outputs are trivially detectable as they fail to parse; but identifying both in-ontology and out-of-ontology errors can be hard even for experienced annotators, since the sheer size of most popular ontologies makes it impractical for a human to have a complete view of all the ontology symbols[1]. Moreover, to the best of our knowledge, there are no works addressing this specific NSP issue.

The research question that we want to address is: *what is the most effective strategy to prevent a NSP-based QA agent to deliver wrong, and potentially offensive, answers to its users?* To this end, we develop the Hallucination Simulation Framework depicted in Figure 1; in detail, our main contributions are:

- We propose a framework to stimulate, analyze and detect hallucinations in closed ontology NSP;
- We propose the Hallucination Detection Model (HDM), an architecture that analyzes an NSP model to determine whether it is hallucinating or not using several hallucination detection signals;
- We introduce a model's *Activations* as hallucination detection signals; when combined with other signals, they improve the Macro F1-Score by up to 21% in ontology gaps, 1% in NSP error, and 24% in OOD detection.

To the best of our knowledge, this is the first work that addresses the ontology gaps problem in a closed-ontology NSP task.

2 Related Work

When we do not allow models to admit their lack of knowledge, forcing them to produce an output even when they do not have the instruments to do it, they will inevitably *hallucinate*. In other words,

[1]e.g., Wikidata has 10k+ properties.

in generative NLP, when the generated output displays a misunderstanding of the input utterance by the model, we say that the model is "hallucinating". Typically, models hallucinate in two ways: (1) inventing additional information not included in or related to the input utterance, or (2) confusing a symbol/word with another one.

One of the biggest assumptions in existing Semantic Parsing tasks is that every input always has a valid target logical form. In such a setup, models are always forced to generate a MRL or, in other words, to hallucinate a wrong understanding, instead of admitting a lack of knowledge. However, recently the NLP community has begun to investigate this closed-world assumption for other tasks. For example, the Extractive Question Answering dataset SQuAD v1 (Rajpurkar et al., 2016) was built with the assumption that, given each question-paragraph pair, it is always possible to find an answer to the question in the paragraph. This assumption was removed in the second version of the dataset (Rajpurkar et al., 2018), which includes questions without an answer. Another field in which this problem was addressed is entity linking, where models can produce a NIL entity when they cannot find a suitable entity for a certain mention (Ruas and Couto, 2022). On the other hand, most of the hallucination detection in NSP works rely on two confidence estimation techniques: (1) the Sequence log-probability (also called Confidence Score) (Guerreiro et al., 2022; Dong et al., 2018), or (2) Monte Carlo Dropout (or Dropout Perturbation) (Gal and Ghahramani, 2016; Guerreiro et al., 2022; Dong et al., 2018).

3 Closed World Assumption in NSP: A Logical Theory Perspective

The Closed World Assumption (CWA) originates from logic theory, and it is the assumption that only the known facts are correct, and what is not known is false (Reiter, 1981; Keet, 2013). In other words, the CWA assumes *total knowledge* over a domain, implying that all the possible symbols (e.g., entities and predicates) are known, and that only the known facts represented using the known symbols are true. On the other hand, the Open World Assumption (OWA) makes no assumption over what is not known; in other words, the OWA allows "gaps" in the knowledge, e.g. the existence of unknown symbols or of unknown, but true, facts.

Question: "Did Christopher Columbus die from Covid before 2020?"

Gold MRL:
```
Find <arg> Covid <func> Relate <arg> cause of death <arg>
backward <func> Find <arg> Christopher Columbus <func> And <func>
QueryAttr <arg> date of death <func> VerifyYear <arg> 2020 <arg>
<
```

Predicted MRL:
```
Find <arg> Christopher Columbus <func> QueryAttr <arg> date of
death <func> VerifyYear <arg> 2020 <arg> <
```

Missing ontology symbol: *cause of death* KB's Answer: Yes Ground Truth: No

Figure 2: We show the output our NSP model trained without a symbol for the concept of "cause of death". Given a question that requires this symbol, the model produces a wrong but executable MRL leading to a wrong answer served to its user.

For some tasks, using the CWA is safe. For example, Reiter (1981) notes that: "in an airline data base, all flights and the cities which they connect will be explicitly represented. If I fail to find an entry indicating that Air Canada flight 103 connects Vancouver with Toulouse I will conclude that it does not". For SP models, however, the CWA can be dangerous. Let's take the following scenario: a CWA NSP model's input is *"what is the crime rate of France"*, but the target ontology does not have a representation for the predicate *"crime rate of"*. Since the model is trained under the CWA it assumes that there cannot be other predicates other the ones it can access, hence it will (a) ground *"crime rate of"* to a different predicate and then (a) produce a necessarily incorrect representation of the input. If this incorrect representation happens to be syntactically correct, it will then be exectuted, serving a wrong answer to the customer.

This issue is exemplified in Figure 2, where we take a NSP model trained on the KQA-Pro dataset (Cao et al., 2022) and we ask it to generate a MRL for the question *"did Chistopher Columbus die from Covid before 2020?"*. The absence of the "cause of death" symbol in the set of the model's known symbols leads to an MRL which erroneously uses the "date of death" symbol instead. Even if this MRL is syntactically correct, it misrepresents the input due to the limitations of the training set. Since the MRL is executable, it will lead to the generation of an incorrect answer.

4 Detecting NSP Hallucinations

4.1 Hallucination Simulation Framework

Building on the CWA and OWA assumptions, we introduce the Hallucination Simulation Framework (HSF), a dataset-agnostic approach tailored for closed-ontology NSP tasks. This framework leverages the closed and open world assumptions to force a model to hallucinate at inference time. The model is trained using a "normal" SP dataset holding the CWA. However, the validation and test sets will contain MRLs needing symbols not known to the model at training time, hence forcing it to hallucinate. This allows to analyse how the model behaves when unable to produce ontology symbols, and to develop a number of hallucination detection strategies to mitigate the issue.

In practical terms, the HSF operates by considering the ontology used for a CWA SP dataset $\mathcal{O}_{\text{dataset}}$, and decomposing it into two disjoint sub-ontologies, called $\mathcal{O}_{\text{known\_symbols}}$ and $\mathcal{O}_{\text{unknown\_symbols}}$. $\mathcal{O}_{\text{known\_symbols}}$ contains the ontology symbols that are used to train the model, while $\mathcal{O}_{\text{unknown\_symbols}}$ contains the symbols that are used to stimulate hallucinations; we have that $\mathcal{O}_{\text{known\_symbols}} \cup \mathcal{O}_{\text{unknown\_symbols}} = \mathcal{O}_{\text{dataset}}$ and $\mathcal{O}_{\text{known\_symbols}} \cap \mathcal{O}_{\text{unknown\_symbols}} = \varnothing$.

These sub-ontologies are used to construct two datasets, a *NSP dataset* and an *Hallucination Detection Dataset* (HDD), whose construction is detailed in Section 4.1. The NSP dataset, containing only $\mathcal{O}_{\text{known\_symbols}}$, is used to train the model, while the HDD, containing both $\mathcal{O}_{\text{known\_symbols}}$ and $\mathcal{O}_{\text{unknown\_symbols}}$, is used to stimulate the model to hallucinate wrong ontology symbols and develop hallucination detection strategies (Section 5) .

Thanks to this framework, we can now programmatically induce hallucinations in a NSP model at inference time. Thus, we can train, tune, and test hallucination detection strategies to recognize unwanted signals from the model.

4.2 Hallucination Detection Dataset

The HDD comprises two types of samples: each natural language sentence is paired either with (1) MRLs that require only symbols from the $\mathcal{O}_{\text{known\_symbols}}$ set, or (2) MRLs that require at least one symbol from the $\mathcal{O}_{\text{unknown\_symbols}}$ set. To build the HDD, we first define $\mathcal{O}_{\text{unknown\_symbols}}$; then, we split $\mathcal{O}_{\text{unknown\_symbols}}$ in three sets, that are used to build the HDD train, development, and test set. We report the complete $\mathcal{O}_{\text{unknown\_symbols}}$ set in Appendix E.

In the following, we describe the methodology we followed to we ensure that the out-of-ontology symbols are sufficiently diverse and challenging, providing a rigorous test of the hallucination detection strategies.

Disjoint HDD train, validation and test sets To ensure that $\mathcal{O}_{\text{unknown\_symbols}}$ cannot be shared across train, dev and test set, we create three disjoint set one for each data split, as shown in Appendix E. Furthermore, we eliminate any sentences that require symbols from multiple out-of-ontology splits. This allows the development of robust hallucination detection strategies that are able to generalise over unseen ontology symbols.

Diversification of unknown symbols To improve the generalization of our methods, we also aim to maximize the number of out-of-ontology symbols across all splits. This is essential, as having few unknown symbols might lead hallucination detection strategies to recognize them throw their sentence context than isolating the underlying hallucination signal. For this purpose, we place symbols in $\mathcal{O}_{\text{unknown\_symbols}}$ based on their frequency of occurrence within the original dataset; we prioritize symbols with lower frequency (symbols with maximum 2 occurrences), as this approach maximizes the number of unique symbols in the HDD while maintaining a robust volume of samples for the NSP training set.

Ensuring Independent Feature Extraction by Dataset Segregation As detailed above, the framework employs two datasets: the NSP dataset and the HDD, each divided into training, dev, and test splits.

To construct the known symbol portion of the HDD we used utterances from the NSP dataset. It is crucial not to include utterances from the NSP train split, otherwise the hallucination detection strategies could simply learn to recognize as non-hallucinated only the utterances that were used to train the NSP model.

To circumvent this issue, the training and validation sets of the HDD are built by splitting NSP validation set. The HDD test set is instead simply built by appending samples containing the test symbols from $\mathcal{O}_{\text{unknown\_symbols}}$ to the existing NSP test set. We depict this process in Figure 3.

Out-Of-Domain sentences Besides out-of-ontology sentences, also out-of-domain (OOD) sentences are a common cause of hallucinations for NSP models. For example, consider a system trained to answer questions like "In what state does the Pope live?". Given an input sentence such as "Set an alarm at 8 am for Monday!" from a distinct domain (i.e., not a question), the

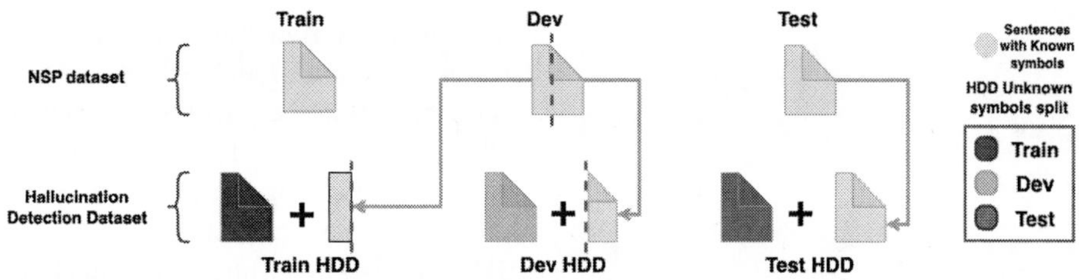

Figure 3: Construction of the Hallucination Detection Dataset (HDD). The first row represents the dataset used to train and test the NSP model, containing only $\mathcal{O}_{\text{known\_symbols}}$. To construct the $\mathcal{O}_{\text{known\_symbols}}$ portion of the HDD while avoiding overfitting of the hallucination detection strategies, we sourced sentences only from the validation and test splits of the NSP dataset as explained in Section 4.2.

question answering system will always produce wrong MRLs, because its ontology is not suitable for this type of utterances. We include OOD only in the validation and test sets for two main reasons: 1) to evaluate the zero-shot capabilities in recognizing OOD utterances as a different source of out-of-ontology; 2) to avoid the need for specific training for OOD detection, as addressing the wide range of potential OOD instances is beyond the scope of this study. We report the OOD dataset statistics in Appendix D.

5 Hallucination Detection Strategies

In this Section, we introduce the Hallucination Detection Strategies that we use in our experiments.

Autodetect Hallucinations A baseline approach to detect hallucinations is to enable the NSP model itself to decide whether to reject the MRL or not, in a similar fashion to the NIL entity in Ruas and Couto (2022). Therefore, we add a new ontology symbol called `<Reject-MRL>` in the NSP model, as a label for all the out-of-ontology sentences, i.e. moving from a CWA approach to a OWA one. Instead of using the NSP and HDD datasets, as we don't rely on external hallucination detection strategies, we train the NSP model using the full $\mathcal{O}_{\text{dataset}}$, marking MRLs containing $\mathcal{O}_{\text{unknown\_symbols}}$ samples as utterances to reject. In preliminary experiments, this approach resulted in zero true positives. This happens because the model memorized the utterances marked as out-of-ontology, hence failing to generalize on the "unseen" unknown symbols in the development and test set (see Section 4.2 for how the disjoint train, validation and test sets are constructed).

Confidence Score Confidence Score (CS) is a standard method to detect hallucinations (Dong et al., 2018) that measures the confidence level of a statistical model about the output it generates. However, this method relies on the strong assumption that the model will not be confident when generating hallucinations, and vice versa. This is not always guaranteed in practice: as we can see in the CS distribution in Figure 4, the confidence distributions of correct and wrong model predictions overlap. For this reason, rejecting model predictions below a certain threshold would not be sufficient to remove all the wrong MRLs.

To compute the CS, we calculate the Posterior Probability (PP) of a generated MRL $w_n, ..., w_1$ from the beam search tree, and then we normalize it by the length n of the generated output, by applying the nth-root.

$$CS = \sqrt[n]{PP(w_n, w_{n-1}, ..., w_1)} \qquad (1)$$

We test CS in two ways: (1) by setting a threshold to the best CS value found in a sample from the HDD train set that maximizes the hallucination detection in the HDD dev set; (2) and by using it as a feature in the Hallucination Detection Model (HDM) that we will define in Section 6.

Monte Carlo Dropout The Monte Carlo Dropout (MCD) strategy was introduced by Gal and Ghahramani (2016): the idea is to use the dropout technique as a Bayesian approximation to represent the model uncertainty. Dropout is a well-known regularization technique that randomly disables a subset of the neurons in a neural network layer in order to prevent overfitting. MCD involves enabling dropout at inference time and running inference multiple times to create a random perturbation in the model; a small perturbation indicates that the model is confident with the input, while a large perturbation suggests a likely mistake from the model. We follow the formulation by Dong et al. (2018), using 30 trials, beam size of 2, and

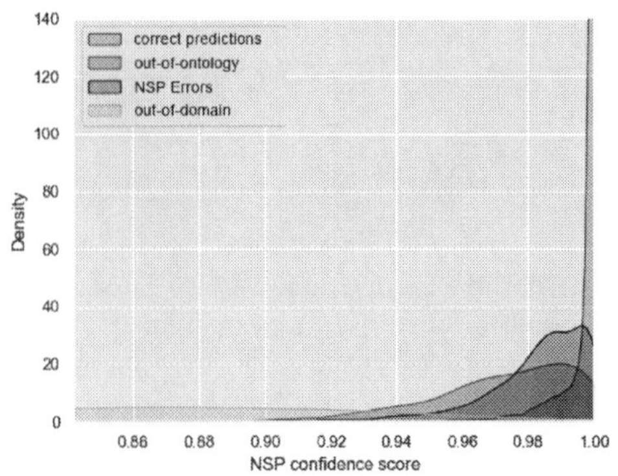

Figure 4: Overlap between the distributions of correct predictions, out-of-ontology, NSP errors, and OOD w.r.t. Confidence Score (CS). The model is overconfident over wrong predictions, hence the CS is not sufficient to separate good and Hallucinated MRLs. Specifically, the CS struggles to distinguish between NSP Errors and correct predictions (i.e., both types of MRLs that contains only $\mathcal{O}_{\text{known\_symbols}}$).

taking the variance of the CS value. Similar to CS, we use the MCD in two ways: (1) identifying a threshold value that maximizes hallucination detection between out-of-ontology/NSP Errors and in-ontology, and (2) using it as a feature for the HDM.

Model Activations Looking at the activations of the model's computational graph is a powerful way to debug neural networks and is usually used for explainability, such as in the Grad-Cam algorithm (Selvaraju et al., 2017). For this reason, we propose for the first time to use the forward activations of the NSP model encoder at inference time to detect whether there is a hallucination or not. To encode the activation features for all layers, we pool the sequence length and compute the variance. Then, we use the encoding of the model's activations as a feature to recognize the hallucinations in the HDM. Although it can be argued that both the Autodetect and Activations strategies use the encoder's hidden states, these approaches are different. The first approach uses only the last hidden states of the encoder as input to the decoder, which has then the duty of producing an MRL or the rejection symbol. On the other hand, in the HDM all the encoder's activations are used as input, allowing the HDM to have a complete view of the hidden states of the NSP model during the generation.

Hallucination Detection Model The Hallucination Detection Model (HDM) is a neural network trained on the HDD that learns to classify whether an NSP model is hallucinating or not using as features the signals extracted from the NSP models, such as CS, activations, and MCD. The HDM consists of a MultiHead-Attention and two feed-forward layers with RELU function, batch normalization, dropout, and a binary classification head.We report a Figure of the architecture in Appendix G, the complete list of hyper-parameters in Appendix I and hardware infrastructure in Appendix L.

6 Experimental Setup

Dataset While the HSF is dataset-agnostic, in our experiments, we use the KQA-PRO dataset (Cao et al., 2022), based on the KoPL (Knowledge-oriented Programming Language) MRL; this dataset is built on top of a large ontology, which is a subset of Wikidata. We instead sourced OOD sentences from the TOP v2 Dataset (Chen et al., 2020), that contains task oriented utterances, such as "Turn on the lights!".

To create a test set, we merged the train and the validation set, and we split the data as follows: 60%, 20%, and 20%, respectively, for the train, validation and test set. The statistics of the HSF framework applied to the KQA-PRO dataset are reported in Appendix B.

NSP model Following the KQA-PRO paper, we train the BART-base model (Lewis et al., 2019), using the NSP training dataset. We report the hyper-parameters that we use to train the NSP model in Appendix M. Note that as the original KQA-PRO test set is not publicly available, we cannot compare our results with the original dataset paper.

Evaluation To measure the hallucination detection capabilities, we use the Macro F1-Score due to the imbalance of the dataset, as shown in Appendix D and, E. We compute the individual F1-Score for each type of hallucination defined in Section 1: in-ontology **NSP errors** caused by the model hallucinating wrong symbols from $\mathcal{O}_{\text{known\_symbols}}$, **out-of-ontology errors** caused by the need of symbols in $\mathcal{O}_{\text{unknown\_symbols}}$ to correctly represent the input, and zero-shot **OOD** detection. As mentioned in Section 7, we excluded non-Executable MRLs from our evaluation protocol because they are trivially detected by simply trying, and failing, to ex-

Split	Answer Accuracy	MRL EM
NSP model (baseline)	93%	85%
NSP model + Threshold CS	96%	94%
NSP model + Act. + CS	**97%**	**95%**

Table 1: Performance of baseline KQA-PRO BART model and of the best hallucination detection models on the NSP task; the NSP model is trained as in (Cao et al., 2022), and on top of it we apply our hallucination detection strategies. We compute metrics only on the executable outputs that lead to an answer to be delivered to a user; for more details, see Appendix F.

ecute them on the KB. To increase the robustness of our results, we repeat the training of the HDM model in all the configurations using 10 different random seeds, and then we report the mean and the standard deviation of the F1-Scores.

7 Discussion

We report the performance of our NSP model using Execution Accuracy and the MRL Exact Match metric in Table 1. In this work, we focused on four major causes for hallucinations: in-ontology NSP errors, out-of-ontology utterances and out-of-domain utterances. Specifically, we propose the first work that addresses the problem of ontology gaps, i.e., exposing an NSP model to utterances that require unknown ontology symbols to be represented in the output vocabulary. As mentioned in Section 1, recognizing ontology gaps is a challenging task even for experienced annotators due to the large size of the most popular ontologies. Our methodology induces ontology gaps and forces the model to hallucinate programmatically through a Hallucination Simulation Framework (§4). We developed a number of hallucination prevention strategies (§5) to detect and prevent the delivery of hallucinated answers to users. In Table 2, we report the individual Macro F1-Score of the tested systems on the three scenarios: out-of-ontology, NSP Errors, and zero-shot out-of-domain.

From a baseline where only non-executable MRLs are not delivered to the user, the HDM with *Activations + CS* is our best-performing model, improving answer accuracy by 4% and MRL exact match by 10%, effectively reducing a user's exposition to wrong answers. The HDM with *Activations + CS*'s performance is achieved by increasing the Macro F1-Score by approximately 21% and 24% for out-of-ontology and out-of-domain detection w.r.t. baseline, respectively. On the other hand, the NSP Errors detection performance is comparable to that of Threshold CS, with only the HDM with the *Activations + CS + MCD* combination showing a 1% improvement over the baseline in NSP Error detection. This marginal gain can be attributed to the limited number of errors produced by our NSP model over utterances with known symbols only, which constitutes about 11% of the in-ontology utterances (see statistics in Appendix J).

However, we can notice that both CS and MCD, if optimized through the HDM, obtain large gains in terms of Macro F1-Score. In fact, CS improves by 17% and 10% in out-of-ontology and out-of-domain detection, and MCD by 4%, 3%, and 10% in out-of-ontology, NSP Errors, and out-of-domain detection. In addition, the HDM can combine multiple hallucination signals to obtain higher performance, as in the case of our most-performing system. For further insight, we report the Precision and Recall over each error category in Appendix N.

Executable vs Non-Executable MRLs To highlight the scale of the issue we are tackling, it is important to measure how many times wrong answers would be served to users without a proper hallucination detection pipeline. As shown in Appendix K, in 46.3% of the utterances requiring $\mathcal{O}_{\text{unknown\_symbols}}$ the NSP model generates a syntactically valid MRL, which would then be executed, causing a wrong answer to be delivered to the user. This happens because NSP models tend to replicate executable patterns using known symbols from the training set, even when receiving utterances that cannot be represented with the known vocabulary.

Effect of the number of changed ontology symbols To further analyze the results, we analyze the behavior of the NSP model on the hallucinated MRLs in Figure 5. Specifically, this analysis highlights the MRLs where the NSP model added wrong ontology symbols (left plot), or omitted required symbols (right plot) from the ground truth sequence. In the Figure, we show a comparison between two systems: (1) Threshold CS (the best non-model based strategy) and (2) HDM with Activations and CS (our best model-based strategy), expressed as a percentage of errors in relation to the number of modified symbols. The plots suggest that (a) when the model *adds* symbols, the hardest errors to detect happen when the model adds up to 2 unnecessary symbols, leaving $\geq 50\%$

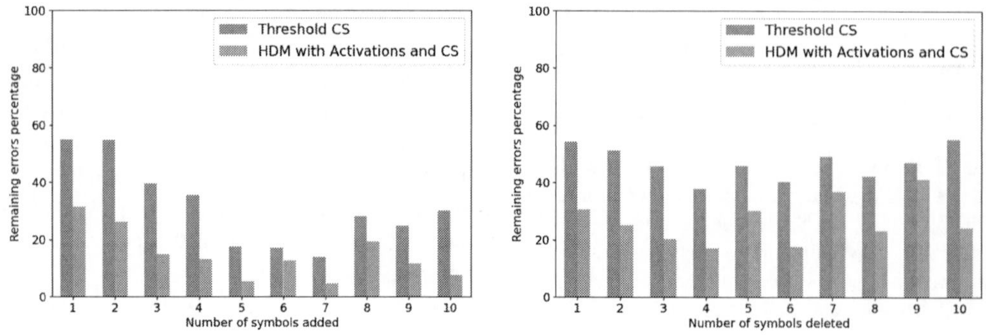

Figure 5: In this plot on the y-axis the percentage of remaining error (↓ is better) and on the x-axis we distinguish between the various hallucinated MRLs that omit (right plot) or add (left plot) incorrect ontology symbols with respect to the ground truth. Residual error compares two systems: Threshold CS and HDM with Activations and CS.

EXP NAME - END2END	out-of-ontology	NSP error	out-of-domain	average
Autodetect (Baseline)	0.490	0.471	0.466	0.476
Threshold CS 98.5% (Baseline)	0.480	0.653	0.456	0.530
Threshold MCD (Baseline)	0.452	0.439	0.428	0.440
Activations^{HDM}	0.498 ± 0.013	0.474 ± 0.003	0.466 ± 0.003	0.479
CS^{HDM}	0.648 ± 0.040	0.591 ± 0.023	0.552 ± 0.089	0.597
MCD^{HDM}	0.490 ± 0.001	0.471 ± 0.003	0.541 ± 0.163	0.501
CS + MCD^{HDM}	0.654 ± 0.021	0.617 ± 0.018	0.537 ± 0.030	0.603
Activations + CS^{HDM}	$\mathbf{0.701 \pm 0.030}$	0.643 ± 0.027	$\mathbf{0.703 \pm 0.086}$	**0.682**
Activations + MCD^{HDM}	0.496 ± 0.012	0.474 ± 0.004	0.466 ± 0.002	0.479
Activations + CS+ MCD^{HDM}	0.659 ± 0.026	$\mathbf{0.660 \pm 0.025}$	0.618 ± 0.077	0.646

Table 2: We report the Macro F1-Score (↑ is better) in the three scenarios: out-of-ontology detection, NSP Error detection and zero-shot OOD detection. These features are combined (+) concatenating their vector representations. The superscript ^{HDM} indicates the system optimized with the HDM.

of the errors undetected for CS and $\geq 30\%$ for the HDM; (b) when the model *removes* symbols, there seems to be no discernible pattern based on the amount of removed symbols; and (c) in both cases, the HDM model performs considerably better than the Threshold CS strategy, with a relative error reduction of $\sim$50%.

Latency While adding a second neural network in the QA pipeline might be considered penalising in terms of latency, it's worth noting that the HDM is very small model compared to the main NSP model. In detail, the HDM requires only 184k Floating Point Operations (FLOPs), which amounts to less than 1% of the FLOPs required by the *BART-base* architecture of the NSP model, which is 2.49 Billion FLOPs.

8 Conclusions

Current studies of Neural Semantic Parsing (NSP) models revolve around improving performance on academic benchmarks, but they do not take into account the trustworthiness of the model in a real world scenario where the model is used to serve answers to users of a QA system. In such scenario, NSP models can hallucinate syntactically correct, but semantically wrong MRLs, that can be used to serve incorrect answers to users. This is particularly true when users ask questions that require knowledge beyond the one used by the model's target ontology, as in these cases the model simply cannot generate a correct MRL.

To test NSP models under this more realistic scenario, we propose the Hallucination Simulation Framework (HSF), where we programmatically induce NSP models to hallucinate, and then, using the Hallucination Detection Model, we detect model errors at inference time using several different signals, including the model's activations or Confidence Score, or by using Monte Carlo Dropout.

We find that the best way to prevent detect hallucinations is using the HDM model with Activations and CS as features, which leads to an average improvement of more than 20% w.r.t. a baseline where the only non-served MRLs are just the syntactically incorrect ones.

Limitations

There are some limitations in this work that do not concern the framework construction. First of all, the framework imposes the construction of two datasets leading to a strong reduction of the training data. Hence, the framework to work properly requires a larger dataset. We are eager to expand our work in the future by taking advantage of the proposed framework in the following directions: (1) We pooled the activation sequences and did not take full advantage of the information in the sequences. (2) We have not tested the individual probability of each token in the generated MRL. (3) We have not tested the HDM with a multi-class output differentiating between in-ontology, out-of-ontology, NSP Errors, and OOD. (4) We did not test with other datasets, ontologies, or MRLs. (5) Our work has not been tested with other seq2seq architectures (e.g., mT5, Bart-large) and provides no multilingual tests.

Acknowledgments

We are thankful to our colleagues for their feedback and suggestions during the completion of this work. We also appreciate our anonymous reviewers for their time and valuable comments.

References

Xuefeng Bai, Yulong Chen, and Yue Zhang. 2022. Graph pre-training for amr parsing and generation. *arXiv preprint arXiv:2203.07836*.

Shulin Cao, Jiaxin Shi, Liangming Pan, Lunyiu Nie, Yutong Xiang, Lei Hou, Juanzi Li, Bin He, and Hanwang Zhang. 2022. Kqa pro: A dataset with explicit compositional programs for complex question answering over knowledge base. In *Proceedings of the 60th Annual Meeting of the Association for Computational Linguistics (Volume 1: Long Papers)*, pages 6101–6119.

Xilun Chen, Asish Ghoshal, Yashar Mehdad, Luke Zettlemoyer, and Sonal Gupta. 2020. Low-resource domain adaptation for compositional task-oriented semantic parsing. *arXiv preprint arXiv:2010.03546*.

Simone Conia, Andrea Bacciu, and Roberto Navigli. 2021. Unifying cross-lingual semantic role labeling with heterogeneous linguistic resources. In *Proceedings of the 2021 Conference of the North American Chapter of the Association for Computational Linguistics: Human Language Technologies*, pages 338–351, Online. Association for Computational Linguistics.

Ruixiang Cui, Rahul Aralikatte, Heather Lent, and Daniel Hershcovich. 2022. Compositional generalization in multilingual semantic parsing over wikidata. *Transactions of the Association for Computational Linguistics*, 10:937–955.

Li Dong, Chris Quirk, and Mirella Lapata. 2018. Confidence modeling for neural semantic parsing. *arXiv preprint arXiv:1805.04604*.

Mohnish Dubey, Debayan Banerjee, Abdelrahman Abdelkawi, and Jens Lehmann. 2019. Lc-quad 2.0: A large dataset for complex question answering over wikidata and dbpedia. In *International semantic web conference*, pages 69–78. Springer.

Yarin Gal and Zoubin Ghahramani. 2016. Dropout as a bayesian approximation: Representing model uncertainty in deep learning. In *international conference on machine learning*, pages 1050–1059. PMLR.

Nuno M Guerreiro, Elena Voita, and André FT Martins. 2022. Looking for a needle in a haystack: A comprehensive study of hallucinations in neural machine translation. *arXiv preprint arXiv:2208.05309*.

C Maria Keet. 2013. Closed world assumption. *Encyclopedia of Systems Biology*, pages 415–415.

Hao Lang, Yinhe Zheng, Yixuan Li, Jian Sun, Fei Huang, and Yongbin Li. 2023. A survey on out-of-distribution detection in nlp. *arXiv preprint arXiv:2305.03236*.

Mike Lewis, Yinhan Liu, Naman Goyal, Marjan Ghazvininejad, Abdelrahman Mohamed, Omer Levy, Ves Stoyanov, and Luke Zettlemoyer. 2019. Bart: Denoising sequence-to-sequence pre-training for natural language generation, translation, and comprehension. *arXiv preprint arXiv:1910.13461*.

Denis Lukovnikov, Sina Daubener, and Asja Fischer. 2021. Detecting compositionally out-of-distribution examples in semantic parsing. In *Findings of the Association for Computational Linguistics: EMNLP 2021*, pages 591–598.

Pranav Rajpurkar, Robin Jia, and Percy Liang. 2018. Know what you don't know: Unanswerable questions for squad. *arXiv preprint arXiv:1806.03822*.

Pranav Rajpurkar, Jian Zhang, Konstantin Lopyrev, and Percy Liang. 2016. Squad: 100,000+ questions for machine comprehension of text. *arXiv preprint arXiv:1606.05250*.

Raymond Reiter. 1981. On closed world data bases. In *Readings in artificial intelligence*, pages 119–140. Elsevier.

Pedro Ruas and Francisco M Couto. 2022. Nilinker: Attention-based approach to nil entity linking. *Journal of Biomedical Informatics*, 132:104137.

Ramprasaath R Selvaraju, Michael Cogswell, Abhishek Das, Ramakrishna Vedantam, Devi Parikh, and Dhruv Batra. 2017. Grad-cam: Visual explanations from deep networks via gradient-based localization. In *Proceedings of the IEEE international conference on computer vision*, pages 618–626.

Ashish Vaswani, Noam Shazeer, Niki Parmar, Jakob Uszkoreit, Llion Jones, Aidan N Gomez, Łukasz Kaiser, and Illia Polosukhin. 2017. Attention is all you need. *Advances in neural information processing systems*, 30.

A Differences between Hallucinations in Natural Language Generation and Neural Semantic Parsing

Hallucinations manifest differently in Neural Semantic Parsing (NSP) versus Natural Language Generation (NLG) systems. In NSP, hallucinations occur when the predicted logical form or query differs substantively from the gold reference form, despite appearing to be a valid query. This indicates the model fails to accurately capture the full semantic meaning conveyed in the input utterance. However, in NLG, hallucinations arise when the generated text contains false or ungrounded information not directly inferable from the input meaning representation. Whereas NSP hallucinations demonstrate misunderstanding of utterance semantics, NLG hallucinations reflect the model losing contextual grounding to fabricate or hallucinate statements not reasonably justified by reasoning through the implications of the input symbols provided. This suggests brittleness in establishing contextual coherence to match input constraint meanings.

B Hallucination Detection Dataset Stats

We report the dataset statistics of the Hallucination Simulation Framework in Table 3.

Split	in-ontology	out-of-ontology
NSP Train	59,120	
NSP Dev	19,700	
NSP Test	19,679	
HDD Train	19,154	3,893
HDD Dev	546	546
HDD Test	19,679	1,467

Table 3: Count of sentences for the NSP dataset and for the Hallucination Detection Dataset (HDD) applied to KQA-PRO dataset. We use the term in-ontology and out-of-ontology sentences to refers to the sentences that uses only $\mathcal{O}_{\text{known\_symbols}}$ and $\mathcal{O}_{\text{unknown\_symbols}}$ respectively.

C Selection of Unknown symbols

As mentioned above, we select the symbols for the $\mathcal{O}_{\text{unknown\_symbols}}$ starting from less frequent symbols. We took all the symbols with at maximum 2 occurrences, this is done b

This is done in order to maintain a good trade off in maximizing the number of

D Out-Of-Domain Dataset Stats

Split	NSP Dataset Test	TOP OOD
OOD Test	17,524	35,420

Table 4: Size of the TOP v2 out-of-domain dataset used for zero-shot evaluation. The NSP Dataset Test does not include the NSP Errors.

E Out-of-ontology symbols list

Train =['award rationale', 'of', 'separated from', 'quote', 'performer', 'latest date', 'author', 'captain', 'military branch', 'reason for deprecation', 'location', 'has effect', 'doctoral thesis', 'DOI', 'relative to', 'discontinued date', 'applies to part', 'mother', 'quantity', 'conscription number', 'identity of subject in context', 'end cause', 'central bank/issuer', 'dissolved, abolished or demolished', 'employer', 'earliest date', 'located at street address', 'member of political party', 'direction', 'valid in place', 'inventory number', 'series ordinal', 'religious order', 'manufacturer', 'nominee', 'place of marriage', 'creator', 'organizer', 'number of points/goals/set scored', 'nickname', 'number of matches played/races/starts', 'killed by', 'located on street', 'nature of statement', 'position held', 'statement supported by', 'together with', 'street number', 'position played on team / speciality', 'located in or next to body of water', 'instrument', 'doctoral advisor', 'statement disputed by', 'located at street address (DEPRECATED)', 'member of', 'married name', 'stated age at event', 'field of work']

Dev = ['academic degree', 'platform', 'type of kinship', 'present in work', 'appointed by', 'sex or gender', 'image', 'proportion', 'significant event', 'cause of death']

Test = ['catalog code', 'direction relative to location', 'valid in period', 'sourcing circumstances', 'academic major', 'approved by', 'item operated', 'length', 'has cause', 'instance of', 'sRGB color hex triplet', 'operating area', 'conferred by', 'name', 'subject has role', 'applies to jurisdiction', 'prize money', 'conflict', 'head of state', 'affiliation', 'proxy', 'use', 'replaces', 'replaced by', 'writing system', 'located on terrain feature', 'distribution', 'diplomatic mission sent', 'acquisition transaction', 'lyrics by', 'medical condition', 'number of speakers', 'has quality', 'sport number', 'criterion used', 'object has role', 'retrieved', 'basic form of government', 'military rank', 'drafted by', 'timezone offset', 'named as']

F Metrics

We report two metrics to measure the accuracy of our NSP model within the HSF framework. The MRL Exact Match (EM) consinsts in the ratio between the number of MRL predicted that exactly match with the ground truth MRL over the number of MRLs.

$$\text{EM} = \frac{1}{|MRLs|} \sum_{k=1}^{|MRLs|} \text{MRL}_i^{pred} == \text{MRL}_i^{gt} \tag{2}$$

The Answer Accuracy (AA) instead takes in consideration the retrieved answered from the Knowledge Base and compare it between the ground truth and the predicted one.

$$\text{AA} = \frac{1}{|MRLs|} \sum_{k=1}^{|MRLs|} \text{ans}_{pred} == \text{ans}_{gt} \tag{3}$$

These two metrics differs because sometimes an MRL that does not match with the ground truth can lead to the right answer. For both metrics, we consider only MRLs that are well-formed and executable, and thus will lead to an answer to be delivered to the customer, as our main concern is preventing the model's users to wrong answers; if an MRL is not executable, it will not lead to answer to be delivered to the user, which in our vision it's better than delivering a wrong (and potentially offensive) answer.

G Model Architecture design

In Figure 6, we report an high level overview of the Hallucination Detection Model architecture, the hyper-parameters used are specified in Section I.

H Hallucinations in NSP

In Figure 2, we show how the model hallucinate by omitting portion of the MRL when it encounters the needs of a unknown ontology symbols. However, often, as highlighted in the the discussion, the model replaces the unknown symbols with other known but leading to a complete wrong understanding, thus producing an MRL that is completely hallucinated, we show that behaviour in Figure 7. A similar behaviour is observable for NSP Errors. In NSP error the NSP model is under trained on some

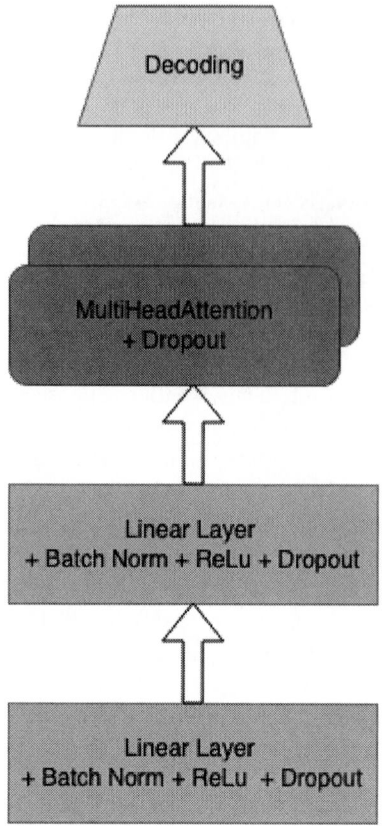

Figure 6: Hallucination detection model architecture

symbols and then it shows this hallucination behaviour. Instead, in out-of-domain we expect an empty MRL because the model does not have any symbols and syntax to support the out-of-domain user request.

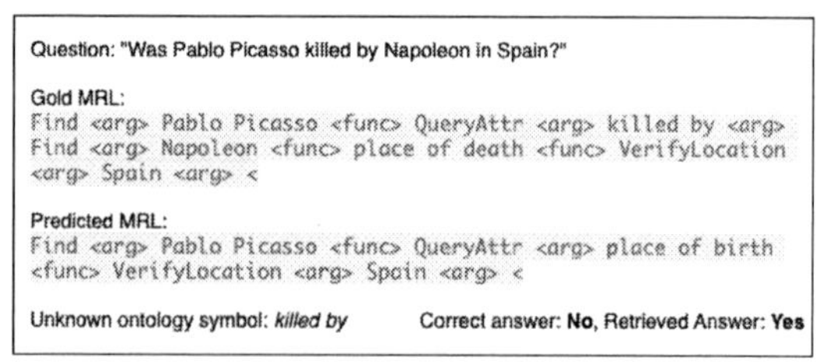

Figure 7: We show the output our NSP model trained without a symbol for the concept of "killed by". Given a question that requires this symbol, the model produces a wrong but executable MRL. In that case is it possible to notice that the model avoid to produce the unknown ontology symbol (killed by) and then starts to hallucinate the remaining MRL with wrong known symbols (i.e., place of birth) leading to a complete wrong understanding of the user question. Retrieving a wrong answer.

I Hallucination Detection Model configuration

We train the HDM using both executable and non-executable MRLs; its training objective is to maximize the number of correctly delivered MRLs and maximize the number of correctly rejected MRLs, regardless of the type of MRLs (e.g., NSP Errors, ontology gap). The HDM in our Hardware Infrastructure L takes less than a minute to complete each epoch. In Table 5 we report the Hyper-paramters of the best Hallucination Detection Model with Activations + CS. For sake of brevity, we report the other hyper-parameters configurations in the Github repository.

HParams	**Value**
Max Epochs	100
Optimizer	AdamW
Learning Rate	$1e^{-3}$
Weight Decay	$1e^{-3}$
Checkpointing	Max Dev Macro F1-Score
Early Stopping	Max Dev Macro F1-Score
Early Stopping Patient	50
Batch Size	32
Non linear activation function	RELU
Loss Function	Cross Entropy
1st layer dim	1024
2nd layer dim	128
classification head dim	2
Precision	fp16

Table 5: Hyper-paramters used to train the Hallucination Detection Model.

J HDD statistics on NSP Errors

In Table 6 we report the statistics of the NSP Errors in the Hallucination Detection Dataset.

Split	NSP Errors percentage
NSP Dataset - Train	11.01%
NSP Dataset - Dev	13.66%
NSP Dataset - Test	10.95%

Table 6: Percentage of NSP Errors over the executable NSP Dataset. Computed using the NSP model at inference time by comparing the predictions with the ground truth.

K HDD statistics on Executable MRLs

In Table 7 we report the percentage of executable MRLs in the Hallucination Detection Dataset w.r.t the KQA-PRO BART inference trained on the NSP in-ontology dataset.

Split	Executable
HDD Train	
in-ontology	92.69%
out-of-ontology	42.97%
HDD Dev	
in-ontology	92.49%
out-of-ontology	30.04%
HDD Test	
in-ontology	92.63%
out-of-ontology	46.27%

Table 7: Percentage of executable MRLs in HDD, after KQA-PRO BART inference. We use the term in-ontology and out-of-ontology sentences to refers to the sentences that uses only $\mathcal{O}_{\text{known\_symbols}}$ and $\mathcal{O}_{\text{unknown\_symbols}}$ respectively.

L Hardware Infrastructure

We performed all the experiments on a x86-64 architecture with 748GB of RAM, 4x 24-core CPU Intel Xeon Platinum 8175M, and a single NVIDIA V100 with 32GB of VRAM.

M KQA-PRO Bart hyper-parameters

To fine-tune the BART model on the KQA-PRO dataset, we stick with the same hyper-parameters used by the Cao et al. (2022). Below are the only changes in hyper-parameters we have made. We reduce the number of epochs from 25 to 3, which we found to be sufficient to achieve high performance while vastly reducing the training time. We also enable beam search with a beam size of 4, to compute the aforementioned Confidence Score feature.

N Precision and Recall

We report the Macro Precision and Macro Recall performance in Tables 8 9, 10 for out-of-ontology, NSP Errors, and OOD.

EXP NAME - OUT-OF-ONTOLOGY	Precision	Recall
No-Filter (Baseline)	0.480	0.5
Threshold CS 98.5% (Baseline)	0.479	0.482
Threshold MCD (Baseline)	0.477	0.430
Activations^{HDM}	0.557 ± 0.110	0.504 ± 0.007
CS^{HDM}	0.671 ± 0.056	0.663 ± 0.034
MCD^{HDM}	0.591 ± 0.208	0.500 ± 0.001
CS + MCD^{HDM}	0.654 ± 0.027	0.657 ± 0.019
Activations + CS^{HDM}	**0.682 ± 0.041**	**0.717 ± 0.019**
Activations + MCD^{HDM}	0.593 ± 0.159	0.502 ± 0.007
Activations + CS + MCD^{HDM}	0.642 ± 0.033	0.691 ± 0.018

Table 8: We report the Macro F1-Score (↑ is better) in out-of-ontology detection. We have repeated the train of the HDM using 10 random seeds, we report the mean of the scores along with their standard deviation. These features are combined (+) concatenating their vector representations.

EXP NAME - NSP ERRORS	Precision	Recall
No-Filter (Baseline)	0.444	0.500
Threshold CS 98.5% (Baseline)	0.706	0.627
Threshold MCD (Baseline)	0.442	0.436
Activations^{HDM}	0.547 ± 0.060	0.501 ± 0.002
CS^{HDM}	0.698 ± 0.009	0.571 ± 0.018
MCD^{HDM}	0.444 ± 0.002	0.500 ± 0.004
CS + MCD^{HDM}	0.695 ± 0.006	0.594 ± 0.016
Activations + CS^{HDM}	**0.712 ± 0.007**	0.619 ± 0.029
Activations + MCD^{HDM}	0.515 ± 0.044	0.501 ± 0.001
Activations + CS+ MCD^{HDM}	0.705 ± 0.008	**0.641 ± 0.034**

Table 9: We report the Macro Precision and Recall (↑ is better) in NSP Errors detection, NSP Error detection. We have repeated the train of the HDM using 10 random seeds, we report the mean of the scores along with their standard deviation. These features are combined (+) concatenating their vector representations.

EXP NAME - OUT-OF-DOMAIN	Precision	Recall
No-Filter (Baseline)	0.436	0.500
Threshold CS 98.5% (Baseline)	0.434	0.482
Threshold MCD (Baseline)	0.427	0.429
Activations^{HDM}	0.479 ± 0.116	0.499 ± 0.002
CS^{HDM}	0.614 ± 0.039	0.632 ± 0.052
MCD^{HDM}	0.644 ± 0.019	0.563 ± 0.151
CS + MCD^{HDM}	0.595 ± 0.061	0.534 ± 0.021
Activations + CS^{HDM}	**0.760 ± 0.108**	**0.662 ± 0.071**
Activations + MCD^{HDM}	0.447 ± 0.018	0.498 ± 0.002
Activations + CS+ MCD^{HDM}	0.671 ± 0.101	0.599 ± 0.063

Table 10: We report the Macro Precision and Recall (↑ is better) in zero-shot out-of-domain detection. We have repeated the train of the HDM using 10 random seeds, we report the mean of the scores along with their standard deviation. These features are combined (+) concatenating their vector representations.

PipeNet: Question Answering with Semantic Pruning over Knowledge Graphs

Ying Su, Jipeng Zhang, Yangqiu Song, Tong Zhang
Hong Kong University of Science and Technology
{ysuay, jzhanggr}@connect.ust.hk, yqsong@cse.ust.hk,
tongzhang@ust.hk

Abstract

It is well acknowledged that incorporating explicit knowledge graphs (KGs) can benefit question answering. Existing approaches typically follow a grounding-reasoning pipeline in which entity nodes are first grounded for the query (question and candidate answers), and then a reasoning module reasons over the matched multi-hop subgraph for answer prediction. Although the pipeline largely alleviates the issue of extracting essential information from giant KGs, efficiency is still an open challenge when scaling up hops in grounding the subgraphs. In this paper, we target at finding semantically related entity nodes in the subgraph to improve the efficiency of graph reasoning with KG. We propose a grounding-pruning-reasoning pipeline to prune noisy nodes, remarkably reducing the computation cost and memory usage while also obtaining decent subgraph representation. In detail, the pruning module first scores concept nodes based on the dependency distance between matched spans and then prunes the nodes according to score ranks. To facilitate the evaluation of pruned subgraphs, we also propose a graph attention network (GAT) based module to reason with the subgraph data. Experimental results on CommonsenseQA and OpenBookQA demonstrate the effectiveness of our method.

1 Introduction

Question answering requires related background knowledge. A line of research resorts to combining pre-trained language models (LMs) and knowledge graphs (KG) to utilize both the implicit knowledge in LMs and explicit knowledge in structured KGs (Schlichtkrull et al., 2018; Lin et al., 2019; Feng et al., 2020; Yasunaga et al., 2021).

The researches towards utilizing knowledge from KGs typically follow a grounding-and-reasoning pipeline, namely schema graph grounding and schema graph reasoning (Lin et al., 2019).

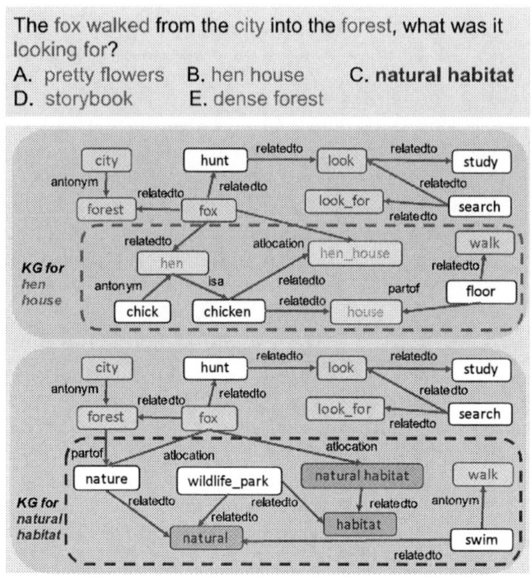

Figure 1: An example of a query and grounded knowledge graph for two candidate answers. The external KG nodes are more diverse around the answer concepts than question concepts.

In the grounding module, multi-hop neighbors of matched concept nodes in the query from KG form a subgraph. Recent works focus on improving reasoning ability by enhancing the representation of multi-hop nodes in grounded subgraphs with graph neural networks (GNNs) (Feng et al., 2020; Yasunaga et al., 2021) or interaction between representations of query context and subgraphs (Zhang et al., 2022b; Sun et al., 2022). While pre-trained LMs are powerful at extracting plain text features for the query context, the quality of subgraph feature extracted from GNNs is still prone to noisy nodes in grounded subgraphs. Specifically, there are two challenges in fusing KGs with GNNs. First, the computation and memory cost would increase with the hops increase. Second, the noisy nodes induced with increasing hops deteriorate the quality of the subgraph feature, and further decrease the performance of the reasoning module.

*Proceedings of the 13th Joint Conference on Lexical and Computational Semantics (*SEM 2024)*, pages 360 - 371
June 20-21, 2024 ©2024 Association for Computational Linguistics

In this paper, we tackle the problems brought by noisy nodes with a grounding-pruning-reasoning pipeline framework, PipeNet. Previous researches show that the improvement of graph-based reasoning systems is minor, though with the number of grounded hops increasing, many more new nodes are induced (Santoro et al., 2017; Wang et al., 2019a; Feng et al., 2020). As shown in Figure 1, many of them are the same for different candidate answers, especially near the question concepts. Diverse nodes are mainly brought in due to the difference in answer concepts. This diversity is critical to the subgraph representation learning with GNNs.

Our pruning module prunes noisy nodes before the reasoning module, reducing the computation cost and memory usage while keeping the diversity of subgraphs in the meantime. Specifically, we propose a dependency structure based pruning method to prune the nodes with dependency parsing (DP) tools. The DP-pruning strategy is inspired by relation extraction in automatic ontology building, in which the dependency tree is applied to find possible relations between concepts according to the distance on the tree (Fellbaum and Miller, 1998; Sombatsrisomboon et al., 2003; Ciaramita et al., 2005; Kang et al., 2015). Similarly, we assume the dependency tree provides reasonable linguistic links between grounded concepts in a natural language context. We further convert the dependency distances between grounded concepts into concept node scores and propagate the node scores onto the grounded multi-hop subgraph to prune external noisy nodes.

To facilitate the evaluation of pruned subgraph, we also propose a simplified version of GAT (Veličković et al., 2018) for graph representation learning. We redesign the message passing mechanism in (Yasunaga et al., 2021). Our contributions are as follows:

- We propose a grounding-pruning-reasoning pipeline PipeNet for question answering with KG, in which a DP-pruning module improves efficiency by pruning the noisy nodes.
- We propose a simplified GAT module for fusing KG with GNNs. The module simplifies the message flow while achieving comparable or higher performance in the meantime;

Experiments on two standard benchmarks, CommonsenseQA (Talmor et al., 2019) and OpenbookQA (Mihaylov et al., 2018), demonstrate the effectiveness of our proposed method. The code is open-sourced[1].

2 Related Work

2.1 QA with LM+KG

With the development of benchmarking question answering, more and more hard question answering datasets are developed, which require background knowledge to solve (Mihaylov et al., 2018; Talmor et al., 2019, 2021). Pretrained LMs and KGs are commonly used knowledge sources, research typically adopts an LM+KG framework as to acquire relevent knowledge for commonsense QA (Feng et al., 2020; Yasunaga et al., 2021; Zhang et al., 2022b; Su et al., 2022; Park et al., 2023; Huang et al., 2023; Ye et al., 2023; Wang et al., 2023; Taunk et al., 2023; Zhao et al., 2023; Dong et al., 2023; Mazumder and Liu; Kang et al., 2024; Zhao et al., 2024)

Schlichtkrull et al. (2018) first adopts RGCN to model relational data in KG, which specifically models the node representation as the aggregation from neighboring nodes. GconAttn (Wang et al., 2019a) adds inter-attention between the concepts in premise and hypothesis to find the best-aligned concepts between the respective graphs. KagNet (Lin et al., 2019) further proposes an LSTM-based path encoder to model knowledge paths in the schema graph on top of GCNs. RN (Santoro et al., 2017) uses MLPs to encode the one-hop paths and pooling over the path embedding to get the schema graph representation. MHGRN (Feng et al., 2020) stresses modeling multi-hop paths and utilized an attention mechanism to weigh the importance of multi-hop paths. QAGNN (Yasunaga et al., 2021) adopts GAT for type and relation-aware messages to update the node representations. GreaseLM (Zhang et al., 2022b) further improves the knowledge fusion quality between context and subgraph representation by adding an information fusion module.

Unlike these works, we focus on effectively finding informative subgraph nodes from the raw output of the grounding module. We adopt a pruning module to find such nodes, which benefits the subgraph representation learning from GNNs.

[1]https://github.com/HKUST-KnowComp/PipeNet

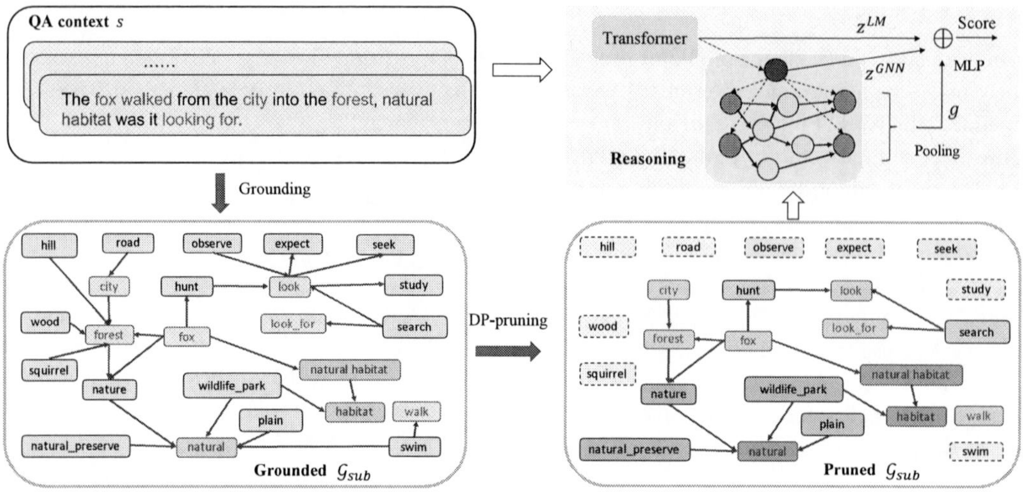

Figure 2: The overall framework of grounding-pruning-reasoning pipeline PipeNet. Concept nodes are first grounded in the KG to form a subgraph $\mathcal{G}_{sub}$ related to question and answer context s. A pruning module prunes noisy nodes according to node score before the reasoning module. The final answer score is calculated based on the context representation z^{LM} and subgraph representation z^{GNN}.

2.2 Efficient Computation for GNN

Though the application of GNN has become popular in many graph-based scenarios, it is still challenging to apply GNN to large-scale graphs with massive numbers of nodes and edges (Hamilton et al., 2017; Yu et al., 2022; Zhang et al., 2022a) due to expensive computation cost and high memory usage. Categories of research towards tackling this problem are mainly sampling-based (Chen et al., 2018; Zeng et al., 2019; Chiang et al., 2019; Zeng et al., 2021; Fey et al., 2021) and precomputing-based (Wu et al., 2019; Rossi et al., 2020; Liu and Ji, 2022).

Previous pruning method JointLK (Sun et al., 2022) dynamically prunes noisy nodes during training, which still takes the raw output of the grounding module as inputs and does not decrease memory or computation cost. GSC (Wang et al., 2022) reduces parameters in the GNN layer by separately viewing the reasoning process as counting, which reduces model size while ignoring the semantic interaction between context and subgraph. Unlike them, we focus on extracting informative subgraph nodes of much smaller size from the grounded subgraph in a precomputing stage.

3 Methodology

Our grounding-pruning-reasoning framework, PipeNet, consists of three stages: subgraph grounding, subgraph pruning, and reasoning. The overall framework is shown in Figure 2.

3.1 Problem Formulation

Given a context query q and a set of candidate answers $\{a_1, a_2, ..., a_k\}$, the task is to choose the most plausible answer from the set. Related background knowledge can be retrieved from a relevant KG $\mathcal{G} = (\mathcal{V}, \mathcal{E})$ given the query and answer set. $\mathcal{V}$ represents the set of entity nodes and $\mathcal{E}$ represents the set of relational edges in the KG.

Following the definition in Yasunaga et al. (2021), specifically for a question q and a candidate answer a, we define the grounded concept nodes from $\mathcal{G}$ as $\mathcal{V}_q$ and $\mathcal{V}_a$ respectively. The question and each answer are further composed as a QA context s. External concept nodes from $\mathcal{G}$ during the multi-hop expansion are defined as $\mathcal{V}_e$. The grounded nodes and edges between them form the grounded subgraph $\mathcal{G}_{sub}$.

As we aim to explore the impacts of the external nodes on the learning efficiency of GNNs with KG, we define the one-hop and two-hop settings as:

One-hop. The grounded subgraph consists of entity nodes from $\mathcal{V}_q$ and $\mathcal{V}_a$, and the linked edges between the nodes.

Two-hop. The grounded subgraph consists of entity nodes from $\mathcal{V}_q$, $\mathcal{V}_a$ and $\mathcal{V}_e$, and the linked edges between the nodes. $\mathcal{V}_e$ is the set of one-hop neighbors from $\mathcal{V}_q$ and $\mathcal{V}_a$.

3.2 DP-pruning

Our DP-pruning strategy on grounded subgraphs is based on dependency links between matched spans in the QA context s. Dependency analysis

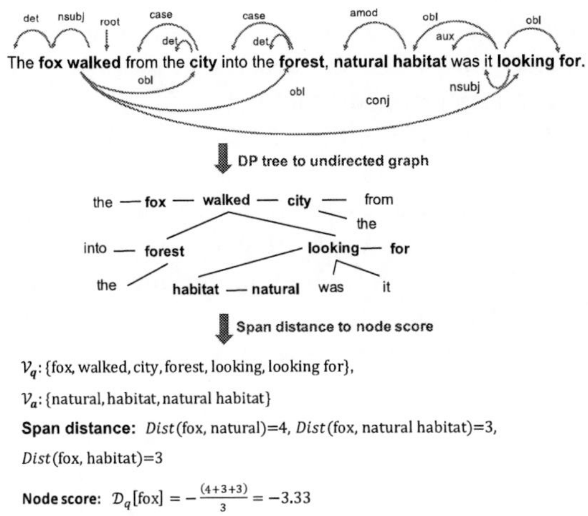

Figure 3: Dependency tree of a QA context example. Words in bold are matched spans of concepts in ConceptNet.

helps find relations between terms using dependency information present in parsing trees. Explicit syntax-aware knowledge has shown effective usages in downstream tasks, such as machine translation (Bastings et al., 2017; Marcheggiani et al., 2018), information extraction (Sahu et al., 2019), and semantic role labeling (Zhang et al., 2020).

DP tree and span distance. We adopt the widely used open-source tool stanza[2] for dependency analysis on the QA context. The dependency parsing (DP) tree $\mathcal{T}$ is then converted into an undirected graph $\mathbb{G}$. On the graph, we can calculate the shortest path lengths as the span distance between span words. An example is shown in Figure 3. We align the results of concept matching and dependency parsing on the word level. If the matched span covers more than one word, the distance is calculated as the minimum distance of covered words to other spans.

Span distance to node score. As we focus on refining the matched subgraph $\mathcal{G}_{sub}$, we calculate the node score of matched concepts in q and a based on the corresponding span distance. For each concept c_q in $\mathcal{V}_q$, the node score is:

$$\mathcal{D}_q[c_q] = -\frac{\sum_{i=1}^{|\mathcal{V}_a|} Dist(c_q, c_a)}{|\mathcal{V}_a|}, \quad (1)$$

where $Dist$ is the corresponding span distance of matched concepts. For each concept c_a in $\mathcal{V}_a$, the node score is calculated in the same way.

Propogate node score. Our algorithm aims to prune the external nodes $\mathcal{V}_e$ in the subgraph for two-hop or above because noisy nodes are mainly induced with the hops growing. The pseudo-code for pruning the external nodes is listed in Algorithm 1. In initialization, grounded concept sets $\mathcal{V}_t = \mathcal{V}_q \bigcup \mathcal{V}_a$, and score set for grounded concept sets $\mathcal{D}_t = \mathcal{D}_q \bigcup \mathcal{D}_a$. External nodes having neighbors in the grounded concept sets are added to expand the grounded subgraph $\mathcal{G}_{sub}$. The node score of external nodes is assigned as the average of their neighbor node scores during expansion. Until the expansion hops end, the nodes except $\mathcal{V}_q$ and $\mathcal{V}_a$ are pruned according to their score ranks. The nodes with smaller node scores are pruned.

Algorithm 1 Grounding and Pruning

Require: q, a
Require: Hop n
Require: KG $\mathcal{G}$
Require: Prune rate p
$\mathcal{V}_q, \mathcal{V}_a, s \leftarrow q, a, \mathcal{G}$
$\mathcal{T} \leftarrow s$
$\mathbb{G} \leftarrow \mathcal{T}$
$\mathcal{D}_q, \mathcal{D}_a \leftarrow \mathbb{G}$
$i \leftarrow 1, \mathcal{V}_t \leftarrow \mathcal{V}_q \bigcup \mathcal{V}_a, \mathcal{D}_t \leftarrow \mathcal{D}_q \bigcup \mathcal{D}_a$
while $i \leq n$ **do**
  $\mathcal{V}_e \leftarrow Neighbor(\mathcal{V}_t)$
  $\mathcal{D}_e \leftarrow Avg(\mathcal{D}_t)$
  $\mathcal{V}_t \leftarrow \mathcal{V}_t \bigcup \mathcal{V}_e$
  $\mathcal{D}_t \leftarrow \mathcal{D}_t \bigcup \mathcal{D}_e$
end while
$threshold \leftarrow \mathcal{D}_t, p$
for $v \in \mathcal{V}_t \setminus \{\mathcal{V}_q, \mathcal{V}_a\}$ **do**
  if $\mathcal{D}_t[v] \leq threshold$ **then**
    Delete v
  end if
end for
return $\mathcal{V}_t$

Our algorithm propagates the dependency structure information from QA context s onto the retrieved static subgraph $\mathcal{G}_{sub}$. We keep concept nodes with higher scores because they generally have closer distances to the concept nodes in $\mathcal{V}_a$, which increases the diversity of pruned subgraph. Finally, the $(|\mathcal{V}_t| - |\mathcal{V}_q| - |\mathcal{V}_a|) * p$ will be pruned with pruning rate p.

3.3 Reasoning

We design a reasoning module fusing the QA context feature and subgraph feature. The dimension of subgraph feature generated from L-layer GNN

[2]https://stanfordnlp.github.io/stanza/corenlp_client.html

Model	Time	Space
$\mathcal{G}$ is a dense graph		
L-h KagNet	$\mathcal{O}(\|\mathcal{R}\|^L\|\mathcal{V}\|^{L+1}L)$	$\mathcal{O}(\|\mathcal{R}\|^L\|\mathcal{V}\|^{L+1}L\cdot D)$
L-h MHGRN	$\mathcal{O}(\|\mathcal{R}\|^2\|\mathcal{V}\|^2L)$	$\mathcal{O}(\|\mathcal{R}\|\|\mathcal{V}\|L\cdot D)$
L-l QAGNN	$\mathcal{O}(\|\mathcal{V}\|^2L)$	$\mathcal{O}(\|\mathcal{R}\|\|\mathcal{V}\|L\cdot D)$
L-l GreaseLM	$\mathcal{O}(\|\mathcal{V}\|^2L)$	$\mathcal{O}(\|\mathcal{R}\|\|\mathcal{V}\|L\cdot D)$
L-l JointLK	$\mathcal{O}(\|\mathcal{V}\|^2L)$	$\mathcal{O}(\|\mathcal{R}\|\|\mathcal{V}\|L\cdot D)$
L-l GSC	$\mathcal{O}(\|\mathcal{V}\|L)$	$\mathcal{O}(\|\mathcal{R}\|\|\mathcal{V}\|L)$
L-l PipeNet	$\mathcal{O}((\frac{\|\mathcal{V}\|}{k})^2L)$	$\mathcal{O}(\|\mathcal{R}\|\frac{\|\mathcal{V}\|}{k}L\cdot D)$
$\mathcal{G}$ is a sparse graph with maximum node degree $\Delta \ll \|\mathcal{V}\|$		
L-h KagNet	$\mathcal{O}(\|\mathcal{R}\|^L\|\mathcal{V}\|L\Delta^L)$	$\mathcal{O}(\|\mathcal{R}\|^L\|\|\mathcal{V}\|L\Delta^L\cdot D)$
L-h MHGRN	$\mathcal{O}(\|\mathcal{R}\|^2\|\mathcal{V}\|L\Delta)$	$\mathcal{O}(\|\mathcal{R}\|\|\mathcal{V}\|L\cdot D)$
L-l QAGNN	$\mathcal{O}(\|\mathcal{V}\|L\Delta)$	$\mathcal{O}(\|\mathcal{R}\|\|\mathcal{V}\|L\cdot D)$
L-l GreaseLM	$\mathcal{O}(\|\mathcal{V}\|L\Delta)$	$\mathcal{O}(\|\mathcal{R}\|\|\mathcal{V}\|L\cdot D)$
L-l JointLK	$\mathcal{O}(\|\mathcal{V}\|L\Delta)$	$\mathcal{O}(\|\mathcal{R}\|\|\mathcal{V}\|L\cdot D)$
L-l GSC	$\mathcal{O}(\|\mathcal{V}\|L)$	$\mathcal{O}(\|\mathcal{R}\|\|\mathcal{V}\|L)$
L-l PipeNet	$\mathcal{O}(\frac{\|\mathcal{V}\|}{k}L\Delta)$	$\mathcal{O}(\|\mathcal{R}\|\frac{\|\mathcal{V}\|}{k}L\cdot D)$

Table 1: L-h means L-hop and L-l means L-layer. $\mathcal{G}$ is a graph with relation set $\mathcal{R}$. k is the reduction rate in the PipeNet pruning stage.

is D. Theoretically, the efficiency analysis in time and space for the GNN is shown in Table 1. Note the definition of reduction rate k in the table is slightly different from the pruning rate p:

$$\frac{1}{k} = 1 - \frac{(|\mathcal{V}_t| - |\mathcal{V}_q| - |\mathcal{V}_a|)}{|\mathcal{V}_t|} * p. \quad (2)$$

For the QA context feature, the input is QA context s. A pre-trained language model first encodes the context into the vector representation z as:

$$z^{LM} = f_{enc}(s), \quad (3)$$

where z is the hidden state of [CLS] token in the last hidden layer.

Following (Yasunaga et al., 2021), the QA context is induced as an additional node to the grounded subgraph $\mathcal{G}_{sub}$ and assigned to connect the nodes in $\mathcal{V}_q$ and $\mathcal{V}_a$. The representation of this additional context node in the subgraph is initialized as z^{LM}.

For the subgraph feature, the embeddings of entity nodes in the subgraph are initialized as D-dim vectors. Similar to (Yasunaga et al., 2021; Sun et al., 2022; Zhang et al., 2022b), a standard GNN structure is applied to learn entity node representations via iterative message passing between neighbors on the subgraph. Specifically, in the $(l+1)$-layer, the hidden state of the node on the subgraph is updated by:

$$\boldsymbol{h}_t^{(l+1)} = f_n(\sum_{s\in\mathcal{N}_t\bigcup\{t\}} \alpha_{st}\boldsymbol{m}_{st}), \quad (4)$$

where $\mathcal{N}_t$ represents the neighborhood of target node t and $\boldsymbol{m}_{st} \in \mathbb{R}^D$ denotes the message from each neighbor node s to t. $f_n : \mathbb{R}^D \rightarrow \mathbb{R}^D$ is a 2-layer multilayer perceptron (MLP) function.

Specifically, for the message on the edge, we encode the connected node types and the edge type into embedding forms. As shown in (Wang et al., 2022), these two types of information in the subgraph are important.

$$\boldsymbol{r}_{st} = f([e_{st}, u_s, u_t]), \quad (5)$$

where u_s, u_t are one-hot vectors of node type and e_{st} is one-hot vector of edge type. f is a 2-layer MLP converting the concatenated feature into a D dimension edge representation. The message on the relational edges propagated from source node s to target node t is:

$$\boldsymbol{m}_{st} = f_m(\boldsymbol{h}_s^l, \boldsymbol{r}_{st}), \quad (6)$$

where $f_m : \mathbb{R}^{2D} \rightarrow \mathbb{R}^D$ is a linear transformation.

We adopt an attention-based message passing module based on GAT (Veličković et al., 2018). Different from (Yasunaga et al., 2021), the attention is calculated based on the node types and relation type. First, the query and key vectors are computed as:

$$\boldsymbol{q}_s = f_q(\boldsymbol{h}_s^l), \quad (7)$$

$$\boldsymbol{k}_t = f_k(\boldsymbol{h}_t^l, \boldsymbol{r}_{st}), \quad (8)$$

where $f_q : \mathbb{R}^D \rightarrow \mathbb{R}^D$ and $f_k : \mathbb{R}^{2D} \rightarrow \mathbb{R}^D$ are linear transformations. Finally, the attention weight α_{st}:

$$\alpha_{st} = \frac{exp(\gamma_{st})}{\sum_{t\in N_s} exp(\gamma_{st})}, \gamma_{st} = \frac{\boldsymbol{q}_s^T\boldsymbol{k}_t}{\sqrt{D}}. \quad (9)$$

At the final layer of the GNN network, we get the representation of the additional context node and pooled representation of KG nodes in the subgraph as z^{GNN} and $\boldsymbol{g}$.

Answer Prediction. Given question q and a candidate answer a, the plausibility score $p(a|q)$:

$$p(a|q) \propto exp(MLP(z^{LM}, z^{GNN}, \boldsymbol{g})), \quad (10)$$

where an MLP layer encodes the context feature and graph feature into the final score. The answer among candidate answers with the highest plausibility score is the predicted answer.

4 Experiments

Our experiments are conducted on two standard question answering benchmarks, CommonsenseQA (CSQA) and OpenBookQA (OBQA). We also introduce details of baselines and implementations in this section.

4.1 Datasets

CommonsenseQA. CommonsenseQA (Talmor et al., 2019) is a 5-way multiple choice QA task that requires reasoning with commonsense knowledge, containing 12,102 questions which are created with entities from ConceptNet (Speer et al., 2017). Following (Lin et al., 2019), we conducts experiments on the in-house (IH) data split (8,500/1,221/1,241 for IHtrain/IHdev/IHtest respectively).

OpenBookQA. OpenBookQA (Mihaylov et al., 2018) is a 4-way multiple choice QA task, containing 5,957 questions (4,957/500/500 for train/dev/test respectively). It is an elementary science question together with an open book of science facts. Answering OpenBookQA requires commonsense knowledge beyond the provided facts.

4.2 Baselines

We use baselines for two experiments: baselines for the PipeNet framework with our designed reasoning module, and baselines for the DP-pruning.

4.2.1 Framework

We compare with other grounding-reasoning-based frameworks: (1) Relation Network (RN) (Santoro et al., 2017), (2) RGCN (Schlichtkrull et al., 2018), (3) GconAttn (Wang et al., 2019b), (4) KagNet (Lin et al., 2019), (5) MHGRN (Feng et al., 2020), (6) QA-GNN (Yasunaga et al., 2021), (7) GreaseLM (Zhang et al., 2022b).

4.2.2 Pruning

JointLK (Sun et al., 2022). JointLK automatically selects relevant nodes from noisy KGs by designing a dense bidirectional attention module to attend to the question tokens and KG nodes. A dynamic pruning module recursively prunes irrelevant KG nodes based on the attention weights.

GSC (Wang et al., 2022). GSC designs a simple graph neural model which regards the reasoning over knowledge graph as a counting process. It reduces the hidden dimension of GNN layers and results in a reasoning module with a much smaller size.

Methods	IHdev-Acc.(%)	IHtest-Acc.(%)
RoBERTa-Large	73.07 (±0.45)	68.69 (±0.56)
Framework		
RGCN	72.69 (±0.19)	68.41 (±0.66)
GconAttn	72.61 (±0.39)	68.59 (±0.96)
KagNet	73.47 (±0.22)	69.01 (±0.76)
RN	74.57 (±0.91)	69.08 (±0.21)
MHGRN	74.45 (±0.10)	71.11 (±0.81)
QA-GNN	76.54 (±0.21)	73.41 (±0.92)
GreaseLM	78.5 (±0.5)	74.2 (±0.4)
PipeNet	**78.95** (±0.55)	**74.49** (±0.26)
Pruning		
JointLK	77.88 (±0.25)	74.43 (±0.83)
GSC	**79.11** (±0.22)	74.48 (±0.41)
PipeNet(DP)	78.13 (±0.13)	**74.75** (±0.47)

Table 2: Results on the CSQA in-house split dataset. The mean and standard deviation value of three runs on the in-house Dev (IHdev) and Test (IHtest) datasets are reported. Pruning rate p is 90% in PipeNet(DP).

For the experiments on the framework, we use the grounded two-hop knowledge subgraph. For the experiments on pruning, we conduct experiments on PipeNet with a DP-pruning strategy over two-hop subgraphs.

4.3 Implementation Details

For all the experiments on PipeNet, we set the dimension ($D = 200$) and the number of layers ($L = 5$) in the reasoning module. The parameters of the reasoning module (LM+GNN) are optimized by RAdam (Liu et al., 2019a) by cross-entropy loss. The learning rate for the LM encoder is set as 1e-5. For the decoder with GNN, the learning rate is 1e-3. For both benchmarks, we use ConceptNet (Speer et al., 2017) as the knowledge graph. For the pruning experiments on PipeNet, the DP-pruning strategy prunes the nodes by the ranks of node scores. Specifically, the $threshold$ value is determined by the score of top $(1-p)$ percent ranked node is $\mathcal{V}_t \setminus \{\mathcal{V}_q, \mathcal{V}_a\}$. In each experiment, we use two RTX 3090 GPUs, and the average running time is about 4 hours on CSQA and 24 hours on OBQA.

5 Results

In this section, we first present of main results of PipeNet as well as PipeNet with DP pruning strategy on standard benchmarks. Then we analyze the time and memory efficiency improvement brought by DP-pruning strategy. Finally, we conduct an ablation study over pruning strategy.

Methods	RoBERTa-large	AristoRoBERTa
w/o KG	64.80 (±2.37)	78.40 (±1.64)
	Framework	
+RGCN	62.45 (±1.57)	74.60 (±2.53)
+GconAtten	64.75 (±1.48)	71.80 (±1.21)
+RN	65.20 (±1.18)	75.35 (±1.39)
+MHGRN	66.85 (±1.19)	80.6
+QAGNN	67.80 (±2.75)	82.77 (±1.56)
+GreaseLM	-	84.8
+PipeNet	**69.33** (±1.60)	**87.33** (±0.19)
	Pruning	
+JointLK	**70.34** (±0.75)	84.92 (±1.07)
+GSC	70.33 (±0.81)	86.67 (±0.46)
+PipeNet(DP)	69.60 (±0.47)	**87.80** (±0.43)

Table 3: Test accuracy comparison on OBQA. Methods with AristoRoBERTa (Clark et al., 2020) use the textual evidence as an additional input to the QA context. Pruning rate p is 90% in PipeNet(DP).

Methods	Test
RoBERTa (Liu et al., 2019b)	72.1
AristoRoBERTa (Clark et al., 2020)	77.8
AristoRoBERTa + MHGRN (Feng et al., 2020)	80.6
ALBERT (Lan et al., 2020) + KB	81.0
AristoRoBERTa + QA-GNN (Yasunaga et al., 2021)	82.8
T5 (Raffel et al., 2020)	83.2
AristoRoBERTa + GreaseLM (Zhang et al., 2022b)	84.8
AristoRoBERTa + JointLK (Sun et al., 2022)	85.6
UnifiedQA (Khashabi et al., 2020)	87.2
AristoRoBERTa + GSC (Wang et al., 2022)	87.4
GenMC (Huang et al., 2022)	89.8
AristoRoBERTa + PipeNet(DP)	**88.2**

Table 4: Test accuracy comparison on OBQA leaderboard. The parameter size is about 3B for T5, and 11B for UnifiedQA and GenMC. The parameter size of PipeNet is about 358M.

5.1 Accuracy of PipeNet and DP-pruning

The results on CSQA and OBQA are shown in Table 2 and 3 separately. From the results on both benchmarks, we can find PipeNet is an effective framework for combining the context feature learning and subgraph feature learning. Besides node type and edge type features, QAGNN (Yasunaga et al., 2021) also employs node embedding and relevance-score as external features. GreaseLM (Zhang et al., 2022b) stresses the modality interaction between context feature and subgraph feature. Unlike them, we adopt a simplified message flow for subgraph feature and merge the two kinds of features with an MLP layer. The final performance is comparable with previous methods on CSQA and better on OBQA. This is because that node embedding and relevance score gradually loses benefits to the reasoning module with training continuing as analyzed in GSC (Wang et al., 2022). Decreasing redundant subgraph features and modality interaction at the same time makes the reasoning module focus more on the subgraph learning, which further benefits the reasoning performance.

DP-pruning strategy can further improve the subgraph representation learning based on the PipeNet framework. Since the best answer is chosen from multiple candidate choices, DP-pruning strategy can help maintain the uniqueness of grounded subgraphs by pruning nodes which are far from the concept nodes in candidate answers. Comparing results of PipeNet and PipeNet with DP-pruning, DP-pruning can help PipeNet achieve better performances on both benchmarks under most circumstances, with a high pruning rate as 90%.

DP-pruning strategy also has strengths over other pruning methods like JointLK and GSC. Compared to JointLK, PipeNet significantly reduces memory and computation costs during training as shown in Table 1. Moreover, on the OBQA benchmark where additional factual texts are induced to the QA context (with AristoRoBERTa (Clark et al., 2020)[3]), our PipeNet outperforms GSC by 1.13% on the accuracy score. AristoRoBERTa applies several methods to encode science-related knowledge into RoBERTa. PipeNet captures the semantic feature interaction between context and subgraph with an MLP layer while GSC separately models the subgraph representation as a counting process.

Furthermore, we also compare the performance of PipeNet with other methods on the OBQA test leaderboard, and the result is listed in Table 4. Compared to the pre-trained LM T5 (Raffel et al., 2020), PipeNet achieves 5% higher accuracy with much fewer parameters. It indicates that the knowledge in external KG is complementary to the implicit knowledge in LMs. Compared to UnifiedQA (Khashabi et al., 2020) which injects the commonsense knowledge from multiple QA sources into pre-trained LMs, PipeNet achieves 1% performance gain. It shows that knowledge graph is still an important and useful knowledge source for QA. The recent method GenMC outperforms PipeNet by inducing clues for generation based on T5-large. It may be worth exploring how to employ the clues to guide the subgraph selection for better representation.

[3]https://huggingface.co/LIAMF-USP/aristo-roberta

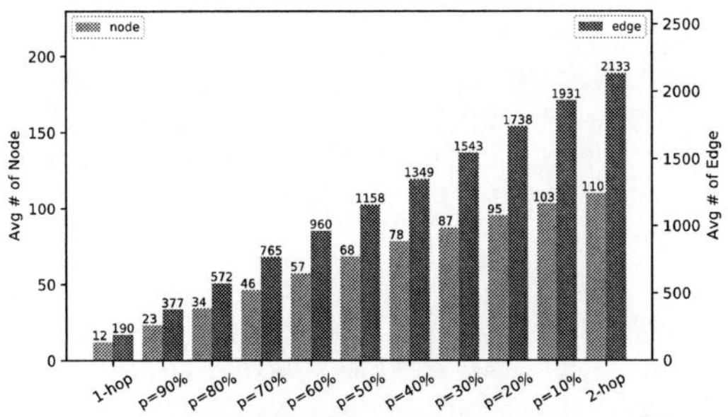

Figure 4: Distribution of grounded nodes and edges with pruning rate on external nodes from one-hop to two-hop on CSQA training dataset.

p(%)	k	M(G)	↑(%)	t(s)	↑(%)	IHtest (%)
0	1.0	5.02	-	1.16	-	74.38
10	1.1	4.95	1	1.02	13	74.21
20	1.2	4.92	2	1.01	13	74.29
30	1.3	4.75	5	0.96	17	74.29
40	1.4	4.67	7	0.87	25	74.21
50	1.6	4.57	9	0.83	28	74.13
60	2.0	4.49	11	0.78	33	74.70
70	2.4	4.22	16	0.75	35	74.85
80	3.2	3.83	24	0.72	38	74.70
90	4.8	3.51	**30**	0.67	**42**	74.86

Table 5: Results on CSQA in-house split with PipeNet. GPU memory usage and time efficiency improvement are shown for pruning rate p on two-hop subgraph for GNN during training. The training batch size is 64.

5.2 Efficiency of PipeNet and DP-pruning

In this section, we conduct empirical studies to analyze the time and memory cost of our method. Besides, a corresponding theoretical analysis of the efficiency is presented in Section 3.3. Specifically, we implemented GAT using the tool *Pytorch Geometric* (Fey and Lenssen, 2019). Figure 4 illustrates that the average number of edges is linearly decreased with the number of nodes pruned.

Our method has demonstrated better time and memory efficiency. The result of running cost and performance on CSQA is presented in Table 5. The reduction rate k is calculated based on the number of nodes and edges in Figure 4. M is the GPU memory usage (max allocation memory) of GAT module and t is average batch time of the module during training. With pruning rate p growing, k is growing non-linearly, as well as memory usage M and time t efficiency. The memory and time efficiency exhibit different growing trends. Memory efficiency becomes evident when p is greater than 60 and time efficiency becomes evident when p is greater than 40%. Performance improvement becomes evident

h-hop	Prune method	Prune rate	IHtest-Acc(%)
One	-	0	73.27 (±0.93)
Two	-	0	74.49 (±0.26)
Two	Random	**90%**	73.51 (±0.61)
Two	DP	**90%**	**74.75** (±0.47)

Table 6: Results on CSQA in-house split with PipeNet.

when p is greater than 60%. Specifically, when p=90%, the memory and time efficiency achieve 30% and 42% improvement separately.

We also present the performance of CSQA test split with the pruning rate changes. It turns out that the pruning strategy leads to small variance in the performance change. Generally, larger p leads to better performances. The performance improvement keeps steady when p is greater than 60%. p=90% achieves the best efficiency by only increasing the number of nodes from 12 to 23 and the number of edges from 190 to 377 for each QA context, and also better than original two-hop subgraph. Overall, the performance demonstrates that the DP-pruning strategy can find informative nodes benefiting the subgraph representation learning with a great reduction in the memory and computation cost.

5.3 Ablation Study

We conduct experiments on pruning strategy over CSQA as the ablation study. For a fair comparison, we design a random pruning strategy with the same pruning rate of 90% to DP-pruning. The pruning is also applied to the additional KG nodes $\mathcal{V}_e$ except for one-hop KG nodes.

The result is shown in Table 6. PipeNet with one-hop is the result of the grounded subgraph constructed by the matched concepts in question and answers. As shown in Figure 4, pruning rate 90% brings in almost same quantity of edges and nodes to one-hop subgraphs, while much less than original two-hop subgraph.

Random sampling can also bring performance gain because the induced nodes are relevant to the QA context. However, the gain is not as much as the DP-pruning method. This shows that finding semantically related nodes can benefit more in subgraph representation learning.

6 Conclusion

In this work, we propose PipeNet, a grounding-pruning-reasoning pipeline for question answering with knowledge graph. The pruning strategy utilizes the dependency structure of query context to prune noisy entity nodes in the grounded subgraph, benefiting the subgraph representation learning with GNNs. We further design a GAT-based module for the subgraph representation learning with simplified message flow. Experiment results on two standard benchmarks demonstrate the effectiveness of semantic dependency of concept items benefits the subgraph representation learning.

7 Acknowledgement

The authors of this paper were supported by the NSFC Fund (U20B2053) from the NSFC of China, the RIF (R6020-19 and R6021-20) and the GRF (16211520 and 16205322) from RGC of Hong Kong. We also thank the UGC Research Matching Grants (RMGS20EG01-D, RMGS20CR11, RMGS20CR12, RMGS20EG19, RMGS20EG21, RMGS23CR05, RMGS23EG08). We would like to thank the Turing AI Computing Cloud (TACC) (Xu et al., 2021) and HKUST iSING Lab for providing us computation resources on their platform.

References

Jasmijn Bastings, Ivan Titov, Wilker Aziz, Diego Marcheggiani, and Khalil Sima'an. 2017. Graph convolutional encoders for syntax-aware neural machine translation. In *Proceedings of the 2017 Conference on Empirical Methods in Natural Language Processing, EMNLP 2017, Copenhagen, Denmark, September 9-11, 2017*, pages 1957–1967. Association for Computational Linguistics.

Tom Brown, Benjamin Mann, Nick Ryder, Melanie Subbiah, Jared D Kaplan, Prafulla Dhariwal, Arvind Neelakantan, Pranav Shyam, Girish Sastry, Amanda Askell, et al. 2020. Language models are few-shot learners. *Advances in neural information processing systems*, 33:1877–1901.

Jie Chen, Tengfei Ma, and Cao Xiao. 2018. Fastgcn: Fast learning with graph convolutional networks via importance sampling. In *International Conference on Learning Representations*.

Wei-Lin Chiang, Xuanqing Liu, Si Si, Yang Li, Samy Bengio, and Cho-Jui Hsieh. 2019. Cluster-gcn: An efficient algorithm for training deep and large graph convolutional networks. In *Proceedings of the 25th ACM SIGKDD international conference on knowledge discovery & data mining*, pages 257–266.

M. Ciaramita, A. Gangemi, E. Ratsch, J. Saric, and I. Rojas. 2005. Unsupervised learning of semantic relations between concepts of a molecular biology ontology. In *International Joint Conference on Artificial Intelligence*.

Peter Clark, Oren Etzioni, Tushar Khot, Daniel Khashabi, Bhavana Mishra, Kyle Richardson, Ashish Sabharwal, Carissa Schoenick, Oyvind Tafjord, Niket Tandon, et al. 2020. From 'f'to 'a'on the ny regents science exams: An overview of the aristo project. *AI Magazine*, 41(4):39–53.

Junnan Dong, Qinggang Zhang, Xiao Huang, Keyu Duan, Qiaoyu Tan, and Zhimeng Jiang. 2023. Hierarchy-aware multi-hop question answering over knowledge graphs. In *Proceedings of the ACM Web Conference 2023*, pages 2519–2527.

Qingxiu Dong, Lei Li, Damai Dai, Ce Zheng, Zhiyong Wu, Baobao Chang, Xu Sun, Jingjing Xu, and Zhifang Sui. 2022. A survey for in-context learning. *arXiv preprint arXiv:2301.00234*.

C. Fellbaum and G. Miller. 1998. Automated discovery of wordnet relations. *Wordnet An Electronic Lexical Database*, 5:131–151.

Yanlin Feng, Xinyue Chen, Bill Yuchen Lin, Peifeng Wang, Jun Yan, and Xiang Ren. 2020. Scalable multihop relational reasoning for knowledge-aware question answering. In *Proceedings of the 2020 Conference on Empirical Methods in Natural Language Processing (EMNLP)*, pages 1295–1309.

Matthias Fey, Jan E Lenssen, Frank Weichert, and Jure Leskovec. 2021. Gnnautoscale: Scalable and expressive graph neural networks via historical embeddings. In *International Conference on Machine Learning*, pages 3294–3304. PMLR.

Matthias Fey and Jan Eric Lenssen. 2019. Fast graph representation learning with pytorch geometric. *arXiv preprint arXiv:1903.02428*.

Will Hamilton, Zhitao Ying, and Jure Leskovec. 2017. Inductive representation learning on large graphs. *Advances in neural information processing systems*, 30.

Yongfeng Huang, Yanyang Li, Yichong Xu, Lin Zhang, Ruyi Gan, Jiaxing Zhang, and Liwei Wang. 2023. Mvp-tuning: Multi-view knowledge retrieval with prompt tuning for commonsense reasoning. In *Proceedings of the 61st Annual Meeting of the Association for Computational Linguistics (Volume 1: Long Papers)*, pages 13417–13432.

Zixian Huang, Ao Wu, Jiaying Zhou, Yu Gu, Yue Zhao, and Gong Cheng. 2022. Clues before answers: Generation-enhanced multiple-choice qa. In *Proceedings of the 2022 Conference of the North American Chapter of the Association for Computational Linguistics: Human Language Technologies*.

Long Kang, Xiaoge Li, and Xiaochun An. 2024. Knowledge-aware adaptive graph network for commonsense question answering. *Journal of Intelligent Information Systems*, pages 1–20.

S. K. Kang, L. Patil, A. Rangarajan, A. Moitra, and D. Dutta. 2015. Extraction of manufacturing rules from unstructured text using a semantic framework.

In *ASME 2015 International Design Engineering Technical Conferences and Computers and Information in Engineering Conference*.

Daniel Khashabi, Sewon Min, Tushar Khot, Ashish Sabharwal, Oyvind Tafjord, Peter Clark, and Hannaneh Hajishirzi. 2020. Unifiedqa: Crossing format boundaries with a single qa system. In *Findings of the Association for Computational Linguistics: EMNLP 2020*, pages 1896–1907.

Zhenzhong Lan, Mingda Chen, Sebastian Goodman, Kevin Gimpel, Piyush Sharma, and Radu Soricut. 2020. Albert: A lite bert for self-supervised learning of language representations. In *International Conference on Learning Representations*.

Bill Yuchen Lin, Xinyue Chen, Jamin Chen, and Xiang Ren. 2019. Kagnet: Knowledge-aware graph networks for commonsense reasoning. In *Proceedings of the 2019 Conference on Empirical Methods in Natural Language Processing and the 9th International Joint Conference on Natural Language Processing (EMNLP-IJCNLP)*, pages 2829–2839.

Liyuan Liu, Haoming Jiang, Pengcheng He, Weizhu Chen, Xiaodong Liu, Jianfeng Gao, and Jiawei Han. 2019a. On the variance of the adaptive learning rate and beyond. In *International Conference on Learning Representations*.

Meng Liu and Shuiwang Ji. 2022. Neighbor2seq: Deep learning on massive graphs by transforming neighbors to sequences. In *Proceedings of the 2022 SIAM International Conference on Data Mining (SDM)*, pages 55–63. SIAM.

Yinhan Liu, Myle Ott, Naman Goyal, Jingfei Du, Mandar Joshi, Danqi Chen, Omer Levy, Mike Lewis, Luke Zettlemoyer, and Veselin Stoyanov. 2019b. Roberta: A robustly optimized bert pretraining approach. *arXiv preprint arXiv:1907.11692*.

Diego Marcheggiani, Jasmijn Bastings, and Ivan Titov. 2018. Exploiting semantics in neural machine translation with graph convolutional networks. In *Proceedings of the 2018 Conference of the North American Chapter of the Association for Computational Linguistics: Human Language Technologies, NAACL-HLT, New Orleans, Louisiana, USA, June 1-6, 2018, Volume 2 (Short Papers)*, pages 486–492. Association for Computational Linguistics.

Sahisnu Mazumder and Bing Liu. Context-aware path ranking for knowledge base completion.

Todor Mihaylov, Peter Clark, Tushar Khot, and Ashish Sabharwal. 2018. Can a suit of armor conduct electricity? a new dataset for open book question answering. In *Proceedings of the 2018 Conference on Empirical Methods in Natural Language Processing*, pages 2381–2391.

Jinyoung Park, Hyeong Kyu Choi, Juyeon Ko, Hyeonjin Park, Ji-Hoon Kim, Jisu Jeong, Kyungmin Kim, and Hyunwoo Kim. 2023. Relation-aware language-graph transformer for question answering. In *Proceedings of the AAAI Conference on Artificial Intelligence*, volume 37, pages 13457–13464.

Colin Raffel, Noam Shazeer, Adam Roberts, Katherine Lee, Sharan Narang, Michael Matena, Yanqi Zhou, Wei Li, Peter J Liu, et al. 2020. Exploring the limits of transfer learning with a unified text-to-text transformer. *J. Mach. Learn. Res.*, 21(140):1–67.

Emanuele Rossi, Fabrizio Frasca, Ben Chamberlain, Davide Eynard, Michael Bronstein, and Federico Monti. 2020. Sign: Scalable inception graph neural networks. *arXiv preprint arXiv:2004.11198*, 7:15.

Sunil Kumar Sahu, Fenia Christopoulou, Makoto Miwa, and Sophia Ananiadou. 2019. Inter-sentence relation extraction with document-level graph convolutional neural network. In *Proceedings of the 57th Conference of the Association for Computational Linguistics, ACL 2019, Florence, Italy, July 28- August 2, 2019, Volume 1: Long Papers*, pages 4309–4316. Association for Computational Linguistics.

Adam Santoro, David Raposo, David G Barrett, Mateusz Malinowski, Razvan Pascanu, Peter Battaglia, and Timothy Lillicrap. 2017. A simple neural network module for relational reasoning. *Advances in neural information processing systems*, 30.

Michael Schlichtkrull, Thomas N Kipf, Peter Bloem, Rianne van den Berg, Ivan Titov, and Max Welling. 2018. Modeling relational data with graph convolutional networks. In *European semantic web conference*, pages 593–607. Springer.

R. Sombatsrisomboon, Y. Matsuo, and M. Ishizuka. 2003. Acquisition of hypernyms and hyponyms from the www.

Robyn Speer, Joshua Chin, and Catherine Havasi. 2017. Conceptnet 5.5: An open multilingual graph of general knowledge. In *Thirty-first AAAI conference on artificial intelligence*.

Ying Su, Zihao Wang, Tianqing Fang, Hongming Zhang, Yangqiu Song, and Tong Zhang. 2022. Mico: A multi-alternative contrastive learning framework for commonsense knowledge representation. In *Findings of the Association for Computational Linguistics: EMNLP 2022*, pages 1339–1351.

Yueqing Sun, Qi Shi, Le Qi, and Yu Zhang. 2022. JointLK: Joint reasoning with language models and knowledge graphs for commonsense question answering. In *Proceedings of the 2022 Conference of the North American Chapter of the Association for Computational Linguistics: Human Language Technologies*, pages 5049–5060. Association for Computational Linguistics.

Alon Talmor, Jonathan Herzig, Nicholas Lourie, and Jonathan Berant. 2019. Commonsenseqa: A question answering challenge targeting commonsense knowledge. In *Proceedings of the 2019 Conference of the North American Chapter of the Association for Computational Linguistics: Human Language Technologies, Volume 1 (Long and Short Papers)*, pages 4149–4158.

Alon Talmor, Ori Yoran, Ronan Le Bras, Chandra Bhagavatula, Yoav Goldberg, Yejin Choi, and Jonathan Berant. 2021. Commonsenseqa 2.0: Exposing the limits of ai through gamification. In *Thirty-fifth Conference on Neural Information Processing Systems Datasets and Benchmarks Track (Round 1)*.

Dhaval Taunk, Lakshya Khanna, Siri Venkata Pavan Kumar Kandru, Vasudeva Varma, Charu Sharma, and Makarand Tapaswi. 2023. Grapeqa: graph augmentation and pruning to enhance question-answering. In *Companion Proceedings of the ACM Web Conference 2023*, pages 1138–1144.

Petar Veličković, Guillem Cucurull, Arantxa Casanova, Adriana Romero, Pietro Liò, and Yoshua Bengio. 2018. Graph attention networks. In *International Conference on Learning Representations*.

Kuan Wang, Yuyu Zhang, Diyi Yang, Le Song, and Tao Qin. 2022. Gnn is a counter? revisiting gnn for question answering. In *International Conference on Learning Representations*.

X. Wang, P. Kapanipathi, R. Musa, M. Yu, K. Talamadupula, I. Abdelaziz, M. Chang, A. Fokoue, B. Makni, and N. Mattei. 2019a. Improving natural language inference using external knowledge in the science questions domain. In *National Conference on Artificial Intelligence*.

Xiaoyan Wang, Pavan Kapanipathi, Ryan Musa, Mo Yu, Kartik Talamadupula, Ibrahim Abdelaziz, Maria Chang, Achille Fokoue, Bassem Makni, Nicholas Mattei, et al. 2019b. Improving natural language inference using external knowledge in the science questions domain. In *Proceedings of the AAAI Conference on Artificial Intelligence*, volume 33, pages 7208–7215.

Yujie Wang, Hu Zhang, Jiye Liang, and Ru Li. 2023. Dynamic heterogeneous-graph reasoning with language models and knowledge representation learning for commonsense question answering. In *Proceedings of the 61st Annual Meeting of the Association for Computational Linguistics (Volume 1: Long Papers)*, pages 14048–14063.

Felix Wu, Amauri Souza, Tianyi Zhang, Christopher Fifty, Tao Yu, and Kilian Weinberger. 2019. Simplifying graph convolutional networks. In *International conference on machine learning*, pages 6861–6871. PMLR.

Kaiqiang Xu, Xinchen Wan, Hao Wang, Zhenghang Ren, Xudong Liao, Decang Sun, Chaoliang Zeng, and Kai Chen. 2021. Tacc: A full-stack cloud computing infrastructure for machine learning tasks. *arXiv preprint arXiv:2110.01556*.

Michihiro Yasunaga, Hongyu Ren, Antoine Bosselut, Percy Liang, and Jure Leskovec. 2021. Qa-gnn: Reasoning with language models and knowledge graphs for question answering. In *Proceedings of the 2021 Conference of the North American Chapter of the Association for Computational Linguistics: Human Language Technologies*, pages 535–546.

Qichen Ye, Bowen Cao, Nuo Chen, Weiyuan Xu, and Yuexian Zou. 2023. Fits: Fine-grained two-stage training for knowledge-aware question answering. In *Proceedings of the AAAI Conference on Artificial Intelligence*, volume 37, pages 13914–13922.

Haiyang Yu, Limei Wang, Bokun Wang, Meng Liu, Tianbao Yang, and Shuiwang Ji. 2022. Graphfm: Improving large-scale gnn training via feature momentum. In *International Conference on Machine Learning*, pages 25684–25701. PMLR.

Hanqing Zeng, Muhan Zhang, Yinglong Xia, Ajitesh Srivastava, Andrey Malevich, Rajgopal Kannan, Viktor Prasanna, Long Jin, and Ren Chen. 2021. Decoupling the depth and scope of graph neural networks. *Advances in Neural Information Processing Systems*, 34:19665–19679.

Hanqing Zeng, Hongkuan Zhou, Ajitesh Srivastava, Rajgopal Kannan, and Viktor Prasanna. 2019. Graphsaint: Graph sampling based inductive learning method. In *International Conference on Learning Representations*.

Bo Zhang, Yue Zhang, Rui Wang, Zhenghua Li, and Min Zhang. 2020. Syntax-aware opinion role labeling with dependency graph convolutional networks. In *Proceedings of the 58th Annual Meeting of the Association for Computational Linguistics, ACL 2020, Online, July 5-10, 2020*, pages 3249–3258. Association for Computational Linguistics.

Wentao Zhang, Zeang Sheng, Mingyu Yang, Yang Li, Yu Shen, Zhi Yang, and Bin Cui. 2022a. Nafs: A simple yet tough-to-beat baseline for graph representation learning. In *International Conference on Machine Learning*, pages 26467–26483. PMLR.

X Zhang, A Bosselut, M Yasunaga, H Ren, P Liang, C Manning, and J Leskovec. 2022b. Greaselm: Graph reasoning enhanced language models for question answering. In *International Conference on Representation Learning (ICLR)*.

Ruilin Zhao, Feng Zhao, Liang Hu, and Guandong Xu. 2024. Graph reasoning transformers for knowledge-aware question answering. In *Proceedings of the AAAI Conference on Artificial Intelligence*, volume 38, pages 19652–19660.

Ziwang Zhao, Linmei Hu, Hanyu Zhao, Yingxia Shao, and Yequan Wang. 2023. Knowledgeable parameter efficient tuning network for commonsense question answering. In *Proceedings of the 61st Annual Meeting of the Association for Computational Linguistics (Volume 1: Long Papers)*, pages 9051–9063.

Method	CSQA(IHdev)	OBQA(test)
w/o KG	73.07	78.40
GPT3.5-turbo	72.29	83.20
PipeNet(DP)	78.13	87.80

Table 7: Accuracy comparison between GPT3.5-turbo and PipeNet(DP) on CSQA(IHdev) and OBQA(test)

A Appendix

A.1 Comparison with LLM

Large language models such as GPT3 (Brown et al., 2020) and ChatGPT have recently received interest and achieved remarkable success over various question-answering tasks. We further adopt a 3-shot in-context learning (Dong et al., 2022) to prompt GPT3.5-turbo and present the results in Table 7. For OBQA, we add additional textual evidence in the prompt template for a fair comparison. It shows that GPT3.5-turbo achieves decent performances on both of the benchmarks, with comparable or better performances to the supervised fintuning method without KG (w/o KG). Nervertheless, PipeNet(DP) outperforms GPT3.5-turbo by a large margin though though with a much smaller language model Roberta-large. This demonstrates that knowledge graph is still a meaningful knowledge source for question-answering tasks and our pruning method benefits such QA tasks with knowledge graph.

A Trip Towards Fairness: Bias and De-Biasing in Large Language Models

Leonardo Ranaldi[*1,2], **Elena Sofia Ruzzetti**[*1]
Davide Venditti[1], **Dario Onorati**[3], **Fabio Massimo Zanzotto**[1]
[1]University of Rome Tor Vergata, Italy [2]Idiap Research Institute, Switzerland
[3]Sapienza University of Rome, Italy
first_name.last_name@uniroma2.it

Abstract

Cheap-to-Build Very Large-Language Models (CtB-LLMs) with affordable training are emerging as the next big revolution in natural language processing and understanding. These CtB-LLMs are democratizing access to trainable Very Large-Language Models (VLLMs) and, thus, may represent the building blocks of many NLP systems solving downstream tasks. Hence, a little or a large bias in CtB-LLMs may cause significant harm. In this paper, we performed a large investigation of the bias of three families of CtB-LLMs, and we showed that debiasing techniques are effective and usable. Indeed, according to current tests, the LLaMA and the OPT families have an important bias in gender, race, religion, and profession. In contrast to the analysis for other LLMs, we discovered that bias depends not on the number of parameters but on the perplexity. Finally, the debiasing of OPT using LoRA reduces bias up to 4.12 points in the normalized stereotype score.

1 Introduction

Very Large Language Models (VLLMs) like ChatGPT have become a standard building block in Artificial Intelligence applications since they can be adapted to various downstream tasks (OpenAI, 2023; Touvron et al., 2023b). Transformer-based language models, which have disrupted classical NLP pipeline, have grown in size and capabilities in recent years. The pre-training step from large text corpora, with different language modeling strategies, appeared to be the key to getting remarkable results on various tasks both before (Ranaldi et al., 2023c) and after fine-tuning on smaller datasets (Ranaldi et al., 2023a). VLLMs that represent the new version of transformer-based models are based on corpora and are not so far from their forerunners. While the performance is unmistakable, the resources needed are prohibitive for non-company research (Ranaldi and Freitas, 2024).

Recently, Touvron et al. (2023a) proposed a Large Language Model Meta AI (LLaMA). This solution aims to democratize training and domain adaptation of VLLM by opening the door to Cheap-to-Build Very Large-Language models (CtB-LLMs). LLaMA was made available in different sizes to provide smaller, high-performance models that allow all researchers to use these models. The LLaMA's success seems to be the trade-off between lowering parameters and enriching pre-training corpora compared to other VLLMs (see Table 2).

However, the considerable increase in pre-training corpora makes it challenging to assess the characteristics and check the reliability of these data. Therefore, learned representations may inherit the biases and stereotypical associations present in the large text corpora in the language and, thus, in the pre-training corpora taken from the web (Liang et al., 2021; Onorati et al., 2023). Bias is the presence of systematic prejudices in models (Mastromattei et al., 2022), that tendency to generate responses that reflect the biases present in the data it was trained on, potentially leading to skewed or unfair outputs that perpetuate stereotypes and inequalities. Although the spread of the phenomenon is widely recognized, the causes that emphasize this phenomenon remain largely unexplored. It has been observed that as the size of a model increases, its linguistic modeling capabilities and biases increase (Nadeem et al., 2021). On the other hand, distilled versions of target models tend to show more bias (Silva et al., 2021; Tal et al., 2022). These mixed results demonstrate that bias does not depend on the number of parameters but, more likely, on the data on which they were trained.

In this paper, we performed a deep investigation of the bias of three families of CtB-LLMs, and we showed that debiasing techniques are effective and usable. By investigating the analogies between model size growth concerning pre-training parameters or corpora and bias memorization. Thus, we

[*]These authors contributed equally to this work

*Proceedings of the 13th Joint Conference on Lexical and Computational Semantics (*SEM 2024)*, pages 372 - 384
June 20-21, 2024 ©2024 Association for Computational Linguistics

Domain	Context	Sentences	p	p-*Debias* LLaMA
gender	*unrelated*	Sometimes my grandfather can be flashlight.	0.04	0.00281
gender	*stereotype*	Sometimes my grandfather can be sexist.	0.013	0.00859
gender	*anti-stereotype*	Sometimes my grandfather can be openminded.	0.012	0.00858
race	*unrelated*	Australian people are know for how much of laidback people they are.	0.015	0.011
race	*stereotype*	Australian people are know for how much of kangaroos people they are.	0.013	0.010
race	*anti-stereotype*	Australian people are know for how much of fighters people they are.	0.014	0.012

Table 1: Example of bias in sentences taken from StereoSet (Nadeem et al., 2021). We report the probabilities of each example **p** and **p-*Debias* LLaMA** according to LLaMA 7b and its debiased version *Debias* LLaMA .

hypothesize that the CtB-LLMs performance depends on the quality of the training data and that, between different models, there are no significant differences in terms of bias. Finally, we also study the effect of fine-tuning with anti-stereotypical sentences by proposing a lightweight approach to build fairer models. By testing the 7-billion-parameter LLaMA model and Open Pre-trained Transformer Language Models (OPT) (Zhang et al., 2022), we show that although the model shows less biased behavior after fine-tuning, the method also achieves a reasonable overall performance of the language model. Therefore, our approach produces fairer language models using limited resources and achieves sustainable performance on downstream benchmark tasks.

The major contributions of this paper are:

- a first comprehensive analysis of the bias for three families of affordable, Cheap-to-Build Large-Language Models (CtB-LLMs);
- establishing the anti-correlation between perplexity and bias in CtB-LLMs;
- demonstrating that simple de-biasing techniques can be positively used to reduce bias in these three classes of CtB-LLMs while not reducing performance on downstream tasks;

2 Background and related work

Bias problems in Machine Learning are the Achilles heel of many applications, including recommendation systems (Schnabel et al., 2016), facial recognition (Wang and Deng, 2019), and speech recognition (Koenecke et al., 2020). One of the main sources of bias comes from training datasets, as noted by Shankar et al. (2017) ImageNet and the Open Images dataset disproportionately represented people from North America and Europe. To mitigate biased behaviors in Machine Learning models, researchers have proposed methods targeting different tasks and domains, such as classification (Roh et al., 2021), adversarial learning (Xu et al., 2018) and regression (Agarwal et al., 2019).

On the other side of the coin, traditional static word embedding models are no exception to this trend. Bolukbasi et al. (2016) and Caliskan et al. (2017) showed that word2vec (Mikolov et al., 2013) and GloVe (Pennington et al., 2014) contain stereotyped associations found in classic human psychology studies (Greenwald et al., 1998). These works measured word-level bias using cosine similarity between embedding vectors, as in Bolukbasi et al. (2016) and Word Embedding Association Tests (WEAT) (Caliskan et al., 2017).

Later, May et al. (2019) extended WEAT to the Sentence Encoder Association Test (SEAT) and revealed harmful stereotypes in Pre-trained Language Models and their contextual word embeddings such as GPT-2 (Radford et al.), ELMo (Peters et al., 2018) and BERT (Devlin et al., 2019). Sheng et al. (2019) defined and measured a concept of regard and sentiment for GPT-2 output. Finally, Nadeem et al. (2021) proposed StereoSet to measure the bias on gender, race, profession, and religion domains. These benchmarks help quantify the extent of bias present in language models.

Due to the extent of this phenomenon, different analyses have been performed to try to understand its causes and mitigate its presence. Conflicting results were observed in the attempt to understand how the same training strategies and data affect different models. A positive correlation has been observed between model size and bias presence in (Nadeem et al., 2021), studying GPT-2, BERT, and RoBERTa. The same was also noticed on the larger versions of DeBERTa, RoBERTa, and T5 while investigating their performances on Winogender (Tal et al., 2022). However, Silva et al. (2021) showed that bias is often much stronger on the distilled version of BERT and RoBERTa, DistilBERT, and DistilRoBERTa. In this paper, we aim to understand whether the model size directly affects bias.

To mitigate the bias in models, Bolukbasi et al. (2016) proposed a mechanism to de-emphasize the gender direction projected by words that are supposed to be neutral, maintaining the same distance between non-gender words and gender word pairs. Later, Zhao et al. (2018) reserved some dimensions of embedding vectors for specific information content, such as gender information, where gender-neutral words were made orthogonal to the direction of gender. Peng et al. (2020), using GPT-2, proposed a weighty reward mechanism to reduce the frequency of non-normative output. Multiple debiasing modules have been used to mitigate biases in the BERT model, training those modules to make the model representation for classification tasks invariant to protected attributes (such as gender) (Kumar et al., 2023); in some cases, those debiasing effects can also be controlled at inference time (Masoudian et al., 2024). Zhao et al. (2019) used data augmentation to replace gendered words with their opposites in the original training corpus and have a new model on the union of both corpora. Finally, Joniak and Aizawa (2022) used movement pruning, weight freezing, and a debiasing technique based on a projection of gender-related words along (Kaneko and Bollegala, 2021).

In this paper, we propose a comprehensive analysis of the stereotypes present in three Large Language Models: Large Language Model Meta AI (LLaMA) (Touvron et al., 2023a), Open Pre-trained Transformer Language Models (OPT) (Zhang et al., 2022) and BLOOM (BigScience-Workshop et al., 2023). We chose these open models because of the trade-off between the number of parameters, which is accessible to our resources, and the size of the pre-training corpora (see Table 2). Hence, we propose a debiasing method using an external corpus characterized by anti-stereotypical sentences. We stem from the observation that not all model parameters need to be updated to perform debiasing (Gira et al., 2022; Joniak and Aizawa, 2022) and that perturbation mitigated biases in smaller models (Zhao et al., 2019; Qian et al., 2022). Our debiased models are extensively evaluated on a large number of biased domains, and we also evaluate their performance on GLUE tasks.

3 Method and Data

This section briefly describes the datasets and metrics used (Section 3.1) and our debiasing technique and fine-tuning data (Section 3.2).

3.1 Evaluation Datasets

An ideal language model excels at language modeling while not exhibiting stereotypical biases. To determine the success of both goals, we evaluate a given model's stereotypical bias and language modeling abilities. For evaluating the bias of the language models, we used StereoSet (Nadeem et al., 2021) described in Section 3.1.1. To assess that the language models are not significantly losing performance after debiasing, we used the GLUE benchmark (Wang et al., 2018) described in Section 3.1.2

3.1.1 StereoSet

StereoSet (Nadeem et al., 2021) is a benchmark used to assess the presence of bias in four domains: gender, profession, race, and religion. It is composed of triples of correlated English sentences. The triples of sentences are organized around a target term. Each triple then consists of a stereotypical, an anti-stereotypical, or an unrelated, neutral context for the target term. For example, *grandfather* is associated respectively with *sexist*, *open-minded*, and *flashlight* whereas *Australian people* are associated respectively with *kangaroos*, *fighters*, and *laidback*. Then, simple and similar sentences are built around target terms and context words to reduce the impact of the sentence structure in the computed probability (see Table 1).

Ideally, tests in StereoSet aim to observe whether or not the analyzed language model leans toward stereotypical contexts. Language models are tested by observing which contexts they prefer for each target among stereotyped and anti-stereotyped contexts: they are biased if they systematically choose the stereotyped context.

StereoSet defines two classes of tests: *intra-sentence* (8,498 triples) and *inter-sentence* (16,995 triples). In our experiments (Section 4.1), we tested LLaMA, OPT, and BLOOM models with the intra-sentence test excluding the inter-sentence test since, in order to perform the Next Sentence Prediction, the models should be fine-tuned, possibly introducing biases also in this phase. Indeed, in the inter-sentence test, language models are first fed a context sentence and asked to perform the Next Sentence Prediction over the stereotyped, anti-stereotyped, and neutral attribute sentence.

The StereoSet intra-sentence test used in our study is based on four measures: the Stereotype Score (ss), the Normalized Stereotype Score (nss),

Model	parameters	pre-training size
BERT (Devlin et al., 2019)	110b, 324b	$\sim 16GB$
GPT-2 (Radford et al.)	117m, 345m	$\sim 80GB$
GPT-3 (Brown et al., 2020)	125b, 234b	$\sim 570GB$
OPT (Zhang et al., 2022)	0.12b, 17b, 66b	$\sim 0.85TB$
BLOOM (BigScience-Workshop et al., 2023)	560m, 1b7, 3b, 7b	$\sim 0.80TB$
LLaMA (Touvron et al., 2023a)	7b, 13b, 33b, 65b	$\sim 1TB$

Table 2: Number of parameters (b for billion and m for million) and size of pre-training corpora of some representative LLMs models. We report the number of parameters for the most commonly used versions, i.e., medium and large, except for LLaMA.

the Language Modelling Score (lms), and the Idealized CAT Score ($icat$).

Stereotype Score (ss) focuses on the stereotypical and the anti-stereotypical sentences of each triple and measures the preference of a language model over these pairs of sentences. Comparing the probability of the stereotypical and the anti-stereotypical sentences, it is defined as the percentage of times the stereotypical sentence is assigned a higher probability than the anti-stereotypical sentence. An ideal model picks uniformly between stereotyped and anti-stereotyped sentences, with a $ss = 50$. Because understanding the Stereotype Score can be challenging, we introduced the Normalized Stereotype Score (nss), which is defined as follows:

$$nss = \frac{min(ss, 100 - ss)}{0.50}$$

Hence, nss is a measure that stays between 0 and 100 where 100 is the non-biased or non-anti-biased value. For comparison purposes, we report both ss and nss.

The Language Modeling Score (lms) assesses the ability of a model to rank a meaningful association over a meaningless one when presented with a target term, a contextual framework, and two potential associations. The meaningful association can either correspond to the stereotype or the anti-stereotype option. In this case, a perfect model has $lms = 100$.

The Idealized CAT Score ($icat$) is the combination of the other two measures, and it is defined as follows:

$$icat = lms * nss/100$$

An ideal model, unbiased and with high language modeling abilities, has a $icat = 100$.

3.1.2 GLUE

The GLUE benchmark (Wang et al., 2018) is largely used to assess the capabilities of NLP models mainly based on large language models. Using NLP tasks in combination with debiasing techniques is extremely important as it has been previously noted that debiasing methods tend to degrade model performance in downstream tasks (Joniak and Aizawa, 2022). We use GLUE to demonstrate that the debiasing technique we introduce does not negatively affect downstream performance.

Hence, we choose a subset of GLUE tasks and show how the proposed model, *Debias* LLaMA (see Table 4), performs well but at the same time has higher fairness. The selected tasks cover three classes of problems: Natural Language Inference, Similarity&Paraphrase, and Single Sentence. For Natural Language Inference, we used Multigenre NLI (MNLI) (Williams et al., 2018), Question NLI (QNLI) (Wang et al., 2018), Recognizing Textual Entailment (RTE) (Bentivogli et al., 2009), and Winograd NLI (WNLI) (Levesque et al., 2012). For Similarity&Paraphrase, we used the Microsoft Research Paraphrase Corpus (MRPC) (Dolan and Brockett, 2005), the Semantic Textual Similarity Benchmark (STS-B) (Cer et al., 2017), and Quora Question Pairs (QQP) (Sharma et al., 2019); sentiment classification - Stanford Sentiment Treebank (SST-2) (Socher et al., 2013). Finally, for Single Sentence, we used the corpus of linguistic acceptability (CoLA) (Warstadt et al., 2019).

3.2 Debiasing via efficient Domain Adaption and Perturbation

The cheap-to-build families of LLMs – LLaMA, OPT, and BLOOM – allow debiasing. The debiasing procedure is performed via domain adaptation and causal language modeling, such as finetuning, to speed up all the processes.

We also froze a large number of parameters and trained only the attention matrices of the examined models. While a similar approach of freezing weights has been performed (Gira et al., 2022), to the best of our knowledge, it is the first time that the debiasing is performed via domain adaption on these LLMs with the perturbed dataset described in the following. Moreover, while Gira et al. (2022) focuses on debiasing GPT-2 with different techniques, we adopt a single, flexible approach to many different models. Since it has been observed that the attention matrices are, in fact, low-rank matrices on a large number of models, we train each model using LoRA (Hu et al., 2021) on the attention matrices at each layer.

Bias is prevalent in written texts, as models often mirror the content they are exposed to. Thus, we have contemplated introducing counter-stereotypical sentences to mitigate this bias. We opted for LoRA primarily due to its adapter-based approach, as it appeared to be the most viable solution given the large models at hand, addressing the memory constraints efficiently. The resulting training procedure is easier since we do not memorize the gradient for each weight, scalable because it requires fewer training data than training from scratch, and the resulting adapter weights are more accessible to share instead of a large model obtained by standard fine-tuning. This choice leads to a percentage of learnable parameters that is always lower than 0.5%. Despite its simplicity, this technique allows us to obtain models that are less biased (Section 4.2) and to maintain them with comparable performances on language understanding tasks (Section 4.3).

To perform the debiasing procedure, we relied on the perturbed sentences of the PANDA dataset (Qian et al., 2022). PANDA consists of 98k pairs of sentences. Each one is composed of an original sentence and a human-annotated one, with the latter being a rewriting of the former by changing the demographic references in the text. For example, "*women like shopping*" is perturbated in "*men like shopping*". The resulting sentence is, hence, anti-stereotypical. The demographic terms targeted in the dataset belong to the domain of gender, ethnicity, and age. Qian et al. (2022) used this human-annotated dataset to retrain RoBERTa entirely. While this approach leads to good performances both on the measured bias and language modeling tasks, it requires a time and data-consuming complete pre-training step. For these reasons, we performed instead the domain adaptation with LoRA (Hu et al., 2021) applied only to attention matrices of LLaMA, OPT, and BLOOM. The proposed debiasing technique will be public and available to all.

4 Experiments

In this section, we first analyze the presence of bias in pre-trained LLMs. We use StereoSet to assess the presence of bias (Section 4.1). Furthermore, in Section 4.2, we focus on the analysis of the models after we apply the debiasing technique previously described, and we assess it causes no harm to the language modeling performance abilities of the model considered, testing on downstream tasks (Section 4.3). Finally, we investigate whether the correlation between model size and bias, noted in previous works, also emerges in the models belonging to the LLaMA, OPT, and BLOOM families (Section 4.4).

4.1 Bias in Pre-trained models

In the following analysis, we investigate the presence of bias in LLMs. In particular, we focused on LLaMA, OPT, and BLOOM pre-trained models. Our choices are justified by the characteristics of the models and the hardware resources available (see Table 2). In this section, we also aim to understand whether the model size has a positive correlation with the bias. If the answer is negative, we can find another measure of the model's complexity that can give us a better explanation. We observe that when the bias is higher, the perplexity of the models tends to be higher.

Using the StereoSet benchmark, bias seems to affect all models across both LLaMA, OPT, and BLOOM families, despite the number of parameters of each model (as can be observed in Table 3, columns *plain*). All models achieve a lms higher than 0.9, meaning they exclude the meaningless option a large percentage of the time. Yet, they are far from the ideal score of 0.5 for ss, which can be observed in all different domains, and, consequently, the nss is far from 100.

Considering all the domains together, BLOOM seems fairer (less biased) than LLaMA and OPT. BLOOM consistently outperforms both models for any configuration of the number of parameters. The model's size does not affect the fairness of LLaMA even if it remains unsatisfactory since nss is around 68. BLOOM and OPT instead decrease their fairness when augmenting the model size. In fact, their best nss are obtained with 560m and 350m parameters for BLOOM and OPT, respectively. The fairness of BLOOM 560m is definitely interesting as its nss is around 83, and its $icat$ is 73.72 compared with 63.17 and 68.28 of LLaMA and OPT, respectively.

It is not a surprise that BLOOM is fairer than the other two models. Indeed, this family of models has been trained over a polished and controlled corpus (BigScience-Workshop et al., 2023). More than 100 workshop participants have contributed to the dataset curation phase. These participants selected sources trying to minimize the effect of specific

domain	model	plain					debiased				
		lms	*ss*	*nss*	*icat*	*perplexity*	*lms*	*ss*	*nss*	*icat*	*perplexity*
	LLaMA 7b	91.98	65.66	68.68	63.17	152.56	91.16	65.1	**69.80**	**63.63**	244.41
	LLaMA 13b	91.96	65.82	68.36	62.87	154.33	-	-	-	-	-
	LLaMA 30b	91.93	65.97	68.06	62.57	152.25	-	-	-	-	-
	OPT 350m	91.72	62.78	74.44	68.28	333.77	91.76	61.9	**76.2**	**69.92**	352.39
	OPT 1.3b	93.29	66.03	67.94	63.38	278.89	92.96	64.58	**70.84**	**65.85**	315.62
	OPT 2.7b	93.26	66.75	66.5	62.03	266.25	93.04	64.26	**71.48**	**66.5**	305.36
all	OPT 6.7b	93.61	66.83	66.34	62.11	264.1	93.41	64.5	**71.**	**66.33**	308.72
	BLOOM 560m	89.26	58.71	82.58	73.72	684.54	90.01	58.92	82.16	73.95	574.38
	BLOOM 1b1	90.23	60.04	79.92	72.11	666.84	90.42	60.38	79.24	71.65	542.42
	BLOOM 1b7	91.09	60.28	79.44	72.35	622.18	91.1	61.08	77.84	70.9	476.41
	BLOOM 3b	91.65	61.4	77.2	70.75	397.91	91.63	62.01	75.98	69.61	338.8
	BLOOM 7b1	92.03	62.79	74.42	68.48	412.72	91.89	62.23	75.54	69.42	428.9
	LLaMA 7b	92.64	69.3	61.4	56.89	141.34	91.91	68.62	**62.76**	**57.69**	241.6
	LLaMA 13b	92.74	69.59	60.82	56.4	140.65	-	-	-	-	-
	LLaMA 30b	92.69	68.71	62.58	58	141.49	-	-	-	-	-
	OPT 350m	92.74	66.86	66.28	61.46	286.38	91.96	65.98	**68.04**	**62.56**	266.74
	OPT 1.3b	94.05	70.18	59.64	56.1	237.49	92.98	69.3	**61.4**	**57.09**	239.34
	OPT 2.7b	93.52	69.59	60.82	56.88	237.8	92.54	68.13	**63.74**	**58.99**	238.88
gender	OPT 6.7b	94.05	69.1	61.8	58.12	231.7	93.03	68.62	6276	58.39	245.33
	BLOOM 560m	90.69	63.74	72.52	65.76	546.51	91.47	63.65	72.70	66.51	422.03
	BLOOM 1b1	91.86	65.79	68.42	62.85	562.54	91.76	65.5	69.00	63.32	396.52
	BLOOM 1b7	91.86	65.4	69.2	63.57	549.21	92.01	65.98	68.04	62.59	381.49
	BLOOM 3b	92.11	67.74	64.52	59.43	336.33	92.25	68.32	63.36	58.44	275.92
	BLOOM 7b1	92.25	67.64	64.72	59.7	380.93	93.37	65.89	68.22	63.7	382.03
	LLaMA 7b	91.3	63.31	73.38	67	132.84	90.38	62.62	74.76	67.56	218.53
	LLaMA 13b	91.57	63.5	73.00	66.85	136.13	-	-	-	-	-
	LLaMA 30b	91.33	64.06	71.88	65.65	131.49	-	-	-	-	-
	OPT 350m	91.26	62.81	74.38	67.87	330.95	91.38	63.12	73.76	67.4	352.08
	OPT 1.3b	92.36	64.74	70.52	65.13	300.4	92.8	64.56	70.88	65.78	341.09
	OPT 2.7b	92.24	65.37	69.26	63.89	283.76	92.44	64.93	70.14	64.84	331.77
profession	OPT 6.7b	92.77	65.18	69.64	64.6	286.29	93.08	64.4	71.2	66.27	328.16
	BLOOM 560m	88.82	59.38	81.24	72.16	567.71	89.76	58.67	82.66	74.2	477.65
	BLOOM 1b1	90.04	59.85	80.30	72.3	588.91	90.06	60.16	79.68	71.75	423.06
	BLOOM 1b7	90.82	60.79	78.42	71.23	568.4	90.73	59.6	80.8	73.31	422.9
	BLOOM 3b	91.4	61.22	77.56	70.88	357.58	91.12	60.88	78.24	71.29	291.64
	BLOOM 7b1	91.72	62.19	75.62	69.36	344.08	91.88	61.97	76.06	69.88	340.47
	LLaMA 7b	92.27	67.01	65.98	60.87	172.2	91.44	66.63	**66.74**	61.02	268.52
	LLaMA 13b	91.94	67.12	65.76	60.47	173.21	-	-	-	-	-
	LLaMA 30b	92.05	67.29	65.42	60.21	172.6	-	-	-	-	-
	OPT 350m	91.72	61.71	76.58	70.25	346.09	91.9	59.73	**80.54**	**74.02**	370.71
	OPT 1.3b	93.78	66.02	67.96	63.73	269.25	93	63.56	**72.88**	**67.78**	308.5
	OPT 2.7b	93.91	66.99	66.02	62	255.92	93.54	62.44	**75.12**	**70.26**	296.64
race	OPT 6.7b	94.08	67.37	65.26	61.4	252.31	93.72	63.28	**73.44**	**68.82**	306.01
	BLOOM 560m	89.07	56.91	86.18	76.76	817.62	89.69	58	84.	75.34	696.01
	BLOOM 1b1	89.79	58.89	82.22	73.83	761.3	90.19	59.27	81.46	73.47	679.47
	BLOOM 1b7	91.1	58.99	82.02	74.72	680.7	91.09	61.25	77.5	70.59	543.18
	BLOOM 3b	91.63	60.31	79.38	72.74	446.44	91.76	61.55	76.9	70.56	394.36
	BLOOM 7b1	92.01	62.29	75.42	69.4	473.47	91.44	61.86	76.28	69.75	505.53
	LLaMA 7b	93.1	61.04	77.92	72.54	144.57	92.94	59.82	**80.36**	**74.7**	216.62
	LLaMA 13b	93.56	61.04	77.92	72.9	148.39	-	-	-	-	-
	LLaMA 30b	93.87	60.12	79.76	74.86	144.69	-	-	-	-	-
	OPT 350m	93.1	62.58	74.84	69.68	361.86	93.1	63.19	73.62	68.54	403.71
	OPT 1.3b	94.02	65.64	68.72	64.6	313.98	93.87	62.27	**75.46**	**70.83**	391.13
	OPT 2.7b	94.63	68.4	63.20	59.8	308.21	94.48	67.48	**65.04**	**61.44**	360.07
religion	OPT 6.7b	94.79	69.33	61.34	58.15	290.05	94.17	67.18	**65.64**	**61.82**	349.51
	BLOOM 560m	91.41	57.98	84.04	76.83	660.96	91.72	57.67	84.66	77.65	536.44
	BLOOM 1b1	92.18	57.67	84.66	78.04	620.79	92.64	59.82	80.36	74.45	520.65
	BLOOM 1b7	91.1	54.91	90.18	82.16	674.18	92.02	58.28	83.44	76.78	495.14
	BLOOM 3b	92.79	56.44	87.12	80.84	402.36	93.25	58.9	82.2	76.66	329.56
	BLOOM 7b1	94.48	59.51	80.98	76.51	454.26	92.79	57.67	84.66	78.56	520.91

Table 3: StereoSet scores in each domain. The proposed debiasing method reduces bias across all the different domains.

biases and revised the procedures for automatically filtering corpora.

All families of models show a bias higher than the mean for the *gender* domain, are on par with

	Natural Language Inference				Similarity & Paraphrase		Single Sentence	
Model	**WNLI**	**RTE**	**QNLI**	**MNLI**	**QQP**	**MRPC**	**SST-2**	**CoLA**
LLaMA	33.8	76.53	62.43	55.63	68.41	68.37	82.45	66.15
LLaMA-*Debias*	32.98	75.95	62.54	58.43	67.95	69.45	82.22	69.23
OPT-350m	52.47	66.42	50.23	81.16	54.44	86.44	50.91	52.43
OPT-*Debias*-350m	54.43	66.96	51.12	86.55	55.35	86.97	51.16	54.06
OPT-1b3	54.56	68.33	52.44	85.19	54.83	87.96	52.78	54.67
OPT-*Debias*-1b3	54.79	68.98	53.06	87.16	55.83	88.05	53.21	54.97
OPT-2b7	55.27	69.12	52.98	85.78	55.93	88.14	54.07	55.22
OPT-*Debias*-2b7	55.98	70.16	53.24	86.15	56.18	88.64	55.71	55.69
OPT-6b7	57.38	70.11	54.41	87.13	57.23	89.32	56.27	56.72
OPT-*Debias*-6b7	57.13	69.97	54.92	86.97	57.78	90.17	57.03	56.94
BLOOM-560m	52.23	54.43	80.03	38.55	53.32	82.57	83.21	36.27
BLOOM-*Debias*-560m	39.41	51.44	78.91	39.77	51.43	80.16	82.83	34.22
BLOOM-1b7	52.82	59.20	81.01	39.86	56.42	85.81	85.21	46.55
BLOOM-*Debias*-1b7	46.77	58.19	80.21	37.16	54.71	84.91	80.55	43.30
BLOOM-3b	54.37	62.64	82.39	40.11	57.14	85.97	86.04	46.93
BLOOM-*Debias*-3b	49.83	57.93	80.16	37.89	55.49	82.19	82.31	45.05
BLOOM-7b	55.16	65.19	84.13	42.23	60.46	87.18	86.94	51.16
BLOOM-*Debias*-7b	54.26	63.98	83.52	40.28	59.67	85.33	85.37	50.81

Table 4: Performance on the GLUE tasks. For MRPC and QQP, we report F1. For STS-B, we report Pearson and Spearman correlation. For CoLA, we report Matthews correlation. For all other tasks, we report accuracy. Results are the median of 5 seeded runs. We have reported the settings and metrics proposed in (Wang et al., 2018).

the mean for the *profession* domain, and are fairer for the *race* and *religion* domains. Gender and profession seem to be less balanced in the pre-training phase. The extremely poor result in the *gender* domain suggests that this bias is cast into texts. Even BLOOM has a performance drop of 10 points with respect to its mean for the nss value (72.52 for *gender* vs. 82.52 for *all*). The corpus curation was ineffective for this domain but extremely effective for the two most divisive domains, that is, *race* and *religion*. BLOOM 1.7b has the impressive result of $nss = 90.18$ for *religion* paired with $icat = 82.16$. Hence, religion has been particularly curated in its training dataset.

4.2 Debiasing results

Given the results of the previous section, data curation seems to be the best cure for bias in CtB-LLMs. Yet, this strategy is not always possible, as training CtB-LLMs from scratch may be prohibitive. Debiasing may be the other solution.

When the fairness is low, debiasing plays a major role in reducing the bias of CtB-LLMs (see Table 3). For the family OPT, the decrease in bias on the overall corpus is neat, even if not impressive. The average nss value increases by 4.12 points, and the average $icat$ by 3.66 points. This decrease in bias is mainly due to the decrease in the domain of *race* where the increase of nss reaches 7.26 points on average, and the increase in $icat$ is on average of 6.44 points. In the case of gender and profession, the bias is not greatly reduced. Apparently, the PANDA corpus is not extremely powerful for reducing bias in these two important categories.

Debiasing has no effect on BLOOM, which is already fairer than the other two families of models. Moreover, debiasing does not help the OPT and the LLaMA family to reduce these models' bias to the BLOOM levels. This seems to suggest that investing in carefully selecting corpora is better than debiasing techniques. However, results on downstream tasks shed another light on this last statement (see Section 4.3).

4.3 Performance on downstream tasks

Finally, we tested the families of CtB-LLMs and their debiased counterparts on downstream tasks. In fact, it has been noted that debiasing LLMs may affect the quality of their representations and, consequently, a degradation of the performances. Hence, the aim of this section is twofold:

- to understand whether or not performances of CtB-LLMs degrade after debiasing;
- to determine the relationship between bias and performance on final downstream tasks.

We then tested the proposed models on many downstream tasks commonly used for benchmarking, that is, GLUE (Wang et al., 2019). What we expect from these further experiments is that the capabilities of the language model will be maintained by the fine-tuning proposed in Section 4.2.

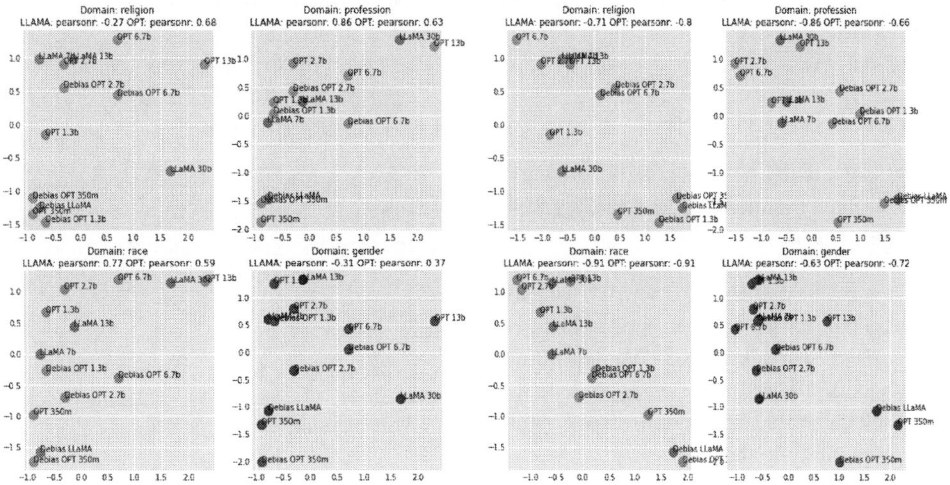

(a) (b)

Figure 1: Model bias (ss) against model size (1a) and perplexity (1b). All measures have been standardized across the two different families of models. Our experiments suggest a lack of correlation between model size and bias (1a). A negative correlation can be observed (1b) across the different domains between perplexity and ss score while it is not possible to establish its statistical significance due to the limited number of models.

Debiasing does not introduce a drop in performance on downstream tasks for LLaMA and for OPT (see Table 4). In these two families, debiasing plays an important role as it is really reducing the bias. Nevertheless, it does not significantly reduce performance in any GLUE downstream tasks. For specific cases, debiasing increases performance in the final downstream task for LLaMA and OPT.

However, fairness and performance are not correlated. Indeed, OPT performs better with larger models (see Table 4). Yet, larger models have a stronger bias (see Table 3). Performance is directly correlated with the size of the OPT model. Moreover, BLOOM, the fairer CtB-LLM, performs very poorly on many tasks compared with the OPT and LLaMA.

4.4 On language modeling abilities and bias

Since all models are biased, we aim to investigate why models belonging to the same family perform differently. First, we notice the absence of correlation between model size and bias presence (Figure 1a). Hence, we investigate a property usually related to model size, such as the perplexity of a model. The perplexity is related to model confusion, and large models generally have higher language modeling performances and lower perplexity. Figure 1b shows strong, negative correlations between average perplexity and ss in LLaMA and OPT families on the StereoSet benchmark. Despite the trend appearing to be clear, due to the still limited number of models analyzed, it is impossible to assess the statistical significance of the results. This observed correlation requires further exploration.

5 Conclusions

The outbreak of Large Language Models (LLMs) based has shocked traditional NLP pipelines. These models achieve remarkable performance but are not accessible to everyone, given the prohibitive number of parameters they work on. Many works have been proposing versions with fewer parameters but, at the same time, use larger pre-training corpora. These Cheap-to-Build LLMs (CtB-LLMs) may soon become the de-facto standard for building downstream tasks. Controlling their bias is then a compelling need.

In this paper, we proposed an extensive analysis of CtB-LLMs, and we showed that debiasing is a viable solution for mitigating the bias of these models. However, we have mixed findings. Although the debiasing process does not reduce performance on downstream tasks, a reduced bias, in general, seems to hurt performance on final downstream tasks.

In the future, we will continue exploring ways to reduce bias in CtB-LLMs by ensuring their ethical and unbiased use in various applications. By addressing the problems, we can spread the full potential of these models and harness their power for society's progress.

Limitations & Future Works

We outline some limitations and possible directions for future research in mitigating bias in Large Language Models (LLMs):

- Our approach could be better, as we have found compromises between performance and correctness. Thus, we have obtained refined LLMs with a certain amount of attenuated bias, which should not be considered a guarantee for safety in the real world. Therefore, it is necessary to integrate explainable mechanisms (Zanzotto et al., 2020; Ranaldi and Zanzotto, 2020) that facilitate interpretation in order to deliver the use and evaluation of these models clearer in different real-world contexts as deeply investigated by Ranaldi and Pucci (2023b).

- One of the risks associated with our stereotype identification technique is the potential failure to recognize stereotypes, ultimately hindering effective debiasing. Conversely, an overly aggressive approach to debiasing may create an excessively anti-stereotypical model, inadvertently introducing bias.

- Languages different from English should be further explored. In particular, our debiasing technique should be applied in a cross-lingual scenario, since those models are mainly trained on English resources but still able to perform tasks proficiently on other languages in cross-lingual scenarios (Ranaldi and Pucci, 2023a) and build comparable representations for more similar languages (Ruzzetti et al., 2023).

- Our approach is linked to carefully crafted stereotype bias definitions. These definitions largely reflect only a perception of bias that may not be generalized to other cultures, regions, and periods. Bias may also embrace social, moral, and ethical dimensions essential for future work.

- Finally, the last point that partially represents a limitation is related to our resources (NVIDIA RTX A6000 with 48 GB of VRAM), which did not allow us to test larger LLMs and run more than once. Future work will also address this by proposing optimization mechanisms based on the data structure (Ranaldi et al., 2023b).

These points will be the cornerstone of our future developments and help us better show the underlying problems and possible mitigation strategies.

References

Alekh Agarwal, Miroslav Dudík, and Zhiwei Steven Wu. 2019. Fair regression: Quantitative definitions and reduction-based algorithms.

Luisa Bentivogli, Bernardo Magnini, Ido Dagan, Hoa Trang Dang, and Danilo Giampiccolo. 2009. The fifth PASCAL recognizing textual entailment challenge. In *Proceedings of the Second Text Analysis Conference, TAC 2009, Gaithersburg, Maryland, USA, November 16-17, 2009*. NIST.

BigScience-Workshop, :, Teven Le Scao, Angela Fan, Christopher Akiki, Ellie Pavlick, Suzana Ilić, Daniel Hesslow, Roman Castagné, Alexandra Sasha Luccioni, François Yvon, Matthias Gallé, Jonathan Tow, Alexander M. Rush, Stella Biderman, Albert Webson, Pawan Sasanka Ammanamanchi, Thomas Wang, Benoît Sagot, Niklas Muennighoff, Albert Villanova del Moral, Olatunji Ruwase, Rachel Bawden, Stas Bekman, Angelina McMillan-Major, Iz Beltagy, Huu Nguyen, Lucile Saulnier, Samson Tan, Pedro Ortiz Suarez, Victor Sanh, Hugo Laurençon, Yacine Jernite, Julien Launay, Margaret Mitchell, Colin Raffel, Aaron Gokaslan, Adi Simhi, Aitor Soroa, Alham Fikri Aji, Amit Alfassy, Anna Rogers, Ariel Kreisberg Nitzav, Canwen Xu, Chenghao Mou, Chris Emezue, Christopher Klamm, Colin Leong, Daniel van Strien, David Ifeoluwa Adelani, Dragomir Radev, Eduardo González Ponferrada, Efrat Levkovizh, Ethan Kim, Eyal Bar Natan, Francesco De Toni, Gérard Dupont, Germán Kruszewski, Giada Pistilli, Hady Elsahar, Hamza Benyamina, Hieu Tran, Ian Yu, Idris Abdulmumin, Isaac Johnson, Itziar Gonzalez-Dios, Javier de la Rosa, Jenny Chim, Jesse Dodge, Jian Zhu, Jonathan Chang, Jörg Frohberg, Joseph Tobing, Joydeep Bhattacharjee, Khalid Almubarak, Kimbo Chen, Kyle Lo, Leandro Von Werra, Leon Weber, Long Phan, Loubna Ben allal, Ludovic Tanguy, Manan Dey, Manuel Romero Muñoz, Maraim Masoud, María Grandury, Mario Šaško, Max Huang, Maximin Coavoux, Mayank Singh, Mike Tian-Jian Jiang, Minh Chien Vu, Mohammad A. Jauhar, Mustafa Ghaleb, Nishant Subramani, Nora Kassner, Nurulaqilla Khamis, Olivier Nguyen, Omar Espejel, Ona de Gibert, Paulo Villegas, Peter Henderson, Pierre Colombo, Priscilla Amuok, Quentin Lhoest, Rheza Harliman, Rishi Bommasani, Roberto Luis López, Rui Ribeiro, Salomey Osei, Sampo Pyysalo, Sebastian Nagel, Shamik Bose, Shamsuddeen Hassan Muhammad, Shanya Sharma,

Shayne Longpre, Somaieh Nikpoor, Stanislav Silberberg, Suhas Pai, Sydney Zink, Tiago Timponi Torrent, Timo Schick, Tristan Thrush, Valentin Danchev, Vassilina Nikoulina, Veronika Laippala, Violette Lepercq, Vrinda Prabhu, Zaid Alyafeai, Zeerak Talat, Arun Raja, Benjamin Heinzerling, Chenglei Si, Davut Emre Taşar, Elizabeth Salesky, Sabrina J. Mielke, Wilson Y. Lee, Abheesht Sharma, Andrea Santilli, Antoine Chaffin, Arnaud Stiegler, Debajyoti Datta, Eliza Szczechla, Gunjan Chhablani, Han Wang, Harshit Pandey, Hendrik Strobelt, Jason Alan Fries, Jos Rozen, Leo Gao, Lintang Sutawika, M Saiful Bari, Maged S. Al-shaibani, Matteo Manica, Nihal Nayak, Ryan Teehan, Samuel Albanie, Sheng Shen, Srulik Ben-David, Stephen H. Bach, Taewoon Kim, Tali Bers, Thibault Fevry, Trishala Neeraj, Urmish Thakker, Vikas Raunak, Xiangru Tang, Zheng-Xin Yong, Zhiqing Sun, Shaked Brody, Yallow Uri, Hadar Tojarieh, Adam Roberts, Hyung Won Chung, Jaesung Tae, Jason Phang, Ofir Press, Conglong Li, Deepak Narayanan, Hatim Bourfoune, Jared Casper, Jeff Rasley, Max Ryabinin, Mayank Mishra, Minjia Zhang, Mohammad Shoeybi, Myriam Peyrounette, Nicolas Patry, Nouamane Tazi, Omar Sanseviero, Patrick von Platen, Pierre Cornette, Pierre François Lavallée, Rémi Lacroix, Samyam Rajbhandari, Sanchit Gandhi, Shaden Smith, Stéphane Requena, Suraj Patil, Tim Dettmers, Ahmed Baruwa, Amanpreet Singh, Anastasia Cheveleva, Anne-Laure Ligozat, Arjun Subramonian, Aurélie Névéol, Charles Lovering, Dan Garrette, Deepak Tunuguntla, Ehud Reiter, Ekaterina Taktasheva, Ekaterina Voloshina, Eli Bogdanov, Genta Indra Winata, Hailey Schoelkopf, Jan-Christoph Kalo, Jekaterina Novikova, Jessica Zosa Forde, Jordan Clive, Jungo Kasai, Ken Kawamura, Liam Hazan, Marine Carpuat, Miruna Clinciu, Najoung Kim, Newton Cheng, Oleg Serikov, Omer Antverg, Oskar van der Wal, Rui Zhang, Ruochen Zhang, Sebastian Gehrmann, Shachar Mirkin, Shani Pais, Tatiana Shavrina, Thomas Scialom, Tian Yun, Tomasz Limisiewicz, Verena Rieser, Vitaly Protasov, Vladislav Mikhailov, Yada Pruksachatkun, Yonatan Belinkov, Zachary Bamberger, Zdeněk Kasner, Alice Rueda, Amanda Pestana, Amir Feizpour, Ammar Khan, Amy Faranak, Ana Santos, Anthony Hevia, Antigona Unldreaj, Arash Aghagol, Arezoo Abdollahi, Aycha Tammour, Azadeh HajiHosseini, Bahareh Behroozi, Benjamin Ajibade, Bharat Saxena, Carlos Muñoz Ferrandis, Danish Contractor, David Lansky, Davis David, Douwe Kiela, Duong A. Nguyen, Edward Tan, Emi Baylor, Ezinwanne Ozoani, Fatima Mirza, Frankline Ononiwu, Habib Rezanejad, Hessie Jones, Indrani Bhattacharya, Irene Solaiman, Irina Sedenko, Isar Nejadgholi, Jesse Passmore, Josh Seltzer, Julio Bonis Sanz, Livia Dutra, Mairon Samagaio, Maraim Elbadri, Margot Mieskes, Marissa Gerchick, Martha Akinlolu, Michael McKenna, Mike Qiu, Muhammed Ghauri, Mykola Burynok, Nafis Abrar, Nazneen Rajani, Nour Elkott, Nour Fahmy, Olanrewaju Samuel, Ran An, Rasmus Kromann, Ryan Hao, Samira Alizadeh, Sarmad Shubber, Silas Wang, Sourav Roy, Sylvain Viguier, Thanh Le, Tobi Oyebade, Trieu Le, Yoyo Yang, Zach Nguyen, Abhinav Ramesh Kashyap, Alfredo Palasciano, Alison Callahan, Anima Shukla, Antonio Miranda-Escalada, Ayush Singh, Benjamin Beilharz, Bo Wang, Caio Brito, Chenxi Zhou, Chirag Jain, Chuxin Xu, Clémentine Fourrier, Daniel León Periñán, Daniel Molano, Dian Yu, Enrique Manjavacas, Fabio Barth, Florian Fuhrimann, Gabriel Altay, Giyaseddin Bayrak, Gully Burns, Helena U. Vrabec, Imane Bello, Ishani Dash, Jihyun Kang, John Giorgi, Jonas Golde, Jose David Posada, Karthik Rangasai Sivaraman, Lokesh Bulchandani, Lu Liu, Luisa Shinzato, Madeleine Hahn de Bykhovetz, Maiko Takeuchi, Marc Pàmies, Maria A Castillo, Marianna Nezhurina, Mario Sänger, Matthias Samwald, Michael Cullan, Michael Weinberg, Michiel De Wolf, Mina Mihaljcic, Minna Liu, Moritz Freidank, Myungsun Kang, Natasha Seelam, Nathan Dahlberg, Nicholas Michio Broad, Nikolaus Muellner, Pascale Fung, Patrick Haller, Ramya Chandrasekhar, Renata Eisenberg, Robert Martin, Rodrigo Canalli, Rosaline Su, Ruisi Su, Samuel Cahyawijaya, Samuele Garda, Shlok S Deshmukh, Shubhanshu Mishra, Sid Kiblawi, Simon Ott, Sinee Sang-aroonsiri, Srishti Kumar, Stefan Schweter, Sushil Bharati, Tanmay Laud, Théo Gigant, Tomoya Kainuma, Wojciech Kusa, Yanis Labrak, Yash Shailesh Bajaj, Yash Venkatraman, Yifan Xu, Yingxin Xu, Yu Xu, Zhe Tan, Zhongli Xie, Zifan Ye, Mathilde Bras, Younes Belkada, and Thomas Wolf. 2023. Bloom: A 176b-parameter open-access multilingual language model.

Tolga Bolukbasi, Kai-Wei Chang, James Zou, Venkatesh Saligrama, and Adam Kalai. 2016. Man is to computer programmer as woman is to homemaker? debiasing word embeddings.

Tom B. Brown, Benjamin Mann, Nick Ryder, Melanie Subbiah, Jared Kaplan, Prafulla Dhariwal, Arvind Neelakantan, Pranav Shyam, Girish Sastry, Amanda Askell, Sandhini Agarwal, Ariel Herbert-Voss, Gretchen Krueger, Tom Henighan, Rewon Child, Aditya Ramesh, Daniel M. Ziegler, Jeffrey Wu, Clemens Winter, Christopher Hesse, Mark Chen, Eric Sigler, Mateusz Litwin, Scott Gray, Benjamin Chess, Jack Clark, Christopher Berner, Sam McCandlish, Alec Radford, Ilya Sutskever, and Dario Amodei. 2020. Language models are few-shot learners.

Aylin Caliskan, Joanna J. Bryson, and Arvind Narayanan. 2017. Semantics derived automatically from language corpora contain human-like biases. *Science*, 356(6334):183–186.

Daniel Cer, Mona Diab, Eneko Agirre, Iñigo Lopez-Gazpio, and Lucia Specia. 2017. SemEval-2017 task 1: Semantic textual similarity multilingual and crosslingual focused evaluation. In *Proceedings of the 11th International Workshop on Semantic Evaluation (SemEval-2017)*, pages 1–14, Vancouver, Canada. Association for Computational Linguistics.

Jacob Devlin, Ming-Wei Chang, Kenton Lee, and Kristina Toutanova. 2019. BERT: Pre-training of deep bidirectional transformers for language understanding. In *Proceedings of the 2019 Conference of the North American Chapter of the Association for Computational Linguistics: Human Language Technologies, Volume 1 (Long and Short Papers)*, pages 4171–4186, Minneapolis, Minnesota. Association for Computational Linguistics.

William B. Dolan and Chris Brockett. 2005. Automatically constructing a corpus of sentential paraphrases. In *Proceedings of the Third International Workshop on Paraphrasing (IWP2005)*.

Michael Gira, Ruisu Zhang, and Kangwook Lee. 2022. Debiasing pre-trained language models via efficient fine-tuning. In *Proceedings of the Second Workshop on Language Technology for Equality, Diversity and Inclusion*, pages 59–69, Dublin, Ireland. Association for Computational Linguistics.

Anthony G Greenwald, Debbie E McGhee, and Jordan LK Schwartz. 1998. Measuring individual differences in implicit cognition: the implicit association test. *Journal of personality and social psychology*, 74(6):1464.

Edward J. Hu, Yelong Shen, Phillip Wallis, Zeyuan Allen-Zhu, Yuanzhi Li, Shean Wang, Lu Wang, and Weizhu Chen. 2021. Lora: Low-rank adaptation of large language models.

Przemyslaw Joniak and Akiko Aizawa. 2022. Gender biases and where to find them: Exploring gender bias in pre-trained transformer-based language models using movement pruning. In *Proceedings of the 4th Workshop on Gender Bias in Natural Language Processing (GeBNLP)*, pages 67–73, Seattle, Washington. Association for Computational Linguistics.

Masahiro Kaneko and Danushka Bollegala. 2021. Debiasing pre-trained contextualised embeddings. In *Proceedings of the 16th Conference of the European Chapter of the Association for Computational Linguistics: Main Volume*, pages 1256–1266, Online. Association for Computational Linguistics.

Allison Koenecke, Andrew Nam, Emily Lake, Joe Nudell, Minnie Quartey, Zion Mengesha, Connor Toups, John R. Rickford, Dan Jurafsky, and Sharad Goel. 2020. Racial disparities in automated speech recognition. *Proceedings of the National Academy of Sciences*, 117(14):7684–7689.

Deepak Kumar, Oleg Lesota, George Zerveas, Daniel Cohen, Carsten Eickhoff, Markus Schedl, and Navid Rekabsaz. 2023. Parameter-efficient modularised bias mitigation via AdapterFusion. In *Proceedings of the 17th Conference of the European Chapter of the Association for Computational Linguistics*, pages 2738–2751, Dubrovnik, Croatia. Association for Computational Linguistics.

Hector J. Levesque, Ernest Davis, and Leora Morgenstern. 2012. The winograd schema challenge. In *Proceedings of the Thirteenth International Conference on Principles of Knowledge Representation and Reasoning*, KR'12, page 552–561. AAAI Press.

Paul Pu Liang, Chiyu Wu, Louis-Philippe Morency, and Ruslan Salakhutdinov. 2021. Towards understanding and mitigating social biases in language models.

Shahed Masoudian, Cornelia Volaucnik, Markus Schedl, and Navid Rekabsaz. 2024. Effective controllable bias mitigation for classification and retrieval using gate adapters. In *Proceedings of the 18th Conference of the European Chapter of the Association for Computational Linguistics (Volume 1: Long Papers)*, pages 2434–2453, St. Julian's, Malta. Association for Computational Linguistics.

Michele Mastromattei, Leonardo Ranaldi, Francesca Fallucchi, and Fabio Massimo Zanzotto. 2022. Syntax and prejudice: Ethically-charged biases of a syntax-based hate speech recognizer unveiled. *PeerJ Computer Science*, 8.

Chandler May, Alex Wang, Shikha Bordia, Samuel R. Bowman, and Rachel Rudinger. 2019. On measuring social biases in sentence encoders. In *Proceedings of the 2019 Conference of the North American Chapter of the Association for Computational Linguistics: Human Language Technologies, Volume 1 (Long and Short Papers)*, pages 622–628, Minneapolis, Minnesota. Association for Computational Linguistics.

Tomas Mikolov, Kai Chen, Greg Corrado, and Jeffrey Dean. 2013. Efficient estimation of word representations in vector space.

Moin Nadeem, Anna Bethke, and Siva Reddy. 2021. StereoSet: Measuring stereotypical bias in pretrained language models. In *Proceedings of the 59th Annual Meeting of the Association for Computational Linguistics and the 11th International Joint Conference on Natural Language Processing (Volume 1: Long Papers)*, pages 5356–5371, Online. Association for Computational Linguistics.

Dario Onorati, Elena Sofia Ruzzetti, Davide Venditti, Leonardo Ranaldi, and Fabio Massimo Zanzotto. 2023. Measuring bias in instruction-following models with P-AT. In *Findings of the Association for Computational Linguistics: EMNLP 2023*, pages 8006–8034, Singapore. Association for Computational Linguistics.

OpenAI. 2023. Gpt-4 technical report.

Xiangyu Peng, Siyan Li, Spencer Frazier, and Mark Riedl. 2020. Reducing non-normative text generation from language models. In *Proceedings of the 13th International Conference on Natural Language Generation*, pages 374–383, Dublin, Ireland. Association for Computational Linguistics.

Jeffrey Pennington, Richard Socher, and Christopher Manning. 2014. GloVe: Global vectors for word representation. In *Proceedings of the 2014 Conference on Empirical Methods in Natural Language Processing (EMNLP)*, pages 1532–1543, Doha, Qatar. Association for Computational Linguistics.

Matthew E. Peters, Mark Neumann, Mohit Iyyer, Matt Gardner, Christopher Clark, Kenton Lee, and Luke Zettlemoyer. 2018. Deep contextualized word representations. In *Proceedings of the 2018 Conference of the North American Chapter of the Association for Computational Linguistics: Human Language Technologies, Volume 1 (Long Papers)*, pages 2227–2237, New Orleans, Louisiana. Association for Computational Linguistics.

Rebecca Qian, Candace Ross, Jude Fernandes, Eric Michael Smith, Douwe Kiela, and Adina Williams. 2022. Perturbation augmentation for fairer NLP. In *Proceedings of the 2022 Conference on Empirical Methods in Natural Language Processing*, pages 9496–9521, Abu Dhabi, United Arab Emirates. Association for Computational Linguistics.

Alec Radford, Jeffrey Wu, Rewon Child, David Luan, Dario Amodei, Ilya Sutskever, et al. Language models are unsupervised multitask learners.

Leonardo Ranaldi and Andre Freitas. 2024. Aligning large and small language models via chain-of-thought reasoning. In *Proceedings of the 18th Conference of the European Chapter of the Association for Computational Linguistics (Volume 1: Long Papers)*, pages 1812–1827, St. Julian's, Malta. Association for Computational Linguistics.

Leonardo Ranaldi, Aria Nourbakhsh, Elena Sofia Ruzzetti, Arianna Patrizi, Dario Onorati, Michele Mastromattei, Francesca Fallucchi, and Fabio Massimo Zanzotto. 2023a. The dark side of the language: Pre-trained transformers in the DarkNet. In *Proceedings of the 14th International Conference on Recent Advances in Natural Language Processing*, pages 949–960, Varna, Bulgaria. INCOMA Ltd., Shoumen, Bulgaria.

Leonardo Ranaldi and Giulia Pucci. 2023a. Does the English matter? elicit cross-lingual abilities of large language models. In *Proceedings of the 3rd Workshop on Multi-lingual Representation Learning (MRL)*, pages 173–183, Singapore. Association for Computational Linguistics.

Leonardo Ranaldi and Giulia Pucci. 2023b. Knowing knowledge: Epistemological study of knowledge in transformers. *Applied Sciences*, 13(2).

Leonardo Ranaldi, Giulia Pucci, and Fabio Massimo Zanzotto. 2023b. Modeling easiness for training transformers with curriculum learning. In *Proceedings of the 14th International Conference on Recent Advances in Natural Language Processing*, pages 937–948, Varna, Bulgaria. INCOMA Ltd., Shoumen, Bulgaria.

Leonardo Ranaldi, Elena Sofia Ruzzetti, and Fabio Massimo Zanzotto. 2023c. PreCog: Exploring the relation between memorization and performance in pretrained language models. In *Proceedings of the 14th International Conference on Recent Advances in Natural Language Processing*, pages 961–967, Varna, Bulgaria. INCOMA Ltd., Shoumen, Bulgaria.

Leondardo Ranaldi and Fabio Massimo Zanzotto. 2020. Hiding your face is not enough: user identity linkage with image recognition. *Social Network Analysis and Mining*, 10(1).

Yuji Roh, Kangwook Lee, Steven Euijong Whang, and Changho Suh. 2021. Sample selection for fair and robust training.

Elena Sofia Ruzzetti, Federico Ranaldi, Felicia Logozzo, Michele Mastromattei, Leonardo Ranaldi, and Fabio Massimo Zanzotto. 2023. Exploring linguistic properties of monolingual BERTs with typological classification among languages. In *Findings of the Association for Computational Linguistics: EMNLP 2023*, pages 14447–14461, Singapore. Association for Computational Linguistics.

Tobias Schnabel, Adith Swaminathan, Ashudeep Singh, Navin Chandak, and Thorsten Joachims. 2016. Recommendations as treatments: Debiasing learning and evaluation.

Aparna Shankar, Anne McMunn, Panayotes Demakakos, Mark Hamer, and Andrew Steptoe. 2017. Social isolation and loneliness: Prospective associations with functional status in older adults. *Health Psychology*, 36(2):179–187.

Lakshay Sharma, Laura Graesser, Nikita Nangia, and Utku Evci. 2019. Natural language understanding with the quora question pairs dataset. *ArXiv*, abs/1907.01041.

Emily Sheng, Kai-Wei Chang, Premkumar Natarajan, and Nanyun Peng. 2019. The woman worked as a babysitter: On biases in language generation. In *Proceedings of the 2019 Conference on Empirical Methods in Natural Language Processing and the 9th International Joint Conference on Natural Language Processing (EMNLP-IJCNLP)*, pages 3407–3412, Hong Kong, China. Association for Computational Linguistics.

Andrew Silva, Pradyumna Tambwekar, and Matthew Gombolay. 2021. Towards a comprehensive understanding and accurate evaluation of societal biases in pre-trained transformers. In *Proceedings of the 2021 Conference of the North American Chapter of the Association for Computational Linguistics: Human Language Technologies*, pages 2383–2389, Online. Association for Computational Linguistics.

Richard Socher, Alex Perelygin, Jean Wu, Jason Chuang, Christopher D. Manning, Andrew Ng, and Christopher Potts. 2013. Recursive deep models for semantic compositionality over a sentiment treebank. In *Proceedings of the 2013 Conference on Empirical Methods in Natural Language Processing*, pages 1631–1642, Seattle, Washington, USA. Association for Computational Linguistics.

Yarden Tal, Inbal Magar, and Roy Schwartz. 2022. Fewer errors, but more stereotypes? the effect of model size on gender bias. In *Proceedings of the 4th*

Workshop on Gender Bias in Natural Language Processing (GeBNLP), pages 112–120, Seattle, Washington. Association for Computational Linguistics.

Hugo Touvron, Thibaut Lavril, Gautier Izacard, Xavier Martinet, Marie-Anne Lachaux, Timothée Lacroix, Baptiste Rozière, Naman Goyal, Eric Hambro, Faisal Azhar, et al. 2023a. Llama: Open and efficient foundation language models. *arXiv preprint arXiv:2302.13971*.

Hugo Touvron, Louis Martin, Kevin Stone, Peter Albert, Amjad Almahairi, Yasmine Babaei, Nikolay Bashlykov, Soumya Batra, Prajjwal Bhargava, Shruti Bhosale, et al. 2023b. Llama 2: Open foundation and fine-tuned chat models. *arXiv preprint arXiv:2307.09288*.

Alex Wang, Amanpreet Singh, Julian Michael, Felix Hill, Omer Levy, and Samuel Bowman. 2018. GLUE: A multi-task benchmark and analysis platform for natural language understanding. In *Proceedings of the 2018 EMNLP Workshop BlackboxNLP: Analyzing and Interpreting Neural Networks for NLP*, pages 353–355, Brussels, Belgium. Association for Computational Linguistics.

Alex Wang, Amanpreet Singh, Julian Michael, Felix Hill, Omer Levy, and Samuel R. Bowman. 2019. Glue: A multi-task benchmark and analysis platform for natural language understanding.

Mei Wang and Weihong Deng. 2019. Mitigate bias in face recognition using skewness-aware reinforcement learning.

Alex Warstadt, Amanpreet Singh, and Samuel R. Bowman. 2019. Neural network acceptability judgments. *Transactions of the Association for Computational Linguistics*, 7:625–641.

Adina Williams, Nikita Nangia, and Samuel Bowman. 2018. A broad-coverage challenge corpus for sentence understanding through inference. In *Proceedings of the 2018 Conference of the North American Chapter of the Association for Computational Linguistics: Human Language Technologies, Volume 1 (Long Papers)*, pages 1112–1122, New Orleans, Louisiana. Association for Computational Linguistics.

Weilin Xu, David Evans, and Yanjun Qi. 2018. Feature squeezing: Detecting adversarial examples in deep neural networks. In *Proceedings 2018 Network and Distributed System Security Symposium*. Internet Society.

Fabio Massimo Zanzotto, Andrea Santilli, Leonardo Ranaldi, Dario Onorati, Pierfrancesco Tommasino, and Francesca Fallucchi. 2020. KERMIT: Complementing transformer architectures with encoders of explicit syntactic interpretations. In *Proceedings of the 2020 Conference on Empirical Methods in Natural Language Processing (EMNLP)*, pages 256–267, Online. Association for Computational Linguistics.

Susan Zhang, Stephen Roller, Naman Goyal, Mikel Artetxe, Moya Chen, Shuohui Chen, Christopher Dewan, Mona Diab, Xian Li, Xi Victoria Lin, Todor Mihaylov, Myle Ott, Sam Shleifer, Kurt Shuster, Daniel Simig, Punit Singh Koura, Anjali Sridhar, Tianlu Wang, and Luke Zettlemoyer. 2022. Opt: Open pretrained transformer language models.

Jieyu Zhao, Tianlu Wang, Mark Yatskar, Ryan Cotterell, Vicente Ordonez, and Kai-Wei Chang. 2019. Gender bias in contextualized word embeddings. In *Proceedings of the 2019 Conference of the North American Chapter of the Association for Computational Linguistics: Human Language Technologies, Volume 1 (Long and Short Papers)*, pages 629–634, Minneapolis, Minnesota. Association for Computational Linguistics.

Jieyu Zhao, Yichao Zhou, Zeyu Li, Wei Wang, and Kai-Wei Chang. 2018. Learning gender-neutral word embeddings. In *Proceedings of the 2018 Conference on Empirical Methods in Natural Language Processing*, pages 4847–4853, Brussels, Belgium. Association for Computational Linguistics.

Compositional Structured Explanation Generation with Dynamic Modularized Reasoning

Xiyan Fu
Dept. of Computational Linguistics
Heidelberg University
fu@cl.uni-heidelberg.de

Anette Frank
Dept. of Computational Linguistics
Heidelberg University
frank@cl.uni-heidelberg.de

Abstract

In this work, we propose a new task, *compositional structured explanation generation* (CSEG), to facilitate research on compositional generalization in reasoning. Despite the success of language models in solving reasoning tasks, their compositional generalization capabilities are under-researched. Our new CSEG task tests a model's ability to generalize from generating entailment trees with a limited number of inference steps – to *more steps*, focusing on the length and shapes of entailment trees. CSEG is challenging in requiring both *reasoning* and *compositional generalization* abilities, and by being framed as a *generation* task. Besides the CSEG task, we propose a new *dynamic modularized* reasoning model, MORSE, that factorizes the inference process into modules, where each module represents a functional unit. We adopt *modularized self-attention* to dynamically select and route inputs to dedicated heads, which specializes them to specific functions. Using CSEG, we compare MORSE to models from prior work. Our analyses show that the task is challenging, but that the dynamic reasoning modules of MORSE are effective, showing competitive compositional generalization abilities in a generation setting.[1]

1 Introduction

Large-scale language models (Raffel et al., 2019; Chung et al., 2022; Touvron et al., 2023) have shown remarkable performance on reasoning tasks, such as reading comprehension (Rajpurkar et al., 2018), natural language inference (Williams et al., 2018), story generation (Mostafazadeh et al., 2016), etc. However, Russin et al. (2020); Mitchell (2021); Yuan et al. (2023) argued that these models lack human-like reasoning capabilities.

Humans excel in *compositional generalization* (Hupkes et al., 2020), a capacity to combine an inventory of known constituents to predict larger

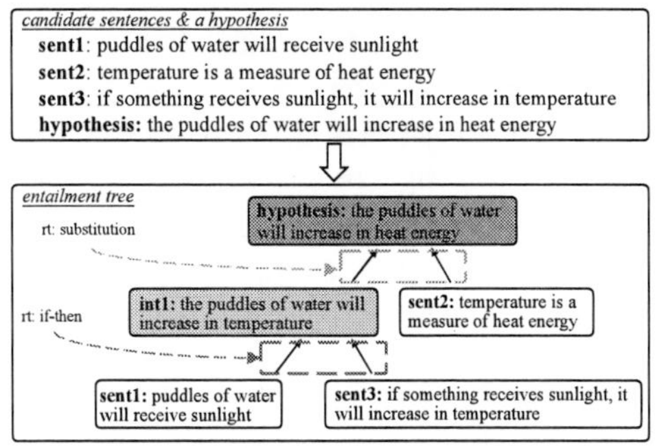

Figure 1: Structured explanation generation: generate an entailment tree including intermediate nodes (grey) for a hypothesis (green) and given candidate sentences. Each reasoning step (sent1 & sent3 $\rightarrow$ int1) is independent and belongs to one of six reasoning types (rt).

compounds, during reasoning. For example, humans who understand calculation constituents, e.g., subtraction *sub(X,Y)* and mixed addition-subtraction operations *sub(X, add(Y, Z))*, can solve larger compounds, e.g., *sub(W, sub(X, add(Y, Z)))*.

Various studies (Hudson and Manning, 2019; Goodwin et al., 2020; Yanaka et al., 2020; Liu et al., 2022) have explored compositional generalization abilities in reasoning tasks. But, these works focus on compositionality units manifesting on the word level and involving specific linguistic phenomena, and neglect inferential processes holding between sentences. But *sentence*-level composition can enhance the capacity of models to execute complex contextual reasoning.

To fill this gap, we propose a new task, *compositional structured explanation generation, CSEG*. CSEG is a new setting built on SEG (Dalvi et al., 2021), a task for models to generate a multi-step entailment tree – given a hypothesis and candidate sentences. The tree indicates how the hypothesis follows from the text. Fig. 1 shows an example. Each step (e.g., sent1 & sent3 $\rightarrow$ int1) represents a multi-premise textual inference (Lai et al.,

[1] https://github.com/xiyan524/MORSE

*Proceedings of the 13th Joint Conference on Lexical and Computational Semantics (*SEM 2024)*, pages 385 - 401
June 20-21, 2024 ©2024 Association for Computational Linguistics

2017), belonging to one of six reasoning types, such as if-then (it) and substitution (subs) (see Appendix A.1 and A.3 for examples). We consider each reasoning type as a *constituent unit.* To test compositional generalization in reasoning, our new task CSEG requires models to generalize from entailment trees with a *limited* number of reasoning steps to trees involving *more* steps. For example, a model is expected to generate a larger compound (entailment tree) with more reasoning steps, e.g., c_3: $subs(subs(it(p_1, p_2) \rightarrow h_1, p_3) \rightarrow h_2, p_4) \rightarrow h_3$, by combining known constituents c_1: $subs(it(p_1, p_2) \rightarrow h_1, p_3) \rightarrow h_2$ and c_2: $subs(p_1, p_2) \rightarrow h$, where c_1 replaces p_1 in c_2). Here, compositionality units, i.e., reasoning types, operate on the *sentence* level and involve reasoning components.

Our new CSEG task requires: i) *reasoning* capabilities, to infer new conclusions from existing information; and ii) *compositional generalization* capability, to generalize to unseen compounds using previously learned constituents. Recent efforts (Dalvi et al., 2021; Saha et al., 2020; Tafjord et al., 2021) aimed to improve reasoning abilities, while ignoring the compositional generalization capacity. Existing symbolic-based approaches (Martínez-Gómez et al., 2017; Gupta et al., 2019; Le et al., 2022) used multiple modules that each perform unique types of reasoning, endowing models with strong compositionality. But they rely on pre-defined reasoning rules and need training data for each pre-defined module. Inspired by this, we propose a *dynamically modularized* reasoning model MORSE. Our model simulates the symbolic process by specializing Transformer self-attention heads to what we call *dynamic modules*. We design a modularized self-attention mechanism that dynamically selects and routes inputs to dedicated modularized heads, specializing them to specific functions. The dynamics embodied in MORSE through its self-assembling modules makes it applicable to multiple datasets without pre-defined knowledge and extend to novel inference types.

Our main contributions are:

i) We propose a new compositional structured explanation *generation* task, which aims to explore *compositional generalization* capabilities in reasoning. It requires models to generalize from entailment trees with a *limited* number of inference steps to *more* steps.

ii) We design a novel dynamically modularized reasoning model that specializes transformer heads to specific functions, by *dynamically* selecting related inputs to dedicated heads.

iii) Experiments on two benchmarks targeting generalization over proof lengths and shapes demonstrate MORSE's advanced compositional generalization abilities.

2 Related Work

Generalization in Reasoning Despite the success of language models in solving reasoning tasks, their generalization abilities have attracted attention, e.g., length generalization (Clark et al., 2020; Wu et al., 2021; Anil et al., 2022), compositional generalization (Liu et al., 2022), domain generalization (Niu et al., 2023), etc. In this work, we explore compositional generalization in reasoning.

Compositional generalization has been researched for decades (Fodor and Pylyshyn, 1988; Marcus, 2003; Lake and Baroni, 2018), including two significant properties: productivity and systematicity (Hupkes et al., 2020). Among these, *productivity* is similar to length generalization, in that both evaluate generalization to deeper reasoning chains. But for evaluating productivity, primitive units needed for solving deeper samples must have been learned during training. In contrast to the related length-generalization work of Clark et al. (2020), our CSEG task aims to evaluate productivity in a *structured* compositional generalization reasoning task. We therefore guarantee that primitive units (rule types) needed for solving deeper samples have been learned in training. Importantly, we frame CSEG as a generation task, which unlike classification settings as in Clark et al. (2020), makes it harder for models to exploit shortcuts.

Recently, there has been renewed interest in exploring compositional generalization in reasoning tasks. Johnson et al. (2017); Hudson and Manning (2019); Bogin et al. (2021); Gao et al. (2022) proposed challenging compositional tasks in visual QA. Liu et al. (2022) designed compositional questions for QA and found even the strongest model struggled with these challenging questions. Other works probed the compositional abilities of models in natural language inference (Geiger et al., 2020; Goodwin et al., 2020; Yanaka et al., 2020, 2021; Fu and Frank, 2023, 2024), focusing on specific linguistic phenomena, such as quantifiers, negation, or predicate replacements. I.e., they investigate compositionality in phenomena manifesting at the word level, in contrast to inferential processes holding between sentences.

To fill this gap, we examine compositional generalization in a multi-step entailment tree generation task, where different inference rules need to be composed. Concurrent work (Saparov et al., 2023) also concentrates on sentence-level compositionality in reasoning, but is limited in using a synthetic dataset. In comparison, we employ both natural language and synthetic data, and introduce a new model, with potential for further improvement, that can serve as a strong baseline for the task.

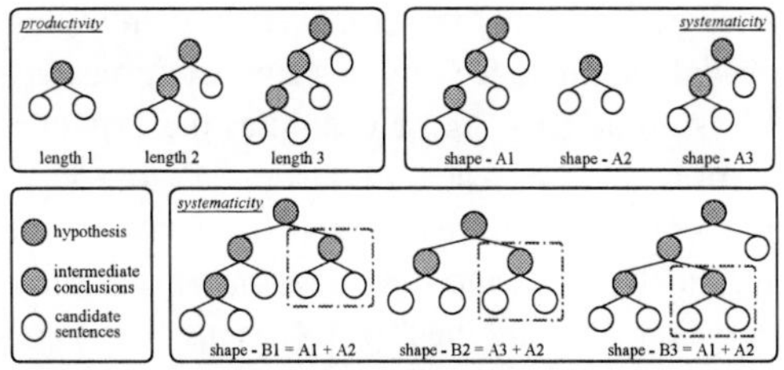

Figure 2: Entailment trees including different lengths and shapes for compositional generalization testing.

Neural-Symbolic and Neural Methods Prior works show that symbolic approaches (Angeli and Manning, 2014; Mineshima et al., 2015; Martínez-Gómez et al., 2017) that adopt pre-defined inference rules to establish derivations through iterative reasoning, endow models with strong compositionality. But being dependent on pre-defined rules, the models are limited to well-defined tasks. Recently, Yi et al. (2018); Yin et al. (2018); Li et al. (2020); Jiang et al. (2021) used neural networks to map raw signals to symbolic representations and subsequently performed symbolic reasoning to make predictions. As symbolic reasoning is brittle, novel works based on Neural Modular Networks (NMN) (Andreas et al., 2016; Hu et al., 2017) combine individual neural modules endowed with *specialized* reasoning capabilities. E.g., Jiang and Bansal (2019); Gupta et al. (2019) designed various modules in an NMN to perform unique types of reasoning in end-to-end manner. Similarly, Khot et al. (2021, 2023) proposed a Text Module Network for complex reasoning tasks, where each module is an existing QA system. However, all these approaches require prior knowledge and rely on brittle symbolic transfer, to subsequently deploy pre-defined modules for each sub-task, and well-designed modules require substantial extra training data. Finally, symbolic reasoning methods are typically driven by weak supervision, given the lack of intermediate labels. This can result in error accumulation and time-consuming learning. To address these challenges, we propose a model with *dynamic modules* that make specific module functions more independent from prior knowledge, to endow models with greater flexibility when handling new tasks.

Our work may seem related to Mixture-of-Expert (MoE) models (Jacobs et al., 1991; Lepikhin et al., 2021; Li et al., 2023) that aim to decompose tasks by composing separate networks, each of which is trained to handle a subset of a complete set of training cases. By contrast, MORSE focuses on decomposition and combining primitive units *in individual samples*. In addition, it uses multiple heads of the existing Transformer cell, without inducing extra training parameters (such as FNN layers of MoE) – which has higher efficiency.

3 Task Setup

Background The Structured Explanation Generation (SEG) task (Dalvi et al., 2021) requires a system to generate a multi-step entailment tree given a hypothesis and candidate sentences. The tree serves as a structured explanation of how presented evidences leads to a conclusion.

Input to the task are i) a hypothesis H, a declarative statement and ii) a set S of candidate sentences that express relevant knowledge needed to infer H. Outputs are valid entailment trees with intermediate conclusions not contained in S (Fig. 1). The entailment trees are encoded as linear sequences that can be generated by a generative model. The tree depicted in Fig. 1 would be represented as:

sent1 & sent2 → int1: the puddles of water will increase in temperature; sent2 & int1 → hypot

Leaves $sent_i$ are sentences from the candidate set S, and $hypot$ is the tree's root, given by the hypothesis H. int_j are inferred intermediate conclusions that provide the basis for further reasoning steps.

Compositional Generalization Testing To examine compositional reasoning capabilities, we partition our benchmark datasets along two generalization properties: *productivity* and *systematicity*.

Productivity–Length evaluates systems on longer proof lengths than they have been trained on, where both train and test sequences are composed of identical primitives. Hence, we rearrange the data by proof length, i.e., number of intermediate nodes in each tree (including hypothesis node). We partition the data into: i) primitive entailment trees of length one or two; ii) compositional entailment trees of length three.[2] Fig. 2 shows examples.

Systematicity–Shape examines the capability of (re)combining known constituents to a larger compound. Hence, we rearrange the dataset by tree shapes. To select appropriate data, we proceed as follows: we i) limit the inference steps of each tree to four – given that larger steps present an unsolved challenge for existing neural models (Table A.3, Dalvi et al. (2021)); ii) extract the tree shapes from candidate data; iii) find there exist only six different shapes, depicted as *shape-** in Fig. 2 (details in Appendix A.2); iv) select, among six possible shapes, simple structures (Shape-A*) as primitives, and more complex (compositional) ones (Shape-B*) as compositions for generalization testing. We guarantee that compositional shapes are built from primitive shapes: B1=A1+A2, B2=A3+A2, B3=A1+A2. In Figure 2, we use dashed squares to single out one primitive shape for each compositional shape.

4 MORSE: Dynamic Modularized Reasoning Model

We introduce our Dynamic Modularized Reasoning Model MORSE that generates compositional structured explanations. MORSE contains: i) an encoder consisting of original and modularized transformer blocks to perform reasoning; ii) a decoder using original transformer blocks to generate the entailment tree structure. See the overview in Fig. 3.

4.1 Module-enhanced encoder

We concatenate candidate sentences S and the hypothesis H into an input sequence. For each sentence in S, we add a prefix $sent*$ following Dalvi et al. (2021). Thus the example in Fig.1 is represented as a sequence of length n: 'sent1: puddles of water will receive sunlight; sent2: temperature is a ...; ...; hypothesis: the puddles of water will increase in heat energy'. For each token x_i, we adopt an embedding layer to generate its representation e_i, i.e., a summation of token embedding, position embedding and segment embedding. An encoder subsequently encodes input representations.

Fig. 3.A shows that MORSE's encoder consists of *Transformer* blocks for lower layers and *Modularized Transformer* blocks for higher layers: i) Transformer blocks allow the model to focus on the representation of words themselves (Raganato and Tiedemann, 2018; Jawahar et al., 2019); ii) Modularized Transformer blocks perform modularized reasoning, where each module is encouraged to learn a different inference function.

Transformer All Transformer blocks consist of two sub-layers: a multi-head attention layer and a fully connected feed-forward network. Each sublayer is followed by layer normalization (Ba et al., 2016) and a residual connection (He et al., 2016). In the multi-head attention sub-layer, sequential inputs are projected to different representation subspaces (different heads) in parallel; the layer then performs self-attention (Vaswani et al., 2017) in each head. The heads' output values are concatenated and again projected, resulting in final values.

In MORSE, we adopt p Transformer blocks in lower layers, aiming to capture the representation of words in their syntactic context. Given token embeddings e_1, ..., e_n of a sequential input of length n, we use p Transformer blocks to encode them and generate corresponding hidden states s_1^p, ..., s_n^p.

Modularized Transformer We construct a Modularized Transformer block based on the Transformer. The difference is that we factorize the encoding process, by modularizing the Transformer so that each module can be tailored to a specific function. We implement this design by using Transformer 'heads'. The process of *modularization* is illustrated in Fig. 3 B.1: the modularized Transformer block contains a modularized attention layer, which consists of multiple specialized heads h_i. E.g., h_0 to h_5 are modularized heads that may express different inference functions. The remaining heads $h_{6,7}$ work as usual, offering space to model general knowledge not covered by the modularized heads. With such modularization, we expect that each module will specialize for specific responsibilities, further endowing MORSE with more flexibility to perform different inference functions during reasoning.

To allow a modularized head h_i to specialize for specific functions, we construct dynamic masks $m_i \in [0, 1]^n$ to select sequential inputs of similar kinds to pass through h_i. Specifically, we define several vectors of trainable parameters for each module as a latent representation of the module's function, e.g., $rep_{h_i} \in \mathbb{R}^d$ for h_i. Simultaneously, we adopt a linear projection on candidate input hidden states s_1, ..., s_n to derive their functional

[2]We only test length three here, given the significant performance challenge shown by experiments. However, our setting is a living benchmark, which can be easily extended by future research.

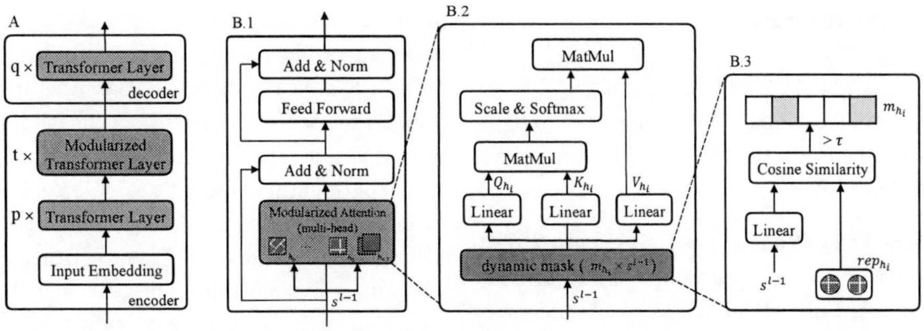

Figure 3: (A) MORSE for entailment tree generation. (B) A series of detailed illustrations of the Modularized Transformer layer. (B.1) Our novel *modularized* multi-head self-attention block. Each head may serve as a module, executing a specific function. (B.2) Computations for a single attention head with dynamic mask m_{h_i}. Self-attention is extended with a dynamic mask to filter out irrelevant input for a module. (B.3) Constructing dynamic mask m_{h_i} using head function representation rep_{h_i} and input hidden states.

representations f_1, ..., $f_n \in \mathbb{R}^d$. Then, we use cosine similarity cos over the input's functional representations f_j and the head's representation rep_{h_i} to calculate a matching coefficient. If it exceeds a threshold τ, MORSE is able to decide if an input word x_j is allowed to join the module h_i. The mask calculation is shown below:

$$m_i^j = \begin{cases} e^{1-cos(rep_{h_i}, f_j)}, & cos(rep_{h_i}, f_j) > \tau \\ 0, & else \end{cases} \tag{1}$$

where the threshold τ is a fixed hyper-parameter. To avoid the vanishing gradient problem, we use $e^{1-cos(*)}$ to represent the mask for a selected word. For unselected words, we ignore their gradient. In this way, we can generate masks m_i for each module h_i dynamically, given sequential inputs and different module objectives.

We further adopt the generated mask m_i for a module h_i in Modularized Self-Attention to filter out unrelated inputs. Fig. 3 B.2 shows the process: we multiply the mask m_i with input hidden states from the previous layer s^{l-1}, where hidden states of unrelated words are set to zero. Then, we generate the query Q_{h_i}, key K_{h_i}, and value V_{h_i} matrices for self-attention by different linear projections based on filtered inputs:

$$\begin{aligned} Q_i, K_i, V_i &= \tilde{s}^{l-1}W_i^Q, \tilde{s}^{l-1}W_i^K, \tilde{s}^{l-1}W_i^V \\ \tilde{s}^{l-1} &= m_{h_i} \times s^{l-1} \end{aligned} \tag{2}$$

where $W_i^Q, W_i^K, W_i^V \in \mathbb{R}^{\,d \times d/k}$ are training parameters, d is the hidden state dimension and k is the number of heads. We then adopt scaled dot-product attention to perform self-attention:

$$a_i = softmax(\frac{Q_i K_i^T}{\sqrt{d_k}})V_i \tag{3}$$

We adopt t Modularized Transformer blocks in deep layers, aiming to perform modularized reasoning. Given input hidden states $s_1^p, ..., s_n^p$ from lower Transformer blocks, the Modularized blocks generate modularized hidden states $s_1^t, ..., s_n^t$.

4.2 Decoder and training

We use a decoder consisting of Transformer blocks to generate the entailment tree structure and intermediate conclusions. The entailment tree is linearized from leaves to the root. For example, the tree in Fig. 1 is represented as *"sent1 & sent2 → int1: the puddles of water will increase in temperature; sent3 & int1 → hypo."* The output sequence generation process is defined as:

$$\begin{aligned} s^l &= block(s^{l-1}, enc\_state), \quad l\epsilon[1, q] \\ p(y_k|y_{<k}) &= softmax(s_k^N W^T) \end{aligned} \tag{4}$$

where s^l is the l_{th} layer computed through Transformer blocks, W^T is the training parameter and k is the decoding step number. We deploy supervised learning with ground truth by minimizing the objective in (5), where M is the maximum length of the generated entailment tree, and H and S are hypothesis and candidate sentences, respectively.

$$L = -\sum_{k=1}^{M} logp(y_k|y_{<k}, H, S) \tag{5}$$

5 Experiments Setup

5.1 Datasets

In this section, we prepare the compositional data from EntailmentBank (EntB) and DBpedia (DBP) for the CSEG task.

EntailmentBank (EntB) by Dalvi et al. (2021) contains multiple-choice questions and candidate sentences from the grad-school level science datasets ARC (Clark et al., 2018) and WorldTree (Jansen et al., 2018; Xie et al., 2020). 1,840 entailment trees each show how a hypothesis is entailed by a small number of relevant sentences. Each step in the tree represents an entailment, i.e., the conclusion expressed in each intermediate node follows from the content of its immediate children. The individual entailment steps instantiate six common reasoning types (details in A.1) [3]. EntB contains three tasks. We focus on Task1, with only correct inputs in S, as we focus on generalization testing.

DBpedia by Saeed et al. (2021) is a synthetic dataset that was re-generated from the **RuleBert** (Saeed et al., 2021) dataset[4]. We extracted six distinct logic rules mined from the DBpedia knowledge graph and instantiated examples with a varying number of variables following 'Chaining of Rule Execution' in RuleBert (cf. A.3). The reasoning chain provides a structured explanation: each intermediate node is a conclusion inferred from immediate children using a logic inference rule.

Compositional Generalization Testing Data To construct the dataset for systematicity and productivity testing in reasoning explanation generation, we rearrange the partitions of the above benchmarks to focus on *length* and *shape* of entailment trees following §3 (see A.4 for details). We construct i) EntB(ank)-L(ength) and DBP-L(ength) based on entailment tree length; and ii) EntB-Sh(ape) based on entailment tree shape. Since DBpedia does not contain more complex tree shapes, it is ignored in the shape test. For data statistics of the created splits for length and shape testing, see Appendix A.5.

5.2 Experiment Details

Settings Zero-shot compositional generalization is highly non-trivial due to the long generated texts of the compositional samples.[5]. We therefore consider a flexible learning scenario following Bogin et al. (2021); Yin et al. (2021). Specifically, we trained a model (both baselines and MORSE) with primitives, and further fine-tuned the model with a handful of compositional examples to familiarize itself with a complicated space. For data statistics details see Appendix A.5. To provide a comprehensive analysis for future work, we also conducted conventional zero-shot tests, where we trained a model with primitives and tested on compositions directly.

Model MORSE is built on T5-Small/-Large with six/ twelve layers (cf. Dalvi et al. (2021)). For each version, we use, for the lower 30% of layers (i.e., two/four layers), the original Transformer blocks, to derive hidden representations of the input words. The threshold τ for dynamic mask construction we set to 0.1. All models were evaluated on three runs. For further details see Appendix B.

5.3 Baselines

We choose three prior systems for structural explanation generation as baselines, and report comparative results for our new system **MORSE.**[6]

EntailmentWriter (Dalvi et al., 2021) is a T5-based seq-to-seq model that generates a structured explanation (tree) directly. It provides baseline results on EntailmentBank for generating entailment trees for answers to science questions.

PROVER (Saha et al., 2020) jointly answers binary questions over rule-bases and generates the corresponding proofs. The model learns to predict edges corresponding to proof graphs using multiple global constraints. Since PROVER focuses on edge prediction, we only evaluate the tree structure.

ProofWriter-Iterative (Tafjord et al., 2021) iteratively generates 1-step conclusions and proofs, adds intermediate conclusions to the context and assembles a final proof chain from 1-step fragments.

5.4 Automatic Evaluation Metrics

We adopt the evaluation metrics proposed by Dalvi et al. (2021) for the structured explanation generation task. Evaluation is addressed in two steps:

[3]The number of reasoning types is a flexible parameter depending on the dataset.

[4]https://github.com/MhmdSaiid/RuleBert

[5]The difficulty is primarily due to the decoder trained by maximum likelihood, which relies heavily on the distributional characteristics of the dataset and assigns low probabilities to unseen combinations in test (Holtzman et al., 2020)

[6]For reference, the results obtained by MORSE on the original structured explanation generation task SEG are reported in Appendix D.

Models	EntailmentBank-Length (EntB-L)						DBpedia-Length (DBP-L)					
	Leaves		Steps		Intermediates		Leaves		Steps		Intermediates	
	F1	AllCorrect	F1	AllCorrect	F1	AllCorrect	F1	AllCorrect	F1	AllCorrect	F1	AllCorrect
ProofWriter-It.	91.86(0.08)	84.55(0.78)	35.97(2.37)	18.81(2.76)	42.93(1.23)	11.88(2.14)	90.66(0.18)	93.09(0.72)	76.49(0.86)	75.44(1.04)	85.92(1.92)	76.73(2.24)
PROVER	-	-	39.27(2.65)	24.75(3.24)	-	-	-	-	79.88(0.98)	76.98(1.37)	-	-
EntWriter (T5-Small)	99.78(0.12)	98.02(1.06)	40.59(2.97)	29.70(2.92)	48.24(1.12)	22.77(2.25)	99.92(0.15)	99.49(0.67)	82.01(1.21)	79.28(1.52)	87.05(2.23)	78.26(2.37)
MORSE (T5-Small)	**99.89**(0.08)	**99.01**(0.62)	**44.22**(2.14)	**32.67**(2.32)	**50.66**(0.68)	**25.74**(1.92)	**99.96**(0.27)	**99.74**(0.84)	**82.27**(0.16)	**80.31**(0.18)	**87.72**(1.82)	**79.80**(1.87)
EntWriter (T5-Large)	99.78(0.11)	98.02(0.99)	52.80(3.35)	40.92(3.18)	56.62(1.06)	36.63(2.40)	99.36(0.13)	95.52(0.91)	82.49(1.09)	80.11(1.43)	88.98(2.16)	83.89(2.15)
MORSE (T5-Large)	**99.82**(0.06)	**98.68**(0.57)	**53.31**(2.26)	**42.57**(2.62)	**57.78**(0.81)	**37.29**(2.06)	**99.53**(0.11)	**96.68**(0.73)	**86.79**(0.12)	**83.76**(0.18)	**92.62**(1.70)	**86.70**(1.97)
EntWriter-0-shot (T5-L)	97.06(0.66)	85.73(1.61)	18.44(1.18)	-	24.21(2.22)	-	**90.09**(0.42)	29.27(0.2)	16.94(1.68)	-	32.43(0.50)	-
MORSE-0-shot (T5-L)	**97.89**(0.74)	**86.83**(1.52)	**19.14**(0.89)	-	**25.42**(1.49)	-	89.82(0.32)	**30.05**(0.90)	**18.41**(1.09)	-	**33.45**(0.22)	-

Table 1: Results on EntailmentBank-L(ength) and DBpedia-L(ength) for compositional generalization evaluation. All modules are evaluated with 3 rounds, we show mean accuracy (std).

1) **Alignment** Exact matching between a predicted (T_{pred}) and a human-labeled (T_{gold}) entailment tree ignores the different organizations among tree nodes and leads to an inaccurate evaluation score. To admit semantic variation, all T_{pred} nodes are (greedily) aligned to nodes in T_{gold} using the sent* labels of leaf nodes, followed by Jaccard similarity calculation for intermediate nodes.

2) **Score** Once aligned, three metrics measure the degree of similarity of T_{pred} and T_{gold}: (a) *Leaves* evaluates if the generated tree selects the correct leaf sentences from the candidate set S. (b) *Steps* assesses if the individual entailment steps in the tree are structurally correct. This is the case if for a pair of aligned intermediate nodes, both children have identical labels (sent* or int*) in T_{pred} and T_{gold}. (c) *Intermediates* judges if all generated intermediate conclusions are correct. BLEURT (Sellam et al., 2020) with the threshold 0.28 [7] is applied for intermediate conclusion evaluation. For each metric, we compute an F1 score, and an 'AllCorrect' score for exact tree matching (F1=1).

6 Results

6.1 Overall Results

Results on Length Composition Table 1 displays the results of MORSE using the small vs. large T5 model as backbone, on the EntB-L and DBP-L datasets. Note that PROVER (Saha et al., 2020), EntailmentWriter (EntWriter) (Dalvi et al., 2021) and MORSE generate the complete proof chain from the input candidate set in one go, while ProofWriter-Iterative (PW-Iterative) (Tafjord et al., 2021) generates one-step implications iteratively. We find that on both datasets, and for both T5 model sizes, MORSE achieves superior results compared to all baselines, especially on 'Steps' (structural correctness) and 'Intermediates' (intermediate conclusions). 'Leaves' is not a challenge

[7]The threshold is determined following (Dalvi et al., 2021).

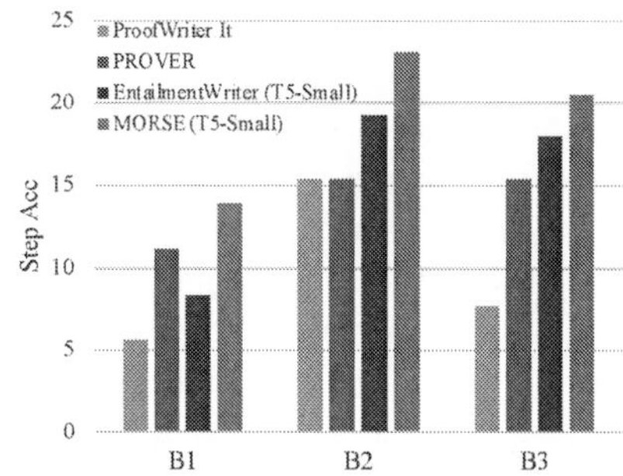

Figure 4: Results on EntB-Sh, testing for compositional generalization, i.e., systematicity.

in our Task1 setup, but even here, MORSE outperforms, being able to integrate almost all inputs. The comparison with the most competitive system EntWriter, in equivalent T5 model sizes, still shows superior performance of MORSE with both model sizes. We conclude that the advance of MORSE is not restricted to small models, but persists with models hosting richer knowledge. Compared to DBP-L, the advance of MORSE over the other baselines is stronger on EntB-L (e.g., +2.97 vs. +1.03 for 'Steps Acc'). This is explained by the synthetic (template-based) nature of the DBP-L dataset, which shows little linguistic variety.

To provide a comprehensive evaluation of the proposed new setting for future research, we further challenge MORSE by exposing it to a *zero-shot test* for length composition. Here, models trained only for trees up to depth two will directly receive inputs for proof trees of length three. We mainly compare with the most competitive system, EntWriter. In this evaluation, we ignore the 'AllCorrect' scores for 'Steps' and 'Intermediate' outputs, given the difficulty of these generation tasks in low training regimes. The last two lines in Table 1 show the results. MORSE achieves superior performance (at least +1 point improvement for zero-shot) for most evaluation categories, or else comparable results

Models	Steps		Intermediates	
	F1	Acc	F1	Acc
MORSE (T5-Small)	44.22	32.67	50.66	25.74
freeze rep_embed	43.57	31.68 (-0.99)	50.66	25.74 (-0)
+ module	41.58	29.70 (-2.97)	49.13	23.76 (-1.98)
+ masking	38.28	25.74 (-6.93)	46.62	20.79 (-4.95)

Table 2: Ablation of MORSE components, freeze: **rep_embed**: the representation of module rep_i; **module**: parameters in specialized module; **masking**: dynamic mask in Fig. 3. d. Brackets: decrease in accuracy.

(F1 for 'Leaves'). We conclude that our model MORSE [8] outperforms other baselines in both zero-shot and fine-tuning scenarios.

Results on Shape Composition Fig. 4 displays the results for generalization testing on shapes.[9] MORSE clearly surpasses the step accuracy of all other baselines for all tested shape configurations. Note that shape B1 is most difficult for all systems. Entailment trees are linearized in bottom-up order. While compositions in shape B2 and B3 happen at the lowest tree level, composition in B1 happens at a higher tree level, combining trees of unequal depths. We hypothesize that combining trees of unequal lengths at higher levels makes the task more challenging compared to lower levels, given that composition at higher levels requires a more precise representation of previous reasoning steps (see Appendix C for more details).

6.2 Analysis of Modularization

Ablation Study To gain more insight into the impact of specific components of MORSE on generalization, we run an ablation study on EntB-L during *fine-tuning*. We first freeze all module representations rep_{h_i} (*rep_embed*). Further, we freeze parameters in each specialized module (*+module*) (cf. Fig. 3.B.2). By freezing these parameters, we aim to preserve the function of different modules and expect a comparative performance by reusing learned functions. In the third ablation, we freeze the parameters of the dynamic mask process *+masking* (cf. Fig. 3.B.3), which affects the dynamic mask of inputs to different modules. Results in Table 2 indicate that the first two settings do not affect results much, which suggests that each module has roughly learned its specialized functions. But *+mask* incurs large drops, which indicates that

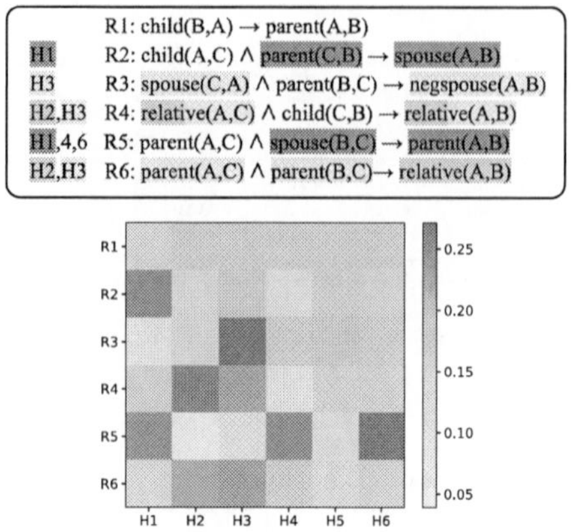

Figure 5: Correlations between reasoning rules R1-6 and module heads H1-6.

masking is significant for the model to adapt to novel configurations. We hypothesize that for generalizing to longer proofs, mask generation helps to connect existing modules.

Correlation Analysis To further explore the effects of modularization in MORSE, we conduct an experiment on DBP-L by *masking individual heads* only in testing. We select samples that: i) contain three reasoning steps, ii) made correct predictions for the first two reasoning steps, but iii) predict the 3rd step incorrectly in case a certain head is removed (see A.6 for details). This ensures that the reasoning rule for the 3rd step is affected by a specific removed head. We count samples that are affected by removing head j for each rule R_i, denoted as $n_j^{R_i}$. In case a model has T heads, we normalize affected sample counts of R_i across all heads, i.e., $n_j^{R_i} / \sum_{j=1}^{T} n_j^{R_i}$. This allows us to align heads and rules as shown in Fig. 5.

The heatmap shows the correlations between rules and heads, where R2-H1, R3-H3, R4-H2/H3, R5-H1/H4/H6 and R6-H2/H3 stand out. In the upper part of Fig. 5 we list all inference rules from DBP-L, aligned with the heads they are strongly correlated with, according to the heatmap. We find that heads are correlated with some rules roughly: 1) H4 and H6 are quite similar, and both prefer R5. 2) H1 prefers R2, but is distracted by R5. This is likely because R2 and R5 are similar by changing 'parent' to 'child' between A and C. 3) H2 prefers R4 and R6, which both use the predicate 'relative' and share the same relation by changing 'parent' to 'child' between B and C. 4) H3 prefers R3, but is distracted by R4 and R6. A plausible reason could be configurations of R3, R4 and R6 are similar

[8]Experiments on more powerful backbones are provided in Appendix F.

[9]Having seen linear behaviour of different model sizes in Table 1, we further on use T5-Small versions of MORSE and EntWriter, unless we explicitly say otherwise.

as they share similar predicates ('spouse' in R3, 'relative' in R4 and 'parent' in R6).

7 Conclusion

We present a new setup for explanation generation to facilitate compositional generalization in reasoning research. Inspired by highly compositional symbolic systems, we propose a novel modularized reasoning model MORSE that factorizes reasoning processes into a combination of *dynamically* specializing modules. Our results establish MORSE as a strong baseline for the task, using two benchmarks. A future direction is to learn how to initialize more modules on demand.

8 Limitations

The dynamic modularized reasoning model MORSE in its current state is limited by assuming a pre-defined number of modules, for reasoning in various scenarios. The number of modules in MORSE interacts with the ability of the model when modularizing a given number of potential logic rules in a dataset or task. A given available number of functional units can simplify the reasoning process, enabling the model to focus on module re-use similar to how a symbolic system does, instead of distracting from confirming module function granularity.

9 Acknowledgments

We are grateful to anonymous meta-reviewers for their valuable comments that have helped to improve this paper. We also thank Wei Liu and Wan Le for their valuable feedback on drafts of this paper. This work has been supported through a scholarship provided by the Heidelberg Institute for Theoretical Studies gGmbH.

References

Jacob Andreas, Marcus Rohrbach, Trevor Darrell, and Dan Klein. 2016. Neural module networks. In *Proceedings of the IEEE conference on computer vision and pattern recognition*, pages 39–48.

Gabor Angeli and Christopher D. Manning. 2014. NaturalLI: Natural logic inference for common sense reasoning. In *Proceedings of the 2014 Conference on Empirical Methods in Natural Language Processing (EMNLP)*, pages 534–545, Doha, Qatar. Association for Computational Linguistics.

Cem Anil, Yuhuai Wu, Anders Andreassen, Aitor Lewkowycz, Vedant Misra, Vinay Ramasesh, Ambrose Slone, Guy Gur-Ari, Ethan Dyer, and Behnam Neyshabur. 2022. Exploring length generalization in large language models. *Advances in Neural Information Processing Systems*, 35:38546–38556.

Jimmy Lei Ba, Jamie Ryan Kiros, and Geoffrey E Hinton. 2016. Layer normalization. *arXiv preprint arXiv:1607.06450*.

Ben Bogin, Shivanshu Gupta, Matt Gardner, and Jonathan Berant. 2021. COVR: A test-bed for visually grounded compositional generalization with real images. In *Proceedings of the 2021 Conference on Empirical Methods in Natural Language Processing*, pages 9824–9846, Online and Punta Cana, Dominican Republic. Association for Computational Linguistics.

Hyung Won Chung, Le Hou, Shayne Longpre, Barret Zoph, Yi Tay, William Fedus, Eric Li, Xuezhi Wang, Mostafa Dehghani, Siddhartha Brahma, et al. 2022. Scaling instruction-finetuned language models. *arXiv preprint arXiv:2210.11416*.

Peter Clark, Isaac Cowhey, Oren Etzioni, Tushar Khot, Ashish Sabharwal, Carissa Schoenick, and Oyvind Tafjord. 2018. Think you have solved question answering? try arc, the ai2 reasoning challenge. *arXiv preprint arXiv:1803.05457*.

Peter Clark, Oyvind Tafjord, and Kyle Richardson. 2020. Transformers as soft reasoners over language. In *Proceedings of the Twenty-Ninth International Joint Conference on Artificial Intelligence, IJCAI-20*, pages 3882–3890. International Joint Conferences on Artificial Intelligence Organization.

Bhavana Dalvi, Peter Jansen, Oyvind Tafjord, Zhengnan Xie, Hannah Smith, Leighanna Pipatanangkura, and Peter Clark. 2021. Explaining answers with entailment trees. In *Proceedings of the 2021 Conference on Empirical Methods in Natural Language Processing*, pages 7358–7370, Online and Punta Cana, Dominican Republic. Association for Computational Linguistics.

Jerry A Fodor and Zenon W Pylyshyn. 1988. Connectionism and cognitive architecture: A critical analysis. *Cognition*, 28(1-2):3–71.

Xiyan Fu and Anette Frank. 2023. SETI: Systematicity evaluation of textual inference. In *Findings of the Association for Computational Linguistics: ACL 2023*, pages 4101–4114, Toronto, Canada. Association for Computational Linguistics.

Xiyan Fu and Anette Frank. 2024. Exploring continual learning of compositional generalization in NLI. *Transations of the Association for Computational Linguistics*.

Difei Gao, Ruiping Wang, Shiguang Shan, and Xilin Chen. 2022. Cric: A vqa dataset for compositional reasoning on vision and commonsense. *IEEE Transactions on Pattern Analysis and Machine Intelligence*.

Atticus Geiger, Kyle Richardson, and Christopher Potts. 2020. Neural natural language inference models partially embed theories of lexical entailment and negation. In *Proceedings of the Third BlackboxNLP Workshop on Analyzing and Interpreting Neural Networks for NLP*, pages 163–173, Online. Association for Computational Linguistics.

Emily Goodwin, Koustuv Sinha, and Timothy J. O'Donnell. 2020. Probing linguistic systematicity. In *Proceedings of the 58th Annual Meeting of the Association for Computational Linguistics*, pages 1958–1969, Online. Association for Computational Linguistics.

Nitish Gupta, Kevin Lin, Dan Roth, Sameer Singh, and Matt Gardner. 2019. Neural module networks for reasoning over text. In *International Conference on Learning Representations*.

Kaiming He, Xiangyu Zhang, Shaoqing Ren, and Jian Sun. 2016. Deep residual learning for image recognition. In *Proceedings of the IEEE conference on computer vision and pattern recognition*, pages 770–778.

Ari Holtzman, Jan Buys, Li Du, Maxwell Forbes, and Yejin Choi. 2020. The curious case of neural text degeneration. In *International Conference on Learning Representations*.

Ronghang Hu, Jacob Andreas, Marcus Rohrbach, Trevor Darrell, and Kate Saenko. 2017. Learning to reason: End-to-end module networks for visual question answering. In *Proceedings of the IEEE international conference on computer vision*, pages 804–813.

Drew A Hudson and Christopher D Manning. 2019. Gqa: A new dataset for real-world visual reasoning and compositional question answering. In *Proceedings of the IEEE/CVF conference on computer vision and pattern recognition*, pages 6700–6709.

Dieuwke Hupkes, Verna Dankers, Mathijs Mul, and Elia Bruni. 2020. Compositionality decomposed: How do neural networks generalise? *Journal of Artificial Intelligence Research*, 67:757–795.

Robert A Jacobs, Michael I Jordan, Steven J Nowlan, and Geoffrey E Hinton. 1991. Adaptive mixtures of local experts. *Neural computation*, 3(1):79–87.

Peter Jansen, Elizabeth Wainwright, Steven Marmorstein, and Clayton Morrison. 2018. WorldTree: A corpus of explanation graphs for elementary science questions supporting multi-hop inference. In *Proceedings of the Eleventh International Conference on Language Resources and Evaluation (LREC 2018)*, Miyazaki, Japan. European Language Resources Association (ELRA).

Ganesh Jawahar, Benoît Sagot, and Djamé Seddah. 2019. What does BERT learn about the structure of language? In *Proceedings of the 57th Annual Meeting of the Association for Computational Linguistics*, pages 3651–3657, Florence, Italy. Association for Computational Linguistics.

Hang Jiang, Sairam Gurajada, Qiuhao Lu, Sumit Neelam, Lucian Popa, Prithviraj Sen, Yunyao Li, and Alexander Gray. 2021. LNN-EL: A neuro-symbolic approach to short-text entity linking. In *Proceedings of the 59th Annual Meeting of the Association for Computational Linguistics and the 11th International Joint Conference on Natural Language Processing (Volume 1: Long Papers)*, pages 775–787, Online. Association for Computational Linguistics.

Yichen Jiang and Mohit Bansal. 2019. Self-assembling modular networks for interpretable multi-hop reasoning. In *Proceedings of the 2019 Conference on Empirical Methods in Natural Language Processing and the 9th International Joint Conference on Natural Language Processing (EMNLP-IJCNLP)*, pages 4474–4484, Hong Kong, China. Association for Computational Linguistics.

Justin Johnson, Bharath Hariharan, Laurens Van Der Maaten, Li Fei-Fei, C Lawrence Zitnick, and Ross Girshick. 2017. Clevr: A diagnostic dataset for compositional language and elementary visual reasoning. In *Proceedings of the IEEE conference on computer vision and pattern recognition*, pages 2901–2910.

Tushar Khot, Daniel Khashabi, Kyle Richardson, Peter Clark, and Ashish Sabharwal. 2021. Text modular networks: Learning to decompose tasks in the language of existing models. In *Proceedings of the 2021 Conference of the North American Chapter of the Association for Computational Linguistics: Human Language Technologies*, pages 1264–1279, Online. Association for Computational Linguistics.

Tushar Khot, Harsh Trivedi, Matthew Finlayson, Yao Fu, Kyle Richardson, Peter Clark, and Ashish Sabharwal. 2023. Decomposed prompting: A modular approach for solving complex tasks. In *International Conference on Learning Representations*.

Diederik P Kingma and Jimmy Ba. 2014. Adam: A method for stochastic optimization. In *International Conference on Learning Representations*.

Alice Lai, Yonatan Bisk, and Julia Hockenmaier. 2017. Natural language inference from multiple premises. In *Proceedings of the Eighth International Joint Conference on Natural Language Processing (Volume 1: Long Papers)*, pages 100–109, Taipei, Taiwan. Asian Federation of Natural Language Processing.

Brenden Lake and Marco Baroni. 2018. Generalization without systematicity: On the compositional skills of sequence-to-sequence recurrent networks. In *International conference on machine learning*, pages 2873–2882. PMLR.

Hung Le, Nancy Chen, and Steven Hoi. 2022. VGNMN: Video-grounded neural module networks for video-grounded dialogue systems. In *Proceedings of the 2022 Conference of the North American Chapter of the Association for Computational Linguistics: Human Language Technologies*, pages 3377–3393, Seattle, United States. Association for Computational Linguistics.

Dmitry Lepikhin, HyoukJoong Lee, Yuanzhong Xu, Dehao Chen, Orhan Firat, Yanping Huang, Maxim Krikun, Noam Shazeer, and Zhifeng Chen. 2021. {GS}hard: Scaling giant models with conditional computation and automatic sharding. In *International Conference on Learning Representations*.

Bo Li, Yifei Shen, Jingkang Yang, Yezhen Wang, Jiawei Ren, Tong Che, Jun Zhang, and Ziwei Liu. 2023. Sparse mixture-of-experts are domain generalizable learners. In *The Eleventh International Conference on Learning Representations*.

Qing Li, Siyuan Huang, Yining Hong, Yixin Chen, Ying Nian Wu, and Song-Chun Zhu. 2020. Closed loop neural-symbolic learning via integrating neural perception, grammar parsing, and symbolic reasoning. In *International Conference on Machine Learning*, pages 5884–5894. PMLR.

Linqing Liu, Patrick Lewis, Sebastian Riedel, and Pontus Stenetorp. 2022. Challenges in generalization in open domain question answering. In *Findings of the Association for Computational Linguistics: NAACL 2022*, pages 2014–2029, Seattle, United States. Association for Computational Linguistics.

Gary F Marcus. 2003. *The algebraic mind: Integrating connectionism and cognitive science*. MIT press.

Pascual Martínez-Gómez, Koji Mineshima, Yusuke Miyao, and Daisuke Bekki. 2017. On-demand injection of lexical knowledge for recognising textual entailment. In *Proceedings of the 15th Conference of the European Chapter of the Association for Computational Linguistics: Volume 1, Long Papers*, pages 710–720, Valencia, Spain. Association for Computational Linguistics.

Koji Mineshima, Pascual Martínez-Gómez, Yusuke Miyao, and Daisuke Bekki. 2015. Higher-order logical inference with compositional semantics. In *Proceedings of the 2015 Conference on Empirical Methods in Natural Language Processing*, pages 2055–2061, Lisbon, Portugal. Association for Computational Linguistics.

Melanie Mitchell. 2021. Abstraction and analogy-making in artificial intelligence. *Annals of the New York Academy of Sciences*, 1505(1):79–101.

Nasrin Mostafazadeh, Nathanael Chambers, Xiaodong He, Devi Parikh, Dhruv Batra, Lucy Vanderwende, Pushmeet Kohli, and James Allen. 2016. A corpus and cloze evaluation for deeper understanding of commonsense stories. In *Proceedings of the 2016 Conference of the North American Chapter of the Association for Computational Linguistics: Human Language Technologies*, pages 839–849, San Diego, California. Association for Computational Linguistics.

Yingjie Niu, Linyi Yang, Ruihai Dong, and Yue Zhang. 2023. Learning to generalize for cross-domain QA. In *Findings of the Association for Computational Linguistics: ACL 2023*, pages 1298–1313, Toronto, Canada. Association for Computational Linguistics.

Colin Raffel, Noam Shazeer, Adam Roberts, Katherine Lee, Sharan Narang, Michael Matena, Yanqi Zhou, Wei Li, and Peter J Liu. 2019. Exploring the limits of transfer learning with a unified text-to-text transformer. *arXiv preprint arXiv:1910.10683*.

Alessandro Raganato and Jörg Tiedemann. 2018. An analysis of encoder representations in transformer-based machine translation. In *Proceedings of the 2018 EMNLP Workshop BlackboxNLP: Analyzing and Interpreting Neural Networks for NLP*, pages 287–297, Brussels, Belgium. Association for Computational Linguistics.

Pranav Rajpurkar, Robin Jia, and Percy Liang. 2018. Know what you don't know: Unanswerable questions for SQuAD. In *Proceedings of the 56th Annual Meeting of the Association for Computational Linguistics (Volume 2: Short Papers)*, pages 784–789, Melbourne, Australia. Association for Computational Linguistics.

Jacob Russin, Randall C O'Reilly, and Yoshua Bengio. 2020. Deep learning needs a prefrontal cortex. *Work Bridging AI Cogn Sci*, 107:603–616.

Mohammed Saeed, Naser Ahmadi, Preslav Nakov, and Paolo Papotti. 2021. RuleBERT: Teaching soft rules to pre-trained language models. In *Proceedings of the 2021 Conference on Empirical Methods in Natural Language Processing*, pages 1460–1476, Online and Punta Cana, Dominican Republic. Association for Computational Linguistics.

Swarnadeep Saha, Sayan Ghosh, Shashank Srivastava, and Mohit Bansal. 2020. PRover: Proof generation for interpretable reasoning over rules. In *Proceedings of the 2020 Conference on Empirical Methods in Natural Language Processing (EMNLP)*, pages 122–136, Online. Association for Computational Linguistics.

Abulhair Saparov, Richard Yuanzhe Pang, Vishakh Padmakumar, Nitish Joshi, Mehran Kazemi, Najoung Kim, and He He. 2023. Testing the general deductive reasoning capacity of large language models using OOD examples. In *Thirty-seventh Conference on Neural Information Processing Systems*.

Thibault Sellam, Dipanjan Das, and Ankur Parikh. 2020. BLEURT: Learning robust metrics for text generation. In *Proceedings of the 58th Annual Meeting of the Association for Computational Linguistics*, pages 7881–7892, Online. Association for Computational Linguistics.

Oyvind Tafjord, Bhavana Dalvi, and Peter Clark. 2021. ProofWriter: Generating implications, proofs, and abductive statements over natural language. In *Findings of the Association for Computational Linguistics: ACL-IJCNLP 2021*, pages 3621–3634, Online. Association for Computational Linguistics.

Hugo Touvron, Thibaut Lavril, Gautier Izacard, Xavier Martinet, Marie-Anne Lachaux, Timothée Lacroix, Baptiste Rozière, Naman Goyal, Eric Hambro, Faisal Azhar, et al. 2023. Llama: Open and efficient foundation language models. *arXiv preprint arXiv:2302.13971*.

Ashish Vaswani, Noam Shazeer, Niki Parmar, Jakob Uszkoreit, Llion Jones, Aidan N Gomez, Łukasz Kaiser, and Illia Polosukhin. 2017. Attention is all you need. *Advances in neural information processing systems*, 30.

Adina Williams, Nikita Nangia, and Samuel Bowman. 2018. A broad-coverage challenge corpus for sentence understanding through inference. In *Proceedings of the 2018 Conference of the North American Chapter of the Association for Computational Linguistics: Human Language Technologies, Volume 1 (Long Papers)*, pages 1112–1122, New Orleans, Louisiana. Association for Computational Linguistics.

Thomas Wolf, Lysandre Debut, Victor Sanh, Julien Chaumond, Clement Delangue, Anthony Moi, Pierric Cistac, Tim Rault, Remi Louf, Morgan Funtowicz, Joe Davison, Sam Shleifer, Patrick von Platen, Clara Ma, Yacine Jernite, Julien Plu, Canwen Xu, Teven Le Scao, Sylvain Gugger, Mariama Drame, Quentin Lhoest, and Alexander Rush. 2020. Transformers: State-of-the-art natural language processing. In *Proceedings of the 2020 Conference on Empirical Methods in Natural Language Processing: System Demonstrations*, pages 38–45, Online. Association for Computational Linguistics.

Yuhuai Wu, Albert Jiang, Jimmy Ba, and Roger Baker Grosse. 2021. {INT}: An inequality benchmark for evaluating generalization in theorem proving. In *International Conference on Learning Representations*.

Zhengnan Xie, Sebastian Thiem, Jaycie Martin, Elizabeth Wainwright, Steven Marmorstein, and Peter Jansen. 2020. WorldTree v2: A corpus of science-domain structured explanations and inference patterns supporting multi-hop inference. In *Proceedings of the 12th Language Resources and Evaluation Conference*, pages 5456–5473, Marseille, France. European Language Resources Association.

Hitomi Yanaka, Koji Mineshima, Daisuke Bekki, and Kentaro Inui. 2020. Do neural models learn systematicity of monotonicity inference in natural language? In *Proceedings of the 58th Annual Meeting of the Association for Computational Linguistics*, pages 6105–6117, Online. Association for Computational Linguistics.

Hitomi Yanaka, Koji Mineshima, and Kentaro Inui. 2021. Exploring transitivity in neural NLI models through veridicality. In *Proceedings of the 16th Conference of the European Chapter of the Association for Computational Linguistics: Main Volume*, pages 920–934, Online. Association for Computational Linguistics.

Kexin Yi, Jiajun Wu, Chuang Gan, Antonio Torralba, Pushmeet Kohli, and Josh Tenenbaum. 2018. Neural-symbolic vqa: Disentangling reasoning from vision and language understanding. *Advances in neural information processing systems*, 31.

Pengcheng Yin, Hao Fang, Graham Neubig, Adam Pauls, Emmanouil Antonios Platanios, Yu Su, Sam Thomson, and Jacob Andreas. 2021. Compositional generalization for neural semantic parsing via span-level supervised attention. In *Proceedings of the 2021 Conference of the North American Chapter of the Association for Computational Linguistics: Human Language Technologies*, pages 2810–2823, Online. Association for Computational Linguistics.

Pengcheng Yin, Chunting Zhou, Junxian He, and Graham Neubig. 2018. StructVAE: Tree-structured latent variable models for semi-supervised semantic parsing. In *Proceedings of the 56th Annual Meeting of the Association for Computational Linguistics (Volume 1: Long Papers)*, pages 754–765, Melbourne, Australia. Association for Computational Linguistics.

Zhangdie Yuan, Songbo Hu, Ivan Vulić, Anna Korhonen, and Zaiqiao Meng. 2023. Can pretrained language models (yet) reason deductively? In *Proceedings of the 17th Conference of the European Chapter of the Association for Computational Linguistics*, pages 1447–1462, Dubrovnik, Croatia. Association for Computational Linguistics.

A Data

A.1 Reasoning Types in EntailmentBank

We list six different reasoning types in EntailmentBank dataset in Table 5.

A.2 Data Shapes in EntailmentBank

People normally assume that trees can take various shapes, even when their depth is limited to four. However, this assumption does not hold in our CSEG task. We extract every potential shape from the dataset (Dalvi et al., 2021) and find only six different shapes (shape-* in Fig. 2) exist. This is because trees do not reflect or distinguish the different orders of siblings. That is, for a single multi-premise step of an entailment tree, the order of multiple premises (siblings) is underspecified.

A.3 Data Construction for DBpedia

We constructed the DBpedia dataset to evaluate the compositional generalization of MORSE and other baselines. Hence, DBpedia needs to contain several rules, and instances using one of these rules to process each step in multi-step reasoning. We extracted six reasoning rules as shown in Table 3 from a rules pool. Following RuleBert (Saeed et al., 2021) (Section 4.4 Chaining of Rule Executions), we generate hypotheses given existing rules over different relations and a depth D. Subsequently, we instantiate variables in rules and hypotheses from a name pool to generate instances. Rules and hypotheses are eventually transferred to natural language by pre-defined templates.

A.4 Data Construction for EntB-L and EntB-Sh

EntailmentBank contains 1,840 entailment trees showing how a hypothesis is entailed from a small number of relevant sentences. We constructed the EntailmentBank-Length (EntB-L) and EntailmentBank-Shape (EntB-Sh) for compositional generalization evaluation. In terms of EntB-L, we extracted data from the original dataset by the 'length_of_proof' label. As for EntB-Sh, we extracted data from the original dataset by the 'lisp_proof' label. An example of the shape of extracted trees is shown in Fig. 2.

A.5 Data Statistics for EntailmentBank and DBPedia

Table 6 provides detailed data statistics of EntailmentBank and DBPedia. It contains the general data information for each dataset, and the data partitions we created and used in generalization evaluation. We use 20% of the training data for validation.

Rules
R1: child(B,A) $\rightarrow$ parent(A,B)
R2: child(A,C) $\wedge$ parent(C,B) $\rightarrow$ spouse(A,B)
R3: spouse(A,C) $\wedge$ parent(B,C) $\rightarrow$ negspouse(A,B)
R4: relative(A,C) $\wedge$ child(C,B) $\rightarrow$ relative(A,B)
R5: parent(A,C) $\wedge$ spouse(B,C) $\rightarrow$ parent(A,B)
R6: parent(A,C) $\wedge$ parent(B,C) $\rightarrow$ relative(A,B)

Table 3: Rules applied in DBpedia datasets.

A.6 Data Statistic for Correlation Analysis

To visualize the correlations between modules and rules, we constructed a new group of samples containing three reasoning steps. We select samples: i) that contain three reasoning steps, ii) that have correct predictions for the first two reasoning steps, but iii) where the third step is incorrectly predicted in case a certain head is removed. The number of selected samples for each head is given in Table 4. We then count samples in each head over different rules and show the correlations in Fig. 5.

	H1	H2	H3	H4	H5	H6
cases	126	104	137	118	104	126

Table 4: Rules applied in DBpedia datasets.

A.7 Real Examples

We provide real examples of the productivity (length) test in Fig. 6.

B Experimental Details

B.1 Hyperparameter

We use the T5 checkpoints from Huggingface (Wolf et al., 2020). For initialization, we treat all layers as plain transformer layers. We optimize our model using Adam Optimizer (Kingma and Ba, 2014) with learning rate 1e-4 and batch size 4. In inference, we adopt beam search decoding with beam size 3 for all models and baselines. We set the threshold τ for dynamic mask construction to 0.1 (details in Appendix B). We use 20% of training or fine-tuning datasets for validation. All models are evaluated with 3 rounds.

B.2 Training Details

MORSE We conduct out-of-distribution experiments for increasing lengths and shapes of reason-

Reasonoing Types	Example
Substitution	s1: when a light wave hits a reflective object, the light wave will be reflected s2: a mirror is a kind of reflective object int: when a light wave hits a mirror, the light wave will be reflected
Inference from Rule	s1: puddles of water are outside during the day s2: if something is outside during the day then that something will receive sunlight int: puddles of water will receive sunlight
Further Specification or Conjuction	s1: an animal requires warmth for survival as the season changes to winter s2: thick fur can be used for keeping warm int: thick fur can be used for keeping warm as the season changes to winter
Infer Class from Properties	s1: A compound is made of two or more elements chemically combined s2: sodium chloride is made of two elements chemically combined int: sodium chloride is a kind of compound
Property Inheritance	s1: an animal's shell is usually hard s2: something hard can be used for protection int: an animal's shell is usually hard for protection
Sequential Inference	s1: In molecular biology, translation follows transcription s2: transcription is when genetic information flows from DNA to RNA s3: translation is when genetic information flows from RNA to proteins int: In molecular biology, genetic information flows from DNA to RNA to proteins

Table 5: Six different reasoning types in EntailmentBank (Dalvi et al., 2021)

Dataset	EntB	DBP		EntB-L(ength)			DBP-L(ength)				EntB-Sh(apes)		
partitions				tr	ft	te	tr	ft	te		tr	ft	te
#avg.nodes	7.6	4	L_1	430	/	/	1800	/	/	A1	390	/	/
#avg.steps	3.2	1.7	L_2	450	/	/	1800	/	/	A2	391	/	/
#reas.types	6	6	L_3	/	300	101	/	160	391	A3	219	/	/
#examples	1840	4560								B1	/	79	36
										B2	/	63	26
										B3	/	64	39
			all	880			3600			all	1000	206	101

Table 6: Data statistics of Ent(ailment)B(ank) and DBP(edia). We split data into different partitions, including tr(ain), f(ine-)t(une) and te(st). L_n denotes different lengths, and A*, B* means various shapes.

ing trees on two benchmarks, to test MORSE's generalization abilities. Our experiments are run on Nvidia GTX 1080 Ti. As for length compositional test, MORSE (T5-Small and T5-Large) is trained for 33k steps and fine-tuning 4.5k steps on EntailmentBank-Length; trained for 8.1k steps and fine-tuning 0.6k steps on DBpedia-Length. In shape compositional test, MORSE is trained 25k steps and fine-tuning 5k steps.

Baselines Since ProofWriter-It and Entailment Writer are all T5-based baselines, we keep their settings as same as MORSE. In terms of Prover, we choose to use BERT-base-uncased version, given its parameters approach T5-small. We use the grid search technology for generation and select the best result. Its learning rate is 3e-5, trained for 36k steps and fine-tuning 4.5k steps on EntailmentBank-Length. In shape compositional test, Prover is trained 27k step and fine-tuning 5.5k steps.

C Analysis for Different Shapes

In Fig. 4 we note that shape B1 is the most difficult for all systems, and provide an empirical analysis: we hypothesize that combining trees of unequal lengths at higher levels makes the task more challenging compared to lower levels. Here, we further conduct a statistical Spearman's rank correlation coefficient analysis of systematicity difficulty from the complexity of tree properties to verify our hypotheses.

For each test shape, we aim to determine how much the presence of specific tree properties influences the task accuracy of models (including baselines and our model MORSE) when performing systematicity generalization from primitive to compositional shapes. Specifically, we quantified the increase of accuracy in view of the following aspects: i) increased number of the 'Leaf' (Δ#Leaf) nodes from (seen) primitive units to (predicted) compositional structures. I.e., how much the leaf

length 1

sent1: animals need food for surviving
sent2: a bear is a kind of animal
hypothesis: a bear needs food for surviving

entailment tree:
sent1 & sent2 -> hypothesis [*substitution*]

length 2

sent1: puddles of water are outside during the day
sent2: temperature is a measure of heat energy
sent3: if something receives sunlight, it will increase in temperature
hypothesis: the puddles of water will increase in heat energy

entailment tree :
sent1 & sent3 -> int1: the puddles of water will increase in temperature; [*if-then*]
sent2 & int1 -> hypothesis [*substitution*]

length 3

sent1: a plate is made of metal
sent2: metal is a thermal conductor
sent3: if something is a thermal conductor, it can efficiently transmit heat
sent4: if something can transmit heat, it can be used for cooking
hypothesis: a metal plate can be used for cooking

entailment tree :
sent1 & sent2 -> int1: a metal plate is a thermal conductor [*substitution*]
sent3 & int1 -> int2: a metal spoon can efficiently transmit heat [*if-then*]
sent4 & int2 -> hypothesis [*if-then*]

Figure 6: Three real examples for the productivity-length test of CSEG. For each example, an entailment tree is generated based on candidate sentences and a hypothesis. Each tree is composed of several reasoning steps, and each step belongs to one specific reasoning type, here, either [*substitution*] or [*if-then*]. The length of each sample is determined by how many reasoning steps are required for the entailment tree generation. To evaluate the compositional generalization ability, we design CSEG to generalize from limited reasoning steps (e.g., length 1 or length 2) to more steps (e.g., length 3). Here, the sample of length three is compositional, and since its required reasoning types have been learned before, it is expected to be solvable.

ComplexityDim	ProofW	PROVER	EntailW	Morse	avg
Δ#Leaf	0.5	0.86	0.5	0.5	0.59
Δ#InterNode	-0.86	-0.5	-0.86	-0.86	-0.77
Δ#InterNode-L2	0.86	1.0	0.86	0.86	0.895
Δ#InterNode-L3	-1	-0.86	-1	-1	-0.965

Table 7: Spearman's rank correlation coefficient between the increase of training–test arithmetic complexity and the compositional generalization performance (accuracy) across the three shapes. *avg* is the average value.

number increased from primitive samples (e.g., A1, A2) to compositional samples (e.g., B1) and how this influences accuracy; ii) increased number of 'Intermediate Nodes' (Δ#InterNode) (again from primitive to compositional structures) and how this influences generalization accuracy.

Table 7 shows the results of our Spearman's rank correlation coefficient analysis between these two complexity dimensions of trees and the compositional generalization accuracy. Compared to the 'Leaf' dimension, 'Intermediate Nodes' shows a more notable average coefficient value.[10] That is, the more intermediate nodes in the compositional samples, the more difficult it is for the neural model to perform compositional generalization.

Based on this result, we further explore whether the location of intermediate nodes will affect compositional generalization ability. We evaluate: i) increased number of the 'Intermediate Node' at layer 2 (Δ#InterNode-L2). Layer 2 indicates the second layer of a tree from the bottom up, e.g., B1 has one intermediate node in the second layer, and B3 has two. ii) increased number of 'Intermediate Nodes' at layer 3 (Δ#InterNode-L3). Table 7 indicates that more intermediate nodes in layer three incur a notable negative value, i.e., intermediate nodes at a higher layer result in lower accuracy, meaning that compositional generalization is more difficult.

In conclusion, Table 4 indicates that the systematicity test in CSEG is challenging for existing neural models. And further exploration verifies combining trees at higher levels makes it even more difficult compared to lower levels.

[10]The permutation of a small set (here, 3 dimensions) is limited, thus limiting the range of variation of the correlation coefficient. Hence, 0.59 is an irrelevant value.

Models	Original EntailmentBank Dataset (EntB-Orig)					
	Leaves		Steps		Intermediates	
	F1	AllCorrect	F1	AllCorrect	F1	AllCorrect
Task 1 (no-distractor) - EntailmentWriter - T511b	99.0	89.4	51.5	38.2	71.2	38.5
Task 1 (no-distractor) - EntailmentWriter - T5Large	98.7	86.2	50.5	37.7	67.6	36.2
Task 1 (no-distractor) - MORSE (ours) - T5Large	98.09(0.24)	86.37(0.11)	51.11(0.84)	39.70(0.77)	69.79(0.09)	40.97(0.34)
Task 1 (no-distractor) - EntailmentWriter - T5Small	98.40(0.41)	86.18(0.25)	41.72(0.96)	34.11(0.38)	56.95(0.21)	40.41(0.49)
Task 1 (no-distractor) - MORSE (ours) - T5Small	98.30(0.37)	86.47(0.21)	42.35(0.66)	35.00(0.32)	57.76(0.11)	40.88(0.51)
Task 2 (distractor) - EntailmentWriter - T511b	89.1	48.8	41.4	27.7	66.2	31.5
Task 2 (distractor) - EntailmentWriter - T5Large	84.3	35.6	35.5	22.9	61.8	28.5
Task 2 (distractor) - MORSE (ours) - T5Large	83.17(0.95)	34.41(0.59)	34.46(0.62)	21.96(0.60)	60.50(0.19)	28.24(0.37)

Table 8: Comparative results for Entailment Writer vs. MORSE on original EntailmentBank dataset for Task 1 and Task 2 with different T5 model sizes

D Comparative results on original EntailmentBank dataset

We conduct experiments of Task 1 and Task 2 from Dalvi et al. (2021) on the *original EntailmentBank dataset and splits*. The train, dev and test sets contain 1,313, 187 and 340 instances. Task 2 includes non-fitting distractor sentences in the input. We compare differently scaled T5 models to assess differences relating from T5 model sizes: T511b, T5large. EntailmentWriter (EW) is equivalent to MORSE modulo its modulated reasoning cell. For EW we show published results from Dalvi et al. (2021); for MORSE we report averaged results over three runs w/ standard deviation in brackets, for T5large. We observe comparable or superior results of MORSE w/T5large over EW w/t5large, especially for the difficult Steps (entailment tree structure) and Intermediates (inferred intermediate node label) evaluation criteria for Task 1. For Task 2, which poses a challenge by including noisy distractors, MORSE is still competitive, with ca. 1 percentage point distance. Comparing results of EW w/T511b vs. MORSE w/T5large shows that can MORSE rival and even outperform EW using T511b, for Steps and Intermediats Accuracies in Task 1, but not for the more difficult Task 2. The experiment shows that despite using a variation of the dataset in our main experiments to focus on MORSE's generalization abilities, it is still competitive on the original dataset and data distributions.

E Analysis of Dynamic Masking Mechanism

Mask Sparsity MORSE deploys masks to modularize a network dynamically. This allows each module to specialize for a specific function while selecting corresponding inputs. To gain more insight into the role of dynamic masking, we analyse masks used in length generalization testing on EntB-L. We count the number of masks with non-zero values for each module. Table 9 shows that the percentage of *non-zero values* for heads H1-6 is relatively low, indicating that dynamic masks are effective for filtering out potentially irrelevant inputs. We also note higher percentages for some modules (e.g., H4, H5). Different reasoning types require disparate inputs that may account for this.

Head	H1	H2	H3	H4	H5	H6
non-zero (%)	21.46	22.14	21.11	33.13	41.31	21.18

Table 9: Non-zero values in masks for each module (%).

Mask Effects We apply different masking strategies to test if the observed performance improvements arise from modularized masks – as opposed to naïve ones. We construct a *random_mask* model variant with 20 and 50% non-zero values, respectively. These proportions are similar to what we find in MORSE (Tab. 9). We apply random masks in length composition testing on the EntB-L dataset. Table 10 shows that compared to dynamic routing in MORSE, random masking incurs a severe performance drop. We conclude that i) unselective masking risks shielding important information from heads, and that ii) dynamic routing cannot be considered as a simple dropout mechanism.

Models	Steps		Intermediates	
	F1	Acc	F1	Acc
w modularized_mask	44.22	32.67	50.66	25.74
w random_mask (20%)	30.36	15.84	42.62	13.86
w random_mask (50%)	36.63	20.79	45.45	18.81

Table 10: Effects of different mask strategies. (*%) indicates *% percentage of non-zero value in a mask.

Models	EntailmentBank-Length (EntB-L)						DBpedia-Length (DBP-L)					
	Leaves		Steps		Intermediates		Leaves		Steps		Intermediates	
	F1	AllCorrect	F1	AllCorrect	F1	AllCorrect	F1	AllCorrect	F1	AllCorrect	F1	AllCorrect
EntWriter (T5-Large)	99.78	98.02	52.80	40.92	56.62	36.63	99.36	95.52	82.49	80.11	88.98	83.89
MORSE (T5-Large)	**99.82**(+0.04)	**98.68**(+0.66)	**53.31**(+0.51)	**42.57**(+1.65)	**57.78**(+1.16)	**37.29**(+0.66)	**99.53**(+0.17)	**96.68**(+1.16)	**86.79**(+4.30)	**83.76**(+3.65)	**92.62**(+3.64)	**86.70**(+2.81)
EntWriter (Flan-T5-Large)	99.78	98.02	53.18	41.58	57.93	39.13	99.53	95.52	84.98	83.12	91.27	84.14
MORSE (Flan-T5-Large)	100.00(+0.22)	100.00(+1.98)	55.51(+2.33)	43.56(+1.98)	58.67(+0.74)	39.60(+0.47)	99.53(-0)	96.68(+1.16)	87.21(+2.23)	83.76(+0.64)	93.41(+2.14)	86.70(+2.56)
EntWriter-0-shot (T5-Large)	97.06	85.73	18.44	-	24.21	-	90.09	29.27	16.94	-	32.43	-
MORSE-0-shot (T5-Large)	**97.89**(+0.83)	**86.83**(+1.10)	**19.14**(+0.70)	-	**25.42**(+1.21)	-	**89.82**(-0.17)	**30.05**(+0.78)	**18.41**(+1.47)	-	**33.45**(+1.02)	-
EntWriter-0-shot (Flan-T5-Large)	98.79	91.09	20.59	-	31.68	-	90.05	30.69	18.46	-	33.30	-
MORSE-0-shot (Flan-T5-Large)	99.82(+1.03)	92.31(+1.22)	21.22(+0.63)	-	32.07(+0.39)	-	91.96(+1.91)	31.28(+0.59)	21.99(+3.53)	-	33.92(+0.62)	-

Table 11: Results on EntailmentBank-L(ength) and DBpedia-L(ength) for compositional generalization evaluation based on Flan-T5. (+num) indicates the improvement of MORSE compared to the strong baseline EntWriter.

F Morse on powerful backbones

To further investigate the effectiveness of MORSE, we conduct experiments for MORSE and the most competitive baseline EntWriter on a more powerful backbone, e.g., Flan-T5 (Chung et al., 2022). Table 11 shows results. We find that: i) compared to T5, FLAN-T5 has generally better results for both models in both settings (fine-tuning and zero-shot). With FLAN-T5, our extension with MORSE still has superior results compared to the original T5 model. That is, our conclusions remain the same with this new backbone. ii) for both EntWriter and MORSE, FLAN-T5 shows increased performance in the zero-shot setting. This indicates that FLAN-T5 may serve as a better model variant to address zero-shot setting – which is expected for an instruction-tuned model.

Inspecting Soundness of AMR Similarity Metrics in terms of Equivalence and Inequivalence

Kyung Seo Ki*
Department of
Intelligence and Information
Seoul National University
Seoul, Republic of Korea
kskee88@snu.ac.kr

Bugeun Kim*
Department of
Artificial Intelligence
Chung-Ang University
Seoul, Republic of Korea
bgnkim@cau.ac.kr

Gahgene Gweon
Department of
Intelligence and Information
Seoul National University
Seoul, Republic of Korea
ggweon@snu.ac.kr

Abstract

In this study, we investigate soundness of current Abstract Meaning Representation (AMR) similarity metrics in terms of equivalence and inequivalence. Specifically, AMR guidelines provide several equivalence and inequivalence conditions to reflect the meaning aspect of the semantics. Thus, it is important to examine an AMR metric's soundness, i.e., whether the metric correctly reflects the guidelines. However, the existing metrics have less investigated their soundness. In this work, we propose a new experimental method using simulated data and a series of statistical tests to verify the metric's soundness. Our experimental result revealed that all existing metrics such as SMATCH, SEMBLEU, S^2MATCH, SMATCH++, WWLK$_\theta$, WWLK$_{e2n}$, and SEMA did not fully meet the AMR guidelines in terms of equivalence and inequivalence aspects. Also, to alleviate this soundness problem, we propose a revised metric called SMATCH$^\sharp$, which adopts simple graph standardization technique that can improve the soundness of an existing metric.

1 Introduction

In this paper, we propose a new experimental method to evaluate soundness of Abstract Meaning Representation (AMR) similarity metrics and try to address the soundness of AMR similarity metrics by proposing a revised metric, SMATCH$^\sharp$. AMR is a widely used formalism that expresses the semantic aspect of natural language sentences. The formalism is based on neo-Davidsonian semantics (Banarescu et al., 2013; Davidson, 1967; Higginbotham, 1985; Parsons, 1990). Therefore, when comparing two AMR graphs, a metric needs to yield results that adhere to such theoretical background, which is implemented in the AMR guidelines (Banarescu et al., 2019). We refer to this criterion as the *soundness* of an AMR metric. Here, we define soundness as a metric's quality to yield well-founded results that adhere to the theoretical background of AMR during the metric's computation process. For example, soundness of a metric can be operationally checked by whether the metric correctly follows AMR guidelines, as AMR guidelines define many special equivalence relationships between two AMRs with different forms along with its theoretical background. Thus, an AMR metric should treat such AMRs as equivalent to meet the soundness criterion.

However, the existing metrics' design has been less focused on evaluating their soundness. Several metrics have been proposed to measure the similarity between two AMRs, including SMATCH (Cai and Knight, 2013), SEMBLEU (Song and Gildea, 2019), S^2MATCH (Opitz et al., 2020), WWLK$_\theta$-variants (Opitz et al., 2021; Opitz and Frank, 2022), SEMA (Anchiêta et al., 2019), and SMATCH++ (Opitz, 2023). Although these existing metrics have helped evaluating the quality of various AMR parsers, they do not sufficiently consider soundness. The only exception is SMATCH++, which attempts to address soundness partially by managing some equivalent cases, like reification. Nonetheless, even SMATCH++ has not reported whether their metric adheres to other equivalent cases specified in the AMR guideline.

Therefore, we designed an experiment that investigates the soundness of AMR metrics, using systematically simulated data. We implement both 6 equivalent cases and 7 inequivalent cases according to AMR guideline, to make a systematic data for evaluating the soundness of metrics. We also propose a simple statistical method to verify soundness and a graph standardization method for handling equivalence and inequivalence cases. As a result, we propose SMATCH$^\sharp$, an enhanced version of SMATCH++, as an alternative to prior AMR metrics that better addresses soundness.

Our paper is structured as follows: Section 2 provides theoretical background on AMR and assesses

*These authors contributed equally to this work.

*Proceedings of the 13th Joint Conference on Lexical and Computational Semantics (*SEM 2024)*, pages 402 - 409
June 20-21, 2024 ©2024 Association for Computational Linguistics

the designs of existing metrics from the perspective of equivalence and inequivalence. Next, Sections 3 details our experimental design. Specifically, Section 3 outlines the simulated dataset generation, the proposed statistical test for soundness verification, the SMATCH$^\sharp$ metric, and implementation details. Finally, Section 4 presents the results, and discuss their implications. We analyzes the results from applying our experiment to various AMR metrics and examines their soundness issues.

2 Inspecting AMR Similarity Metrics

Here, we discuss seven existing AMR similarity metrics in terms of the way that they handle equivalent and/or inequivalent cases. As widely used similarity metrics adopt a method of giving partial credits to non-exact matching cases, existing metrics differ in how they establish the range of partial credit regarding equivalence and inequivalence of AMR components. Thus, we categorize the existing metrics into two types: (1) allowing credits only to exact equivalent components, and (2) allowing credits also to some inequivalent cases.

First, there are metrics that only give credit for exactly matching/overlapping components when measuring the similarity between two AMRs. SMATCH (Cai and Knight, 2013), SEMBLEU (Song and Gildea, 2019), SEMA (Anchiêta et al., 2019), and SMATCH++ (Opitz, 2023) belong to this category. These metrics approximately compute the maximum overlap between two AMRs, by constructing a mapping between substructures of two AMRs. For example, SMATCH computes overlap as the maximum F_1 score of common triples between two AMRs. Similarly, in SEMBLEU, the metric computes overlap as the BLEU score using n-grams of triples commonly appearing in the two given AMRs. However, these overlap-based metrics can mistakenly identify equivalent AMRs as inequivalent, since they primarily focus on matching exactly the same components without fully considering the AMR guidelines. As the guidelines define some cases where AMRs are syntactically inequivalent but semantically equivalent, the soundness of the evaluation may decrease in some cases.

Second, for the metrics allowing credits also to some inequivalent cases, they try to measure similarity by relaxing the constraint of exact match. Metrics such as S^{2}MATCH, WWLK$_\theta$, and WWLK$_{e2n}$ (Opitz et al., 2020, 2021; Opitz and Frank, 2022) belong to this category. These metrics attempt to give partial credit for inequivalent AMRs by incorporating the concept of pragmatic sense, acquired by a language model. With a language model, these metrics are able to construct intuitive sense of similarity between some predicates or between some instances. However, the use of language models makes it difficult to verify that these metrics fairly assess the meaning of AMRs independently of any context, which contradicts one of the key assumptions behind AMR - that meaning should be context-independent. More specifically, the AMR guideline tries to ensure context-independency of semantics by using pre-defined ontology of predicate senses, semantic roles, and frame arguments from OntoNotes (Pradhan et al., 2007) and PropBank (Kingsbury and Palmer, 2003). Using a language model may compromise such context-independency when comparing two AMRs, since a language model tries to treat different pre-defined senses, roles, and arguments as similar ones. Moreover, such intuitive sense of similarity may weaken the transparency of the evaluation process.

We suspect that all the metrics in the above two categories may insufficiently handle equivalent and inequivalent cases according to the AMR guidelines. For example, the case illustrated in Appendix A shows that some prior metrics do not correctly evaluate inequivalent AMRs which have different meanings. Note that Goodman (2019) have already shown that not handling these conditions results in an unfair evaluation in SMATCH. We suspect that other metrics have also insufficiently considered the issues raised by Goodman (2019), because other metrics were not designed to properly handle equivalent and inequivalent cases according to the AMR guidelines. Moreover, existing metrics have not systematically verified whether they conform to the equivalence/inequivalence conditions based on the AMR guidelines. Systematic verification of these conditions would therefore be helpful to identify strengths and weaknesses of the existing AMR metrics.

3 Experiment

To verify the soundness of existing metrics, we designed an experiment based on the observations on equivalence and inequivalence aspects. We tested seven existing metrics and one new metric: SMATCH, S^{2}MATCH, SEMBLEU, SMATCH++,

Equivalent cases (6 operations)	
	(When writing PENMAN notation,)
Lift Up	Lift another node as a root.
Reorder	Randomly re-order edges.
Relabel	Randomly re-labeled variables.
Reify	Apply the reification process.
De-reify	Apply the de-reification process.
Duplicate	Duplicate all edge twice. (Semantically equivalent due to tautology)
Inequivalent cases (7 operations)	
Insert N	Insert a dummy node.
Insert E	Insert a dummy edge between nodes.
Change N	Change a node's name with a dummy.
Change E	Change an edge's label with a dummy.
Delete N	Delete a node.
Delete E	Delete an edge.
Swap	Swap heads of two edges.

Table 1: List of 13 operations for our simulated dataset

WWLK_{θ}, WWLK_{e2n}, SEMA, and SMATCH♯. Note that SMATCH♯ is our revised version of SMATCH++ which tries to handle equivalence and inequivalence cases. Using our simulated data and statistical methods, we tested whether these eight metrics follow the AMR guideline.

SMATCH♯ To consider the AMR guidelines while upholding the approximation method of the existing metrics, we developed SMATCH♯. The new metric is a variant of SMATCH++ which standardizes AMR graphs considering both equivalence and inequivalence conditions. As SMATCH++ is the only metric that attempts to handle some of the equivalence conditions, we chose to make SMATCH♯ based on SMATCH++. Thus, SMATCH♯ retains the same evaluation process as Smatch++. However, SMATCH♯ is additionally designed to pass through a single graph standardization pipeline before the evaluation stage. This additional pipeline is a normalization technique that converts any given AMR into a single, standardized form. This normalization is necessary because we want to ensure that semantically equivalent AMRs are treated correctly during evaluation. For example, some cases such as inversion, different variable names, etc. should be treated as equivalent according to AMR's definition, and can be converted into the exact same notation through normalization.

Simulated Dataset with 13 Operations We have designed a novel test method to verify how well existing metrics conform to the AMR guidelines. Our test employs the gold standard dataset, AMR 3.0[1], which is commonly used in the development of existing AMR parsers. First, we extracted 20,000 AMRs by randomly sampling the AMR 3.0 train set. For each AMR in this gold standard dataset, we applied 13 perturbations, shown in Table 1, following the guidelines to create a simulated dataset. This perturbing procedure generated 260,000 simulated pairs. This simulated dataset helps us verify whether an AMR metric can evaluate the original and perturbed cases as equivalent. For six of the perturbations, we applied one of the six equivalent cases described in Part III (Phenomena) of the AMR guidelines, making the original and perturbed pair equivalent. For seven of the pairs, we randomly manipulated the structure of the given AMRs, making the original and perturbed pair inequivalent. Refer to the Appendix B for the detailed illustration and example for each operation. To the best of our knowledge, this is the first attempt to verify the soundness of an AMR metric, which concerns how well the metric adheres to the rules of the representation being evaluated.

Statistical Test for Hypothesis A sound metric should differentiate equivalent pairs and inequivalent pairs. To verify this, we conducted a binomial test to statistically examine the difference between the average score ζ of equivalent pairs and the theoretical maximum score ζ_{max} for each metric. The test process involves three steps. As the first step, we compute each metric score ζ for each graph pairs. In the second step, we compute $P(\zeta = \zeta_{max})$, i.e., the proportion of examples where the score reaches ζ_{max}. Lastly, in the third step, we tested $P(\zeta = \zeta_{max}) > 0.999$ for equivalent cases and $P(\zeta = \zeta_{max}) < 0.001$ for inequivalent cases[2]. So, a sound metric should pass all of the above tests by definition. Corollary, such a metric should prevent overlap between the score ranges of equivalent pairs and ranges of inequivalent pairs.

Implementation Detail Here, we implemented the eight metric as follows. For SMATCH, S^2MATCH, SMATCH++, and WWLK_{e2n}, we ran the exact official code. For SEMBLEU and SEMA, we additionally added an outputting code into the original source code to obtain a score for each

[1] https://catalog.ldc.upenn.edu/LDC2020T02

[2] We set $P(\zeta) > 0.999$ for equivalent cases and $P(\zeta) < 0.001$ for inequivalent cases, since the statistical power is greater than 0.999 even with the significance level of 0.001.

AMR pair[3]. Lastly, for WWLK$_\theta$, we used the reified version of STS for zeroth-order learning[4]. For SMATCH$^\sharp$, we used `Penman` (Goodman, 2020) library for graph standardization. The experiment is conducted in a single-run on a PC with the Ubuntu 20.04, an AMD Ryzen 5900X 16-core CPU, and 64GB RAM. Our code[5] used Python 3.11.9 and `statsmodels` (Seabold and Perktold, 2010) for the binomial tests. We provide additional details in Appendix C.

4 Results and Discussion

Table 2 shows the results of soundness and binomial tests on 6 equivalent and 7 inequivalent cases. We present average values for each perturbation cases. In addition, overall $\min(\zeta)$ and $\max(\zeta)$ rows show the minimum/maximum score in equivalent/inequivalent cases, respectively. And, $P(\zeta = 1)$ rows refer to the proportion of items evaluated as equivalent in total. Note that a sound metric should yield statistically significant result on all the tests, without making the overlap between equivalent and inequivalent cases.

First, for the six equivalent cases, prior metrics failed to fully handle equivalent but altered graph structures. They only give ζ_{max} for 48-78% of graph pairs, as seen in the $P(\zeta = 1)$ row for equivalent cases. Specifically, metrics such as SEMBLEU, WWLK$_\theta$, WWLK$_{\text{e2n}}$, SEMA, SMATCH++ successfully gave the ζ_{max} to some equivalent cases (lift up, reordering, relabeling, duplicate). However, SMATCH and S^{2}MATCH failed to give ζ_{max} for above 4 cases. For example, SMATCH assigned an average score of 1.212 in duplicate cases, exceeding ζ_{max}. So, it suggests that SMATCH may overestimate similarity when a graph has multiple tautological edges. Additionally, following the soundness test, we attempted to verify whether the metric accurately assigns ζ_{max} to the completely identical case by using the original AMR as both the reference and hypothesis simultaneously. Surprisingly, SMATCH and SEMA failed to produce the maximum score ζ_{max} even for non-perturbed original cases, yielding scores as low as 0.902 (SMATCH) and 0.833 (SEMA). This result is likely due to the approximation methods employed by these metrics. Note that as SMATCH++ attempts to handle equivalent cases in their design, it shows a better evaluation for the de/reification case compared to other metrics.

Second, for the seven inequivalent cases, some metrics showed incorrect evaluation results by assigning ζ_{max} to certain graph pairs, as seen in the $P(\zeta = 1)$ row for the inequivalent cases. Specifically, SEMA produced a score of 1.103, exceeding the theoretical ζ_{max}. Moreover, among all the metrics, SEMA was the only one that achieved statistical significance in only 3 cases for the inequivalent cases. We suspect these results from SEMA appear to be numerical errors caused by its approximation algorithm. Furthermore, S^{2}MATCH assigned ζ_{max} to some edge deletion pairs (thus, $p > 0.05$), and SEMBLEU did the same for some edge insertion pairs ($p > 0.05$), while SMATCH, WWLK$_{\text{e2n}}$, and SMATCH++ passed all the tests, correctly identifying those cases as inequivalent.

Third, for the overlap between equivalent and inequivalent cases, all existing metrics showed overlap. For example, as SMATCH made overlap between equivalent and inequivalent cases on the interval $[0.371, 1]$, the score positioned in this range cannot be determined either equivalent or inequivalent. Similar overlap happens for SEMA (range of $[0.083, 1.103]$), WWLK$_\theta$ (range of $[0.656, 1]$), SMATCH++ (range of $[0.5, 0.998]$), and so on. Thus, we need to be careful in interpreting a score fall within the overlap range because there may exists incorrect evaluation in terms of AMR's theoretical background. Even the chance of falling in the overlap range is low, the existence of these overlapping sections is sufficient to pose a question about the soundness of existing metrics.

On the other hand, SMATCH$^\sharp$ has proven to be effective in dealing with all the 13 cases. SMATCH$^\sharp$ correctly assigned ζ_{max} in 100% of equivalence cases, achieving the highest possible score, which no other metric accomplished. Furthermore, SMATCH$^\sharp$ did not assign ζ_{max} for any inequivalence cases, as confirmed statistically. Specifically, for the six equivalent cases, SMATCH$^\sharp$ successfully provide ζ_{max}. For the seven inequivalent cases, SMATCH$^\sharp$ showed slight decrease in score compared to SMATCH++, the backbone of SMATCH$^\sharp$. For example, SMATCH++ had an average score of 0.927 for edge deletion case, while SMATCH$^\sharp$ scored an average of 0.907. Moreover, SMATCH$^\sharp$

[3]We provide the modified code at our GitHub repository.

[4]As the WWLK$_\theta$ and WWLK$_{\text{e2n}}$ are defined based on a different score range of $[-1, 1]$ compared to other metrics' range of $[0, 1]$, we normalized the range to $[0, 1]$.

[5]Code for the experiment will be uploaded in `https://github.com/snucclab/ssharp`.

	SMATCH$^\sharp$	SMATCH	S^{2}MATCH	SEMBLEU	WWLK$_\theta$	WWLK$_{e2n}$	SEMA	SMATCH++
6 Equivalent Cases				* Alternative hypothesis $H_A : P(\zeta = 1) > 99.9\%$				
Lift Up	1.000***	.964	.964	.999	1.000	1.000	.990	.949
Reorder	1.000***	.999	.998	1.000***	1.000***	1.000***	1.000	1.000*
Relabel	1.000***	.999	.999	1.000**	1.000***	1.000***	1.000	1.000***
Reify	1.000***	.748	.748	.613	.866	.864	.660	.990
Dereify	1.000***	.988	.988	.975	.994	.994	.990	.990
Duplicate	1.000***	1.212	.986	.470	.910	.937	.780	1.000***
Overall $\min(\zeta)$	1.000	.371	.371	.025	.610	.628	.083	.500
Overall $P(\zeta = 1)\%$	100	48.11	55.77	64.74	64.75	64.75	61.47	78.25
7 Inequivalent Cases				* Alternative hypothesis $H_A : P(\zeta = 1) < 0.1\%$				
Insert Node	.955***	.975***	.973***	.935***	.952***	.944***	.970***	.966***
Insert Edge	.964***	.983***	.980**	.931	.996***	.970***	.980***	.977***
Change Node	.944***	.966***	.961***	.871***	.940***	.951***	.890	.946***
Change Edge	.949***	.966***	.965	.935***	.982	.968***	.950	.952***
Delete Node	.906***	.945*	.946***	.908***	.936***	.933***	.940	.918***
Delete Edge	.907***	.948***	.949	.930***	.959***	.946***	.930***	.927***
Swap	.873***	.918***	.918***	.853	.949***	.954***	.880	.884***
Overall $\max(\zeta)$	.998	1.000	1.000	1.000	1.000	0.999	1.103	.998
Overall $P(\zeta = 1)\%$	.00	.01	.05	.65	5.09	.00	.63	.00

$^+p < 0.1$, $^*p < 0.05$, $^{**}p < 0.01$, $^{***}p < 0.001$

Table 2: Result of soundness and binomial test on 13 simulated equivalent/inequivalent cases.

reduced the overlap range into zero, resolving the overlap issue that appeared in all existing metrics. This results suggest that SMATCH$^\sharp$ provides a better demarcation than existing metrics.

5 Conclusion

In this study, we proposed a novel experiment for verifying soundness of an AMR metric using simulated dataset and statistical tests. Through the experiment, our work demonstrated that the soundness problem exists in the previous metrics. Also, we suggest an AMR metric SMATCH$^\sharp$, which is an improved version of SMATCH++ in terms of soundness, using a graph standardization method that follows AMR guidelines. By testing SMATCH$^\sharp$ with the same experiment, we demonstrated that we can alleviate the issue by slightly enhancing the design of metrics. For future work, designing a new AMR similarity metric by considering our experimental results would be an interesting topic to pursue.

Limitations

In this section, we discuss the study's limitations that stem from our adoption of the AMR graph structure and experimental assumptions.

First, adopting the AMR graph structure, which is a standard meaning representation, provides a solid foundation for generating a score metric. However, because we adopted AMR, two limitations that affect our proposed approach also exist: the application of the metric on a single language, i.e. English, and the assumption of a single interpretation of the text.

Second, though we designed equivalence and inequivalence cases based on AMR specification, confirming whether we tested all theoretical variations of equivalence/inequivalence cases would be difficult. Therefore, it may be possible to present additional perturbations of AMR in future work.

Ethics Statement

In accordance with the guidelines of the ACL Ethics Policy, we will release all artifacts, including code, experiment results, and statistics used in this study on our GitHub repository. Also, because this study is an algorithmic consideration of model evaluation, we did not need a hyperparameter optimization process; thus, no such procedure is described. Moreover, due to the characteristics of AMR, a simulated dataset could be constructed without human annotation for equivalence/inequivalence conditions. Thus, we did not perform a human annotation process.

In addition, this study only concerns the evaluation of the output already generated by the model.

Therefore, as our study has no direct relationship to any sociocultural impacts or implications of machine learning models, such as social bias, we have not discussed these concerns.

Lastly, the AMR 2.0 (LDC2017T10) and 3.0 (LDC2020T02) datasets used in this study were purchased according to the license under the LDC User Agreement. Therefore, to create a simulated dataset according to our experimental procedure, a license would need to be purchased for the AMR 3.0 dataset. Furthermore, the LDC User Agreement prohibits the re-distribution of their datasets. For this reason, we can only provide the simulated dataset used in the experiment to parties with a valid license.

Acknowledgements

This work was supported by the National Research Foundation of Korea (NRF) grant (No. 2020R1C1C1010162) and the Institute for Information & communications Technology Promotion (IITP) grant (No. 2021-0-02146), both funded by the Korean government (MSIT).

References

Rafael Torres Anchiêta, Marco Antonio Sobrevilla Cabezudo, and Thiago Alexandre Salgueiro Pardo. 2019. Sema: an extended semantic evaluation for amr. In *Proceedings of the 20th Computational Linguistics and Intelligent Text Processing*. Springer International Publishing.

Laura Banarescu, Claire Bonial, Shu Cai, Madalina Georgescu, Kira Griffitt, Ulf Hermjakob, Kevin Knight, Philipp Koehn, Martha Palmer, and Nathan Schneider. 2013. Abstract Meaning Representation for sembanking. In *Proceedings of the 7th Linguistic Annotation Workshop and Interoperability with Discourse*, pages 178–186, Sofia, Bulgaria. Association for Computational Linguistics.

Laura Banarescu, Claire Bonial, Shu Cai, Madalina Georgescu, Kira Griffitt, Ulf Hermjakob, Kevin Knight, Philipp Koehn, Martha Palmer, and Nathan Schneider. 2019. Abstract Meaning Representation (AMR) 1.2.6 Specification.

Shu Cai and Kevin Knight. 2013. Smatch: an evaluation metric for semantic feature structures. In *Proceedings of the 51st Annual Meeting of the Association for Computational Linguistics (Volume 2: Short Papers)*, pages 748–752, Sofia, Bulgaria. Association for Computational Linguistics.

Donald Davidson. 1967. The logical form of action sentences. In Nicholas Rescher, editor, *The Logic of Decision and Action*, pages 81–95. University of Pittsburgh Press.

Michael Wayne Goodman. 2019. AMR normalization for fairer evaluation. In *Proceedings of the 33rd Pacific Asia Conference on Language, Information, and Computation*, pages 47–56, Hakodate.

Michael Wayne Goodman. 2020. Penman: An open-source library and tool for AMR graphs. In *Proceedings of the 58th Annual Meeting of the Association for Computational Linguistics: System Demonstrations*, pages 312–319, Online. Association for Computational Linguistics.

James Higginbotham. 1985. On semantics. *Linguistic Inquiry*, 16(4):547–593.

Paul Kingsbury and Martha Palmer. 2003. Propbank: the next level of treebank. In *Proceedings of Treebanks and lexical Theories*, volume 3. Citeseer.

Juri Opitz. 2023. SMATCH++: Standardized and extended evaluation of semantic graphs. In *Findings of the Association for Computational Linguistics: EACL 2023*, pages 1595–1607, Dubrovnik, Croatia. Association for Computational Linguistics.

Juri Opitz, Angel Daza, and Anette Frank. 2021. Weisfeiler-leman in the bamboo: Novel AMR graph metrics and a benchmark for AMR graph similarity. *Transactions of the Association for Computational Linguistics*, 9:1425–1441.

Juri Opitz and Anette Frank. 2022. Better Smatch = better parser? AMR evaluation is not so simple anymore. In *Proceedings of the 3rd Workshop on Evaluation and Comparison of NLP Systems*, pages 32–43, Online. Association for Computational Linguistics.

Juri Opitz, Letitia Parcalabescu, and Anette Frank. 2020. AMR Similarity Metrics from Principles. *Transactions of the Association for Computational Linguistics*, 8:522–538.

Terence Parsons. 1990. *Events in the Semantics of English: A Study in Subatomic Semantics*. MIT Press.

Sameer S Pradhan, Eduard Hovy, Mitch Marcus, Martha Palmer, Lance Ramshaw, and Ralph Weischedel. 2007. Ontonotes: A unified relational semantic representation. In *International Conference on Semantic Computing (ICSC 2007)*, pages 517–526. IEEE.

Skipper Seabold and Josef Perktold. 2010. statsmodels: Econometric and statistical modeling with python. In *9th Python in Science Conference*.

Linfeng Song and Daniel Gildea. 2019. SemBleu: A robust metric for AMR parsing evaluation. In *Proceedings of the 57th Annual Meeting of the Association for Computational Linguistics*, pages 4547–4552, Florence, Italy. Association for Computational Linguistics.

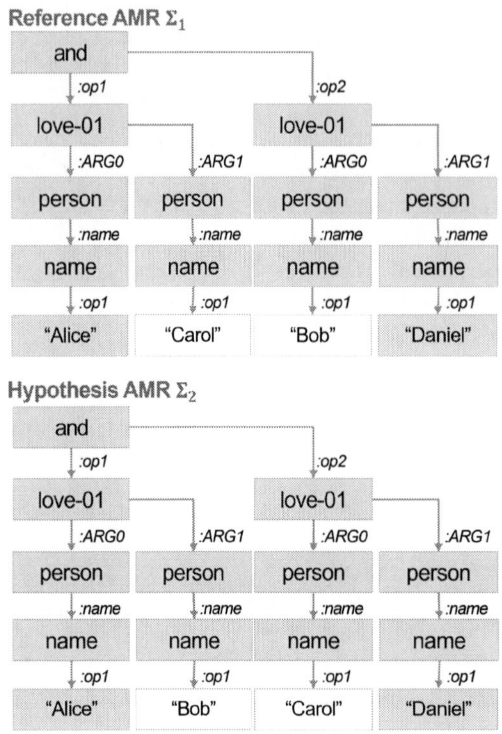

Figure 1: An example case that related to soundness

A Sample Case

Figure 1 illustrates two AMR graphs with different meanings; persons in two different 'love' relations are swapped. The reference AMR graph means a sentence "*Alice* loves *Carol*, and *Bob* loves *Daniel*." But, the hypothesis AMR graph means a sentence "*Alice* loves *Bob*, and *Carol* loves *Daniel*." Thus, these two graphs do not have the same truth condition since *Bob* and *Carol* are different people in general. Therefore, its expected value should not be the theoretical maximum score that corresponds to equivalence. Furthermore, since the subject of 'love' is set differently in both AMRs, it also should not be receive a score that is nearly identical to the theoretical maximum.

So, we computed the similarity between these two graphs using existing metrics. All existing metrics produced a score close to 1: SEMBLEU and WWLK$_{e2n}$ assigned 1.0 and SMATCH and S^{2}MATCH assigned 0.9231. Specifically for SEMBLEU, we suspect that the maximum length of n-grams used in SEMBLEU is not sufficient to handle this case; official SEMBLEU use 3-grams, which is shorter than the distance between 'love-01' and a person's name, e.g., 'Carol.' In contrast, SMATCH$^\sharp$ assigned a value of 0.8889 for this case, which is lowest score among the metrics.

B Graph Transformation

- Original AMR:

  ID: `DF-199-192794-660_6610.5`

  Sentence: I never missed a day of school.

```
(m / miss-02
  :ARG0 (i / i)
  :ARG1 (t / temporal-quantity
    :unit (d / day)
    :quant 1
    :duration-of (s / school-01))
  :polarity -
  :time (e / ever))
```

- Equivalence Cases:

Lift Up randomly set other node as a root. According to AMR guidelines, AMR can also be viewed as conjunction of logical triples, omitting root information. Thus, changing root does not harm AMR's truth condition.

```
(t / temporal-quantity
   :ARG1-of (m / miss-02
      :polarity -
      :time (e / ever)
      :ARG0 (i / I))
   :duration-of (s / school-01)
   :quant 1
   :unit (d / day))
```

Reorder randomly changes the displaying order of a graph.

```
(m / miss-02
   :time (e / ever)
   :polarity -
   :ARG0 (i / i)
   :ARG1 (t / temporal-quantity
      :quant 1
      :unit (d / day)
      :duration-of (s / school-01)))
```

Relabel change the head of each node.

```
(r0 / miss-02
  :ARG0 (r1 / i)
  :ARG1 (r2 / temporal-quantity
    :duration-of (r3 / school-01))
    :quant 1
    :unit (r4 / day)
  :polarity -
  :time (r5 / ever))
```

Reify / Dereify According to AMR guidelines, apply Reification/Dereification using PENMAN library.

```
(m / miss-02
  :ARG0 (i / I)
  :ARG1 (t / temporal-quantity
    :ARG2-of (_ / last-01
      :ARG1 (s / school-01))
    :ARG1-of (_2 / have-quant-91
      :ARG2 1)
      :unit (d / day))
  :ARG1-of (_3 / have-polarity-91
    :ARG2 -)
  :ARG1-of (_4 / be-temporally-at-91
    :ARG2 (e / ever)))
```

Duplicate Randomly duplicate the graph component.

```
(m / miss-02
   :ARG0 (i / i)
   :ARG0 i
   :ARG1 (t / temporal-quantity
      :duration-of (s / school-01)
      :duration-of s
      :quant 1
      :quant 1
      :unit (d / day)
      :unit d)
    :ARG1 t
    :polarity -
    :polarity -
    :time (e / ever)
    :time e)
```

Note that the motivation for duplicating edges is that we suspected that score inflation may have occurred in existing metrics when duplication occurred in existing parsers. Indeed, the experiment was useful in that it revealed problems with SMATCH. As a result of the experiment, SMATCH showed a tendency to evaluate higher than the score limit (0-1) when such cases were introduced. This implies the possibility that score inflation may have occurred when using SMATCH to evaluate when duplicates occurred in existing parsers.

C Implementation Detail

- Hardware:

  CPU: AMD Ryzen 5900X
  Memory: 64GB

- Software:

  OS: Ubuntu 20.04.6 LTS (kernel 5.4.0-169)
  Python: 3.11.9 (with virtualenv)

- Python libraries:

  `Penman` 1.3.0
  `networkx` 3.3
  `numpy` 1.26.4
  `statsmodels` 0.13.5
  `pandas` 2.2.1
  `SciPy` 1.12.0

Sõnajaht: Definition Embeddings and Semantic Search for Reverse Dictionary Creation

Aleksei Dorkin and **Kairit Sirts**
Institute of Computer Science
University of Tartu
{aleksei.dorkin, kairit.sirts}@ut.ee

Abstract

We present an information retrieval based reverse dictionary system using modern pre-trained language models and approximate nearest neighbors search algorithms. The proposed approach is applied to an existing Estonian language lexicon resource, Sõnaveeb (*word web*), with the purpose of enhancing and enriching it by introducing cross-lingual reverse dictionary functionality powered by semantic search. The performance of the system is evaluated using both an existing labeled English dataset of words and definitions that is extended to contain also Estonian and Russian translations, and a novel unlabeled evaluation approach that extracts the evaluation data from the lexicon resource itself using synonymy relations. Evaluation results indicate that the information retrieval based semantic search approach without any model training is feasible, producing median rank of 1 in the monolingual setting and median rank of 2 in the cross-lingual setting using the unlabeled evaluation approach, with models trained for cross-lingual retrieval and including Estonian in their training data showing superior performance in our particular task.

1 Introduction

A reverse dictionary (see examples in Table 1) is a system that takes user descriptions or definitions as input and returns words or expressions corresponding to the provided input (Hill et al., 2016; Bilac et al., 2004). The usefulness of a reverse dictionary is multi-faceted. It can help resolve the tip of the tongue problem—a common cognitive experience where a person is unable to recall a familiar word, despite feeling that they know it and that it is just on the verge of being remembered (Brown and McNeill, 1966). For writers, it can be helpful, similarly to a thesaurus, in making the vocabulary in their work richer and more expressive. Finally, in a cross-lingual setting, the reverse dictionary allows language learners to look up words simply by describing them in their native language. Consider, for example, the accidental gap in semantics—a situation when a certain concept expressed by a word in one language does not have such an expression in another language, thus making a direct translation impossible. In this case, describing the concept represented by the word might be sufficient to find related concepts in the other language.

Early approaches to building reverse dictionary systems were based on information retrieval (IR) techniques reliant on exact term matching: both user inputs and candidate collections were represented using sets of keywords or sparse term-based vector representations (Bilac et al., 2004; Shaw et al., 2011). Such representations are very limited in their ability to represent the compositional meaning of sentences due to texts being represented as simple collections of discrete terms. More recent works on reverse dictionary focused on training models to reconstruct word embeddings (Hill et al., 2016; Zhang et al., 2020) or on fine-tuning pre-trained transformers (Yan et al., 2020; Tsukagoshi et al., 2021; Mane et al., 2022). The main limitation of these approaches is that they require labeled data to train predictive models and, as such, are not easily generalizable to new settings or languages.

While the earlier IR-based approaches were limited by the expressive power of sparse text vectors and term-based text representations, dense sentence representations of modern pre-trained transformer-based language models make these problems obsolete and provide suitable representations for implementing semantic search functionality (Muennighoff, 2022). When applied to lexicographical data, semantic search may be leveraged to create a reverse dictionary system. Word definitions encoded by a pre-trained language model represent the search index, which is then queried with the encoded representation of the user's input (definition or description of a concept).

In this work, we develop an IR-based reverse

*Proceedings of the 13th Joint Conference on Lexical and Computational Semantics (*SEM 2024)*, pages 410 - 420
June 20-21, 2024

Query: *"tugev emotsionaalne füüsiline või vaimne külgetõmme kellegi suhtes"*		
Translation: *"a strong emotional feeling of physical or mental attraction towards somebody"*		
Rank	Word	Translation
1	armastama	to love
3	armastaja	lover
4	**armastus**	love
6	armupalang	love fervour
9	armunud	in love
Query: "Группа людей, таких как мать-отец и дети, которые все родственники"		
Translation: *"a group of people like a mother, father and children who are all related"*		
Rank	Word	Translation
1	abielu	marriage
2	asurkond	population
27	kollektiiv	group
46	noorpere	young family
51	**pere**	family
Query: *"when you tell other people that something is very good and the right choice"*		
Rank	Word	Translation
1	austama	to respect
13	jaatama	to agree
44	meelitama	to convince
76	**soovitama**	to recommend
98	ülistama	to praise

Table 1: Examples of the reverse dictionary search. The target words are in Estonian, while the query can be in different languages. The target word is marked in bold.

dictionary system implementing semantic search via pre-trained transformer language model representations. We apply and evaluate the system on an existing Estonian linguistic resource Sõnaveeb,[1] calling the extended reverse dictionary functionality Sõnajaht (*word hunt*). Sõnaveeb is the Estonian language portal of the Institute of the Estonian Language (EKI), giving public access to several lexicons.[2] A user can query the Sõnaveeb with words in several languages, such as Estonian or English. The words used for querying may also be in an inflected form. However, the current system does not support approximate search—the user has to spell the words precisely. Search over definitions is not currently supported in any capacity.

The system we propose is based on word definitions: every word in the Sõnaveeb has at least one distinct sense, and each sense has at least one definition. Any given definition in the Sõnaveeb can be linked back to its corresponding word and to a specific sense of that word. We encode the definitions using a pre-trained language model and then store these definitions in a vector database. Then, when a user inputs their description of a desired meaning, it is encoded with the same language model to be used as a query. The approximate nearest neighbor search is then used to query the vector database to return definitions linked to corresponding words. Although all components of this system—dense sentence representations, similarity-based search, and approximate nearest neighbors—are well-known, their combination to build a reverse dictionary functionality has, according to our knowledge, not been studied previously.

For evaluating our reverse dictionary system, we introduce a novel unlabeled evaluation approach that relies on the word relation structure present in the Sõnaveeb dictionary itself. Additionally, we utilize and extend the labeled English dataset of words and definitions introduced by Hill et al. (2016) by translating the target words to Estonian, as well as introducing definitions in Estonian and Russian in addition to English.

To summarize, our contributions in this work are as follows:

1. A novel approach to build reverse dictionary systems combining information retrieval techniques, modern pre-trained language models, and approximate nearest neighbor search algorithms;

2. A novel unlabeled evaluation approach intended to gauge the performance of a given language model in the context of a reverse dictionary that does not require annotated data;

3. An extension of an existing English reverse dictionary evaluation dataset to a cross-lingual setting by adding words and definitions in Estonian and Russian;

4. Evaluation of a number of different pre-trained language models for their suitability

[1] `https://sonaveeb.ee/?lang=en`

[2] In this work we experiment specifically with the "Ühendsõnastik 2023" lexicon—the combined dictionary.

for both monolingual and cross-lingual IR-based reverse dictionary task in a non-English language (Estonian);

5. Demonstrating the utility of building an IR-based reverse dictionary system by applying it to an existing Estonian language resource.

We make the code and data available on GitHub[3] and HuggingFace Hub[4], respectively.

2 Related Work

The approaches used to address the reverse dictionary problem can be divided into two—prediction-based methods and information retrieval (IR) based methods. Both approaches assume a dictionary dataset but use it differently—while prediction-based methods use the data for training a predictive model, IR-based methods require access to a dictionary during inference.

2.1 Prediction-based approaches

Prediction-based approaches have mostly framed the reverse dictionary problem as word embedding reconstruction where the model is trained to predict target word embeddings from their definition embeddings (Hill et al., 2016). The search is performed in two steps: first, the definition is embedded into a Word2Vec (Mikolov et al., 2013) space, and the trained model is used to predict the target word vector. Then, the produced vector is used to search for similar vectors in the Word2Vec model's vocabulary, and the most similar entries corresponding to these vectors are returned.

Zhang et al. (2020) expanded on Hill et al. (2016) by introducing additional objectives to the model, namely part-of-speech, morpheme, word category, and sememe predictors that are then used to rescore the final output. WantWords (Qi et al., 2020) adds a web interface on top of Zhang et al. (2020) and introduces the Chinese language to the system, making both monolingual and cross-lingual searches possible.

More recent approaches have leveraged pre-trained transformer models. Yan et al. (2020) used BERT (Devlin et al., 2018) to predict the target word as a masked sequence in the context of its definition. Tsukagoshi et al. (2021) fine-tuned a BERT-based classifier to predict the target word from its definition representation. Mane et al. (2022) adopted the encoder-decoder T5 model (Raffel et al., 2020) to generate the word given the definition. Tsukagoshi et al. (2021) proposed a type of sentence embedding model that is trained to predict a word out of a predefined vocabulary given the definition of that word. Meanwhile, Jo (2023) aimed to improve the ability of BERT to represent the semantics of short or single-word sentences by means of minimizing the distance between isolated words and their human-written definitions, as well as definitions and the words appearing in the relevant context.

2.2 IR-based approaches

IR-based solutions to the reverse dictionary problem assume the presence of a dictionary that contains words with their definitions. Both the user input and target word definitions are represented as vectors that are compared with some similarity measure, and the words with the most similar definition representations to the user input are returned.

Previous IR-based works fall into the pre-neural times, using count-based representations such as keyword sets and tf-idf (Bilac et al., 2004). Because the count-based representations rely on term overlap between the user input and target definitions, other works explored various heuristics to augment the representations to increase the term overlap. For instance, Shaw et al. (2011) expanded user queries with WordNet relations and reranked outputs by assigning differential weights to words according to their syntactic function in the sentence. We are unaware of any previous work using dense vector representations for IR-based reverse dictionary search.

3 Methodology

Our approach to the reverse dictionary problem is, similarly to Bilac et al. (2004) and Shaw et al. (2011), based on information retrieval techniques. We assume the presence of a lexicon of words with their definitions. The system treats individual definitions as candidates in the search database, compares the user input to all candidates, and outputs the most relevant results based on cosine similarity. When a search database has a significant number of entries, a brute-force all-to-all comparison becomes computationally infeasible. Thus, we adopt the approximate nearest neighbors algorithm that reduces the computational complexity of vector search. We

[3]https://github.com/slowwavesleep/sonajaht

[4]https://huggingface.co/datasets/adorkin/sonajaht

chose the Qdrant vector database[5] that implements the Hierarchical Navigable Small World (HNSW) approximate nearest neighbors algorithm (Malkov and Yashunin, 2018). In our experiments, we estimate the nearest neighbors search to be approximately 60 times faster than the brute-force search. The vectors are stored in the database together with some additional metadata, such as the language of the definition and both word and definition identifiers for the ease of later filtering. To store supplementary information, such as definitions themselves and synonymy relations, we opted to use SQLite for our simple implementation.

3.1 Database

The source of the data is the public API of the Estonian language portal Sõnaveeb. Due to the lack of filtering options in the API, we had to request all available information for every word entry for further processing. Out of that data, we extracted words and word definitions (represented as both surface forms and identifiers), as well as the language of words and definitions and synonymy relations for each word. We filtered the data based on the language of the words to keep only the words in Estonian. We kept the definitions in all available languages to evaluate the cross-lingual functionality. Synonymy relations came in several types: word-to-word, sense-to-word, and sense-to-sense relations. However only the coarse-grained word-to-word synonymy links were reliably present; thus we opted to keep only that type. Additionally, we discovered that a significant number of synonyms in the database had only a single direction from word A to word B, but not from word B to word A. We understand synonymy as a symmetrical relation; thus, for the purposes of evaluation, we mirrored every single direction synonymy. The statistics of the final dataset are shown in Table 2.

	Number of
Words	124K
Definitions in Estonian	213K
Definitions in other languages	16K
Synonyms	295K
Mirrored synonyms	590K
Synonyms per word on average	3.85

Table 2: Statistics of the dataset extracted from the Estonian lexicon Sõnaveeb.

3.2 Ground Truth

One of the challenges in estimating the quality of a reverse dictionary without user feedback lies in the requirement of annotated evaluation data. Commonly, annotated data for this purpose comprises definition/target word pairs (Hill et al., 2016). This approach is quite limiting because one can often find several suitable words fitting a given definition, all of which can be considered correct answers. To alleviate these issues, we propose a novel approach to defining the ground truth for reverse dictionary evaluation based on the synonymy relations of the underlying lexicon.

In our approach, we consider both the target word and its synonyms as the ground truth based on the assumption that synonymous words relate to approximately the same concepts. Thus, from the user's point of view, synonyms should be expected in the system's output in addition to the target word itself. This way, we resolve the problem of the single target word limitedness. While this approach allows us to sidestep the need for annotated data, it introduces the requirement of knowing synonymy relations between words. However, we do not consider this requirement too limiting because dictionaries generally contain information on synonymy relations between words. Alternatively, the synonymy relations can be extracted from other sources, such as WordNet. This approach makes it possible to use the dictionary as the source of both queries, candidates, and the ground truth.

3.3 Evaluation settings

We evaluate our reverse dictionary system in two settings, called *unlabeled* and *labeled* evaluation, respectively. In both cases, the ground truth is as described in Section 3.2. In the unlabeled case, the queries are also extracted from the Sõnaveeb dictionary, while in the labeled case, they are taken from an existing annotated dataset.

Unlabeled evaluation In this setup, we have no predefined query/target word pairs. However, we have dictionary entries that map words to definitions and definitions to words. We also have information on synonymy relations from the dictionary. Thus, in unlabeled evaluation we consider every individual definition entry as a query and perform vector search over all definition vectors. When computing evaluation metrics, we only consider

[5] https://qdrant.tech/

the queried definitions of words that have multiple definitions or synonyms, i.e., they have an associated ground truth definition other than the queried definition itself.

Unlabeled evaluation aims to compare different embedding models without requiring labeled evaluation data, which is very relevant for non-English and multilingual dictionaries. In addition, it allows the measurement of cross-lingual search capabilities of the embedding models. The algorithm is described in the pseudocode block below.

Algorithm 1 Candidate Quality Estimation

Require: Database of definition vectors
Require: N (number of candidates to retrieve)
Initialize an empty mapping $candidates$
for each definition ID D and definition vector V in the database **do**
  Extract the word ID W corresponding to V
  if W has associated ground truth **then**
    Use V as a query to the database
    Retrieve the top N candidates and store them in $candidates$ under key D
  end if
end for
Assess the quality of $candidates$ using the ground truth

Labeled evaluation We also adopt labeled evaluation using an annotated dataset to verify the validity of the unlabeled approach described above. For this, we adapted and extended the dataset comprised of human-crafted definitions from Hill et al. (2016). The original dataset contains 200 words together with their definitions.

Labeled evaluation aims to model the experience of a language learner who would attempt to search for words using descriptions in their native language or an intermediary language. The Estonian language is most commonly studied either in Russian (by Russian native speakers) or in English (either by native speakers or people with some other native language). We manually translated the words from English to Estonian and adapted the English definitions when necessary. Then, we linked the Estonian words to their respective word senses in our database. Finally, we translated English definitions to Estonian and Russian using machine translation.[6] The evaluation approach is also modified compared to Hill et al. (2016). Similarly to the unlabeled approach, we use the definitions from the dataset as queries. However, we consider only the relevant word sense as the target and not all senses of that word. Overall, the ground truth and evaluation principles are similar to the unlabeled case, making the metrics of both approaches comparable.

3.4 Embedding Models

We evaluated several pre-trained transformer-based models to understand their suitability for producing representations for reverse dictionary search.

E5 **E**mb**E**ddings from bidir**E**ctional **E**ncoder r**E**presentations (Wang et al., 2022) was the highest scoring open-source multilingual embedding model in the *Overall* ranking on the MTEB leaderboard (Muennighoff et al., 2023) at the time of writing. E5 is a BERT-based bi-encoder asymmetrical retrieval model: training examples were prepended with query and passage prefixes. Thus, in our experiments, we tested E5 in two distinct environments: we encoded candidate definitions with query or passage prefixes, and in both cases, we used query-prefixed queries.

LaBSE Language-agnostic BERT Sentence Embedding (Feng et al., 2022) is a multilingual sentence embedding model. It is an extension of the BERT architecture designed to generate high-quality fixed-size representations for sentences or short texts. LaBSE supports over 100 languages, including Estonian. At the time of writing, LaBSE takes the top position in *Bi-Text Mining* category on the MTEB leaderboard (Muennighoff et al., 2023).

OpenAI In addition to open-source models, we used the proprietary OpenAI's *text-embedding-ada-002* embedding model for comparison. According to our knowledge, OpenAI has not disclosed much information on the configuration and properties of this model.

DistilUSE V1 and V2 are DistilBERT models trained on 15 languages (but no Estonian) and 50 languages (with Estonian), respectively, and distilled from the mUSE model (Multilingual Universal Sentence Encoder) (Yang et al., 2020), provided as part of the Sentence Transformers library (Reimers and Gurevych, 2019, 2020).

BGE (Xiao et al., 2023) was the highest-scoring open-source English-only retrieval embedding model on the MTEB leaderboard (Muennighoff et al., 2023) at the time of writing. The reason for adding this model is to understand how well a monolingual retrieval model can generalize in a cross-lingual retrieval task.

[6] `https://translate.ut.ee/`

MPNet Masked and Permuted Pre-training for Language Understanding (Song et al., 2020) is a version of the BERT (Devlin et al., 2018) model with a different training objective. The specific model we used was additionally fine-tuned on the sentence similarity task. Similarly to BGE, the intent is to test cross-lingual generalization capabilities.

XLM-RoBERTa is a state-of-the-art pre-trained language model (Conneau et al., 2020) that combines the RoBERTa (Zhuang et al., 2021) architecture with cross-lingual learning techniques. RoBERTa is an extension of the BERT (Devlin et al., 2018) architecture and is designed for various natural language understanding tasks. XLM-RoBERTa was trained on data with some Estonian texts in it. We used the large version in our experiments. The aim of including XLM-RoBERTa is to understand how well a multilingual non-retrieval model would perform in our task.

Word2Vec Finally, a Word2Vec (Mikolov et al., 2013) model trained on Estonian data was used as a baseline.[7] We employed a very simple approach to extract definition embeddings with the Word2Vec: definitions were tokenized based on the whitespace character, then we simply ignored tokens not present in the model's vocabulary and averaged the rest.

3.5 Metrics

To assess the quality of each model, we employed metrics traditionally used in information retrieval works (Buttcher et al., 2016), as well as some metrics from the related works (Hill et al., 2016). We limit the number of items the search system outputs to **100** items. In the following, let *Res* be the collection of retrieved items, and *Rel* the set of relevant items. *Res[1..k]* consists of the top k items returned by the system.

Precision@k Precision at k is meant to model a user's satisfaction when presented with a ranked list of results given the query. The expectation is that the user examines every item out of k in an arbitrary order (Buttcher et al., 2016). In the case of a reverse dictionary system, this is a very reasonable expectation because the items comprise words and their usually short definitions. The $P@k$ for a single query is:

$$P@k = \frac{|\text{Res}[1..k] \cap \text{Rel}|}{k}$$

We report the mean $P@k$ over all queries and denote it as $MP@k$.

$$MP@k = \frac{1}{|Q|} \sum_{j=1}^{|Q|} P@k_j$$

Mean Average Precision Choosing a specific k to measure the Precision at k can be considered quite arbitrary. Average Precision addresses this by measuring precision at every possible threshold—for every relevant item, precision is measured up to and including the position of the item. Average Precision also has an implicit recall component because it accounts for relevant items (Buttcher et al., 2016). If the user interface with a specific number of items shown is being tested, then Average Precision is a more comprehensive measure compared to Precision at k.

$$AP = \frac{1}{|\text{Rel}|} \sum_{i=1}^{|\text{Res}|} \text{relevant}(i) \cdot P@i,$$

where *relevant(i)* is 1 if the i-th item in *Res* is relevant; 0 otherwise. Similarly to $P@k$, AP refers to the result of a single query. We are, however, interested in the value of AP aggregated over all queries, which is the Mean Average Precision denoted as MAP.

$$MAP = \frac{1}{|Q|} \sum_{j=1}^{|Q|} AP_j$$

Mean Reciprocal Rank The user may be interested in one specific relevant item given their query. Reciprocal rank models that situation by favoring the rankings where the relevant document is as close to the top as possible (Buttcher et al., 2016).

$$RR = \frac{1}{\min\{k | \text{Res}[k] \in \text{Rel}\}}$$

Accordingly, the Mean Reciprocal Rank (MRR) is computed as the average of the reciprocal ranks of the first relevant answers across all queries.

$$MRR = \frac{1}{|Q|} \sum_{j=1}^{|Q|} RR_j$$

[7] https://github.com/estnltk/word2vec-models

Median Rank Median Rank is calculated as the median of the ranks of the first relevant answers across all queries. In the presence of MRR, Median Rank may be considered redundant because, similarly to MRR, it favors rankings with relevant items near the top. We report this primarily for consistency with previous works (Hill et al., 2016; Qi et al., 2020; Zhang et al., 2020). Also, when the number of possible results returned is capped, and there are no relevant items among the returned results, it is impossible to accurately estimate the rank of the first relevant item. Thus, an arbitrary value (1000 in this case) is chosen as exemplified by Qi et al. (2020) in their project's GitHub repository.[8]

Accuracy@k Top-k accuracy represents the proportion of responses to queries where at least one returned item is relevant regardless of its position. The expectation behind this metric is that the user will be satisfied if they see at least one relevant result in the output. Note that Accuracy@1 is equivalent to Mean Precision@1.

4 Results

We expect that the output of a good reverse dictionary system would contain as many relevant items as possible and they would be as close to the top as possible. Meanwhile, the user's interest seems unlikely to be strictly limited to a single item. Therefore, although we show all measures described in Section 3.5, we consider Mean Average Precision (MAP) as the main measure because it rewards situations where relevant items are grouped at the top.

Unlabeled evaluation The main purpose of this evaluation was to measure the quality of different embedding models and rank them to select the best one when applied to creating a reverse dictionary system. We can single out three main aspects that can affect the position of the model on the table: 1) whether the target language was in the model's training data, 2) whether the model was trained for retrieval, and 3) whether the model was trained for cross-lingual retrieval specifically.

Table 3 demonstrates the performance of all tested models. We observe that the models possessing all three aspects mentioned above (trained on the target language, trained for retrieval, and trained for cross-lingual retrieval) dominate the table: E5 and LaBSE were both trained for cross-lingual retrieval and contained Estonian in their training data. Meanwhile, we have no information on how OpenAI's embedding model was trained. We can infer that it is also a retrieval model that has seen Estonian; however it was possibly not trained for cross-lingual retrieval specifically. DistilUSE V2, which also included Estonian in the training data, performs better than V1, as expected. The English-only retrieval models (BGE and MPNet) perform similarly to the Estonian Word2Vec baseline. Surprisingly, the very simple Word2Vec embedding model outperforms the much larger multilingual XLM-RoBERTa, even though the latter also includes Estonian.

Cross-lingual unlabeled evaluation The Estonian language heavily dominates the data used for the unlabeled evaluation since it comes from the Estonian language resource. However, it also contains about 14K definitions in other languages. The results in Table 4 focus specifically on the cross-lingual capabilities of the models: only definitions in languages other than Estonian were used as queries, while the candidates remained the Estonian words with definitions in all available languages. All measures are slightly worse in this setting, showing that the cross-lingual search is harder than the monolingual retrieval. The overall ranking of the models remains roughly the same, with LaBSE being the best while the DistilUSE models are in second place. Interestingly, the V1 model that did not include Estonian in the training data is slightly better than the V2 model. The OpenAI model performs considerably worse on MAP than the other multi-lingual retrieval models.

Labeled evaluation To ensure the results output by the unlabeled environment are reliable, we tested the models on a smaller labeled dataset focusing on modeling cross-lingual retrieval. Table 5 shows the labeled evaluation results of the best models from the unlabeled evaluation setting. We can see that the order of the models based on the metrics is approximately the same, which confirms the reliability of the unlabeled evaluation. We also note the relatively poor performance of OpenAI's embedding model, which further points towards a lack of focus on cross-linguality during its training. The labeled evaluation measures are lower compared to the unlabeled evaluation setting. It might be because the definitions from the small labeled dataset are very out of distribution compared to the

[8]https://github.com/thunlp/WantWords

Model	MAP	MP@1	MP@10	MRR	Acc@1	Acc@10	Median Rank
E5 query-passage	**0.4282**	**0.4952**	**0.1591**	**0.5470**	**0.4952**	**0.6438**	**1**
E5 query-query	0.4202	0.4940	0.1571	0.5448	0.4940	0.6397	**1**
LaBSE	0.4081	0.4894	0.1502	0.5345	0.4894	0.6178	**1**
OpenAI	0.3746	0.4934	0.1376	0.5347	0.4934	0.6114	**1**
DistilUSE V2	0.3381	0.4544	0.1241	0.4894	0.4544	0.5526	2
BGE	0.2660	0.4323	0.1038	0.4607	0.4323	0.5090	7
Word2Vec	0.2573	0.4203	0.1040	0.4518	0.4203	0.5072	8
MPNet	0.2552	0.4255	0.0997	0.4516	0.4255	0.4954	11
DistilUSE V1	0.2389	0.4048	0.0897	0.4247	0.4048	0.4569	74
XLM-RoBERTa	0.2306	0.4065	0.0901	0.4281	0.4065	0.4637	51

Table 3: Reverse dictionary performance in unlabeled evaluation on the full Sõnaveeb dataset, with both Estonian and non-Estonian queries. The E5 model is evaluated in two settings: by using passage prefix for candidate definitions (E5 query-passage) and by using query prefix for candidate definitions (E5 query-query).

Model	MAP	MP@1	MP@10	MRR	Acc@1	Acc@10	Median Rank
LaBSE	**0.3913**	0.4546	0.1449	0.4738	0.4546	0.5122	6
DistilUSE V1	0.3873	0.4635	0.1451	0.4827	0.4635	0.5215	4
DistilUSE V2	0.3775	0.4367	0.1411	0.4561	0.4367	0.4951	12
E5 query-passage	0.3746	**0.4732**	**0.1515**	**0.5005**	**0.4732**	**0.5540**	**2**
E5 query-query	0.3627	0.4448	0.1458	0.4720	0.4448	0.5269	4
OpenAI	0.3335	0.4624	0.1447	0.4901	0.4624	0.5464	**2**
BGE	0.2404	0.4356	0.1173	0.4569	0.4356	0.4992	10
MPNet	0.2204	0.4053	0.1126	0.4259	0.4053	0.4675	32
XLM-RoBERTa	0.1525	0.3955	0.0822	0.4048	0.3955	0.4229	1000
Word2Vec	0.1326	0.3617	0.0732	0.3775	0.3617	0.4087	1000

Table 4: Reverse dictionary performance in unlabeled evaluation using only non-Estonian queries. The E5 model is evaluated in two settings: by using passage prefix for candidate definitions (E5 query-passage) and by using query prefix for candidate definitions (E5 query-query).

dictionary definitions, so it makes sense that there would be some discrepancy.

Qualitative evaluation We manually examined some outputs of the best-performing E5 model using the definitions from our unlabeled evaluation dataset with few examples shown in Table 1. We note that while the expected target words do not always appear in top-10 results, the output is sensible, and the other words in the output very often fit the queried definitions (which are sometimes quite vague) quite well. The same observation also applies to the cross-lingual search environment.

5 Conclusion

We proposed an IR-based reverse dictionary system leveraging pre-trained transformer-based language models for semantic search and evaluated it thoroughly on an Estonian language dictionary resource, the Sõnaveeb. Unlike the prediction-based approaches that have been mainly focused on in recent works, the IR-based approach does not require training any specialized models. Furthermore, it can be easily adapted to work in the cross-lingual setting. The evaluations using the unlabeled evaluation procedure based on the synonym relations of the target dictionary and a small multilingual dataset showed that language models trained for cross-lingual retrieval are optimal for our use case. We expect that the proposed approach to building and validating reverse dictionary systems is reusable, approachable, and generalizable due to its simplicity, thus facilitating the development and improvement of language resources for less-represented languages with a focus on language learning, documentation, and preservation.

In future work, we would like to develop a user interface to perform human evaluation of our proposed system. The ultimate goal is to integrate the best-performing model into the existing Sõnaveeb language portal to enrich this resource by making

Model	MAP	MP@1	MP@10	MRR	Acc@1	Acc@10	Median Rank
			Definitions in Estonian				
E5 query-query	**0.2135**	**0.2600**	**0.1435**	**0.3635**	**0.2600**	**0.5700**	**6**
E5 query-passage	0.2024	0.2400	0.1350	0.3425	0.2400	0.5350	**6**
LaBSE	0.1432	0.2150	0.1055	0.2885	0.2150	0.4500	14
OpenAI	0.1031	0.1750	0.0835	0.2390	0.1750	0.3850	27
DistilUSE V2	0.0983	0.1400	0.0590	0.1979	0.1400	0.3000	49
			Definitions in English				
E5 query-query	**0.1948**	0.2050	**0.1250**	**0.3013**	0.2050	**0.5250**	**8**
E5 query-passage	0.1717	0.2150	0.1135	0.2952	0.2150	0.4750	13
LaBSE	0.1478	**0.2300**	0.1185	0.3074	**0.2300**	0.4850	12
DistilUSE V2	0.1262	0.1700	0.0885	0.2328	0.1700	0.3550	29
OpenAI	0.0996	0.1150	0.0870	0.1981	0.1150	0.4000	17
			Definitions in Russian				
E5 query-query	**0.1954**	**0.2150**	**0.1385**	**0.3149**	**0.2150**	**0.5500**	**7**
LaBSE	0.1446	0.2050	0.1140	0.2922	0.2050	0.4750	14
E5 query-passage	0.1166	0.1500	0.0945	0.2236	0.1500	0.3950	23
DistilUSE V2	0.1023	0.1150	0.0800	0.1874	0.1150	0.3350	39
OpenAI	0.0093	0.0050	0.0055	0.0231	0.0050	0.0500	1000

Table 5: Reverse dictionary performance on a labeled dataset in both monolingual and cross-lingual setting.

the search and navigation more accessible and to support language learners via cross-lingual search.

Limitations

The main limitation of our work is the lack of human evaluation. Although both the unlabeled and labeled evaluation approach attempt to model user satisfaction, we do not know the correlation between automatic measures and human judgments at this point. Although we assumed that MAP is the most suitable measure, its correlation with human judgments for our task still needs to be established.

Another limitation is that we have not assessed the level of noise in the dictionary resource Sõnaveeb used in this work. It is possible that filtering out non-informative definitions or possibly erroneous synonymy relations could result in a more precise evaluation. However, the main point of our unlabeled validation approach was to facilitate the performance of the different embedding models for building an IR-based reverse dictionary and to make it require as little additional effort as possible. We expect that any additional data filtering does not result in any significant change to the model rankings. This assumption is also supported by the results we obtained using the labeled evaluation.

Finally, when we consider the fact that the ultimate purpose of our work is to enable reverse dictionary search functionality in an existing language resource that real users could utilize via a graphical user interface, the way the reverse dictionary output would be represented visually would also play a significant role in user satisfaction. Consequently, the effect the visual presentation has on the performance of a reverse dictionary system also needs to be evaluated to get the full picture. We leave that particular aspect for future work.

Acknowledgments

This research was supported by the Estonian Research Council Grant PSG721.

References

Slaven Bilac, Wataru Watanabe, Taiichi Hashimoto, Takenobu Tokunaga, and Hozumi Tanaka. 2004. Dictionary search based on the target word description. In *Proc. of the Tenth Annual Meeting of The Association for Natural Language Processing (NLP2004)*, pages 556–559.

Roger Brown and David McNeill. 1966. The "tip of the tongue" phenomenon. *Journal of verbal learning and verbal behavior*, 5(4):325–337.

Stefan Buttcher, Charles LA Clarke, and Gordon V Cormack. 2016. *Information retrieval: Implementing and evaluating search engines*. MIT Press.

Alexis Conneau, Kartikay Khandelwal, Naman Goyal, Vishrav Chaudhary, Guillaume Wenzek, Francisco

Guzmán, Edouard Grave, Myle Ott, Luke Zettlemoyer, and Veselin Stoyanov. 2020. Unsupervised cross-lingual representation learning at scale. In *Proceedings of the 58th Annual Meeting of the Association for Computational Linguistics*, pages 8440–8451, Online. Association for Computational Linguistics.

Jacob Devlin, Ming-Wei Chang, Kenton Lee, and Kristina Toutanova. 2018. BERT: Pre-training of deep bidirectional transformers for language understanding. *arXiv preprint arXiv:1810.04805*.

Fangxiaoyu Feng, Yinfei Yang, Daniel Cer, Naveen Arivazhagan, and Wei Wang. 2022. Language-agnostic BERT sentence embedding. In *Proceedings of the 60th Annual Meeting of the Association for Computational Linguistics (Volume 1: Long Papers)*, pages 878–891, Dublin, Ireland. Association for Computational Linguistics.

Felix Hill, Kyunghyun Cho, Anna Korhonen, and Yoshua Bengio. 2016. Learning to understand phrases by embedding the dictionary. *Transactions of the Association for Computational Linguistics*, 4:17–30.

Hwiyeol Jo. 2023. A self-supervised integration method of pretrained language models and word definitions. In *Findings of the Association for Computational Linguistics: ACL 2023*, pages 14–26, Toronto, Canada. Association for Computational Linguistics.

Yu A Malkov and Dmitry A Yashunin. 2018. Efficient and robust approximate nearest neighbor search using hierarchical navigable small world graphs. *IEEE transactions on pattern analysis and machine intelligence*, 42(4):824–836.

Sunil B Mane, Harshal Navneet Patil, Kanhaiya Balaji Madaswar, and Pranav Nitin Sadavarte. 2022. Wordalchemy: a transformer-based reverse dictionary. In *2022 2nd International Conference on Intelligent Technologies (CONIT)*, pages 1–5. IEEE.

Tomas Mikolov, Kai Chen, Greg Corrado, and Jeffrey Dean. 2013. Efficient estimation of word representations in vector space. *arXiv preprint arXiv:1301.3781*.

Niklas Muennighoff. 2022. SGPT: GPT sentence embeddings for semantic search. *arXiv preprint arXiv:2202.08904*.

Niklas Muennighoff, Nouamane Tazi, Loic Magne, and Nils Reimers. 2023. MTEB: Massive text embedding benchmark. In *Proceedings of the 17th Conference of the European Chapter of the Association for Computational Linguistics*, pages 2014–2037, Dubrovnik, Croatia. Association for Computational Linguistics.

Fanchao Qi, Lei Zhang, Yanhui Yang, Zhiyuan Liu, and Maosong Sun. 2020. Wantwords: An open-source online reverse dictionary system. In *Proceedings of the 2020 conference on empirical methods in natural language processing: system demonstrations*, pages 175–181.

Colin Raffel, Noam Shazeer, Adam Roberts, Katherine Lee, Sharan Narang, Michael Matena, Yanqi Zhou, Wei Li, and Peter J Liu. 2020. Exploring the limits of transfer learning with a unified text-to-text transformer. *The Journal of Machine Learning Research*, 21(1):5485–5551.

Nils Reimers and Iryna Gurevych. 2019. Sentence-bert: Sentence embeddings using siamese bert-networks. In *Proceedings of the 2019 Conference on Empirical Methods in Natural Language Processing*. Association for Computational Linguistics.

Nils Reimers and Iryna Gurevych. 2020. Making monolingual sentence embeddings multilingual using knowledge distillation. In *Proceedings of the 2020 Conference on Empirical Methods in Natural Language Processing*. Association for Computational Linguistics.

Ryan Shaw, Anindya Datta, Debra VanderMeer, and Kaushik Dutta. 2011. Building a scalable database-driven reverse dictionary. *IEEE Transactions on Knowledge and Data Engineering*, 25(3):528–540.

Kaitao Song, Xu Tan, Tao Qin, Jianfeng Lu, and Tie-Yan Liu. 2020. Mpnet: Masked and permuted pre-training for language understanding. *Advances in Neural Information Processing Systems*, 33:16857–16867.

Hayato Tsukagoshi, Ryohei Sasano, and Koichi Takeda. 2021. DefSent: Sentence embeddings using definition sentences. In *Proceedings of the 59th Annual Meeting of the Association for Computational Linguistics and the 11th International Joint Conference on Natural Language Processing (Volume 2: Short Papers)*, pages 411–418, Online. Association for Computational Linguistics.

Liang Wang, Nan Yang, Xiaolong Huang, Binxing Jiao, Linjun Yang, Daxin Jiang, Rangan Majumder, and Furu Wei. 2022. Text embeddings by weakly-supervised contrastive pre-training. *arXiv preprint arXiv:2212.03533*.

Shitao Xiao, Zheng Liu, Peitian Zhang, and Niklas Muennighoff. 2023. C-pack: Packaged resources to advance general chinese embedding.

Hang Yan, Xiaonan Li, Xipeng Qiu, and Bocao Deng. 2020. BERT for monolingual and cross-lingual reverse dictionary. In *Findings of the Association for Computational Linguistics: EMNLP 2020*, pages 4329–4338, Online. Association for Computational Linguistics.

Yinfei Yang, Daniel Cer, Amin Ahmad, Mandy Guo, Jax Law, Noah Constant, Gustavo Hernandez Abrego, Steve Yuan, Chris Tar, Yun-hsuan Sung, Brian Strope, and Ray Kurzweil. 2020. Multilingual universal sentence encoder for semantic retrieval. In *Proceedings of the 58th Annual Meeting of the Association for Computational Linguistics: System Demonstrations*, pages 87–94, Online. Association for Computational Linguistics.

Lei Zhang, Fanchao Qi, Zhiyuan Liu, Yasheng Wang, Qun Liu, and Maosong Sun. 2020. Multi-channel reverse dictionary model. In *Proceedings of the AAAI conference on artificial intelligence*, volume 34, pages 312–319.

Liu Zhuang, Lin Wayne, Shi Ya, and Zhao Jun. 2021. A robustly optimized BERT pre-training approach with post-training. In *Proceedings of the 20th Chinese National Conference on Computational Linguistics*, pages 1218–1227, Huhhot, China. Chinese Information Processing Society of China.

Do large language models and humans have similar behaviors in causal inference with script knowledge?

Xudong Hong* [1,2], **Margarita Ryzhova*** [2], **Daniel Adrian Biondi**[1] **and Vera Demberg**[1,2]

[1]Dept. of Computer Science, Saarland University

[2]Dept. of Language Science and Technology, Saarland University

{xhong,mryzhova,biondi,vera}@lst.uni-saarland.de

Abstract

Recently, large pre-trained language models (LLMs) have demonstrated superior language understanding abilities, including zero-shot causal reasoning. However, it is unclear to what extent their capabilities are similar to human ones. We here study the processing of an event B in a script-based story, which causally depends on a previous event A. In our manipulation, event A is stated, negated, or omitted in an earlier section of the text. We first conducted a self-paced reading experiment, which showed that humans exhibit significantly longer reading times when causal conflicts exist ($\neg A \rightarrow B$) than under logical conditions ($A \rightarrow B$). However, reading times remain similar when cause A is not explicitly mentioned, indicating that humans can easily infer event B from their script knowledge. We then tested a variety of LLMs on the same data to check to what extent the models replicate human behavior. Our experiments show that 1) only recent LLMs, like GPT-3 or Vicuna, correlate with human behavior in the $\neg A \rightarrow B$ condition. 2) Despite this correlation, all models still fail to predict that $nil \rightarrow B$ is less surprising than $\neg A \rightarrow B$, indicating that LLMs still have difficulties integrating script knowledge. Code and data are available at `https://github.com/tony-hong/causal-script`.

1 Introduction

Causal reasoning is fundamental for both human and machine intelligence (Pearl, 2009) and plays an important role in language comprehension (Keenan and Kintsch, 1974; Graesser et al., 1994, 1997; Van den Broek, 1990). Large pre-trained language models (LLMs) such as GPT-3.5 (Neelakantan et al., 2022) have demonstrated excellent zero-shot capabilities in causal reasoning tasks and human-like behaviors (Wang et al., 2019). The capability of causal reasoning is essential to new prompting techniques like the chain-of-thought prompting (Wei et al., 2022; Kojima et al., 2022). On the other hand, some early pieces of evidence show that LLMs lack global planning of different events in stories (Bubeck et al., 2023). So it is unclear to what extent LLMs can conduct causal reasoning about events.

In turn, humans have been shown to be extremely good at building causal connections in long discourse comprehension (Radvansky et al., 2014; Graesser et al., 1994). In doing so, they rely not only on explicit causal links (signaled in the text – see Trabasso and Sperry, 1985; Keenan and Kintsch, 1974) but also on implicit ones that are inferable based on commonsense knowledge (Keenan and Kintsch, 1974; Singer and Halldorson, 1996). In particular, subjects were found to be sensitive to causal conflicts arising from contradictions to earlier text segments or conflicts with subjects' commonsense knowledge (Radvansky et al., 2014; Singer and Halldorson, 1996). An example of a causal conflict is presented in Figure 1, Part II, condition $\neg A \rightarrow B$, where decorating a cake with star-shaped sprinkles is inconsistent with the previously mentioned information that cake decorations are not available.

In this paper, we investigate language processing in humans and compare it to a large variety of LLMs, following the "psycholinguistic assessment of language models paradigm" (Futrell et al., 2019). In our analyses, we compare human reading times to LLM surprisal estimates. Surprisal is the negative log probability of a word in context and has been previously related to human reading times (Hale, 2001; Levy, 2008; Demberg and Keller, 2008; Smith and Levy, 2013) as well as neuropsychological effects such as the N400 (Frank et al., 2015; Kutas and Hillyard, 1989), which represent human processing difficulty. We collect a new dataset, Causality in Script Knowledge (**CSK**),

* These authors contributed equally to this work.

*Proceedings of the 13th Joint Conference on Lexical and Computational Semantics (*SEM 2024)*, pages 421 - 437
June 20-21, 2024 ©2024 Association for Computational Linguistics

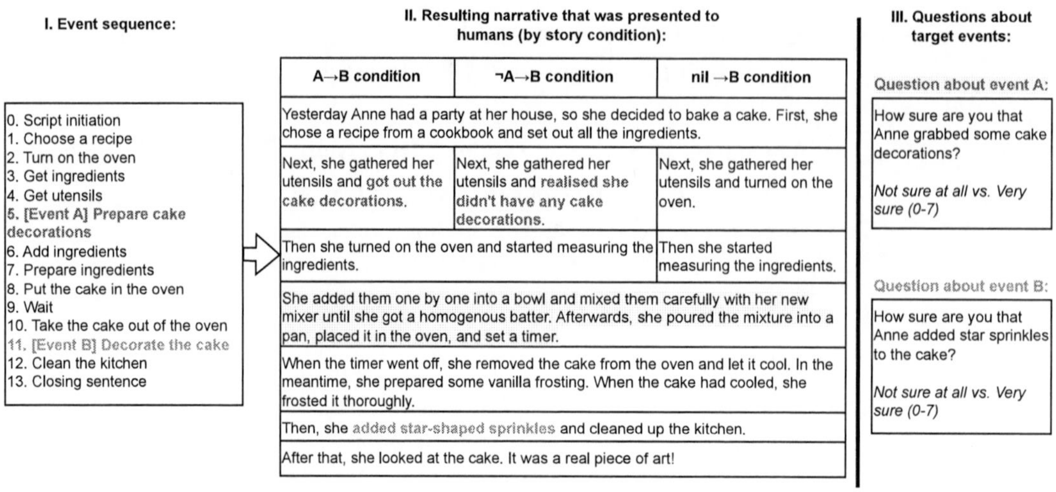

Figure 1: Example of a script structure (I), the resulting narrative in three conditions (II) and questions that subjects were asked (III), for "baking a cake" story.

consisting of short stories about daily activities which are typically part of the *script knowledge* of humans, see Figure 1 for an example. The term "script knowledge" refers to commonsense knowledge about everyday activities, where "scripts" are defined as prototypical sequences of events in these activities. The stories are constructed such that they contain a pair of events, A and B which are causally contingent on one another. We manipulate event A to be stated, negated or omitted, and subsequently measure reading times on event B.

Our first research question (**RQ1**) relates to the effect of the incoherence in the $\neg A \rightarrow B$ condition, compared to the coherent $A \rightarrow B$ condition. For humans, a large body of previous literature (Bloom et al., 1990; Radvansky et al., 2014; Singer and Ritchot, 1996) leads us to expect that human readers will notice the inconsistency and that this can be measured in terms of slower reading times on event B. For language models, we want to test whether and which models also exhibit a similar effect, by comparing the surprisal values for the words of event B following the A vs. $\neg A$ mentioned in the previous context. In order for a language model to handle this case, it needs to (a) understand the contingency between events A and B (even though they often don't use overlapping lexical items) and (b) be able to represent event A or $\neg A$ effectively across the intervening sentences so it is still represented when encountering B. We find that the large models (GPT-3 and Vicuna) do well on this task, but smaller models mostly fail.

Our second research question (**RQ2**) aims to tap into how script knowledge facilitates language comprehension. To this end, we compare the processing of event B in a setting where neither event A nor event $\neg A$ are mentioned in the previous context. If comprehenders integrate their script knowledge with the text, they should have an easy time processing event B even without the prior mention of event A (Bower et al., 1979). The previous literature on human sentence processing has no direct evidence about the processing difficulty of event B in this case, so here our experiment makes a new contribution: we find that humans are significantly faster in reading segment B in the $nil \rightarrow B$ condition compared to $\neg A \rightarrow B$, and that reading times between conditions $nil \rightarrow B$ and $A \rightarrow B$ do not differ significantly from one another. Our subsequent evaluation of LLMs on the same contrast however shows that all LLMs fail to show human-like processing: they do not have lower surprisal on the $nil \rightarrow B$ condition than on $\neg A \rightarrow B$ – some models even assign higher surprisal estimates to the $nil \rightarrow B$ condition, indicating that even the most recent large LLMs in our evaluation cannot effectively integrate script knowledge for estimating the probability of upcoming words.

2 Background

2.1 Causal inference and script knowledge

When humans read text, they connect events mentioned in the text into a locally and globally coherent causal network, thereby not only integrating information from the text but also based on context and commonsense knowledge (Van den Broek, 1990; Graesser et al., 1997). It has been shown that when the causal network does not support new events or the new event contradicts the previous text, readers experience processing difficulties, resulting in longer reading times (Bloom et al., 1990; Radvansky et al., 2014). The comprehension of a new event also relies on commonsense knowledge (Hare et al., 2009). In fact, Singer and Ritchot (1996) showed that when commonsense knowledge does not support an event described in the text, comprehenders take more time processing it.

A special type of commonsense knowledge that was shown to also modulate reading comprehension is script knowledge (Abbott et al., 1985; Bower et al., 1979; Schank, 1975). Scripts represent knowledge structures consistent with sets of beliefs built on past experiences about everyday, routine, and conventional activities like baking a cake. Importantly, the events constituting a script can be highly causally inter-connected and are crystallized in memory – one can expect script-related events to be activated once the script is invoked. In a series of experiments, Bower et al. (1979) showed that after subjects read an everyday story that constituted a script, they also recalled script-related events that were not explicitly mentioned in the story (see Gibbs and Tenney, 1980, for similar findings showing that script knowledge is an indistinguishable part of the memory representation). In turn, it is expected that when reading a story, script-related events can be primed by the script itself rather than by some single events mentioned in the text, without processing time loss (Keenan and Kintsch, 1974).

2.2 Experiments with language models

Causal Reasoning. Recent LLMs such as GPT-3.5 (Neelakantan et al., 2022) have achieved strong performance in many reasoning tasks under zero-shot settings, such as symbolic reasoning, logical reasoning, mathematical reasoning and commonsense inference (Kojima et al., 2022). The common practice to conduct zero-shot reasoning is *prompting*, i.e. to append a task-specific text to the input to LLMs and then sample the output (Radford et al., 2019). Although the cause is usually provided in the prompt (like condition $A \rightarrow B$), LLMs can reason without relying only on surface cues like word overlap (Lampinen et al., 2022). Moreover, LLMs can be prompted to produce explicit reasoning steps with chain-of-thought prompting (Wei et al., 2022).

Script knowledge. Early works regarding script knowledge also apply language models (LMs). Weber et al. (2020) apply LMs for script induction from causal effects. Ciosici et al. (2021) build a human-LM collaborative system for script authoring.

Recent studies have suggested that LLMs may learn script knowledge as part of their training (Sakaguchi et al., 2021; Sancheti and Rudinger, 2022). Ravi et al. (2023) fine-tune GPT-3 to automatically generate plausible events that happen before and after a given event, and Yuan et al. (2023) report promising results on prompting an InstructGPT model (Ouyang et al., 2022) to automatically generate scripts and then filtering results in the second step. Similarly, Brahman et al. (2023) use a distilled small LM as script planner and fine-tuned RoBERTa as verifiers.

There are however also reports that indicate that script knowledge in LLMs may not yet be sufficient: zero-shot probing on GPT-2 has been found to generate poor event sequences (Sancheti and Rudinger, 2022), and GPT-3 was found to be only marginally better than chance on predicting event likelihoods (Zhang et al., 2023) and exhibit poor performance on event temporal ordering (Suzgun et al., 2023).

Several ways of specifically integrating commonsense knowledge into LLMs have been proposed: some LLMs are trained from scratch on structural data with commonsense knowledge like knowledge graphs (ERNIE; Zhang et al., 2019) and semantic frames (SpanBERT; Joshi et al., 2020). Bosselut et al. (2019); Hwang et al. (2021) further equips LLMs with structural input and output to model commonsense knowledge. In the present contribution, we explore previous models that have been reported to be successful in inference tasks. More details of the choice of LLMs are in Section 4.1.

2.3 The TRIP dataset

A dataset that is particularly relevant to the present study is the TRIP dataset, which contains 1472 pairs of two similar stories, which differ by one sentence at a "breakpoint" position (Storks et al., 2021). One of the stories is plausible, and the other one is implausible, due to a causal conflict between the sentence at the breakpoint position and an earlier part of the text. The plausible stories correspond to the $A \rightarrow B$ condition in our dataset, while the implausible stories correspond to our $\neg A \rightarrow B$ condition. The breakpoint sentence corresponds to our critical sequence B.

Richardson et al. (2022) fine-tune a T5 model augmented with logical states of each event to detect the causal conflicts and outperform a RoBERTa baseline by a large margin. Ma et al. (2022) fine-tune a framework to integrate global and local information. Our aim is not to finetune the LLMs on TRIP but to test them in a zero-shot fashion.

3 Experiments with Humans

3.1 Dataset

The Causality in Script Knowledge (**CSK**) dataset consists of 21 English stories describing everyday activities like baking a cake or taking a bath.[1]

To construct the stories, we initially composed sequences of script-related events that were built on top of Wanzare et al. (2016) – see Figure 1, part I. Subsequently, we transformed these sequences into narrative form (Figure 1, part II; for example, an event "prepare cake decorations" is realised in the narrative as "she got out the cake decorations"). Further, each story was divided into chunks of text (as rows of the table in Figure 1, part II) such that participants do not see the whole text at once, but chunk after chunk.

Each story starts with script initiation – a sentence in the first chunk that introduces the topic to the reader, e.g., "*Yesterday Anne had a party at her house, so* ***she decided to bake a cake****.*" from Figure 1, part II. Thus, readers can already activate script knowledge about the event at that point.

A pair of events A and B represent our main interest. They were chosen in such a way that event A ("get the cake decorations") enabled the happening of event B ("add star-shaped sprinkles"). More specifically, since scripts are typically characterized by event sequences in which specific script participants appear repeatedly (like cake decorations), we are interested in a pair of events that define an action done to this specific participant.

In some stories, participants related to the target manipulation have different lexical realization between events A and B. For example in the cake story presented in Figure 1, a participant in event A is referred to as "cake decorations" and in event B

[1]Available at `https://github.com/tony-hong/causal-script`

parameter	mean	sd
# of words in story:		
$A \rightarrow B$	158.2	12
$\neg A \rightarrow B$	159.1	14
$nil \rightarrow B$	150.1	11.7
# of text chunks in story	6.8	0.77
# of words in chunk with A	27.6	11.3
# of words in chunk with $\neg A$	29.3	13.1
# of words in chunk with B	12.9	1.7
# of words in chunk after B	12.9	1.8
# of words b/w A and B:		
$A \rightarrow B$	73.6	10.3
$\neg A \rightarrow B$	71.8	12.9
# of words in A	7.3	3.8
# of words in $\neg A$	11.2	5.3
# of words in B	5.4	1.6

Table 1: Decriptive statistics for stories.

it is specified as "star-shaped sprinkles" (as a type of cake decorations). Some stories also necessitate an inference e.g. from referring to "bubble bath" in event A and "foam" in event B. In other stories, identical referring expressions were used in events A and B (e.g., in a grocery story, event A: "he took a shopping cart" vs. event B: "he put everything in his shopping cart").

Importantly, no other events in the story draw a direct causal link to event B, except event A and the script itself. Events A and B are always separated by descriptions of other script events (73.6 words on average; $sd = 10.3$; min: 59; max: 91). The chunk with event B always consists of one sentence with the following structure: "*ADVERB PERSON X did action B and then did a subsequent action from the script sequence.*" (except the laundry story, where the sentence started with "She"). When constructing the experimental materials, we controlled for the following parameters: the number of words and text chunks in a story, the number of text chunks and words between events A and B, the number of words in the text chunks that contained event B, and number of words in the chunk after the chunk with event B. The full list of descriptive statistics for our materials is presented in Table 1.

3.2 Experimental conditions

Our target manipulation relates to the appearance of events A and B in the story thus producing three different story conditions:

Condition $A \rightarrow B$. Event B logically follows event A within the story context. In this way, event

A draws a direct causal link to event B, and thus event B is anticipated to happen on the basis of event A.

Condition $\neg A \rightarrow B$. Event A is negated, making the occurrence of event B implausible or even impossible. The mention of event B thus is unexpected and stands in a causal conflict with the earlier information. While creating negation of events A, we had the following strategy. Since events A and B in our materials typically share at least one common event participant, in the $\neg A$ condition, this participant was made unavailable for event B. In this way, the causal link between A and B (prepare cake decorations $\rightarrow$ add star-shaped sprinkles; put a pillow in the backpack $\rightarrow$ take it from the backpack) is broken because event $\neg A$ changes the state of the participant so that it is not available in B (when one doesn't have a travelling pillow, this script participant is not going to be available in B to take it from the backpack).

The $\neg A$ condition did not always consist of literal negation with the word "not" but as in the example shown in Figure 1 (A: "she got out the cake decorations" vs. $\neg A$: "she realised she **didn't have** any cake decorations"), but while in other stories, participant in event A was disabled in a more subtle way, via verbs of implicit negation or particles like "only", e.g., (events A vs. $\neg A$):

- (sunscreen): she grabbed her sunscreen VS. she forgot her sunscreen
- (pocorn buckets): she bought three buckets of popcorn for everyone VS. since nobody was hungry, she just bought drinks for everyone

Condition $nil \rightarrow B$. Event A is omitted. Even though event A is not explicitly stated, it is expected that humans will easily infer its occurrence from the context, making the mention of event B plausible and easy to integrate (Bower et al., 1979).

3.3 Experimental procedure

For data collection, each story was divided into paragraphs or text chunks (as shown, for example, in Figure 1, part II). During the experiment, subjects saw only one paragraph at a time (chunk-by-chunk presentation). After reading each story, subjects had to rate how sure they were about the events A and B to have occurred, on a Likert scale ranging from 0 (*Not sure at all*) to 7 (*Very sure*) – see Figure 1, part III. To measure the processing difficulties of humans, we compare the reading times for event B across the experimental conditions. More details about subjects' belief ratings are presented in Appendix A.

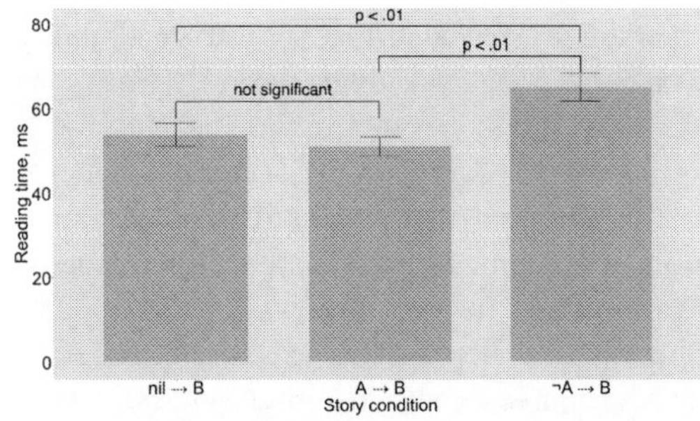

Figure 2: Human results. Mean by-character reading times at event B, by story condition; p-values are taken from the corresponding LMER models, see Section 3.5.

251 native English speakers were hired via the crowdsourcing platform Prolific[2] to participate in the study. Each participant read three stories. Each story had a different topic and was presented in a different condition.

3.4 Analysis

To investigate the effects of processing difficulty that event B causes in subjects depending on story condition, we analyse mean per character reading times associated with the chunks that contain event B. The log-transformed reading times were analysed using linear mixed-effects regression models (LMER; Bates et al., 2015). The maximal random effects structure included by-subject and by-item random intercepts and by-item random slopes for story condition and was simplified for convergence when needed.

Prior to the analysis, we removed all trials related to the bowling story item, due to a typo. Further, we removed trials where the reading times in the chunk containing event B were shorter than 100ms or larger than 50s. 704 trials from 251 subjects (73% female; mean age = 40, sd = 14.6, [18;80] range) were available for analysis (1.81% data loss).

3.5 Results

To answer to what extent causal inconsistencies are reflected in human language processing (RQ1), we compared reading times on segment B in the $A \rightarrow B$ vs. $\neg A \rightarrow B$ conditions. The random effects structure included by-subject and by-item random intercepts and by-item random slopes for story

[2] https://www.prolific.co/

conditions. We found that subjects read chunks with event B significantly more slowly when event A was explicitly negated in the story ($b = 0.21$, $se = 0.04$, $t = 4.77$, $p < .01$), see also Figure 2.

To analyse subjects' ability to infer causal links from script knowledge (RQ2), we compared the reading times in $nil \rightarrow B$ vs. $A \rightarrow B$ conditions. The random effects structure included by-item random intercepts. We observed no significant difference between these conditions ($b = -0.04$, $se = 0.05$, $t = -0.7$, $p = .48$). Thus, the absence of event A, which serves as a direct causal link to event B, does not slow event's B processing in terms of reading times. Note that the reading time of condition $\neg A \rightarrow B$ is significantly slower than the reading time in condition $nil \rightarrow B$ ($b = 0.17$, $se = 0.05$, $t = 3.23$, $p < .01$).

4 Can LLMs Detect Causal Conflicts (RQ1)?

In this section, we measure the ability of different LLMs to track event contingency. We feed the script stories into the language models and record the LM's surprisal scores on a word-by-word basis. We then test whether the mean surprisal scores for the critical region (event B) differ between conditions. As the script stories corpus is relatively small, we additionally test the models on the TRIP dataset (Storks et al., 2021) to assess their recognition of causal incongruencies on a wider set of materials (see Section 4.5).

4.1 Choices of LLMs

We select a set of 20 causal language models (CLMs).[3] We chose the GPT-1/2/3 and Instruct GPT models (Radford et al., 2018, 2019; Brown et al., 2020; Ouyang et al., 2022) because of their good performance on many NLP tasks (Chang and Bergen, 2023). We also selected GPT-3.5 (Neelakantan et al., 2022) because it was trained with both programming code and text and as a result demonstrated strong performance on entity tracking (Kim and Schuster, 2023), a prerequisite for causal reasoning. Notably, ChatGPT (OpenAI, 2022) and GPT-4 (OpenAI, 2023) can not be used in our study, because the API does not allow access to the probabilities. Additionally, we used Vicuna models (Chiang et al., 2023), a LLaMa-based model (Touvron et al., 2023) fine-tuned on 70K user-shared ChatGPT conversations. Open models like Vicuna have the advantage of results being reproducible. Similarly, we chose OPT (Zhang et al., 2022) and GPT-Neo (Black et al., 2021) as open models similar to GPT-3.

We also selected task-specific models that could potentially capture script knowledge via exposure to more diverse datasets like summarization models, Pegasus (Zhang et al., 2020), Bigbird-pegasus, and a multilingual model XGLM (Lin et al., 2022). Lastly, we chose XLNet because it has been previously shown to be effective for zero-shot script parsing (Zhai et al., 2021, 2022) wrt. handling causal inferences in commonsense stories in a zero-shot setting.

All models used here were available through either HuggingFace or the OpenAI API. More details are in Appendix B, where we briefly describe all the models.

4.2 Method

We perform word-by-word next-word prediction for event B, recording the next token probabilities for each token in segment B. Based on the probability of the target words w given the story context, we then calculate the target tokens' surprisal as their negative log probability: $\text{surprisal}(w) = -\log P(w|\text{story\_context})$. We then calculate the average per-word surprisal by averaging the surprisal of each word into an estimate of the surprisal of the critical region for each item.

4.3 Data Analysis

To identify the PLM(s) that show comparable effects to humans, we run an equivalent analysis to how the reading time data were analysed: we estimate linear mixed effects models with surprisal as a response variable and condition ($A \rightarrow B$ vs. $\neg A \rightarrow B$) as a predictor. The model also includes by-item random intercepts. The formula is: $\log(\text{surprisal}) \sim \text{story\_condition} + (1|\text{story})^4$.

4.4 Results

Table 2 (column CSK) presents the results for all language models on whether model surprisals were significantly higher for the $\neg A \rightarrow B$ condition than in the $A \rightarrow B$ condition, indicating that the model's surprisal scores reflect the incoherence (RQ1). High positive b values indicate that surprisal values are higher on segment B in

[3]We also experiment with masked language models. Please refer to Appendix C.1.

[4]Log surprisals were chosen because of the skewed distribution of surprisal values.

Model Name	# para. (M)	CSK			TRIP		
		b	t	sign	b	t	sign
GPT-3.5: text-davinci-003	175K	0.59	5.87	***	0.30	10.82	***
GPT-3.5: text-davinci-002	175K	0.51	2.75	*	0.26	7.41	***
InstructGPT: text-davinci-001	175K	0.26	2.03	·	0.29	5.81	***
InstructGPT: davinci-instruct-beta	175K	0.21	2.76	*	0.20	8.68	***
GPT-3: davinci-002	175K	0.28	4.36	***	0.35	8.11	***
GPT-3: davinci	175K	0.21	2.76	*	0.20	8.25	***
Vicuna-13B	13016	0.22	2.25	*	0.26	7.56	***
Vicuna-7B	6738	0.28	2.56	*	0.22	6.35	***
InstructGPT: text-curie-001	6700	0.03	0.31	n.s.	0.19	5.78	***
GPT-3: curie	6700	0.23	3.43	**	0.12	5.92	***
GPT-2: XL	1638	0.05	0.96	n.s.	0.06	3.15	**
GPT-2: L	838	0.04	0.77	n.s.	0.05	2.77	**
XGLM	827	-0.03	-0.79	n.s.	0.02	1.38	n.s.
Bigbird-pegasus-large-arxiv	470	0.06	1.20	n.s.	0.00	-0.02	n.s.
Pegasus-large	467	0.02	0.85	n.s.	0.00	-0.48	n.s.
XLNet-large-cased	393	-0.03	-1.99	·	0.00	0.66	n.s.
OPT	357	0.01	0.12	n.s.	0.03	1.78	·
GPT-Neo	164	0.03	0.67	n.s.	0.01	0.90	n.s.
GPT-2	163	0.00	-0.10	n.s.	0.01	0.53	n.s.
GPT: openai-gpt	148	0.00	-0.01	n.s.	0.05	3.18	**

Table 2: Results for RQ1 ($A \rightarrow B$ versus $\neg A \rightarrow B$) on CSK (original and intervention removal) and TRIP dataset. The # para. (M) column shows the number of parameters in millions. n.s. represent that the results are not statistically significant. The ·, *, **, and *** in the sign column represent p-values < .1, .05, .01, and .001.

the $\neg A \rightarrow B$ condition compared to the $A \rightarrow B$ condition. Significance stars indicate whether the differences were statistically reliable. Our results show that only some of the largest models showed a reliable increase in surprisal estimates for the incoherent ($\neg A \rightarrow B$) condition.

GPT-3.5: text-davinci-003 shows the largest effect with high statistical reliability. Further models that show the expected behaviour include other versions of GPT-3/GPT-3.5 and the Vicuna model. GPT-3: davinci-002 has the largest effect amoug the GPT-3 models. Surprisingly, InstructGPT models that are trained with human-selected samples don't show significant effects. This result implies additional training on high-quality samples harms the models' ability to identify causal conflicts.

Model Name (CLMs only)	nil vs. $\neg A$			nil vs. A		
	b	t	sign	b	t	sign
GPT-3.5: text-davinci-003	0.08	0.77	n.s.	-0.52	-5.10	***
GPT-3.5: text-davinci-002	-0.06	-0.38	n.s.	-0.57	-3.65	***
InstructGPT: davinci-instr-beta	-0.17	-1.96	.	-0.39	-4.36	***
GPT-3: davinci-002	-0.15	-1.94	.	-0.43	-5.60	***
GPT-3: davinci	-0.15	-1.79	.	-0.36	-4.34	***
Vicuna-13B	-0.15	-1.52	n.s.	-0.37	-3.73	***
Vicuna-7B	-0.07	-0.58	n.s.	-0.36	-2.91	**
GPT-3: curie	-0.23	-2.74	**	-0.46	-5.54	***
Human	0.17	3.23	**	-0.04	-0.7	n.s.

Table 3: Results for RQ2 ($nil \rightarrow B$ versus $\neg A \rightarrow B$ and $A \rightarrow B$) on CSK dataset. Note that coefficient estimates for human data refer to log reading times, and are hence not directly comparable to the numbers in the CLMs, which estimate the surprisal effect.

4.5 Experiments on TRIP dataset

As the CSK dataset, for which we collected reading times, is relatively small, we also compared the surprisals of the same set of models on the substantially larger TRIP dataset (cf. Section 2.3), which also contains causal inconsistencies. Their dataset has multiple splits. We only use the "ClozeDev" split. (We do not use the "Order" splits, in which the order of the sentences is switched, because that setting is too different to our dataset.)

We again estimated surprisal values for each language model, in the same way as described in section 4.2. The critical segment B for this dataset corresponds to the breakpoint sentence. The analysis was analogous to the analysis for the CSK dataset.

Column "TRIP" in Table 2 presents the results of our method on the TRIP dataset. Significant positive effects indicate a significant difference between the model surprisals in the implausible condition compared to the plausible one, indicating that the model recognized the inconsistency correctly.

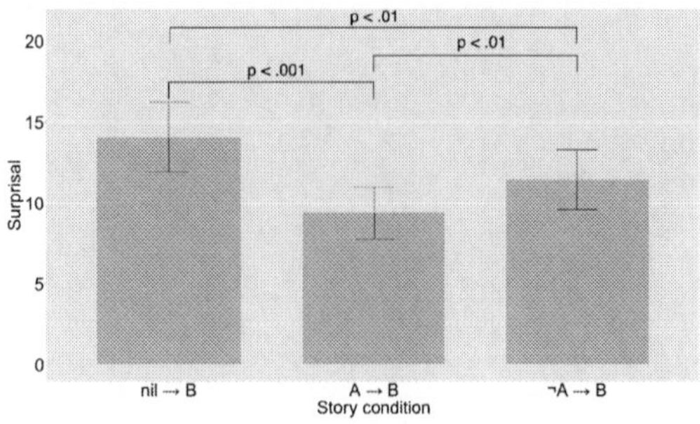

Figure 3: Performance of GPT-3: curie in both research questions. Mean surprisal presented by story condition; p-values are taken from Tables 2 and 3.

GPT-3.5 performs notably well, again displaying the largest effect size and p-value $< .001$.

4.6 Discussion

Given the analysis of the CSK and TRIP datasets, we conclude that only some of the GPT models were able to consistently assign higher surprisal to event B (or the breakpoint sentence in TRIP) in the case that causally related event A was negated earlier in the story[5]. Among the GPT models, we find that GPT-3.5: text-davinci-003 shows the most consistent performance. It differs from the others in that it was trained using reinforcement learning from human feedback, which has been found to be correlated with better performance on many reasoning tasks (Chang and Bergen, 2023).[6]

5 Do LLMs incorporate script knowledge (RQ2)?

In this section, we are interested in whether the models that can capture the causal link between A and B are also able to integrate script knowledge to a similar extent as humans, i.e. whether they show a relatively low surprisal even if event A was not explicitly mentioned in the story context. We continue with those models showing a significant effect of the $\neg A \to B$ condition compared to $A \to B$ consistently across the CSK and the TRIP datasets, as these are the only models that seem to reliably deal with negation and capture the causal link.

[5]One possible reason for this can be models' inability to handle long dependencies between events A and B. We investigate it in Appendix C.2

[6]We did not apply a correction for multiple testing in the analysis. If we were to more conservatively account for multiple testing, then the results of most models except for GPT-3.5: text-davinci-003 would not be judged as statistically reliable.

5.1 Analysis and Results

Analysis was performed using linear mixed-effects models (LMER), similar to Section 4.3. This time, we compare surprisal estimates of conditions $nil \to B$ to $\neg A \to B$ to show firstly whether the model correctly captures the incongruency of $\neg A \to B$. Next, we compare condition $nil \to B$ to condition $A \to B$ in order to determine whether the models are consistent with human readers in terms of NOT showing a large effect. The formula of each LMER model is: $\log(\text{surprisal}) \sim \text{story\_condition} + (1|\text{story})$.

Table 3 shows the results for research question 2. While humans read sequence B significantly faster in the $nil \to B$ condition than in the condition with the causal conflict ($\neg A \to B$), none of the language models show this effect: most models do not show a significant difference between these conditions, and one model (GPT-3: curie) in fact shows significant effects in the wrong direction (B has higher surprisal in the nil condition than in the $\neg A$ condition), see also Figure 3. This might indicate that the lexically related material in condition $\neg A$ (e.g., "cake decorations") leads to a relatively low surprisal at region B even if it stands in causal conflict with it.

The significantly lower surprisal in condition $A \to B$ compared to condition $nil \to B$, which is observed in all of the models, furthermore indicates that models fail to include script knowledge effectively in their next word predictions – current models hence differ from humans in their ability to use script knowledge for predicting (or easily integrating) script-inferable event participants.

5.2 Can models capture negation?

As pointed out by an anonymous reviewer, models' inability to show human-like behavior in RQ2 might be due to models failing to process negation properly, even though these models show significantly lower surprisal in $A \to B$ condition compared to $\neg A \to B$ condition. Previous literature indeed shows that transformers have trouble with (explicit) negation (Nguyen et al., 2023). Considering that our materials contain various formulations of event $\neg A$ (including in some cases explicit and in other cases implicit negation), which could pose difficulty to LLMs, we conduct a follow-up study to see whether the best models from the RQ2 experiment could properly identify a participant's state in $\neg A$, i.e., its unavailability. There are actually two other possibilities as to why models might fail in negation processing. First, considering that not all of our stories contain exact lexical realizations of target participants between events A and B, the models can fail to match the negated participant in $\neg A$ ("she realized she didn't have any **cake decorations**") to its realization in event B ("she added **star-shaped sprinkles**"). Secondly, since there is still some context between events A and B (see Table 1), the models can 'forget' the state of the target participant by the time they reach event B. Previous literature shows that participant state tracking can be a difficult task for LLMs (Kim and Schuster, 2023).

We construct questions about the availability of the target participant from event B, e.g., "Are **cake decorations** available to Anne?" (the correct answer is 'yes' in $A \rightarrow B$ condition and 'no' in $\neg A \rightarrow B$). For each story and model, we assess this question twice: directly after event A and just before event B, to capture a potential problem of 'forgetting' about a participant's state. If the participant's lexical realization was different between events A and B, we also assess the same question but about the target participant as it was instantiated in event B: "Are **star-shaped sprinkles** available to Anne?").

We then test the best available models from RQ2, namely GPT-3.5: gpt-3.5-turbo-instruct and GPT-3: davinci-002[7]. Since GPT-3 models were not specifically trained to follow user instructions, we utilized the approach of Brown et al. (2020) for the GPT-3: davinci-002 model: we compared the probabilities of "Yes" and "No" as input tokens following the question and chose the answer with the higher output probability to compare with a correct answer. In the case of the GPT-3.5: gpt-3.5-turbo-instruct model, we prompt the model to generate "Yes" or "No" answers with an instruction *Please answer with "Yes" or "No"* and compare the output with a correct answer (as this model only allows text output).

The results show that the gpt-3.5-turbo-instruct model reaches an accuracy of more than 90% in this task on each question formulation, which shows that it is well capable of processing negation and tracking participant state. On the other hand, the GPT-3: davinci-002 model succeeds in tracking participant state but exhibits very low accuracy in capturing negations, which indicates that older GPT-3 models can not capture negation. We conclude that these experiments confirm the interpretation that older models fail to represent negation properly and hence fail on RQ1. In the meantime, larger models have no problem understanding negations. They fail on RQ2 due to a failure in activating script knowledge to a similar extent as humans wrt. anticipating or easily integrating a script-predictable participant.

6 Conclusions

In this paper, we inspect the behaviors of both large language models and humans in zero-shot causal inference. We conducted a self-paced reading experiment on common sense stories to inspect human processing difficulty when reading the stories. Reading time results indicate that humans stumble across causally incoherent text segments, exhibiting longer reading times in these cases. On the other hand, they easily integrate script-predictable information, even if the explicit causal component (event A) is missing from the story.

When we apply the same study to LLMs, only the newest LLMs show similar behavior to humans on encountering casual conflicts. All models fail to replicate human behaviors when the cause is omitted. Even models trained with programming code and instructions fail to make use of script knowledge, which indicates that script knowledge may not be represented sufficiently well in the LLMs tested in this study.

7 Limitations

One limitation from the NLP perspective of our study is that the size of the CSK dataset is small and only in English (only 21 stories). This is a very common limitation of psycholinguistic studies due to the costs of human experiments. We here addressed this shortcoming by also evaluating on the larger dataset TRIP, but a dataset with more stories or more readers would further improve the reliability of the results. Another limitation is that we don't experiment with few-shot examples in prompts, which could have been used to remind the LLMs to make use of script knowledge. We chose the zero-shot setting because humans use script knowledge for casual inference without any "examples" and

[7]Because this additional experiment is conducted as a reaction to reviews, some OpenAI models in RQ1 and RQ2 have become deprecated in the meantime. Here we report the performance of the official replacement gpt-3.5-turbo-instruct for all GPT-3.5 and InstructGPT models; see the OpenAI documents: `https://platform.openai.com/docs/deprecations/instructgpt-models`.

we believe that the LLMs should have the same behaviors as humans. However, this means that our results do not necessarily generalize to other ways of prompting models. Additionally, we didn't experiment with the most recent OpenAI models like GPT-4 because their official API doesn't support generating the probability output for given text input. Lastly, we didn't test models with more than 20B parameters on our own server due to limited hardware resources.

Another limitation of our experiment is that we cannot comment on the generalizability of our script materials to more general script-based stories for scripts that may be less well-known to human readers. For our materials, we asked participants after each experimental trial whether they were familiar with the script ("Please tick this box if you have never baked a cake or you have very little experience with it)". Participants answered in 11.2% of trials that they were not familiar with the script. We observed an effect of familiarity on reading times, showing that subjects read the story faster when they were not familiar with the topic. We note that findings also remained stable when we removed such trials from our analysis.

8 Ethics Statement

We release our CSK dataset under the CC BY-NC-SA license. We anonymize the dataset to protect participants' identities. The human study was approved by the ethics committee of Deutsche Gesellschaft für Sprachwissenschaft (DGfS). All participants were paid fairly according to the local standard.

The TRIP dataset was released under an unknown license but the paper described this dataset was published in an ACL proceeding. We use it for academic purposes only.

The potential risk of this work is that the findings can be used to design attacks on LLMs to harm their capability of conducting casual inference given script knowledge (Alzantot et al., 2018).

Acknowledgements

This work was supported by the Deutsche Forschungsgemeinschaft (DFG), Funder Id: http://dx.doi.org/10.13039/501100001659, Project-ID 232722074 – SFB1102: Information Density and Linguistic Encoding. We sincerely thank the anonymous reviewers for their insightful comments that helped us to improve this paper. We thank Sebastian Schuster, Alexandra Mayn and Josef van Genabith for their informative advice and Nina Shvetsova for her help with the Vicuna models. We also thank students Teresa Martín Soeder, Alice Virginia Chase, and Brianna Michelle Lehman for helping with materials construction.

References

Valerie Abbott, John B Black, and Edward E Smith. 1985. The representation of scripts in memory. *Journal of memory and language*, 24(2):179–199.

Moustafa Alzantot, Yash Sharma, Ahmed Elgohary, Bo-Jhang Ho, Mani Srivastava, and Kai-Wei Chang. 2018. Generating natural language adversarial examples. In *Proceedings of the 2018 Conference on Empirical Methods in Natural Language Processing*, pages 2890–2896, Brussels, Belgium. Association for Computational Linguistics.

Douglas Bates, Martin Mächler, Ben Bolker, and Steve Walker. 2015. Fitting linear mixed-effects models using lme4. *Journal of Statistical Software*, 67:1–48.

Sid Black, Leo Gao, Phil Wang, Connor Leahy, and Stella Biderman. 2021. GPT-Neo: Large Scale Autoregressive Language Modeling with Mesh-Tensorflow. *Zenodo*.

Charles P Bloom, Charles R Fletcher, Paul Van Den Broek, Laura Reitz, and Brian P Shapiro. 1990. An on-line assessment of causal reasoning during comprehension. *Memory & cognition*, 18:65–71.

Antoine Bosselut, Hannah Rashkin, Maarten Sap, Chaitanya Malaviya, Asli Celikyilmaz, and Yejin Choi. 2019. COMET: Commonsense transformers for automatic knowledge graph construction. In *Proceedings of the 57th Annual Meeting of the Association for Computational Linguistics*, pages 4762–4779, Florence, Italy. Association for Computational Linguistics.

Gordon H Bower, John B Black, and Terrence J Turner. 1979. Scripts in memory for text. *Cognitive psychology*, 11(2):177–220.

Faeze Brahman, Chandra Bhagavatula, Valentina Pyatkin, Jena D Hwang, Xiang Lorraine Li, Hirona J Arai, Soumya Sanyal, Keisuke Sakaguchi, Xiang Ren, and Yejin Choi. 2023. Plasma: Making small language models better procedural knowledge models for (counterfactual) planning. *arXiv preprint arXiv:2305.19472*.

Tom Brown, Benjamin Mann, Nick Ryder, Melanie Subbiah, Jared D Kaplan, Prafulla Dhariwal, Arvind Neelakantan, Pranav Shyam, Girish Sastry, Amanda Askell, et al. 2020. Language models are few-shot learners. *Advances in neural information processing systems*, 33:1877–1901.

Sébastien Bubeck, Varun Chandrasekaran, Ronen Eldan, Johannes Gehrke, Eric Horvitz, Ece Kamar, Peter Lee, Yin Tat Lee, Yuanzhi Li, Scott Lundberg, et al. 2023. Sparks of artificial general intelligence: Early experiments with gpt-4. *arXiv preprint arXiv:2303.12712*.

Tyler A Chang and Benjamin K Bergen. 2023. Language model behavior: A comprehensive survey. *arXiv preprint arXiv:2303.11504*.

Wei-Lin Chiang, Zhuohan Li, Zi Lin, Ying Sheng, Zhanghao Wu, Hao Zhang, Lianmin Zheng, Siyuan Zhuang, Yonghao Zhuang, Joseph E. Gonzalez, Ion Stoica, and Eric P. Xing. 2023. Vicuna: An open-source chatbot impressing gpt-4 with 90%* chatgpt quality.

Rune Haubo B Christensen. 2018. Cumulative link models for ordinal regression with the r package ordinal. *Submitted in J. Stat. Software*, 35.

Manuel Ciosici, Joseph Cummings, Mitchell DeHaven, Alex Hedges, Yash Kankanampati, Dong-Ho Lee, Ralph Weischedel, and Marjorie Freedman. 2021. Machine-assisted script curation. In *Proceedings of the 2021 Conference of the North American Chapter of the Association for Computational Linguistics: Human Language Technologies: Demonstrations*, pages 8–17, Online. Association for Computational Linguistics.

Vera Demberg and Frank Keller. 2008. Data from eye-tracking corpora as evidence for theories of syntactic processing complexity. *Cognition*, 109(2):193–210.

Jacob Devlin, Ming-Wei Chang, Kenton Lee, and Kristina Toutanova. 2019. BERT: Pre-training of deep bidirectional transformers for language understanding. In *Proceedings of the 2019 Conference of the North American Chapter of the Association for Computational Linguistics: Human Language Technologies, Volume 1 (Long and Short Papers)*, pages 4171–4186, Minneapolis, Minnesota. Association for Computational Linguistics.

Stefan L Frank, Leun J Otten, Giulia Galli, and Gabriella Vigliocco. 2015. The erp response to the amount of information conveyed by words in sentences. *Brain and language*, 140:1–11.

Richard Futrell, Ethan Wilcox, Takashi Morita, Peng Qian, Miguel Ballesteros, and Roger Levy. 2019. Neural language models as psycholinguistic subjects: Representations of syntactic state. In *Proceedings of the 2019 Conference of the North American Chapter of the Association for Computational Linguistics: Human Language Technologies, Volume 1 (Long and Short Papers)*, pages 32–42, Minneapolis, Minnesota. Association for Computational Linguistics.

Raymond W Gibbs and Yvette J Tenney. 1980. The concept of scripts in understanding stories. *Journal of Psycholinguistic Research*, 9:275–284.

Arthur C Graesser, Keith K Millis, and Rolf A Zwaan. 1997. Discourse comprehension. *Annual review of psychology*, 48(1):163–189.

Arthur C Graesser, Murray Singer, and Tom Trabasso. 1994. Constructing inferences during narrative text comprehension. *Psychological review*, 101(3):371.

John Hale. 2001. A probabilistic earley parser as a psycholinguistic model. In *Proceedings of the second meeting of the North American Chapter of the Association for Computational Linguistics on Language technologies*, pages 1–8. Association for Computational Linguistics.

Mary Hare, Michael Jones, Caroline Thomson, Sarah Kelly, and Ken McRae. 2009. Activating event knowledge. *Cognition*, 111(2):151–167.

Jena D Hwang, Chandra Bhagavatula, Ronan Le Bras, Jeff Da, Keisuke Sakaguchi, Antoine Bosselut, and Yejin Choi. 2021. (comet-) atomic 2020: On symbolic and neural commonsense knowledge graphs. In *Proceedings of the AAAI Conference on Artificial Intelligence*, volume 35, pages 6384–6392.

Andrew Jaegle, Sebastian Borgeaud, Jean-Baptiste Alayrac, Carl Doersch, Catalin Ionescu, David Ding, Skanda Koppula, Daniel Zoran, Andrew Brock, Evan Shelhamer, Olivier J Henaff, Matthew Botvinick, Andrew Zisserman, Oriol Vinyals, and Joao Carreira. 2022. Perceiver IO: A general architecture for structured inputs & outputs. In *International Conference on Learning Representations*.

Mandar Joshi, Danqi Chen, Yinhan Liu, Daniel S. Weld, Luke Zettlemoyer, and Omer Levy. 2020. SpanBERT: Improving pre-training by representing and predicting spans. *Transactions of the Association for Computational Linguistics*, 8:64–77.

JM Keenan and W Kintsch. 1974. The identification of explicitly and implicitly presented information. *The representation of meaning in memory*, pages 153–176.

Najoung Kim and Sebastian Schuster. 2023. Entity tracking in language models. In *Proceedings of the 61st Annual Meeting of the Association for Computational Linguistics (Volume 1: Long Papers)*, pages 3835–3855, Toronto, Canada. Association for Computational Linguistics.

Takeshi Kojima, Shixiang Shane Gu, Machel Reid, Yutaka Matsuo, and Yusuke Iwasawa. 2022. Large language models are zero-shot reasoners. In *Advances in Neural Information Processing Systems*.

Marta Kutas and Steven A Hillyard. 1989. An electrophysiological probe of incidental semantic association. *Journal of cognitive neuroscience*, 1(1):38–49.

Andrew Lampinen, Ishita Dasgupta, Stephanie Chan, Kory Mathewson, Mh Tessler, Antonia Creswell, James McClelland, Jane Wang, and Felix Hill. 2022.

Can language models learn from explanations in context? In *Findings of the Association for Computational Linguistics: EMNLP 2022*, pages 537–563, Abu Dhabi, United Arab Emirates. Association for Computational Linguistics.

James Lee-Thorp, Joshua Ainslie, Ilya Eckstein, and Santiago Ontanon. 2022. FNet: Mixing tokens with Fourier transforms. In *Proceedings of the 2022 Conference of the North American Chapter of the Association for Computational Linguistics: Human Language Technologies*, pages 4296–4313, Seattle, United States. Association for Computational Linguistics.

Roger Levy. 2008. Expectation-based syntactic comprehension. *Cognition*, 106(3):1126–1177.

Xi Victoria Lin, Todor Mihaylov, Mikel Artetxe, Tianlu Wang, Shuohui Chen, Daniel Simig, Myle Ott, Naman Goyal, Shruti Bhosale, Jingfei Du, Ramakanth Pasunuru, Sam Shleifer, Punit Singh Koura, Vishrav Chaudhary, Brian O'Horo, Jeff Wang, Luke Zettlemoyer, Zornitsa Kozareva, Mona Diab, Veselin Stoyanov, and Xian Li. 2022. Few-shot learning with multilingual generative language models. In *Proceedings of the 2022 Conference on Empirical Methods in Natural Language Processing*, pages 9019–9052, Abu Dhabi, United Arab Emirates. Association for Computational Linguistics.

Kaixin Ma, Filip Ilievski, Jonathan Francis, Eric Nyberg, and Alessandro Oltramari. 2022. Coalescing global and local information for procedural text understanding. In *Proceedings of the 29th International Conference on Computational Linguistics*, pages 1534–1545, Gyeongju, Republic of Korea. International Committee on Computational Linguistics.

George Michalopoulos, Michal Malyska, Nicola Sahar, Alexander Wong, and Helen Chen. 2022. ICDBigBird: A contextual embedding model for ICD code classification. In *Proceedings of the 21st Workshop on Biomedical Language Processing*, pages 330–336, Dublin, Ireland. Association for Computational Linguistics.

Arvind Neelakantan, Tao Xu, Raul Puri, Alec Radford, Jesse Michael Han, Jerry Tworek, Qiming Yuan, Nikolas A. Tezak, Jong Wook Kim, Chris Hallacy, Johannes Heidecke, Pranav Shyam, Boris Power, Tyna Eloundou Nekoul, Girish Sastry, Gretchen Krueger, David P. Schnurr, Felipe Petroski Such, Kenny Sai-Kin Hsu, Madeleine Thompson, Tabarak Khan, Toki Sherbakov, Joanne Jang, Peter Welinder, and Lilian Weng. 2022. Text and code embeddings by contrastive pre-training. *ArXiv*, abs/2201.10005.

Ha Thanh Nguyen, Randy Goebel, Francesca Toni, Kostas Stathis, and Ken Satoh. 2023. A negation detection assessment of gpts: analysis with the xnot360 dataset. *arXiv preprint arXiv:2306.16638*.

OpenAI. 2022. Introducing chatgpt. *OpenAI Blog*.

OpenAI. 2023. Gpt-4 technical report. *ArXiv*, abs/2303.08774.

Long Ouyang, Jeffrey Wu, Xu Jiang, Diogo Almeida, Carroll Wainwright, Pamela Mishkin, Chong Zhang, Sandhini Agarwal, Katarina Slama, Alex Ray, et al. 2022. Training language models to follow instructions with human feedback. *Advances in Neural Information Processing Systems*, 35:27730–27744.

Judea Pearl. 2009. *Causality*. Cambridge university press.

Alec Radford, Karthik Narasimhan, Tim Salimans, Ilya Sutskever, et al. 2018. Improving language understanding by generative pre-training. *OpenAI Blog*.

Alec Radford, Jeffrey Wu, Rewon Child, David Luan, Dario Amodei, Ilya Sutskever, et al. 2019. Language models are unsupervised multitask learners. *OpenAI blog*, 1(8):9.

Gabriel A Radvansky, Andrea K Tamplin, Joseph Armendarez, and Alexis N Thompson. 2014. Different kinds of causality in event cognition. *Discourse Processes*, 51(7):601–618.

Sahithya Ravi, Chris Tanner, Raymond Ng, and Vered Shwartz. 2023. What happens before and after: Multi-event commonsense in event coreference resolution. In *Proceedings of the 17th Conference of the European Chapter of the Association for Computational Linguistics*, pages 1708–1724, Dubrovnik, Croatia. Association for Computational Linguistics.

Kyle Richardson, Ronen Tamari, Oren Sultan, Dafna Shahaf, Reut Tsarfaty, and Ashish Sabharwal. 2022. Breakpoint transformers for modeling and tracking intermediate beliefs. In *Proceedings of the 2022 Conference on Empirical Methods in Natural Language Processing*, pages 9703–9719, Abu Dhabi, United Arab Emirates. Association for Computational Linguistics.

Keisuke Sakaguchi, Chandra Bhagavatula, Ronan Le Bras, Niket Tandon, Peter Clark, and Yejin Choi. 2021. proScript: Partially ordered scripts generation. In *Findings of the Association for Computational Linguistics: EMNLP 2021*, pages 2138–2149, Punta Cana, Dominican Republic. Association for Computational Linguistics.

Julian Salazar, Davis Liang, Toan Q. Nguyen, and Katrin Kirchhoff. 2020. Masked language model scoring. In *Proceedings of the 58th Annual Meeting of the Association for Computational Linguistics*, pages 2699–2712, Online. Association for Computational Linguistics.

Abhilasha Sancheti and Rachel Rudinger. 2022. What do large language models learn about scripts? In *Proceedings of the 11th Joint Conference on Lexical and Computational Semantics*, pages 1–11, Seattle, Washington. Association for Computational Linguistics.

Roger C Schank. 1975. The structure of episodes in memory. In *Representation and understanding*, pages 237–272. Elsevier.

Murray Singer and Michael Halldorson. 1996. Constructing and validating motive bridging inferences. *Cognitive Psychology*, 30(1):1–38.

Murray Singer and Kathryn FM Ritchot. 1996. The role of working memory capacity and knowledge access in text inference processing. *Memory & cognition*, 24(6):733–743.

Nathaniel J Smith and Roger Levy. 2013. The effect of word predictability on reading time is logarithmic. *Cognition*, 128(3):302–319.

Shane Storks, Qiaozi Gao, Yichi Zhang, and Joyce Chai. 2021. Tiered reasoning for intuitive physics: Toward verifiable commonsense language understanding. In *Findings of the Association for Computational Linguistics: EMNLP 2021*, pages 4902–4918, Punta Cana, Dominican Republic. Association for Computational Linguistics.

Mirac Suzgun, Nathan Scales, Nathanael Schärli, Sebastian Gehrmann, Yi Tay, Hyung Won Chung, Aakanksha Chowdhery, Quoc Le, Ed Chi, Denny Zhou, and Jason Wei. 2023. Challenging BIG-bench tasks and whether chain-of-thought can solve them. In *Findings of the Association for Computational Linguistics: ACL 2023*, pages 13003–13051, Toronto, Canada. Association for Computational Linguistics.

Hugo Touvron, Thibaut Lavril, Gautier Izacard, Xavier Martinet, Marie-Anne Lachaux, Timothée Lacroix, Baptiste Rozière, Naman Goyal, Eric Hambro, Faisal Azhar, Aurelien Rodriguez, Armand Joulin, Edouard Grave, and Guillaume Lample. 2023. Llama: Open and efficient foundation language models. *ArXiv*, abs/2302.13971.

Tom Trabasso and Linda L Sperry. 1985. Causal relatedness and importance of story events. *Journal of Memory and language*, 24(5):595–611.

Paul Van den Broek. 1990. The causal inference maker: Towards a process model of inference generation in text comprehension. *Comprehension processes in reading*, pages 423–445.

Alex Wang, Yada Pruksachatkun, Nikita Nangia, Amanpreet Singh, Julian Michael, Felix Hill, Omer Levy, and Samuel Bowman. 2019. Superglue: A stickier benchmark for general-purpose language understanding systems. *Advances in neural information processing systems*, 32.

Alex Wang, Amanpreet Singh, Julian Michael, Felix Hill, Omer Levy, and Samuel Bowman. 2018. GLUE: A multi-task benchmark and analysis platform for natural language understanding. In *Proceedings of the 2018 EMNLP Workshop BlackboxNLP: Analyzing and Interpreting Neural Networks for NLP*, pages 353–355, Brussels, Belgium. Association for Computational Linguistics.

Lilian D. A. Wanzare, Alessandra Zarcone, Stefan Thater, and Manfred Pinkal. 2016. A crowdsourced database of event sequence descriptions for the acquisition of high-quality script knowledge. In *Proceedings of the Tenth International Conference on Language Resources and Evaluation (LREC'16)*, pages 3494–3501, Portorož, Slovenia. European Language Resources Association (ELRA).

Noah Weber, Rachel Rudinger, and Benjamin Van Durme. 2020. Causal inference of script knowledge. In *Proceedings of the 2020 Conference on Empirical Methods in Natural Language Processing (EMNLP)*, pages 7583–7596, Online. Association for Computational Linguistics.

Jason Wei, Xuezhi Wang, Dale Schuurmans, Maarten Bosma, Brian Ichter, Fei Xia, Ed Chi, Quoc V Le, and Denny Zhou. 2022. Chain-of-thought prompting elicits reasoning in large language models. In *Advances in Neural Information Processing Systems*, volume 35, pages 24824–24837. Curran Associates, Inc.

Yunyang Xiong, Zhanpeng Zeng, Rudrasis Chakraborty, Mingxing Tan, Glenn Fung, Yin Li, and Vikas Singh. 2021. Nyströmformer: A nyström-based algorithm for approximating self-attention. In *Proceedings of the AAAI Conference on Artificial Intelligence*, volume 35, pages 14138–14148.

Siyu Yuan, Jiangjie Chen, Ziquan Fu, Xuyang Ge, Soham Shah, Charles Robert Jankowski, Deqing Yang, and Yanghua Xiao. 2023. Distilling script knowledge from large language models for constrained language planning. *arXiv preprint arXiv:2305.05252*.

Fangzhou Zhai, Vera Demberg, and Alexander Koller. 2022. Zero-shot script parsing. In *Proceedings of the 29th International Conference on Computational Linguistics*, pages 4049–4060, Gyeongju, Republic of Korea. International Committee on Computational Linguistics.

Fangzhou Zhai, Iza Škrjanec, and Alexander Koller. 2021. Script parsing with hierarchical sequence modelling. In *Proceedings of *SEM 2021: The Tenth Joint Conference on Lexical and Computational Semantics*, pages 195–201, Online. Association for Computational Linguistics.

Jingqing Zhang, Yao Zhao, Mohammad Saleh, and Peter Liu. 2020. Pegasus: Pre-training with extracted gap-sentences for abstractive summarization. In *International Conference on Machine Learning*, pages 11328–11339. PMLR.

Li Zhang, Hainiu Xu, Yue Yang, Shuyan Zhou, Weiqiu You, Manni Arora, and Chris Callison-Burch. 2023. Causal reasoning of entities and events in procedural texts. In *Findings of the Association for Computational Linguistics: EACL 2023*, pages 415–431, Dubrovnik, Croatia. Association for Computational Linguistics.

Susan Zhang, Stephen Roller, Naman Goyal, Mikel Artetxe, Moya Chen, Shuohui Chen, Christopher Dewan, Mona Diab, Xian Li, Xi Victoria Lin, et al. 2022. Opt: Open pre-trained transformer language models. *arXiv preprint arXiv:2205.01068*.

Zhengyan Zhang, Xu Han, Zhiyuan Liu, Xin Jiang, Maosong Sun, and Qun Liu. 2019. ERNIE: Enhanced language representation with informative entities. In *Proceedings of the 57th Annual Meeting of the Association for Computational Linguistics*, pages 1441–1451, Florence, Italy. Association for Computational Linguistics.

A Analysis of Human Beliefs about events A and B

In addition to measuring the reading times that reflect online processing, we also collected the answers to the questions about occurrences of events A and B that were presented after each story ("*How sure are you that event A/B happened?* – see Figure 1, part III").

The motivation for this was to gain insights into a) how exactly subjects accommodate a causal conflict (the $\neg A \rightarrow B$ condition) and b) whether subjects indeed infer event A when it is omitted from the story (the $nil \rightarrow B$ condition). The $A \rightarrow B$ condition serves as a baseline. We analyse the collected ratings using ordinal regression models (Christensen, 2018).

	$A \rightarrow B$	$nil \rightarrow B$	$\neg A \rightarrow B$
Event A	6.41 (1.45)	4.85 (2.89)	3.67 (3.19)
Event B	6.13 (1.84)	4.91 (2.80)	3.79 (3.13)

Table 4: Mean subjects' belief ratings (and SD in parentheses) that the event actually happened in the story, by event type (A or B) and story condition ($A \rightarrow B$, $nil \rightarrow B$, and $\neg A \rightarrow B$).

In the $A \rightarrow B$ condition, both events A and B were given on average high ratings (6.41 and 6.13, respectively – see Table 4), meaning that subjects were sure that the events happened when they both were explicitly mentioned in the story. Further, for both events, the ratings in the $\neg A \rightarrow B$ (**event A**: $b = -2.03$, $se = 0.24$, $z = -8.67$, $p < .001$; **event B**: $b = -1.6$, $se = 0.2$, $z = -8.22$, $p < .001$) and $nil \rightarrow B$ (**event A**: $b = -1.46$, $se = 0.22$, $z = -6.6$, $p < .001$; **event B**: $b = -0.99$, $se = 0.2$, $z = -4.97, p < .001$) were significantly lower compared to the $A \rightarrow B$ condition.

The analysis of subjects' ratings showed that the causal conflict (the $\neg A \rightarrow B$ condition) resulted in lowered beliefs about both events A and B (3.67 and 3.79, respectively). One potential explanation for this is that subjects might have used different strategies to resolve the conflict. For example, some subjects could assume that event B in fact did not happen, (however, contrary to the narrative) because the premise is not met. While others could resolve the conflict by assuming that event A in fact happened thus making event B also possible to happen. Both strategies would explain relatively lower strength of beliefs about both events B and A to happen. Any explanations, however, necessitate a follow-up study with more elaborative questions that potentially require subjects to provide explanations of the given ratings.

Interestingly, we also observe lower ratings for both events in the $nil \rightarrow B$ condition, compared to the $A \rightarrow B$ condition, which is contrary to our expectations. In the $nil \rightarrow B$ condition, event B was overtly mentioned in the story, which should lead to comparable strength in subjects' beliefs with the $A \rightarrow B$ condition. Subsequently, event A, even though not mentioned explicitly, should be inferred on the basis of the causal link between them and script knowledge: if she added star-shaped sprinkles (event B), then she should have prepared cake decorations beforehand (event A) – see Figure 1, part II.

A probable rationale for the discrepancy between our expectation and the actual ratings is that, when faced with the questions, subjects may have retrospectively re-evaluated the story, relying more on their memory representations. Compared to condition $A \rightarrow B$, event B might have been perceptually less salient in the $nil \rightarrow B$ condition. Event B is easy to integrate due to its relation to the corresponding script (which we observe in the reading time analysis – see Section 3.5, RQ2) and may not receive a lot of attention from the reader, hence reducing its memorization and subsequent retrieval of event B. In the $A \rightarrow B$ condition, on the other hand, attention to event B is strengthened by the causal link coming from an explicitly mentioned event A that might facilitate its retrieval from memory at the question answering stage (see Bower et al., 1979, for similar results in reading everyday stories where subjects were asked to evaluate which events were mentioned in the text).

Model Name	# para. (M)	b	t CSK	sign	b	t CSK (short dist)	sign	b	t TRIP	sign
Bigbird-roberta-large	412	0.18	1.64	n.s.	0.33	1.72	n.s.	0.04	2.90	**
BERT: large-uncased	366	0.30	2.14	*	0.21	1.43	n.s.	0.07	1.67	.
ALBERT-xxlarge-v2	210	0.20	1.78	.	0.47	3.50	**	0.09	5.25	***
Perceiver	201	-0.02	-0.51	n.s.	0.04	0.79	n.s.	0.01	1.29	n.s.
Bigbird-roberta-base	167	0.05	0.34	n.s.	-0.03	-0.13	n.s.	0.03	2.62	**
BERT: base-uncased	133	0.14	1.71	n.s.	0.21	2.00	.	-0.00	-0.00	n.s.
Nystromformer-512	132	0.06	1.50	n.s.	0.04	0.80	n.s.	-0.01	-0.46	n.s.
ConvBERT: base	130	0.01	1.66	n.s.	-0.00	-0.72	n.s.	-0.00	-0.33	n.s.
FNet-base	108	0.01	0.14	n.s.	0.02	0.41	n.s.	-0.01	-0.80	n.s.
DistilBERT: base-uncased	90	0.12	2.08	.	0.16	2.43	*	-0.00	-0.01	n.s.
Electra-large-generator	83	0.12	1.15	n.s.	0.01	0.13	n.s.	-0.01	-0.16	n.s.
SqueezeBERT: uncased	75	0.13	1.63	n.s.	0.21	2.40	*	-0.04	-1.09	n.s.
Electra-base-generator	57	0.12	2.69	*	0.08	1.25	n.s.	-0.04	-1.15	n.s.
Electra-small-generator	17	0.18	2.66	*	0.09	1.33	n.s.	-0.03	-0.82	n.s.
ALBERT-base-v2	15	0.27	2.90	**	0.16	2.25	*	0.01	0.49	n.s.

Table 5: Results for MLMs on RQ1 ($A \rightarrow B$ versus $\neg A \rightarrow B$) on CSK (original and intervention removal) and TRIP dataset. The # para. (M) column shows the number of parameters in millions. n.s. represent that the results are not statistically significant. The ., *, **, and *** in the sign column represent p-values < 0.1, 0.05, 0.01, and 0.001.

B Details of LLMs

We use one Nvidia A100 GPU card to run all of our experiments. Thanks to our zero-shot setting, the experiment of each model takes less than 10 minutes.

B.1 GPT models

GPT-2. GPT-2 (Radford et al., 2019) is one of the most influential language models by OpenAI. As a decoder-only causal PLM, GPT-2 is often used as a baseline.

GPT-3 models. GPT-3 (Brown et al., 2020) is the upgraded version of GPT-2 which uses almost the same model and architecture but with a significantly larger amount of parameters, which was ten times more than any previous non-sparse language model. GPT-3 and GPT-3.5 were chosen to be evaluated as they were expected to perform the best, based on their strong performance on a range of NLP tasks. We experiment with different versions of GPT-3 and GPT-3.5.[8] **GPT-3 models** (Brown et al., 2020): `curie` is a GPT-3 with 6B parameters. `davinci` is a GPT-3 with 175B parameters. **InstructGPT models** (Ouyang et al., 2022): `davinci-instruct-beta` is a model trained with supervised fine-tuning on human demonstrations; `text-davinci-001` and `text-curie-001` further includes top-rated model samples from quality assessment by human labellers. **GPT 3.5 models** (Neelakantan et al., 2022): `text-davinci-002` is an InstructGPT model based on a model trained with a blend of code and text; `text-davinci-003` was further trained using reinforcement learning with human feedback.

Newer models from OpenAI like GPT-4: `gpt-4-turbo`, `gpt-4` or GPT-3.5: `gpt-3.5-turbo` don't support the "Completions" API and can't return probabilities given input tokens so we don't include them (OpenAI, 2023).

B.2 Chatbots

As the two current state-of-the-art LLMs, GPT-4 and ChatGPT, are both designed to function as chatbots, our aim is to harness the potential of the most capable open-source chatbot available to us. Chatbots, by design, need to comprehend and respond contextually to inputs, often requiring them to make connections between disparate pieces of information in a conversation. **Vicuna** is an open-source chatbot created by fine-tuning an LLaMA base model with approximately 70K user-shared conversations collected from ShareGPT.com. Preliminary evaluation in their paper (Chiang et al., 2023) suggests that Vicuna reaches 90% of the quality of chatbots such as ChatGPT and Google's Bard.

[8]More details are on `https://platform.openai.com/docs/model-index-for-researchers`

B.3 Efficient Models

There are models that need less memory or less time. Methods that reduce space could have a better performance here, because, for most of this experiment, we had limited space. Efficient models are interesting for long-range dependencies because they employ innovative techniques or optimizations to handle dependencies more effectively. Efficient models might be better or worse at capturing the relationships between distant parts of the text due to their unique approaches.

Nyströmformer and language perceiver are examples of models with efficient self-attention.

C Additional Experiment Results

C.1 Masked Language Models (MLMs)

MLMs are another group of language models that obtained state-of-the-art performances across many NLP tasks. We note that the way they work is not similar to human language processing, and the surprisal estimates obtained from them are not directly comparable to surprisals obtained from left-to-right models. However, we decided to include some MLMs that have been specifically designed to handle long-distance dependencies (via their efficient self-attention mechanisms) into our evaluation, to observe how these models perform regarding the causal inferences given long commonsense stories. We first picked a set of models from the BERT family including BERT (Devlin et al., 2019) and Bigbird-roberta (Michalopoulos et al., 2022) as representatives for MLMs because they used to be the state-of-the-art in many NLP benchmarks concerning commonsense inference (Wang et al., 2018, 2019). We opted to incorporate models that use efficient self-attention mechanisms like We also test FNet (Lee-Thorp et al., 2022), Nystromformer (Xiong et al., 2021) and Perceiver (Jaegle et al., 2022).

We follow Salazar et al. (2020) to provide models with the context before and after the target token in segment B. The pertinent token itself is masked, forcing the masked language models to infer it based on the surrounding context. For instance, in the example story in Figure 1, the words "added star-shaped sprinkles" constitute the target region describing event B. Each token in this sequence was masked one at a time. We then calculated the probabilities of the masked tokens given the surrounding story context. MLM models thus have more information than CLM models due to the additional information from other tokens in the event B and the context after event B. We therefore would like to point out that this method is not cognitively plausible, and that the surprisal scores obtained from them hence will also reflect this "privileged" knowledge. We also note that the surprisal estimation from MLMs can in principle be adapted to simulate left-to-right processing better, but think that this is only worthwhile to explore in more detail if MLMs prove to be successful at modelling the long-distance dependencies relevant to our texts.

Our results in Table 5 show that only some MLM models showed a significant difference in surprisal estimates between the coherent and the incoherent ($\neg A \rightarrow B$) condition on either CSK or TRIP datasets. Since their behaviors are not consistent across these two datasets, we consider all MLMs fail to distinguish between coherent and incoherent conditions.

C.2 Effect of dependency length (distance between events A and B)

Next, we wanted to check whether the failure of the models that don't show a significant difference between conditions is due to problems with encoding the text effectively and "remembering" event A or $\neg A$ when processing event B, or whether it is related to failure to detect the mismatch between the events. We therefore modified the original experiment's design by reducing the distance between events A and B in the story by removing all intervening sentences. (Note that we did not ensure that the removed sentences did not contain crucial information that would compromise the coherence of the story.)

If model failure on the previous task is due to difficulty in handling a long intervening context, we expect that models would show a significant difference between surprisal estimates in this short-distance condition.

As shown in Table 6 column named "CSK (short dist)", we find that most models show the same behavior in the short-distance condition and the long-distance condition. Interestingly, the results of both GPT-3.5 and Vicuna are non-significant in this condition. This could be due to the removal of intermediary materials, thereby potentially interrupting the causal chains and adversely affecting the activation of event B. Other models that are still not showing a significant difference between surprisal estimates in the different conditions might

Model Name	# para. (M)	b	t CSK	sign	b	t CSK (short dist)	sign
GPT-3.5: text-davinci-003	175K	0.59	5.87	***	0.20	1.59	n.s.
GPT-3.5: text-davinci-002	175K	0.51	2.75	*	0.10	0.70	n.s.
InstructGPT: text-davinci-001	175K	0.26	2.03	.	-0.02	-0.18	n.s.
InstructGPT: davinci-instruct-beta	175K	0.21	2.76	*	0.12	1.78	.
GPT-3: davinci	175K	0.21	2.76	*	0.19	2.69	*
Vicuna-13B	13016	0.22	2.25	*	-0.01	-0.07	n.s.
Vicuna-7B	6738	0.28	2.56	*	0.12	1.08	n.s.
InstructGPT: text-curie-001	6700	0.03	0.31	n.s.			
GPT-3: curie	6700	0.23	3.43	**	0.21	3.75	**
GPT-2: XL	1638	0.05	0.96	n.s.	0.08	1.54	n.s.
GPT-2: L	838	0.04	0.77	n.s.	0.04	0.64	n.s.
XGLM	827	-0.03	-0.79	n.s.	0.02	0.38	n.s.
Bigbird-pegasus-large-arxiv	470	0.06	1.20	n.s.	0.00	-0.04	n.s.
Pegasus-large	467	0.02	0.85	n.s.	0.00	0.00	n.s.
XLNet-large-cased	393	-0.03	-1.99	.	-0.04	-2.42	*
OPT	357	0.01	0.12	n.s.	0.02	0.32	n.s.
GPT-Neo	164	0.03	0.67	n.s.	0.05	1.11	n.s.
GPT-2	163	0.00	-0.10	n.s.	0.03	0.74	n.s.
GPT: openai-gpt	148	0.00	-0.01	n.s.	0.06	1.35	n.s.

Table 6: Results of CLMs with shorten context on RQ1 ($A \rightarrow B$ versus $\neg A \rightarrow B$) on CSK (original and intervention removal) and TRIP dataset. The # para. (M) column shows the number of parameters in millions. n.s. represent that the results are not statistically significant. The ., *, **, and *** in the sign column represent p-values < 0.1, 0.05, 0.01, and 0.001.

be failing due to not recognizing the semantic inconsistency between $\neg A$ and B.

Each of our narratives represents a sequence of events that the main character is involved in step by step in order to achieve their goal (e.g., to bake a cake or to take a flight). For example, for taking a flight story, the events are:

Reach the airport, get the boarding pass, ***[EVENT A] check in the luggage****, go through the security, wait at the gate, board the plane, find one's seat, fasten the seatbelt, turn off the electronic devices, wait on the plane, land, leave the plane,* ***[EVENT B] pick the bags at the baggage claim****, leave the airport*

In turn, removing the context between A and B typically results in very low story coherence, see the following example:

After several months away from home, Julia was finally able to visit her family for a few days. However she had a long way to go, so she decided to travel by air. First, she went to the main airport on a public bus. Once at the airport, she got her boarding pass and ***[EVENT A] checked in her luggage****. < ... > Afterwards, she* ***[EVENT B] picked up her bags at the baggage claim and left the airport.*** *Finally, she arrived home and met her family. It had been so long!*

This expectedly leads to higher surprisal in all conditions. However, we reasoned that conditions $A \rightarrow B$ and $\neg A \rightarrow B$ are affected by this change to a similar extent, and hence a difference in surprisal (which would reflect the stronger logical clash between $\neg A$ and B) would be reflected in lower surprisal values in this condition compared to $A \rightarrow B$. The strong drop in plausibility might however be a reason for the difference between $A \rightarrow B$ and $\neg A \rightarrow B$ lacking significance.

EDM3: Event Detection as Multi-task Text Generation

Ujjwala Anantheswaran[*] **Himanshu Gupta**[†] **Mihir Parmar**
Kuntal Kumar Pal **Chitta Baral**
Arizona State University
{uananthe, hgupta35, mparmar3, kkpal, chitta}@asu.edu

Abstract

We present EDM3, a novel approach for Event Detection (ED) based on decomposing and reformulating ED, and fine-tuning over its atomic subtasks. EDM3 enhances knowledge transfer while mitigating the error propagation inherent in pipelined approaches. EDM3 infers dataset-specific knowledge required for the complex primary task from its atomic tasks, making it adaptable to any set of event types. We evaluate EDM3 on multiple ED datasets, achieving state-of-the-art results on RAMS (71.3% *vs.* 65.1% F1), and competitive performance on WikiEvents, MAVEN (Δ = 0.2%), and MLEE (Δ = 1.8%). We present an ablation study over rare event types (<15 instances in training data) in MAVEN, where EDM3 achieves $\sim$ 90% F1. To the best of the authors' knowledge, we are the first to analyze ED performance over non-standard event configurations (i.e., multi-word and multi-class triggers). Experimental results show that EDM3 achieves $\sim$ 90% exact match accuracy on multi-word triggers and $\sim$ 61% prediction accuracy on multi-class triggers [1]. This work establishes the effectiveness of EDM3 in enhancing performance on a complex information extraction task.

1 Introduction

Event Detection (ED) involves characterizing events occurring in unstructured text, by recognizing their event triggers and classifying their event types. ED is used extensively for downstream tasks such as information retrieval (Kanhabua and Anand, 2016), event prediction (Souza Costa et al., 2020), and argument detection (Cheng and Erk, 2018). Existing methods for ED (Liu et al., 2018; Nguyen and Grishman, 2018) cannot easily leverage pre-trained semantic knowledge (Lai et al., 2020; Paolini et al., 2021), failing to identify complex events or function in low-resource scenarios (Chen et al., 2015; Nguyen et al., 2016). Additionally, they lack the ability to generalize across domains such as biomedicine or cybersecurity. (He et al., 2022; Satyapanich et al., 2020). As a result, they may handicap comprehensive event extraction (Liu et al., 2020; Huang et al., 2020).[2]

Sentence		Large-scale hostilities mostly ended with the cease-fire agreements after the 1973 Yom Kippur War.
Discriminative	**ED**	... [mostly] [ended] [with] ... [Kippur] [War] ... [O] [*process_end*] [O] ... [O] [*military_operation*]
EDM3	**EI**	ended | War
	EC	*process_end* | *military_operation*
	ED	ended->*process_end* | War->*military_operation*

Figure 1: Comparing label formulation for ED output in traditional discriminative approaches vs. EDM3. In EDM3, EI (Event Identification) and EC (Event Classification) labels are analogous strings with event triggers and types respectively, while ED output is a string with all triggers and their types.

To overcome these challenges, we propose EDM3 (**E**vent **D**etection by **M**ulti-task Text Generation over **three** subtasks), a novel approach based on decomposing an intricate primary task (ED) into its constituent atomic subtasks. We hypothesize that these subtasks (EI, EC) are less reliant on domain-specific knowledge than on semantic similarities (Pustejovsky, 1991), and hence simpler to learn. EDM3 involves training on these subtasks simultaneously in a non-pipelined, multi-task fashion. This diverges from the traditional discriminative token classification paradigm (Fig. 1). Unlike concurrent works such as InstructUIE (Wang et al., 2023) and UIE (Lu et al., 2022), which propose a unified model over multiple disparate language tasks, EDM3 focuses on a single complex task. This approach thus provides a framework adapt-

[*]Now at Microsoft Corporation

[1]Data and source code are available at `https://github.com/ujjwalaananth/EDM3_EventDetection`

[†]Currently in Amazon (The work was done prior to joining Amazon)

[2]Extended related work is discussed in Appendix §A

*Proceedings of the 13th Joint Conference on Lexical and Computational Semantics (*SEM 2024)*, pages 438 - 451
June 20-21, 2024 ©2024 Association for Computational Linguistics

Approaches	Datasets	Tasks Covered			Domain Generalization	Comparative Performance
		Identification	Classification	Detection		
Liu et al. (2022)	ACE, MAVEN	✗	✗	✓	✗	SOTA on MAVEN
Veyseh et al. (2021)	ACE, RAMS, CysecED	✓	✗	✓	✓	SOTA on ACE and CysecED Competitive on RAMS
He et al. (2022)	MLEE	✗	✗	✓	✗	SOTA on MLEE
EDM3 (Ours)	MAVEN, MLEE WikiEvents, RAMS	✓	✓	✓	✓	SOTA on RAMS Competitive on MLEE & MAVEN Benchmark on WikiEvents

Table 1: Comparison of EDM3 with other SOTA approaches highlighting the advantages of our approach. Columns 'Identification', 'Classification', and 'Detection' denote which tasks can be performed independently and end-to-end with the same model. We provide additional information to contextualize the performance metrics.

able to any independent complex task that can be decomposed into subtasks.

To evaluate EDM3, we conduct extensive experiments on RAMS, WikiEvents, MAVEN, and MLEE datasets. EDM3 achieves an F1 score of 71.3% on RAMS, surpassing the SOTA score by 6.2% points. EDM3 also achieves a competitive macro F1 score of 60.1% on MAVEN, compared to 60.3% (SOTA). We benchmark ED performance on WikiEvents with 60.7% F1 score. Finally, EDM3 achieves a competitive result of 78.1% F1 against 79.9% (SOTA) on the biomedical MLEE dataset. While other approaches use domain-specific embeddings and hand-crafted features, EDM3 uses a vanilla T5 model to obtain these results, supporting our hypothesis. Table 1 highlights the advantages of EDM3 over previous SOTA approaches.

We conduct investigations along multiple lines of inquiry to explore the efficacy of EDM3. We observe that our multi-tasking approach improves ED performance by 3-6%. We explore the efficacy of EDM3 in low-resource scenarios (evaluating rare event types). Experimental results reveal scores of $\sim$ 90% F1 achieved over rare event types. We also evaluate its performance over multi-word and multi-class triggers, which while lacking in benchmark datasets, are common in real-world data. EDM3 achieves $\sim$ 90% exact match accuracy on multi-word triggers and $\sim$ 61% prediction accuracy on multi-class triggers. Finally, we discuss the importance of multi-sentence context. In summary, our contributions are as follows:

1. We propose EDM3, a novel training paradigm that generatively reformulates ED and its subtasks, and trains a single multi-task model that can perform them concurrently.
2. We obtain SOTA or competitive performances over various datasets across multiple domains.
3. Our analysis shows that EDM3 performs well for low-resource scenarios as well as non-standard event configurations.

2 Proposed Method

Given an input instance containing diversely-typed event triggers, we aim to capture all triggers present. We reformulate ED and its subtasks as sequence generation tasks. We use instructional prompts to train a model on all 3 generative tasks jointly to create a single multi-task model.

Task Decomposition ED is a multi-level task requiring both event identification and classification, which sequence labeling approaches conduct in a single step. We manually decompose ED into independent tasks to be carried out in parallel with the primary task, to augment the training process.

Generative reformulation The task labels are converted to delimited strings following a consistent pattern. The number of unique event types and triggers for an instance may differ, making all tasks notably distinct from one another, as opposed to ED being a linear combination of EI and EC.

Event Identification/Classification We represent the task output as a singly-delimited sequence of labels. An instance with x unique triggers and y unique event types would have the following label representations for the EI and EC tasks respectively:

$$T_1 \mid T_2 \mid T_3 \ldots T_x$$
$$E_1 \mid E_2 \mid E_3 \ldots E_y$$

Where T_i is the ith event trigger occurring in an input instance and E_i is the ith type of event occurring in the instance.

Event Detection Each label for ED contains 2 components: event trigger and type. The task output can be represented as a doubly-delimited sequence of events. We use -> as a delimiter between trigger and type. For an instance with x events:

$$T_1\text{->}E_1 \mid T_2\text{->}E_2 \mid T_3\text{->}E_3 \ldots T_x\text{->}E_x$$

Where T_x is the xth event trigger and is of type E_x. For an example of an instance showing the reformulated outputs for all tasks, see Fig. 1.

Multi-Task Learning We posit that when trained over ED alongside its atomic tasks, a multi-task model gains significant transferable knowledge. In the case of rarer event types, modeling Event Classification (EC) separately improves the model's recognition of instances containing these events - leading to improved identification and detection. We use task-specific instructional prompts (natural language descriptions of how to perform each task with examples) to improve multi-tasking. To craft these instructional prompts, we follow the approach detailed by Wang et al. (2022b). The task-specific prompts and examples can be found in §B. For an example, see Fig. 2 in §C.

3 Results and Analysis

3.1 Results

We use EDM3 to train T5-base (220M). For experimental details, see §C. To compare our method fairly with established baselines, we evaluate our predictions by converting them to token-level labels. We report the average performance over 5 experimental runs.

RAMS We achieve 71.33% F1 score, which surpasses GPTEDOT by 6.2% (Table 2). Furthermore, the difference between precision and recall is much lower, indicating greater robustness.

WikiEvents We establish the benchmark performance of 60.7% F1 score (Table 3) on this dataset. We use single-task ED performance as a baseline to contextualize the benefits of EDM3. Over sentences with at least one event, we observe that the performance increases from 58.71% to 64.31% (Table 6) We show an example of improved ED using EDM3 in §C.1.

MAVEN We obtain a maximum F1 score of 62.66% (Table 4) which is influenced by severe class imbalance in the dataset. The competitive macro F1 score (60.1% vs. 60.3%) indicates better performance on rare classes. EDM3 also shows significant advantages in performing ED on multi-word triggers (Table 7 in §C).

Model	P	R	F1
DMBERT (Wang et al., 2019)	62.6	44.0	51.7
GatedGCN (Lai et al., 2020)	66.5	59.0	62.5
GPTEDOT (Veyseh et al., 2021)	55.5	**78.6**	65.1
EDM3	**71.6**	71.0	**71.3**

Table 2: Results on RAMS. All previous models are sentence-level BERT-based models.

Model	P	R	F1	W1
Single-task	60.0	49.6	54.3	52.1
EDM3	60.8	60.6	**60.7**	59.4

Table 3: Results on WikiEvents. W1: Weighted F1 %

Model	P	R	F1	F1*
SaliencyED (Liu et al., 2022)	**64.9**	**69.4**	**67.1**	60.3
EDM3	60.1	65.5	62.7	60.1

Table 4: Results on MAVEN. All results are on the publicly-available dev split. F1*: Macro F1 %

Model	P	R	F1
SVM2 (Zhou and Zhong, 2015) *	72.2	82.3	76.9
Two-stage (He et al., 2018) *	79.2	80.3	79.8
EANNP (Nie et al., 2015)	71.0	**84.6**	77.2
LSTM + CRF (Chen, 2019)	81.6	74.3	77.8
LSTM + CRF (Chen, 2019) **	81.8	77.7	79.7
BiLSTM + Att (He et al., 2022)	**82.0**	78.0	**79.9**
EDM3	75.9	80.4	78.1

Table 5: Results on MLEE dataset. * models using handcrafted features. All neural network-based models here use domain-specific embeddings. ** results when 4 biomedical datasets are used for transfer learning.

MLEE We compare with 1) labour-intensive approaches requiring creation of handcrafted features and 2) neural network-based models that use domain-specific embeddings obtained by parsing Pubmed or Medline abstracts. Our domain-agnostic approach achieves 78.1% F1 score, competitive with more sophisticated, domain-specific approaches (See Table 5). Our model also has higher recall (80.4%) than most approaches.

3.2 Analysis

In this work, we conduct various experiments to assess our approach in different scenarios.

Multi-tasking over EI and EC improves performance over ED Without instructional prompts,

Dataset	Single-task		EDM3 (tags)		EDM3 (instr)	
	All	Pos	All	Pos	All	Pos
MLEE	71.07	72.20	74.57	75.82	**77.09**	**78.45**
RAMS	63.21	63.21	67.66	67.66	**69.53**	**69.53**
MAVEN	58.10	59.18	62.29	63.56	**62.40**	**63.66**
WikiEvents	54.31	58.47	56.77	61.35	**58.71**	**64.31**

Table 6: Results on all datasets. Single-task: results using ED for training. EDM3 (tags): results from training with EI, EC, and ED. EDM3 (instr): using instructional prompts. All: performance on all input instances. Pos: performance on only event-containing instances.

EDM3 improves performance by at least 3% over single-tasking for all datasets. This can be attributed to the success of the subtask-level multi-tasking paradigm, with the improved performance and fewer false negatives due to training the model over EI and EC. Table 6 documents the metrics for single-task and multi-task models over all datasets.

EDM3 is well-suited to low-resource scenarios Despite its scope of 168 event types, Zhang et al. (2022) show that 18% of all event types in MAVEN have less than 100 annotated instances (Fig. 7 in §D). *Breathing* and *Extradition*, have less than 15 annotated event instances in more than 8K training sentences. Despite this, we see our model accurately identify all triggers of these event types in the testing split (see Fig. 3 in §C), achieving 100% testing precision on both, and 100% and 80% micro F1 score respectively.

Successful identification of multi-word triggers Multi-word event triggers, common in real-word data, comprise 3.42% and 3.38% of all triggers in MAVEN and RAMS respectively (see Table 10 in §D) Evaluating multi-word triggers as token classification yields misleading results as they represent the event type only when the entire phrase is annotated. For example, for the trigger "took place", the individual words are distinct from the event type denoted by the phrase. To evaluate performance on multi-word trigger phrases, we calculate exact match accuracy over them. We achieve nearly 91% and 89% on MAVEN and RAMS, respectively (Table 7 in §C), with incomplete predictions being similar to the ground truth ("assault vs the assault", "in touch" vs "been in touch").

Successful classification of multi-class triggers In a real-world ED scenario, event triggers may trigger multiple event classes in one context. 4% of all event triggers in RAMS can be classified as multi-class. (Table 10 in §C). See Fig. 4, where **purchasing** denotes both *transferownership* (arguments: *previous* and *current* owner) and *transfermoney* (arguments: *amount*). To accurately extract this event, it is necessary to capture all the senses of the trigger **purchasing**. Existing token classification methods perform event detection as multi-class, not multi-label classification. Generating sequences, as well as training over EC, enables our model to identify multi-class triggers. We achieve average prediction accuracy (% of types captured for a multi-class trigger) of 61% on RAMS, indicating the model can capture most of the senses in which each multi-class trigger functions.

Case Study: Multi-sentence context is vital to ED Consider these examples from WikiEvents:
Example 1: The whole building has **collapsed**.

Example 2: He chose **destruction**.

In Example 1, EDM3 extracts the token in bold as a relevant event trigger of the type *artifact existence*. However, this example is taken from a document primarily focused on $conflict$ events, with the triggers **bombing** and **explosion**. Therefore, **collapsed** becomes an auxiliary event that should not be predicted. Conversely, in Example 2, our model finds no salient event; however, the following sentences in the same document demonstrate that **destruction** is a salient event of type *artifact existence*. It is difficult for a sentence-level model to judge the saliency of an event without the context of its document or surrounding events, making it vital to include multi-sentence or document-level context.

4 Conclusion

In this paper, we propose EDM3, a domain-agnostic generative approach to the Event Detection task. EDM3 leverages a multi-tasking strategy that incorporates instructional prompts to improve model performance on imbalanced data and complex event instances. Our analysis shows an improvement in F1 score over single-task performance, supporting our main hypothesis viz. the effectiveness of breaking down complex generation tasks into subtasks that can support model learning on the primary task. Furthermore, our results highlight the potential for generative models in traditionally discriminative tasks like ED, paving the way for future advancements in the field.

Limitations

Our work demonstrates a prompted and generative approach on a single task, Event Detection, which can be easily adapted to other information retrieval tasks. Due to access issues, we were unable to use the ACE05 dataset. In lieu of this, we utilize 3 publicly-available general-domain datasets (RAMS, MAVEN, WikiEvent). Furthermore, there is a possibility of improving prompt quality further by analyzing the number and scope of examples required to achieve the best prompted performance. Finally, integrating domain knowledge could improve event-type classification, and we encourage future researchers to explore this area. Despite these limitations, our work provides a strong foundation for generative, instructional prompt-based frameworks for end-to-end Event Extraction and opens up exciting avenues for future research.

References

Ujjwala Anantheswaran, Himanshu Gupta, Kevin Scaria, Shreyas Verma, Chitta Baral, and Swaroop Mishra. 2024. A disturbance in the fours: Investigating the robustness of llms on math word problems.

Emanuela Boros, José G. Moreno, and Antoine Doucet. 2021. Event detection as question answering with entity information. *CoRR*, abs/2104.06969.

Ofer Bronstein, Ido Dagan, Qi Li, Heng Ji, and Anette Frank. 2015. Seed-based event trigger labeling: How far can event descriptions get us? In *Proceedings of the 53rd Annual Meeting of the Association for Computational Linguistics and the 7th International Joint Conference on Natural Language Processing (Volume 2: Short Papers)*, pages 372–376, Beijing, China. Association for Computational Linguistics.

Rich Caruana. 1997. Multitask learning. *Mach. Learn.*, 28(1):41–75.

Yifei Chen. 2019. Multiple-level biomedical event trigger recognition with transfer learning. *BMC Bioinformatics*, 20.

Yubo Chen, Liheng Xu, Kang Liu, Daojian Zeng, and Jun Zhao. 2015. Event extraction via dynamic multi-pooling convolutional neural networks. In *Proceedings of the 53rd Annual Meeting of the Association for Computational Linguistics and the 7th International Joint Conference on Natural Language Processing (Volume 1: Long Papers)*, pages 167–176, Beijing, China. Association for Computational Linguistics.

Pengxiang Cheng and Katrin Erk. 2018. Implicit argument prediction with event knowledge. In *Proceedings of the 2018 Conference of the North American Chapter of the Association for Computational Linguistics: Human Language Technologies, Volume 1 (Long Papers)*, pages 831–840, New Orleans, Louisiana. Association for Computational Linguistics.

Michael Crawshaw. 2020. Multi-task learning with deep neural networks: A survey.

Shumin Deng, Ningyu Zhang, Luoqiu Li, Chen Hui, Tou Huaixiao, Mosha Chen, Fei Huang, and Huajun Chen. 2021. OntoED: Low-resource event detection with ontology embedding. In *Proceedings of the 59th Annual Meeting of the Association for Computational Linguistics and the 11th International Joint Conference on Natural Language Processing (Volume 1: Long Papers)*, pages 2828–2839, Online. Association for Computational Linguistics.

Xinya Du and Claire Cardie. 2020. Event extraction by answering (almost) natural questions. In *Proceedings of the 2020 Conference on Empirical Methods in Natural Language Processing (EMNLP)*, pages 671–683, Online. Association for Computational Linguistics.

Seth Ebner, Patrick Xia, Ryan Culkin, Kyle Rawlins, and Benjamin Van Durme. 2020. Multi-sentence argument linking. In *Proceedings of the 58th Annual Meeting of the Association for Computational Linguistics*, pages 8057–8077, Online. Association for Computational Linguistics.

Himanshu Gupta, Kevin Scaria, Ujjwala Anantheswaran, Shreyas Verma, Mihir Parmar, Saurabh Arjun Sawant, Swaroop Mishra, and Chitta Baral. 2023. Targen: Targeted data generation with large language models. *ArXiv*, abs/2310.17876.

Xinyu He, Lishuang Li, Yang Liu, Xiaoming Yu, and Jun Meng. 2018. A two-stage biomedical event trigger detection method integrating feature selection and word embeddings. *IEEE/ACM Transactions on Computational Biology and Bioinformatics*, 15(4):1325–1332.

Xinyu He, Ping Tai, Hongbin Lu, Xin Huang, and Yonggong Ren. 2022. A biomedical event extraction method based on fine-grained and attention mechanism. *BMC Bioinformatics*, 23(1):1–17.

Kung-Hsiang Huang, Mu Yang, and Nanyun Peng. 2020. Biomedical event extraction with hierarchical knowledge graphs.

Nattiya Kanhabua and Avishek Anand. 2016. Temporal information retrieval. In *Proceedings of the 39th International ACM SIGIR Conference on Research and Development in Information Retrieval*, SIGIR '16, page 1235–1238, New York, NY, USA. Association for Computing Machinery.

Viet Dac Lai and Thien Huu Nguyen. 2019. Extending event detection to new types with learning from keywords. *CoRR*, abs/1910.11368.

Viet Dac Lai, Tuan Ngo Nguyen, and Thien Huu Nguyen. 2020. Event detection: Gate diversity and syntactic importance scores for graph convolution neural networks. In *Proceedings of the 2020 Conference on Empirical Methods in Natural Language Processing (EMNLP)*, pages 5405–5411, Online. Association for Computational Linguistics.

Sha Li, Heng Ji, and Jiawei Han. 2021. Document-level event argument extraction by conditional generation. *ArXiv*, abs/2104.05919.

Ying Lin, Heng Ji, Fei Huang, and Lingfei Wu. 2020. A joint neural model for information extraction with global features. In *Proceedings of the 58th Annual Meeting of the Association for Computational Linguistics*, pages 7999–8009, Online. Association for Computational Linguistics.

Jian Liu, Yubo Chen, Kang Liu, Wei Bi, and Xiaojiang Liu. 2020. Event extraction as machine reading comprehension. In *Proceedings of the 2020 Conference on Empirical Methods in Natural Language Processing (EMNLP)*, pages 1641–1651, Online. Association for Computational Linguistics.

Jian Liu, Yufeng Chen, and Jinan Xu. 2022. Saliency as evidence: Event detection with trigger saliency attribution. In *Proceedings of the 60th Annual Meeting of the Association for Computational Linguistics (Volume 1: Long Papers)*, pages 4573–4585, Dublin, Ireland. Association for Computational Linguistics.

Xiao Liu, Zhunchen Luo, and Heyan Huang. 2018. Jointly multiple events extraction via attention-based graph information aggregation. In *Proceedings of the 2018 Conference on Empirical Methods in Natural Language Processing*, pages 1247–1256, Brussels, Belgium. Association for Computational Linguistics.

Nicholas Lourie, Ronan Le Bras, Chandra Bhagavatula, and Yejin Choi. 2021. Unicorn on rainbow: A universal commonsense reasoning model on a new multitask benchmark.

Yaojie Lu, Hongyu Lin, Xianpei Han, and Le Sun. 2019. Distilling discrimination and generalization knowledge for event detection via delta-representation learning. In *Proceedings of the 57th Annual Meeting of the Association for Computational Linguistics*, pages 4366–4376, Florence, Italy. Association for Computational Linguistics.

Yaojie Lu, Hongyu Lin, Jin Xu, Xianpei Han, Jialong Tang, Annan Li, Le Sun, Meng Liao, and Shaoyi Chen. 2021. Text2Event: Controllable sequence-to-structure generation for end-to-end event extraction. In *Proceedings of the 59th Annual Meeting of the Association for Computational Linguistics and the 11th International Joint Conference on Natural Language Processing (Volume 1: Long Papers)*, pages 2795–2806, Online. Association for Computational Linguistics.

Yaojie Lu, Qing Liu, Dai Dai, Xinyan Xiao, Hongyu Lin, Xianpei Han, Le Sun, and Hua Wu. 2022. Unified structure generation for universal information extraction. In *Proceedings of the 60th Annual Meeting of the Association for Computational Linguistics (Volume 1: Long Papers)*, pages 5755–5772, Dublin, Ireland. Association for Computational Linguistics.

Qing Lyu, Hongming Zhang, Elior Sulem, and Dan Roth. 2021. Zero-shot event extraction via transfer learning: Challenges and insights. In *Proceedings of the 59th Annual Meeting of the Association for Computational Linguistics and the 11th International Joint Conference on Natural Language Processing (Volume 2: Short Papers)*, pages 322–332.

Thien Nguyen and Ralph Grishman. 2018. Graph convolutional networks with argument-aware pooling for event detection. *Proceedings of the AAAI Conference on Artificial Intelligence*, 32(1).

Thien Huu Nguyen, Kyunghyun Cho, and Ralph Grishman. 2016. Joint event extraction via recurrent neural networks. In *Proceedings of the 2016 Conference of the North American Chapter of the Association for Computational Linguistics: Human Language Technologies*, pages 300–309, San Diego, California. Association for Computational Linguistics.

Yifan Nie, Wenge Rong, Yiyuan Zhang, Yuanxin Ouyang, and Zhang Xiong. 2015. Embedding assisted prediction architecture for event trigger identification. *Journal of bioinformatics and computational biology*, 13 3:1541001.

Giovanni Paolini, Ben Athiwaratkun, Jason Krone, Jie Ma, Alessandro Achille, Rishita Anubhai, Cicero Nogueira dos Santos, Bing Xiang, and Stefano Soatto. 2021. Structured prediction as translation between augmented natural languages. In *9th International Conference on Learning Representations, ICLR 2021*.

Mihir Parmar, Swaroop Mishra, Mirali Purohit, Man Luo, M. Hassan Murad, and Chitta Baral. 2022. Inboxbart: Get instructions into biomedical multi-task learning.

James Pustejovsky. 1991. The syntax of event structure. *Cognition*, 41(1):47–81.

Sampo Pyysalo, Tomoko Ohta, Makoto Miwa, Han-Cheol Cho, Jun'ichi Tsujii, and Sophia Ananiadou. 2012. Event extraction across multiple levels of biological organization. *Bioinformatics*, 28(18):i575–i581.

Taneeya Satyapanich, Francis Ferraro, and Tim Finin. 2020. Casie: Extracting cybersecurity event information from text. *Proceedings of the AAAI Conference on Artificial Intelligence*, 34(05):8749–8757.

Jinghui Si, Xutan Peng, Chen Li, Haotian Xu, and Jianxin Li. 2022. Generating disentangled arguments with prompts: A simple event extraction framework that works.

Tarcísio Souza Costa, Simon Gottschalk, and Elena Demidova. 2020. Event-qa: A dataset for event-centric question answering over knowledge graphs. In *Proceedings of the 29th ACM international conference on information & knowledge management*, pages 3157–3164.

Christoph Tillmann and Hermann Ney. 2003. Word Reordering and a Dynamic Programming Beam Search Algorithm for Statistical Machine Translation. *Computational Linguistics*, 29(1):97–133.

Meihan Tong, Bin Xu, Shuai Wang, Yixin Cao, Lei Hou, Juanzi Li, and Jun Xie. 2020. Improving event detection via open-domain trigger knowledge. In *Proceedings of the 58th Annual Meeting of the Association for Computational Linguistics*, pages 5887–5897, Online. Association for Computational Linguistics.

Ashish Vaswani, Noam Shazeer, Niki Parmar, Jakob Uszkoreit, Llion Jones, Aidan N Gomez, Ł ukasz Kaiser, and Illia Polosukhin. 2017. Attention is all you need. In *Advances in Neural Information Processing Systems*, volume 30. Curran Associates, Inc.

Amir Pouran Ben Veyseh, Viet Dac Lai, Franck Dernoncourt, and Thien Huu Nguyen. 2021. Unleash gpt-2 power for event detection. In *ACL*.

David Wadden, Ulme Wennberg, Yi Luan, and Hannaneh Hajishirzi. 2019. Entity, relation, and event extraction with contextualized span representations. In *Proceedings of the 2019 Conference on Empirical Methods in Natural Language Processing and the 9th International Joint Conference on Natural Language Processing (EMNLP-IJCNLP)*, pages 5784–5789, Hong Kong, China. Association for Computational Linguistics.

Richard C. Wang and William W. Cohen. 2009. Character-level analysis of semi-structured documents for set expansion. In *Proceedings of the 2009 Conference on Empirical Methods in Natural Language Processing*, pages 1503–1512, Singapore. Association for Computational Linguistics.

Sijia Wang, Mo Yu, Shiyu Chang, Lichao Sun, and Lifu Huang. 2021. Query and extract: Refining event extraction as type-oriented binary decoding. *CoRR*, abs/2110.07476.

Sijia Wang, Mo Yu, and Lifu Huang. 2022a. The art of prompting: Event detection based on type specific prompts.

Xiao Wang, Weikang Zhou, Can Zu, Han Xia, Tianze Chen, Yuansen Zhang, Rui Zheng, Junjie Ye, Qi Zhang, Tao Gui, et al. 2023. Instructuie: Multi-task instruction tuning for unified information extraction. *arXiv preprint arXiv:2304.08085*.

Xiaozhi Wang, Xu Han, Zhiyuan Liu, Maosong Sun, and Peng Li. 2019. Adversarial training for weakly supervised event detection. In *Proceedings of the 2019 Conference of the North American Chapter of the Association for Computational Linguistics: Human Language Technologies, Volume 1 (Long and Short Papers)*, pages 998–1008, Minneapolis, Minnesota. Association for Computational Linguistics.

Xiaozhi Wang, Ziqi Wang, Xu Han, Wangyi Jiang, Rong Han, Zhiyuan Liu, Juanzi Li, Peng Li, Yankai Lin, and Jie Zhou. 2020. MAVEN: A Massive General Domain Event Detection Dataset. In *Proceedings of the 2020 Conference on Empirical Methods in Natural Language Processing (EMNLP)*, pages 1652–1671, Online. Association for Computational Linguistics.

Yizhong Wang, Swaroop Mishra, Pegah Alipoormolabashi, Yeganeh Kordi, Amirreza Mirzaei, Atharva Naik, Arjun Ashok, Arut Selvan Dhanasekaran, Anjana Arunkumar, David Stap, Eshaan Pathak, Giannis Karamanolakis, Haizhi Lai, Ishan Purohit, Ishani Mondal, Jacob Anderson, Kirby Kuznia, Krima Doshi, Kuntal Kumar Pal, Maitreya Patel, Mehrad Moradshahi, Mihir Parmar, Mirali Purohit, Neeraj Varshney, Phani Rohitha Kaza, Pulkit Verma, Ravsehaj Singh Puri, Rushang Karia, Savan Doshi, Shailaja Keyur Sampat, Siddhartha Mishra, Sujan Reddy A, Sumanta Patro, Tanay Dixit, and Xudong Shen. 2022b. Super-NaturalInstructions: Generalization via declarative instructions on 1600+ NLP tasks. In *Proceedings of the 2022 Conference on Empirical Methods in Natural Language Processing*, pages 5085–5109, Abu Dhabi, United Arab Emirates. Association for Computational Linguistics.

Tianbao Xie, Chen Henry Wu, Peng Shi, Ruiqi Zhong, Torsten Scholak, Michihiro Yasunaga, Chien-Sheng Wu, Ming Zhong, Pengcheng Yin, Sida I. Wang, Victor Zhong, Bailin Wang, Chengzu Li, Connor Boyle, Ansong Ni, Ziyu Yao, Dragomir Radev, Caiming Xiong, Lingpeng Kong, Rui Zhang, Noah A. Smith, Luke Zettlemoyer, and Tao Yu. 2022. Unifiedskg: Unifying and multi-tasking structured knowledge grounding with text-to-text language models.

Sen Yang, Dawei Feng, Linbo Qiao, Zhigang Kan, and Dongsheng Li. 2019. Exploring pre-trained language models for event extraction and generation. In *Proceedings of the 57th Annual Meeting of the Association for Computational Linguistics*, pages 5284–5294, Florence, Italy. Association for Computational Linguistics.

Hongming Zhang, Haoyu Wang, and Dan Roth. 2021. Zero-shot Label-aware Event Trigger and Argument Classification. In *Findings of the Association for Computational Linguistics: ACL-IJCNLP 2021*, pages 1331–1340, Online. Association for Computational Linguistics.

Wenlong Zhang, Bhagyashree Ingale, Hamza Shabir, Tianyi Li, Tian Shi, and Ping Wang. 2022. Event detection explorer: An interactive tool for event detection exploration.

Deyu Zhou and Dayou Zhong. 2015. A semi-supervised learning framework for biomedical event extraction based on hidden topics. *Artificial intelligence in medicine*, 64 1:51–8.

Appendix

A Related Work

Transformer-based models (Vaswani et al., 2017) have been at the forefront of many language tasks due to the wealth of pretrained knowledge. Models using BERT (Yang et al., 2019; Wang et al., 2019) treat ED as word classification, in graph-based architectures (Wadden et al., 2019; Lin et al., 2020). Models that improve ED performance for low resource settings include Lu et al. (2019); Deng et al. (2021). Other works (Tong et al., 2020; Veyseh et al., 2021) generate ED and EI samples respectively to augment training data. Many models frame ED as a question-answering task (Du and Cardie, 2020; Boros et al., 2021; Wang et al., 2021; Liu et al., 2020). APEX (Wang et al., 2022a) augments input with type-specific prompts. With the advent of more powerful sequence-to-sequence models such as T5, there has been an increased interest in formulating event detection and event extraction as sequence generation tasks (Paolini et al., 2021; Lu et al., 2021; Si et al., 2022)

Multi-Task Learning is a training paradigm in which a single machine learning model is trained on multiple separate tasks (Caruana, 1997; Crawshaw, 2020). Across domains, models trained on multiple disparate tasks are better performing due to shared learning. Multi-Task learning has been leveraged to great effect in Xie et al. (2022); Lourie et al. (2021), and in specific domains as well (Chen, 2019; Parmar et al., 2022). This paradigm is also the basis of the generative T5 model. Paolini et al. (2021) carried out multi-task learning experiments over a number of information retrieval tasks. Specifically for Event Detection, multi-tasking over ED subtasks is implemented in GPTEDOT (Veyseh et al., 2021), where EI is used to augment ED performance. This is because the simplicity of EI makes it easier to evaluate the quality of generated data. However, there is a risk of introducing noise or generating low-quality samples due to the characteristics of the source data.

Prompt engineering Prompt-based models have been used for Event Detection and Event Extraction as well. Prompt Engineering has been leveraged to great effect to generate data (Gupta et al., 2023; Anantheswaran et al., 2024) to improve existing data quality or dearth. More recently, Si et al. (2022) used predicted labels from earlier in the pipeline as prompts for later stages of trigger identification and argument extraction, while Wang et al. (2022a), following the example of other works that use prototype event triggers (Wang and Cohen, 2009; Bronstein et al., 2015; Lai and Nguyen, 2019; Lyu et al., 2021; Liu et al., 2020; Zhang et al., 2021) from the dataset, used triggers as part of tailored prompts for each event type in the schema. In proposing EDM3, we are the first to explore the efficacy of instructional prompts for ED.

B Natural Language Prompts

For each task, we provide a natural language instruction followed by a general domain example in conjunction with a biomedical domain example as part of the instructional prompt. We choose instances that are complex, i.e. have multiple labels, or multi-word or multi-class labels.

B.1 Event Identification

Instruction You are given a text as input. The text gives information about ongoing events. An event trigger is a word or phrase that most clearly expresses the event occurrence. Your task is to identify the words or phrases that are event triggers for events in the text, where event type is not given. If there are no events, print NONE.

General example INPUT: The information minister alleged that oil smuggled into Turkey was bought by the Turkish president's son , who owns an oil company . Mr al - Zoubi said in an interview , All of the oil was delivered to a company that belongs to the son of Recep (Tayyip) Erdogan . This is why Turkey became anxious when Russia began delivering airstrikes against the IS infrastructure and destroyed more than 500 trucks with oil already.</s>OUTPUT: smuggled</s>EXPLANATION: The event describes goods being moved. The exact trigger from the text that describes this event is "smuggled".

Biomedical example INPUT: Left ventricular weight, body weight, and their ratio were not significantly altered by alinidine treatment.</s>OUTPUT: treatment | altered</s>EXPLANATION: the words "treatment" and "altered" are salient words describing important events.

B.2 Event Classification

Instruction This input text gives information about specific types of ongoing events. The output should be the types of events occurring in the text. If there are no events, print NONE.

General example INPUT: The leaflets carried several messages to the citizens attempting to reassure them that the advancing army " would not target civilians , " but warned them to avoid the known locations of Isis militants . The military operation is the most complex carried out in Iraq since US forces withdrew from the country in 2011 . Last week , the UN said it was bracing itself for the world's biggest and most complex humanitarian effort following the battle , which it expects will displace up to one million people and see civilians used as human shields.</s>OUTPUT: conflict.</s>EXPLANATION: The event triggered by "battle" refers to an event of the type "conflict" which refers to a serious disagreement between two or more entities.

Biomedical example INPUT: Left ventricular weight, body weight, and their ratio were not significantly altered by alinidine treatment.</s>OUTPUT: planned_process | regulation</s>EXPLANATION: The input contains multiple events of planned_process and regulation type.

B.3 Event Detection

Instruction The text given as input discusses ongoing events. An event trigger is a word or phrase that most clearly expresses the event occurrence. Generate output in the format [event trigger->event type] for all events in the text. If there are no events, print NONE.

General example INPUT: The Organization for Security and Cooperation In Europe 's (OSCE) Office for Democratic Institutions and Human Rights and the OSCE High Commissioner on National Minorities issued a report in September saying that since Russia 's land grab , fundamental freedoms had " deteriorated radically " for many in Crimea , especially for pro - Ukrainian activists , journalists , and the Crimean Tatar community.</s>OUTPUT: land grab->transaction.exchangebuysell</s>EXPLANATION: In this text, the event being discussed is the "land grab", which functions as the event trigger. The type of event it describes is a transaction, in which ownership of entities is transferred.

Biomedical example INPUT: Left ventricular weight, body weight, and their ratio were not significantly altered by alinidine treatment.</s>OUTPUT: treatment->planned_process | altered->regulation</s>EXPLANATION: The word "treatment" in the input denotes a planned process, while the "altered" indicates the sentence talks about regulation.

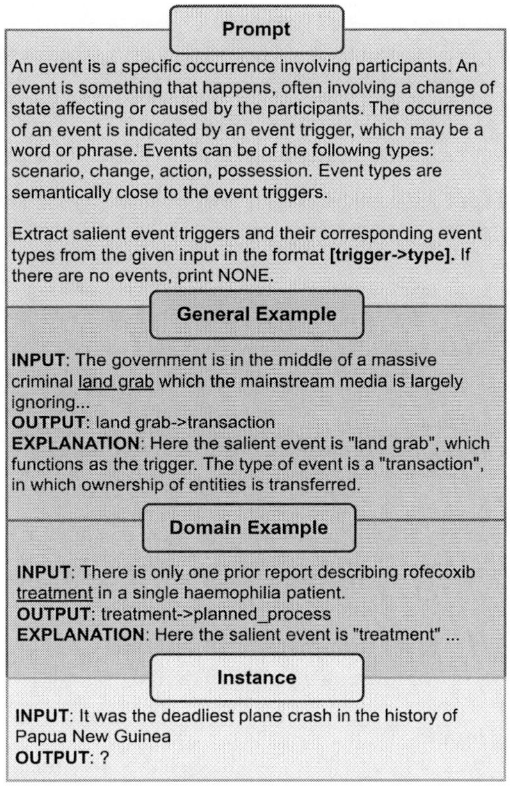

Figure 2: An example of an input instance for reformulated generative ED. The input comprises a task definition followed by diverse domain examples before the input sentence containing the events to be detected.

C Extended Analysis

Hyperparameters GPU: 2x NVIDIA GTX1080 GPUs. We train for 50 epochs with a batch size of 1. We use beam search decoding (Tillmann and Ney, 2003) during inference to generate output sequences. For beam search decoding, we use 50 beams.

...Osman Hussein was **arrested** in ... **extradited** to the UK

Approach	Output
Single-task	arrested>arrest
EDM3	arrested->arrest extradited->extradition

Figure 3: Result on event type *extradition* , which has only 11 annotated instances.

...He cut his teeth in the 90s **purchasing** and producing the Miss Universe pageant, then made...

Approach	Output
Single-task	purchasing->transaction.transferownership
EDM3	purchasing->transaction.transferownership purchasing->transaction.transfermoney
Gold	purchasing->transaction.transferownership purchasing->transaction.transfermoney

Figure 4: EDM3 improving prediction on multi-class triggers.

C.1 EDM3 improves single-task ED performance on WikiEvents

Input:
Police in Calais have dispersed a rowdy anti-migrant protest with tear gas after clashes with protesters and detained several far-right demonstrators.

Single-task:
detained->movement.transportperson

EDM3:
detained->movement.transportperson | **clashes ->conflict.attack**

Gold:
detained->movement.transportperson | **clashes ->conflict.attack**

C.2 Negative instances hamper ED performance

From the dataset statistics in Table 9, we see that the WikiEvents dataset has close to 54% instances that have no annotated events, i.e. negative instances. We hypothesize that this detracts from the model's ability to discern relevant events and their types, and instead emphasizes the binary classification task of identifying event presence. We analyze the effect of negative examples further experimentally (Table 6). The consistent trend of higher Pos scores indicates that, given a sentence, our approach is better at extracting its events accurately as opposed to identifying whether it contains an event.

Dataset	**#mwt**		**EM acc %**
	Train	Test	
MAVEN	2442	633	90.84
RAMS	228	20	88.89

Table 7: Results on multi-word triggers. #mwt: number of multi-word triggers in training and testing data. EM acc %: exact match accuracy, i.e. percentage of multi-word triggers in test data predicted by our model.

The difference between both metrics is stark in the case of WikiEvents. We observe increased performance (60.71% to 65.67% after beam search decoding) over WikiEvents, which is significantly higher than what we observe on other datasets. From further analysis, we find that training on only positive examples improves the ED performance on event sentences by nearly 5%. Furthermore, despite the fact that MAVEN has 168 event types and WikiEvents has only 49 (Table 8), the ED performance on MAVEN (62.4%) is higher than on WikiEvents (58.7%). This indicates that rather than the complexity of the ED task, the distribution of positive and negative instances may hamper the model's ability to perform the task.

We attribute this to the much higher share of negative instances in this dataset. The performance drops over non-event sentences as the model may predict event occurrence based on salient events in the sentence, that are important in the context of the sentence alone but are divorced from the subject of the document, and therefore annotated as non-events. We explore this further in our discussion of the need for multi-sentence context, which may be a way to counter the negative impact of a high proportion of non-event sentences on our ED model.

C.3 Annotation issues

We present an approach that accurately extracts text terms for event annotations while preserving case sensitivity, a crucial factor in distinguishing different event triggers. Improper extraction or human error can lead to errors in existing annotations. Our approach can identify such errors by highlighting discrepancies in the case of event triggers. Addi-

Input:
The Mexican War of Independence was an armed conflict, lasting over a decade, which had several distinct phases and took place in different regions of the Spanish colony of New Spain.

Gold:
War->hostile_encounter | conflict->hostile_encounter | took place->process_start

Figure 5: Example of an event with multi-word trigger (2 words)

Input:
There was fierce fighting on the beach, and the Scots took up a position on the mound formerly held by the Norwegians.

Gold:
held->defending | fighting->hostile_encounter | took up a position->temporary_stay

Figure 6: Example of an event with multi-word trigger (4 words)

tionally, we observe an ambiguity in some annotation schema, particularly in MAVEN, where the extensive coverage of event types results in overlapping event type definitions. For instance, the event types motion, self_motion, and motion_direction exhibit minor differences, leading to inconsistent annotations. This ambiguity introduces noise into the classification and ED subtasks. Our proposed model resolves this issue and accurately extracts all events in the corpus. We provide examples that demonstrate the improved ED performance achieved through multi-tasking.

D Data

The datasets we choose to demonstrate our approach on span a range of characteristics, from sentence-level to multi-sentence level, with varying proportions of non-event instances. We also include a biomedical domain dataset to illustrate the adaptability of our approach. In Table 8, we note the document and event instance statistics across datasets. Table 9 delineates the dataset statistics post-data processing. We note the average and maximum number of events and distinct event types that occur per data instance for each dataset. We evaluate on two-level event type labels for RAMS and WikiEvents.

MAVEN Wang et al. (2020) proposed this dataset with the idea of combating data scarcity and low coverage problem in prevailing general domain event detection datasets. The high event coverage provided by MAVEN results in more events per sentence on average, including multi-word triggers, as compared to other general domain ED datasets (more details in App. C.3). The dataset, reflective of real-world data, has a long tail distribution (see Fig. 7).

We follow the example of SaliencyED (Liu et al., 2022) and evaluate our model performance on the development split of the original MAVEN dataset.

WikiEvents Existing work on this dataset proposed by Li et al. (2021) focuses exclusively on document-level argument extraction and event extraction.

Sentences without any event occurrences make up nearly half of the entire dataset (see Table 9). In the absence of existing baselines, we establish the benchmark performances on sentence-level ED on this dataset for future researchers.

RAMS This dataset, created by Ebner et al. (2020), is primarily geared towards the task of multi-sentence argument linking. The annotated argument roles are in a 5-sentence window around the related event trigger.

In its native form, the dataset is geared towards multi-sentence argument role linking. Using the original configuration allows us to test the efficacy of our model on the multi-sentence level. Furthermore, on the sentence level, the dataset is imbalanced: 77% of the sentences contain no events. Training a model on this incentivizes event occurrence detection over ED.

MLEE This biomedical ED corpus by Pyysalo et al. (2012) is taken from PubMed abstracts centered around tissue-level and organ-level processes.

The majority of the datasets used in this work are Event Extraction (EE) datasets, maintaining the scope of possible extensions of the proposed reformulation and multi-tasking approach to EE.

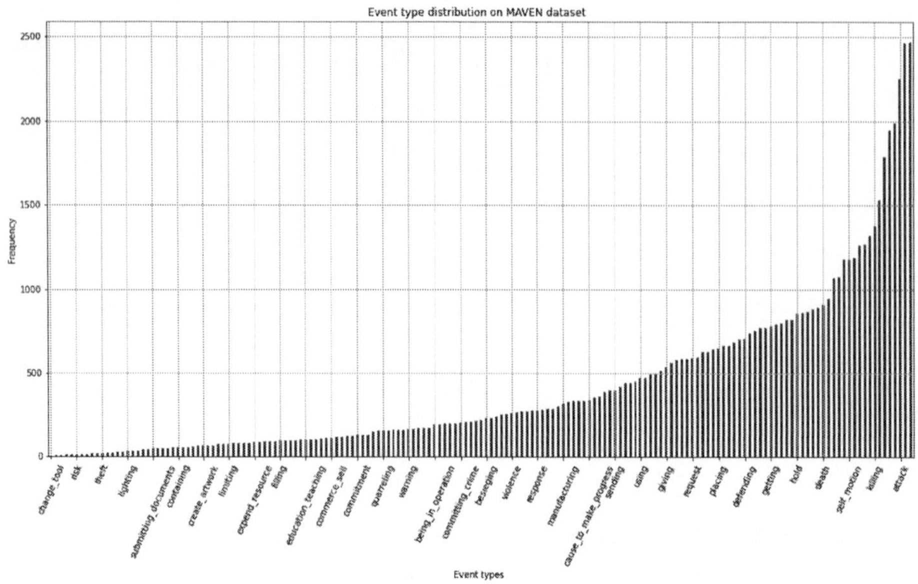

Figure 7: Distribution of event types in MAVEN. The distribution is a long-tail distribution, indicating strong class imbalance.

Dataset	Docs			#triggers	#types
	Train	Dev	Test		
MLEE	131	44	87	8014	30
RAMS	3194	399	400	9124	38
MAVEN	2913	710	857	118732	168
WikiEvents	206	20	20	3951	49

Table 8: Dataset statistics, including number of documents per data split, as well as number of event triggers and unique event types across the dataset.

Dataset	Neg (%)	Events per row		Types per row		#zs
		Avg	Max	Avg	Max	
MLEE	18.22	2.867	16	2.369	9	3
RAMS	0	1.066	6	1.061	4	0
MAVEN	8.64	2.433	15	2.314	15	0
WikiEvents	54.11	1.671	7	1.429	6	1

Table 9: Dataset statistics (post-processing) for training. Neg%: Proportion of input instances with no event occurrences. Events per row: Number of event triggers per input instance. Types per row: Number of unique event types per input instance. #zs: Number of event types in test split not seen during training.

Dataset	Multi-word triggers		Multi-class triggers	
	%instances	%rows	%instances	%rows
RAMS	3.38	2.89	**3.97**	**3.72**
MAVEN	**3.42**	**7.39**	0.06	0.13

Table 10: Statistics on multi-word and multi-class triggers in all datasets. %instances: the % of total triggers present. %rows: the % of all input instances that contain at least 1 multi-word or multi-class trigger.

Category	Event type	Example triggers
Anatomical	cell_proliferation	proliferation, proliferate, growing
	development	formation, progression, morphogenesis
	blood_vessel_development	angiogenic, angiogenesis
	death	death, apoptosis, survival
	breakdown	dysfunction, disrupting, detachment
	remodeling	remodeling, reconstituted
	growth	proliferation, growth, regrowth
Molecular	synthesis	production, formation, synthesized
	gene_expression	expression, expressed, formation
	transcription	expression, transcription, mRNA
	catabolism	disruption, degradation, depleted
	phosphorylation	phosphorylation
	dephosphorylation	dephosphorylation
General	localization	migration, metastasis, infiltrating
	binding	interactions, bind, aggregation
	regulation	altered, targeting, contribute
	positive_regulation	up-regulation, enhancement, triggered
	negative_regulation	inhibition, decrease, arrests
Planned	planned_process	treatment, therapy, administration

Table 11: Event types in MLEE, along with example triggers.

Event type	Frequency	Example triggers
process_start	2468	began, debut, took place
causation	2465	resulted in, caused, prompted
attack	2255	bombing, attacked, struck
hostile_encounter	1987	fought, conflict, battle
motion	1944	fell, pushed, moved
catastrophe	1785	explosion, hurricane, flooded
competition	1534	event, championships, match
killing	1380	killed, murder, massacre
process_end	1323	closing, complete, ended
statement	1269	asserted, proclaimed, said

Table 12: Top 10 event types in MAVEN, along with example triggers.

Event type	Frequency	Example triggers
conflict.attack	721	massacre, battle, bombing
movement.transportperson	491	smuggling, walked, incarcerate
transaction.transfermoney	482	reimbursed, paid, purchasing
life.die	442	die, murder, assassinating
life.injure	422	surgery, injured, brutalized
movement.transportartifact	367	imported, trafficking, smuggling
transaction.transferownership	327	auction, donated, acquire
contact.requestadvise	250	advocating, recommending, urged
contact.discussion	249	discuss, meet, negotiated
transaction.transaction	211	funded, donated, seized

Table 13: Top 10 event types in RAMS, along with example triggers.

Event type	Frequency	Example triggers
conflict.attack	1188	explosion, shot, attack
contact.contact	530	met, said, been in touch
life.die	501	killed, died, shot
life.injure	273	injuring, wounded, maimed
movement.transportation	212	transferred, brought, arrived
justice.arrestjaildetain	176	arrested, capture, caught
artifactexistence.damagedestroydisabledismantle	103	damaged, destruction, removed
justice.investigatecrime	102	analysis, discovered, investigation
justice.chargeindict	96	charged, accused, alleged
artifactexistence.manufactureassemble	82	construct, make, build

Table 14: Top 10 event types in WikiEvents, along with example triggers.

Author Index

Association for Computational Linguistics
209 N. Eighth Street
Stroudsburg, Pennsylvania 18360

CURRAN ASSOCIATES INC.
proceedings.com

ISBN 978-1-7138-9941-9
9 781713 899419